Introduction to AutoCAD 2027 for Civil Engineering Applications

Nighat Yasmin
Clemson University

SDC
PUBLICATIONS

SDC Publications
P.O. Box 1334
Mission, KS 66222
913-262-2664
www.SDCpublications.com
Publisher: Stephen Schroff

ISBN-13: 978-1-63057-823-7
ISBN-10: 1-63057-823-1

Printed and bound in the United States of America.

Dedication

This book is dedicated to

my parents Shamim and Wajid

my Family

my siblings and

my students!

Acknowledgment

I wish to acknowledge the patience and continuous support of my husband, Abdul, and my children Nayel, Haaris, and Kirin and my granddaughters Aleena and Afiyah during the countless hours I spent in preparation of the manuscript.

I would greatly appreciate hearing your comments and suggestions to improve future editions, or any problem related to this edition.

Nighat Yasmin, PhD

yasmin@clemson.edu

Preface

A picture is worth a thousand words! This is an old saying that means an engineer describes every idea with a drawing. Visual representation often clarifies engineering concepts more effectively than text alone. As computing power and drafting software have advanced, integrating computer-aided design instruction into engineering curricula has become essential. This book aims to present engineering graphics principles clearly while teaching practical use of AutoCAD 2027. Illustrations throughout were produced using AutoCAD 2027 and Paint, and examples follow the ribbon-interface workflow common to current CAD applications. The material targets civil engineering students, emphasizing fundamental theory, standard drafting procedures, and hands-on exercises to build proficiency with CAD tools and efficient drawing practices

Several enhancements were implemented in this edition. The most notable changes are the addition of new examples for Chapters 11 through 19 covering civil engineering applications. Chapter 23, Suggested In-Class Activities, now includes classroom exercises; some initial activities feature drawing examples with step-by-step instructions, and additional problems have been added. Across the book, chapter content and illustrations have been refined, and the index has been improved to aid navigation and reference.

Each chapter begins with clear learning objectives, followed by a concise introduction. The bulleted objectives offer an overview of the key concepts discussed. Chapters are divided into well-defined sections with detailed, step-by-step instructions accompanied by graphical illustrations demonstrating AutoCAD commands. This layout helps students understand both how to execute commands and the reasoning behind their use, reinforcing practical skills and conceptual understanding for effective applications.

This book has been categorized into 14 parts.

Part 1: Chapters 1-4: -------- Introduction to AutoCAD 2027 ribbon interface
Part 2: Chapters 5: ----------- AutoCAD and annotative objects
Part 3: Chapters 6-8: -------- AutoCAD and layers, layouts, and template files
Part 4: Chapters 9-10: ------- Dimensions and tolerance using AutoCAD 2027
Part 5: Chapters 11-12: ------Use of AutoCAD in land survey data plotting
Part 6: Chapters 13-14: ------Use of AutoCAD in hydrology
Part 7: Chapters 15-16: ------Transportation engineering and AutoCAD
Part 8: Chapters 17-19: ----- AutoCAD and architecture technology
Part 9: Chapter 20: ----------- Introduction to working drawings
Part 10: Chapter 21: ---------- Plotting from AutoCAD
Part 11: Chapter 22: ---------- External Reference Files (Xref)
Part 12: Chapters 23-24: ----- Suggested drawing problems
Part 13: Chapter 25: ---------- Bibliography
Part 14: Chapter 26: ---------- Index

1. The 1st chapter, *Introduction to Engineering Graphics*, provides a relationship between engineering problems and engineering graphics.

2. The 2nd chapter, *Getting Started with AutoCAD 2027*, explains the basics of AutoCAD 2027. The emphasis is on the drawing area (save or delete), ribbons, tabs (add, remove, and relocate), panels (add, remove, and relocate), command line, and file operations (open, close, save, and plot). This chapter also explains the basic features of a new file and provides their default values. Furthermore, the chapter explains how the grid and snap points in the x-y plane help a user during the drawing creation process.

3. The 3rd chapter, *Two-Dimensional Drawings*, begins with the details of the dynamic input capabilities. Most of this chapter is devoted to the commands' description for two-dimensional objects, such as point, lines, circles, ellipse, rectangles, polygons, polylines, arcs, and appearance of object (color, line thickness, and line style). The remaining part of the chapter focuses on creating tables.

4. The 4th chapter, *Two-Dimensional Drawing's Editing*, begins with object selection and de-selection methodology. This chapter discusses object snap capabilities: fast and easy access to the strategic points on a two-dimensional object. The major emphasis of the chapter is the explanation of the *Modify* commands (erase, delete, duplicate objects, mirror, copy, move, rotate, offset, trim, extend, fillet, chamfer, scale, break, join, oops, and explode) to modify two-dimensional objects. An alternate method, the use of grips points, to modify an object is discussed as well. This chapter also explains the process of creating rectangular, polar, and path arrays. Finally, the last topic of the chapter explains the use of the property sheet for object editing.

5. The 5th chapter, *Annotative Objects*, describes annotative objects with the focus on multiline text, hatch, and qleaders. That is, how text, hatch, and qleaders can be created such that their size can be independent of the viewport scale.

6. The 6th chapter, *Layers*, explains the advantages of layers and art of creating, using, and modifying layers.

7. The 7th chapter, *Blocks*, explains how to create and insert different types of blocks. This chapter also discusses the Design Center.

8. The 8th chapter, *Layouts and Template files* explains how to manipulate layouts and how to create a template file.

9. The 9th chapter, *Dimensioning Techniques*, explains the art of creating and reading a dimensioned drawing. This chapter provides the basics of annotative dimensioning techniques, placement of dimensions, and choice of dimensions. This chapter also explains the concept of smart dimensions and quick dimensions.

10. The 10th chapter, *Tolerance*, explains the art of adding tolerance to the dimensions of a drawing. This chapter provides the basics of tolerance techniques, types of tolerance, and choice of tolerance.

11. The 11th chapter, *Land Survey*, describes parcels, deeds, display angles (azimuth and bearing), open and close traverse, and different types of survey systems.

12. The 12th chapter, *Contours*, introduces the basic terminology used in contour maps. It also provides step-by-step instructions to draw and label contour maps.

13. The 13th chapter, *Drainage Basin*, explains the characteristics of a drainage basin. At the end, it provides step-by-step instructions to delineate channels and their drainage basins on a contour map.

14. The 14th chapter, *Floodplains*, explains characteristics of a channel and its floodplain. At the end, it provides step-by-step instructions to delineate a channel and its floodplain on a contour map.

15. The 15th chapter, *Road design*, explains how to draw PnP (plan and profile) and cross-sections drawing for a proposed road on a contour map.

16. The 16th chapter, *Earthwork*, explains how to use a plan and profile (PnP) drawing to delineate an earthwork for a road design.

17. The 17th chapter, *Floor Plan*, explains how to create an architectural drawing of a residential building using simple commands such as point, polyline, circle, trim, extend, offset, and hatch. It also makes use of the blocks from the Design Center.

18. The 18th chapter, *Elevation*, describes the techniques used to create elevation by projecting lines from a floor and roof plans. It also provides step-by-step instructions to create side elevation by projecting lines from a floor and roof plans and from front elevation using 45° miter lines. It provides step-by-step instructions to create hip and gable roofs used in the elevation, too.

19. The 19th chapter, *Site Plan*, provides step-by-step instructions to draw and label a site map of the residential building created in Chapter 17.

20. The 20th chapter, *Construction Drawings*, briefly describes a family of drawings.

21. The 21st chapter, *Plotting From AutoCAD 2027*, explains commands for hard and soft copies. That is paper printing from both the Model space and the layouts and a PDF file creation.

22. The 22nd chapter, *External Reference Files (Xref)*, explains commands for referencing external drawing, image, and PDF files.

23. The 23rd chapter, *Suggested In-Class Activities*, provides a list of design problems for the in-class activities or labs.

24. The 24th chapter, *Homework Drawings*, provides a list of design problems for the homework assignments.

25. The 25th chapter, *Bibliography*, provides a list of the books and papers referenced in the preparation of the manuscript.

26. Finally, the 26th chapter, *Index*, provides an alphabetical list of the major topics discussed in the book.

TABLE OF CONTENTS

8. LAYOUTS AND TEMPLATE 386

9. DIMENSIONS 418

1. Introduction to Engineering Graphics

1.1. Learning Objectives

After completing this chapter, the students will show proficiency in the following areas:

- What is a computer graphic?
- What is a technical drawing?
- How to enlarge or shrink a drawing?

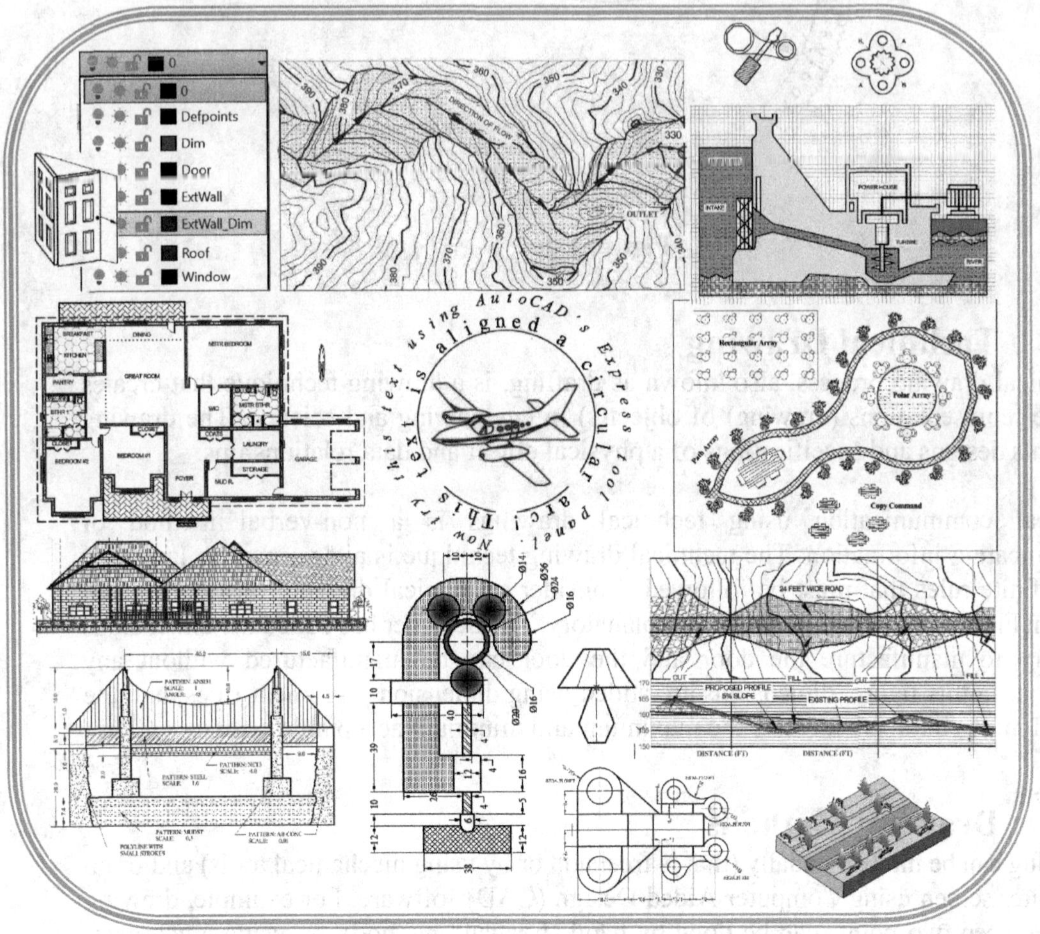

1.2. Engineering Problem

Extensive studies have shown that engineering problem solving techniques are complicated processes. A solution to most engineering problems requires a combination of organization, analysis, problem solving principles, communication skills, and graphical representations of the problem. The concept map shown in Figure 1-1 represents a simplified version of the interaction and complexities involved in the solution processes. The focus of this book is the graphical representations of the problem that can be used to find a solution.

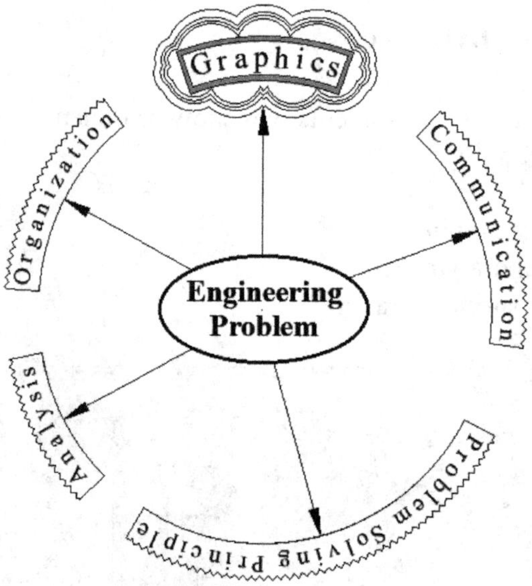

Figure 1-1

1.3. Technical Drawing

A technical drawing process, also known as drafting, is a drawing technique that creates accurate representations (drawing) of object(s) in engineering and science. The drawing represents designs and specifications of a physical object and data relationships.

Graphical communication using technical drawings is a non-verbal method of communicating information. The technical drawing technique is a clear precise language with definite rules that must be followed. Consider a technical drawing of a door panel shown in Figure 1-2. The figure is self-explanatory. The designer has added the dimensions necessary to manufacture the door and the door can be manufactured without any confusion. In this figure, dimensions are added using dimension placement rules; and the plus and minus numbers indicate the maximum and minimum acceptable errors.

1.4. Drawing Methods

A drawing can be made manually (that is freehand or by using mechanical tools) and/or on a computer screen using Computer Aided Design (CAD) software. For example, drawing a line between two points can be done by hand (freehand method), by using a compass, protractor, rulers, etc. (mechanical method), or on a computer using software (CAD software). Figure 1-3a shows a freehand sketch and Figure 1-3b shows the mechanical drawing of the door panel, respectively. Figure 1-3c is the drawing of the same door created using CAD software.

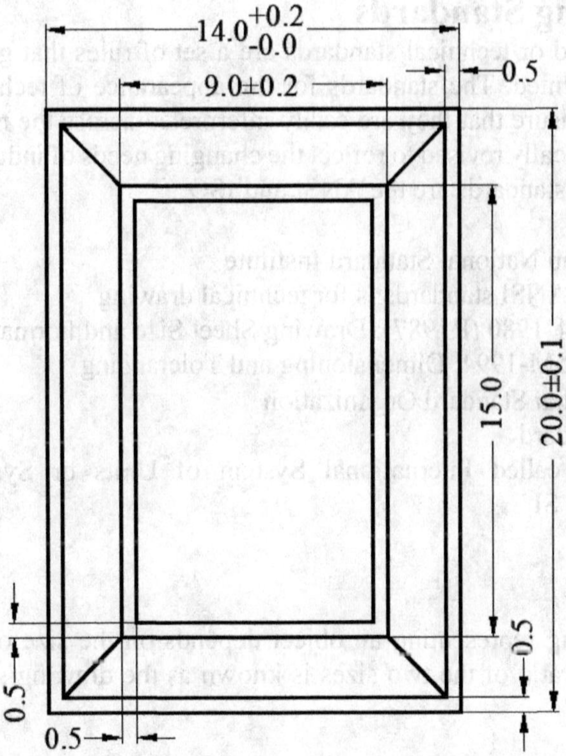

Figure 1-2

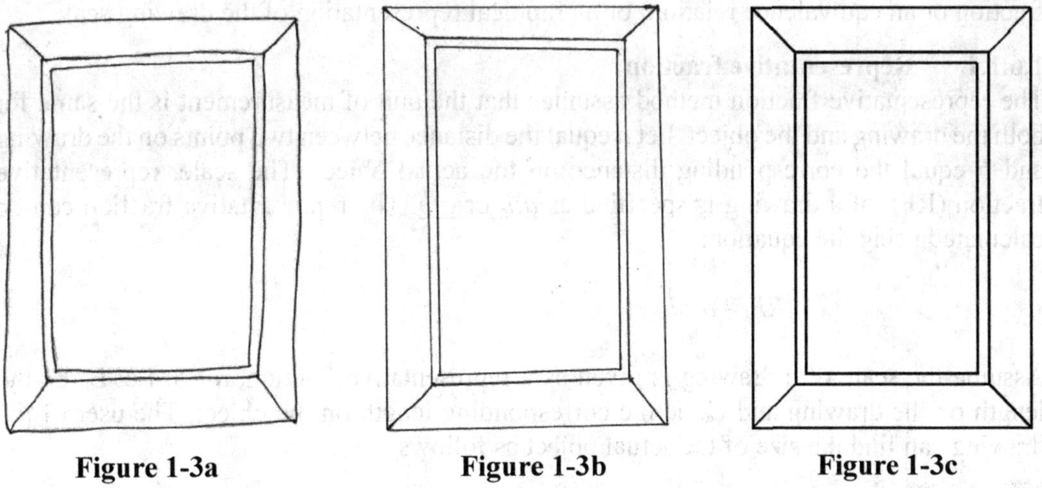

Figure 1-3a **Figure 1-3b** **Figure 1-3c**

The appearances of the three drawings shown in Figure 1-3 indicate that freehand sketches are good candidates for the brainstorming session. On the other hand, a CAD drawing should be delivered to the client on the completion of the project. One of the major advantages of a CAD drawing is that the editing process is fast compared to manual methods. The focus of this book is AutoCAD 2027, a Computer Aided Design software.

1.5. Drawing Standards

The drawing standard or technical standards are a set of rules that govern how technical drawings are represented. The standards for the appearance of technical drawings have been developed to ensure that they are easily interpreted across the nation and the world. Standards are periodically revised to reflect the changing needs of industry and technology. The commonly used standards are the ANSI and ISO.

- ANSI: American National Standard Institute
  - Y series of ANSI standards is for technical drawing
  - ANSI Y14.1-1980 (R1987): Drawing Sheet Size and Format
  - ANSI Y14.5M-1994: Dimensioning and Tolerancing
- ISO: International Standard Organization
  - Metric standard
  - System is called International System of Units or System Internationale, abbreviated SI

1.6. Scale

The size of a drawing representing an object depends on the size of the object and the drawing paper. The ratio of the two sizes is known as the drawing's scale or simply the scale.

1.6.1. Type of scale

The scale of a drawing can be represented as a mathematical relation (representative fraction or an equivalence relation) or a graphical representation of the drawing scale.

1.6.1.1. Representative fraction

The representative fraction method assumes that the unit of measurement is the same for both the drawing and the object. Let *a* equal the distance between two points on the drawing and *b* equal the corresponding distance on the actual object. The scale, representative fraction (RF), of a drawing is specified as $\underline{a:b}$ or $\underline{a/b}$. The representative fraction can be calculated using the equation:

$$RF = a : b$$

Assume the scale of a drawing is given as a representative fraction, $a\ /\ b$. Let L_d be the length on the drawing and L_o be the corresponding length on the object. The user of the drawing can find the size of the actual object as follows.

1. <u>Measure the length of an object on the drawing (L_d)</u>: If the object is straight then a ruler can be used to find its length (or distance between two points). If the object is not straight, then (i) take a string and place it on top of the object and then (ii) measure the length of the string.

2. Calculate the object length (L_o): Calculate the length of the object using the equation:

$$L_d / L_o = a/b \qquad \text{Implies} \qquad L_o = (b/a) * L_d$$

- Example #1: Let the scale equal 1:240 (that is *a* = *1* inch and *b* = *240 inches*), and L_d = 25 inches then
  $L_o = (240/1) * 25 = 6000$ *inches*

- Example #2: Let the scale equal 50:1 (that is *a* = *50* inches and *b* = *1 inch*), and L_d = 250 inches then
  $L_o = (1/50) * 250 = 5$ *inches*

1.6.1.2. Equivalence relation

The equivalence relation method assumes that the units of measurement are different on the drawing and the object. The equivalence relation is also known as an engineer's scale. Assume *a inches* is the distance between two points on the drawing and *b feet* is the corresponding distance on the actual object. The scale, equivalence relation (ER), of a drawing is specified as *a" = b'*.

Assume the scale of a drawing is given as an equivalence relation. Let L_d be the length on the drawing and L_o be the corresponding length on the object. The user of the drawing can find the size of the object as follows.

1. Measure the length on the drawing (L_d): If the object is straight then a ruler can be used to find the distance between two points. If the object is not straight, then take a string and place it on the top of the drawing and then measure the length of the string.
2. Calculate the object length (L_o): Calculate the length of the object using the equation:

$$a" = b' \text{ and } L_d \text{ inches} = L_o \text{ feet}$$
$$\Longrightarrow \quad L_d / a = L_o / b$$
$$\Longrightarrow \quad L_o \text{ feet} = (b \text{ feet}) * [(L_d \text{ inches})/(a \text{ inches})]$$

- Example #1: Let the scale be 1" = 240' (that is *a* = *1* inch, *b* = *240* feet), and L_d = 25 inches; then
  $L_o = 240 * 25 = 6000$ *feet*

- Example #2: Let the scale be 50" = 1' (that is *a* = *50* inches, *b* = *1* foot), and L_d = 250 inches; then
  $L_o = (1/50) * 250 = 5$ *feet*

1.6.1.3. Converting RF to ER

A representative fraction (RF) scale can be converted into an equivalence relation (ER) and vice versa. An RF scale can be converted into an ER using the methodology explained in the following example.

Example #1: The RF scale is 1:600 and the units of measurement are inches. Find the corresponding ER.

1. Convert the right side of the scale into feet. The conversion of inches of the scale into feet is shown here.

   600 inches = (600/12) feet = 50 feet

2. Hence, the RF scale of 1:600 can be written in ER format as 1" = 50'

1.6.1.4. Graphical representation

The graphical representation is known as graphical or bar scale. Generally, the graphical scales are used for large-scale maps. In this representation, a ruler is drawn on the map as shown in Figure 1-4. In this representation, the bar is divided into two parts: the left and right part. In the left part (*Part 1* in Figure 1-4), the scale is divided into tenths and in the right part (*Part 2* in Figure 1-4), the scale is marked in full units. This representation assumes that the unit of measurement is the same on both the drawing and the object. For the current example, assume that the unit of measurement is inch.

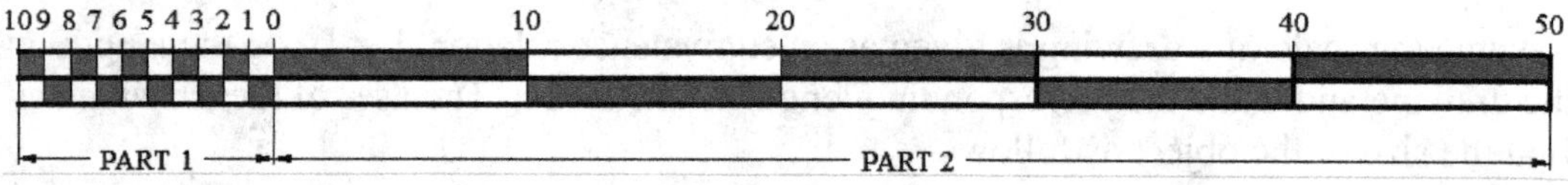

Figure 1-4

Example #1: Assume the scale of a drawing is given as a ruler shown in Figure 1-4. Let L_m be the distance between two points on the map and L_G be the corresponding distance on the ground. The user of the map can find the distance on the ground as follows.

1. Measure the distance of an object on the drawing (L_m): If the path is straight then any straight edge object can be used to find the distance between two stations. If the path is not straight, then take a string and place it on the top of the path and then measure the length of the string. Assume the user of the map (Figure 1-5a) desired to measure the straight-line distance between two points A and B. The user will use a piece of paper and will mark two points on the straight edge, one point at the starting station (A) and the second point at the destination station (B), Figure 1-5b. For the demonstration purpose, the marks at A and B are represented as small line segments; the segments are highlighted by displaying their grip points.

2. Find the object distance of the drawing (L_G): Now place the straight edge on the graphical scale as shown in Figure 1-5c. The distance between stations A and B is 11.3 inches.

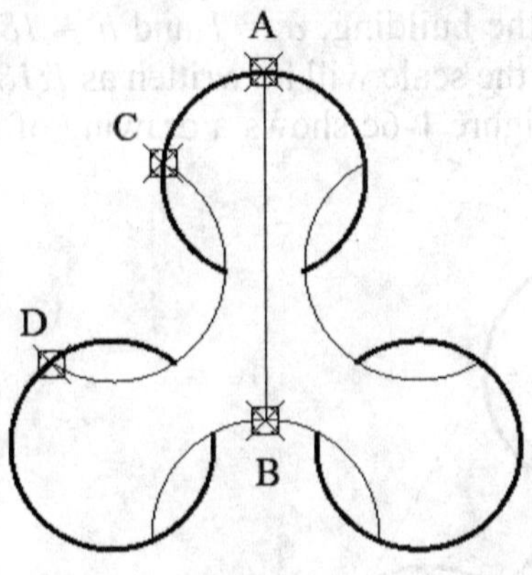

Figure 1-5a

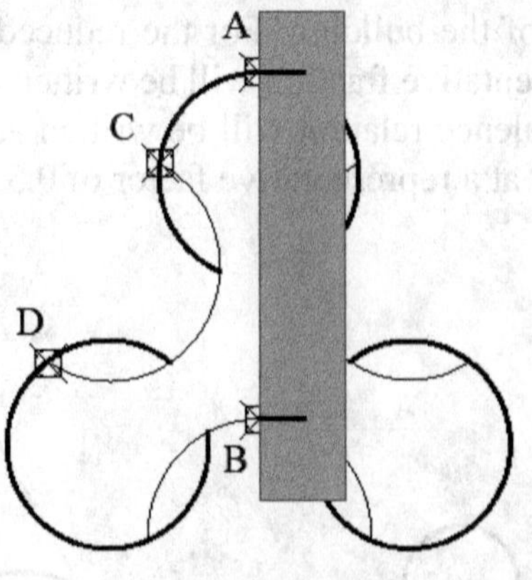

Figure 1-5b

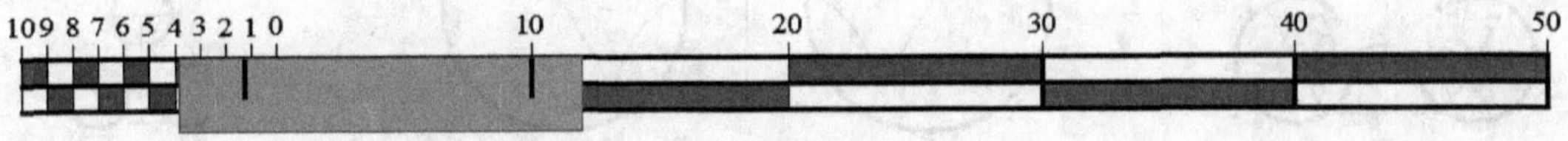

Figure 1-5c

1.7. Scale Of A Drawing

Generally, drawings are drawn to a scale, because the object is either too large or too small to draw on a drawing sheet. Hence, a drawing can be smaller or larger than the object itself.

1.7.1. Full scale

The scale of a drawing is full if the drawing of an object is of the same size as the object. That is, one unit on the drawing will represent one unit on the object. For example, a drawing of an average calculator (which is 6 inches long and 2.75 inches wide) can be a full-scale drawing. For full-scale drawings, $a = 1$ and $b = 1$. The representative fraction will be written as 1/1 and the scale will be written *1:1* or *FULL*. Figure 1-6a shows a drawing of a plate drawn at full scale.

1.7.2. Large scale

The scale of a drawing is large, if the drawing of an object is larger than the actual size of the object. That is, one unit on the drawing will represent a fraction of a unit on the object. For example, a printed circuit board of a computer chip may be 36 times the actual size; that is, 36 units on the drawing is actually 1 unit on the circuit board. For the enlarged drawing of the computer chip, $a = 36$ and $b = 1$. The representative fraction will be written as 36/1 and the scale will be written as *36:1*. The equivalence relation will be written as *3' = 1"*. Figure 1-6b shows a drawing of a plate drawn at a representative factor of 2 (Scale 2:1).

1.7.3. Small scale

The scale of a drawing is small, if the drawing of an object is smaller than the actual size of the object. That is, one unit of the object will be represented by a fraction of a unit on the drawing. Consider a drawing of a building. One unit of drawing may represent 180 units of the building. For the reduced drawing of the building, $a = 1$ and $b = 180$. The representative fraction will be written as 1/180, and the scale will be written as *1:180*. The equivalence relation will be written as *1" = 15'*. Figure 1-6c shows a drawing of a plate drawn at a representative factor of 0.5 (Scale 1:2).

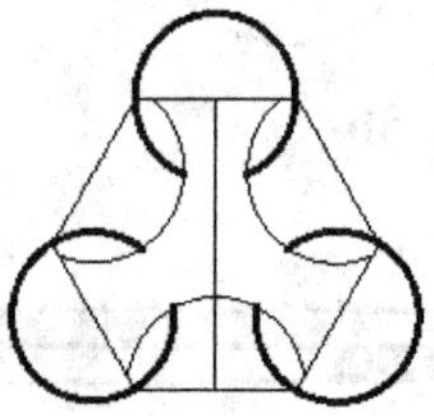

Scale 1:1

Figure 1-6a

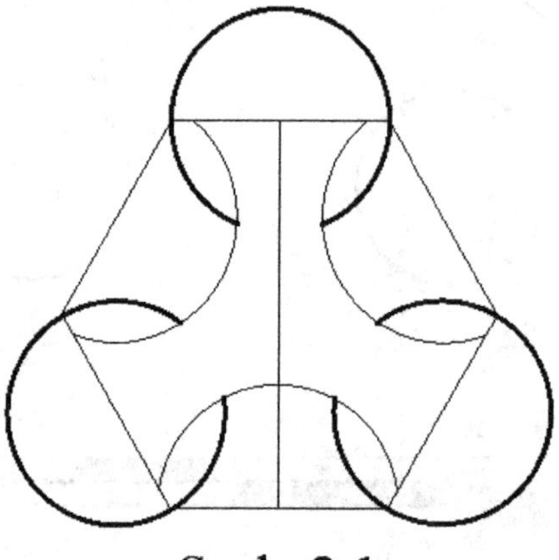

Scale 2:1

Figure 1-6b

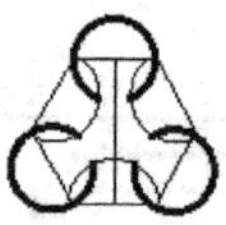

Scale 1:2

Figure 1-6c

1.8. Computer Aided Graphics

Computer Aided Design (commonly abbreviated as CAD) software provides the capability to create graphics, hence the name computer graphics. The graphics created can be used to analyze, modify, and finalize a graphical solution for the problem being studied. The focus of this book is AutoCAD 2027.

1.8.1. AutoCAD 2027

AutoCAD is a suite of popular CAD software products for two- and three-dimensional design and drafting developed and sold by Autodesk.

1.8.2. AutoCAD and drawing scale

A drafter creating a drawing on a drawing sheet using mechanical equipment needs to decide about the drawing scale before starting the drawing. The selected scale will depend upon the size of the object and the paper, such that the drawing will fit on the drawing sheet. On the other hand, in AutoCAD, every drawing is drawn to full-scale (that is 1:1). Generally, a drafter starts a drawing in AutoCAD without thinking about the scale and chooses the scale when s/he decides to print the drawing. However, it is important to think about the plotting scale early in the drawing process because the text size, line thickness, and line style (linetype scale) will be affected by changing the drawing scale.

AutoCAD provides both the representative factors and the equivalence relation techniques. The software provides a long list of scale factors, Figure 1-7. Also, the user can make more entries in the list or can delete the existing scale factors. This dialog box is discussed in detail in *Chapter 8* (Section 8.3).

The user can create graphical scales using *Line*, *Hatch*, and *Text* commands. These commands are discussed in detail in *Chapter 3*.

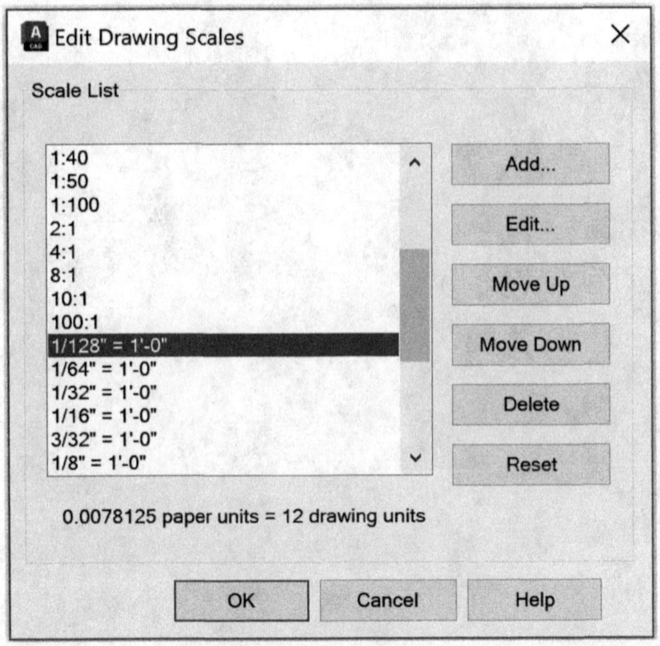

Figure 1-7

Notes:

2. Getting started with AutoCAD 2027

2.1. Learning Objectives

After completing this chapter, the students will show proficiency in the following areas:

- Features of AutoCAD 2027 interface
  - The drawing area
  - The ribbon
  - Tabs and panels of the ribbon
  - The command line window
- Workspace manipulation
  - Customizing workspace
  - Renaming a workspace
  - Save/delete a workspace
- File manipulation
  - Open a new file and/or pre-existing file
  - Make a file a current file
  - Save a new file and/or previously saved file
- The basic features of a new file
- The grid and snap capabilities

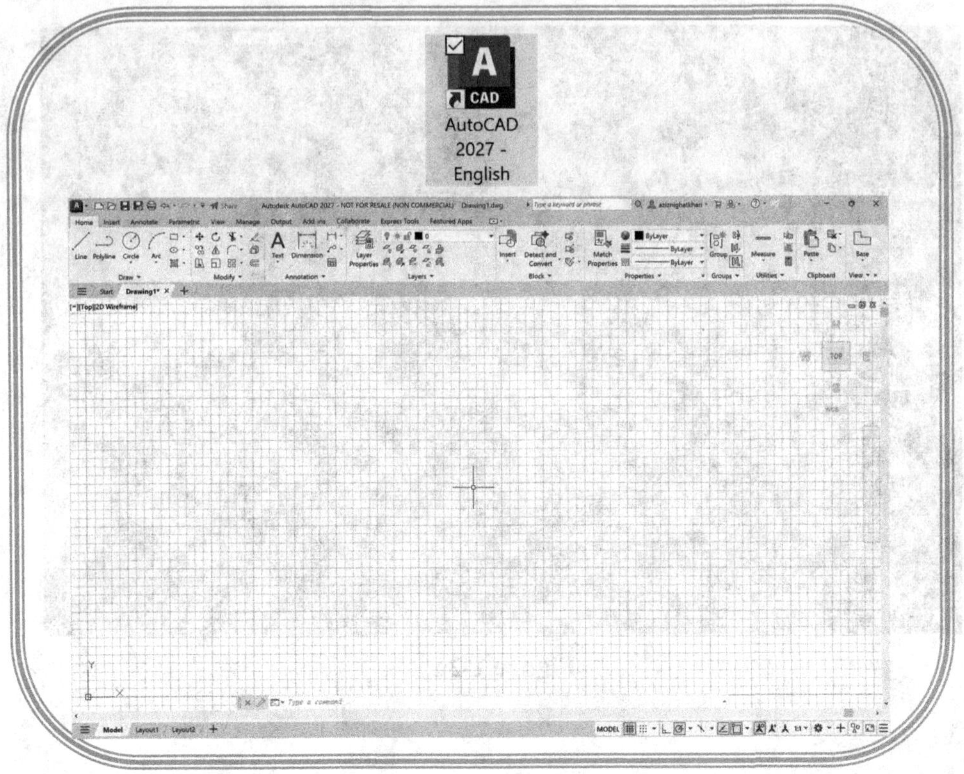

2.2. Introduction

Initially a general-purpose 2D drafting program, AutoCAD has evolved into a family of products that provides a platform for 2D and 3D computer-aided design (CAD). Currently, civil engineers, land developers, architects, mechanical engineers, interior designers, and medical and other design professionals use it.

AutoCAD can be launched by either double clicking on the AutoCAD icon (Figure 2-1a) on the desktop or clicking *Start* → *All Programs* → *Autodesk* → *AutoCAD 2027*→ *AutoCAD 2027*. If the software is installed at a different location on your computer, follow that specific path.

For the first launch of the software, if the AutoCAD interface displays the *Autodesk Data collection* dialog box, *Autodesk Licensing* dialog box, and/or *DWG Association* options list, click on appropriate options. Once the license validation process is complete, the *Autodesk AutoCAD 2027* interface is launched as shown in Figure 2-2a. Click the *Learning & Insights* label on the left side of the interface, Figure 2-2a; the screen shown in Figure 2-2b will appear. This screen provides access to video and online resources. Click the *RECENT* label on the left side of the interface, Figure 2-2b and the screen shown in Figure 2-2a will reappear.

Figure 2-1

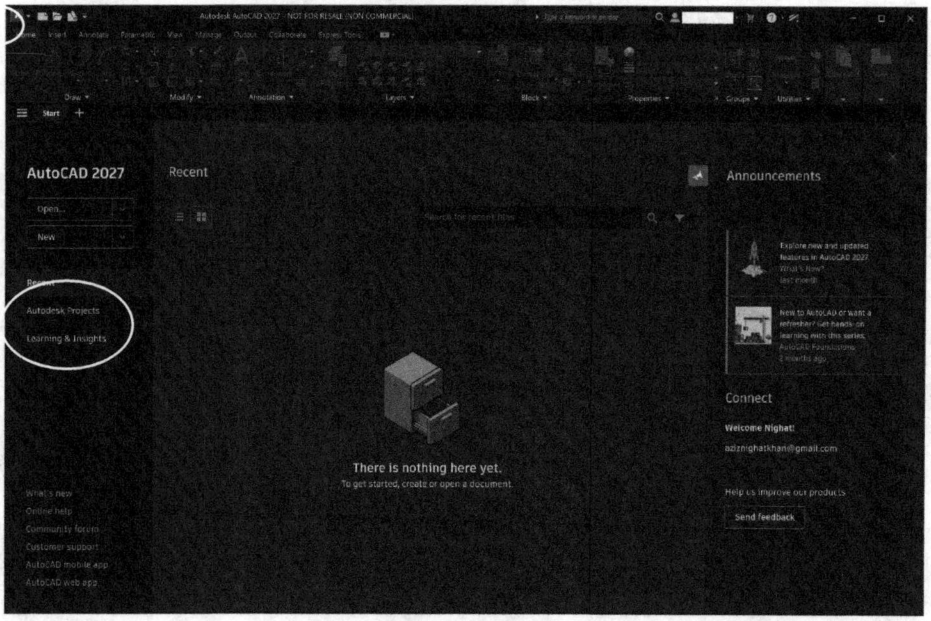

Figure 2-2a

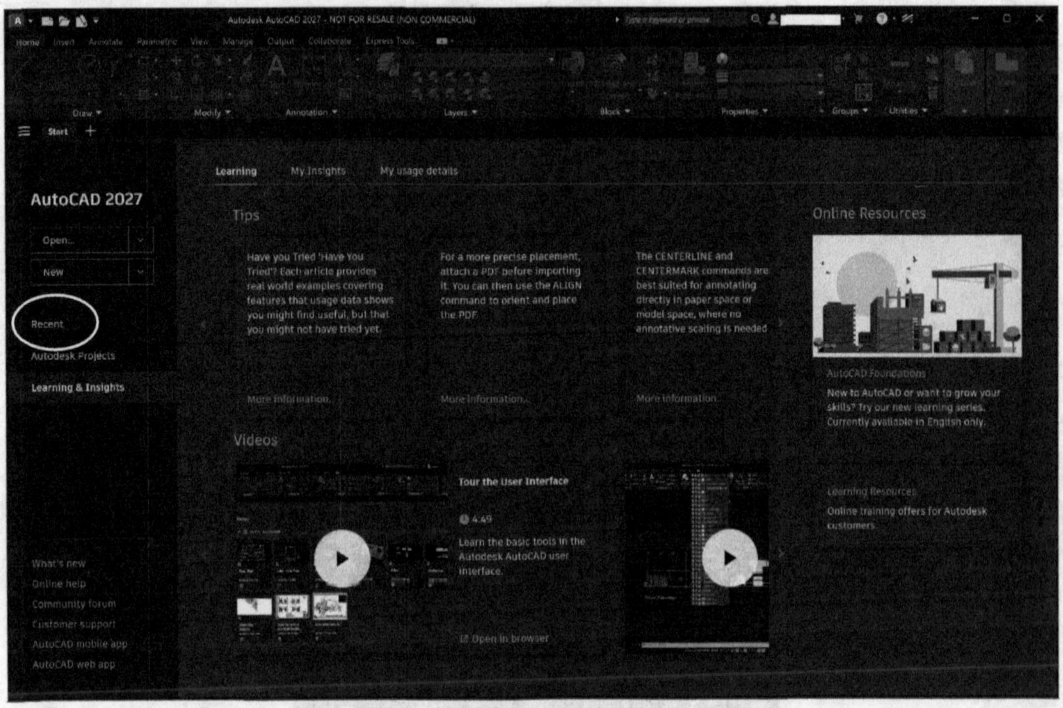

Figure 2-2b

Click the down-arrow on the right side of *A* (the AutoCAD symbol) in the upper left corner of the interface, Figure 2-2a and Figure 2-2c. A dropdown list, Figure 2-2d, will appear on the screen. Click the *New* button, and *Select Template* dialog box will open, Figure 2-2e.

Figure 2-2c

Click the *acad.dwt* option on the *Select Template* dialog box, Figure 2-2e. Now click the *Open* button. This closes the dialog box and opens a new file, Figure 2-3a.

In AutoCAD, commands are executed by pressing the *Enter* key on the keyboard, left button of the mouse, and/or right button of the mouse. Hence, in this text unless otherwise mentioned, the terms *click* or *clicking* mean press the left button of the mouse. In addition, in this text "a → b" means click "a" followed by clicking at "b".

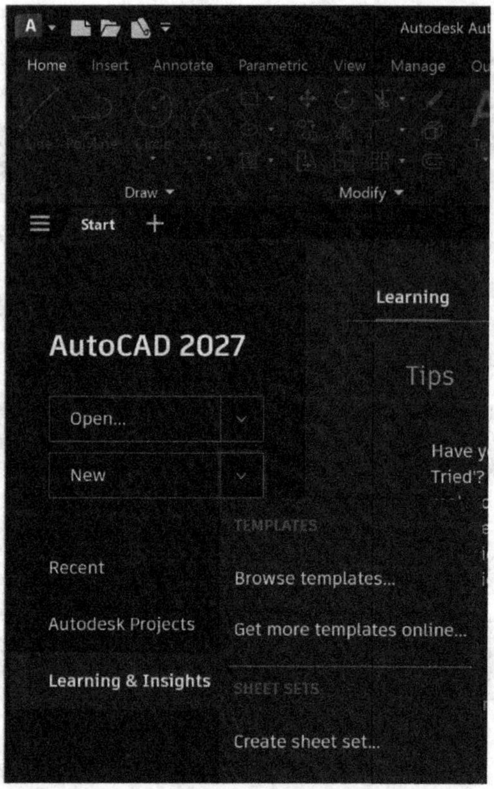

Figure 2-2d

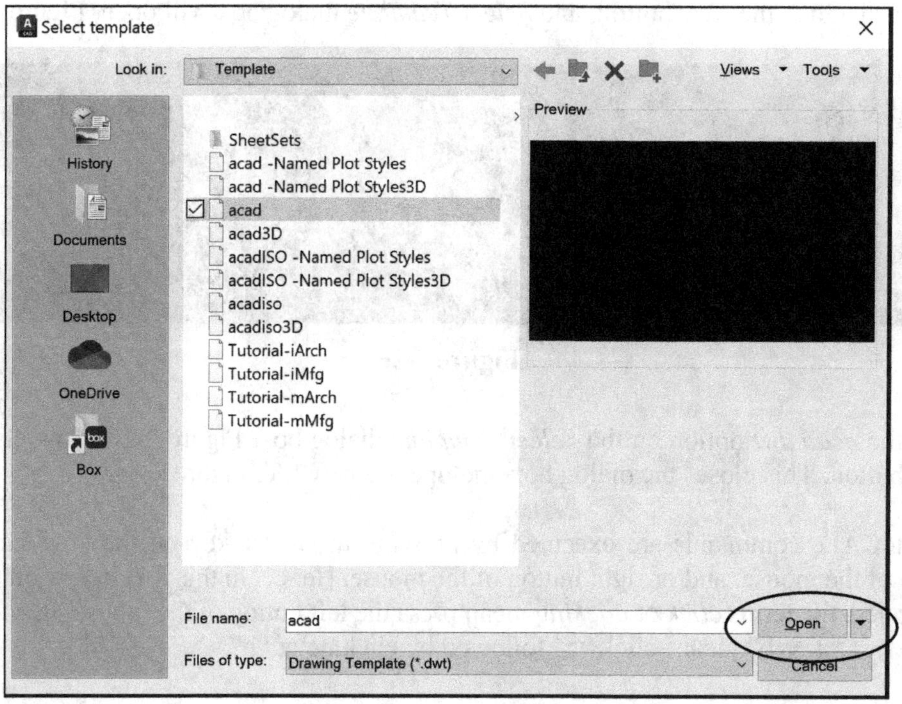

Figure 2-2e

2.3. Focus Of The Book

The focus of this book is to create and edit two-dimensional drawings using *Drafting and Annotation* workspace. For the first time launch, AutoCAD is in the *Drafting & Annotation* interface, Figure 2-3a. However, a user can switch to the other interfaces using the following method.

- Click the small downward arrow on the *Workspace Switching* wheel in the lower right corner of the interface, Figure 2-3a. A small window displaying various options will appear on the screen, Figure 2-3b.
- The user can select one of the three options: *Drafting & Annotation*, *3D Basics*, and *3D Modeling*. A checkmark will appear beside the selected option. Click the desired option and the interface is switched to the selected format. Figure 2-3b shows the selection of *Drafting and Annotation* option.

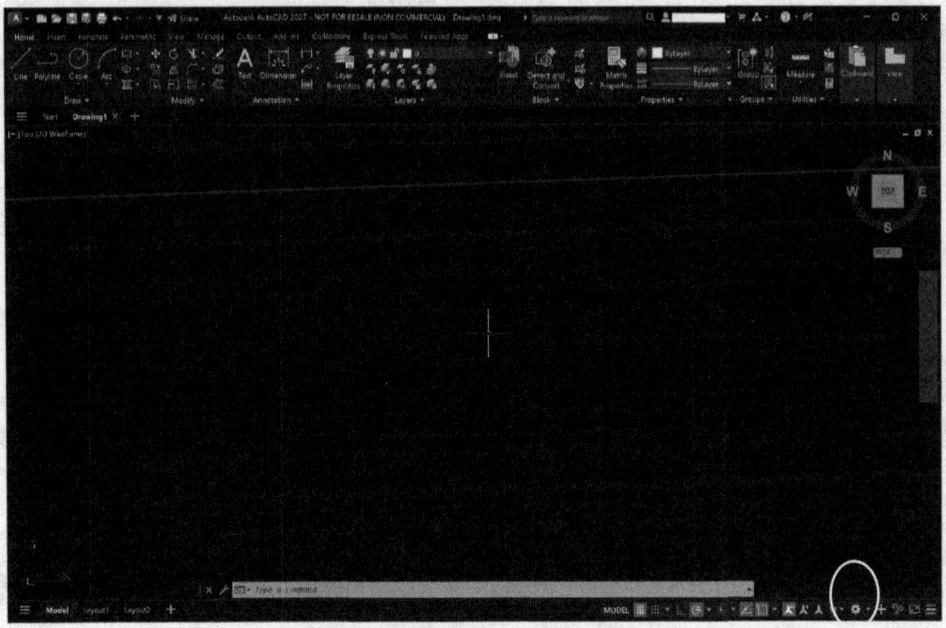

Figure 2-3a

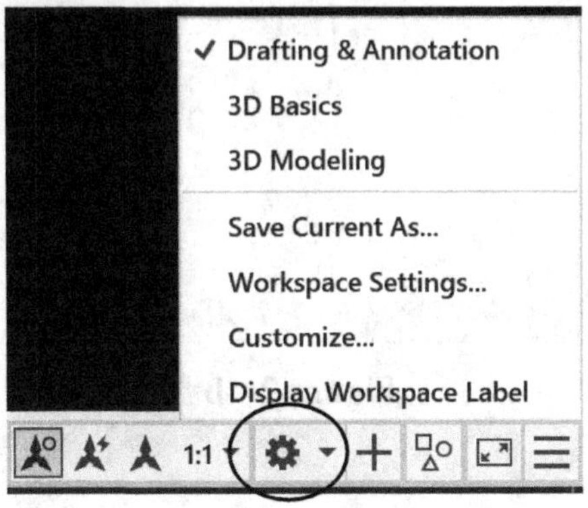

Figure 2-3b

2.4. Initial Setup

For the demonstration purpose, the ribbon color (*top portion of the interface with command buttons*) and the background color of the drawing area (*the big rectangular area*) is changed to a lighter color, Figure 2-4a; and the grid is turned off, Figure 2-4b. The drawing area, color setup, ribbons, and grid will be discussed in Sections 2.5 – 2.21.

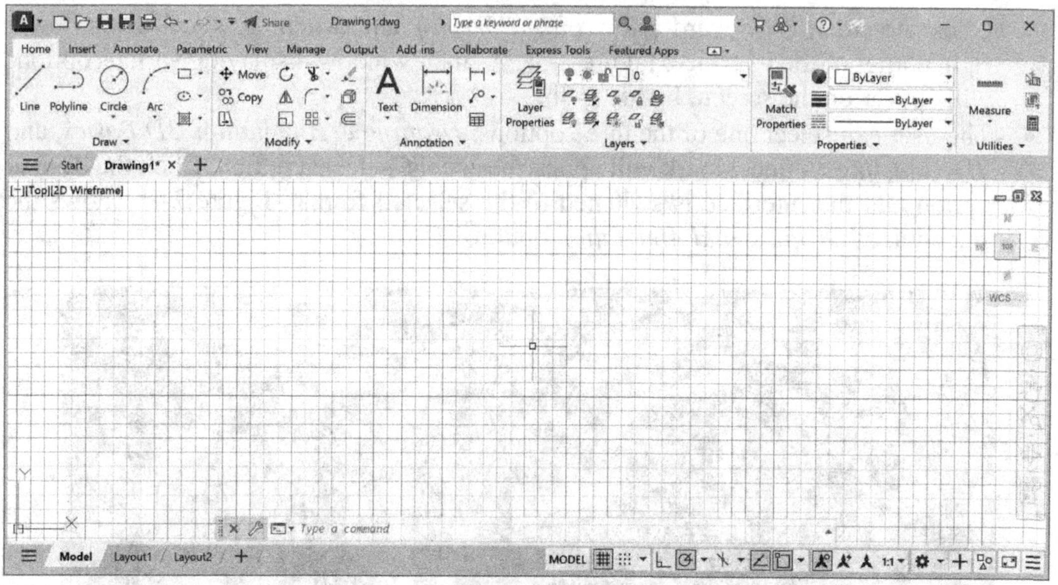

Figure 2-4a

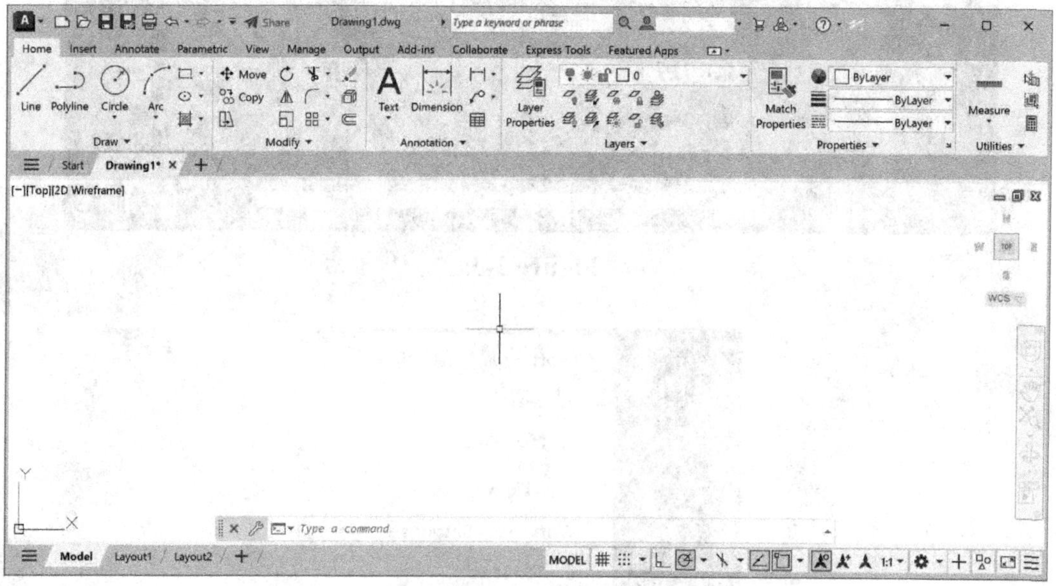

Figure 2-4b

2.5. Typical Window Screen

Technically, the AutoCAD interface is called a workspace. A typical (*Drafting and Annotation Interface*) window screen (Figure 2-5a and Figure 2-5b) displays the drawing area, cursor, World coordinate system, viewcube, navigation bar, drawing display format, scroll bars, command line, status bar, and the ribbon (its tabs and panels), etc. These features are grouped and organized based on the drawing environment and the user requirements.

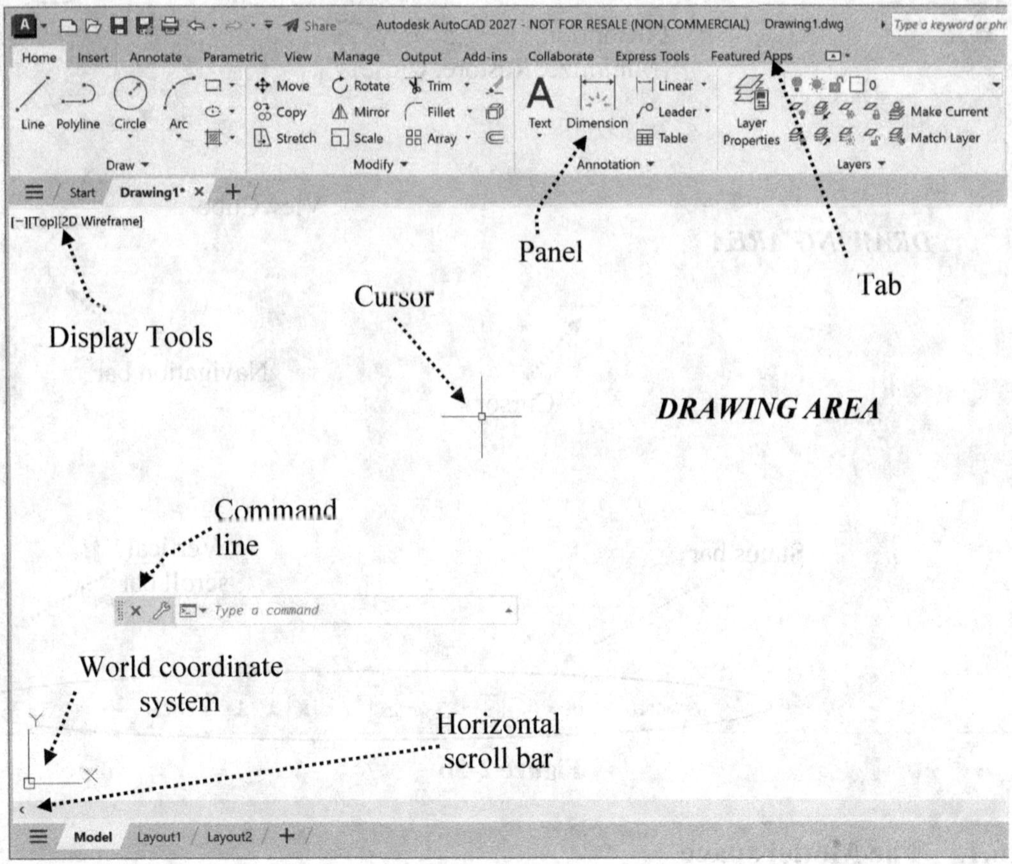

Figure 2-5a

2.6. Drawing Area

The drawing area is the empty blank rectangular area in Figure 2-5a and Figure 2-5b that is used to create a new drawing or modify a previously created drawing. Although the drawing area is unlimited, the size of the drawing window depends on various factors such as the size of the computer screen, AutoCAD's window, and other displayed features.

The drawing area is classified as a Model space and paper space. The user can switch to the Model space or the paper space, Figure 2-5a and Figure 2-6, by selecting the *Model* or *Layout* (*Layout1* or *Layout2*) tabs, respectively, located in the lower left corner of the interface.

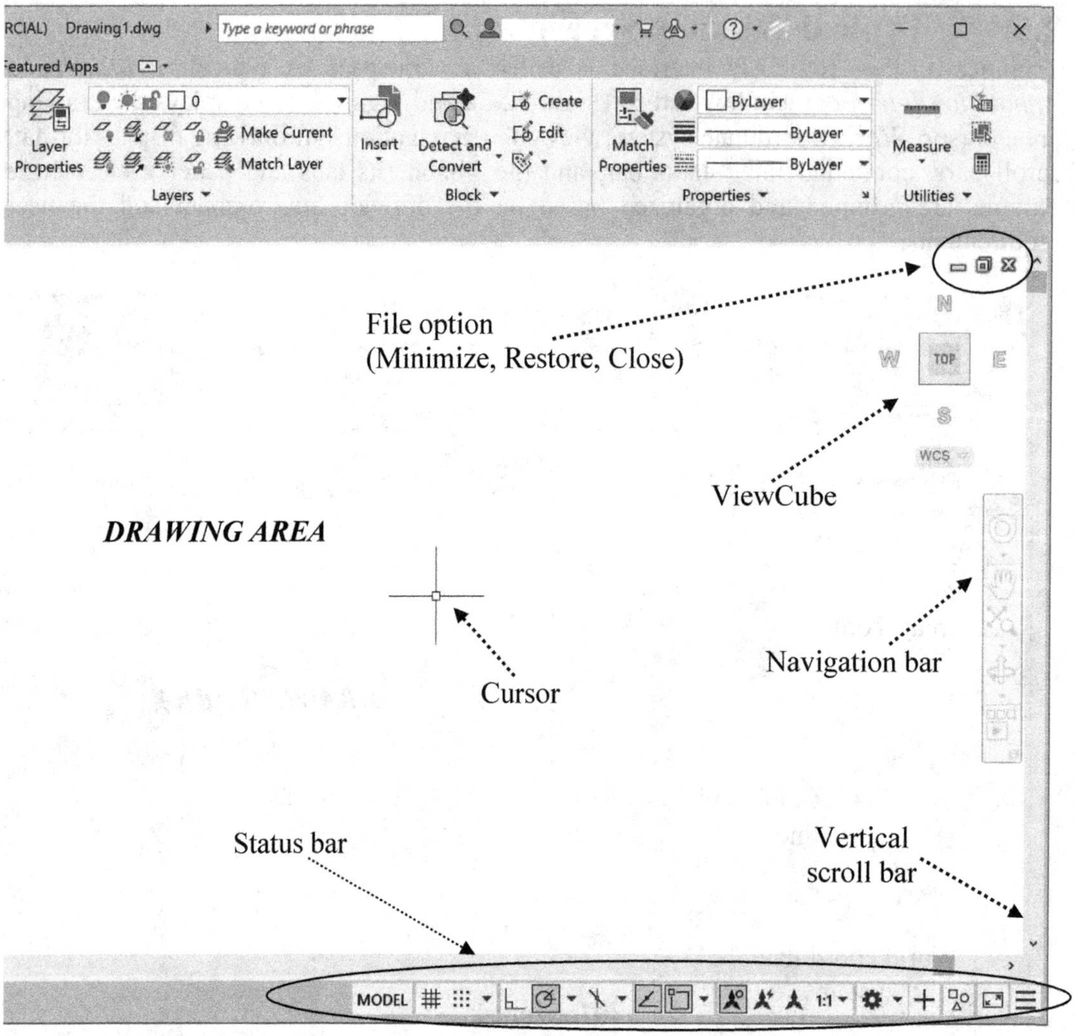

Figure 2-5b

2.6.1. The Model space

Generally, the Model (workspace) space is used to create two- or three-dimensional models. The default color of the Model space can be changed as follows:

- Click with the right button in the *Drawing area* and select the *Options* option, Figure 2-7a or type *Options* on the command line and press the *Enter* key. The *Options* dialog box shown in Figure 2-7b appears on the screen.
- Click the *Display* tab of the *Options* dialog box.
- Press the *Color* button in the *Window Elements* panel to open the *Drawing Window Colors* (Figure 2-7c) dialog box.

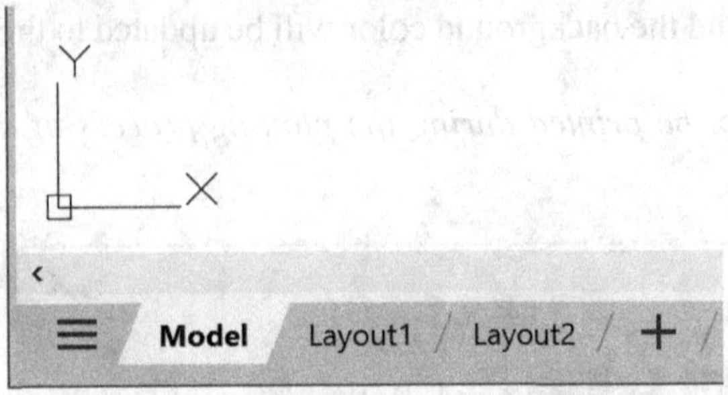

Figure 2-6

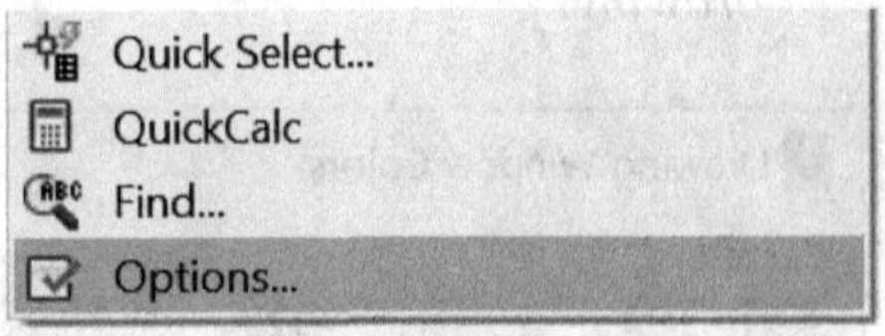

Figure 2-7a

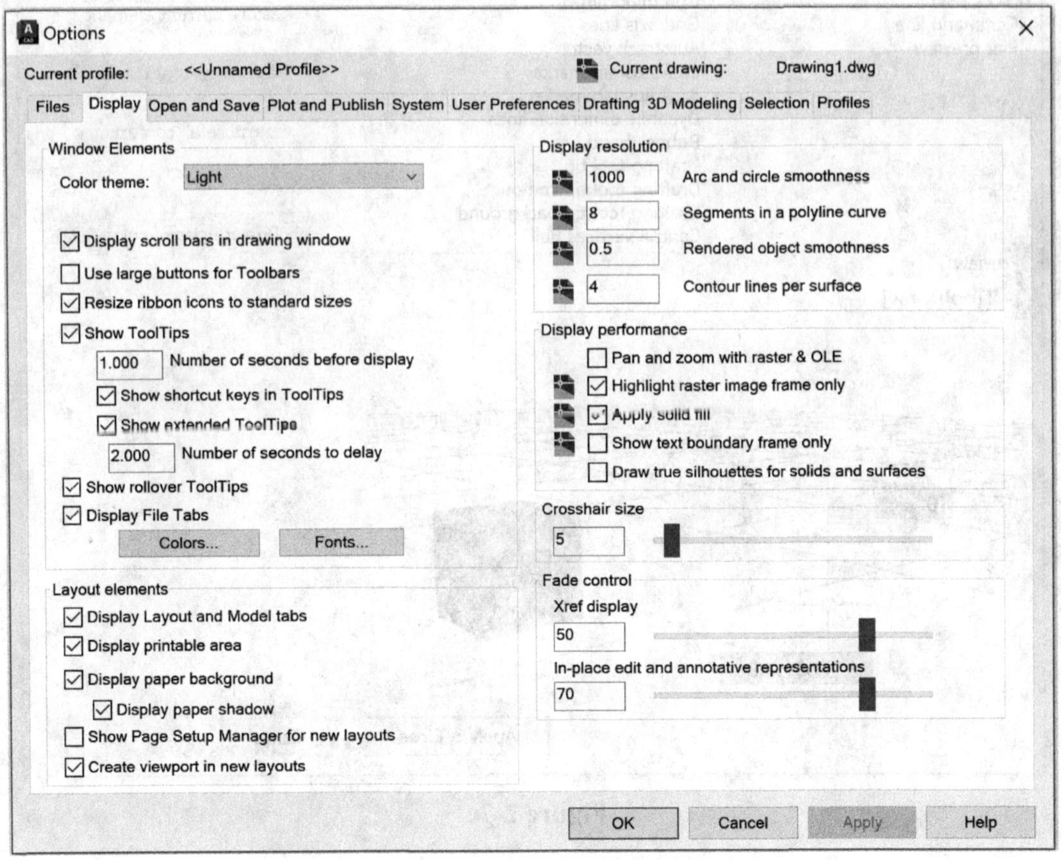

Figure 2-7b

- In the *Drawing Window Colors* dialog box, under the *Context* panel choose *2D Model space*, under the *Interface element* panel choose *Uniform background*, and under the *Color* options panel select the desired color; the selection is highlighted. In the current example, color *White* is chosen; in the *Preview* window, the color of the model changes to the selected color.
- Click the *Apply & Close* button of the *Drawing Window Colors* dialog box.
- Finally, click the *OK* button of the *Options* dialog box.

- Both the dialog boxes will be closed, and the background color will be updated to the selected color.
- *NOTE: The background color will not be printed during the plotting process of a drawing.*

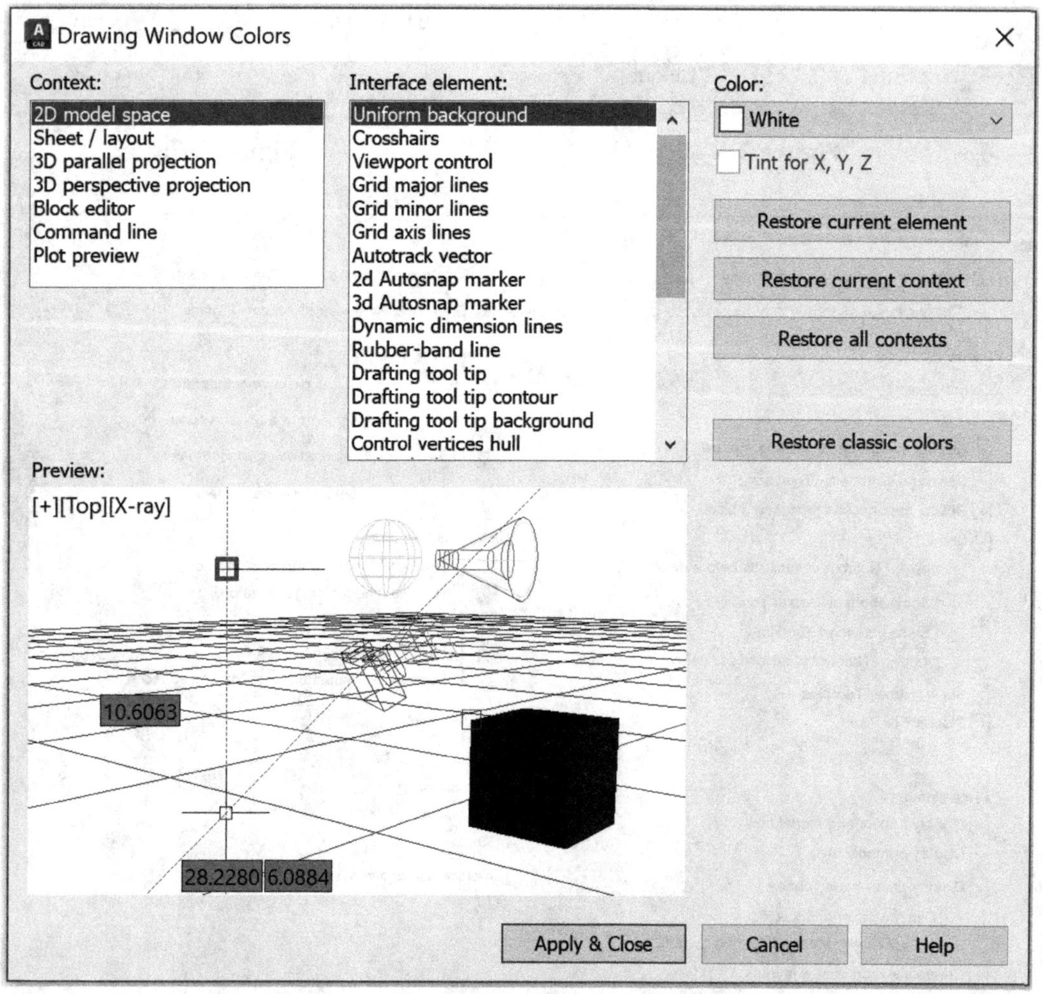

Figure 2-7c

2.6.2. Paper space and layout

The layouts are also known as paper space. By default, AutoCAD creates two layouts, Figure 2-6; however, more layouts can be created for each drawing. When a user clicks on a layout tab, the drawing area appears as shown in Figure 2-8a. Generally, layouts are not used for drafting or design work; the layouts are used for printing or plotting the drawing. The self-explanatory options for a layout are shown in the *Layout elements* of Figure 2-8b (the lower left quarter of Figure 2-7b). Layouts are discussed in detail in *Chapter 8*.

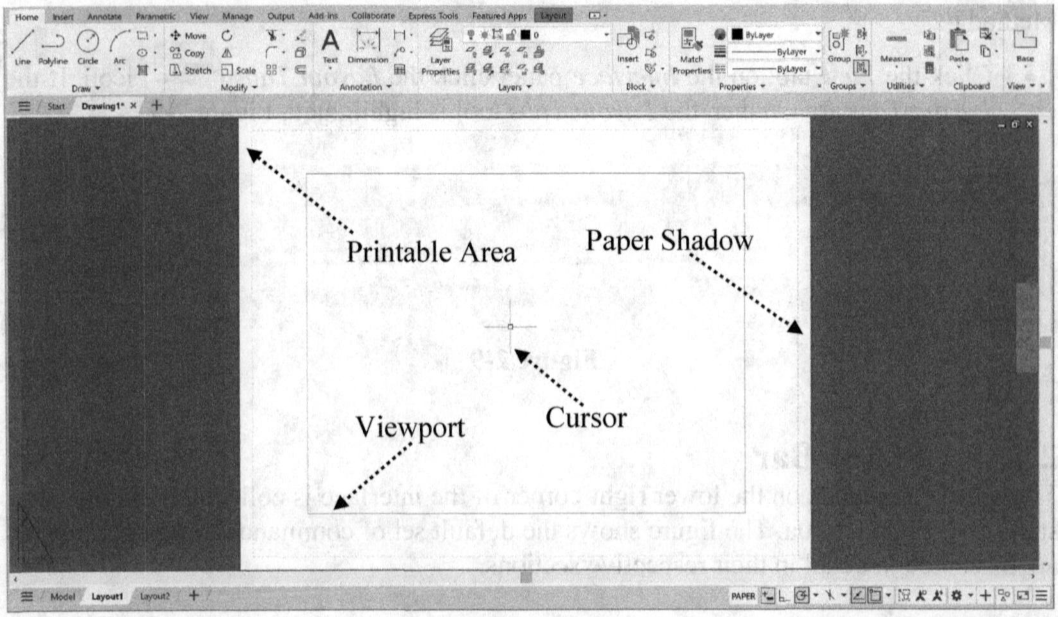

Figure 2-8a

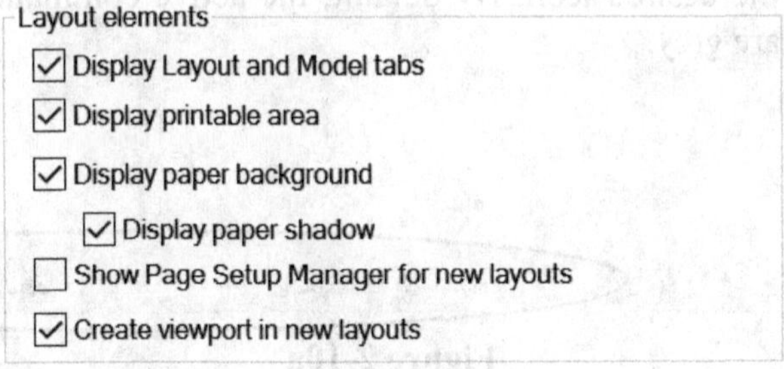

Figure 2-8b

2.6.3. Display/hide model and layout tabs

A user can display/hide the *Model* and *Layout* tabs using one of the following methods.

Method #1

- Click with the right button of the mouse in the *Drawing area* and select the *Options* option or type *Options* on the command line and press the *Enter* key.
- The *Options* dialog box appears on the screen.
- Click the *Display* tab of the *Options* dialog box.
- Check or clear the *Display Layout and Model tabs* box in the *Layout elements* panel, Figure 2-8b, to display or hide the tabs, respectively.
- Click the *Apply* or *OK* button. The *Apply* button does NOT close the *Options* dialog box but hides the tabs and the *OK* button closes the *Options* dialog box and hides the tabs.

Method #2

- Click the *View* tab; on the *Interface* panel click the *Layout Tabs* () icon. If the *Layout Tabs* are *On* then the *Layout Tabs* tool is highlighted, Figure 2-9.

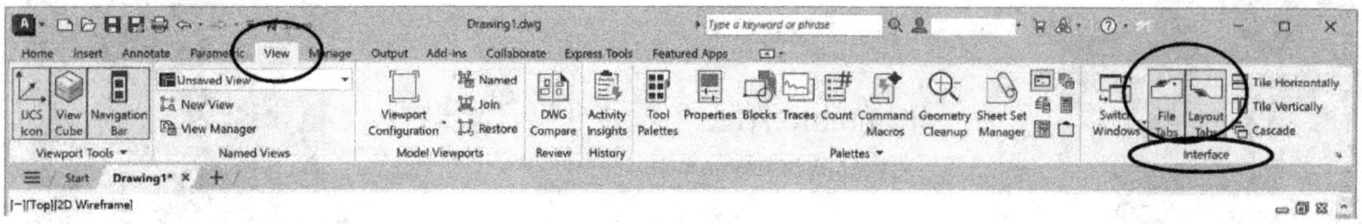

Figure 2-9

2.7. Status Bar

The set of commands on the lower right corner of the interface is collectively known as a status bar, Figure 2-10a. The figure shows the default set of commands. These commands are discussed in detail in their respective sections.

A user can activate commands from the status bar during the execution of the other commands (drawing, editing, etc.). A user can activate/deactivate the status bar commands by simply clicking the desired icon. By default, the active commands are blue, and the inactive commands are grey.

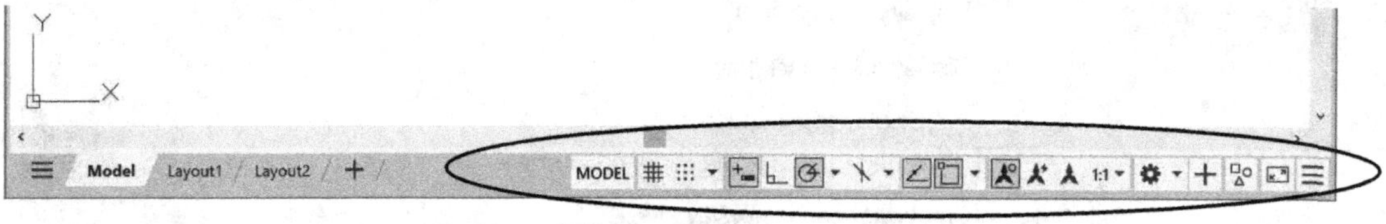

Figure 2-10a

A user can add more commands or remove the existing commands using the customization button () at the lower right corner of the interface as follows.

- Click the customization button, Figure 2-10a and Figure 2-10b.
- A list of commands appears as shown in Figure 2-10b.
- A check mark on the left side of a command indicates that the command is available on the status bar.
- To add/remove a command from the status bar, click on the command's name.
- To exit customization mode, click in the drawing area. This hides the commands list, and the customization mode is turned off.

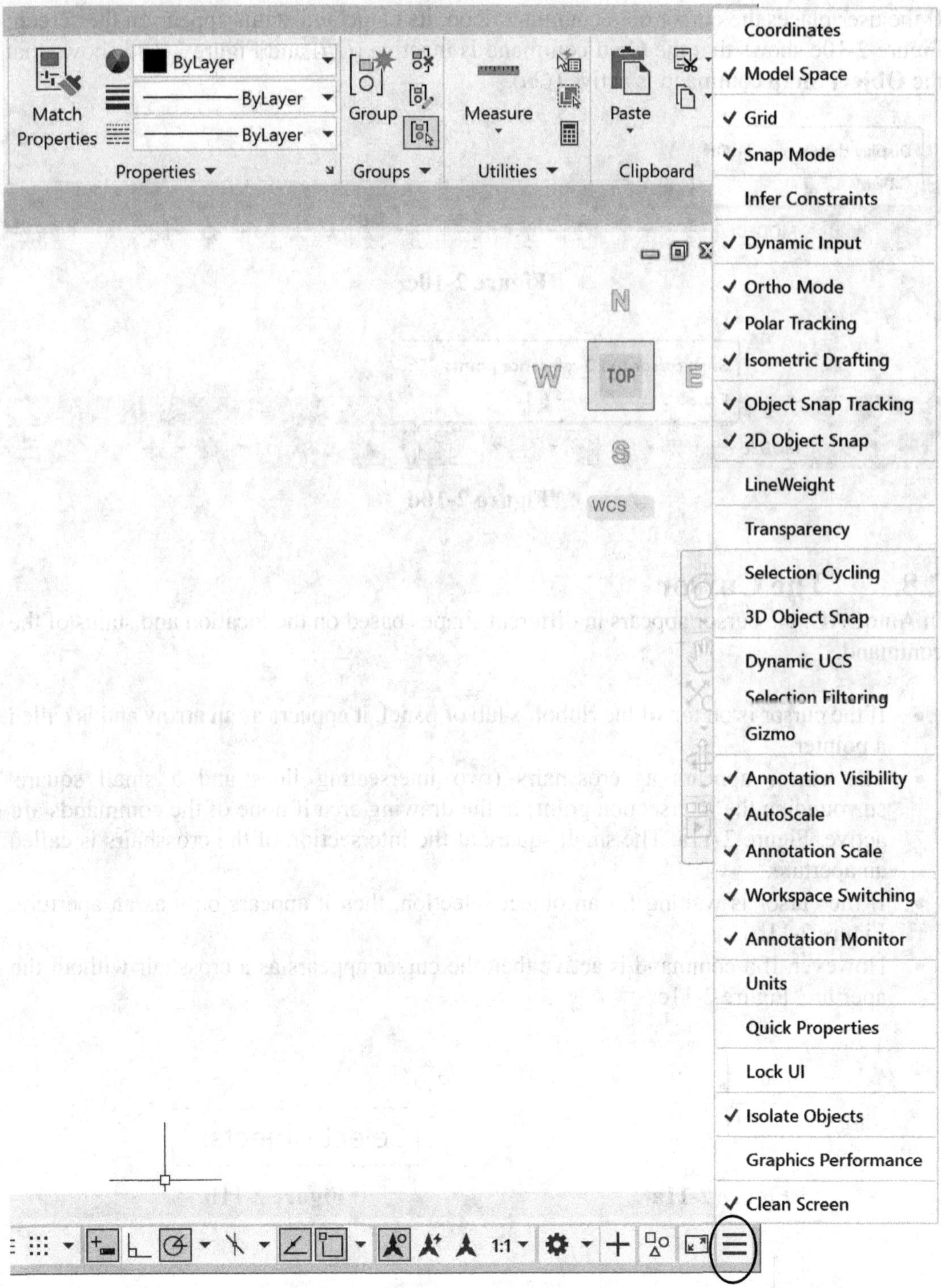

Match Properties
ByLayer
ByLayer
ByLayer
Properties
Group
Groups
Measure
Utilities
Paste
Clipboard
N
W
TOP
E
S
WCS
Coordinates
✓ Model Space
✓ Grid
✓ Snap Mode
Infer Constraints
✓ Dynamic Input
✓ Ortho Mode
✓ Polar Tracking
✓ Isometric Drafting
✓ Object Snap Tracking
✓ 2D Object Snap
LineWeight
Transparency
Selection Cycling
3D Object Snap
Dynamic UCS
Selection Filtering
Gizmo
✓ Annotation Visibility
✓ AutoScale
✓ Annotation Scale
✓ Workspace Switching
✓ Annotation Monitor
Units
Quick Properties
Lock UI
✓ Isolate Objects
Graphics Performance
✓ Clean Screen
1:1

Figure 2-10b

If the user places the cursor on a command icon, its name and status appear on the screen; Figure 2-10c shows that the **Grid** command is inactive (*Off*) and Figure 2-10d shows that the **Object Snap** command is active (*On*).

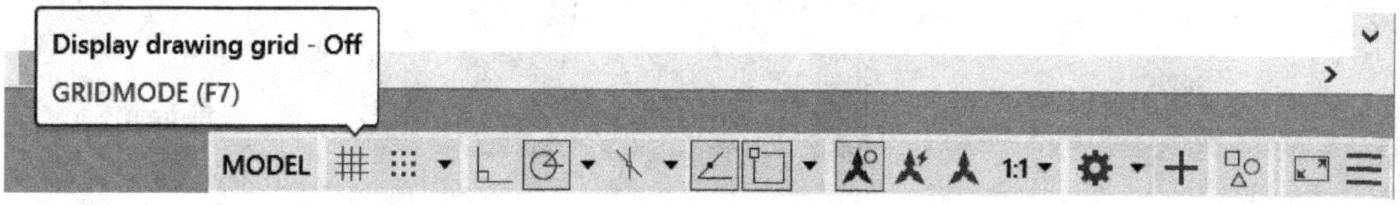

Figure 2-10c

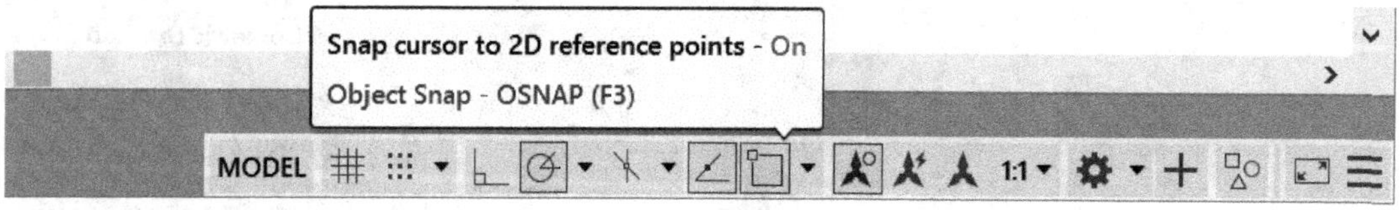

Figure 2-10d

2.8. The Cursor

In AutoCAD, the cursor appears in different shapes based on the location and status of the command.

- If the cursor is on top of the ribbon's tab or panel, it appears as an arrow and is called a pointer.
- The cursor appears as crosshairs (two intersecting lines and a small square surrounding the intersection point) in the drawing area if none of the commands are active, Figure 2-11a. The small square at the intersection of the crosshairs is called an aperture.
- If the cursor is waiting for an object selection, then it appears only as an aperture, Figure 2-11b.
- However, if a command is active then the cursor appears as a crosshair without the aperture, Figure 2-11c.

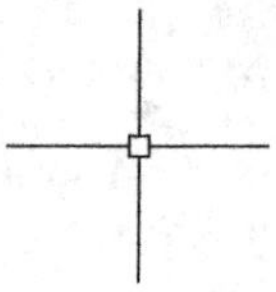

Figure 2-11a

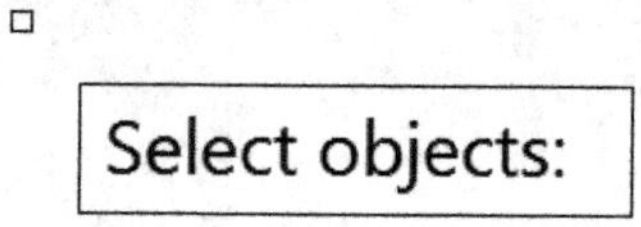

Figure 2-11b

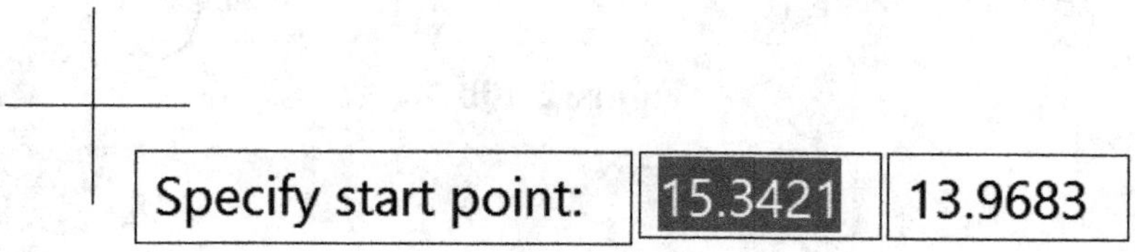

Figure 2-11c

2.8.1. Location of the cursor

As the cursor moves in the drawing area its position coordinates (x, y, z) change; for two-dimensional drawing, the z-coordinate is always zero. By default, the position of the cursor (that is, the coordinates) is not displayed on the workspace. However, it is good drawing practice to display the coordinates of the cursor's location in the drawing area. The user can display the coordinates as follows.

- Click the *Customization* button; it is located on the lower right corner of the workspace, Figure 2-10b.
- A selection list will appear on the screen; Figure 2-10b shows the list.
- Select the *Coordinates* option; it is at the top of the list.
- This will close the list, and the coordinates of the cursor will appear on the status bar, Figure 2-12. In the figure, note that the z-coordinate is zero.

Figure 2-12

2.8.2. Size of the intersecting lines

The size of the intersecting lines of the cursor's crosshairs can be changed from the *Options* dialog box as follows.

- Click with the right button of the mouse in the *Drawing area* and select the *Options* option or type *Options* on the command line and press the *Enter* key.
- The *Options* dialog box will appear on the screen.
- Click the *Display* tab of the *Options* dialog box.
- Change the size of the intersecting lines using one of the following methods:
  1. Move the slider of the *Crosshair size* to the right or left (to increase or decrease), Figure 2-13. The slider is in the lower right quarter of the dialog box.
  2. Enter the desired value (1 - 100) in the small box; this value represents the size of the crosshairs as a percentage of the drawing screen.
- Press the *Apply* or *OK* button or press the *Enter* key. The *Apply* button makes the change permanent and the dialog box remains open. The *OK* button or the *Enter* key makes the changes permanent and closes the dialog box, too.
- The size of the crosshair does not influence the accuracy of the drawing. However, it is not a good practice to keep the crosshair's size larger than 10.

Figure 2-13

2.8.3. Size of the aperture

The size of the aperture of the crosshairs of the cursor can be changed from the *Options* dialog box as follows.

- Click with the right button of the mouse in the *Drawing area* and select the *Options* option or type *Options* on the command line and press the *Enter* key.
- The *Options* dialog box will appear on the screen.
- Click the *Drafting* tab of the *Options* dialog box.
- To increase the size of the aperture, move the slider of the *Aperture Size* to the right, Figure 2-14. The slider is in the right side of the dialog box.
- The aperture size does not influence the accuracy of the drawing. However, it is not a good practice to keep the aperture's size too large or too small.
- Press the *Apply* or *OK* button or press the *Enter* key. The *Apply* button will make the change permanent and the dialog box will remain open. The *OK* button and the *Enter* key will make the change permanent and will close the dialog box simultaneously.

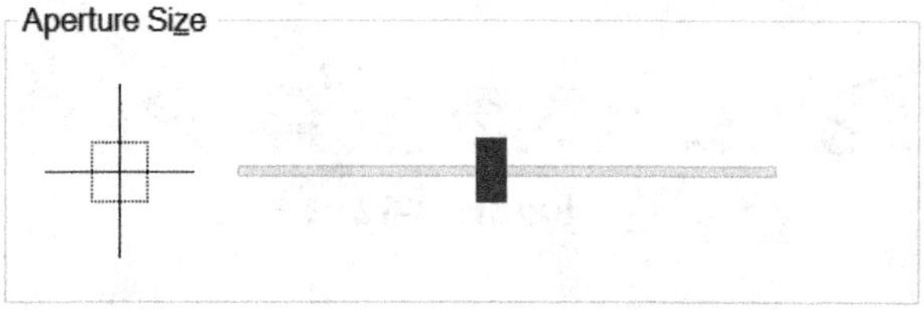

Figure 2-14

2.8.4. Color of the cursor

The color of the crosshairs of the cursor in Model space or layout can be changed from the *Options* dialog box as follows.

- Click with the right button of the mouse in the *Drawing area* and select the *Options* option or type *Options* on the command line and press the *Enter* key.
- The *Options* dialog box will appear on the screen.
- Click the *Display* tab of the *Options* dialog box.
- Press the *Color* button in the *Window Elements* panel to open the *Drawing Window Colors* dialog box, Figure 2-15.
- In the *Drawing Window Colors* dialog box, under the *Context* choose *2D Model space*, under the *Interface element* choose *Crosshairs*, and under the *Color* option choose the desired color. The selection will be highlighted. In the current example, the *Magenta* color is selected. In the *Preview* window, the color of the cursor will change to the selected color.
- Finally, click the *Apply & Close* button to close the dialog box.
- In the 2D Model space, the color of the cursor will change to the selected color.

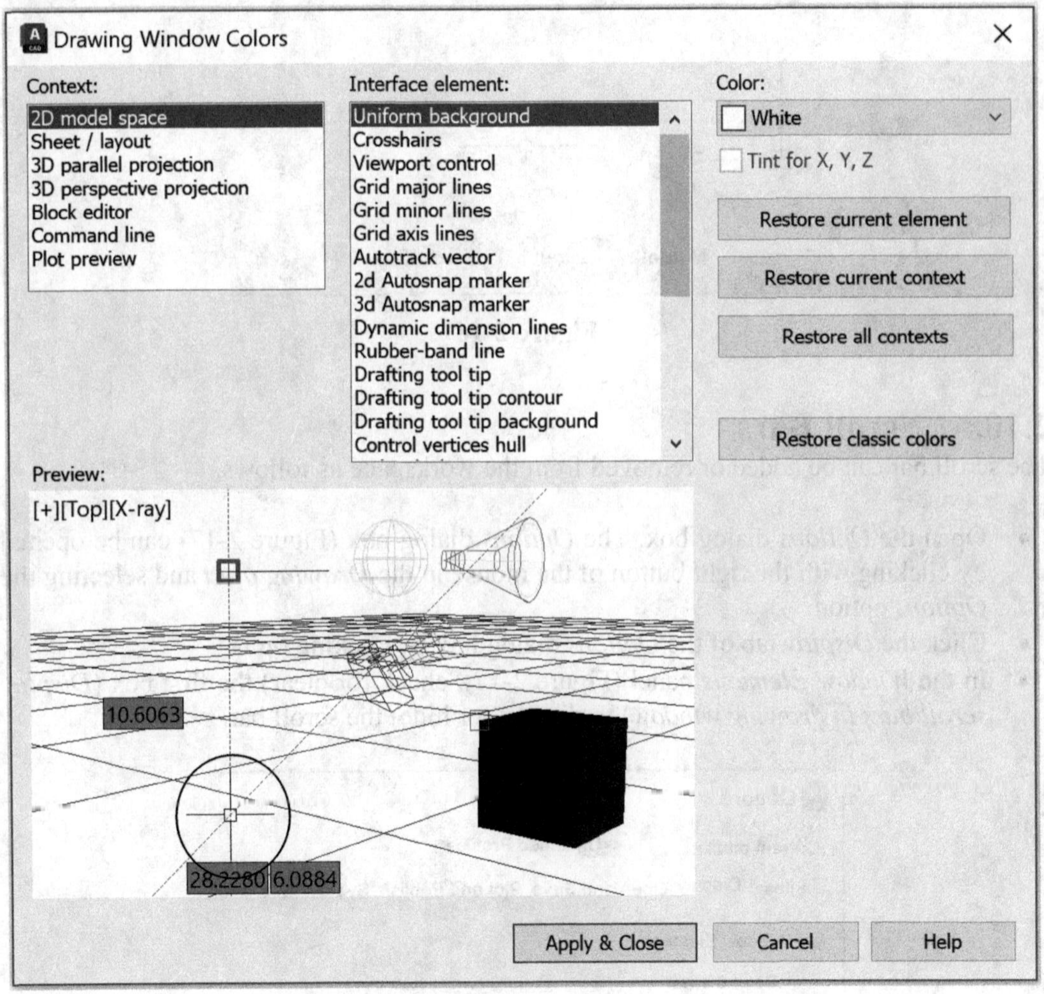

Figure 2-15

2.9. World Coordinate System (WCS)

In AutoCAD, there are two types of coordinate systems. (i) A fixed Cartesian system named the *World Coordinate System* (WCS), Figure 2-16; the WCS is used as the base for defining the drawing object. (ii) A movable Cartesian coordinate system called the *User Coordinate System* (UCS); a UCS is defined relative to the WCS.

In both the WCS and UCS, the Z-axis is always perpendicular to the XY-plane. In the default setting for 2D drawings, the WCS's X-axis is horizontal, the Y-axis is vertical, and the origin is located at the intersection of the X- and Y-axis (Figures 2-16). **Note the box at the origin; this box indicates that the coordinate system is WCS.**

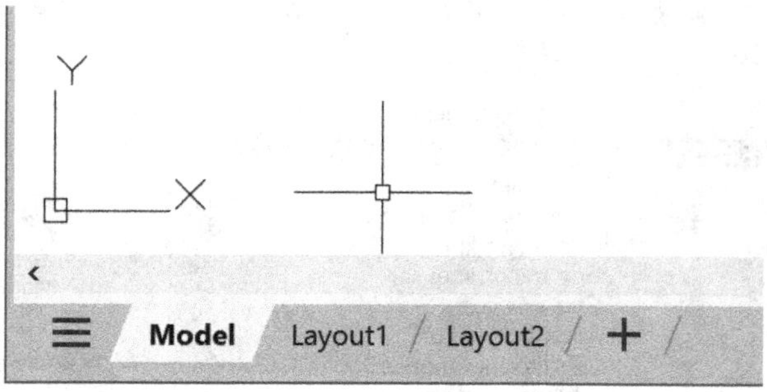

Figure 2-16

2.10. Scroll Bars

The scroll bar can be added or removed from the workspace as follows.

- Open the *Options* dialog box. The *Options* dialog box (Figure 2-17) can be opened by clicking with the right button of the mouse in the *Drawing area* and selecting the *Options* option.
- Click the *Display* tab of the *Options* dialog box by clicking on it.
- In the *Window Elements* panel (Figure 2-17), check (or clear) the first box (*Display scroll bars in drawing window*) to display (or hide) the scroll bar.

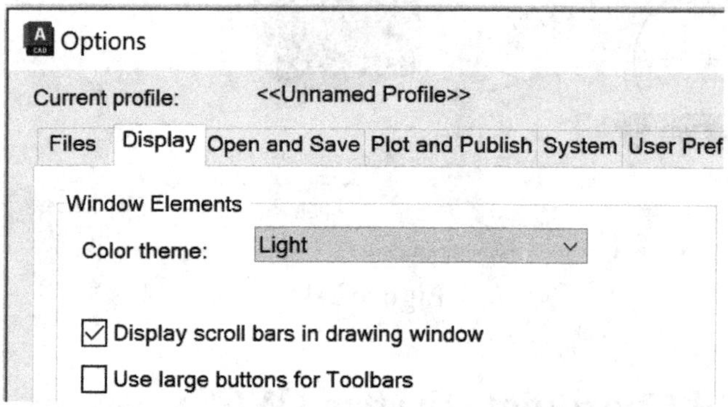

Figure 2-17

2.11. ViewCube 

The *ViewCube* is a navigational tool. It is displayed in 2D or 3D visual style, both in Model space and layouts. By default, the tool is on, inactive, and semi-transparent. The *ViewCube* tool contains a coordinate system (WCS) and a compass (NSWE), Figure 2-18a. By default, it is in the upper right corner of the drawing area. In 2D Model space, the default view is the top view as shown in Figure 2-18a. A sample cube with its sides labeled is shown in Figure 2-18b.

The *ViewCube* can be turned *On*/*Off* by using one of the following methods:

1. Panel method: From the *View* tab and *Viewport Tools* panel click the *ViewCube* tool. If the tool was *off* then it turns *on* or vice versa.
2. Command line method: Type "navvcube", "Navvcube", or "NAVVCUBE" in the command line and press the *Enter* key; and the option list shown in Figure 2-18c appears. Click the desired option.

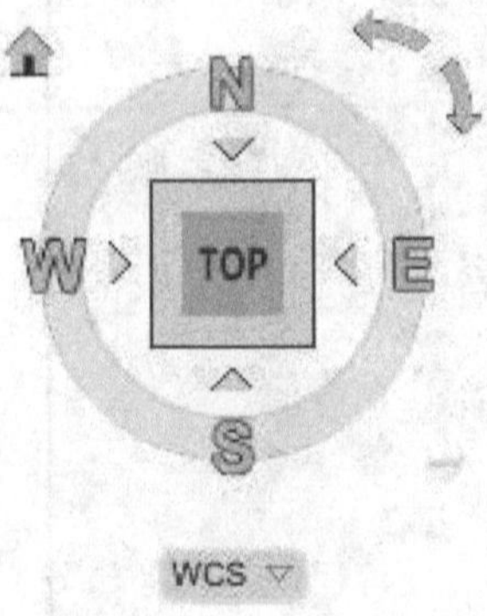

Figure 2-18a

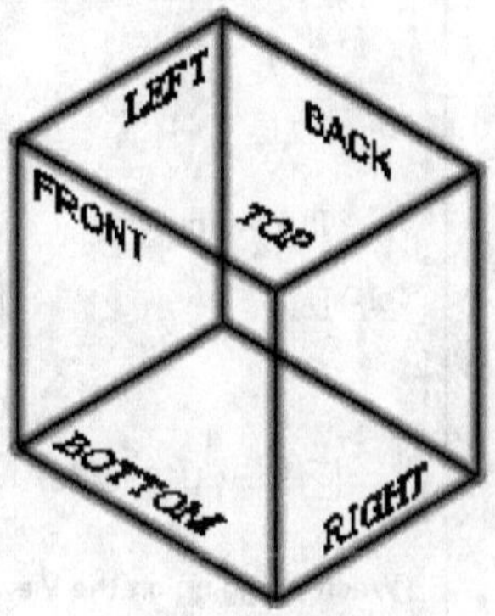

Figure 2-18b

2.11.1. ViewCube settings

The various features of the ViewCube can be changed from the *ViewCube Settings* dialog box. The self-explanatory dialog box is shown in Figure 2-18c. The dialog box can be opened using one of the two methods.

- Type "navvcube", "Navvcube", or "NAVVCUBE" in the command line and press the *Enter* key. The option list shown in Figure 2-18c appears. Click on the *Settings* option.
- (i) Bring the cursor on the NESW circle of the *ViewCube*, (ii) press the right button of the mouse, and (iii) select the *ViewCube Settings* option, Figure 2-18d.

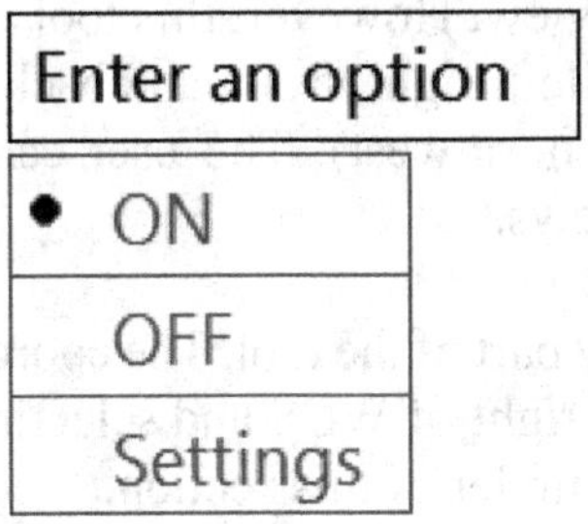

Figure 2-18c

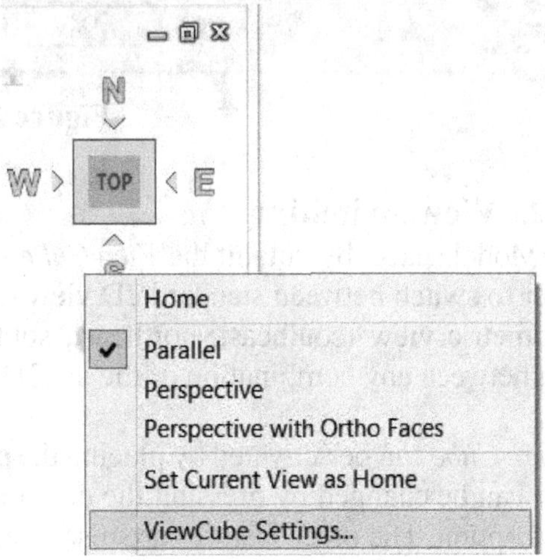

Figure 2-18d

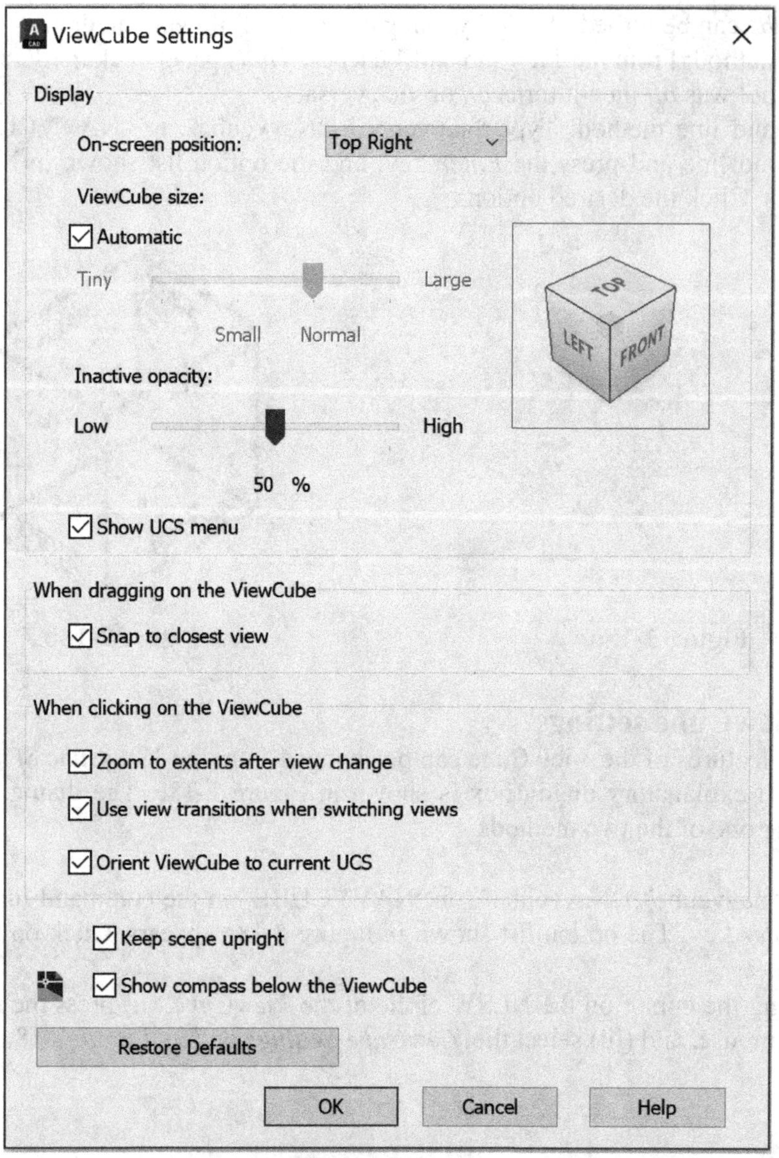

Figure 2-18e

2.11.2. View switching

In 2D Model space, by default the *ViewCube* is in the top view. However, this tool allows the user to switch between standard 2D view (top, bottom, left, right, front, and back), and 3D isometric view (southeast, northeast, southwest, and northwest). The user can also switch between any combination of the six 2D standard views.

The *ViewCube* can be activated by placing the cursor on any part of the tool. The coordinate system can be changed by pressing the down-arrow to the right of WCS and selecting the desired option. The other features are discussed in the remainder of this section.

The user can switch from one view to the other as follows.

- Click on a quadrant of the compass (W is selected in Figure 2-19a) or a face of the square and the view changes to the corresponding standard view, Figure 2-19b.
- Click an edge of the square (Figure 2-19c) and the view changes to the corresponding standard view, Figure 2-16d.

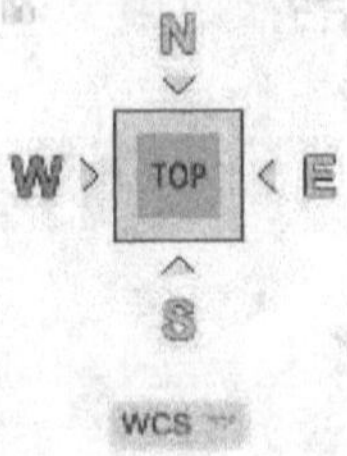

Figure 2-19a

Figure 2-19b

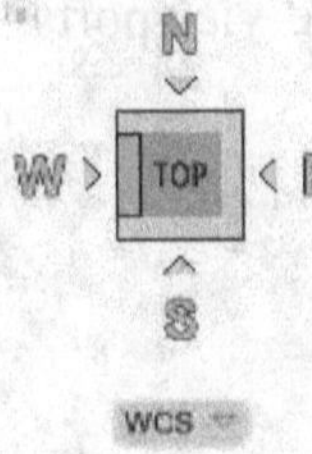

Figure 2-19c

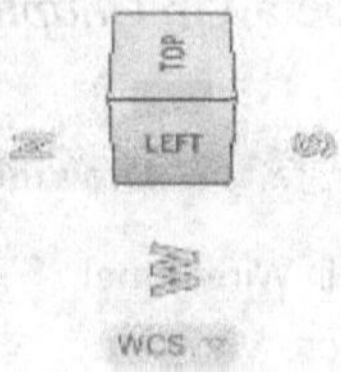

Figure 2-19d

- Click a corner of the square (Figure 2-19e) and the view changes to the corresponding 3D view, Figure 2-19f.

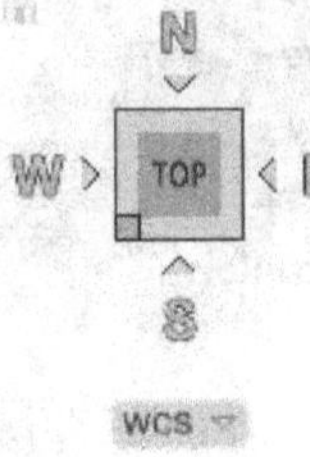

Figure 2-19e

Figure 2-19f

2.12. Drawing Display Format

The three tools (*[-] [Top] [2D Wireframe]*) in the upper left corner of the drawing area represent the drawing display format, Figure 2-20a: *[-]* represents viewport control, *[Top]* represents view control, and *[2D Wireframe]* represents the visual style control. Click on the desired tool to explore the available options. This section briefly discusses the display tools.

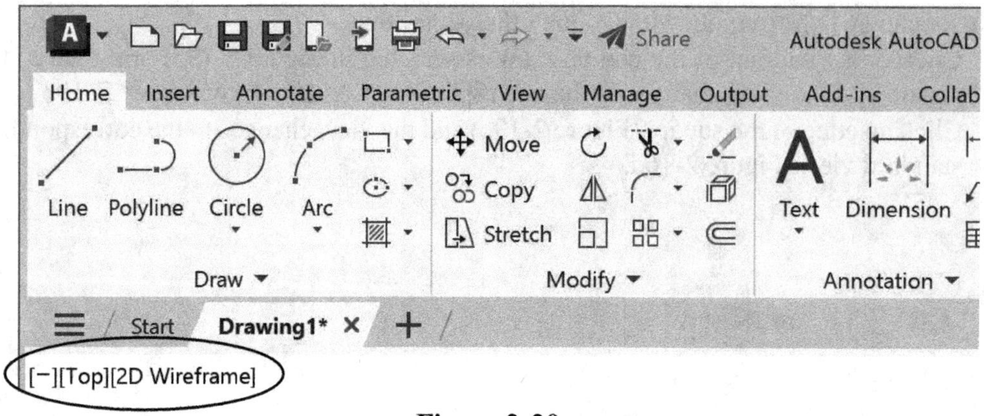

Figure 2-20a

- Viewport control: The *Viewport control* allows the user to manipulate the viewports in Model space and layouts, Figure 2-20b. The user can use single (the default option) or multiple viewports; and how to arrange multiple viewports. The viewports are discussed in detail in *Chapter 8*.

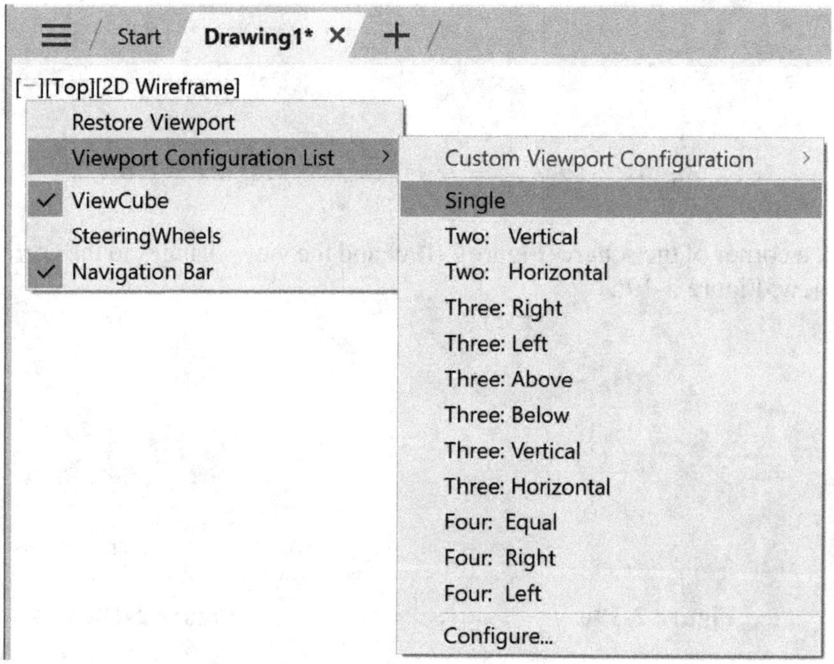

Figure 2-20b

- View control: The *View control* allows the user to switch between standard 2D view (top, bottom, left, right, front, and back), and 3D isometric view SW, SE, NE, and NW, Figure 2-20c. In this figure, N, S, E, and W represent north, south, east, and west, respectively. Generally, the 2D drawings are looked at from the top and other styles are used to display the 3D models.

- Visual style control: The *Visual style control* allows the user to switch between various visual styles, Figure 2-20d. Generally, the 2D drawings are in *2D Wireframe* style and the other styles are used to display the 3D models.

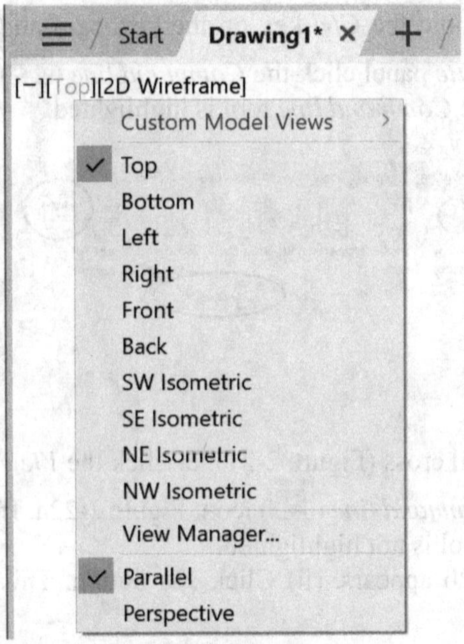

Figure 2-20c

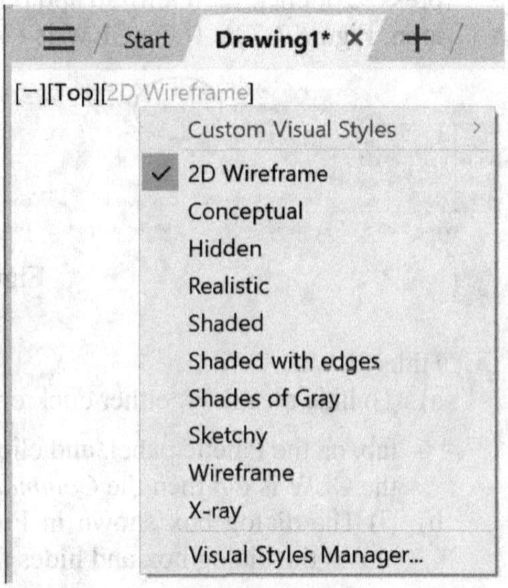

Figure 2-20d

2.13. Command Line Window

The command line window (CLW) is a text area reserved for the prompts, keyboard input, and error messages, Figure 2-21. By default, the CLW is *On*, located at the bottom of AutoCAD's window.

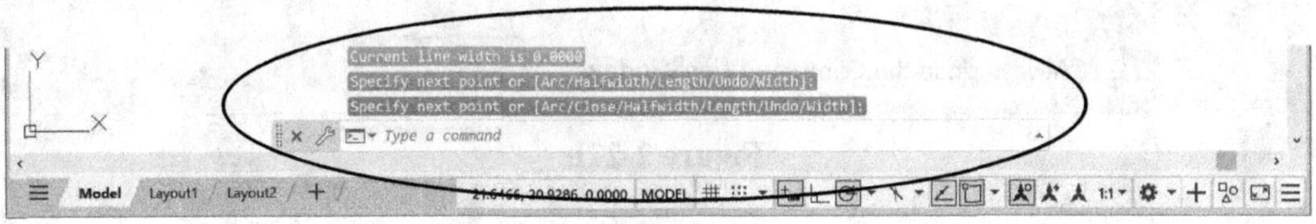

Figure 2-21

2.13.1. Move the CLW

The user can move the command line window on the interface.

- Bring the cursor on the left gray end of the CLW, Figure 2-21.
- Press the left button of the mouse.
- Keep pressing the left button and move the cursor.
- The CLW will appear as a light gray box.
- Keep holding down the left button and move the cursor to the new location.
- Release the left button and CLW moves to the new location.

2.13.2. Display/hide the CLW

By default, the CLW is displayed on the interface. However, the user can display the CLW on the interface or hide from the interface.

- Display CLW: To display the CLW, either hold the *Ctrl* key on the keyboard and press 9; or click the *View* tab and on the *Palette* panel click the *Command line* () icon, Figure 2-22a. If the CLW is *On* then the *Command line* tool is highlighted.

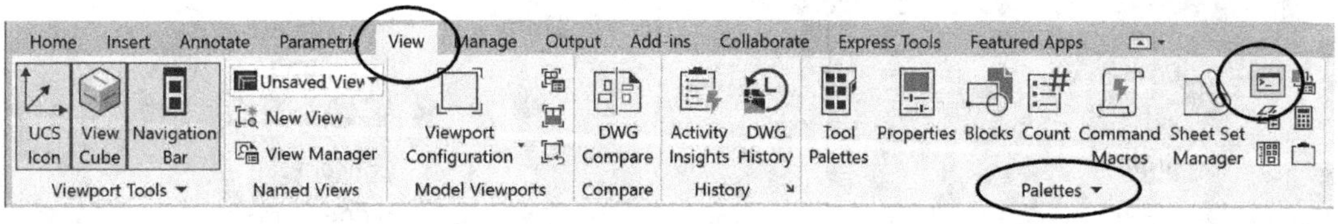

Figure 2-22a

- Hide CLW:
  a) To hide the CLW, either click on the small cross (Figure 2-21); or click the *View* tab, on the Palette panel, and click the *Command line* () icon, Figure 2-22a. If the CLW is *Off* then the *Command line* tool is not highlighted.
  b) (i) The dialog box shown in Figure 2-22b appears. (ii) Click *Yes* button. This closes the dialog box and hides the CLW.

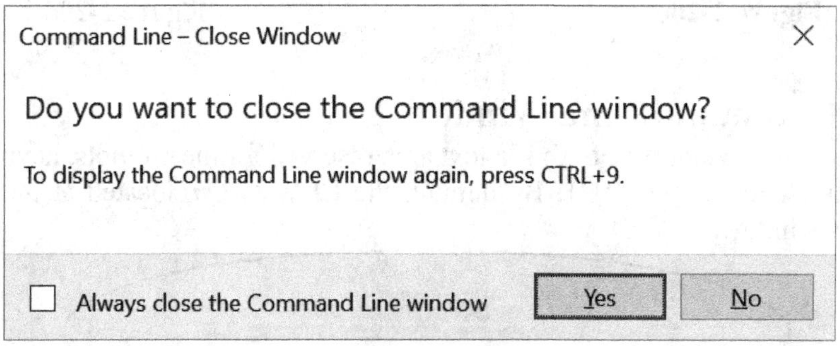

Figure 2-22b

2.13.3. Resize the CLW

By default, only one command can be written in the CLW, and three commands are displayed above the CLW, Figure 2-23a. However, the user can resize the CLW as follows.

- Bring the cursor on the top edge of the CLW and a double-headed arrow appears.
- Press and hold the left button of the mouse and move the cursor. The CLW expands as the cursor moves upward or contracts as the cursor moves downward. In the current example, the cursor is moved upward, Figure 2-23b.
- Release the left button of the mouse to resize the CLW.
- Similarly, the width can be increased or decreased. In the current example, the width is reduced, Figure 2-23b.

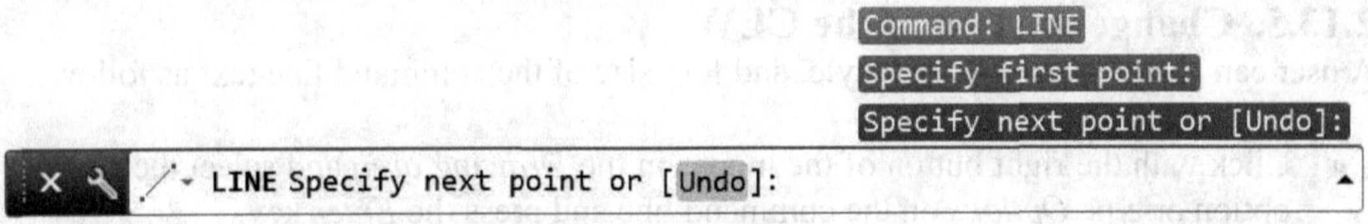

Figure 2-23a

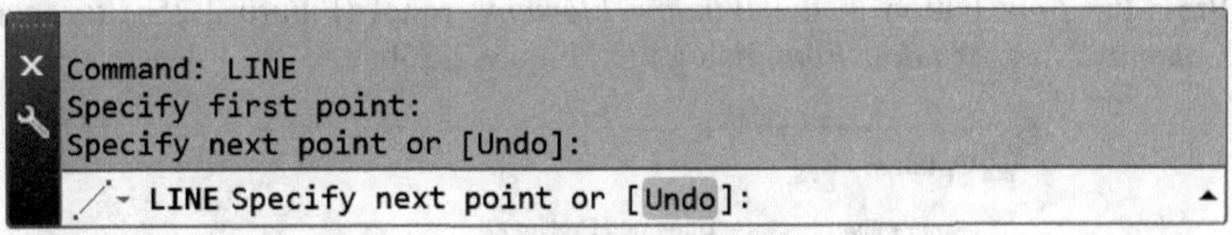

Figure 2-23b

2.13.4. Change the color of the CLW

A user can change the background and the text color of the command line window as follows.

- Click with the right button of the mouse in the *Drawing area* and select the *Options* option or type *Options* on the command line and press the *Enter* key.
- The *Options* dialog box appears on the screen.
- Click the *Display* tab of the *Options* dialog box.
- Press the *Color* button in the *Window Elements* panel to open the *Drawing Window Colors* dialog box.
- In the *Drawing Window Colors* dialog box, Figure 2-24, under the *Context* choose the *Command line*, under the *Interface elements* choose the *Command history background* to change the color of the background, and under the *Color* option choose the desired color. The selection is highlighted. In the current example, the *Yellow* color is selected. In the *Preview* window, the color of the CLW changes to the selected color.
- Finally, click the *Apply & Close* button to close the dialog box.
- The color of the CLW changes to the selected color.
- Similarly, change the color of the text of the CLW.

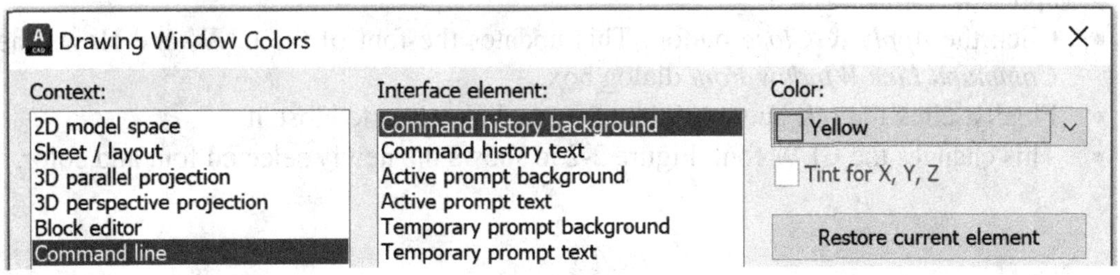

Figure 2-24

2.13.5. Change the font of the CLW

A user can change the font, font style, and font size of the command line text as follows.

- Click with the right button of the mouse in the *Drawing area* and select the *Options* option or type *Options* on the command line and press the *Enter* key.
- The *Options* dialog box appears on the screen.
- Click the *Display* tab of the *Options* dialog box.
- Press the *Font* button in the *Window Elements* panel (Figure 2-25a) to open the *Command Line Window Font* dialog box, Figure 2-25b.

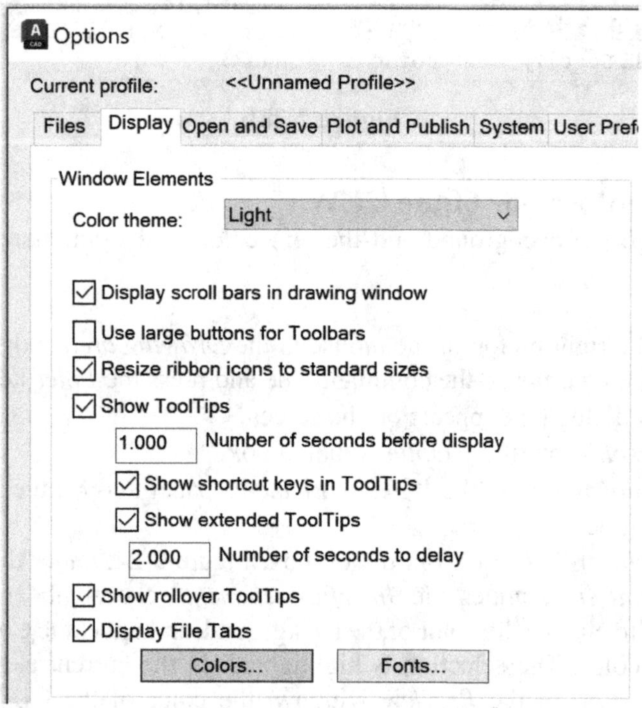

Figure 2-25a

- Select the desired *Font*, *Font Style*, and *Size*; in the current example, *Courier New*, *Regular*, and *10* are selected, respectively. In the *Preview* panel, the selected font appears.
- Click the *Apply & Close* button. This updates the font of the CLW and closes the *Command Line Window Font* dialog box.
- Finally, click the *OK* button of the *Options* dialog box to close it.
- This changes the CLW font. Figure 2-25c shows the newly selected font and color.

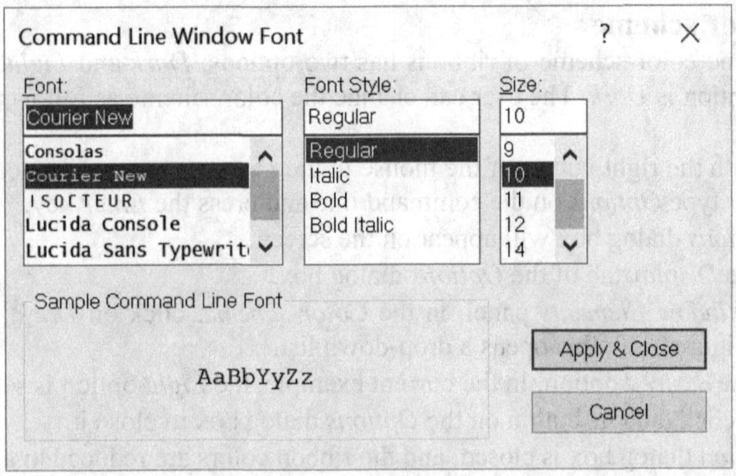

Figure 2-25b

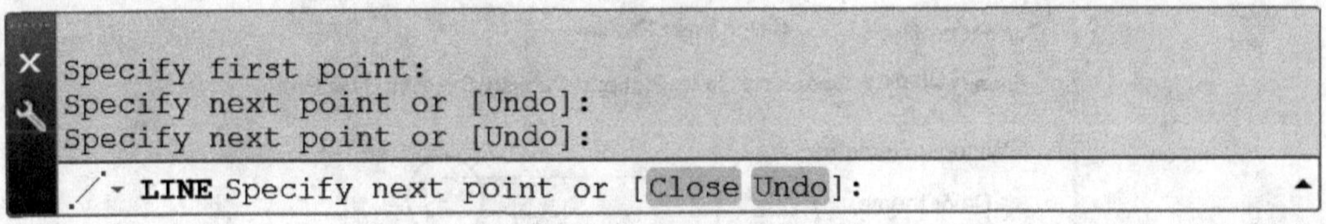

Figure 2-25c

2.14. Ribbon

Ribbon is an important part of the AutoCAD's interface. It is a collection of tabs, panel and tools. Figure 2-26 shows the selection of the *Home* tab, *Modify* panel, and the *Offset* command tool. A tab is a collection of panels. A panel is a collection of tools. A tool is a pictured icon that represents an AutoCAD command; that is, a tool is a graphical representation of a command. In this text "Tab → Panel → Command tool" means first select the "Tab" then from the desired "Panel" click the "Command tool" icon.

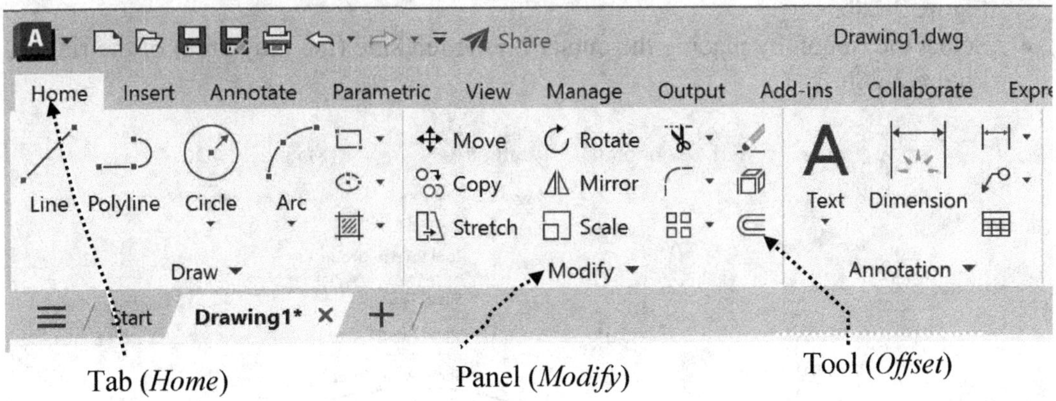

Figure 2-26

2.14.1. Color scheme

The background color scheme of ribbons has two options: *Dark* and *Light*, Figure 2-27. The default option is *Dark*. The user can change the color scheme as follows.

- Click with the right button of the mouse in the *Drawing area* and select the *Options* option or type *Options* on the command line and press the *Enter* key.
- The *Options* dialog box will appear on the screen.
- Click the *Display* tab of the *Options* dialog box.
- In the *Window Elements* panel, in the *Color scheme*, click on *Dark*, or the down-arrow, Figure 2-27; this opens a drop-down list.
- Select the *desired* option. In the current example, the *Light* option is selected.
- Finally, click the *OK* button on the *Options* dialog box to close it.
- The *Option* dialog box is closed, and the ribbon colors are reduced to a lighter color.

Figure 2-27

2.14.2. Relocate

By default, the ribbon is docked above the drawing area, Figure 2-26. However, the user can move the ribbon to the left or right side of the interface as follows.

- Undock the ribbon: (i) Bring the cursor in the tabs area and click with the right button of the mouse, Figure 2-28a. (ii) The selection list shown in Figure 2-28a appears. Select the *Undock* option. (iii) This closes the option list and undocks the ribbon, Figure 2-28b.
- Select the ribbon by placing the cursor on the left side (the gray area) of the ribbon, Figure 2-28b.

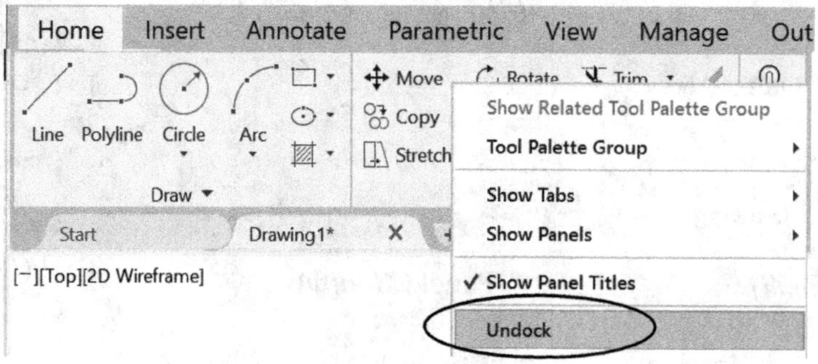

Figure 2-28a

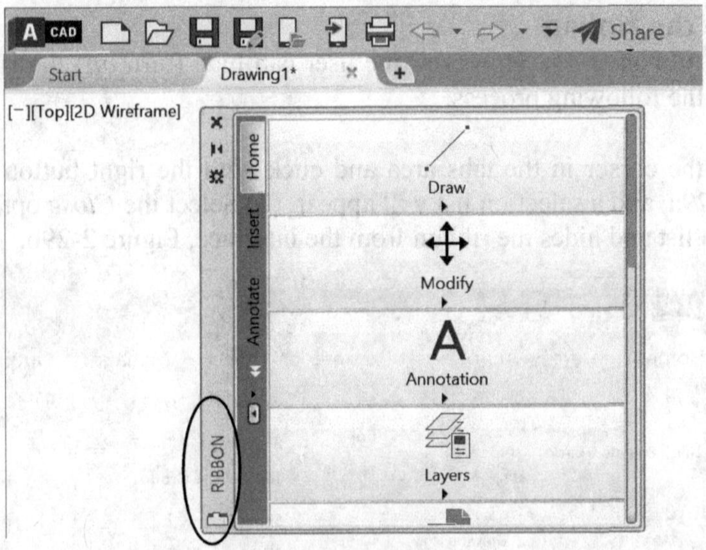

Figure 2-28b

- Press and hold down the left button of the mouse.
- Keep pressing the left button, move the cursor to the left or right side of the interface. In the current example, the ribbon is moved to the left.
- Move the cursor to the left of the AutoCAD window; the ribbon will appear as a light gray box.
- Release the left button of the mouse and the gray box will be replaced by the ribbon, Figure 2-28c. The ribbon is docked on the left side of the interface.

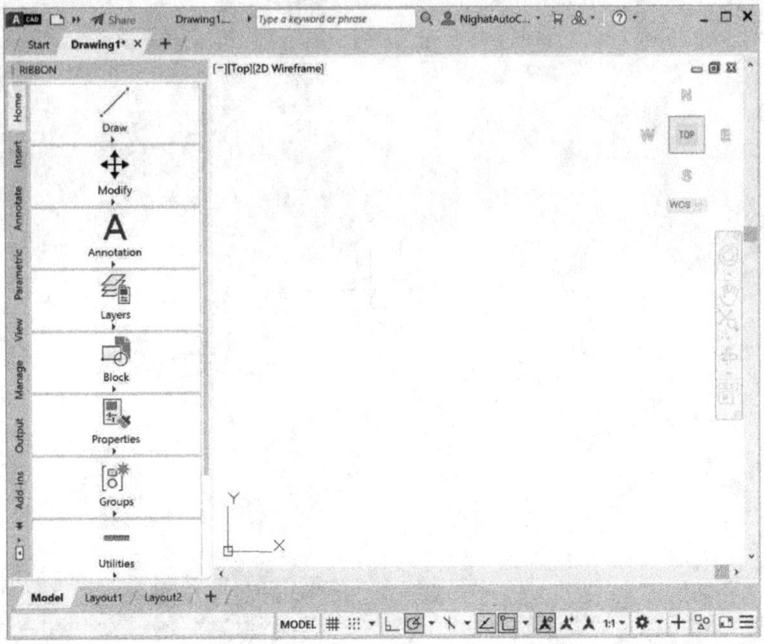

Figure 2-28c

2.14.3. Hide the ribbon

By default, the ribbon is *On*. However, the user can hide (turn *off*) the ribbon from the interface using the following process.

- (i) Bring the cursor in the tabs area and click with the right button of the mouse, Figure 2-29a, and a selection list will appear. (ii) Select the *Close* option; this closes the option list and hides the ribbon from the interface, Figure 2-29b.

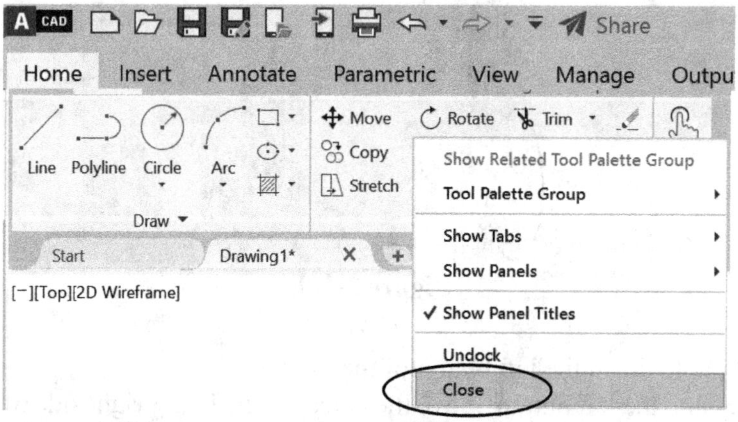

Figure 2-29a

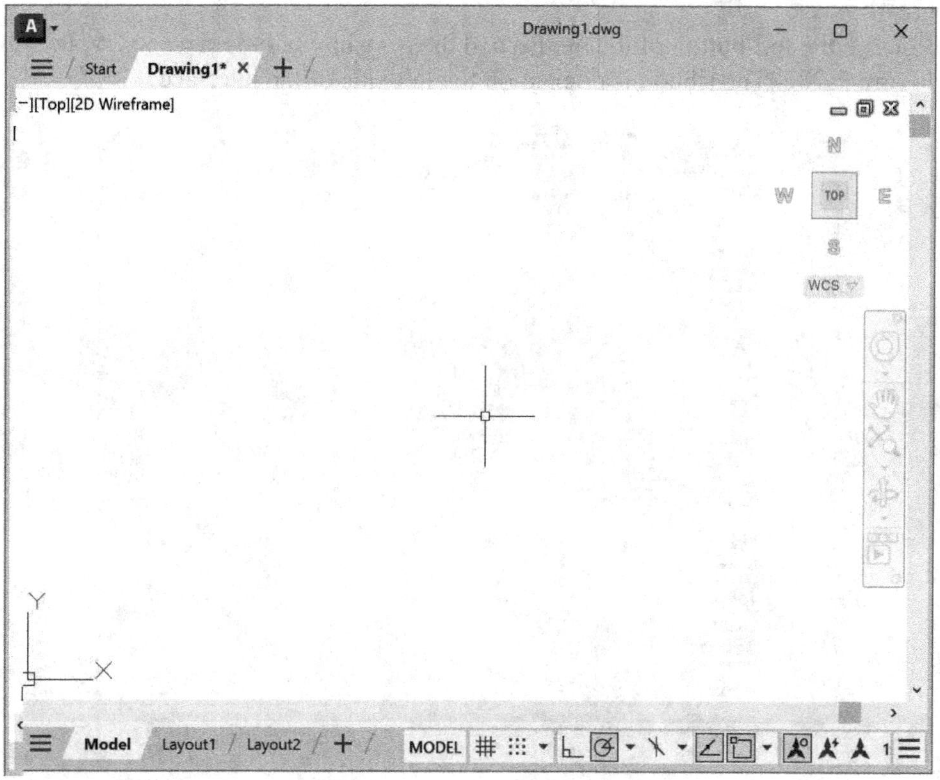

Figure 2-29b

2.14.4. Display the ribbon

The user can display (turn *on*) the ribbon on the interface using one of the following two methods.

- **Method 1:** The ribbon is displayed in a two-step process.
  a) Switch to a different interface: (i) Click on the small triangular arrow on the right side of the workspace switching icon, Figure 2-30a, and a selection list appears. (ii) Click on *3D Basics* or *3D Modeling* interface. (iii) This closes the options list, and the interface is switched.
  b) Switch back to the *Drafting & Annotation* interface: (i) Click again on the small triangular arrow on the right side of workspace switching icon, Figure 2-30b, and a selection list appears. (ii) Click on the *Drafting & Annotation* interface. (iii) This closes the options list, and the interface is switched to the *Drafting & Annotation* interface and the ribbon is visible.

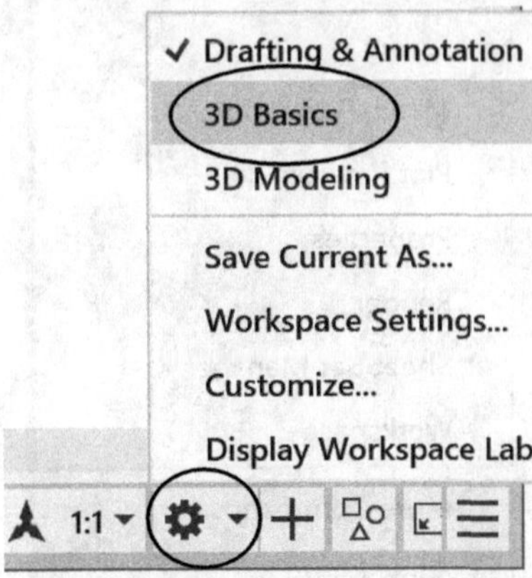

Figure 2-30a

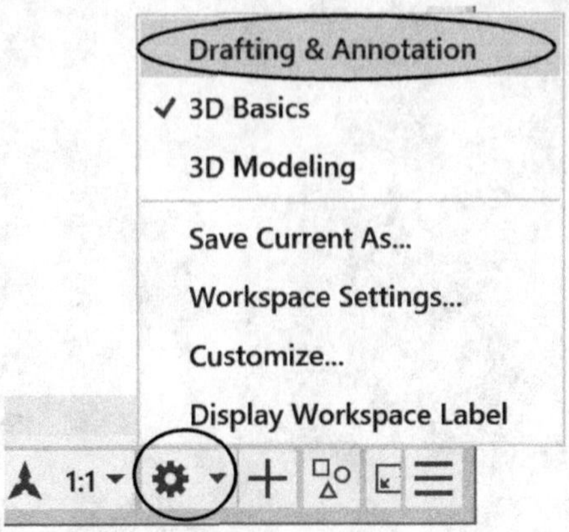

Figure 2-30b

- **Method 2:** The ribbon is displayed in a three steps process.
  a) Display the menu bar: (i) Click on the small triangular arrow on the upper left corner of the interface, Figure 2-30c and a selection list appears. (ii) Select the *Show Menu Bar* option. (iii) This closes the option list and displays the menu bar, Figure 2-30d.

  b) Display the ribbon: Refer to Figure 2-30e. (i) On the menu bar, select the *Tool* menu and a selection list appears. (ii) Select the *Palettes* option and another selection list appears. (iii) Finally, select the *Ribbon* option. (iv) This closes the two selection lists and displays the ribbon on the interface, Figure 2-30f.

  c) Hide the menu bar: (i) Bring the cursor on the menu bar and click with the right button of the mouse. The *Show Menu Bar* option appears on the screen, Figure 2-30g. (ii) Clear the check box; this closes the option list and hides the menu bar.

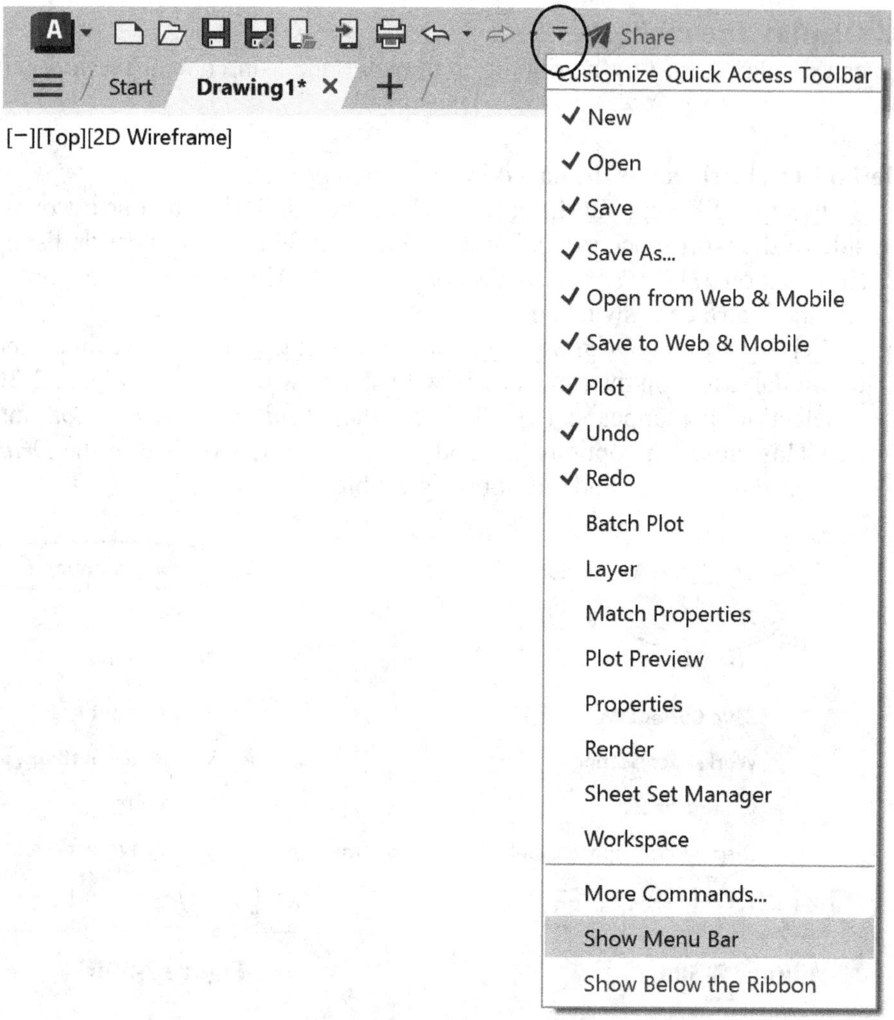

Figure 2-30c

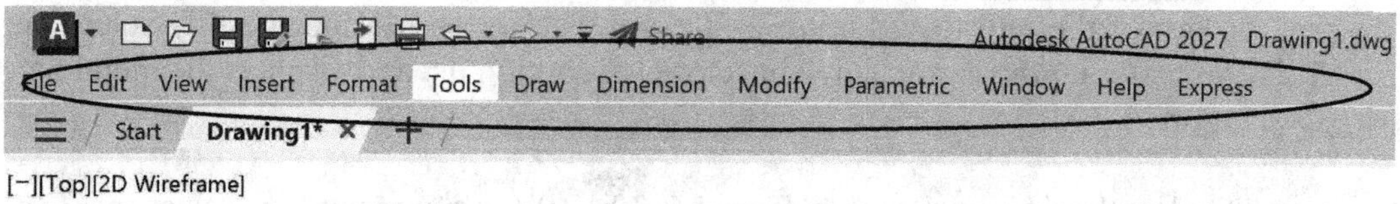

Figure 2-30d

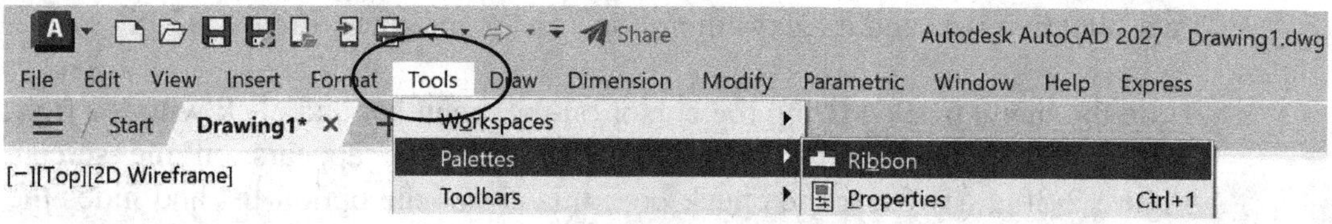

Figure 2-30e

Figure 2-30f

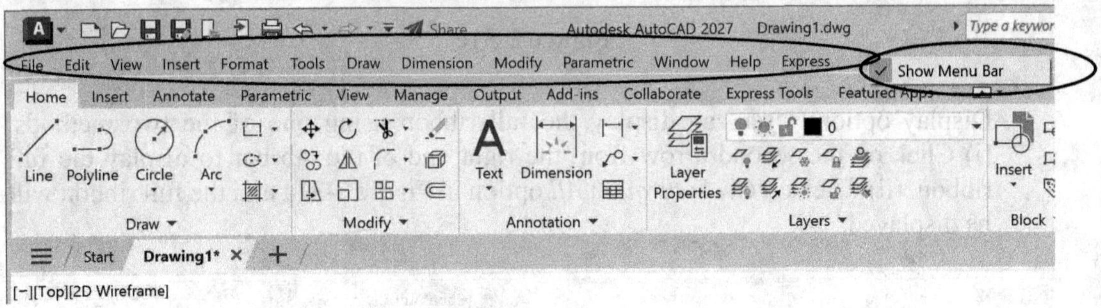

Figure 2-30g

2.14.5. States

By default, the ribbon is *On* and the tabs, the panels, and the panel names are displayed, Figure 2-31a. However, the user can display/hide any of the tabs, panels, and/or panel names using the two arrows on the right end of the tab bar.

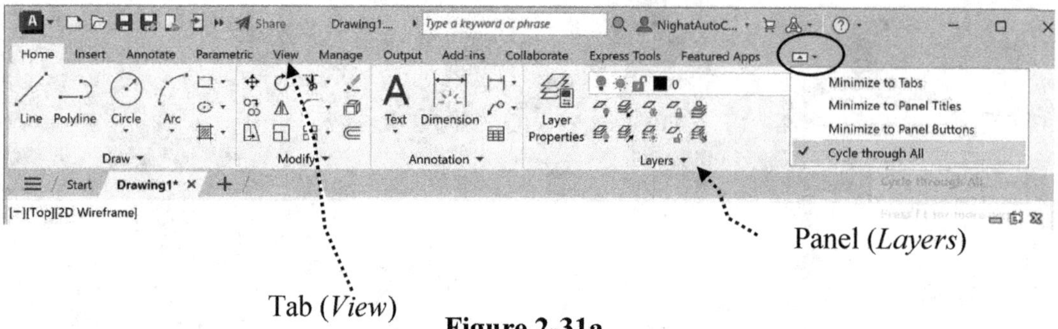

Figure 2-31a

- Hide option: Click on the arrow at the right end of the tab bar (Figure 2-31a) and select the desired option. Figure 2-31b shows only the tabs; Figure 2-31c shows the tabs and the panel names; and Figure 2-31d shows the tab's name and the panel buttons.

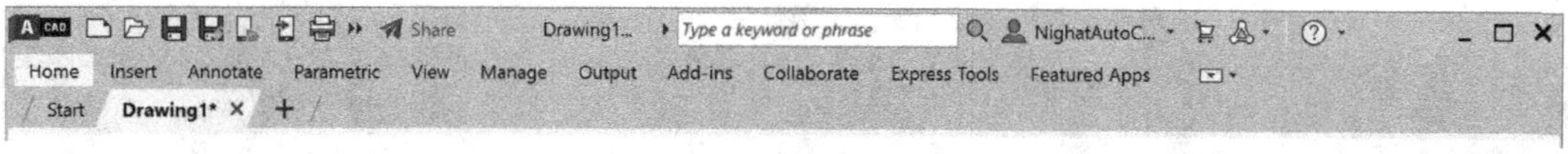

Figure 2-31b

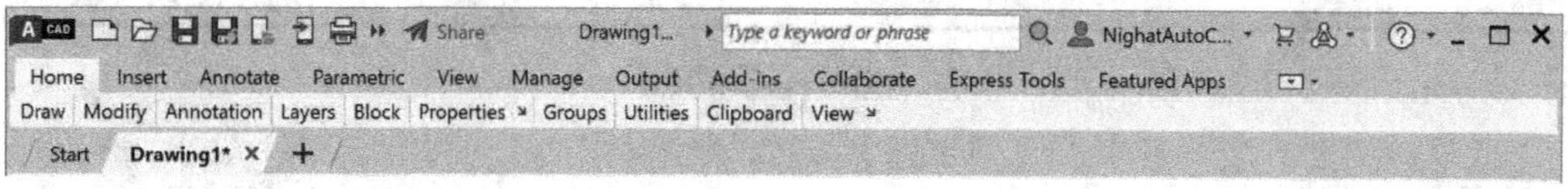

Figure 2-31c

- Display option: User can display the full ribbon using one of the two methods. (i) Click on the second arrow from the right end of the tab bar to display the full ribbon. (ii) Click on *Cycle through All* option in Figure 2-31a and the full ribbon will be displayed.

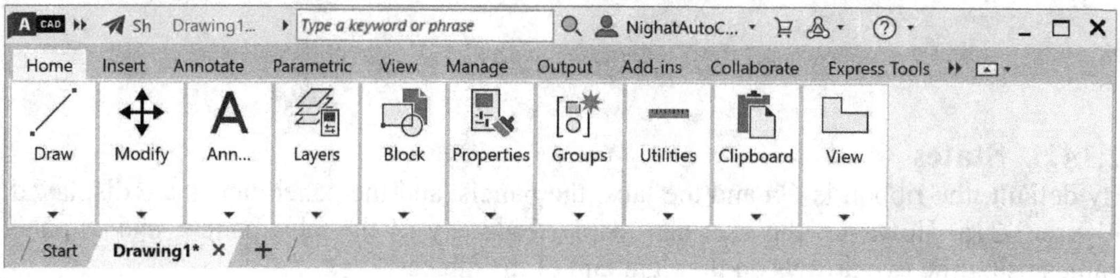

Figure 2-31d

2.14.6. Ribbon's tab

The ribbon tabs are not used for command execution; these tabs are used to display the panel. A user can display or hide and relocate the default tabs and can create new tabs.

2.14.6.1. Display or hide tabs

By default, the tabs of the ribbon are *On*. However, the user can hide (turn *off*) the tabs from the ribbon or display (turn *on*) the tabs on the ribbon.

- Display a tab: Refer to Figure 2-32. (i) Bring the cursor in the tab area and click with the right button of the mouse. A selection list will appear. (ii) Select the *Show Tabs* option. This opens a tab's list. If a tab is displayed on the ribbon, then it has a check mark on the left side of its name. (iii) To display a tab, click on a tab without a check mark, *3D Tools* in the current example. (iv) This closes the option lists and displays the selected tab and associated panels on the ribbon.

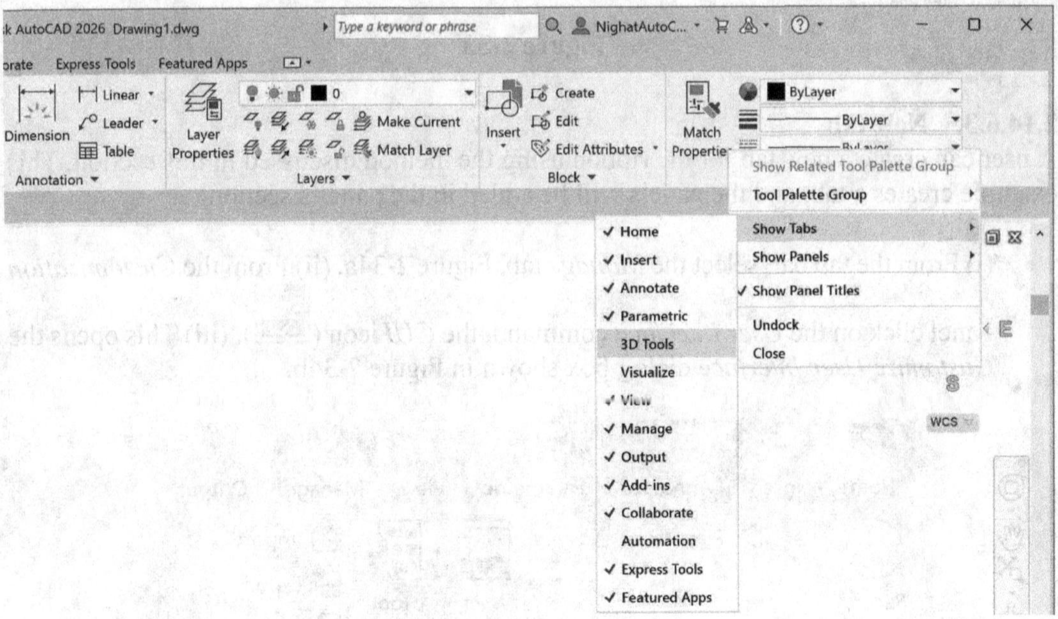

Figure 2-32

- Hide a tab: Refer to Figure 2-32. (i) Bring the cursor to the tab area and click with the right button of the mouse. The selection list will appear. (ii) Select the *Show Tabs* option. (iii) This will open a tab's list. If a tab is displayed on the ribbon, then it has a check mark on the left side of its name, Figure 2-32. (iv) To hide a tab, click on the tab with a check mark, *Express Tools* in the current example. (v) This closes the option lists and hides the selected tab.

2.14.6.2. Tab relocation

A user can relocate a tab of the ribbon using a drag and drop method. By default, the *Home* tab is on the left end of the tab bar, Figure 2-32. This example will move the *Home* tab to the right end.

- (i) Click on the *Home* tab with the left button of the mouse, (ii) keep pressing the left button, and (iii) move the cursor to the desired location. A grayed tab appears at the new location, Figure 2-33, after the *View* tab in the current example.

- Release the left button of the mouse and the tab is moved to the new location. Figure 2-33 shows the new location of *Home* tab, the right end of the tab bar in the current example.

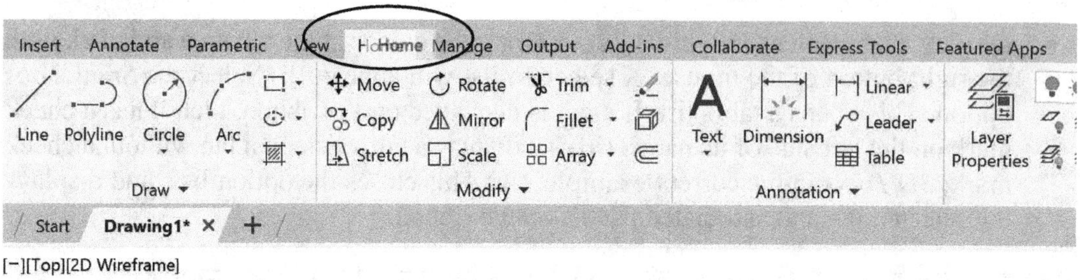

Figure 2-33

2.14.6.3. New tab

A user can create a new tab for the ribbon using the method discussed in this section. This example creates a tab, and the panels will be added in the panel's section.

- (i) From the tab bar, select the *Manage* tab, Figure 2-34a. (ii) From the *Customization* panel click on the *User Interface* command, the *CUI* icon (). (iii) This opens the *Customize User Interface* dialog box shown in Figure 2-34b.

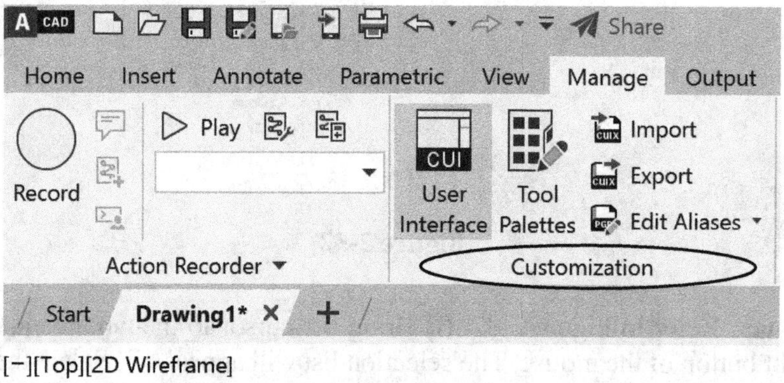

Figure 2-34a

- From the *Customize User Interface* dialog box, Figure 2-34b, select the *Customize* tab. The tab is located on the upper left corner of the dialog box. The figure also shows that *Drafting & Annotation* is the current workspace.

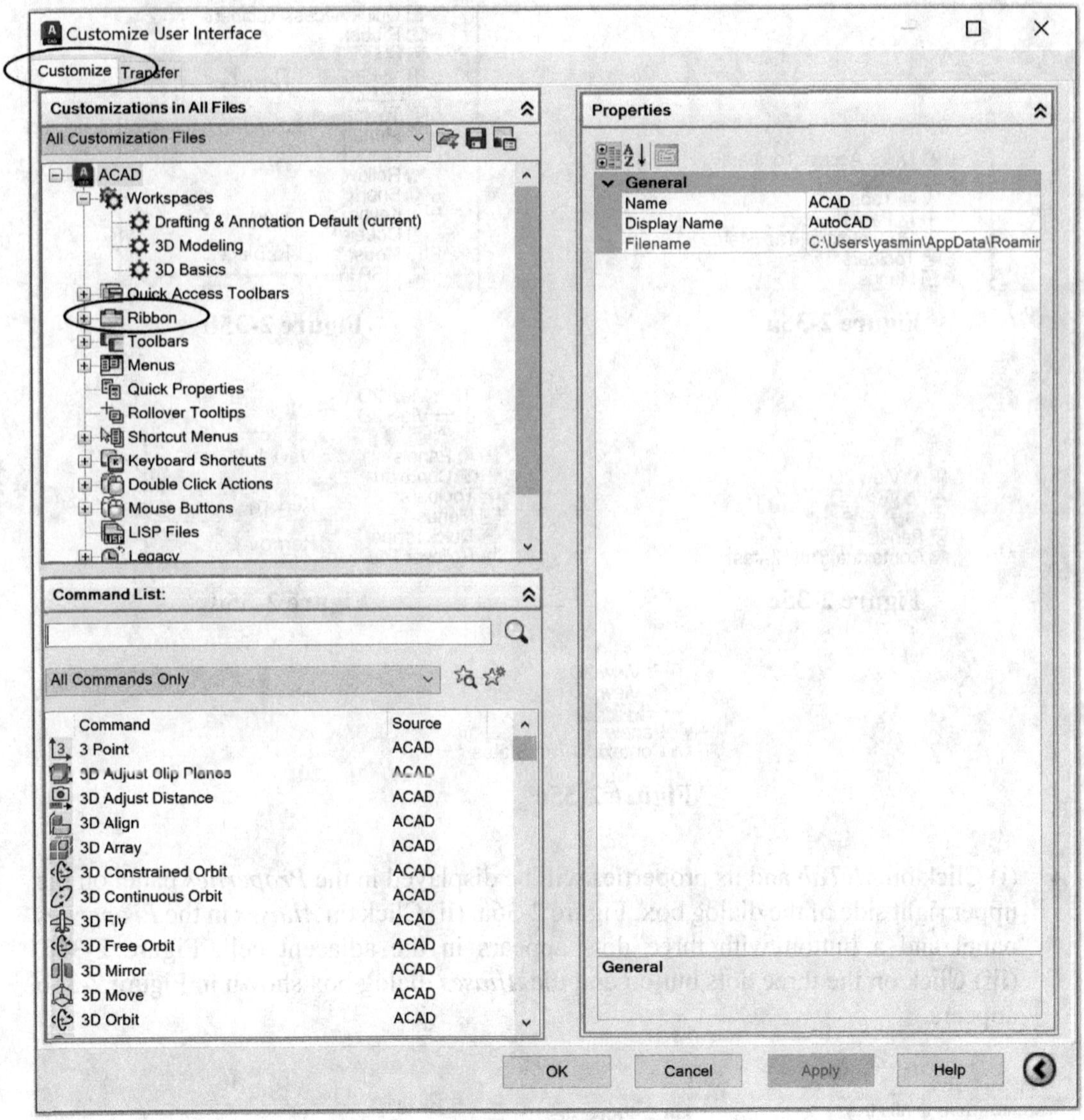

Figure 2-34b

- In the upper left quadrant, Figure 2-34b, click on the '+' adjacent to the *Ribbon* label. This displays an option list, Figure 2-35a.
- (i) Select the *Tab* option, Figure 2-35a. (ii) Click with the right button of the mouse on the *Tab* option. (iii) This displays an option list. (iv) Select the *New Tab* option.
- This closes the option list and creates a new tab labeled *New Tab* at the lower end of the *Tab* options list. Move the scrollbar downward to display the *New Tab*, Figure 2-35b.
- (i) Select the *New Tab*, (ii) Press the right button of the mouse and the options list will appear, Figure 2-35c, (iii) select the *Rename* option from the list, (iv) rename *New Tab* to *MyTab*, Figure 2-35d.

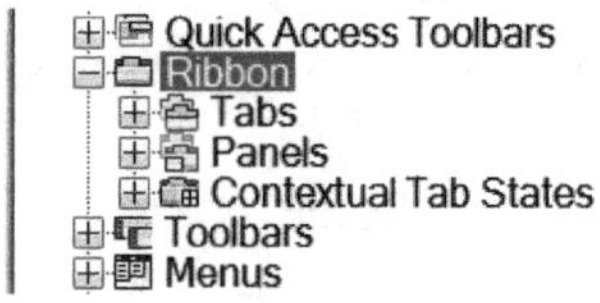

Figure 2-35a

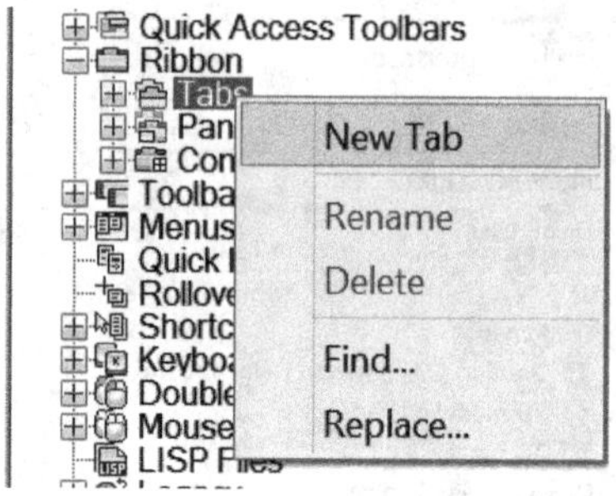

Figure 2-35b

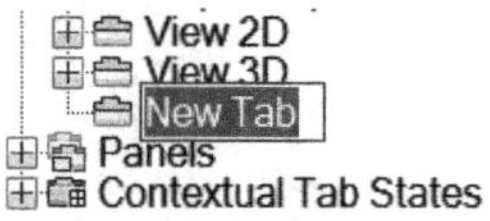

Figure 2-35c

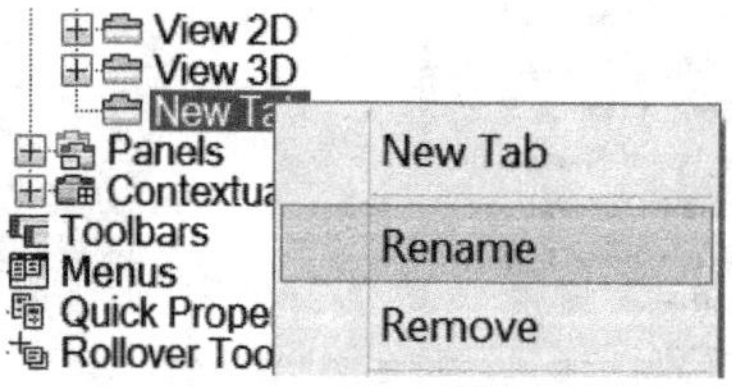

Figure 2-35d

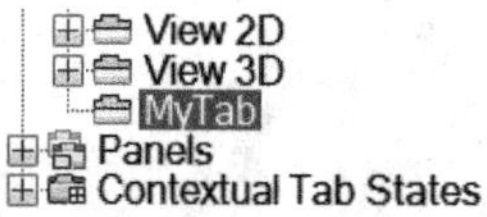

Figure 2-35e

- (i) Click on *MyTab* and its properties will be displayed in the *Properties* panel on the upper right side of the dialog box, Figure 2-36a. (ii) Click on *Aliases* in the *Properties* panel and a button with three dots appears in the adjacent cell, Figure 2-36a. (iii) Click on the three dots button and the *Aliases* dialog box shown in Figure 2-36b appears.

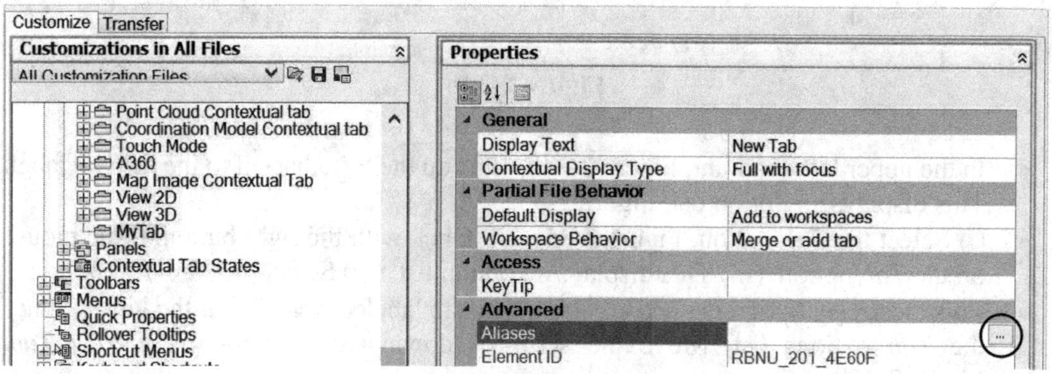

Figure 2-36a

- Enter the alias's name, Figure 2-36b, and press the *OK* button. This closes the *Aliases* dialog box and the alias appears in the *Properties* panel, Figure 2-36c.

- Under *General* and for the *Display Text*, enter *MyTab*, Figure 2-36c.

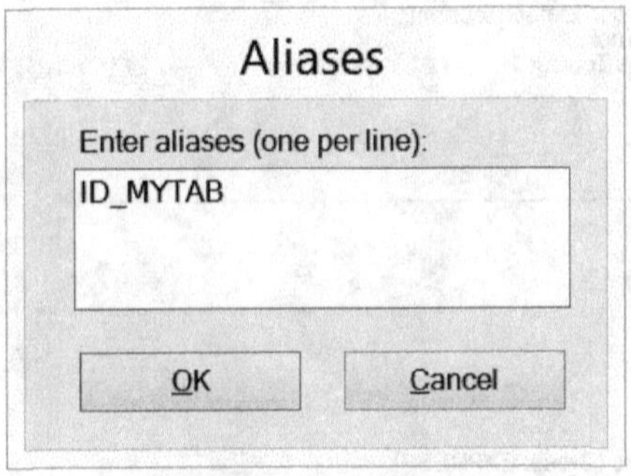

Figure 2-36b

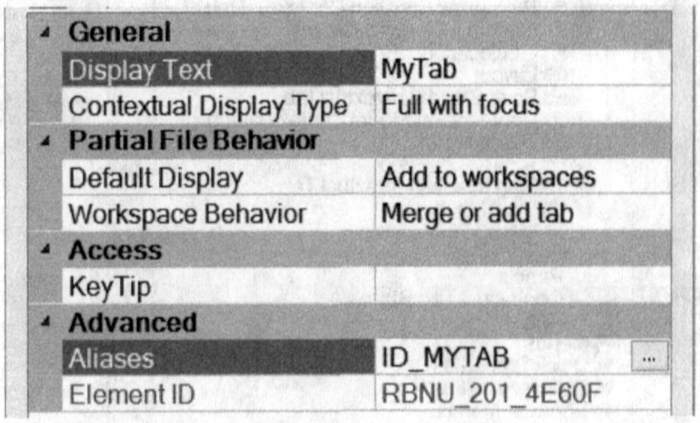

Figure 2-36c

- Double click on *Drafting & Annotation* under *Workspaces*, Figure 2-36d, and the list of workspace content will appear on the right side of the dialog box.
- On the right side of the dialog box, click on the '+' adjacent to the *Ribbon Tabs* label. This displays an option list shown in Figure 2-36d.

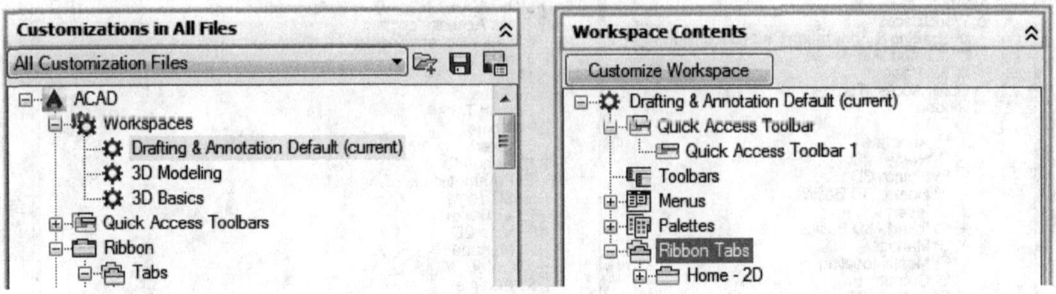

Figure 2-36d

- Click on *MyTab* and keep pressing the left button of the mouse; the selected tab will be highlighted, Figure 2-37a.
- (i) Keep pressing the left button of the mouse, (ii) move the cursor to the right side of the dialog box under the *Ribbon Tabs*, Figure 2-37a, (iii) click anywhere below the *Ribbon Tabs* and above *Performance* (the last tab), and (iv) release the left button of the mouse. The figure shows the cursor below the *Home* tab.
- The new tab is added to the *Ribbon Tabs* list, Figure 2-37b. By default, the tab is always added at the end of the list (independent of the location selected). If necessary, move the new tab to the desired location.
- Click the *OK* button of the dialog box. This closes the dialog box and creates the new tab (*MyTab*) in the tab bar of the workspace, Figure 2-37c. The new tab is at the end of the tab bar. If the newly created tab does not appear in the tab list, then complete the next step.

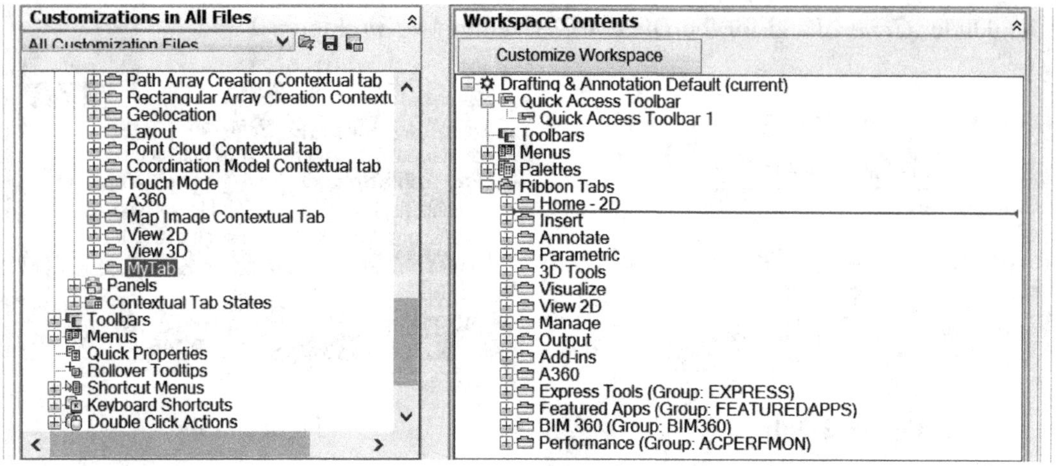

Figure 2-37a

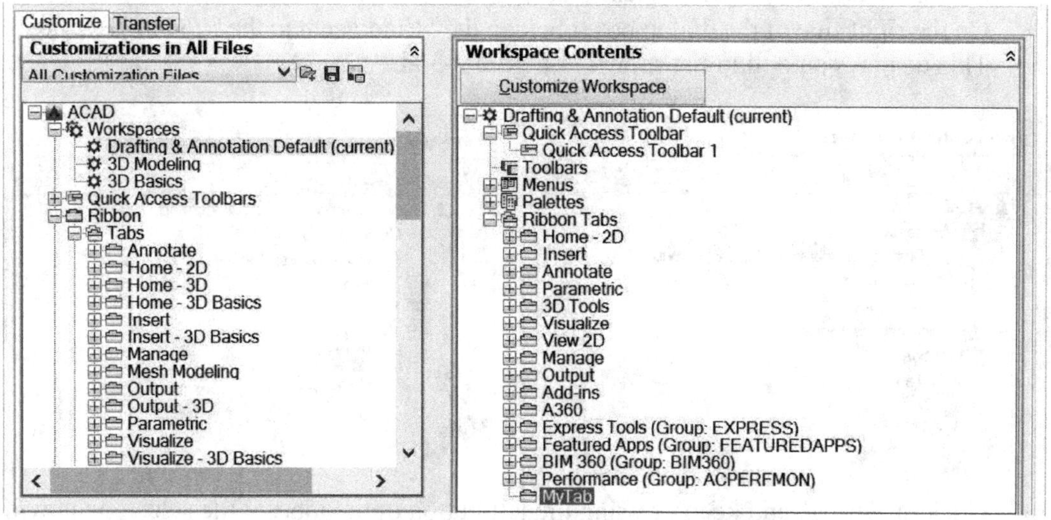

Figure 2-37b

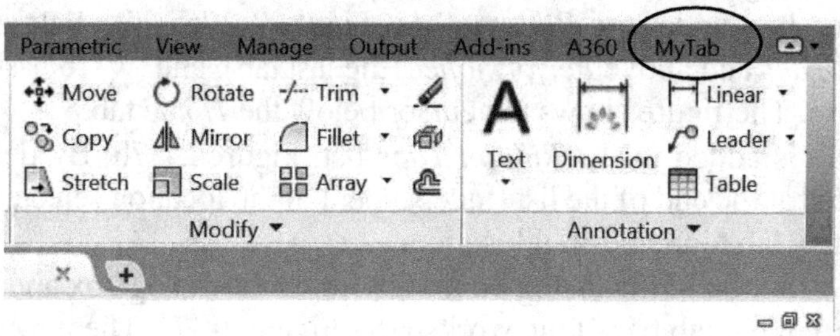

Figure 2-37c

- If the newly created tab does not appear in the tab list, then refresh the modeling environment using the following steps: (i) Click on the small arrow located at the right side of *Workspace Switching* wheel, Figure 2-37d. The wheel is located on the lower right corner of the interface. (ii) Select the *3D Basics* or *3D Modeling* environment. This closes the list and changes the drawing environment to the selected option. (iii) Repeat step (i) and (ii). However, select *Drafting & Annotation* option in step (ii). The new tab appears at the end of the tab bar.

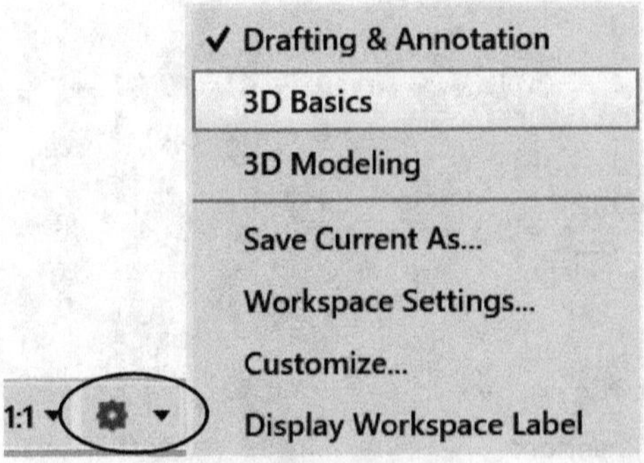

Figure 2-37d

2.14.7. Ribbon's panel

The ribbon panels are used to display the commands. Some of the panels also provide access to the corresponding dialog box. A user can display or hide and relocate the default panel and can create new panels.

2.14.7.1. Panel components

Every panel shows three rows of commands icons, Figure 2-38a. If a panel's commands cannot be accommodated in three rows, then those commands can be accessed through the panel expander, Figure 2-38a. If a command has several options available through a dropdown menu, then those options can be accessed through the command expander; and the command icon displays the most recently used option.

- Panel expander: (i) Bring the cursor on the tiny arrow near the panel label, Figure 2-38a and (ii) click with the left button of the mouse and the panel expands, Figure 2-38b. However, if the user moves the cursor, then the panel collapses to the original size. However, the user can pin the panel expansion using the *Pin* command.

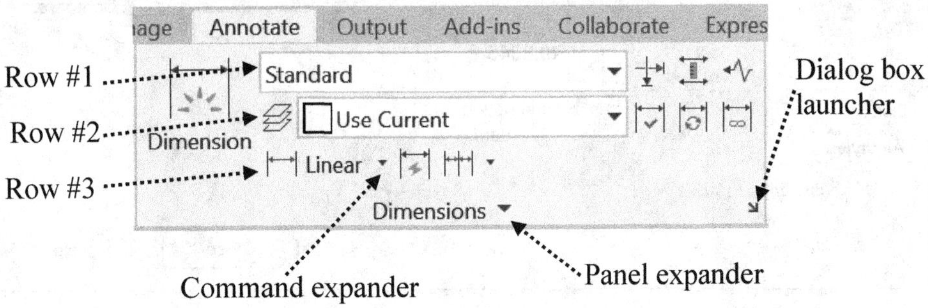

Figure 2-38a

- Pin the panel: The user can pin the panel expansion using the *Pin* command. The pin command is located in the lower left corner of the expanded panel, Figure 2-38b. (i) The pin command is executed by clicking on the pin icon, Figure 2-38b. (ii) Figure 2-38c shows that the panel is pinned. Carefully note the difference in the appearance of the pin in the two figures.

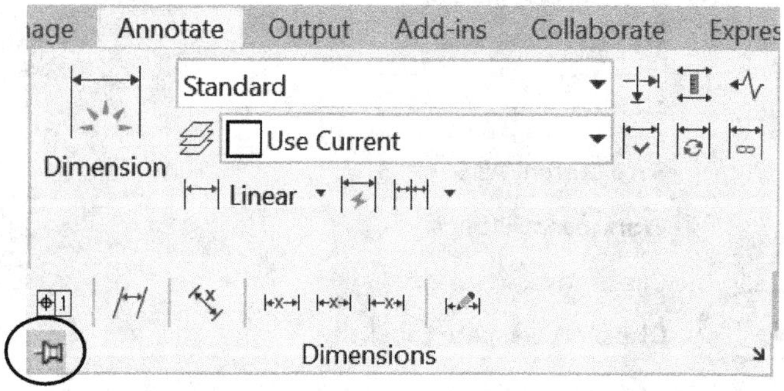

Figure 2-38b

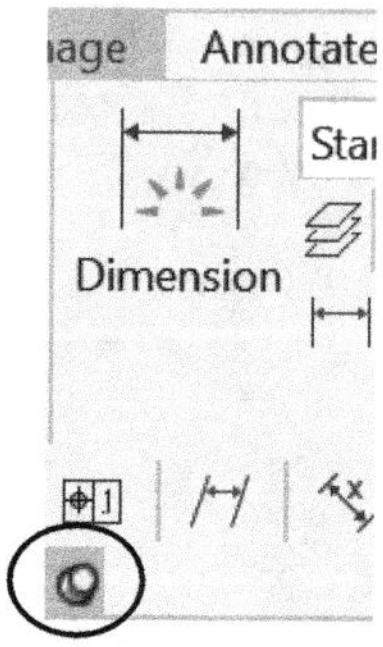

Figure 2-38c

- Dialog box launcher: (i) Bring the cursor on the tiny arrow near the lower right corner of the panel, Figure 2-38a, and (ii) click the arrow and the *Dimension Style Manager* dialog box will appear, Figure 2-38d. This dialog box is discussed in detail in *Chapter 9*. Click the *Close* button to close the dialog box.

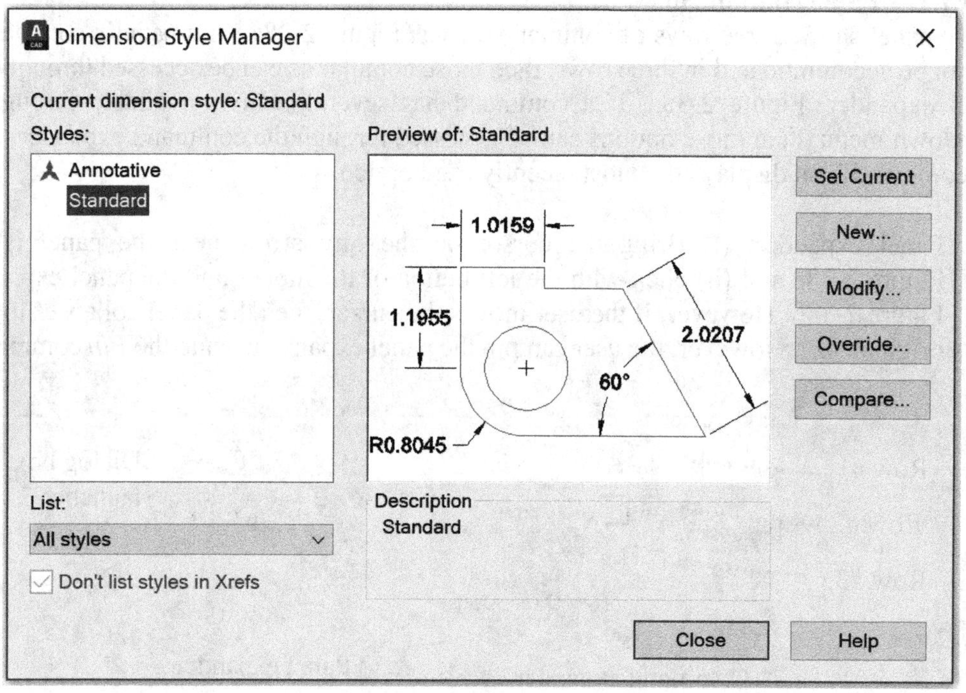

Figure 2-38d

- Command expander: (i) Bring the cursor on the tiny arrow below the command label, Figure 2-38a and Figure 2-38e, (ii) click with the left button of the mouse and the panel will expand, Figure 2-38e. (iii) The user can click on any command; this will close the list and execute the selected command. The figure shows the selection of the *Radius* dimension command. (iv) The user can cycle through the list using the down-arrow key of the keyboard and can close the list by clicking the same arrow again.

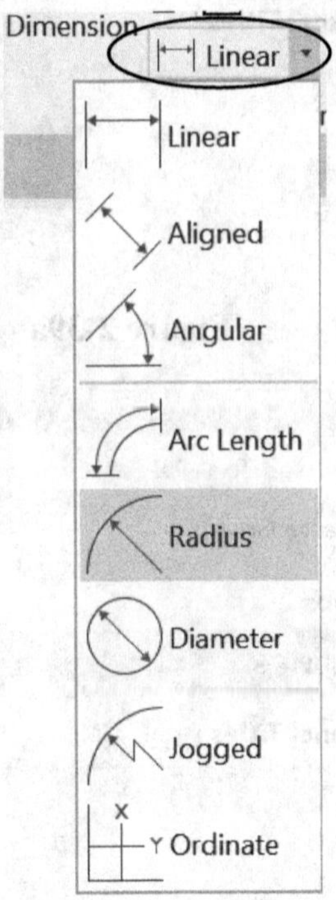

Figure 2-38e

2.14.7.2. Display or hide panel

By default, the panels of the ribbon are *On*. However, the user can hide (turn *off*) the panels from the ribbon or display (turn *on*) the panels on the ribbon.

- Display a panel: (i) Bring the cursor in the tab area and click with the right button of the mouse, Figure 2-39a. (ii) The selection list shown in Figure 2-39a appears. Select the *Show Panels* option. This opens a panel's list for the selected tab. In the current example, the panels under the *Home* tab are displayed. If a panel is displayed on the ribbon, then it shows a check mark on the left side of its name, Figure 2-39b. (iii) To display a panel, click on a panel without a check mark, *Properties* in the current example. This closes both the option lists and displays the selected panel on the ribbon and a check mark appears on the left side of its name, Figure 2-39b.

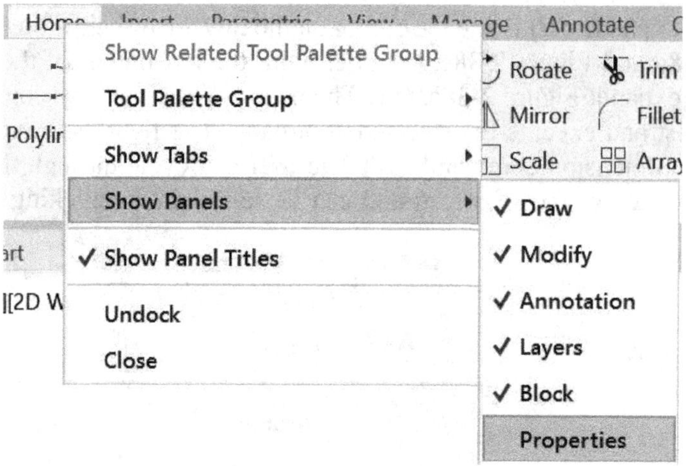

Figure 2-39a

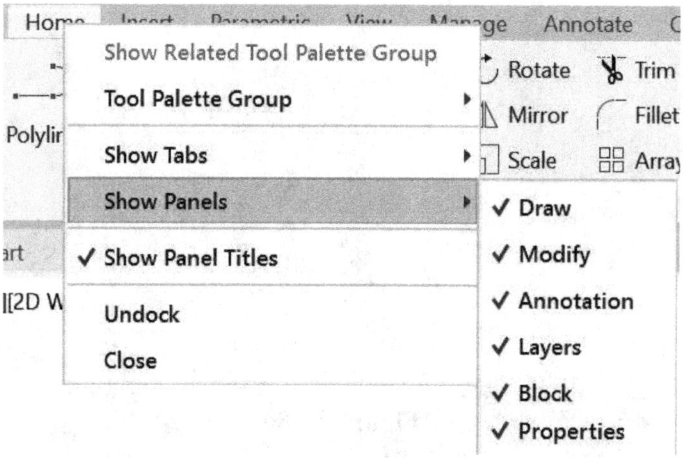

Figure 2-39b

2.14.7.3. Panel relocation

A user can relocate a panel of the ribbon using a drag and drop method. In the *Home* tab, by default the *Draw* panel is on the left end of the ribbon, Figure 2-40a. This example moves the *Draw* panel on the right side of the *Modify* panel using the following steps.

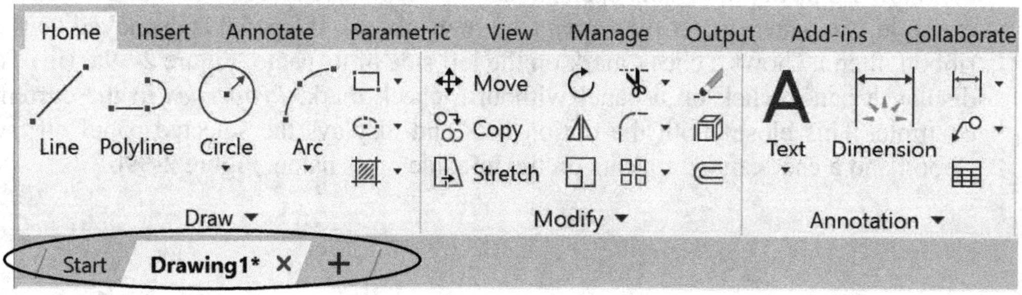

Figure 2-40a

- Select the *Home* tab.
- Click on the *Draw* panel's name area with the left button of the mouse.
- Keep pressing the left button and move the cursor to the desired location. A grayed panel appears at the new location, and a rectangular space is created; in the current example, on the right end of the *Modify* panel, Figure 2-40b.
- Release the left button of the mouse and the panel is moved to the new location. Figure 2-40c shows the new location of the *Draw* panel.

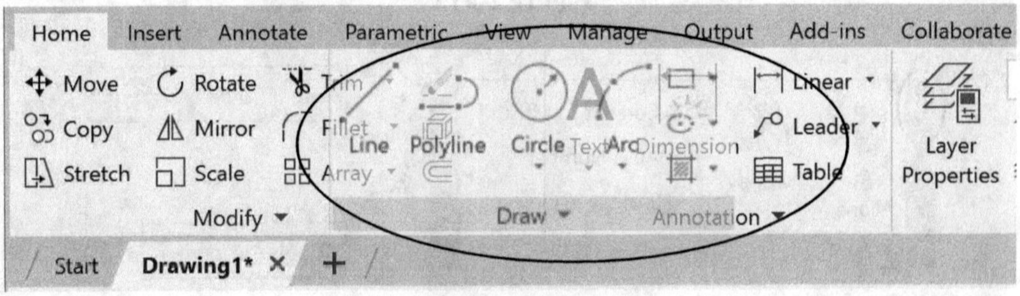

Figure 2-40b

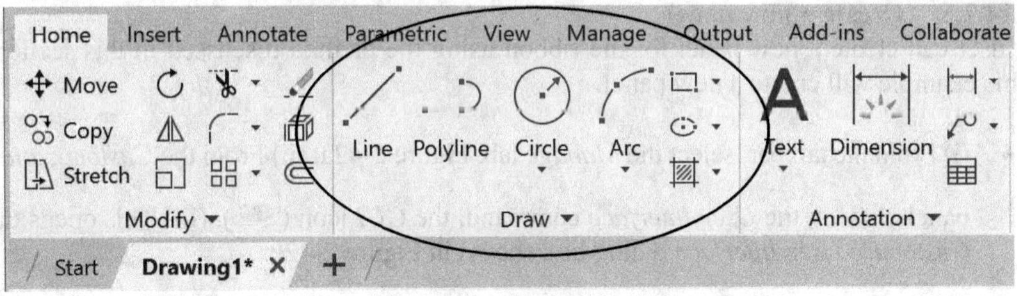

Figure 2-40c

2.14.7.4. Floating panel

If a user drags and drops a panel in the drawing area, then it is called a floating panel. A panel can be converted to a floating panel using the following steps.

- (i) Bring the cursor on the panel's name, Figure 2-41a. (ii) Select the panel's label bar by pressing the left button. (iii) Keep pressing the left button and move the cursor to the drawing area. For the current example, *Text* panel under the *Express Tools* tab is selected.
- Release the left button of the mouse and the panel becomes the floating panel. The panel stays in the drawing area until it is returned to the ribbon. The user can return the panel back to the ribbon using one of the two methods.
    - Click at *Return Panels to Ribbon* button, Figure 2-41b, and the panel is moved to its location on the tab.
    - (a) Click at the two dotted parallel lines on the left side of the panel. (b) Press the left button. (c) Keep pressing the left button of the mouse. (d) Move and release the cursor at the desired location on the ribbon.

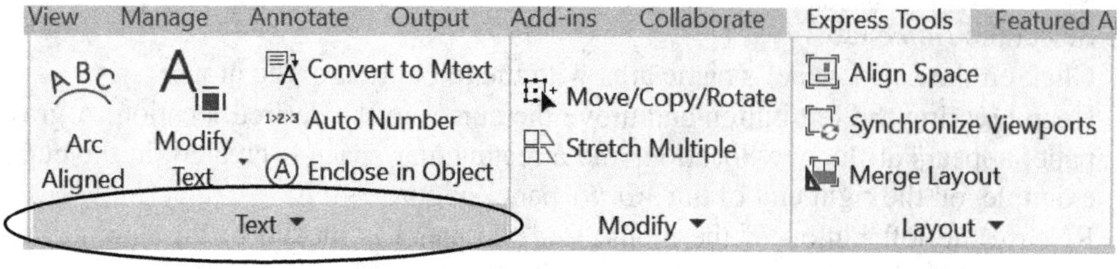

Figure 2-41a

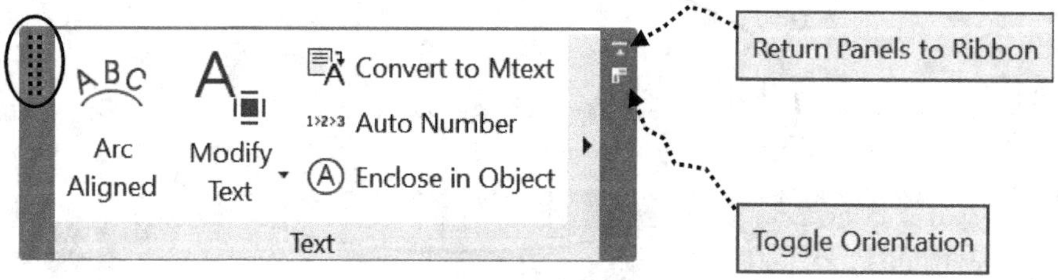

Figure 2-41b

2.14.7.5. Create a new panel

A user can create a new panel for the ribbon using the method discussed in this section. This example will create a new panel.

- (i) From the tab bar, select the *Manage* tab, Figure 2-42a. (ii) From the *Customization* panel click on the *User Interface* command, the *CUI* icon (CUI). (iii) This opens the *Customize User Interface* dialog box shown in Figure 2-42b.

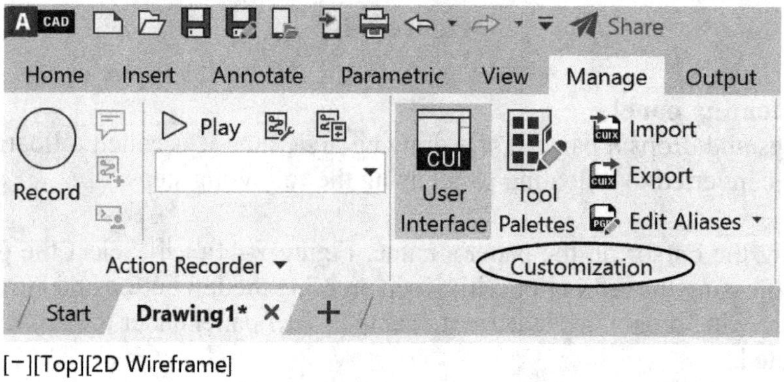

Figure 2-42a

- From the *Customize User Interface* dialog box, Figure 2-42b, select the *Customize* tab. The tab is located on the upper left corner of the dialog box. The figure also shows the selection of *Drafting & Annotation* under the Workspace.

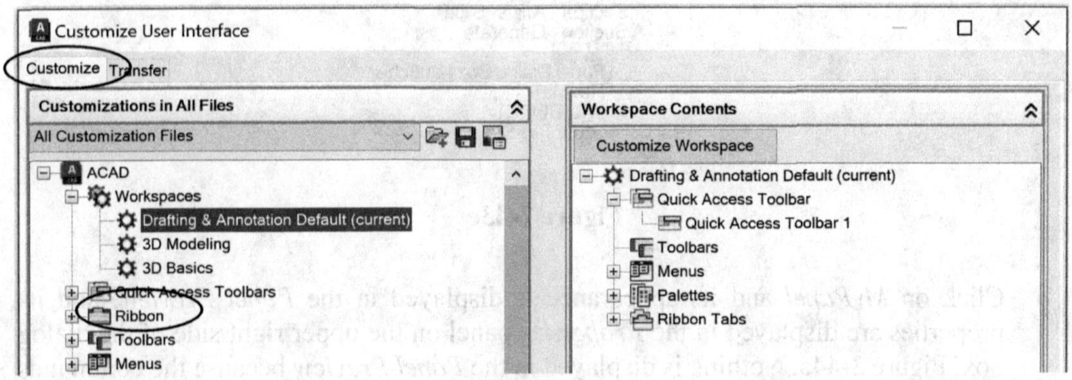

Figure 2-42b

- In the upper left quadrant, Figure 2-42b, click on the '+' adjacent to the *Ribbon* label. This displays an option list, Figure 2-43a.
- (i) Select the *Panel* option, Figure 2-43b. (ii) Click with the right button of the mouse on the *Panel* option; this displays an option list, Figure 2-43b. (iii) Select the *New Panel* option.

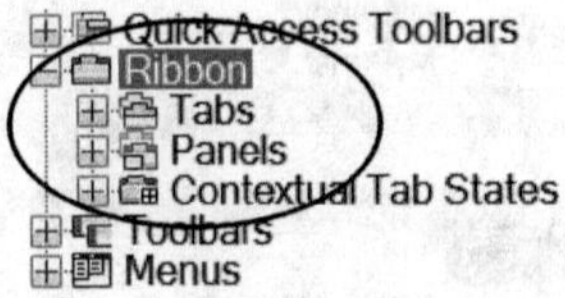

Figure 2-43a

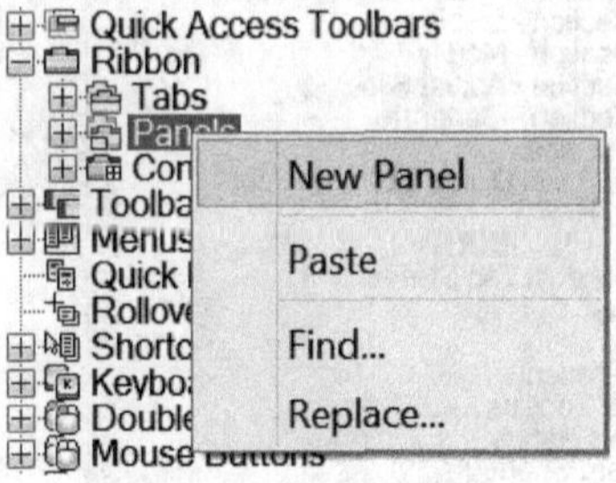

Figure 2-43b

- This closes the option list and creates a new panel labeled *Panel1* at the lower end of the *Panel* options list, Figure 2-43c. Move the scroll bar downward to display the new panel, *Panel1*.
- (i) Select the *Panel1*, (ii) Press the right button of the mouse and the options list appears, Figure 2-43d. (iii) Select the *Rename* option from the list, (iv) and rename *Panel1* to *MyPanel*, Figure 2-43e.

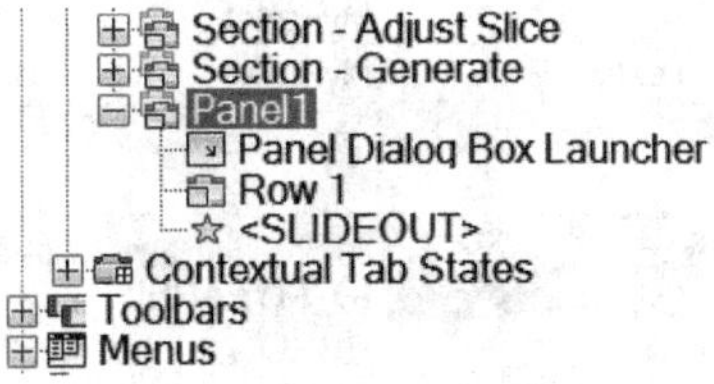

Figure 2-43c

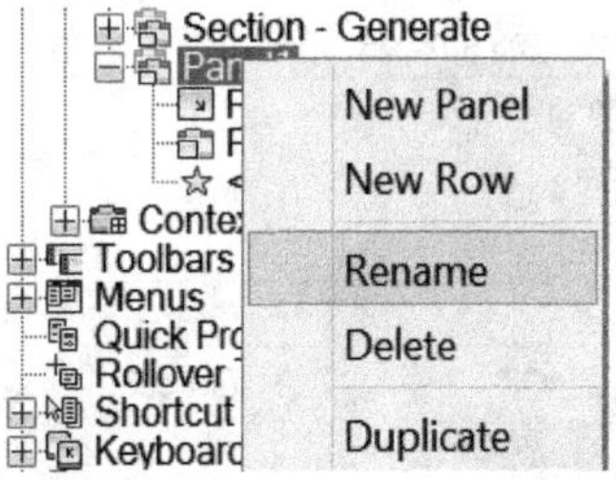

Figure 2-43d

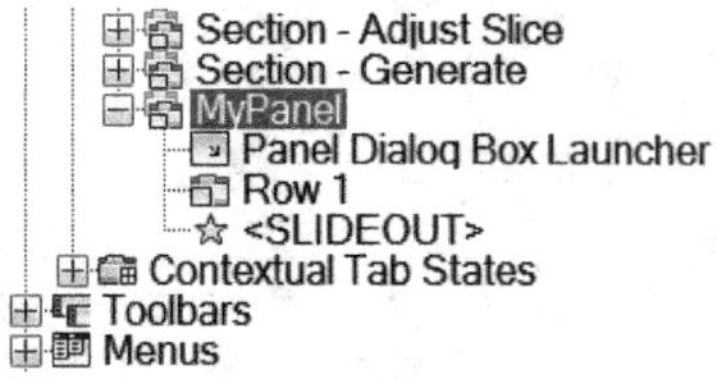

Figure 2-43e

- Click on *MyPanel* and its appearance is displayed in the *Panel Preview,* and its properties are displayed in the *Properties* panel on the upper right side of the dialog box, Figure 2-44a. Nothing is displayed in the *Panel Preview* because the commands are not added to the panel.
- Click on *Aliases* in the *Properties* section (lower right end of the dialog box) and a button with three dots appears in the adjacent cell, Figure 2-44a.

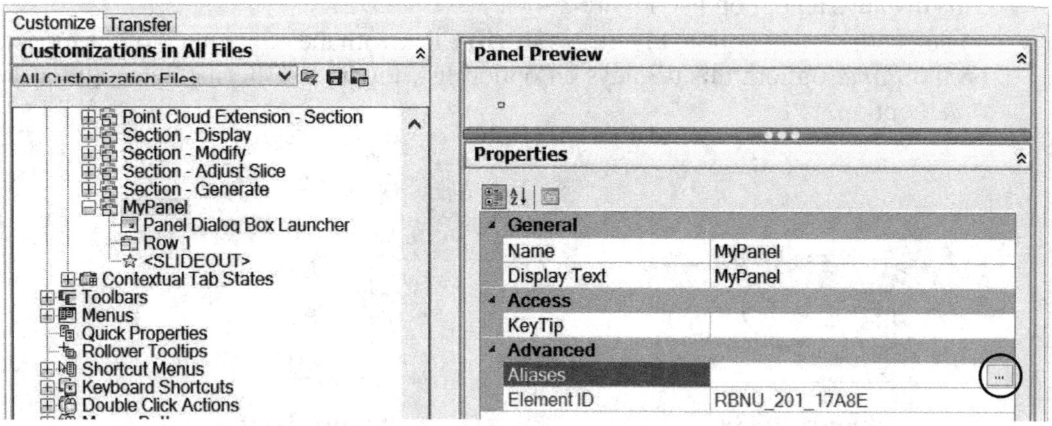

Figure 2-44a

- Click on the three dots button and the *Aliases* dialog box, Figure 2-44b, appears.
- Type the alias's name, Figure 2-44b, and press the *OK* button. This closes the *Aliases* dialog box and the alias's name appears in the *Properties* section, Figure 2-44c.

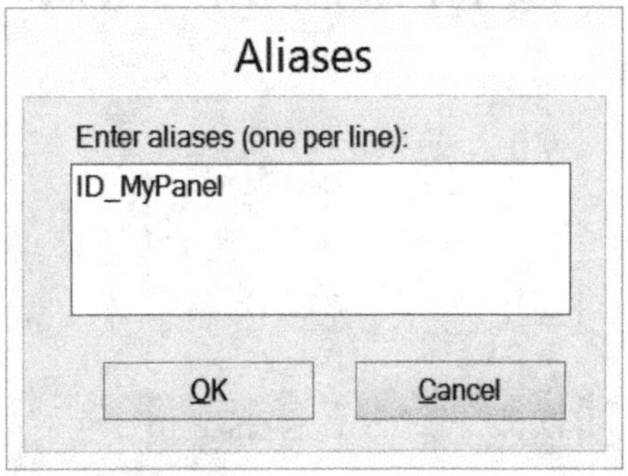

Figure 2-44b

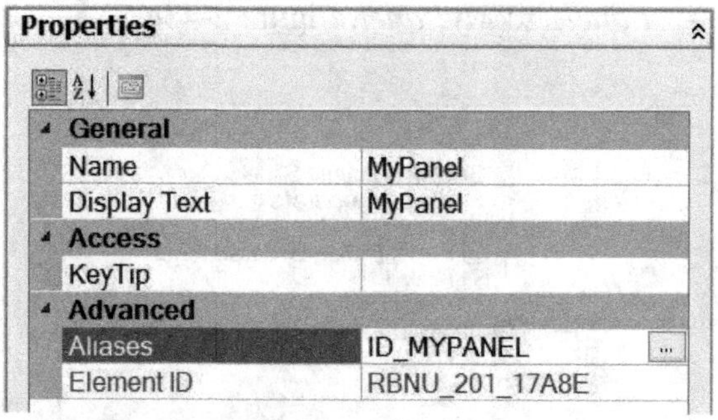

Figure 2-44c

2.14.7.6. Add panel to a tab

A user can add a panel to a tab using the method discussed in this section. This example adds the newly created panel, *MyPanel*, to *MyTab* (this tab was created in the section *New Tab*).

- (i) From the tab bar, select the *Manage* tab. (ii) From the *Customization* panel click on the *User Interface* command, the *CUI* icon (). (iii) This opens the *Customize User Interface* dialog box.
- In the upper left quadrant, click on the '+' adjacent to the *Ribbon* label. This displays an option list.
- The move process described in this step is not necessary; however, it makes the process discussed in the next step easier to understand. (i) Click on the '+' adjacent to the *Panel* label. This displays the list of panels with *MyPanel* at the lower end of the panel list (the newly created panel). (ii) Click on *MyPanel*. (iii) Press the left button of the mouse and keep pressing. (iv) Move the cursor upward. (v) Release the cursor when it is on the top of the panel list, Figure 2-45a.
- Click on the '+' adjacent to the *Tab* label. This displays the list of tabs with *MyTab* at the lower end of the tab list (the previously created tab), Figure 2-45a.
- (i) Select *MyPanel* again. (ii) Press the left button of the mouse and keep pressing. A light grey rectangle appears at the tail of the pointer and is not shown in the figure. (iii) Move the cursor upward to *MyTab*; a small blue arrowhead appears beside *MyTab*, Figure 2-45b. (iv) Release the cursor when it is on *MyTab*.
- The newly created panel is added to the previously created tab, Figure 2-45c.

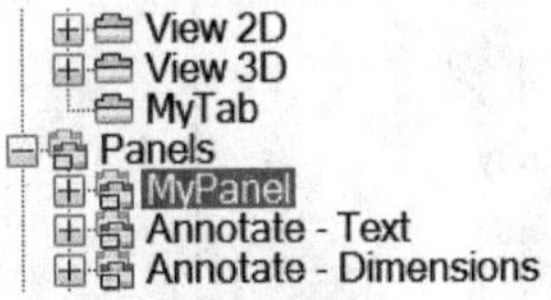

Figure 2-45a

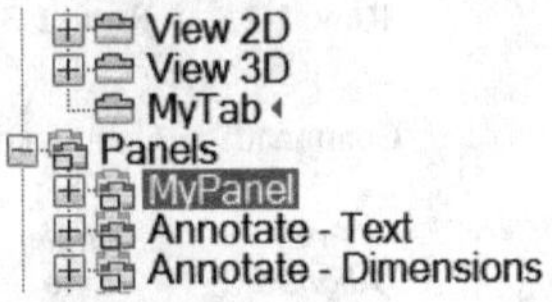

Figure 2-45b

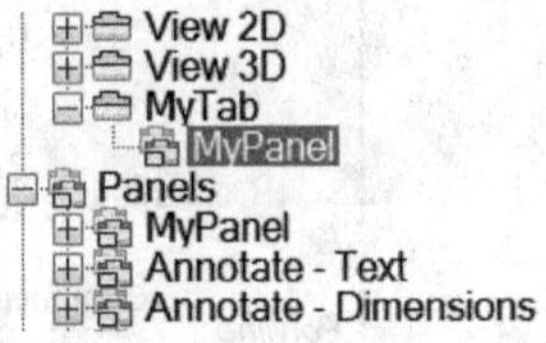

Figure 2-45c

2.14.7.7. Add commands to a panel

A user can add commands to a panel arranged in rows, sub-panel, and drop-down menus. A row can be further subdivided into rows, sub-panel, and drop-down menus.

This section creates two rows in *MyPanel*, Figure 2-46 and Figure 2-52. *Row_1* contains two commands and a sub-panel. The sub-panel is further subdivided into three rows: *Row_1-1* contains three commands and *Row_1-2* and *Row_1-3* contain one command each. *Row_2* contains one drop-down menu and is named *Array*, and the menu contains three commands. The remainder of this section describes the step-by-step process to add commands to a panel.

- (i) From the tab bar, select the *Manage* tab. (ii) From the *Customization* panel click on the *User Interface* command, the *CUI* icon (

). (iii) This opens the *Customize User Interface* dialog box.
- In the upper left quadrant, click on the '+' adjacent to the *Ribbon* label. This displays an option list, Figure 2-47a.
- In the upper left quadrant, click on the '+' adjacent to the *Panel* label. This displays an option list, Figure 2-47a.
- In the upper left quadrant, click on the '+' adjacent to the *MyPanel* label. This displays an option list. The newly created panel has three components as shown in Figure 2-47.

- **Add a row:** (i) Select *Row_1*, Figure 2-48a, and (ii) click with the right button of the mouse. A selection list shown in Figure 2-48a appears. (iii) Click on the *New Row* option. This closes the option list and creates a new row, *Row_2*, Figure 2-48b.

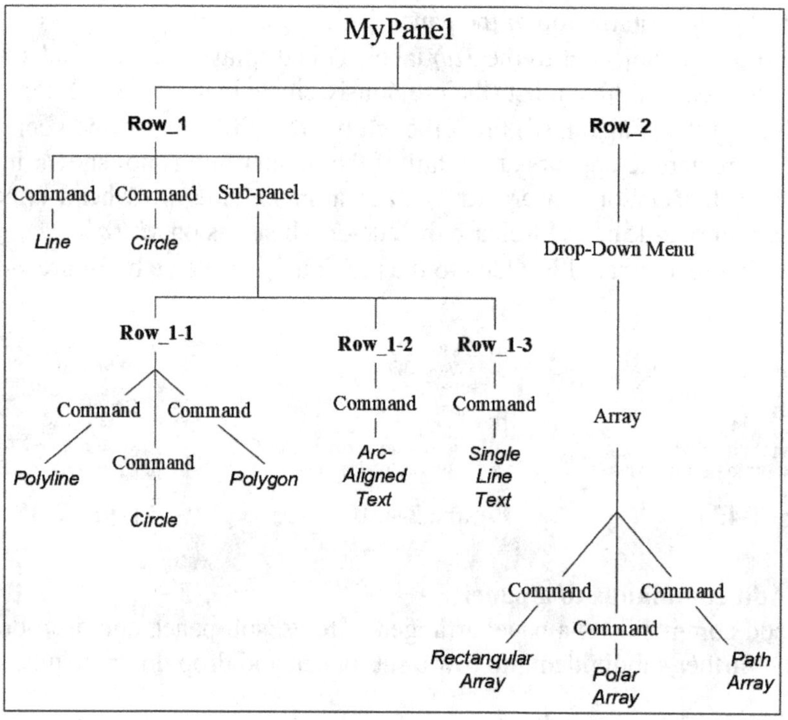

Figure 2-46

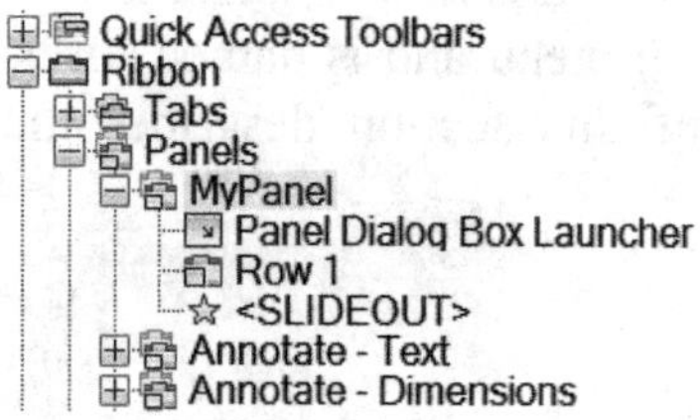

Figure 2-47

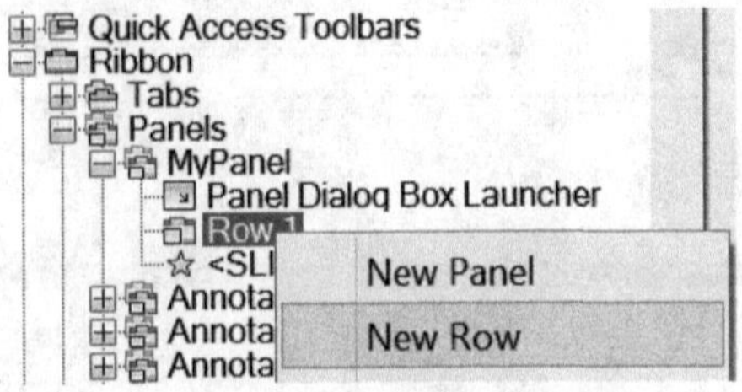

Figure 2-48a

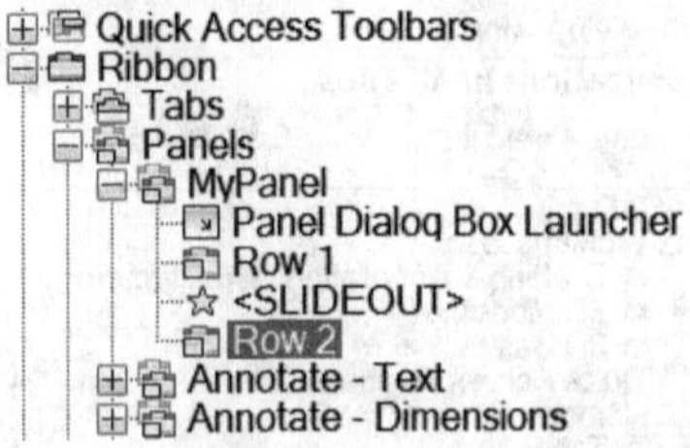

Figure 2-48b

- **Add a command:** Now add the *Line* command to *Row_1*.
  - Type *Line* in the search command list, Figure 2-49a. The command list box displays all the commands containing the word "Line".
  - Locate the *Line* command and select it, Figure 2-49a.
  - Press the left button of the mouse and keep pressing.
  - Move the cursor to *Row_1*. A small arrow appears beside *Row_1*, Figure 2-49a.
  - Release the left button and the *Line* command is added to *Row_1*, Figure 2-49b.
  - Click on the *Line* under *Row_1* and its properties are displayed on the right side of the dialog box, Figure 2-49b.

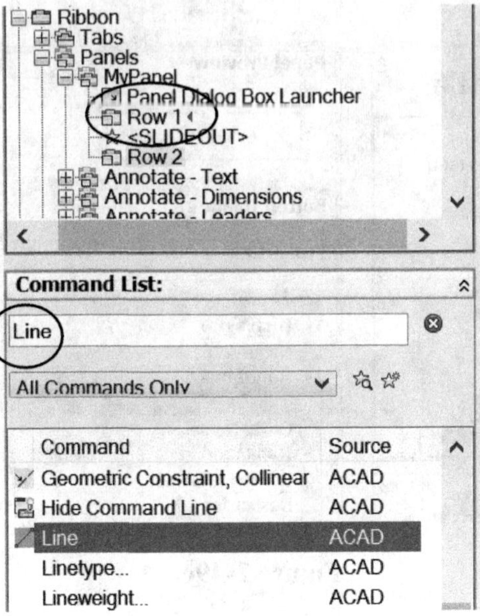

Figure 2-49a

  - In the *Properties* group, under *Appearance*, click on *Button Style* and a dropdown-arrow appears in the right cell.
  - Press the down-arrow and select *SmallWithText* option, Figure 2-49b. The command picture and label are displayed in the *Panel Preview* window; they are on the upper right corner of the dialog box, Figure 2-49b.

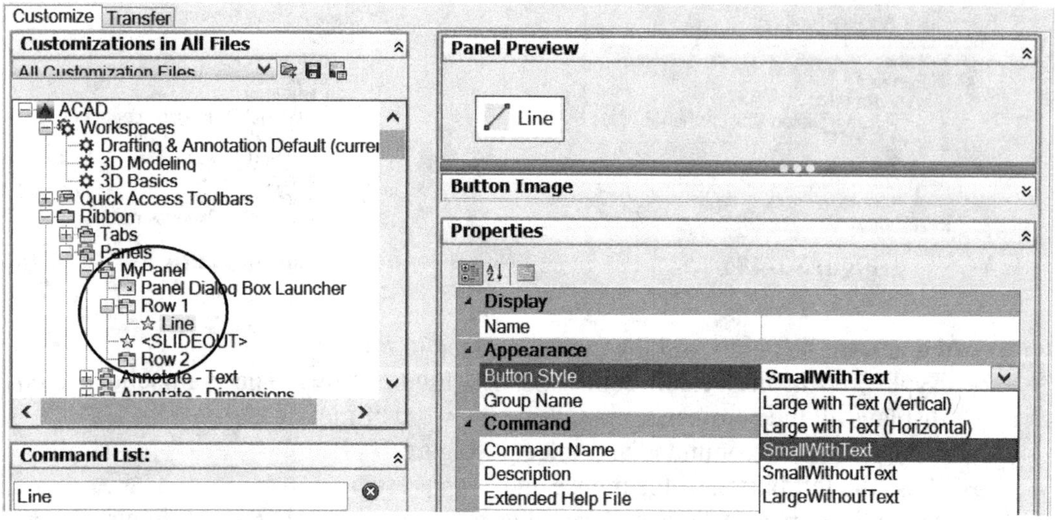

Figure 2-49b

- Similarly, add the circle command, Figure 2-49c.

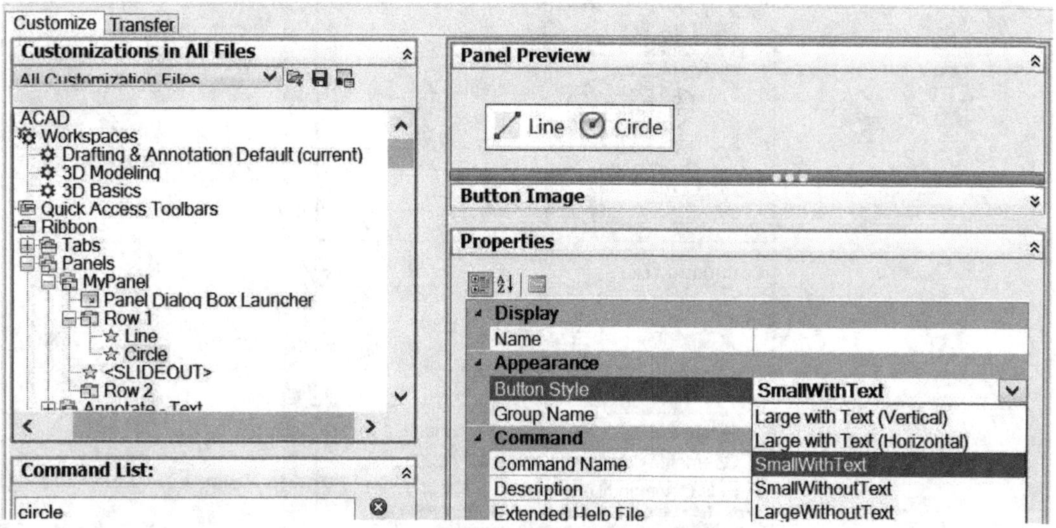

Figure 2-49c

- **Add a sub-panel:**
  - Select *Row_1*, Figure 2-50a.
  - Click with the right button of the mouse and a selection list will appear.
  - Click on the *New Sub-Panel* option. This closes the option list and a new sub-panel, *Sub-Panel 1*, is created, Figure 2-50b. The sub-panel is created with one unnamed row.
  - Now add two more rows and commands to the rows, Figure 2-50c. The command picture and label are displayed in the *Panel Preview* window; they are on the upper right corner of the dialog box, Figure 2-50c.

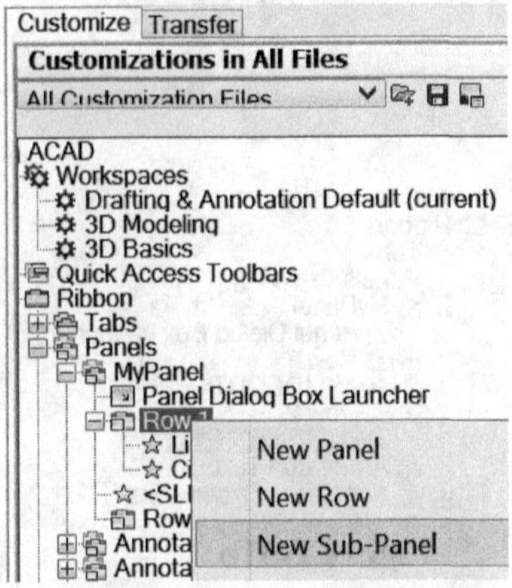

Figure 2-50a

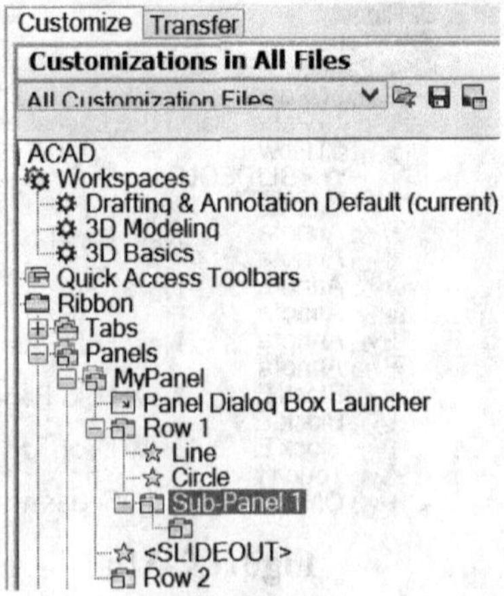

Figure 2-50b

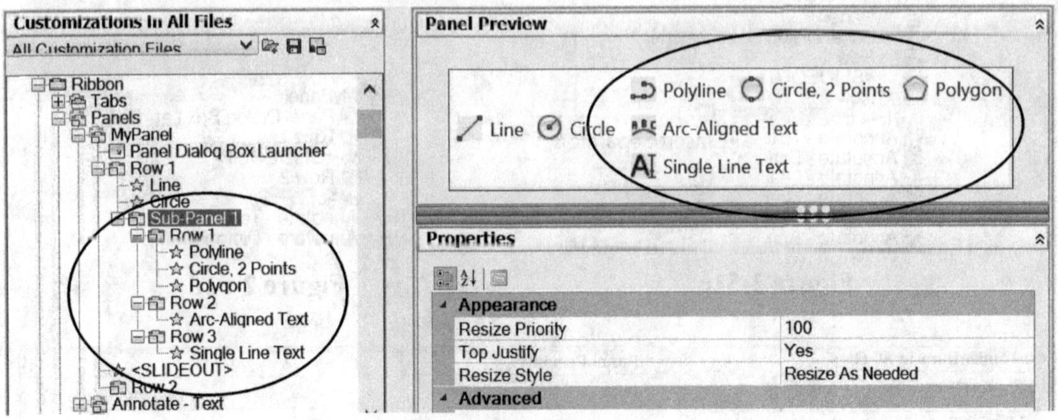

Figure 2-50c

- **Add a drop-down:**
  - Select *Row_2*, Figure 2-51a.
  - Click with the right button of the mouse. A selection list shown in Figure 2-51a appears.
  - Click on the *New Drop-Down* option. This closes the option list and a new drop-down menu, *Drop-Down 1*, is created, Figure 2-51b.
  - Select the New Drop-Down and press the right button of the mouse. A selection list appears. Select the Rename option, Figure 2-51c.
  - Rename the drop-down to Array, Figure 2-51d.
  - Now add three commands to the drop-down as shown in Figure 2-51e and discussed in the corresponding steps. The command picture and label are displayed in the *Panel Preview* window; they are on the upper right corner of the dialog box, Figure 2-51e.

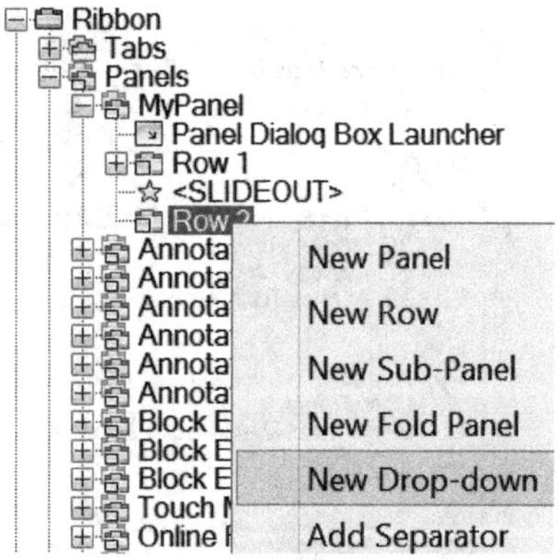

Figure 2-51a

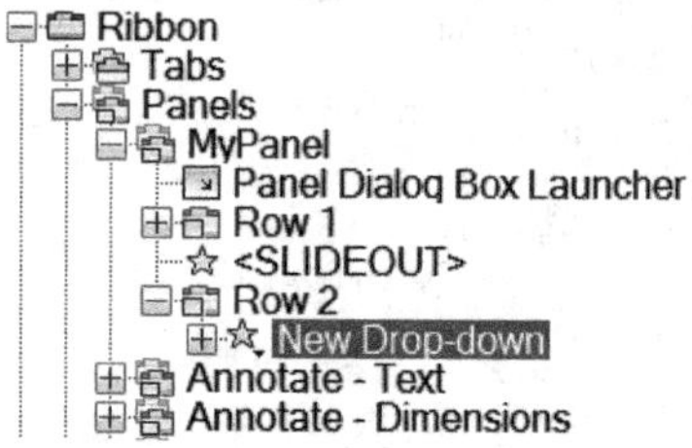

Figure 2-51b

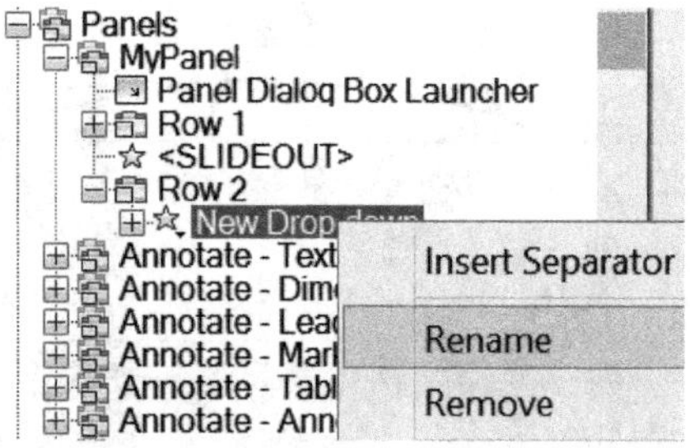

Figure 2-51c

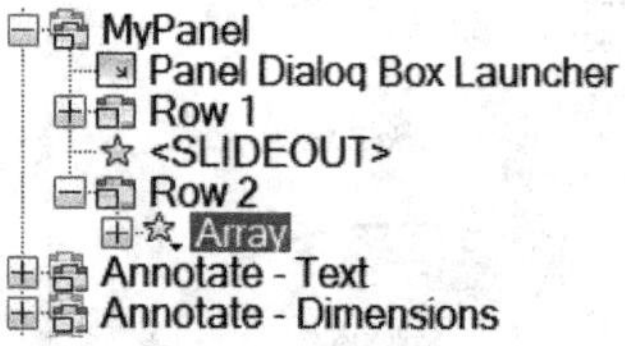

Figure 2-51d

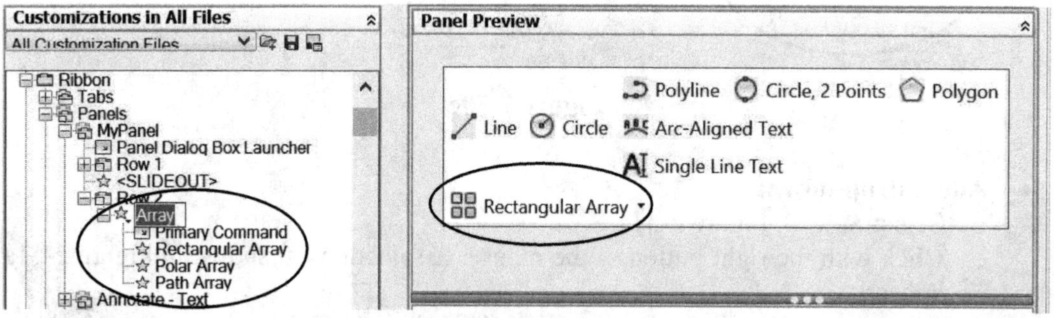

Figure 2-51e

- Figure 2-52 shows the selection of *MyTab* and *MyPanel*. The figure also shows the expanded *Array* drop-down menu.

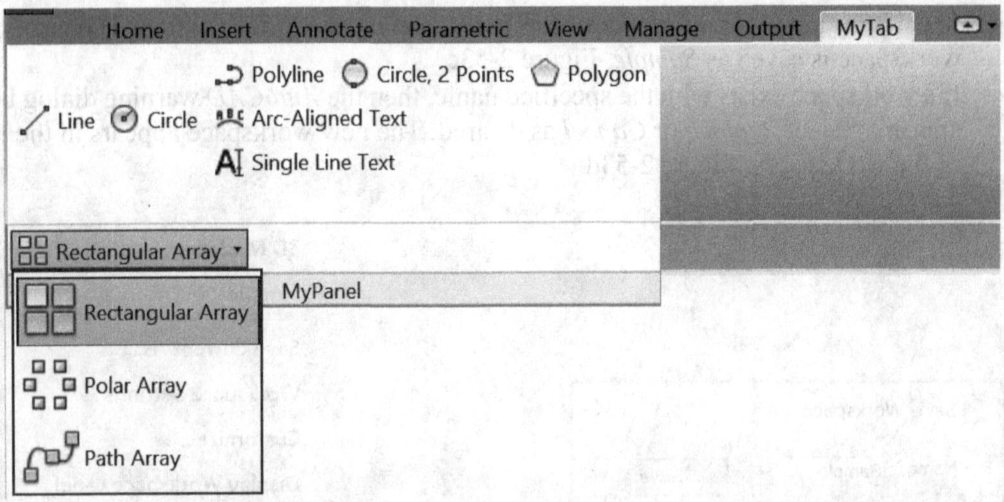

Figure 2-52

2.15. Workspace

The collection of the drawing area, cursor, World coordinate system, viewcube, drawing display format, scroll bars, ribbon, pull down menus, command line, status bar, toolbars, and dockable windows is known as workspace, but the ribbon panels, set of toolbars, and menus used in 2D and 3D drawings are different. Hence, to increase efficiency and productivity, a user can customize and save the workspace according to the project.

2.15.1. Save a workspace

A workspace can be saved as follows:

- Press the down-arrow (▾) on *Workspace Switching* wheel, Figure 2-53a; it is located on the lower right side of the workspace. An option list appears; click on the *Save Current As* option, Figure 2-53b, to open the *Save Workspace* dialog box, Figure 2-50c.

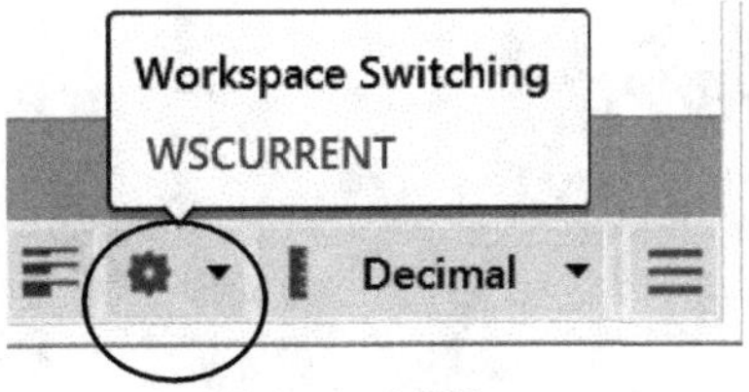

Figure 2-53a

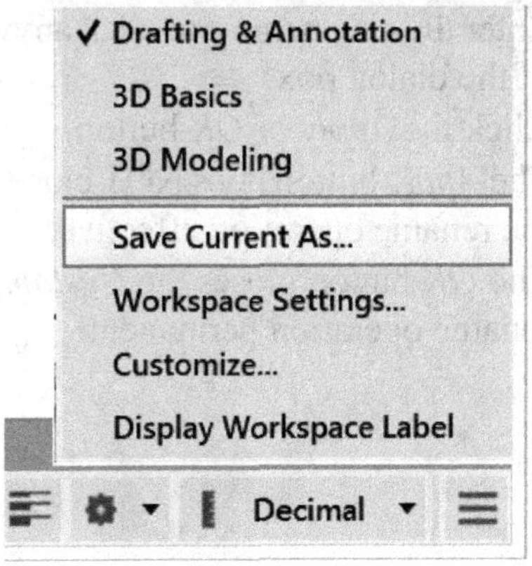

Figure 2-53b

- Specify the name for the workspace, *Sample*, and press the *Save* button. The example workspace is saved as *Sample*, Figure 2-53c.
- If a workspace exists with the specified name, then the *AutoCAD* warning dialog box appears. Select *Replace* or *Cancel* as desired. The new workspace appears in the list of the workspaces, Figure 2-53d.

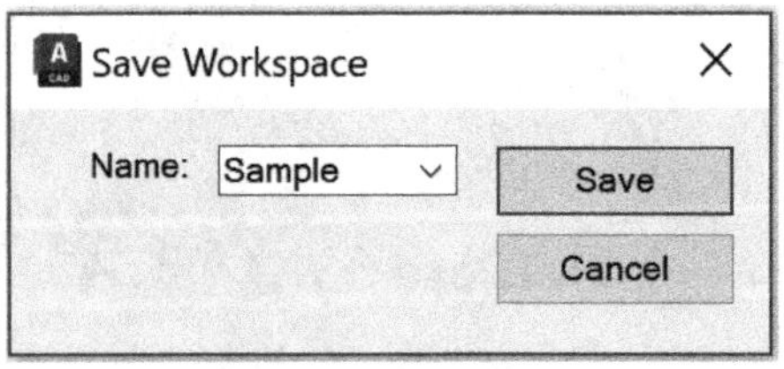

Figure 2-53c

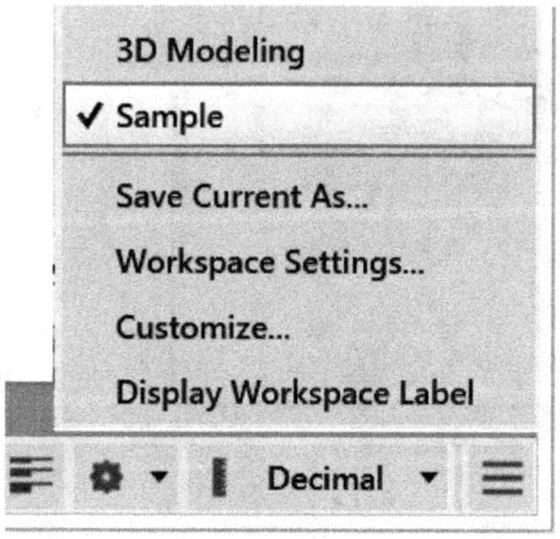

Figure 2-53d

2.15.2. Rename a workspace

A workspace can be renamed as follows.

- (i) From the tab bar, select the *Manage* tab. (ii) From the *Customization* panel click on the *User Interface* command, the *CUI* icon ( ). (iii) This opens the *Customize User Interface* dialog box.
- Click on the *Customize* tab of the *Customize User Interface* dialog box, Figure 2-54.
- Click on the workspace to be renamed, *Sample* in our example.
- Press the right button of the mouse; an options list shown in Figure 2-54 appears on the screen.
- Select the *rename* option.
- This closes the options list and the name (to be changed) is highlighted.
- Enter the new name and click anywhere on the screen. This activates the *Apply* button of the dialog box.
- Click the *Apply* or *OK* button.
- The *Apply* button does NOT close the *Customize User Interface* dialog box but makes the rename operation effective.
- The *OK* button closes the *Customize User Interface* dialog box as well as makes the rename operation permanent.

2.15.3. Switch a workspace

A workspace can be switched as follows. In this example, the current workspace, *Drafting & Annotation*, is switched to the *3D Basics* workspace.

- Press the down-arrow (▾) on *Workspace Switching* wheel, Figure 2-55a; it is located on the lower right side of the workspace. An option list appears; click on the desired workspace, *3D Basics*, Figure 2-55b.
- The list is closed and the workspace is switched.

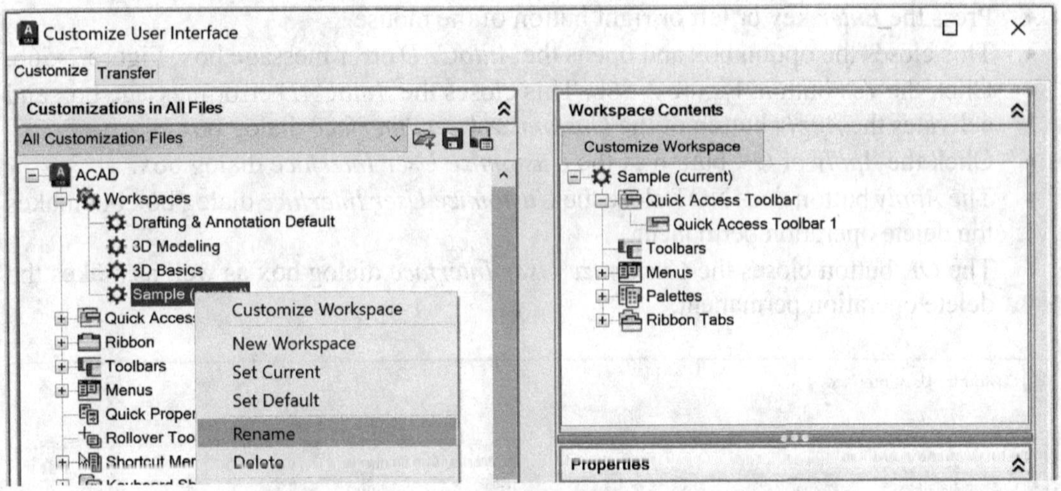

Figure 2-54

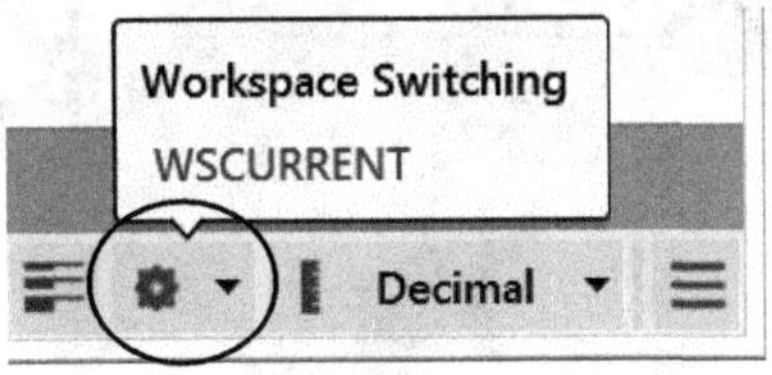

Figure 2-55a

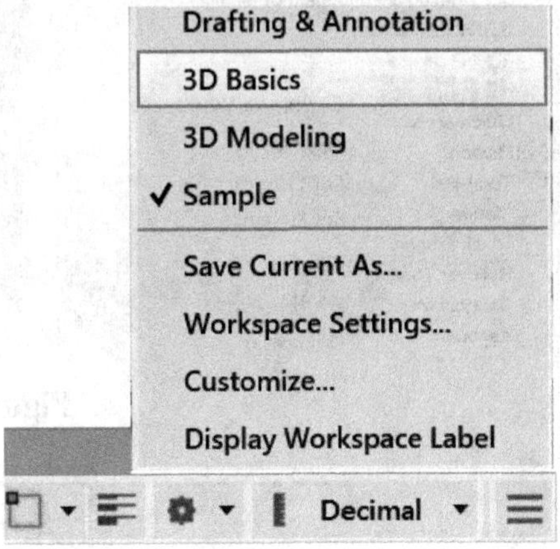

Figure 2-55b

2.15.4. Delete a workspace

A workspace can be deleted as follows.

- Figure 2-52 shows the selection of *MyTab* and *MyPanel*. The figure also shows the expanded *Array* drop-down menu.

- (i) From the tab bar, select the *Manage* tab. (ii) From the *Customization* panel click on the *User Interface* command, the *CUI* icon (). (iii) This opens the *Customize User Interface* dialog box.
- Click on the *Customize* tab of the *Customize User Interface* dialog box.
- Click on the workspace to be deleted, 'Sample' in our example, Figure 2-56a.
- Press the right button of the mouse; the option box shown in Figure 2-56a appears on the screen.
- Select the *Delete* option.
- Press the *Enter* key or left or right button of the mouse.
- This closes the option box and opens the *AutoCAD* error message box, Figure 2-56b.
- Click the *Yes* button, Figure 2-56b. This closes the *AutoCAD* error message box and activates the *Apply* button of the *Customize User Interface* dialog box.
- Click the *Apply* or *OK* button of the *Customize User Interface* dialog box.
- The *Apply* button does NOT close the *Customize User Interface* dialog box but makes the delete operation permanent.
- The *OK* button closes the *Customize User Interface* dialog box as well as makes the delete operation permanent.

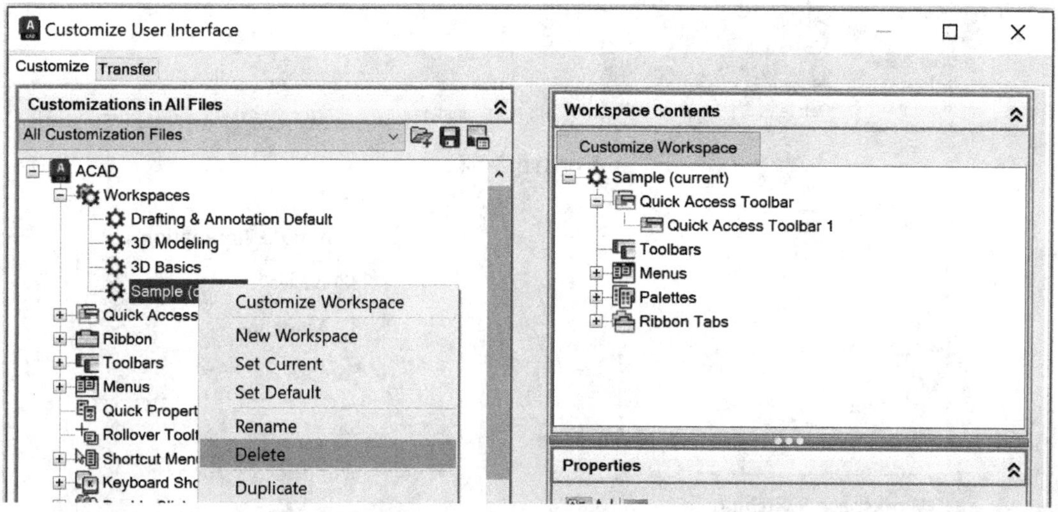

Figure 2-56a

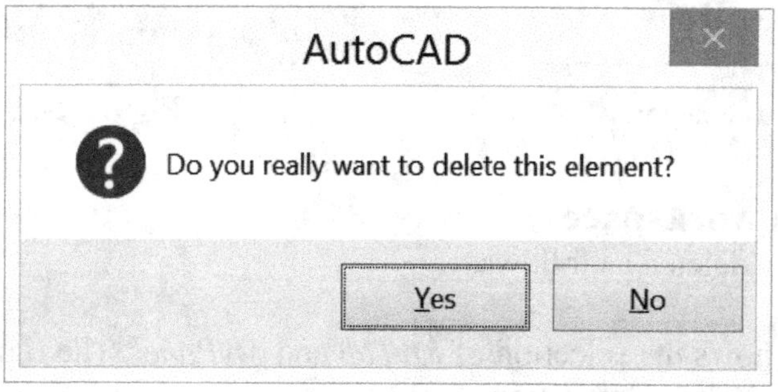

Figure 2-56b

2.16. New Drawing 

In AutoCAD, a new drawing can be opened using one of the following methods.

1. Menu method: Click on the down-arrow from the *Application* pull-down menu, Figure 2-57a, and select the *New* option.
2. Toolbar method: Select the new drawing tool (), Figure 2-57b, in the quick access toolbar. It is located on the upper left corner of the dialog box.
3. From the **Start** tab of interface: Click the down-arrow for the New option and select the **Browse templates...** option as shown in Figure 2-57c.
4. Command line method: Type "new", "New", or "NEW" in the command line, Figure 2-57d, and press the *Enter* key.
5. Keyboard method: Hold down the control "Ctrl" key and type "N".
6. From the interface: Click with the **right** button of the mouse on the "+" sign as shown in Figure 2-57e, and select the *New* option.

The methods 1 - 5 discussed above open the *Select template* dialog box shown in Figure 2-58a and Figure 2-58b, whereas method 6 opens the default file.

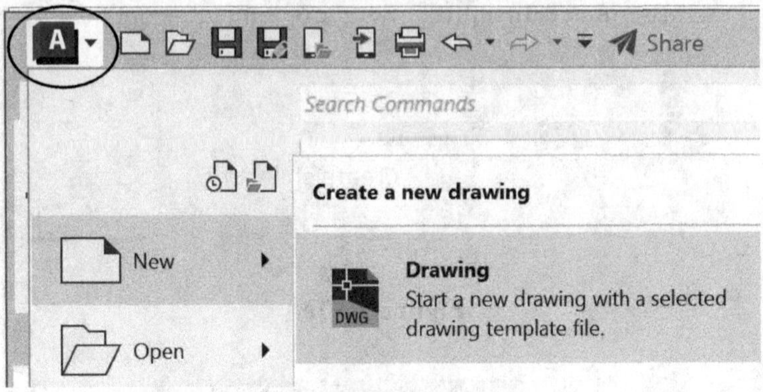

Figure 2-57a

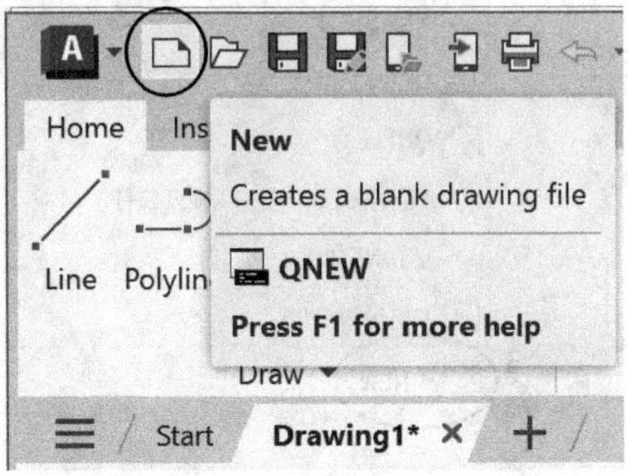

Figure 2-57b

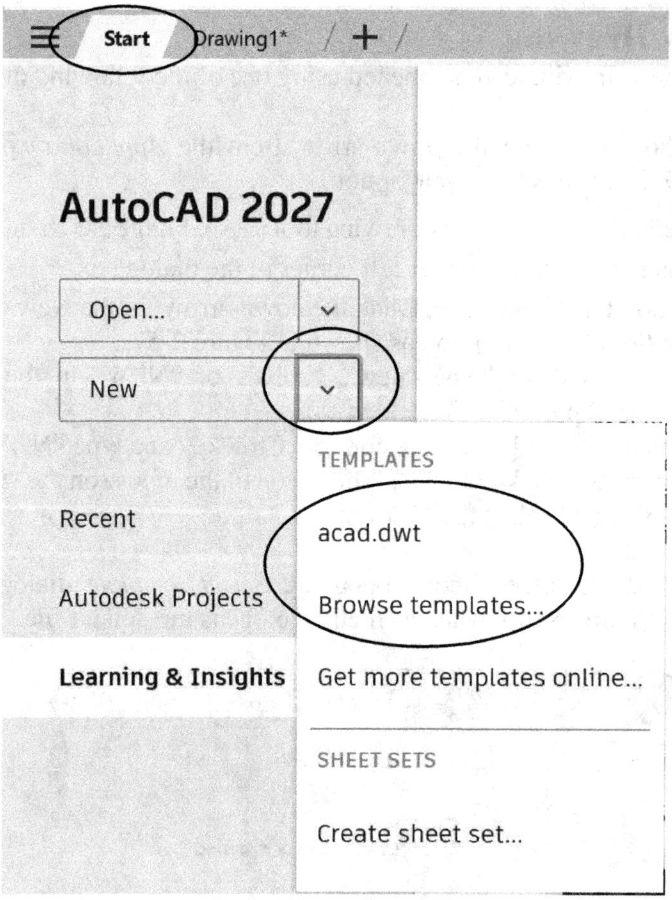

Figure 2-57c

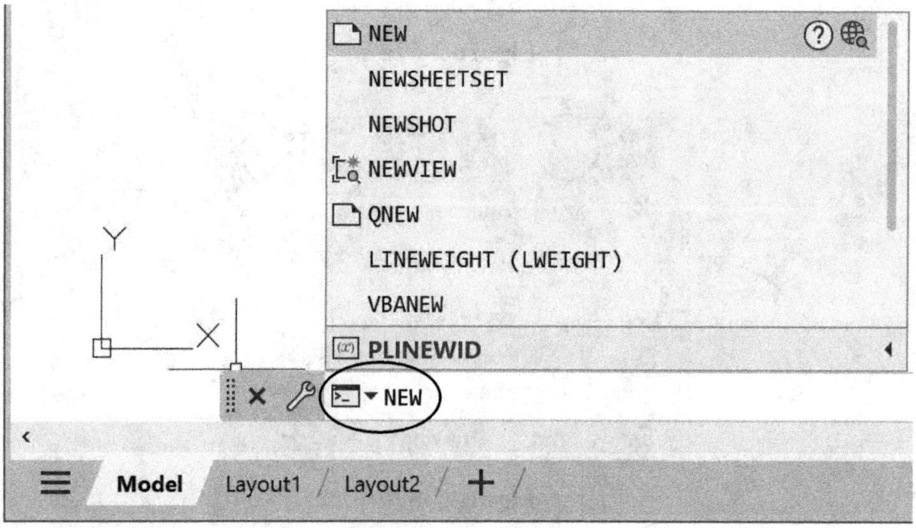

Figure 2-57d

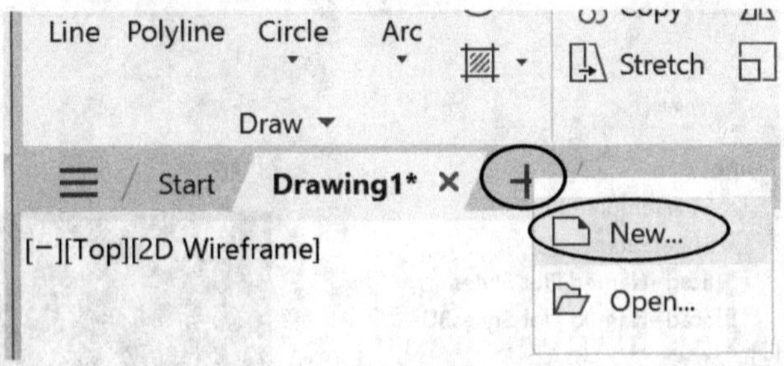

Figure 2-57e

2.16.1. Drawing units

Every object in AutoCAD is measured in drawing units. Before starting the drawing, the user must decide on the type of units. The input type can be ANSI or ISO.

2.16.1.1. ANSI units

In ANSI units, the linear dimensions (lengths, distance, height, etc.) are measured in terms of inches, feet, miles, etc. The *Select template* dialog box shown in Figure 2-58a shows the selection of the "acad" template, giving the drawing ANSI (inch) units and ANSI style dimensions.

To create a new drawing file for ANSI units, use the following steps: (i) select an ***acad*** template file; and (ii) click the *Open* button of the dialog box. This closes the dialog box and creates a new file.

In AutoCAD, a new drawing file is opened with the default values. For example, its name is Drawing1, Drawing2, etc.; its units are decimal; the drawing limits are 12 x 9 inches; and the default values for both the grid and snap are 0.5 inches.

2.16.1.2. ISO units

In ISO units, the linear dimensions (lengths, distance, height, etc.) are measured in terms of millimeter, centimeter, kilometers, etc. The *Select template* dialog box shown in Figure 2-58b shows the selection of the "acadiso" template, giving the drawing ISO (millimeters) units and ISO style dimensions.

To create a new drawing file for ISO units, use the following steps: (i) select an ***acadiso*** template file based; and (ii) click the *Open* button of the dialog box. This closes the dialog box and creates a new file.

In AutoCAD, a new drawing file is opened with the default values. For example, its name is Drawing1, Drawing2, etc.; its units are decimal; the drawing limits are 420 x 290 millimeters; and the default values for both the grid and snap are 10 millimeters.

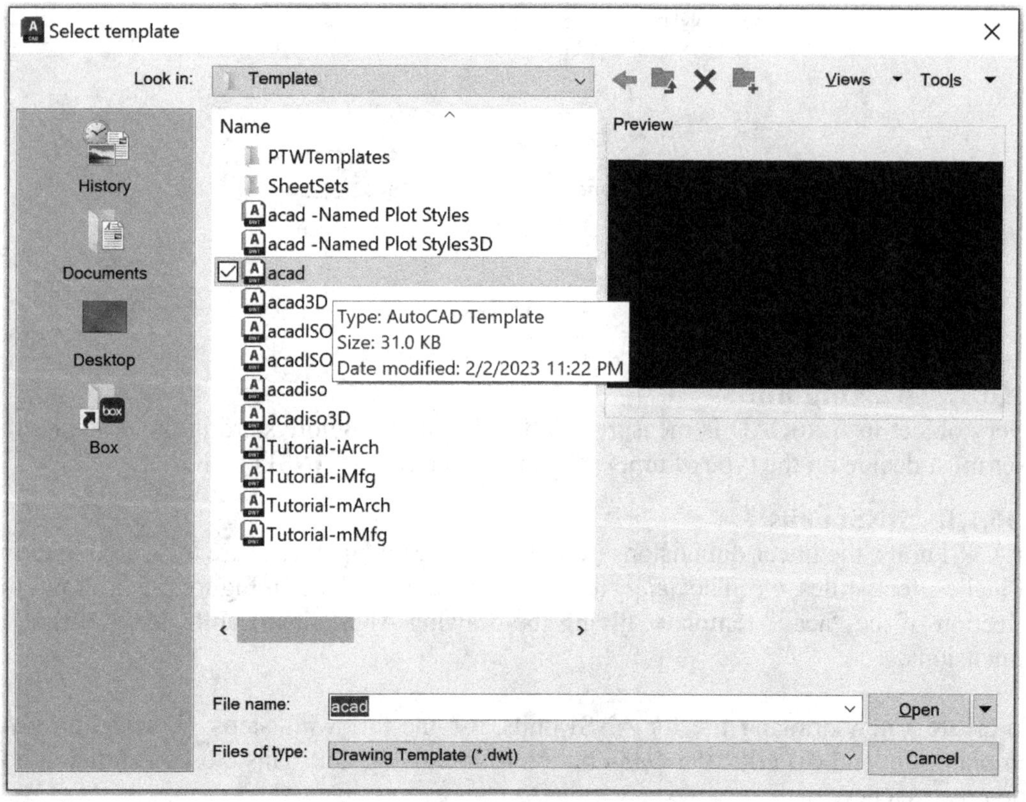

Figure 2-58a

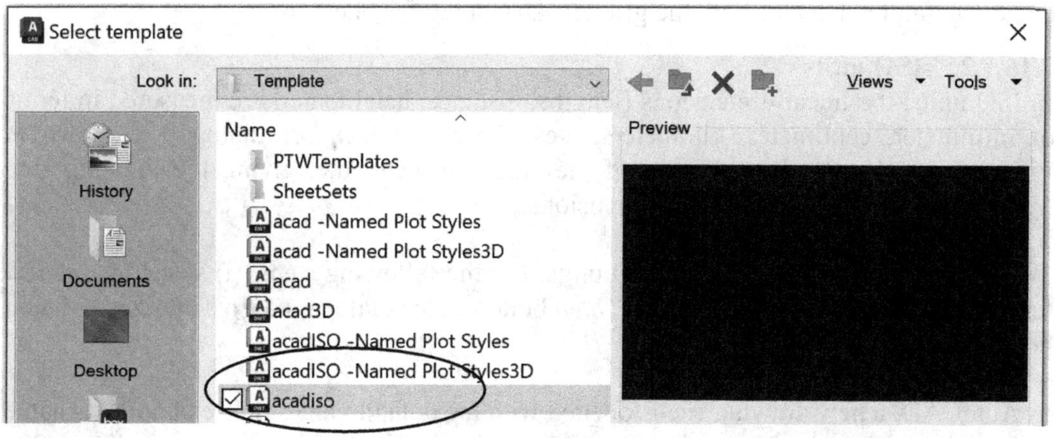

Figure 2-58b

2.16.2. Convert a drawing from ISO to ANSI (and vice versa)

Based on the type, a user should open the correct type of template file (acad for ANSI or acadiso for ISO). However, if a user opens an incorrect file type and realizes the mistake after drawing a part (or complete) drawing, then the user can fix the mistake using *Copy* and *Scale* command. The *Copy* and *Scale* commands are discussed in *Chapter 4*.

Since 1 inch = 2.54 cm, therefore, to convert a drawing unit from inches to centimeters, a scale factor of 2.54 must be used; and to convert from centimeters to inches, the scale factor of 1/2.54 or 0.3937 must be used.

Convert a drawing from inches to centimeters

The drawing conversion from ANSI to ISO or vice versa is a two-step process: (i) make a copy of the drawing, and (ii) scale the copied drawing. *Note: Mac users should use Command key instead of Ctrl key.*

i. *Make a copy of the drawing:*
   - Select every object of the source drawing: hold the *Ctrl* key and press the '*A*' key of the keyboard.
   - Copy the content of the source drawing: hold the *Ctrl* key and press the '*C*' key of the keyboard.
   - Open a new acad file: the target file.
   - Click in the drawing area of the target file.
   - Paste the contents in the target drawing: hold the *Ctrl* key and press the '*V*' key of the keyboard.

ii. *Scale the target drawing:*
   - Activate the *Scale* () command using one of the following techniques:
     - o Ribbon method: From the *Home* tab and the *Modify* panel select the *Scale* tool.
     - o Command line method: Type "scale", "Scale", or "SCALE" in the command line and press the *Enter* key.
   - The prompt shown in Figure 2-58c appears on the screen.

Figure 2-58c

   - At the *Select Objects* prompt, click on every object and then press the *Enter* key. All objects in the target drawing are selected for scaling. The prompt shown in Figure 2-58d appears.

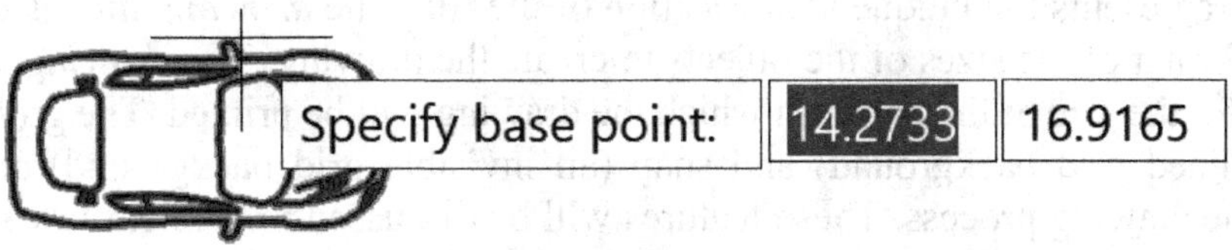

Figure 2-58d

- A base point is the point which does not change its location after the completion of the scaling process. In this example, the right corner of the side view mirror is selected as the base point as shown in Figure 2-58d; click at the right corner of the side view mirror. The prompt shown in Figure 2-58e appears.
- Enter a scale factor of 2.54, Figure 2-58e, and press the *Enter* key.
- All the objects in the drawing are now 2.54 times larger than the source file, Figure 2-58f.
- Scaling is relative to the world coordinate system origin, and the location of the drawing origin remains at the WCS origin.

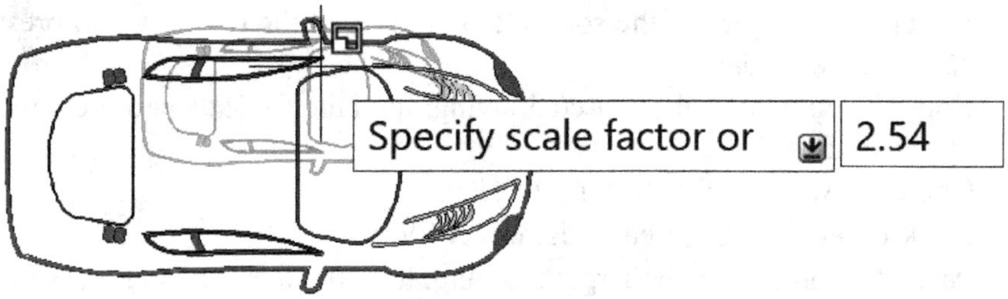

Figure 2-58e

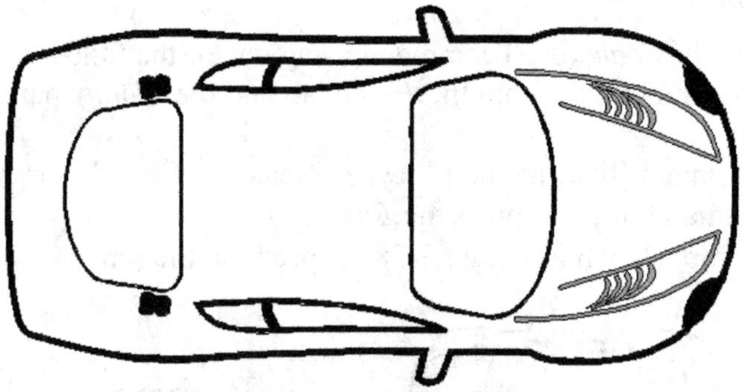

Figure 2-58f

2.17. Basics Of A Drawing File

The basic features of any drawing are its drawing units (discussed in Section 2.16), name, input units' format, drawing limits and grid and snap spacing. The user can select the default values when a new file is opened or reset as needed.

The *name* represents the unique identification of the file. The *drawing units* is used to set the input format of the sizes of the objects to create the drawing. The *drawing limit* is the metaphor for the size of the paper on which the drawing will be printed. The grid (a visible dotted or lined grid background) and snap (an invisible grid background) are used to improve the drawing process. These features will be discussed in the next few sections of this chapter.

2.18. Drawing's Name

A drawing should always be assigned with a short and meaningful name. For example, the file named *Angles_NS* contains angles and north-south direction representation. A drawing name can be 256 characters long, and it can be any combination of letters (both upper and lower case), numbers, and symbols. Although the user is allowed to use the characters $, %, and *, these characters should not be used. For example, YourName_1.dwg, ENGR2100_1.dwg are legitimate names but not 1_%.dwg or *.*.dwg.

2.19. Data Input Format

As the name suggests, The *Units* command is used to set the input format of the dimensions of the objects to create the drawing, that is, the style of the input values. For example, in ANSI style dimensions, the efficiency of the drafter can be increased if the lengths could be specified in architectural units (feet and inches) for drawing a floor plan. ***A user must remember that the Units command is used to set the input format; the type of the units ANSI or ISO is set when a new file is open as "acad" or "acadiso" template file, respectively.***

Activate the *Units* command using the command line method.

a. Command line method: Type "units", "Units", or "UNITS" on the command line and press the *Enter* key.

The *Units* command opens the *Drawing Units* dialog box shown in Figure 2-59. Using the *Length* and *Angle* panels, the dialog box allows for setting the type and precision of the linear and angular measurements.

By default, AutoCAD sets the length in decimal format with precision of four decimal places; that is, length appears in the form 0.0000. The angular unit precision is set to whole degrees, that is, an angle appears in the form 0°. The dialog box also provides the capability to change the units of measurement for blocks and drawings that are inserted into the current drawing under *Insertion scale* panel.

2.19.1. Length

The *Length* panel specifies the format and the precision for the linear measurement of the current drawing. The linear measurements can be in five different formats, Figure 2-60a. The various options for length units (Figures 2-60a) can be visualized by clicking on the down arrowhead () for *Type* window in the *Length* panel of the *Drawing Units* dialog box, Figure 2-60a.

- To change the format, click on the desired format. This updates the format and closes the dropdown list. The example figure shows the selection of *Architectural* units.
- To close the dropdown list without changing the format, either press the *Esc* key or click outside the length panel.
- Similarly, the precision can be modified, Figure 2-60b. The example figure shows the precision for the *Architectural* units.

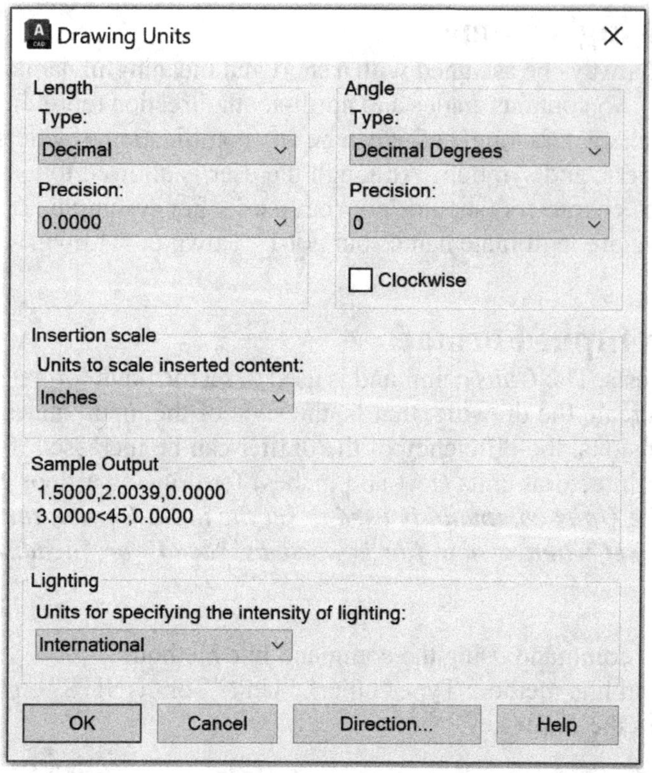

Figure 2-59

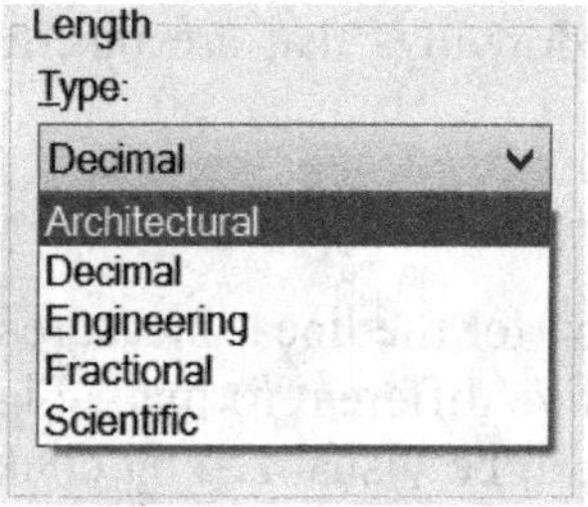

Figure 2-60a

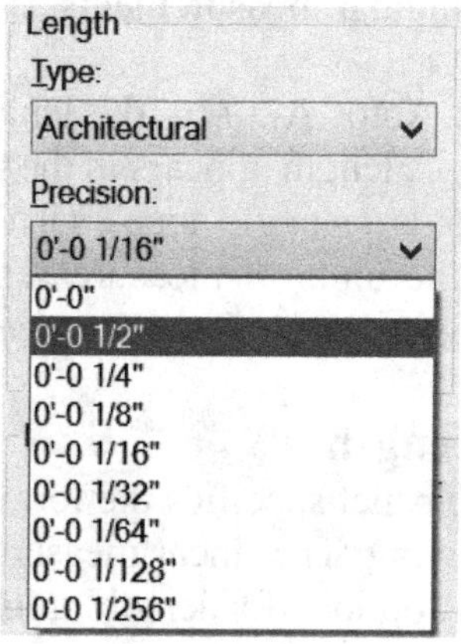

Figure 2-60b

Each of the linear measurement's formats can be specified to nine degrees of precision, Table #1. The *Engineering* and *Architectural* formats produce feet-and-inches displays and assume that each drawing unit represents one inch. The other three can be used for both the SI and ANSI systems to represent any real-world units. The *Decimal* formats produce a scale broken down into 10's. This is the default unit system in AutoCAD. The *Fractional* formats produce a scale in a mixed number format. The *Scientific* formats use exponential notation to display very large or small numbers.

Table #1: Linear measurements

Format	*Precision*
Architectural	0′-0″ to 0′-1/256″
Decimal	0 to 0.00000000
Fractional	0′-0″ to 0′-1/256″
Engineering	0′-0″ to 0′-0.00000000″
Scientific	0E+01 to 0.00000000E+01

2.19.2. Angle

The *Angle* panel specifies the format and the precision for the current angular measurement of the current drawing. The angular measurement can be in five different formats, Figure 2-61a. The various options for an angle, shown in Figure 2-61a, can be visualized by clicking on the down arrowhead (▾) for *Type* window in the *Angle* panel of the *Drawing Units* dialog box, Figures 2-59.

- To change the angle format, click on the desired format. This will update the format and close the dropdown list. Figure 2-61a shows the selection of the *Decimal Degree*.
- To close the drop-down list without changing the format, either press the *Esc* key or click outside the *Angle* panel.
- Similarly, the precision can be modified, Figures 2-61b. The figure shows the precision for the *Decimal Degree*.

Each of the angular measurements can be specified to seven degrees of precision, Table #2. **Remember** the conversion! 400 grads are equal to 360 degrees and 2 Pi radians are equal to 360 degrees (2 π = 360° = 400 grad).

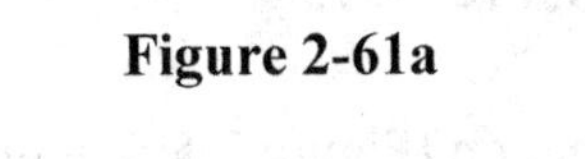

Figure 2-61a

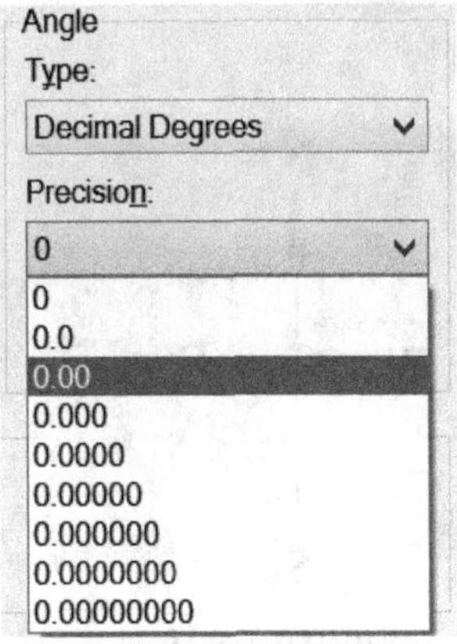

Figure 2-61b

Each of the angular measurements can be specified to seven degrees of precision, Table #2. **Remember** the conversion! 400 grads are equal to 360 degrees and 2 Pi radians are equal to 360 degrees (2 π radians = 360° = 400 grad).

Table #2: Angular measurements

Format	*Precision*
Decimal degree	0 to 0.00000000
Deg/Min/Sec	0d to 0d00′00.0000″
Grads	0g to 0.00000000g
Radian	0r to 0.00000000r
Surveyor's Units	N 0d E to N 0d00′00.0000″ E

- An angle appears as a decimal number in the *Decimal* format.
- The *Deg/Min/Sec* format is represented with suffixes "d", "'", and """ for degrees, minutes, and seconds, respectively.
- A lowercase "g" suffix is used for the *Grads* formats.
- A lowercase "r" suffix is used for the *Radians* formats.
- The *Surveyor's Units* show angles as bearings (angle always less than 90 degrees) measured from north or south towards east or west, Figures 2-61c. This representation has three parts: (i) N or S for north or south, (ii) angle's numerical value in degrees/minutes/seconds for how far from east or west, and (iii) E or W for east or west, for example N 35° 24′ 19″ W. If the angle is precisely north, south, east, or west, then only the single letter representing the compass point is displayed.

By default, AutoCAD starts with the zero angles at the 3 o'clock position (East) with angles increasing in the counterclockwise direction, Figure 2-61c and Figure 2-61d. To change the direction of angular measurement, check the *Clockwise* check box in the *Angle* panel of the *Drawing Units* dialogue box, Figure 2-59. When this box is checked, positive angles are measured in a clockwise direction.

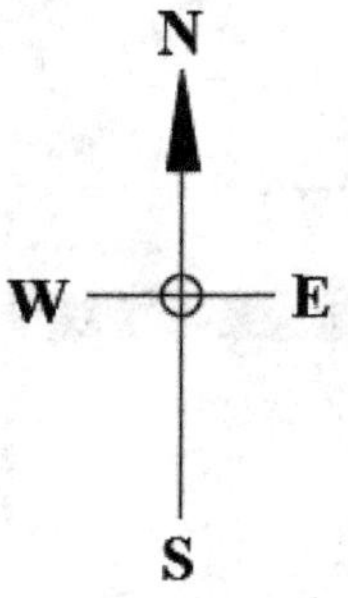

Figure 2-61c

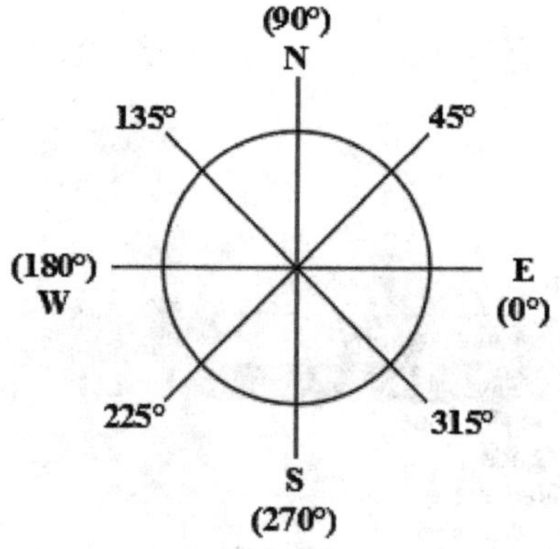

Figure 2-61d

To change the start angle, click on the "Direction..." button (Figure 2-59) in the *Drawing Units* dialogue box. The *Direction Control* dialogue box appears. The user can set the *Base Angle* to any one of the four major directions by clicking on the appropriate radio button or can set it to a specific angle with the "Other" option, Figure 2-61e. The user can enter a specific angle into the edit box. To change the directions of angular measurement (to E, N, S, or W) simply click on the appropriate radio button.

2.19.3. Insertion scale

The insertion scale is the ratio of the units used in the source drawing and the units used in the target drawing. That is, it controls the units of measurement for a drawing (source) that is inserted into the current drawing (target). If no scaling is desired then choose the *Unitless* option, Figure 2-62. The various options for insertion scale are shown in Figure 2-59 and can be visualized by clicking on the down arrowhead ( ) in the *Insertion scale* panel of the *Drawing Units* dialog box, Figure 2-62.

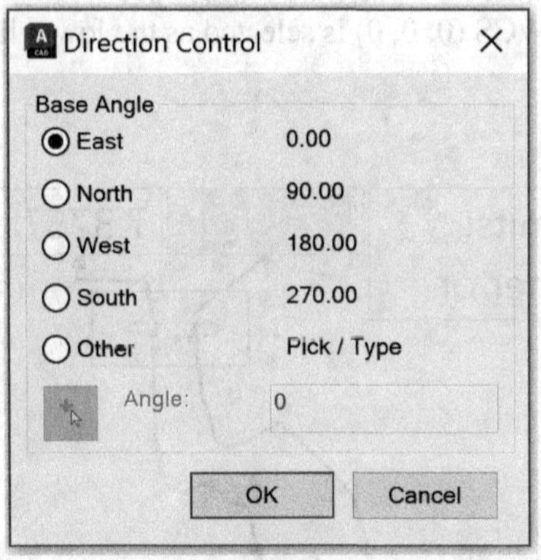

Figure 2-61c

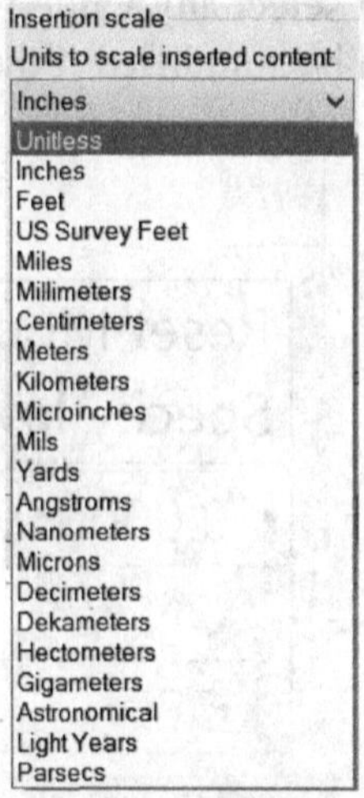

Figure 2-62

2.20. Drawing Limits

Generally, the *drawing limits* is the metaphor for the size of the paper on which the drawing will be printed. The *Limits* command is used to set the boundaries of the drawing or grid display in the current *Model* or *Layout* tab. Generally, limits are set to match the size of the paper (on which the drawing will be printed). Figure 2-63a shows the standard size drawing papers for the engineering and architectural applications.

Standard Drawing Sheet Sizes – Millimeters

A4 = 210 * 297
A3 = 297 * 420
A2 = 420 * 594
A1 = 594 * 841
A0 = 841 * 1189

Standard Drawing Sheet Sizes – Inches

A = 8.5 * 11.0
B = 11.0 * 17.0
C = 17.0 * 22.0
D = 22.0 * 34.0
E = 34.0 * 44.0

Figure 2-63a

The default drawing limits are 12 x 9 inches in the ANSI system and 420 x 290 millimeters in the ISO system. The following section provides step by step instruction for setting the drawing limits.

1. Activate the drawing limits command *Limits* using the command line method.
   a. Command line method: Type "limits", "Limits", or "LIMITS" in the command line and press the *Enter* key.
2. This displays the prompt for the lower left corner shown in Figure 2-63b. The user can select any value for the lower limits. However, the *Limits* specification process can be simplified if the origin of the WCS (0, 0, 0) is selected as the lower limits.

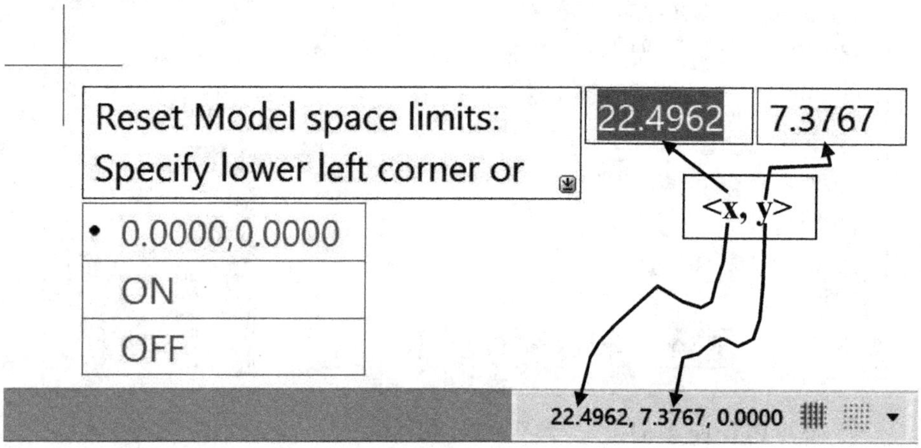

Figure 2-63b

3. Press the down-arrow key on the keyboard to reveal the various options. The *On* option restricts entering points outside the drawing limits. However, portions of objects such as circles can extend outside the drawing limits because limits check only test points that are entered. The default is *Off* (no limits checking).
4. Press the up-arrow key on the keyboard to hide the various options.
5. To choose the default values (for either of the lower left and upper right corners) just press the *Enter* key on the keyboard.
6. Specify the coordinates of the lower left corner using one of the following methods. This example uses (0, 0) for the lower left corner.
   a. (i) Type '0' at the prompt, (ii) press the 'TAB' key on the keyboard, the cursor moves to the second cell, (iii) type '0', and (iv) press the *Enter* key.
   b. (i) Specify the x,y (no space) coordinates in the command line and (ii) press the *Enter* key.
   c. Click with the left button of the mouse at the desired location.
7. The prompt for the upper right corner appears, Figure 2-63c. Specify (10, 12) the coordinates for this point as follows. (i) Type '10' at the prompt, (ii) press the 'TAB' key on the keyboard, the cursor moves to the second cell, (iii) type '12', and (iv) press the *Enter* key.

8. Turn on the *Grid* to check the drawing limits; the *Grid* command is discussed in the next section. Figure 2-63d and Figure 2-63e show the lower left corner (0, 0, 0) and upper right corner (10, 12, 0) of the drawing limits, respectively.

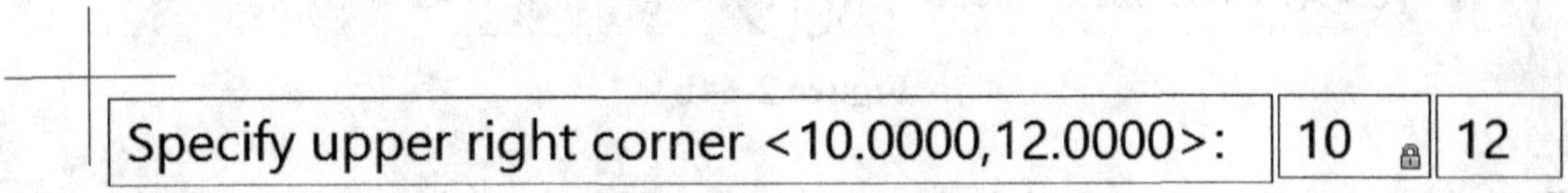

Figure 2-63c

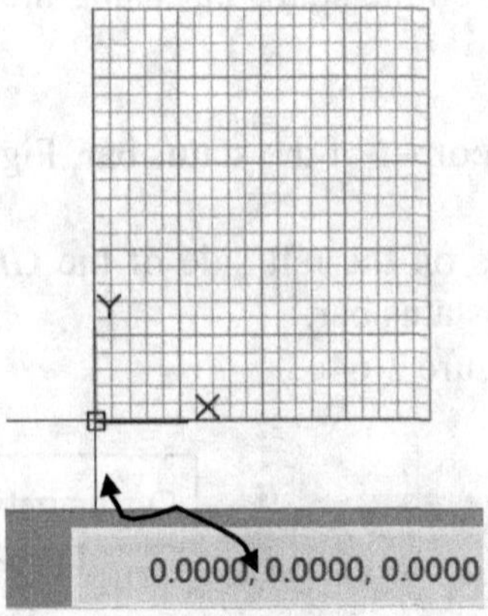

Figure 2-63d

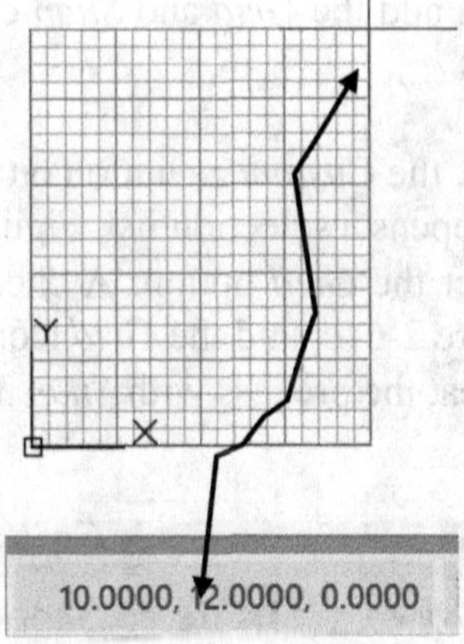

Figure 2-63e

2.21. Grid ( ) And Snap ( ) Commands

The *Grid* command is used to display a visible grid (similar to graph or engineering paper) background on the drawing screen. The *Snap* command is used to set an invisible grid background on the drawing screen and to limit the movement of the cursor to the snap grid's points only. The snap grid is completely independent of the visible grid. However, the grid spacing and snap spacing are usually set to the same value to avoid confusion. The default *Grid* and *Snap* setting for an acad template is 0.50 inch and for an acadiso template is 10 millimeters. By default, the *Grid* (Figure 2-64a) and *Snap* (Figure 2-64b) commands icons are located on the status bar. Notice the difference in appearance of *On* and *Off* commands. However, if the commands icons are not available from the status bar, Figure 2-64c, then the user must add the icon using *Customization* command.

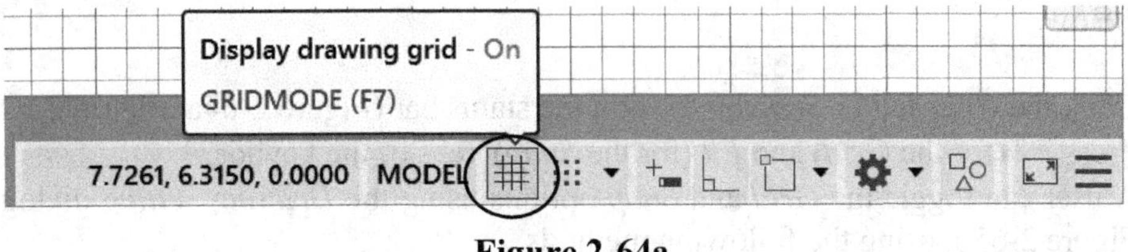

Figure 2-64a

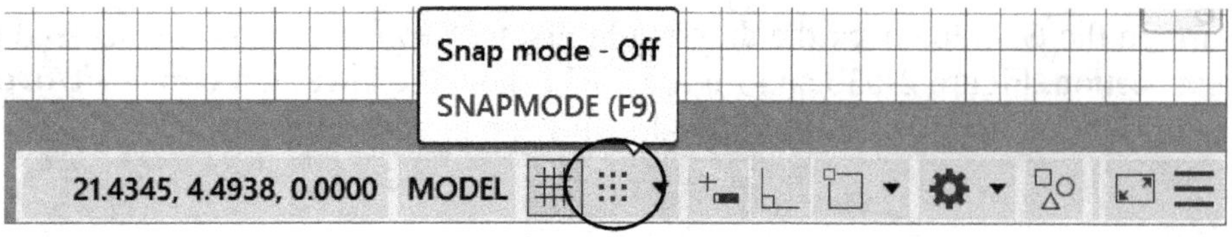

Figure 2-64b

By default, the grid appears both in the drawing area of the Model space and in the layouts. However, the user can set the grid and snap properties independently in the Model space and layouts. In addition, every layout can be set to its own style.
A user can add the *Grid* and *Snap* commands icons on the status bar using the following techniques.

- Click the *Customize* button on the lower right corner of the status bar, Figure 2-64c; this opens a selection list, Figure 2-64d.
- Select the *Grid* option. A check mark appears on the left side of the *Grid* option, Figure 2-64e; and the *Grid* icon appears in the status bar.
- Repeat the process with *Snap Mode* option, Figure 2-64e.

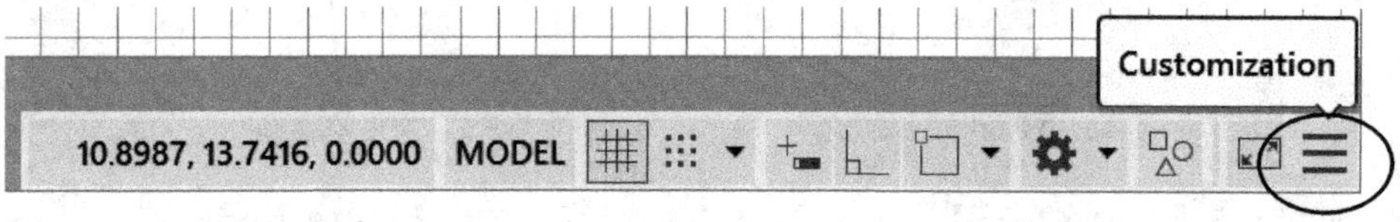

Figure 2-64c

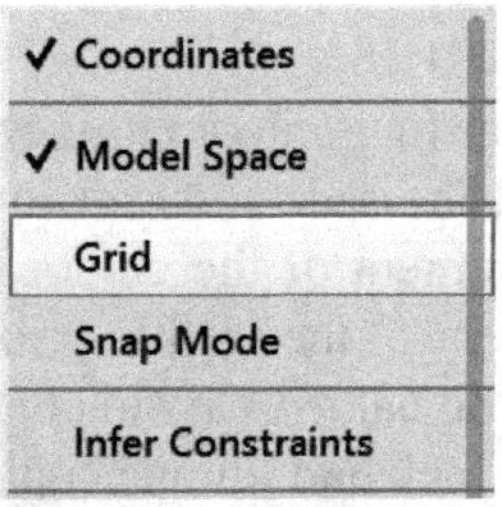

Figure 2-64d

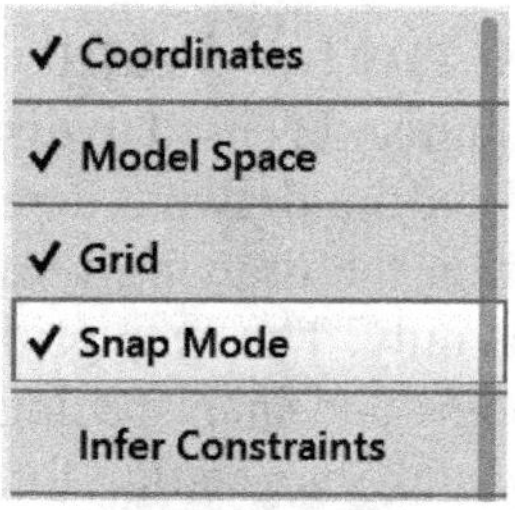

Figure 2-64e

2.21.1. Toggle grid and snap in the Model space

A user can toggle the *Grid* and *Snap* options in the Model space using one of the techniques listed below.

- Click the *Grid* and/or *Snap* buttons on the status bar (Figure 2-64a, Figure 2-64b).
- Press *F7* (for the *Grid*) and *F9* (for the *Snap*) keys of the keyboard.
- A user can toggle the *Grid* and *Snap* options using the *Drafting Setting* dialog box, Figure 2-65b, using the following methods.

- Open the *Drafting Setting* dialog box using one of the following methods.
  - Bring the cursor on the *Grid* button on the status bar and click with the **right** button of the mouse, Figure 2-65a.
  - Bring the cursor on the *Snap* button on the status bar and click with the **right** button of the mouse, Figure 2-65b.
  - Bring the cursor on the small arrow on the *Snap* button on the status bar and click with the **left** button of the mouse, Figure 2-65b.
- On the dialog box, click the *Snap and Grid* tab.
- Finally, check or clear the boxes to the left of *Snap On* and *Grid On* to turn *On* or *Off* the corresponding option, Figure 2-65c.

Figure 2-65a

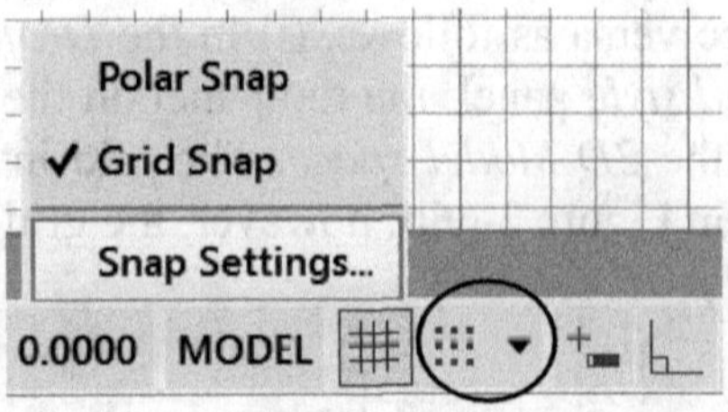

Figure 2-65b

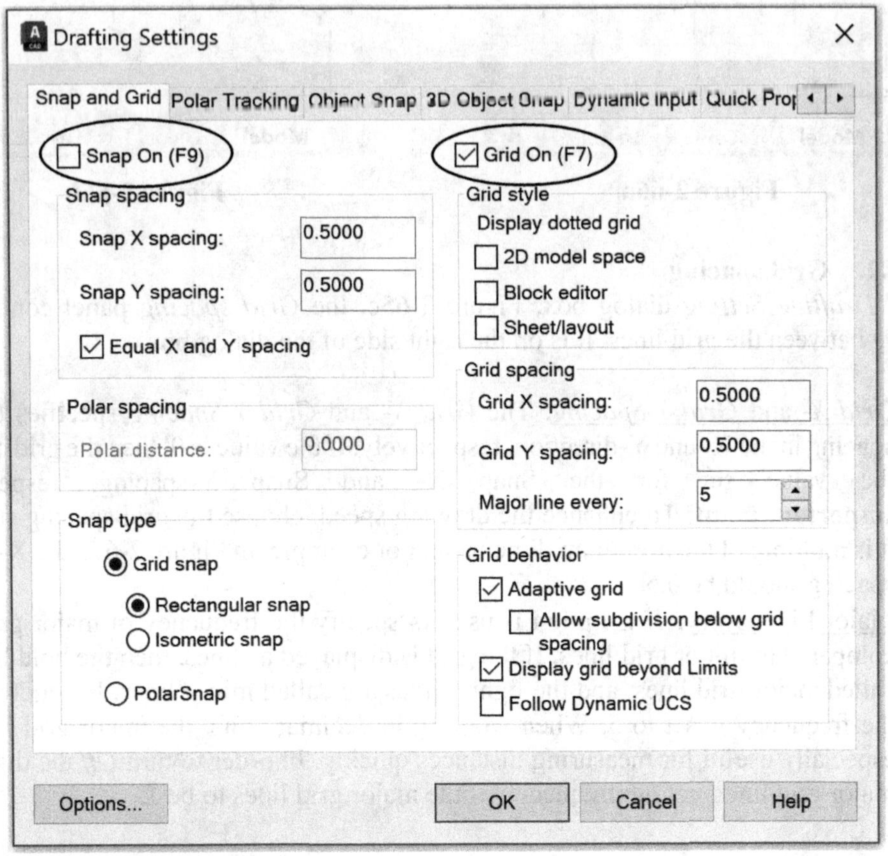

Figure 2-65c

2.21.2. Toggle the grid and snap in the layout

In order to toggle the *Grid* and *Snap* buttons in a layout, double click in the viewport (the solid rectangle); this makes the solid rectangle bold and the WCS appears in the viewport. Now toggle the grid and snap following the options discussed for the Model space.

2.21.3. Grid properties

The grid properties (style, spacing, behavior, and color) can be set using the *Drafting Setting* dialog box, Figure 2-65c.

2.21.3.1. Grid style

A user can convert the solid grid lines (Figure 2-66a) into the dotted line (Figure 2-66b) and vice versa as follows. (i) In the *Drafting Setting* dialog box, Figure 2-66c, (ii) under the *Grid style* panel, the top panel on the right side of the dialog box, (iii) check the box beside the *2D Model space*. The grid in the Model space will change its appearance as shown in Figure 2-66b; however, the grid in the layout will not be changed.

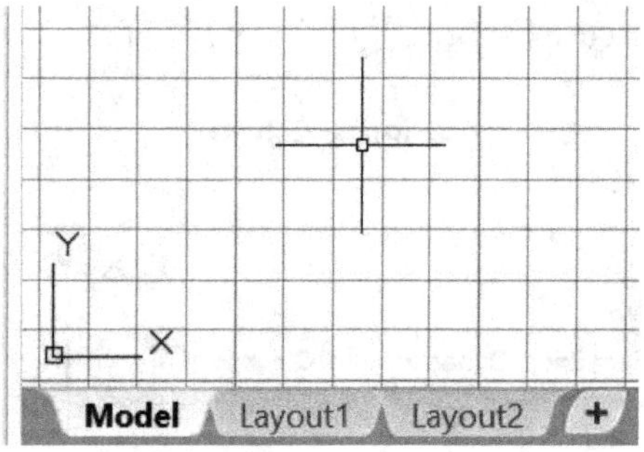

Figure 2-66a

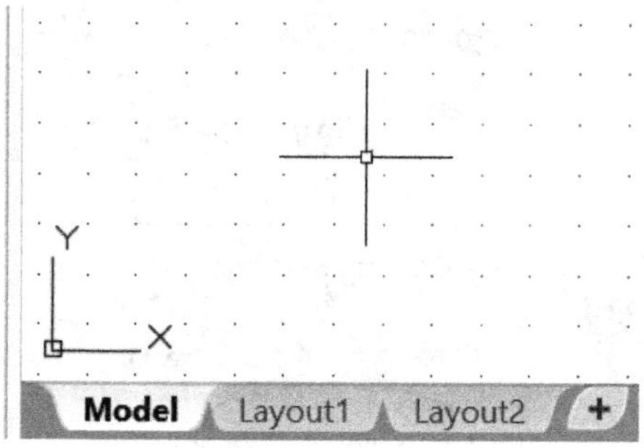

Figure 2-66b

2.21.3.2. Grid spacing

In the *Drafting Setting* dialog box, Figure 2-65c, the *Grid spacing* panel controls the spacing between the grid lines. It is on the right side of the dialog box.

- Grid X- and Grid Y-Spacing: The *Grid X-* and *Grid Y-Spacing* specifies the grid spacing in the X- and Y-direction, respectively. If the value is 0, then the grid assumes the value set for the Snap X- and Snap Y-spacing, respectively. **Important point**: To enhance the drawing speed, choose the grid spacing such that it is multiple of the minimum dimension. For example, in Figure 2-67a the X- and Y-spacing should be 0.5.
- Major Line Every: This option is used to specify the frequency of major grid lines compared to minor grid lines. If the grid is displayed as lines, then the bold lines are called major grid lines, and the lighter lines are called minor lines. In Figure 2-67b, the frequency is set to 5. When working in decimal units, the major grid lines are especially useful for measuring distances quickly. In order to turn *Off* the display of major grid lines, set the frequency of the major grid lines to be 1.

2.21.3.3. Grid behavior

In the *Drafting Setting* dialog box, Figure 2-65c, the *Grid behavior* panel controls the appearance of the grid lines. It is the bottom panel on the right side of the dialog box. In case of the dotted grid, the grid dots are displayed only for the major grid lines.

- Adaptive grid: If the *Adaptive Grid* box is checked, then the density of the grid lines is updated when zooming options are used.
- *Allow subdivision below grid spacing*: This option generates additional grid lines when zoomed in. The frequency of these additional lines is determined by the frequency of the major grid lines.
- Display grid beyond limits: This option displays the grid beyond the area specified by the drawing limits.
- Follow Dynamic UCS: This option changes the grid plane to follow the XY plane of the dynamic UCS.

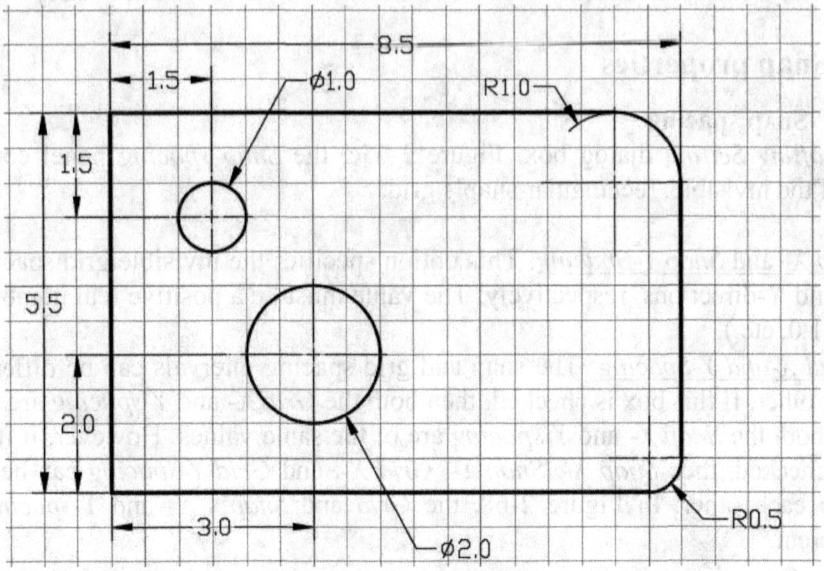

Figure 2-67a

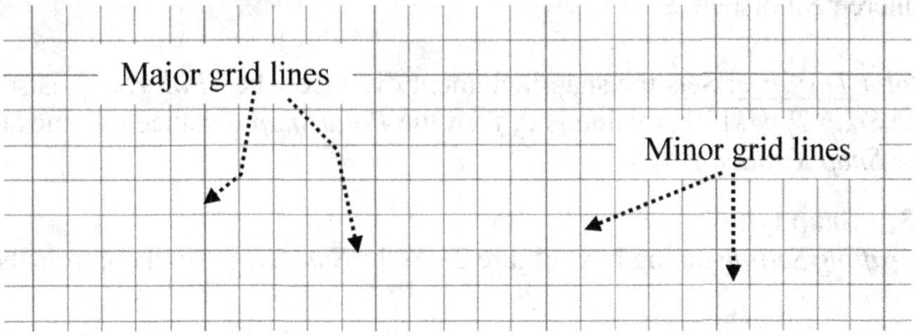

Figure 2-67b

2.21.3.4. Grid color

The dotted grid's color is the same as the cursor color. The grid color can be changed as follows:

- Click with the right button in the *Drawing area* and select the *Options* option or type *Options* on the command line and press the *Enter* key.
- The *Options* dialog box will appear on the screen.
- Click the *Display* tab of the *Options* dialog box by clicking on it.
- Press the *Color* button in the *Window Elements* panel to open the *Drawing Window Colors* dialog box.
- In the *Drawing Window Colors* dialog box, under *Context* panel choose *2D Model space*, under *Interface element* panel choose *Grid major line*, and under the *Color* options panel select the desired color. The selection is highlighted. In the *Preview* window, the color of the grid will change to the selected color.
- Similarly, change the colors of the *Grid minor line* and *Grid axes line*.

2.21.4. Snap properties

2.21.4.1. Snap spacing

In the *Drafting Setting* dialog box, Figure 2-65c, the *Snap spacing* panel controls the spacing of the invisible, rectangular snap's grid.

- <u>*Snap X-* and *Snap Y-Spacing*</u>: This option specifies the invisible grid spacing in the X- and Y-directions, respectively. The value must be a positive real number (that is 0.5, 1.0, etc.).
- <u>*Equal X-and Y-Spacing*</u>: The snap and grid spacing intervals can be different from each other. If this box is checked, then both the *Grid X-* and *Y-spacing* are the same; and both the *Snap X-* and *Y-spacing* are of the same values. However, if this box is not checked, then *Snap X-*, *Snap Y-*, *Grid X-*, and *Grid Y-spacing* can be different from each other. In Figure 2-68, the *Grid* and *Snap*'s *X-* and *Y-spacing* are all different.

2.21.4.2. Polar spacing

In the *Drafting Setting* dialog box, Figure 2-68, the *Polar spacing* panel controls the polar snap's increment distance.

- <u>*Polar Distance*</u>: Sets the snap increment distance when *PolarSnap* is selected under the *Snap Type*. If this value is 0, then the *PolarSnap* distance assumes the value for the *Snap X spacing*.

2.21.4.3. Snap type

In the *Drafting Setting* dialog box, Figure 2-68, the *Snap type* panel controls the type of the snap.

- <u>*Grid snap*</u>: This option sets the snap type to the *Grid*. In this case, the cursor snaps along vertical or horizontal grid points. This type is further subdivided into two groups.

- <u>Rectangular snap</u>: This radio button sets the snap style to a rectangular snap mode. Now, the cursor snaps to the rectangular snap grid, Figure 2-69a.
- <u>Isometric snap</u>: This radio button sets the snap style to the isometric snap mode. Now, the cursor snaps to an isometric snap grid, Figure 2-69b.

- *<u>PolarSnap</u>*: Sets the snap type to *Polar*. When *Snap* mode is *On* and the user specifies points with polar tracking turned *On*, the cursor snaps along polar alignment angles set on the *Polar Tracking* tab relative to the starting polar tracking point.

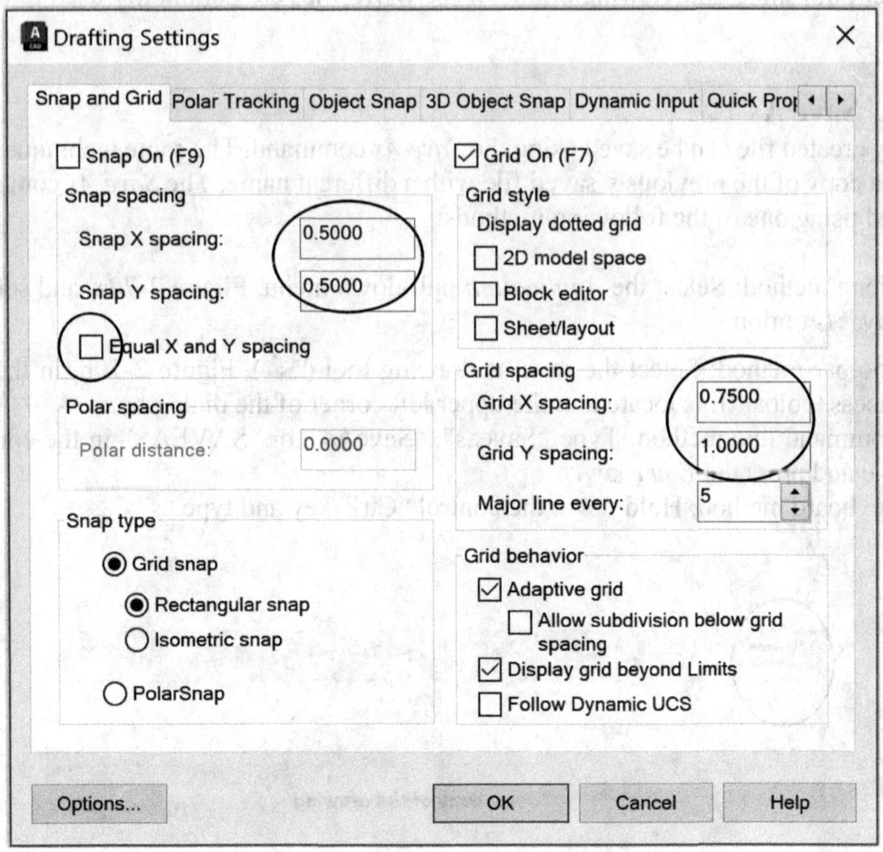

Figure 2-68

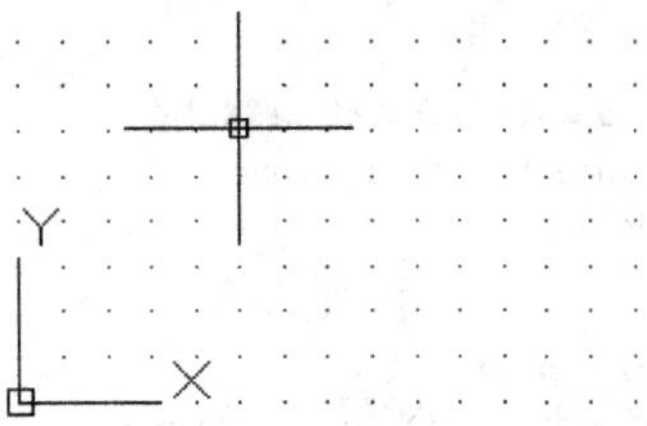

Figure 2-69a

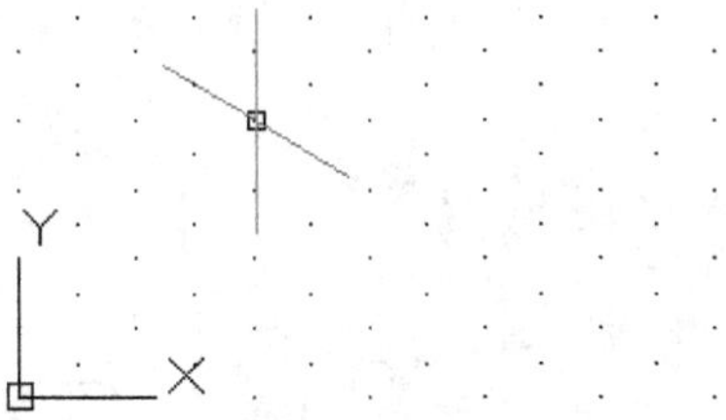

Figure 2-69b

2.22. Save A File

In AutoCAD, a file can be saved using the *Save As* or *Save* command. AutoCAD's native/standard file format is DWG; that is, files are saved with the extension '.dwg'. For example, a file named as *My_First_Drawing* will be saved as *My_First_Drawing.dwg*. AutoCAD allows file interchange to (and/or from) other CAD applications. The commonly used formats are DXF (Drawing Exchange Format), DWF (Design Web Format), and WMF (Window Metafile Format). DXF is an ASCII or binary file for exporting/importing drawings to/from other applications. DWF is a compressed file created from a DWG file for faster publishing and viewing on the Web. WMF files are commonly used to produce clip art.

2.22.1. Save As 

A newly created file can be saved using the *Save As* command. The same technique is used to save a copy of the previously saved file with a different name. The *Save As* command is activated using one of the following methods:

1. Menu method: Select the *Application* pull-down menu, Figure 2-70a, and select the *Save As* option.
2. Toolbar method: Select the save as drawing tool (), Figure 2-70b, in the quick access toolbar. It is located on the upper left corner of the dialog box.
3. Command line method: Type "Saveas", "SaveAs", or "SAVEAS" in the command line and press the *Enter* key.
4. Keyboard method: Hold down the control "Ctrl" key and type "s".

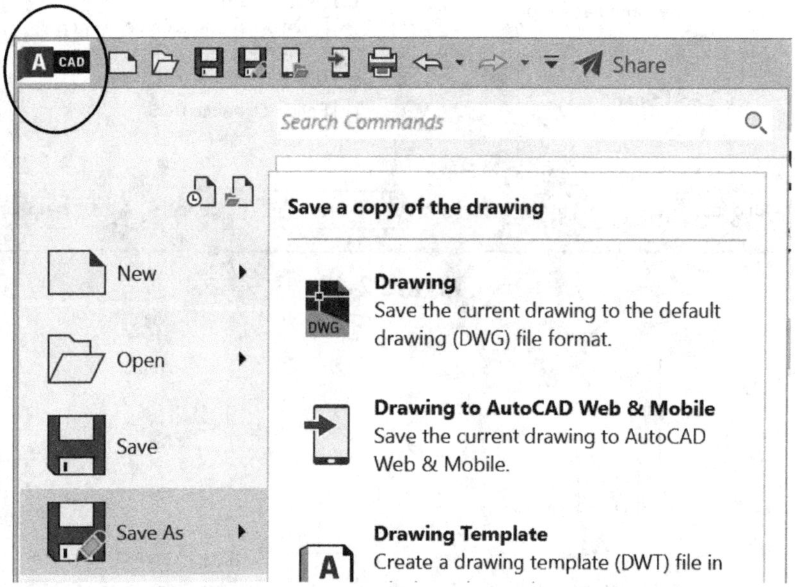

Figure 2-70a

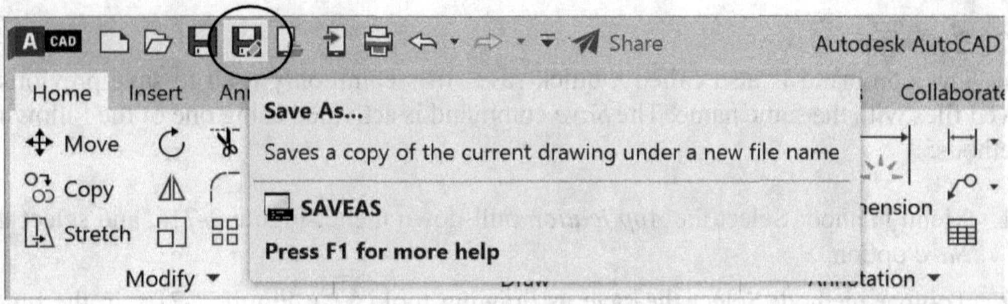

Figure 2-70b

Any of the four methods discussed above opens the *Save Drawing As* dialog box, Figure 2-70c. The dialog box shows the default name, *Drawing1*. To save a file, specify the name in the *File Name* box using the naming convention and press the *Save* button. The AutoCAD files are automatically saved with the *dwg* extension. For example, if the user specifies the name Ex_2_1, then it is saved as Ex_2_1.dwg. If necessary, the user can select the desired file type by pressing the down-arrow key for the *Files of type* option.

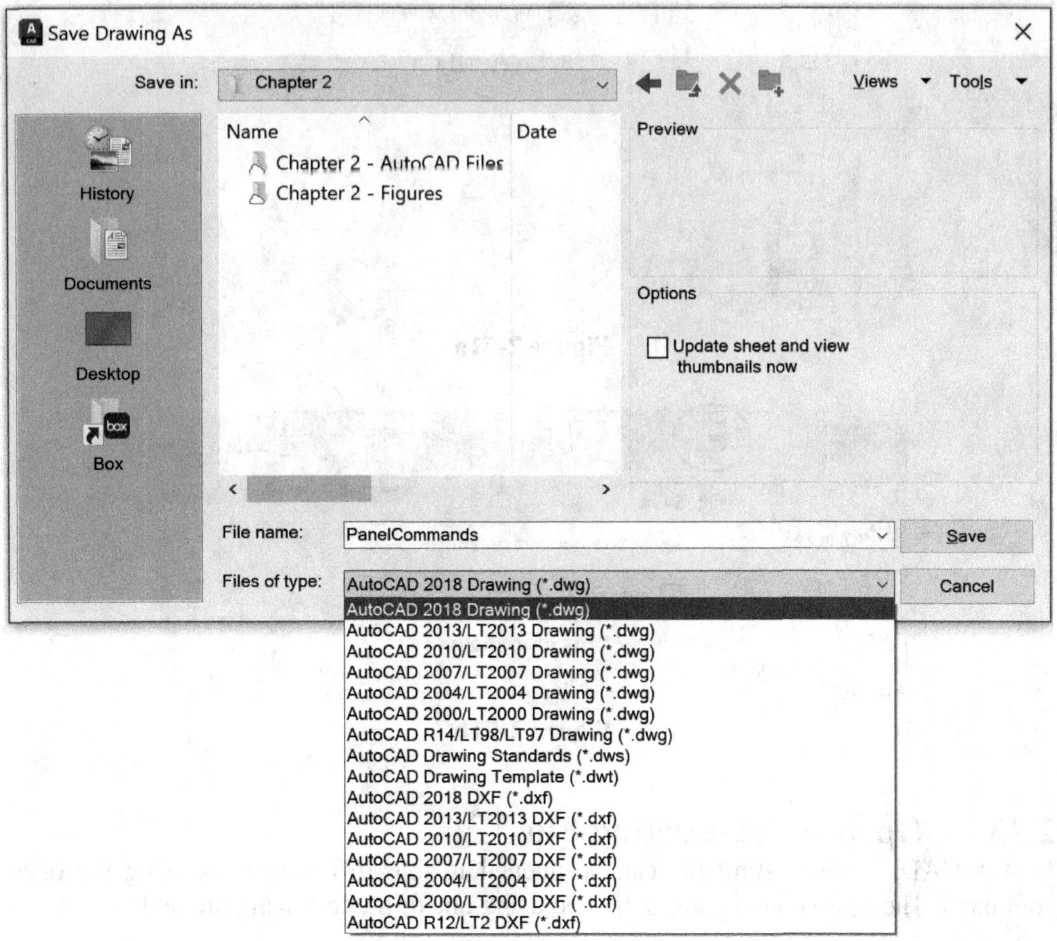

Figure 2-70c

2.22.2. Save

The *Save* command is also called a quick save. It is commonly used to save previously saved files with the same name. The *Save* command is activated using one of the following methods:

1. Menu method: Select the *Application* pull-down menu, Figure 2-71a, and select the *Save* option.
2. Toolbar method: Select the save as drawing tool ( ), Figure 2-71b, in the quick access toolbar. It is located on the upper left corner of the dialog box.
3. Command line method: Type "Save", "Save", or "SAVE" in the command line and press the *Enter* key.
4. Keyboard method: Hold down the control "Ctrl" key and type "s".

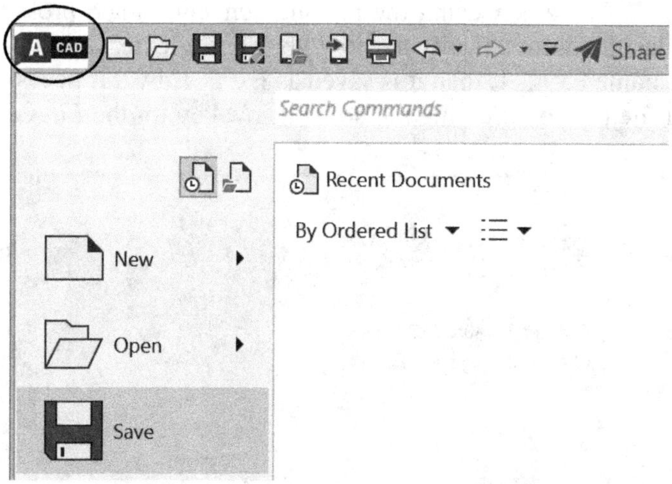

Figure 2-71a

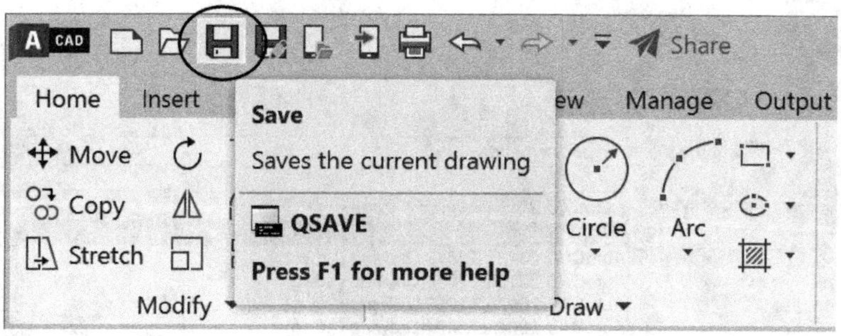

Figure 2-71b

2.23. Open A Pre-existing File

In AutoCAD, a pre-existing file can be opened in four different ways using the open command. The *Open* command is activated using one of the following methods.

1. Menu method: Select the *Application* pull-down menu, Figure 2-72a, and select the *Open* option.
2. Toolbar method: Select the open drawing tool ( ), Figure 2-72b, in the quick access toolbar. It is located on the upper left corner of the dialog box.
3. Command line method: Type "open", "Open", or "OPEN" in the command line and press the *Enter* key.
4. Keyboard method: Hold down the control "Ctrl" key and type 'o' or 'O'.

Any of the four methods discussed above will open the *Select File* dialog box shown in Figure 2-72c. The dialog box lists all of the drawing files in the folder. If the *Thumbnail* option under the *View* menu is selected, then thumbnails are displayed. If the *Preview* option under the *View* menu is selected, then a bitmap of the selected file is displayed in the *Preview* window. The *Preview* window is blank if none of the files are selected. The preview option is the default method and is shown in Figure 2-72c.

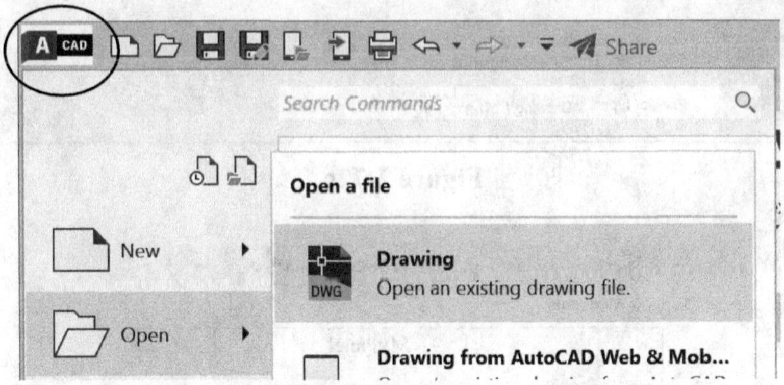

Figure 2-72a

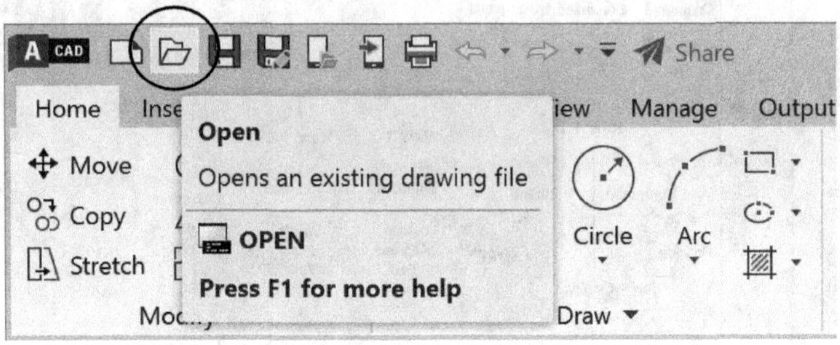

Figure 2-72b

2.24. Current file

In AutoCAD 2027, the open files (new or previously created) appear as tabs in the workspace, Figure 2-73. In the figure, a tab (*Start*) and two files (*Drawing1* and *PanelCommands*) are open. A file can be made current by clicking its tab. The current file (*PanelCommands*) is highlighted, and the other file (*Drawing1*) and the *Start* are grayed. The asterisk symbol indicates that the file contents are changed, and the changes are not saved.

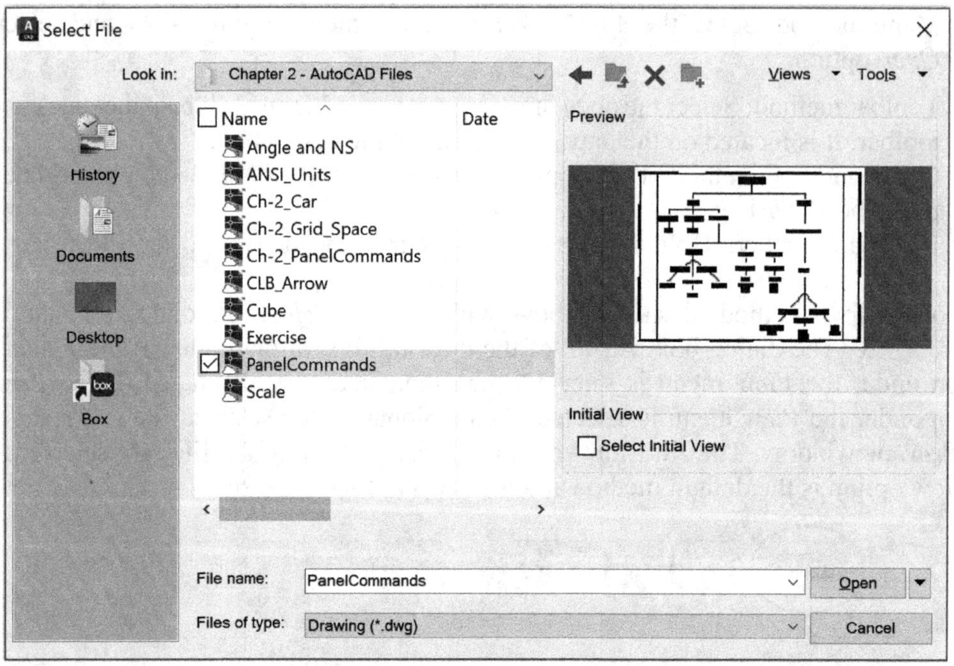

Figure 2-72c

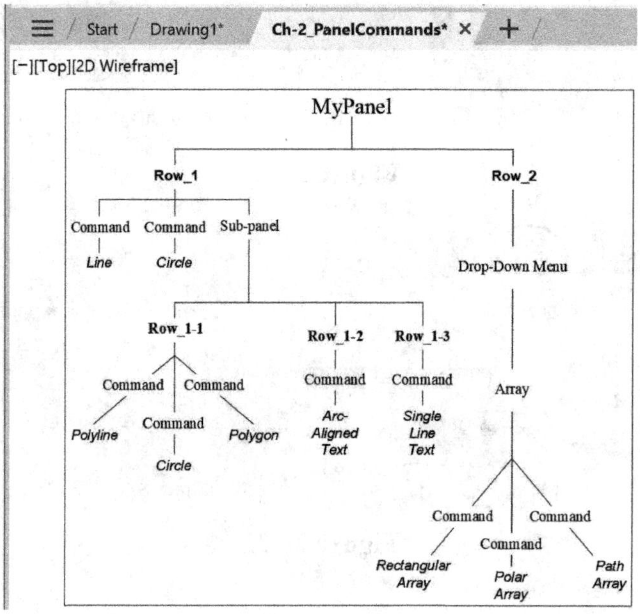

Figure 2-73

2.25. Close A File

In AutoCAD, an open file can be closed via the *Close* command. The command is activated using one of the following methods:

1. Menu method: (i) Select the *Application* pull-down menu, Figure 2-74a; (ii) select the *Close* option; and (iii) click on *Current Drawing* or *All Drawings* as needed.
2. Interface method: Click on the "x" sign on the right side of the file name as shown in Figure 2-74b.
3. From the file: Click on the "x" sign on the upper right corner of the file as shown in Figure 2-74c.
4. Command line method: Type "close", "Close", or "CLOSE" in the command line and press the *Enter* key.

The above methods either close the file (if it was saved after the last modification) or the file save error message (Figure 2-74d) appears. In case of an error message, click the appropriate button and follow the prompts.

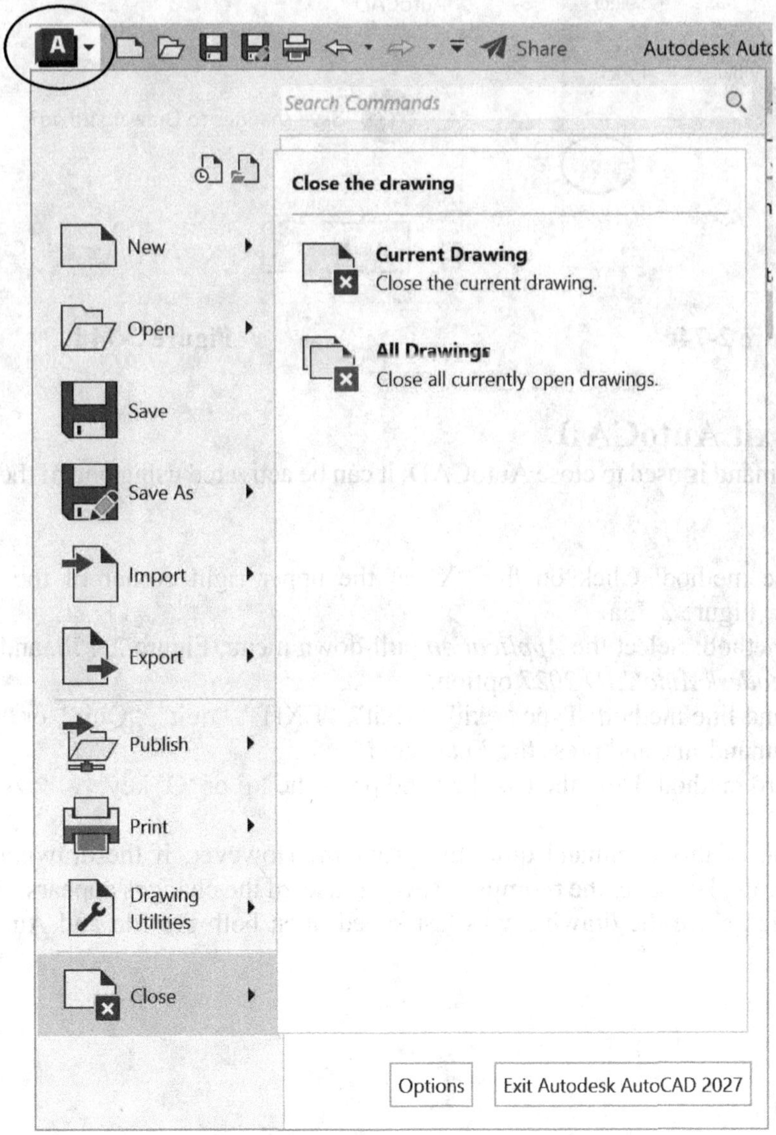

Figure 2-74a

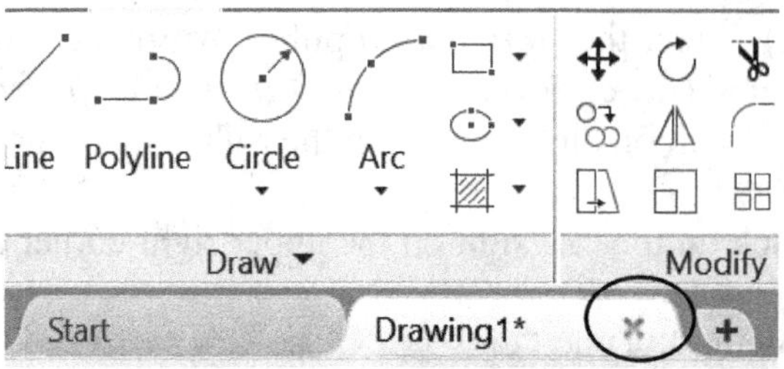

Figure 2-74b

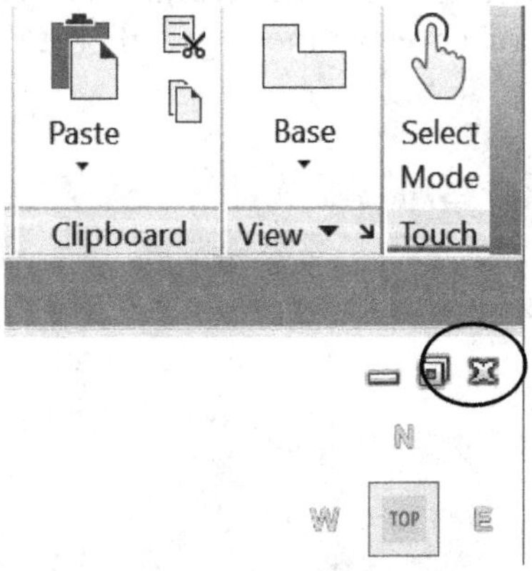

Figure 2-74c

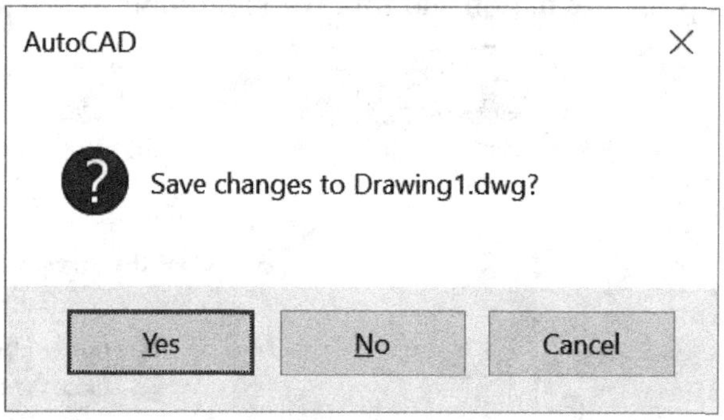

Figure 2-74d

2.26. Exit AutoCAD

The *Exit* command is used to close AutoCAD; it can be activated using one of the following techniques.

1. Interface method: Click on the "X" at the upper right corner of the AutoCAD window, Figure 2-75a.
2. Menu method: Select the *Application* pull-down menu, Figure 2-75b, and select the *Exit Autodesk AutoCAD 2027* option.
3. Command line method: Type "exit", "Exit", "EXIT", "quit", "Quit", or "QUIT" on the command line and press the *Enter* key.
4. Keyboard method: Hold the *Ctrl* key and press the 'q' or 'Q' key.

The activation of this command quits the program! However, if the drawing has been modified after the last save, the prompt to save or discard the changes appears. If there has been no change since the drawing was last saved, then both the file and AutoCAD are closed.

Figure 2-75a

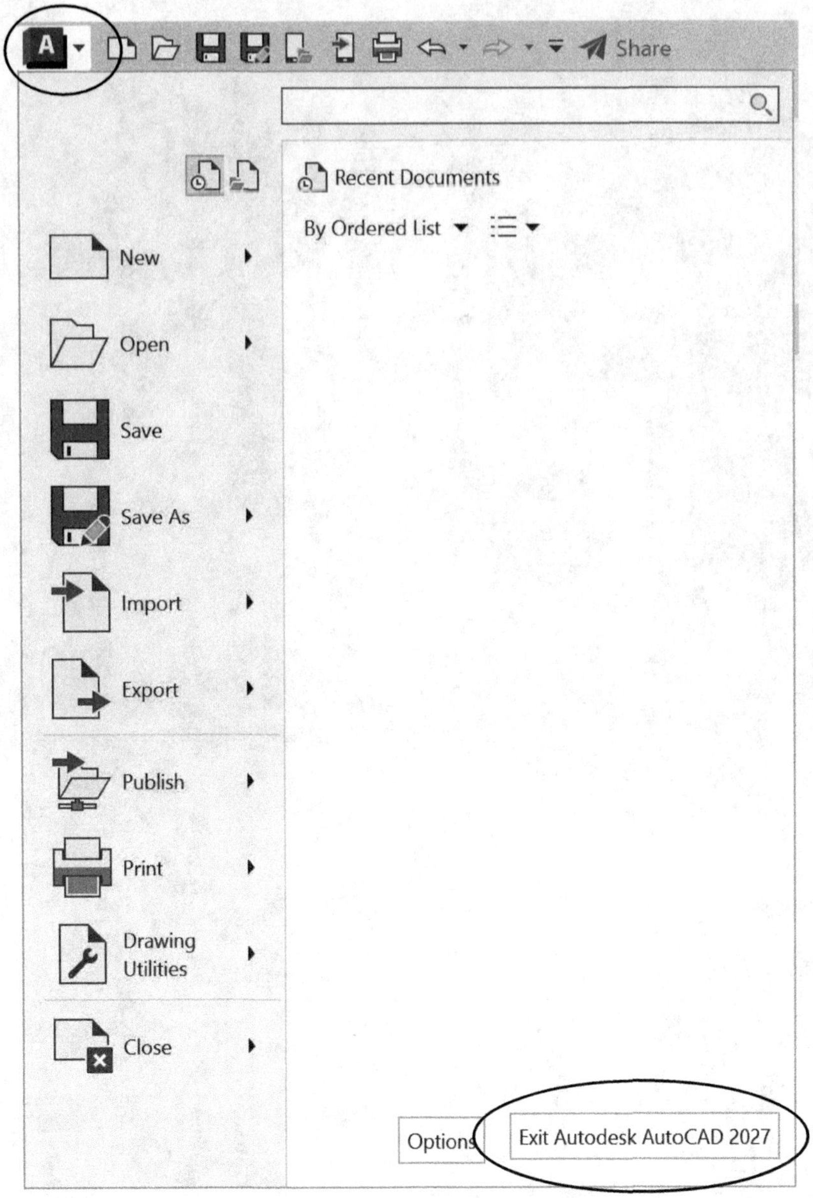

Figure 2-75b

Notes:

3. Two-Dimensional Drawings

3.1. Learning Objectives

After completing this chapter, the students will show proficiency in the following areas:

- Features of AutoCAD 2027 interface
- The dynamic input capabilities
- Draw commands
    - o Line, Polyline, Circle, Rectangle, Polygon, Ellipse, Arcs, Point, Point Measure, and Cloud
- Object appearance
    - o Color, line thickness, and line pattern (dotted, dashed, phantom, etc.)
- Table

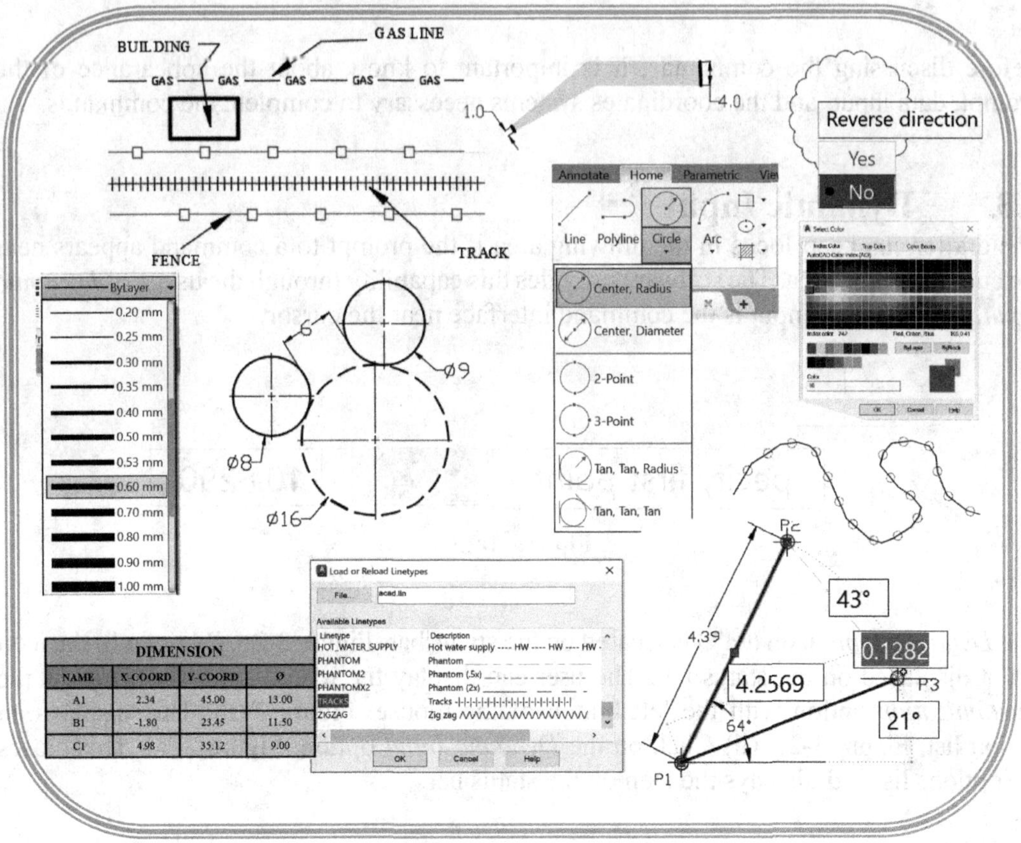

3.2. Introduction

A drafter can create unlimited designs by creating new drawings and editing existing drawings. The focus of this chapter is the AutoCAD capabilities to draw two-dimensional drawing objects. To achieve these functionalities, AutoCAD provides the *Draw* panel from the *Home* tab, Figure 3-1. The figure shows the expanded and pinned (check the pin at the lower left corner) panel.

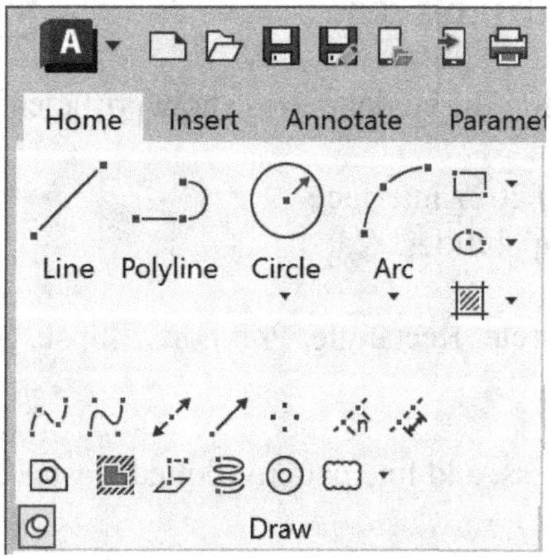

Figure 3-1

Before discussing the commands, it is important to know about the appearance of the prompt, data input, and the coordinates systems necessary to complete the commands.

3.3. Dynamic Input

The drafter can keep focus in the drawing area if the prompt to a command appears near the cursor, Figure 3-2a. The software provides this capability through the usage of *Dynamic Input*. The dynamic input is the command interface near the cursor.

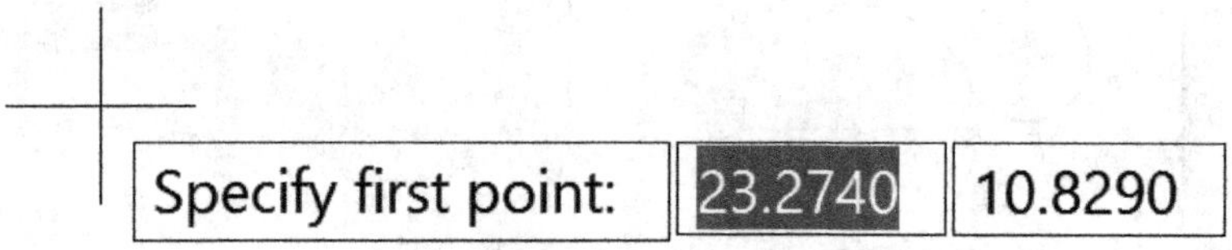

Figure 3-2a

The *Dynamic Input* icon ( ) is located on the status bar, Figure 3-2b. By default, the icon is not displayed on the status bar. The user can display the icon as follows: (i) Press the *Customization* option with the left button of the mouse, Figure 3-2b. This displays an option list, Figure 3-2c. (ii) Click on the *Dynamic Input* option, Figure 3-2d. This closes the options list and displays the icon on the status bar.

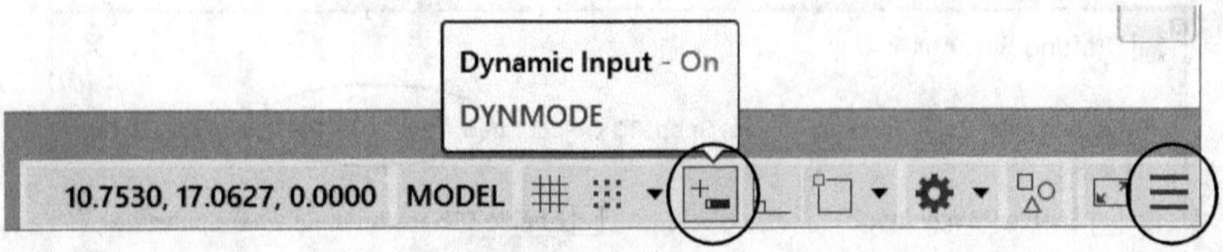

Figure 3-2b

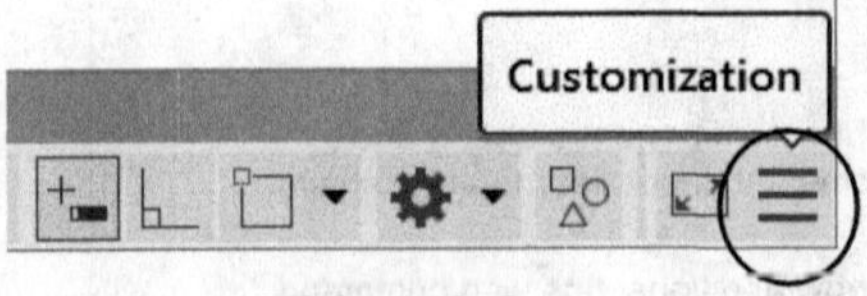

Figure 3-2c

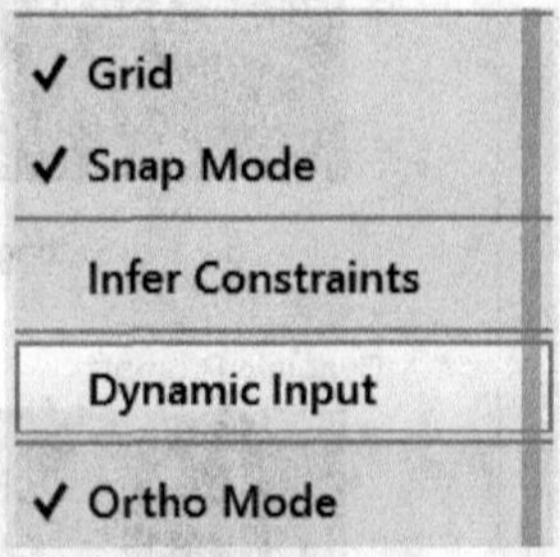

Figure 3-2d

3.3.1. Toggle dynamic input

The dynamic input option can be activated by clicking the *Dynamic Input* button on the status bar or by pressing the *F12* key. However, the dynamic input option can be deactivated by clicking the *Dynamic Input* button on the status bar.

3.3.2. Components of a dynamic input

A user can set the dynamic input properties from the *Drafting Settings* dialog box shown in Figure 3-3b. The *Drafting Settings* dialog box can be opened as follows:

- (i) Bring the cursor on the *Dynamic Input* button. (ii) Right click and select the *Dynamic Input Settings* option, Figure 3-3a. This opens the *Drafting Settings* dialog box. (iii) Select the *Dynamic Input* tab of the dialog box, Figure 3-3b.

Figure 3-3a

The *Dynamic Input* tab, Figure 3-3b, of the *Drafting Settings* dialog box contains three major components: *Pointer Input*, *Dimension Input*, and *Dynamic Prompts*. The dialog box also contains four check boxes; all the boxes should be checked as shown in Figure 3-3b. The details of these boxes are provided in their respective sections.

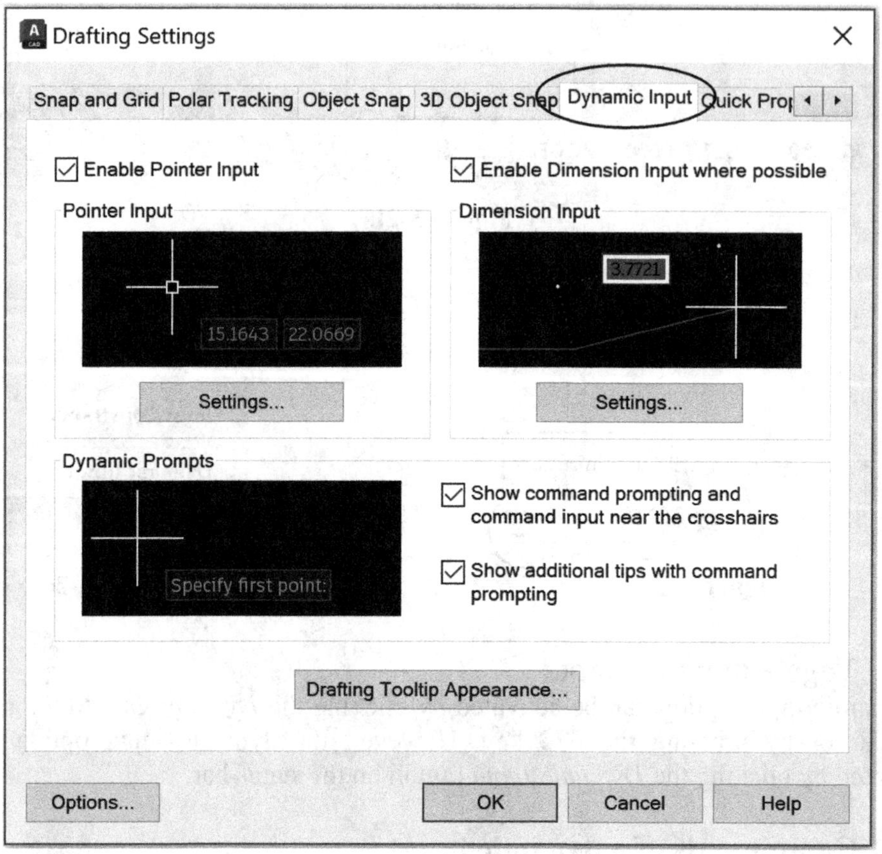

Figure 3-3b

3.3.2.1. Pointer input

To check the capabilities of the pointer input, click the *Settings* button in the *Pointer Input* panel, Figure 3-3b; this opens the *Pointer Input Settings* dialog box, Figure 3-4a. The *Pointer Input Settings* dialog box is used to change the coordinates' format: polar or Cartesian and relative or absolute; the coordinates are discussed in the next section. This dialog box also controls the pointer input tooltips display.

If the *Enable Pointer Input* box (Figure 3-3b) is checked and in Figure 3-4a under the *Visibility* panel the last option (*Always*) is selected, then the location of the crosshairs is displayed as coordinates in the tooltip near the cursor, Figure 3-4b. To avoid confusion, it is good drawing practice to use the *When a command asks for a point* option, Figure 3-4a under the *Visibility* panel.

Note: The user must check the *Enable Pointer Input* box in Figure 3-3b. Otherwise, the capabilities discussed in this section are NOT effective!

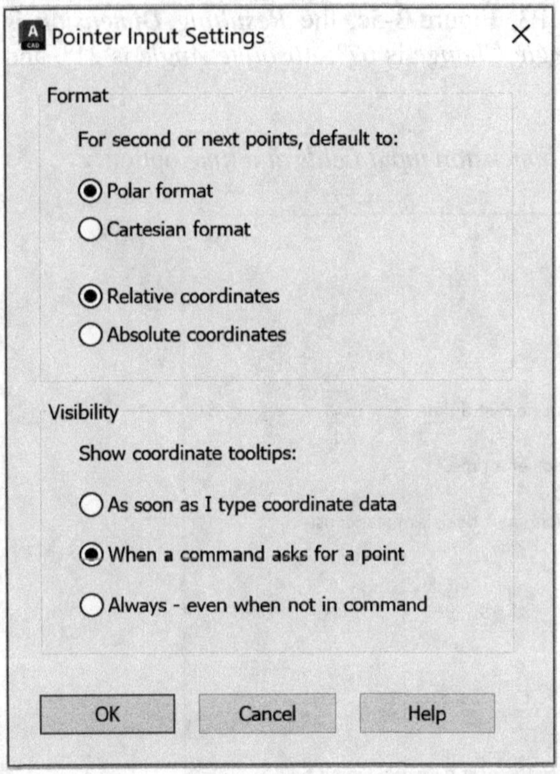

Figure 3-4a

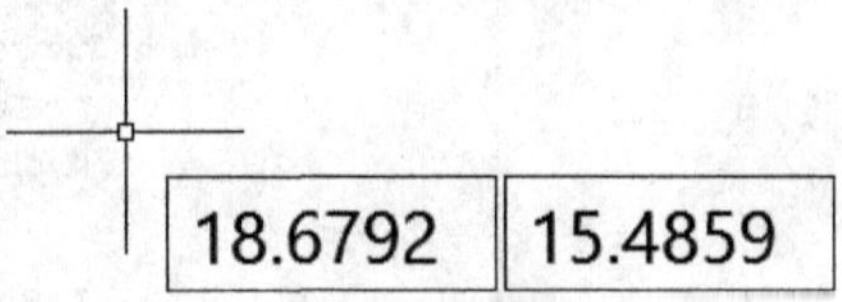

Figure 3-4b

3.3.2.2. Dimension input

To check the capabilities of the dimension input, click the *Enable Dimensional Input where possible* box, Figure 3-3b. This option is used to display the dimensions' values when a command demands a second point. The value in the dimensional tooltip changes as the cursor moves.

The user can set the dimensional input characteristics from the *Dimension Input Settings* dialog box, Figure 3-5a. The dialog box can be opened by clicking the *Settings* button in the *Dimension Input* panel, Figure 3-3b. The line P1-P2 of length 4.39 at an angle of 64° with the x-axis and point P3 shown in Figure 3-5b are used to explain the behavior of the options of the dialog box. The remainder of this section discusses the *Dimension Input Settings* dialog box.

- *Show only 1 dimension input field at a time*: If this option is selected then only the change in length (0.1282) is displayed when point P2 of the line P1-P2 is stretched to point P3, Figure 3-5c.
- *Show 2 dimension input fields at a time*: If this option is selected then the change in length (0.1282) and the new length (4.2569) are displayed when point P2 of the line P1-P2 is stretched to point P3, Figure 3-5d.
- *Show the following dimension input fields simultaneously*: This option displays a combination of the dimensions by checking the appropriate boxes. When point P2 of

the line P1-P2 is stretched to point P3, Figure 3-5e, the *Resulting Dimension* is 4.2569, *Length Change* is 0.1282, *Angle Change* is 67°, *Absolute Angle* is 21°, and *Arc Radius* is 43°.

Note: The best option to use is the *Show 2 dimension input fields at a time* option.

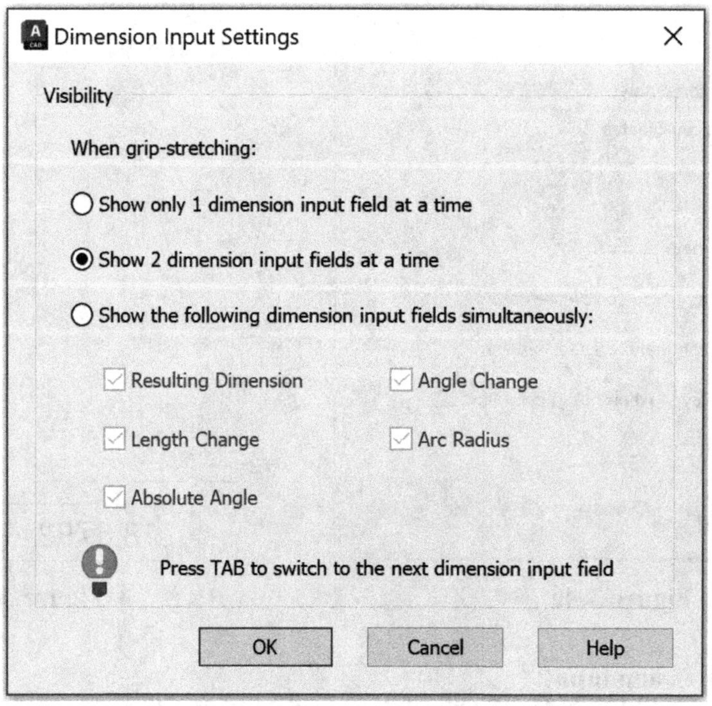

Figure 3-5a

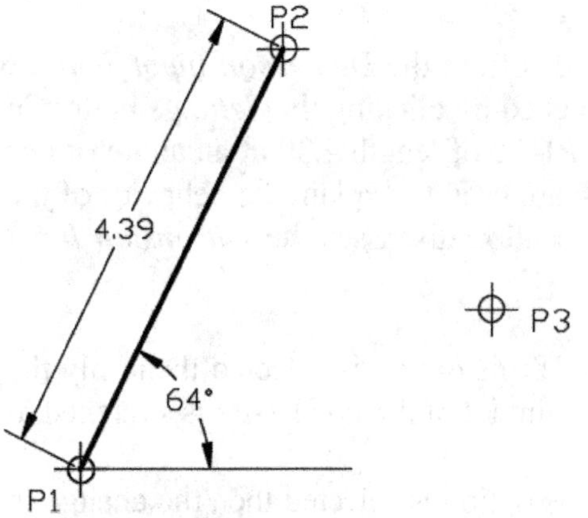

Figure 3-5b

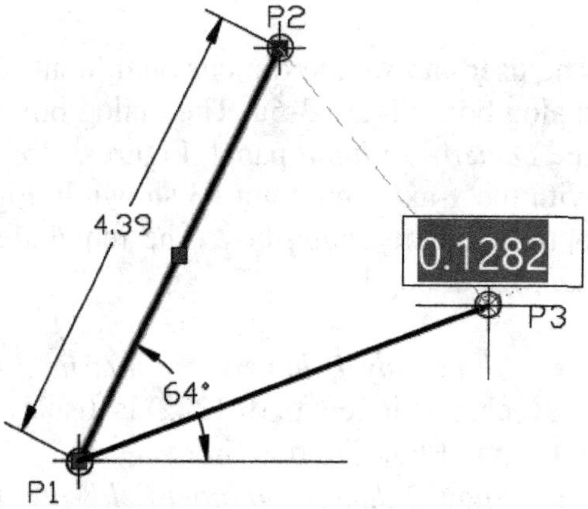

Figure 3-5c

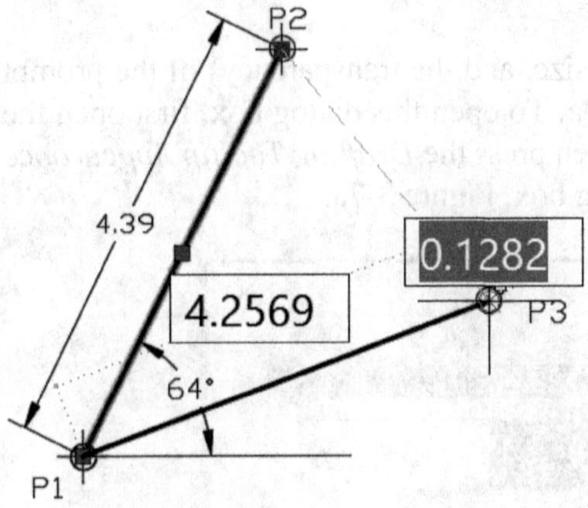

Figure 3-5d

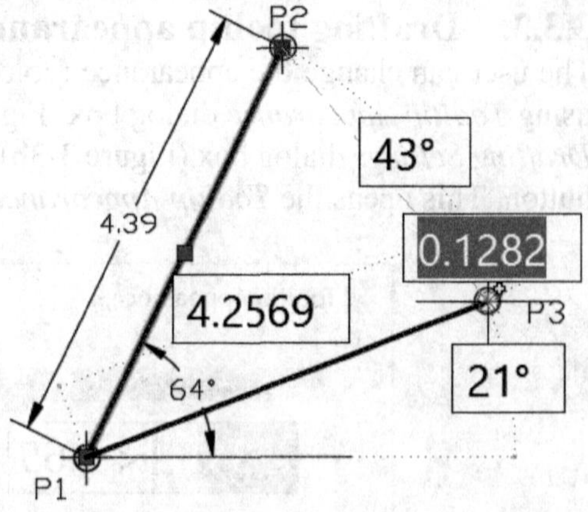

Figure 3-5e

3.3.2.3. Dynamic prompts

To display the dynamic prompt, in the *Dynamic Prompts* panel, click the check box in the *Show command prompting and command input near the crosshairs* (Figure 3-3b). If the box is checked then the prompts are displayed in a tooltip near the cursor. Figure 3-6a shows a command's prompt near the cursor.

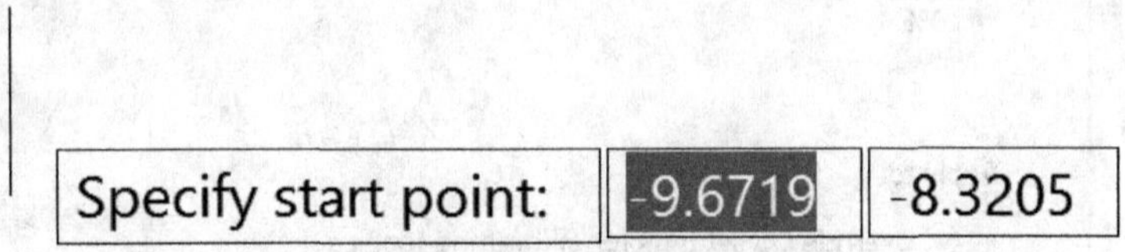

Figure 3-6a

On some of the prompts, the down-arrow (⯆) indicates that the current prompt has multiple options. To display the options list, press the down-arrow key of the keyboard. Figure 3-6b shows the commands to hatch an area after pressing the down-arrow key. The down-arrow key of the keyboard and/or the left button of the mouse can be used to select the options. The figure shows the selection of the *Undo* option.

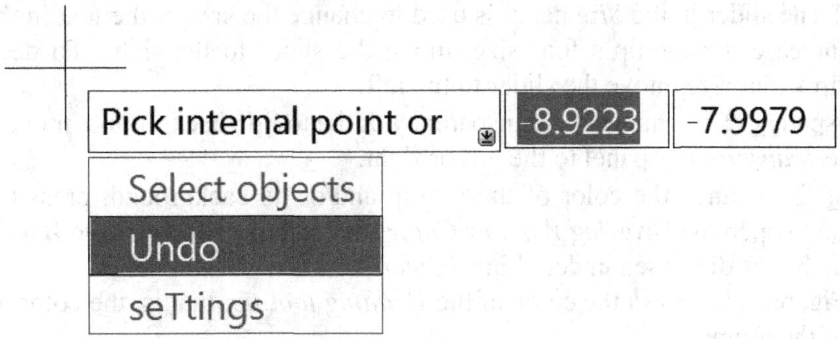

Figure 3-6b

3.3.3. Drafting tooltip appearance

The user can change the appearance (color, text size, and the transparency) of the prompt using *Tooltip Appearance* dialog box, Figure 3-7a. To open this dialog box, first open the *Drafting Settings* dialog box (Figure 3-3b) and then press the *Drafting Tooltip Appearance* button. This opens the *Tooltip Appearance* dialog box, Figure 3-7a.

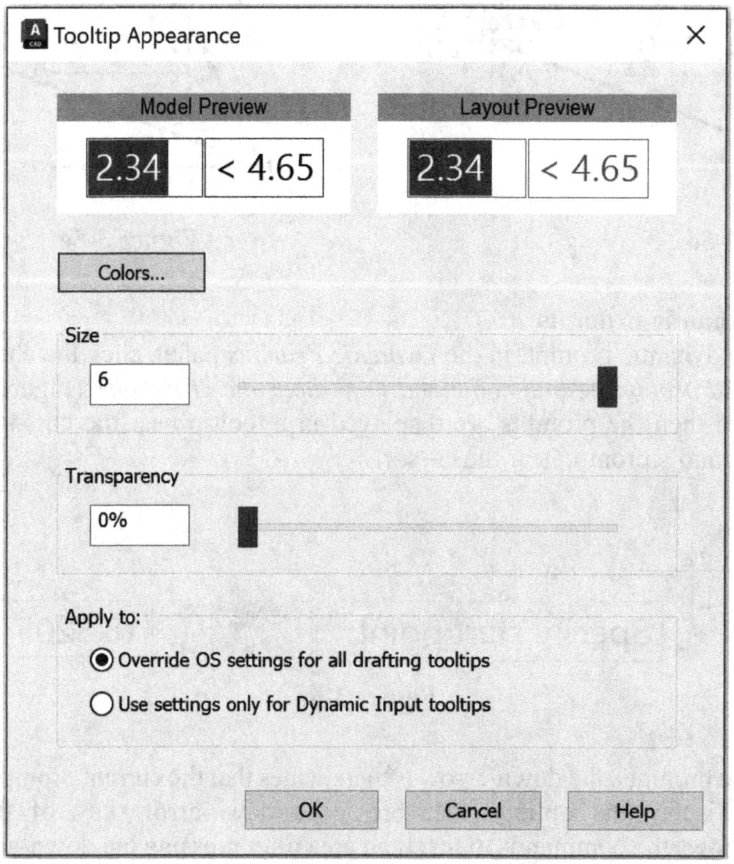

Figure 3-7a

- Size: The slider in the *Size* panel is used to change the size of the text in the tooltip. To increase the tooltip's font size, move the slider to the right. To decrease the tooltip's font size, move the slider to the left.
- Transparency: To change the transparency of the tooltip background, move the slider in the *Transparency* panel to the left or right.
- Color: To change the color of the tooltip and/or its background, press the *Colors* button to open the *Drawing Window Colors* dialog box. The *Drawing Window Color* dialog box is discussed in detail in *Chapter 2*.
    - Figure 3-7b shows the color of the *Drafting tool tip*, that is, the color of the text of the prompt.
    - Figure 3-7c shows the color of the *Drafting tool tip contour*, that is, the rectangular outline of the prompt.
    - Figure 3-7d shows the color of the *Drafting tool tip background* used in the text.

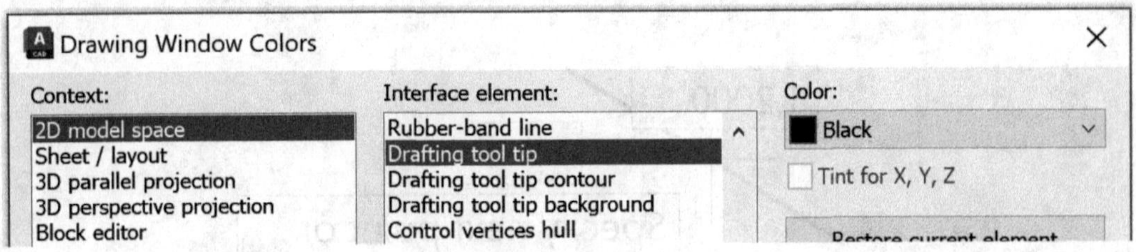

Figure 3-7b

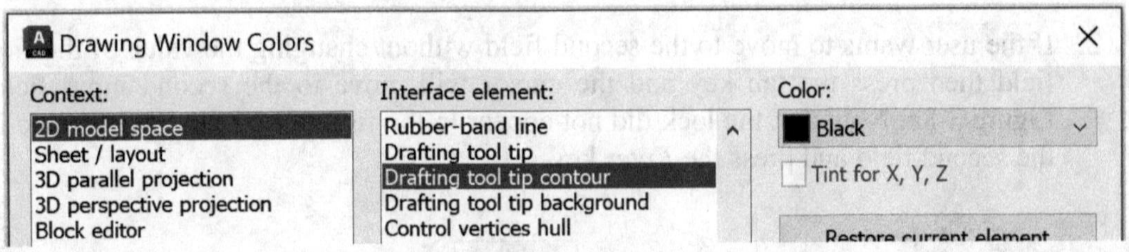

Figure 3-7c

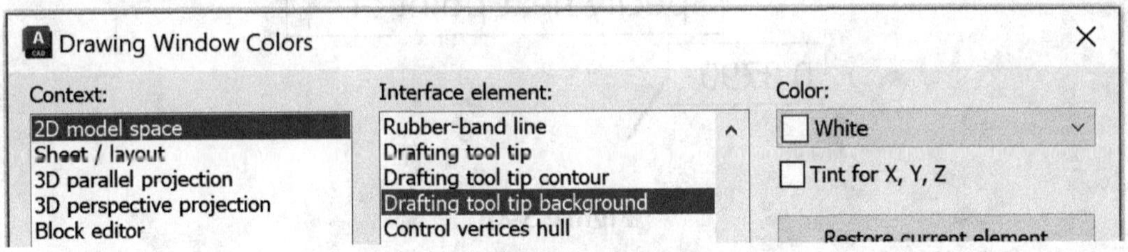

Figure 3-7d

3.4. Input Data

The input prompt of Figure 3.6a contains two input fields. The cursor can be moved from one input field to the other using the ***Tab***, ",", or "<" keys of the keyboard. Type a value in an input field and press one of the three keys. However, if a value is typed followed by pressing the *Enter* key, then the second and subsequent input fields will be ignored.

3.4.1.1. Tab key

The tab key is used for entering the polar (length, angle) coordinates.

1. Type a value in an input field and press the tab key; the field will display a lock icon (Figure 3-8a) and the cursor is constrained by the value just entered. The cursor also moves to the second input field. Finally, type in the value in the second field and press the *Enter* key.

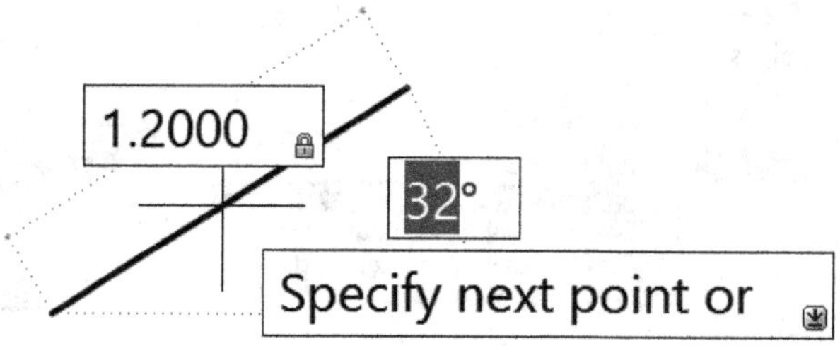

Figure 3-8a

2. If the user wants to move to the second field without changing the value of the first field then press the tab key and the cursor will move to the second input field, Figure 3-8b. Note that the lock did not appear in the first field. Type in the value in the second field and press the *Enter* key.

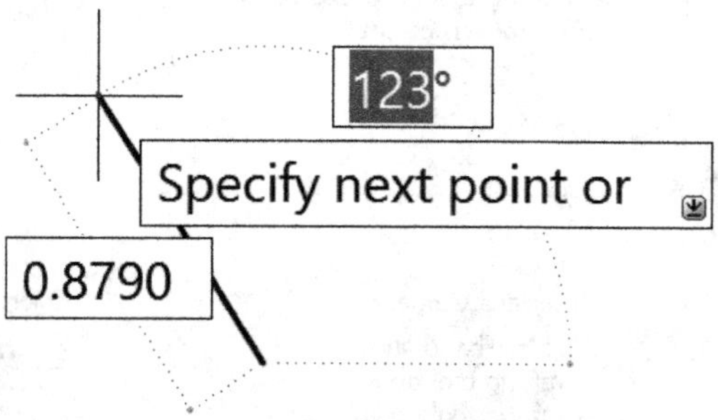

Figure 3-8b

3.4.1.2. Comma key

The comma "," key is used for entering the Cartesian coordinates, 2D (x, y) or 3D (x, y, z).

1. Type a value in an input field and press the comma key; the field displays a lock icon (Figure 3-8c) and the cursor is constrained by the value just entered. The cursor also moves to the second input field. Type the value in the second field. For the 2D drawing, press the *Enter* key. For the 3D drawing, repeat the process of second input field and then press the *Enter* key.
2. If the user wants to move to the second field without changing the value of the first field then first move the cursor to the right end of the input field and then press the comma key; the cursor will move to the second input field, Figure 3-8c. Type in the value in the second field and press the *Enter* key.

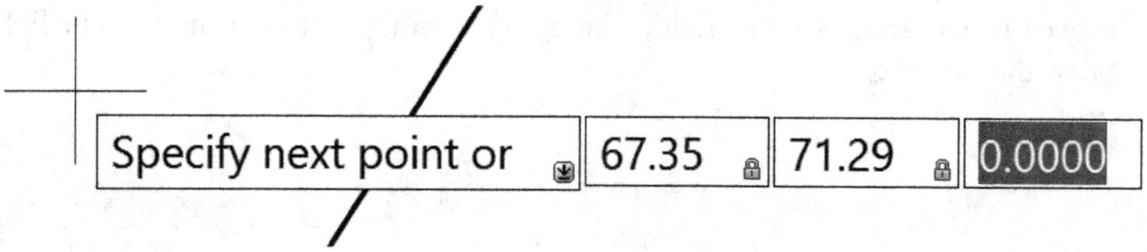

Figure 3-8c

3.4.1.3. Less than key

The less than (<) key is used for entering the polar (length, angle) coordinates.

1. Type a value in an input field and press the "<" key; the field displays a lock icon (Figure 3-8d) and the cursor is constrained by the value just entered. The cursor, also, moves to the second input field. Finally, type in the value in the second field and press the *Enter* key.

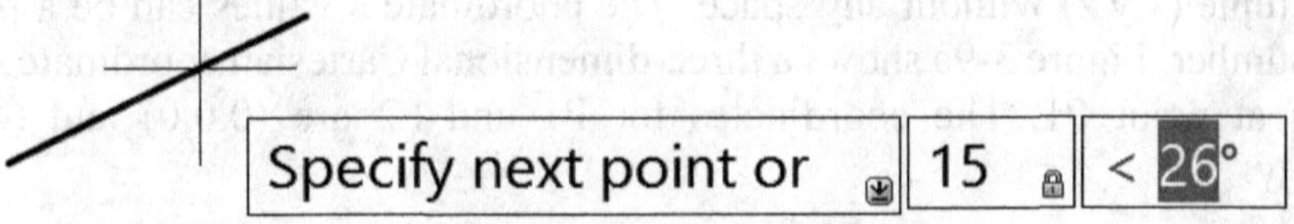

Figure 3-8d

2. If the user wants to move to the second field without changing the value of the first field then first move the cursor to the right end of the input field and then press the "<" key and the cursor moves to the second input field, Figure 3-8e. Note the difference in the prompts of Figure 3-8d and Figure 3-8e. In Figure 3-8e, the length of the line is not displayed. Type in the value in the second field and press the *Enter* key.

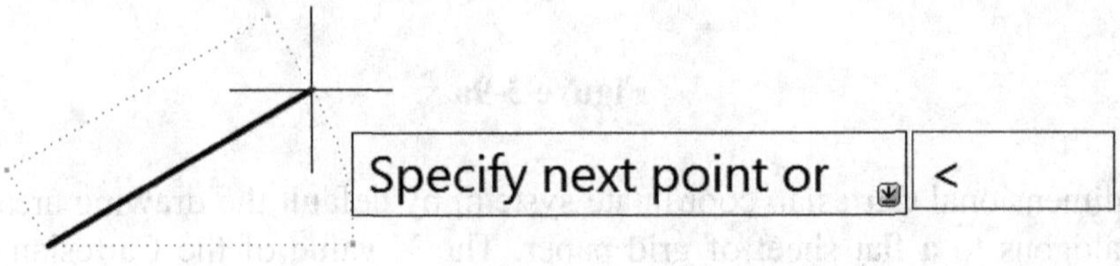

Figure 3-8e

3.4.1.4. Remove typing errors from the dynamic input tooltips

If there is an error in the dynamic input then the tooltip displays the red outline, Figure 3-8f. To remove the error, type over the selected text to replace it and continue the command.

Figure 3-8f

3.5. Reference System

For the two-dimensional drawing, AutoCAD provides two reference systems: Cartesian coordinates and polar coordinates systems.

3.5.1. Cartesian coordinates

A Cartesian (also known as a rectangular) coordinate system has three mutually perpendicular and intersecting axes, X, Y, and Z. The origin (0, 0, 0) is the location where the three axes intersect. The x-coordinate value indicates a point's distance in units and its direction, positive or negative, along the X-axis with respect to the origin. This principle also applies to the Y- and Z- axes.

In AutoCAD, the three-dimensional Cartesian coordinates values are specified as a comma separated tuple (x,y,z) without any space. The coordinate's values can be a positive or a negative number. Figure 3-9a shows a three-dimensional Cartesian coordinate system with the origin at point P1. The coordinates for P1 and P2 are (0,0,0) and (4.0,5.0,3.0), respectively.

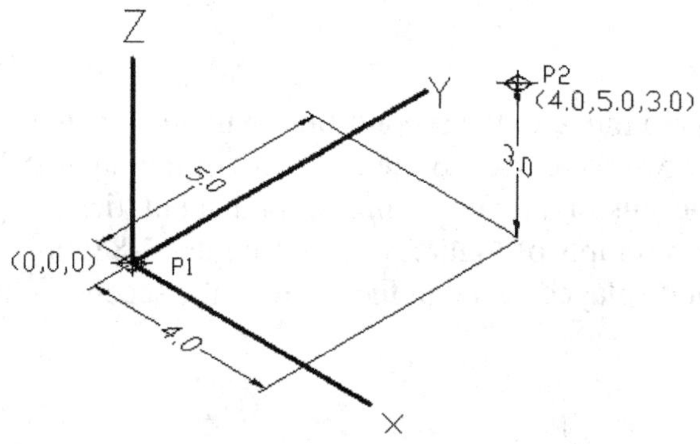

Figure 3-9a

In a two-dimensional Cartesian coordinate system, by default the drawing area is the XY plane, analogous to a flat sheet of grid paper. The X value of the Cartesian coordinate specifies the horizontal distance, and the Y value specifies the vertical distance. Figure 3-9b shows a two-dimensional Cartesian coordinate system with the origin at point P1. The coordinates for P1 and P2 are (0,0) and (3.4,2.9), respectively.

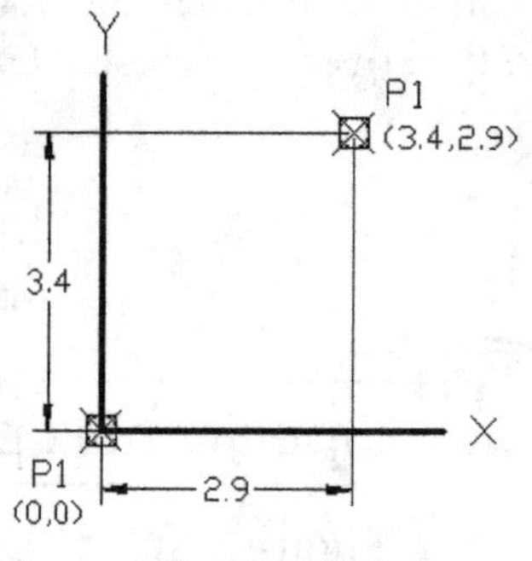

Figure 3-9b

3.5.2. Polar coordinates

A polar system uses a distance and an angle to locate a point. Figure 3-9c shows a polar coordinate system with its origin at point P1. The angle is measured with respect to a reference axis. For polar coordinates, the coordinate values are specified as an ordered pair (distance, angle). The coordinates for P1 and P2 are (0,0) and (6.6,34°), respectively.

In AutoCAD, the coordinate values are specified as an ordered pair separated by an angle bracket, (Length<Angle). By default, the angle increases in the counterclockwise direction and decreases in the clockwise direction. To specify a clockwise direction, enter a negative value for the angle. For example, (6.6<34) and (6.6<-326) locates the same point.

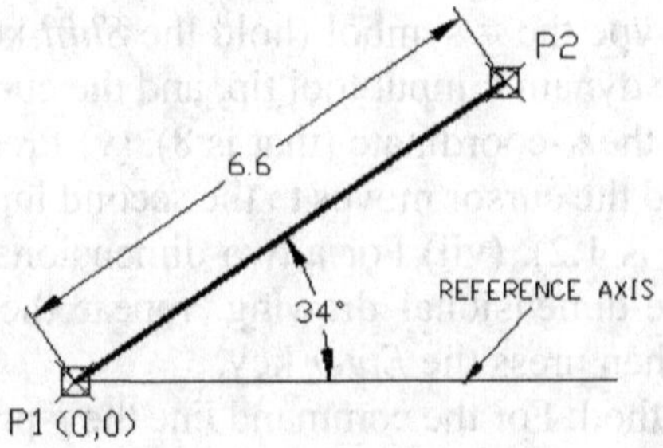

Figure 3-9c

3.5.3. AutoCAD and the coordinate systems

Distance is always measured from a benchmark or a reference point. Based on the benchmark, there are two types of coordinate system, absolute and relative. The absolute coordinates are always measured from the benchmark, whereas the relative coordinates are measured with respect to the previous point. Both the Cartesian and polar coordinates can be measured either as absolute coordinates or as relative coordinates.

In Figure 3-10, point P1 (0,0) is the benchmark. The figure shows the absolute coordinates of the points P2 (4.5,3.2) and P3 (8.0,1.2). The figure also shows the relative coordinates of point P3 (3.5,-2.0) with respect to point P2.

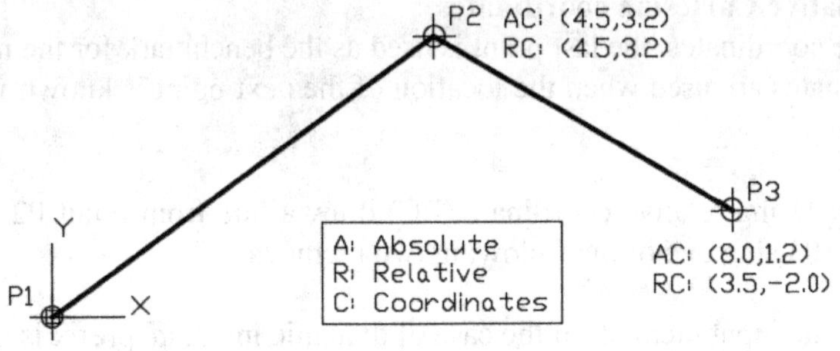

Figure 3-10

In AutoCAD, both the absolute and relative coordinates can be specified on the command line or on the tooltip of the dynamic input.

3.5.3.1. Absolute Cartesian coordinates

In AutoCAD, the origin of the WCS is used as the benchmark for the absolute coordinates. The absolute Cartesian coordinates are used when the precise location of x- and y-coordinates of a point are known. In the dynamic input, the absolute coordinates are specified using the # prefix. However, for the command line the prefix is not used.

- ***Example:*** Using absolute coordinate (AC) draw a line from point P2 to point P3 of Figure 3-10 using one of the following two methods.

  1. Dynamic input method: In the case of dynamic input, # prefix is used to specify the absolute coordinates, Figure 3-11a. (i) Activate the *Line* command. (ii) Click at point P2. (iii) Type the # symbol (hold the *Shift* key and press # key). The # sign appears in the dynamic input tool tip, and the cursor moves to the first input field. (iv) Type in the x-coordinate (that is 8). (v) Press the comma key; the first entry is locked, and the cursor moves to the second input field. (vi) Now, type the y-coordinate (that is 1.2). (vii) For a two-dimensional drawing, press the *Enter* key. For the three-dimensional drawing, repeat the step (v) and (vi) for the z-coordinate and then press the *Enter* key.
  2. Command line method: For the command line the # prefix is not used. Type 8,1.2 (no space) and press the *Enter* key.

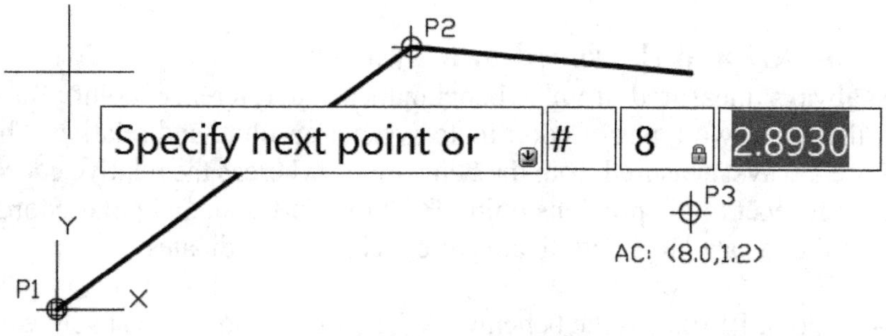

Figure 3-11a

3.5.3.2. Relative Cartesian coordinates

For the relative coordinates, the last point is used as the benchmark for the next point. The relative coordinates are used when the location of the next point is known with respect to the previous point.

- ***Example:*** Using relative coordinate (RC) draw a line from point P2 to point P3 of Figure 3-10 using one of the following two methods.

  1. Dynamic input method: In the case of dynamic input, @ prefix is used to specify the relative coordinates, Figure 3-11b. (i) Activate the *Line* command. (ii) Click at point P2. (iii) Type the @ symbol (hold the *Shift* key and press @ key). The @ sign appears in the dynamic input tool tip and the cursor will move to the first input field. (iv) Type in the x-coordinate (that is 3.5). (v) Press the comma key; the first entry is locked, and the cursor moves to the second input field. (vi) Now, type the y-coordinate (that is -2.0). (vii) For the two-dimensional drawing, press the *Enter* key. For the three-dimensional drawing, repeat the steps (v) and (vi) for the z-coordinate and then press the *Enter* key.

2. Command line method: For the command line the @ is used. Type @3.5,-2.5 (no space) and press the *Enter* key.

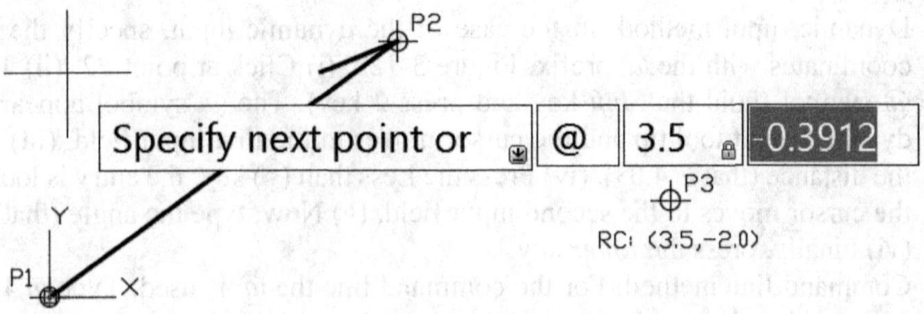

Figure 3-11b

3.5.3.3. Absolute Polar coordinates

In AutoCAD, the origin of the WCS is used as the benchmark for the absolute coordinates. The absolute polar coordinates are used when the precise distance and angle coordinates of a point are known.

- ***Example:*** Draw a line from point P2 to point P3. The absolute polar coordinates of point P3 are (8.09,9°) using one of the following two methods.

1. Dynamic input method: In the case of dynamic input, specify the absolute coordinates with the # prefix, Figure 3-12a. (i) Activate the *Line* command. (ii) Click at point P2. (iii) Type the # symbol (hold the *Shift* key and press # key). The # sign appears in the dynamic input tool tip, and cursor moves to the first input field. (iv) Type in the distance (that is 8.09). (v) Press the Less than (<) key; the entry is locked and the cursor moves to the second input field. (vi) Now, type the angle (that is 9). (vii) Finally, press the *Enter* key.
2. Command line method: For the command line the # is not used. Type 8.09<9 (no space) and press the *Enter* key.

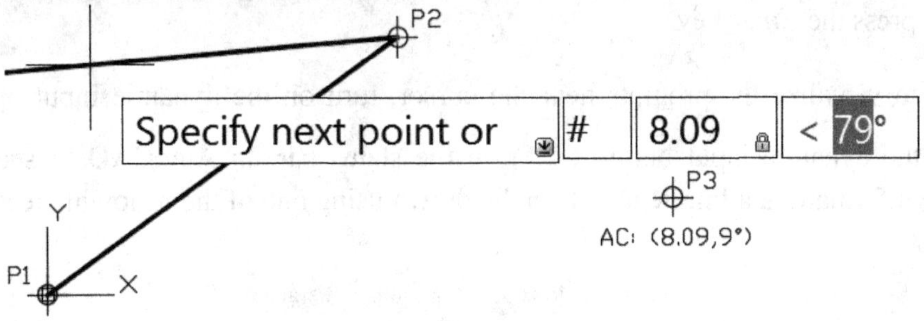

Figure 3-12a

3.5.3.4. Relative Polar coordinates

For the relative coordinates, the last point is used as the benchmark for the relative coordinates of the next point. The relative coordinates are used when the location of the next point is known with respect to the previous point.

- ***Example:*** Draw a line from point P2 to point P3. The relative polar coordinates of point P3 with respect to P2 are (4.03, -30°) using one of the following two methods.

  1. Dynamic input method: In the case of the dynamic input, specify the relative coordinates with the @ prefix, Figure 3-12b. (i) Click at point P2. (ii) Type the @ symbol (hold the *Shift* key and press 2 key). The @ symbol appears in the dynamic input tool tip and the cursor moves to the first input field. (iii) Type in the distance (that is 4.03). (iv) Press the Less than (<) key; the entry is locked and the cursor moves to the second input field. (v) Now, type the angle (that is -30). (vi) Finally, press the *Enter* key.
  2. Command line method: For the command line the @ is used. Type @4.03<-30 (no space) and press the *Enter* key.

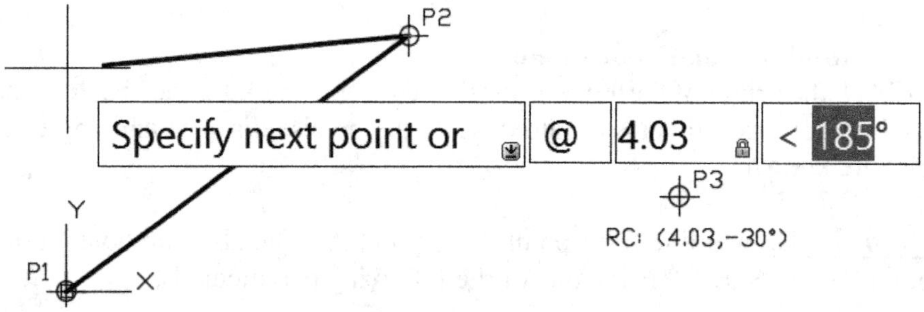

Figure 3-12b

3.6. Line

The *Line* command is used to draw a straight line between two points.

- The *Line* command is activated using one of the following methods.
  1. Panel method: From the *Home* tab and *Draw* panel, select the *Line* tool, Figure 3-13a.
  2. Command line method: Type "line", "Line", or "LINE" on the command line and press the *Enter* key.

In order to visualize the prompts near the cursor, turn on the dynamic input option by clicking the dynamic input button ( ) on the status bar. In AutoCAD, based on the available information, a line segment can be drawn using one of the following techniques.

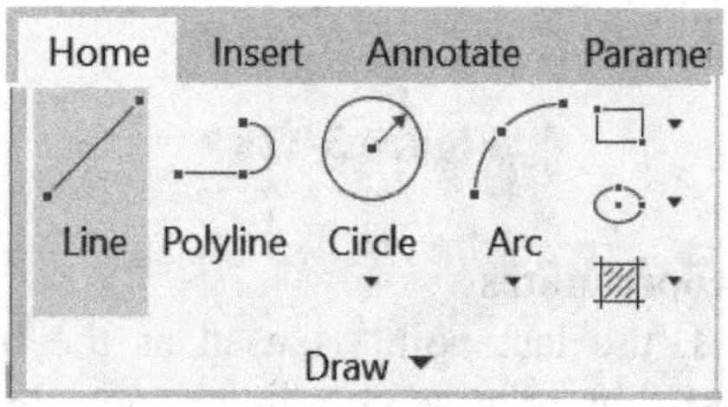

Figure 3-13a

3.6.1. Points selection

In point selection method, lines are drawn by clicking at the points in the drawing area. The drafter may or may not draw the points before drawing the lines.

Example: Assume a surveyor has drawn four stations (A, B, C, and D) on a map, Figure 3-13b. Now, the stations are required to be connected by straight roads. The desired roads can be drawn on the map as follows:

1. Activate the *Line* command.
2. Click at station A; press the down-arrow key of the keyboard to check the available options. Only the *Undo* option is available. Press the up-arrow key of the keyboard to exit the selection list.
3. Click at station B; a line segment is drawn from station A to station B. Press the down-arrow key of the keyboard to check the available options; now *eXit* option is available, too, Figure 3-13b. Press the up-arrow key of the keyboard to exit the selection list.

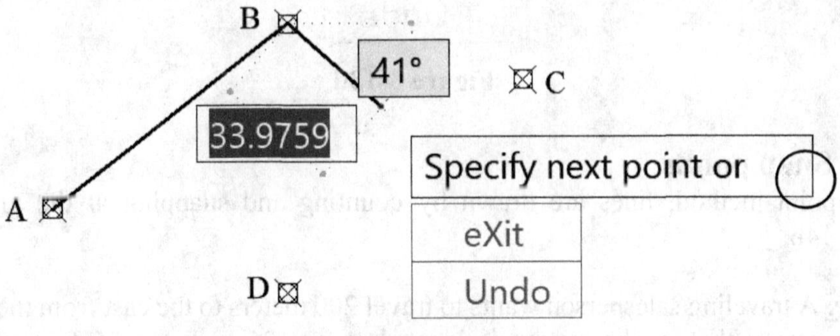

Figure 3-13b

4. Now, click at station C, a line segment is drawn from station B to station C, Figure 3-13c. Press the down-arrow key from the keyboard to check the available options. Now, the *Close* option is available, too. The close option is available only after the user has clicked at least three points (that is, has drawn two lines segments).

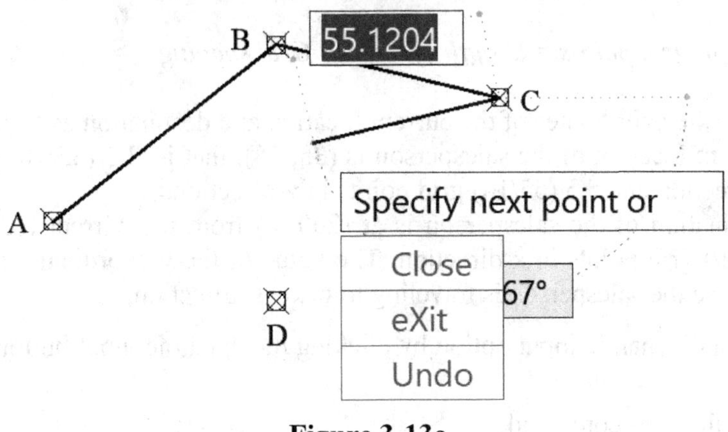

Figure 3-13c

5. Repeat step (3) to draw a line from station C to station D.
6. Press the down-arrow key from the keyboard and click on the *Close* option, Figure 3-13d. The selection of the *Close* option automatically draws a line from D to A and terminates the *Line* command.
7. To exit the command without creating a closed area, either select *eXit* option or press the *Esc* or the *Enter* key.

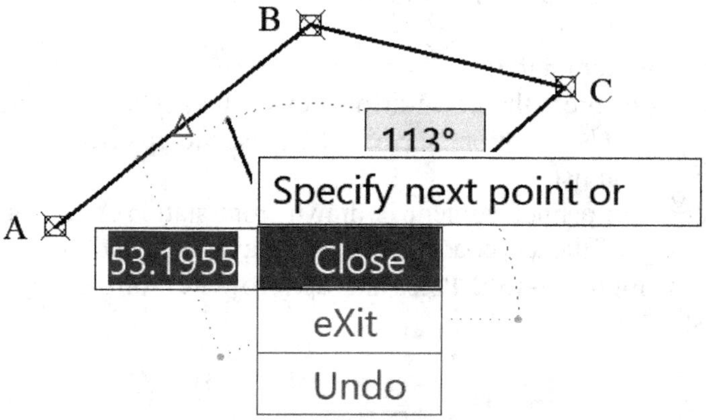

Figure 3-13d

3.6.2. Snap points

In snap point method, lines are drawn by counting and snapping at the grid points, Figure 3-14b.

Example: A traveling salesperson wants to travel 200 meters to the east from the station at (35, 55) meters; that is, the station is located at x = 35 and y = 55 from the origin, Figure 3-14a. The salesperson's current location and destination can be drawn as follows.

1. Turn on the *Grid* ( ) and *Snap* ( ) options by clicking the respective buttons on the status bar. Now, the user is allowed to click only at the snap points.
2. Set the *Grid spacing* to be 10.0 and the *Snap spacing* to be 5.0.
3. The number of grid points can be accurately counted as:

No. of grid points = Length of a line / Grid spacing

4. Calculate the coordinates of the current location and destination as follows:
   - Current location of the salesperson is (35, 55); that is, 3.5 (35/10) grid points in x-direction and 5.5 (55/10) grid points in y-direction.
   - Destination of the salesperson is at (200, 0) from the current location; that is, 200/10 grid points in x-direction. The value of the y-coordinate is not changed because the salesperson is traveling to the east direction.
5. Turn on the dynamic input option by clicking the dynamic input button ( ) on the status bar.
6. Activate the *Line* command.

7. For the current location of the salesperson (first point of the line), Figure 3-14a, click at (35, 55); that is, 3.5 and 5.5 grid points in x- and y-direction, respectively.
8. For the salesperson's destination, click at (200, 0) from the current location; that is, 20 and 0 grid points in x- and y-direction, respectively, Figure 3-14b.
9. Press the *Enter* key to exit the command.

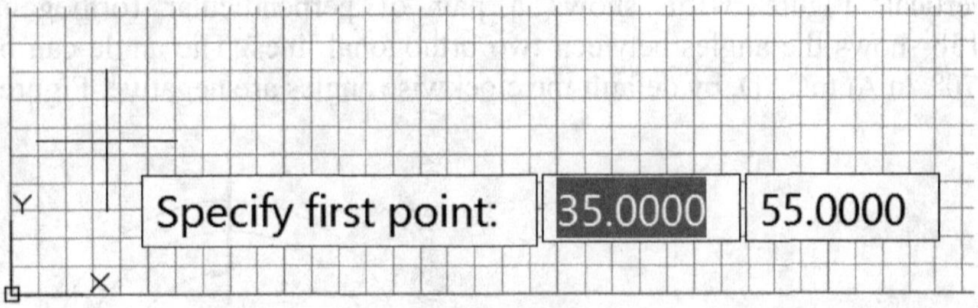

Figure 3-14a

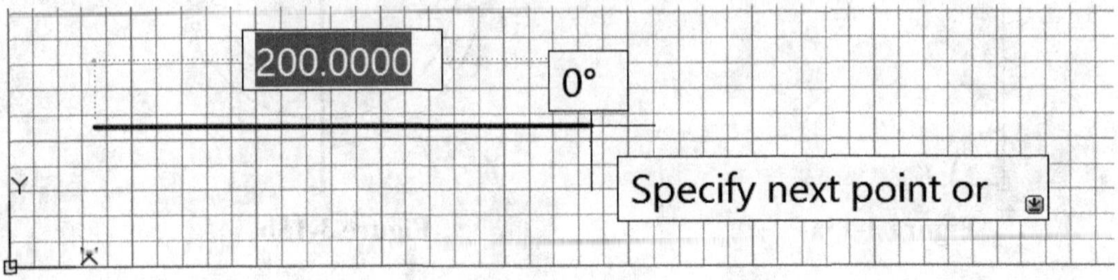

Figure 3-14b

3.6.3. Cartesian coordinates

In Cartesian coordinate's method, lines are drawn by specifying the x-, y-, and z-coordinates of their endpoints.

Example: Draw a line from P2 to P3 using absolute and relative Cartesian coordinates.

1. Refer to Section 3.5.3.1 for the absolute Cartesian coordinates.
2. Refer to Section 3.5.3.2 for the relative Cartesian coordinates.

3.6.4. Polar coordinates

In polar coordinates method, lines are drawn by specifying their lengths and angles from a reference axis.

Example: Draw a line from P2 to P3 using absolute and relative polar coordinates.

1. Refer to Section 3.5.3.3 for the absolute polar coordinates.
2. Refer to Section 3.5.3.4 for the relative polar coordinates.

3.6.5. Orthogonal command

The orthogonal lines mean that lines are perpendicular. Since X- and Y-axes are right angles with respect to each other, lines parallel to X- and Y-axes are perpendicular lines. In AutoCAD terminology, orthogonal command means that the lines are parallel to X- and Y-axis. By default, for the two-dimensional drawings, the X-axis is horizontal and the Y-axis is vertical. Figure 3-15a shows a pair of perpendicular (orthogonal) lines. Figure 3-15b shows the angles between two orthogonal lines. The angle can be 0°, 90°, 180°, or 270°. In AutoCAD, by default the clockwise angles are negative, Figure 3-15b.

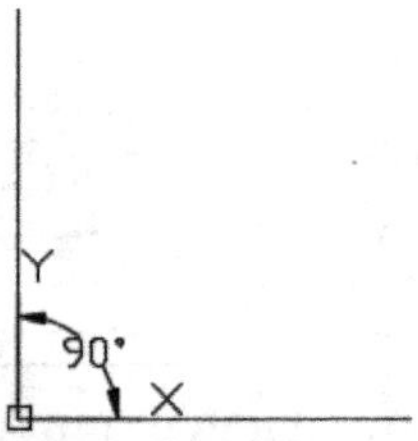

Figure 3-15a

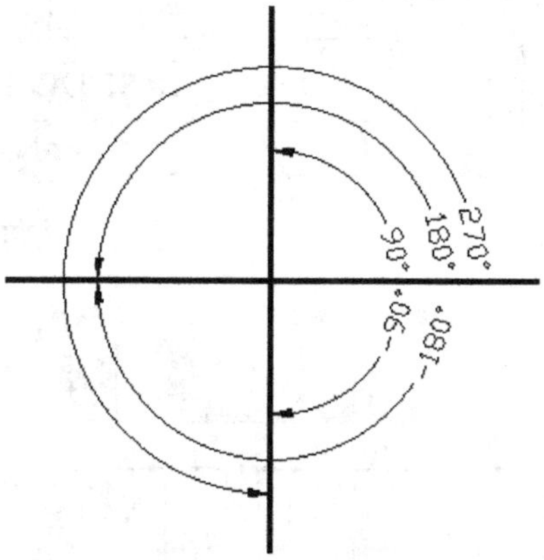

Figure 3-15b

Example: Draw the object shown in Figure 3-16a using polar coordinates and orthogonal command. Recall that the polar coordinate needs length and angle. In the current example, there are 14 line segments. Hence, the user needs to specify 14 lengths and 14 angles. Since the lines are either horizontal or vertical, the AutoCAD user can increase productivity by using the *Ortho* command. This command allows the user to draw the orthogonal lines by specifying the lengths only, thus saving 50% of the time required to draw the drawing!

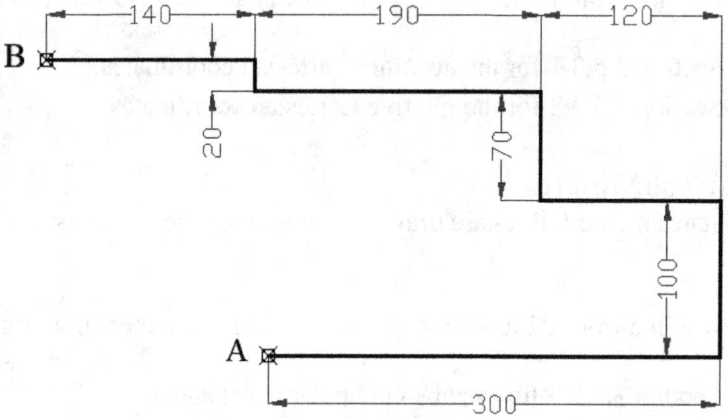

Figure 3-16a

The user can draw the given shape using the following steps:

1. Turn *On* the dynamic input option by clicking the dynamic input button () on the status bar.
2. Turn *On* the *Ortho* mode by clicking on the orthogonal mode button () on the status bar.
3. Activate the *Line* command.
4. The drawing can be started at point A or B. However, in the current example, the drawing starts at point A.
5. To begin the drawing, click at a random point near the WCS.
6. Move the cursor in the direction of the line to be drawn, Figure 3-16b.

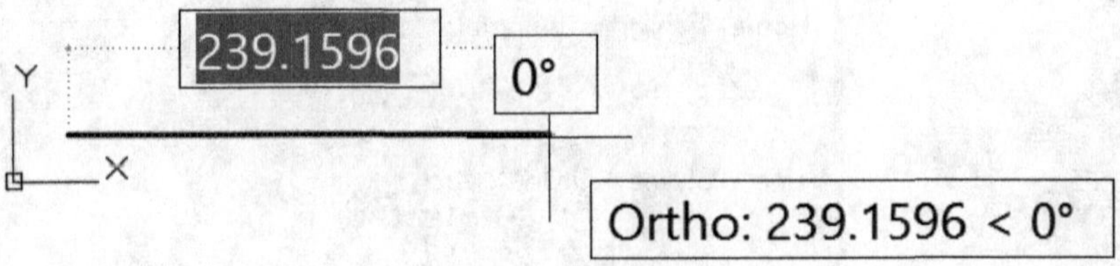

Figure 3-16b

7. Specify the length (300) and press the *Enter* key. **No need to specify the angle.** Now, move the cursor in the direction of the next line to be drawn, Figure 3-16c.

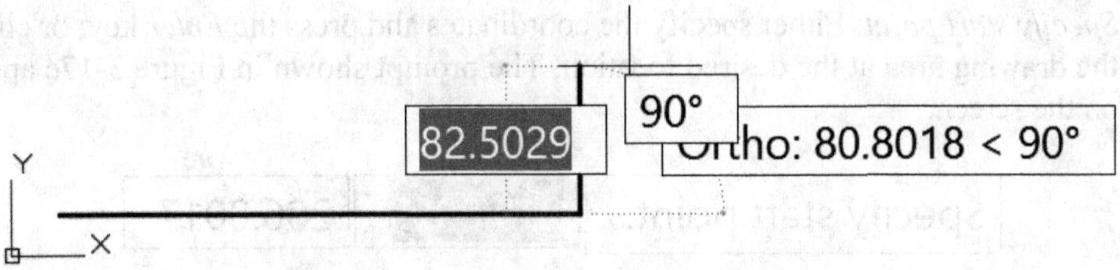

Figure 3-16c

8. Specify the length (100) and press the *Enter* key. No need to specify the angle. Now, move the cursor in the direction of the next line to be drawn, Figure 3-16d.
9. Repeat the above process and complete the drawing as shown in Figure 3-16a.

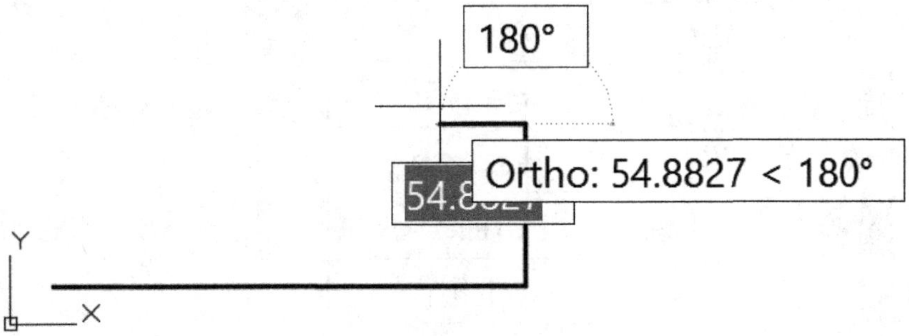

Figure 3-16d

3.7. Polyline

The *Polyline* command is used to draw an object composed of one or more connected line segments or circular arcs. The resultant polyline is a single entity; that is, one of its segments cannot be modified independently. A polyline can be converted to multiple entities using *Explode* command (the *Explode* command is discussed in *Chapter 4*).

- The *Polyline* command is activated using one of the following methods:
  1. Panel method: From the *Home* tab and *Draw* panel, select the *Polyline* tool, Figure 3-17a.
  2. Command line method: Type "pline", "Pline", or "PLINE" in the command line and press the *Enter* key.

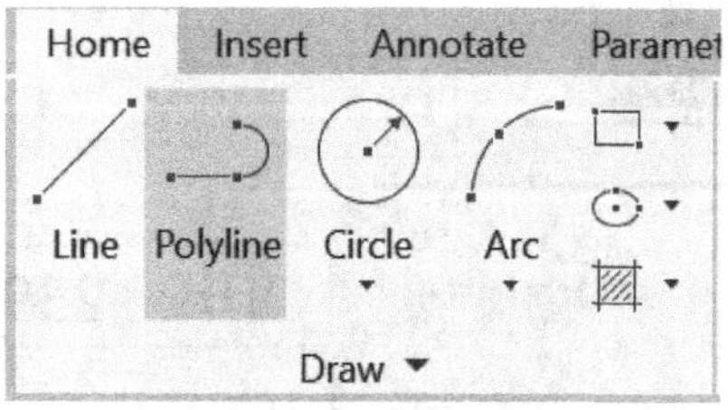

Figure 3-17a

- The activation of the command results in the prompt to specify the start point, Figure 3-17b.
- *Specify start point*: Either specify the coordinates and press the *Enter* key; or click in the drawing area at the desired location. The prompt shown in Figure 3-17c appears on the screen.

Figure 3-17b

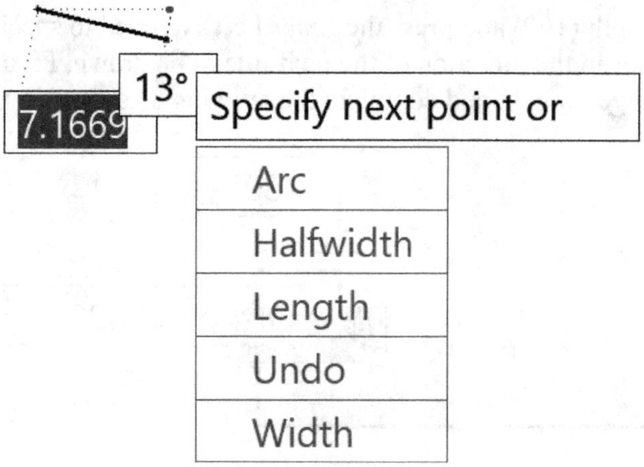

Figure 3-17c

- Arc option: The arc option creates arc segments in a polyline. Click on the *Arc* option in Figure 3-17c. The prompt shown in Figure 3-18 appears on the screen. Either specify the endpoint of the arc or press the down-arrow key from the keyboard to display the options list, Figure 3-18.

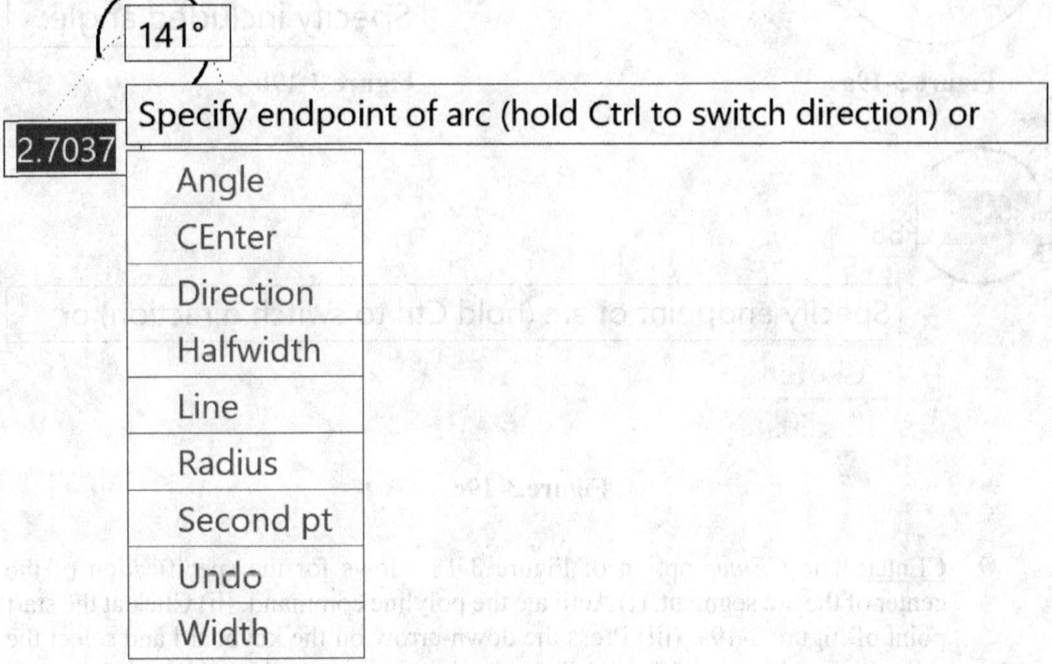

Figure 3-18

1. Angle: The *Angle* option of Figure 3-18 allows for the specification of the included angle of the arc segment from the start point. A positive angle creates a counterclockwise arc segment, and a negative angle creates a clockwise arc segment. (i) Activate the polyline command. (ii) Click at the Start point of Figure 3-19a. (iii) Press the down-arrow on the keyboard and select the *Arc* option in Figure 3.17c. (iv) Press the down-arrow on the keyboard and select the *Angle* option in Figure 3.18. The prompt shown in Figure 3-19b appears on the screen. (v) Specify the angle and press the *Enter* key, Figure 3-19c. (vi) For the *endpoint* option, click at the Endpoint of Figure 3-19a. For the *CEnter* option, click at the CEnter of Figure 3-19a. For the *Radius* option, specify its value. (vii) Press the *Enter* key. The resultant arc is shown in Figure 3-19a. The user is ready to draw the next command.

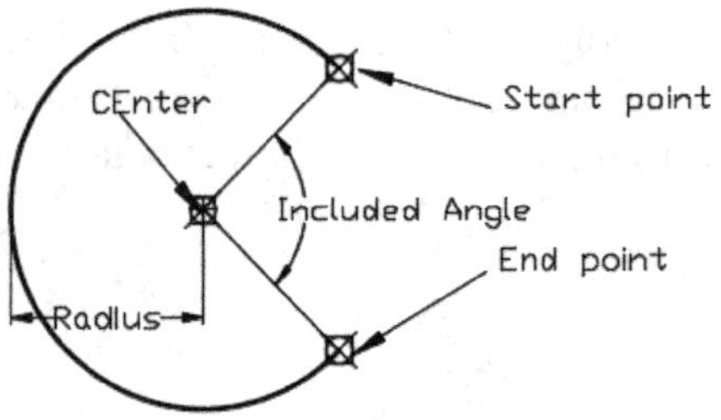

Figure 3-19a

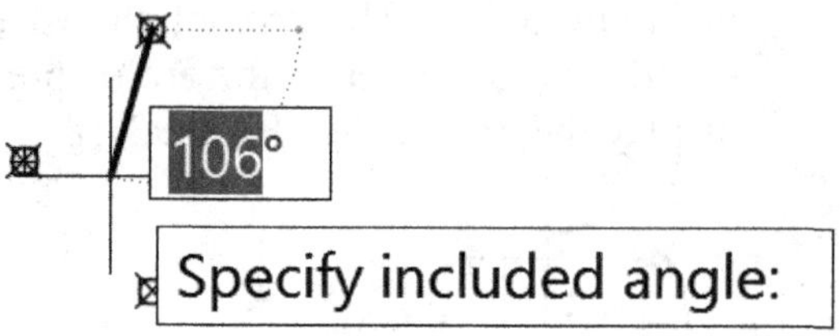

Figure 3-19b

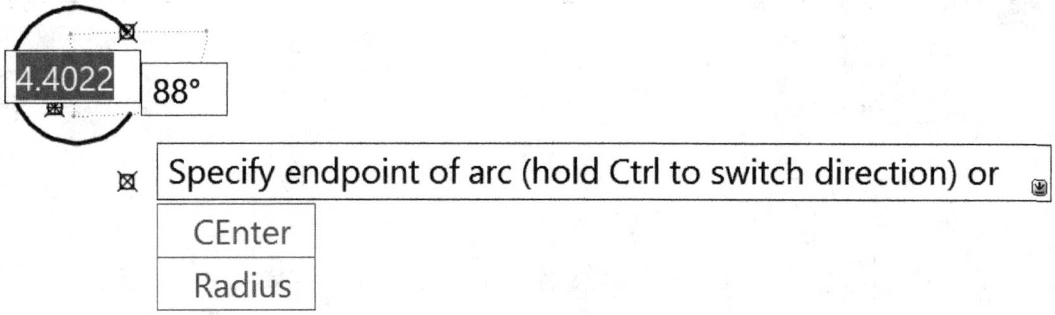

Figure 3-19c

2. CEnter: The *CEnter* option of Figure 3-18 allows for the specification of the center of the arc segment. (i) Activate the polyline command. (ii) Click at the start point of Figure 3-19a. (iii) Press the down-arrow on the keyboard and select the *Arc* option in Figure 3.17c. (iv) Press the down-arrow on the keyboard and select the *CEnter* option in Figure 3.18. (v) Specify the center of the arc segment, either through the coordinates or by clicking in the drawing area, Figure 3-20a. (vi) Choose endpoint, angle, or length option, specify the value, and press the *Enter* key, Figure 3-20b. For the current example, select the angle option, Figure 3-20c. (vii) Specify the included angle, Figure 3-20c. (viii) Press the *Enter* key. The resulting arc is shown in Figure 3-20d. Note that the positive angle resulted in a counterclockwise arc. The user is ready to draw the next command.

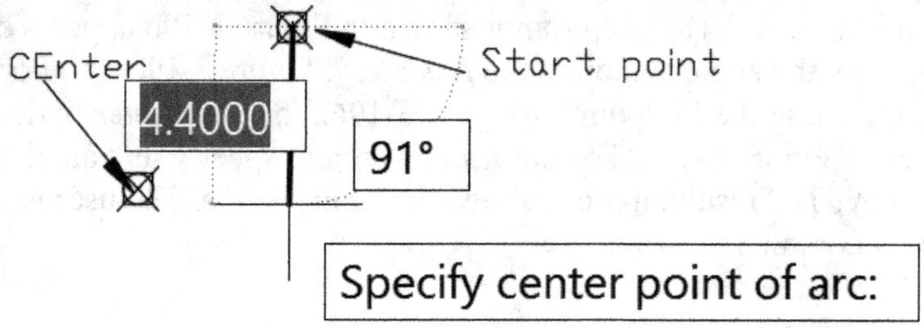

Figure 3-20a

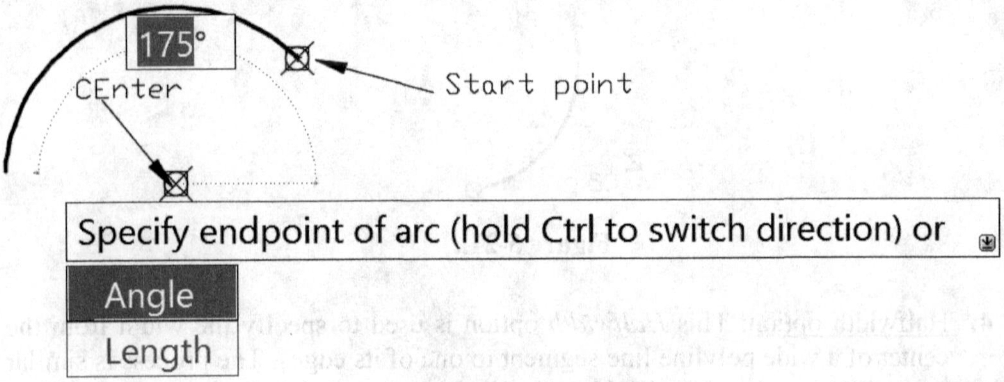

Figure 3-20b

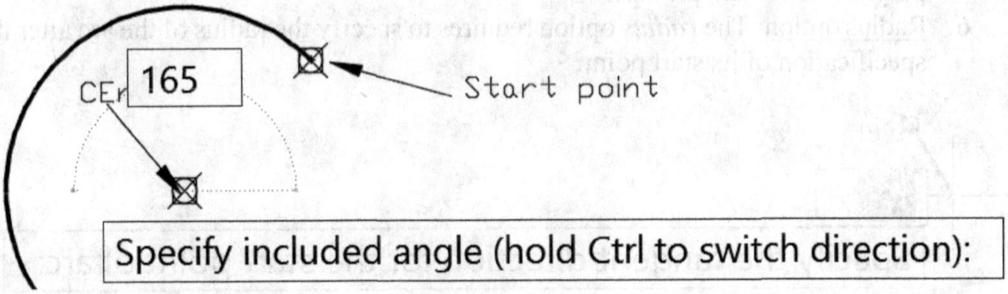

Figure 3-20c

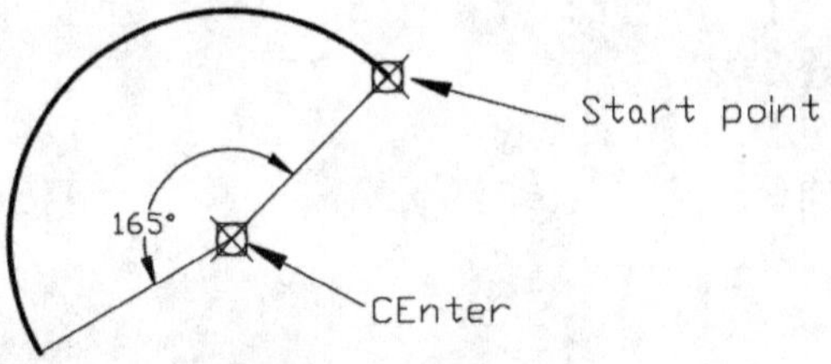

Figure 3-20d

3. <u>Direction</u>: The *Direction* option of Figure 3-18 allows for the specification of the direction of the arc segment. (i) Draw three points as shown in Figure 3-21a. Do NOT label the points. (ii) Activate the polyline command. (iii) Click at point P1 for the start point. (iv) Press the down-arrow on the keyboard and select the *Arc* option in Figure 3.17c. (v) Press the down-arrow key on the keyboard and select the *Direction* option in Figure 3.18. (vi) Specify the starting direction for the arc segment. In order to draw an arc from point P1 to P3 as shown in Figure 3-21a, point P2 should be clicked for the tangent direction, Figure 3-21b. (vii) Finally, for the endpoint, click at P3, Figure 3-21c. (viii) Press the *Enter* key. The resulting arc is shown in Figure 3-21a. The user is ready to draw the next command.

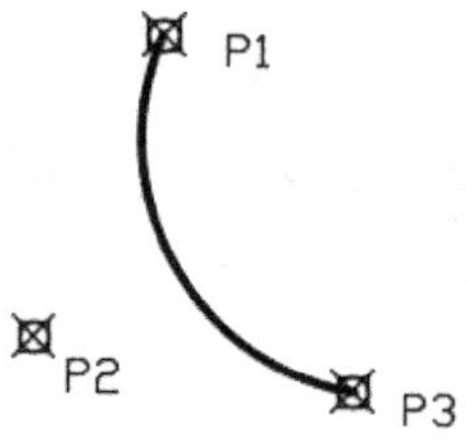

Figure 3-21a

4. Halfwidth option: This *Halfwidth* option is used to specify the width from the center of a wide polyline line segment to one of its edges. The process is similar to the *Width* option. The *Width* option is the last option discussed in this section.
5. Line: This option allows the user to exit the *Arc* option and returns to the initial polyline command prompts.
6. Radius option: The *radius* option requires to specify the radius of the arc after the specification of its start point.

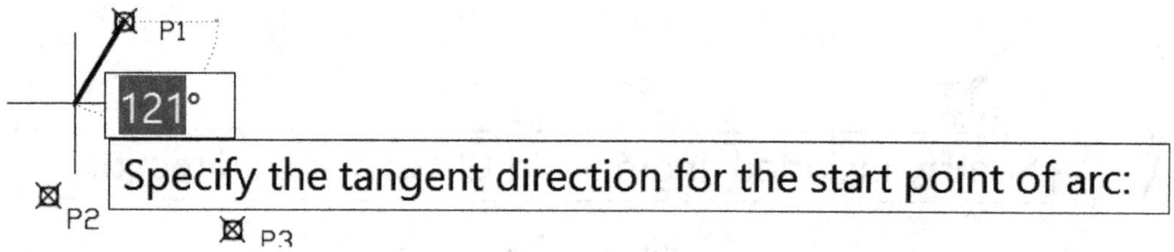

Figure 3-21b

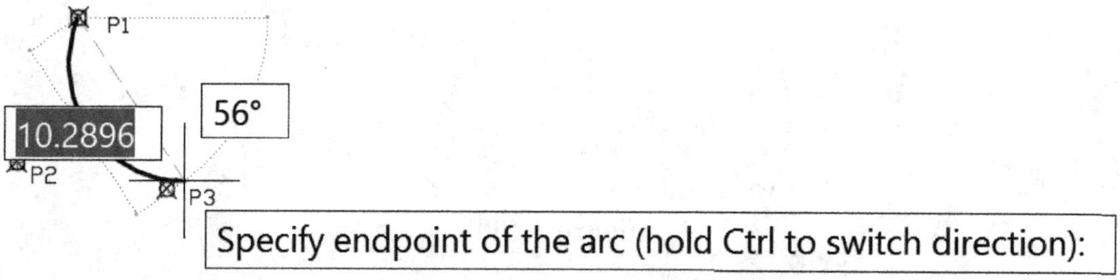

Figure 3-21c

7. Second pt: Specifies the second point and endpoint of a three-point arc.
8. Undo option: The *Undo* option deletes the most recent line segment added to the polyline.
9. Width option: The *Width* option specifies the width of the next line segment of the polyline. (i) Activate the polyline command. (ii) Press the down-arrow on the keyboard and select the *Arc* option in Figure 3.17c. (iii) Press the down-arrow key from the keyboard and select the *Width* option in Figure 3.18. (iv) *Specify starting width*: Enter a value and press the *Enter* key, Figure 3-22a. (v) *Specify ending width*: Enter a value and press the *Enter* key, Figure 3-22b. (vi) The ending width is the uniform width for all the subsequent segments until the width is changed again, Figure 3-22c.

Specify starting width <0.0000>:	1

Figure 3-22a

Specify ending width <1.0000>:	4

Figure 3-22b

Figure 3-22c

3.8. Circle

The user can draw a circle using six different methods (Figure 3-23a) using the *Circle* command. The circle command is used to draw a circle by specifying its center and the radius or diameter; a circle can also be drawn with two or three points on its circumference; and a circle of a known radius and tangent to two objects or a circle tangent to three objects can be drawn, too.

- The *Circle* command is activated using one of the following methods:
  1. Panel method: From the *Home* tab and *Draw* panel, select the *Circle* tool, Figure 3-23a. Use the down-arrow key from the keyboard to display the various options; select the desired option and the prompt for the selected option open.
  2. Command line method: Type "circle", "Circle", or "CIRCLE" in the command line and press the *Enter* key.

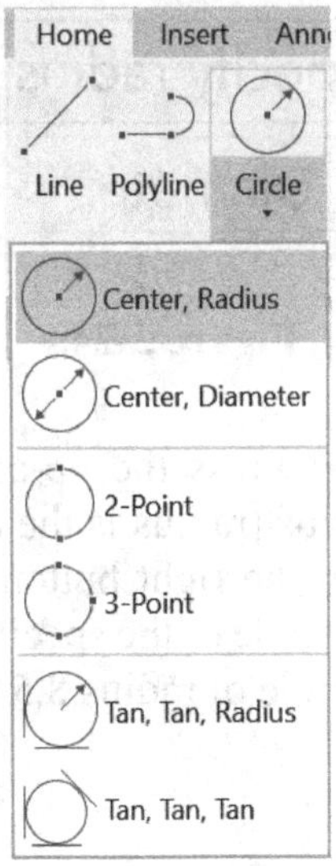

Figure 3-23a

- The activation of the command results in the prompt shown in Figure 3-23b. Use the down-arrow key from the keyboard to display the various options. The user can use the left button of the mouse or drop-down-arrow to select a particular option. However, if the user expands the *Circle*'s drop-down menu from the *Draw* panel, Figure 3-23a, then the user can select the desired option and the prompt for the selected option will appear.

- The remainder of this section explains how to use Circle command to draw a circle.

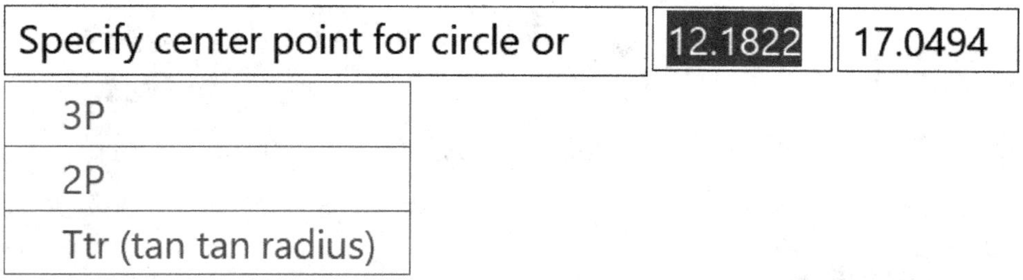

Figure 3-23b

- Center point (default) option: This option draws a circle based on the center point and the radius or the diameter of the circle.
  1. *Specify center point for circle or*: Either click at the desired location in the drawing area or specify the coordinates of the center of the circle and press the *Enter* key. The prompt to specify the radius appears on the screen, Figure 3-24a. Click the down-arrow and check the available option. To draw the circle with radius option, complete step #2 and skip step #3; and for diameter option skip step #2 and complete step #3.

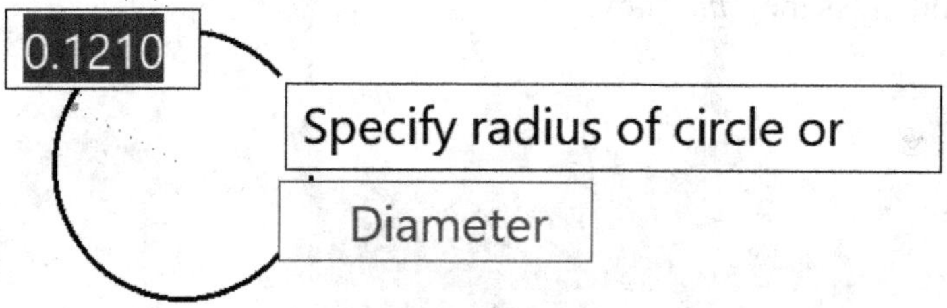

Figure 3-24a

  2. *Specify radius of circle or*: Press the up-arrow to hide the options shown in Figure 3-24a. Type the radius (radius is the default option), Figure 3-24b. Press the *Enter* key or click with the right button of the mouse and select the *Enter* option from the menu. The circle of the specified radius will appear on the screen. In the current example, a circle of radius 8.5 units is drawn.

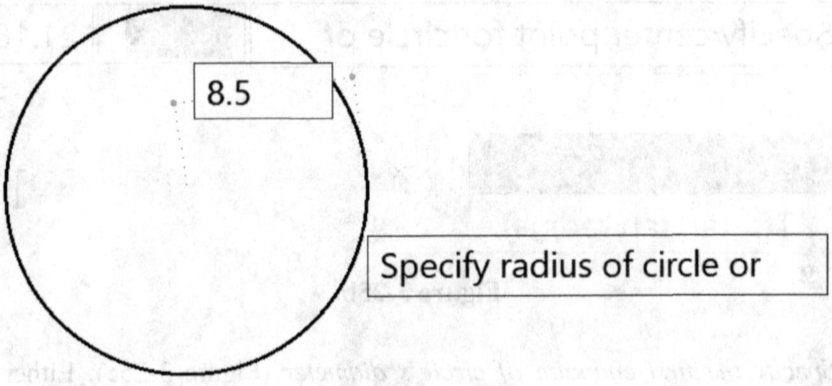

Figure 3-24b

3. *Diameter option*: In Figure 3-24a, click the *Diameter* option. The prompt shown in Figure 3-24c appears. Type the diameter and press the *Enter* key. The circle of the specified diameter will appear on the screen. In the current example, a circle of diameter 8.5 units is drawn.

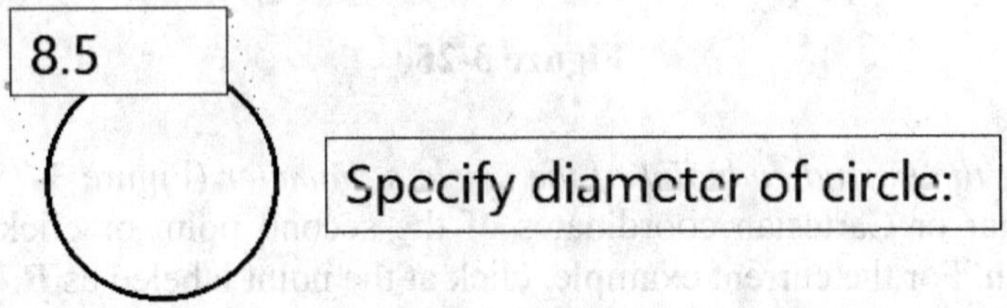

Figure 3-24c

- Two points' option: This option draws a circle based on the two endpoints of the diameter. The advantage of this command is that the user is not required to know the location of the center of the circle and its radius or diameter. This demonstration will use points ***A*** and ***B*** to draw the circle with *2P* option, Figure 3-25a.

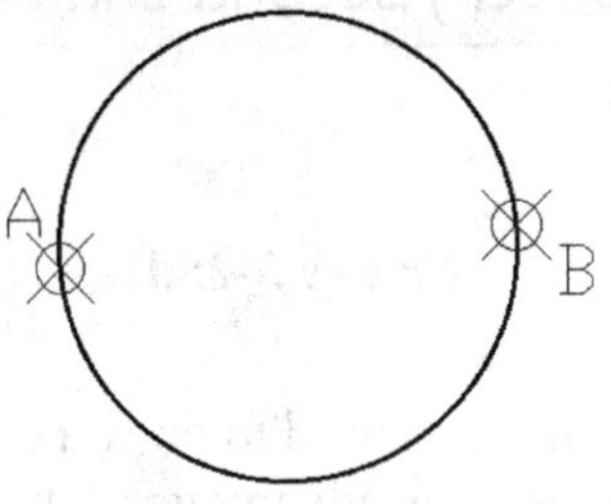

Figure 3-25a

1. Draw two points, ***A*** and ***B***. Do not label them.
2. Activate *Object Snap* command with *Node* option selected.
3. Activate the *Circle* command. Either press the down-arrow and click on *2P* option, Figure 3-25b, or choose *2P* option from Figure 3-23a.

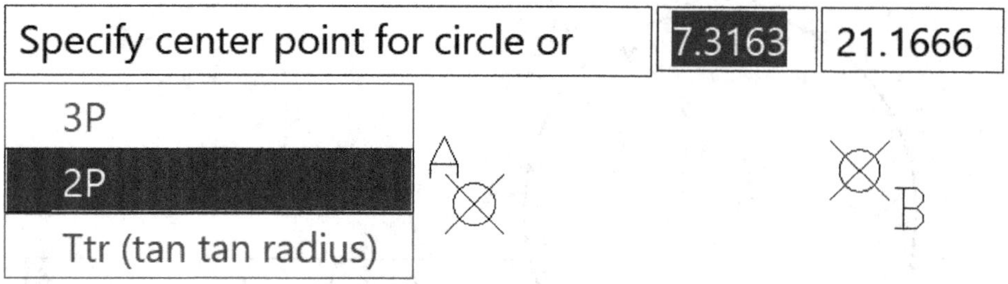

Figure 3-25b

4. *Specify the first endpoint of circle's diameter* (Figure 3-25c): Either type the comma separated coordinates of the first point or click at the desired location. For the current example, click at the point labeled as ***A***.

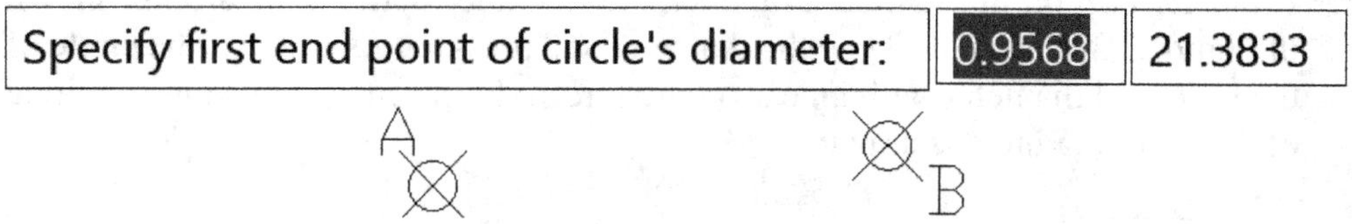

Figure 3-25c

5. *Specify the second endpoint of the circle's diameter* (Figure 3-25d): Either type the polar or Cartesian coordinates of the second point or click at the desired location. For the current example, click at the point labeled as ***B***.
6. The resultant circle is shown in Figure 3-25a.

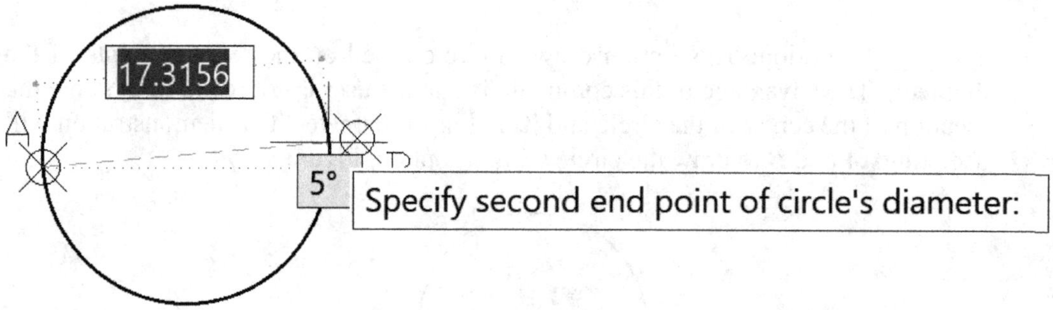

Figure 3-25d

- <u>Three points' option</u>: This option is used to draw a circle based on the three points on the circumference of the circle. The advantage of this command is that the user is not required to know the location of the center of the circle and its radius or diameter. This demonstration will use points ***A***, ***B***, and ***C*** to draw the circle with *3P* option, Figure 3-26a.

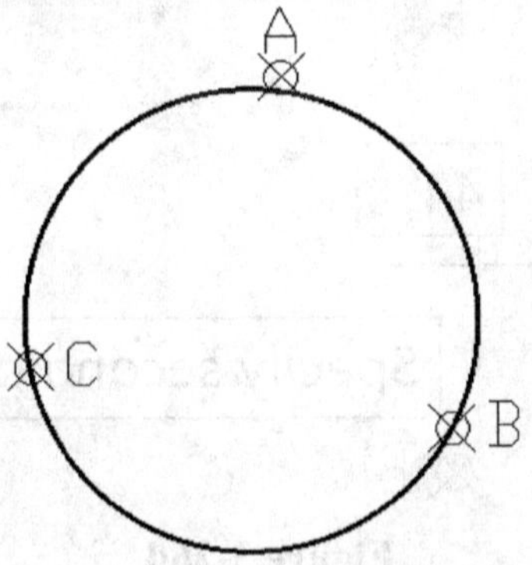

Figure 3-26a

1. Draw three points, ***A***, ***B*** and ***C***. Do not label them.
2. Activate *Object Snap* command with *Node* option selected.
3. Activate the *Circle* command. Either press the down-arrow and click on *3P* option, Figure 3-26b; or choose *3P* option from Figure 3-23a.

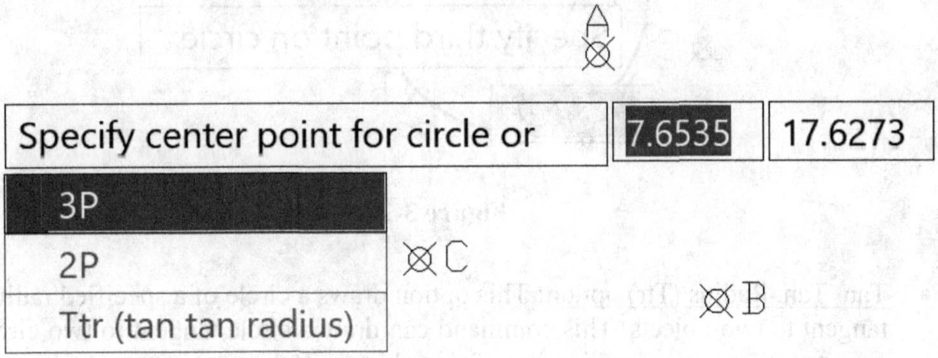

Figure 3-26b

4. *Specify the first point on circle* (Figure 3-26c): Either type the comma separated coordinates of the first point or click at the desired location. In the current example, click at the point labeled as ***A***.

Figure 3-26c

5. *Specify the second point on circle* (Figure 3-26d): Either type the polar or Cartesian coordinates of the second point or click at the desired location. In the current example, click at the point labeled as ***B***.
6. *Specify third point on circle* (Figure 3-26e): Either type the polar or Cartesian coordinates of the third point or click at the desired location. In the current example, click at the point labeled as ***C***.
7. The resultant circle is shown in Figure 3-26a.

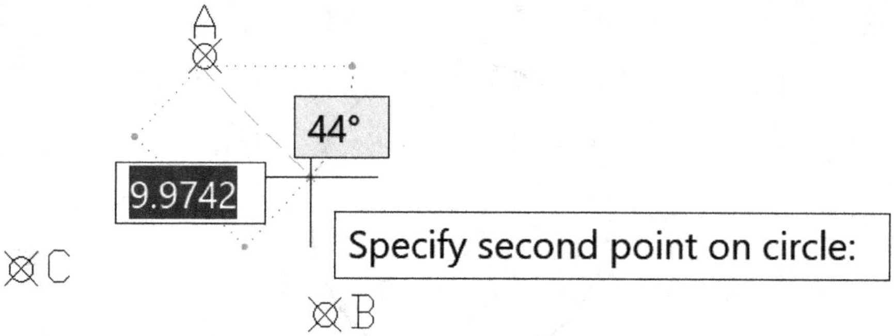

Figure 3-26d

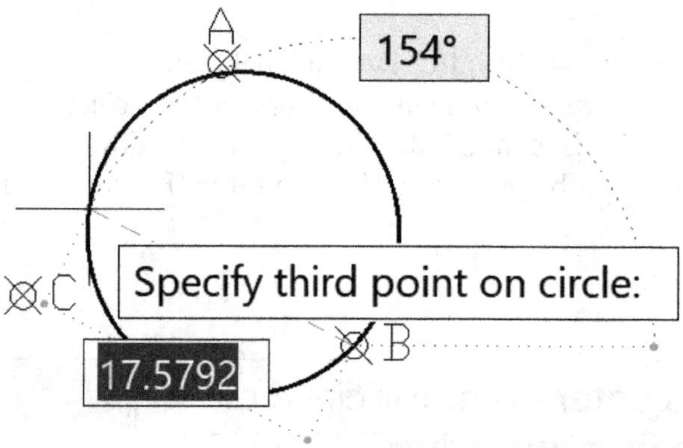

Figure 3-26e

- Tan, Tan, Radius (Ttr) option: This option draws a circle of a specified radius that is tangent to two objects. This command can draw a circle tangent to two circles, two arcs, two lines, or a combination of two objects. The current example draws a circle tangent to a circle and a line.

1. Open an "acad" file and draw a 10 inches diameter circle; draw a 16 inches long line originating at the center of the circle; choose any value for the angle, Figure 3-27a. Do not draw the labels *A* and *B*; these labels are used only for reference.
2. Activate the *Circle* command.
3. Press the down-arrow and choose the "*Ttr*" option, Figure 3-27b. The prompt shown in Figure 3-29c appears on the screen.

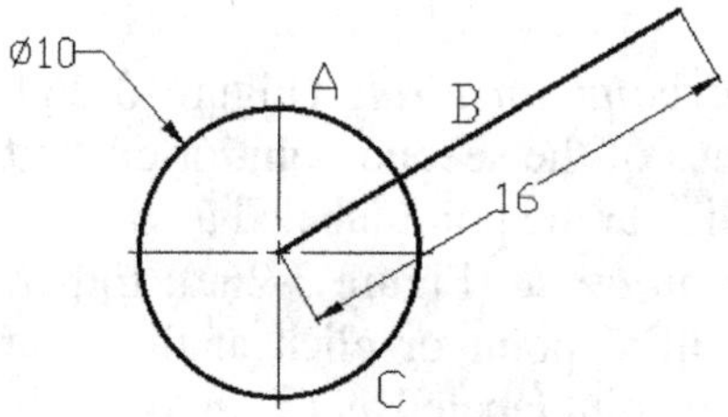

Figure 3-27a

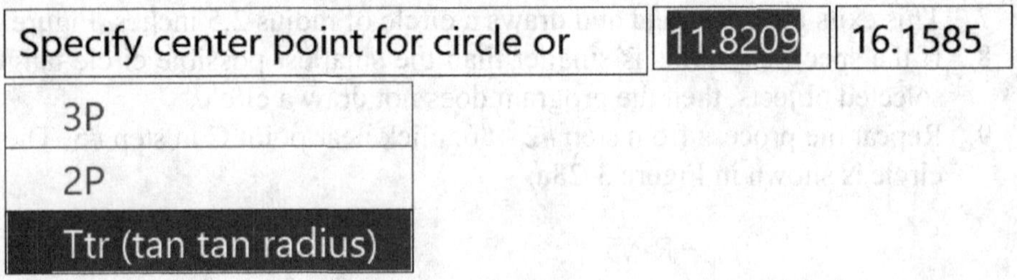

Figure 3-27b

4. *Specify point on the object for first tangent of circle* (Figure 3-27c). Either enter the comma separated coordinates of the tangent on the first object or click roughly in the vicinity of the tangent. In this example, click near label ***A*** on the circle.
5. *Specify point on object for second tangent of circle* (Figure 3-27d). Either enter the coordinates (Cartesian or polar) of the tangent on the second object or click roughly in the vicinity of the tangent. In this example, click near ***B*** on the line.

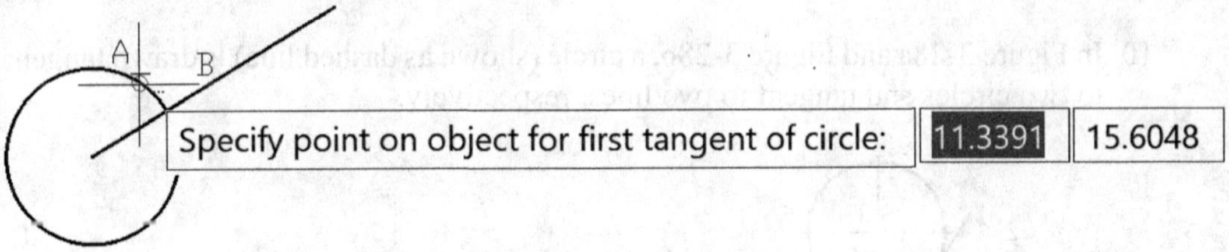

Figure 3-27c

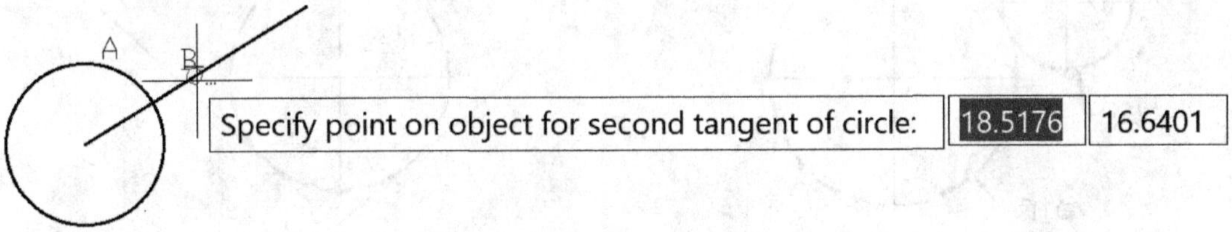

Figure 3-27d

6. *Specify radius of circle* (Figure 3-27e). Specify the radius to be 2.5 and press the *Enter* key.

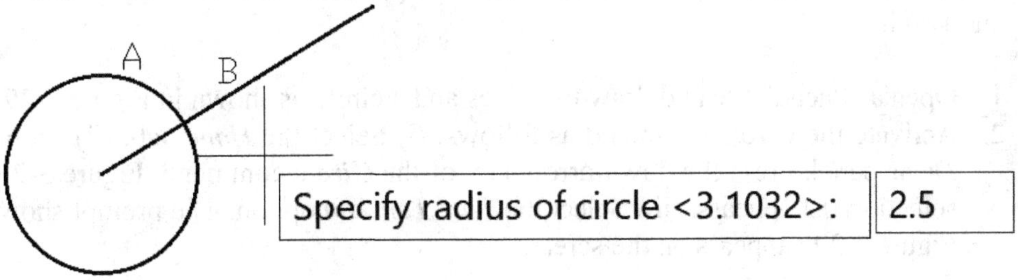

Figure 3-27e

7. This exits the command and draws a circle of radius 2.5 inches, Figure 3-27g.
8. If the specified radius is smaller than the smallest possible circle tangent to the selected objects, then the program does not draw a circle.
9. Repeat the process from step #2 - #6; click near point C in step #5. The resulting circle is shown in Figure 3-28a.

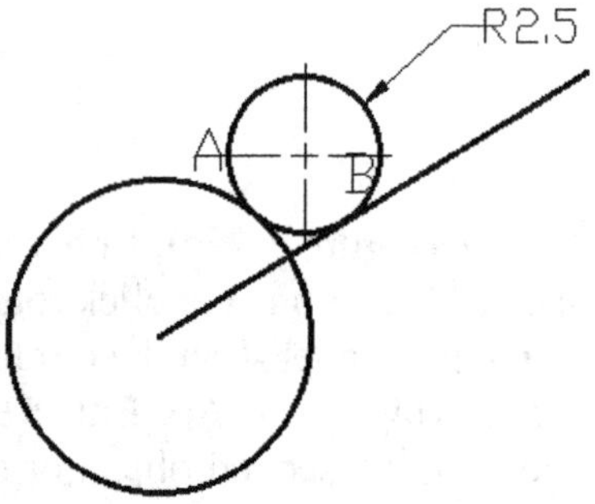

Figure 3-27f

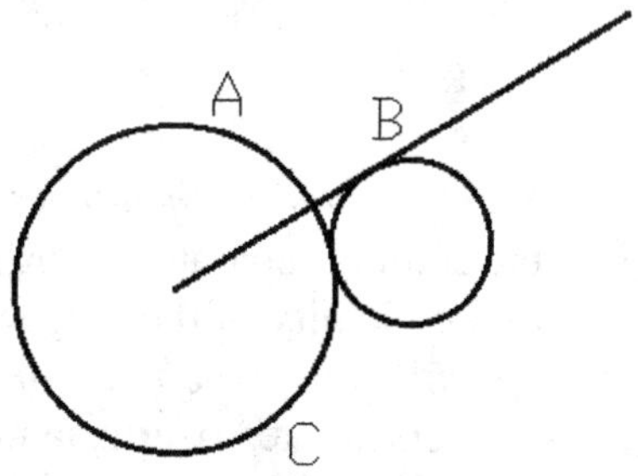

Figure 3-27g

10. In Figure 3-28a and Figure 3-28b, a circle (shown as dashed line) is drawn tangent to two circles and tangent to two lines, respectively.

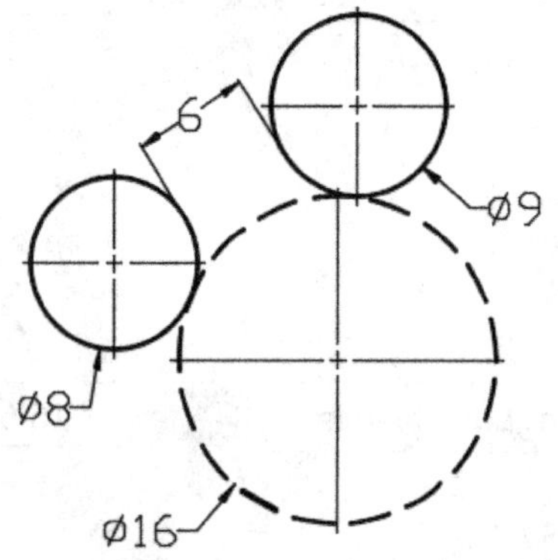

Figure 3-28a

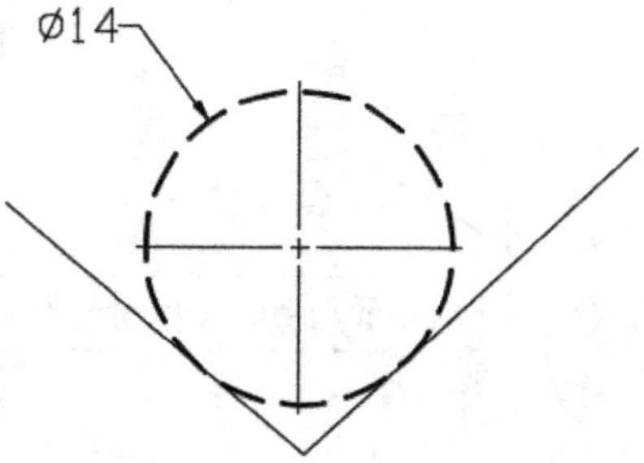

Figure 3-28b

- Tan, Tan, Tan option: This option draws a circle that is tangent to three objects. This command can draw a circle tangent to three circles, three arcs, three lines, or combination of three objects. The current example draws a circle tangent to a circle and two lines.

1. Open an "acad" file and draw two lines and a circle as shown in Figure 3-29a.
2. Activate the *Circle* command as follows: (i) Select the *Home* tab. (ii) From the *Draw* panel, press the down-arrow key of the *Circle* command, Figure 3-29a; a selection list appears. (iii) Select the *Tan, Tan Tan* option. The prompt shown in Figure 3-29c appears on the screen.

3. *Specify first point on circle: to* (Figure 3-29c). Either enter the comma separated coordinates of the tangent on the first object or click roughly in the vicinity of the tangent. In this example click as shown in Figure 3-29c.

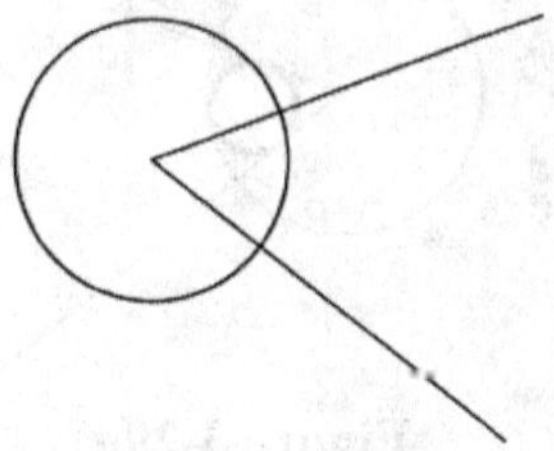

Figure 3-29a

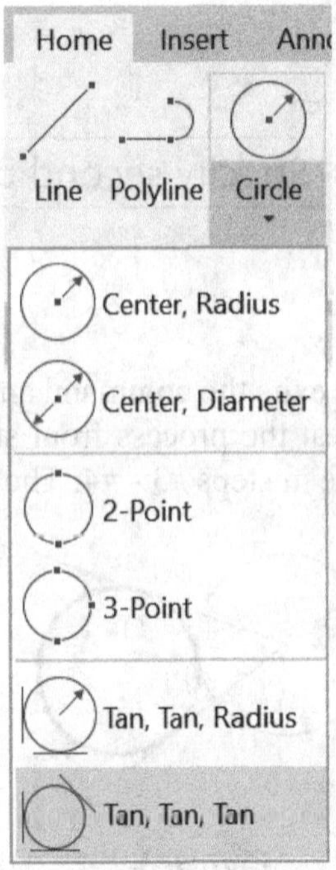

Figure 3-29b

4. *Specify second point on circle: to* (Figure 3-29d). Either enter the coordinates (Cartesian or polar) of the tangent on the second object or click roughly in the vicinity of the tangent. In this example click as shown in Figure 3-29d.

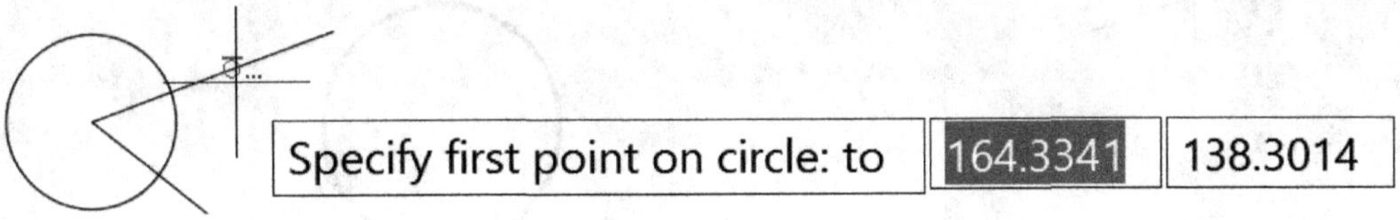

Figure 3-29c

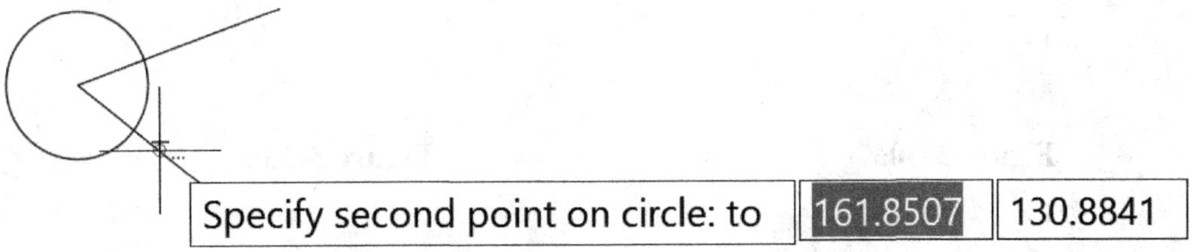

Figure 3-29d

5. *Specify third point on circle: to* (Figure 3-29e). Either enter the coordinates (Cartesian or polar) of the tangent on the second object or click roughly in the vicinity of the tangent. In this example click as shown in Figure 3-29e.

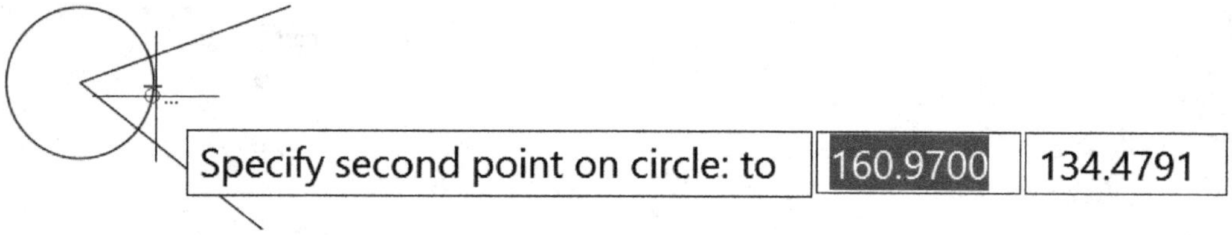

Figure 3-29e

6. This exits the command and draws the circle, Figure 3-29f.
7. Repeat the process from step #2 - #6; click near the end of the lines inside the circle in steps #3 - #4. The resulting circle is shown in Figure 3-29g.

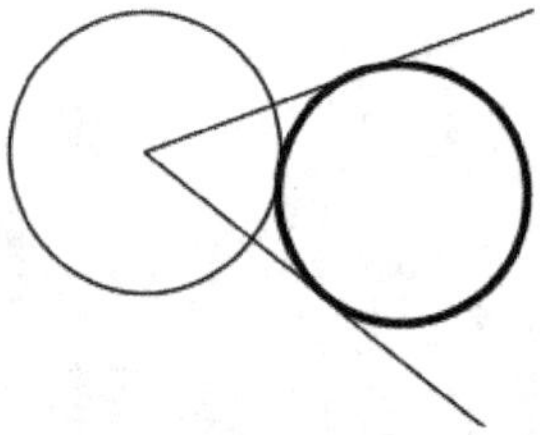

Figure 3-29f

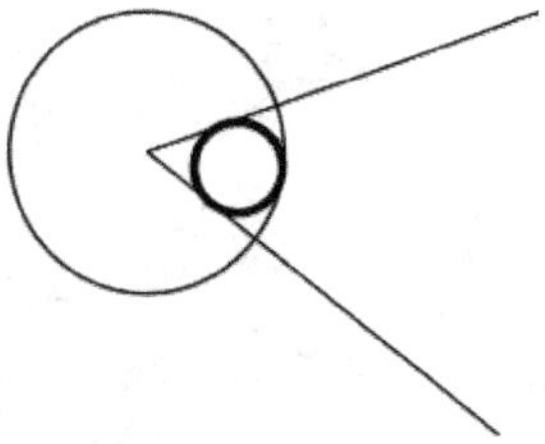

Figure 3-29g

8. If the circle cannot be drawn tangent to the three objects, then it is drawn tangent to one or two objects. Figure 3-30a shows three lines and the tangent points; and Figure 3-30b shows a circle that is tangent to two lines.

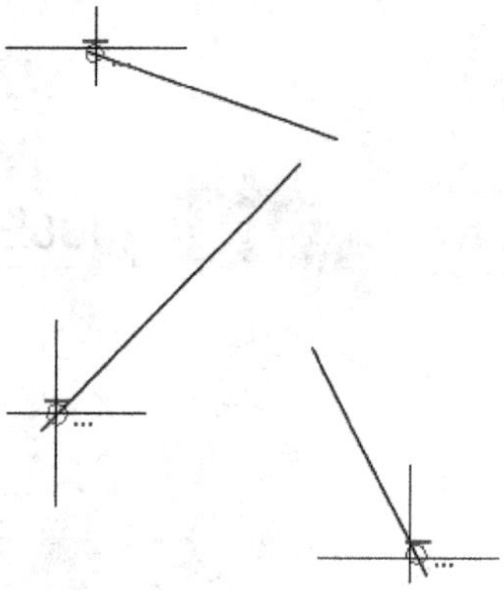

Figure 3-30a

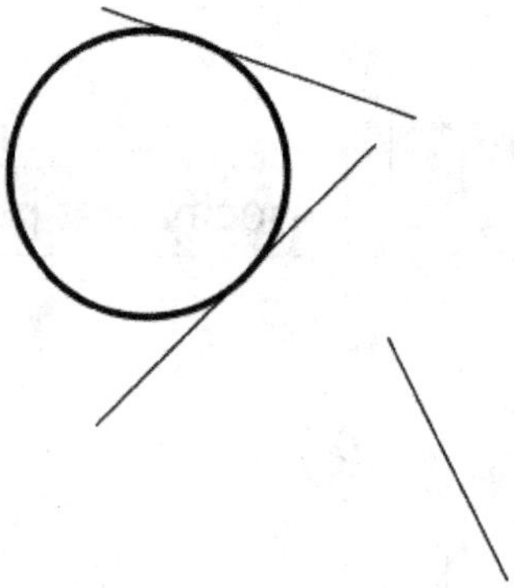

Figure 3-30b

3.9. Rectangle

The *Rectangle* command is used to draw a rectangular shape. Under this command, a rectangle is created by specifying the distance between points diagonally apart. The resultant rectangle is a single entity; that is, one of its sides cannot be erased. A rectangle can be converted to multiple entities using the *Explode* command (the *Explode* command is discussed in *Chapter 4*).

- The *Rectangle* command is activated using one of the following methods:
  1. Panel method: From the *Home* tab and *Draw* panel, select the *Rectangle* tool, Figure 3-31a.
  2. Command line method: Type "rectangle", "Rectangle", or "RECTANGLE" in the command line and press the *Enter* key.

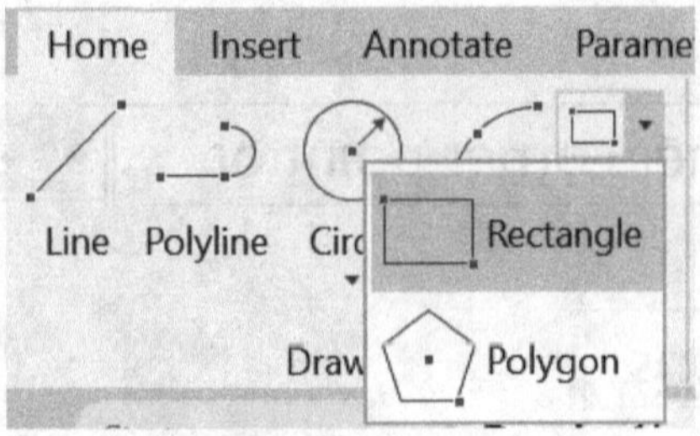

Figure 3-31a

- The activation of the command results in the prompt shown in Figure 3-31b. Use the down-arrow key to display the various options. The *Elevation* and *Thickness* options are useful for 3D modeling. The *width* option specifies the width of the polyline used to draw a rectangle and is discussed in the polyline section. The *Chamfer* and *Fillet* options control the type of corners for the rectangle and are discussed in *Chapter 4*.

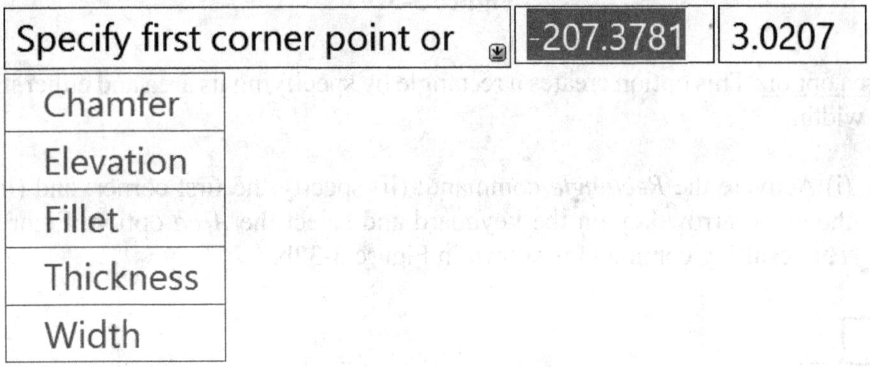

Figure 3-31b

- Corner option: This is the default option. This option creates a rectangle by specifying its diagonally opposite corners.

  1. Activate the *Rectangle* command; the resulting prompt is shown in Figure 3-31c.
  2. *Specify the first corner point*: Either enter the coordinate's values and press the *Enter* key or click at the desired location. The next prompt is shown in Figure 3-31d. Press the down-arrow key from the keyboard to check the option.

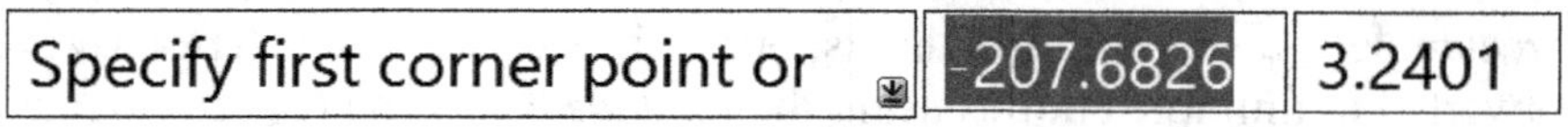

Figure 3-31c

3. *Specify the other corner point*: Press the up-arrow on the keyboard to hide the option in Figure 3-31d. Either specify the coordinates of the diagonally opposite corner or click at the desired location. The resulting Rectangle is shown in Figure 3-31e.

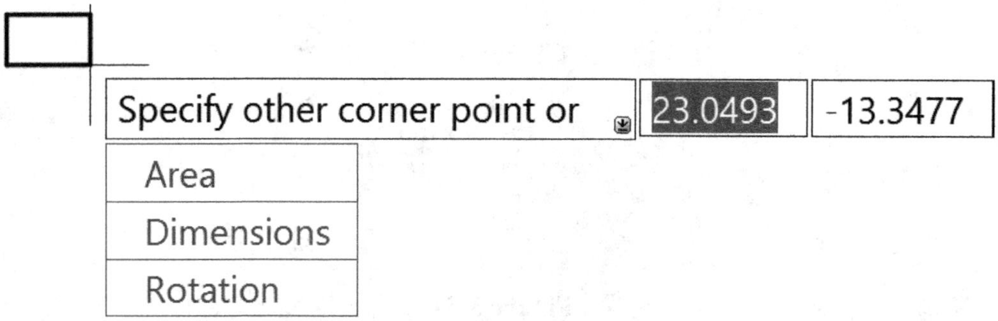

Figure 3-31d

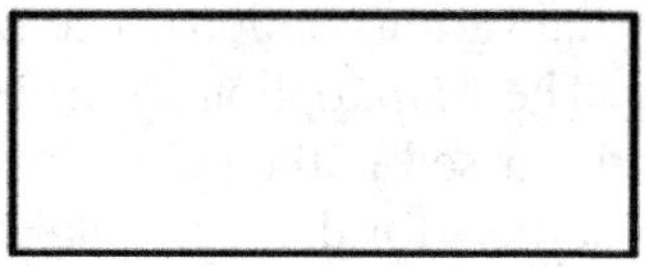

Figure 3-31e

- Area option: This option creates a rectangle by specifying its area and either its length or width.

    1. (i) Activate the *Rectangle* command; (ii) specify the first corner; and (iii) press the down-arrow key on the keyboard and select the *Area* option, Figure 3-32a. The resulting command is shown in Figure 3-32b.

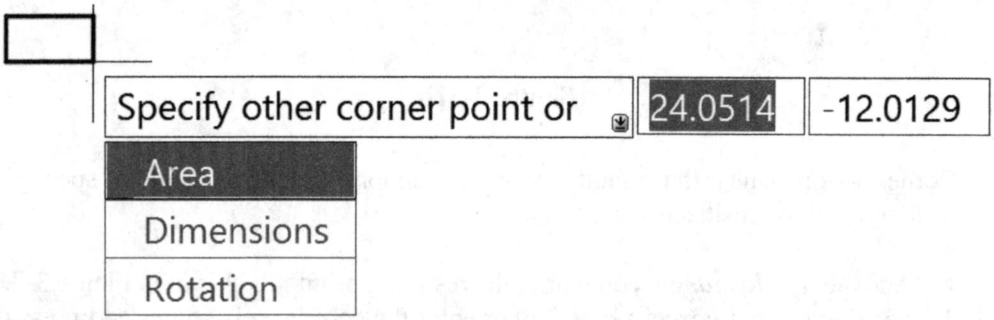

Figure 3-32a

2. *Enter area of a rectangle*: Specify area as a positive number (375 in this example) and press the *Enter* key. The resulting prompt is shown in Figure 3-32c.

Figure 3-32b

3. *Calculate rectangle dimensions based on*: Press the down-arrow key from the keyboard, Figure 3-32c. Select the *Length* or *Width* option. This example selects *Length* option. The resulting prompt is shown in Figure 3-32d.

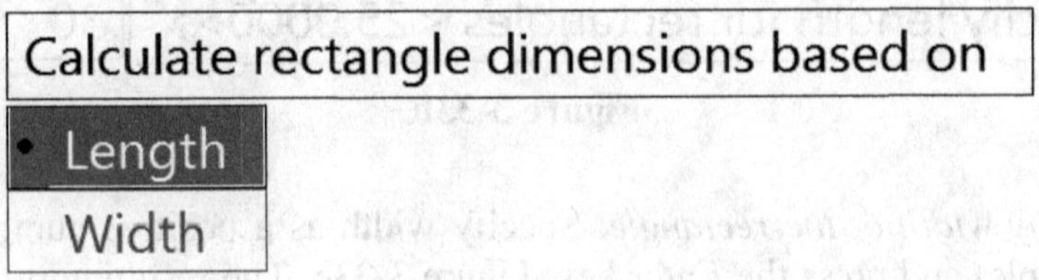

Figure 3-32c

4. *Enter rectangle length*: Specify length as a positive number and press the *Enter* key. This example chooses 25 units, Figure 3-32d.

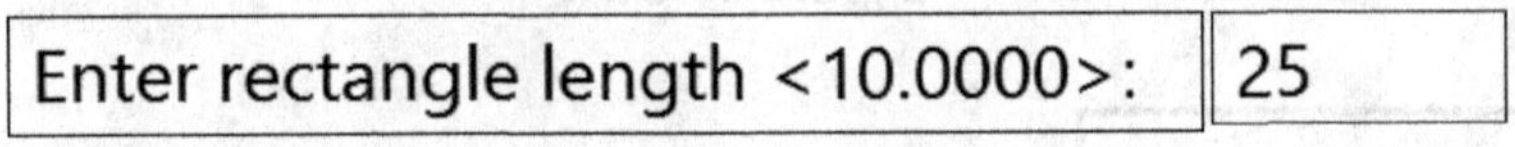

Figure 3-32d

5. The resultant rectangle of area 375 and length 25 is created, Figure 3-32e.

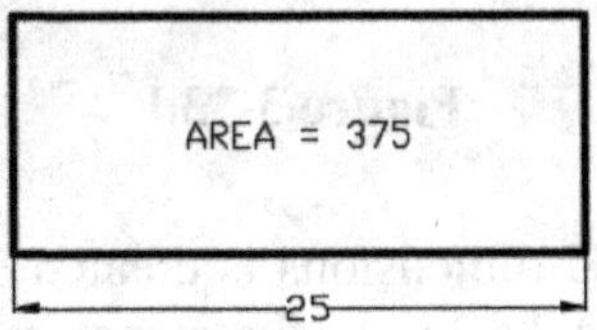

Figure 3-32e

- Dimensions option: This option creates a rectangle by specifying its length and width.

1. (i) Activate the *Rectangle* command; (ii) specify the first corner; and (iii) press the down-arrow on the keyboard and select the *Dimensions* option, Figure 3-33a. The resulting prompt is shown in Figure 3-33b.
2. *Specify length of the rectangle*: Specify length as a positive number (30 in this example) and press the *Enter* key, Figure 3-33b. The resulting prompt is shown in Figure 3-33c.

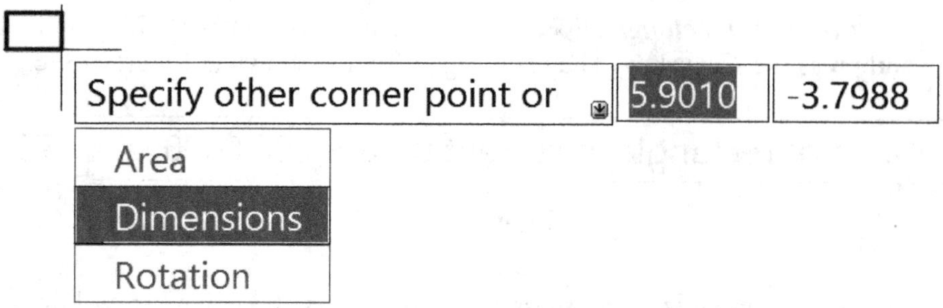

Figure 3-33a

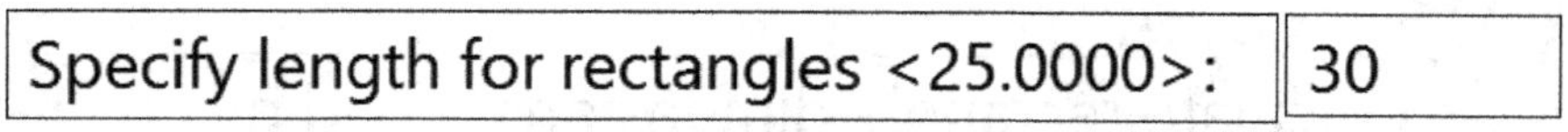

Figure 3-33b

3. *Specify width of the rectangle*: Specify width as a positive number (20 in this example) and press the *Enter* key, Figure 3-33c. The resulting prompt is shown in Figure 3-33d.

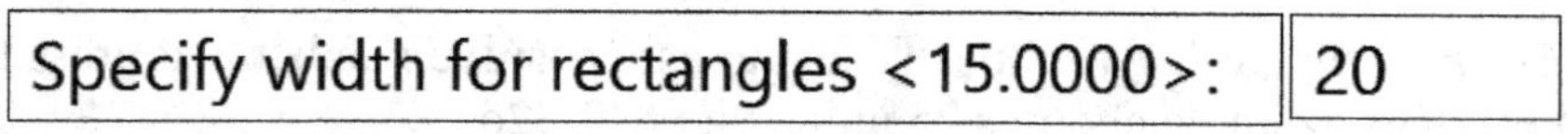

Figure 3-33c

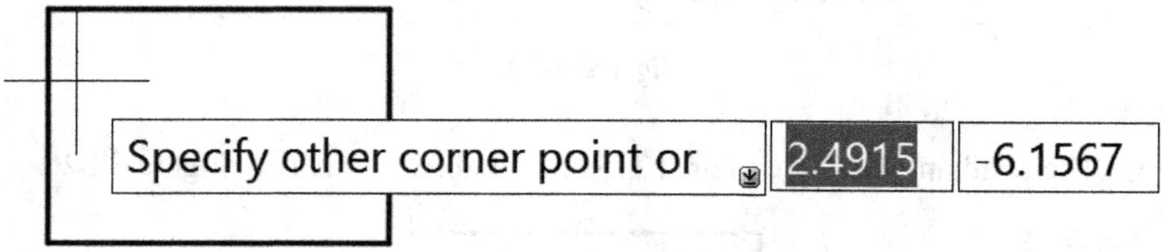

Figure 3-33d

4. A rectangle of specified dimensions is created and is pinned at the first corner point, point *C* in Figure 3-33e. As the cursor moves, the rectangle flips around the first corner point.
5. Click in the desired direction. In this example, click on the diagonally opposite corner. The resulting rectangle of length = 25 and width = 20 is created and is shown in Figure 3-33e.

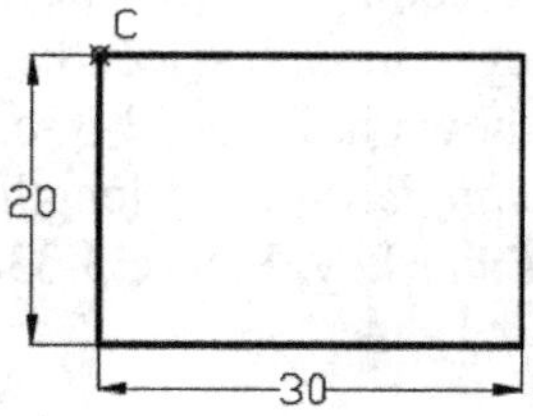

Figure 3-33e

- Rotation option: This option creates a rectangle at a specified rotation angle.

1. (i) Activate the *Rectangle* command; (ii) specify the first corner; and (iii) press the down-arrow on the keyboard and select the *Rotation* option, Figure 3-34a. The resulting prompt is shown in Figure 3-34b.

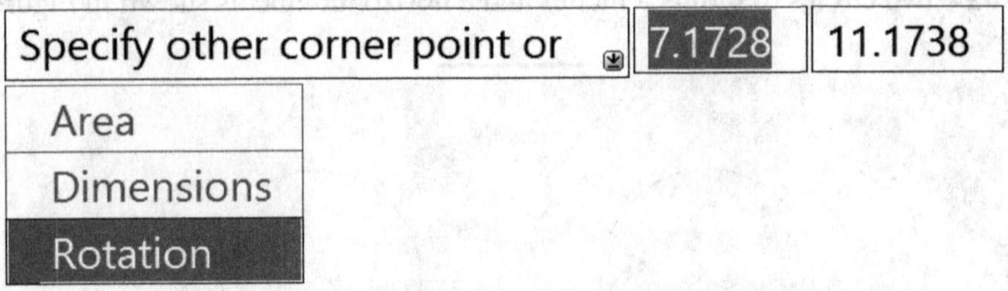

Figure 3-34a

2. *Specify rotation angle*: The default angle is 0°; and positive angle rotates the rectangle counterclockwise (Figure 3-34b) and the negative angle rotates the rectangle clockwise (Figure 3-34c). Specify the rotation angle and press the *Enter* key. In this example, type 135—no need to type degree symbol.

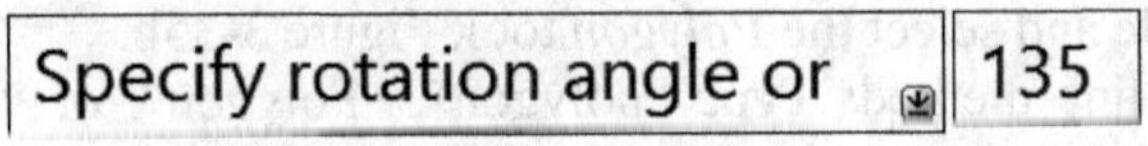

Figure 3-34b

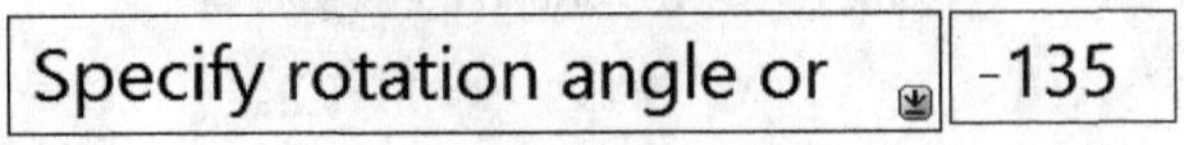

Figure 3-34c

3. Create the rectangle using *Area* or *Dimensions* options. Note that the positive angle creates the rectangle rotated counterclockwise, Figure 3-34d; and the negative angle creates the rectangle rotated clockwise, Figure 3-34e.

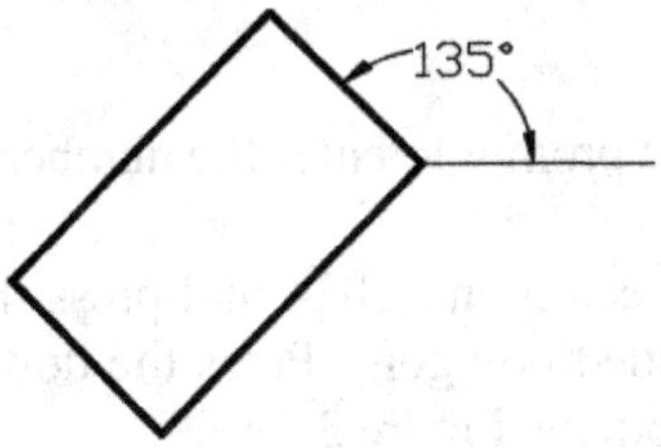

Figure 3-34d

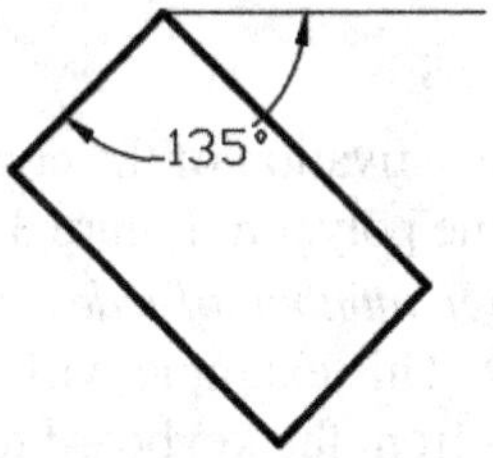

Figure 3-34e

3.10. Polygon

The *Polygon* command is used to draw a regular polygon, that is, a polygon with equal sides. The resultant polygon is a single entity (that is, its one side cannot be modified or erased) unless it is exploded using *Explode* command (the *Explode* command is discussed in *Chapter 4*). For the demonstration of the polygon command, open a new *acad* template file and draw two circles of radius 3 inches and a horizontal line as shown in Figure 3-35a.

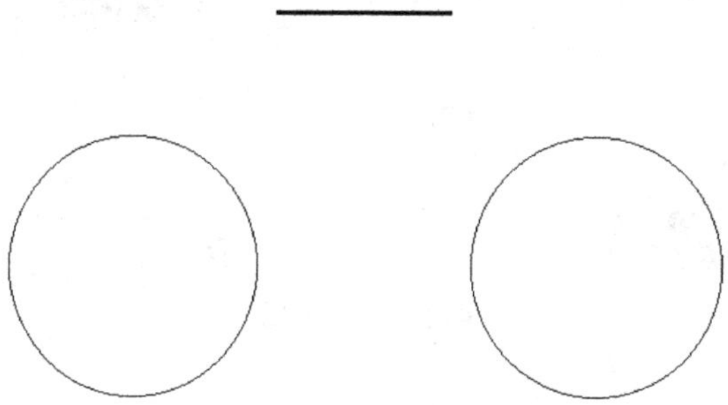

Figure 3-35a

- The *Polygon* command is activated using one of the following methods:
  1. Panel method: From the *Home* tab and *Draw* panel, press the down-arrow beside the rectangle and select the *Polygon* tool, Figure 3-35b.
  2. Command line method: Type "polygon", "Polygon", or "POLYGON" in the command line and press the *Enter* key.

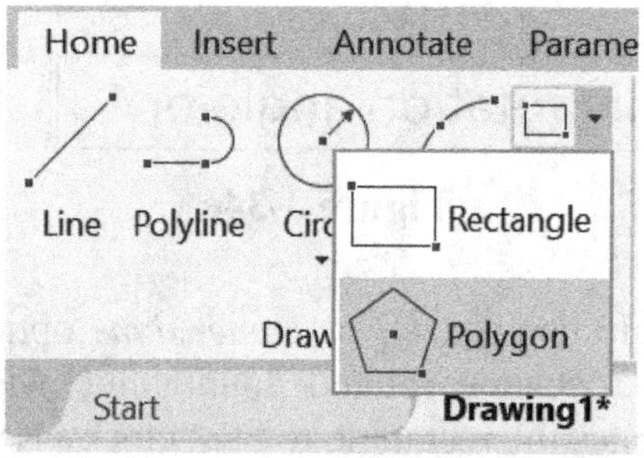

Figure 3-35b

- The activation of the command will result in the prompt to enter the number of sides of the polygon, Figure 3-36a.
- *Enter number of sides*: Specify a number between 3 and 1024 and press the *Enter* key. This example will create an octagon (8-sided polygon). Press the down-arrow key from the keyboard to display the various options, Figure 3-36b.
- The user either specifies the center of the polygon or chooses the edge option.

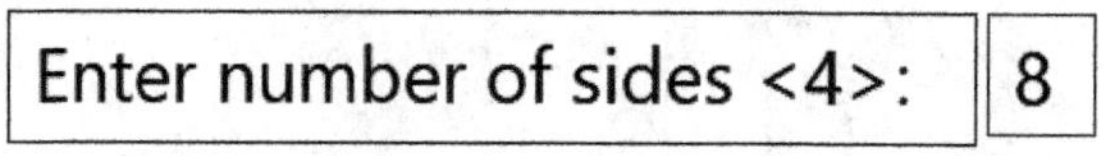

Figure 3-36a

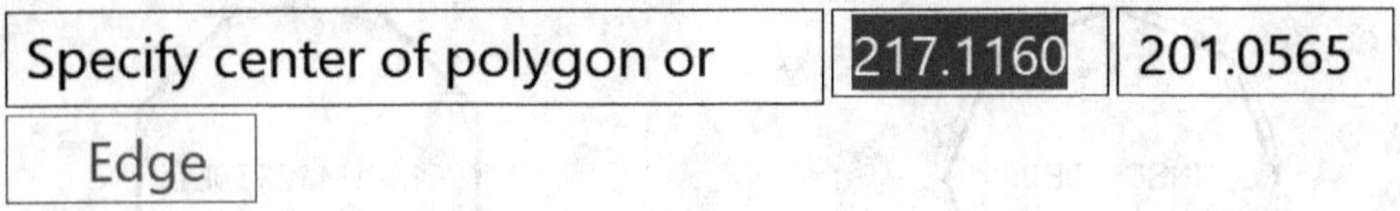

Figure 3-36b

- Center option: This option creates a polygon by specifying its center (the user had already specified the number of edges), Figure 3-36a.
    1. *Specify center of polygon*: Either specify the coordinates of the center point and press the *Enter* key; or click in the drawing area at the desired location. For this example, click at the center point of one of the circles drawn earlier. The next prompt is shown in Figure 3-36c.
    2. *Enter an option [Inscribed in circle/Circumscribed about circle]* Figure 3-36c. Click on the *Inscribed in Circle* option. The prompt shown in Figure 3-36d appears on the screen.
    3. *Specify radius of circle*: Specify the radius (type 3 for the radius), Figure 3-36d, and press the *Enter* key.
    4. The *Inscribed in Circle* option specifies the radius of a circle on which all the vertices of the polygon lie (that is, the polygon is drawn inside the circle), Figure 3-37a. *Circumscribed about Circle* option specifies the distance from the center of the polygon to the midpoints of the edges of the polygon (that is, the polygon is drawn outside the circle), Figure 3-37b.

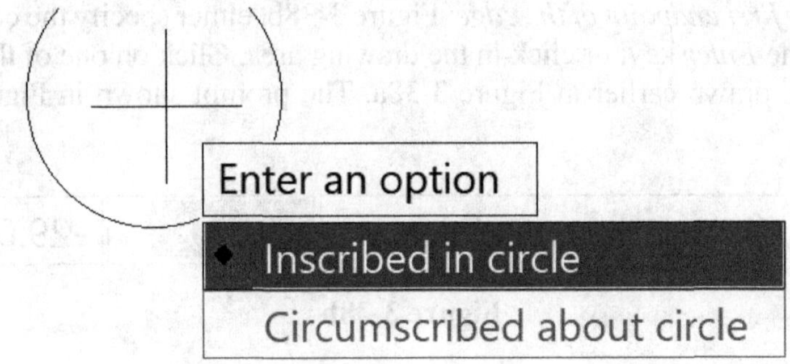

Figure 3-36c

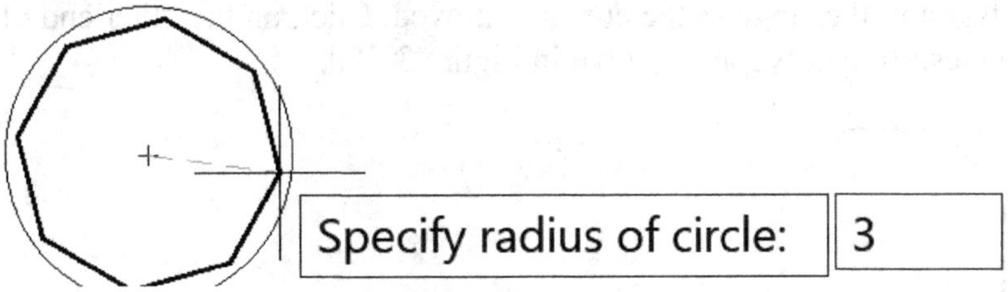

Figure 3-36d

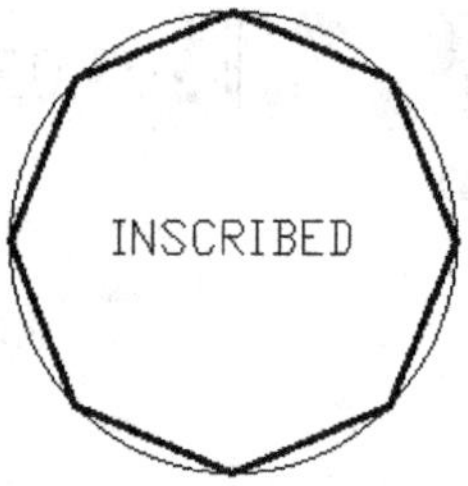

Figure 3-37a

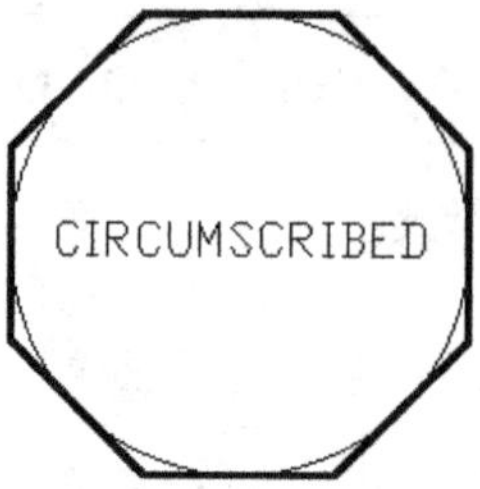

Figure 3-37b

- Edge option: This option creates a polygon by specifying the endpoints of one of the edges (the user had already specified the number of edges). This example creates an 8-sided polygon using the *Edge* command.

1. Click on the edge option as shown in Figure 3-38a. The prompt shown in Figure 3-38b appears.

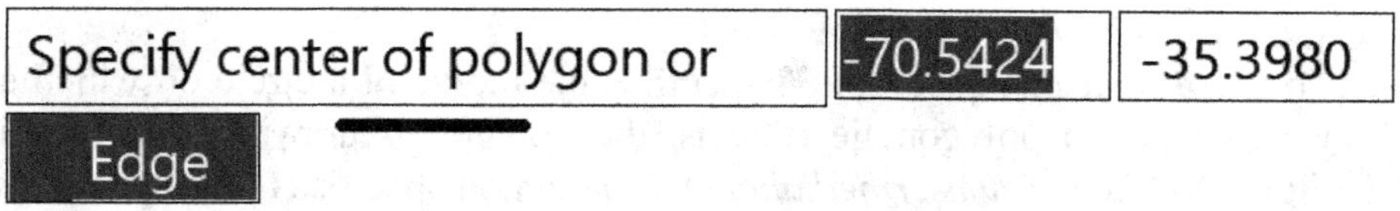

Figure 3-38a

2. *Specify first endpoint of the edge*: Figure 3-38b, either specify the coordinates and press the *Enter* key; or click in the drawing area. Click on one of the two ends of the line drawn earlier in Figure 3-38a. The prompt shown in Figure 3-38c will appear.

Figure 3-38b

3. *Specify the second endpoint of the edge*: Figure 3-38c, either specify the coordinates and press the *Enter* key or click in the drawing area. The size of the polygon will change as the cursor is moved. Click on the other end of the line.
4. The resulting polygon is shown in Figure 3-38d.

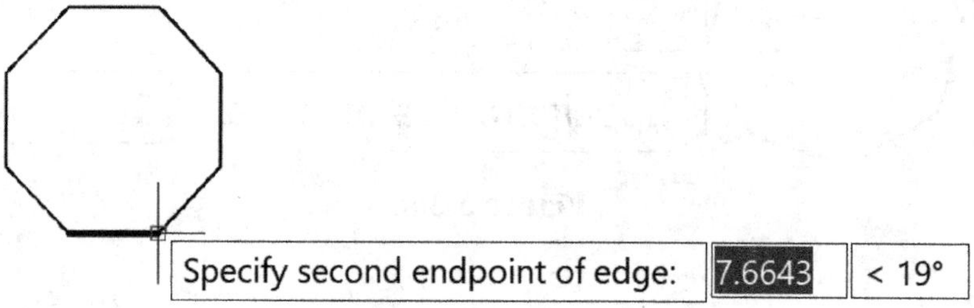

Figure 3-38c

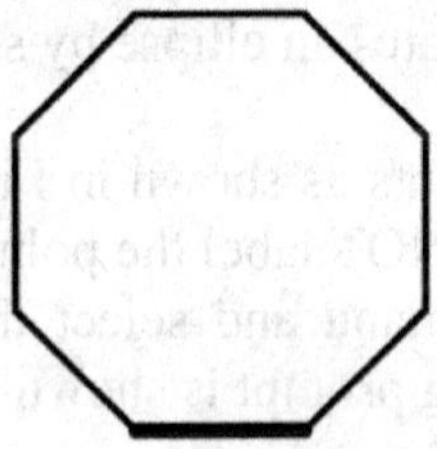

Figure 3-38d

3.11. Ellipse 

The *Ellipse* command is used to draw elliptical shapes. An ellipse is determined by its two axes: the major (longer) and the minor (shorter) axis, Figure 3-39a.

- The *Ellipse* command is activated using one of the following methods:
  1. Panel method: From the *Home* tab and *Draw* panel, select the desired *Ellipse* tool, Figure 3-39b.
  2. Command line method: Type "ellipse", "Ellipse", or "ELLIPSE" in the command line and press the *Enter* key.

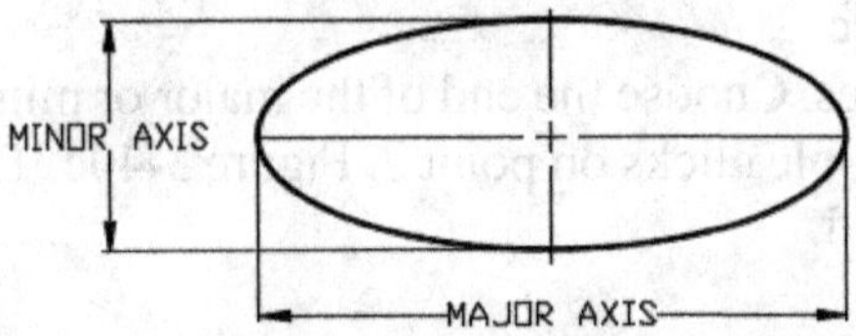

Figure 3-39a

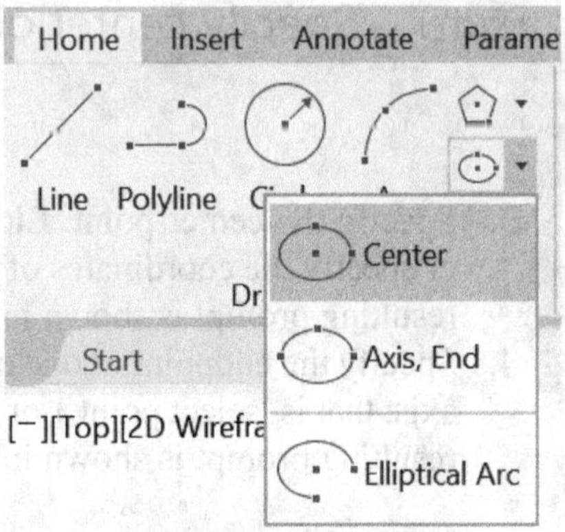

Figure 3-39b

- If the *Ellipse* command is activated from the command line, then the prompt shown in Figure 3-39c appears. Press the down-arrow and select the desired option. However, if the user expands the *Ellipse*'s drop-down menu, Figure 3-39b, then the user can select the desired option, and the prompt is for the selected option.

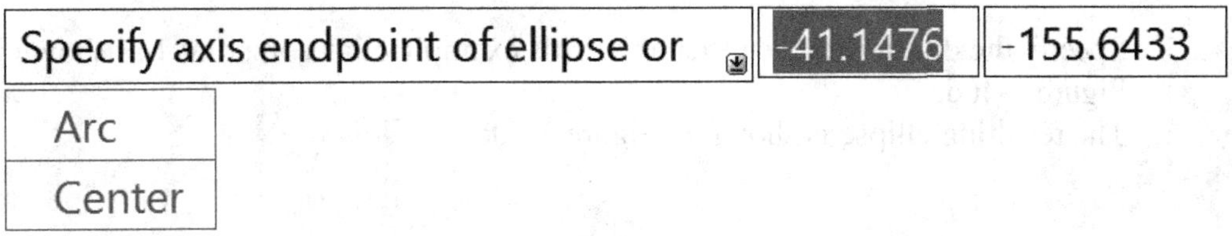

Figure 3-39c

- Center option: This option creates an ellipse by specifying its center.

1. The user can draw the points as shown in Figure 3-40a before the activation of the *Ellipse* command. Do NOT label the points.
2. Activate the *Ellipse* command and select the *Center* option, Figure 3-39b or Figure 3-39c. The resulting prompt is shown in Figure 3-40b.

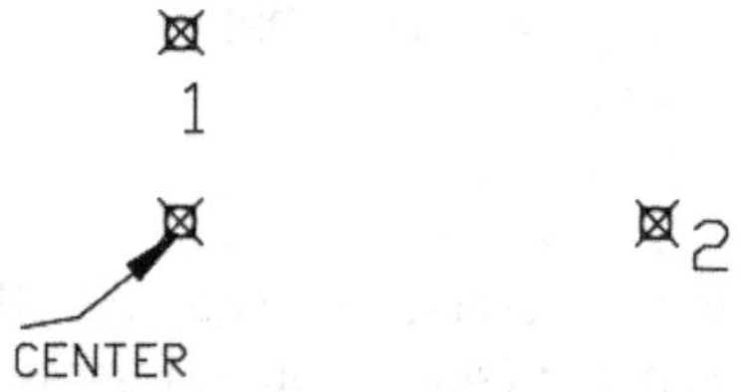

Figure 3-40a

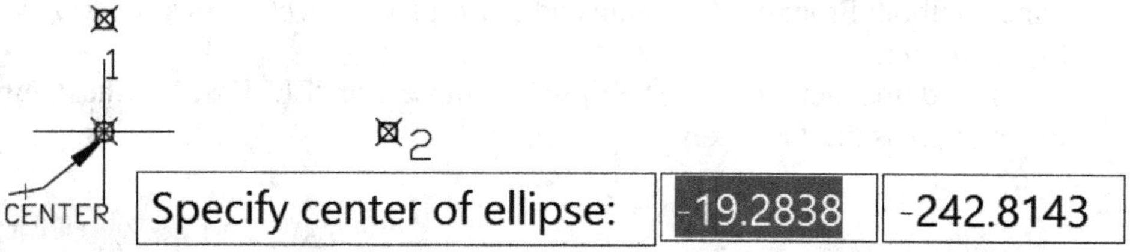

Figure 3-40b

3. Specify the center point. Either click at the desired location in the drawing area or specify the coordinates of the center of the ellipse and press the *Enter* key. The resulting prompt is shown in Figure 3-40c.
4. Specify the endpoint of one of the two axes. Choose the end of the major or minor axis; that is, select point 1 or 2. This example clicks on point 2, Figure 3-40c. The resulting prompt is shown in Figure 3-40d.

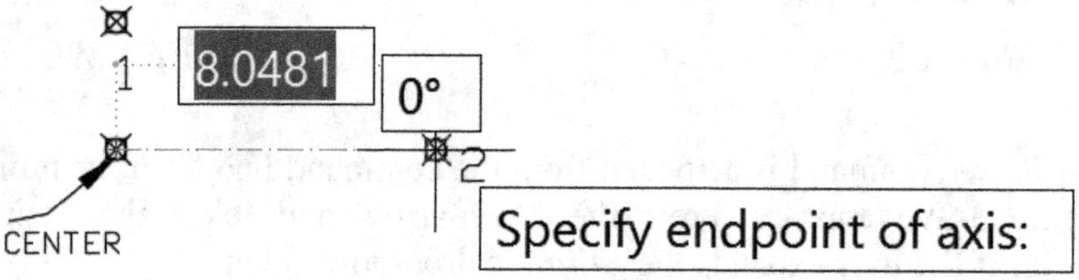

Figure 3-40c

5. Specify the distance to the other axis. This example clicks on point 1 as shown in Figure 3-40d.
6. The resulting ellipse is shown in Figure 3-40e.

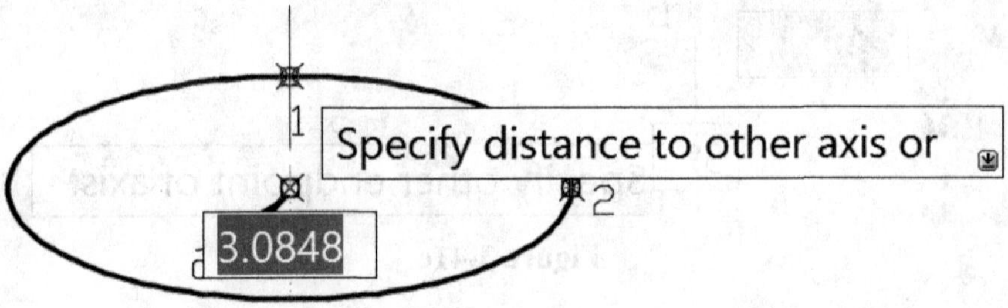

Figure 3-40d

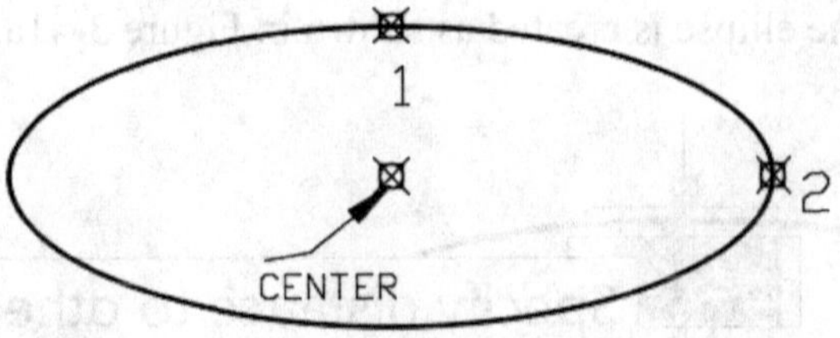

Figure 3-40e

- Axis endpoint option: This option draws an ellipse by specifying the endpoints of the two axes. **Note**: The order of the points' selection is important.

1. The user can draw the three endpoints as shown in Figure 3-41a or draw two perpendicular straight lines, representing the major and minor axes before the activation of the *Ellipse* command.

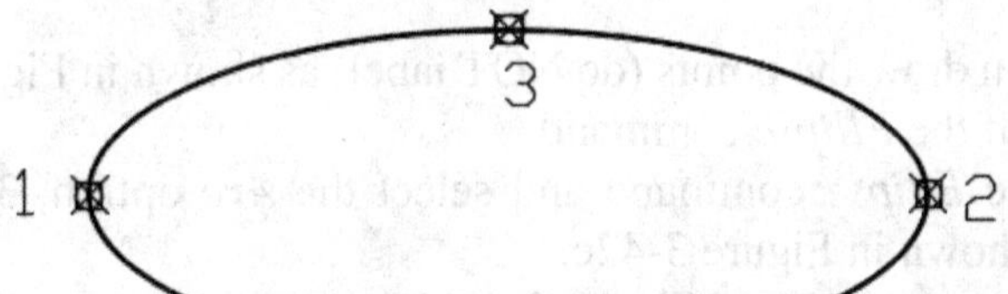

Figure 3-41a

2. Activate the *Ellipse* command and select the *Axis endpoint* option, Figure 3-40b or Figure 3-40c. The resulting prompt is shown in Figure 3-41b.

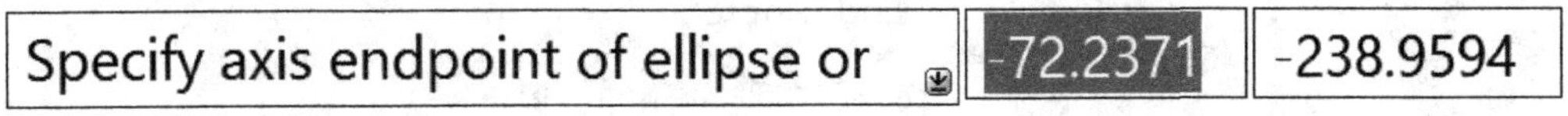

Figure 3-41b

3. Either click at point 1 of Figure 3-41a or specify its coordinates and press the *Enter* key. The prompt shown in Figure 3-41c appears.

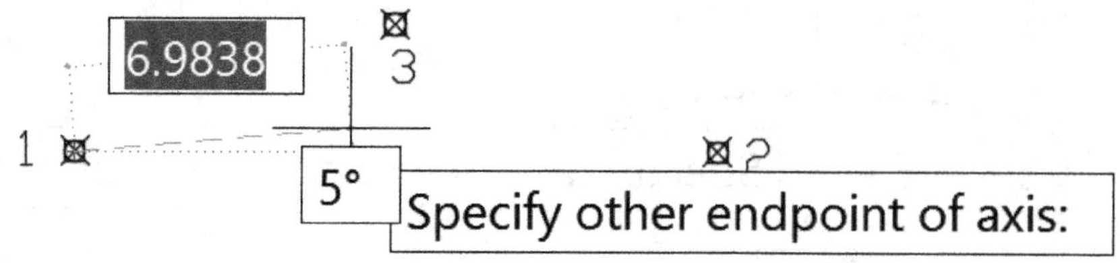

Figure 3-41c

4. Either click at point 2 of Figure 3-41a or specify its coordinates and press the *Enter* key. The prompt shown in Figure 3-41d appears.
5. Either click at point 3 of Figure 3-41a or specify its coordinates and press the *Enter* key. The ellipse is created as shown in Figure 3-41a.

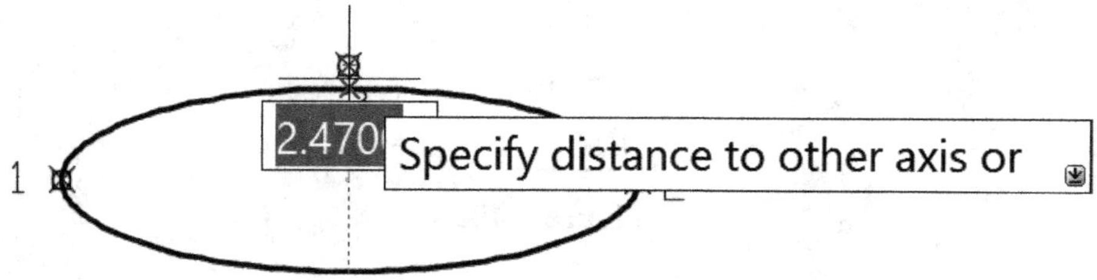

Figure 3-41d

- Arc option: This option draws an elliptical arc. The order of the points' selection is important.

- ***Example:*** Draw an elliptical arc between points 6 and 7 of Figure 3-42a as follows.

1. The user can draw the points (do NOT label) as shown in Figure 3-42a before the activation of the *Ellipse* command.
2. Activate the *Ellipse* command and select the *Arc* option, 3-37b. The resulting prompt is shown in Figure 3-42c.
3. Either click at point 3 of Figure 3-42c or specify its coordinates and press the *Enter* key. The resulting prompt is shown in Figure 3-42d.

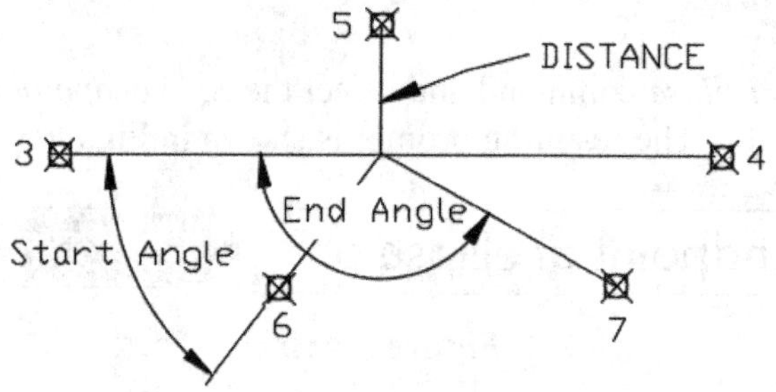

Figure 3-42a

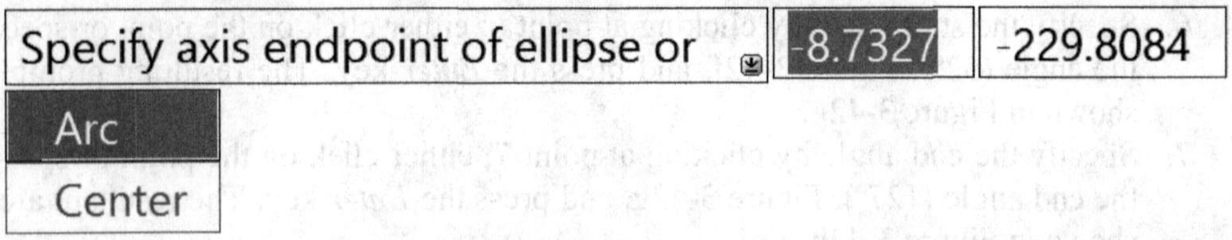

Figure 3-42b

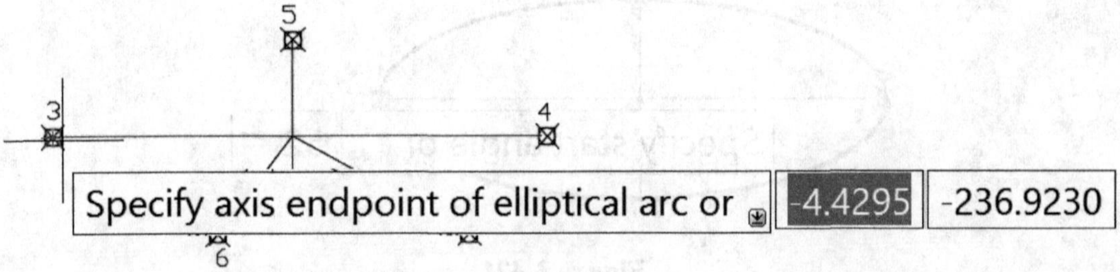

Figure 3-42c

4. Either click at point 4 of Figure 3-42d or specify its coordinates and press the *Enter* key. The resulting prompt is shown in Figure 3-42e.

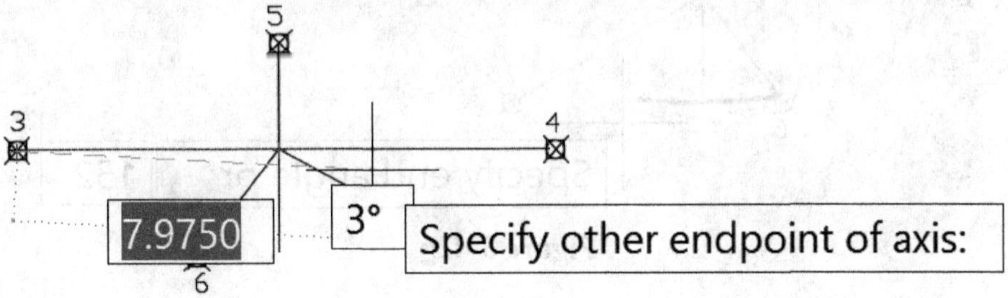

Figure 3-42d

5. Specify the distance to the other axis by either clicking at point 5 of Figure 3-42e or specifying its coordinates and pressing the *Enter* key. The resulting prompt is shown in Figure 3-42f.

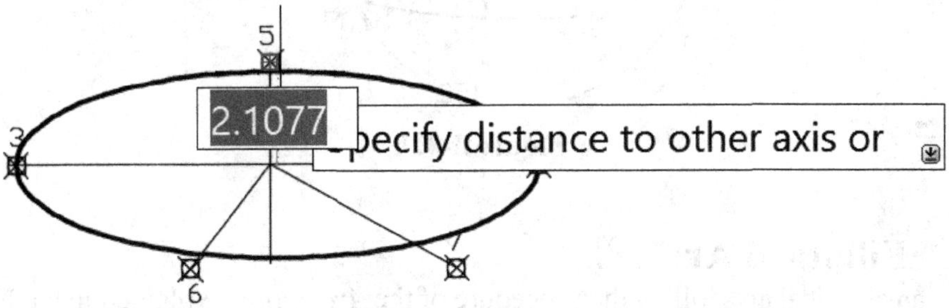

Figure 3-42e

6. Specify the start angle by clicking at point 6; either click on the point or specify the angle (52°), Figure 3-42f, and press the *Enter* key. The resulting prompt is shown in Figure 3-42g.
7. Specify the end angle by clicking at point 7; either click on the point or specify the end angle (127°), Figure 3-42g, and press the *Enter* key. The resultant arc is shown in Figure 3-42h.

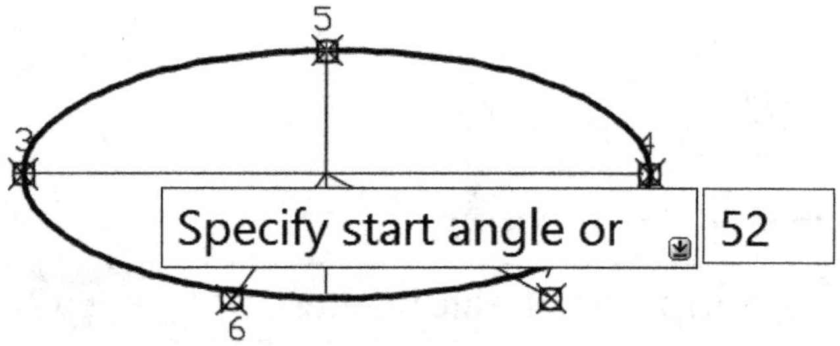

Figure 3-42f

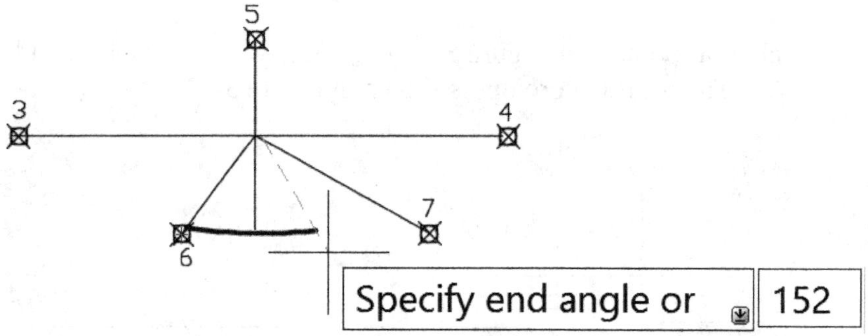

Figure 3-42g

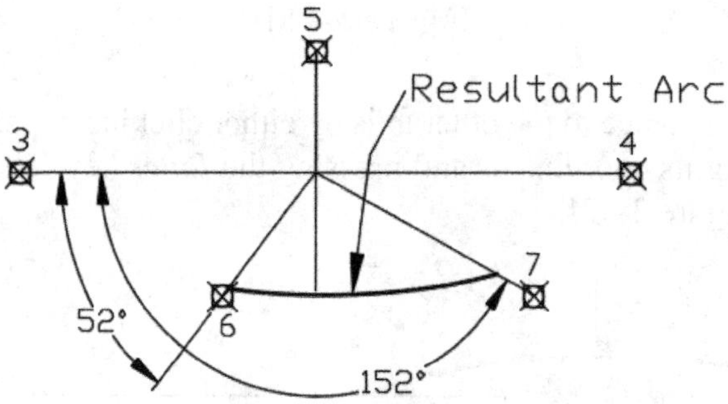

Figure 3-42h

3.12. Elliptical Arc

To create an elliptical arc, follow the procedure of the *Arc option* explained in the Ellipse's section.

3.13. Circular Arc 

To create a circular arc, follow the procedure of the *Arc option* explained in the Ellipse's section. However, the distance to point 5 should be equal to half of the distance between points 3 and 4.

3.14. Point 

Figure 3-43a shows an electric circuit with bulbs; in this circuit, points represent bulbs. In AutoCAD, points are drawn using the *Point* command. AutoCAD's *Point* command makes a distinction between drawing a single point and multiple points. The multiple points command can be used to draw a single point; however, the single point command cannot be used to draw multiple points.

- The *Point* command is activated using one of the following methods.
  1. Panel method: From the *Home* tab and *Draw* panel, select the *Point* tool to activate the option to draw multiple points, Figure 3-43b.
  2. Command line method: Type "point", "Point", or "POINT" in the command line and press the *Enter* key to activate an option to draw a single point.

- The activation of the command results in the prompt to specify a point, Figure 3-43c. A point can be drawn using one of the following three methods.
  1. Click at a random point on the screen.
  2. Specify the coordinates on the command line: (i) type in the values of the point as x,y (no space); and (ii) press the *Enter* key.
  3. Specify the coordinates as a dynamic input.
     a. To specify the (x, y) coordinates (i) type the value of the x-coordinate in the first field; (ii) press the "," key; (iii) type the y-coordinate; and (iv) finally press the *Enter* key.
     b. To specify the (x, y, z) coordinates (i) type the value of the x-coordinate in the first field; (ii) press the "," key; (iii) type the y-coordinate; (iv) press the "," key; (v) type the z-coordinate; (vi) and finally press the *Enter* key.
     c. To specify the polar coordinates (length and angle), (i) type the value of length in the first field; (ii) press "<" or "tab" key; (iii) type the angle in the second field; and (iv) finally press the *Enter* key.

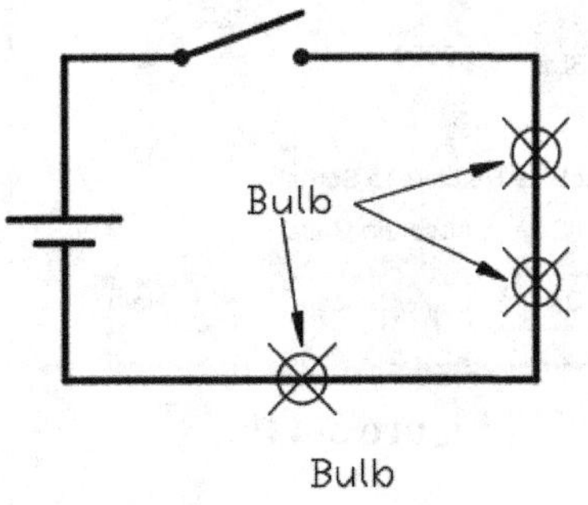

Figure 3-43a

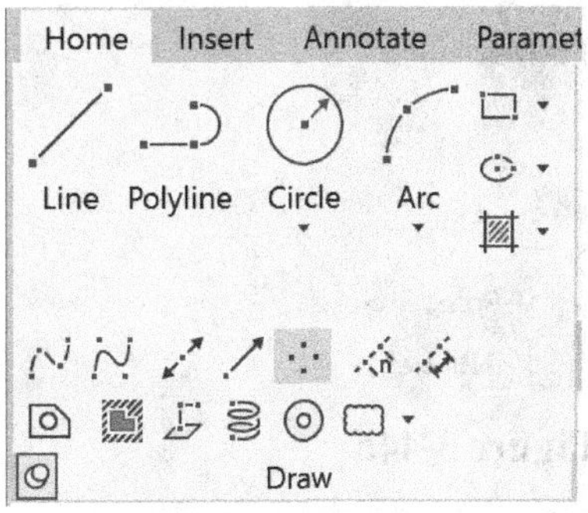

Figure 3-43b

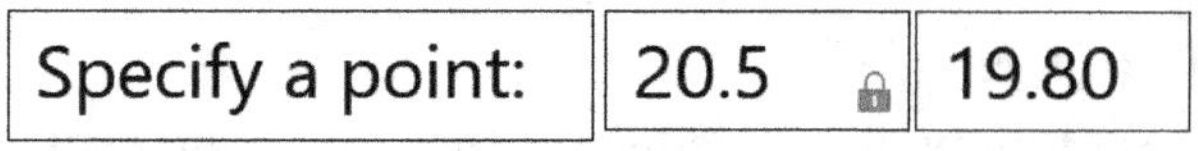

Figure 3-43c

- **Note**: To change a locked value, Figure 3-43c, cycle through the input field using the *Tab* key to reach to the desired field, and then follow the procedure discussed above.
- To **Exit** the command, press the *Esc* key from the keyboard. Do **NOT** press the *Enter* key on the keyboard.

3.14.1. Change style and size of a point

To change the appearance and size of a point, from the *Home* tab and *Utilities* panel select the *Point Style* option, Figure 3-44a, to open the *Point Style* dialog box, Figure 3-44b. This dialog box is used to change the style and size of a point.

3.14.1.1. Style

Changing the style makes the points more visible and easier to differentiate from the grid dots. To change the style, click on the desired shape and press the *OK* button. This will close the dialog box and change the appearance of every point in the current drawing to the selected shape.

3.14.1.2. Point size

This option allows for changing the size of the points. The *Set Size Relative to Screen* option sets the point display size as a percentage of the screen size. The *Set Size in Absolute Units* option sets the point display size as the actual units. In order to keep the point size independent of the zooming effect, choose the second option.

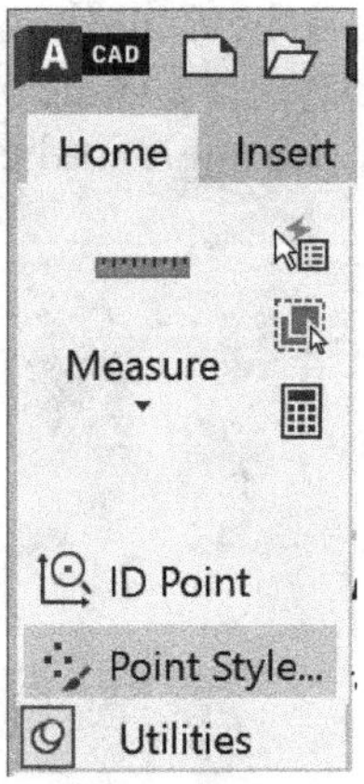

Figure 3-44a

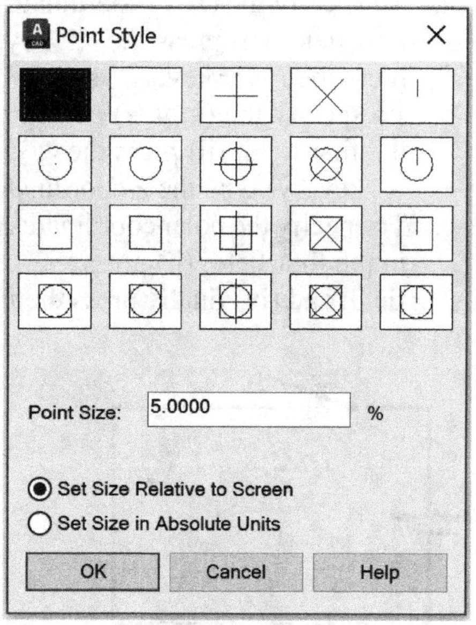

Figure 3-44b

3.15. Point Measure

Figure 3-45a shows a series of equidistant points representing gauging stations along the centerline of a river. In AutoCAD, equidistant points are drawn using the *Measure* command.

- Change the point style and size.
- The *Measure* command is activated using one of the following methods.
  1. Panel method: From the *Home* tab and *Draw* panel, select the *Measure* tool to activate the option to draw equidistant points, Figure 3-45a.
  2. Command line method: Type "measure", "Measure", or "MEASURE" in the command line and press the *Enter* key to activate an option to draw equidistant points.

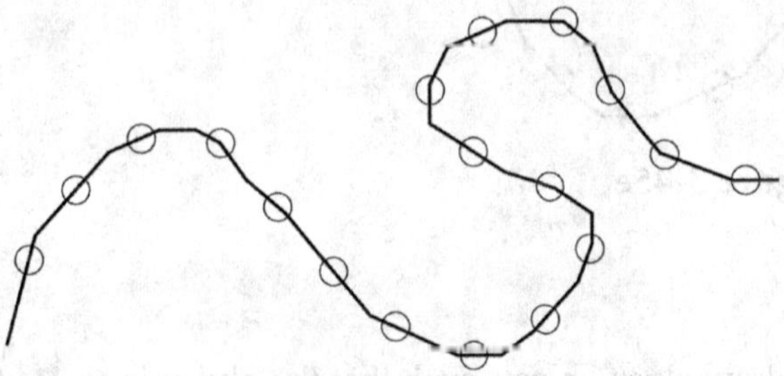

Figure 3-45a

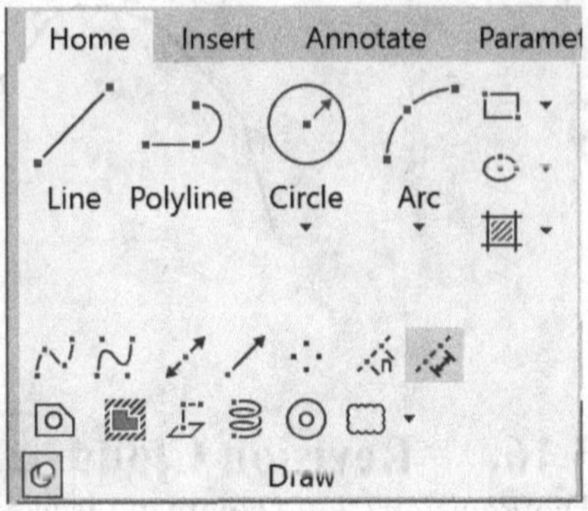

Figure 3-45b

- The activation of the command results in the prompt to specify equidistant points, Figure 3-45c.
  1. Click on the desired polyline. In the current example, click on the left edge of the centerline, Figure 3-45c.
  2. The prompt shown in Figure 3-45d appears.

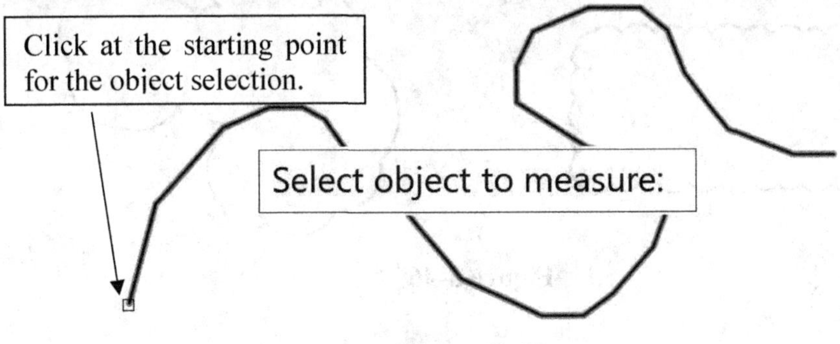

Figure 3-45c

  3. Specify the distance between the stations (points) and press the *Enter* key. In the current example the distance is 75 inches, Figure 3-45d. The software assumes that the distance between the points is constant.

4. The equidistant points appear on the centerline. The first point is 75 inches from the beginning of the polyline, Figure 3-45e.
5. If necessary, draw a point (using the *Point* command) at the beginning of the centerline.

Figure 3-45d

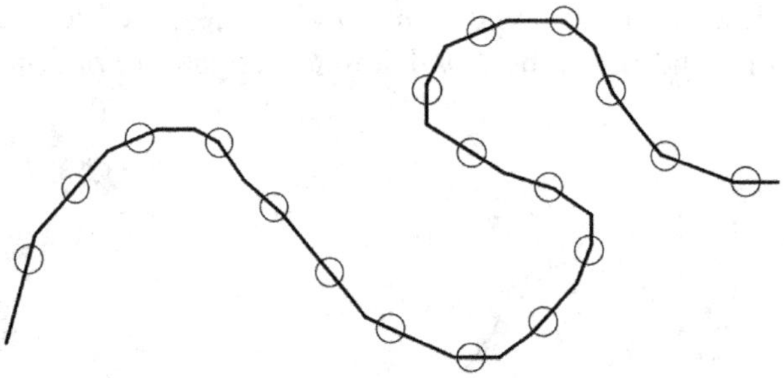

Figure 3-45e

3.16. Revision Cloud

The *Revision Cloud* command is used to draw close objects such that the object is created by conjoined arcs, Figure 3-46. The resultant cloud object is a single entity; that is, one of its arcs cannot be erased. This command can also be used to convert polyline and closed objects (circles, rectangles, and polygons) to a cloud object. The user can draw a revision cloud using three different methods. A cloud object can be converted to multiple arcs using the *Explode* command (*Explode* command is discussed in *Chapter 4*).

Figure 3-46

3.16.1. RevCloudArcVariance system variable

This variable controls the size of the arcs of the cloud objects. By default, this variable is *On* (or 1) and the cloud object is created with variable arc lengths.

The user can turn *Off* (or 0) this variable and the cloud object is created with generally equal arc lengths, however, some of the arc length will be different depending on the size and shape of the cloud object, Figure 3-47a.

The user can change the *RevCloudArcVariance* system variable as follows: (i) Type ***RevCloudArcVariance*** in the drawing area or in command line window. (ii) Press the *Enter* key from the keyboard. The prompt shown in Figure 3.47b will appear. (iii) Type the desired value. (iv) Press the *Enter* key from the keyboard. This will reset the variable value and exits the command.

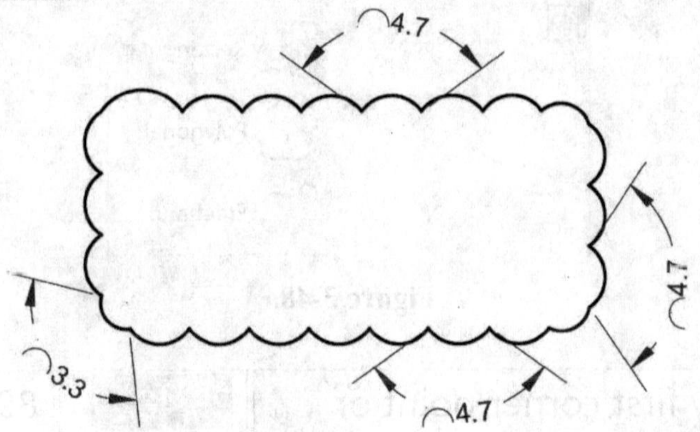

Figure 3-47a

Enter new value for REVCLOUDARCVARIANCE <ON>:	OFF

Figure 3-47b

3.16.2. The RevCloud Command

- The *Revision Cloud* command is activated using one of the following methods:
  1. Panel method: From the *Home* tab and *Draw* panel, select the *Revision Cloud* tool, Figure 3-48a. Use the down-arrow key from the keyboard to display the various options; select the desired option and the prompt for the selected option will appear.
  2. Command line method: Type "revcloud", "Revcloud", or "REVCLOUD" in the command line and press the *Enter* key.

- The activation of the command results in the prompt shown in Figure 3-48b. However, this prompt may be different for *Polygonal* and *Freehand* options.

- *Specify first corner point or*: Either click at the desired location in the drawing area or specify the coordinates of the center of the circle and press the *Enter* key; or use the down-arrow key from the keyboard to display the various options, Figure 3-48b. The user can use the left button of the mouse or the drop-down-arrow to select the desired option.

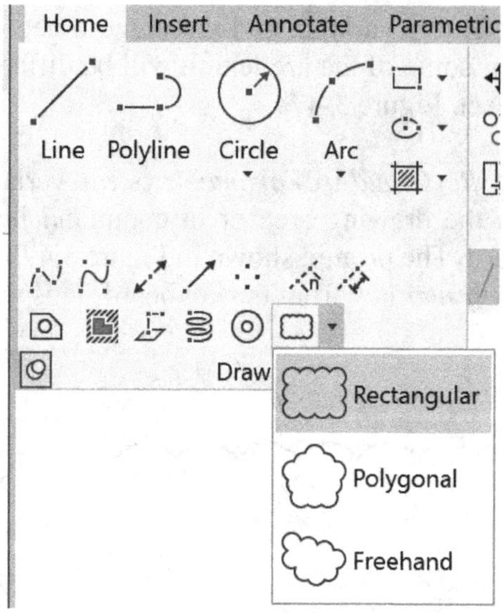

Figure 3-48a

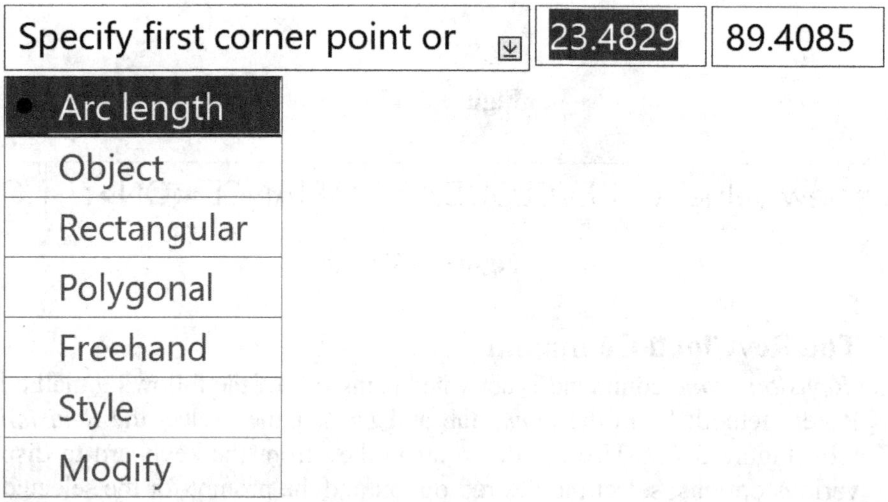

Figure 3-48b

- The remainder of this section explains how to use the options from the dropdown list of Figure 3-48b.

- Arc length option, Fig 3-48b: This option is used to set an approximate arc length for the cloud arcs of the cloud object.
  1. If the user selects the *Arc length* option, then the prompt to specify the approximate length of arc, Figure 3-49, appears on the screen.
  2. Specify the length and press the *Enter* key from the keyboard.
  3. Now the user is ready to create a revision cloud.

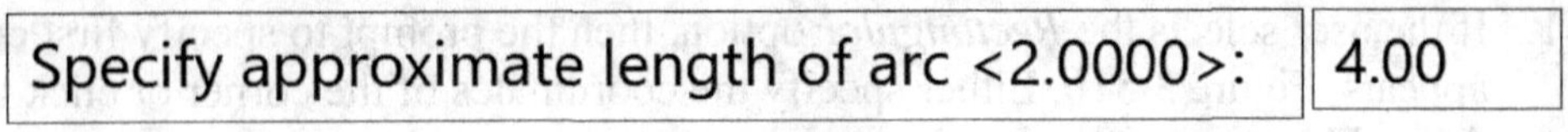

Figure 3-49

- Object, Fig 3-48b: This option is used to convert non-cloud object (Figure 3-50a) to a cloud object (Figure 3-50b).

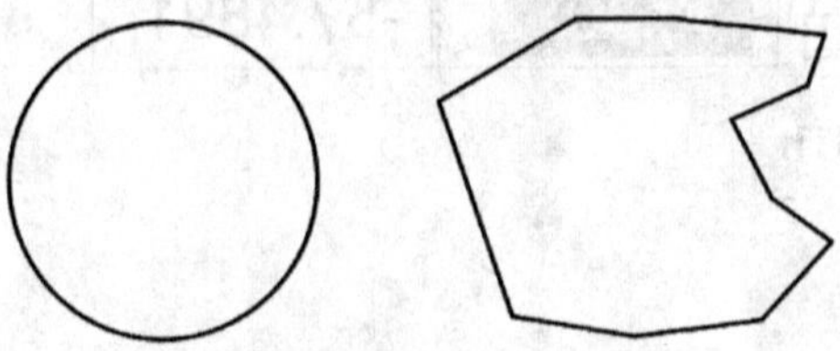

Figure 3-50a

Figure 3-50b

1. If the user selects at the *Object* option, then the prompt to select object appears, Figure 3-50c.
2. Click on the circle and the prompt shown in Figure 3-50d appears; the user selected the *No* option.
3. Repeat the *Object* option on the closed polyline, Figure 3-50e, and select the *Yes* option.

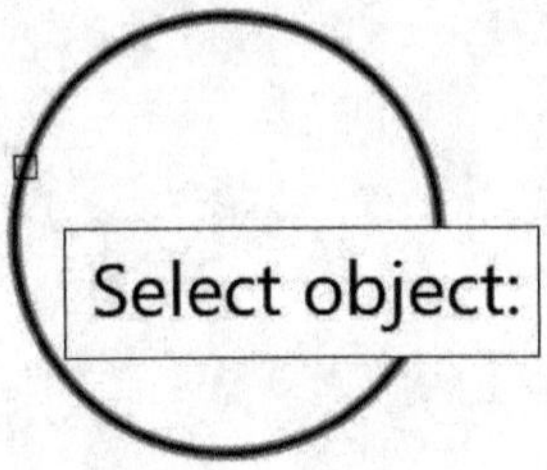

Figure 3-50c

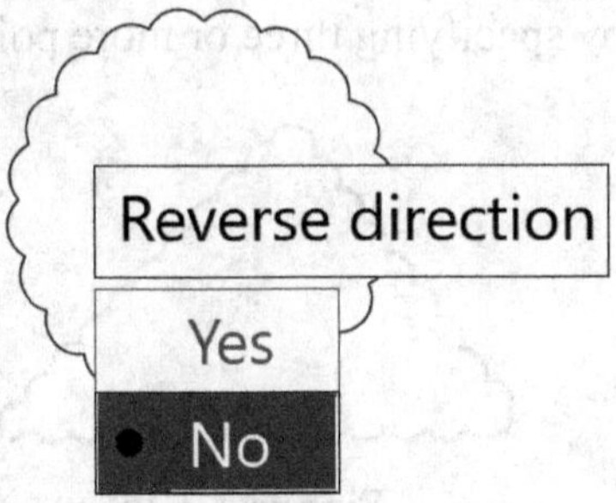

Figure 3-50d

Figure 3-50e

- Rectangular, Fig 3-48a-b: This option is used to create a rectangular cloud object by specifying diagonally opposite corners, Figure 3-51a.

Figure 3-51a

1. If the user selects the *Rectangular* option, then the prompt to specify first corner appears, Figure 3-51b. Either specify the coordinates of the corner or click at the desired location in the drawing area.
2. The prompt to specify the opposite corner appears, Figure 3-51c. Either specify the coordinates of the corner or click at the desired location in the drawing area.
3. This completes the command, and a rectangular cloud object is created.

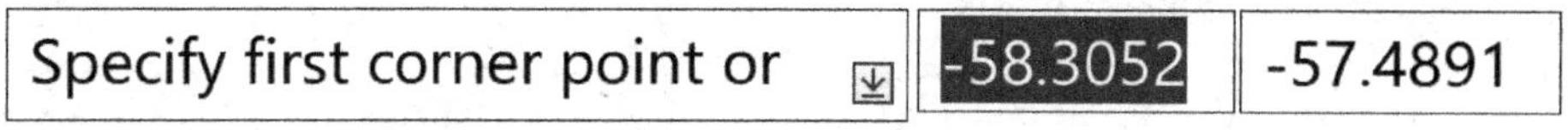

Figure 3-51b

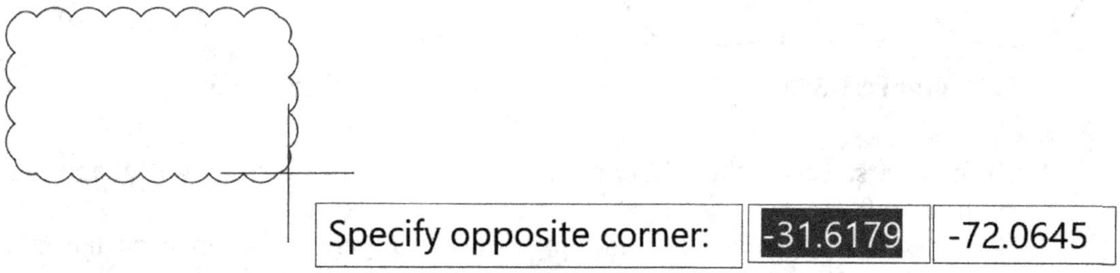

Figure 3-51c

- Polygonal, Fig 3-48a-b: This option is used to create a polygonal (three or more sided closed) cloud object by specifying three or more points, Figure 3-52a.

Figure 3-52a

1. If the user selects the *Polygonal* option, then the prompt to specify start point appears, Figure 3-52b. Either specify the coordinates of the corner or click at the desired location in the drawing area.
2. The prompt to specify the next point appears, Figure 3-52c. Either specify the coordinates of the corner or click at the desired location in the drawing area.
3. Repeat Step 2 as needed.
4. Press the *Enter* key from the keyboard. This completes the command, and a polygonal cloud object is created.

Figure 3-52b

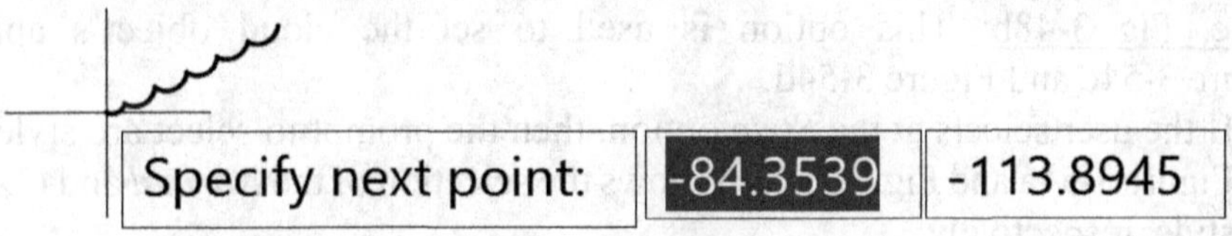

Figure 3-52c

- Freehand, Figure 3-48a-b: This option is used to create a freehand cloud object by specifying its path, Figure 3-53d.
  1. If the user selects the *Freehand* option, then the prompt to specify first point appears, Figure 3-53b. Either specify the coordinates of the corner or click at the desired location in the drawing area.
  2. The prompt to guide the cloud path appears, Figure 3-53b. Either specify the polar coordinates of the next point on the path or click at the desired location in the drawing area.
  3. Repeat Step 2 as needed.
  4. Press the *Enter* key from the keyboard.
  5. The prompt to select the arc direction appears, Figure 3-53c. Select the desired direction.
  6. This completes the command, and a freehand cloud object is created, Figure 3-53d.

Figure 3-53a

Figure 3-53b

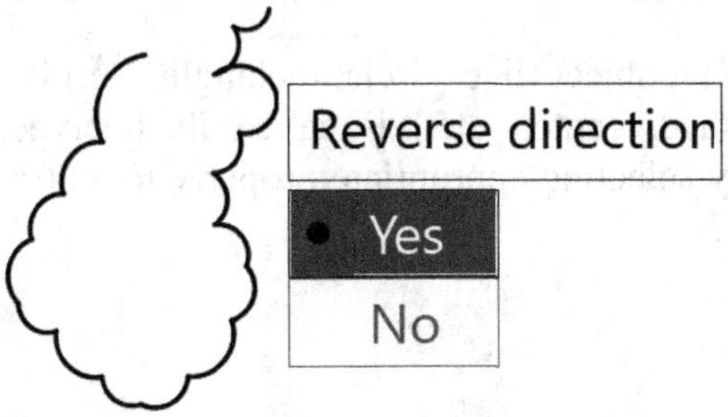

Figure 3-53c

Figure 3-53d

- Style, Fig 3-48b: This option is used to set the cloud object's appearance, Figure 3-54c and Figure 3-54d.
  1. If the user selects at the *Style* option, then the prompt to select arc style appears, Figure 3-54a and Figure 3-54b shows the selection of the *Normal* and *Calligraphy* style, respectively.
  2. Select the style and draw the cloud object as needed.
  3. Figure 3-54c and Figure 3-54d show the *Normal* and *Calligraphed* cloud objects, respectively.

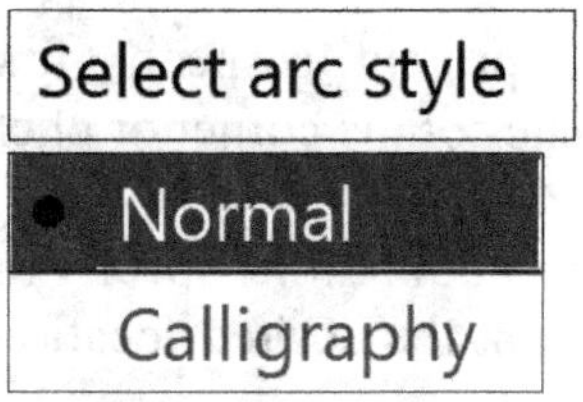

Figure 3-54a

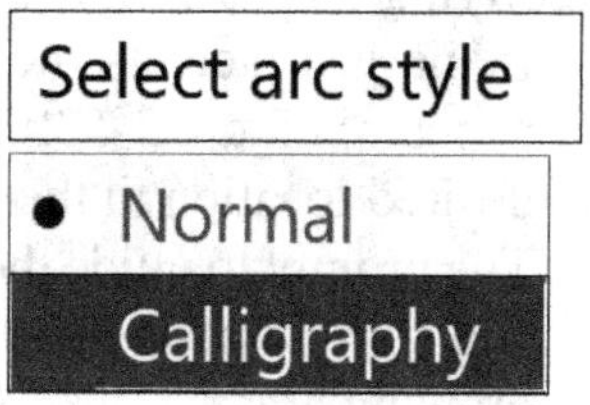

Figure 3-54b

Figure 3-54c

Figure 3-54d

3.17. Object Appearance

The usage of different line style and/or line thickness visually distinguishes objects from one another. Figure 3-55a and Figure 3-55b are two representations of the same drawing, a building, railway track, fences, and a gas line. In Figure 3-55a every object is drawn using the same line style and thickness. However, the drawing shown in Figure 3-55b is easily readable because objects are drawn using different line style, color and thickness.

In AutoCAD terminology, the thickness of an object (line, circle, rectangle, etc.) is called its lineweight and the style (dotted, dashed, center, etc.) is called its linetype. The appearance of an object can be changed by selecting appropriate property tools from the *Home* tab and *Properties* panel, Figure 3-55c.

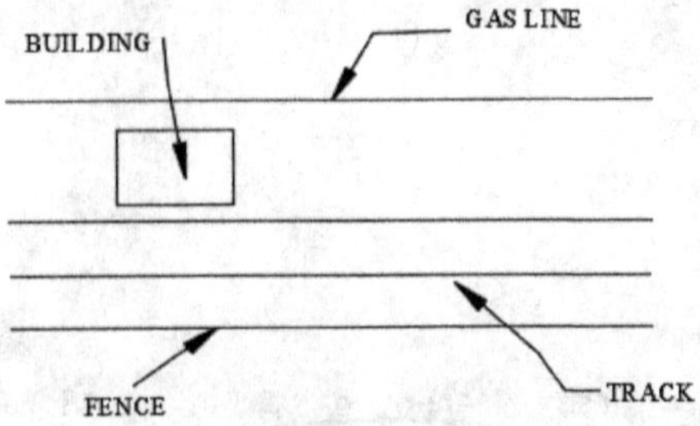

Figure 3-55a

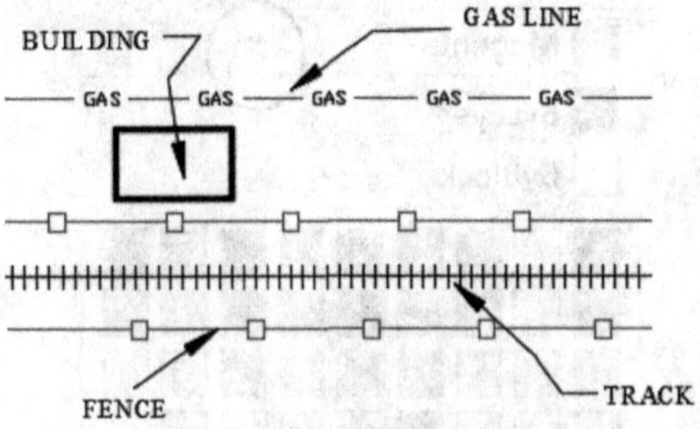

Figure 3-55b

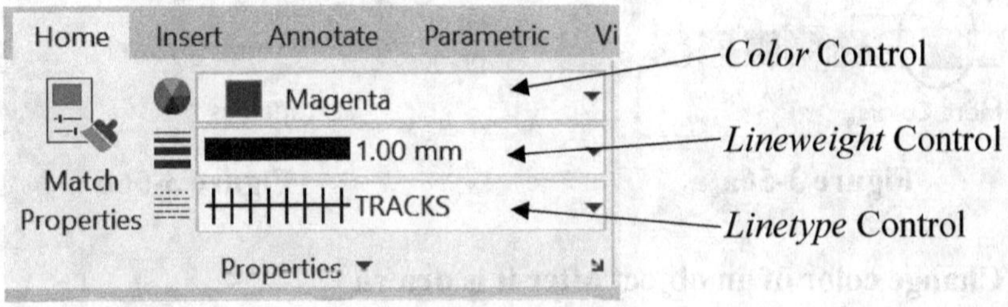

Figure 3-55c

3.17.1. Color Control

Figure 3-56a shows the available options under *Color Control*. The figure shows only some of the colors available in AutoCAD. However, the user can select the colors not shown in the list, too. The color of most of the two-dimensional objects can be changed in two ways: (i) set the color before drawing the object or (ii) change the color after the object is drawn. This section uses a line to demonstrate *Color Control*.

3.17.1.1. Set color of an object before it is drawn

The color of a line before it is drawn is changed as follows:

1. Under *Home* tab and in the *Properties* panel, click on the down-arrow () of the *Color Control*. A dropdown list appears on the screen, Figure 3-56a.
2. Bring the cursor on the desired color and it is highlighted. In the example, *Green* color is selected.
3. Click on the highlighted color; this closes the list and the selected color appears in *Color Control*, Figure 3-56b.
4. Now draw a line; the line is drawn with the selected color.
5. If the desired color is not listed in the color list, then click on *More Color* option of Figure 3-56a. The *Select Color* dialog box shown in Figure 3-56c appears on the screen. Click on the desired color and press the *OK* button and proceed with the drawing. In the example, color 10 is selected.

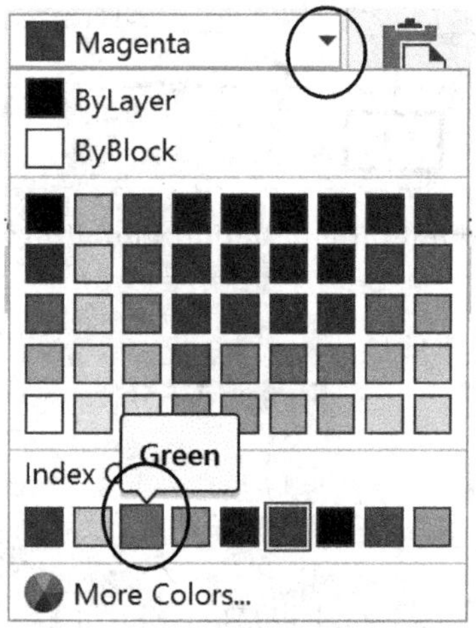

Figure 3-56a

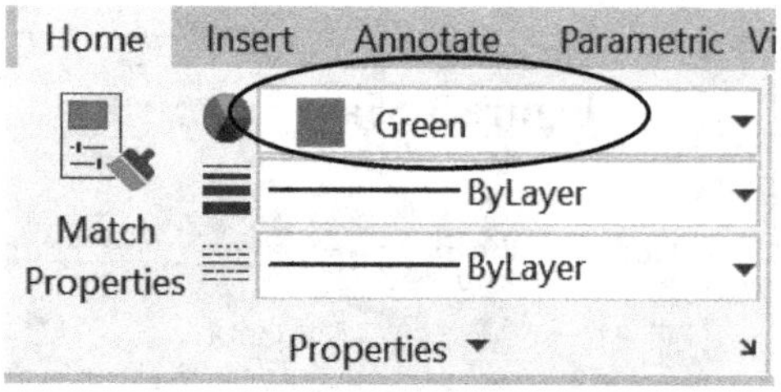

Figure 3-56b

3.17.1.2. Change color of an object after it is drawn

The user can change the color of the object after it is drawn as follows.

1. Draw a line (the line labeled as *Before* in Figure 3-56d).
2. Select the line by clicking with the left button of the mouse (the line with three square boxes in Figure 3-56e). The three blue squares are called grip points.
3. Click on the arrow (▾) of the *Color Control* dropdown list of the *Properties* panel; the color list appears on the screen, Figure 3-56a.
4. Bring the cursor on the desired color and it is highlighted.
5. Click on the highlighted color; this closes the list and color of the selected object changes to the selected color (the line labeled as *After* in Figure 3-56d).

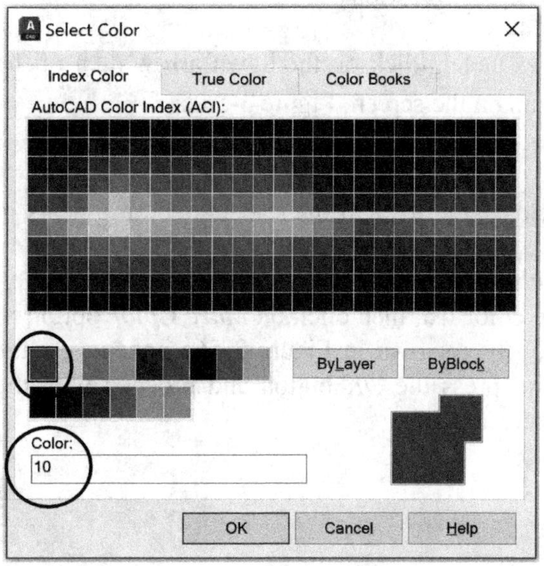

Figure 3-56c

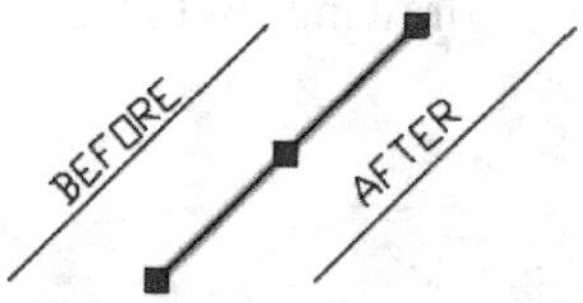

Figure 3-56d

3.17.2. Lineweight control

Figure 3-58a shows the available options under the *Lineweight Control*. The figure shows all the possible lineweights available in AutoCAD. The lineweight (that is, line thickness) for most of the two-dimensional objects can be changed in two ways: (i) set the lineweight before drawing the object or (ii) change the lineweight after the object is drawn. This section uses a line to demonstrate the *Lineweight Control*.

In order to display thickness of an object in the drawing area, click the lineweight button ( ) on the status bar. The thickness of most of the two-dimensional objects can be changed in two ways.

3.17.2.1. Change thickness of a line before it is drawn

The thickness of a line before it is drawn is changed as follows:

1. In the *Properties* panel (under *Home* tab), click on the down-arrow ( ) of the *Lineweight Control*. A dropdown list appears on the screen, Figure 3-57a.
2. Bring the cursor on the desired thickness and it is highlighted.
3. Click on the highlighted thickness; this closes the list and the selected thickness appears in the *Properties* toolbar, Figure 3-57b.
4. Now draw a line; the line is drawn with the selected thickness.
5. The user can set the lineweight properties using *Lineweight Settings* dialog box, Figure 3-57c. This dialog box can be opened by clicking the *Lineweight Settings* option on Figure 3-57a. **Set the default line weight to *0.0*.**

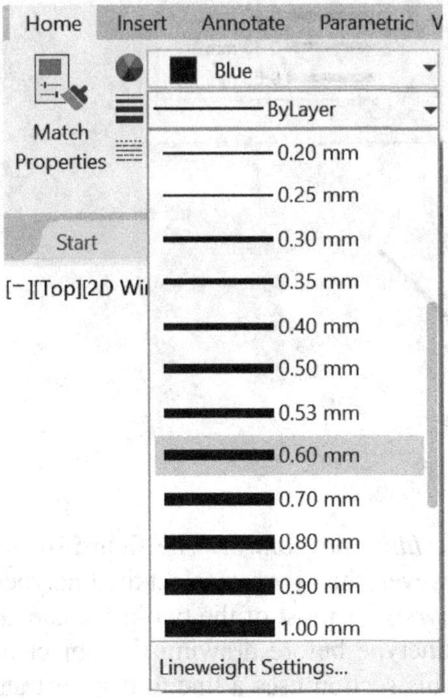

Figure 3-57a

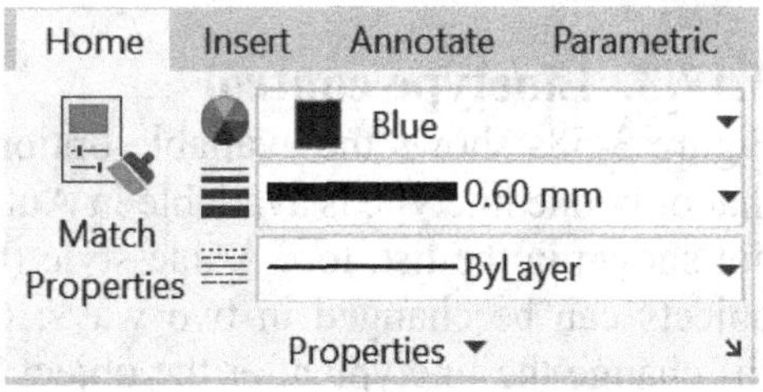

Figure 3-57b

3.17.2.2. Change thickness of a line after it is drawn

The step-by-step process to change the thickness of a line after it is drawn is shown in Figure 3-58c.

1. Draw a line (the line labeled as *Before* in Figure 3-57d).
2. Select the line by clicking with the left button of the mouse (the line with three square boxes in Figure 3-57d). The three blue squares are called grip points.
3. Click on the arrow (▾) of the *Lineweight Control* dropdown list in the *Properties* panel; the thickness list appears on the screen, Figure 3-57a.
4. Bring the cursor on the desired thickness and it is highlighted.
5. Click on the highlighted thickness; this closes the list and the lineweight of the selected object changes to the selected thickness of the selected object (the line labeled as *After* in Figure 3-57d).

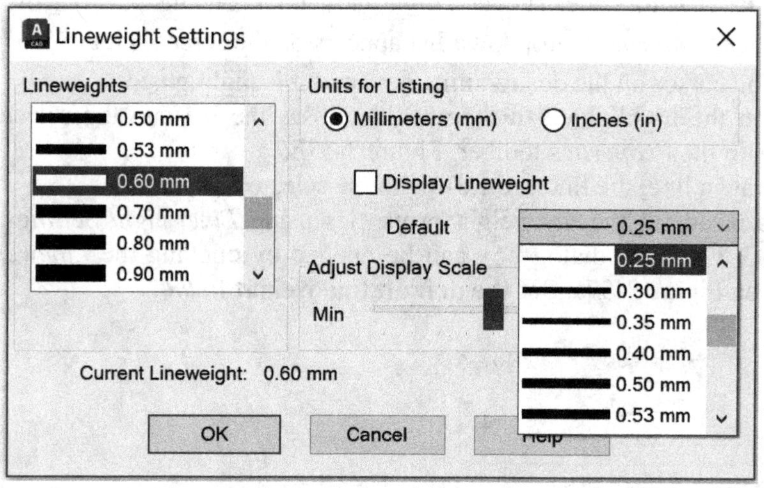

Figure 3-57c

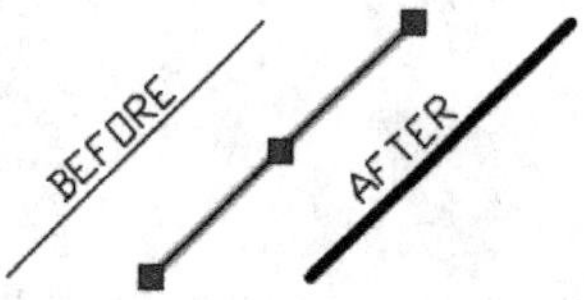

Figure 3-57d

3.17.3. Linetype control

Figure 3-58a shows the available options under the *Linetype Control*. The figure shows that only one linetype is available in AutoCAD. However, the user can select the linetypes not shown in the list, too. A line style (that is, linetype) for most of the two-dimensional objects can be changed in two ways: (i) set the linetype before drawing the object or (ii) change the linetype after the object is drawn. This section uses a line to demonstrate the *Linetype Control*. However, the user needs to load the desired line type before using it.

3.17.3.1. Load a linetype

- (i) Expand the *Linetype control*'s drop-down list, Figure 3-58a. (ii) Select the *Other* option; this opens a *Linetype Manager* (Figure 3-58b) dialog box.
- In the *Linetype Manager* dialog box, click the *Load* button; this opens a *Load or Reload Linetypes* (Figure 3-58c) dialog box.

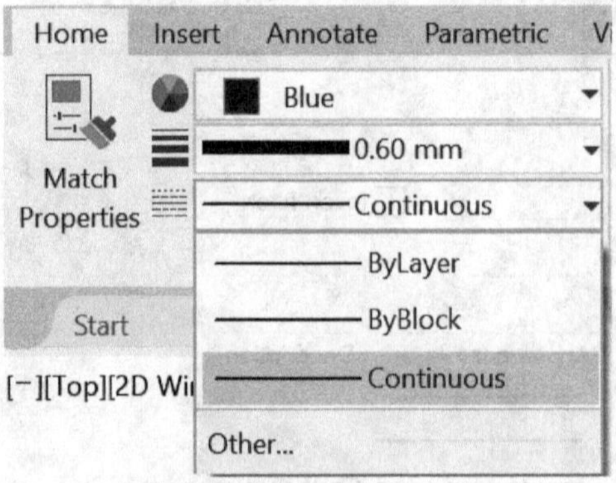

Figure 3-58a

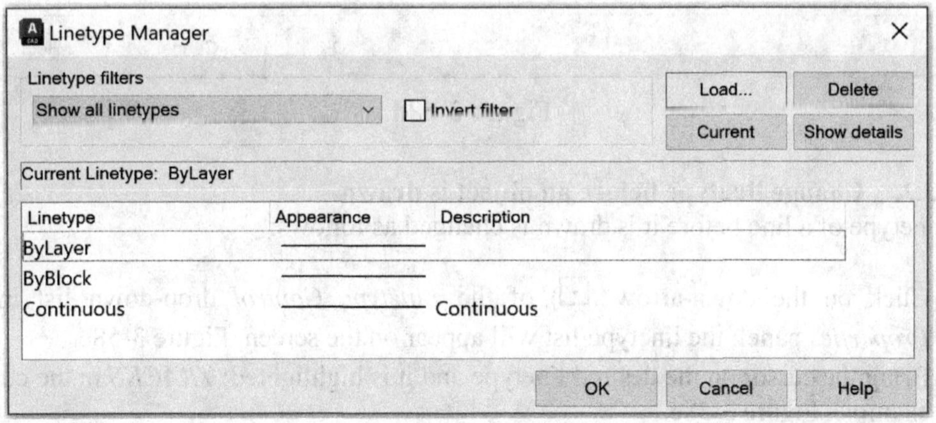

Figure 3-58b

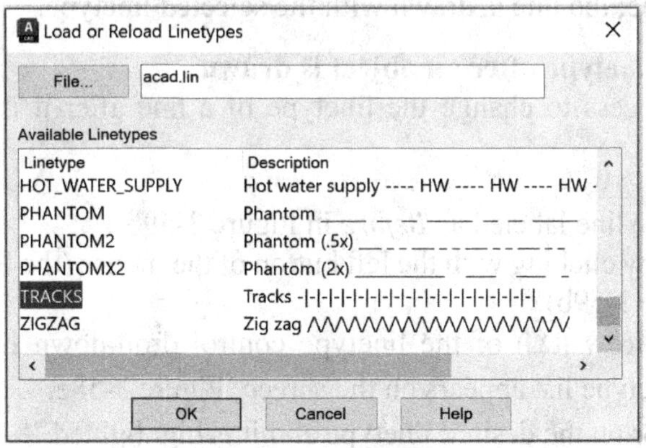

Figure 3-58c

- In the *Load or Reload Linetypes* dialog box, select a linetype and click the *OK* button. This closes the *Load or Reload Linetypes* dialog box and the selected line type appears in the *Linetype Manager* Dialog box, Figure 3-58d. This example selects the *TRACKS* pattern.
- In the *Linetypes Manager* dialog box, click the *OK* button. This closes the dialog box, and the *Tracks* pattern appears in the linetype control, Figure 3-58d.

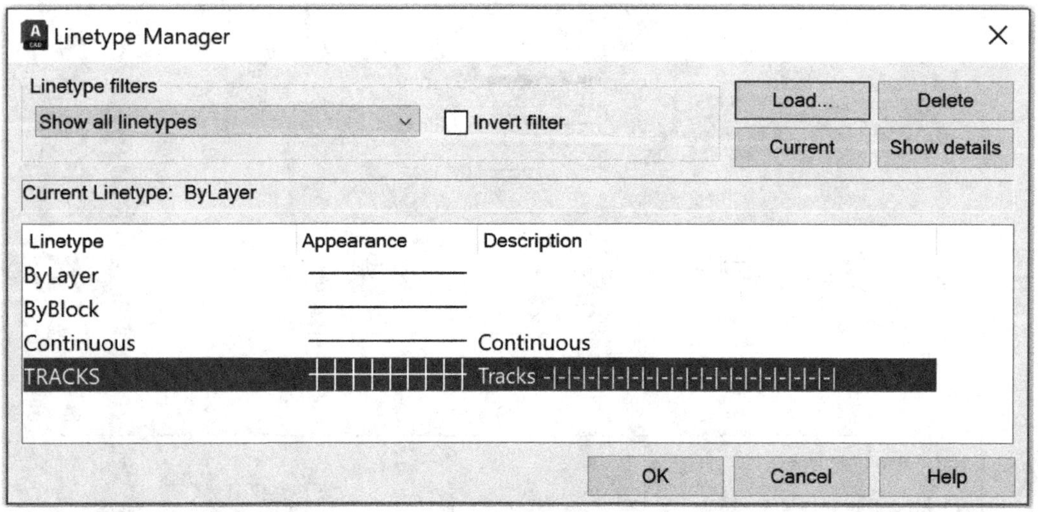

Figure 3-58d

3.17.3.2. Change linetype before an object is drawn

The linetype of a line before it is drawn is changed as follows:

1. Click on the down-arrow (▾) of the *Linetype Control* drop-down list in the *Properties* panel; the linetype list will appear on the screen, Figure 3-58e.
2. Bring the cursor on the desired linetype and it is highlighted; *TRACKS* in the current example, Figure 3-58e.
3. Click on the highlighted linetype; this closes the list and the selected linetype appears in the *Properties* toolbar, Figure 3-59a.
4. Now draw a line; the line is drawn with the selected linetype.

3.17.3.3. Change linetype after an object is drawn

The step-by-step process to change the linetype of a line after it is drawn is shown in Figure 3-59c.

1. Draw a line (the line labeled as *Before* in Figure 3-59b).
2. Select the line by clicking with the left button of the mouse (the line with three square boxes in Figure 3-59b).
3. Click on the arrow (▾) of the linetype control drop-down list in the *Properties* toolbar; the linetype list appears on the screen, Figure 3-58e.
4. Bring the cursor on the desired linetype and it is highlighted.

5. Click on the highlighted linetype; this closes the list and the linetype of the selected line changes to the selected linetype; the line is labeled as *After* in Figure 3-59b.
6. In Figure 3-59c every object is drawn using *Phantom* linetype; however, the pattern is not visible for some of the segments. A user can change the linetype scale to make the pattern visible.

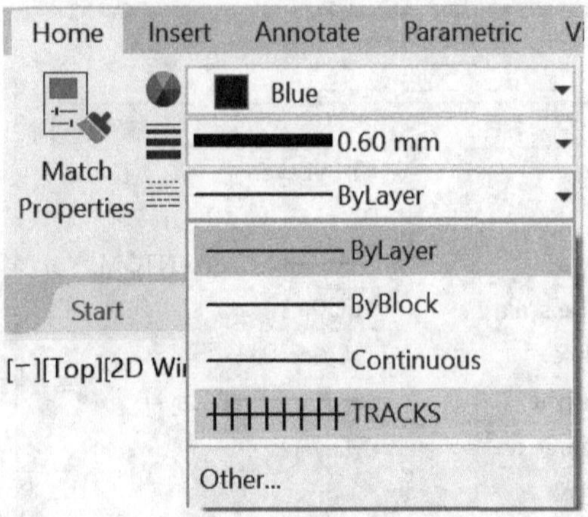

Figure 3-58e

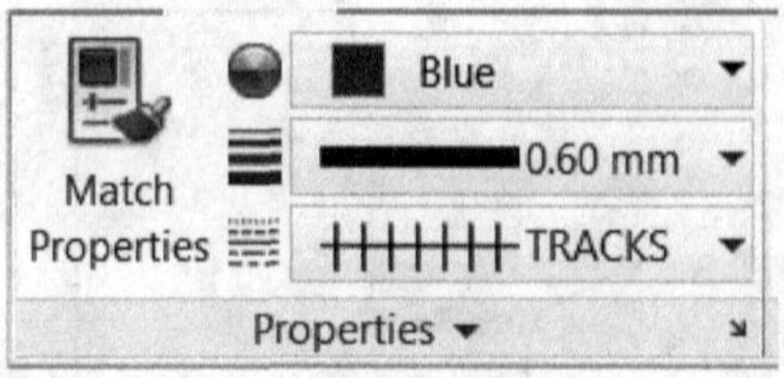

Figure 3-59a

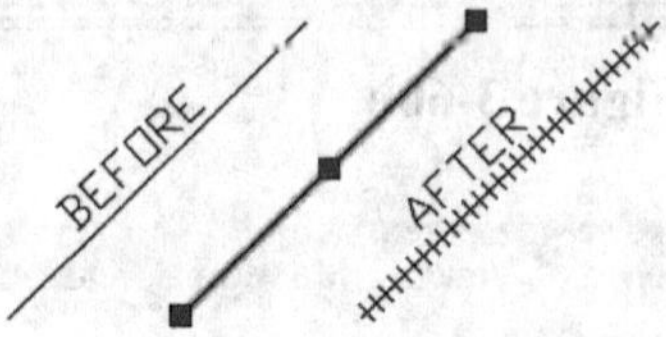

Figure 3-59b

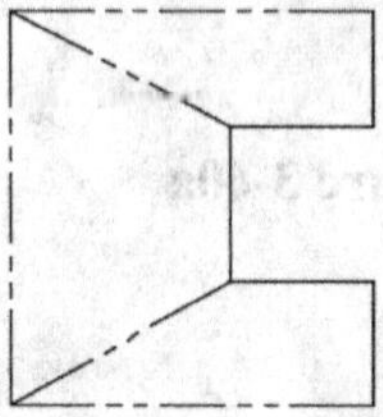

Figure 3-59c

3.17.3.4. Linetype scale

The *Linetype scale* capability is used to change the appearance of a pattern. In Figure 3-60d every object is drawn using *Phantom* linetype; however, the pattern is not visible for some of the segments. A user can change the linetype scale to make the pattern visible as follows:

- Select the lines by clicking with the left button of the mouse, Figure 3-60a.
- Open the *Properties* palette (Figure 3-60b) using one of the techniques listed below.
  1. Panel method: Open the *Properties* palette using one of the two panel methods.
     a. From the *Home* tab and *Properties* panel, click on the dialog box launcher (a small arrow on the lower right corner of the panel), Figure 3-60c.
     b. From the *View* tab and *Palette* panel, click on *Properties* icon, Figure 3-60d.
  2. Object method: (i) Click on the object(s). (ii) Press the right button of the mouse and choose the *Properties* option, Figure 3-60e.

- Any of the above three methods open the *Properties* palette of the selected object. On the upper left corner of the *Properties* palette, the type and number of the object (5 Lines in current example) is displayed. On the *Properties* palette, some of the properties are greyed indicating that those properties could not be changed. The properties palette is discussed in detail in *Chapter 4*.

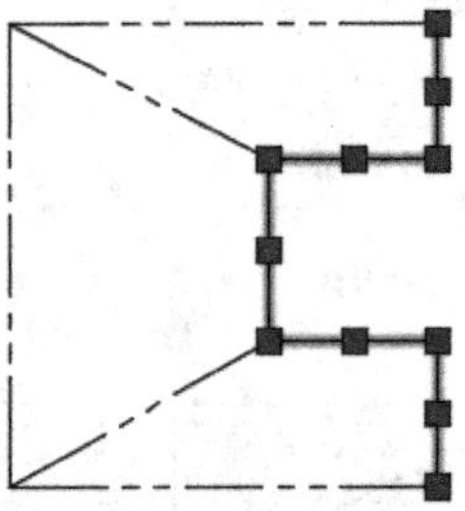

Figure 3-60a

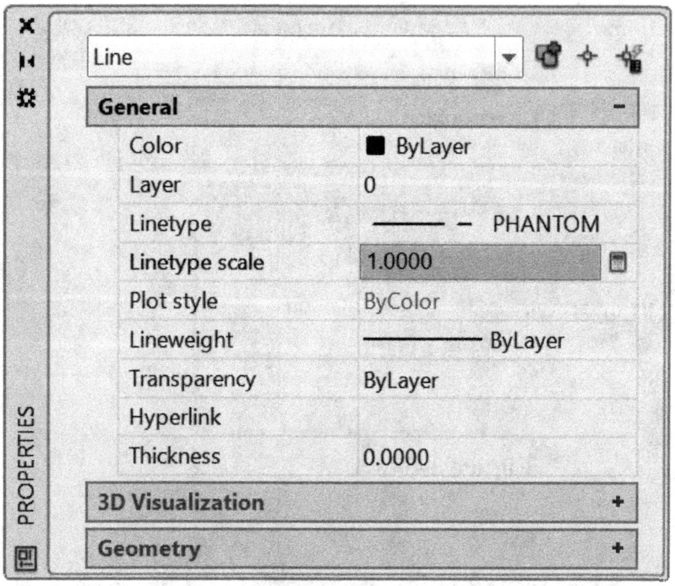

Figure 3-60b

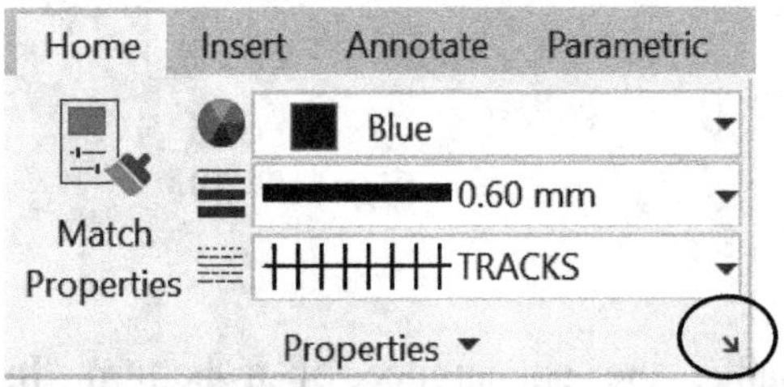

Figure 3-60c

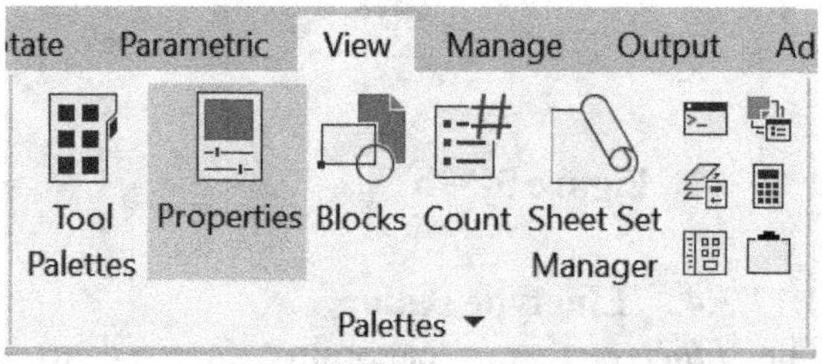

Figure 3-60d

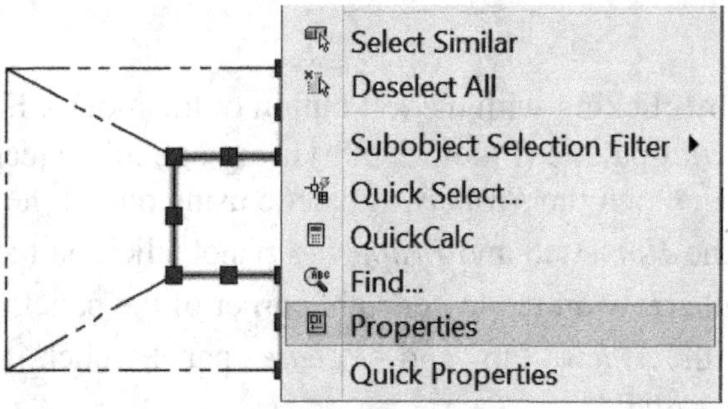

Figure 3-60e

- Select the *Linetype scale* (Figure 3-60f) and change the value to 0.6. If necessary, change the scale of other lines.
- The resultant drawing is shown in Figure 3-60g.
- **Important Note**: The user may need to reset the linetype scale in the layout.

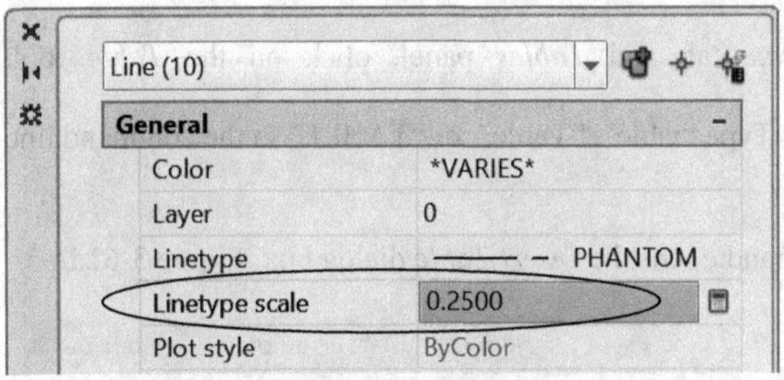

Figure 3-60f

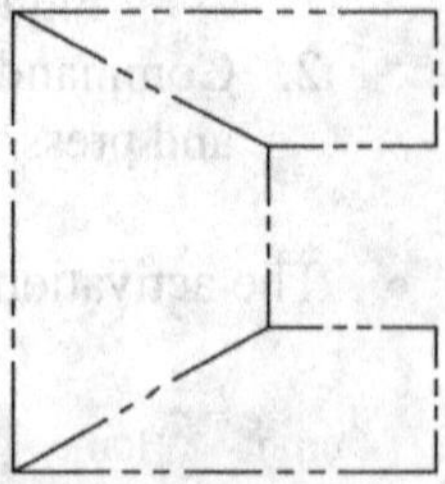

Figure 3-60g

3.18. Table

A table is an object that is used to organize data in rows and columns as shown in Figure 3-61a. Commonly, tables (in drawings) are used for the dimensions of objects with multiple holes, to define coordinate data, to create part lists, and to create doors and windows schedules. In a table, every entry must be written with caps lock or upper case.

In AutoCAD, the *Table* command is used to create a table. Initially, the table is blank; however, it is populated as needed. If the height or width of a table is changed then the rows or columns change proportionally. If the width of a column is changed then the table widens or narrows to accommodate the change.

- ***Example:*** Create the table shown in Figure 3-61a.

DIMENSION			
NAME	X-COORD	Y-COORD	Ø
A1	2.34	45.00	13.00
B1	-1.80	23.45	11.50
C1	4.98	35.12	9.00

Figure 3-61a

- The *Table* command is activated using one of the following methods:

  1. Panel method: The *Table* commands can be activated using one of the two panel methods:
     a. From the *Home* tab and *Annotation* panel, click on the *Table* tool, Figure 3-61b.
     b. From the *Annotate* tab and *Tables* panel, click on the *Table* tool, Figure 3-61c.
  2. Command line method: Type "table", "Table", or "TABLE" in the command line and press the *Enter* key.

- The activation of the command opens the *Insert Table* dialog box, Figure 3-61d.

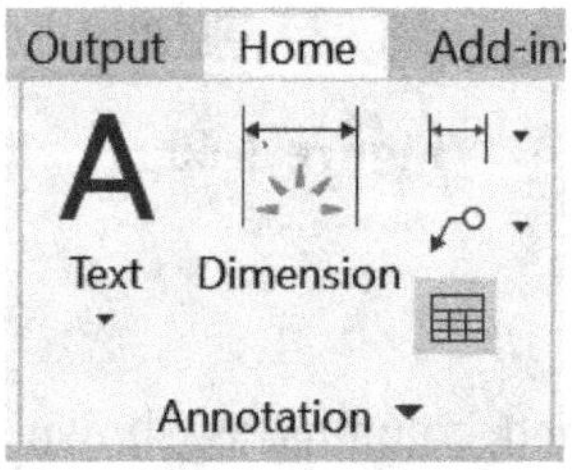

Figure 3-61b

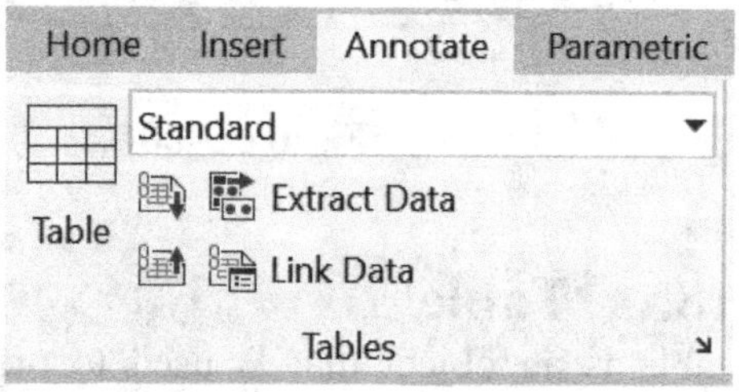

Figure 3-61c

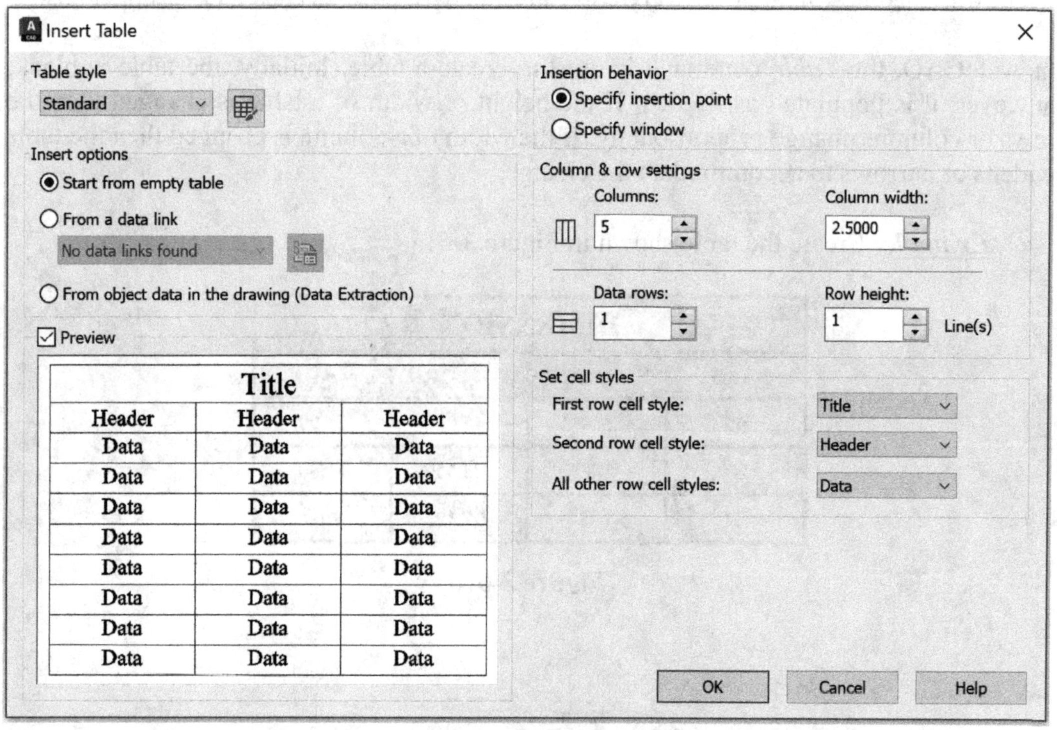

Figure 3-61d

3.18.1. Create a table

- A user can create a new table using *Insert Table* dialog box, Figure 3-61d, as follows:

    - From the *Table style* window, select a style from the list or click the  button to create a new table style.
    - In the *Insert option* panel, select *Start from empty table* option to create a table without any entries.
    - In the *Insertion behavior* panel, select *Specify insertion point* option to insert the table in the drawing area.
    - In the *Column & row settings* panel, set the number of columns and rows. For the current example, set the number of columns to 4 and number of data rows to 3. Assume the default values for the column width and row height.
    - For the *Specify window* insertion method in *Insertion behavior* panel, the user can enter only the number of columns and the rows height.
    - Finally, click the *OK* button. This closes the dialog box and the prompt to specify the insertion point appears, Figure 3-61e.

- Specify the insertion point in the drawing area by clicking at the desired location. The resulting table is shown in Figure 3-61f.

Figure 3-61e

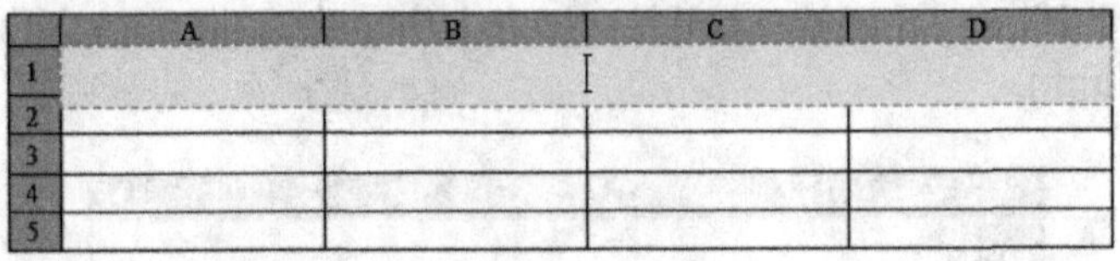

Figure 3-61f

3.18.2. Table resize

This section uses grips point to resize the table. Grips are small, solid-filled squares that are displayed at strategic points on the selected objects. Grips are discussed in detail in *Chapter 4*.

- Grip points can be used to reshape a table. To select a single cell, click inside the cell, Figure 3-62a. For multiple cells selection, use one of the following methods:
    - Click inside a cell. Hold down the *Shift* key and click inside another cell to select those two cells and all the cells between them.
    - Click inside the selected cell. Hold the left button of the mouse. Drag to the desired cell, Figure 3-62b, and release the button.

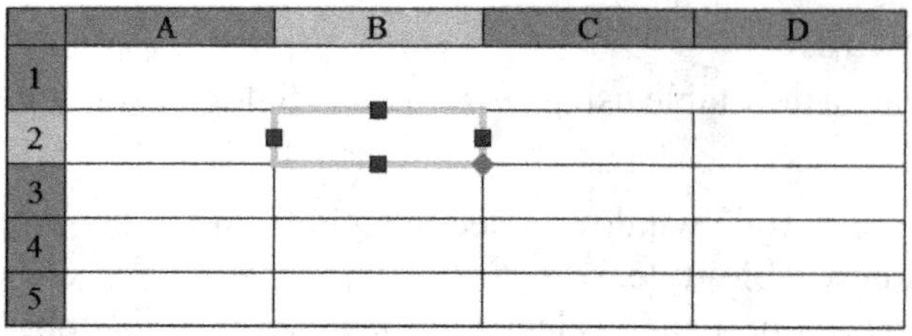

Figure 3-62a

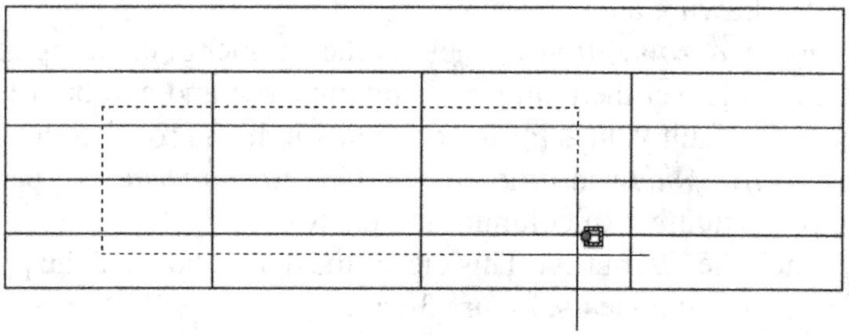

Figure 3-62b

- Change the row height: To change the row height of the selected cell, drag the top or bottom grips point upward or downward, respectively. The resized table is shown in Figure 3-62c. If more than one cell is selected, then the row height changes equally for each row.

- Change the column width: To change the column width of the selected cell, drag the left or right grips point to the left or right, respectively. The resized table is shown in Figure 3-62c. If more than one cell is selected, then the column width changes equally for each column.

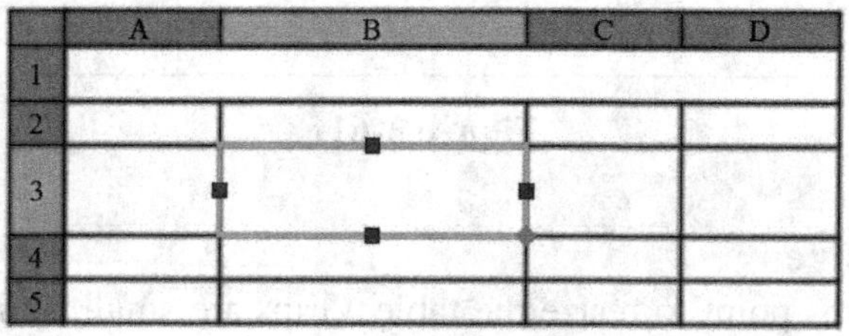

Figure 3-62c

- Resize table: Select the table. To stretch/shrink uniformly: use the grips point at upper right corner to change the width, lower left corner to change the height, and lower right corner to change both the width and height of the table, Figure 3-62d. That is, all the rows and/or columns will be stretched by the same amount. Although Figure 3-62d shows multiple options selection, the software does not allow for multiple options selection simultaneously.

- Press the *Esc* key from the keyboard to remove the selection.

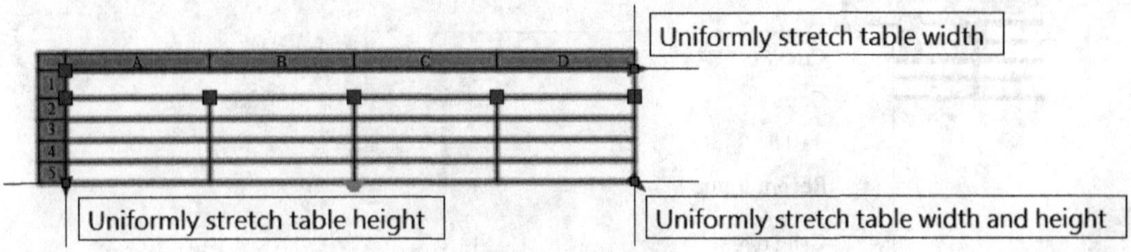

Figure 3-62d

- Move the table: Select the table; use the grips point at the upper left corner to move the table, Figure 3-62e.

- Break the table: Select the table; use the lower middle (light blue) grip point to break the table, Figure 3-62f. The user should avoid using this option.

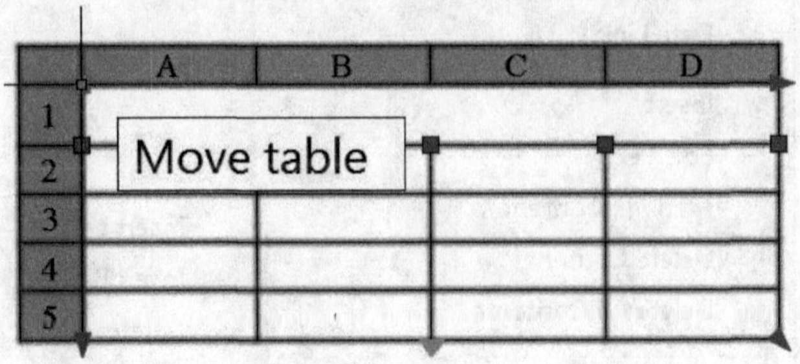

Figure 3-62e

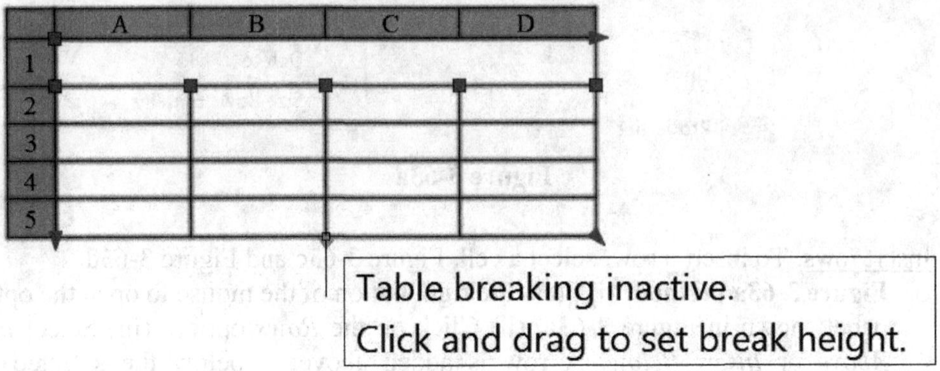

Figure 3-62f

3.18.3. Modify table's shape

Figure 3-63a shows the various options available to reshape the table. Bring the cursor on one of the cells and press the right button of the mouse and select the desired option. The figure shows the selection of multiple options simultaneously. However, the software does not allow for multiple options selection. These options are also available from the *Table Cell* tab shown in Figure 3-63b; this tab appears on the screen when a cell in a table is selected.

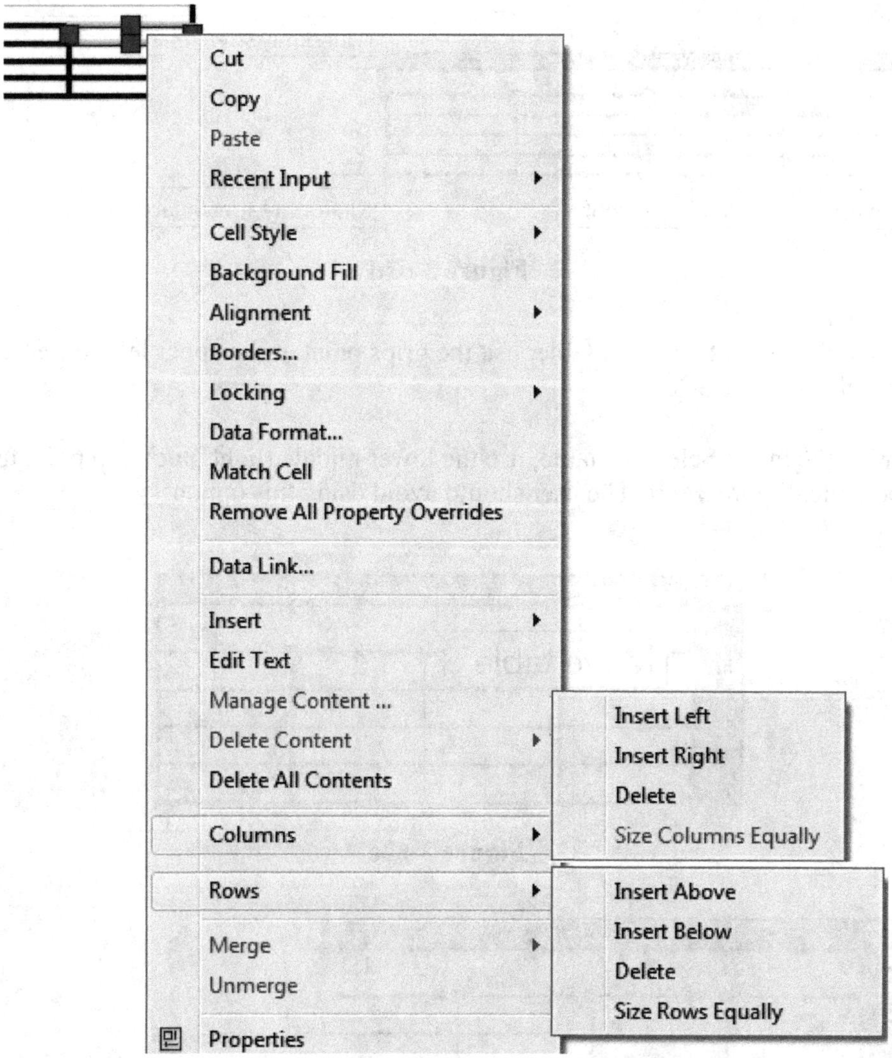

Figure 3-63a

- Insert rows: To insert a row, select a cell, Figure 3-63c and Figure 3-63d.
  - **Figure 3-63a method:** (i) press the right button of the mouse to open the options panel shown in Figure 3-63a. (ii) Click on the *Rows* option. (iii) Select *Insert Above* or *Insert Below*. A row is added above or below the selected cell, respectively. In the current example, a row is added above the selected cell, Figure 3-63c. If '*n*' cells are selected, then '*n*' rows are inserted, where n >1.
  - **Figure 3-63b method:** Press the desired tool from the *Row* panel. In the current example, a row is added above the selected cell, Figure 3-63c. If '*n*' cells are selected, then '*n*' rows will be inserted, where n >1.

- Insert Columns: The procedure to insert a column is similar to the row insertion process.

- <u>Delete rows</u>: To delete a row, select a cell in the row to be deleted.
  - **Figure 3-63a method:** (i) Press the right button of the mouse to open the options panel shown in Figure 3-63a. (ii) Click on the *Rows* option. (iv) Select the *Delete* option. A row will be deleted containing the selected cell. If '*n*' cells are selected then '*n*' rows will be deleted, where '*n*' >1.
  - **Figure 3-63b method:** Press the desired tool from the *Row* panel. A row will be deleted containing the selected cell. If '*n*' cells are selected, then '*n*' rows will be deleted, where '*n*' >1.

- <u>Delete columns</u>: To delete a column, select a cell in the column to be deleted.
  - Same as deleting a row.

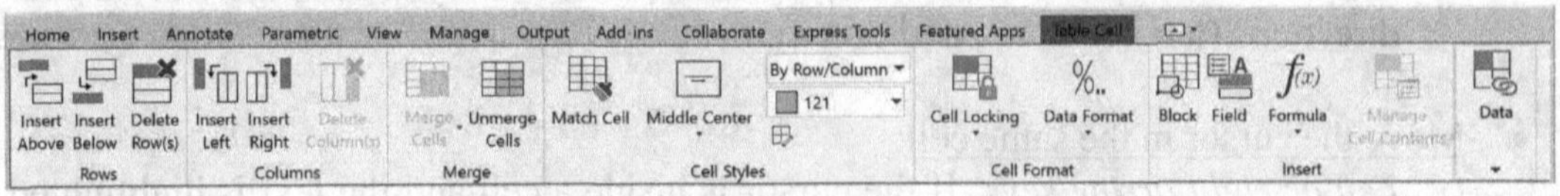

Figure 3-63b

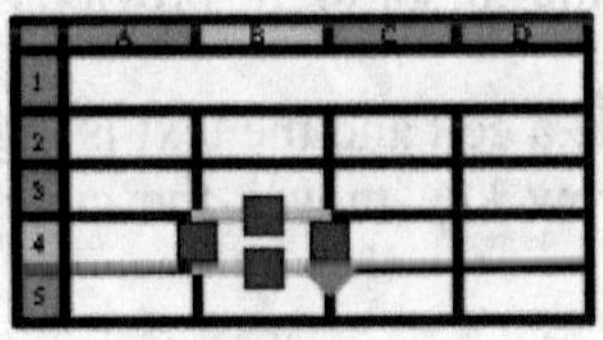

Figure 3-63c

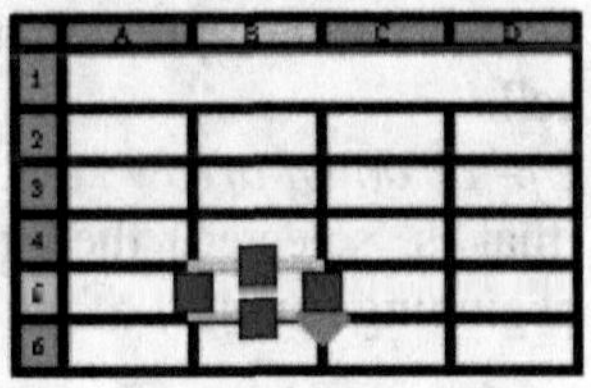

Figure 3-63d

- <u>Merge cells</u>: To merge multiple cells, select the cells to be merged.
  - *By Row* option merges the cells horizontally by removing the vertical gridlines and leaving the horizontal gridlines intact.
  - *By Column* option merges the cells vertically by removing the horizontal gridlines and leaving the vertical gridlines intact, Figure 3-63d.
  - **Figure 3-63a method:** (i) Press the right button of the mouse to open the options panel shown in Figure 3-63a. (iii) Click on the *Merge* option and click on *By Row*. The selected cells will be merged into one cell. Similarly merge the cells in a *Column*, or *All* (both direction, that is, row and column). Figure 3-63d shows the merge of cells using different options.
  - **Figure 3-63b method:** Press the desired tool from the *Merge* panel. The selected cells will be merged into one cell. Similarly merge cells in a *Column*, or *All* (both direction, that is, row and column). Figure 3-63e and Figure 3-63f shows a table and the merging of cells using different options.

- <u>Split cells</u>:
  - Cells cannot be split EXCEPT the cells that were merged previously.

- Press the *Esc* key from keyboard to remove the selection.

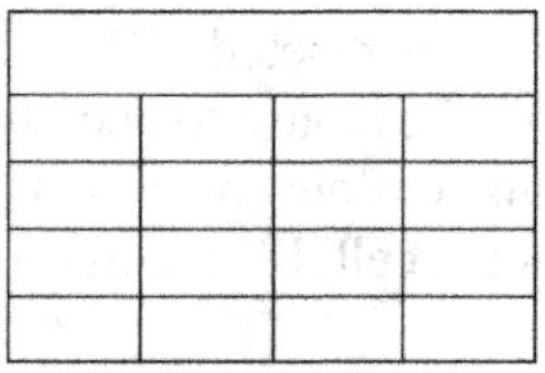

Figure 3-63e

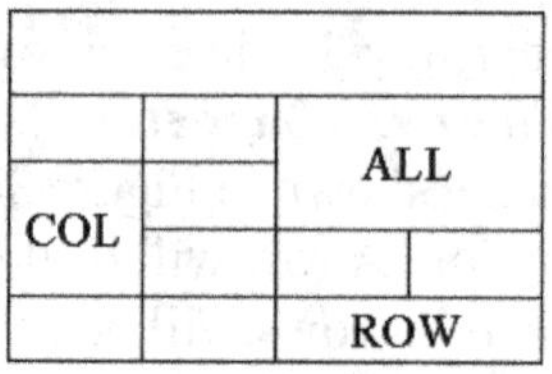

Figure 3-63f

3.18.4. The cursor movement

- Move the cursor to the next cell:
  - If the cursor is inside a cell and the text is NOT selected, then to move the cursor to the next cell press the *TAB* key or use the arrow keys to navigate in all four directions (left, right, up, and down).

- Move the cursor in the same cell:
  - *Left or right arrow keys:* If the cursor is inside a cell and the text is highlighted (that is, selected) then the left (or right) arrow key moves the cursor one character in the left (or right) direction. However, if the cursor is in the beginning (or end) of the text, then pressing the arrow key moves the cursor to the previous (or next) cell.
  - *Up- or down-arrow keys:* If the cursor is inside a cell and the text is highlighted (that is, selected) then the up (or down) arrow key moves the cursor to the beginning (or end) of the highlighted text.

3.18.5. Insert a multiline text in a cell

The row height of the selected cell increases to accommodate the number of lines of the text. If the length of the single line text is longer than the width of a cell, then the text wraps automatically to the next line. If the user presses the *Enter* key on the keyboard, the cursor moves to the next cell, Figure 3-64.

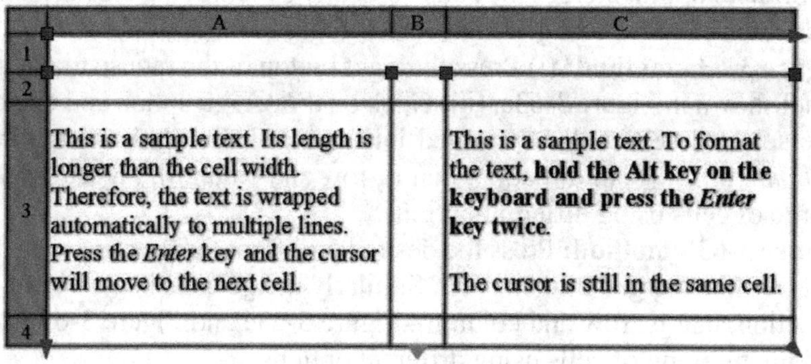

Figure 3-64

If a user desires to create multiline line text objects in a cell, then hold the *Alt* key and press the *Enter* key to move the cursor to the next line. To format the text as shown in the right column of the table in Figure 3-64, the *Alt- Enter* keys are used twice to create a blank line between the two paragraphs.

3.18.6. The data type

The data in a table cell can be a text, a block, or a field. Select three cells of a column in the table and press the right button of the mouse; an options list appears on the screen, Figure 3-65a. Click on the *Data Format*, and the *Table Cell Format* dialog box appears on the screen, Figure 3-65b. In the current example, for the angle *Data type*, the Surveyor's units are used. The content of the *Preview* panel represents the selection of the *Data type*.

Figure 3-65c shows the entries in the table are converted to Surveyor's units. Remember that the angles are measured counterclockwise from the east. To enter the data (i) type the data as decimal number; (ii) press the *Enter* key from the keyboard, and the data will appear in selected data format (the Surveyor's units).

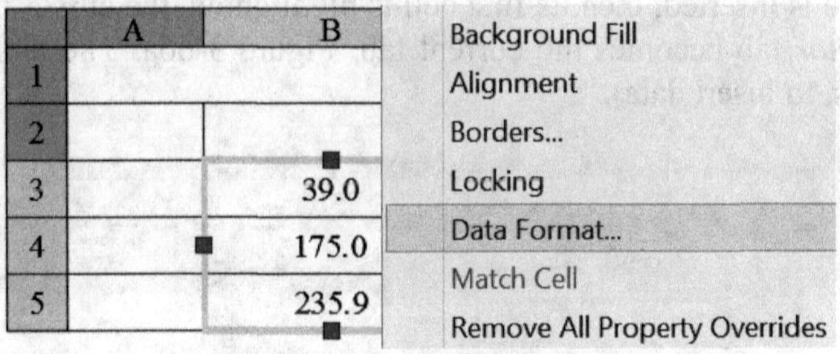

Figure 3-65a

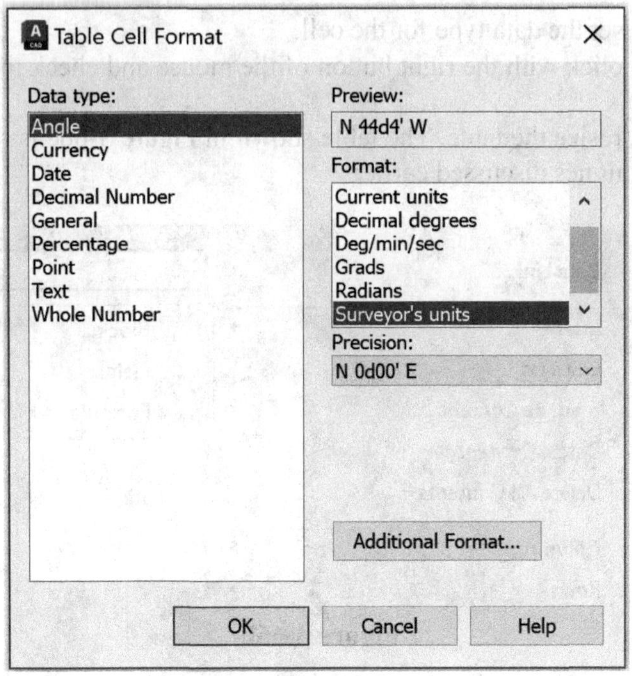

Figure 3-65b

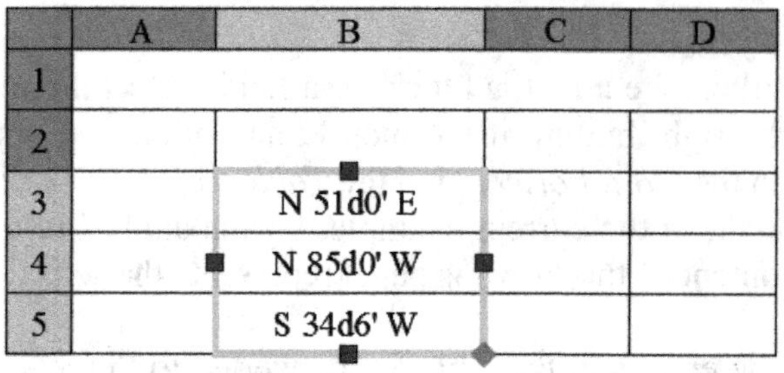

Figure 3-65c

3.18.7. Populate the table

When a new table is inserted, then its first cell is highlighted, the cursor is in the first cell, and the *Text Editor* tab becomes the current tab, Figure 3-66a. The table is ready to be populated (that is, to insert data).

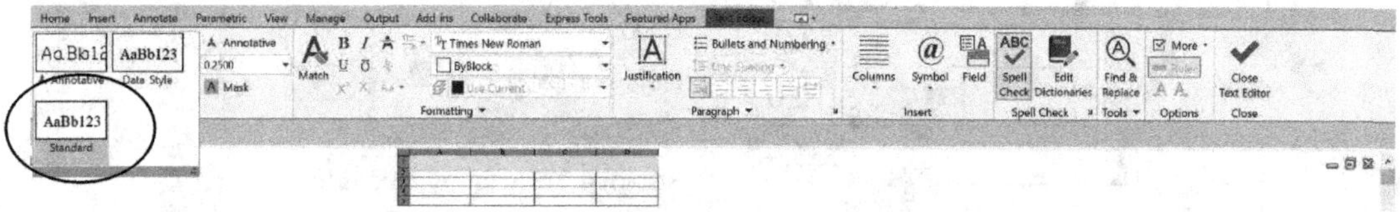

Figure 3-66a

- If necessary, set the data type for the cell.
- If necessary, click with the right button of the mouse and check the various options, Figure 3-66b.
- If necessary, resize the table. The table shown in Figure 3-66c is resized using table resizing techniques discussed earlier.

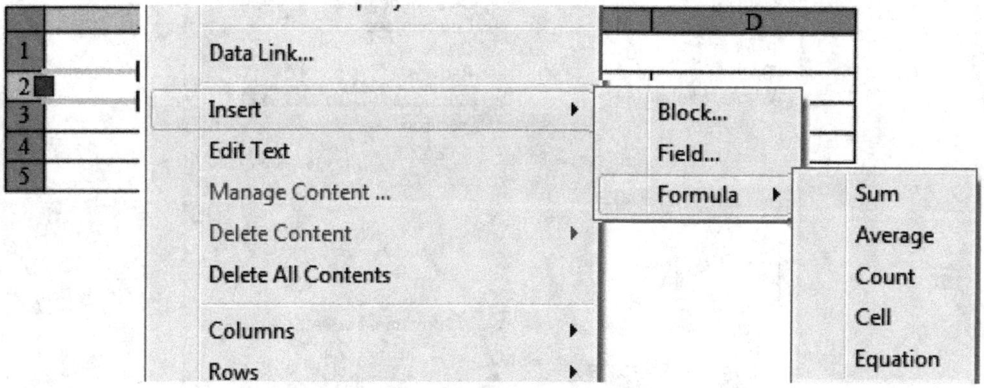

Figure 3-66b

- Populate the table using the cursor movement and multiline text (select the ***Standard*** option from the text editor, Figure 3-66a) and insert the information shown in the table of Figure 3-66c.

DIMENSION			
NAME	X-COORD	Y-COORD	Ø
A1	2.34	45.00	13.00
B1	-1.80	23.45	11.50
C1	4.98	35.12	9.00

Figure 3-66c

3.18.8. Modify the contents of a table

Suppose a user has created the table shown in Figure 3-66c and wants to modify it to the format shown in Figure 3-67. In the table of Figure 3-67, the *Title* cell is shaded blue, the *Header* cells are shaded orange, and the *Data* cells are shaded yellow. The line weight of the border is set to 0.5. The content of the table is aligned in the middle center. The font is set to Times New Roman. The text height is 0.20 for the *Title* cell and 0.15 for the *Header* and the *Data* cells. The contents of the *Title* and the *Header* cells are set to *Bold* style, whereas the contents of the *Data* cells are kept plain.

DIMENSION			
NAME	**X-COORD**	**Y-COORD**	**Ø**
A1	2.34	45.00	13.00
B1	-1.80	23.45	11.50
C1	4.98	35.12	9.00

Figure 3-67

There are multiple techniques to change the table format: (i) Use of the *Table Style* dialog box. This method changes the format of every table in the current drawing. (ii) Use of the property palette. This method only changes the format of the selected table. (iii) Update one cell at a time (long and exhaustive approach).

3.18.8.1. Table Style dialog box

This section uses the *Table Style* dialog box, Figure 3-68c, to change the table format. However, every table in the current drawing will be reformatted to the current style.

- Open the *Table Style* dialog box, using one of the following methods:
  1. Panel method: (i) From the *Home* tab and expanded *Annotation* panel, select the *Table Style* tool, Figure 3-68a. (ii) From the *Annotate* tab and *Table* panel, click the dialog box launcher (a small arrow on the lower right corner of the panel).
  2. Dialog box method: (i) From the *Home* tab and *Annotation* panel, select the *Table* tool. (ii) In the *Insert Table* dialog box Figure 3-68b, from the *Table style* panel click on the button to open the *Table Style* dialog box.
  3. Command line method: Type "tablestyle", "Tablestyle", or "TABLESTYLE" in the command line and press the *Enter* key.

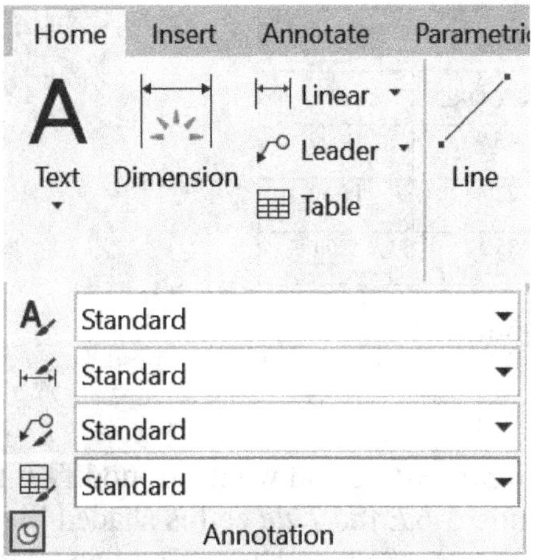

Figure 3-68a

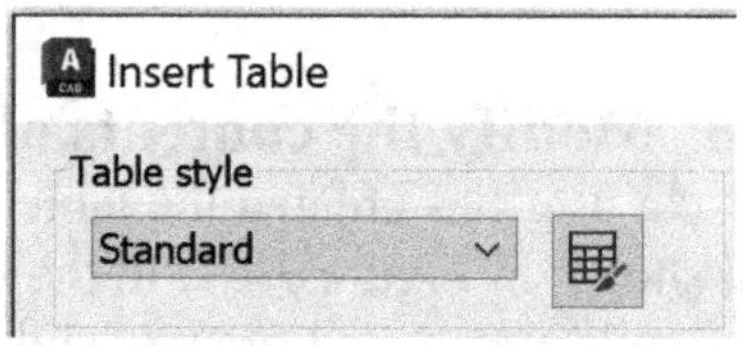

Figure 3-68b

- Click on the *Modify* button of the *Table Style* dialog box to open the *Modify Table Style: Standard* dialog box, Figure 3-68d.

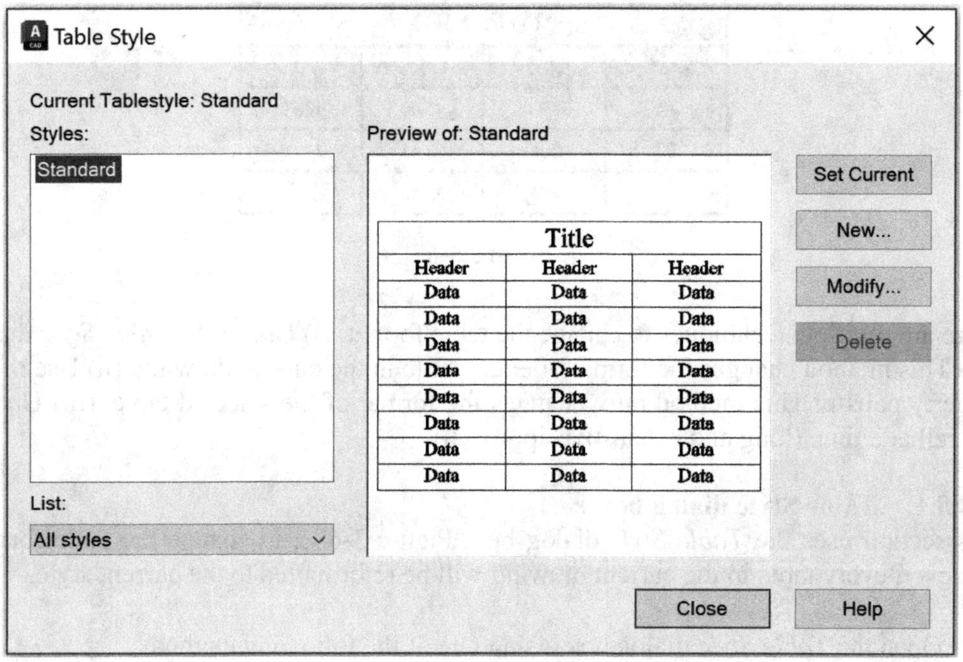

Figure 3-68c

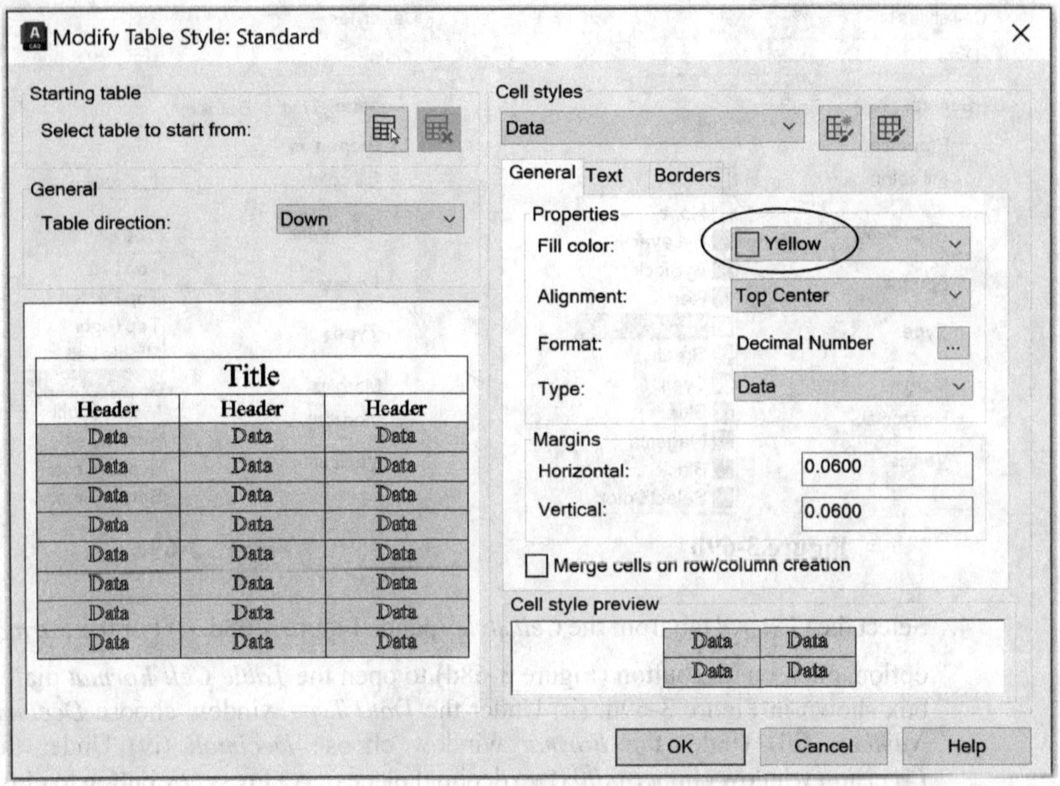

Figure 3-68d

- On the *Modify Table Style: Standard* dialog box, perform the following actions.

  1. From the *Cell styles* panel (Figure 3-68d), click on the down-arrow and select the *Data* option, Figure 3-69a.

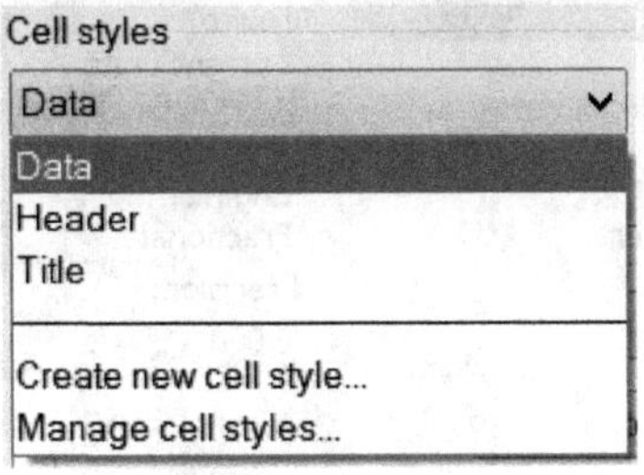

Figure 3-69a

  2. Select the *General* tab from the *Cell styles* panel and under the *Fill color* option, choose the desired color Figure 3-69b or click on *Select Color* option to display more colors. In the current example, the yellow color is chosen.
  3. Select the *General* tab from the *Cell styles* panel and under the *Alignment* option, choose *Middle Center* option, Figure 3-69c.

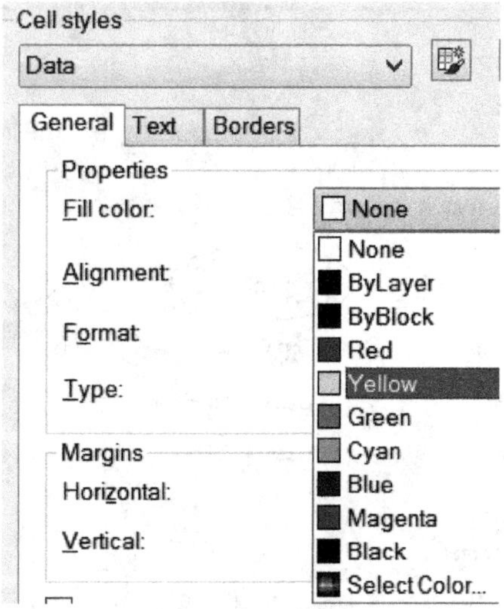

Figure 3-69b

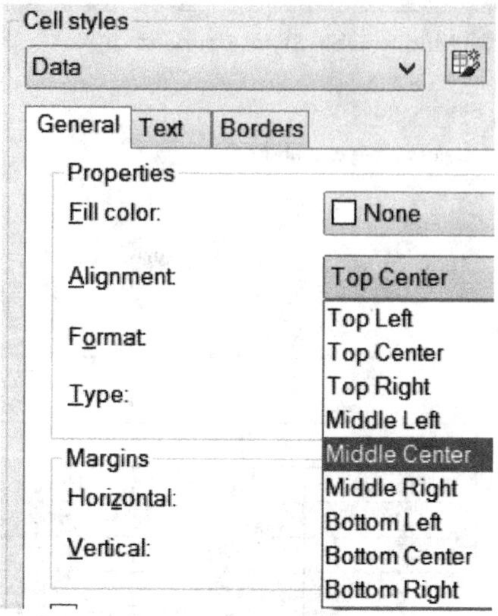

Figure 3-69c

4. Select the *General* tab from the *Cell styles* panel, Figure 3-68d. (i) For the *Format* option, click on button (Figure 3-68d) to open the *Table Cell Format* dialog box shown in Figure 3-69d. (ii) Under the *Data Type* window choose *Decimal Number*. (iii) Under the *Format* window choose *Decimal*. (iv) Under the *Precision* window choose *0.00* (two decimal places). (v) Press *OK* button to close this dialog box.

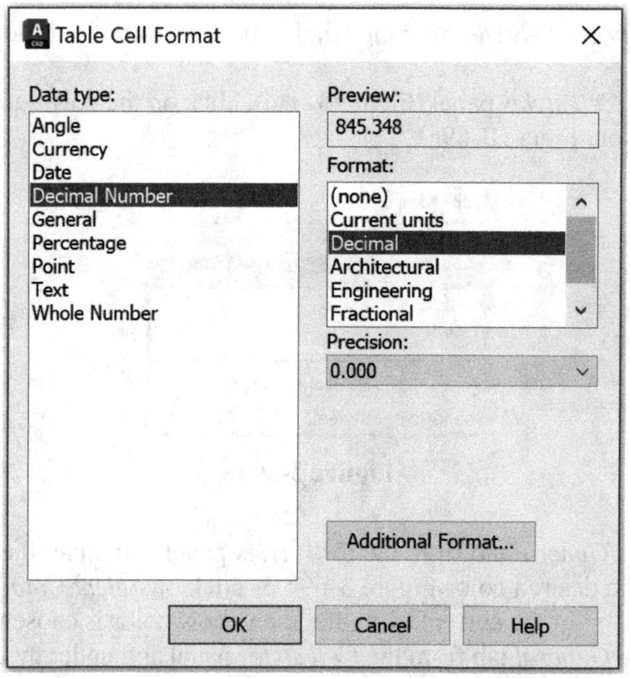

Figure 3-69d

5. Select the *General* tab from the *Cell styles* panel, Figure 3-68d. Under the *Type* option, choose *Data*, Figure 3-69e.

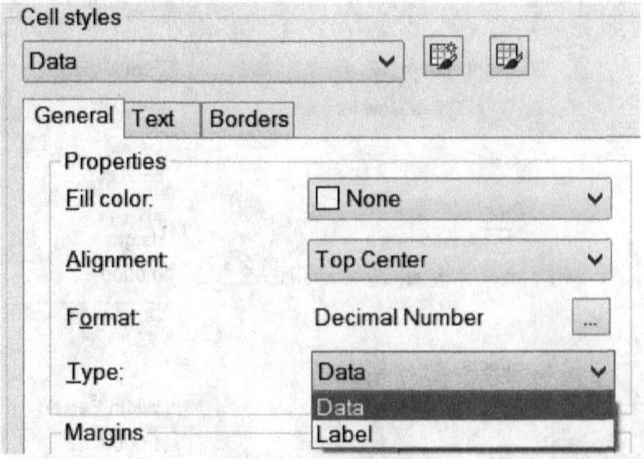

Figure 3-69e

6. Select the *Text* tab from the *Cell styles* panel, Figure 3-68d. Choose the options shown in Figure 3-70a. To set the font information, in Figure 3-68a, click on the  button to open the *Text Style* dialog box, Figure 3-70b.

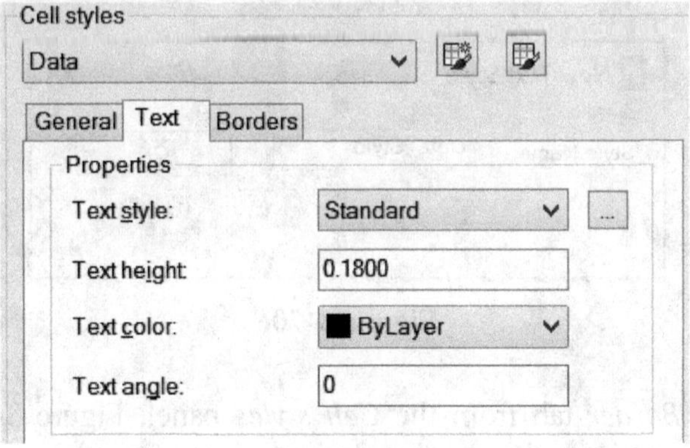

Figure 3-70a

The *Text Style* dialog box shown in Figure 3-70b is used to set the properties of the text. (i) In the dialog box, choose the *Times New Roman* font under the *Font Name*. (ii) To create a new style, click on the *New* button and this opens the *New Text Style* box, Figure 3-70c. (iii) Name the style with an easily recognizable name (*Data_Style* in the current example), save the style, and press the *OK* button. (iv) This closes the *New Text Style* box and activates the *Apply* button on the *Text Style* dialog box and converts the *Cancel* button to the *Close* button. (v) Press the *Apply* button followed by the *Close* button.

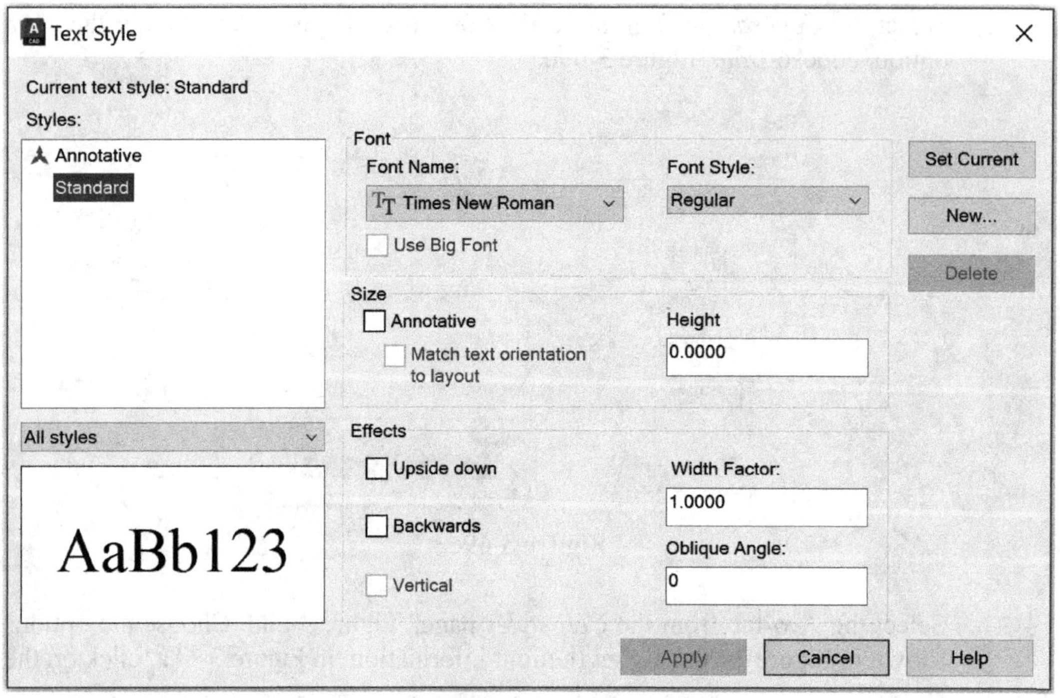

Figure 3-70b

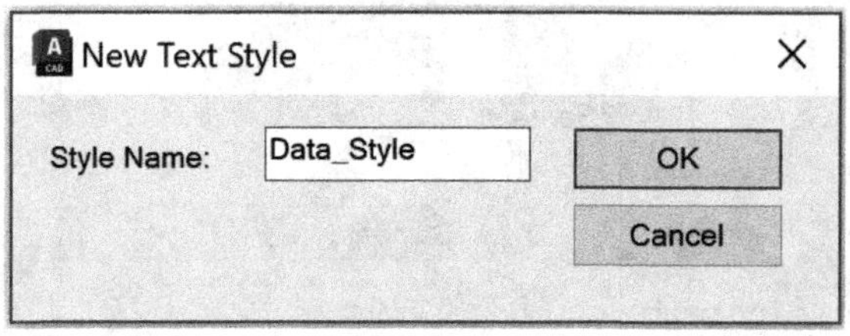

Figure 3-70c

7. Select the *Border* tab from the *Cell styles* panel, Figure 3-68d. (i) Under the *Lineweight* option, choose the desired thickness (0.3mm in the example). (ii) Under the *Linetype* and *Color* options, select the *By Layer* option. The preview window on the lower left corner of the dialog box displays the changes.
8. Repeat the steps #1 - #7 for the *Header* and *Title* cells.
9. The resultant table is shown in Figure 3-67. For the reader's convenience, the figure is shown again on the next page.

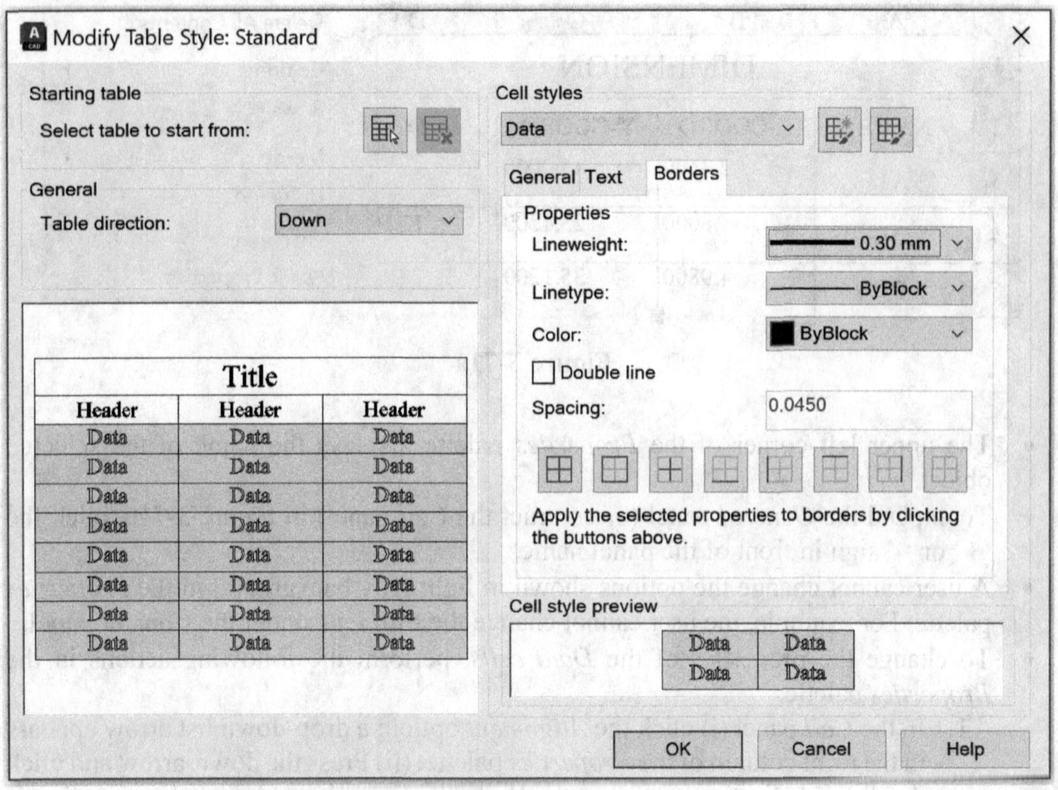

Figure 3-70d

3.18.8.2. Table update using the property palette

A table can also be updated using the *Properties* palette. The advantage of this technique is that only the selected table's format is changed. This section shows the process to modify the contents of the *Data cells*. The user can use the same process to modify the contents of the *Title cell* and the *Header cells*.

DIMENSION			
NAME	X-COORD	Y-COORD	Ø
A1	2.34	45.00	13.00
B1	-1.80	23.45	11.50
C1	4.98	35.12	9.00

Figure 3-67

- To open the *Properties* palette, use one of the following methods:
  1. Select all of the data cells, Figure 3-71a, press the right button of the mouse, and select the *Properties* option from the list of options.
  2. From the View tab and Palettes pane, select the *Properties* tool ( ). The *Properties* palette is shown in Figure 3-71b.

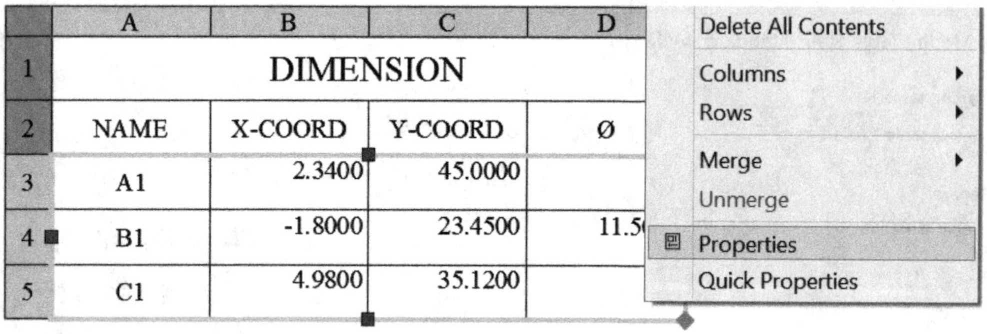

Figure 3-71a

- The upper left corner of the *Properties* palette displays the name of the selected object.
- To expand the *General* panel (or contract the *Cell* panel) in Figure 3-71b, click the '+' or '-' sign in front of the panel name.
- A user cannot change the options shown in light gray background in the *Properties* palette. For example, the user cannot change the *Cell type* under the *Content* panel.
- To change the properties of the *Data cells*, perform the following actions in the *Properties* palette.
    1. In the *Cell* panel (i) click the *Alignment* option; a drop-down list arrow appears in the right column of the *Properties* palette. (ii) Press the down-arrow and click the desired alignments, Figure 3-71b. In the figure, the *Middle Center* option is selected. (iii) The drop-down list is closed, and the contents of the data cell move in the middle center.
    2. In the *Cell* panel (i) select the *Background fill* option; a drop-down list arrow appears in the right column of the *Properties* palette. (ii) Press the down-arrow and click the desired color, Figure 3-71b. In the figure, the *Yellow* color is selected. (iii) The drop-down list is closed, and the background color of the data cell is changed to the selected color.
    3. In the *Cell* panel (i) select the *Border Lineweight* option; the *Choose* button ( ) appears in the right column of the properties' palette. (ii) Click the button and the *Cell Border Properties* dialog box appears, Figure 3-71c. (iii) For the border, select *All Border* option. (iv) Under the *Lineweight* option, choose the desired thickness (0.3mm in the example). (v) Under the *Linetype* and *Color* options, select the *By Layer* option. (vi) Click the OK button of the dialog box. This closes the dialog box; the *Choose* button disappears from the *Properties palette* and the border of the *Data cell* changes to the selected options.
    4. In the *Content* panel (i) select the *Text style* option; a dropdown list arrow appears in the right column of the *Properties* palette. (ii) Press the down-arrow and select the desired style. The *Data_Style* is a user defined style, and the previous section describes the creation process. In this example, the *Data_Style* is selected. (iii) The drop-down list is closed, and the background color of the data cell will change to the selected style.
    5. In the *Content* panel (i) select the *Text height* option, Figure 3-71b. (ii) Type the desired height in the right column. (iii) Press the *Enter* key on the keyboard.

(iv) The selection is cleared and size of the content of the data cell will change to the selected height.

6. Repeat the steps #1 - #5 for the *Header* and *Title* cells.
7. The resultant table is shown in Figure 3-67. For the reader's convenience, the figure is shown here again.

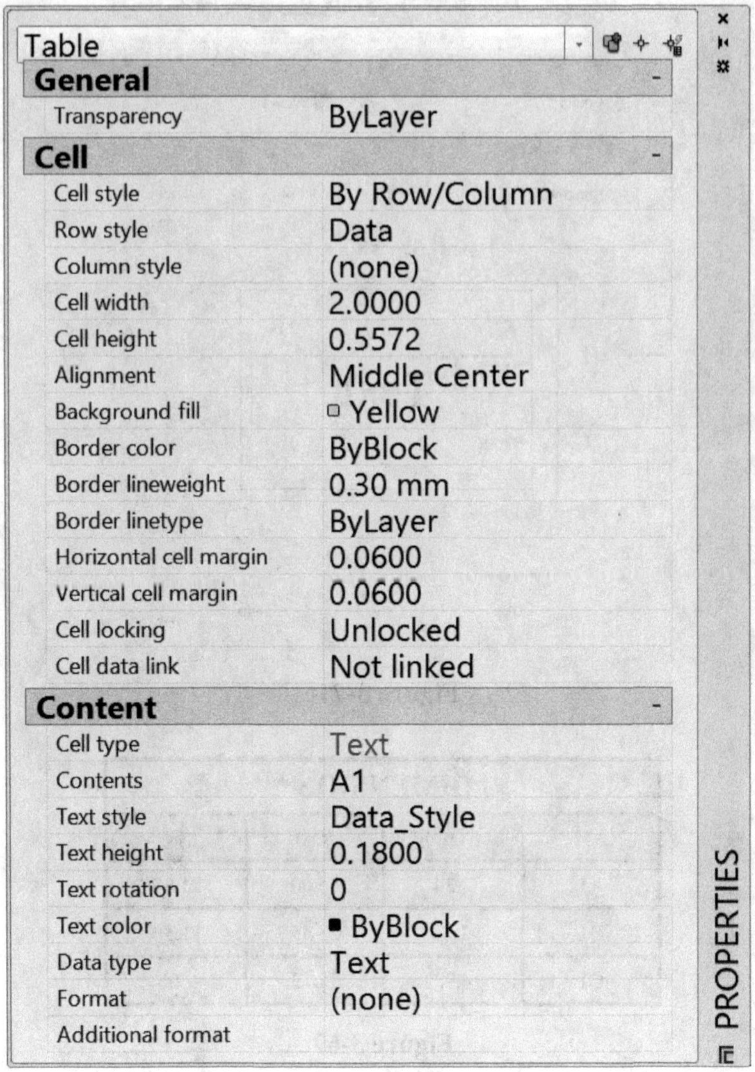

Figure 3-71b

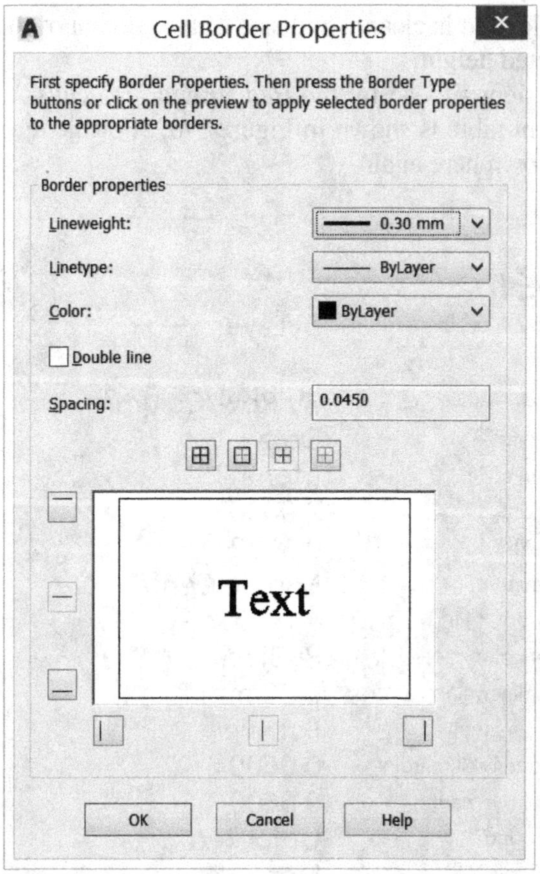

Figure 3-71c

DIMENSION			
NAME	X-COORD	Y-COORD	Ø
A1	2.34	45.00	13.00
B1	-1.80	23.45	11.50
C1	4.98	35.12	9.00

Figure 3-67

Notes:

4. Two-Dimensional Drawings' Editing

4.1. Learning Objectives

After completing this chapter, the students will show proficiency in the following areas:

- Grips points
- Object selection and de-selection
- Pan and Zoom capabilities
- Draw order (move object in front of or behind other objects)
- Object snap
- Editing commands
    - *Cancel*, *Erase*, *Delete Duplicates*, *Undo*, *Redo*, *Oops*, *Copy*, *Array*, *Mirror*, *Offset*, *Move*, *Rotate*, *Scale*, *Stretch*, *Break*, *Explode*, *Join*, *Fillet*, *Chamfer*, *Trim*, *Extend*, and *Polyline Edit*
- Properties Palette

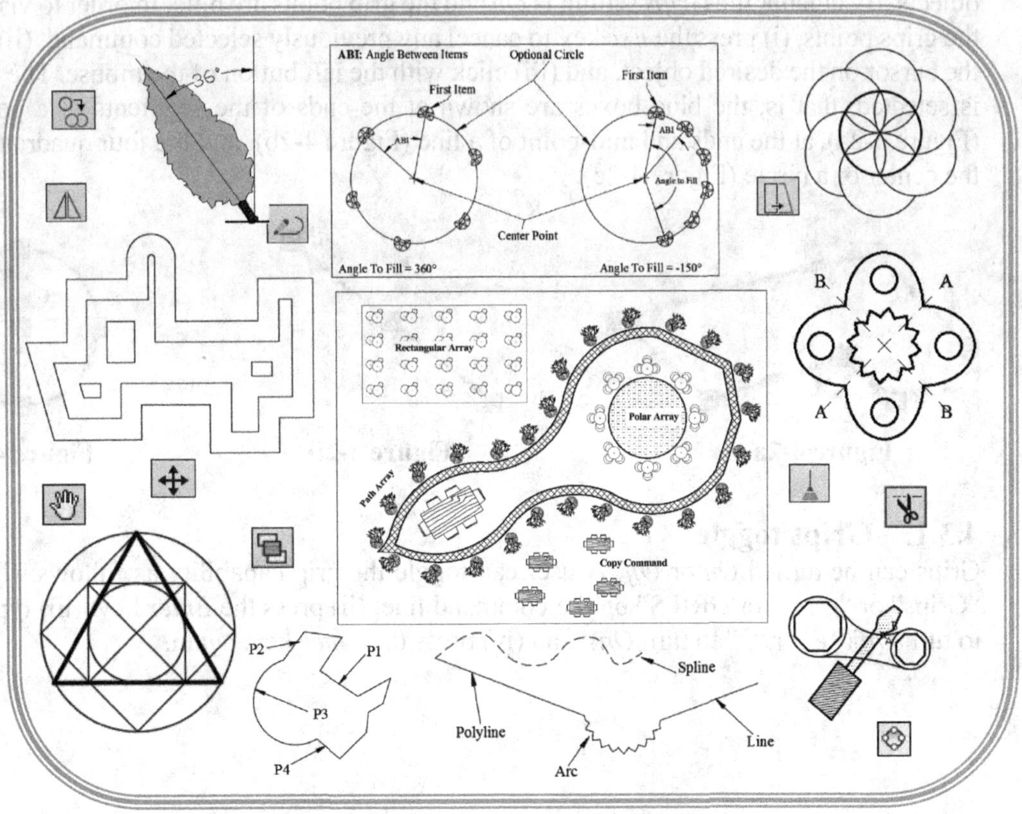

4.2. Introduction

A drafter can create unlimited designs by creating new drawings and editing existing drawings. The focus of this chapter is the AutoCAD capabilities to edit two-dimensional drawing objects. To achieve these capabilities, AutoCAD provides the *Modify* panel from the *Home* tab (Figure 4-1), grip points, and the property palette. Figure 4-1 shows the expanded and pinned (check the pin at the lower left corner) *Modify* panel.

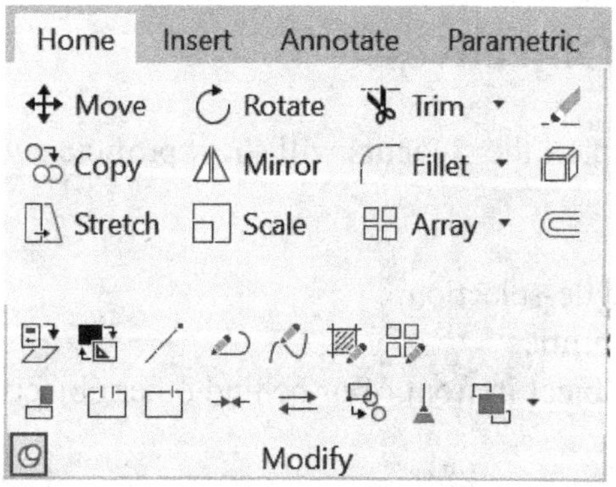

Figure 4-1

4.3. Grips

Grips are small, solid-filled squares that are displayed at strategic points on the selected objects. By default, the *Grips* setting is *On* and the grip points are blue. In order to visualize the grips points, (i) press the *Esc* key to cancel any previously selected command, (ii) place the cursor on the desired object, and (iii) click with the left button of the mouse. The object is selected, that is, the blue boxes are shown at the ends of the segments of a polyline (Figure 4-2a), at the ends and mid-point of a line (Figure 4-2b), and the four quadrants and the center of a circle (Figure 4-2c).

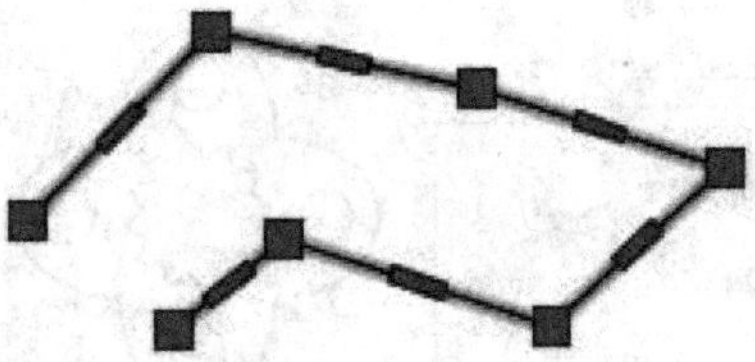

Figure 4-2a

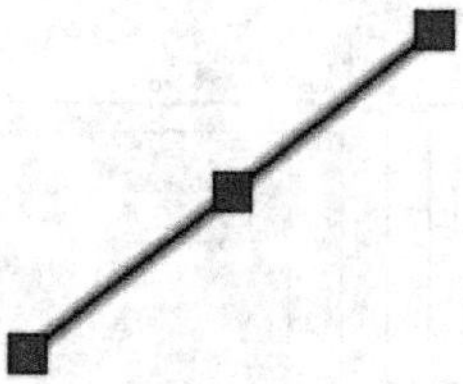

Figure 4-2b

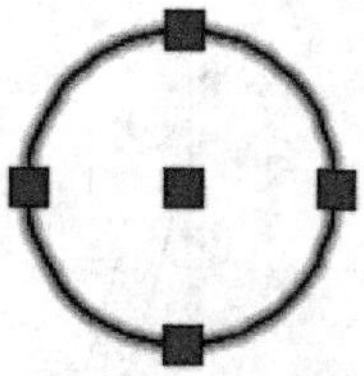

Figure 4-2c

4.3.1. Grips toggle

Grips can be turned *On* or *Off*. A user can toggle the grip capability as follows: (i) type "Grips" or "grips" or GRIPS" on the command line; (ii) press the *Enter* key; (iii) type "0" to turn *Off* ("1" or "2" to turn *On*); and (iv) press the *Enter* key, again.

4.3.2. Change the size and color of the grips

The size and color of the grip points can be changed from the *Options* dialog box as follows:

- Open the *Options* dialog box (Figure 4-3a) using one of the two methods.
  1. Click with the right button in the *Drawing area* and select the *Options* option. The *Options* dialog box appears on the screen.
  2. Command line method: Type "options", "Options", or "OPTIONS" in the command line and press the *Enter* key.
- Click on the *Selection* tab of the *Options* dialog box.
- The slider in the *Grip size* panel, Figure 4-3a, is used to change the size of the grip points. Move the slider to the right (or left) to increase (or decrease) the size.
- Click on the *Grip Colors* button, Figure 4-3a, in the *Grip* panel to open *Grip Colors* dialog box, Figure 4-3b. Make the desired changes and click *OK* button on both dialog boxes.

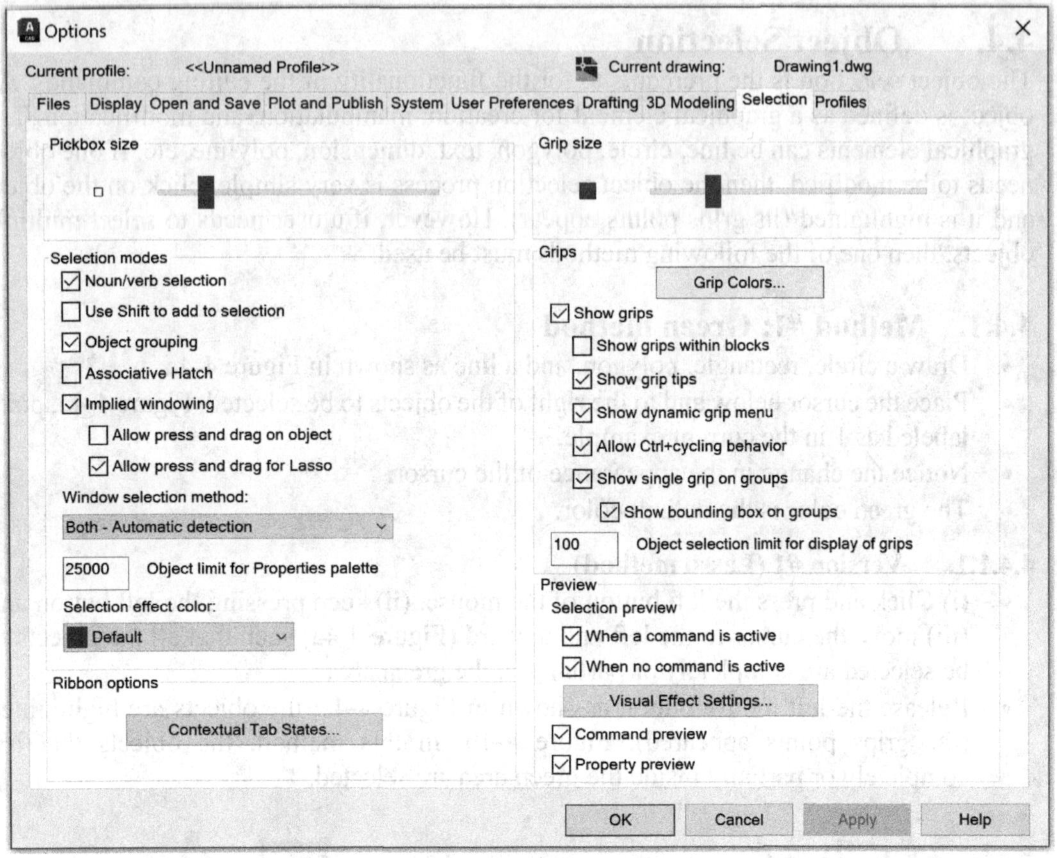

Figure 4-3a

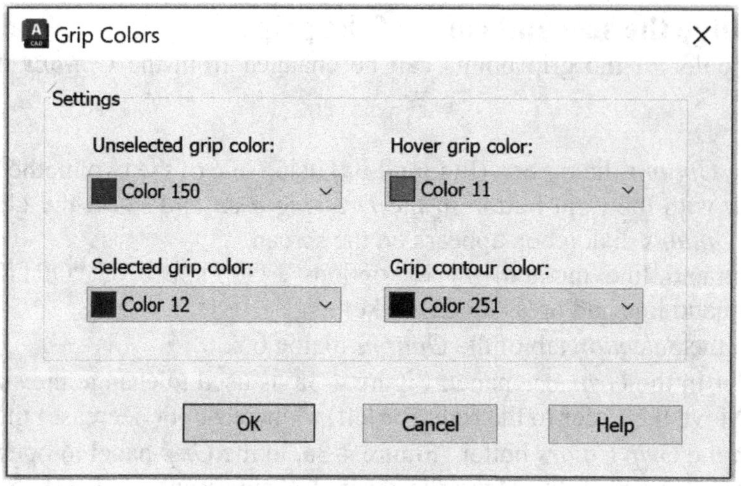

Figure 4-3b

4.4. Object Selection

The object selection is the prerequisite for the functionality of the editing commands. An object is defined as a graphical element for creation, manipulation, and modification. The graphical elements can be line, circle, polygon, text, dimension, polyline, etc. If one object needs to be modified, then the object selection process is very simple; click on the object and it is highlighted (its grips points appear). However, if a user needs to select multiple objects, then one of the following methods must be used.

4.4.1. Method #1: Green method

- Draw a circle, rectangle, polygon, and a line as shown in Figure 4-4a.
- Place the cursor below and to the right of the objects to be selected, Figure 4-4a, point labeled as 1 in the current example.
- Notice the change in the appearance of the cursor.
- The green color is the default color.

4.4.1.1. Version #1 (Lasso method)

- (i) Click and press the left button of the mouse, (ii) keep pressing the left button and (iii) move the cursor to the left and upward (Figure 4-4a) such that all the objects to be selected are completely or partially in the green area.
- Release the left mouse button as shown in Figure 4-4a; the objects are highlighted (the grips points appeared), Figure 4-4b. In this method, the objects that are completely or partially inside the green area are selected.

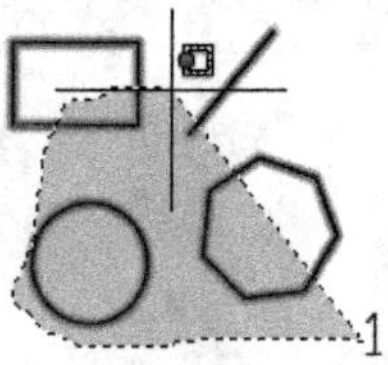

Figure 4-4a

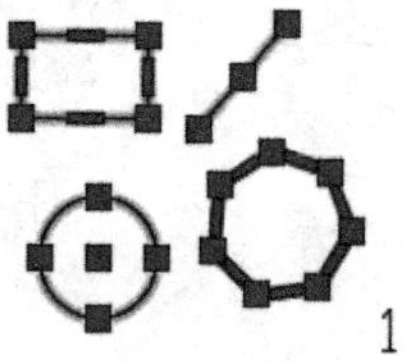

Figure 4-4b

4.4.1.2. Version #2 (Rectangle method)

- (i) Click the left button of the mouse and the prompt shown in Figure 4-4c appears; (ii) move the cursor to the left and upward (Figure 4-4c) such that all the objects to be selected are completely or partially in the green rectangle.
- Click the left button again as shown in Figure 4-4c. In this method, the objects that are completely or partially inside the green rectangle are selected.

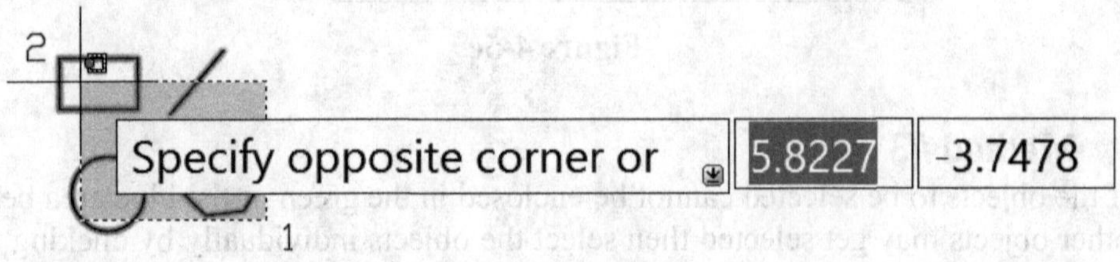

Figure 4-4c

4.4.2. Method #2: Blue method

- Draw a circle, rectangle, polygon, and a line as shown in Figure 4-5a.
- Place the cursor above and to the left of the objects to be selected, Figure 4-5a, point labeled as 2 in the current example.
- Notice the change in the appearance of the cursor.
- The blue color is the default color.

4.4.2.1. Version #1 (Lasso method)

- (i) Press the left button of the mouse, (ii) keep pressing the left button and (iii) move the cursor to the right and downward towards the point labeled as 1, such that all the objects to be selected are completely in the blue area.
- Release the left mouse button as shown in Figure 4-5a; the objects are highlighted (the grips points appeared), Figure 4-5b. In this method, the objects that are completely inside the blue area are selected.

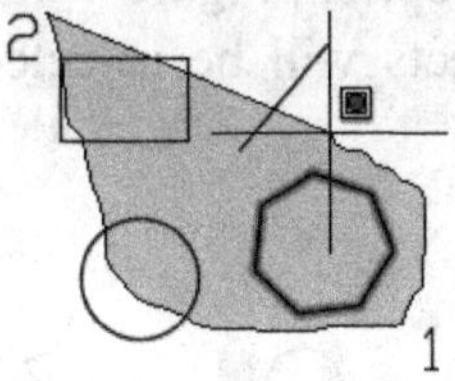

Figure 4-5a

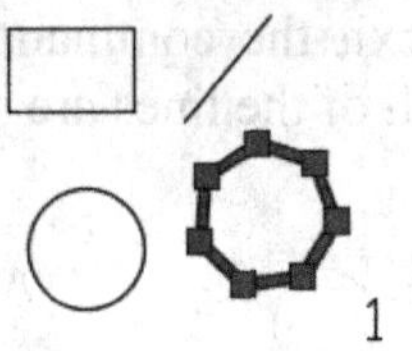

Figure 4-5b

4.4.2.2. Version #2 (Rectangle method)

- (i) Click the left button of the mouse and the prompt shown in Figure 4-5c appears, (ii) move the cursor to the right and downward (Figure 4-5c) such that all the objects to be selected are completely in the blue area.
- Click the left button again as shown in Figure 4-5c. In this method, the objects that are completely inside the blue area are selected, Figure 4-5d.

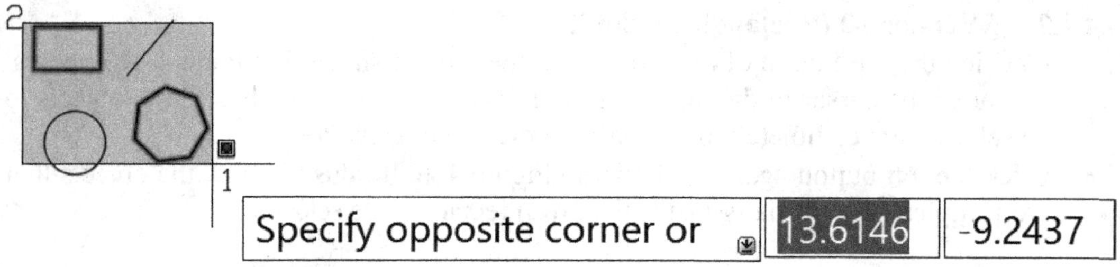

Figure 4-5c

4.4.3. Method #3

- If the objects to be selected cannot be enclosed in the green or the blue area because other objects may get selected then select the objects individually by clicking them, Figure 4-5e and Figure 4-5f.

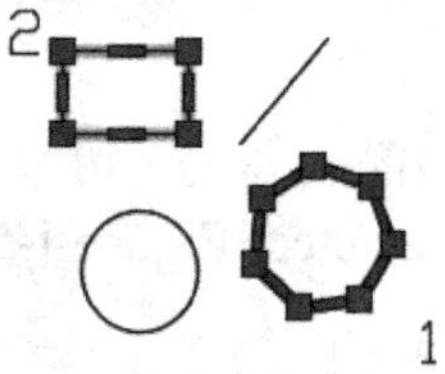

Figure 4-5d

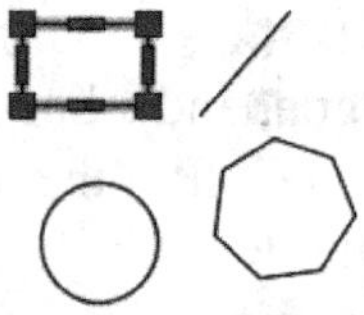

Figure 4-5e

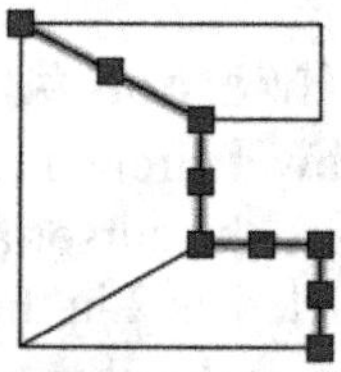

Figure 4-5f

4.5. Similar Object Selection

This command can select multiple similar objects in one activation of the command.

- Draw a few circles, lines, and texts objects as shown in Figure 4-4h.
- Select one of the objects (in the current example, one of the lines is selected) and press the right button of the mouse; an option list will appear, Figure 4-4g.
- From the option list, click on the *Select Similar* option, Figure 4-4g.
- This will exit the command, and similar objects will be selected; in the current example, all of the lines are selected.

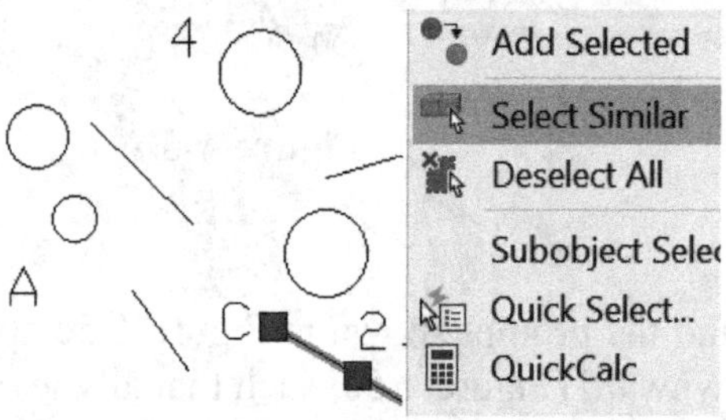

Figure 4-5g

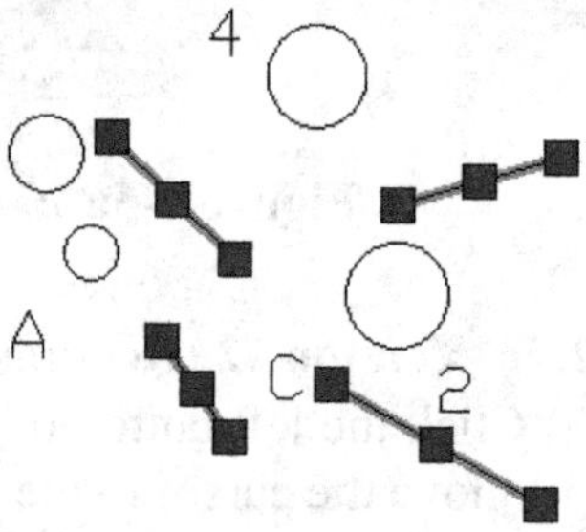

Figure 4-5h

4.6. Object De-Selection

Although object selection is the prerequisite for the functionality of the editing commands, the object de-selection is equally important. Figure 4-6a shows the selection of four objects. The user can de-select the entire selection by pressing the *Esc* key from the keyboard; Figure 4-6b shows the effect of pressing the *Esc* key. However, if the user wants to de-select a few objects from the set (for example wants to deselect the square), then hold the Shift key and click with the left button of the mouse on the desired object (the square in the example). The result is shown in Figure 4-6c.

Figure 4-6a

Figure 4-6b

Figure 4-6c

4.7. Zoom Capabilities

The zoom capabilities are used to change the magnification of the objects in the drawing area. The user accesses the zoom commands from the *View* tab and *Navigate* panel and clicks on the desired tool, Figure 4-7b. In the figure, the down-arrow key is pressed to display the various options. Notice the change in the appearance of the cursor when zoom commands are activated.

By default, the *Navigate* panel is hidden. Therefore, the user must first display the navigate panel using the three-step process listed here, Figure 4-7a. (i) Right click in the grey area after the last panel; (ii) click *Show Panels* option; and (iii) click *Navigate*. Figure 4-7b shows the addition of the *Navigate* panel.

4.7.1. Zoom window 

The *Zoom window* command is used to display the part of the drawing enclosed in a rectangular window. (i) Activate the *Zoom window* command by clicking the  button, Figure 4-7b. The prompt shown in Figure 4-8a appears. (ii) Click below and to the right of the drawing as shown in Figure 4-8a. The prompt shown in Figure 4-8b appears. (iii) Click above and to the left of the drawing as shown in Figure 4-8b. This exits the command and the object is zoomed in. The first point can be any of the four corners of the rectangular window; however, the second point must be the diagonally opposite corner.

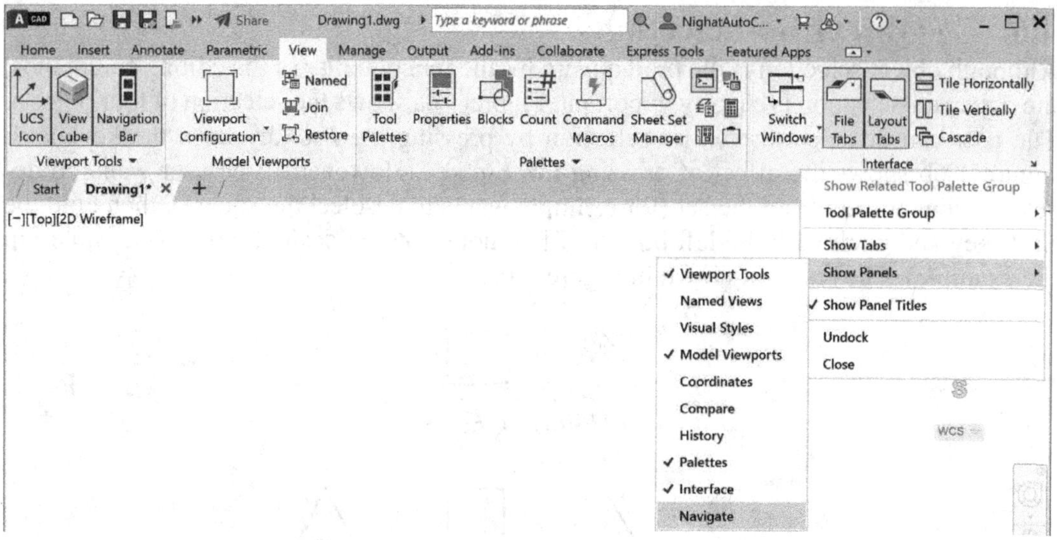

Figure 4-7a

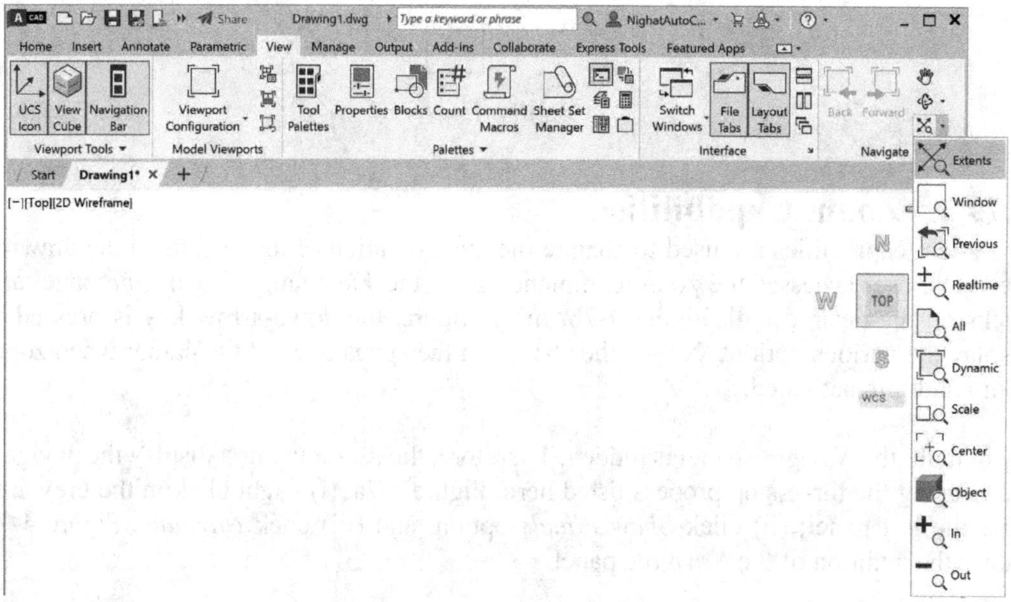

Figure 4-7b

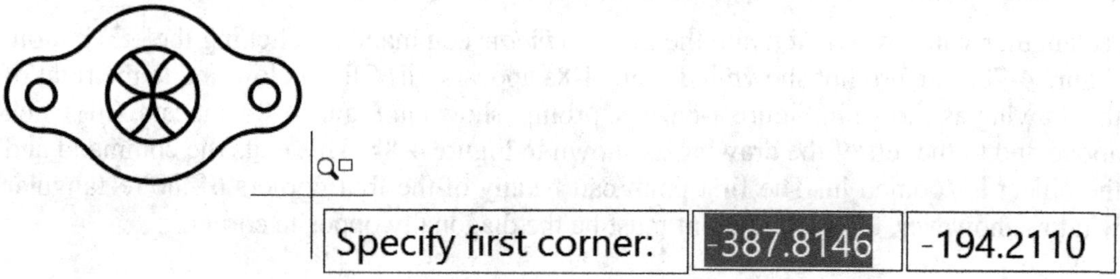

Figure 4-8a

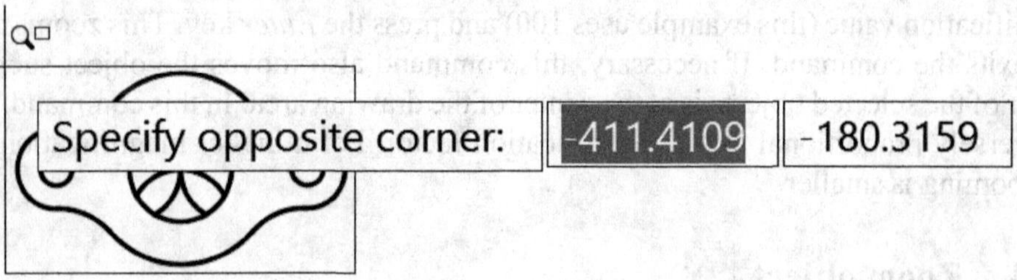

Figure 4-8b

4.7.2. Zoom scale

The *Zoom scale* command is used to zoom (in or out) using the scale factor. (i) Activate the *Zoom scale* command by clicking the button, Figure 4-7b. The prompt shown in Figure 4-9a appears. (ii) Specify the desired value. The value in Figure 4-9b (1.5x) makes every object in the drawing appear one and a half times as big as the original size. In Figure 4-9b the '*x*' implies that the scaling is relative to the current view. (iii) Figure 4-9c shows the original object whereas Figure 4-9d shows the scaled object.

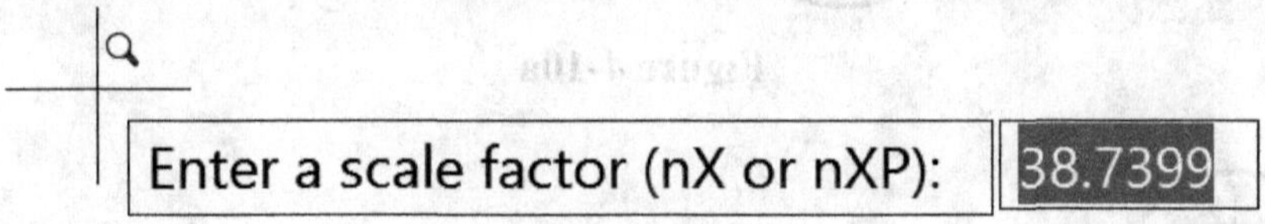

Figure 4-9a

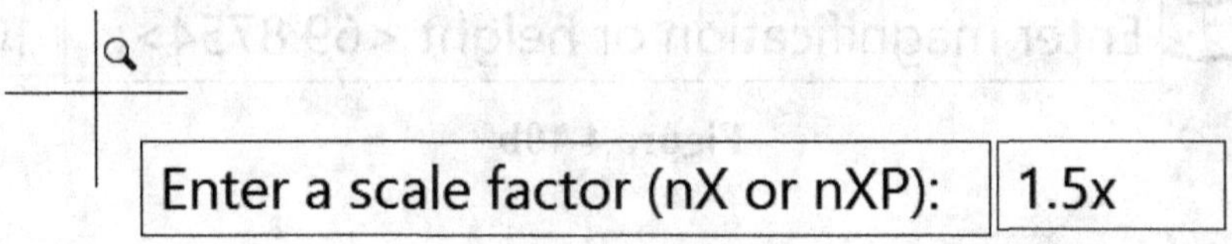

Figure 4-9b

Figure 4-9c

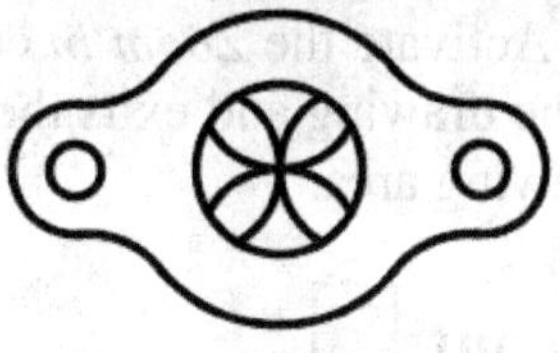

Figure 4-9d

4.7.3. Zoom center

The *Zoom center* command is used to zoom the center of the drawing using the scale factor. (i) Activate the *Zoom center* command by clicking the button, Figure 4-7b. The prompt shown in Figure 4-10a appears. (ii) Either specify the coordinates of the center of the desired object or click in the center. This example clicks at the center of the inner circle shown in Figure 4-10a. The prompt shown in Figure 4-10b appears. (iii) Specify the desired magnification value (this example uses 100) and press the *Enter* key. This zooms the object and exits the command. If necessary, this command also moves the object such that the center of the selected objects is at the center of the drawing area. In this command, zooming is inversely proportional to the magnification factor. For a higher magnification number, the zooming is smaller.

4.7.4. Zoom object

The *Zoom object* command is used to zoom the selected object(s). (i) Activate the *Zoom object* command by clicking the button, Figure 4-7b. The prompt to select object appears. (ii) Click on the desired object and press the *Enter* key. This will zoom-in the object and exit the command. The center of the object is at the center of the drawing area, and the object appears as large as possible.

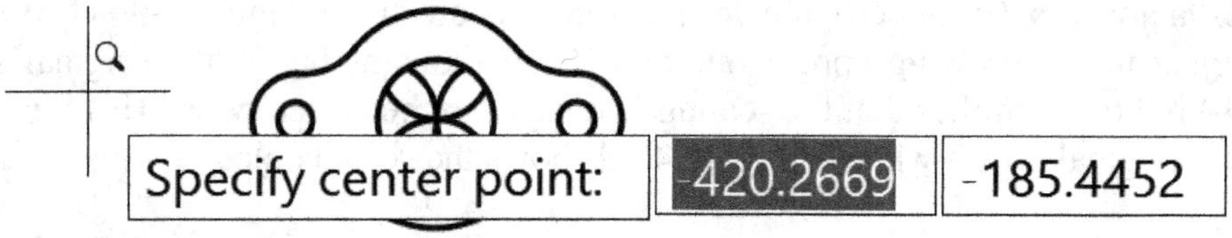

Figure 4-10a

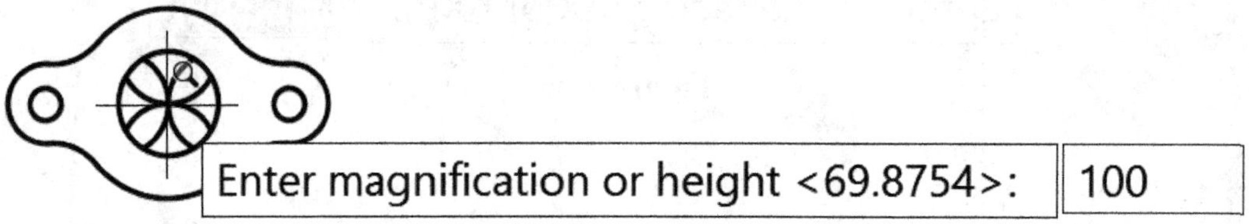

Figure 4-10b

4.7.5. Zoom in

The *Zoom in* command is used to make the size of the drawing appear twice as big as the current size. (i) Activate the *Zoom in* command by clicking the button, Figure 4-7b. This zooms in the drawing and exits the command. The center of the drawing stays in the center of the drawing area.

4.7.6. Zoom out

The *Zoom out* command is used to make the size of the drawing appear half of the current size. (i) Activate the *Zoom out* command by clicking the button, Figure 4-7b. This will zoom out the drawing and exit the command. The center of the drawing stays at the center of the drawing area.

4.7.7. Zoom-wheel

The *Zoom wheel* command is NOT available through the *Navigate* panel. This command is ONLY available through the command line. This command is used to relate the magnification with the wheel of the mouse. Type *Zoomwheel* on the command line and press the *Enter* key.

0: Move wheel forward for zoom-in and backward for zoom-out
1: Move wheel backward for zoom-in and forward for zoom-out

4.7.8. Zoom all

The *Zoom all* command is used to make every object in the drawing appear in the viewing area of the drawing. (i) Activate the *Zoom all* command by clicking the button, Figure 4-7b. This makes every object in the drawing appear in the viewing area of the drawing and exits the command. The center of the drawing stays in the center of the drawing area.

4.8. Pan

The pan capabilities are used to change the view without changing the viewing direction and /or magnification of the objects in the drawing. The user accesses the *Pan* command from the *View* tab and *Navigate* panel and clicks on the pan tool, Figure 4-11. Notice the change in the appearance of the cursor.

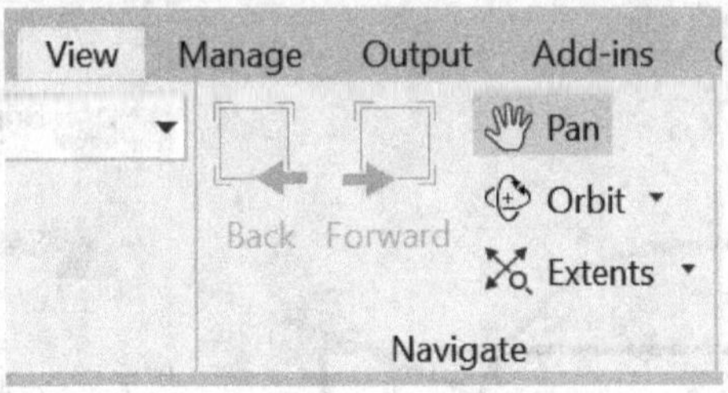

Figure 4-11

- The *Pan* command is activated as follows:
  1. Panel method: (i) From the *View* tab and *Navigate* panel, click on the pan tool.
  2. Command line method: Either type "pan", "Pan", or "PAN" and press the *Enter* key.
- The activation of the command changes the crosshairs to the palm appearance.
- Click at a point and keep pressing the left button of the mouse; this will change the palm appearance to .
- Click at the second point. Let d be the distance between the two clicks.
- Every object in the drawing is moved by distance d in the direction from the first point to the second point.
- Press *Esc* key on the keyboard to exit the command.

4.9. Draw Order

The draw order capabilities are used to change the relative positions of overlapping objects. To understand the *Draw order* commands, draw overlapping objects and change their color and LWT, Figure 4-12a. This example uses four overlapping objects of different colors and different line thickness. The draw-order capabilities are discussed in the remainder of this section.

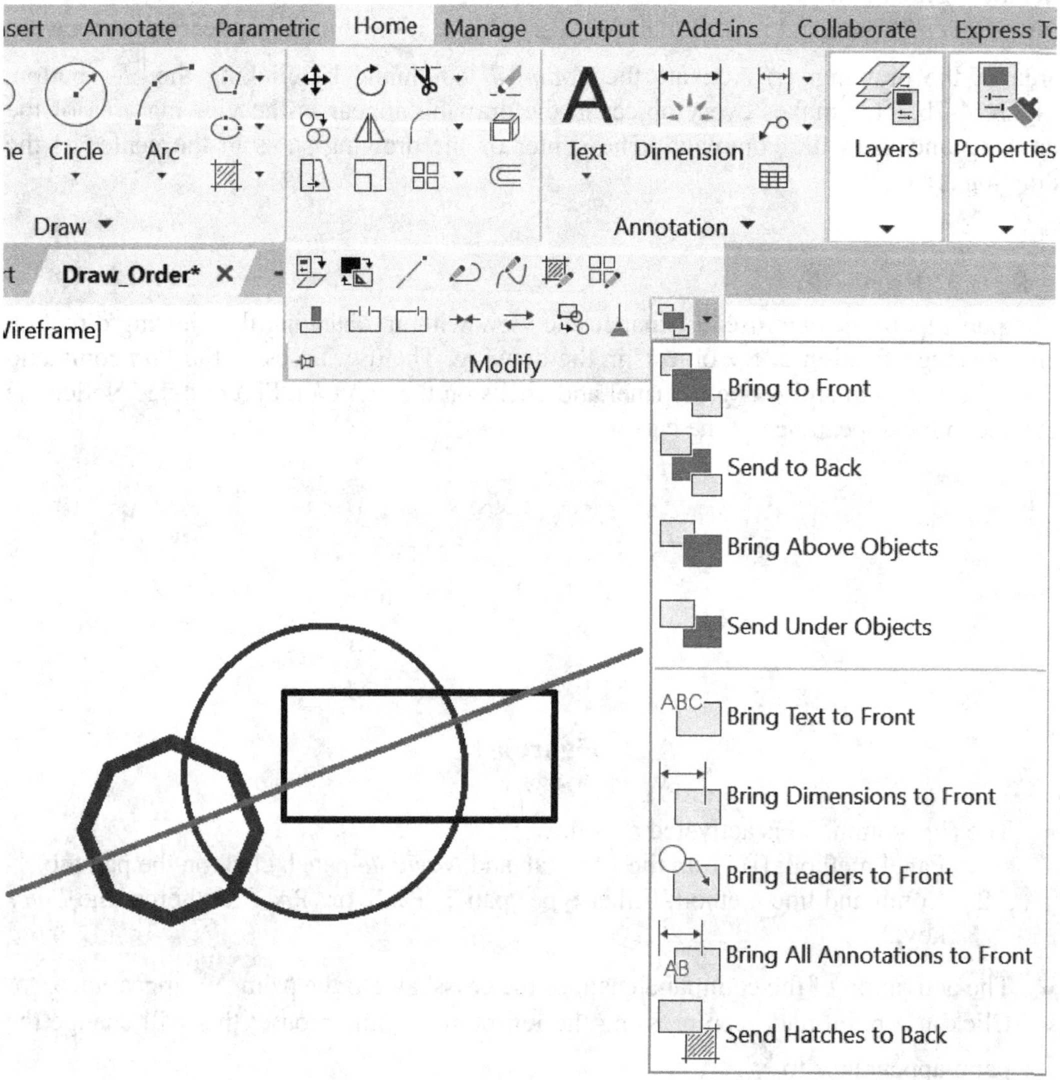

Figure 4-12a

4.9.1. Bring to front 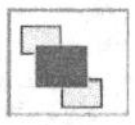

The *Bring to Front* command is used to bring the desired object in front of every other object.

- Select the desired object from the overlapping objects.

- The *Bring to Front* command is executed using one of the following methods:
  1. Panel method: (i) From the *Home* tab and *Modify* panel, Figure 4-12a, expand the *Draw order* drop-down menu, and select the *Bring to Front* tool. (ii) Click on the desired object, circle in the current example. (iii) Press the *Enter* key. This closes the list and brings the selected object to the front.
  2. Selection list method: (i) Click on the desired object, circle in the current example. (ii) Press the right button of the mouse. A selection list, Figure 4-12b, appears. (iii) Click on the desired option, *Bring to Front* in current example. This closes the list and brings the selected object to the front.

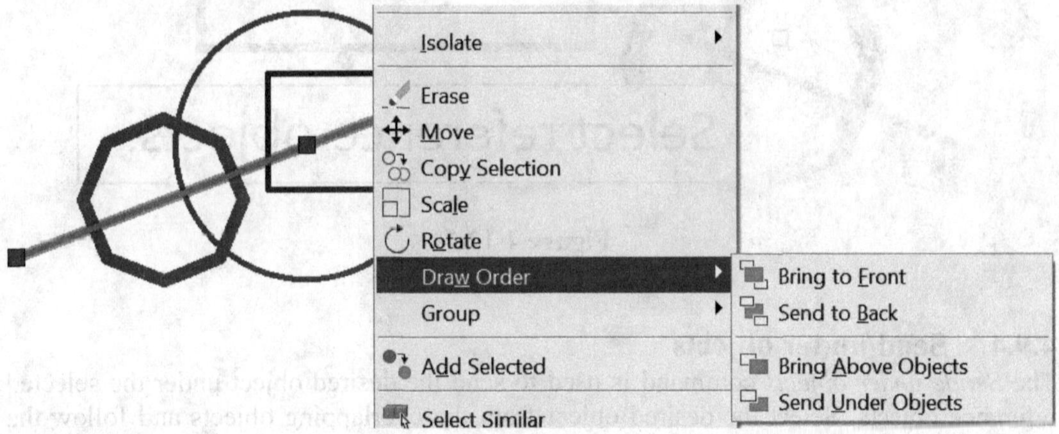

Figure 4-12b

4.9.2. Send to back 

The *Send to Back* command is used to send the desired object behind every other object. Select the desired object from the overlapping objects and follow the procedure discussed in *Bring to front* section.

4.9.3. Bring above objects 

The *Bring above objects* command is used to bring the desired object above the selected reference objects.

- Select the desired object from the overlapping objects.
- Activate the *Bring above objects* command using one of the following methods:
  1. Panel method: (i) From the *Home* tab and *Modify* panel, expand the *Draw order* drop-down menu, Figure 4-12a, and select *Bring above objects* tool. This closes the list and changes the prompt to select the reference objects, Figure 4-12c.
  2. Selection list method: (i) Click on the desired object. (ii) Press the right button of the mouse. A selection list, Figure 4-12b, appears. (iii) Click on *Bring above objects* tool. This closes the list and changes the prompt to select the reference objects, Figure 4-12c.
- Select the reference objects from the overlapping objects. In the current example, the circle and polygon are selected, Figure 4-12c,

- Press the *Enter* key from the keyboard. This will complete the command, and the desired object is placed above the reference objects.

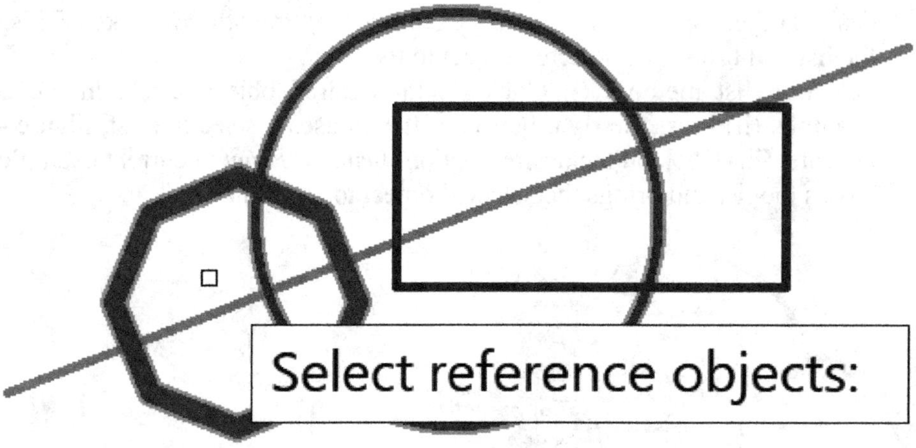

Figure 4-12c

4.9.4. Send under objects

The *Sende under objects* command is used to send the desired object under the selected reference objects. Select the desired object from the overlapping objects and follow the procedure discussed in *Send above objects* section.

4.10. Object Snap

The *Object Snap* command allows snapping at strategic points on the selected objects in the drawing area, for example, the end and mid points of a line, center and quadrant points of a circle, and point of intersection of two objects.

The *Drafting Setting* dialog box provides fourteen object snap modes. However, the user should select the modes related to the drawing objects in the current drawing. Turning *On* all the modes is NOT a good drawing practice.

4.10.1. Toggle object snap

Toggle the *Object snap* option using one of the following methods.

- Click the *Object Snap* button ( ) on the status bar.
- Press the *F3* key on the keyboard.
- (i) Bring the cursor on the *Object Snap* button of the status bar. (ii) Click the down-arrow key adjacent to the icon. This opens a selection list. (iii) Click on the *Object Snap Settings* option; the *Drafting Settings* dialog box will open, Figure 4-13a (the *Object Snap* tab selected). (iv) Finally, check the *Object Snap On* box on the dialog box.

- Type "dsettings" or "osnap" on the command line and press the *Enter* key. This opens the *Drafting Setting* dialog box with the *Object Snap* tab selected. Finally, check the *Object Snap On* box, Figure 4-13a.

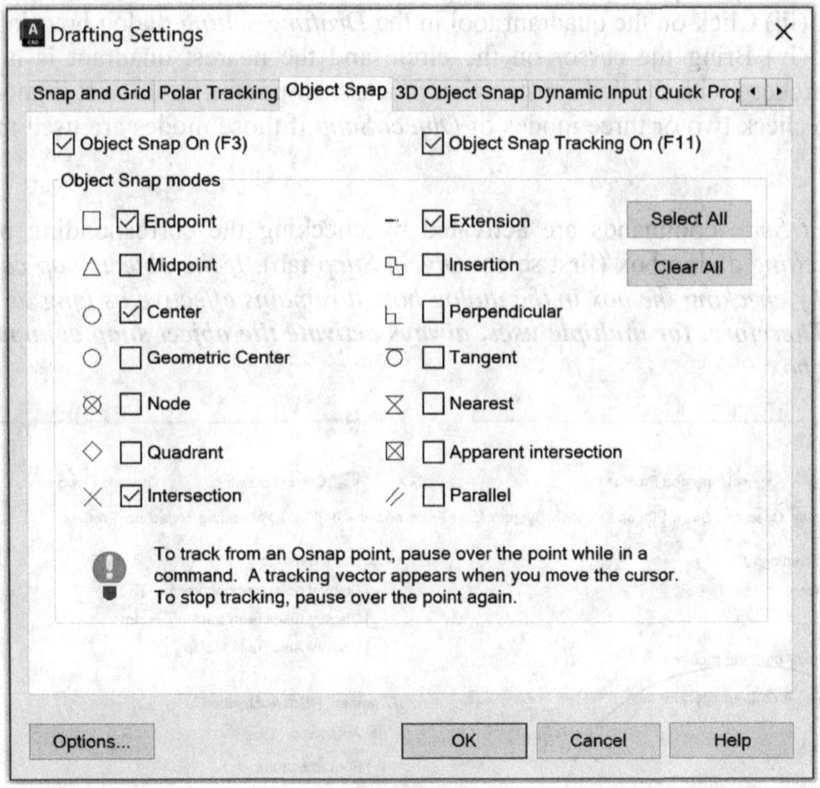

Figure 4-13a

The *Drafting Setting* dialog box provides fourteen object snap modes, Figure 4-13a. In order to distinguish various object snap points, AutoCAD provides different patterns for each mode. This dialog box can be open during the execution of a command from the status bar, too; (i) bring the cursor on the *Object Snap* button of the status bar; (ii) click the down-arrow key adjacent to the icon. This opens a selection list. (iii) Click on the *Object Snap Settings* option; the *Drafting Settings* dialog box with the *Object Snap* tab is selected.

4.10.2. Size and color of the object snap cursor

The user can change the size and color of the object snap cursor box. To change the size and color of the cursor box for the object snap, click on the *Options* (lower left corner) button in the *Drafting Setting* dialog box (Figure 4-13a) and the *Options* dialog box is opened. In the *Options* dialog box, select the *Drafting* tab, Figure 4-13b, and make the desired changes.

4.10.3. Object snap commands

Most of the *Object Snap* commands do not work independently but work in conjunction with other commands. For example, to draw a line starting at a quadrant point of a circle, use the following steps. (i) Activate the *Line* command. (ii) Activate the *object snap* command. (iii) Click on the quadrant tool in the *Drafting setting* dialog box (in the object snap tab). (iv) Bring the cursor on the circle and the nearest quadrant is highlighted. (v) Now, proceed with the line construction process. **Important points**: It is good drawing practice to check two or three modes of *Object Snap* if those modes are used most of the time.

The *Object Snap* commands are activated by checking the corresponding box in the *Drafting setting* dialog box (first select *Object Snap* tab). *If the object snap command is activated by checking the box in the dialog box, it remains effective as long as the box is checked.* ***Therefore, for multiple uses, always activate the object snap commands from the dialog box.***

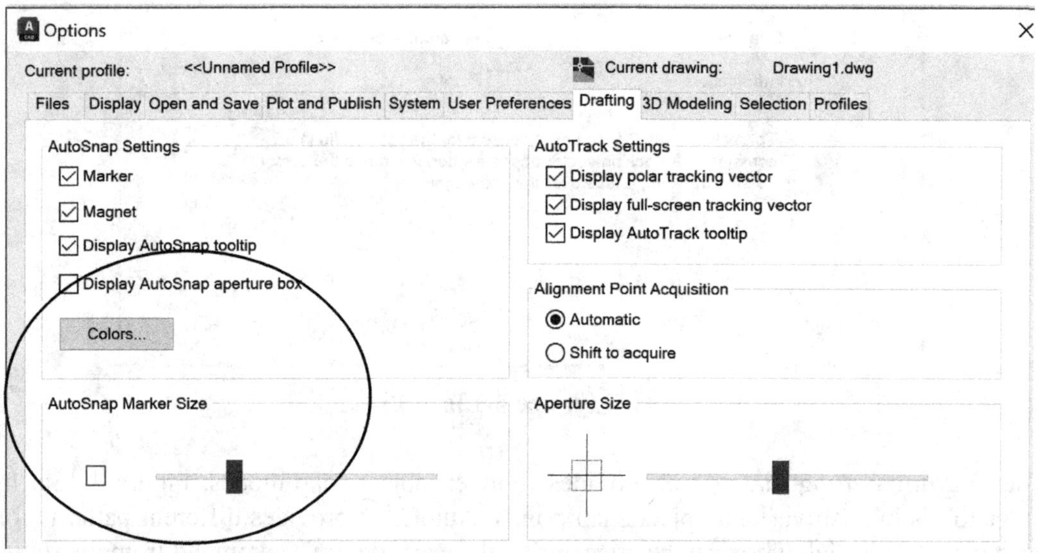

Figure 4-13b

4.10.3.1. Endpoint 

The object snap's *Endpoint* mode snaps to the closest endpoint of an existing entity, for example, ends of a line (Figure 4-14a), an arc (Figure 4-14b), and a polyline. The snap's point appears as a small square.

Example: Draw a circle with its center located at the endpoint of an existing line.

The solution drawing can be created by using the following steps:

1. Draw a line.
2. Activate the *Circle* command.
3. Activate the object snap command and check the *Endpoint* box from the *Drafting setting* dialog box.

4. Bring the cursor near the end of the line, Figure 4-14a; the end of the line is automatically highlighted.
5. Click at the highlighted endpoint.
6. Continue with the *Circle* command.

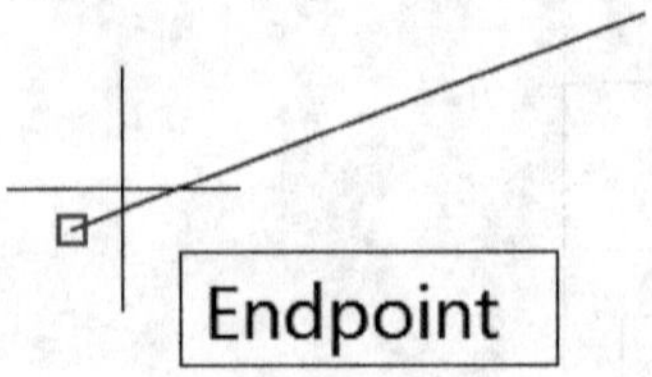

Figure 4-14a

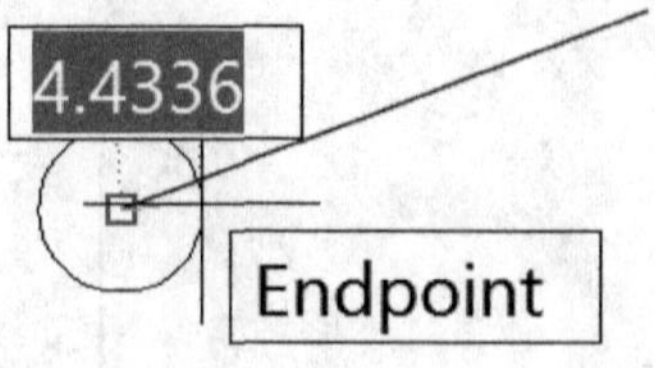

Figure 4-14b

4.10.3.2. Midpoint

The object snap's *Midpoint* mode snaps to the midpoint of an existing entity. For example, midpoint of a line (Figure 4-14c), an arc (Figure 4-14d), and a polyline. The snap's point appears as a small triangle.

Example: Draw a circle with its center located at the midpoint of an existing line.

The solution drawing can be created by using the following steps:
1. Draw a line.
2. Activate the *Circle* command.
3. Activate the object snap command and check the *Midpoint* box from the *Drafting setting* dialog box.
4. Bring the cursor near the mid of the line, Figure 4-14c; the midpoint of the line is automatically highlighted.
5. Click at the highlighted midpoint.
6. Continue with the *Circle* command.

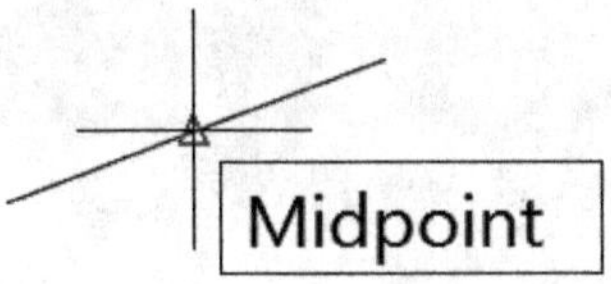

Figure 4-14c

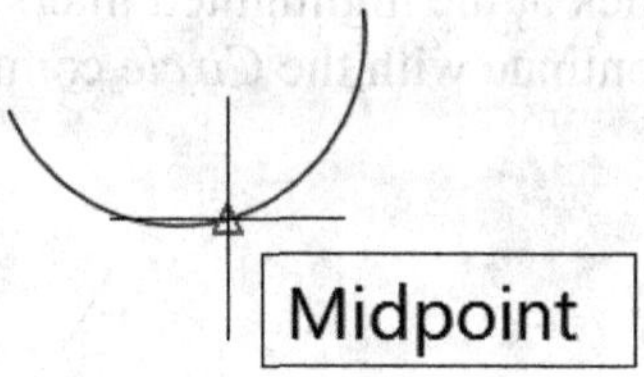

Figure 4-14d

4.10.3.3. Node

The object snap's *Node* mode snaps to a point, Figure 4-15a. The figure shows three points. The snap's point appears as a small circle.

Example: Draw a circle with its center located at a given point.

The solution drawing can be created by using the following steps:
1. Draw a point.
2. Activate the *Circle* command.

3. Activate the object snap command and check the *Node* box from the *Drafting setting* dialog box.
4. Bring the cursor near the point, Figure 4-15; the point is automatically highlighted.
5. Click at the highlighted point.
6. Continue with the *Circle* command.

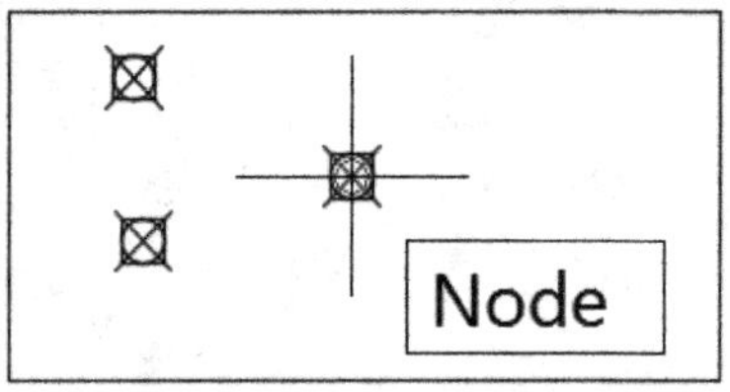

Figure 4-15a

4.10.3.4. Intersection

The object snap's *Intersection* mode snaps to the intersection of two or more existing entities (arc, circle, line, polyline combination), Figure 4-15b. The figure shows the intersection of a circle and a line segment. The snap's point appears as a small x mark.

Example: Draw a circle with its center located at the intersection of a circle and a line.

The solution drawing can be created by using the following steps:

1. Draw a circle and a line.
2. Activate the *Circle* command.
3. Activate the object snap command and check the *Intersection* box from the *Drafting setting* dialog box.
4. Bring the cursor near the intersection of the circle and the line, Figure 4-15b; the intersection point is automatically highlighted.
5. Click at the highlighted intersection.
6. Continue with the *Circle* command.

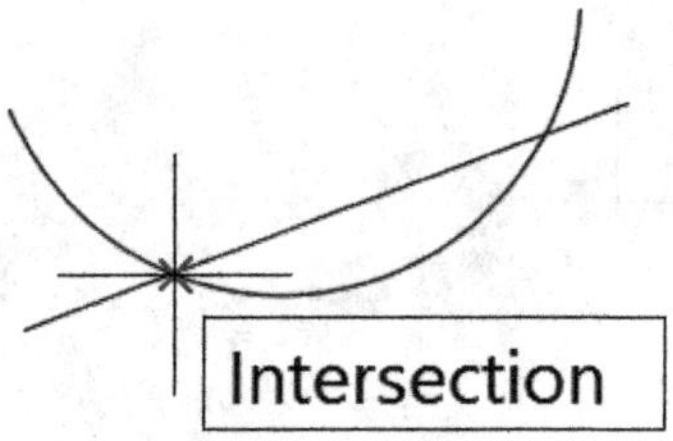

Figure 4-15b

4.10.3.5. Extension

The object snap's *Extension* mode creates a temporary extension of the object on its natural path. Figure 4-16a, Figure 4-16b, and Figure 4-16c show the extension of a circular arc, an elliptical arc, and a straight line, respectively. The snap's point appears as a small x mark.

Example: Draw a circle with its center located at the extension point of an object.

The solution drawing can be created by using the following steps:

1. Draw the object (circular arc, elliptical arc, and a straight line).
2. Activate the *Circle* command.
3. Activate the object snap command and check the *Extension* box from the *Drafting setting* dialog box.
4. Bring the cursor near the end of the object and move the cursor on the natural path of the object, Figure 4-16a (circular arc), Figure 4-16b (parabolic arc), and Figure 4-16c (line).
5. The extension point is automatically highlighted.
6. Extend the object to the desired point.
7. Click at the extended point.
8. Continue with *Circle* command.

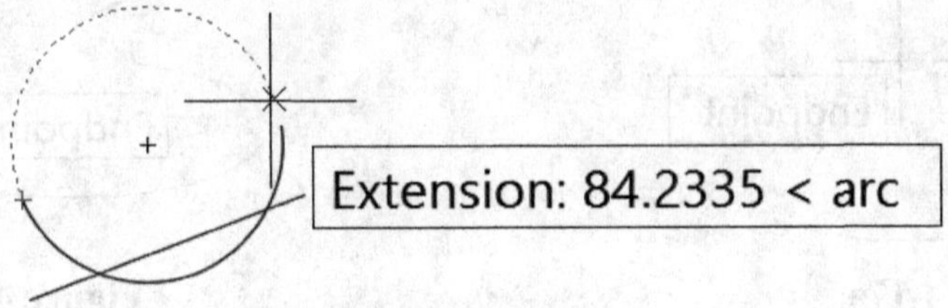

Figure 4-16a

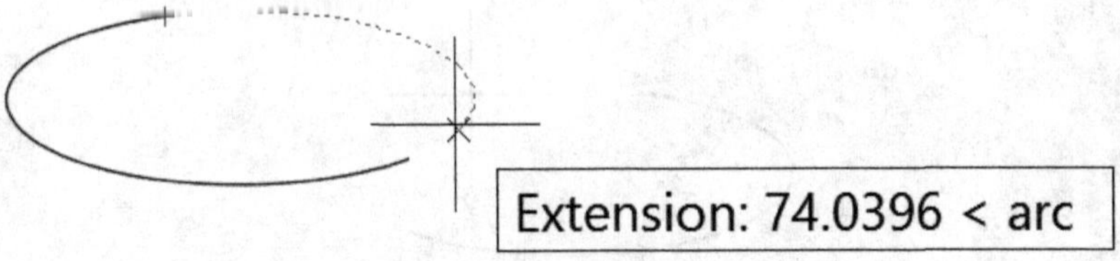

Figure 4-16b

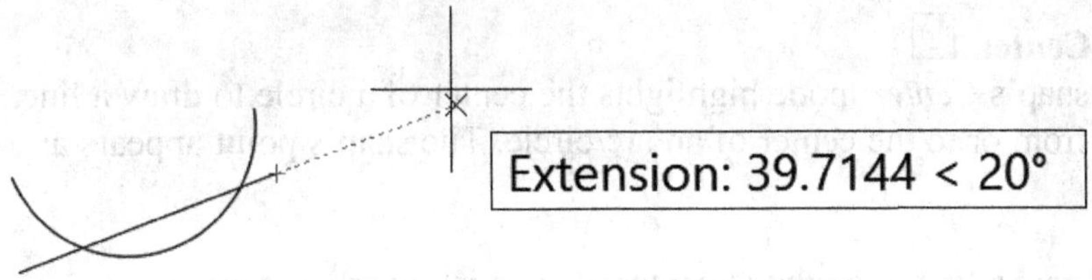

Figure 4-16c

4.10.3.6. Apparent intersection

The object snap's *Apparent Intersection* mode snaps to the imaginary intersection of the two existing entities that would intersect if they were extended along their natural paths, Figure 4-17b. The snap's point appears as a small x mark.

Example: Draw a circle at the apparent intersection of a line and parabolic arc.

The solution drawing can be created by using the following steps:

1. Draw a line and parabolic arc as shown in Figure 4-17a.
2. Activate the object snap command and check the *Apparent Intersection* and *Endpoint* commands box from the *Drafting setting* dialog box.
3. Activate the *Circle* command.
4. Bring the cursor on the line and its endpoint appears, Figure 4-17a.
5. Bring the cursor on the arc and its endpoint appears, Figure 4-17b; also, a small '+' mark appears at the selected end of the first line.
6. Move the cursor towards the apparent intersection of the two lines and a small 'x' mark appears at the apparent intersection, Figure 4-17c.
7. Click at the apparent intersection.
8. Continue with the *Circle* command.

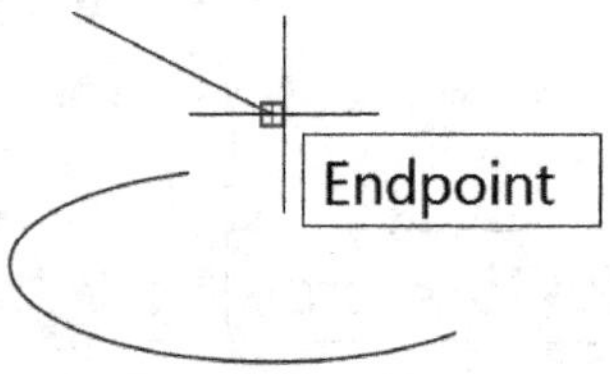

Figure 4-17a

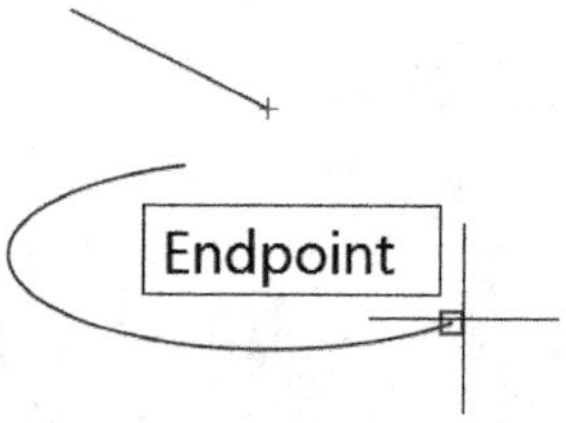

Figure 4-17b

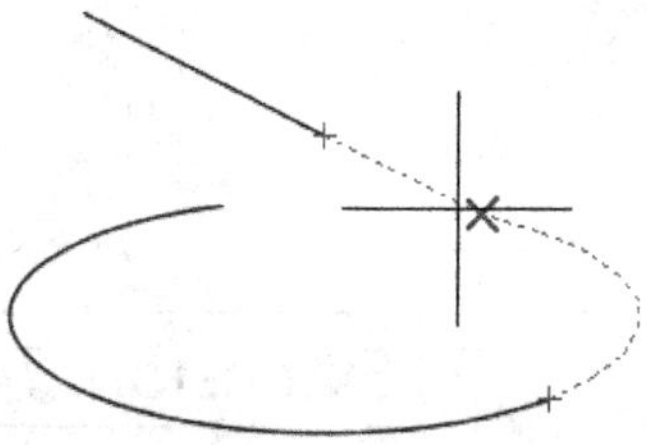

Figure 4-17c

4.10.3.7. Center

The object snap's *Center* mode highlights the center of a circle to draw a line, arc, circle, and ellipse from or to the center of an arc/circle. The snap's point appears as a small plus sign.

Example: Draw a line through the center of an existing arc or a circle.

The solution drawing can be created by using the following steps:

1. Draw an arc or a circle.
2. Activate the *Line* command.
3. Activate the object snap command and check the *Center* box from the *Drafting setting* dialog box.
4. Bring the cursor on the circumference of the circle, Figure 4-18a; the center of the circle is automatically selected.
5. Click at the highlighted center.
6. Continue with *Line* command.

4.10.3.8. Quadrant

The object snap's *Quadrant* mode is used to snap directly to one of the quadrants of an existing arc or a circle. The snap's point appears as a small diamond mark.

Example: Draw a line between two quadrants of a circle as follows:

The solution drawing can be created by using the following steps:

1. Draw a circle.
2. Activate the *Line* command.
3. Activate the object snap command and check the *Quadrant* box from the *Drafting setting* dialog box.
4. Bring the cursor on the circumference of the circle (Figure 4-18b); the closest quadrant is highlighted.
5. Click at the highlighted quadrant.
6. Continue with *Line* command.
7. If in the *Drafting setting* dialog box both the *Center* and *Quadrant* boxes are checked, then the center and the closed quadrant are highlighted as the cursor is moved on the circumference, Figure 4-18c.

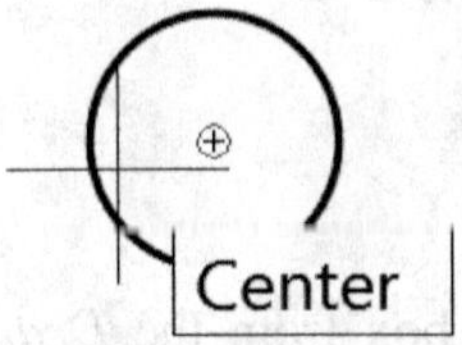

Figure 4-18a

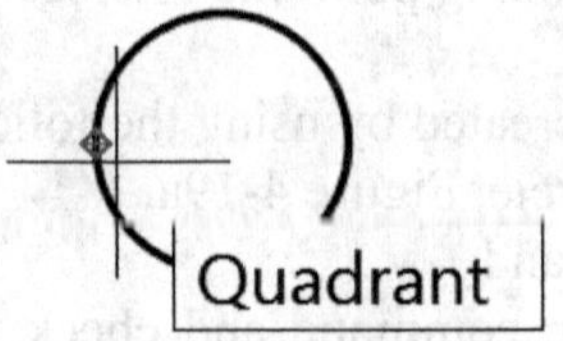

Figure 4-18b

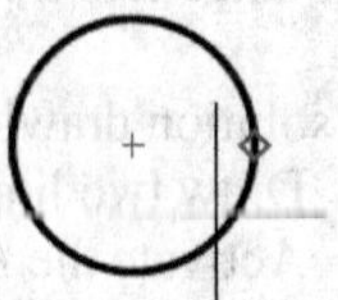

Figure 4-18c

4.10.3.9. Geometric center

In AutoCAD terminology, the *Geometric Center* is the centroid or center of area of closed polylines or polygons. The object snap's *Geometric Center* mode highlights the geometric center of a closed polyline to draw a line, arc, circle, and ellipse from or to the center of the closed polyline. The snapped point appears as a small asterisk enclosed in a circle. Note: Geometric center command does not highlight the center of a circle.

Example: Draw a line through the center of existing closed polylines or polygons.

The solution drawing can be created by using the following steps:

1. Draw closed polylines and polygons as shown in Figure 4-18d, Figure 4-18e, and Figure 4-18f.
2. Activate the *Line* command.
3. Activate the object snap command and check the *Geometric Center* box from the *Drafting setting* dialog box.
4. Bring the cursor on the boundary of the closed polyline and the centroid of the selected object is automatically selected, Figure 4-18d, Figure 4-18e, and Figure 4-18f.
5. Click at the highlighted geometric center.
6. Continue with *Line* command.

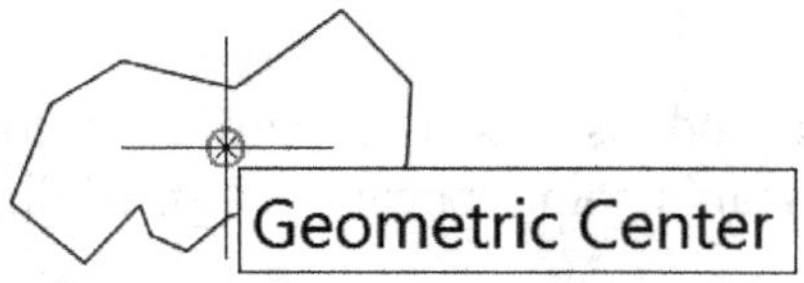

Figure 4-18d

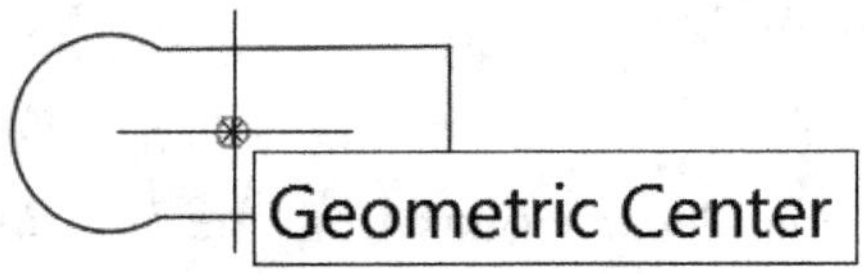

Figure 4-18e

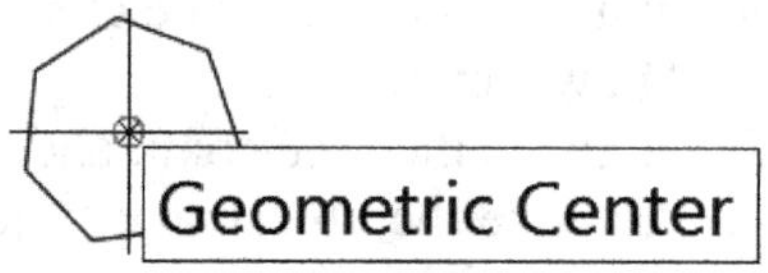

Figure 4-18f

4.10.3.10. Tangent 

The object snap's *Tangent* mode is used to draw an object tangent to an existing arc or a circle. The snap's point appears as a small circle with a horizontal line on top.

Example: Draw a line (the line's grip points are displayed in Figure 4-19a) with the starting point tangent to a circle and ending point the intersection of two lines.

The solution drawing can be created by using the following steps:

1. Draw two lines and a circle, Figure 4-19a.
2. Activate the *Line* command.
3. Activate the object snap command and check the *Tangent* box from the *Drafting setting* dialog box.
4. Bring the cursor on the circumference of the circle, Figure 4-19a. The point at the cursor location is highlighted.
5. Click for the start of the line.
6. The starting point or tangent is called deferred, Figure 4-19a, because this is not the actual start of the line. If the cursor is moved around the circumference, then the start point moves, too (Figure 4-19b).

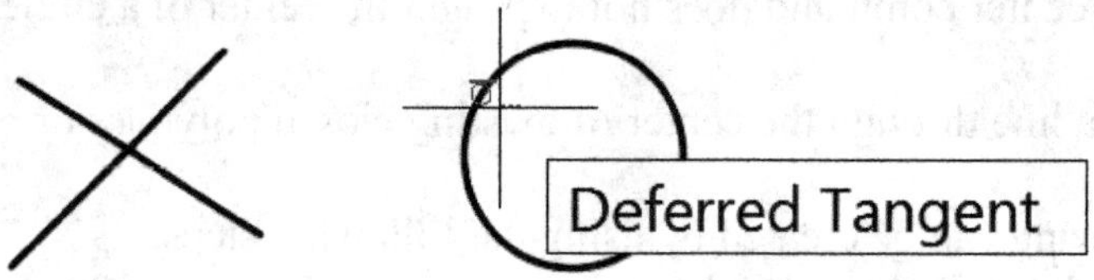

Figure 4-19a

7. The location of the start point of the tangent is determined by the location of the endpoint.
8. Click at the intersection of the two lines for the endpoint of the line under construction. Notice how the starting point has moved, Figure 4-19c.

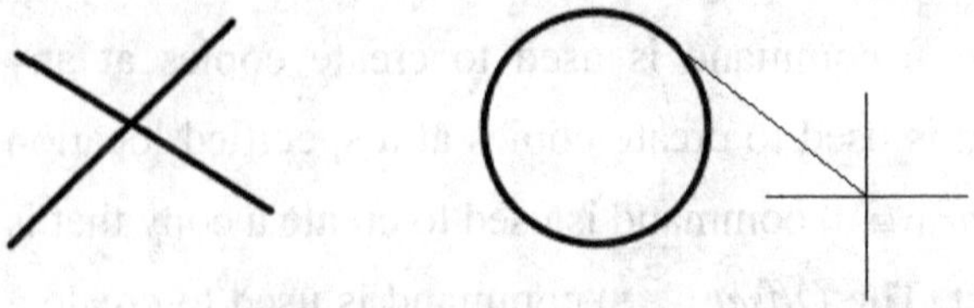

Figure 4-19b

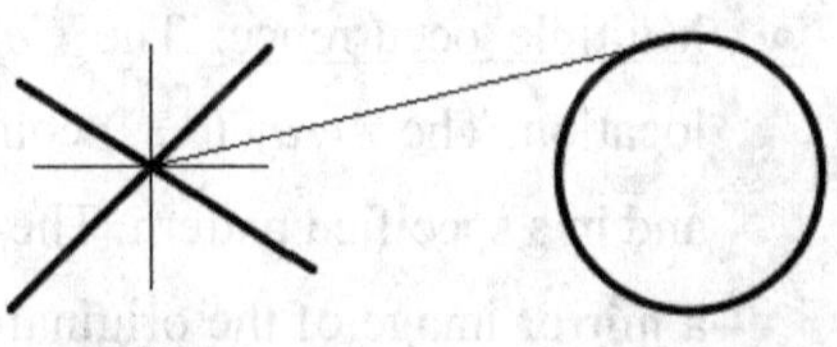

Figure 4-19c

4.10.3.11. Perpendicular

The object snap's *Perpendicular* mode is used to draw a line perpendicular to an existing object. The snap's point appears as two small lines intersecting at 90° and parallel to the World coordinates system.

Example: Draw a line perpendicular to another line.

The solution drawing can be created by using the following steps:

1. Draw a line.
2. Activate the *Line* command.
3. Activate the object snap command and check the *Perpendicular* box from the *Drafting setting* dialog box.
4. Bring the cursor on the line. The point at the cursor location is highlighted.
5. Click for the start of the line.
6. The starting point is called deferred, Figure 4-20a, because this is not the actual start of the line. The location of the starting point of the perpendicular depends on the location of the ending point of the perpendicular. If the cursor is moved on the line then the starting point also moves, Figure 4-20b.

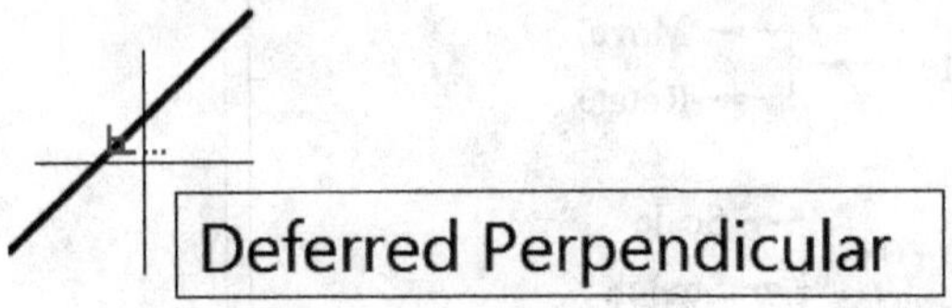

Figure 4-20a

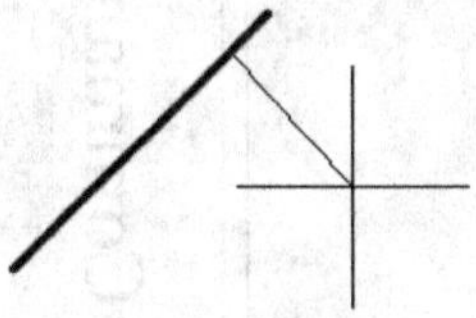

Figure 4-20b

4.11. The Editing Commands

This section introduces the editing commands discussed in the remainder of this chapter. Based on the command functionality, Figure 4-21 shows the classification of the editing command.

- Correction: Most of the commands are obvious from their names. The *Cancel* command is used to exit the currently active command and the *Erase* ( ) command is used to erase the selected object(s). The *Oops* command is used to restore the object(s) deleted by the last erase command. The *Undo* ( ) command is used to reverse the effect of the one or more previous commands. The *Redo* ( ) command is used to reverse the effect of one or more previous *Undo* commands.

- Multiple occurrence: The *Copy* ( ) command is used to create copies at any location. The *Array* ( ) command is used to create copies at a specified location and in a specified pattern. The *Mirror* ( ) command is used to create a copy that is a mirror image of the original object. The *Offset* ( ) command is used to create a smaller or larger copy inside or outside the original object.
- Relocate: The *Move* ( ) command is used to move the selected object to a new location. The *Rotate* ( ) command is used to rotate the object; the entire object is rotated (relocated) except the point of rotation.
- Resize: The *Scale* ( ) command is used to enlarge or shrink an object. The *Stretch* ( ) command is used to stretch the selected part of the object.

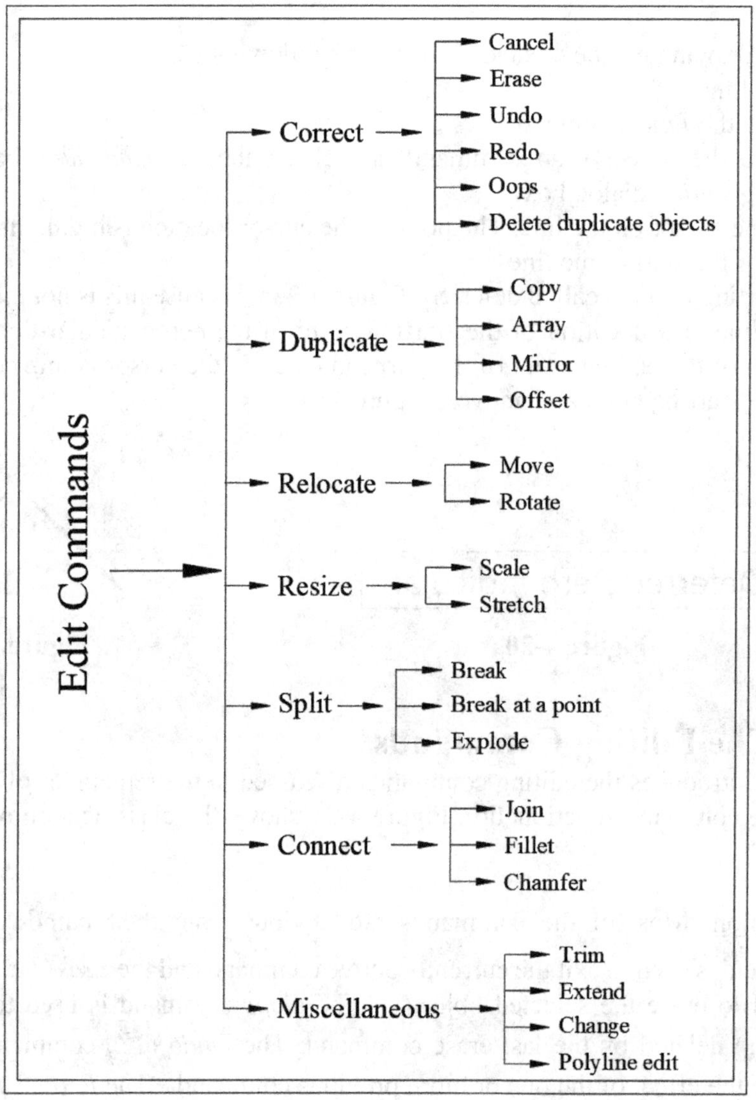

Figure 4-21

- Split: The *Break* () command is used to break the selected object between two points. The *Break at a point* () command is used to break the selected object at a single point. The *Explode* () command is used to break the selected object into its basic components.
- Object Connection: The *Join* () command is used to connect multiple linear or curved objects to create a single object. The *Fillet* () command is used to connect two objects with an arc of the specified radius such that the arc is tangent to both the objects. The *Chamfer* () command is used to bevel the corners of objects or connect two non-parallel objects with a straight line.
- Miscellaneous: The *Delete duplicate objects* () command is used to retain one object if multiple overlapping objects exist. The *Trim* () and the *Extend* () commands are used to trim and extend the edges of an object to meet the selected object, respectively. The *Polyline edit* () command is used to edit a polyline.

4.12. Cancel

A user of AutoCAD can cancel any active command. If the user has activated a command intentionally or unintentionally and needs to exit without completing it, then simply press the *Esc* key on the keyboard and the command is canceled.

4.13. Erase

The *Erase* command is used to delete the selected objects from the drawing. A user can delete one or more objects using the methods discussed in this section.

4.13.1. Erase one object

4.13.1.1. Using delete key

- Click on the object to be deleted and the object is highlighted (that is, its grips points appear), Figure 4-22a.
- Press the *Delete* key on the keyboard, and the selected object is erased.

4.13.1.2. Using Erase tool

- The *Erase* command is activated using one of the following methods:
  1. Panel method: From the *Home* tab and *Modify* panel select the *Erase* tool.
  2. Command line method: Type "erase", "Erase", or "ERASE" in the command line and press the *Enter* key.

- The *Erase* command can be used in two ways.
  Method #1:

- o Click on the object to be deleted, Figure 4-22a.
- o Activate the *Erase* tool.
- o The activation of the command erases the selected object.

Method #2:

- o Activate the *Erase* tool.
- o The *Select objects* prompt appears, Figure 4-22b.
- o Click on the object to be deleted, Figure 4-22b.
- o **Note:** The object to be deleted is faded to light gray color.
- o Press the *Enter* key or press the right button of the mouse to complete the erase process.

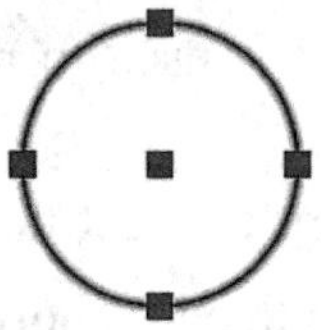

Figure 4-22a

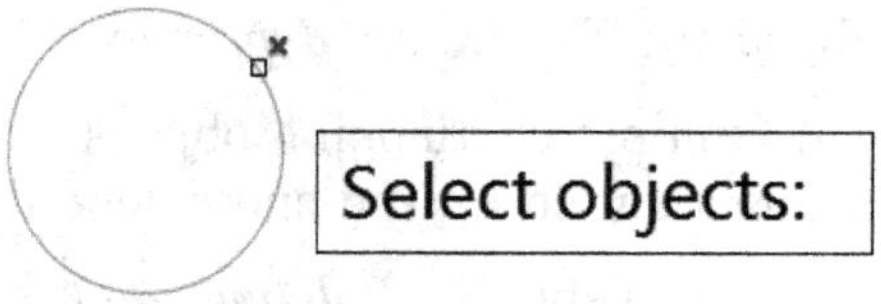

Figure 4-22b

4.13.2. Erase multiple objects simultaneously

Multiple objects can be erased using the same procedure as used for erasing one object. The main difference is instead of selecting one object at a time, select multiple objects simultaneously using selection methods discussed earlier.

4.14. Undo

The *Undo* command is used to reverse the effect of one or more of the previous commands. However, the commands such as *Plot*, *Save*, *Open*, *Export* cannot be undone.

4.14.1. Undo one command

The following methods of undo are available during the activation of another command. For example, if a user is drawing a polyline, then the previous segment can be deleted using one of the two following methods.

- Hold the *Ctrl* key and press the '*z*' key on the keyboard. The most recent command is undone.
- Press the '*u*' or '*U*' key on the keyboard and press the *Enter* key. The most recent command is undone.

4.14.2. Undo several commands

The following methods of undo are available only if none of the other commands are active.

- Command line method: (i) Type "undo", "Undo", or "UNDO" in the command line and press the *Enter* key. The prompt shown in Figure 4-23a appears. (ii) Enter the number of commands to be undone. (iii) Press the *Enter* key.

- Tool bar method: (i) Click the down-arrow of the *Undo* tool ( ) located on the upper left corner of the interface, Figure 4-23b. A drop-down list appears. (ii) Click the commands to be undone. The figure shows the selection of three commands.

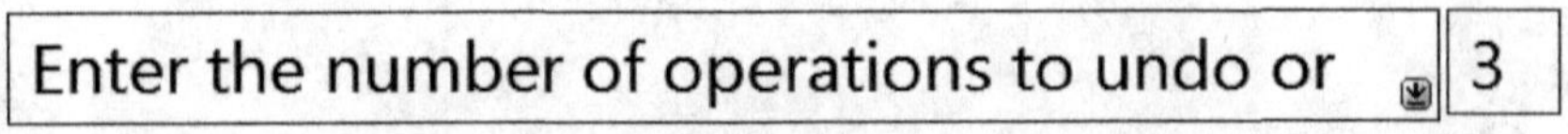

Figure 4-23a

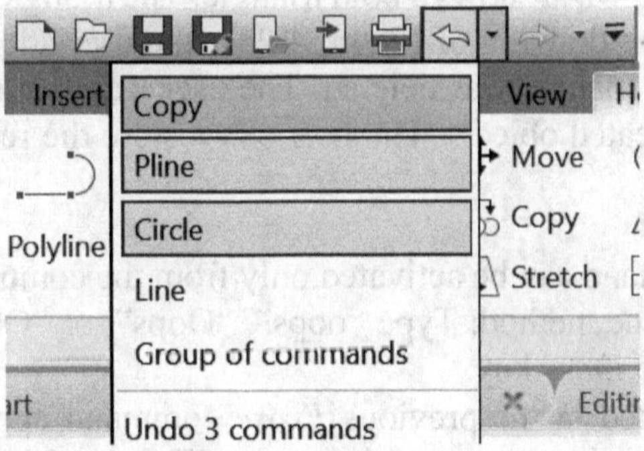

Figure 4-23b

4.15. Redo

The *Redo* command is used to reverse the effect of one or more previous *Undo* commands. However, the commands must be activated immediately after the *Undo* command, Figure 4-23c.

4.15.1. Redo one command

Hold the *Ctrl* key and press the '*y*' key on the keyboard. The most recent *Undo* command is redone.

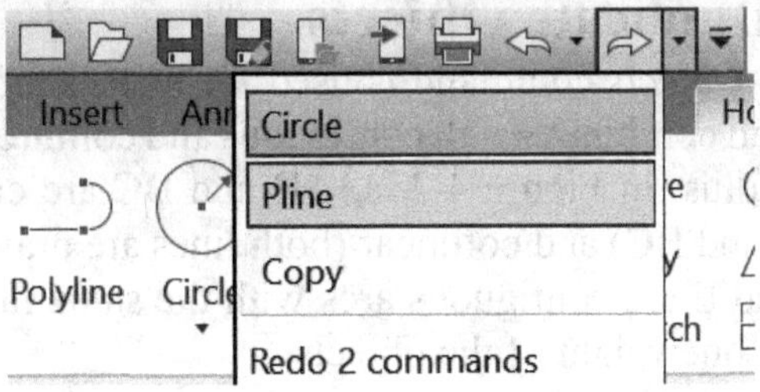

Figure 4-23c

4.15.2. Redo several commands

The following method of redo is available only if none of the other commands are active.

- Command line method: Type "redo", "Redo", or "REDO" in the command line and press the *Enter* key.

- Tool bar method: (i) Click the down-arrow of the *Undo* tool () located on the upper left corner of the interface. A drop-down list appears. (ii) Click the commands to be redone.

4.16. Oops

The *Oops* command is used to restore only object(s) deleted from the last *Erase* command. The drawing of Figure 4-24a shows a bold triangle. The triangle is erased from the drawing of Figure 4-24b. In the drawing of Figure 4-24c, the user added a few more objects and realized that the bold triangle was deleted. The user wants to restore the triangle without deleting the newly created objects. The user can restore the recently deleted object using the *Oops* command.

- The *Oops* command can be activated only from the command line.
  1. Command line method: Type "oops", "Oops", or "OOPS" in the command line and press the *Enter* key.
- The object deleted in the previous *Erase* command appears on the screen. In the example, the triangle appears on the screen, Figure 4-24d.

Figure 4-24a

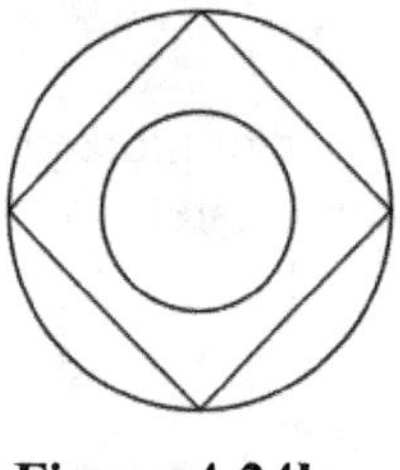

Figure 4-24b

Figure 4-24c

Figure 4-24d

4.17. Delete Duplicate Objects 

The *Delete Duplicate Objects* command is used for housekeeping. This command erases overlapping objects and combines small contiguous and collinear line, polyline, contiguous arcs with the same radius. In Figure 4-25a, AB and BC are contiguous (that is, B is the common point in AB and BC) and collinear (both lines are drawn at the same angle) lines. In Figure 4-25b, D and E are contiguous arcs with the same radius. Notice the difference in color, linetype, and lineweight of the objects.

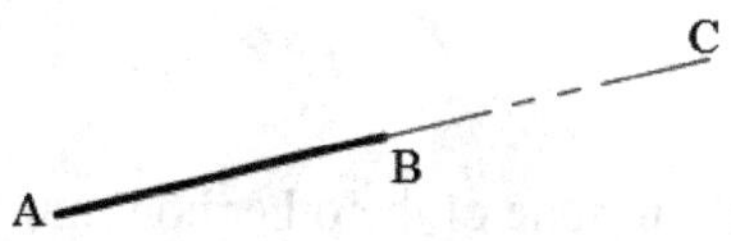

Figure 4-25a

Figure 4-25b

- The *Delete Duplicate Objects* command can be activated using one of the following methods:
  1. Panel method: From the *Home* tab and *Modify* panel select the *Delete Duplicate Objects* tool.
  2. Command line method: Type "overkill", "Overkill", or "OVERKILL" in the command line and press the *Enter* key.

- The activation of the command leads to the object selection prompt. Use one of the object selection methods discussed earlier, Figure 4-25c. Finally, press the *Enter* key to complete the object selection. This completes the object selection process and opens the *Delete Duplicate Objects* dialog box, Figure 4-25d.

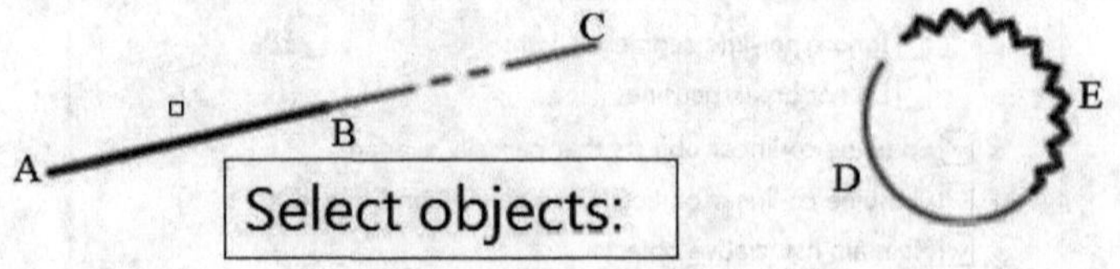

Figure 4-25c

- *Delete Duplicate Objects* dialog box: The self-explanatory dialog box is shown in Figure 4-25e. The outcome of the command is shown in Figure 4-25d; notice the color, linetype, and lineweight of the object. The resultant object adopts to the properties of the first component.

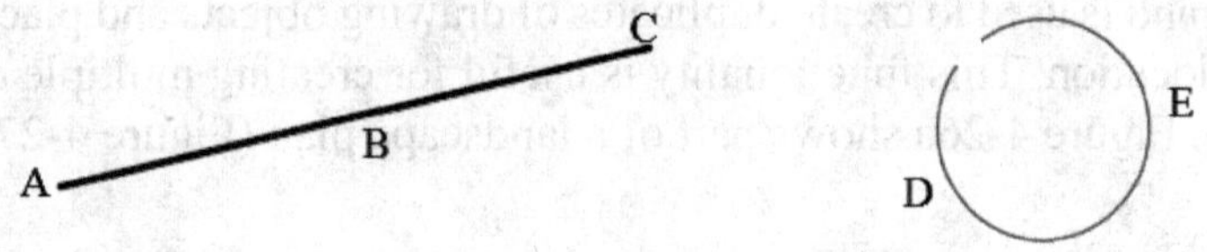

Figure 4-25d

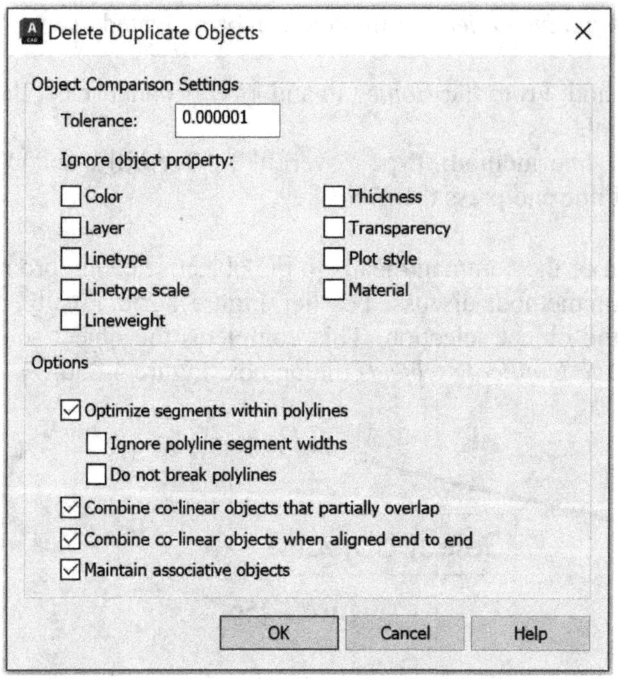

Figure 4-25e

4.18. Copy

The *Copy* command is used to create duplicates of drawing objects and place the duplicates at the specified location. This functionality is useful for creating multiple copies at a non-uniform spacing. Figure 4-26a shows part of a landscape plan (Figure 4-27).

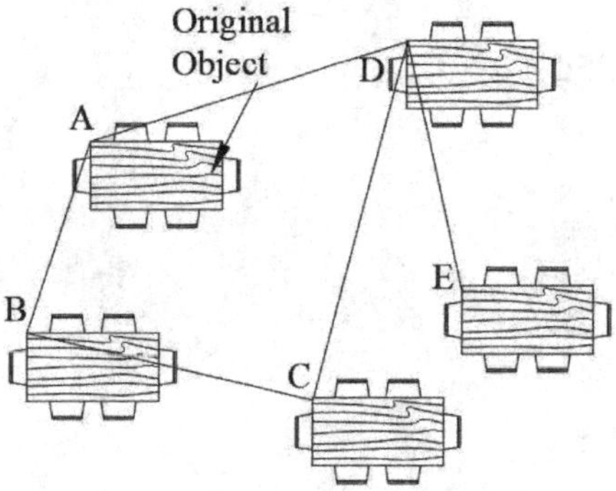

Figure 4-26a

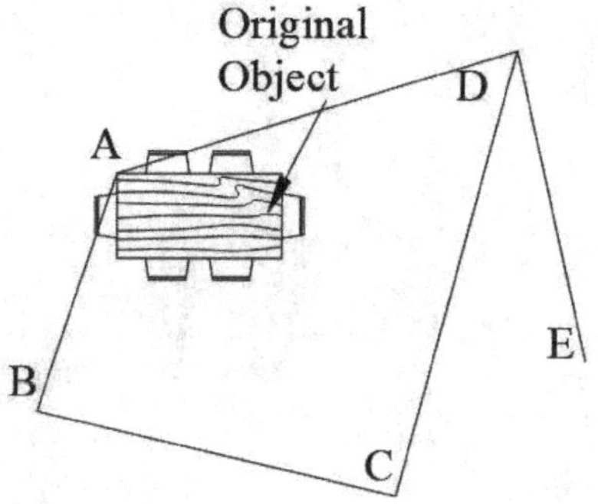

Figure 4-26b

The drafter can create the drawing of the plants shown in 4-26a by creating each plant's drawing individually, a time-consuming exhaustive technique! The most efficient technique to complete the drawing is to use the *Copy* command. For practice, the user can create a simple object and follow the instructions.

Example: The user is designing part of a landscape plan, Figure 4-26a. The user can develop part of the landscape plan by drawing one table and drawing four more copies of the original table and placing them at the desired locations using the following steps. (i) *Draw the original object and the lines,* Figure 4-26b; (ii) *label the ends of the lines A, B, C, D, and E; and* (iii) *use Copy command to create copies at the desired locations.*

This section explains the Copy command.

- Activate the *Copy* command using one of the following methods:
  1. Panel method: From the *Home* tab and *Modify* panel select the *Copy* tool.
  2. Command line method: Type "copy", "Copy", or "COPY" in the command line and press the *Enter* key.

- The most efficient technique is to use the *Copy* command with the *Object snaps* mode *On* (copy-paste objects with precision).

- The activation of the command leads to the object selection prompt, Figure 4-26c. Select the original object using one of the object selection methods discussed earlier and press the *Enter* key to complete the object selection. **Notice the change in the appearance of the cursor**, Figure 4-26f.

Figure 4-26c

- *Specify the base point*, Figure 4-26d: Either click on a point in the drawing or specify its coordinates (use the "," key to move from x's to y's input field) and press the *Enter* key. As a rule of thumb, the base point should be a point such that the copy can be pasted easily and precisely at its new location. In this example, the upper left corner is selected as the base point, 4-26e.

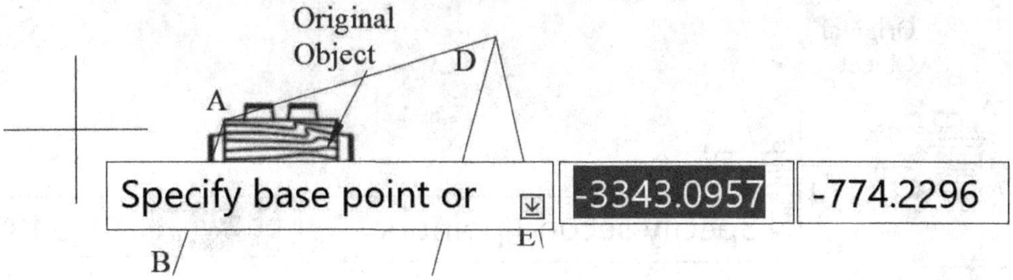

Figure 4-26d

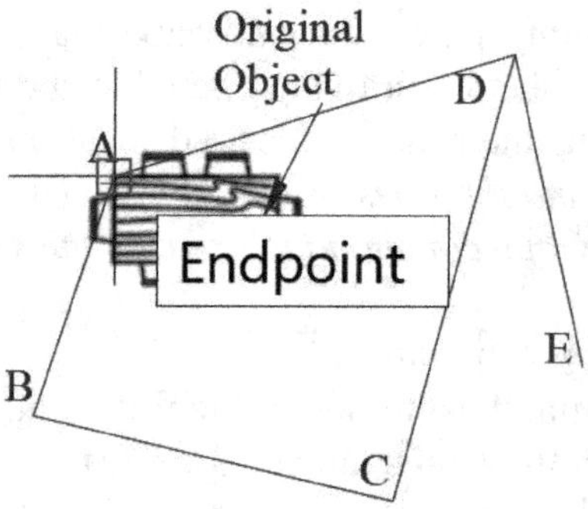

Figure 4-26e

- *Specify the second point*, Figure 4-26f: The second point is the location of the copy. Either click at the location of the copy or specify its coordinates and press the *Enter* key. The coordinates of the second point are relative coordinates with respect to the base point. However, in the current example, click at point B of the line, AB, Figure 4-26g. This completes the process of creating the first copy. The prompt to create the second and subsequent copies is shown in Figure 4-26h.

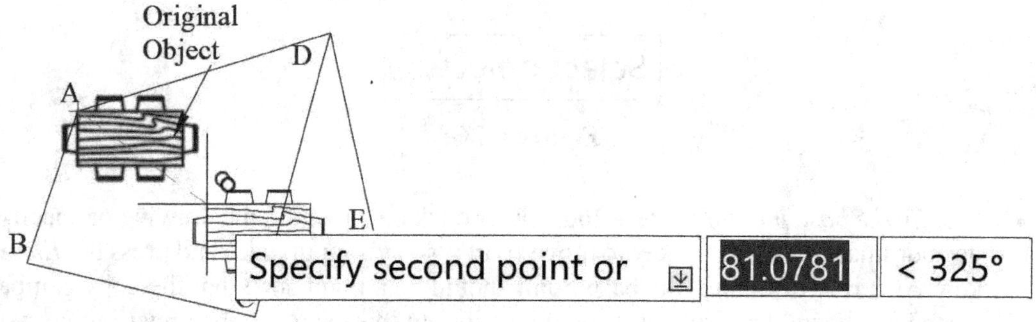

Figure 4-26f

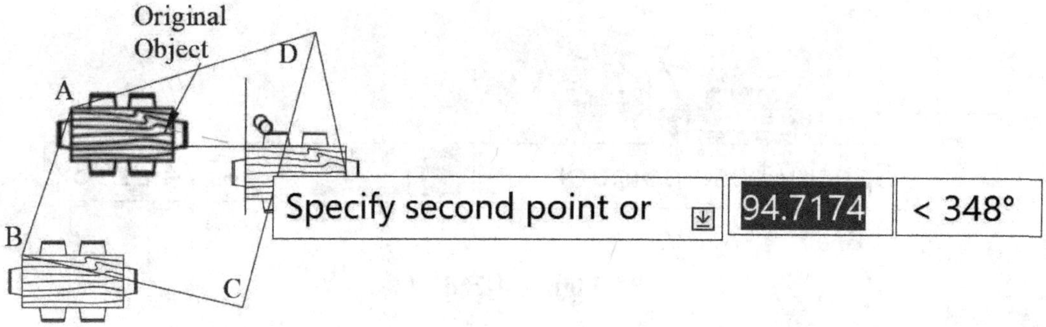

Figure 4-26g

- Make another copy, Figure 4-26h: To create another copy, repeat the process of the specification of the second point. To exit the command, press the *Esc* or *Enter* key.

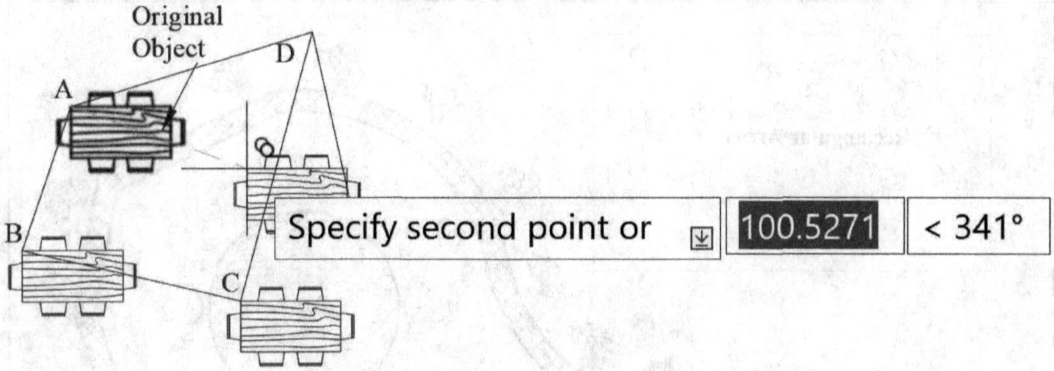

Figure 4-26h

4.19. Array

The *Array* command creates multiple copies of an object and arranges the copies in a specific pattern. The objects can also be copied and arranged in a similar pattern using the *Copy*, *Rotate*, and *Move* commands combination, too. However, the drawing accuracy is increased, and its creation duration is significantly reduced if the *Array* command is used to create multiple copies in a pattern.

AutoCAD provides three different pattern options. The *Rectangular* array command can be used to create copies arranged in a rectangular pattern of rows and columns; *Polar* array command to create copies arranged in a circular pattern; and *Path* array command to create copies along a specified path, Figure 4-27.

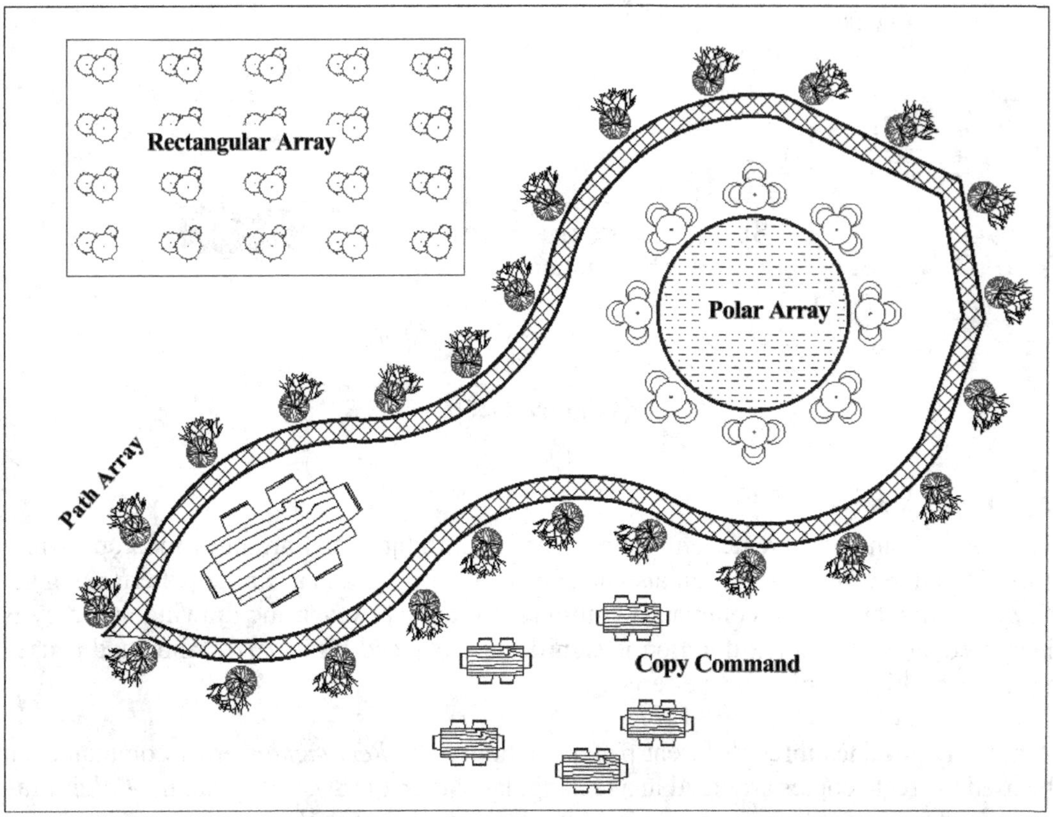

Figure 4-27

4.19.1. Rectangular Array

The *Rectangular Array* command creates a rectangular array of the selected object. In a rectangular array, objects are arranged in rows and columns of an array. If an array contains one row, then it must have more than one column and vice versa. By default, the maximum number of array elements generated in one command is 100,000. The default number of elements in an array is 12 (3 rows and 4 columns).

- The ***ArrayRectangular*** command is activated using one of the following methods:

1. Panel method: From the *Home* tab and *Modify* panel, expand the *Array* drop-down menu and select the *Rectangular Array* tool, Figure 4-28a.
2. Command line method: Either type "array", "Array", or "ARRAY" and select the *ARRAYRECT* option; or type "arrayrect", "Arrayrect", or "ARRAYRECT" in the command line and press the *Enter* key.

Example: Create a 4x5 grid of 20 plants; that is, create a drawing for a landscape plan with four rows and each row with five plants as shown in Figure 4-29a. The figure also shows the definition of the row and column spacing.

Basic Element in the example: Create a simple shape as shown in Figure 4-28b or insert the *Clum of trees or bushes* block, from the Design Center, shown in Figure 4-28c. Do not add dimensions.

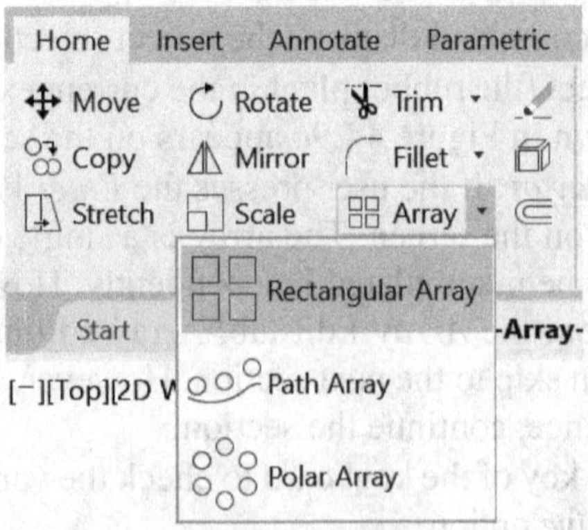

Figure 4-28a

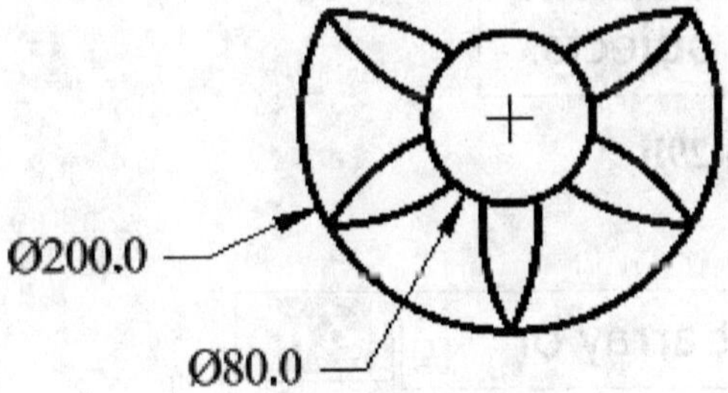

Figure 4-28b

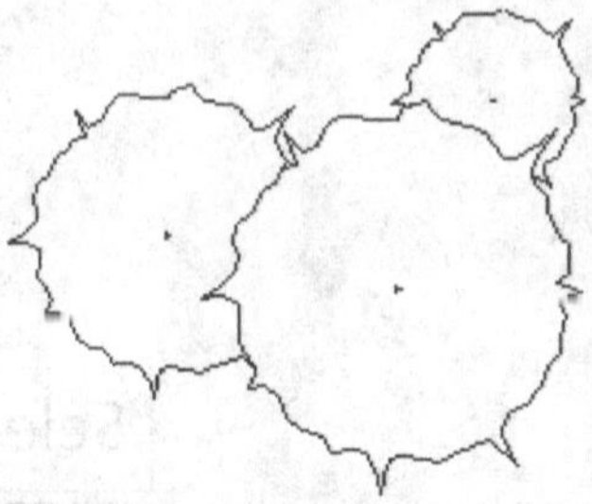

Figure 4-28c

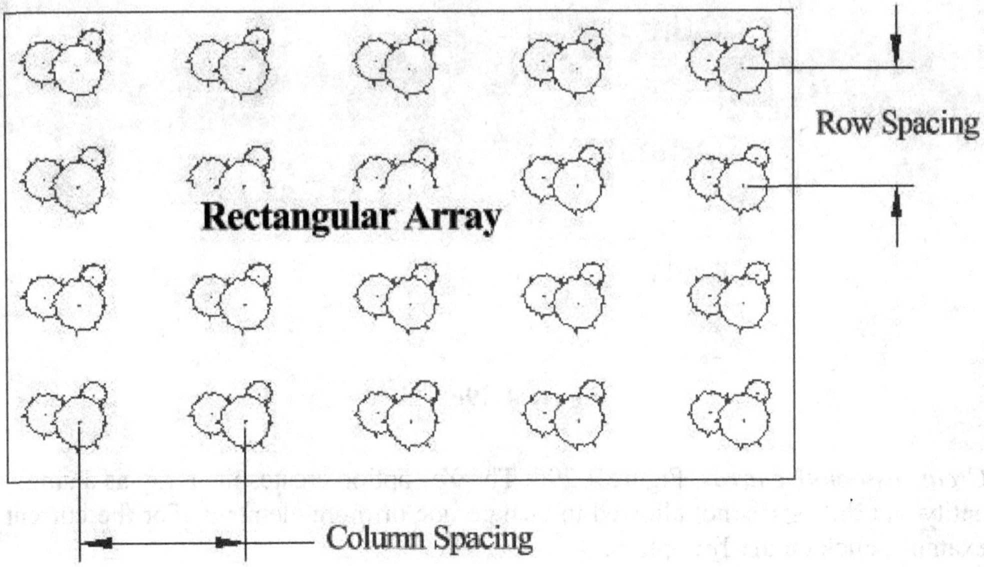

Figure 4-29a

The solution drawing can be created by using the following steps:

- Create the basic element of the array. The current example is based on the Design Center's block.
- Activate the *Array Rectangular* command.
- The activation of the command displays the object selection prompt, Figure 4-29b.
- Select the desired object (the rubber plant in the current example) and press the *Enter* key. The prompt shown in Figure 4-29c appears on the screen.
- *Select grip to edit array or*: If the user presses the *Enter* key, then the array shown in Figure 4-29c appears on the screen. The array is a single entity, that is, the elements of the array could not be manipulated independently. However, the user can edit the array using panels from the *Array* Edit tab. Array editing is discussed later. If this option is selected, then skip to the next section. However, in the current example, this option is not used. Hence, continue the section.
- Press the down-arrow key of the keyboard to check the various options, Figure 4-29c. Click on the *ASsociative* option.

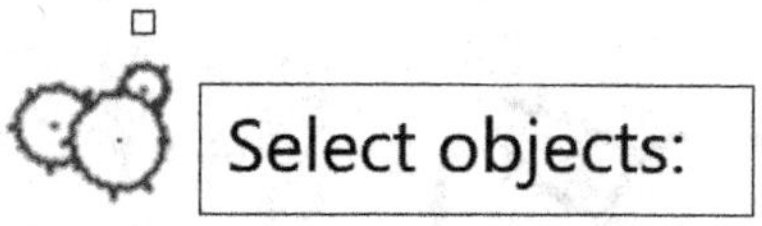

Figure 4-29b

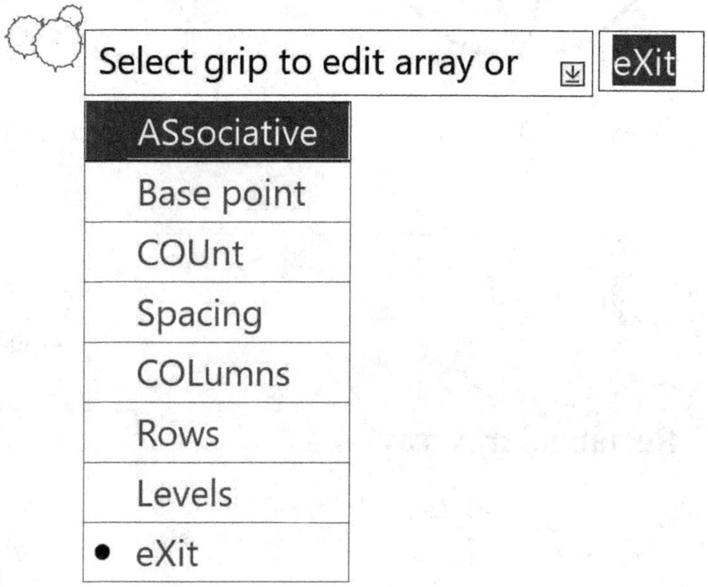

Figure 4-29c

- *Create associative array*, Figure 4-29d: The *Yes* option creates the array as a single entity and the user is not allowed to change one or more elements. For the current example, click on the *Yes* option.

- *Select grip to edit array or*, Figure 4-29e: Press the down-arrow key of the keyboard and click on the *COUnt* option.

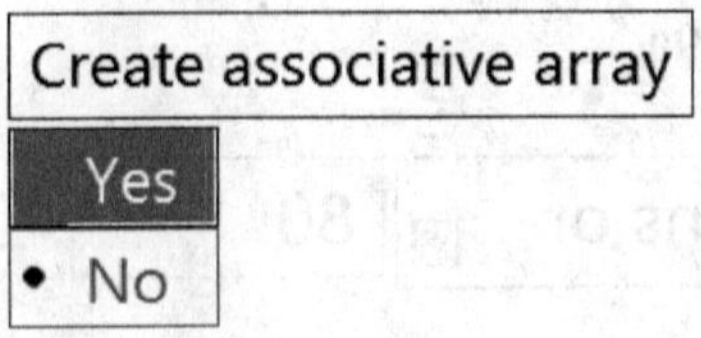

Figure 4-29d

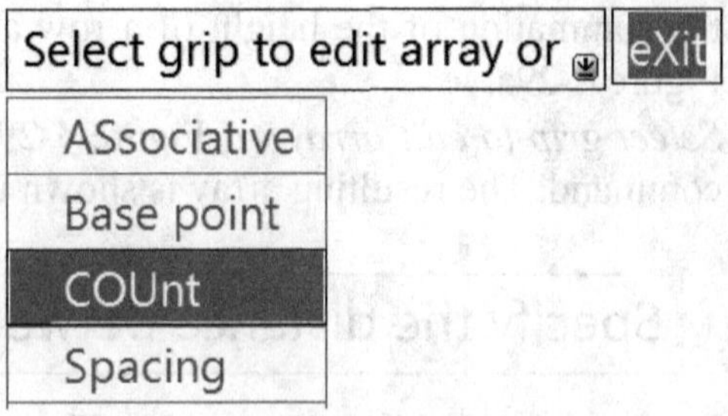

Figure 4-29e

- *Enter number of Columns*, Figure 4-29f: Specify the number of columns in the array (for the current example array, type 5). Press the *Enter* key.
- *Enter number of rows*, Figure 4-29f: Specify the number of rows in the array (for the current example array, type 4). Press the *Enter* key.

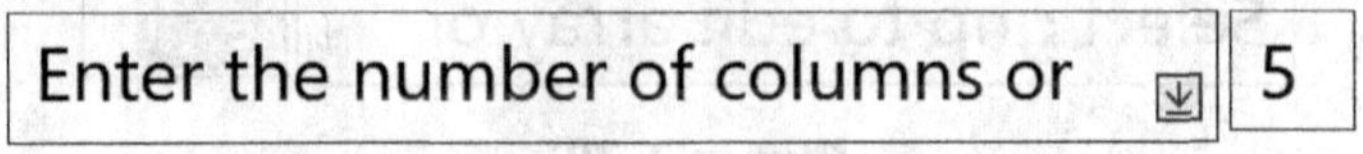

Figure 4-29f

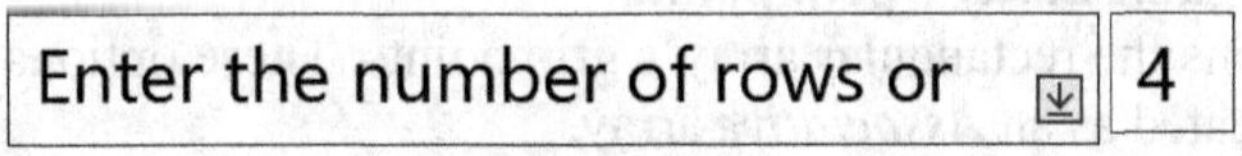

Figure 4-29g

- *Select grip to edit array or*, Figure 4-29h: Press the down-arrow key of the keyboard and click on the *Spacing* option.

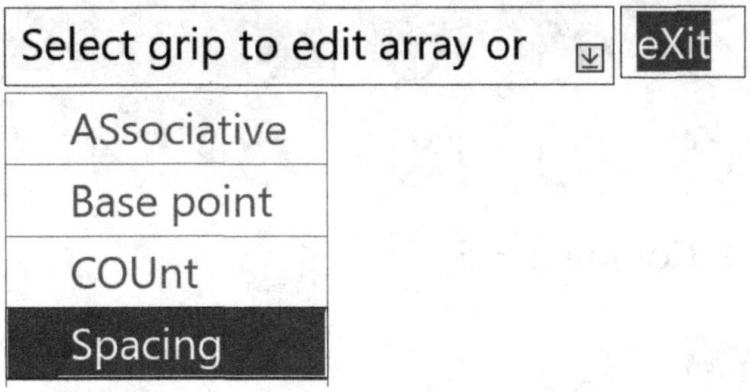

Figure 4-29h

- *Specify the distance between columns or*, Figure 4-29i: Specify the spacing between the columns (for the current example array, type 80). Press the *Enter* key. The column spacing is the summation of the width of a column and the space between two consecutive columns, Figure 4-29a.

- *Specify the distance between rows or*, Figure 4-29i: Specify the spacing between the rows (for the current example array, type 55). Press the *Enter* key. The row spacing is the summation of the height of a row and the space between two consecutive rows, Figure 4-29a.
- *Select grip to edit array or*, Figure 4-29k: Press the *Enter* key to complete the array command. The resulting array is shown in Figure 4-29a.

Figure 4-29i

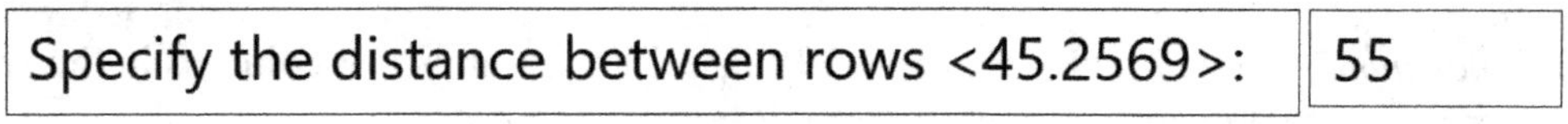

Figure 4-29j

Figure 4-29k

4.19.1.1. Rectangular array's grip points

This section explains the rectangular array's grip points. These options are available only if the array was created as an ***Associative*** array.

- To use the options shown in Figure 4-30a to Figure 4-30f (i) bring the cursor on the desired grip point and it is highlighted (its color is changed) and its options appear; (ii) move the cursor to the desired option; (iii) finally, either press the *Enter* key or click with the left button of the mouse and follow the prompts.

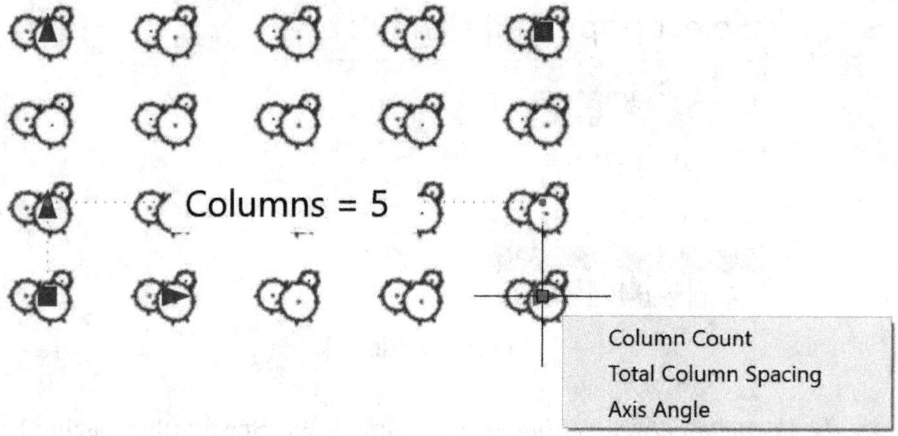

Figure 4-30a

- The triangular grip point near the lower end of the first column, Figure 4-30b, can be used to change the columns' spacing.

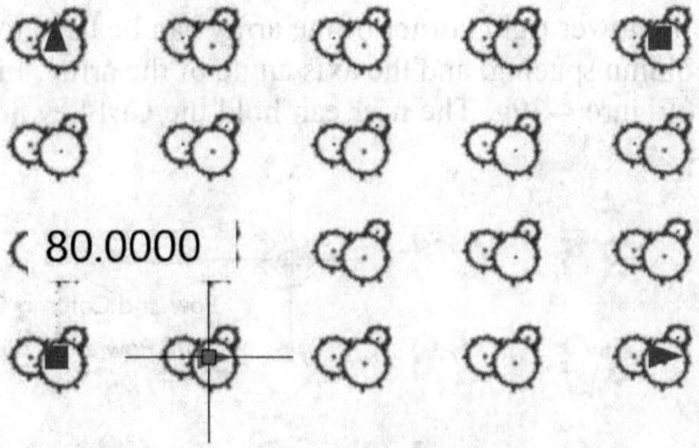

Figure 4-30b

- The grip point at the upper left corner of the array can be used to change the number of rows, the row spacing, and the axis angle of the array, Figure 4-30c.

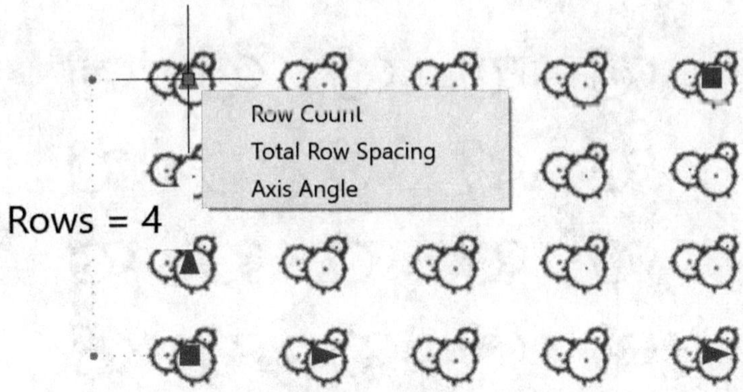

Figure 4-30c

- The triangular grip point near the left end of the first row, Figure 4-30d, can be used to change the rows' spacing.

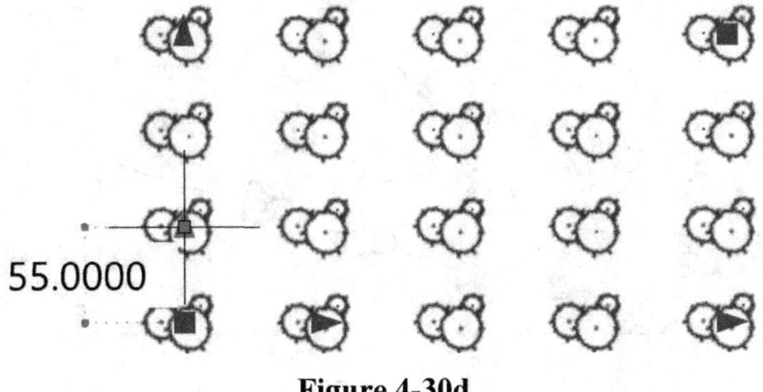

Figure 4-30d

- The grip point at the upper right corner of the array can be used to change the number of rows and columns, and the row and column spacing of the array, Figure 4-30e.
- The grip point at the lower left corner of the array can be used to move the array.
- The grip point at the lower right corner of the array can be used to change the number of columns, the column spacing, and the axis angle of the array, Figure 4-30a; the axis angle is shown in Figure 4-30g. The user can hold the Ctrl key and cycle through the available options.

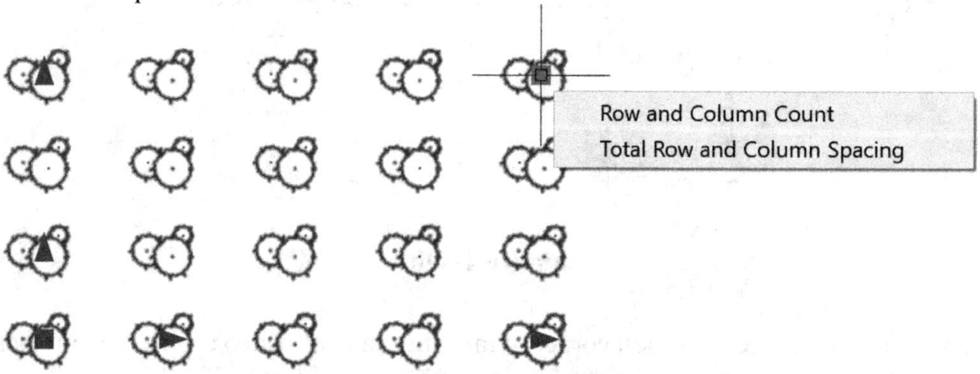

Figure 4-30e

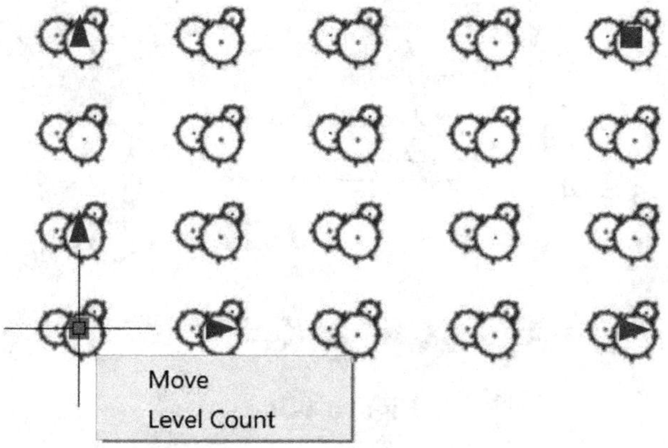

Figure 4-30f

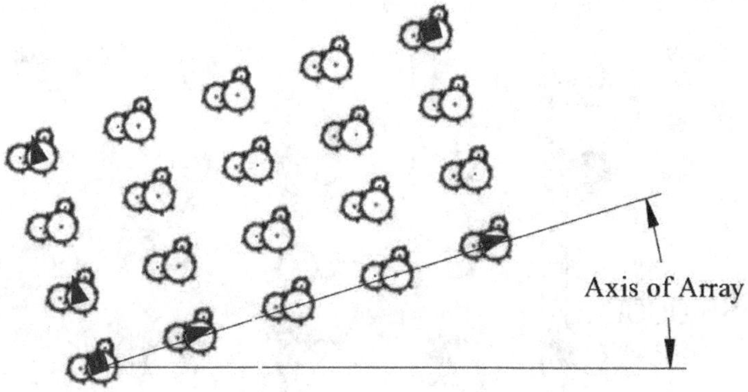

Figure 4-30g

4.19.2. Polar array

The *Polar Array* command creates a circular array of the selected objects around a specified center point. In addition, the objects are rotated to face the center point. This section explains the options available to create a polar array. Figure 4-31a shows basic terminology of a polar array.

- The ***ArrayPolar*** command is activated using one of the following methods:
  1. Panel method: From the *Home* tab and *Modify* panel, expand the *Array* drop-down menu and select the *Polar Array* tool, Figure 4-31b.
  2. Command line method: Either type "array", "Array", or "ARRAY" and select the *ARRAYPOLAR* option; or type "arraypolar", "Arraypolar", or "ARRAYPOLAR" in the command line and press the *Enter* key.

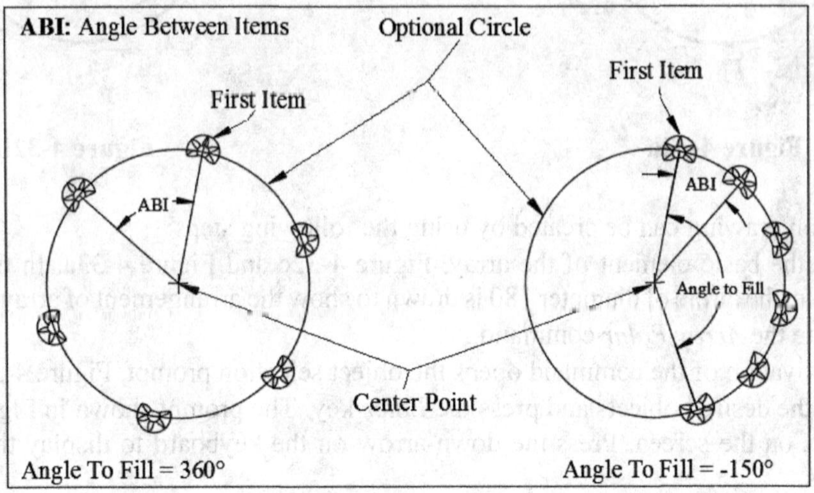

Figure 4-31a

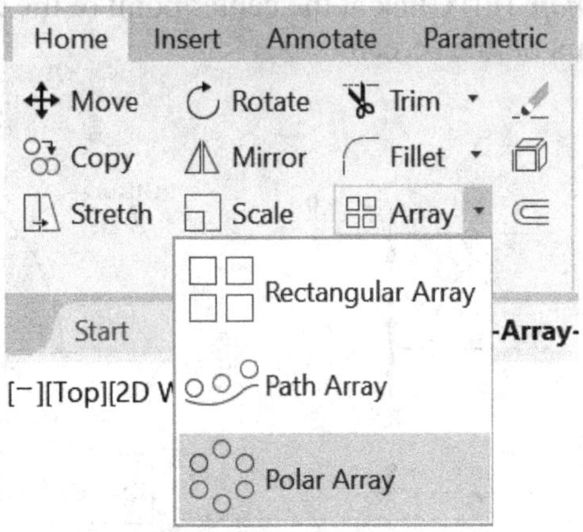

Figure 4-31b

Example: Create a circular arrangement of seven chairs occupying three quarters of a circle and facing towards the center as shown in Figure 4-32a or Figure 4-32b. The two figures represent slightly different polar arrays. Figure 4-32a is created using the fill angle of 270°; and Figure 4-32b is created using the angle between items of 40°.

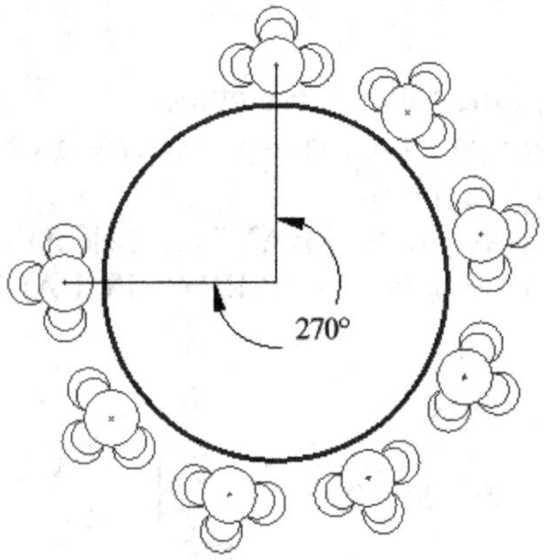

Figure 4-32a

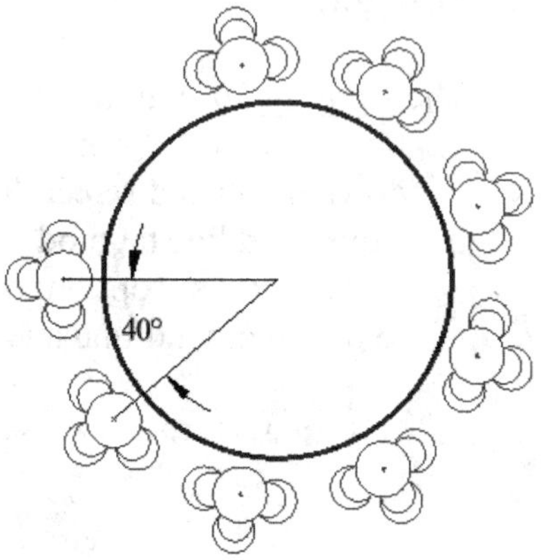

Figure 4-32b

The solution drawing can be created by using the following steps:

- Create the basic element of the array, Figure 4-32c and Figure 4-33a. In the current example, the circle of diameter 180 is drawn to show the arrangement of array elements.
- Activate the *Array Polar* command.
- The activation of the command opens the object selection prompt, Figure 4-33a.
- Select the desired objects and press the *Enter* key. The prompt shown in Figure 4-33b appears on the screen. Press the down-arrow on the keyboard to display the various options.
- *Specify center point of array or*, Figure 4-33b: This example uses the *Center* option. (i) Press the up-arrow of the keyboard to hide the option list. (ii) Turn *On* the *Center* option in the *Object snap*. (iii) Click at the center point of the circle. The prompt shown in Figure 4-33c appears on the screen.

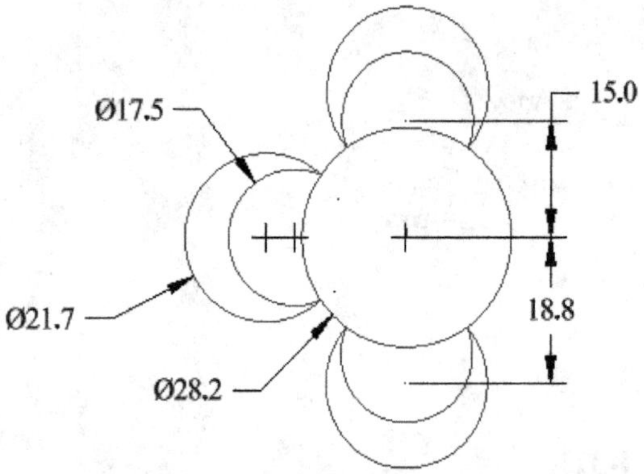

Figure 4-32c

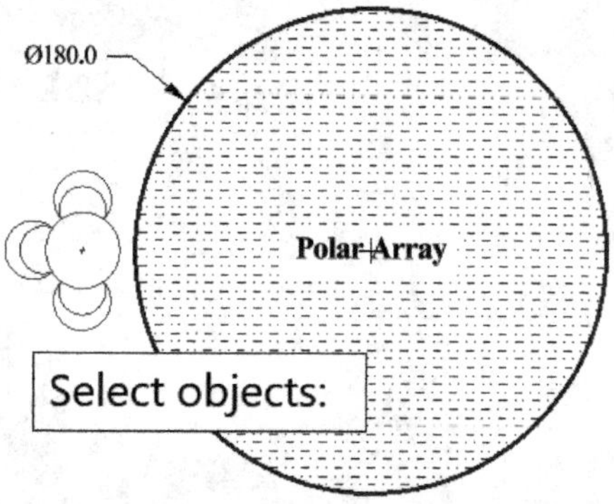

Figure 4-33a

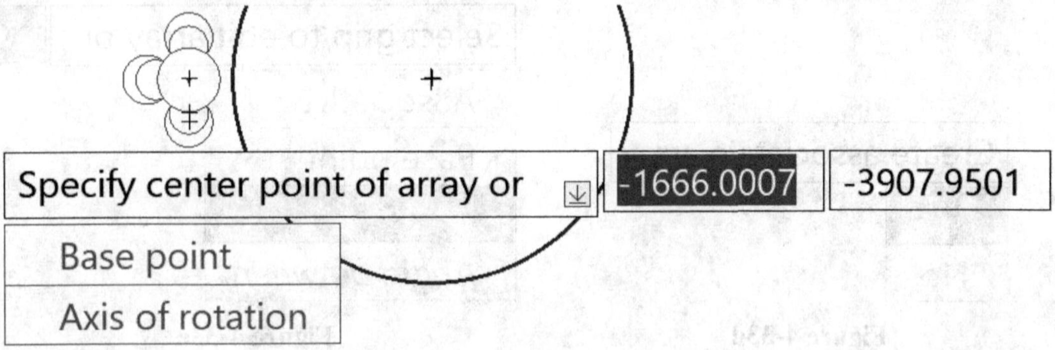

Figure 4-33b

- *Select grip to edit array or*, Figure 4-33c: If the user presses the *Enter* key then the array shown in Figure 4-33c appears on the screen; and the user should neglect the remaining bullets in this section. However, the user can edit the array using panels from the *Edit* tab. Array editing is discussed later. In the current example, press the down-arrow key of the keyboard to check the various options.

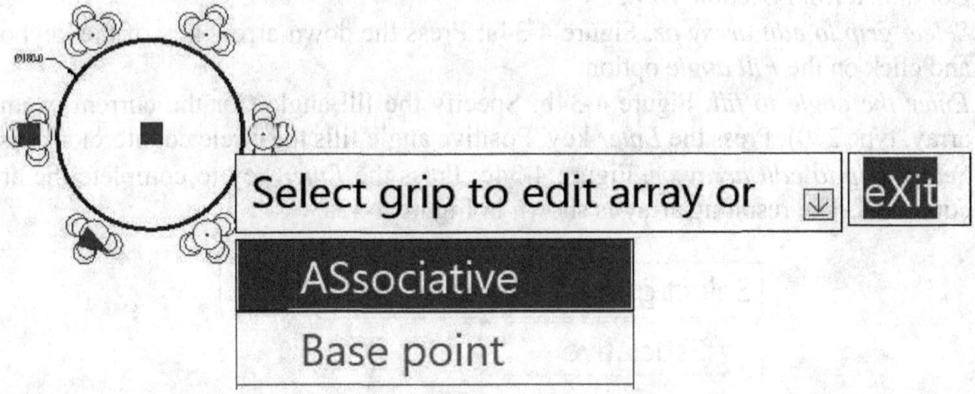

Figure 4-33c

- Select the *ASsociative* option, Figure 4-33d.
- *Create associative array* Figure 4-33d: The *Yes* option creates the array as a single entity; that is, the elements of the array could not be manipulated independently. The user may need to change one or more elements. However, for the current example, click on the *Yes* option.
- *Select grip to edit array or*, Figure 4-33e: Press the down-arrow key of the keyboard and click on the *Items* option.
- *Enter number of items in array or*, Figure 4-33f: Specify the number of items (for the current example array, type 8). Press the *Enter* key.

The next two subsections describe the *Fill angle* and the *Angle between* options, and the user should follow the desired option.

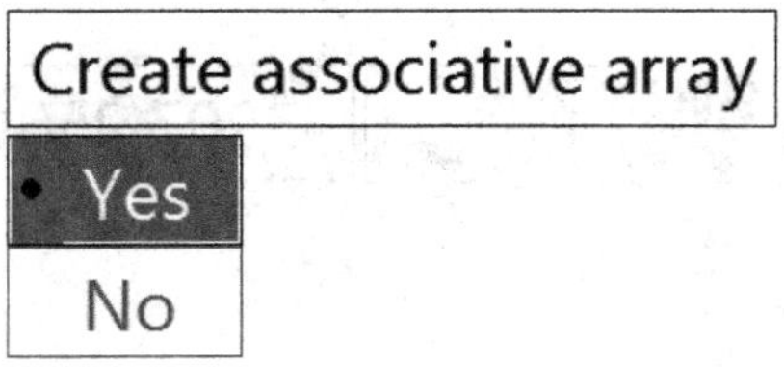

Figure 4-33d

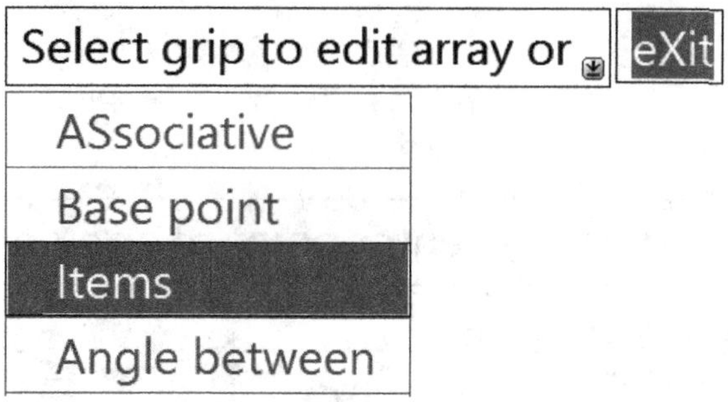

Figure 4-33e

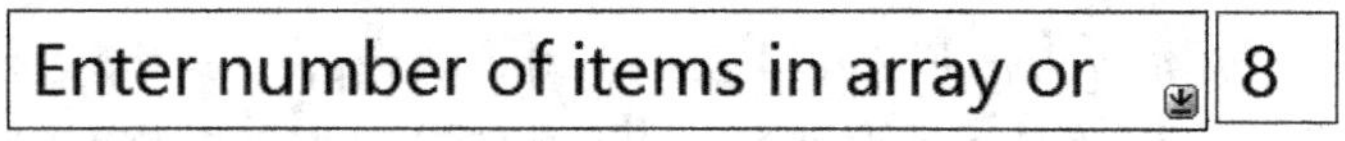

Figure 4-33f

4.19.2.1. Fill angle

- Continued from Section 4.19.2.
- *Select grip to edit array or*, Figure 4-34a: Press the down-arrow key of the keyboard and click on the *Fill angle* option.
- *Enter the angle to fill*, Figure 4-34b: Specify the fill angle (for the current example array, type 270). Press the *Enter* key. Positive angle fills the circle counterclockwise.
- *Select grip to edit array or*, Figure 4-34c: Press the *Enter* key to complete the array command. The resulting array is shown in Figure 4-32a.

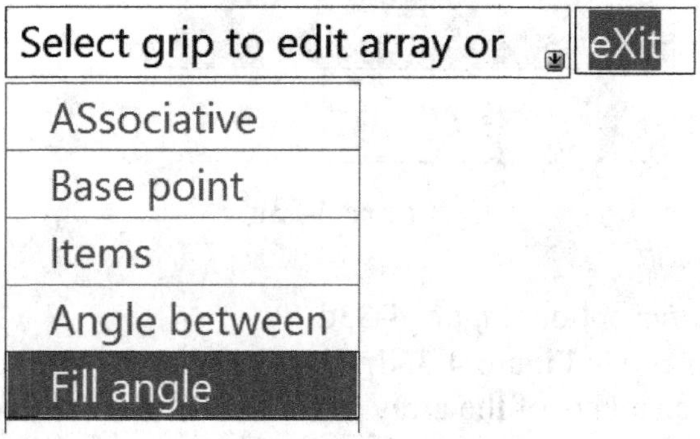

Figure 4-34a

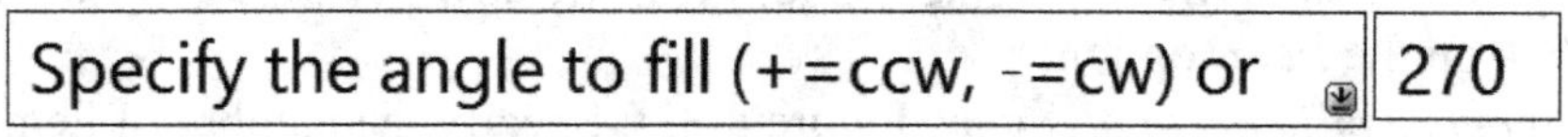

Figure 4-34b

Figure 4-34c

4.19.2.2. Angle between

- Continued from Section 4.19.2.
- *Select grip to edit array or*: Press the down-arrow key of the keyboard and click on the *Angle between* option, Figure 4-35a.

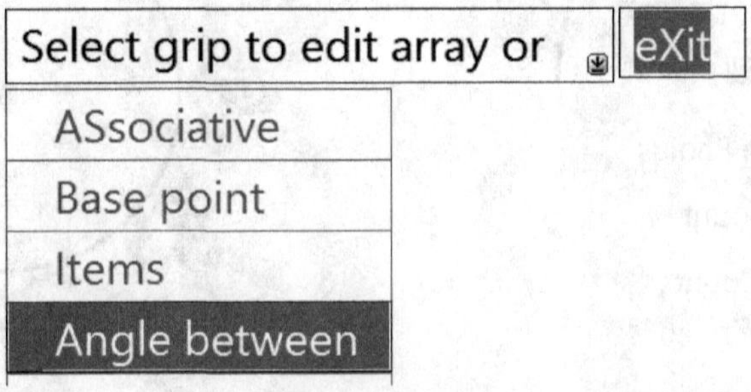

Figure 4-35a

- *Specify angle between items or*: Figure 4-35b. Specify the angle between two consecutive elements. For the example array, type 38.57. The positive angle creates a counterclockwise array. Press the *Enter* key.
- *Select grip to edit array or*, Figure 4-35c: Press the *Enter* key to complete the array command. The resulting array is shown in Figure 4-32b.

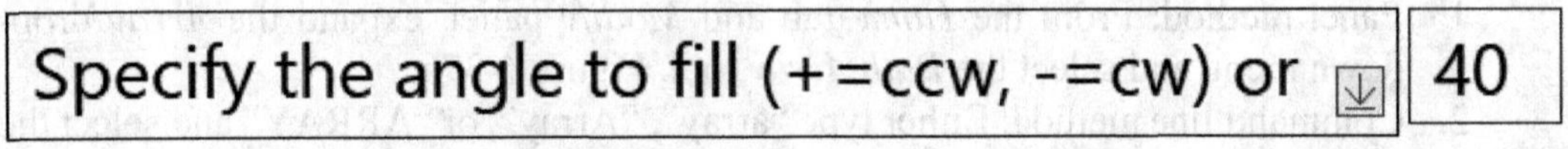

Figure 4-35b

Figure 4-35c

4.19.2.3. Polar array and grip points

- To use the options shown in Figure 4-36a (i) bring the cursor on the desired grip point and it is highlighted (its color changes) and its options appear; (ii) move the cursor to the desired option; (iii) finally, either press the *Enter* key or click with the left button of the mouse and follow the prompts.
- Figure 4-36b shows the behavior of the grip point at the basic element of the array. These grip points can be used to change the number of items (*Item Count*) and the fill angle (*Fill Angle*) of the polar array. It is also used to change the radius (*Stretch Radius*) and the number of circles in the polar array using *Row Count* option.

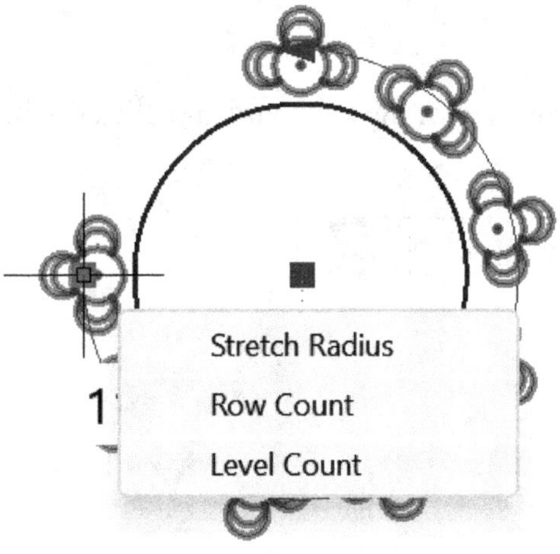

Figure 4-36a

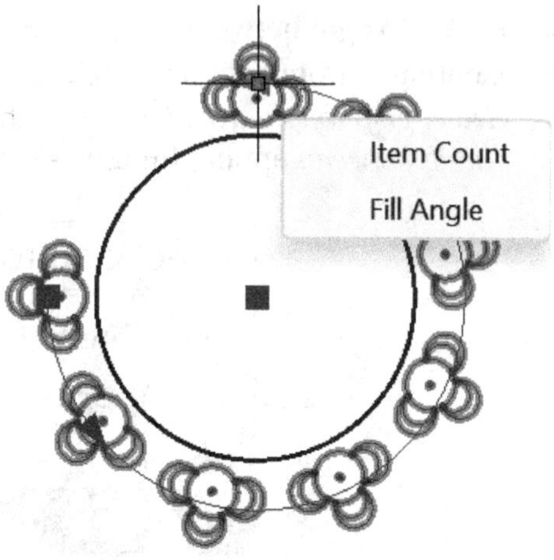

Figure 4-36b

4.19.3. Path array

The *Array Path* command distributes the desired number of objects (to be arrayed) evenly along a path; and the array members are rotated to follow the path. The path can be a line, polyline, spline, helix, arc, circle, or ellipse. In the current example the path is created using a polyline.

- The ***ArrayPath*** command is activated using one of the following methods:
  1. Panel method: From the *Home* tab and *Modify* panel, expand the *Array* drop-down menu and select the *Path Array* tool, Figure 4-37a.
  2. Command line method: Either type "array", "Array", or "ARRAY" and select the *ARRAYPATH* option; or type "arraypath", "Arraypath", or "ARRAYPATH" in the command line and press the *Enter* key.

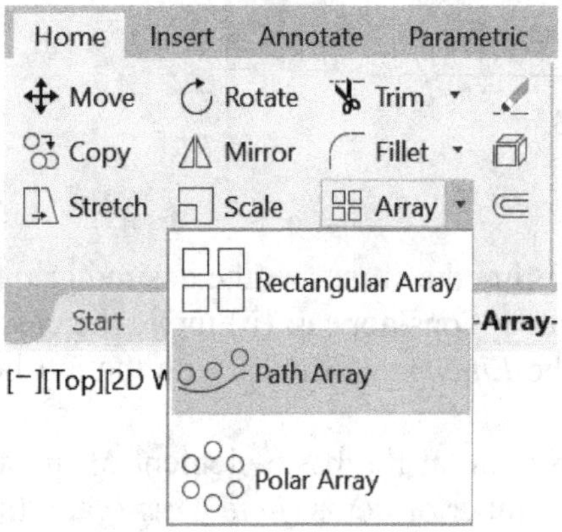

Figure 4-37a

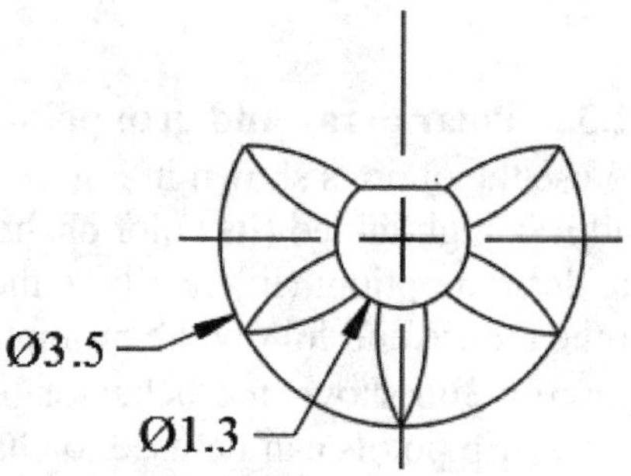

Figure 4-37b

Example: Show 16 deciduous trees along a curved path as shown in Figure 4-38a. This drawing can be created by using a basic element and a path and path array command.

Basic Element in the example: Create a simple shape as shown in Figure 4-28b or insert the *Tree deciduous* and *Shrub* blocks, from the Design Center. Do not add dimensions. For the current example, create the path and the basic element of the array at the beginning of the path, Figure 4-38b and Figure 4-38b1.

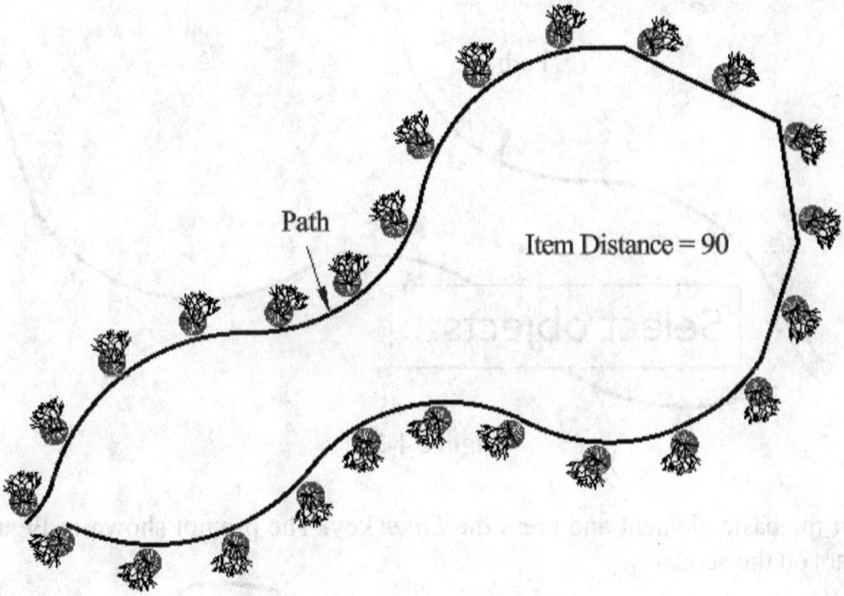

Figure 4-38a

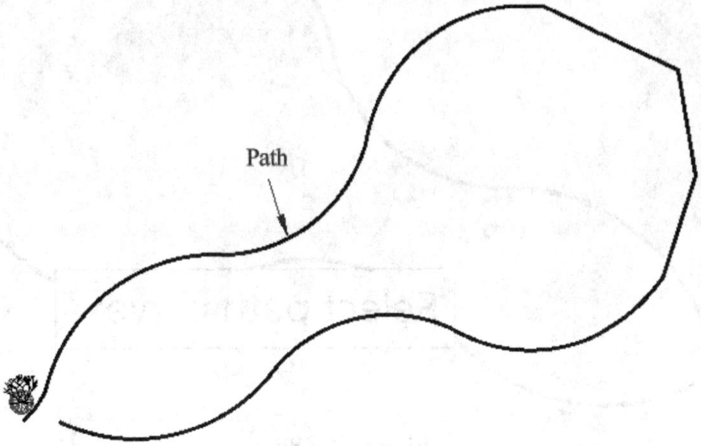

Figure 4-38b

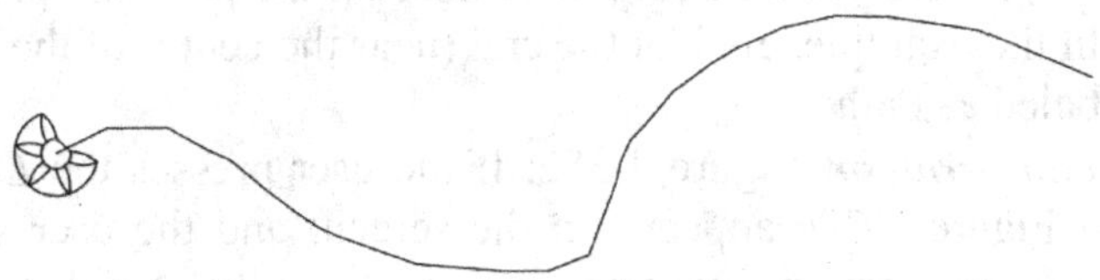

Figure 4-38b1

The solution drawing can be created by using the following steps:

- Create the basic element of the array. The current example is based on the Design Center's block.
- Activate the *Path Array* command.
- The activation of the command opens the object selection prompt, 4-38c.

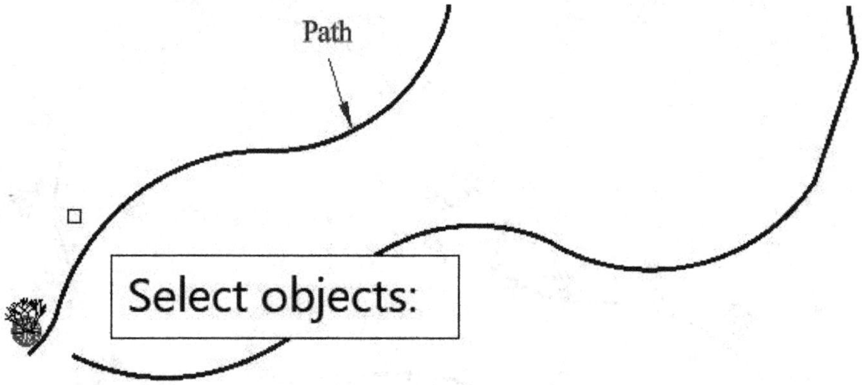

Figure 4-38c

- Select the basic element and press the *Enter* key. The prompt shown in Figure 4-38d appears on the screen.

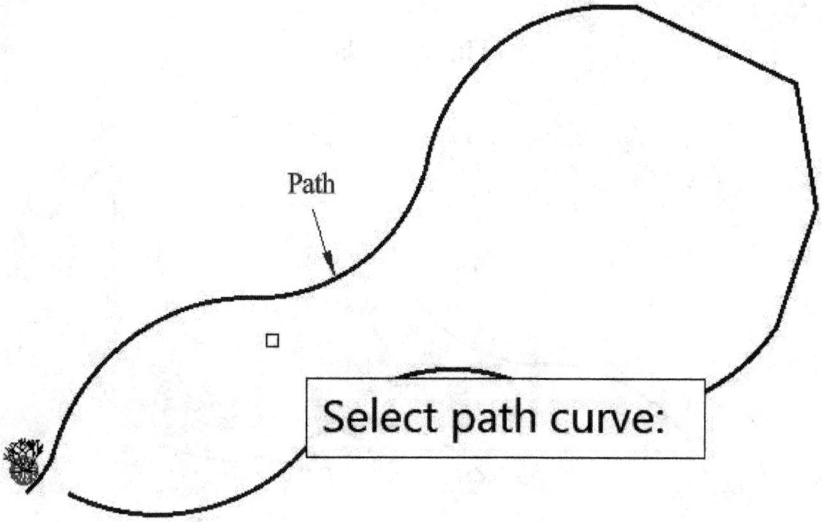

Figure 4-38d

- *Select path curve*, Figure 4-38d: Bring the cursor on the path and press the left button of the mouse. In the example, click at the end (near the center of the basic element) of the polyline labeled as Path.
- *Select grip to edit array or*, Figure 4-38e: If the user presses the *Enter* key then the array shown in Figure 4-38e appears on the screen; and the user should ignore the remaining steps in this section. The array is a single entity, that is, the elements of the

array could not be manipulated independently. However, the user can edit the array using panels from the *Edit* tab. Array editing is discussed later.

- In the current example, press the down-arrow key of the keyboard to check the various options, Figure 4-38e. Click on the *ASsociative* option.
- *Select grip to edit array or*, Figure 4-39b: Press the down-arrow key of the keyboard and click on the *Items* option.

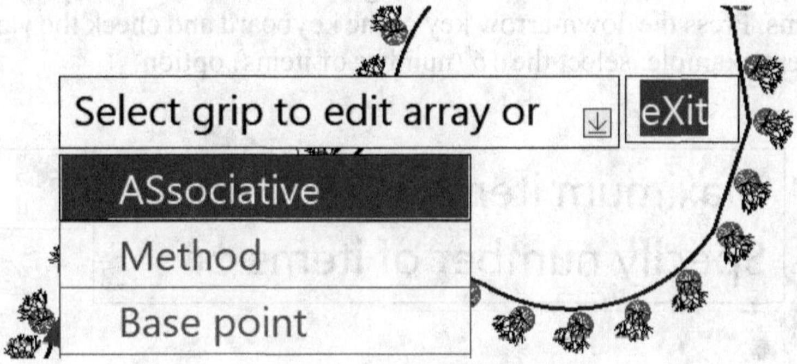

Figure 4-38e

- *Create associative array*, Figure 4-39a: The *Yes* option creates the array as a single entity. The user may need to change one or more elements. However, for the current example, click on the *Yes* option.
- *Specify the distance between items along path or*, Figure 4-39b: Press the down-arrow key of the keyboard and check the various options. However, in this example specify the distance to be 65, Figure 4-39c. Press the *Enter* key.

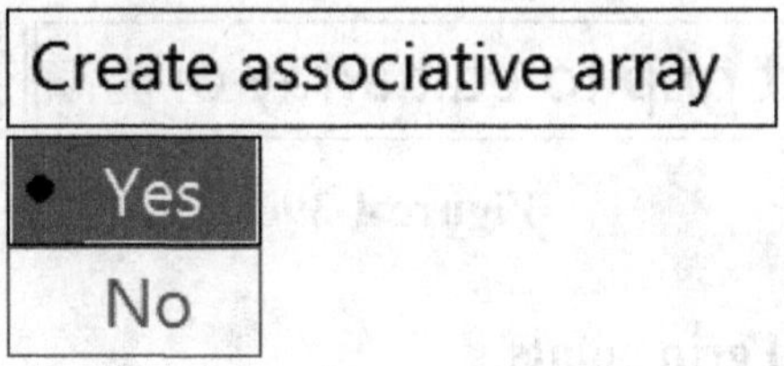

Figure 4-39a

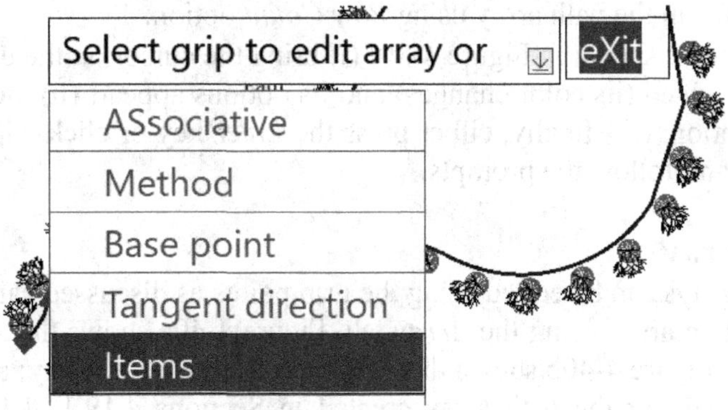

Figure 4-39b

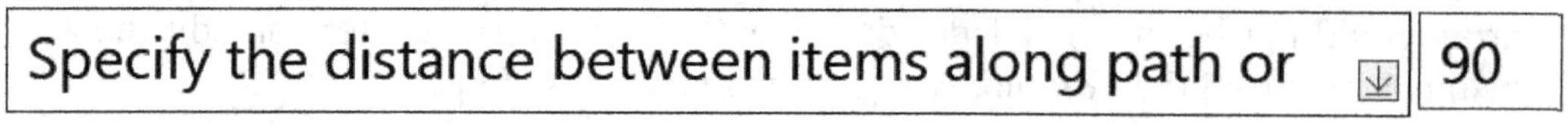

Figure 4-39c

- *Specify number of items or*, Figure 4-39d: The prompt displays the maximum number of items (Figure 4-39d) calculated as the length of the path divided by distance between the two items. Press the down-arrow key of the keyboard and check the various options. In the current example, select the *16* (number of items) option.

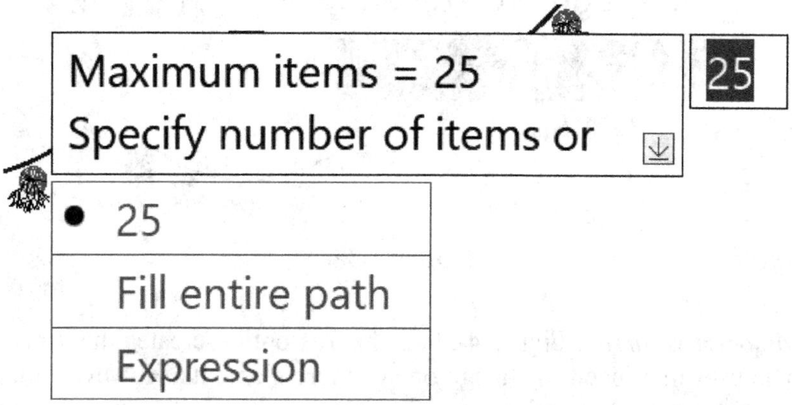

Figure 4-39d

- Press the *Enter* key again to complete the command. The resulting array is shown in Figure 4-38a.

Figure 4-39e

4.19.3.1. Path array and grip points

- Figure 4-39f shows the behavior of the grip point at the basic element of the array. These grip points can be used to move the array to a different location (*Move*) and the number of paths in the path array using *Row Count* option.
- To use the options shown in Figure 4-39f (i) bring the cursor on the desired grip point and it is highlighted (its color changes) and its options appear; (ii) move the cursor to the desired option; (iii) finally, either press the *Enter* key or click with the left button of the mouse and follow the prompts.

4.19.4. Edit array

The *associative* arrays can be edited using the grip points as discussed earlier. However, a user can also edit an array using the *Array* tab. Figure 4-40a shows the *Array* tab for the rectangular array; Figure 4-40b shows the *Array* tab for the polar array; and Figure 4-40c shows the *Array* tab for the path array created in Sections 4.19.1, 4.19.2, and 4.19.3, respectively.

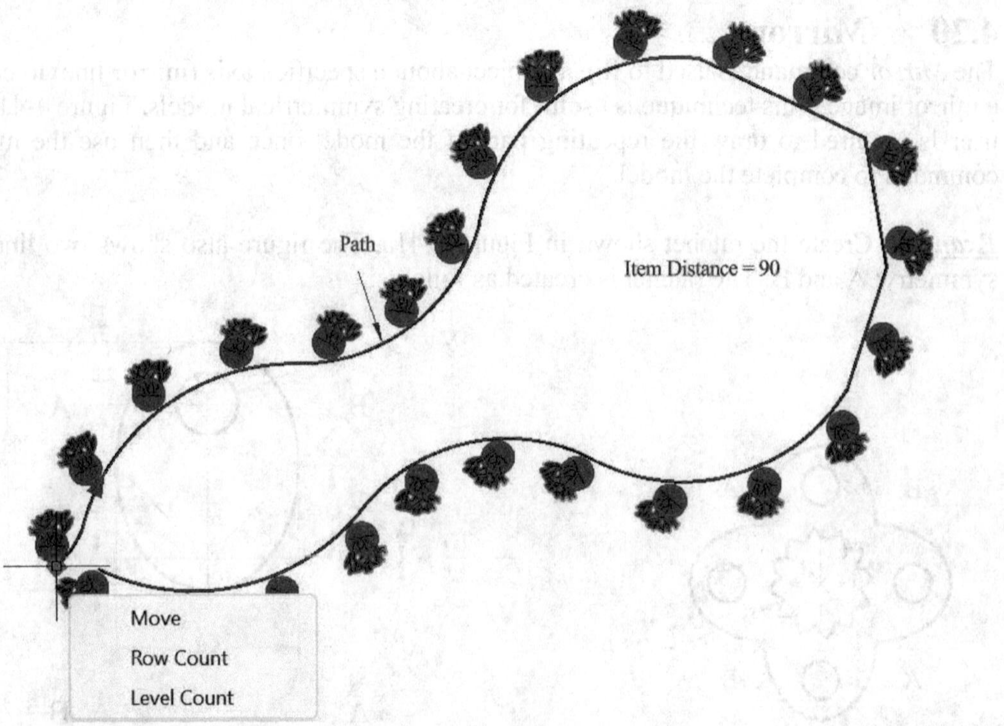

Figure 4-39f

A user can edit an array using the *Array* tab as follows: (i) Click the array that needs to be edited then the *Array* tab becomes the current tab. (ii) Now edit the array using the desired tool from the Array's panels and following the prompts.

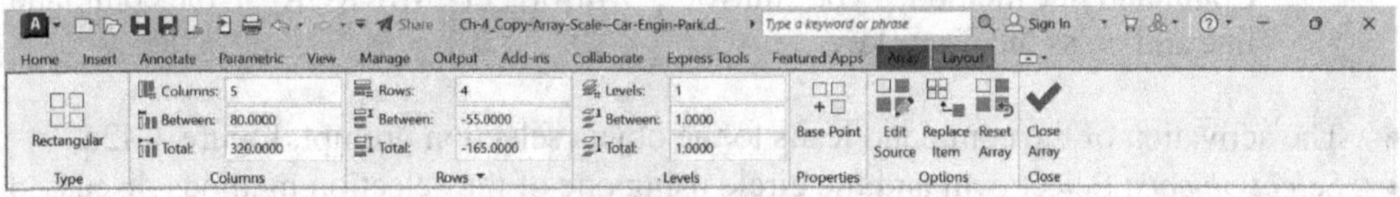

Figure 4-40a

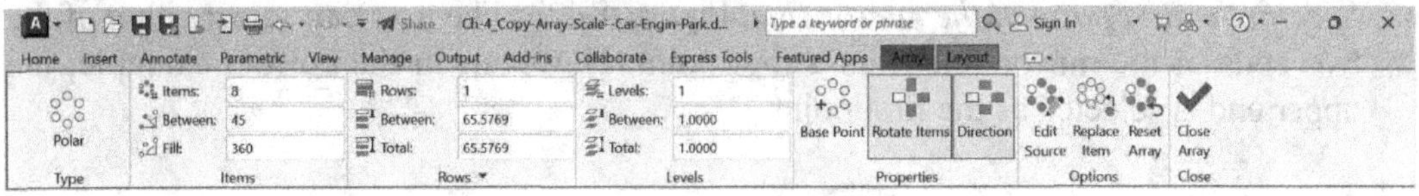

Figure 4-40b

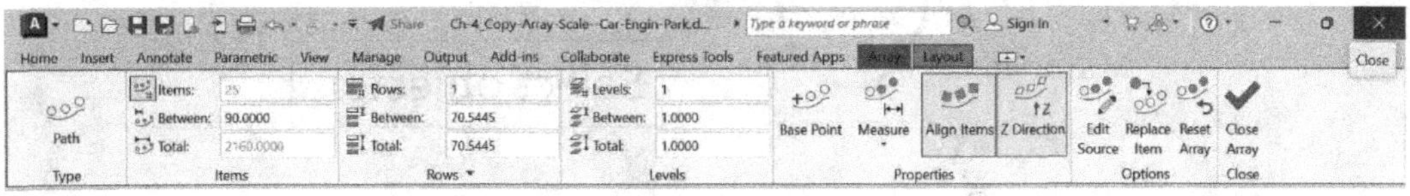

Figure 4-40c

4.20. Mirror

The *Mirror* command is used to flip an object about a specified axis (mirror line) to create a mirror image. This technique is useful for creating symmetrical models, Figure 4-41; the user is required to draw the repeating part of the model once and then use the mirror command to complete the model.

Example: Create the ratchet shown in Figure 4-41a. The figure also shows two lines of symmetry: A and B. The ratchet is created as follows:

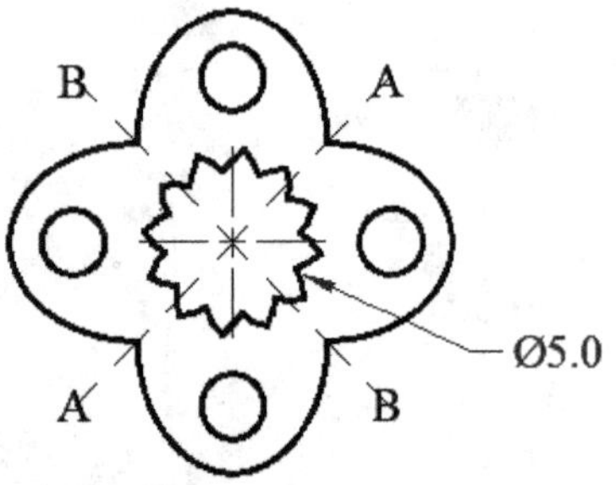

Figure 4-41a

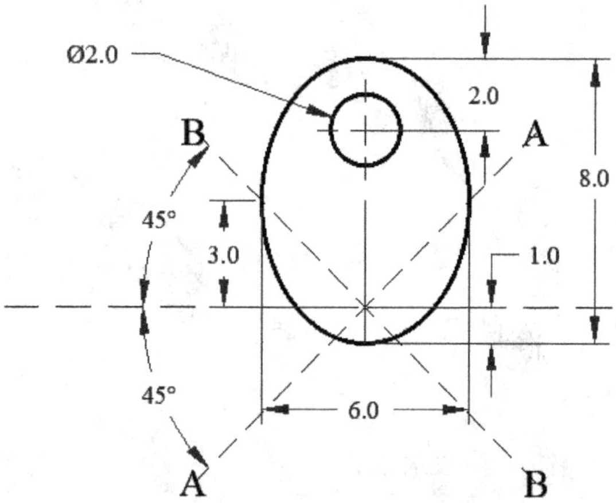

Figure 4-41b

- Draw the basic unit shown in Figure 4-41b. Do not add dimensions and the label *A*.
- Activate the *Mirror* command using one of the following methods:
  1. Panel method: From the *Home* tab and *Modify* panel select the *Mirror* tool.
  2. Command line method: Type "mirror", "Mirror", or "MIRROR" in the command line and press the *Enter* key.

- The activation of the command leads to the object selection prompt, Figure 4-42a.
- *Select objects*: Select oval and the circle using one of the selection methods discussed earlier in this chapter; press the *Enter* key to complete the object selection. The prompt shown in Figure 4-42b appears.
- *Specify the first point of the mirror line*, Figure 4-42b: The user can select either of the two ends of the mirror line *A* as a first point. However, in the current example, the upper end is selected as the first point.

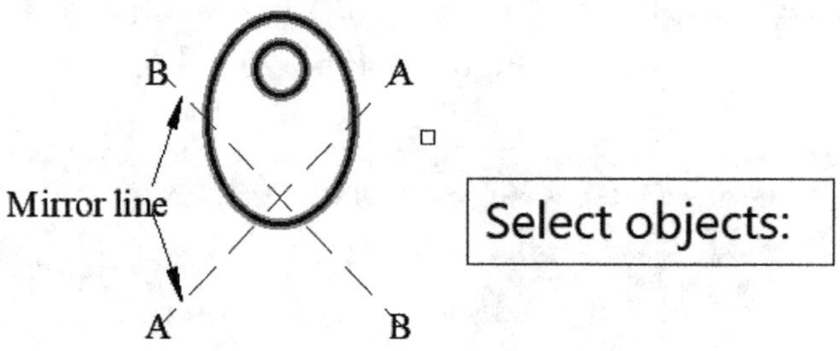

Figure 4-42a

- Either click on the upper end of the mirror line (follow the prompt) or specify its coordinates (use the "," key to move from x's to y's input field) and press the *Enter* key.

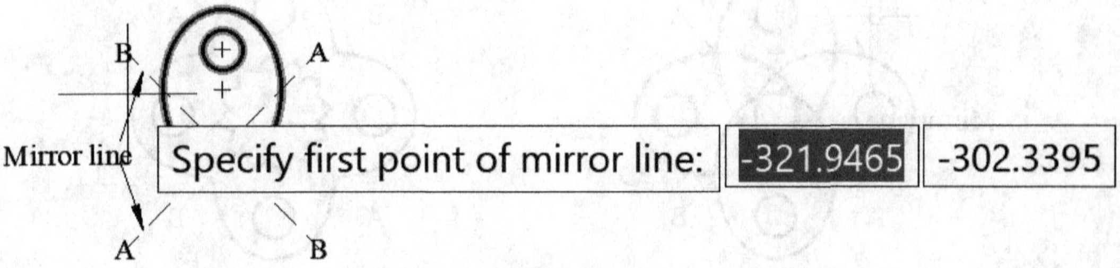

Figure 4-42b

- *Specify the second point of the mirror line*, Figure 4-42c: Either click on the lower end of the mirror line (follow the prompt) or specify the coordinates (use the "," key to move from x's to y's input field) and press the *Enter* key.
- *Erase source objects? [Yes or No]*, Figure 4-42d: Click on *No*; the *No* option is used to flip the image by placing the mirrored image into the drawing and retaining the original objects. The *Yes* option is used to flip the image by placing the mirrored image into the drawing and erasing the original objects. Figure 4-42e shows the result of the mirror command.

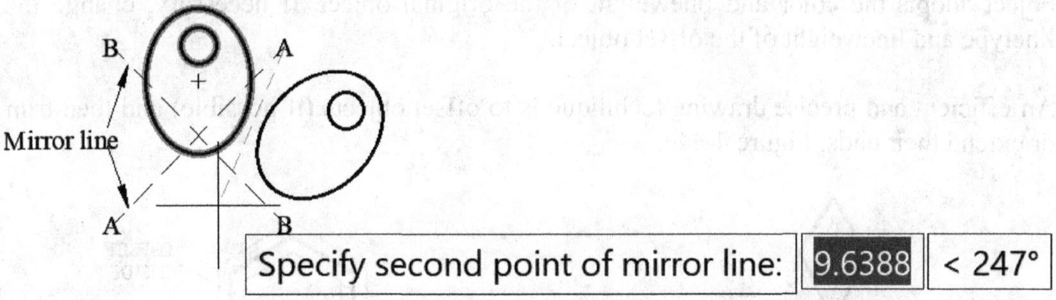

Figure 4-42c

Figure 4-42d

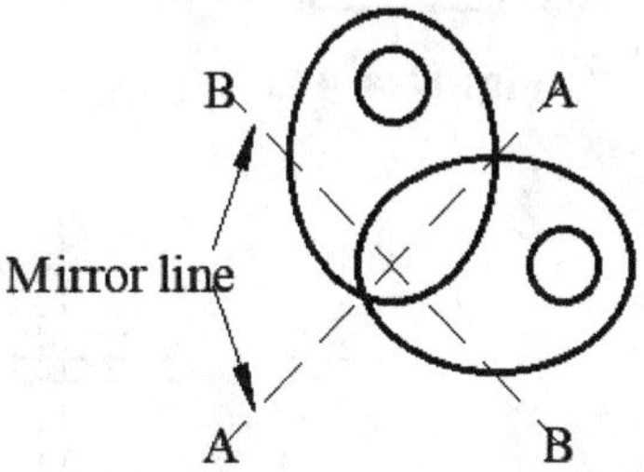

Figure 4-42e

- Repeat the mirror process using the mirror line BB. The resulting drawing is shown in Figure 4-43a.

- Using the trim command, remove the unnecessary parts of the ellipses, draw the circle, and change its linetype to complete the ratchet, Figure 4-43b.

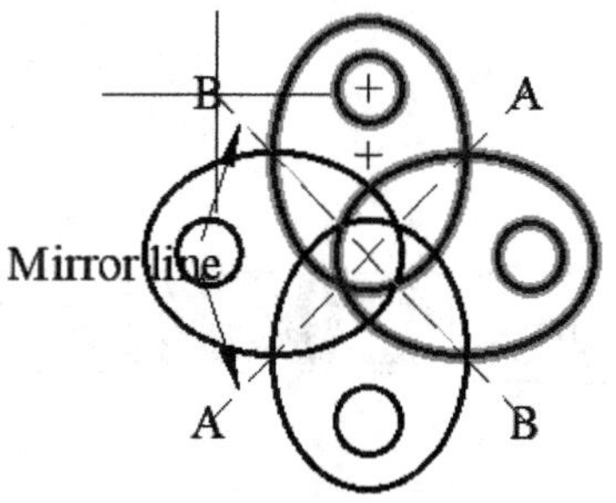

Figure 4-43a

Figure 4-43b

4.21. Offset

The *Offset* command creates a new object whose shape is parallel to the shape of the selected object. A user can offset lines, arcs, circles, ellipses, polylines, construction lines, splines, and rays. Offsetting closed shapes and arcs creates smaller or larger shapes or arcs if offset is inside or outside, respectively (Figure 4-44a and Figure 4-44b).

2D polylines and splines are trimmed automatically when the offset shape is larger than can be accommodated inside the polyline or spline, Figure 4-44a. However, the offset object adopts the color and lineweight of the original object. If necessary, change the linetype and lineweight of the offset object.

An efficient and precise drawing technique is to offset objects (if possible) and then trim or extend their ends, Figure 4-44c.

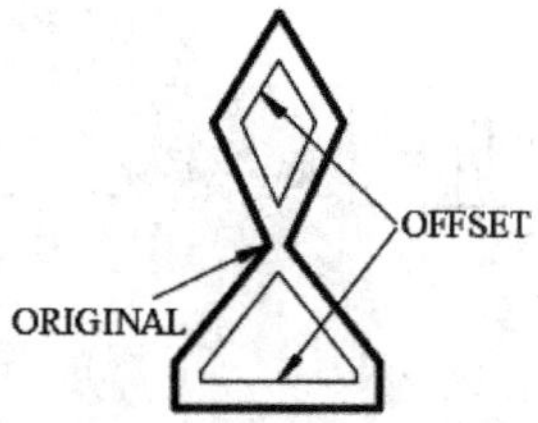

Figure 4-44a

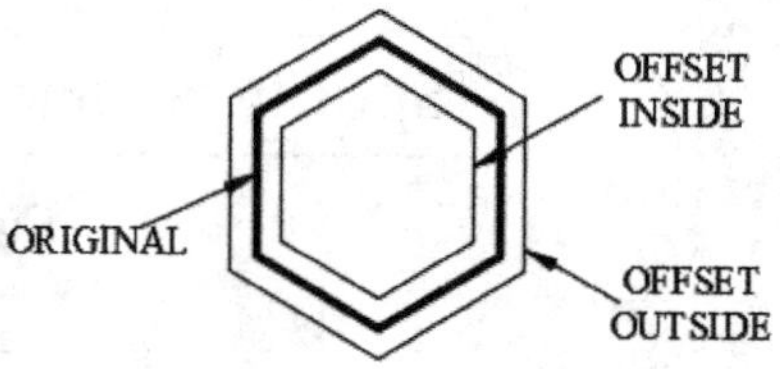

Figure 4-44b

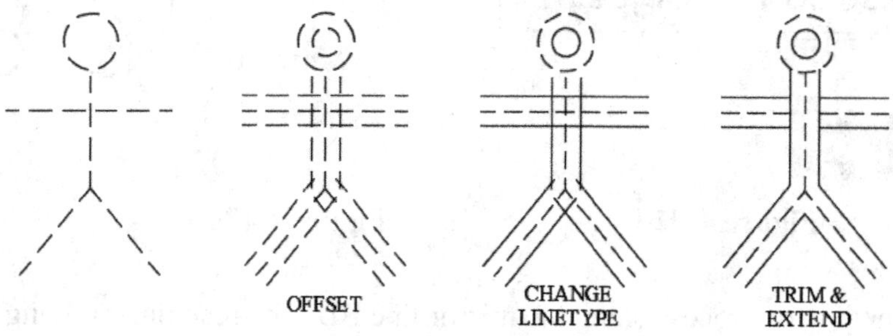

Figure 4-44c

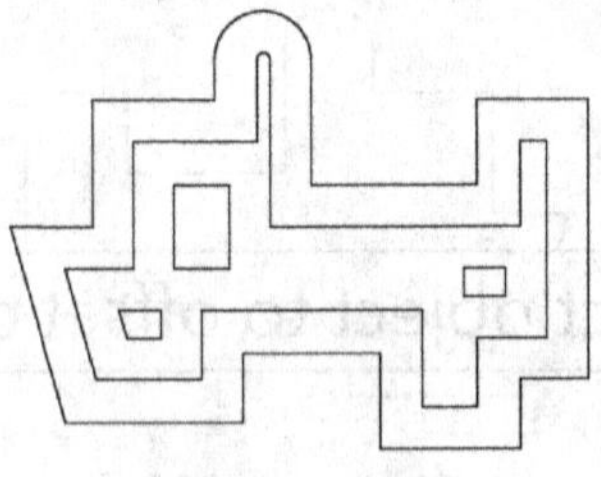

Figure 4-45a

Example: Create the shape shown in Figure 4-45a, using the offset command.

- Open a new "acad" file.
- Draw the basic shape using *Polyline* command as shown in Figure 4-45b. If necessary, use the *Join* command to connect the segments.

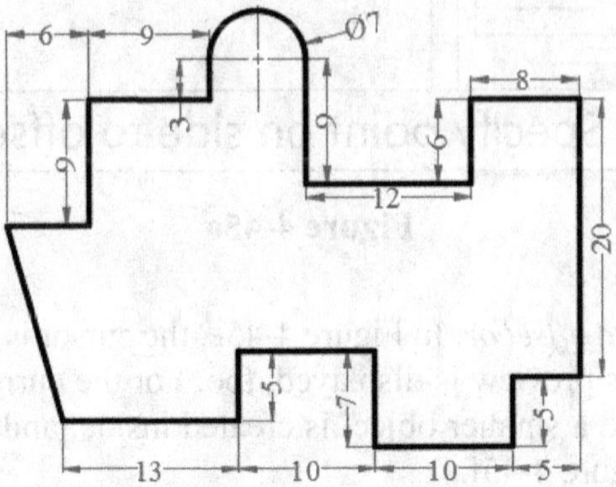

Figure 4-45b

- Activate the *Offset* command using one of the following methods:
  1. Panel method: From the *Home* tab and *Modify* panel select the *Offset* tool.
  2. Command line method: Type "offset", "Offset", or "OFFSET" in the command line and press the *Enter* key.

- The activation of the command leads to the offset distance specification prompt, Figure 4-45c.
- *Specify the offset distance or*, Figure 4-45c: Enter the offset distance and press the *Enter* key. In this example, the offset distance is 3.0. The prompt to select the object to offset (Figure 4-45d) appears.

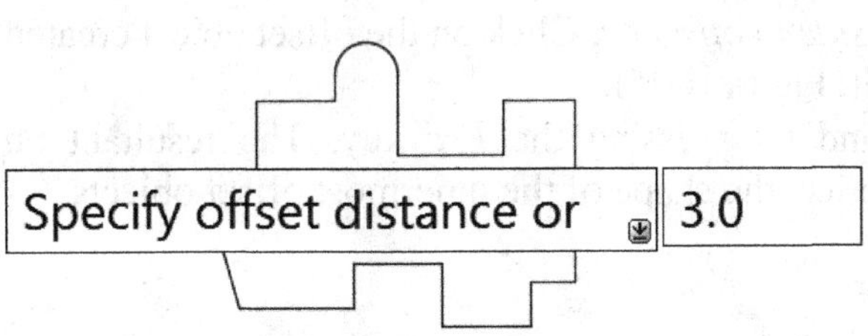

Figure 4-45c

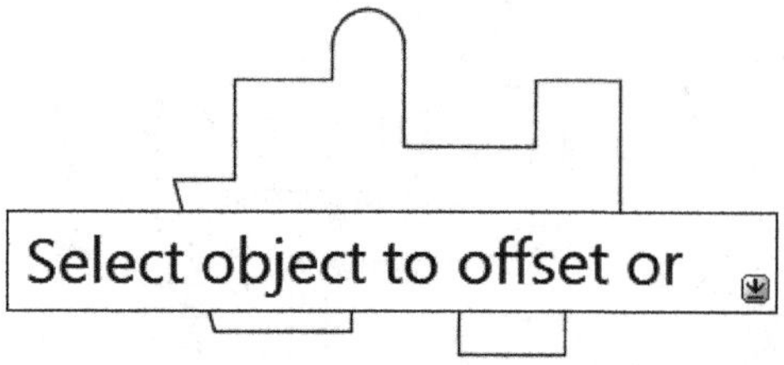

Figure 4-45d

- *Select object to offset or*, Figure 4-45d: In order to select the object to offset, bring the cursor on the object and press the left button of the mouse, Figure 4-45e. The original object's color and appearance changes.

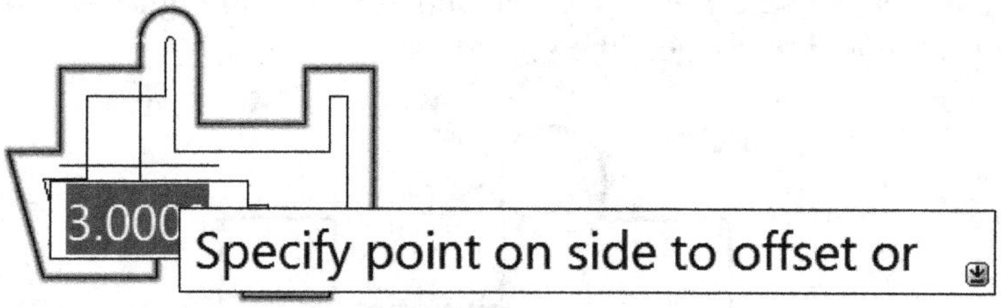

Figure 4-45e

- *Specify point on side to offset or*: In Figure 4-45e, the cursor is inside the selected object and the offset object's preview is displayed, too. For the current example, click inside the original object and a smaller object is created inside; and the prompt goes back to creating an offset, Figure 4-45f.
- Either click for another offset or exit the command by pressing the *Esc* key. However, in the current example, click on the offset object to create a new offset inside the previous offset, Figure 4-45g.

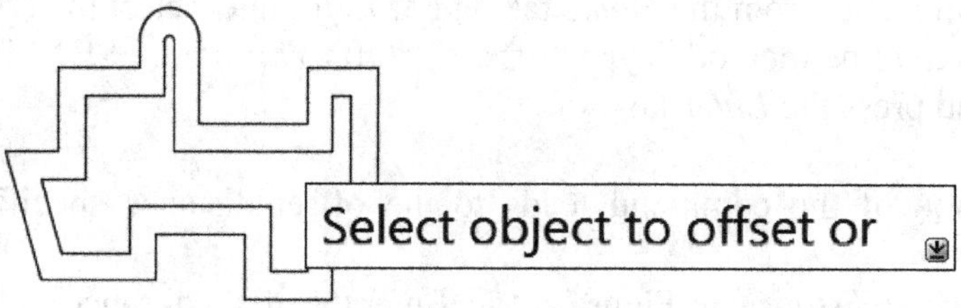

Figure 4-45f

- *Specify point on side to offset or*: Click on the offset object created in the previous step and click inside it, Figure 4-45f.
- Exit the command by pressing the *Esc* key. The resultant objects are shown in Figure 4-45a. Notice, the shape of the innermost offset objects.

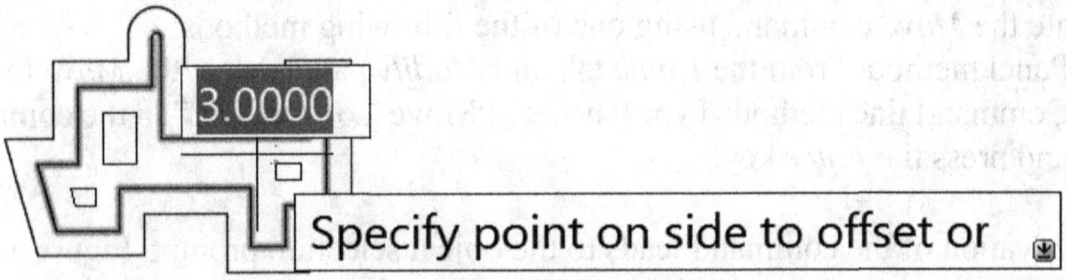

Figure 4-45g

4.22. Move

The *Move* command is used to relocate an object in a specified direction and at a specified distance from the original position. The user must activate the object snap command to move the objects with precision.

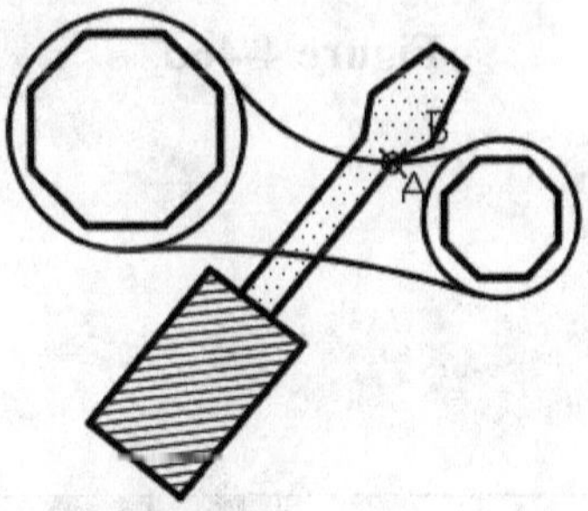

Figure 4-46a

Example: Move the screwdriver (Figure 4-46b) near the wrench (Figure 4-46c) as shown in Figure 4-46a using the *Move* command.

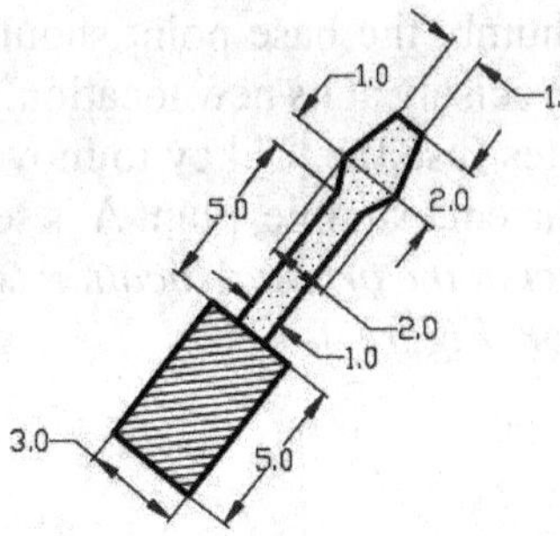

Figure 4-46b

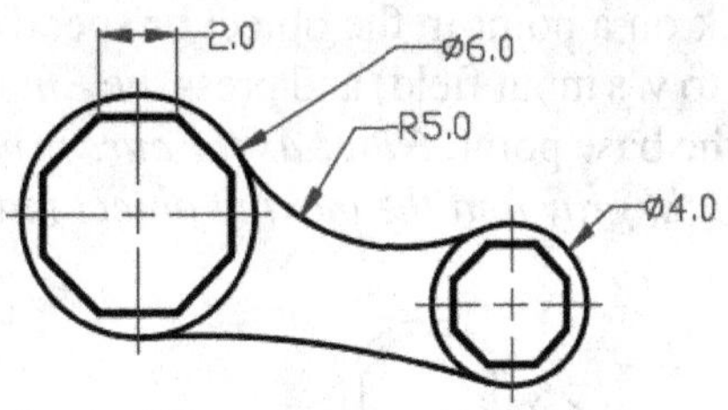

Figure 4-46c

- Open a new "acad" file.
- Draw the screwdriver (Figure 4-46b) near the wrench (Figure 4-46c) using the basic drawing commands. The ϕ symbol represents the diameter. No need to add dimensions. The remainder of this section explains the move process.

- Activate the *Move* command using one of the following methods:
  1. Panel method: From the *Home* tab and *Modify* panel select the *Move* tool.
  2. Command line method: Type "move", "Move", or "MOVE" in the command line and press the *Enter* key.

- The activation of the command leads to the object selection prompt, Figure 4-46d. Use one of the object selection methods discussed earlier. Finally, press the *Enter* key to complete the object selection. Notice the change in the appearance of the cursor. The prompt shown in Figure 4-46e appears.

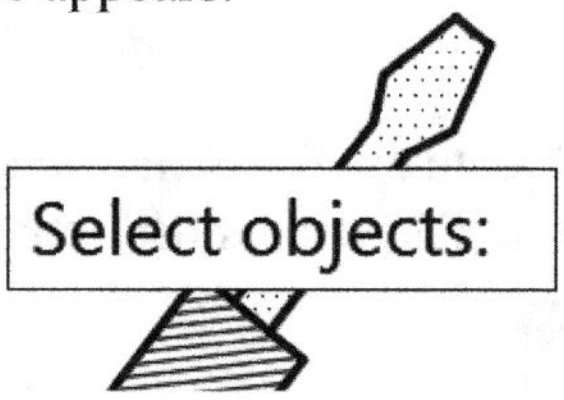

Figure 4-46d

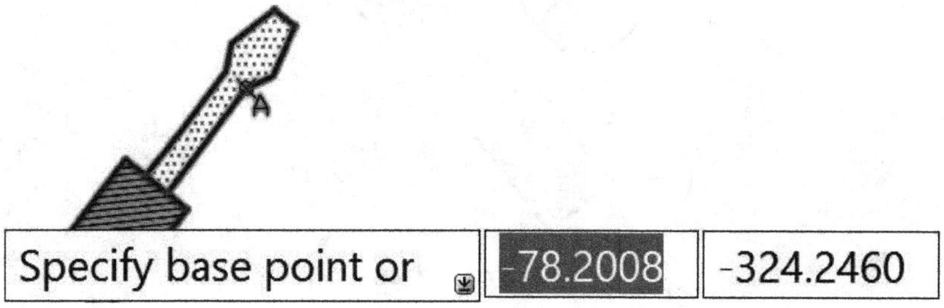

Figure 4-46e

4.22.1. Move in xy-plane

- *Specify the base point*, Figure 4-46e: As a rule of thumb, the base point should be a point such that the object can be relocated easily and precisely at its new location. Either click on a point in the object or specify the coordinates (use the "," key to move from x's to y's input field) and press the *Enter* key. In the current example, point A is selected as the base point. ***Note:*** *As the cursor moves, the object at the original location is faded to light gray and the moving object maintains its color, Figure 4-47a.*

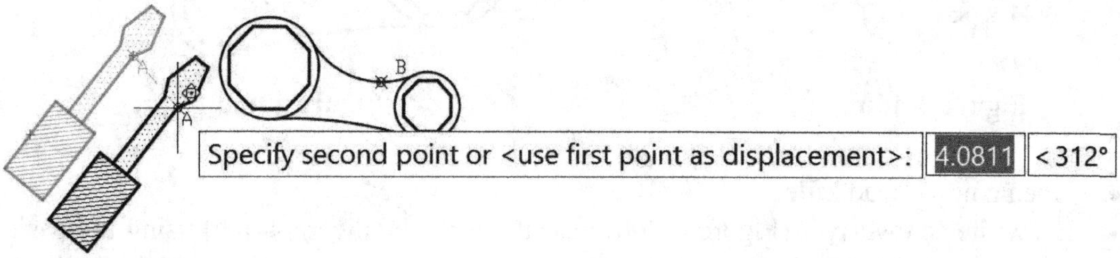

Figure 4-47a

- *Specify the second point*, Figure 4-47a: The second point is the new location of the object. Either click at the new location or specify its coordinates (use the "," key to move from x's to y's input field) and press the *Enter* key. The coordinates of the second point are relative coordinates with respect to the base point. This completes the process of moving the object from the original location to the new location and exits the command, too. For the current example, click at point B on the wrench. The resultant objects are shown in Figure 4-46a.
- The distance from the original to the new location is determined by the distance and direction between the base and second points.

4.22.2. Move in z-direction

The *Move* command can also be used to change the elevation of a drawing.

- Activate the *Move* command.
- Complete the object selection process and press the *Enter* key.
- *Specify the base point*, Figure 4-47b: Press the down-arrow key on the keyboard. Select the *Displacement* option by clicking the left button of the mouse.

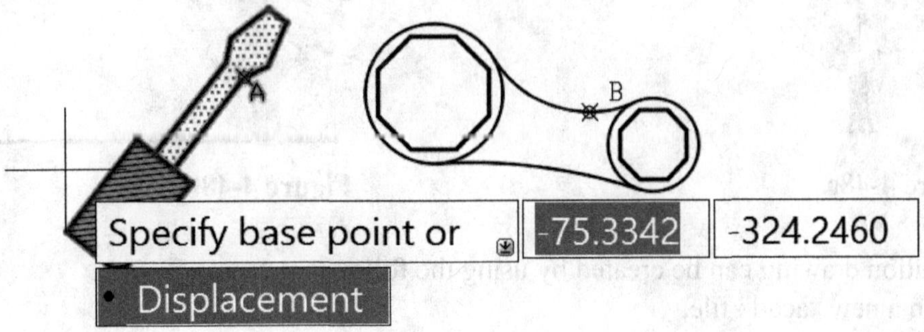

Figure 4-47b

- *Specify displacement*, Figure 4-47c: Specify the coordinates, use the "," key to move from one input field to the next, and press the *Enter* key. In the example, for the vertical displacement x and y are set to "0" and 75 is entered for the z coordinate.

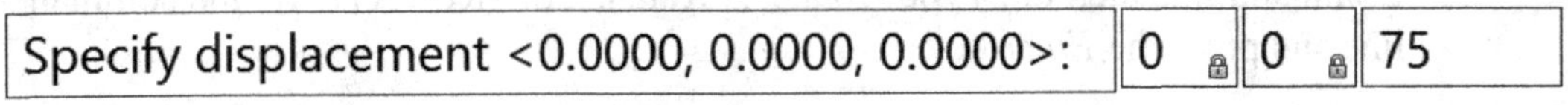

Figure 4-47c

- The base point's elevation (and every point's elevation) is incremented by 75. Initially, the elevation was zero. To check the elevation (or Z value) of the base point, (i) Activate the *Line* command, (ii) bring the cursor on the base point, and (iii) check the coordinate in the lower left corner of the workspace.

4.23. Rotate

The *Rotate* command is used to rotate objects in a drawing about a specified base point. The user must activate object snaps to rotate objects with precision.

Example: Figure 4-48e shows a tree rotated at 36 degrees counterclockwise from its original position, Figure 4-48b. The turned position can be shown using the *Rotate* command. Notice the change in the appearance of the cursor.

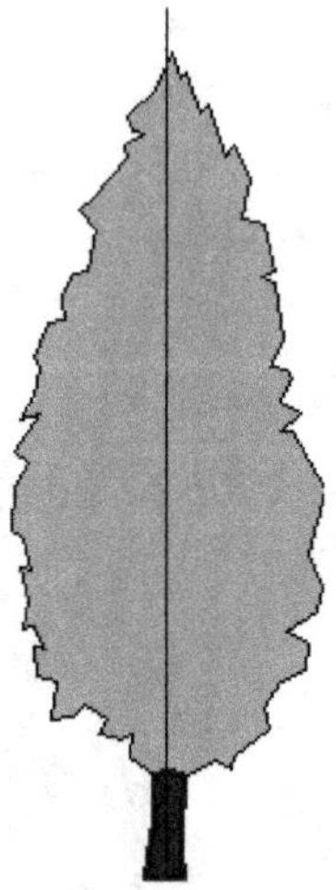

Figure 4-48a

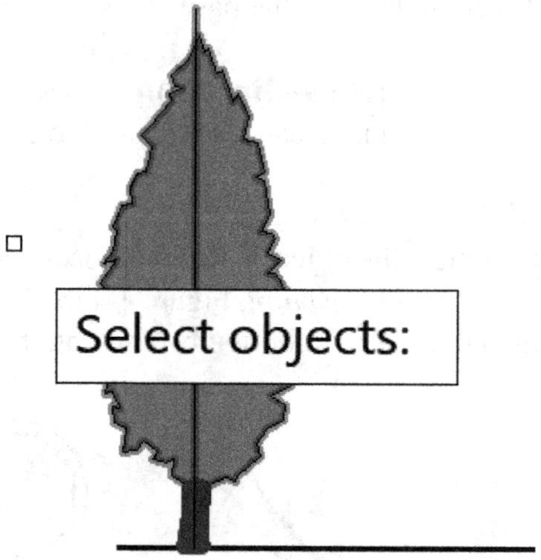

Figure 4-48b

The solution drawing can be created by using the following steps:

- Open a new "acad" file.
- Draw the basic element. For the practice, insert the *Tree – Type 2 Deciduous* block, from the Design Center as shown in Figure 4-48a. Draw two overlapping vertical lines passing through the center of the tree and a horizontal line connecting the bottom ends of the trunk.
- Activate the *Rotate* command using one of the following methods:
  1. Panel method: From the *Home* tab and *Modify* panel select the *Rotate* tool.
  2. Command line method: Type "rotate", "Rotate", or "ROTATE" in the command line and press the *Enter* key.

- The activation of the command leads to the object selection prompt, Figure 4-48b. Select the tree, one of the vertical lines, and the horizontal line; and press the *Enter* key to complete the object selection.

- *Specify the base point*, Figure 4-48c: In *Rotate* command, the base point is the pivot to rotate the object. Either click on a point in the object or specify the coordinates (use the "," key to move from x's to y's input field) and press the *Enter* key. In this example, click at the midpoint of the horizontal line drawn to connect the bottom ends of the trunk, Figure 4-48d. ***Note:*** *As the cursor moves, the object at the original position fades to light gray and the rotated object maintains its color, Figure 4-48d.*

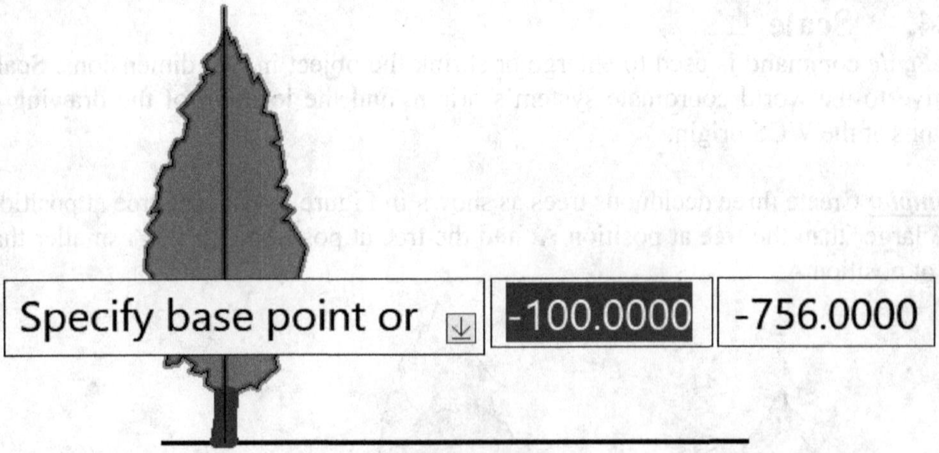

Figure 4-48c

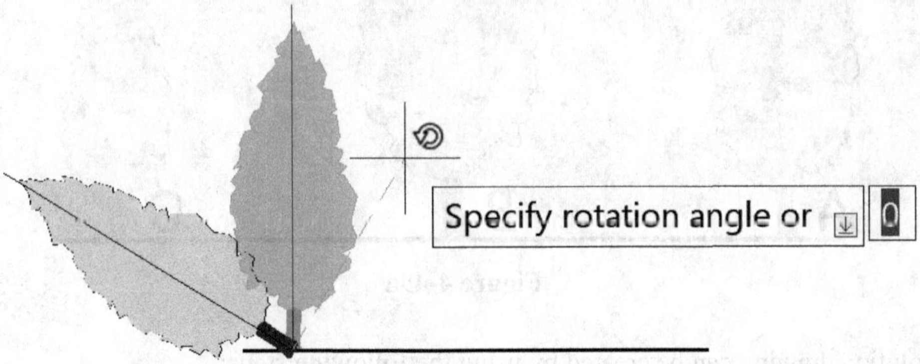

Figure 4-48d

- *Specify rotation angle*, Figure 4-48d: Either click at the desired orientation or specify its value and press the *Enter* key. Positive angle rotates the object counterclockwise, and the negative angle rotates the object clockwise. In the example, the rotation angle is set to 36 degrees. Figure 4.48e shows the rotated tree.

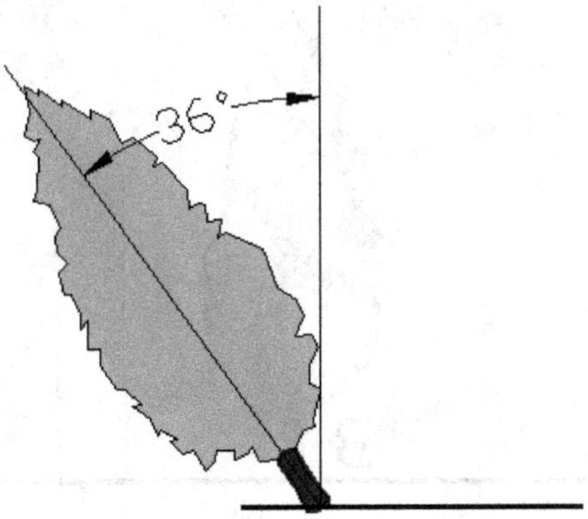

Figure 4-48e

4.24. Scale 

The *Scale* command is used to enlarge or shrink the object in two dimensions. Scaling is relative to the world coordinate system's origin; and the location of the drawing origin remains at the WCS origin.

Example: Create three deciduous trees as shown in Figure 4-49a. The tree at position B is 25% larger than the tree at position A; and the tree at position C is 25% smaller than the tree at position A.

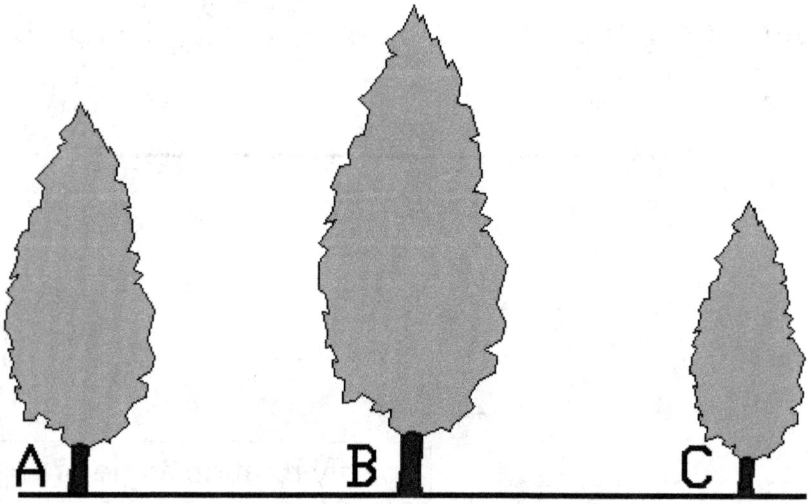

Figure 4-49a

The solution drawing can be created by using the following steps:

- **Basic Element**: Use the screwdriver as shown in Figure 4-48a.
- Open a new "acad" file.
- Draw the basic element.
- Use *Copy* command to create the two copies and place them at position B and C, Figure 4-49b. The tree at position B will be used for the illustration of the *Scale* command.

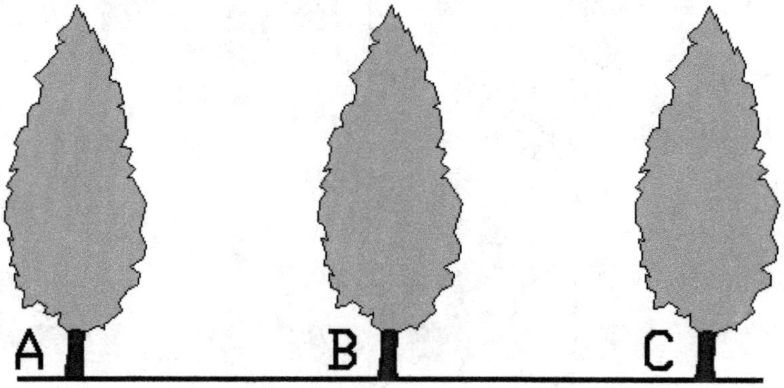

Figure 4-49b

- Activate the *Scale* command using one of the following methods:
    1. Panel method: From the *Home* tab and *Modify* panel select the *Scale* tool.
    2. Command line method: Type "scale", "Scale", or "SCALE" in the command line and press the *Enter* key.
- The activation of this command leads to the object selection prompt, Figure 4-49c.
- Select the object (the tree at position B) to scale and press the *Enter* key to complete the object selection, Figure 4-49d.

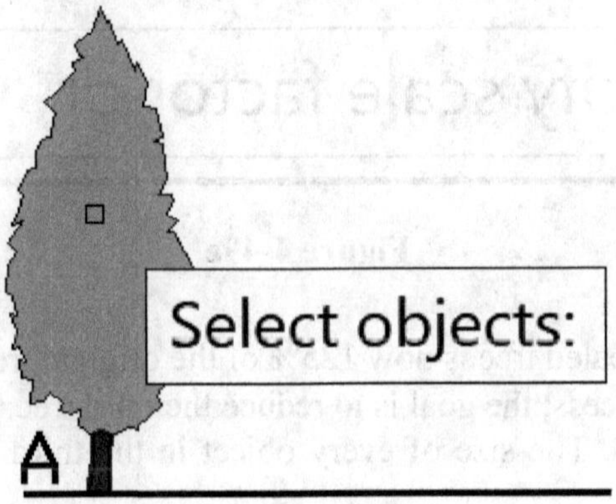

Figure 4-49c

- *Specify the base point*, Figure 4-49d: When an object is scaled up or down, every point in the object moves from its current location except one point (the base point). For the *Scale* command, the base point is the point that stays at its original location. Either click at a point in the object or specify its coordinates and press the *Enter* key. In this example, the midpoint of the horizontal line drawn to connect the bottom ends of the trunk is chosen as the base point. Turn on the object snap and click at the selected point.
- *Specify scale factor*, Figure 4-49e: **Notice the change in the appearance of the cursor**. The tree at the original scale is faded to light gray and the scaled tree maintains its color. Enter the desired value and press the *Enter* key. In this example, the goal is to increase the second tree by 25%. Therefore, the scale factor of 1.25 is used (not shown in the figure).

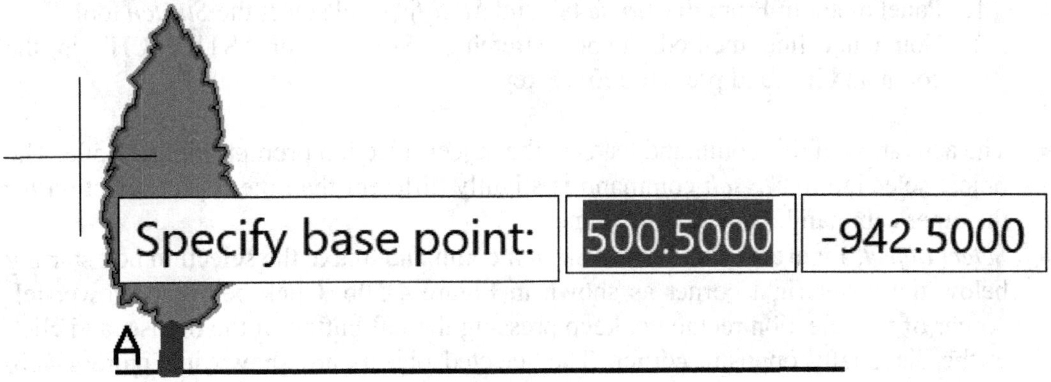

Figure 4-49d

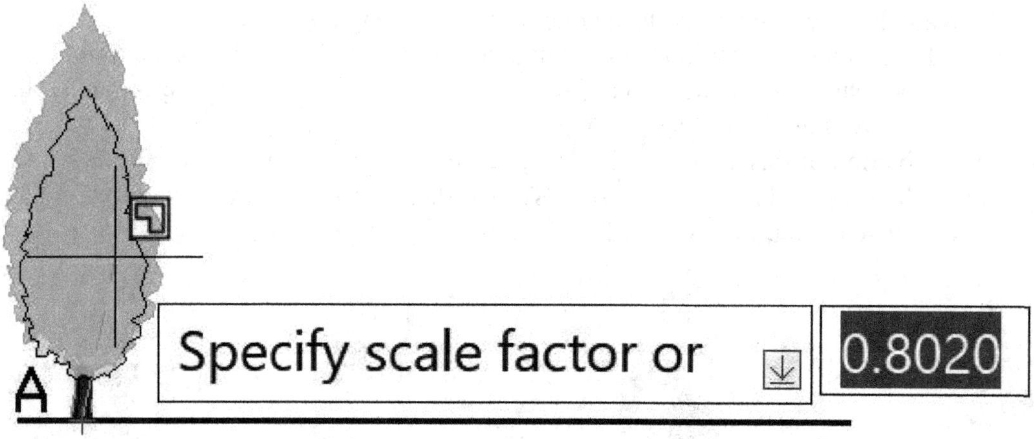

Figure 4-49e

- Every object in the scaled tree is now 125% of the original tree, Figure 4-49a.
- Repeat the above process; the goal is to reduce the third tree by 25%. Hence, the scale factor would be 0.75. The size of every object in the third tree is reduced by 25%, Figure 4-49f.
- Note: The *Scale* command does not save the history of the sizes; it applies the scale factor to the current size.

4.25. Stretch

The *Stretch* command is used to lengthen or shorten an object (change in one-dimension).

Example: Stretch the model such that the right side is stretched from point A to point B, Figure 4-50a.

The solution drawing can be created by using the following steps:

- Open a new "acad" file.
- Draw the objects shown in Figure 4-50a.
- Activate the *Stretch* command using one of the following methods:
  1. Panel method: From the *Home* tab and *Modify* panel select the *Stretch* tool.
  2. Command line method: Type "stretch", "Stretch", or "STRETCH" in the command line and press the *Enter* key.

- The activation of this command leads to the object selection prompt, Figure 4-50a. The object selection in *Stretch* command is slightly different than the object selection for the other command on the *Modify* panel.
- *Select object*, Figure 4-50b: For the *Stretch* command, make the selection box starting below the lower right corner as shown in Figure 4-50b. Click below the lower left corner of the selection rectangle, keep pressing the left button of the mouse, and click at the diagonally opposite corner. The selected objects are shown in Figure 4-50b. Finally, press the *Enter* key.

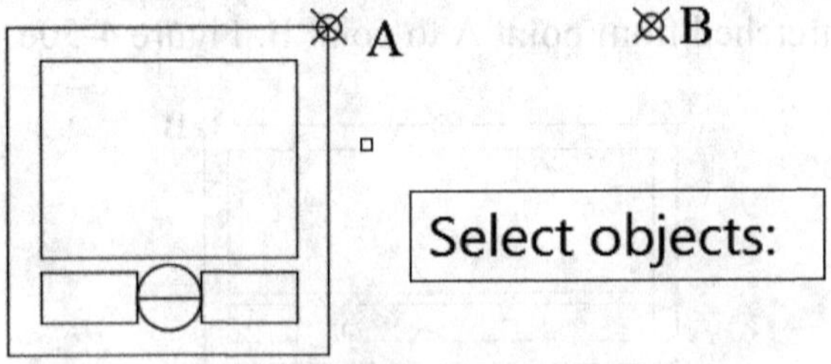

Figure 4-50a

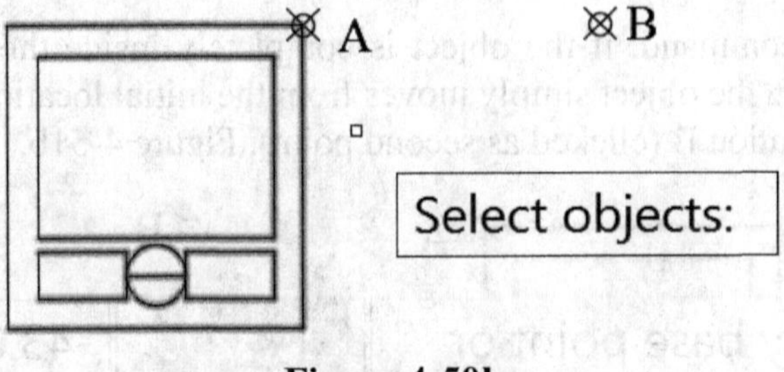

Figure 4-50b

- *Specify the base point*, Figure 4-50c: For the *Stretch* command, the base point should be the point that needs to be stretched to the new location. Either click on the point or specify its coordinates and press the *Enter* key. In this example, click at point A.

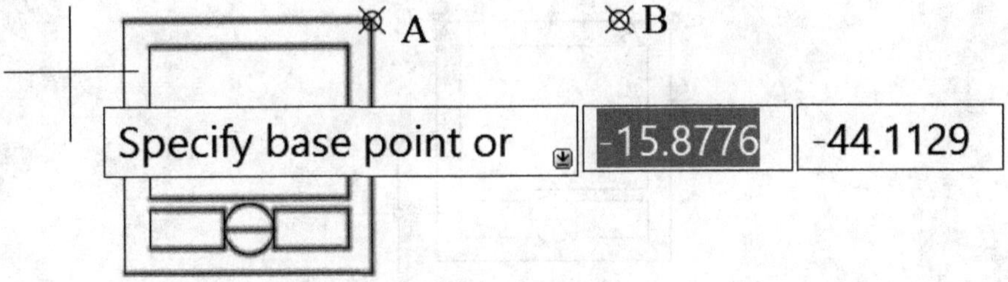

Figure 4-50c

- *Specify second point*, Figure 4-50d: For the *Stretch* command, the second point is the new location of the base point. Either click on the point or specify its coordinates and press the *Enter* key. In this example, click at point B. ***Note: As the cursor moves, the original object is faded to light gray and the new object (that is, the stretched object) maintains its color, Figure 4-50d.***

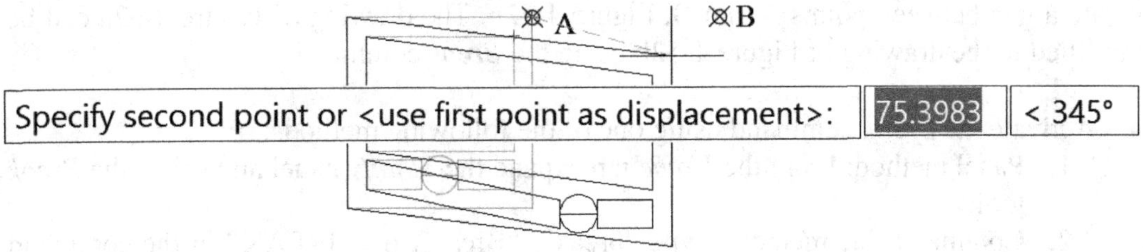

Figure 4-50d

- The right side is stretched from point A to point B, Figure 4-50e.

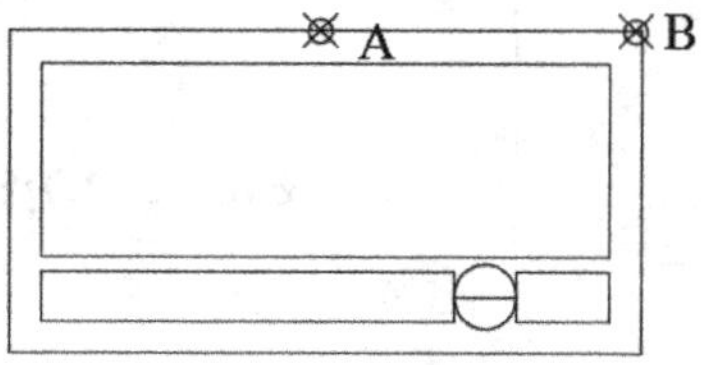

Figure 4-50e

- For the *Stretch* command, if the object is completely inside the selection rectangle, Figure 4-51a, then the object simply moves from the initial location A (clicked as base point) to new location B (clicked as second point), Figure 4-51b.

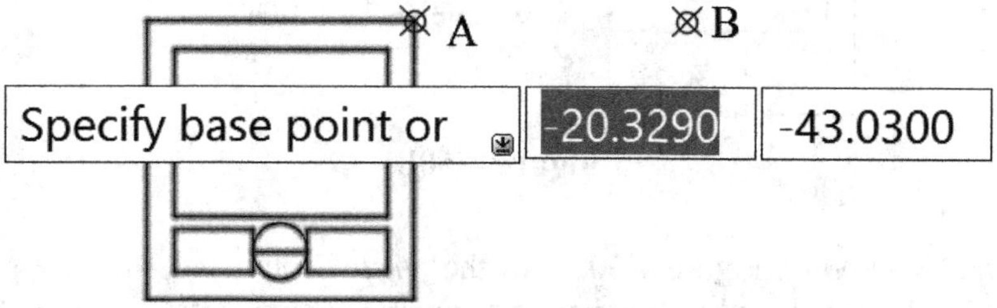

Figure 4-51a

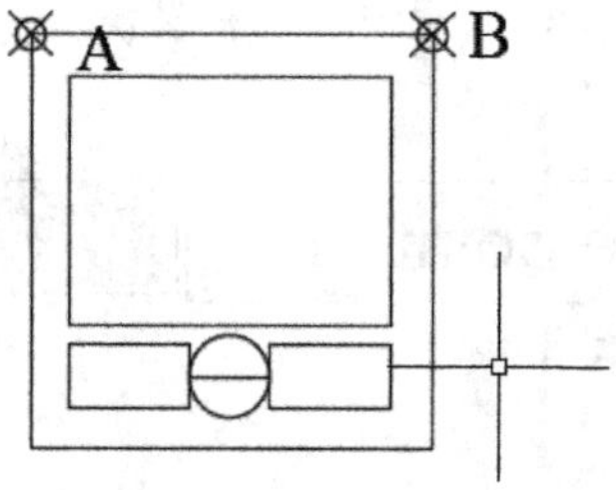

Figure 4-51b

4.26. Break

The *Break* command is used to create a gap or open space in the given object by specifying two points on the object.

Example: Consider a drafter drew the drawing shown in Figure 4-52a and now wants to create a gap between points A and B, Figure 4-52b. The drawing of Figure 4-52a can be modified to the drawing of Figure 4-52b using the *Break* command.

- Activate the *Break* command using one of the following methods:
    1. Panel method: From the *Home* tab expand the *Modify* panel and select the *Break* tool.
    2. Command line method: Type "break", "Break", or "BREAK" in the command line and press the *Enter* key.

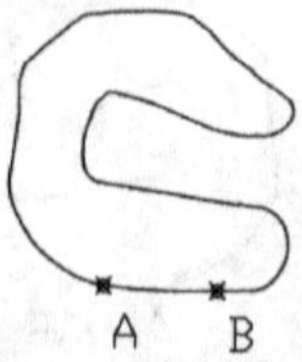

Figure 4-52a

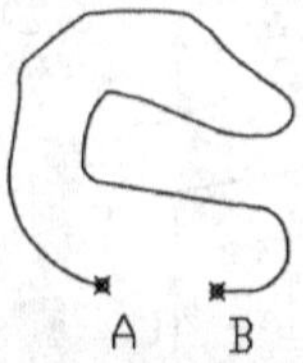

Figure 4-52b

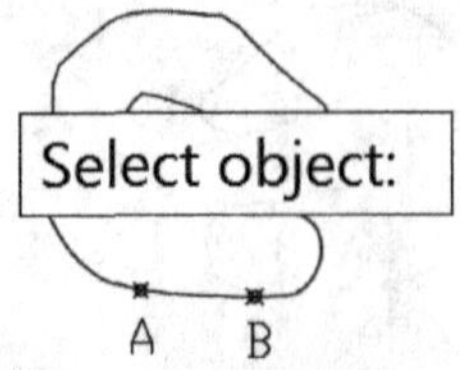

Figure 4-53a

- The activation of the command displays the prompt to select the object, Figure 4-53a.
- *Select object*, Figure 4-53a: Bring the cursor on the object and click with the left button of the mouse. The prompt shown in Figure 4-53b appears.

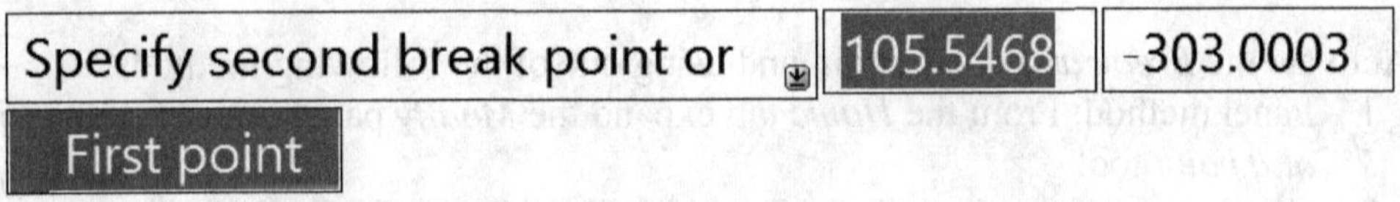

Figure 4-53b

- *Specify second break point or*, Figure 4-53b: Press the down-arrow key on the keyboard to display the available options. Select the First point option. The prompt shown in Figure 4-53c appears.
- *Specify first break point or*, Figure 4-53c: Either click at the desired point or specify its coordinate and press the *Enter* key. In the current example, click at point A.

Figure 4-53c

- *Specify second break point or*, Figure 4-53d: Either click at the desired location or specify its coordinates and press the *Enter* key. In the current example, click at point B.

Figure 4-53d

- The gap between point A and B is created as shown in Figure 4-52b.
- The same effect can also be created by (i) drawing two temporary lines at points A and B, Figure 4-54a; (ii) using the *Trim* command trim the object between the two lines, Figure 4-54b, and (iii) Deleting the lines using *Erase* command, Figure 4-54c.

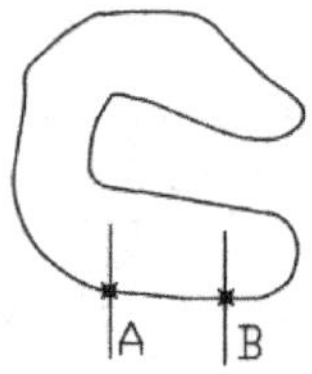

Figure 4-54a

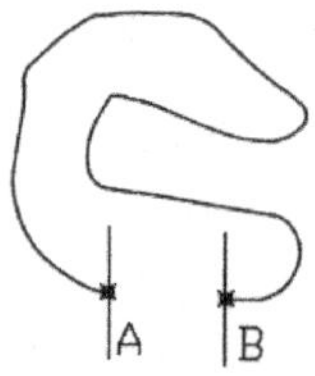

Figure 4-54b

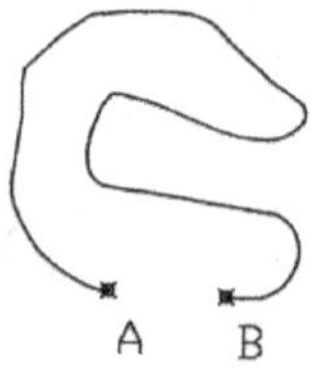

Figure 4-54c

4.27. Break At A Point

The *Break at a point* command is used to break objects (line, polyline, and arcs) without creating a gap or open space in the object.

- Activate the *Break at a point* command using one of the following methods:
    1. Panel method: From the *Home* tab expand the *Modify* panel and select the *Break at a point* tool.
    2. Command line method: Type "break", "Break", or "BREAK" in the command line and press the *Enter* key.

- The activation of the command displays the prompt to select the object.
- After the object selection, click at the desired point. The object is broken without creating a gap. *The same functionality can be achieved using the Break command. The user must click at the same point for both the first and second break points.*

4.28. Explode

The *Explode* command is used to break a compound object into its basic component objects. The exploded objects cannot be joined to create the original object. To practice the command, create a rectangle, pentagon, circle, a closed polyline, and a dimension using the *Rectangle*, *Polygon*, *Circle*, *Polyline*, and *Dimension* commands, respectively, as shown in the left column of Table #1. Only one side of the rectangle is dimensioned.

- Activate the *Explode* command using one of the following methods:
    1. Panel method: From the *Home* tab and *Modify* panel select the *Explode* tool.
    2. Command line method: Type "explode", "Explode", or "EXPLODE" in the command line and press the *Enter* key.
- The activation of the command leads to the object selection prompt. Select the object (bring the cursor on the rectangle) and press the *Enter* key. The object is broken into its basic component.
- The *Explode* command does not change the appearance of the object, left column of Table #1. However, if the original and the exploded object are selected, then their grip points are different. The middle column of Table #1 shows the original objects, whereas the right column of Table #1 shows the exploded objects.
- A circle cannot be exploded.
- The rectangle, pentagon, and the closed polyline are broken into line segments.
- The dimension is exploded into extension and dimension lines, the text, and the arrows.

Table #1: Explode command demonstration

Object	Original	Exploded
	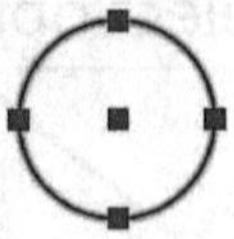	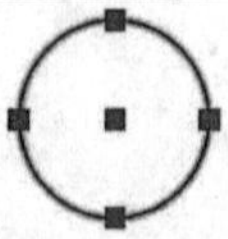 Circle cannot be exploded
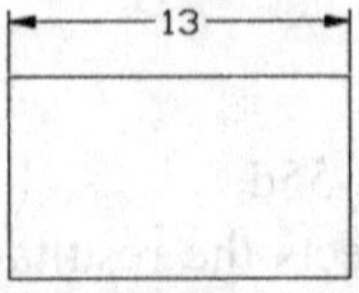		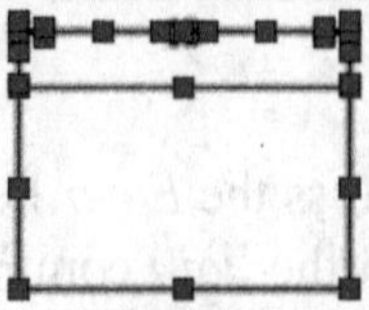
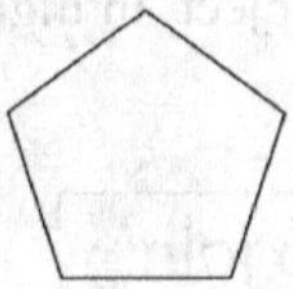	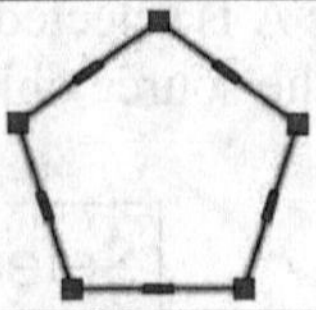	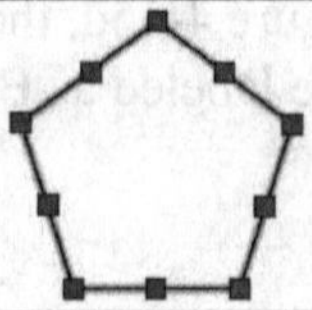
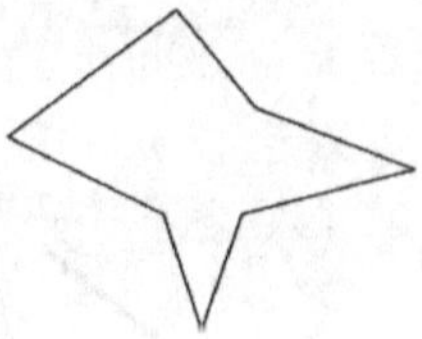	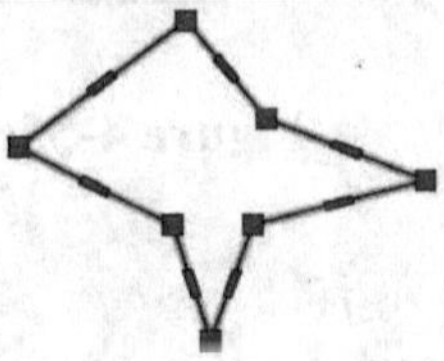	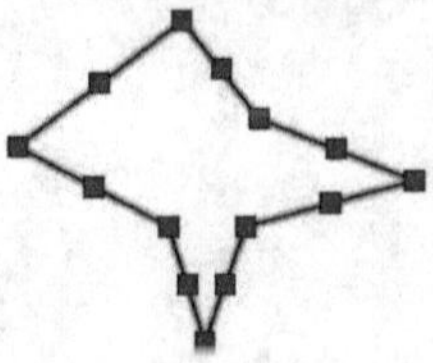

4.29. Join 

The *Join* command is used to connect multiple linear or curved objects to create a single object. The command can be used to connect lines, circular arcs, elliptical arcs, polylines, splines, and their combination. However, the command cannot be used to connect close objects. The order of the object selection affects the resultant object.

- Activate the *Join* command using one of the following methods:
  1. Panel method: From the *Home* tab expand the *Modify* panel and select the *Join* tool.
  2. Command line method: Type "join", "Join", or "JOIN" in the command line and press the *Enter* key.
- The activation of the command leads to the source object selection prompt.
- *Select source object*, Figure 4-55a: Click the source object with the left button of the mouse. In this example, click on the line labeled as A.

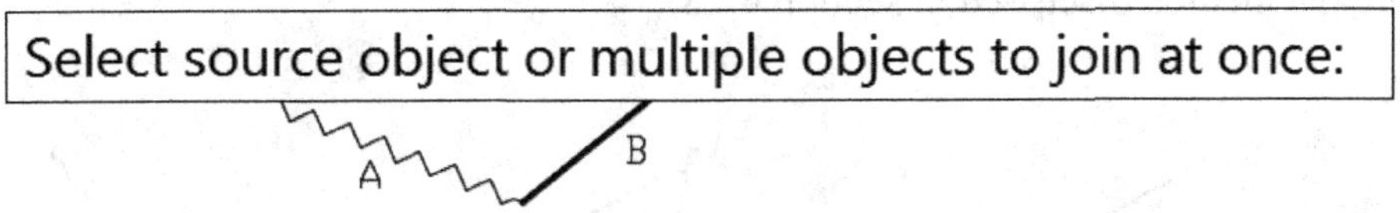

Figure 4-55a

- *Select object to join*, Figure 4-55b: Click the object to be connected with the left button of the mouse, Figure 4-55c. In this example, click on the line labeled as B.

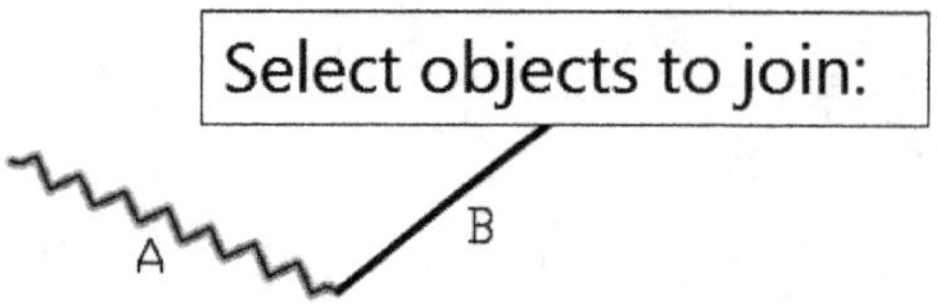

Figure 4-55b

- Press the *Enter* key. The joined object is shown in Figure 4-55d.
- In the *Join* command the order of the object selection affects the resultant object. In Figure 4-55d, the line labeled as A is selected as the source object. In Figure 4-55e, the line labeled as B is selected as the source object.

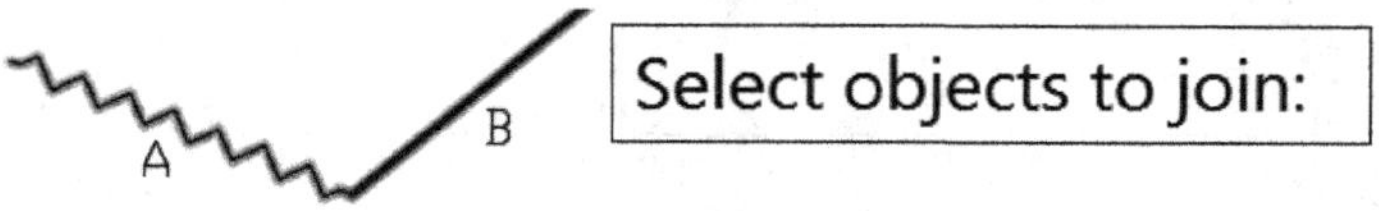

Figure 4-55c

Figure 4-55d

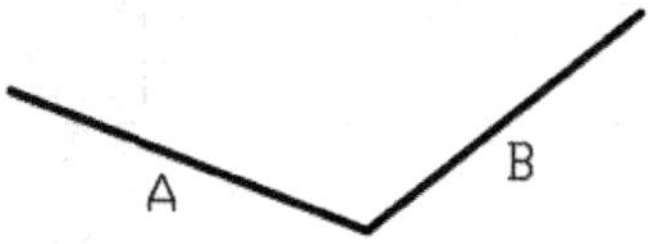

Figure 4-55e

4.29.1.1. Lines

The *Join* command can connect non-intersecting collinear and coplanar lines with or without gaps. The collinear lines are in the same direction. The coplanar lines are in the same plane, that is, they have the same elevation. The resultant object is a single line.

Example: Connect A to B, C to D, and E to F.

- **A and B**: Two collinear and coplanar lines with a gap, Figure 4-56a. Lines A and B can be joined using the method discussed in section 4.28.
- **C and D**: Two collinear and coplanar lines without a gap, Figure 4-56b. Lines C and D can be joined using the method discussed in section 4.28.
- **E and F**: Two coplanar lines without a gap, Figure 4-56c. Lines E and F can be joined using the method discussed in section 4.28.

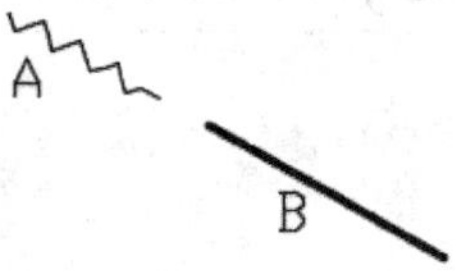

Figure 4-56a

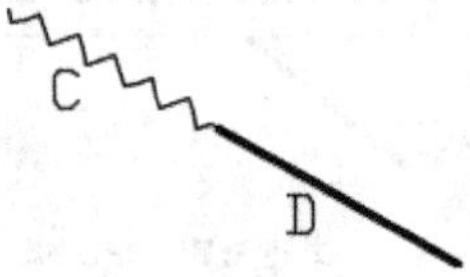

Figure 4-56b

Figure 4-56c

4.29.1.2. Circular arc

The *Join* command can connect circular arcs with the same radius and same center point. The resultant object is an arc or a circle. The arcs are connected in a counterclockwise direction starting from the source arc.

Example: Connect the arcs A to B and C to D, Figure 4-57a. The figure shows four arcs. Arcs labeled as A, B, and C have the same radius. Although the arc D has the same center, its radius is different. Therefore, it cannot be joined to any arc of the figure.

- **A and B**: Figure 4-57a, the arcs A and B can be joined using the method discussed in section 4.28. In this figure, A is the source arc. Arcs are connected in the counterclockwise direction starting from the source arc, Figure 4-57b.

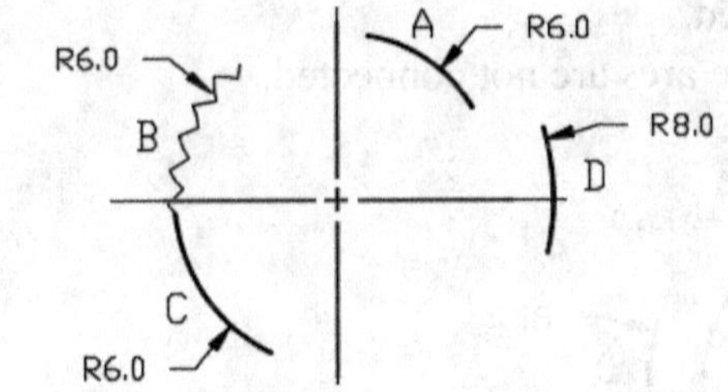

Figure 4-57a

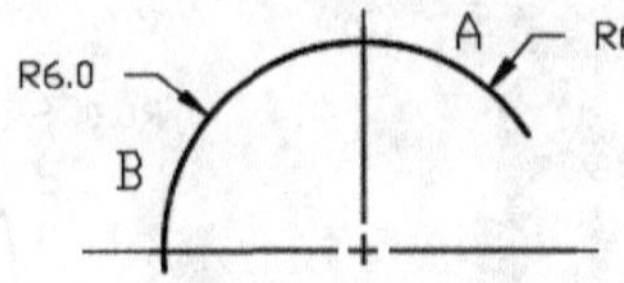

Figure 4-57b

- **B and A**: Figure 4-57a, the arcs B and A can be joined using the method discussed in section 4.28. In this figure, B is the source arc. Arcs are connected in the counterclockwise direction starting from the source arc, Figure 4-57c.
- **Note** the difference in the appearance and size of resultant arcs of Figure 4-57b and Figure 4-57c.
- In Figure 4-57d, arcs A, B, and C have the same radius and same center. The three arcs can be connected as follows: (i) activate the *Join* command; (ii) click on A (source arc); (iii) click on B; (iv) click on C; and (v) finally, press the *Enter* key.

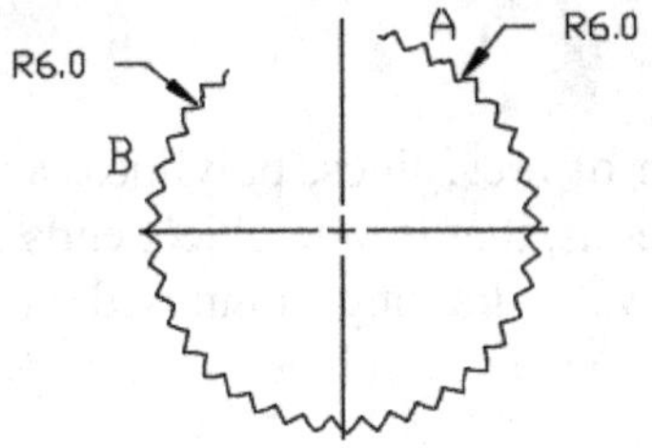

Figure 4-57c

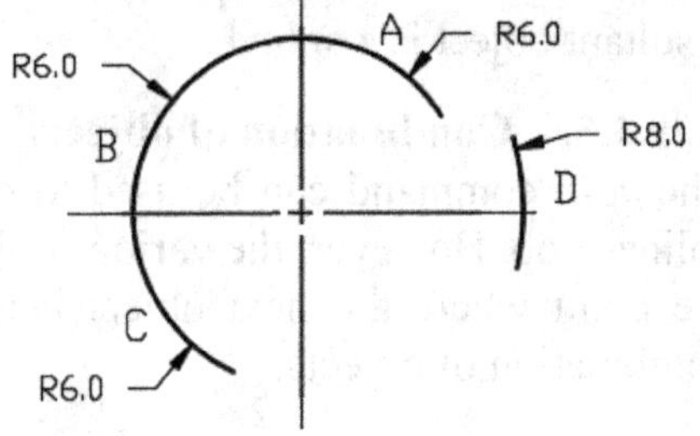

Figure 4-57d

- However, in Figure 4-57a, if the user desires to connect the arcs by setting C as the source arc, then after selecting C, A, and B and pressing the *Enter* key, the prompt shown in Figure 4-58a appears.

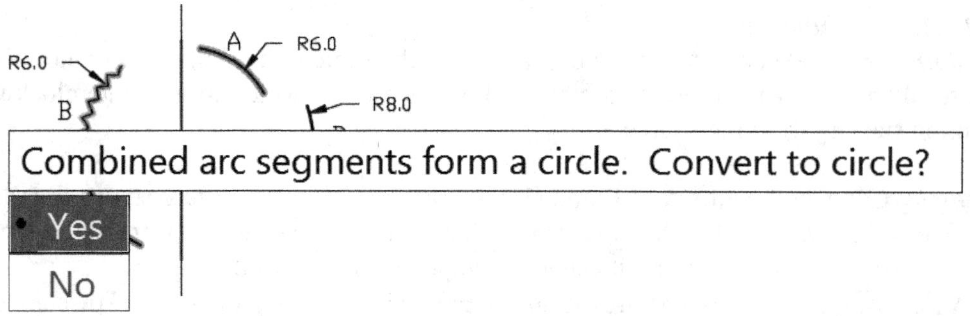

Figure 4-58a

- Since there is no gap between B and C, if the user selects *Yes* option (Figure 4-58a) then the circle shown in Figure 4-58b is created.
- However, if the user selects *No* option then the arcs are not connected.

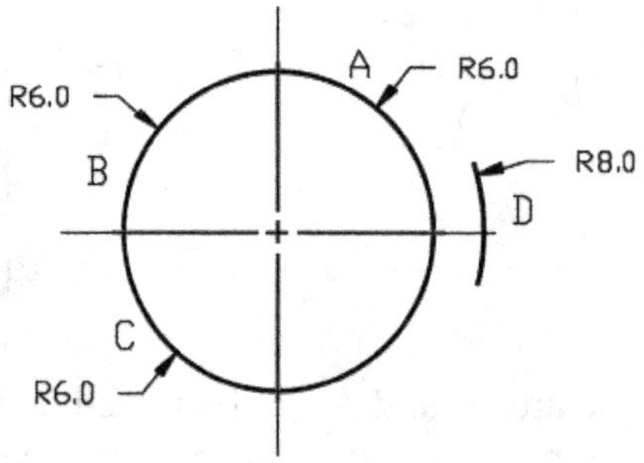

Figure 4-58b

4.29.1.3. Polyline

The process to connect polylines is the same as the process of connecting the lines. The resultant object is a polyline.

4.29.1.4. Spline

The process to connect splines is the same as the process of connecting the lines. The resultant object is a spline.

4.29.1.5. Combination of objects

The *Join* command can be used to connect a combination of arcs, lines, polylines, and splines, too. However, the various objects should be contiguous, that is, one object ends at the point where the next object begins. Figure 4-59 shows a drawing composed of a combination of objects.

- Join line and arc: The resultant object is a polyline.
- Join polyline and arc: The resultant object is a polyline.
- Join line, polyline, and arc: Resultant object is a polyline.
- Join spline and arc: The resultant object is a spline.
- Join line, spline, and arc: The resultant object is a spline.
- Join line, polyline, spline, and arc: The resultant object is a spline.

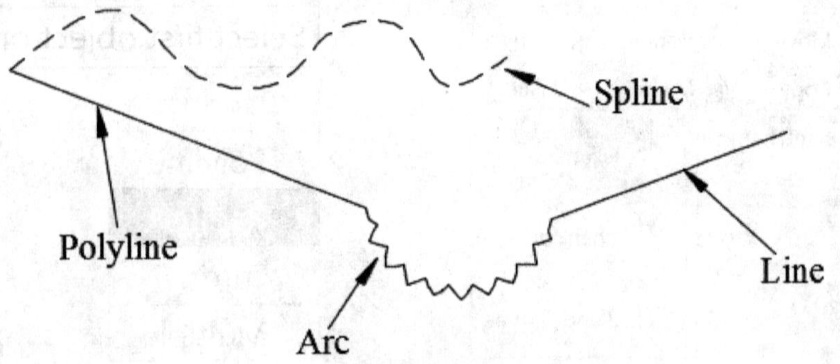

Figure 4-59

4.30. Fillet

The *Fillet* command is used to connect two objects with an arc of the specified radius such that the arc is tangent to both objects. The connecting objects can be arcs, circles, ellipses, elliptical arcs, lines, polylines, rays, splines, or a combination of any two.

Example: To follow the *Fillet* command, draw the lines and circles as shown in Figure 4-60a and Figure 4-60b. In the figure, the symbol ϕ represents the diameter.

- Activate the *Fillet* command using one of the following methods:
  1. Panel method: From the *Home* tab and *Modify* panel expand the *Fillet* drop-down menu and select the *Fillet* tool, Figure 4-61a.
  2. Command line method: Type "fillet", "Fillet", or "FILLET" in the command line and press the *Enter* key.

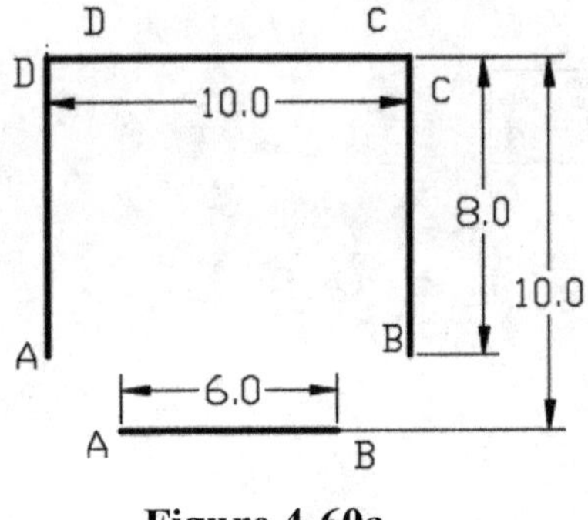

Figure 4-60a

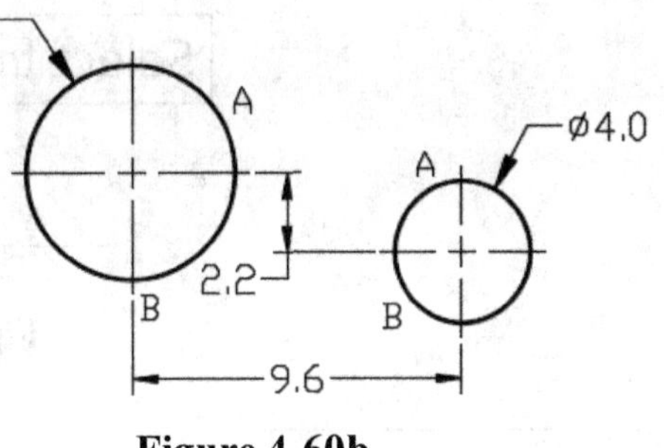

Figure 4-60b

- The activation of the command leads to the first object selection prompt, Figure 4-61b. (i) Press the down-arrow key, (ii) click on the Radius option with the left button of the mouse.
- *Specify fillet radius*: Specify the radius and press the *Enter* key, Figure 4-61c. In the current example, the radius is 2.
- The remainder of this section describes how to fillet lines and circles.

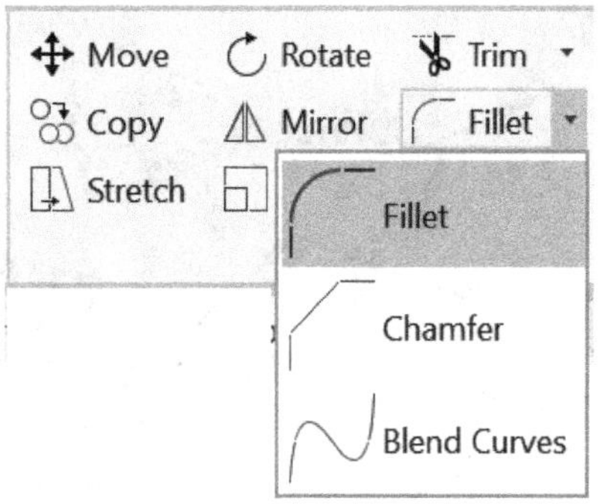

Figure 4-61a

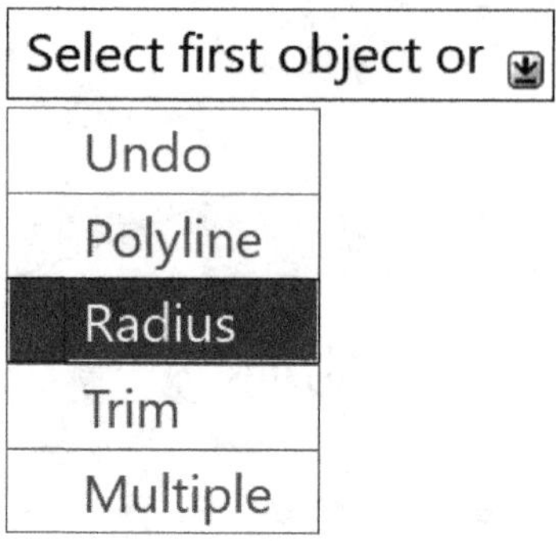

Figure 4-61b

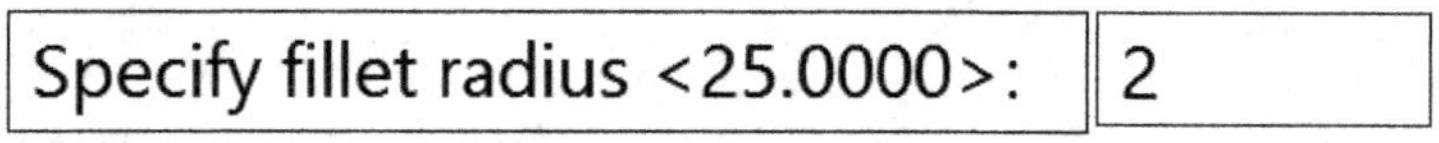

Figure 4-61c

- <u>Fillet lines</u>: The *Fillet* command draws the arc that meets the lines smoothly. If necessary, the command will also trim the corner (fillet at corner D in Figure 4-62c and Figure 4-62d).

1. Activate the *Fillet* command, if it is not active.
2. Specify the radius (in this example, the radius is 2).
3. For the first object, click in the vicinity of point A on the line AD, Figure 4-62a.
4. For the second object, click in the vicinity of point A on line AB, Figure 4-62b.

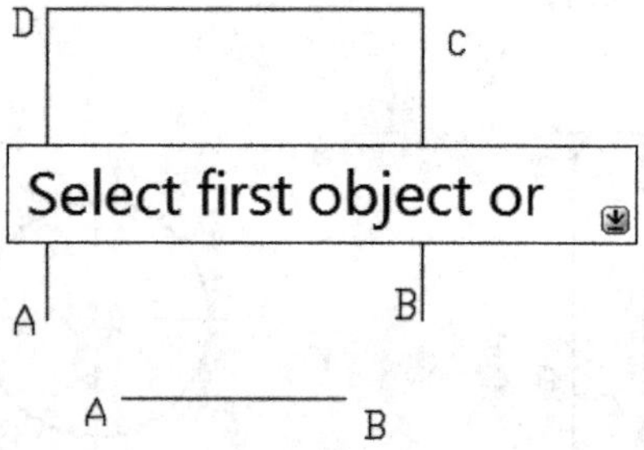

Figure 4-62a

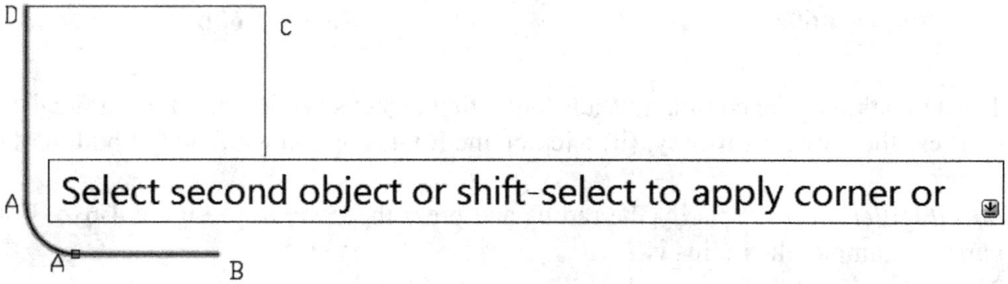

Figure 4-62b

5. An arc (of radius 2) is created from A to A that is tangent to lines AB and AD, Figure 4-62c.
6. Repeat the process from step #1 - #4 near points D. An arc (of radius 2) is created from D to D which is tangent to lines DA and DC. The corners of the lines are also trimmed, Figure 4-62d.
7. Repeat the process from step #1 - #4 near points B. At step #2, specify a radius of 0.0. An arc (of radius 0) is created from B to B tangent to lines BA and BC, Figure 4-62d. Notice the difference between arc for *radius* > *0* and *radius* = *0*.

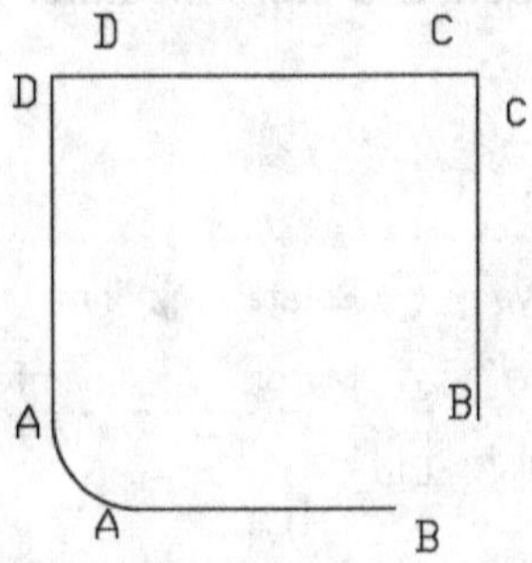

Figure 4-62c

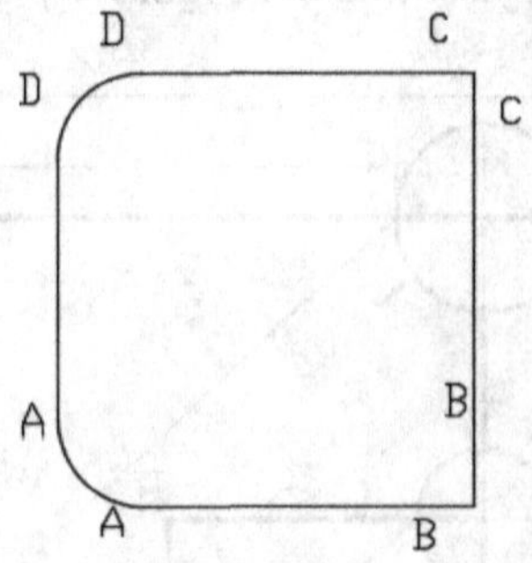

Figure 4-62d

- <u>Fillet Circles</u>: The *Fillet* command does not trim the circles. However, the command draws an arc that meets the circles smoothly.

1. Activate the *Fillet* command, if it is not active.
2. Create a fillet with a specific radius (5 in the example), Figure 4-62e, by clicking near points labeled as A on both circles.
3. Create a fillet with a specific radius (25 in the example), Figure 4-62e, by clicking near points labeled as B on both circles.

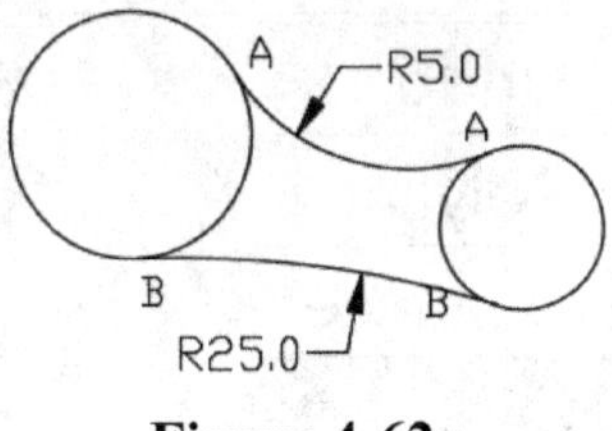

Figure 4-62e

4.31. Chamfer 

The *Chamfer* command is used to connect two objects with a straight line. The connecting objects can be lines and polylines or a combination of any two.

<u>Example:</u> To follow the *Chamfer* command, draw the lines and circles as shown in Figure 4-63a; the symbol ϕ represents the diameter. The figure also shows the angle and chamfer length for the corners A and B.

- Activate the *Chamfer* command using one of the following methods:
  1. Panel method: From the *Home* tab and *Modify* panel expand the *Fillet* drop-down menu and select the *Chamfer* tool, Figure 4-63b.
  2. Command line method: Type "chamfer", "Chamfer", or "CHAMFER" in the command line and press the *Enter* key.

- The activation of the command leads to the prompt shown in Figure 4-64a. Press the down-arrow key to check the options list.
- *Select first line or*, Figure 4-64a: Select the *Angle* option, and press the *Enter* key.

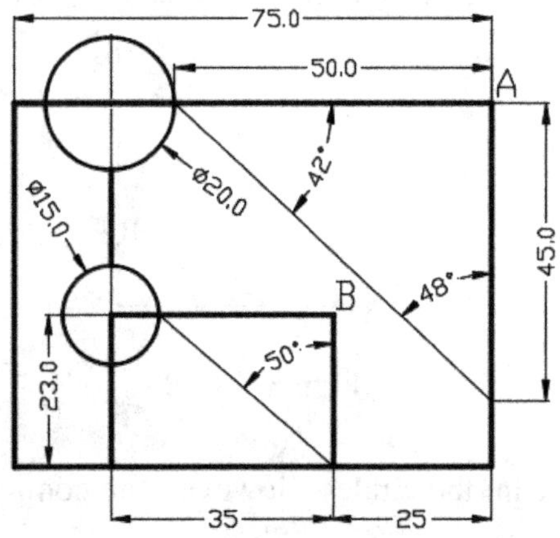

Figure 4-63a

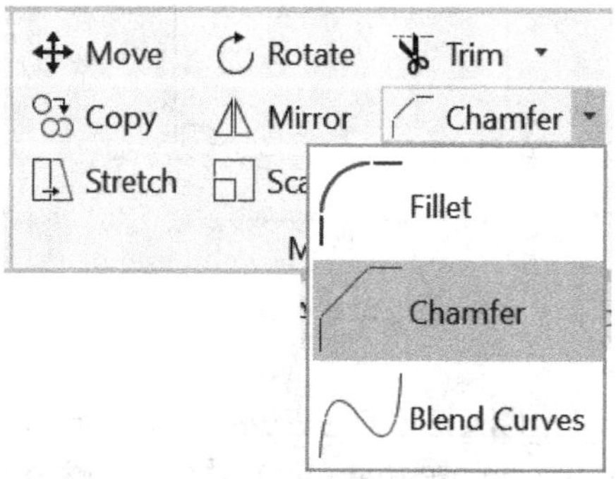

Figure 4-63b

- *Specify chamfer length on the first line*, Figure 4-64b: Specify the length and press the *Enter* key. In the example, for corner *A* the length is 45.

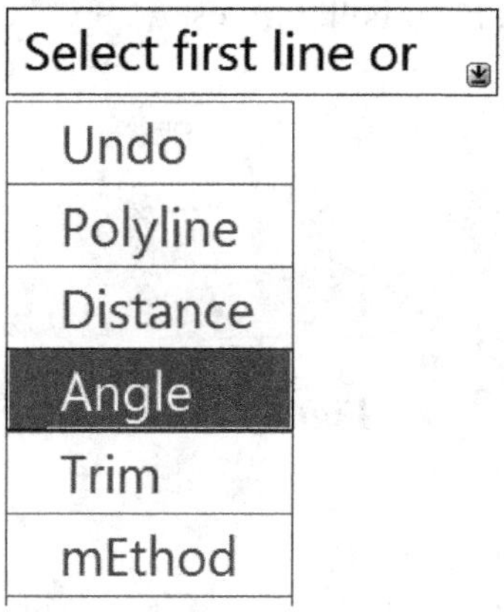

Figure 4-64a

- *Specify chamfer angle from the first line*, Figure 4-64c: Specify the angle and press the *Enter* key. In the example, for corner *A* the angle is 48.

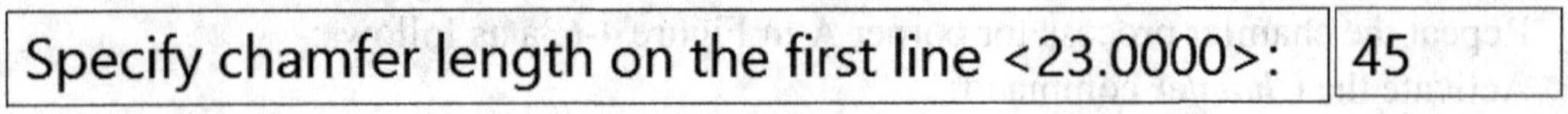

Figure 4-64b

Figure 4-64c

- *Select the first line or*, Figure 4-64d: Click on the vertical line at corner A. The line changes its appearance, Figure 4-64e.

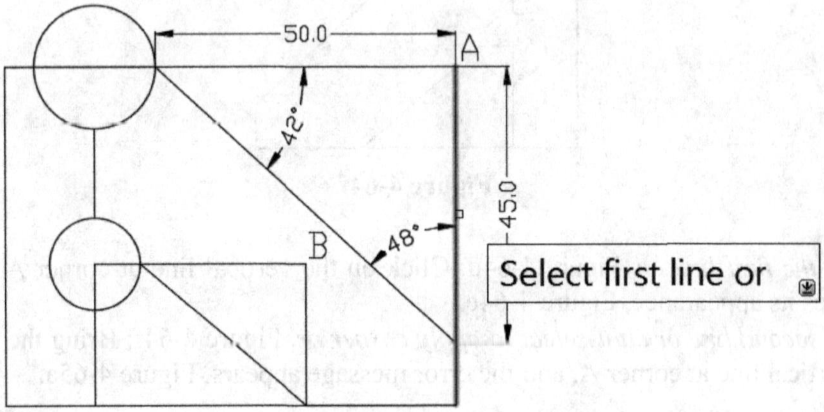

Figure 4-64d

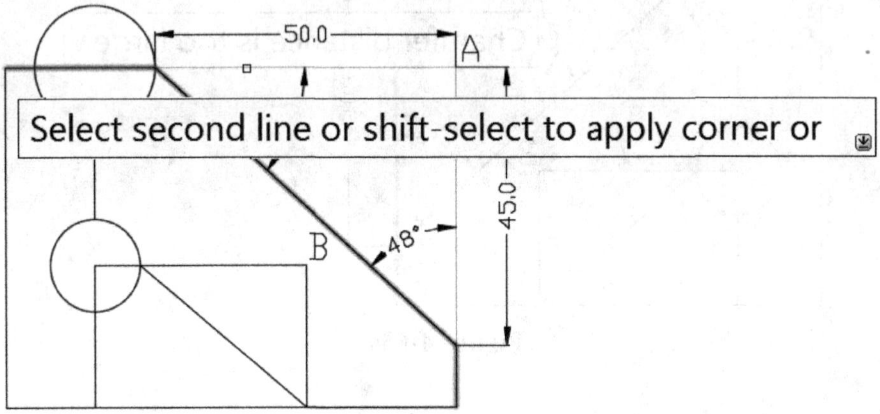

Figure 4-64e

- *Select second line or shift-select to apply corner or*, Figure 4-64f: Bring the cursor on the horizontal line at corner A and the chamfer appears.
- *Select second line or shift-select to apply corner or*, Figure 4-64e: Click on the horizontal line at corner A. The chamfer line replaces the corner at A, Figure 4-64f.
- Repeat the chamfer process for corner B, Figure 4-64f.

- Repeat the chamfer process for corner A in Figure 4-63a as follows:
- Activate the *Chamfer* command.
- *Select first line or*, Figure 4-64a: Select the *Angle* option, and press the *Enter* key.
- *Specify chamfer length on the first line*, Figure 4-64b: Specify the length and press the *Enter* key. In the example, for corner *A* the length is 65.
- *Specify chamfer angle from the first line*, Figure 4-64c: Specify the angle and press the *Enter* key. In the example, for corner *A* the angle is 48.

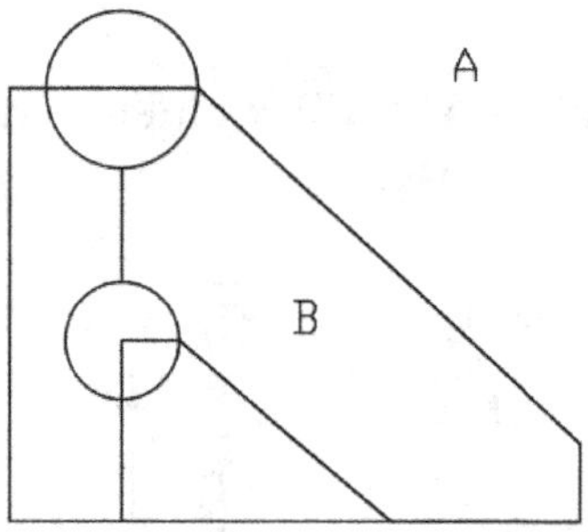

Figure 4-64f

- *Select the first line or*, Figure 4-64d: Click on the vertical line at corner A. The line changes its appearance, Figure 4-64e.
- *Select second line or shift-select to apply corner or*, Figure 4-64f: Bring the cursor on the vertical line at corner A, and the error message appears, Figure 4-65a.

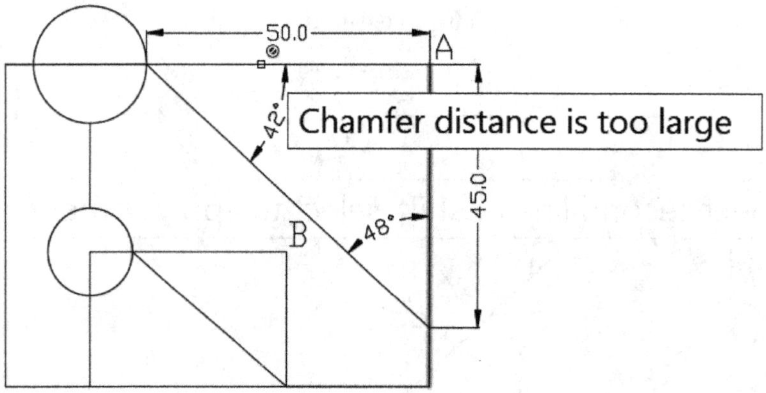

Figure 4-65a

- Click on the horizontal line at corner A. The error message shown in Figure 4-65b appears.
- Correct the error by specifying correct length!

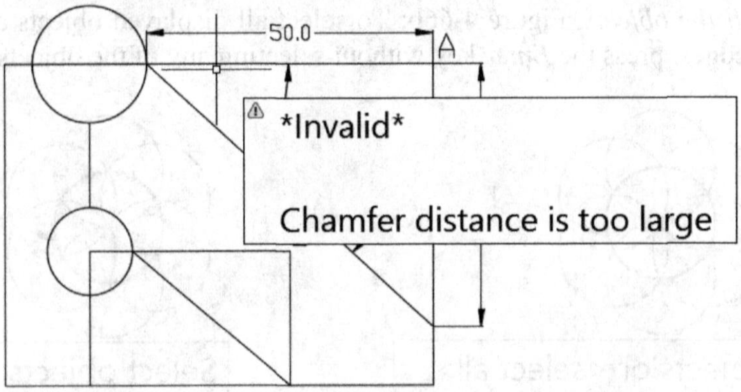

Figure 4-65b

4.32. Trim

The *Trim* command is used to trim objects at a cutting edge. The cutting edge is defined by other objects. The concept of trim command can be better understood by comparing it to hair trimming at a barber shop. The barber holds the customer's hair in their hands and then trims the hair (above the fingers) with reference to their fingers. In this example, the barber fingers are the cutting edge, and "above the fingers" is the desired side for trimming. The difference in the trim command and hair trimming is that the barber cuts the hair above their fingers. However, AutoCAD allows trimming on either side of the cutting edge.

Example: Create the top of a patio umbrella (Figure 4-67a) using circles and trim commands.

The solution drawing can be created by using the following steps:

- Draw the circles as shown in Figure 4-66b.
- Activate the *Trim* command using one of the following methods:
  1. Panel method: From the *Home* tab and *Modify* panel expand the *Trim* drop-down menu and select the *Trim* tool, Figure 4-66a.
  2. Command line method: Type "trim", "Trim", or "TRIM" in the command line and press the *Enter* key.

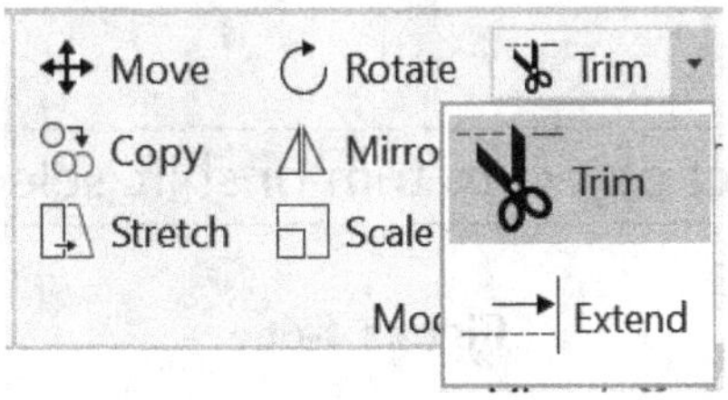

Figure 4-66a

- The activation of this command leads to the object selection prompt to choose which object serves as the cutting edge.

1. *Select all the objects*, Figure 4-66b: To select all displayed objects as potential cutting edges, press the *Enter* key without selecting any of the objects.

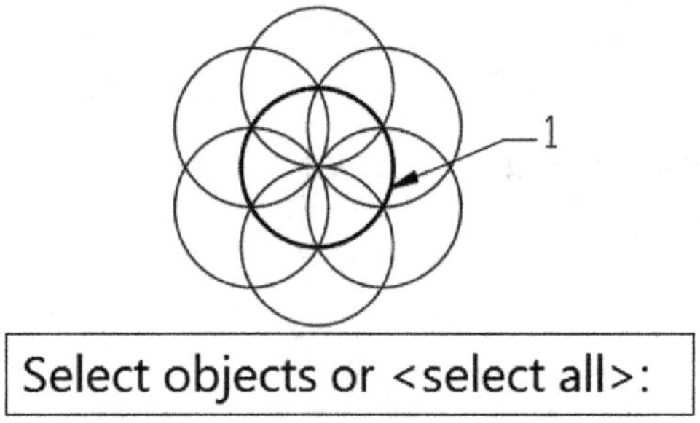

Figure 4-66b

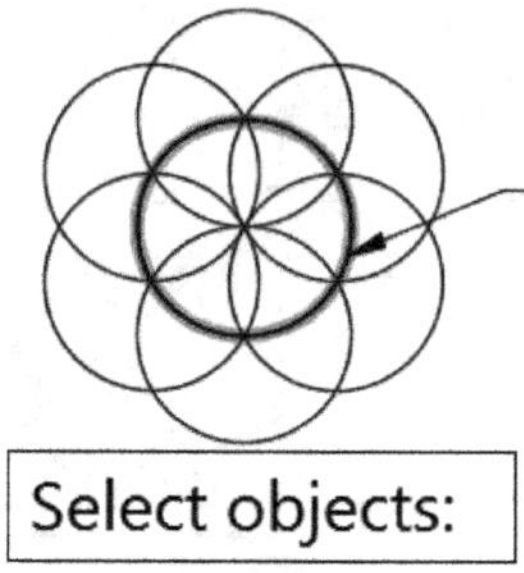

Figure 4-66c

2. *Select one object*, Figure 4-66c: In the figure the circle #1 is selected as the cutting edge. (i) Bring the cursor on top of the circle and the circle is highlighted. (ii) Click the circle with the left button of the mouse. (iii) Press the *Enter* key, or the right button, to complete the object selection. The prompt shown in Figure 4-66d appears. If the *Enter* key or right button is pressed without pressing the left button of the mouse, then the selection process is complete, but the object does not change its appearance.

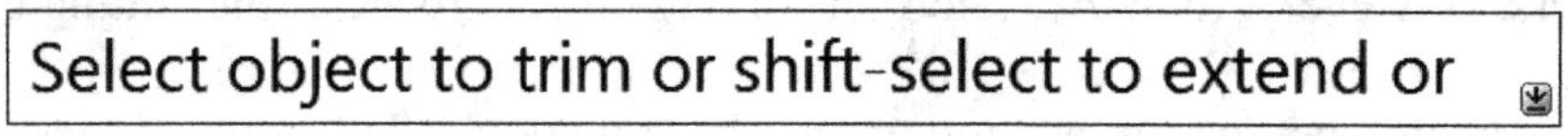

Figure 4-66d

- *Select the objects to trim*, Figure 4-66d: Bring the cursor on the top of the object to be trimmed. To create the object shown in Figure 4-67a, the part of the circles outside the circle #1 needs to be removed. Therefore, bring the cursor on the outside part of circle #2, Figure 4-66e and Figure 4-66f.

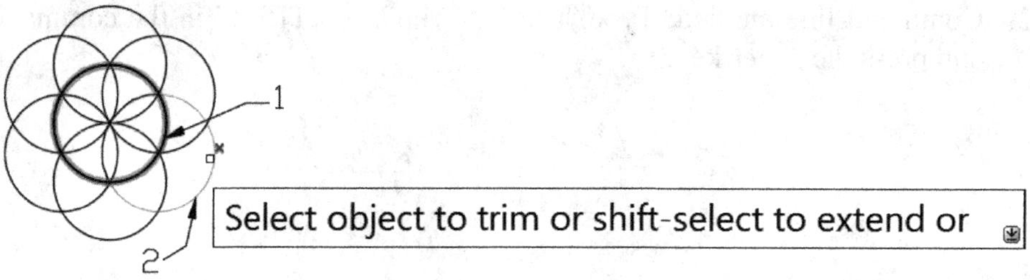

Figure 4-66e

- Repeat the previous step with the other circles to create the patio umbrella as shown in Figure 4-67a.
- Press the *Esc* or the *Enter* key to exit the command.
- Figure 4-67b and Figure 4-67c are created from the circles of Figure 4-66a. In these examples, every circle represents the cutting edge for one or more circles.

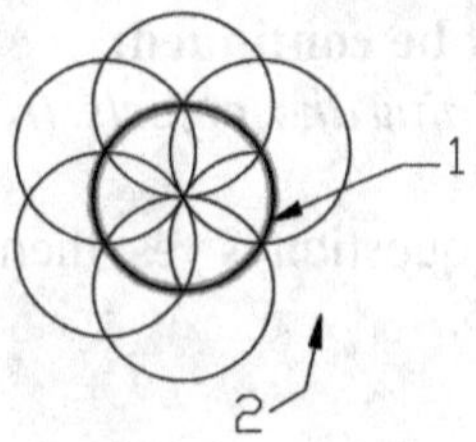

Figure 4-66f

Figure 4-67a

Figure 4-67b

Figure 4-67c

4.32.1. Trim: FAQ

If the *Trim* command is not creating the desired effect, then do one or more of the following methods:

1. **If the object exists after the *Trim* command is executed once, then:**
   a. *Check if there are multiple objects lying on top of each other?*
   b. If the answer to the above question is **yes**, then delete the underlying objects until only the object to be trimmed is left using *Delete Duplicate Objects* command.

2. **If the *Trim* command is executed but the desired result is not created, then:**
   a. *Check if the reference object and the object to be trimmed are clicked in correct order?*
   b. If the answer to the above question is **no**, then do the following steps:
   c. The object(s) clicked after the activation of the *Trim* command are reference objects.
   d. Press the *Enter* key.
   e. The objects clicked after step d are the objects to be trimmed.

3. **If the *Trim* command is executed but the desired result is not created, then:**
   a. *Check if there is a clear space between objects (reference and to be trimmed) visible or invisible to the human eye?*
   b. If the answer to the above question is **yes**, then do the following steps:
   c. Activate the *Extend* command.
   d. Extend the object to be trimmed to the reference object. *Extend* command is discussed in next section.
   e. Now, perform the *Trim* command.

4. **If the trim command cannot be continued:**
   a. *Check if the layer containing the objects (reference and/or to be trimmed) is locked?*
   b. If the answer to the above question is **yes**, then unlock the layers and trim. Layers are discussed in *Chapter 6*.

4.33. Extend

The *Extend* command is used to extend an object to reach another object. The *Extend* command extends the object on its natural path. For example, a circular arc changes to a circle, an elliptical arc changes to an ellipse, a horizontal line remains horizontal, etc. The extend command is executed in a manner similar to the *Trim* command.

Example: In order to follow the extend capability, draw the lines (L1, 12, and L3), circular arcs (CA1 and CA2), elliptical arc (EA1), and a circle (C1) as shown in Figure 4-68. In the figure, the symbol ϕ represents the diameter.

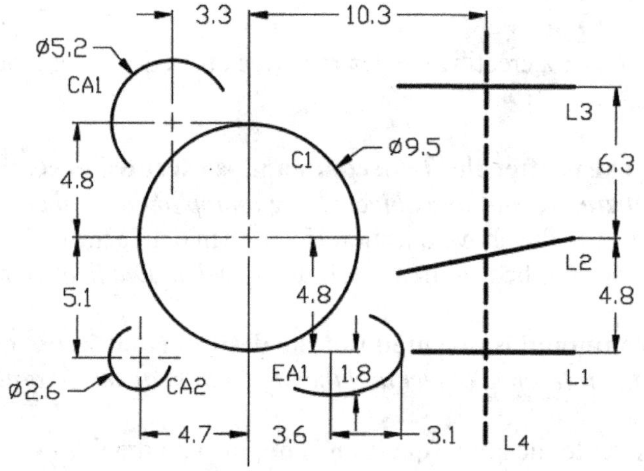

Figure 4-68

- Activate the *Extend* command using one of the following methods:
  1. Panel method: From the *Home* tab and *Modify* panel expand the *Trim* drop-down menu and select the *Extend* tool, Figure 4-69.
  2. Command line method: Type "extend", "Extend", or "EXTEND" in the command line and press the *Enter* key.

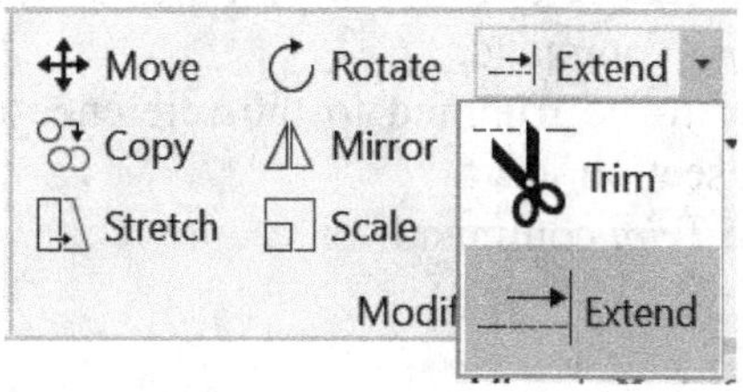

Figure 4-69

- The activation of the command leads to choosing the object that serves as the bounding edge to which the other objects are extended, Figure 4-70a.

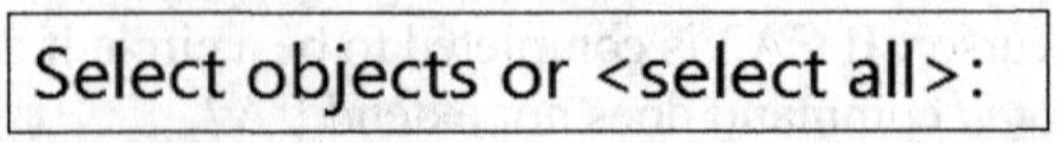

Figure 4-70a

- *Select objects*, Figure 4-70b: In the figure, the circle C1 is selected as the bounding edge. In this example, every line and arc is extended to the circle. (i) Bring the cursor on top of the reference object (circle in the example) and it is highlighted. (ii) Click the circle with the left button of the mouse, and it changes its appearance (becomes a thick line). (iii) Press the *Enter* key or right button to complete the reference object selection. If the *Enter* key or right button is pressed without pressing the left button of the mouse, the selection process is complete, but the object does not change its appearance.

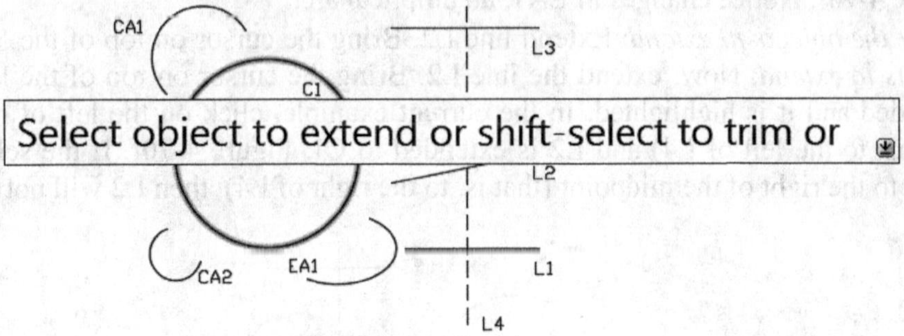

Figure 4-70b

- *Select the objects to extend*, Figure 4-70c: Bring the cursor on top of the object to be extended. For the arcs click near the ends of the arcs. In the example, the circular arc CA1 is selected. Bring the cursor near the end of the arc (Figure 4-70c) and press the left button of the mouse; the arc is extended to the circle, Figure 4-70d.

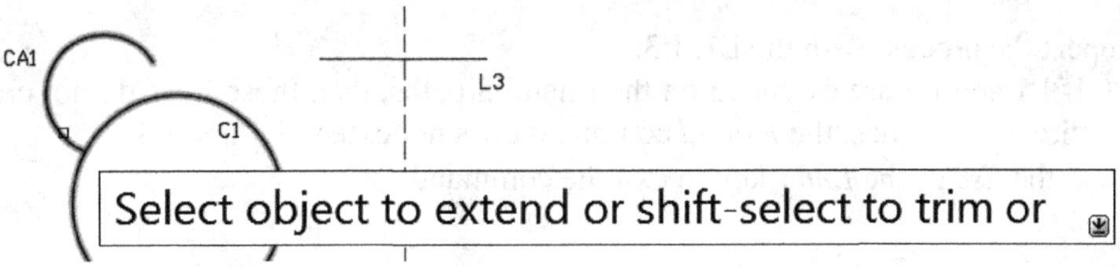

Figure 4-70c

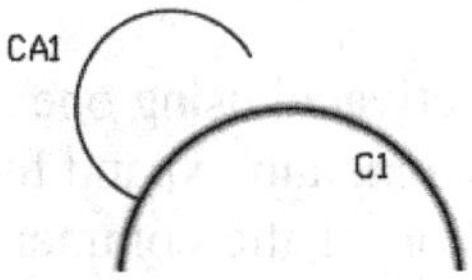

Figure 4-70d

- *Select the objects to extend*: Repeat the process with the arc CA2, Figure 4-70e.
- *Select the objects to extend*: Now, extend the arc CA2 to the circle C1. Bring the cursor on the end of the arc and an error message (Figure 4-70e) appears; notice the appearance of the cursor. If CA2 is completed to be a circle it does not touch the circle C1. Hence, the *Extend* command does not extend CA2.

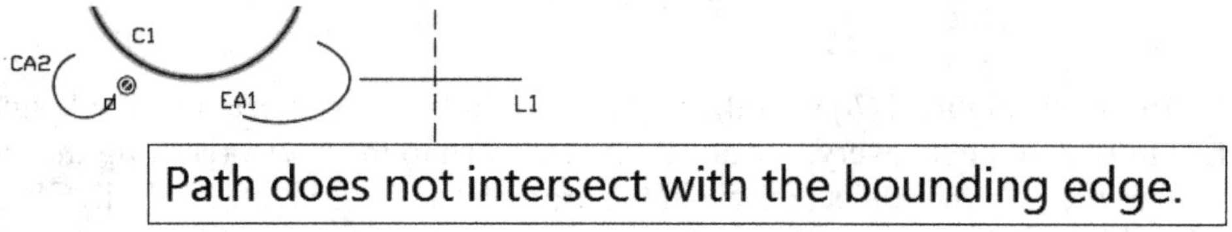

Figure 4-70e

- *Select the objects to extend*: Extend the other edge of CA1, and both edges of EA1, Figure 4-70f. Notice changes in EA1, an elliptical arc.
- *Select the objects to extend*: Extend line L2. Bring the cursor on top of the *Select the objects to extend*: Now, extend the line L2. Bring the cursor on top of the line to be extended and it is highlighted. In the current example, click on the left of midpoint, (that is, to the left of L4) and L2 is extended to C1, Figure 4-70f. If the selection is made to the right of the midpoint (that is, to the right of L4), then L2 will not extend.

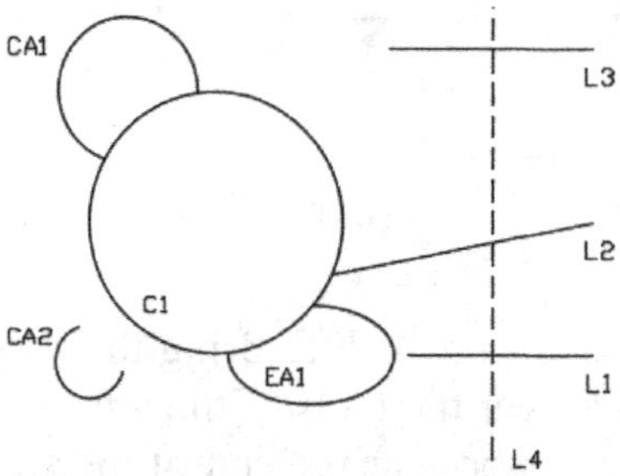

Figure 4-70f

- Repeat the process with the L1, L3.
  - If L1 and L3 are extended on their natural paths, then these lines do not cross the circle C1. Hence, the *Extend* command does not extend L1 and L3.
- Press the *Esc* or the *Enter* key to exit the command.

4.34. Polyline Edit

The polyline edit capabilities allow the drafter to modify the existing polylines.

- The *Edit Polyline* command is activated using one of the following methods:
  1. *Panel method:* From the *Home* tab expand the *Modify* panel and select the *Edit Polyline* tool. The activation of the command results in the polyline selection prompt, Figure 4-71a. Click on a polyline and an options list appears, Figure 4-72.

2. Command line method: (i) Type “pedit”, “Pedit”, or “PEDIT” in the command line and press the *Enter* key. The prompt shown in Figure 4-71b appears; follow one of the following two methods.
   - (i) Type *m* (to modify multiple polylines simultaneously), (ii) press the *Enter* key, (iii) click on multiple polylines, and (iv) press the *Enter* key. This opens the options list shown in Figure 4-72.
   - (i) Press the *Enter* key, and (ii), select the polyline. This opens the options list shown in Figure 4-72.

3. Polyline method: (i) Select a polyline, Figure 4-71c. (ii) Press the right button and select the *Polyline* option. (iii) Select the *Edit Polyline* option. (iv) This opens the options list shown in Figure 4-72.

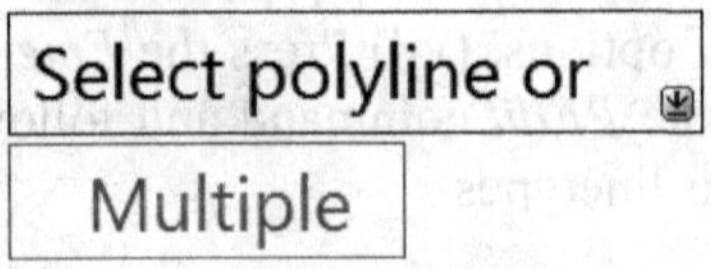

Figure 4-71a

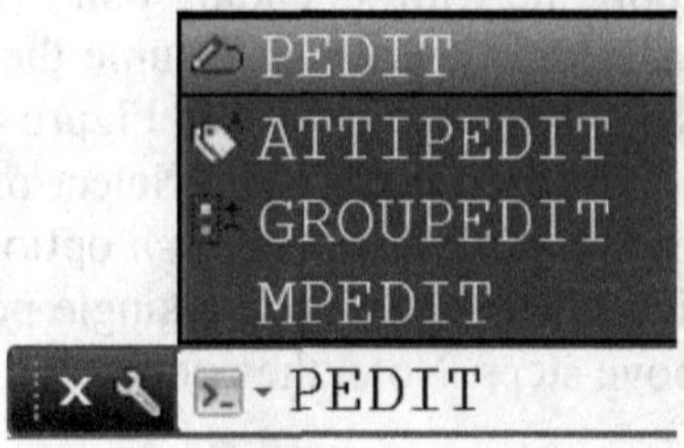

Figure 4-71b

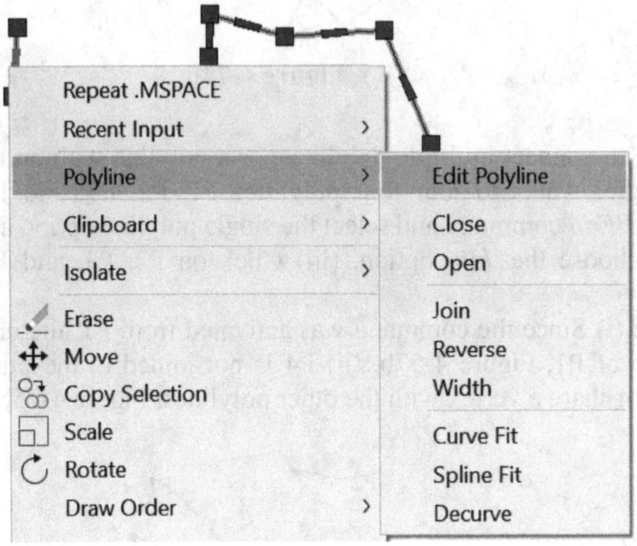

Figure 4-71c

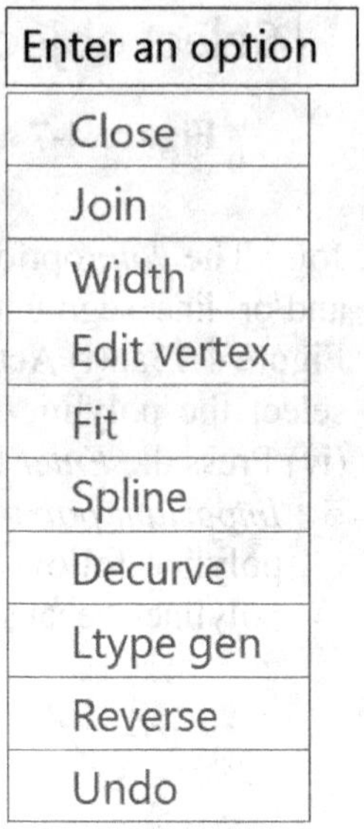

Figure 4-72

- Close: The *Close* option is used to connect the starting point of a polyline with its ending point by drawing a straight segment between the two points. The selected polyline must contain at least two segments. Assume the drafter wants to close multiple segments polyline. (i) Draw two polylines as shown in Figure 4-73a. (ii) Activate the *PEdit* command. (iii) Choose the *Multiple* option. (iv) Select multiple polylines,

Figure 4-73a. (v) Press the *Enter* key. (vi) Click on the *Close* option from the list of options, Figure 4-72. (vii) Press the *Enter* key. The closed polylines are shown in Figure 4-73b. To close a single polyline, activate the *PEdit* command and follow the above steps. Note, the closed polylines maintain their linetypes.

Figure 4-73a

Figure 4-73b

- Open: The *Open* option is used to remove the segment connecting the starting point of a polyline with its ending point. The selected polyline must be closed and contain at least three segments. Assume the drafter wants to open multiple polylines. (i) Draw two polylines as shown in Figure 4-74a. (ii) Activate the *PEdit* command. (iii) Choose the *Multiple* option. (iv) Select multiple polylines, Figure 4-74a. (v) Press the *Enter* key. (vi) Click on the *Open* option from the list of options. (vii) Press the *Enter* key, Figure 4-74b. To open a single polyline, activate the *PEdit* command and follow the above steps. Note, the open polylines maintain their linetypes.

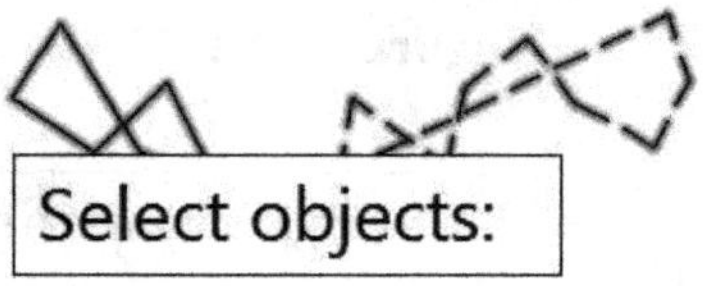

Figure 4-74a

Figure 4-74b

- Join: The *Join* option is used to connect multiple polylines, or a polyline with an arc and/or line segments. A drafter wants to join four polylines P1, P2, P3, and P4, Figure 4-75a. (i) Activate the *PEdit* command and select the single polyline option and select the polyline P1. (ii) Choose the *Join* option. (iii) Click on P2, P3, and P4. (iv) Press the *Enter* key twice.
  - *Important point to notice*: (i) Since the command was activated from P1, the new polyline follows the style of P1, Figure 4-57b. (ii) P4 is not joined to the other polylines because it did not share a vertex with the other polylines, Figure 4-75b.

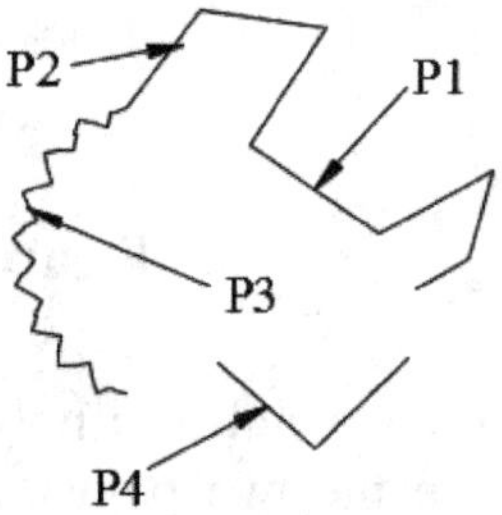

Figure 4-75a

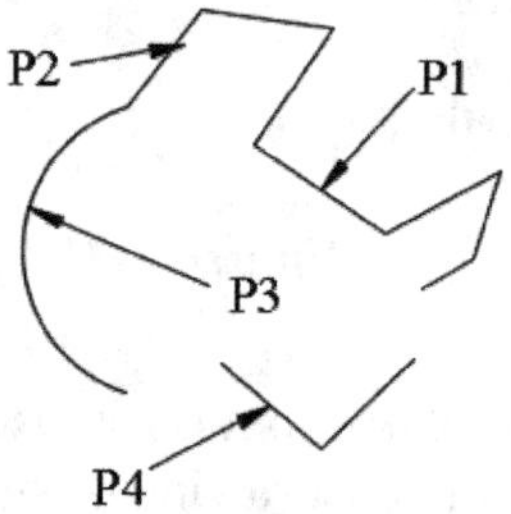

Figure 4-75b

- o *Join P4 with the other polylines*: (i) Activate the *PEdit* command. (ii) Choose the *Multiple* option. (iii) Click on both polylines. (iv) Press the *Enter* key. (v) Choose the *Join* option. (vi) The prompt shown in Figure 4-75c appears; press the down-arrow to display the other options. (vii) Click on *Jointype*. (viii) Choose *Both* option from Figure 4-75d. (ix) The fuzz distance prompt appears, Figure 4-75e. (x) Specify a number (in the example 10 is used). (xi) Finally, press the *Enter* key, TWICE.
- o The new polyline is shown in Figure 4-75f. Since the polyline P1-P2-P3 was selected first in step (ii) above, the new polyline follows its style.

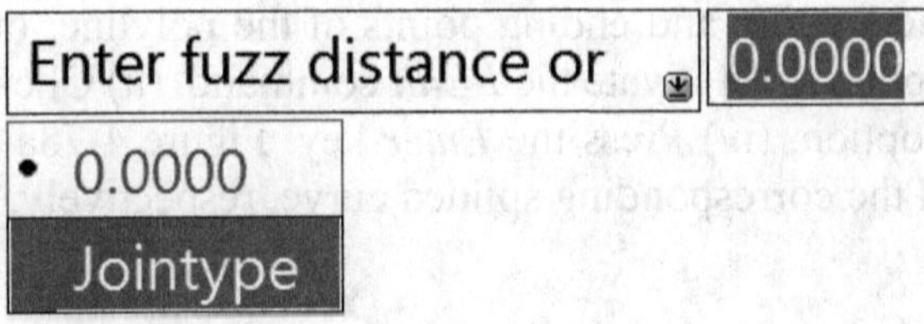

Figure 4-75c

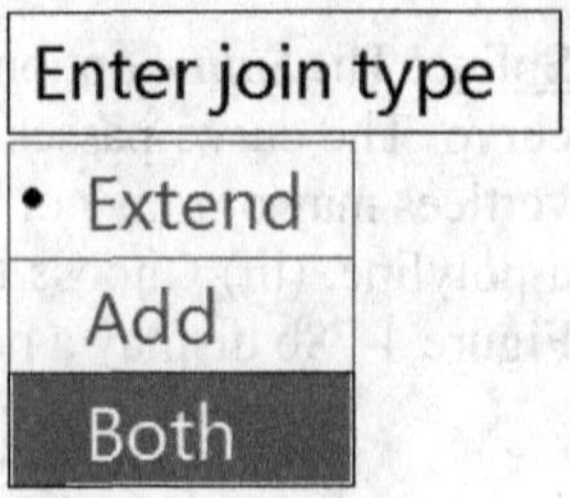

Figure 4-75d

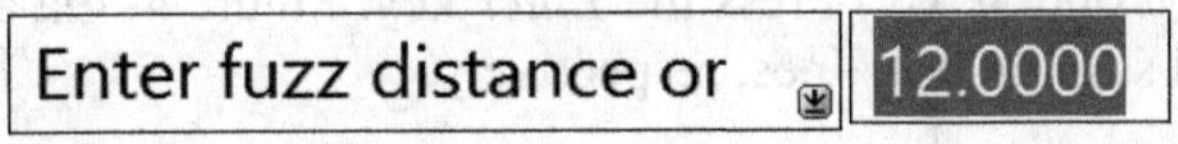

Figure 4-75e

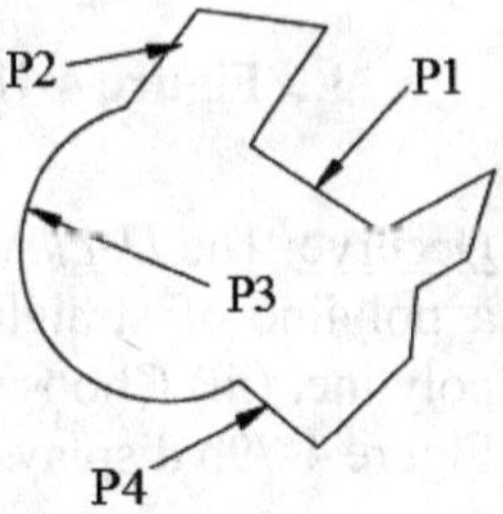

Figure 4-75f

- Width: The *Width* option is used to change the width of a polyline: (i) Activate the *PEdit* command. (ii) Click on a polyline. (iii) Choose the *Width* option. (iv) Specify the new width, Figure 4-76a. (iv) Press the *Enter* key, twice. The width of the polyline is changed. The width of the polyline shown in Figure 4-76a is increased to 2.2 and is shown in Figure 4-76b.

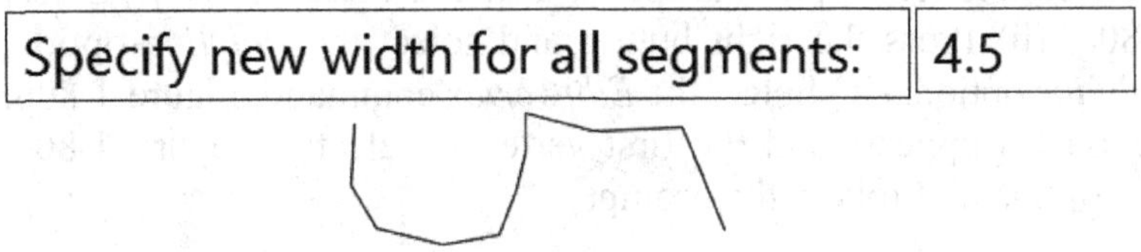

Figure 4-76a

Figure 4-76b

- Fit: The *Fit* option is used to replace the selected polyline with a smooth curve. The fitted curve passes through each vertex of the polyline. (i) Activate the *PEdit* command. (ii) Click on a polyline. (iii) Choose the *Fit* option. (iv) Press the *Enter* key.

Figure 4-77a displays an original polyline and Figure 4-77b displays the polyline transformed into a fitted curve.

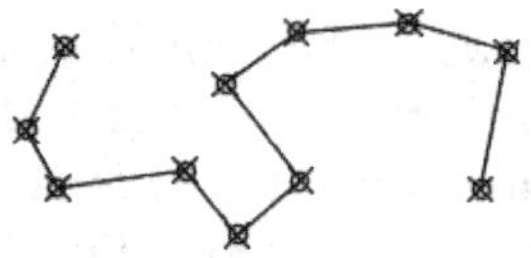

Figure 4-77a

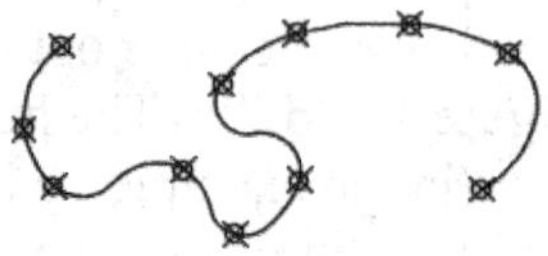

Figure 4-77b

- Spline: The *Spline* option is used to replace the selected polyline with a quadratic spline curve. The curve passes through the starting and ending points of the polyline; other vertices may or may not be on the spline. (i) Activate the *PEdit* command. (ii) Click on a polyline. (iii) Choose the *Spline* option. (iv) Press the *Enter* key. Figure 4-78a and Figure 4-78b display a polyline and the corresponding splined curve, respectively.

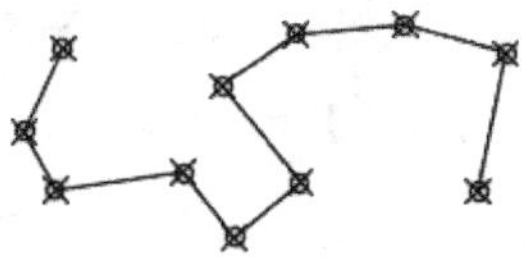

Figure 4-78a

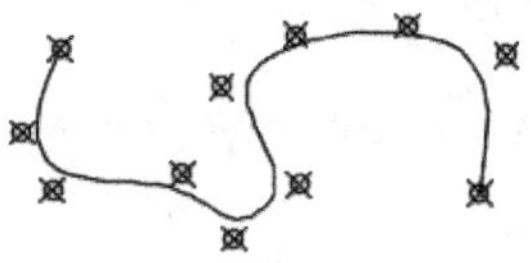

Figure 4-78b

- Decurve: The *Decurve* option is used to replace a curve fitted or splined polyline with a polyline of straight segments. (i) Activate the *PEdit* command. (ii) Click on a polyline. (iii) Choose the *Decurve* option. (iv) Press the *Enter* key. Figure 4-79a and Figure 4-79b displays curved and straight polylines, respectively.

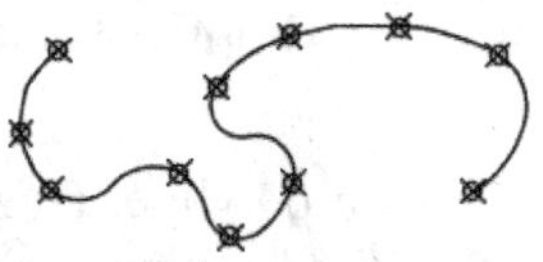

Figure 4-79a

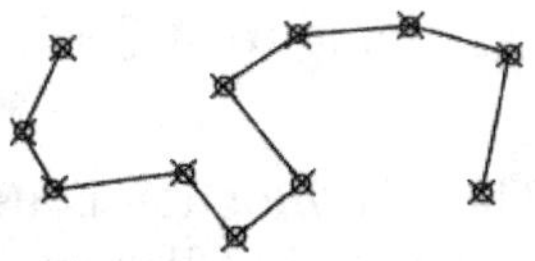

Figure 4-79b

- Edit vertex: The *Edit vertex* option is available only if the *Edit polyline* command is activated using a single polyline. This option is used to edit a selected vertex. (i) Select a polyline, Figure 4-80a. (ii) Press the right button and select the *Polyline* option. (iii) Select the *Edit Polyline* option. (iv) Select the *Edit vertex* command, Figure 4-80b. (v) Vertex editing option list appears and the first vertex is selected, Figure 4-80c. (vi) Choose the desired option and follow the prompt.

- Undo: As the name suggests, the *Undo* option cancels out the previous step.

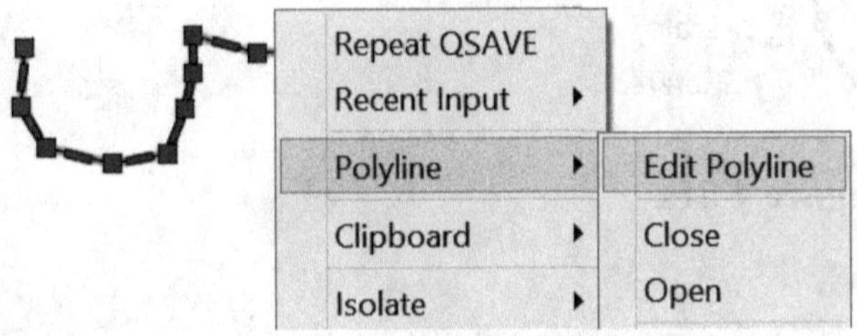

Figure 4-80a

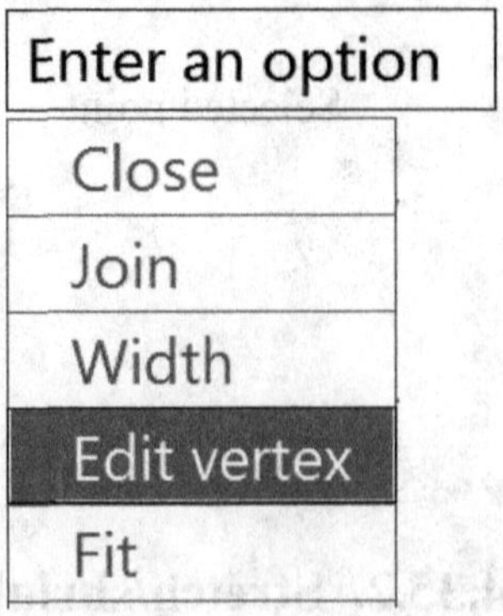

Figure 4-80b

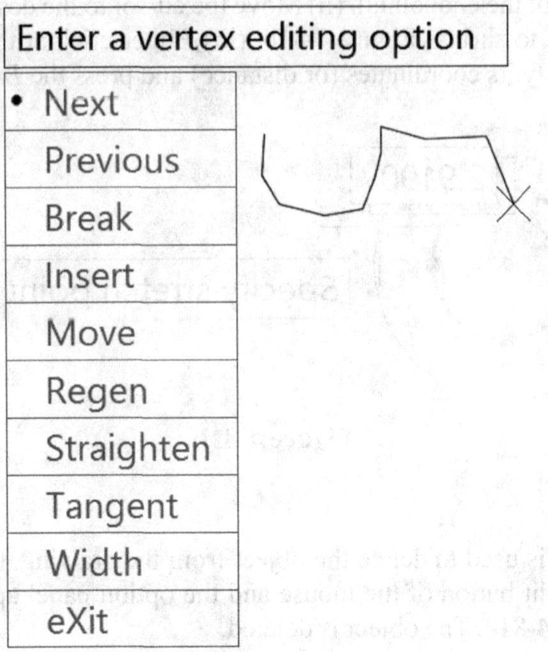

Figure 4-80c

4.35. Grip Points And Object Editing

The selection of an object results in displaying its grip points. These grip points can be used to edit the object using the pointing device instead of entering the respective commands. Some of the editing capabilities activated when grips are displayed on an object are stretch, move, rotate, copy, erase, and scale.

4.35.1. Select a point

(i) Select an object. (ii) Place the cursor on any of the grip points and its color changes to RED, Figure 4-81a. (iii) Click with the right button of the mouse and a list of commands appears. The commands are object and grip point dependent. (iv) Click with the left button of the mouse on the desired command and follow the prompts.

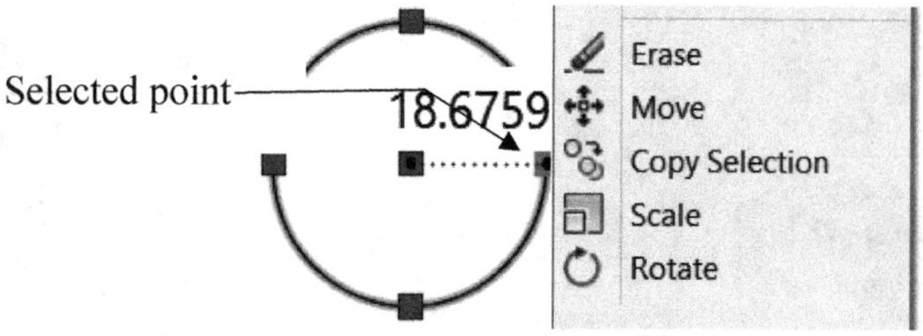

Figure 4-81a

4.35.2. Stretch/shrink

Although the *Stretch/shrink* command does not appear in the list of commands in Figure 4-81a, it is used to resize the object. (i) For a circle, select one of the quadrant points (for a line, select one of the endpoints). (ii) Move the cursor to the desired location, outward to stretch and inward to shrink, Figure 4-81b. (iii) Either click at the new location in the drawing area or specify its coordinates (or distance) and press the *Enter* key.

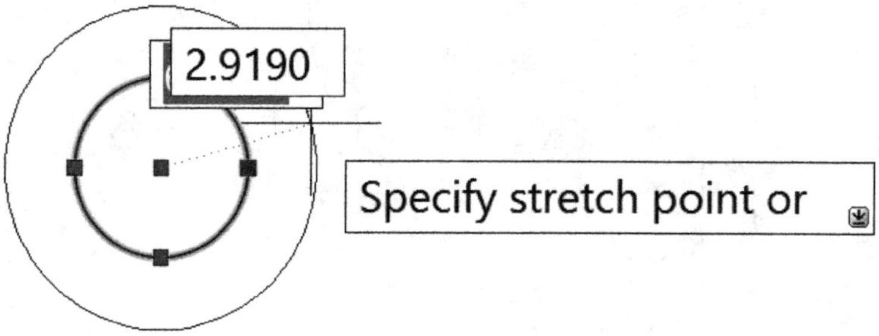

Figure 4-81b

4.35.3. Erase

The *Erase* command is used to delete the object from the drawing. (i) Select a grip point. (ii) Click with the right button of the mouse and the option panel appears. (iii) Select the *Erase* option, Figure 4-81c. The object is deleted.

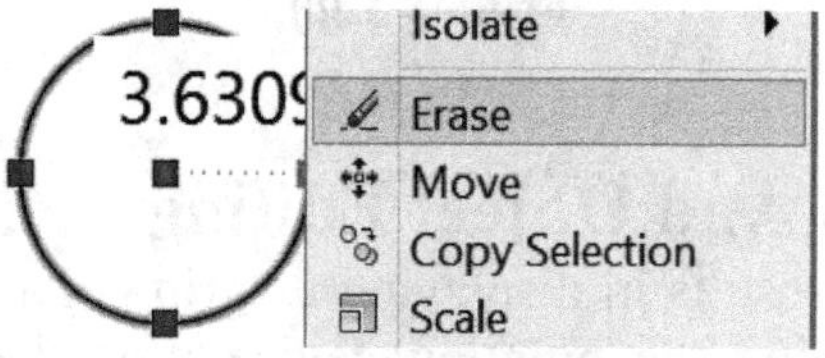

Figure 4-81c

4.35.4. Move

The *Move* command is used to relocate the object. (i) For a circle, select the center point (for a line, select the midpoint). (ii) Move the cursor to the desired location, Figure 4-81d. (iii) Either click at the new location in the drawing area or specify its coordinates (or distance) and press the *Enter* key.

Figure 4-81d

4.35.5. Scale

The *Scale* command is used to resize the object. (i) Select a grip point. (ii) Click with the right button of the mouse and the option list appears. (iii) Select the *Scale* option, Figure 4-81e. (iv) The prompt to select the base point (the point that does not change its location) appears. (v) Click at the desired location. The command scales the selected object relative to the base point. (vi) The prompt to specify the scale factor appears. (vii) Increase the size of an object by dragging the cursor outward or decrease the size by dragging inward. Alternatively, specify the scale factor for the relative scaling (Figure 4-81f) and press the *Enter* key.

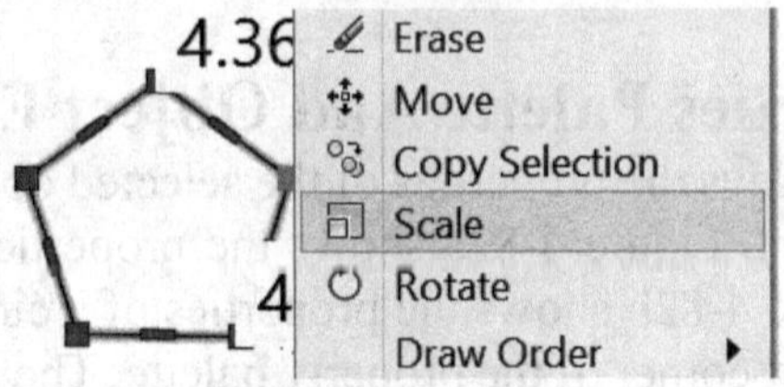

Figure 4-81e

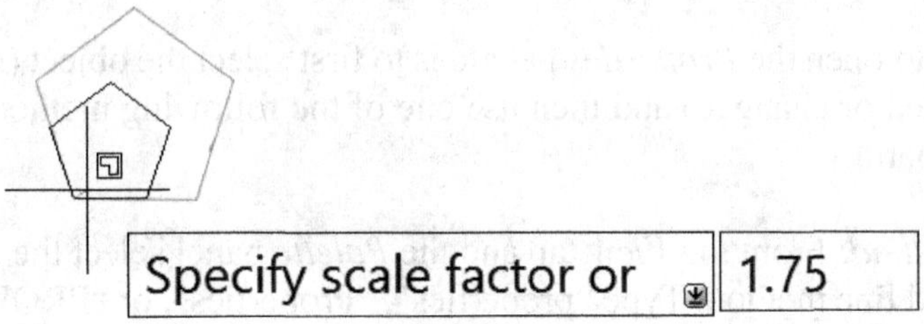

Figure 4-81f

4.35.6. Rotate

As the name suggests, the *Rotate* command is used to rotate the object about a point. (i) Select a grip point. (ii) Click with the right button of the mouse and the options panel appears, Figure 4-81a. (iii) Select the *Rotate* option. (iv) The prompt to select the base point (point of rotation) appears. (v) Click at the desired location. (vi) The prompt to specify the angle of rotation appears, Figure 4-81g. (vii) Rotate the selected object around the base point by moving the cursor. Alternatively, specify the angle value (Figure 4-81h) and press the *Enter* key. This is an excellent method for rotating block references.

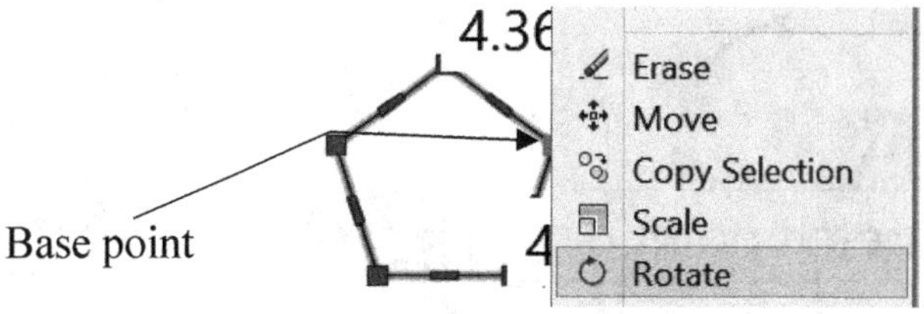

Figure 4-81g

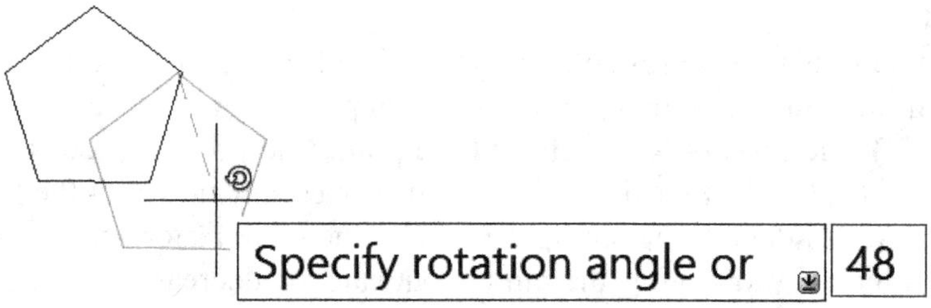

Figure 4-81h

4.36. The Properties Palette And Object Editing

The *Properties* palette displays the properties of the selected object(s). The contents of the palette are object dependent. Figure 4-82a shows the properties of a table created in the previous chapter and Figure 4-82b shows the properties of a circle. The type of the object is displayed in the upper left corner of the property palette. The *Properties* palette not only displays the selected properties of the selected object; it allows the user to modify some of the properties of the selected object.

The prerequisite to open the *Properties* palette is to first select the object (whose properties need to be checked or changed) and then use one of the following methods to activate the *Properties* command.

1. *Panel method:* From the *View* tab and the *Palette* panel select the *Properties* tool.
2. Command line method: Type "properties", "Properties", or "PROPERTIES" in the command line and press the *Enter* key.
3. Hold the *Ctrl* key and press 1.
4. Press the right button of the mouse and choose the *Properties* option from the option panel.

Some of the characteristics of the *Properties* are listed here.

- The down and left arrows buttons (,) are used to hide or display the options under a particular heading, Figure 4-82a.
- The content of the greyed fields cannot be altered. For example, in Figure 4-82a, under the *Table* heading, the number of rows and columns cannot be changed.

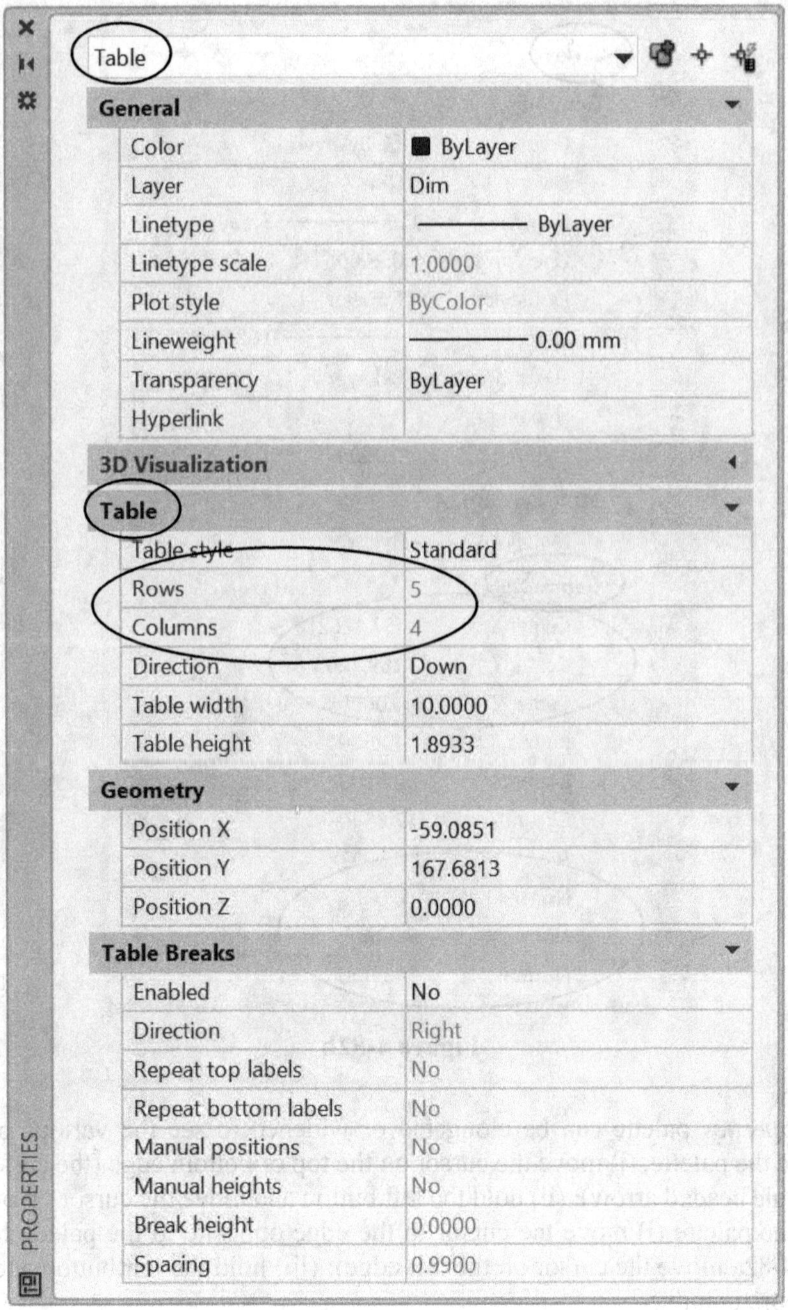

Figure 4-82a

- If desired, the content of the other fields can be altered. Type or choose the new value and press the *Enter* key. For example, in the property sheet for a circle under the *Geometry* heading, Figure 4-82b, *Center X*, *Center Y*, and *Center Z* can be changed; and *Normal X*, *Normal Y*, and *Normal Z* cannot be changed.

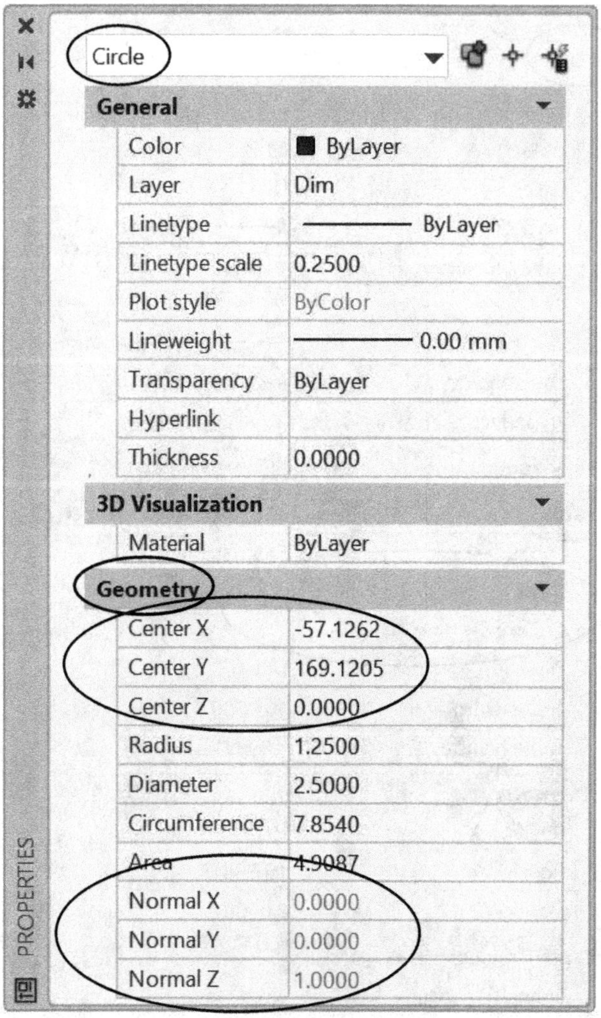

Figure 4-82b

- The *Properties* palette can be elongated or widened to see the various options. To **elongate** the palette, (i) move the cursor on the top or bottom edge (the cursor changes to a double headed arrow); (ii) hold the left button and move the cursor up or down. To **widen** the palette (i) move the cursor to the edge opposite to the palette heading (in Figure 4-82a move the cursor on the left edge); (iii) hold the left button and move the cursor horizontally.
- The columns width of the *Properties* palette can be changed (without changing the properties palette's width) to display the various options. To change the column's width, (i) move the cursor on the line dividing the palette in two columns and the cursor changes to two vertical parallel lines with a horizontal arrow on either side; (ii) hold the left button and move the cursor to the left or right.
- To select another object (without closing the palette, (i) click on the  (*Select object*) button located in the upper right corner, (ii) click on the object(s), and (iii) press the

Enter key. The *Properties* palette is updated to display the properties of the newly selected object.

- The property palette can be moved to a new location using the following. (i) Place the cursor in the grey area of the label, right side in Figure 4-82b. (ii) Press the left button of the mouse. (iii) Keep pressing the left button, move the cursor to the new location. (iv) Release the cursor at the new location and the property palette moves to the new location.

Notes:

5. Annotative Objects

5.1. Learning Objectives

After completing this chapter, the students will show proficiency in the following areas:

- Basics of annotative objects
- Create annotative
    - multiline texts
    - hatches
    - qleaders
    - dimensions
- Annotation buttons and status bar

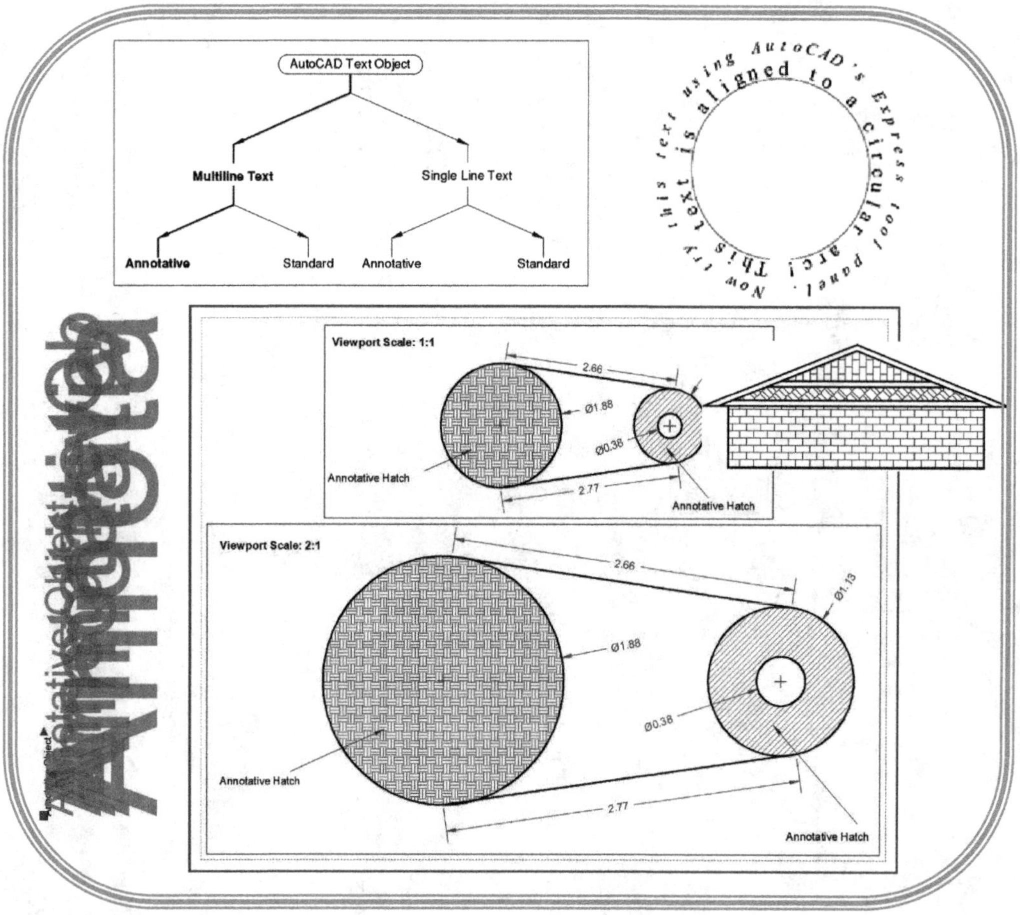

5.2. Introduction

According to Webster New Collegiate Dictionary, the word **annotate** is defined as "*to make or furnish critical or explanatory notes or comments*" and the word **annotation** is defined as "*the act of annotating something*". Thus, annotate and/or annotation in technical drawing refers to the comments, dimensions, hatch, labels, notes, tables, etc.

In AutoCAD, "*annotative objects*" are the objects (texts, hatches, qleaders, and dimensions) for which the annotative ( ) property is activated. The annotative objects are used to control the size at which the annotative objects are displayed in the Model space and layouts. The annotative objects always appear to be of the same size regardless of the viewport scale.

This chapter explains the techniques to create annotative text, hatch, and the qleader objects in layouts. This chapter also describes how linetype appearance can be independent of the viewport scale. The annotative dimensions are discussed in *Chapter 9*. Annotative table option is not available in AutoCAD 2027; therefore, tables are not discussed in this chapter. Tables are discussed in *Chapter 3*.

5.3. Characteristics Of Annotative Objects

This section describes the basic characteristics of an annotative object (text, hatch, and the qleader).

- Annotation objects can be displayed at different scale factors. When the user creates an annotative object, the *Select Annotation Scale* dialog box, Figure 5-1, appears. The user can select the desired scale from the drop-down list or select *OK* button to create objects at full scale (1:1). *Recommended style: 1:1.*

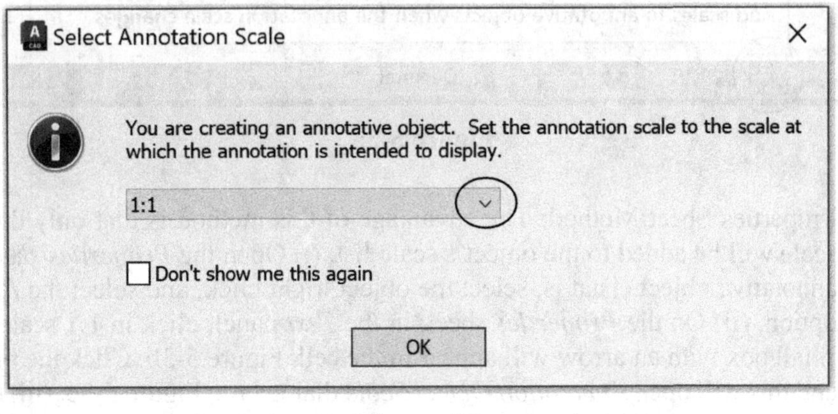

Figure 5-1

- Bring the cursor over an annotative object, and the cursor will appear as shown in Figure 5-02a. This cursor indicates that the object is annotative, and it is linked to only one scale factor. However, if the cursor appears as shown in Figure 5-2b, it means that multiple scale factors are associated with the annotative object.

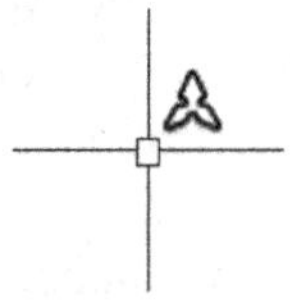

Figure 5-2a

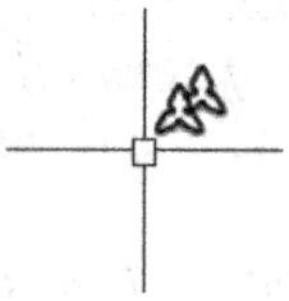

Figure 5-2b

- To display the annotative objects in Model Space and/or Layout, the user must activate (from the *Status bar*) the annotation visibility  option, Figure 5-2c.

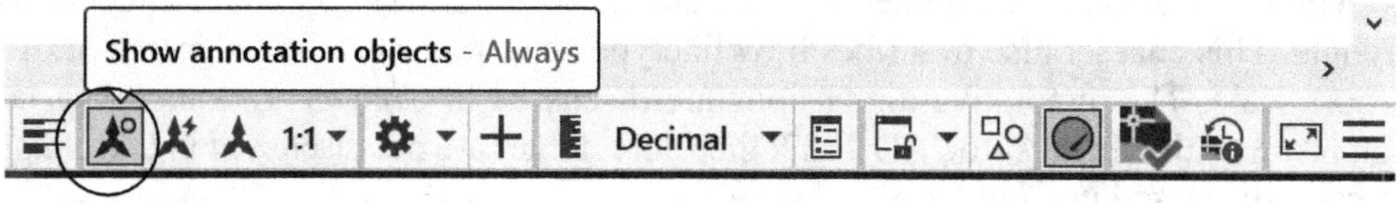

Figure 5-2c

5.3.1. Add a scale factor to the annotative object's scale list

- The user can add scale to annotative objects using one of the following methods.
  1. Status bar method: The advantage of this method is that it is automatic and quick; however, the drawback is that every scale will be added to the object's scale list. From the *Status bar*, activate the annotation auto scale  option, Figure 5-3a.

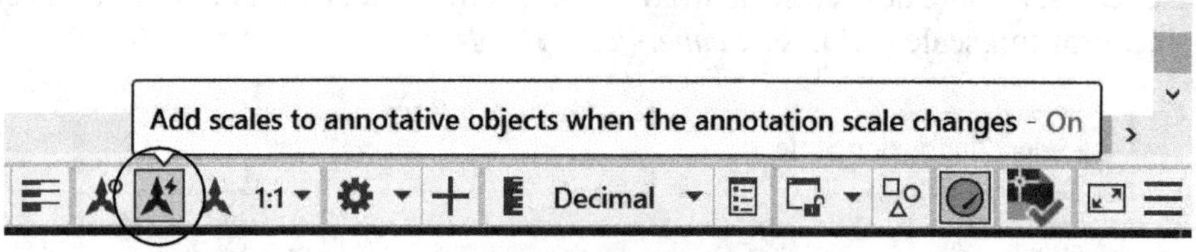

Figure 5-3a

  2. Properties Sheet Method: The advantage of this method is that only the desired scale will be added to the object's scale list. (i) Open the *Properties sheet* for the annotative object. That is, select the object, right click, and select the *Properties* option. (ii) On the *Properties* sheet, in the *Text* panel, click in 1:1 scale cell and small box with an arrow will appear in the cell, Figure 5-3b. Click the tiny arrow and this will open *Annotation Object Scale* dialog box, Figure 5-3c. (iii) Click the *Add* button on the dialog box; this will open *Add Scales to Objects* dialog box, Figure 5-3d. (iv) Select the desired scale and click the *OK* button. This will close the *Add Scales to Objects* dialog box and the selected scale (1:8 in the current example) will appear in *Annotation Object Scale* dialog box, Figure 5-3e. (v) Click the *OK* button. This will close the *Annotation Object Scale* dialog box and the selected scale (1:8 in the current example) is added to the selected

annotative object, Figure 5-3f. The smaller text is linked to the 1:1 scale and the bigger text is linked to the 1:8 scale.

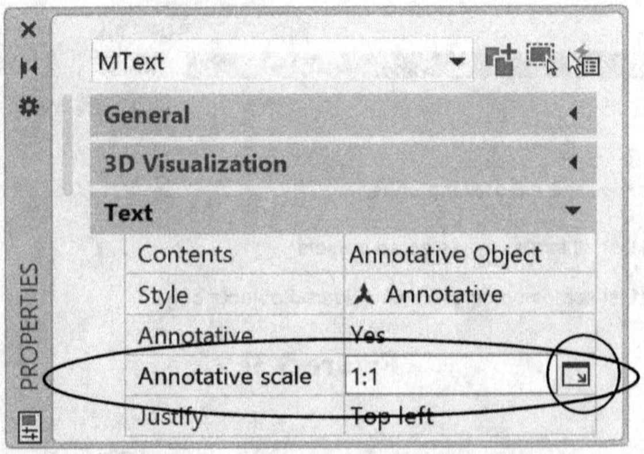

Figure 5-3b

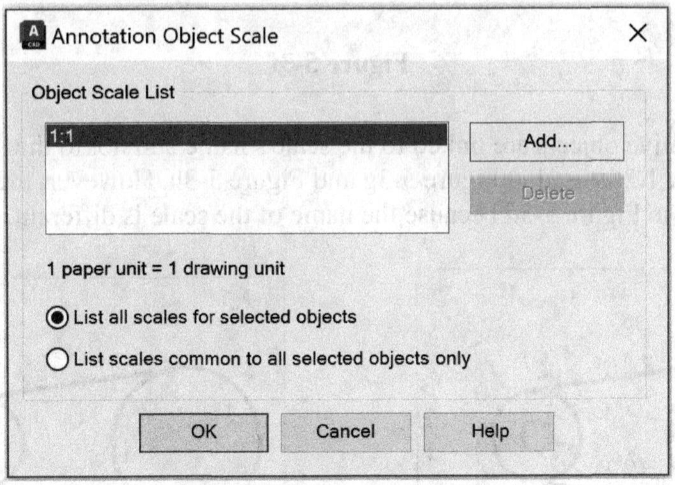

Figure 5-3c

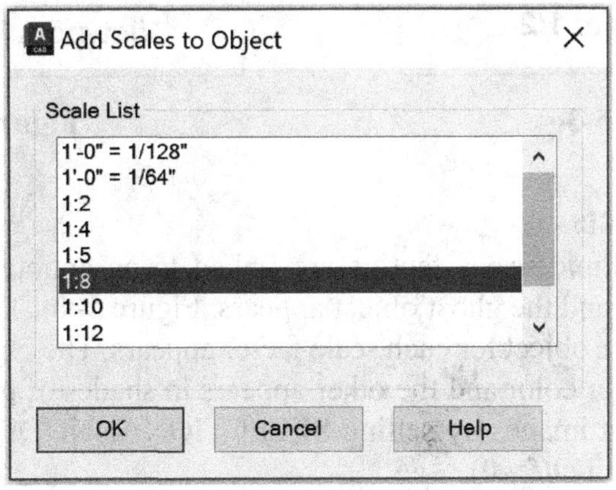

Figure 5-3d

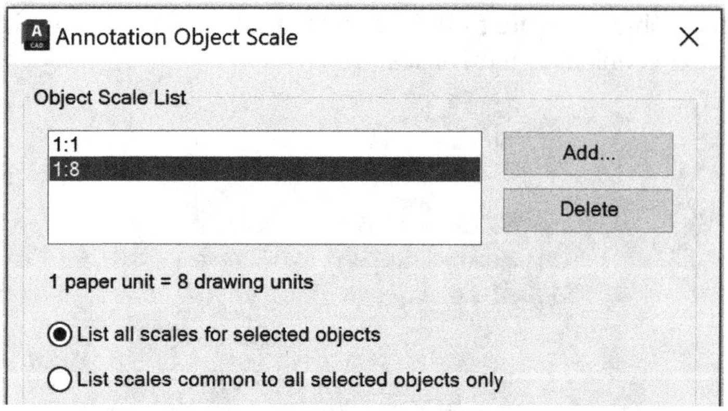

Figure 5-3e

Figure 5-3f

- The annotative objects are linked to the scale's name and not to the scale factor. The scale factor 1:2 is used in Figure 5-3g and Figure 5-3h. However, the dimensions are not visible in Figure 5-3d because the name of the scale is different.

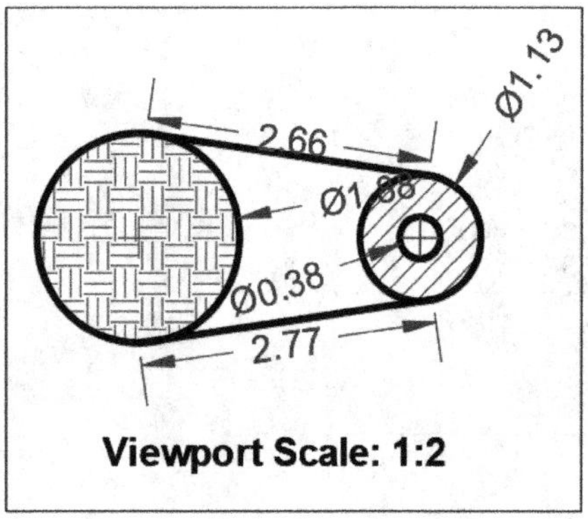

Figure 5-3g

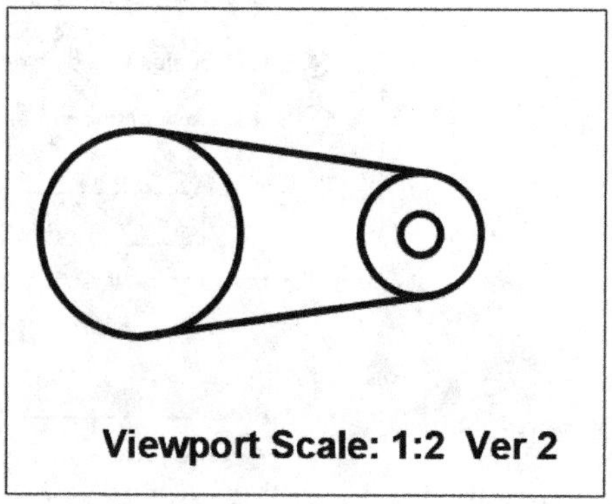

Figure 5-3h

5.3.2. Ghost objects

- Assume that multiple scales factors are linked to an annotative object. Select the annotative object and the ghost object appears, Figure 5-4a. That is, the image of the selected annotative object for each scale factor appears. The object at the current scale appears in the layer color and the other appears in shades of grey and blue. The user can hide the ghost images by setting SELECTIONANNODISPLAY variable value to zero (*On* = 1 and *Off* = 0).

Figure 5-4a

- Every ghost object has its grip points. The user can relocate each ghost individually using its grip point; do NOT use the move command. Figure 5-4b shows that the 1.88 diameter is shown at three different locations in the three different layouts. However, the user can use ANNORESET variable to show the annotative object at the same location in all of the viewports.

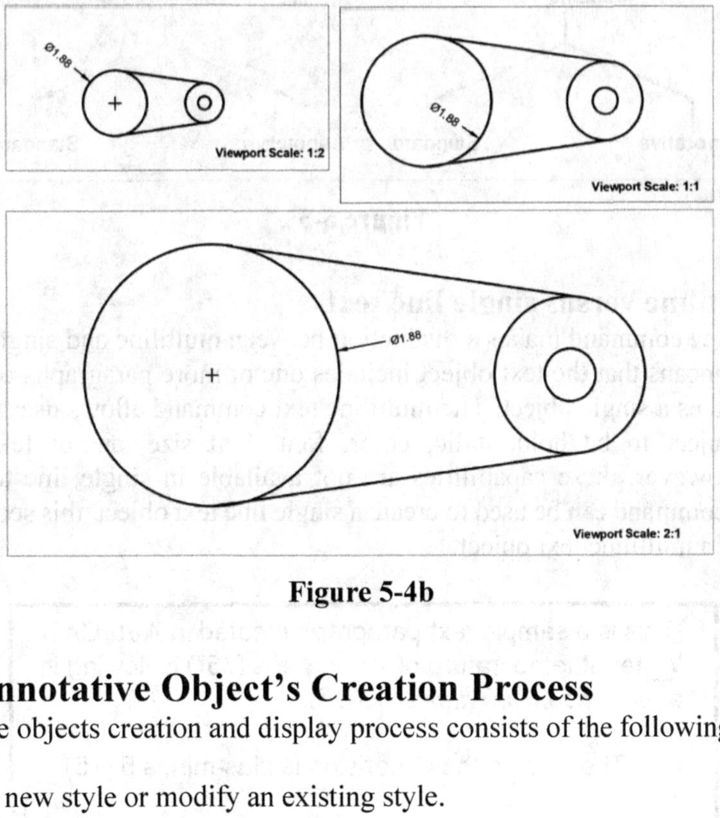

Figure 5-4b

5.4. Annotative Object's Creation Process

The annotative objects creation and display process consists of the following steps.

5. Create a new style or modify an existing style.
6. Make the desired style current.
7. Create the annotative object at full scale (1:1).
8. Add the desired scale to the annotative object scale list.
9. Activate the annotative objects visibility.
10. If working from the Model Space, then make the desired scale to be the current scale. If working from layouts, then first make the desired layout to be the current layout and then change the viewport scale.
11. If necessary, delete the unused styles and scales.

5.5. Text

All technical drawings contain dimensions and may also contain notes. The text (dimensions and notes) in a drawing should be clearly visible and readable. AutoCAD provides the *Text* command to add notes and dimension commands for adding the dimensions. AutoCAD users can create single and/or multi- line text with the standard and/or annotative style, Figure 5-5. This section discusses multiline annotative text, and the dimensions are discussed in detail in *Chapter 9*.

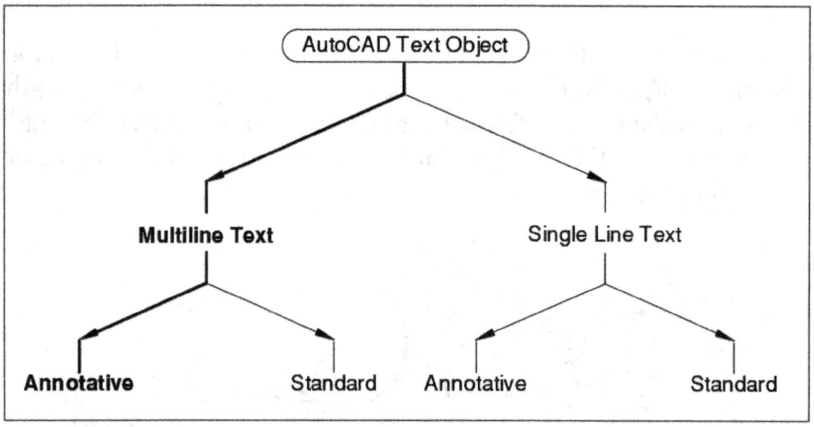

Figure 5-5

5.5.1. Multiline versus single line text

AutoCAD's *Text* command makes a distinction between multiline and single line texts. A multiline text means that the text object includes one or more paragraphs of text that can be manipulated as a single object. The multiline text command allows user to change part of the text object to be bold, italic, color, font, font size, and/or text alignments, Figure 5-6. However, these capabilities are not available in single line text. Since the multiline text command can be used to create a single line text object, this section discusses the creation of a multiline text object.

> This is a sample text paragraph created in **AutoCAD**. Water at temperature of 75 degrees (75°) is flowing in a *pipe of 5 inches diameter* (Ø5).
>
> - The error in the dimension is plus-minus 5 (±5).
> - The center line (℄) of the road is shown yellow.

Figure 5-6

5.5.2. Standard versus annotative text

The annotative objects are used to control the size at which the annotative objects are displayed in the Model space and layouts. The annotative objects always appear to be of the same size regardless of the viewport scale. Figure 5-7 shows two text objects *Non-Annotative Text* created using Standard style and *Annotative Text* created using Annotative style.

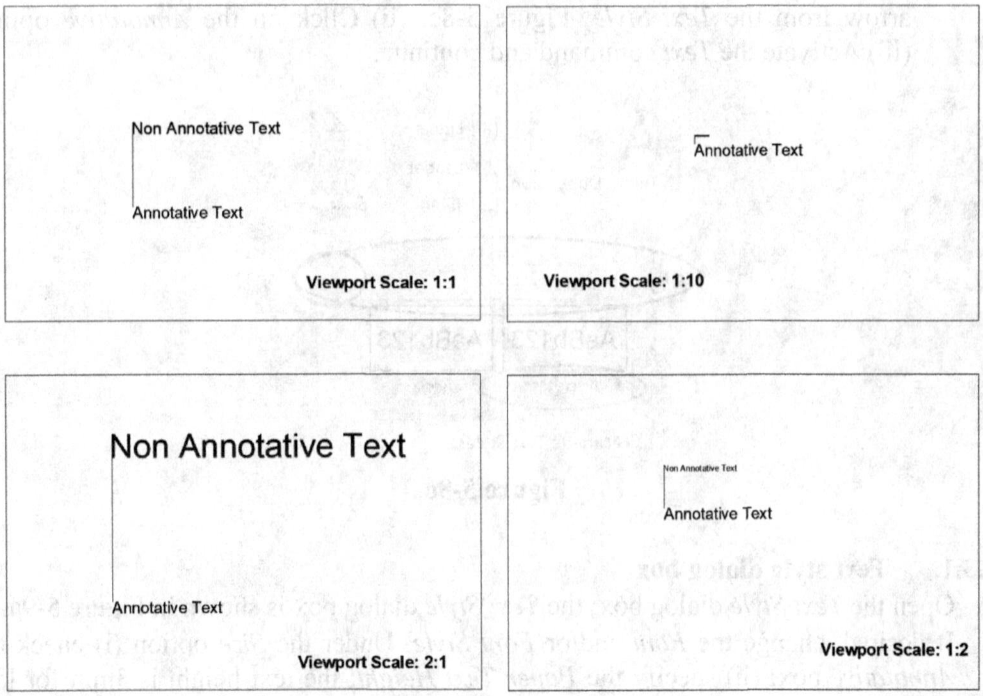

Figure 5-7

5.5.3. Annotative text style

This section provides step-by-step instruction on how to create an annotative text style.

- A user can create annotative text using one of the following methods.
  1. Panel method 1: This is the best method. (i) From the *Home* tab and the *Annotate* panel, click on the down-arrow from the *Text Style*, Figure 5-8a. (ii) Click on the *Manage Text Styles...* option. This will open *Text Style* dialog box, Figure 5-9a. (iii) Create an annotative text style.

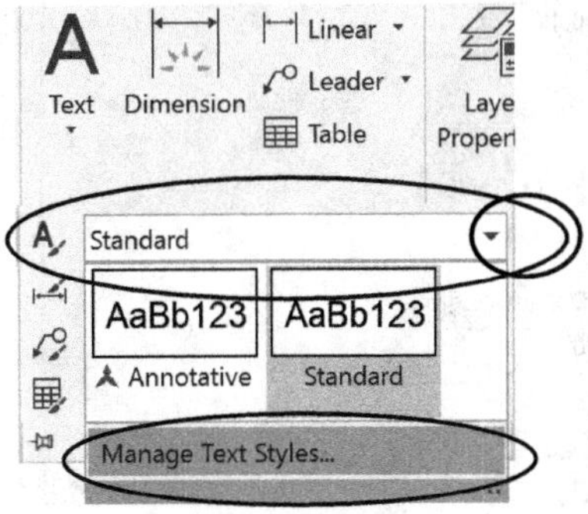

Figure 5-8a

Figure 5-8b

2. Panel method 2: (i) From the *Home* tab and the *Annotate* panel, click on the *Multiline Text* tool. (ii) Create a text box. (iii) Activate *Annotative* option. (iv) Set the text height. (v) Create the desired text, Figure 5-8b.
3. Panel method 3: (i) From the *Home* tab and the *Annotate* panel, click on the down-arrow from the *Text Style*, Figure 5-8c. (ii) Click on the *Annotative* option. (iii) Activate the *Text* command and continue.

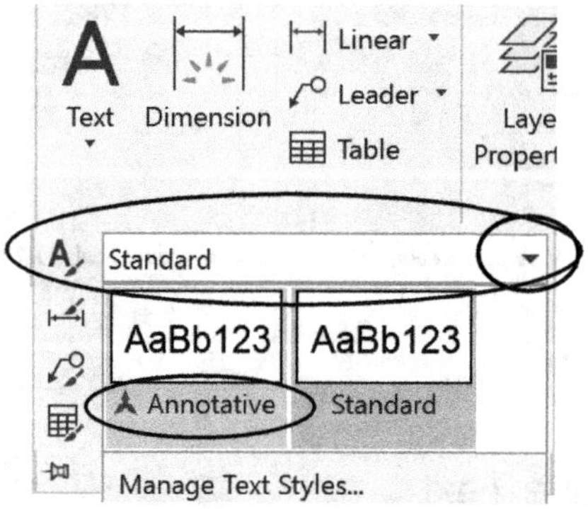

Figure 5-8c

5.5.3.1. Text style dialog box

- Open the *Text Style* dialog box; the *Text Style* dialog box is shown in Figure 5-9a.
- If desired, change the *Font* and/or *Font Style*. Under the *Size* option (i) check the *Annotative* box; (ii) specify the *Paper Text Height*; the text height is 3mm for ISO units (acadiso template file) and 0.12" – 0.125" for ANSI units (acad template file); (iii) click the *New* button and this will open AutoCAD confirmation dialog box.

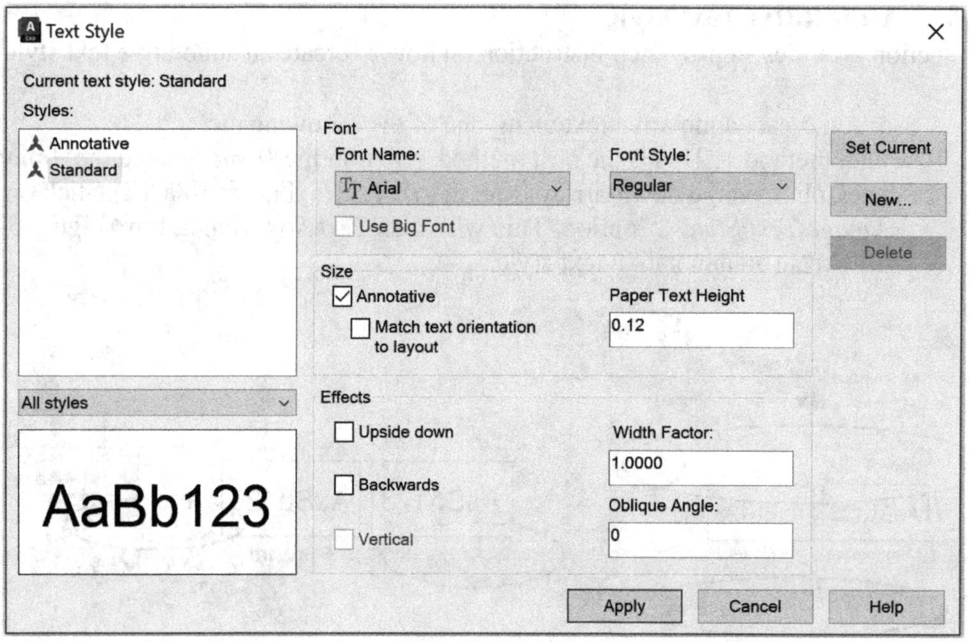

Figure 5-9a

- Click the *No* button from AutoCAD confirmation dialog box, Figure 5-9b. This will open *New Text Style* dialog box.
- In the *New Text Style* dialog box, Figure 5-9c, (i) specify the style name, (ii) click the *OK* button. In the current example, AST (**A**nnotative **S**tyle **T**ext) is the style name.
- The newly created style (AST) will appear in the *Text Style* dialog box, Figure 5-9d.
- Click the *Close* button of *Text Style* dialog box, Figure 5-9d.

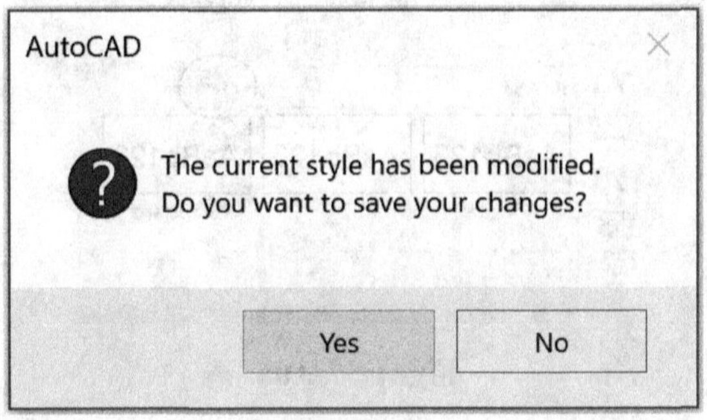

Figure 5-9b

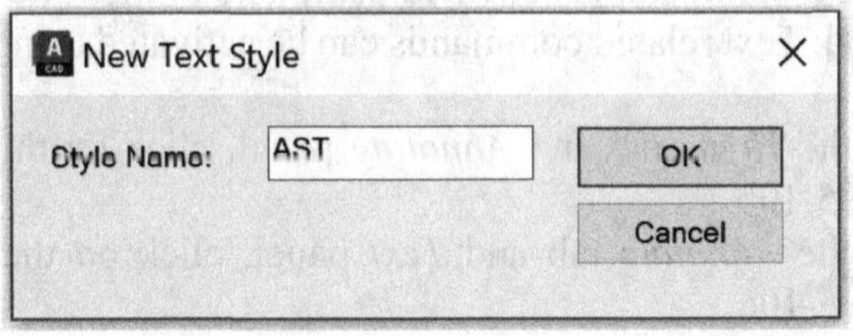

Figure 5-9c

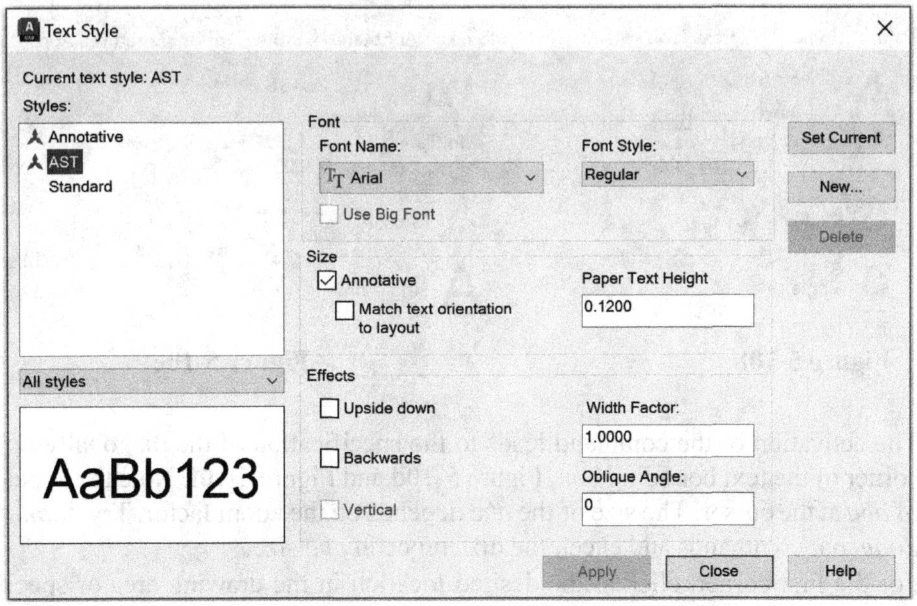

Figure 5-9d

5.5.4. Create multiline annotative text

This section assumes that the user has created an annotative text style. From the *Home* tab and *Annotate* panel, select the desired style, Figure 5-10a.

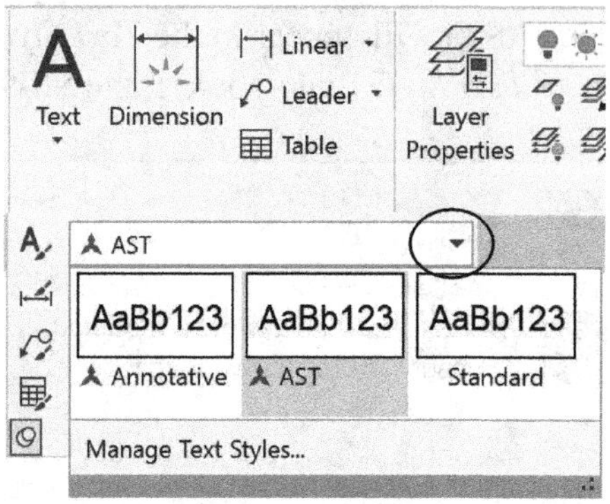

Figure 5-10a

To create a new annotative text, follow the method discussed below.

- The *Multiline Text* command is activated using one of the following methods:
  1. Panel method: Text related commands can be activated using one of the two panel methods:
     a. From the *Home* tab and *Annotate* panel, click on the *Multiline Text* tool, Figure 5-10b.
     b. From the *Annotate* tab and *Text* panel, click on the *Multiline Text* tool, Figure 5-10c.
  2. Command line method: Type "mtext", "MText", or "MTEXT" in the command line and press the *Enter* key to activate an option to create a multiline text.

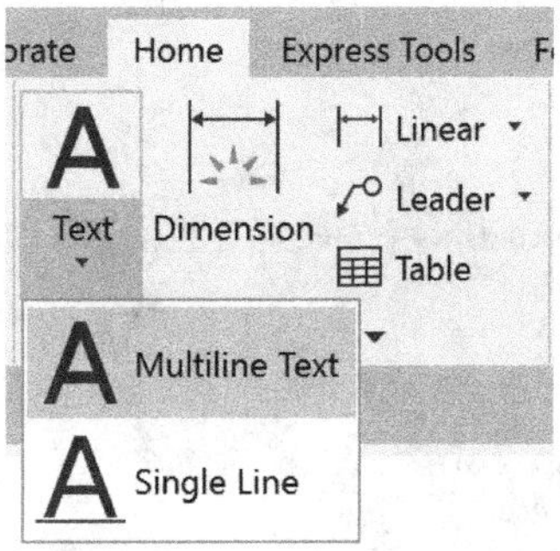

Figure 5-10b

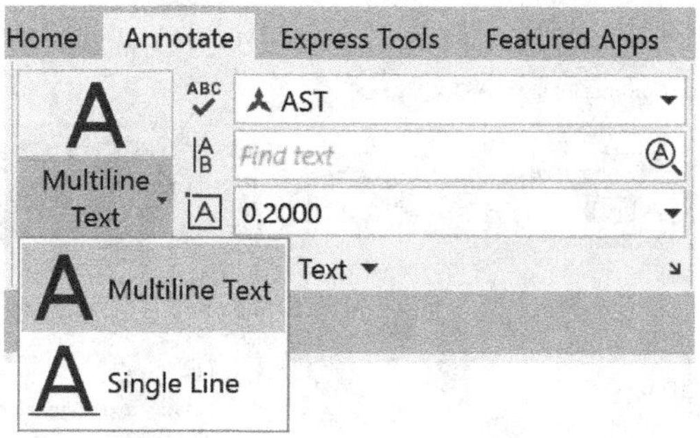

Figure 5-10c

- The activation of the command leads to the specification of the diagonally opposite corner of the text bounding box, Figure 5-10d and Figure 5-10f. Note the appearance of *abc* at the cursor. The size of the *abc* depends on the zoom factor. Try *Zoom in* and *Zoom out* commands and check the difference in *abc* size.
- For the first corner, click at the desired location in the drawing area or specify the coordinate of the point and press the *Enter* key, Figure 5-10e.

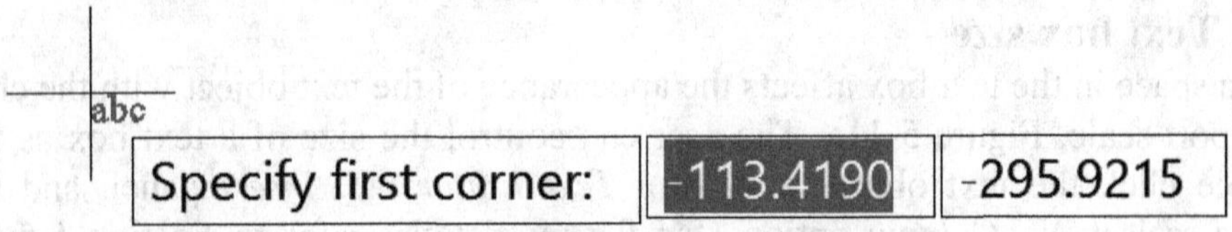

Figure 5-10d

- For the specification of the second point, click at a diagonally opposite corner. This will create a bounding box, Figure 5-10e, and open the text insertion box, Figure 5-10f. Also, the *Text Editor* tab becomes the current tab. The details of the *Text Editor* are discussed in the next section.

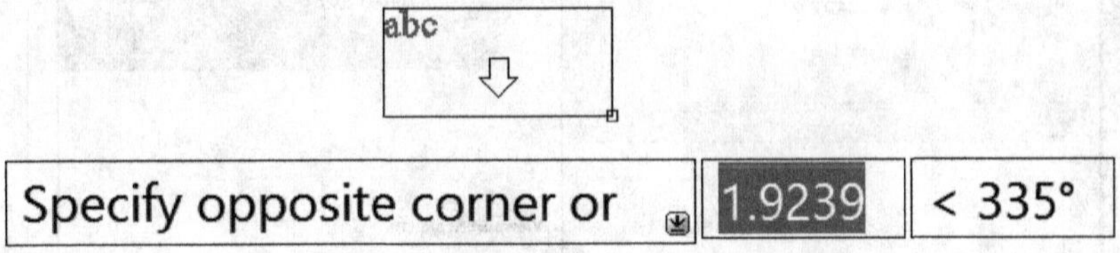

Figure 5-10e

- Type in the text and click in the drawing area. The box will disappear, and the text will appear in the drawing area.

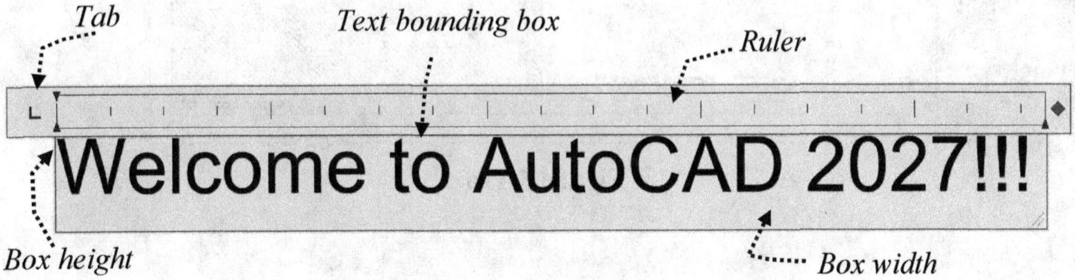

Figure 5-10f

- If the newly created text is not visible and/or too small/big, the user can make the annotative text visible and adjust its size using the following steps. These commands are available from the status bar and discussed in detail in Section 5.10. (i) Activate the *Annotation Visibility* to display the annotative text, Figure 5-10g. (ii) Activate the *Annotation Auto scale* to automatically add the viewport scale to the annotative text scale list. (iii) Change the *Annotation scale* factor to display the annotative text at a desired scale.

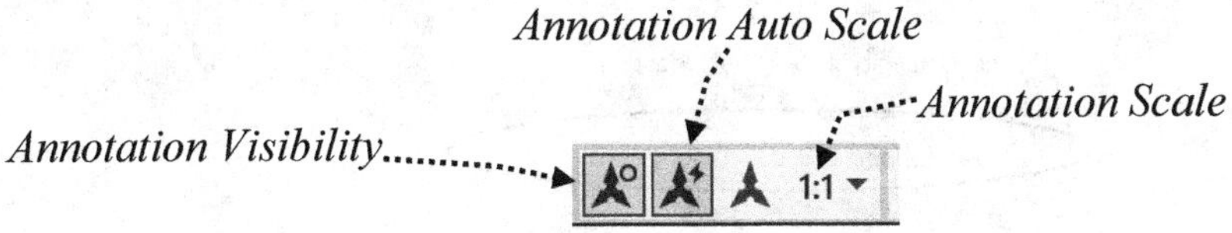

Figure 5-10g

5.5.5. Text box size

The extra space in the text box affects the appearance of the text object with the change in the viewport scale, Figure 5-11a. The user can control the size of a text box as follows: (i) Double click the text object, and from *Text Editor* tab, *Insert* panel, and Column command, select *No Column* option (for further details, refer to Section 5.5.5.6.4.1). (ii) Close the *Text Editor*. (iii) select the text object in question. (iv) Right click and open the *Properties* sheet. (v) from the *Text* tab, set the *Paper defined width* to 0.0, Figure 5-11b.

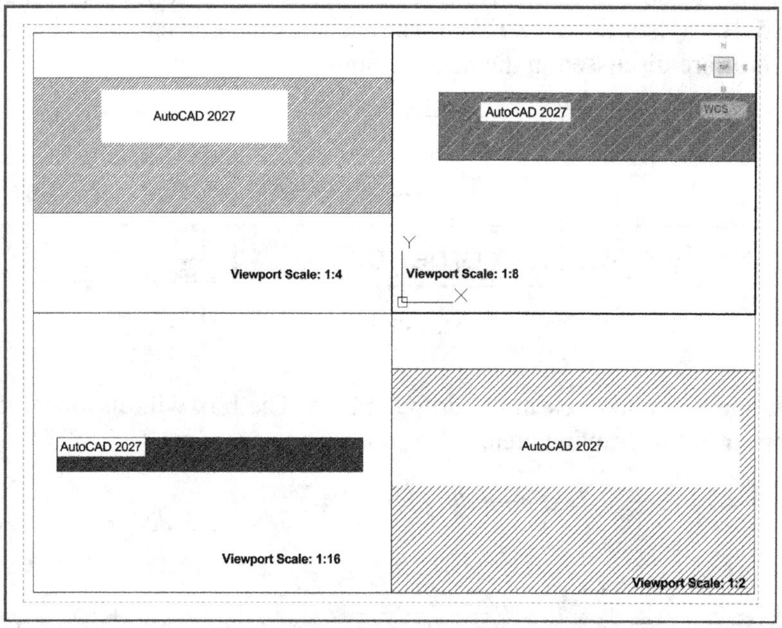

Figure 5-11a

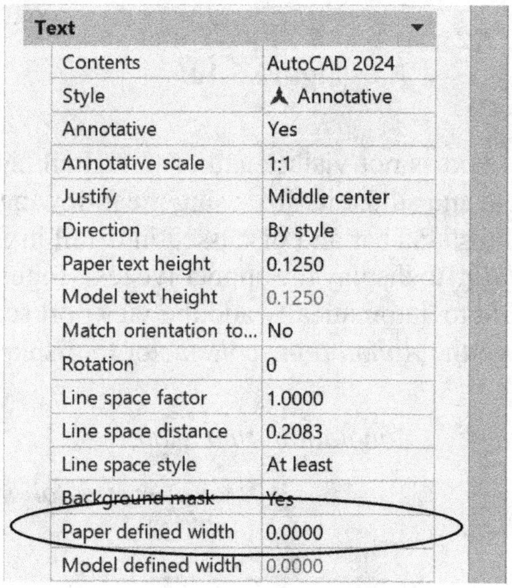

Figure 5-11b

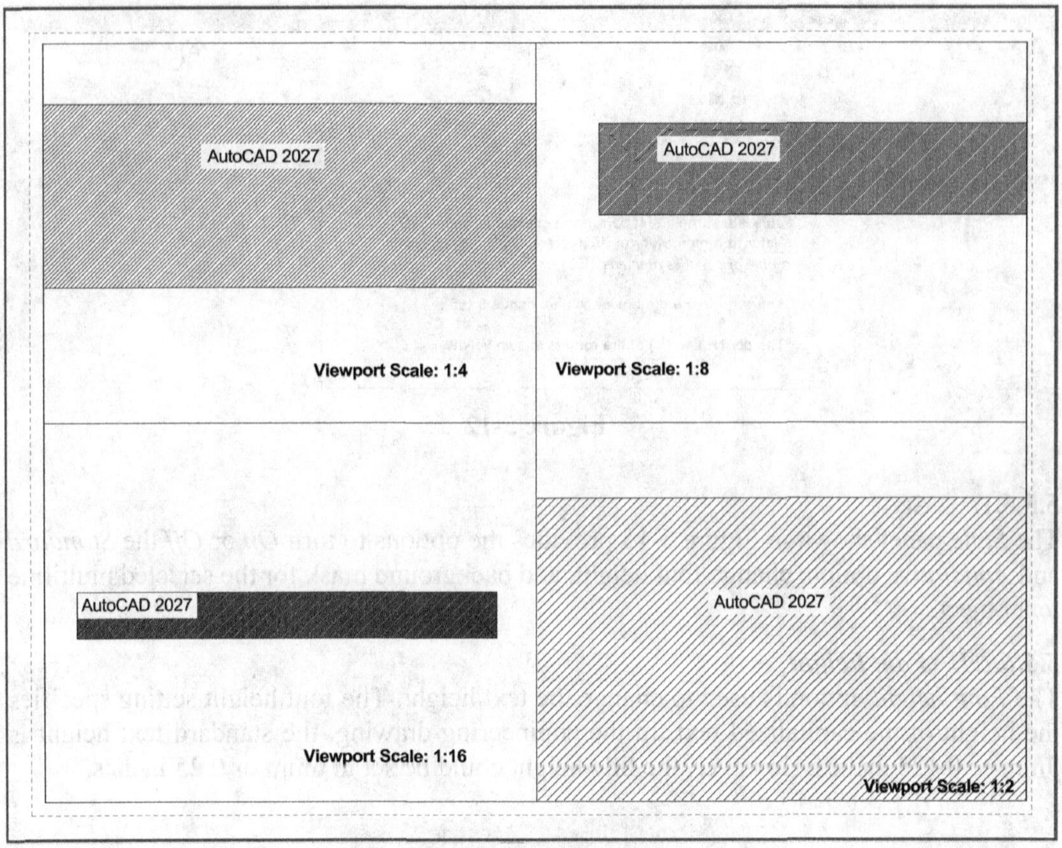

Figure 5-11c

5.5.6. Text editor

The *Text Editor* tab, Figure 5-12, provides the options to modify the style, format, paragraph properties, etc. of the selected multiline text object. These capabilities are available through the *Style*, *Formatting*, *Paragraph*, *Insert*, *Spell Check*, *Tools*, *Options*, and *Close* panels. The editor is available only if the text is open as shown in Figure 5-12 (double click on the text and the text editor opens). When the text editor is open, AutoCAD does not allow the user to access any other functionality. Exit the editor mode by clicking outside the text's bounding box or by pressing the *Esc* key from the keyboard.

The changes are in effect only for the selected text and the current text style is not changed. That is, the user must select the text to be changed and then select the facilities provided by the various panels. For example, in Figure 5-12 to make the word "AutoCAD" bold, the user should first select the text and then apply the bold option to the selected text. Most of the characteristics discussed in the remainder of this section can be updated using properties palette, too.

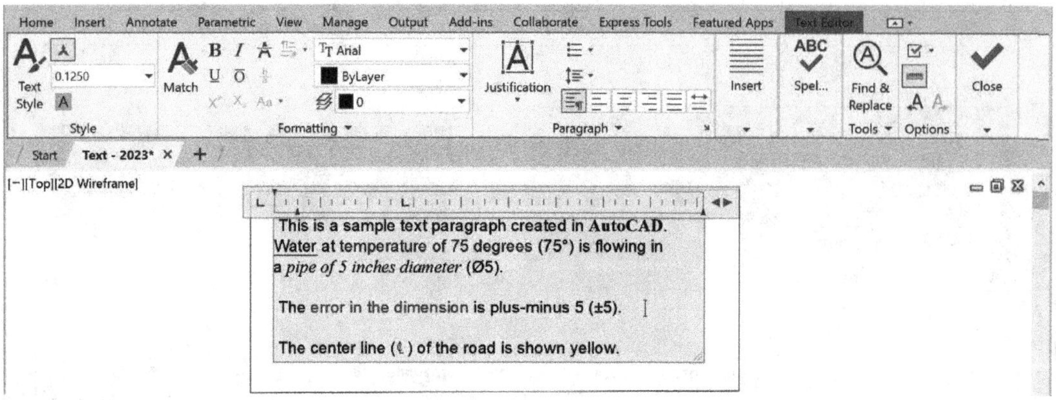

Figure 5-12

5.5.6.1. Style

The *Style* panel shown in Figure 5-13 provides the options to turn *On* or *Off* the *Standard* and *Annotative* option, change font height, and background mask for the selected multiline text object.

5.5.6.1.1. Font height

The *Font height* option is used to change the text height. The font height setting specifies the height of the capitalized text. In the engineering drawing, the standard text height is 3mm or 0.125 inches. However, the title height could be set to 6mm or 0.25 inches.

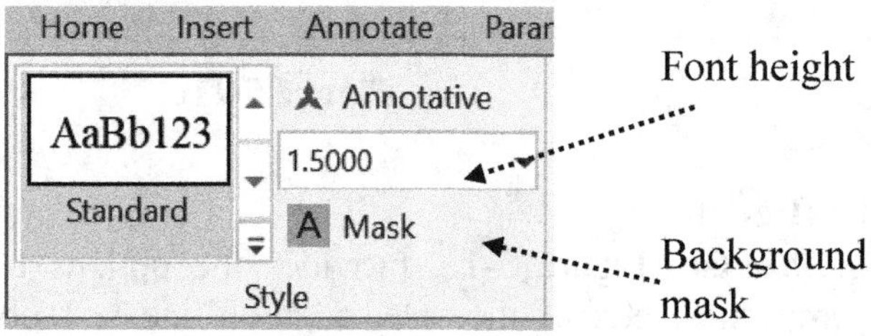

Figure 5-13

5.5.6.1.2. Background mask

Notice the difference between Figure 5-14a and Figure 5-14b. A drafter can convert Figure 5-14a into Figure 5-14b by masking the background using the *Mask* command; this command hides the objects behind the text. A user can mask the background using one of the following two methods.

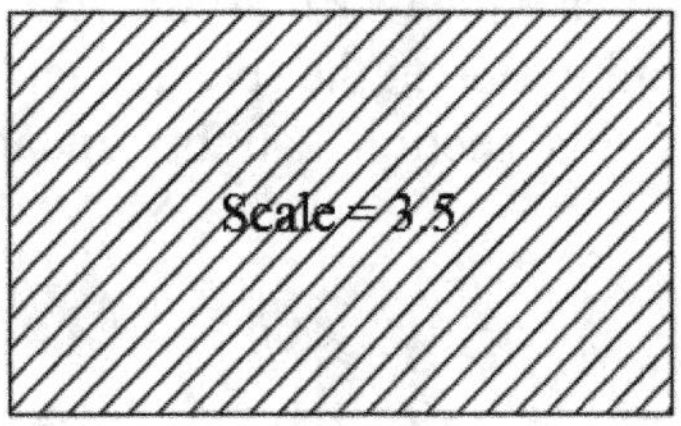

Figure 5-14a

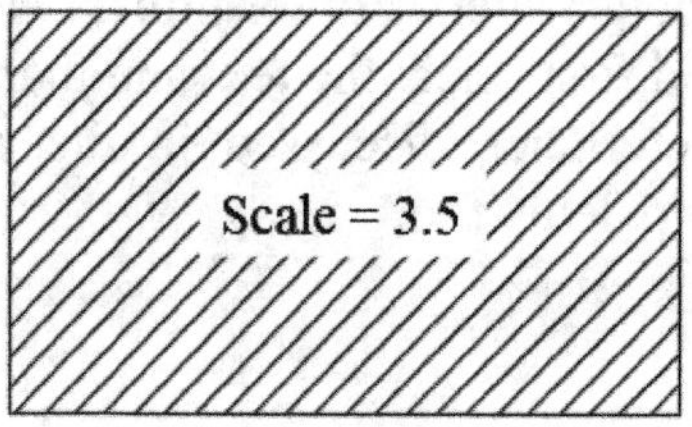

Figure 5-14b

Dialog box method:

The background can be masked from the Background Mask dialog box as follows: (i) Double click the multiline text of Figure 5-14a and the *Text Editor* appears on the screen. (ii) From the *Style* panel, click the *Mask* option and the *Background Mask* dialog box appears on the screen, Figure 5-14c. (iii) Check both boxes on the *Background Mask* dialog box. (iv) Finally, click the *OK* button. The resultant masked text is shown in Figure 5-14b.

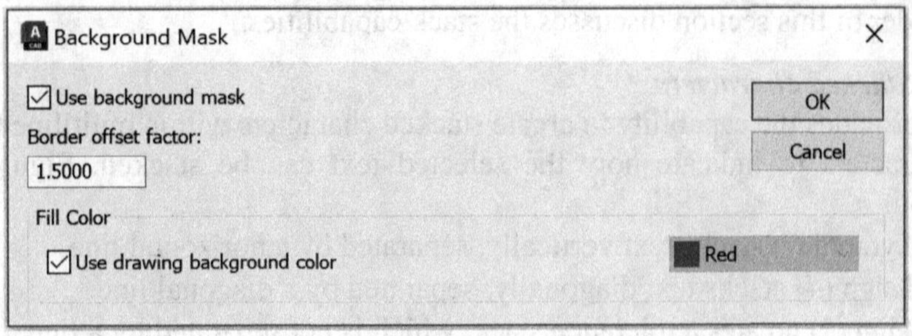

Figure 5-14c

Property palette method:

The background can be masked from the property palette as follows. (i) Select the multiline text. (ii) Press the right button. (iii) Choose the *Properties* option (the last option) to open the properties palette. (iv) From the *Text* panel of the property palette, select the *Background mask* option (Figure 5-14d) and ▭ appears in the left column. (v) Click on the ▭ button and the *Background Mask* dialog box appears on the screen, Figure 5-14c. (vi) Check both boxes on the *Background Mask* dialog box. (vii) Finally, click the *OK* button. The resultant masked text is shown in Figure 5-14b.

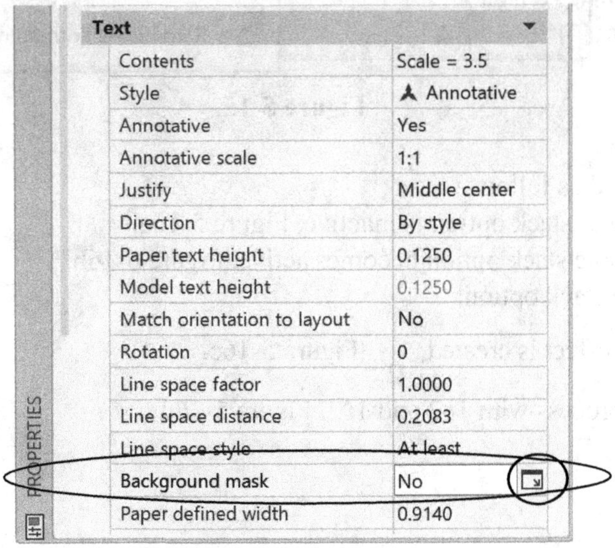

Figure 5-14d

5.5.6.2. Formatting

The expanded *Formatting* panel with the expanded *Clear* menu is shown in Figure 5-15. The user must select the text and then click on the desired command. This panel provides the options to change the font type and color of the selected text. The boldface and italics options are available for some of the fonts. The selected text can also be underlined, over lined, and/or strike through. The case change option allows the user to convert the lowercase to uppercase and vice versa by pressing the down-arrow key from the keyboard and choosing the appropriate option. The *Clear* options remove the selected formatting. The remainder of this section discusses the stack capabilities.

5.5.6.2.1. Stacked characters

AutoCAD provides the capability to create stacked characters within multiline text. It uses special characters to indicate how the selected text can be stacked. Figure 5-16a to Figure 5-16d.

- Slash symbol (/) stacks text vertically, separated by a horizontal line.
- Pound sign (#) stacks text diagonally, separated by a diagonal line.
- Carat sign (^) creates a tolerance stack, which is not separated by a line.

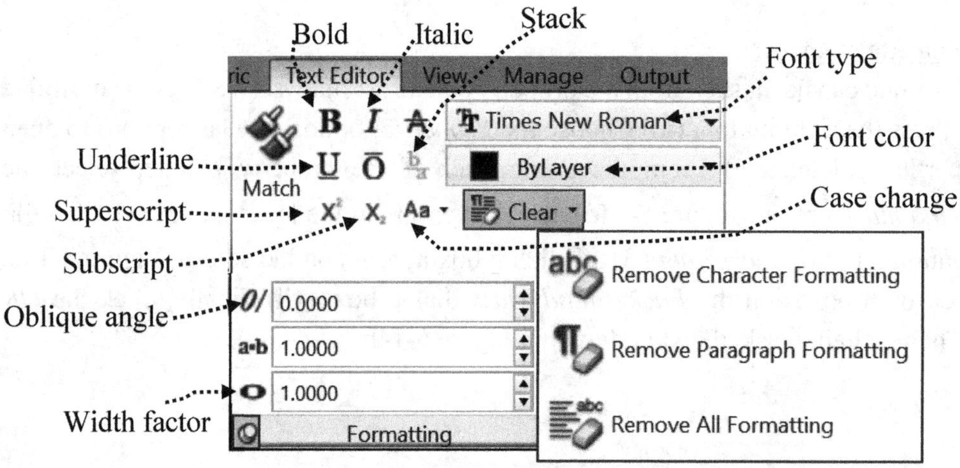

Figure 5-15

Text can be stacked as follows:

- Write 1/2, note stack option is inactive, Figure 5-16a.
- Select 1/2, note stack option becomes active, Figure 5-16b.
- Click on the stack option.
- The desired effect is created, $\frac{1}{2}$, Figure 5-16c.
- Repeat the process with 1#2 and 1^2, Figure 5-16d.

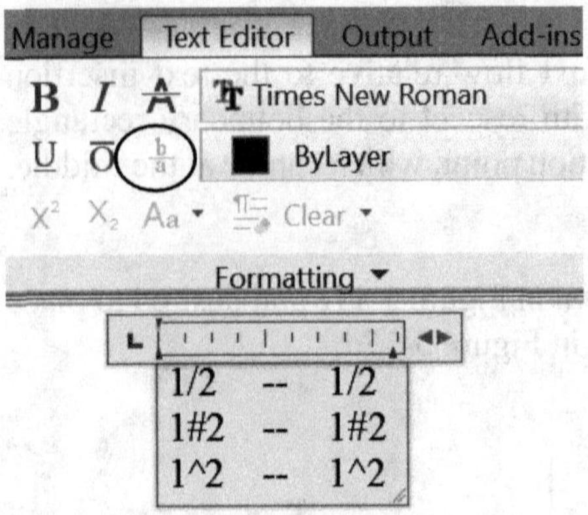

Figure 5-16a

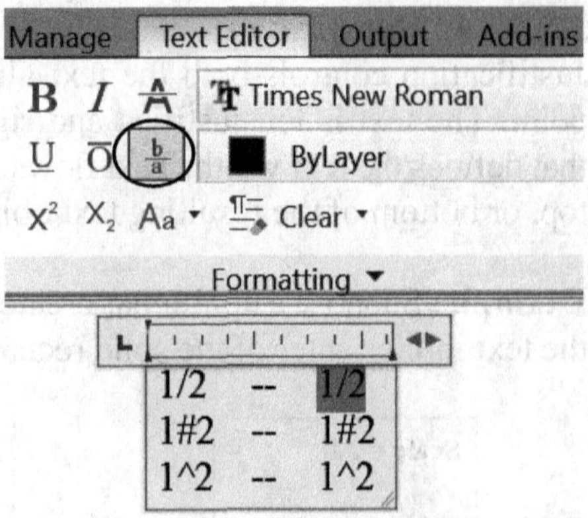

Figure 5-16b

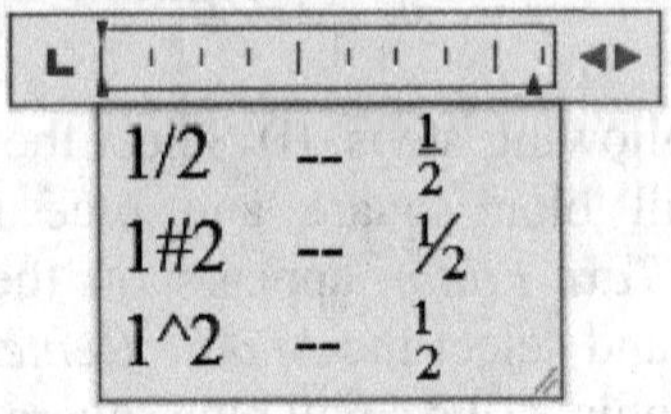

Figure 5-16c

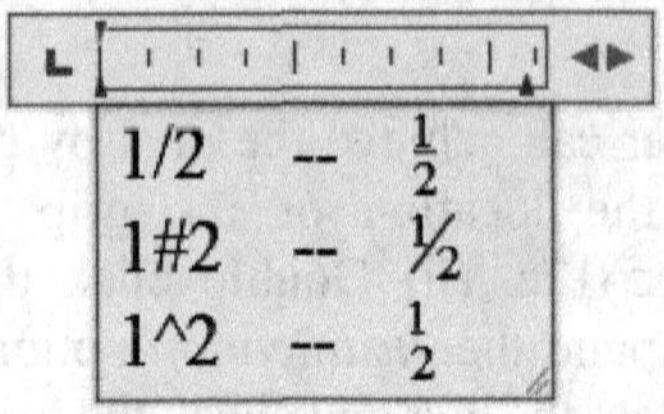

Figure 5-16d

5.5.6.3. Paragraph

The *Paragraph* panel is shown in Figure 5-17a. This panel provides the options to change the paragraph properties of the selected text. Press the down-arrow under *Justification* on the *Paragraph* panel and check the various options, Figure 5-17b.

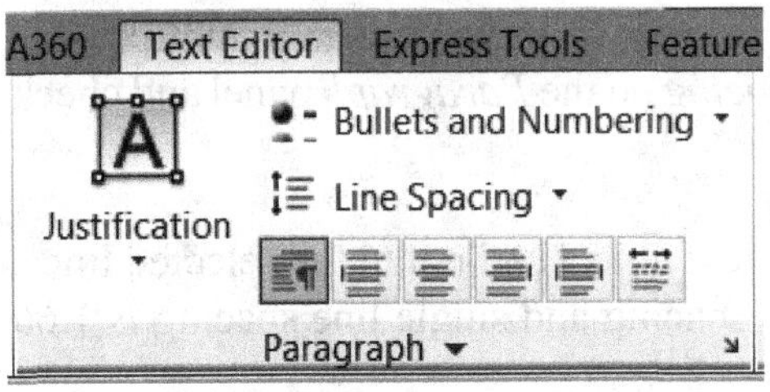

Figure 5-17a

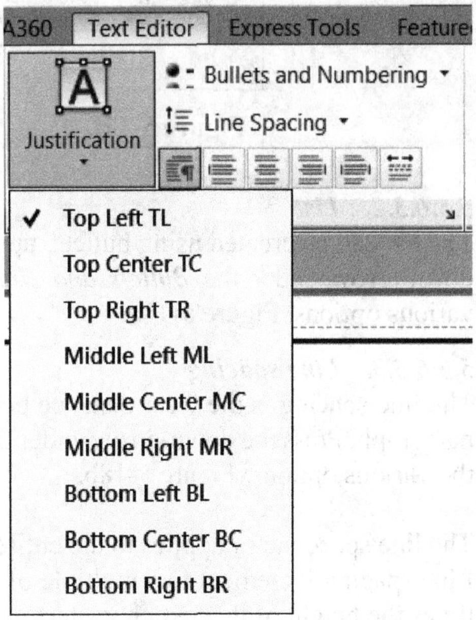

Figure 5-17b

5.5.6.3.1. Justification

Justification controls both the text alignment and text flow relative to the text insertion point. The text is left-justified and right-justified with respect to the boundary rectangle that defines the text width. Text flows from the insertion point, which can be at the middle, top, or bottom of the resulting text object.

Example: Suppose a drafter has created the text shown in Figure 5-17c and desired to place the text in the center of the solid rectangle as shown in Figure 5-17d.

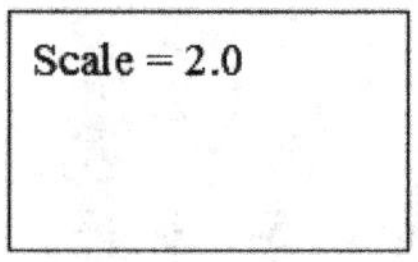

Figure 5-17c

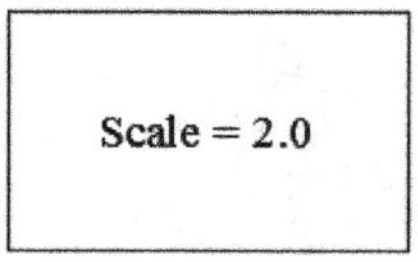

Figure 5-17d

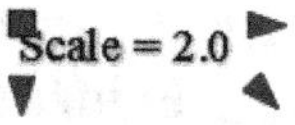

Figure 5-17e

The user can achieve the goal by performing the following steps. (i) Select the text and check the location of the grip points (the small blue square and blue triangle), Figure 5-17e. (ii) Double click the text and the *Text Editor* appears on the screen. (iii) Expand the *Justification* option, Figure 5-17b, and select the *Middle Center* option. (iv) Select the text and check the location of the grip points (the small blue square and blue triangle), Figure 5-17f. (v) Match the four arrows with the corresponding corner of the rectangle, Figure 5-17g. Click on one of the triangular grip points, keep pressing the left button, move the cursor to the nearest corner and repeat the process with the diagonally opposite grip point. The resultant text is shown in Figure 5-17g. (vi) Click the *Esc* key from the keyboard to exit the command, Figure 5-17d.

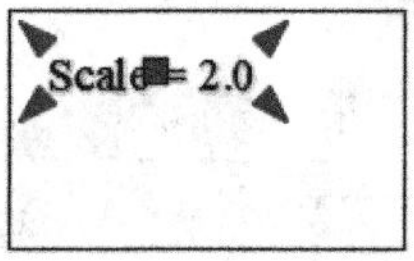

Figure 5-17f

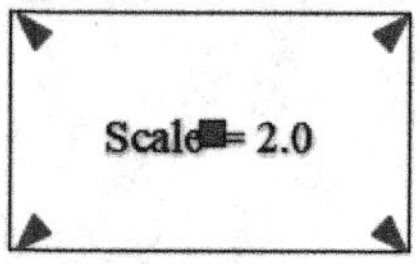

Figure 5-17g

5.5.6.3.2. List

The list can be created using bullets, uppercase or lowercase letters, or numbers. Press the down-arrow under the *Bullets and Numbering* on the *Paragraph* panel and check the various options, Figure 5-18a.

5.5.6.3.3. Line spacing

The line spacing is the clear distance between the two consecutive lines in a multiple line paragraph. Press the down-arrow under the *Line Spacing* on the *Paragraph* panel and check the various options, Figure 5-18b.

The line space factor applies to the entire multiline text object and not to the selected lines. Line spacing increment to a multiple of single line spacing and single line spacing is 1.66 times the height of the text characters.

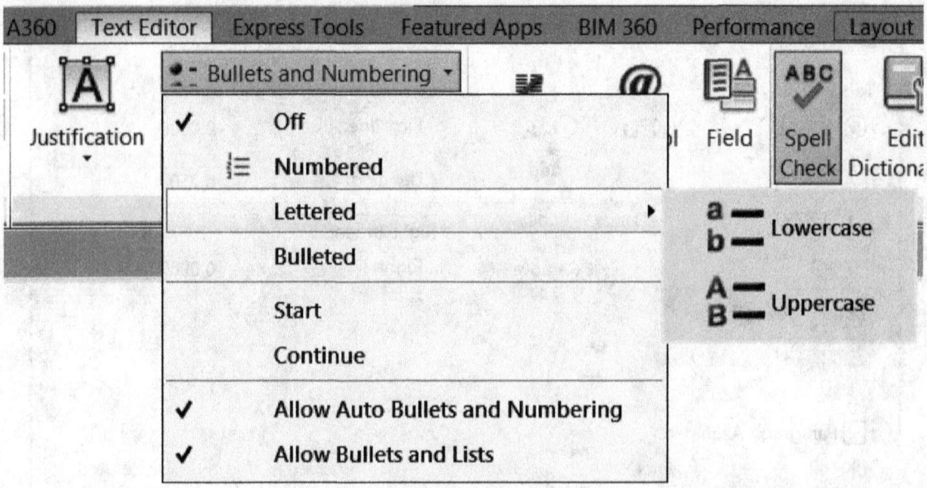

Figure 5-18a

To change the line spacing, (i) click on the drop-down-arrow in line spacing option, Figure 5-18b, and (ii) select the *Line space factor*. The line spacing of the multiline text is updated.

The line spacing can also be changed as follows: (i) select the multiline text, (ii) press the right button, (iii) choose the *Properties* option to open the properties palette, (iv) set the *Line space factor* field (for the example, to 1.5), and (v) press the *Enter* key.

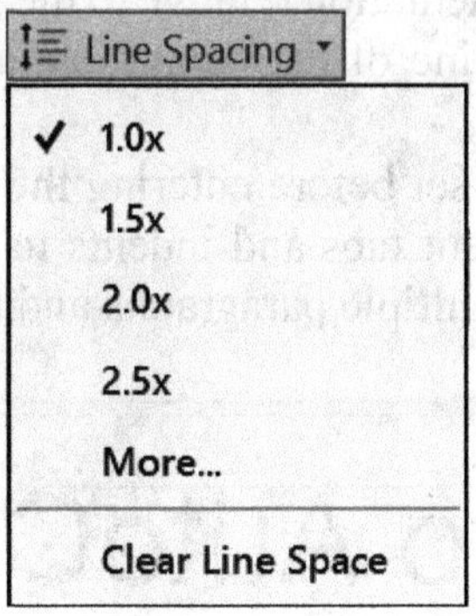

Figure 5-18b

5.5.6.3.4. Paragraph dialog box

The *Paragraph* dialog box, Figure 5-18c, can be opened by clicking the dialog box launcher (a small arrow on the lower right corner of the panel) in the *Paragraph* panel. The dialog box is used to set the tabs, indentations, and paragraphs spacing and alignment.

- Multiline text can be indented using tabs. The ruler in the in-place text editor shows the settings for the current paragraph, Figure 5-18d.

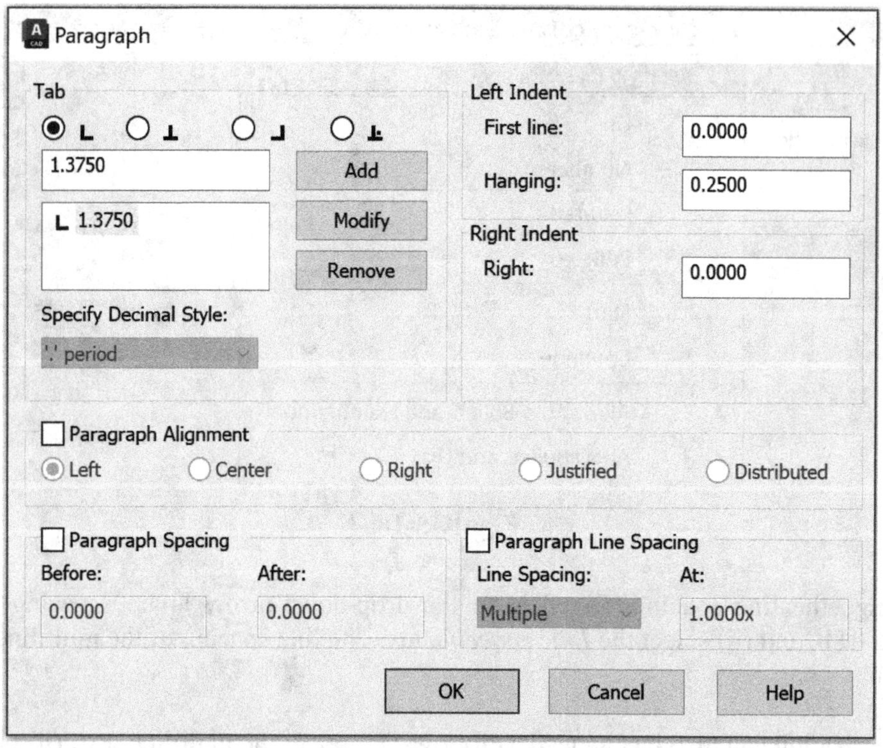

Figure 5-18c

- Sliders on the ruler show indentation relative to the left side of the bounding box. The top slider indents the first line of the paragraph, and the bottom slider indents the other lines of the paragraph.
- Tabs and indents which are set before entering the text apply to the whole multiline text object. To apply different tabs and indents to individual paragraphs, click in a single paragraph or select multiple paragraphs and then change the settings.

Figure 5-18d

5.5.6.4. Insert

The *Insert* panel is shown in Figure 5-19a. This panel provides the options to insert columns and symbols in the multiline text.

5.5.6.4.1. Column

The user can create and edit multiple columns. The various options are shown in the expanded *Columns* drop-down menu, Figure 5-19b.

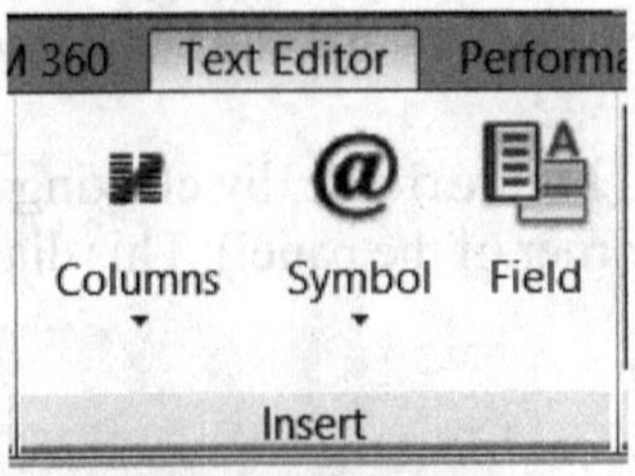

Figure 5-19a

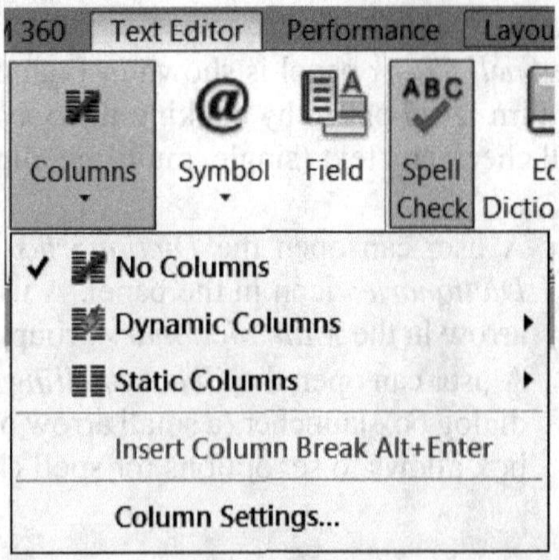

Figure 5-19b

5.5.6.4.2. Symbol

The user can create several symbols in the text. The various options are shown in the expanded *Symbol* drop-down menu, Figure 5-19c. The most used symbols are listed below and Figure 5-19d demonstrates their usage.

- Enter %%C in a text box to create ∅ (diameter symbol)
- Enter %%P in a text box to create ± (Plus Minus)
- Enter %%D in a text box to create ° (degree symbol)
- Set font to "gdt" and type q (centerline symbol)
- To create the almost equal symbol, expand the *Symbol* drop-down menu and select *Almost Equal \U+2248* option, Figure 5-19c.

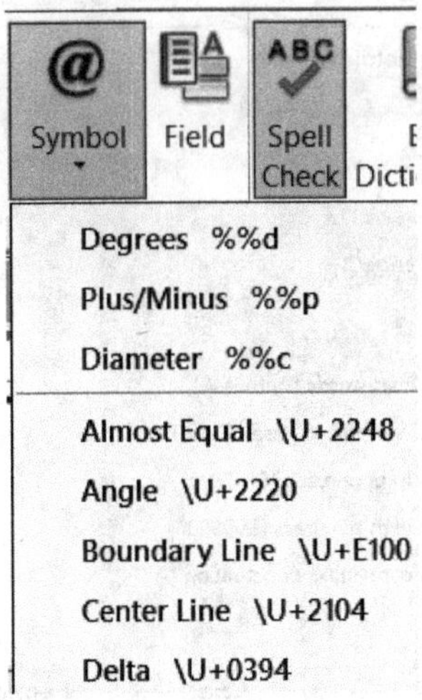

Figure 5-19c

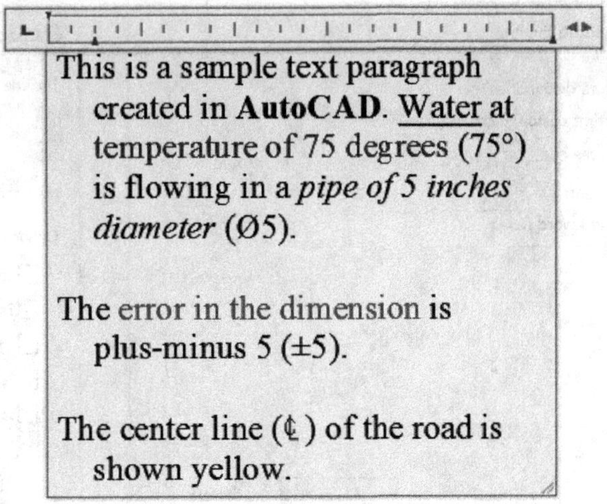

Figure 5-19d

5.5.6.5. Spell check

The *Spell Check* panel is shown in Figure 5-20a. By default, the spell check is *On*; a user can turn it *Off* or *On* by clicking the *Spell Check* icon. This panel provides the options to spell check any text (single, multiline, dimension, qleader, etc.).

- A user can open the *Dictionaries* dialog box, Figure 5-20b, by clicking the *Edit Dictionaries* icon in the panel. A user can select a dictionary by pressing the down-arrow in the *Main dictionary* group.
- A user can open the *Check Spelling Setting* dialog box, Figure 5-20c, by clicking the dialog box launcher (a small arrow on the lower right corner of the panel). This dialog box allows to set options for spell checking.

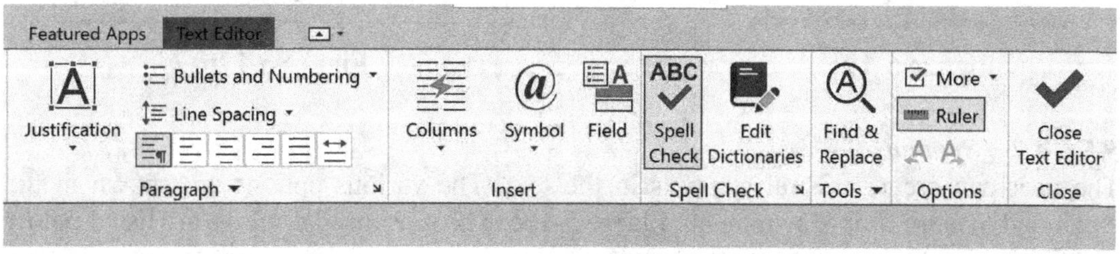

Figure 5-20a

5.5.6.6. Tools

The expanded *Tool* panel is shown in Figure 5-21. This panel provides the options to find and replace a text, import text from other files, and type the uppercase text.

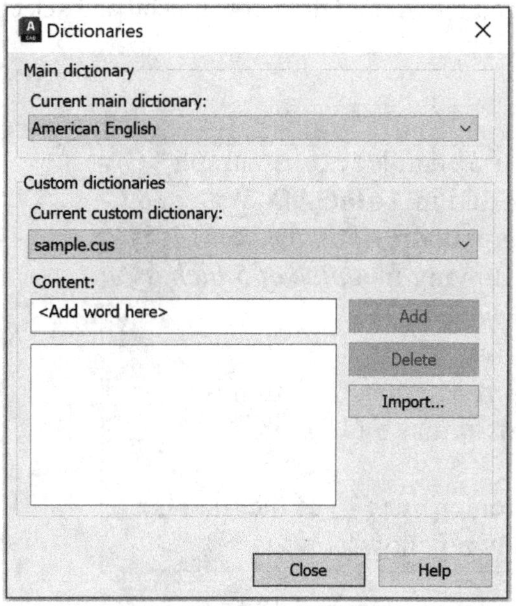

Figure 5-20b

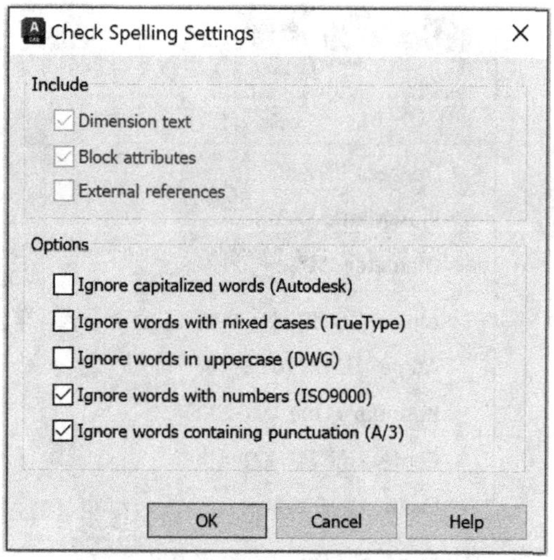

Figure 5-20c

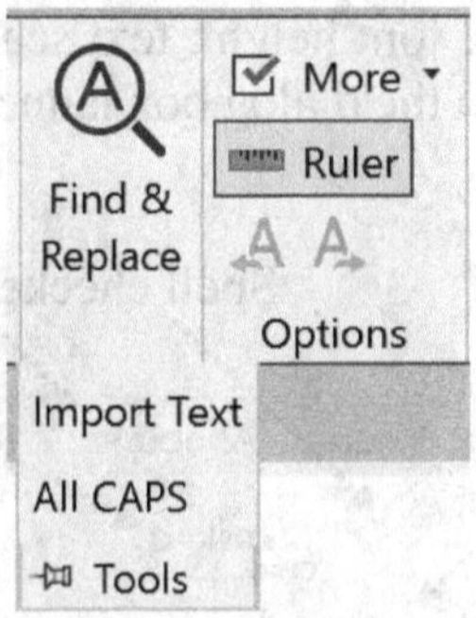

Figure 5-21

5.5.6.7. Options

The expanded *Options* panel is shown in Figure 5-22a. This panel provides the options to select a character set, display or hide the ruler on top of the text bounding box (Figure 5-19d), *Do*, and *Undo* buttons. Click on the down-arrow beside *More*, Figure 5-22b, and expand the *Character Set* to display the available character sets. In the current example, *Western* character set is used.

5.5.6.8. Close

The *Close* panel, Figure 5-22c, is used to close the *Text Editor*. Click on the *Close Text Editor*, and the editor is closed. The user can also exit the editor mode by clicking outside the text's bounding box or by pressing the *Esc* key from the keyboard.

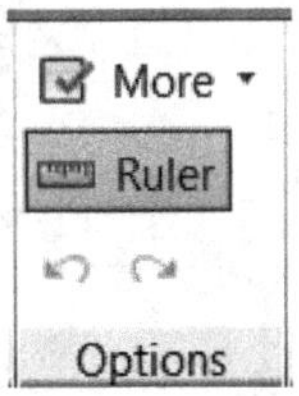

Figure 5-22a

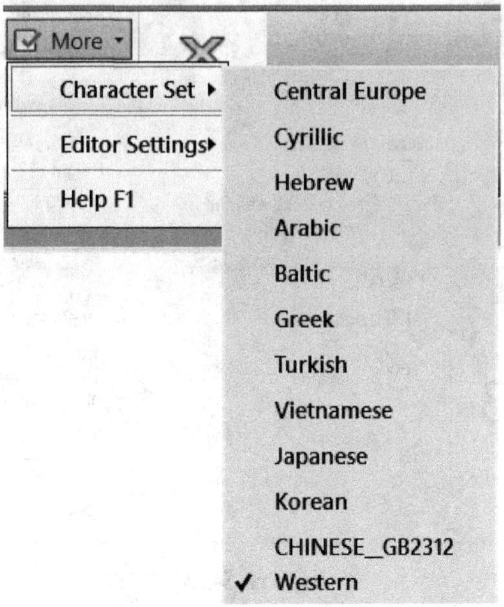

Figure 5-22b

Figure 5-22c

5.5.7. Annotate tab and Text panel

The expanded *Text* panel from the *Annotate* tab is shown in Figure 5-23a. This panel provides the options to create a single and multiline text, spell checker, text alignment, justification, text style, text search, font height, text scaling, and layer selection. The user can open *Text Style* dialog box from the dialog box launcher (small arrow in the lower right corner of the panel), Figure 5-23b.

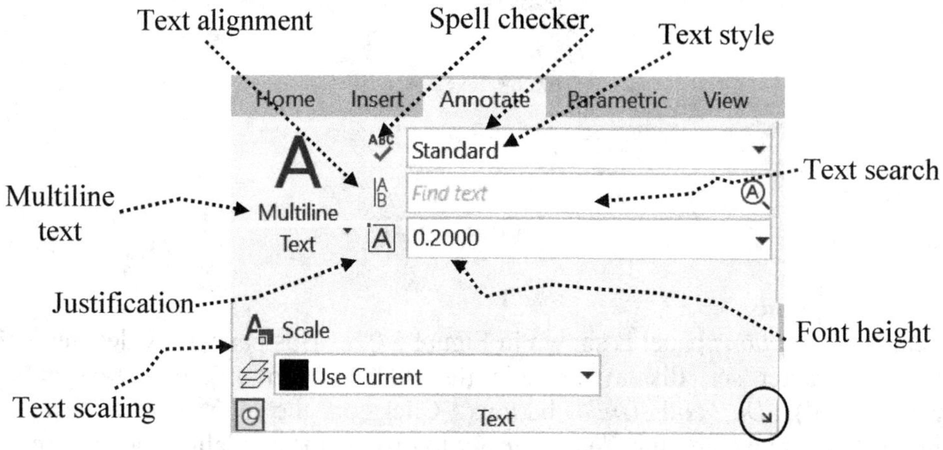

Figure 5-23a

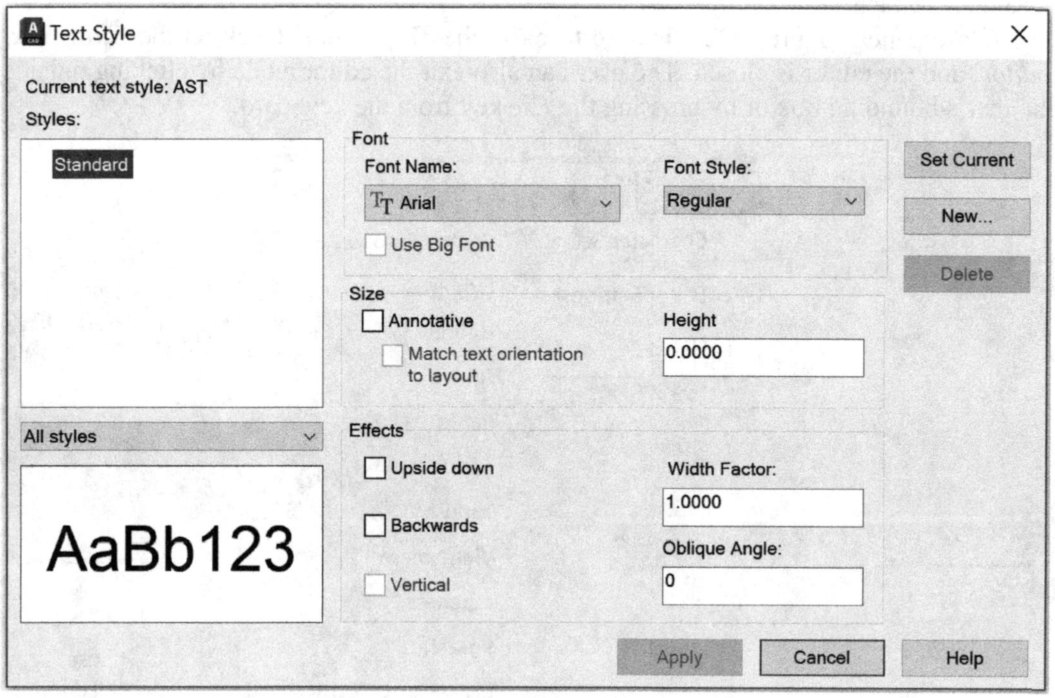

Figure 5-23b

5.5.8. Modify multiline annotative text

To modify an existing text, double click on the text and the text editor opens. Modify the text as needed.

5.5.9. Delete text style

An unused text style can be deleted as follows:

- Make sure that the style to be deleted is not the current style and is not used for any of the text objects.
- Open the *Text Style* dialog box, Figure 5-24a.
    - Select the style to be deleted. In the current example, **style 1** will be deleted.
    - Right click and select the *Delete* option. This will open *acad Alert* dialog box, Figure 5-24b.
    - Click the *OK* button from *acad Alert* dialog box. This will delete the selected style, close the *acad Alert* dialog box, and *Cancel* button of *Text Style* dialog box will change to *Close*.
    - Click the *Close* button from *Text Style* dialog box.

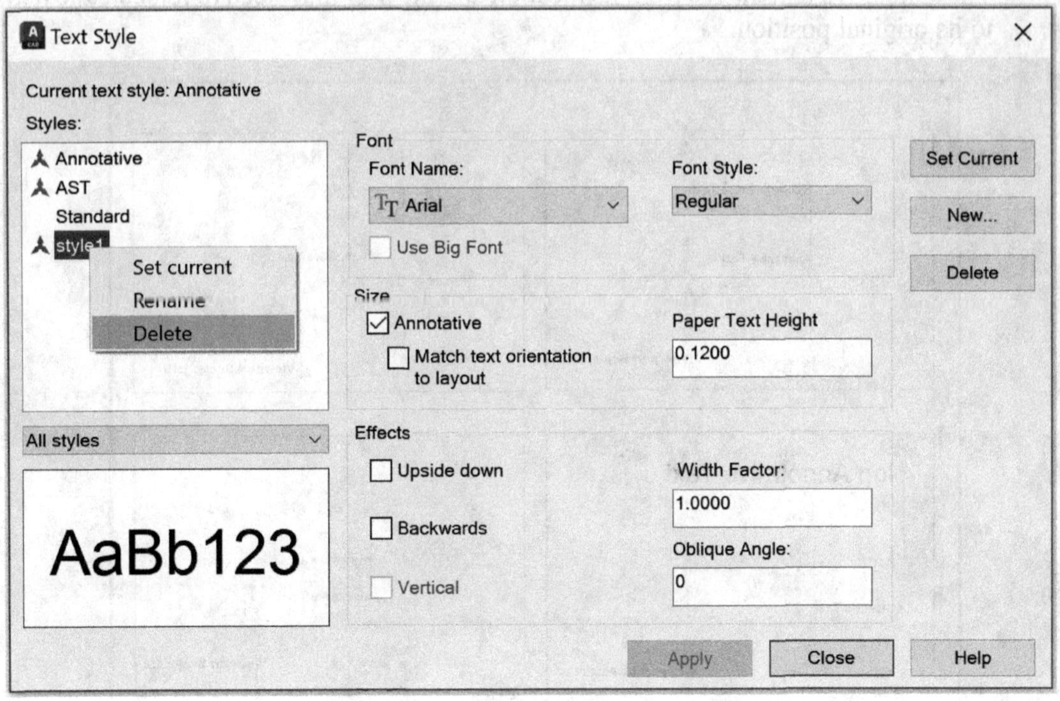

Figure 5-24a

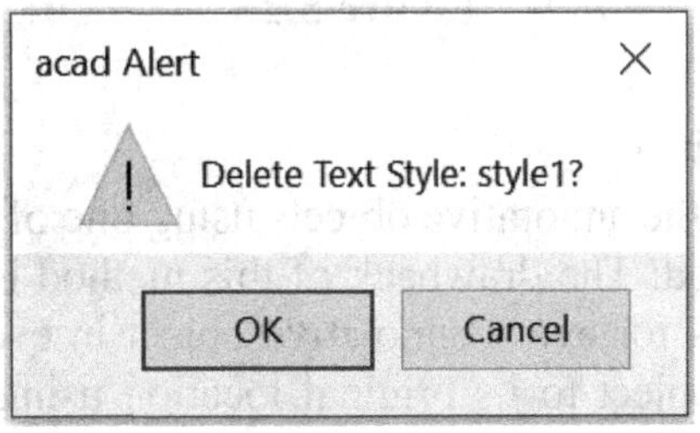

Figure 5-24b

5.5.10. Add the scales to the text properties

The process of adding multiple scale factors to an annotative object is explained in *Section 5.3.1*.

5.5.11. Annotative text and viewport scale

Figure 5-25 shows four viewports with different viewport scales. The scales are shown in the lower right corners of the viewports. The user can either practice with multiple layouts or create multiple viewports in the same layout (for detail, refer to *Chapter 8*).

It is clear from the figure that:

- The non-annotative (*Standard*) text size changes with the change in viewport scale.
- The annotative text size is independent of the viewport scale.
- The annotative text moves from its location and the user may need to relocate the text to its original position.

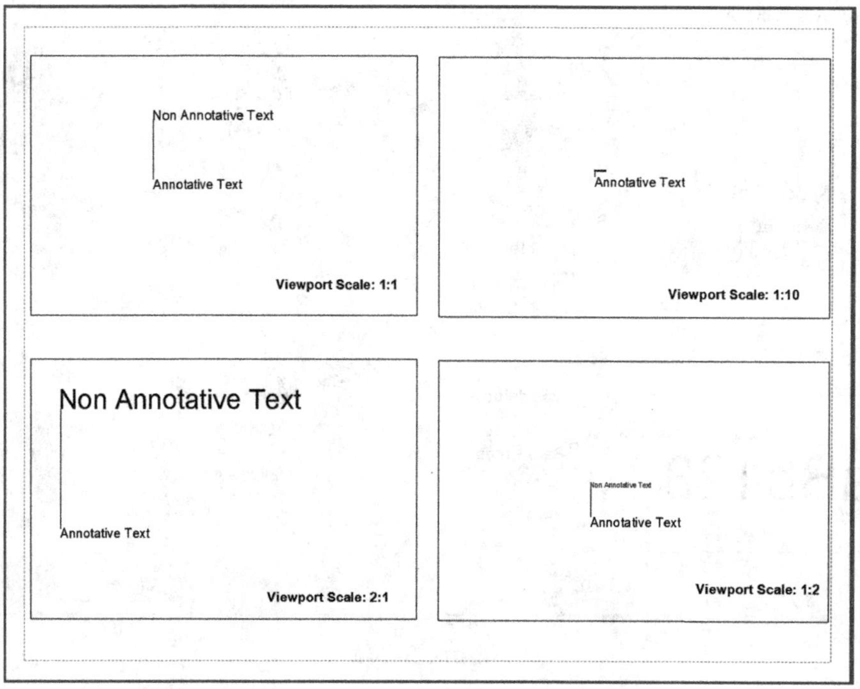

Figure 5-25

5.5.12. Text relocation

- The user can relocate the annotative objects using one of the following methods.
  1. Grip Points Method: The drawback of this method is that the user may need to repeat this process for every annotative object in every viewport. The user can relocate the text object to its original location using the grip point as follows: (i) Click at the text's grip point, Figure 5-26a. (ii) Keep pressing the left mouse button, move the cursor to the original location, Figure 5-26b. (iii) Finally, release the left mouse button.

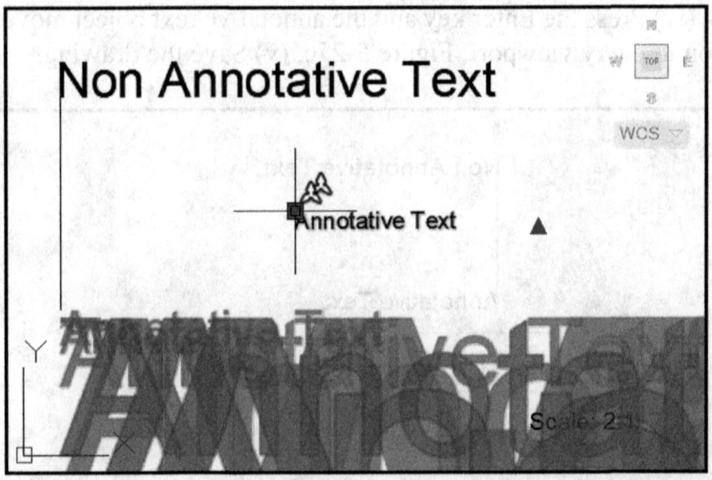

Figure 5-26a

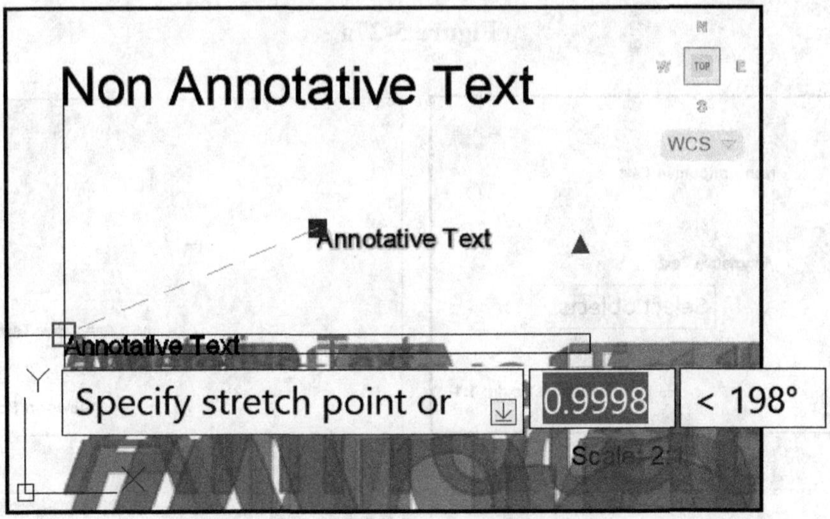

Figure 5-26b

2. The advantage of this method is that the user may need to execute the above process only once for the annotative object in every viewport. The ANNORESET command resets the locations of the annotative text in every viewport simultaneously. The *ANNORESET* command is activated using the following method. Activate the command from the viewport with the correct location of the annotative object. In the current example, the command is activated from the viewport with the scale of 1:1, Figure 5-27a. (i) Command line method: Type "annoreset," "Annoreset," or "ANNORESET" on the command line and press the *Enter* key. (ii) The activation of the command leads to the object selection prompt, Figure 5-27b. (iii) Select the annotative text object. In the current example, **Annotative Text** is selected and the text is highlighted in all of the

views. (iv) Press the Enter key and the annotative text object moves to the correct location in every viewport, Figure 5-27c. (v) Save the drawing.

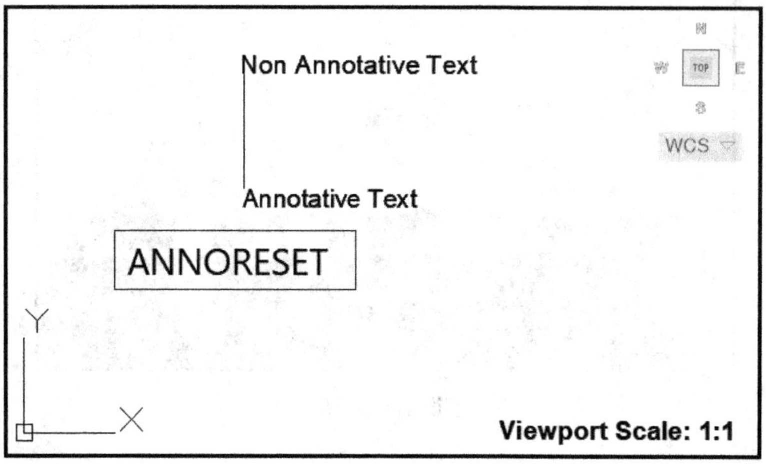

Figure 5-27a

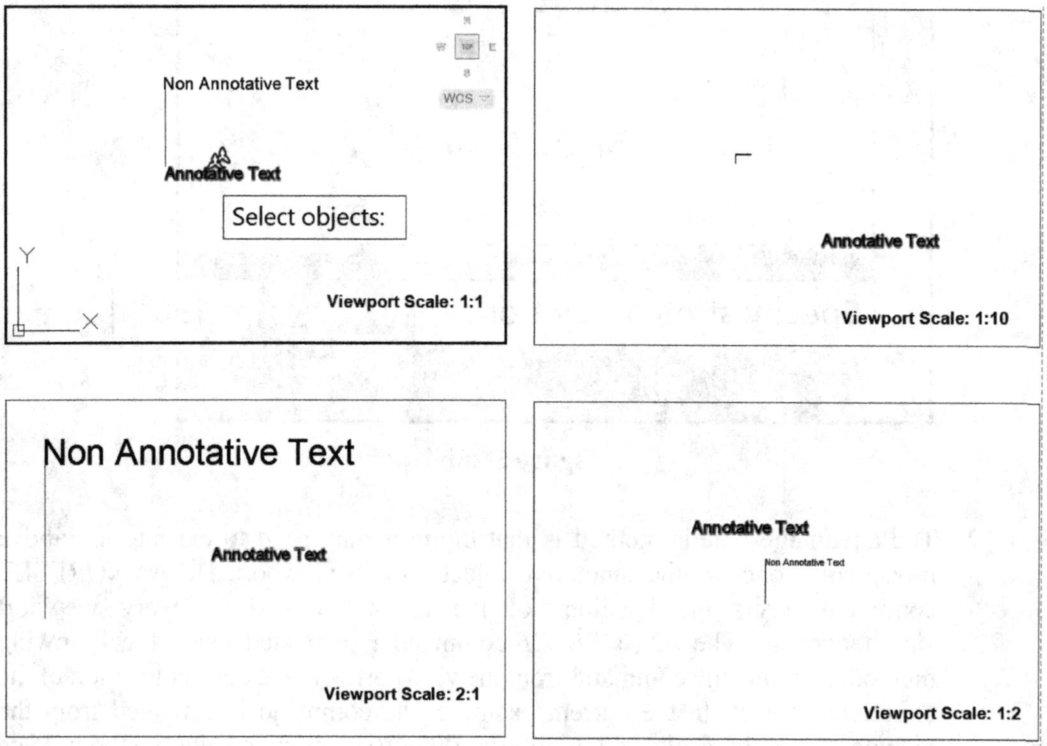

Figure 5-27b

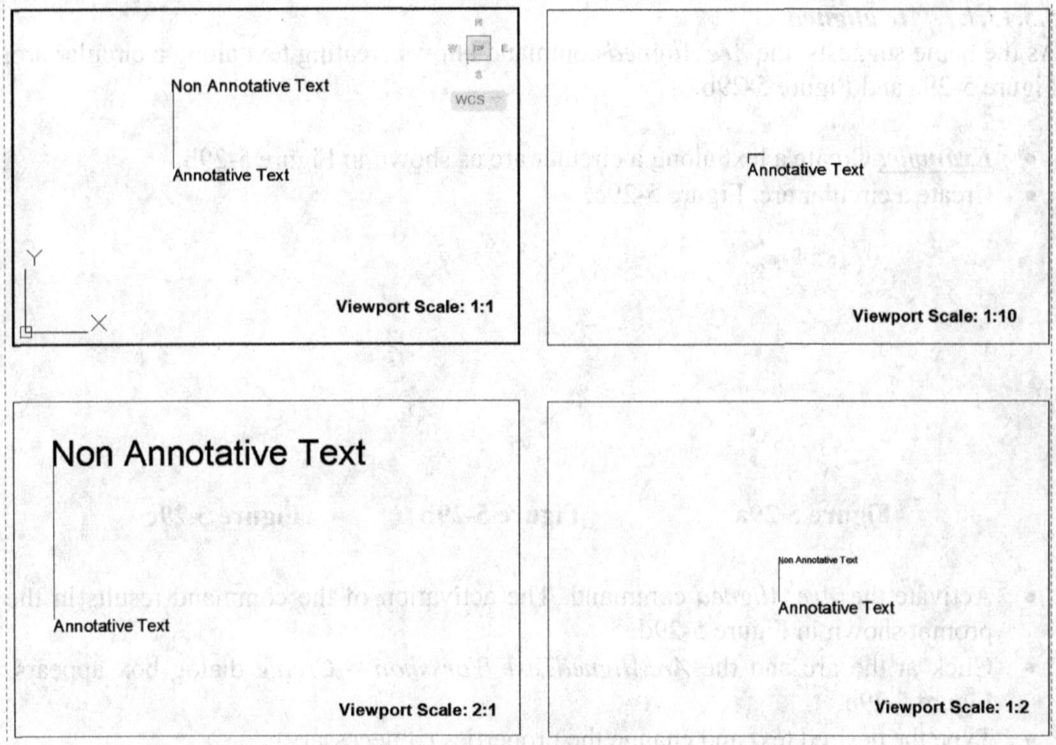

Figure 5-27c

5.5.13. Express Tools tab and Text panel

The expanded *Text* panel from the *Express Tools* tab is shown in Figure 5-28. Some of the commands on this panel are available only for the *Standard* text. This panel provides the options to mask and unmask and modify (press the down-arrow and check the options) the text. Some of these options were discussed earlier. This panel also provides the options to create text along an arc and to enclose a text object in a circle, rectangle, or slots. These two options are discussed here in detail.

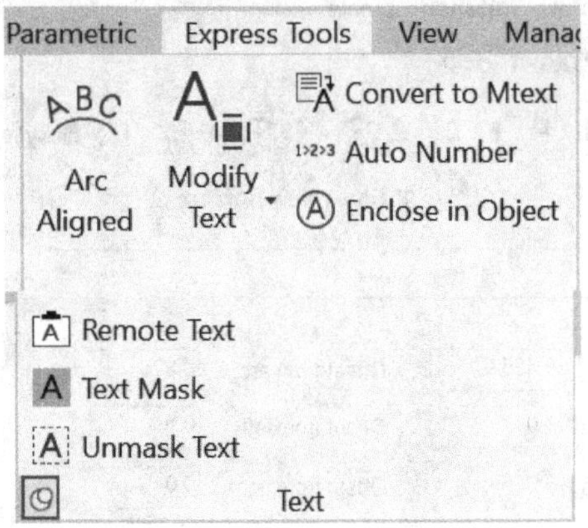

Figure 5-28

5.5.13.1.1. Arc aligned

As the name suggests, the *Arc Aligned* command allows creating text along a circular arc, Figure 5-29a and Figure 5-29b.

- ***Example:*** Create a text along a circular arc as shown in Figure 5-29b.
- Create a circular arc, Figure 5-29c.

Figure 5-29a

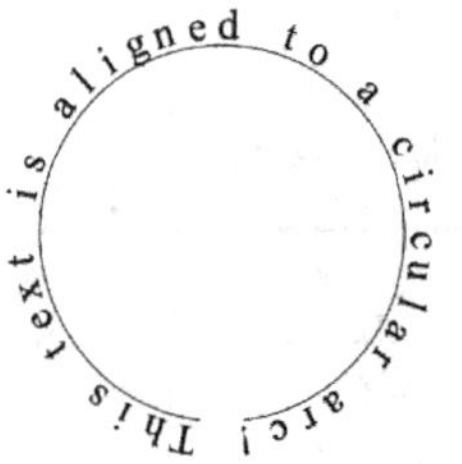

Figure 5-29b

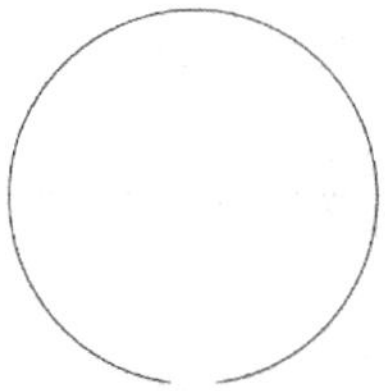

Figure 5-29c

- Activate the *Arc Aligned* command. The activation of the command results in the prompt shown in Figure 5-29d.
- Click at the arc and the *ArcAlignedText Workshop – Create* dialog box appears, Figure 5-29e.
- Type the desired text and change the properties (if necessary).
- Click the *OK* button. This closes the dialog box, and the text appears along the arc, Figure 5-29b.
- To edit the arc aligned text, double click at the text and the property palette appears on the screen, Figure 5-29f. Now the user can make the desired changes.

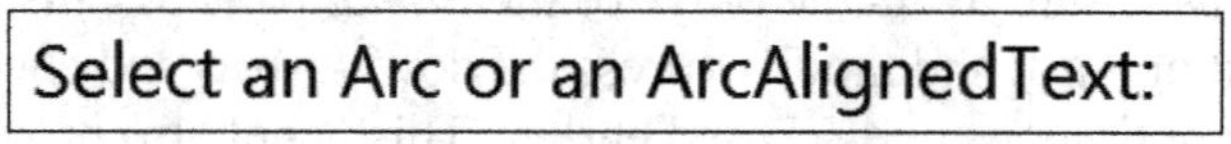

Figure 5-29d

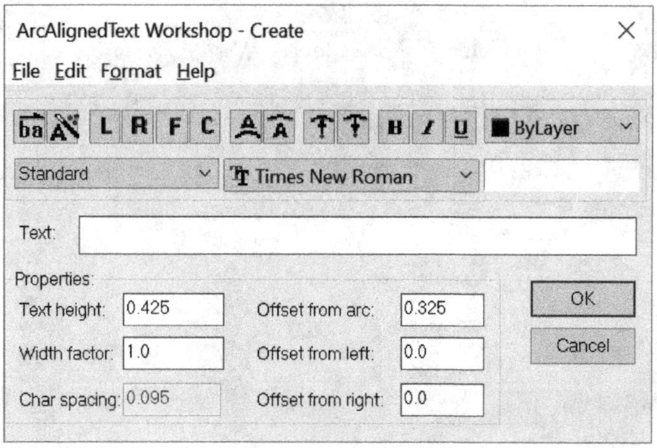

Figure 5-29e

- The user should try to create the second text shown in Figure 5-29a. The *Offset from arc* distance should be the sum of *Text height* of the first row, *Offset from* arc for the first row, and space between the two rows.

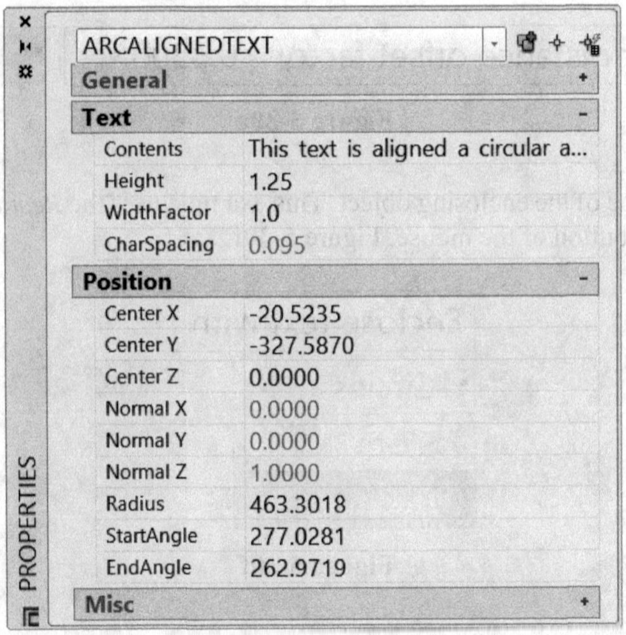

Figure 5-29f

5.5.13.1.2. Enclose in object

The *Enclose in Object* command can be used to enclose single or multiline text objects in a circle, rectangle, and a slot.

- ***Example:*** Enclose the text inside a slot (Figure 5-30a), circle (Figure 5-30b), and rectangle (Figure 5-30c).

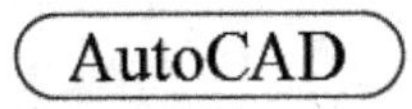

Figure 5-30a

Figure 5-30b

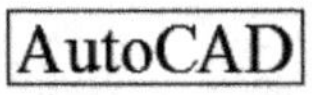

Figure 5-30c

- Create the desired text.
- Activate the *Enclose in object* command. The activation of the command results in the prompt shown in Figure 5-30d.
- Click at the text and press the *Enter* key from the keyboard, Figure 5-30e.
- Specify the offset factor. It is the space between the text and outline of the enclosing object. Press the *Enter* key of the keyboard, Figure 5-30f.

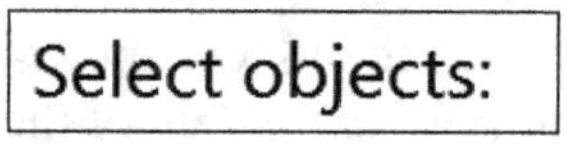

Figure 5-30d

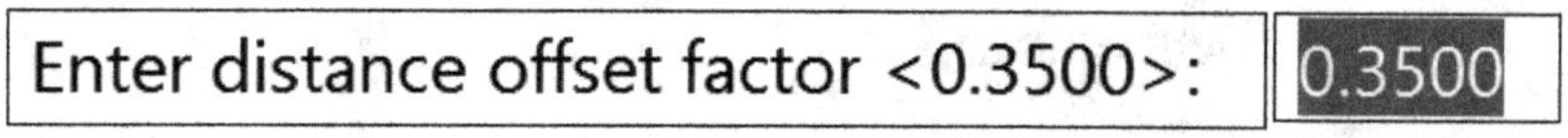

Figure 5-30e

- Select the type of the enclosing object. This example uses the *Rectangle* option. Click with the left button of the mouse, Figure 5-30f.

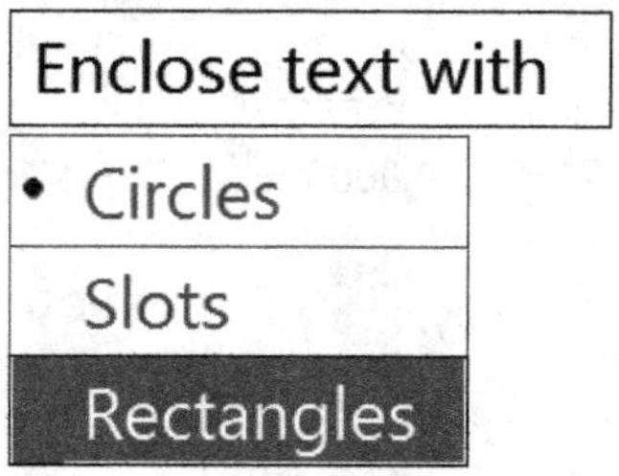

Figure 5-30f

- Select the *Constant* option for the size. Click with the left button of the mouse, Figure 5-30g.
- Select the *Both* option for maintaining the object, Figure 5-30h. Press the *Enter* key of the keyboard.
- The text is enclosed in a rectangle, Figure 5-30a.
- Repeat the process for the slot (Figure 5-30a) and circle (Figure 5-30b).

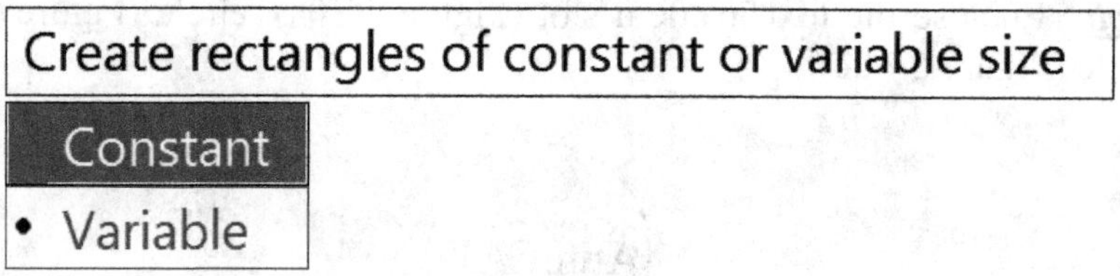

Figure 5-30g

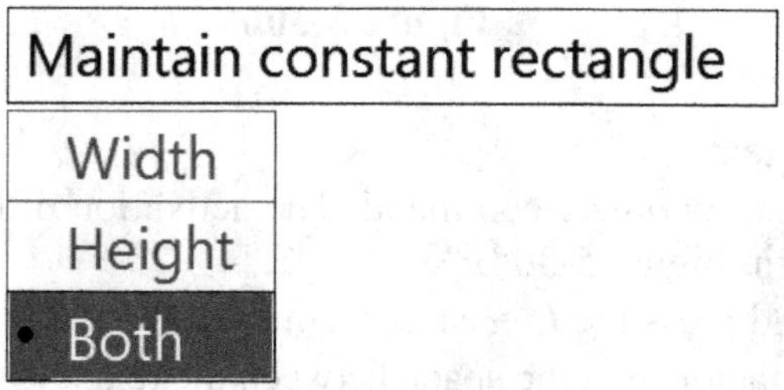

Figure 5-30h

5.5.14. Summary of annotative text creation process

This section summarizes the annotative multiline text creation process. For details, refer to the respective sub-section under Section 5.5. Use the following step-by-step instructions to create multiline annotative text.

5. From *Home* tab and *Annotate* panel; press the down-arrow and select the *Annotative* option, Figure 5-31a.
6. From *Home* tab and *Annotate* panel; press the down-arrow and select the *Text Style* option, Figure 5-31b. This will open the *Text Style Dialog Box*.

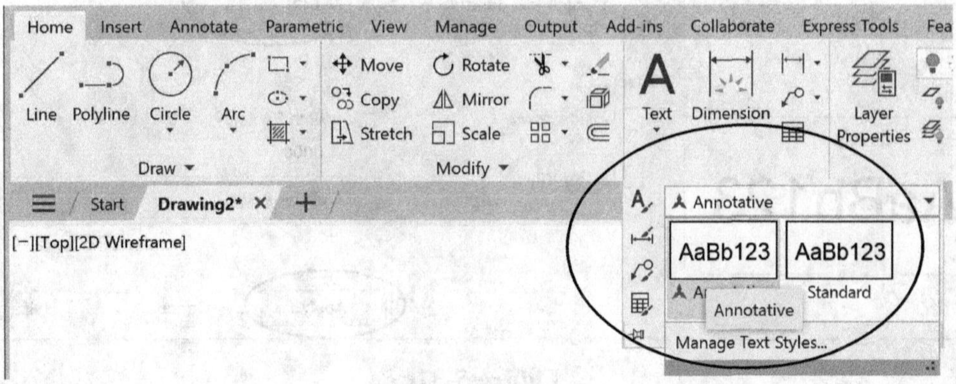

Figure 5-31a

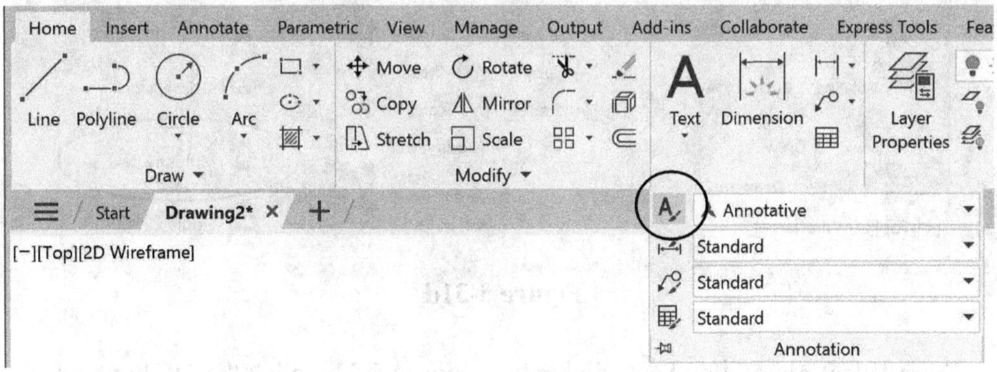

Figure 5-31b

7. Set the *Text Style Dialog* Box options as shown in Figure 5-31c:
   a. Styles: Annotative
   b. Size: Annotative box checked
   c. Paper Text Height: 0.125
   d. Click the *Apply* button. This will make the update and replace the *Cancel* button by the *Close* button.
   e. Finally, click the *Close* button not shown in the figure.

8. From *Home* tab and *Annotate* panel; press the down-arrow and select the *Multiline Text* option, Figure 5-31d, and the *Select Annotation Scale* dialog box appears.

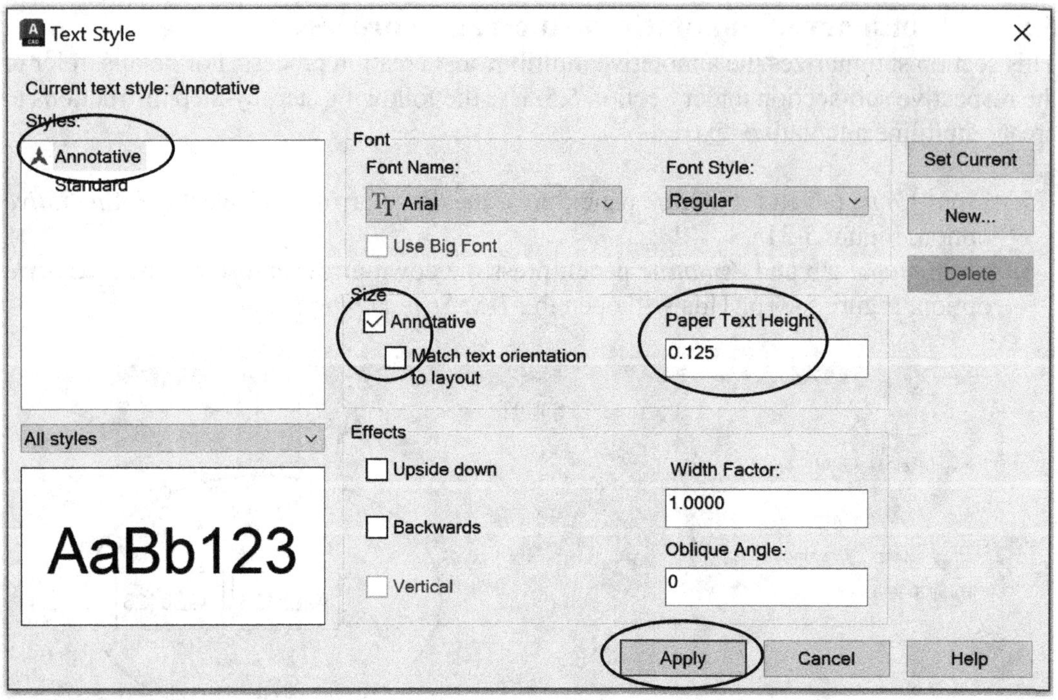

Figure 5-31c

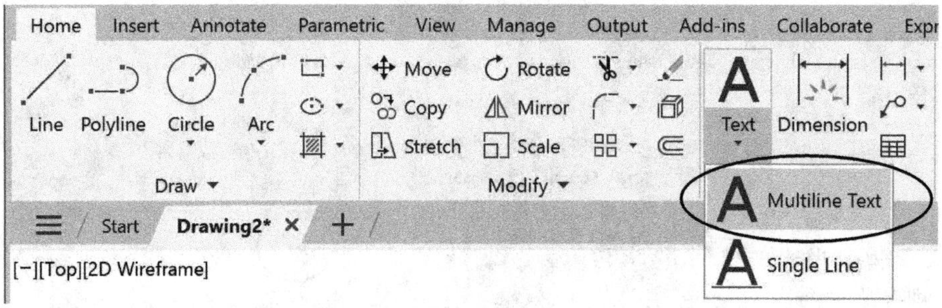

Figure 5-31d

9. From *Select Annotation Scale* dialog box, Figure 5-31e, click the *OK* button and create the desired annotative text object.

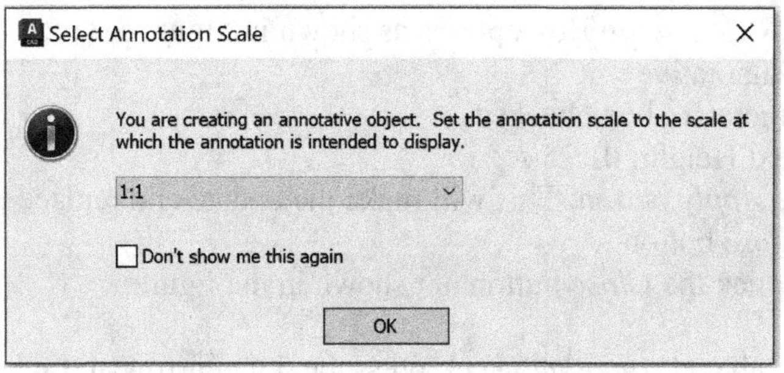

Figure 5-31e

10. Double click the text object created in the previous step, and *Text Editor* tab appears. From the *Text Editor* tab and *Insert* panel, select the *No Column* option, Figure 5-31f. If necessary, from the *Paragraph* panel, set the *Justification*, and other options.

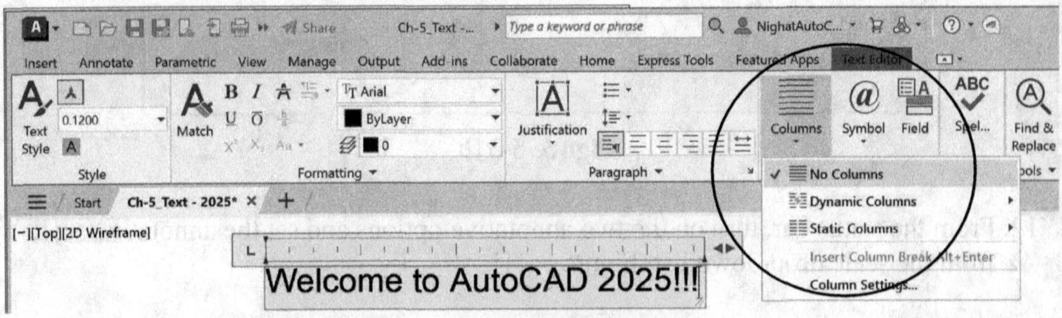

Figure 5-31f

11. Open the *Properties Sheet* for the newly created text object, Figure 5-31g.
    a. From the *Text* tab, set the *Paper defined width* to 0. This option will not be available if *No Column* option was not selected in the previous step (go back and complete the previous step).
    b. From the *Text* tab, apply the background mask, Figure 5-31h.

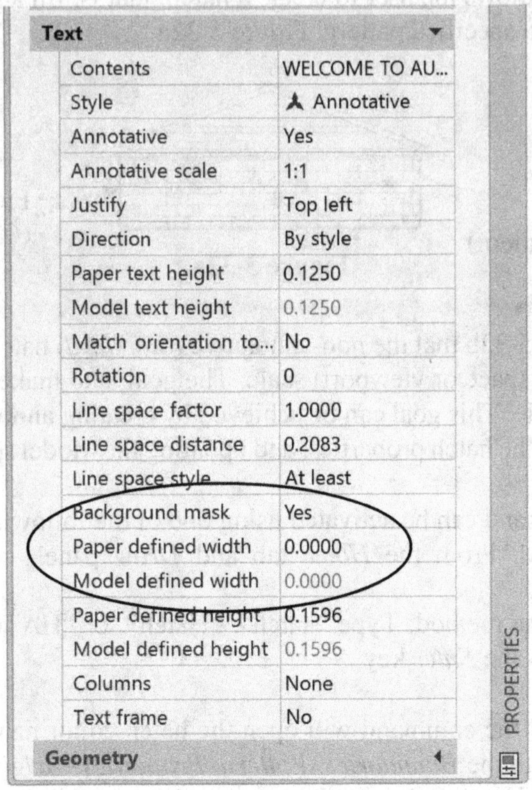

Figure 5-31g

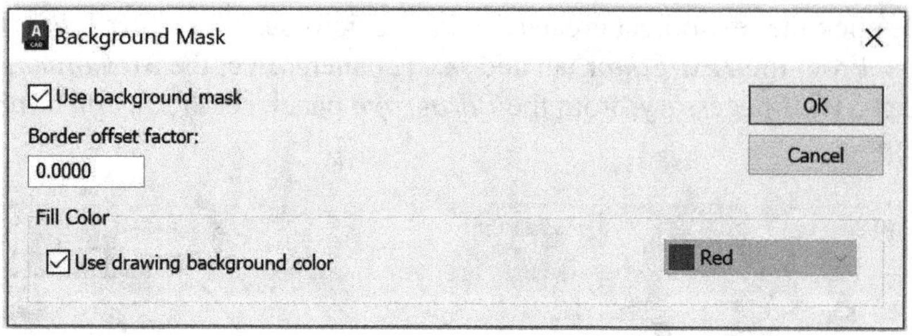

Figure 5-31h

12. From the status bar, turn on the two annotative options and set the annotative scale from the scale drop-down list, Figure 5-31i.

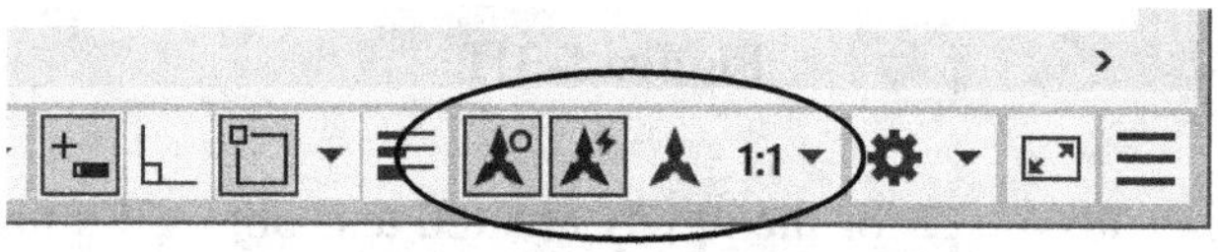

Figure 5-31i

5.6. Hatch

The *Hatch* command allows the user to create a hatch, that is, fill a space surrounded by a closed boundary with a specified pattern, Figure 5-32a.

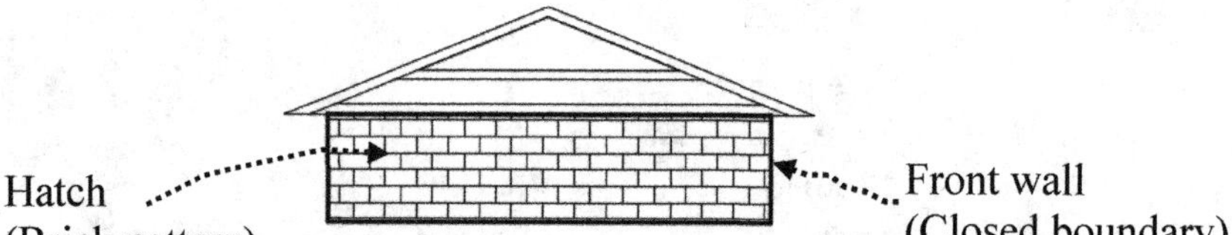

Figure 5-32a

It is clear from Figure 5-32b that the non-annotative (*Standard*) hatch appearance depends on the display (Model space or viewport) scale. The goal is to make the hatch appearance independent of the scale. This goal can be achieved by creating annotative hatches, adding the annotative scale to the hatch properties, and updating the Model space / viewports scale.

- The *Hatch* command can be activated using one of the following methods:
  1. Panel method: From the *Home* tab and *Draw* panel, select the *Hatch* tool, Figure 5-33a.
  2. Command line method: Type "hatch", "Hatch", or "HATCH" in the command line and press the *Enter* key.

- The activation of the command will open the hatch editor named *Hatch Editor* tab, Figure 5-33b, with the *Boundaries*, *Pattern*, *Properties*, *Origin*, *Options*, and *Close* panels. Also, the *Hatch Editor* tab becomes the current tab.

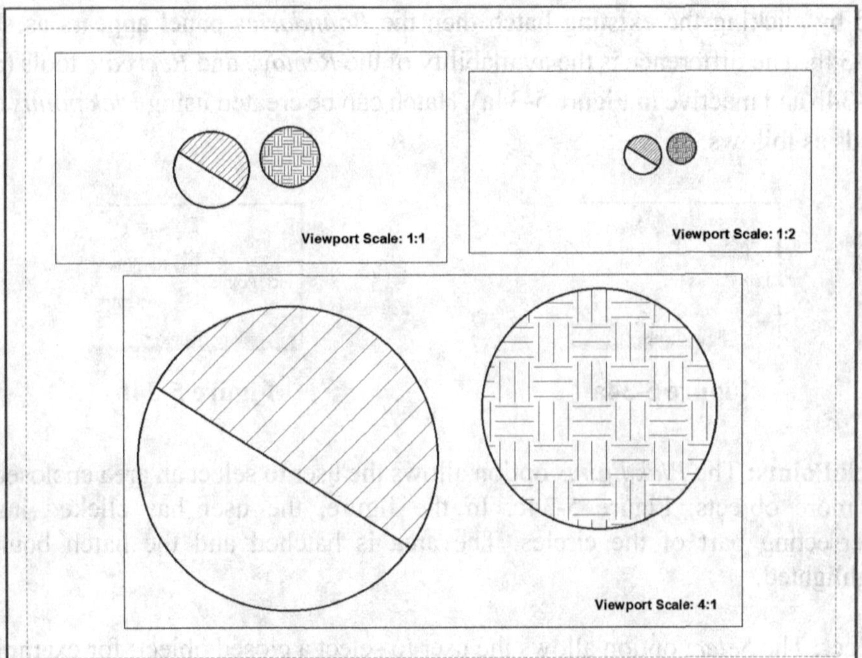

Figure 5-32b

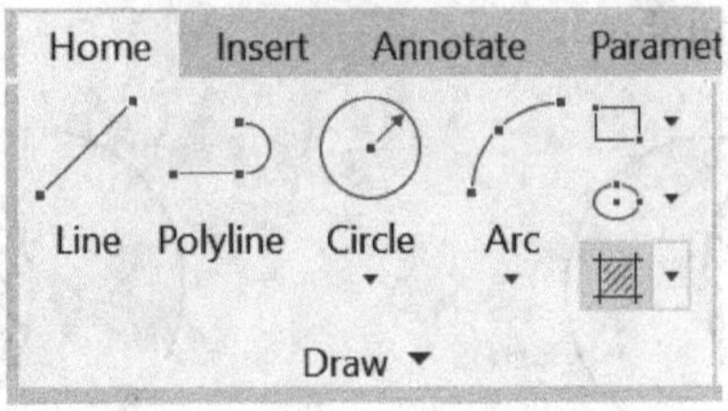

Figure 5-33a

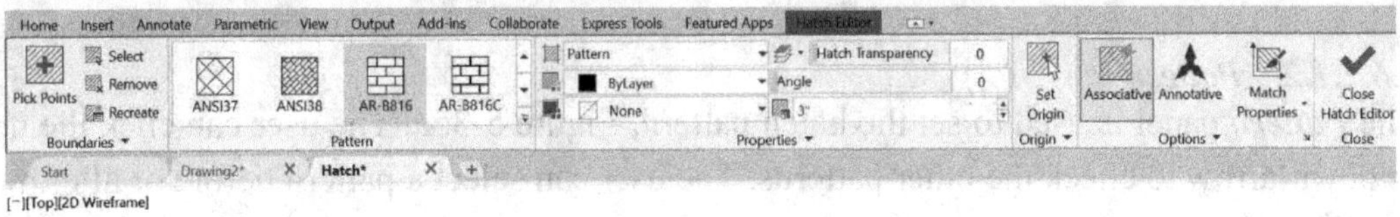

Figure 5-33b

5.6.1. Hatch editor tab

This section describes the basics of hatch process by explaining most of the commands on the *Hatch Editor* tab's panels.

5.6.1.1.1. Boundaries

The *Boundaries* panel is used to set the boundaries for creating a new hatch or modifying an existing hatch. When the *Hatch* command is activated from the *Draw* panel, then the *Boundaries* panel appears as shown in Figure 5-34a. However, when the command is activated by clicking the existing hatch then the *Boundaries* panel appears as shown in Figure 5-34b. The difference is the availability of the *Remove* and *Recreate* tools (active in Figure 5-34b and inactive in Figure 5-34a). Hatch can be created using *Pick points* or *Select* commands as follows:

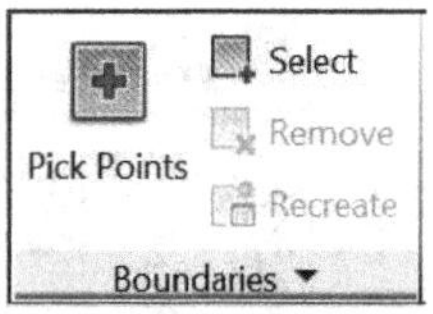

Figure 5-34a

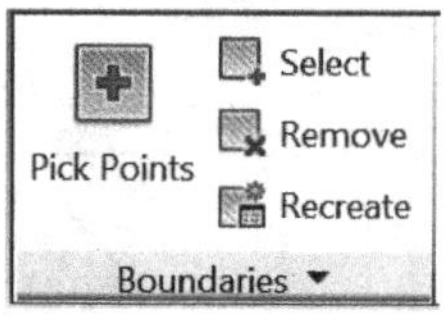

Figure 5-34b

- **Pick Points:** The *Pick Points* option allows the user to select an area enclosed by one or more objects, Figure 5-34c. In the figure, the user has clicked inside the intersecting part of the circles. The area is hatched and the hatch boundary is highlighted.

- **Select:** The *Select* option allows the user to select a closed object; for example, close shape created using polyline, circle, polygon, etc., Figure 5-34d. In this figure, the user has clicked at the boundary of the circle on the right. Therefore, the part of the left circle inside the selected circle is hatched. The selected circle is hatched, and the hatch boundary is highlighted.

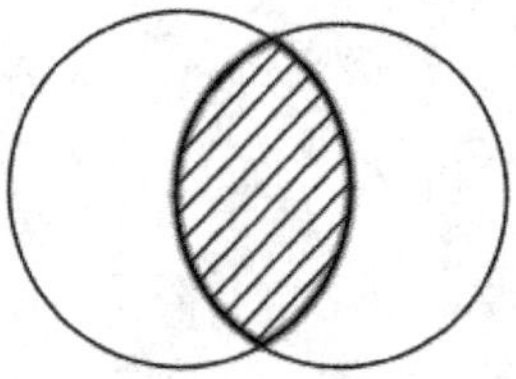

Figure 5-34c

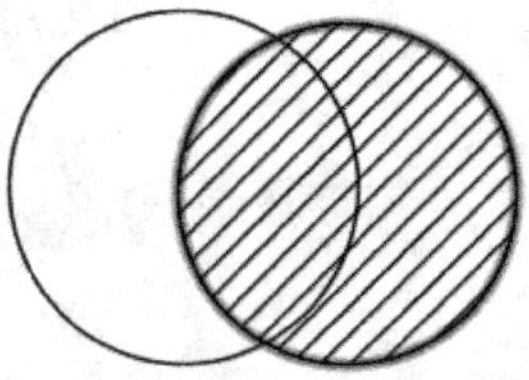

Figure 5-34d

5.6.1.1.2. Pattern

The *Pattern* panel is used to set the hatch pattern, Figure 5-35a. The user can click the up or down-arrow to check the other patterns. The user can select a pattern before or after the hatch is created.

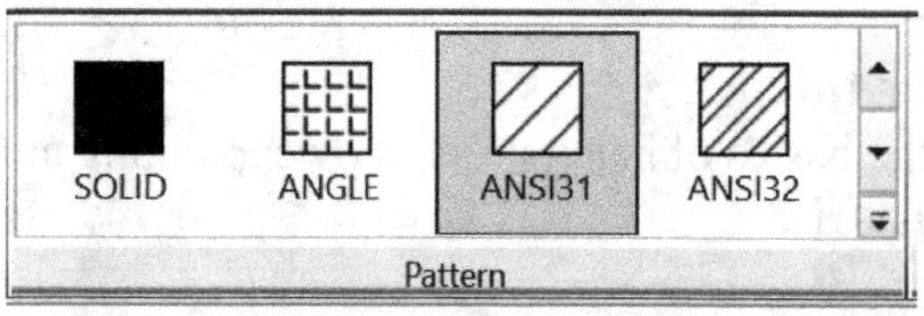

Figure 5-35a

- The user can change the pattern before the hatch command by clicking on the desired pattern.

- The user can change the pattern after the hatch command using the following steps: (i) Click on the hatch and a circular grip point appears, Figure 5-35b. (ii) Select the desired pattern. (iii) Press the *Esc* key from the keyboard. DO NOT PRESS THE *ENTER* KEY. The hatch appearance changes to the selected pattern, Figure 5-35c.

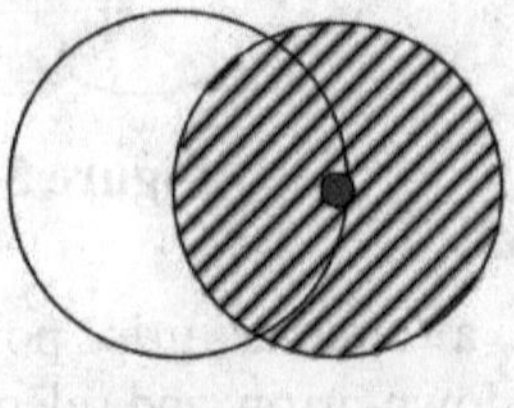
Figure 5-35b

Figure 5-35c

5.6.1.1.3. Properties

The *Properties* panel is used to set hatch color, background color, angle, and scale of the selected hatch, Figure 5-36.

- The user can change the pattern properties before the hatch command by selecting the desired properties.
- The user can also change the pattern properties after the hatch command using the following steps.

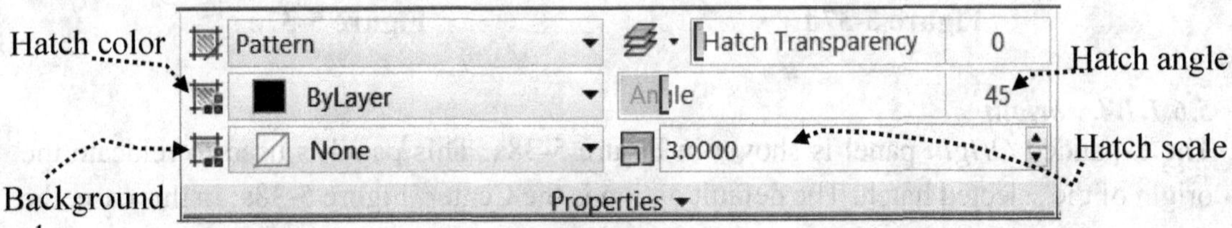

Figure 5-36

  - **Hatch color:** (i) Click on the hatch and a circular grip point appears, Figure 5-37a. (ii) Press the down-arrow and select the desired color. (iii) Press the *Esc* key from the keyboard. DO NOT PRESS THE *ENTER* KEY. The hatch color changes to the selected color, Figure 5-37b. Similarly, change the background color, Figure 5-37c.

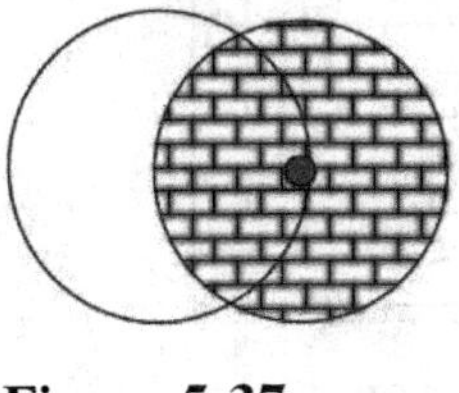
Figure 5-37a

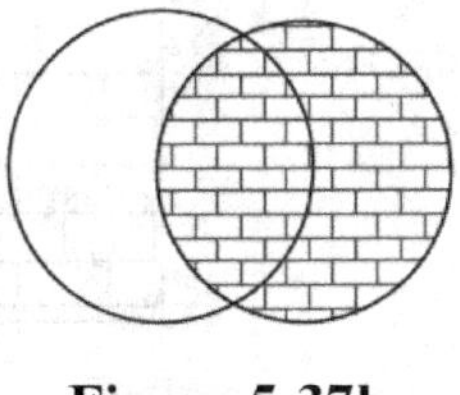
Figure 5-37b

Figure 5-37c

- **Hatch angle:** (i) Click on the hatch and a circular grip point appears, Figure 5-37a (angle = 0). (ii) Click at the *Angle* button and type the desired angle. (iii) Press the *Esc* key from the keyboard. DO NOT PRESS THE *ENTER* KEY. The hatch angle changes to the selected angle, Figure 5-37d (angle = 45°).

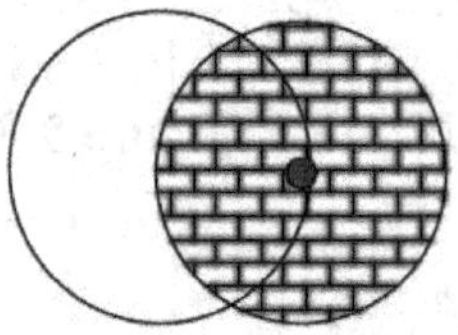

Figure 5-37a

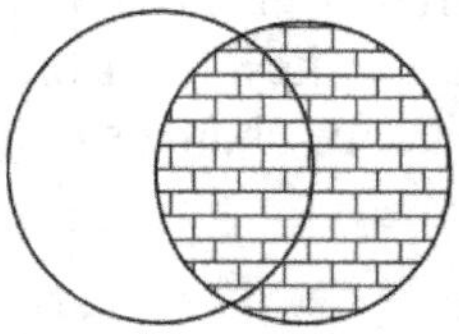

Figure 5-37b

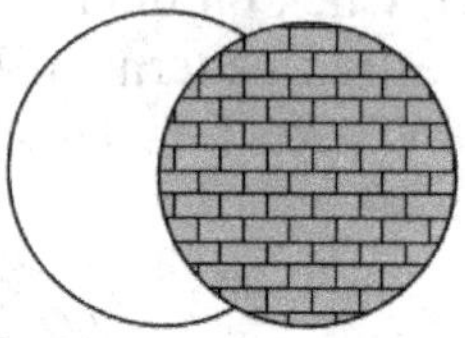

Figure 5-37c

- **Hatch scale:** (i) Click on the hatch and a circular grip point appears, Figure 5-37a (scale factor = 3.0). (ii) Press the down-arrow and select the desired scale factor. (iii) Press the *Esc* key from the keyboard. DO NOT PRESS THE *ENTER* KEY. The hatch scale changes to the selected scale, Figure 5-37e (scale factor = 1.0). The scale factor should be selected such that the pattern is clearly visible.

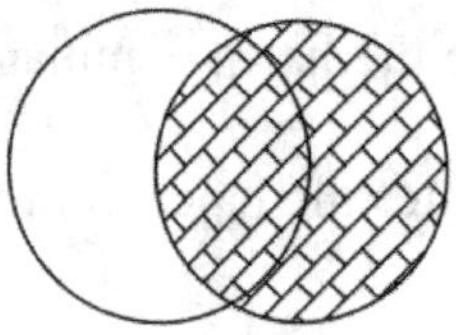

Figure 5-37d

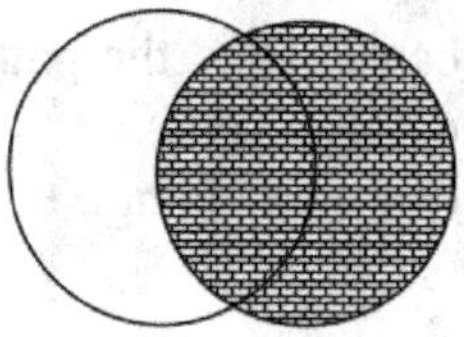

Figure 5-37e

5.6.1.1.4. origin

The expanded *Origin* panel is shown in Figure 5-38a. This panel is used to relocate the origin of the selected hatch. The default option is the Center, Figure 5-38a; in this case, the pattern begins in the center and the partial pattern is evenly distributed on all four edges, Figure 5-38b. Figure 5-38c shows the selection of the *Bottom Right* option; in this case, the pattern begins in the bottom right corner of the closed boundary and the partial pattern is distributed on the top and left edges, Figure 5-38d.

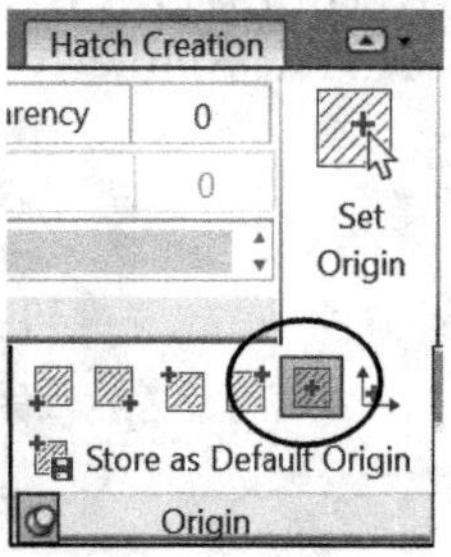

Figure 5-38a

Figure 5-38b

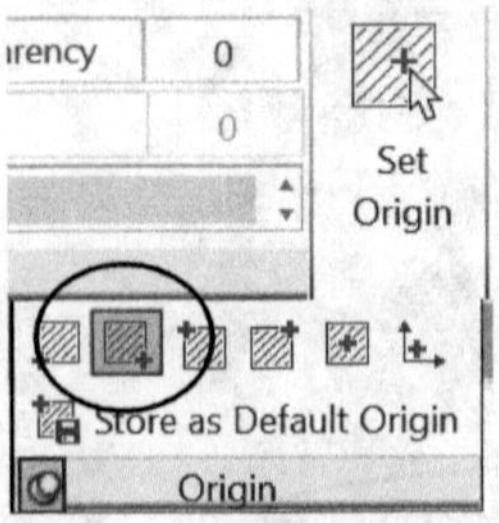

Figure 5-38c

Figure 5-38d

5.6.1.1.5. Options

The *Options* panel, Figure 5-39a, is used to set various hatch properties.

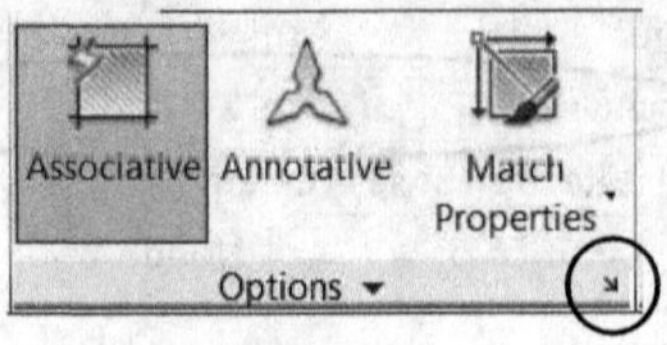

Figure 5-39a

- **Associative:** Active *Associative* hatch option means that the hatch is attached to the closed boundary used to create the hatch.
  - o Any change in the boundaries will update the fill to fit the new boundaries. By default, this option is active. Figure 5-39b and Figure 5-39c show associative and non-associative hatches and Figure 5-39d and Figure 5-39d show the effect on hatch by changing the boundary.

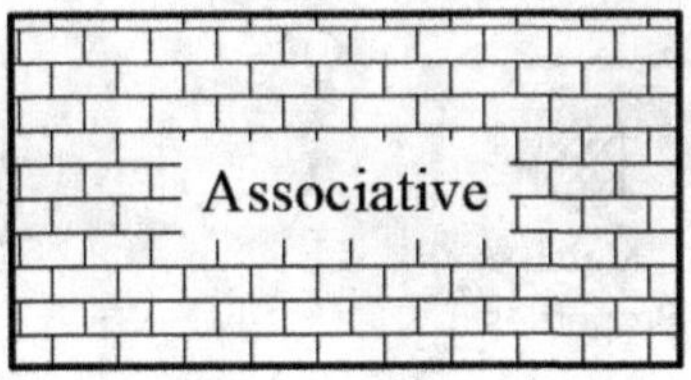

Figure 5-39b

Figure 5-39c

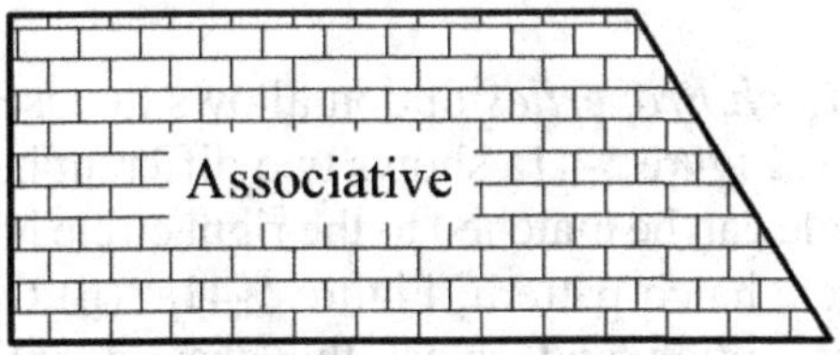

Figure 5-39d

Figure 5-39e

  - o A user can convert non-associative hatch to associative from the *Properties sheet*, Figure 5-39f.

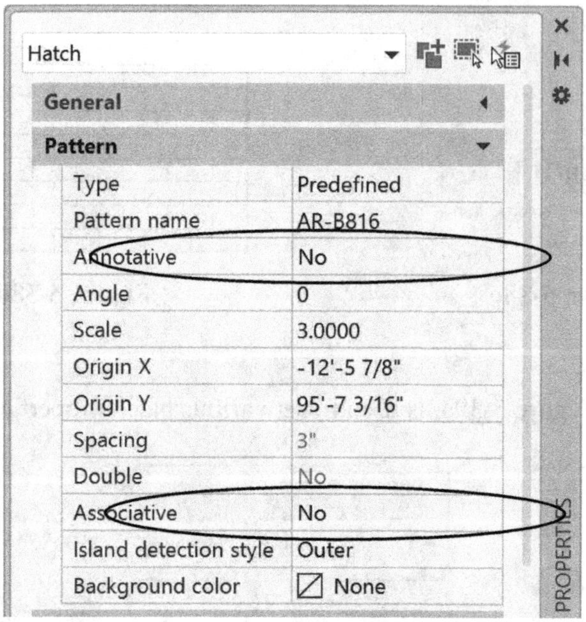

Figure 5-39f

- **Annotative:** Active *Annotative* hatch option, Figure 5-40a, means that the hatch will be automatically updated with the change in the Model Space or viewport scale.
  - o Figure 5-40b shows the hatch in three different viewport scales.
  - o A user can convert non-annotative hatch to annotative hatch using one of the following two techniques. (i) If the *Associative* hatch option is active then activate the *Annotative* hatch option from *Options* panel, Figure 5-40a. (ii) If the *Associative* hatch was inactive then use the *Properties sheet*, Figure 5-39f.

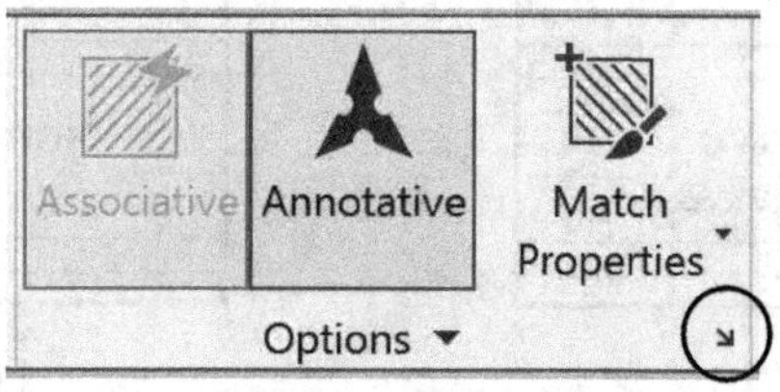

Figure 5-40a

- **Match Properties:** The selection of the *Match Properties* option allows the user to match the properties of two existing hatches. Figure 5-41a shows two different hatch patterns. The hatch properties of the left circle can be matched to the right circle hatch properties as follows: (i) Click the left circle hatch pattern, Figure 5-41a. (ii) Click the down-arrow of the *Match Properties* option and select the desired option, Figure 5-41b. (iii) Click the right circle hatch pattern, Figure 5-41c. (iv) Finally, press the Enter key from the keyboard; and the left circle hatch is matched to the right circle hatch, Figure 5-41c.

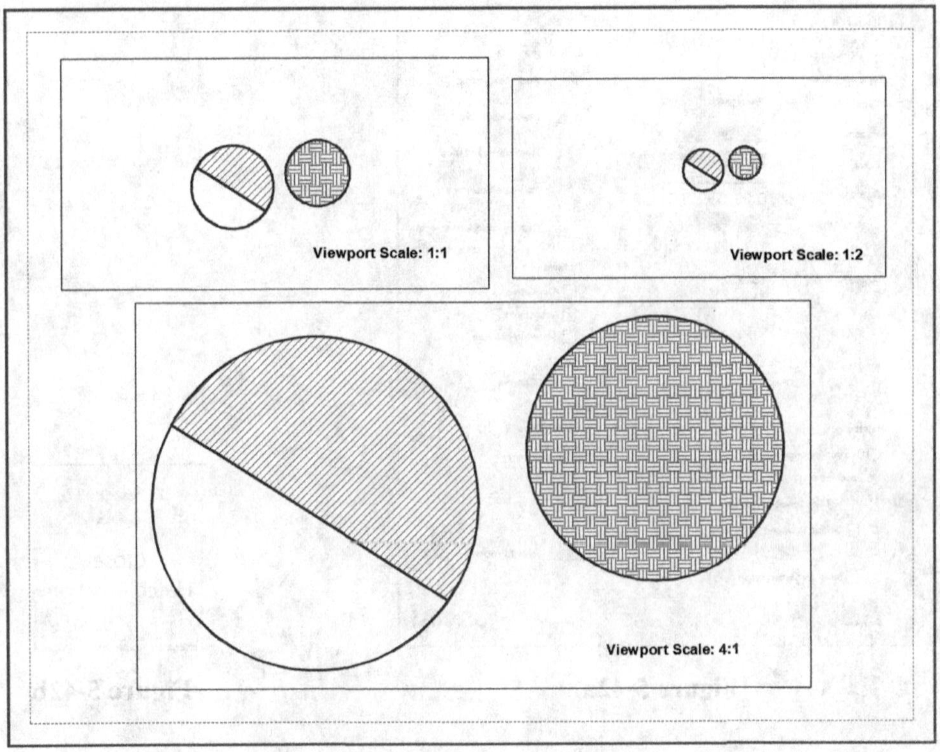

Figure 5-40b

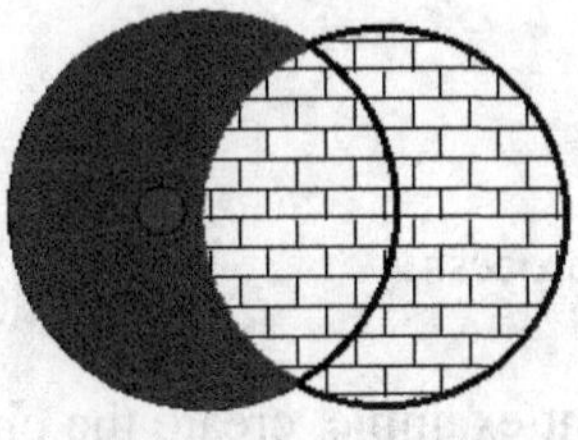

Figure 5-41a

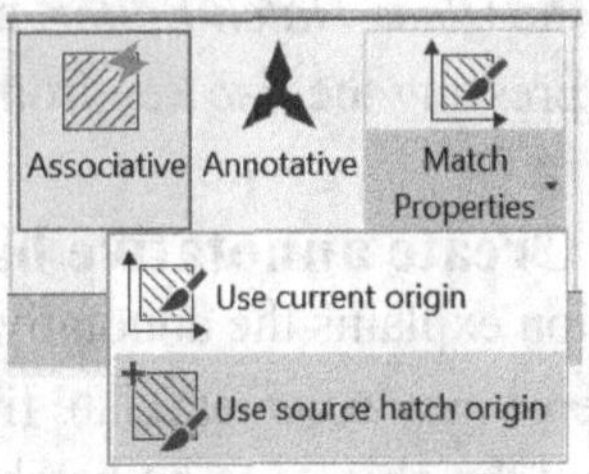

Figure 5-41b

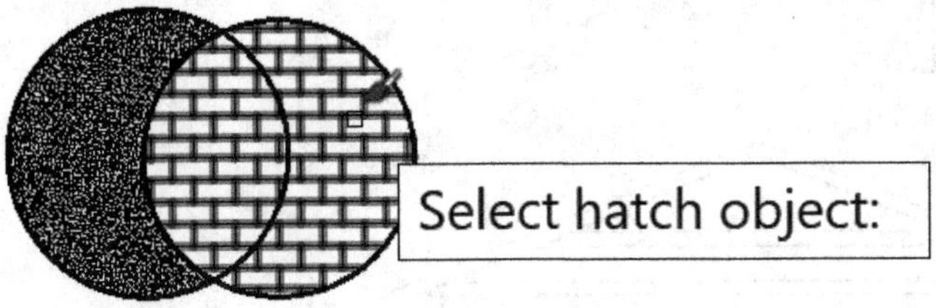

Figure 5-41c

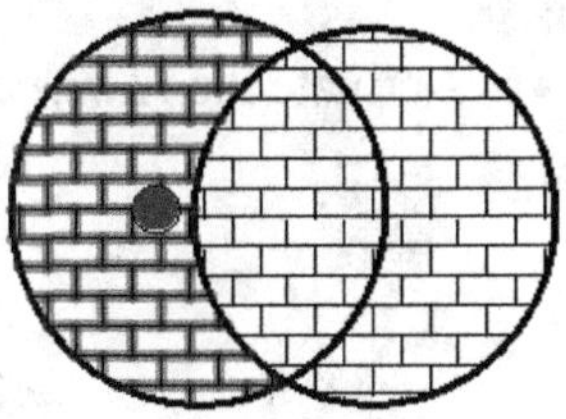

Figure 5-41d

- The user can open the *Hatch Editor* dialog box (Figure 5-42a) from dialog box launcher (a small arrow on the lower right corner of the panel), Figure 5-40a. The sections in the dialog box are similar to the panels in the *Hatch Creation* tab or *Hatch Editor*.

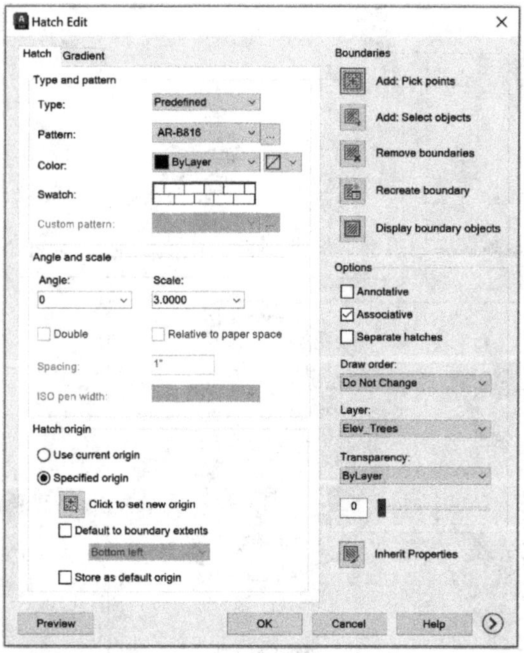

Figure 5-42a

Figure 5-42b

5.6.1.1.6. Close

The *Close* panel, Figure 5-42b, is used to close the *Hatch Creation* tab or *Hatch Editor*. Click on the *Close Hatch Editor*, and the editor is closed. The user can also exit the editor mode by pressing the *Esc* key from the keyboard.

5.6.2. Create annotative hatch

This section explains the annotative hatch creation process.

- Open a new *acad* template file.
- Draw the objects to be hatched. For the current example, create the circles and line as shown in Figure 5-40b or create the building as shown in Figure 5-43a or something similar.
- Activate the *Hatch* command.

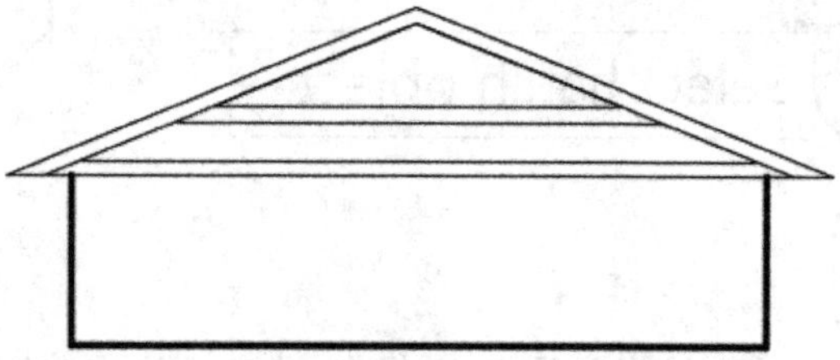

Figure 5-43a

- The activation of the command opens the *Hatch Editor* and the prompt shown in Figure 5-43b or Figure 5-43c appears on screen.
  - o Figure 5-43b: Press the down-arrow key from the keyboard and check the various options. This example uses the *pick internal point* option; press the up-arrow and close the option list.
  - o Figure 5-43c: Press the down-arrow key from the keyboard and check the various options. This example uses the *pick internal point* option; click on the desired option. This closes the option list and the prompt shown in Figure 5-43c appears.

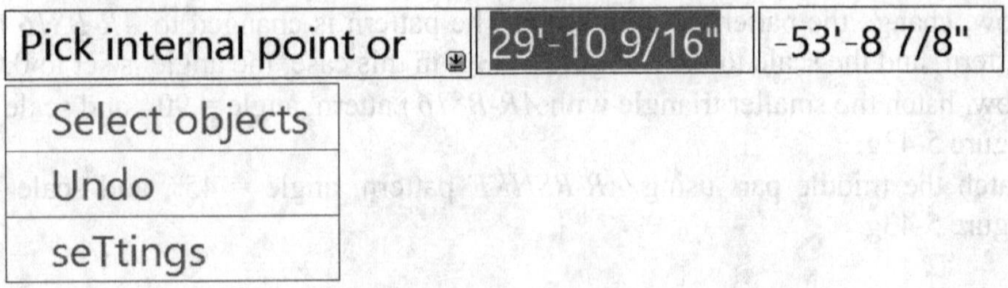

Figure 5-43b

- Bring the cursor inside the large rectangle and the hatch pattern appears. However, if the hatch appears as shown in Figure 5-43d, then set the *Scale* factor in *Properties* panel to higher number. For the current example, the *Scale* is changed from 1 to 75.

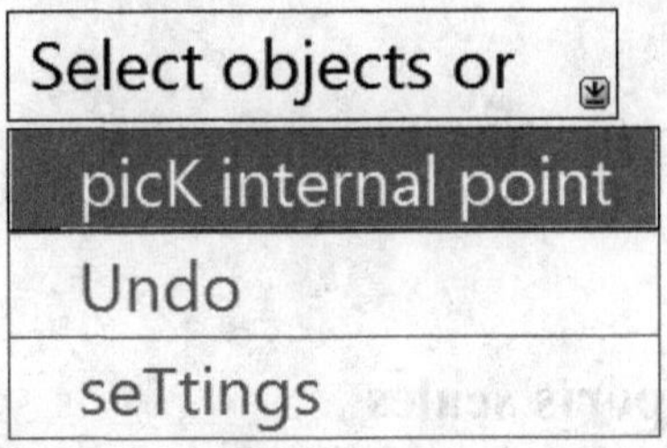

Figure 5-43c

- Now, bring the cursor inside the large rectangle and the hatch pattern appears as shown in Figure 5-43e. If necessary, change the scale factor; otherwise, press the *Enter* key and the hatch command is complete, Figure 5-43f.

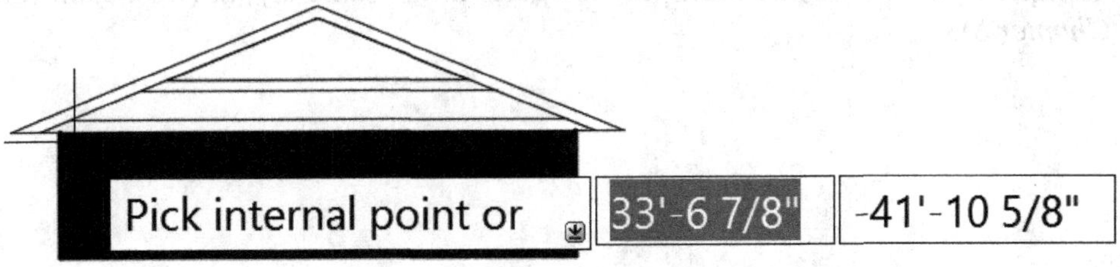

Figure 5-43d

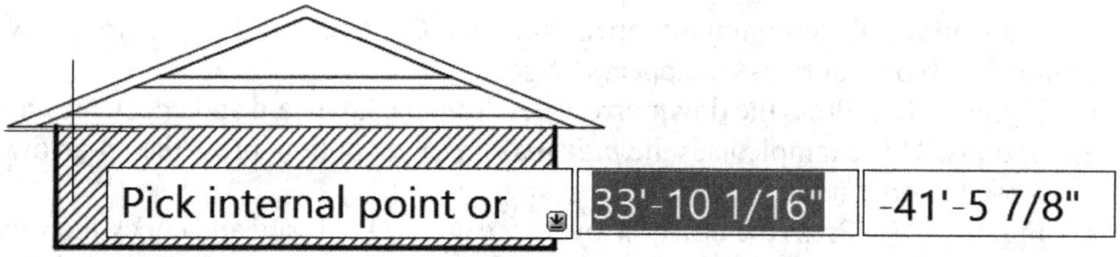

Figure 5-43e

- Now, change the pattern and its scale. The pattern is changed to *AR-B816* (a brick pattern) and the scale to 0.01, Figure 5-43g; in this case, the angle is set to 0.0°.
- Now, hatch the smaller triangle with *AR-B816* pattern, angle = 90°, and scale = 0.01, Figure 5-43g.
- Hatch the middle part using *AR-RSHKE* pattern, angle = 45°, and scale = 0.01, Figure 5-43g.

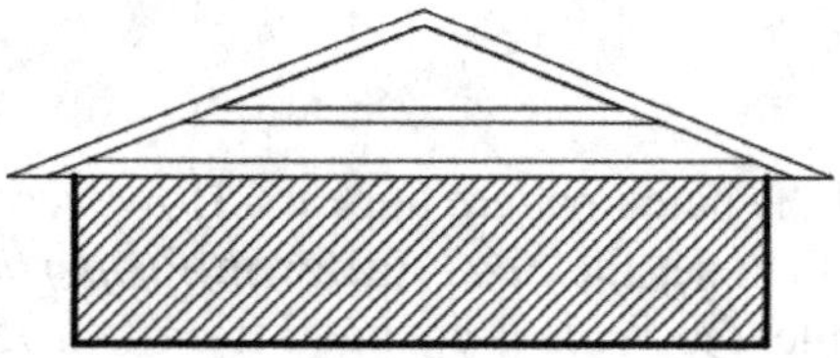

Figure 5-43f

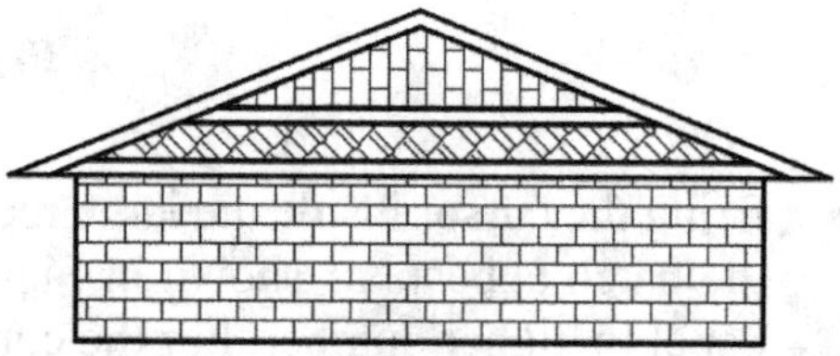

Figure 5-43g

5.6.3. Add the scales to the hatch properties

The process of adding multiple scale factors to an annotative object is explained in *Section 5.3.1*.

5.6.4. Update the viewports scales

If necessary, update the viewport scale as follows:

- Double click inside the viewport.
- Change the scale to the desired viewport scale.
- Figure 5-44 shows three viewports with different viewport scales. The scales are shown in the lower right corners of the viewports. The user can either practice with multiple layouts or create multiple viewports in the same layout (for detail, refer to *Chapter 8*).

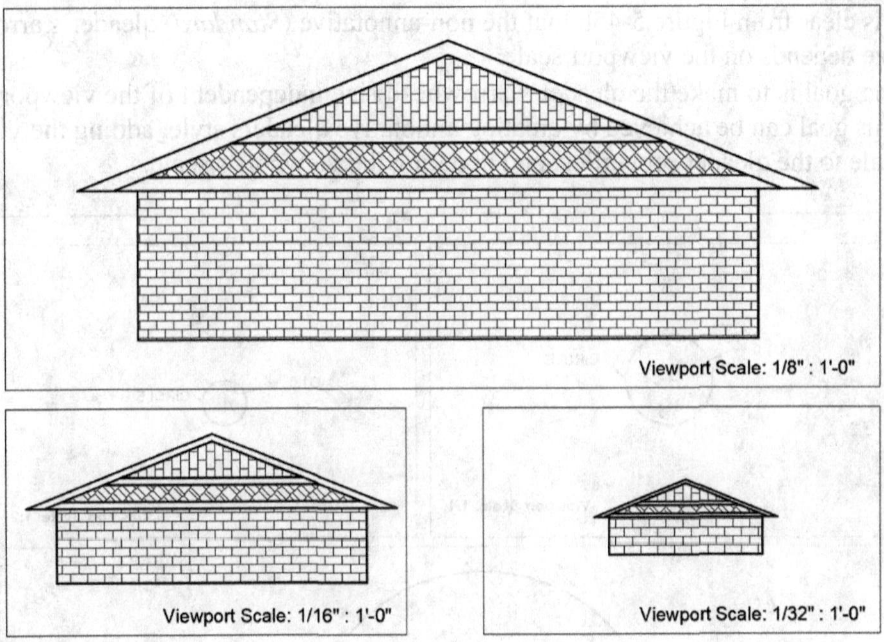

Figure 5-44

5.7. Leader Lines

The *Leader* command is used to create a line that connects an annotation to a feature. Leader line is also known as QLeader (or Quick Leader). A leader line has three parts, Figure 5-45a: (i) an arrowhead at the starting end of the line (A to B in the figure), (ii) a line, (B to C in the figure) and (iii) a multiline text near the other end of the line (text at point C in the figure).

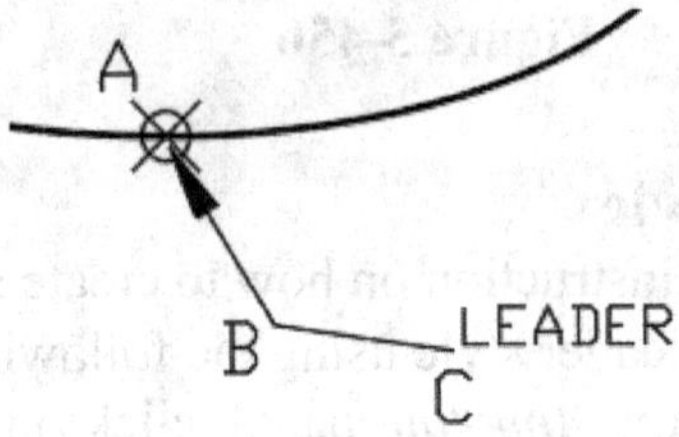

Figure 5-45a

- Open a new *acad* template file.
- Create the circle, the annotative objects (label, dimension, and hatch), and a qleader as shown in Figure 5-45b.
- The figure shows three viewports with different viewport scales. The scales are shown in the lower right corners of the viewports. The user can either practice with multiple layouts or create multiple viewports in the same layout (for detail, refer to *Chapter 8*).

- It is clear from Figure 5-45b that the non-annotative (*Standard*) qleader's arrowhead size depends on the viewport scale.
- The goal is to make the qleader's arrowhead size independent of the viewport scale. This goal can be achieved by creating annotative qleaders style, adding the viewport scale to the qleader properties, and updating the viewport's scale.

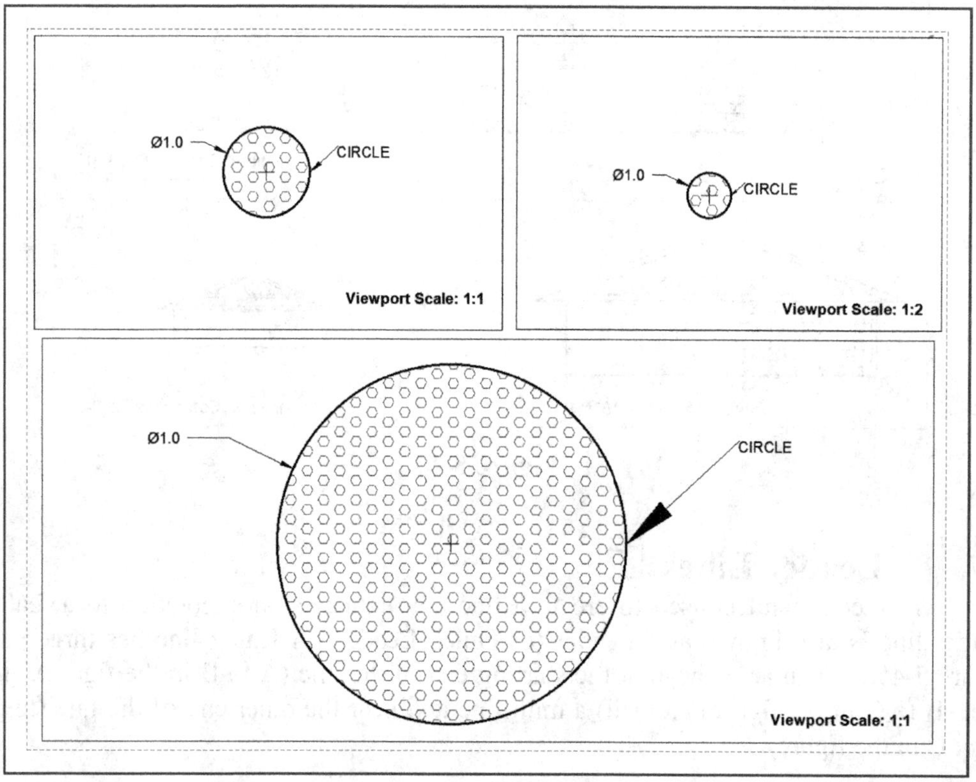

Figure 5-45b

5.7.1. Annotative leader style

This section provides step-by-step instruction on how to create an annotative leader style.

- A user can create annotative leader style using the following method.
  1. From the *Home* tab and the *Annotate* panel, click on the down-arrow from the *Multileader Style*. Select (i) *Annotative* option and (ii) click on *Manage Multileader Styles ...* Figure 5-46a. This will open *Multileader Style Manager* dialog box, Figure 5-46b.
  2. From *Multileader Style Manager* dialog box, select the *Annotative* option (if it was not selected in the previous step) and click the *Modify* button; this will open *Modify Multileader Style: Annotative* dialog box, Figure 5-46c.

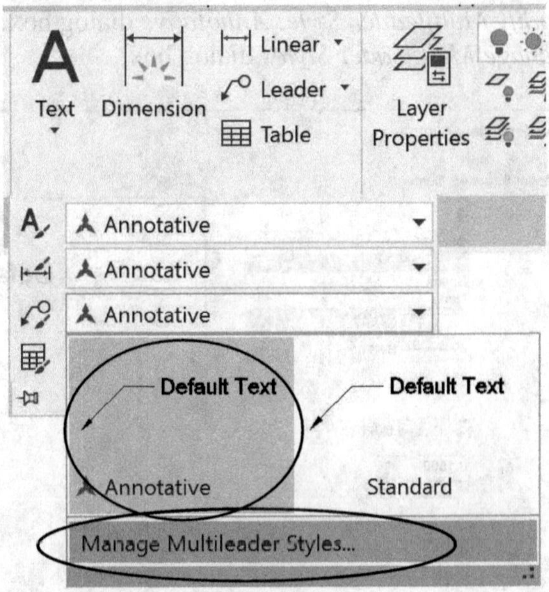

Figure 5-46a

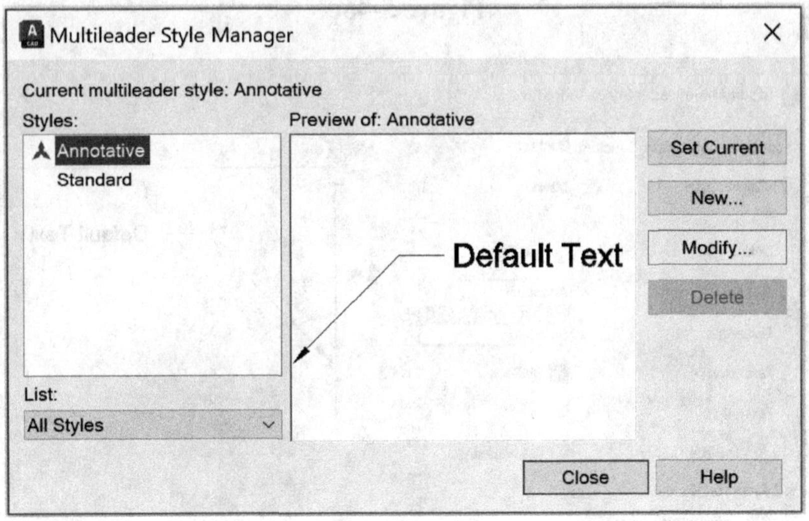

Figure 5-46b

3. From the *Modify Multileader Style: Annotative* dialog box
   a. Select *Leader Format* tab, Figure 5-46c: (i) Under the *General* option, specify the *Type* to be *Straight*. (ii) Under the *Arrowhead* option, specify the arrow size; the arrow size is 5mm for ISO units (acadiso template file) and 0.15" for ANSI units (acad template file).
   b. Select Content tab, Figure 5-46d: Under the *Multileader Type* and option, specify the *Text Style* to be *Annotative*. Confirm that *Text height* is grayed and its value is 0.125 for acad template files and 3 for acadiso template files. If necessary, refer to the annotative text details.

4. Close the *Modify Multileader Style: Annotative* dialog box.
5. Close the *Manage Multileader Styles* dialog box.

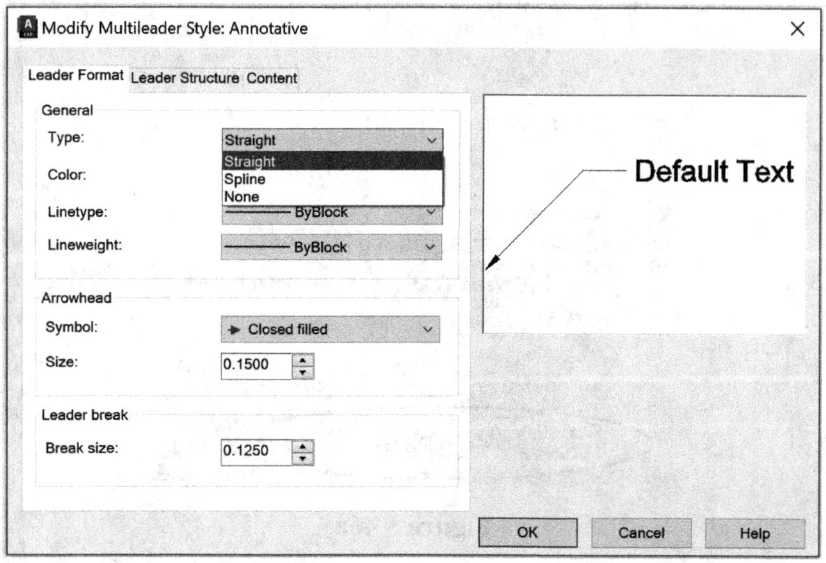

Figure 5-46c

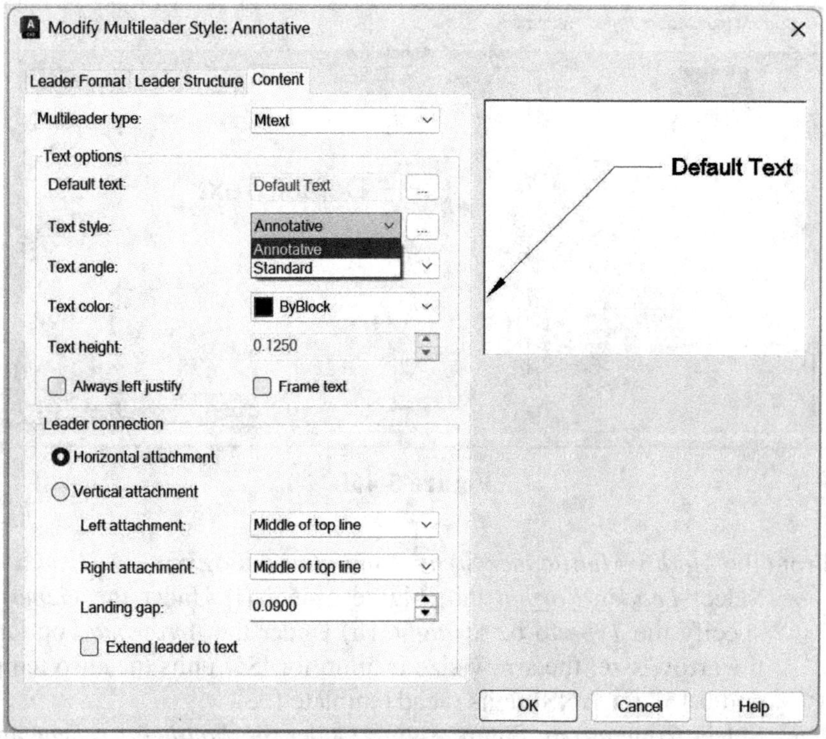

Figure 5-46d

5.7.2. Create annotative leader

This section assumes that the user has created an annotative leader style.

- The *Leader* command is activated using one of the following methods: However, the prompts by the two methods are slightly different.

  1. Panel method: From the *Home* tab and *Annotation* panel click the *Leader* tool, Figure 5-47a. The activation of the command opens *Select Annotation Scale* dialog box. Specify the scale to be 1:1; and the prompt shown in Figure 5-47b appears on the screen.

  2. Command line method: Type "qleader," "Qleader" or "QLEADER" on the command line and press the *Enter* key. The activation of the command leads to the prompt shown in Figure 5-47b.

  3. Specify first leader point, or, Figure 5-47b: Click on the desired location. The arrowhead is created at the first point. This example creates a leader to point *A*; therefore, click at point *A*.

- Specify next point, Figure 5-47c: This point represents the first limb of the arrow in the current example, line AB. Click in the vicinity of point B, Figure 5-47c. The prompt shown in Figure 5-47d appears.

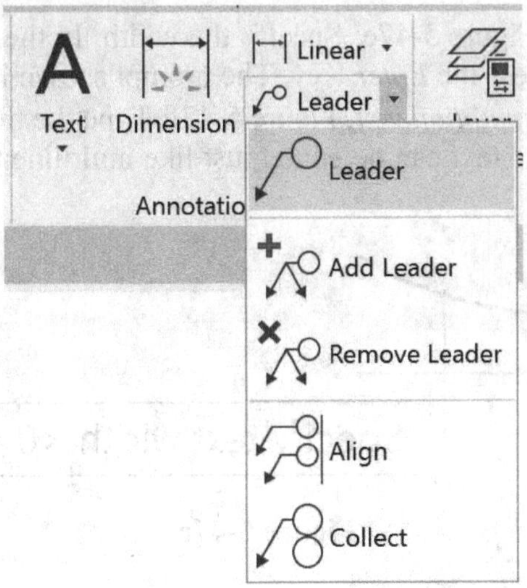

Figure 5-47a

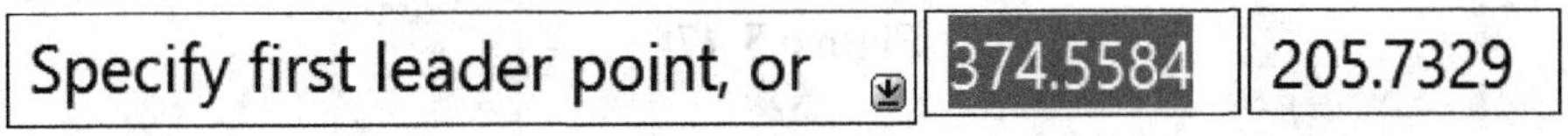

Figure 5-47b

Figure 5-47c

- <u>*Specify next point*</u>, Figure 5-47d: This point represents the second limb of the arrow in the current example, line BC. Click in the vicinity of point C, Figure 5-47d. The prompt shown in Figure 5-47e appears.

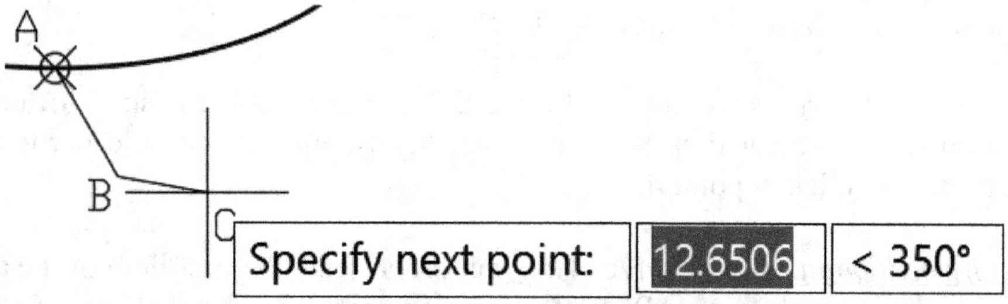

Figure 5-47d

- <u>*Specify text width*</u>, Figure 5-47e: Specify the width. In the current example, use the default value and press the *Enter* Key. The prompt shown in Figure 5-47f appears.
- <u>*Enter first line of annotation text*</u>, Figure 5-47f: Type the multiline text and press the *Enter* key twice. The text can be edited just like multiline text. The leader is shown in Figure 5-47g.

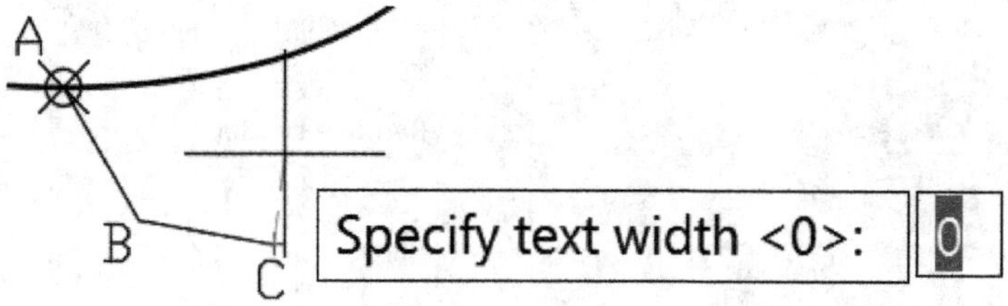

Figure 5-47e

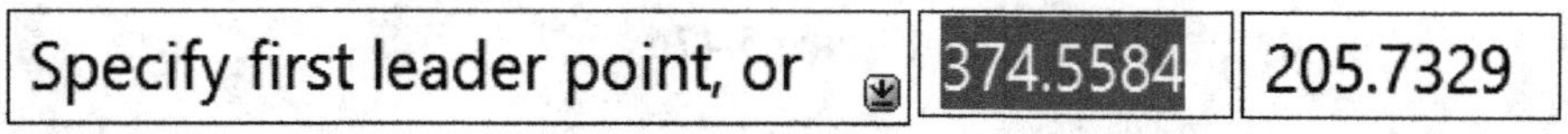

Figure 5-47f

- Figure 5-47g also shows the grip point. Click at a grip point, keep pressing the left button, and move the cursor. Note the behavior of the various grip points.

Figure 5-47g

5.7.3. Add the scales to the leader properties

The process of adding multiple scale factors to an annotative object is explained in *Section 5.3.1*.

5.7.4. Update the viewports scales

If necessary, update the viewport scale as follows:

- Double click inside the viewport.
- Change the scale to the desired viewport scale.
- Figure 5-48 shows three viewports with different viewport scales. The scales are shown in the lower right corners of the viewports. The user can either practice with multiple layouts or create multiple viewports in the same layout (for detail, refer to *Chapter 8*).

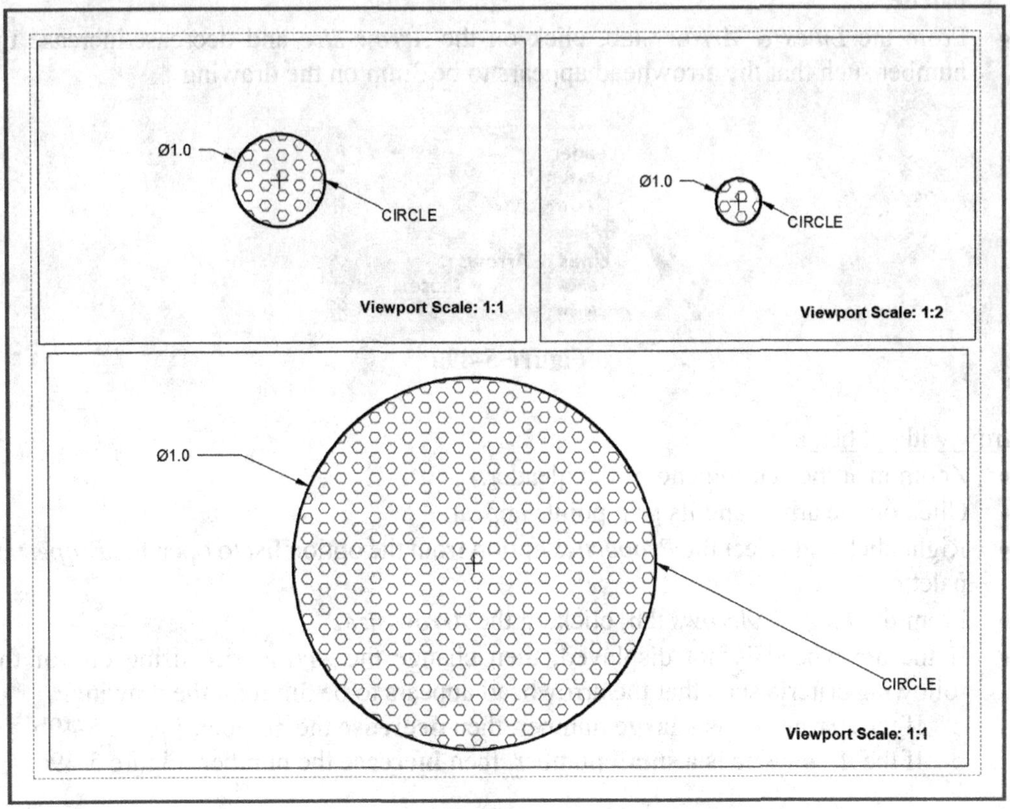

Figure 5-48

5.7.5. Arrow

The user can draw an arrow (without the text) using the *Leader* command as follows.

- Activate the annotative *Leader* command.
- *Specify first leader point*, Figure 5-47b: The arrowhead is created at the first point. Click on the desired location. This example creates a leader to point *A*; therefore, click at point *A*.
- *Specify next point*, Figure 5-47c: This point represents the first limb of the arrow in the current example, line AB. Click in the vicinity of point B, Figure 5-47c. The prompt shown in Figure 5-47d appears.
- **Press the *Esc* key on the keyboard to exit the *Leader* command without writing the text.**

5.7.6. Arrowhead size

The arrowhead size depends on the length of the segment AB and the lineweight of the arrow. This section explains the process to adjust the head size if it is too big/small or not visible.

Head size too big/small, Figure 5-49a:

- Click on the arrow and its grip points appear.
- Right click and select the *Properties* option from the option list to open the *Properties* palette.
- From the *Lines & Arrows* tab, click on the *Arrow size* and decrease/increase the number such that the arrowhead appears to be 3mm on the drawing.

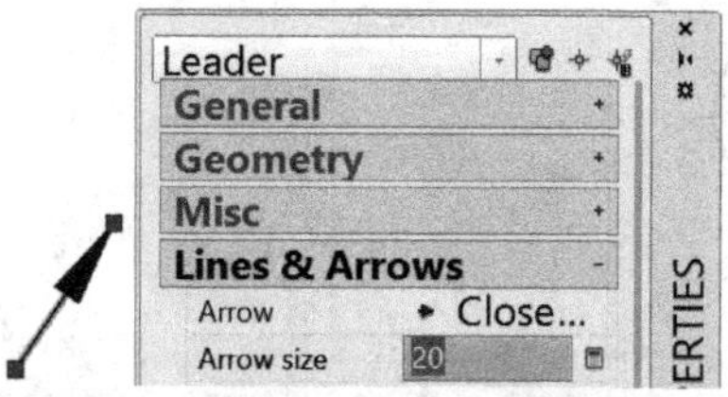

Figure 5-49a

Arrow without head:

- Zoom in at the starting end of the qleader.
- Click on the arrow and its grip points appear.
- Right click and select the *Properties* option from the option list to open the *Properties* palette.
- From the *Lines & Arrows* tab, click on the *Arrow size*.
- If the arrowhead is not displayed, then change the *Arrow size* using one of the following criteria such that the arrowhead appears to be 3mm on the drawing.
  - If the *Arrow size* is a **large** number, then **decrease** the number, Figure 5-49b.
  - If the *Arrow size* is a **small** number, then **increase** the number, Figure 5-49c.

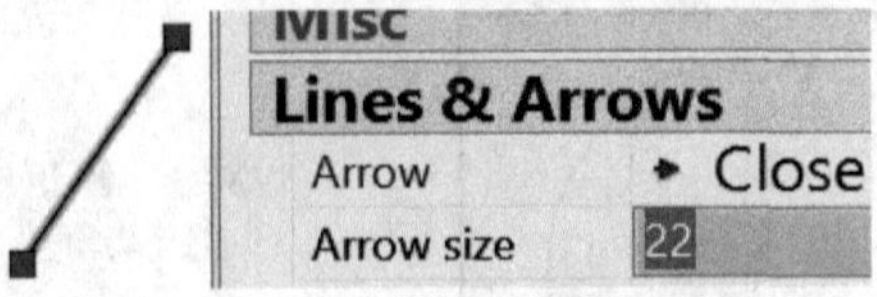

Figure 5-49b

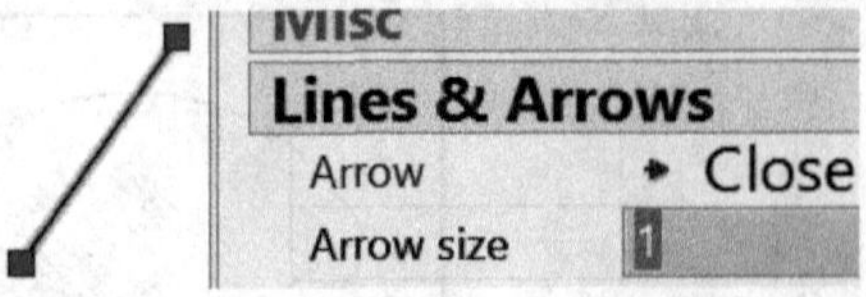

Figure 5-49c

5.8. Annotation – Status Bar Button

Figure 5-50a and Figure 5-50b show annotation *Status Bar* buttons for the Model Space and a layout's viewport, respectively. If the button is in blue state, it means that the command is active and if the button is in grey state, it means that the command is inactive. The *Status Bar* is discussed in *Chapter 2*. The remainder of this chapter describes the functionalities of these buttons.

Figure 5-50a

Figure 5-50b

5.8.1. Annotation visibility 

As the name suggests, the Annotation Visibility (AV) button controls the visibility of the annotative objects. *This button should always be active.*

- **Assumption:** The layers containing the annotative objects are on.
- **On:** Every annotative object is visible.
- **Off:** Only the annotative object for which the annotative scale is the same as the current annotative scale.

- **Example:**
    - The fully hatched circle's hatch scale is 4:1 and the viewport scale is 3:1.
    - Figure 5-51a: Since the AV command is active, the fully hatched circle's hatch is visible.
    - Figure 5-51b: Since the AV command is inactive, the fully hatched circle's hatch is not visible.

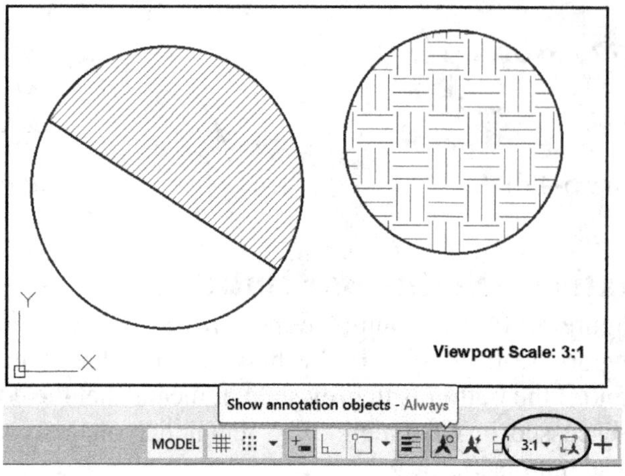

Figure 5-51a

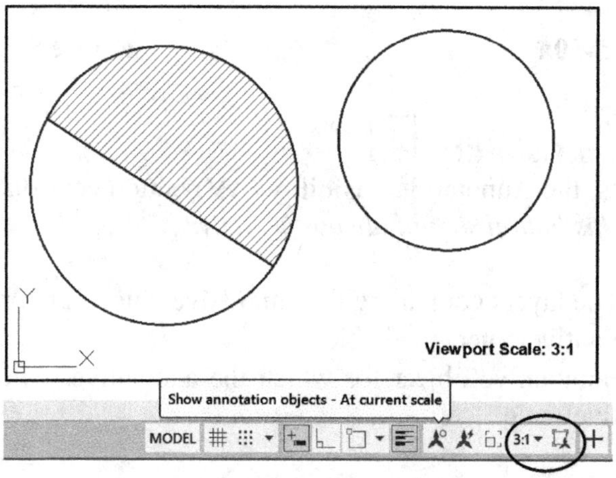

Figure 5-51b

5.8.2. Annotation auto scale

As the name suggests, the Annotation Auto Scale (AAS) button controls the addition of the viewport scale to the annotative objects' annotation scale list. *This button should always be active.*

- **Assumption:** The layers containing the annotative objects are on.
- **On:** The viewport scale is automatically added to the annotative objects' annotation scale list.
- **Off:** The viewport scale is NOT added to the annotative objects' annotation scale list.

- **Example:**
  - The viewport scale of 1:3 is not added to the fully hatched circle's annotative hatch scale list.
  - Figure 5-52a: Since the AAS command is active, the viewport scale of 1:3 is automatically added to the fully hatched circle's annotative hatch scale list.

- Figure 5-52b: Since the AAS command is inactive, the viewport scale of 1:3 is NOT added to the fully hatched circle's annotative hatch scale list.

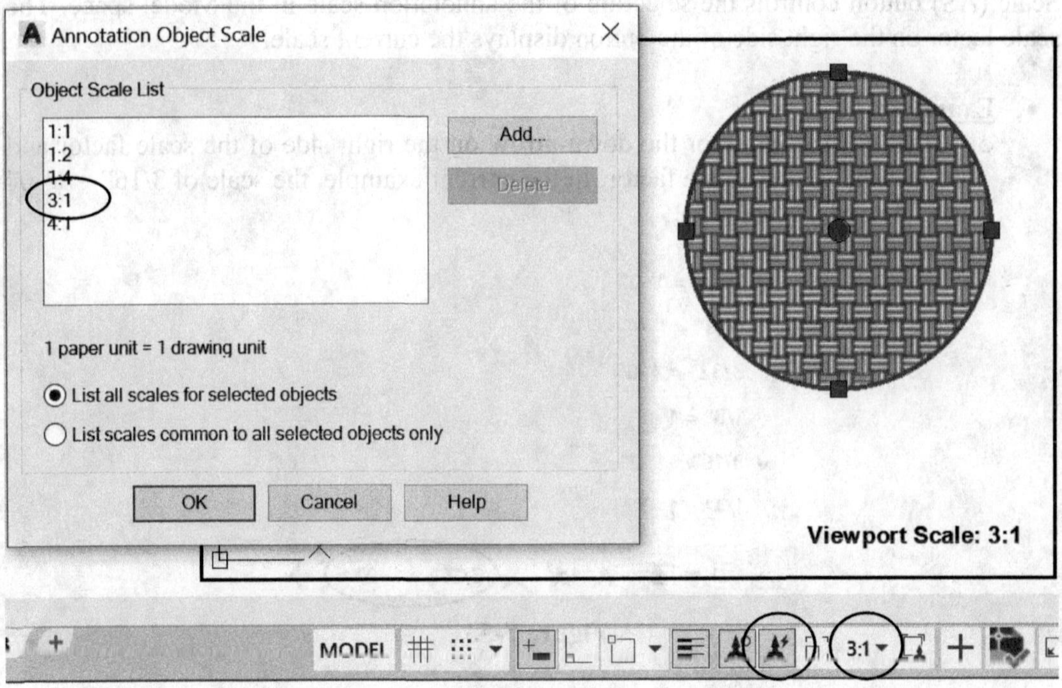

Figure 5-52a

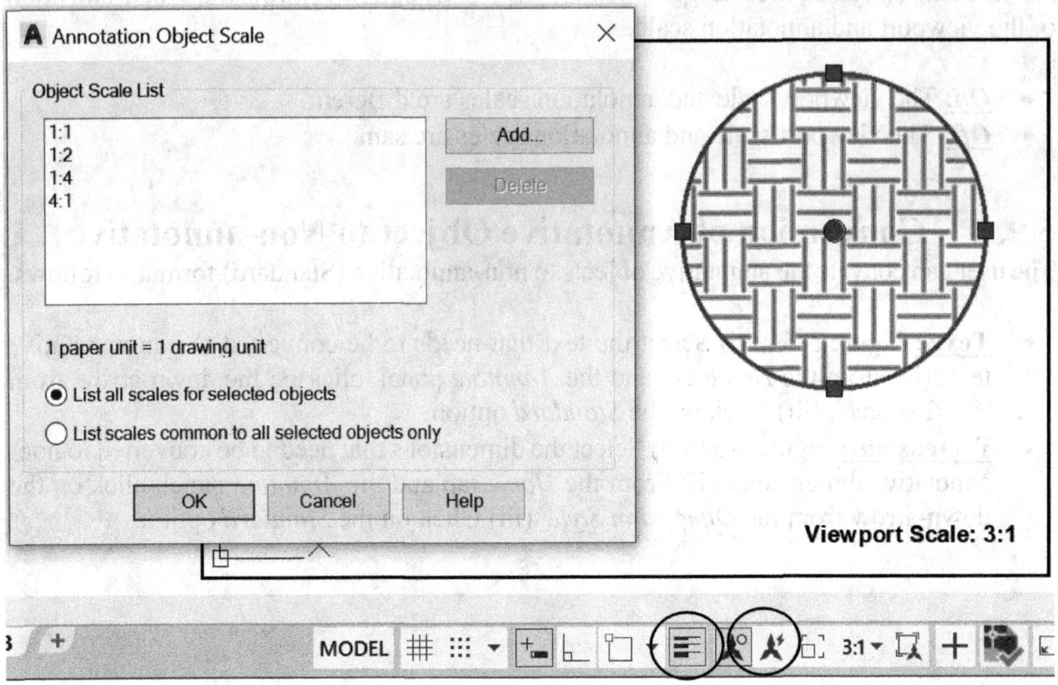

Figure 5-52b

5.8.3. Annotation scale 

This button is available only in the Model Space. As the name suggests, the Annotation Scale (AS) button controls the selection of the annotation scale in the Model space. The scale factor on the right side of the button displays the current scale.

- **<u>Example:</u>**
  - Click on AS button or the down-arrow on the right side of the scale factor and select the desired scale factor. In the current example, the scale of 3/16" = 1'-0" is selected, Figure 5-53.

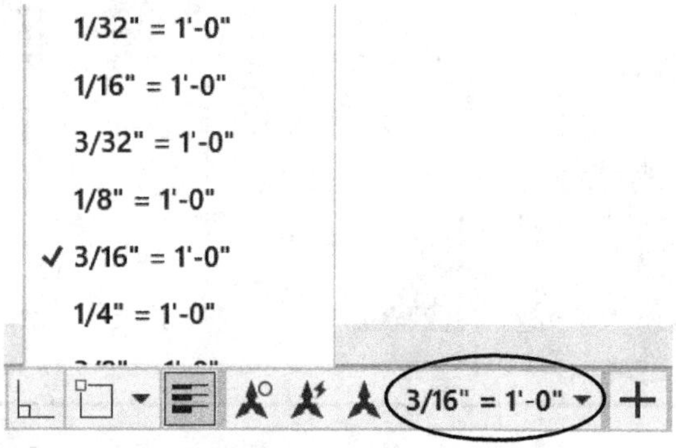

Figure 5-53

5.8.4. Viewport scale sync 

As the name suggests, the Viewport Scale Sync (VSS) button controls the synchronization of the viewport and annotation scale.

- ***<u>On</u>*:** The viewport scale and annotation scales are different.
- ***<u>Off</u>*:** The viewport scale and annotation scales are same.

5.9. Conversion of Annotative Object to Non-annotative

The user can convert the annotative objects to non-annotative (Standard) format as follows.

- **<u>Texts:</u>** Figure 5-54a (i) Select the text that needs to be converted to non-annotative text. (ii) From the *Home* tab and the *Annotate* panel, click on the down-arrow from the *Text Style*. (iii) Click on the *Standard* option.
- **<u>Dimensions:</u>** Figure 5-54b (i) Select the dimensions that need to be converted to non-annotative dimensions. (ii) From the *Home* tab and the *Annotate* panel, click on the down-arrow from the *Dimension Style*. (iii) Click on the *Standard* option.

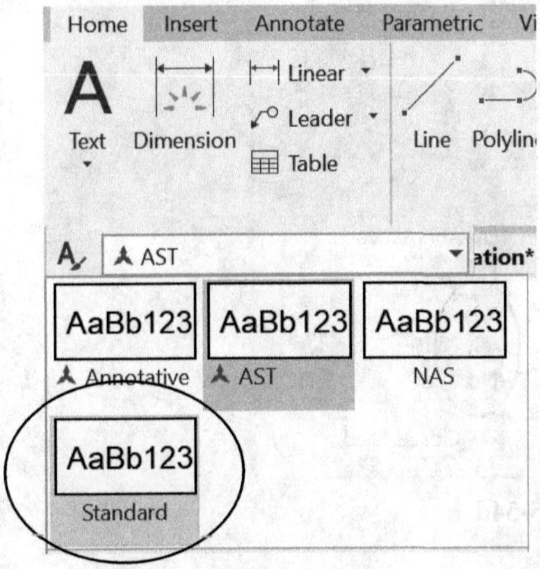

Figure 5-54a

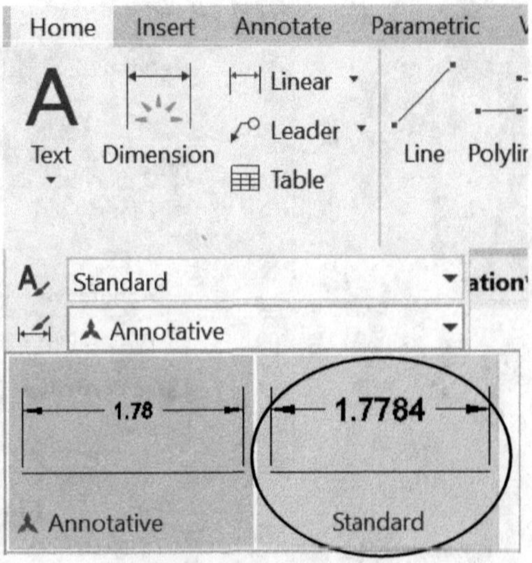

Figure 5-54b

- **<u>Hatches:</u>** Figure 5-54c (i) Select the hatches that need to be converted to non-annotative hatches. (ii) Open the *Properties* sheet for the desired hatches. (iii) On the *Properties* sheet under the *Pattern* tab, verify that the right column for the *Annotative* is set to *No*.
- **<u>Qleaders:</u>** Figure 5-54d (i) Select the qleaders that need to be converted to non-annotative qleaders. (ii) Open the *Properties* sheet for the desired qleaders. (iii) On the *Properties* sheet under the *Misc* tab, verify that the right column for the *Annotative* is set to *No*.

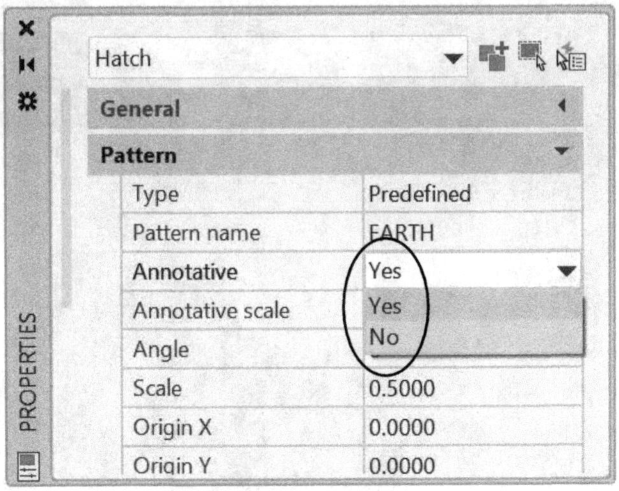

Figure 5-54c

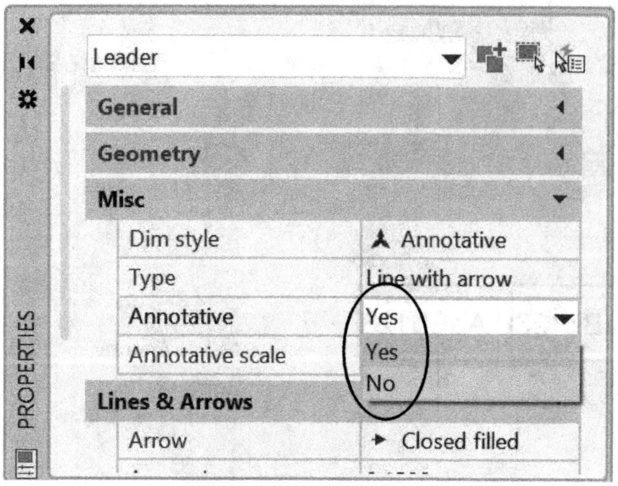
Leader
General
Geometry
Misc
Dim style
Annotative
Type
Line with arrow
Annotative
Yes
Annotative scale
Yes
No
Lines & Arrows
Arrow
Closed filled
PROPERTIES

Figure 5-54d

Notes:

6. Layers

6.1. Learning Objectives

After completing this chapter, the students will show proficiency in the following areas:

- Basics of a layer
- Layer properties manager
- Layers manipulation (create, delete, rename, and update)
- Creating drawings with layers
- Moving Objects from one layer to the other
- Objects' visibility and layers

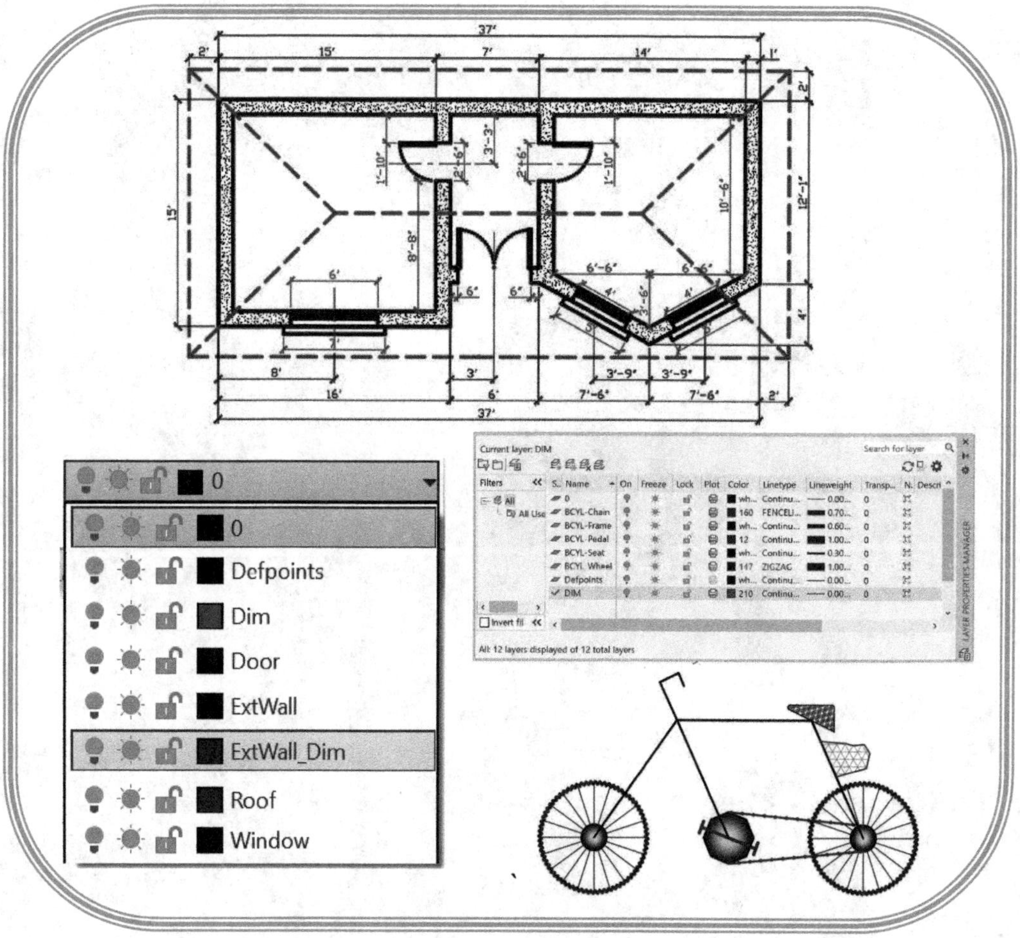

6.2. Introduction

Prior to computer use in drafting, architects drew different parts of the drawing on transparent overlays. The base drawing and the overlays maintained matching points for the alignment. Figure 6-1a demonstrates the base drawing (floor plan) and the roof overlay; and both the base drawing and the roof overlay have four matching points (A, B, C, and D). Figure 6-1b shows the roof overlay placed on the base drawing by aligning the matching points.

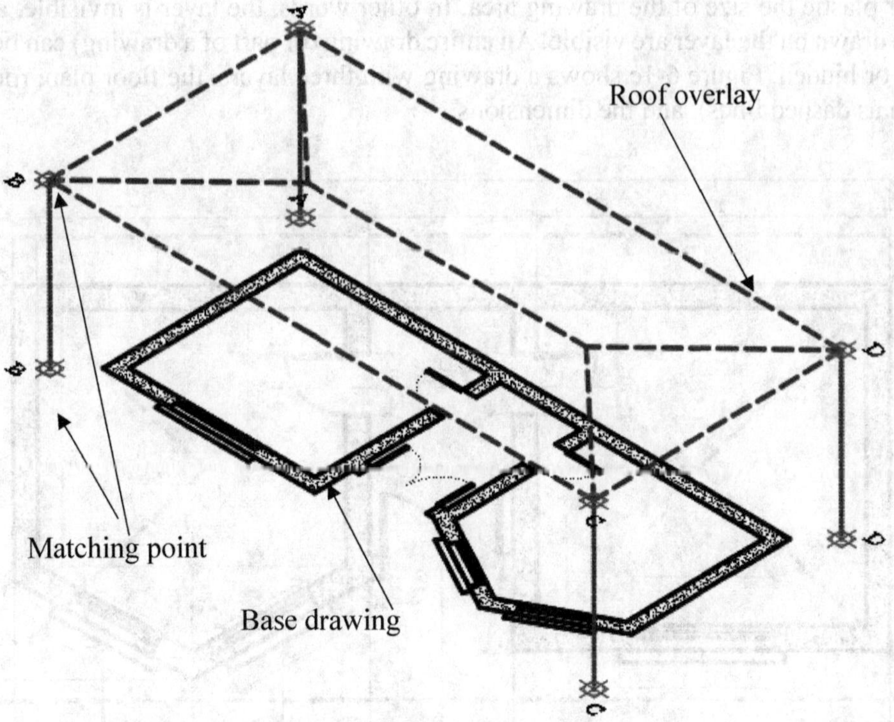

Figure 6-1a

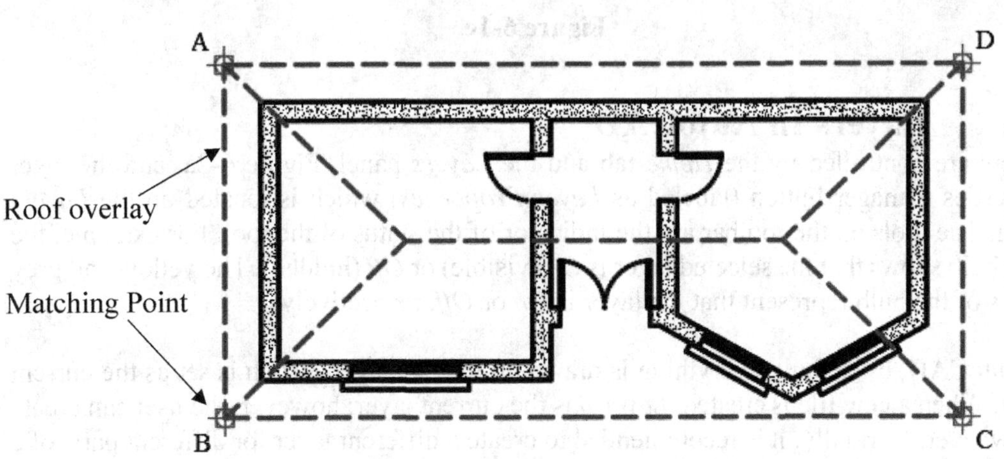

Figure 6-1b

The use of overlays provided a technique of managing, organizing, and controlling the visual layout of a drawing. To see the drawing more clearly, the drafter may want to remove all the text and dimensions from the drawing. **The drafter prefers retaining the information but hides it from view in certain situations to protect the context.** Deleting the information would not be appropriate as the drafter would lose all the work. Hence, just hiding the selected overlays would solve the problem.

In AutoCAD, an overlay is replaced by a layer. A layer can be thought of as a large piece of clear plastic the size of the drawing area. In other words, the layer is invisible, and the objects drawn on the layer are visible. An entire drawing (or part of a drawing) can be made visible or hidden. Figure 6-1c shows a drawing with three layers, the floor plan, roof plan (shown as dashed lines), and the dimensions.

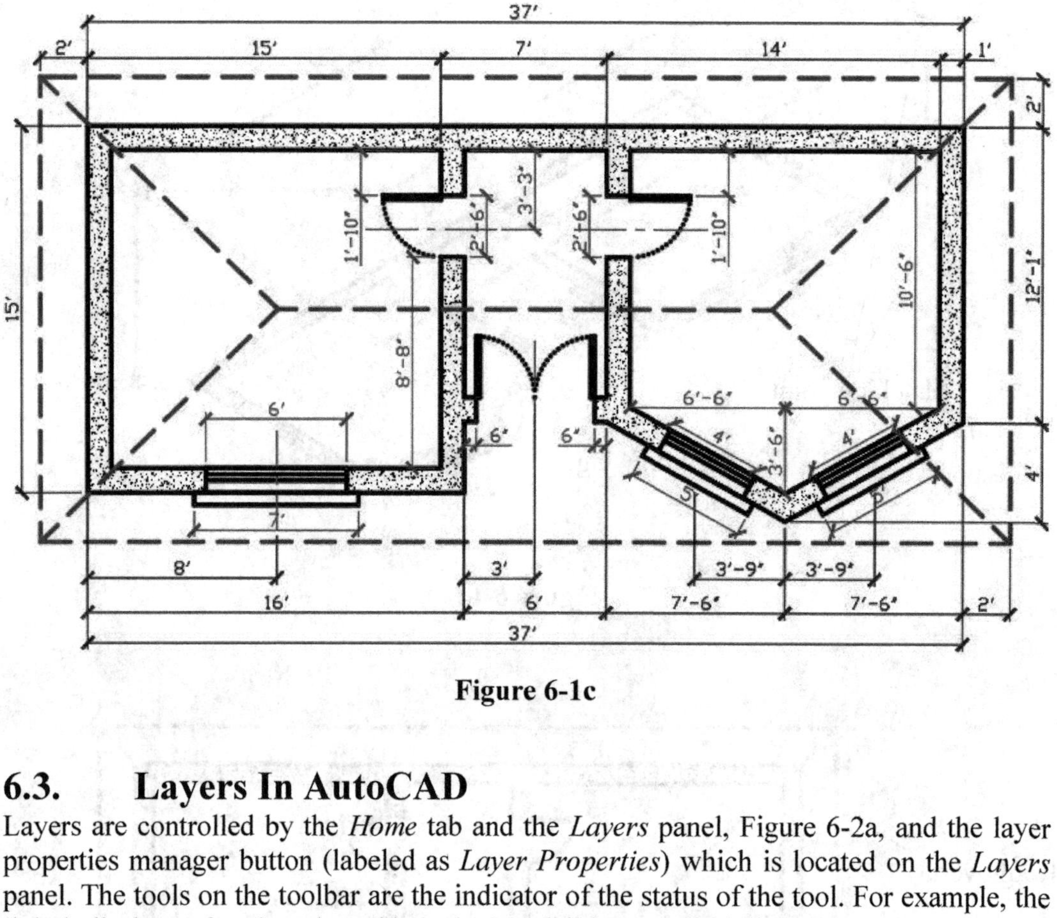

Figure 6-1c

6.3. Layers In AutoCAD

Layers are controlled by the *Home* tab and the *Layers* panel, Figure 6-2a, and the layer properties manager button (labeled as *Layer Properties*) which is located on the *Layers* panel. The tools on the toolbar are the indicator of the status of the tool. For example, the light bulb shows that the selected layer is *On* (visible) or *Off* (hidden). The yellow and grey colors of the bulb represent that the layer is *On* or *Off*, respectively.

In AutoCAD, by default, everything is drawn on the "0" layer, which is set as the current layer. When a new file is created, *Layer 0* is the current layer; however, the user can create a new layer. Normally, it is recommended to create a different layer for different parts of a drawing. Each layer should be assigned to its own color, linetype, and line thickness so that every object drawn on that layer appears in the same color, linetype, and line thickness. Figure 6-2b shows the layers created for the drawing shown in Figure 6-1c. Figure 6-2c shows the basic characteristic of a layer.

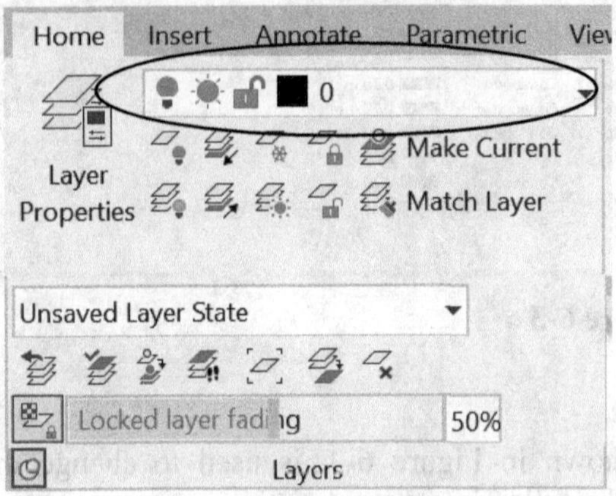

Figure 6-2a

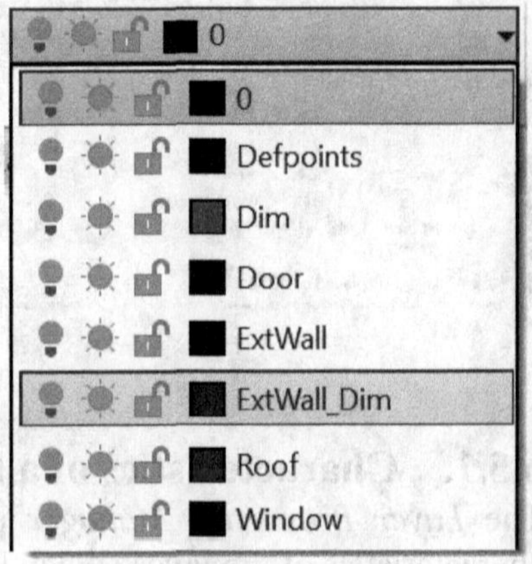

Figure 6-2b

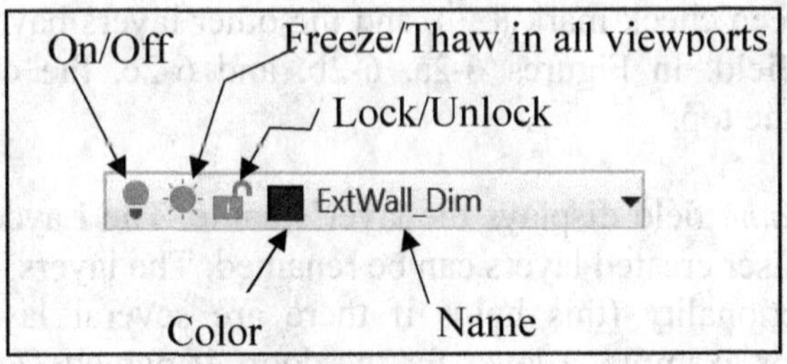

Figure 6-2c

6.4. Layer Command

The *Layer* command is used to create new layers and modify the existing layers.

- The *Layer* command is activated using one of the following methods:
  1. Panel method: From the *Home* tab and the *Layers* panel click on the *Layer Properties* tool ( ).
  2. Command line method: Type "layer," "Layer," or "LAYER" on the command line and press the *Enter* key.

- The activation of the command opens the *Layer Properties Manager* palette as shown in Figure 6-3.

6.5. Layer Properties Manager

The *Layer Properties Manager* palette for the drawing of Figure 6-1c is shown in Figure 6-3. This palette is used to create a new layer, delete an empty layer, and change the characteristics of new and existing layers.

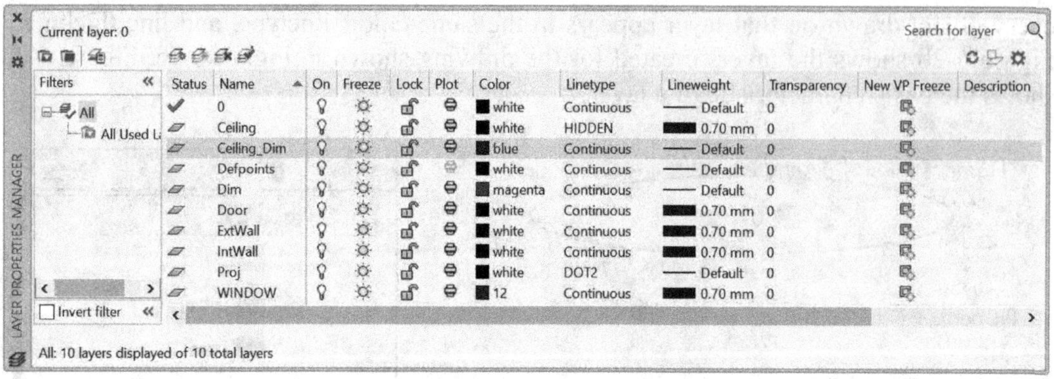

Figure 6-3

6.5.1. Characteristics of a layer

The *Layer Properties Manager* palette, shown in Figure 6-3, is used to change the characteristics of the layers. Each layer has the following characteristics.

1. <u>*Status*</u>: The *Status* field shows if a layer is the current layer. In Figure 6-3, the current layer has a green check mark ( ), and the other layers have a small parallelogram ( ) in this field. In Figures 6-2a, 6-2b, and 6-2c, the current layer's name is displayed on the top.

2. <u>*Name*</u>: The *Name* field displays the layer's name. The Layer *0* cannot be renamed; however, the user created layers can be renamed. The layers' names should be based on their functionality (this helps if there are several layers), Figure 6-2b and Figure 6-3. For example, a layer for the doors is named *Door*. To rename a layer, (i) press the *F2* key or click inside the name field, (ii) type the new name, and (iii) press the *Enter* key.

3. <u>*On*</u>: The *On* option controls the visibility of a layer. Select the light bulb ( ) to turn the layer *Off* on the drawing. The drawing of an *On* layer is visible and available for plotting. The drawing of an *Off* layer is invisible and is unavailable for drawing and plotting. The visibility can be switched by using one of the following two methods.
   a. Click the bulb button in *Layer Properties Manager* palette, Figure 6-3.
   b. Press the down-arrow of the *Layer* toolbar and click the bulb icon of the desired layer, Figure 6-2b and Figure 6-2c.

4. <u>*Freeze*</u>: This option is available for layouts. The layouts are discussed in *Chapter 8*. The *Freeze or thaw in current view port* option ( ) is used to hide a layer for a longer period of time. If a layer is turned *Off* in the *Model* space, then it disappears from the *Model* space and from all the viewports, too. However, freezing a layer in a particular viewport will only hide the contents of the layer in question in the selected viewport. Freezing of layers improves the performance and reduces the object regeneration time. The freeze option should be used only for those layers that need to be invisible for long periods. Otherwise, the *On/Off* option should be used. **Before freezing the layer, the viewport must be selected. The viewport is selected by double clicking**

inside the viewport. For the selected viewport, its boundary's line thickness and the coordinate system appear in the viewport. The freezing option can be set by using one of the following two methods.

   a. Click the *Freeze* button in *Layer Properties Manager* palette.
   b. Press the down-arrow of the *Layer* toolbar and click the *Freeze* icon of the desired layer.

5. <u>*Lock*</u>: The *Lock* option ( ) is used to lock a layer. The contents of a lock layer cannot be modified. The lock option can be set by using one of the following two methods.
   a. Clicking the lock button in *Layer Properties Manager* palette.
   b. Press the down-arrow of the *Layer* toolbar and click the lock icon of the desired layer.

6. <u>*Color*</u>: The *Color* option is used to set the color of the objects drawn on the layer. To change the color (i) open the *Layer Properties Manager* palette, Figure 6-3, (ii) click on the small colored box ( ) under the *Color* column to open the *Select Color* dialog box, Figure 6-4a, (iii) select the desired color from the *Select Color* dialog box, and (iv) press the *OK* button of the *Select Color* dialog box. This closes the *Select Color* dialog box and changes the color of the small box to the selected color. All the objects drawn on the layer are displayed in the chosen color, provided that the *Color Control*'s setting in the *Properties* panel of *Home* tab is set to *By Layer*, Figure 6-4b.

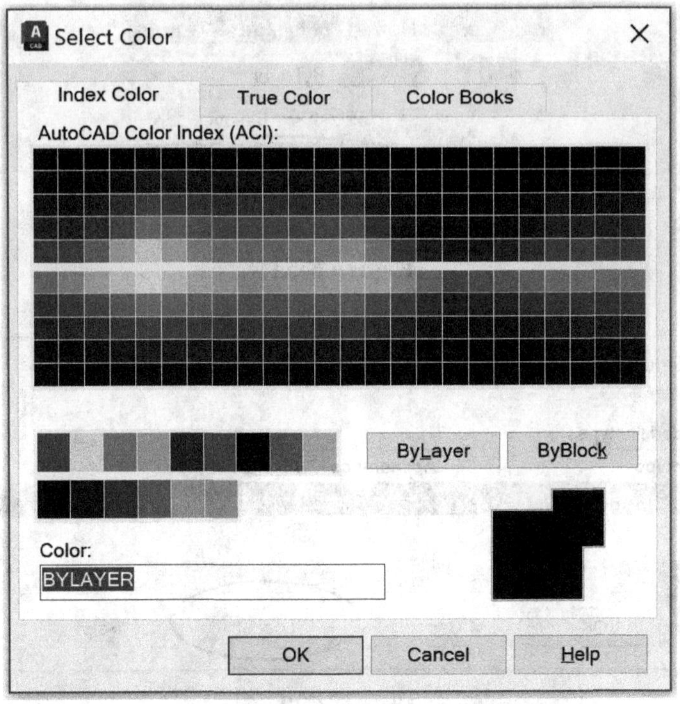

Figure 6-4a

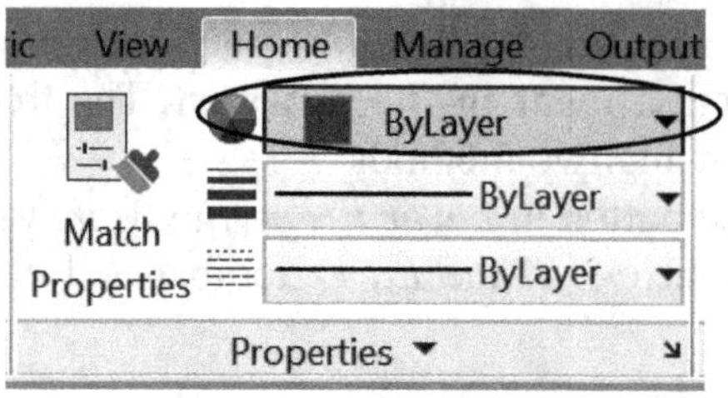

Figure 6-4b

7. Linetype: The *Linetype* option sets the default linetype for all the objects drawn on the layer. All objects drawn on the layer are displayed in the chosen linetype style, provided that the *Line Type Control*'s setting in the *Properties* panel of *Home* tab is set to *By Layer*, Figure 6-5a. Linetype is discussed in detail in *Chapter 3*. The linetype of a layer can be changed as follows. (i) Open the *Layer Properties Manager* palette, Figure 6-3. (ii) Click on *Continuous* under the *Linetype* column to open the *Select Linetype* dialog box, Figure 6-5b. (iii) Click on the *Load* button to open the *Load or Reload Linetype* dialog box, Figure 6-5c. (iv) Select the desired linetype (Figure 6-5b shows the selection of *Phantom*) and press the *OK* button. The *Phantom* linetype appears in the *Select Linetype* dialog box, Figure 6-5d. (v) Select the *Phantom* linetype and press the *OK* button. This closes the *Load or Reload Linetype* dialog box and changes the linetype to the selected style.

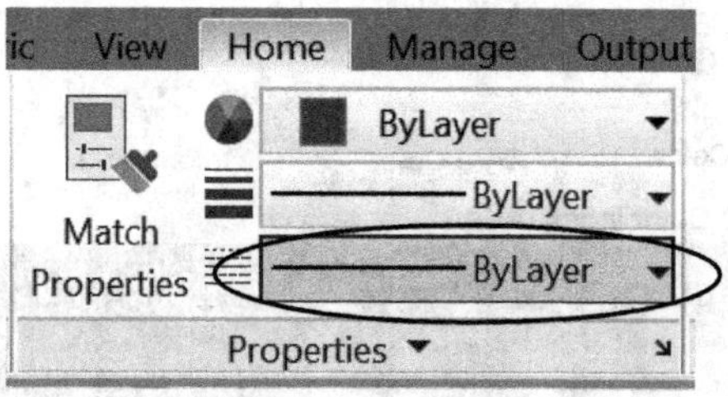

Figure 6-5a

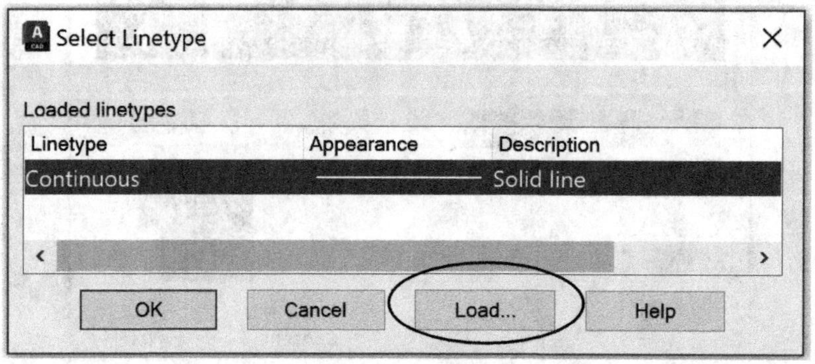

Figure 6-5b

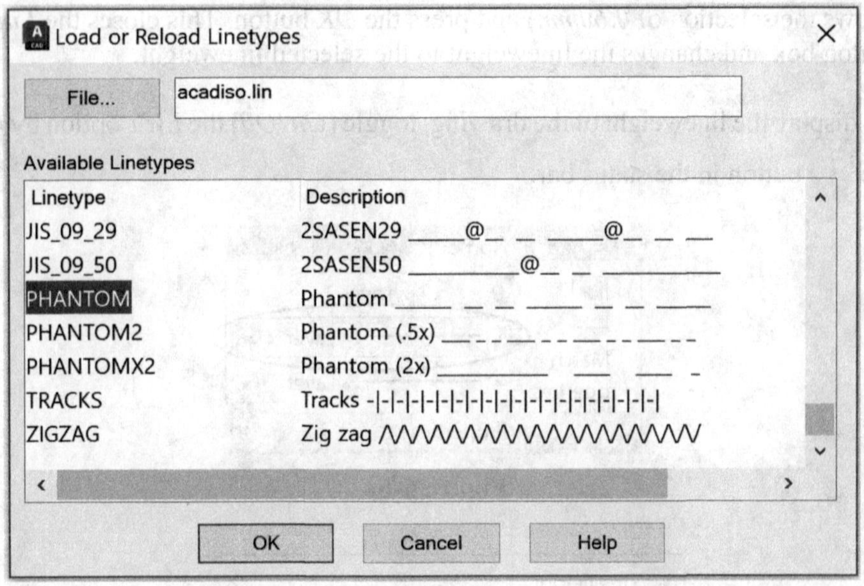

Figure 6-5c

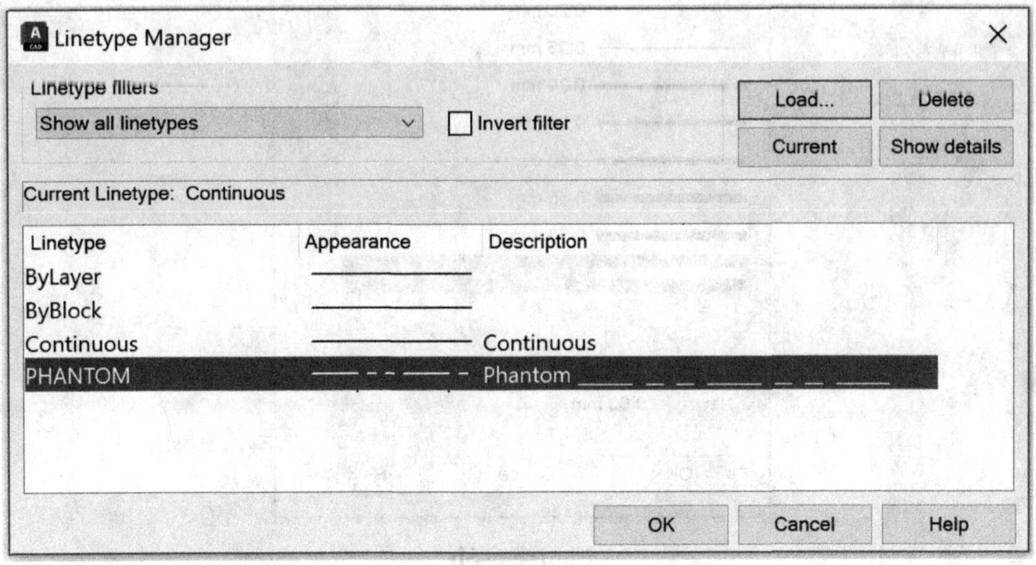

Figure 6-5d

8. Lineweight: The *Lineweight* option sets the thickness of the lines drawn on the layer. All objects drawn on the layer are displayed in the chosen lineweight, provided that the *Line Weight Control*'s setting in the *Properties* panel of the *Home* tab is set to *By Layer*, Figure 6-6a. Lineweight is discussed in detail in *Chapter 3*. The lineweight of a layer can be changed as follows. (i) Open the *Layer Properties Manager* palette, Figure 6-3. (ii) Click on the *Default* under the *Lineweight* column to open the *Lineweight* dialog box, Figure 6-6b, (iii) select the desired lineweight (Figure 6-6b

shows the selection of *0.60mm*) and press the *OK* button. This closes the *Lineweight* dialog box and changes the lineweight to the selected lineweight.

To display the lineweight of the drawing, toggle (*On* /*Off*) the *LWT* option by pressing the button in the status bar.

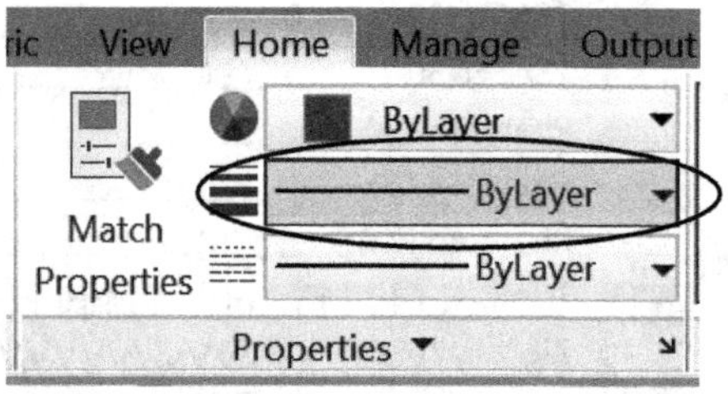

Figure 6-6a

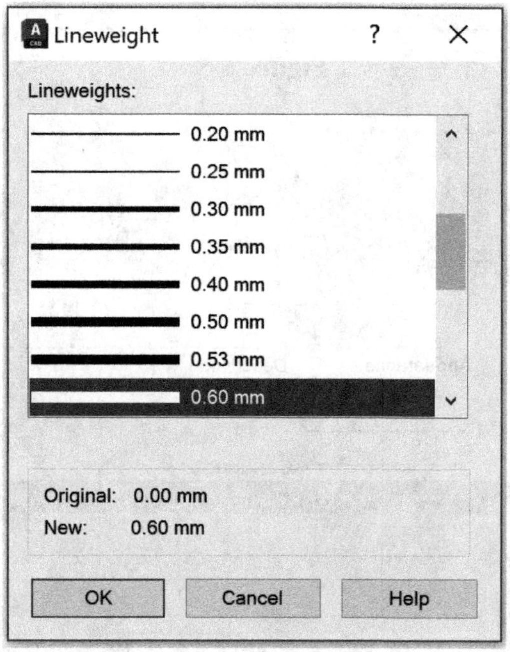

Figure 6-6b

9. Plot: The *Plot* option ( ) is used to allow the objects on the layer to be printed. To turn off the printer, click the printer icon and its appearance changes to . If the printer is off for a layer, then the user (i) cannot print/plot the content of the layer and (ii) if the drawing is exported as a pdf, the content of the layer will not be visible in the pdf file. The user can turn on *Plot* option of the layer by simply clicking the and it will change to .

6.5.2. Create a new layer

To create a new layer, in the *Layer Properties Manager* palette shown in Figure 6-3, click on the *New Layer* button ( ). The new layer inherits the properties of the current layer, Figure 6-7. If necessary, change the properties of the new layer. By default, the new layers are named *Layer1*, *Layer2*, etc. To rename a layer, (i) press the *F2* key or click inside the name field, (ii) type the new name, and (iii) press the *Enter* key, Figure 6-7. To make the change permanent, close the *Layer Properties Manager* palette by clicking the cross on the upper left corner of the toolbar.

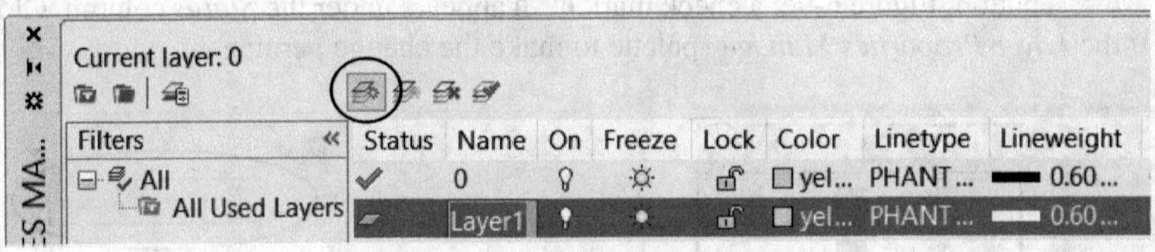

Figure 6-7

6.5.3. Delete an existing layer

To delete a layer, in the *Layer Properties Manager* palette shown in Figure 6-3, (i) select the layer by clicking on it; (ii) click on the *Delete Layer* button ( ) in the *Layer Properties Manager* palette, Figure 6-8a. The selected layer is deleted only if it is not one of the layers shown in Figure 6-8b. Close the *Layer Properties Manager* palette to make the change permanent.

Figure 6-8a

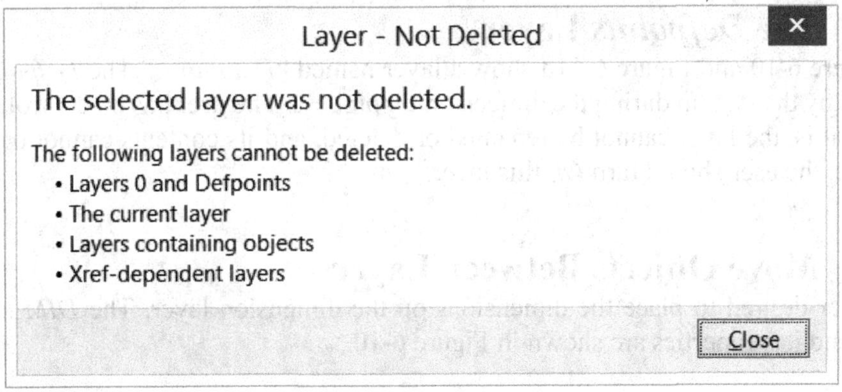

Figure 6-8b

6.5.4. Make a layer to be a current layer

AutoCAD provides three ways to make a layer the current layer.

1. Use the down-arrow in *Layer* toolbar (*Home* tab and *Layer* panel) to display the layers in the drawing, and choose the desired layer, Figure 6-9a.
2. Click on the *Make Current* tool ( ) in the *Layer* panel from *Home* tab, Figure 6-9b, and follow the prompts.
3. In the *Layer Properties Manager* palette, click on a layer, and click on the *Set Current* ( ) button, Figure 6-9c; a check mark ( ) appears under the *Status* column. Close the *Layer Properties Manager* palette to make the change permanent.

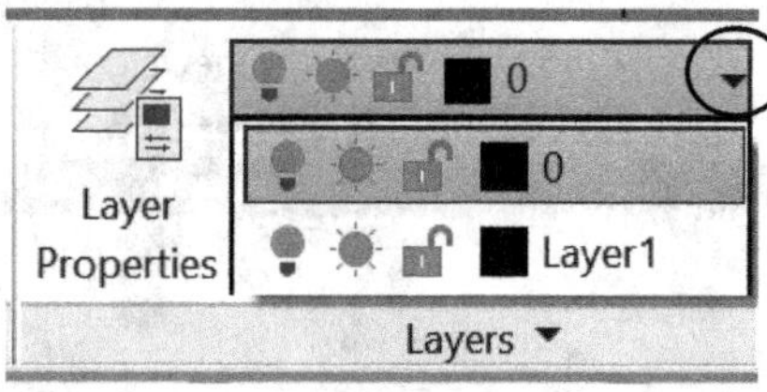

Figure 6-9a

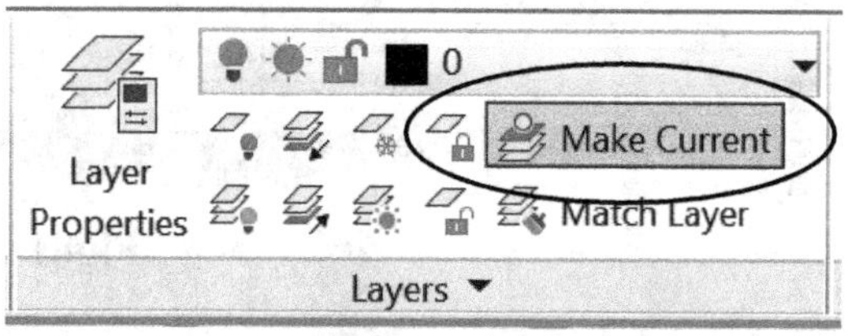

Figure 6-9b

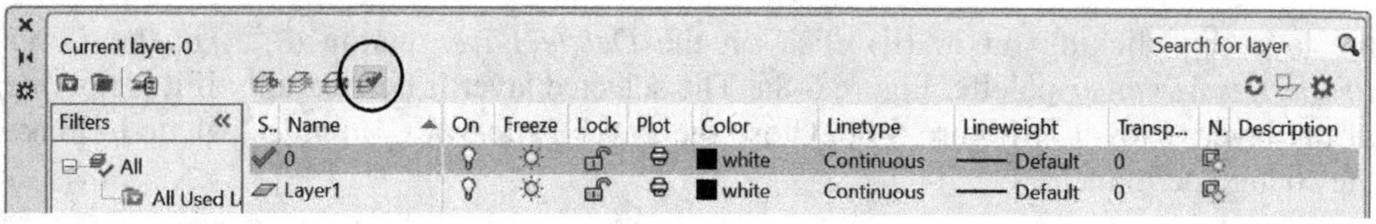

Figure 6-9c

6.6. Drawing And Layers

To draw on a specific layer, the drafter must make the desired layer to be a current layer and then draw on it. Also, **remember** to turn *On* and *thaw* (not freeze) the current layer before drawing any object.

6.7. The *Defpoints* Layer

Both Figure 6-10 and Figure 6-11d show a layer named "*Defpoints.*" The *Defpoints* layer is created by the system during the dimensioning process. The user has no control over this layer. That is, the layer cannot be renamed or deleted, and its contents cannot be printed. Therefore, the user should turn *Off* this layer.

6.8. Move Objects Between Layers

The drafter desired to place the dimensions on the dimension layer. The *DIM* layer was created, and its properties are shown in Figure 6-10.

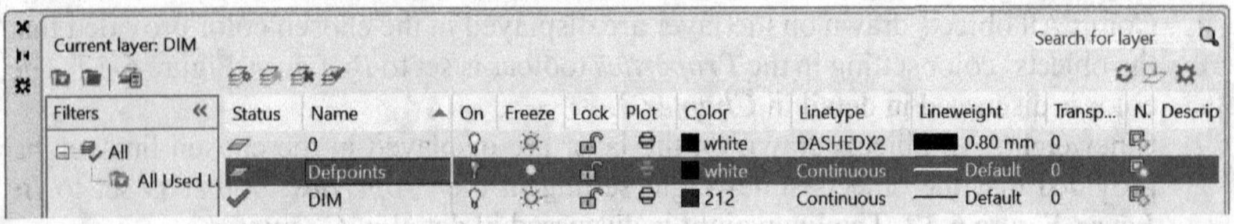

Figure 6-10

After drawing the objects and adding the dimension, Figure 6-11a, the drafter realized that the dimensions are not on the DIM layer. The drafter can correct the mistake by moving the dimensions to the DIM layer, Figure 6-11b.

Figure 6-11a

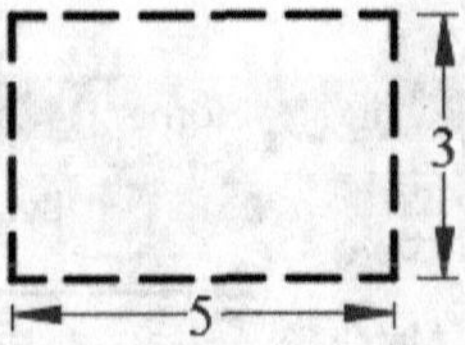

Figure 6-11b

If objects are created on one layer, and later it is necessary to move them to another layer, then use the following steps to move the objects.

1. Select the objects to be moved, Figure 6-11c, dimensions in the example.
2. Select the layer as shown in Figure 6-11d, that is, press the down-arrow in the *Layers* toolbar and click on the desired layer.
3. The selected objects (dimensions in the example) move to the selected layer (DIM layer in the example). The dimensions were created on *Layer 0* but are now moved to the *DIM* layer.
4. The objects (dimensions) are moved to the desired layer (DIM), Figure 6-11d; however, the current layer is still *Layer 0*.
5. ***Check***: To make sure that the objects have moved to the selected layer, turn *Off* the selected layer and if the objects disappear then it means that the objects have moved. If the objects do not disappear then repeat steps #1 - #3.

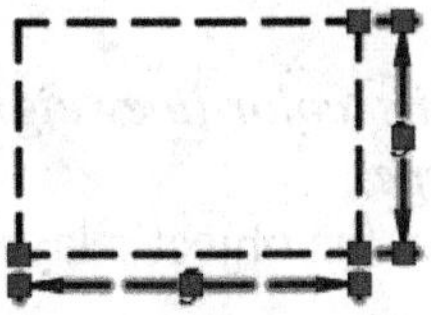

Figure 6-11c

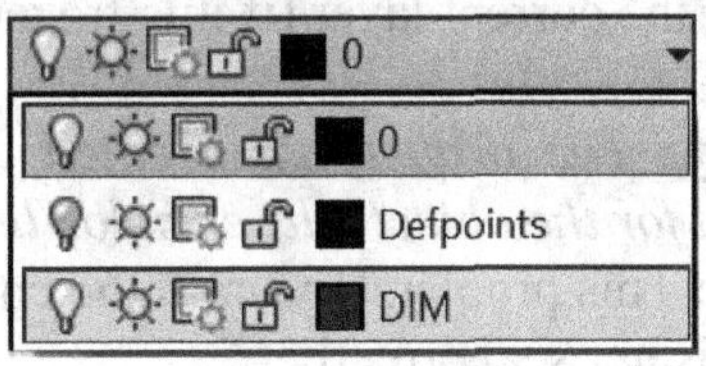

Figure 6-11d

6.9. Update Layer Properties

In order to draw on specific layers with the layer properties, it is important that on the *Properties* panel, the color, linetype, and lineweight are set to *By Layer*, Figure 6-12 (shown below). Any update for these properties using *Layer Properties Manager* palette is reflected in the drawing.

1. Color: All objects drawn on the layer are displayed in the chosen color provided that the objects' color setting in the *Properties* toolbar is set to *By Layer*, Figure 6-12. The color is discussed in detail in *Chapter 3*.
2. Lineweight: All objects drawn on the layer are displayed in the chosen lineweight, provided that the objects' lineweight setting in the *Properties* toolbar is set to *By Layer*, Figure 6-12. The lineweight is discussed in detail in *Chapter 3*.
3. Linetype: All objects drawn on the layer are displayed in the chosen linetype, provided that the objects' linetype setting in the *Properties* toolbar is set to *By Layer*, Figure 6-12. The linetype is discussed in detail in *Chapter 3*.

If the properties of the object drawn are not set *By Layer*, then any change in the layer properties will **NOT** reflect on the drawing.

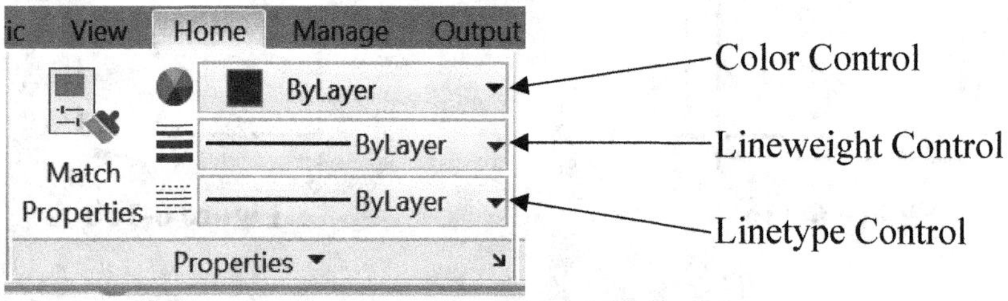

Figure 6-12

6.10. Layers: FAQ

The user may come across one or more problems during a drawing creation, modification, and plotting using layers. This section describes some of the problems and their solution. **Remember** that the drafter can DRAW ONLY on the CURRENT layer and objects appear based on the options selected in the controls of the *Properties* toolbar.

1. **Problem:** *The drafter is creating an object, but it is not appearing on the screen in the drawing area.*
   Reason: This problem occurs if the current layer is either *Off* or frozen.
   Solution: This problem can be solved by turning *On* the current layer (if it is *Off*) or thawing the current layer (if it is frozen).

2. **Problem:** *The drafter has created an object but its color/lineweight/linetype is different for the object's layer color/lineweight/linetype.*
   Reason: This problem occurs if the current layer is not the object's layer or the layer toolbar is not set correctly.

   Solution: This problem can be solved as follows:
   1. If the object is not drawn on the correct layer, then move the object to its layer.
   2. If the *Properties* toolbar is not set correctly, then select the object and set the *color/lineweight/linetype* controls to *By Layer*. Also, make sure that the three controls are set to *By Layer* before drawing the objects.

3. **Problem:** *The drafter is changing the layers color/lineweight/linetype in the Layer Properties Manager palette, but the objects are not changing their color/lineweight/linetype in the drawing area.*
   Reason: This problem occurs if the *color/lineweight/linetype* of the *Properties* toolbar is not set to the *By Layer* option.
   Solution: This problem can be solved as follows: (i) Select the objects; (ii) press the down-arrow of the *color/lineweight/linetype Control* in the *Properties* toolbar; and (iii) select the *By Layer* option.

4. **Problem:** *The drafter can see the objects but cannot plot them.*
   Reason: This problem occurs if the objects in question are drawn in the *defpoints* layer or the layer's plot option is *Off* ( ).
   Solution: This problem can be solved as follows:
   1. If the objects are drawn on the *defpoints* layer, then move them to their respective layers and the drafter will be able to plot the objects.
   2. If the objects are drawn on their respective layer, then open the *Layer Properties Manager* palette. If the layer's (containing the objects in question) plot option is *off*, that is, the layer's printer icon shows the no entry sign ( ) then simply click on the printer icon. The no entry sign disappears ( ) and the drafter will be able to plot the drawing.

6.11. Illustrative Example

Example: Draw the bicycle shown in Figure 6-13a using layers. The drafter can use the following commands to create the drawing.

- Units: Millimeters
- Open a new acadiso template file.
- Create five layers and name them *BCYL_Chain*, *BCYL_Frame*, *BCYL_Pedal*, *BCYL_Seat*, and *BCYL_Wheel*. Set the properties (color, linetype, and lineweight) of the layers as shown in Figure 6-13b.
- In order to draw on different layers with the layer properties, it is important that on the *Properties* toolbar, the *Color*, *Linetype*, and *Lineweight* controls must be set to *By Layer*, Figure 6-12.
- Make the *BCYL_Frame* layer to be the current layer and draw the frame of the Bicycle.
- Make the *BCYL_Seat* layer to be the current layer and draw the seat of the Bicycle.
- Make the *BCYL_Wheel* layer to be the current layer and draw the wheels of the Bicycle.
- Make the *BCYL_Seat* layer to be the current layer and draw the seat of the Bicycle.
- Make the *BCYL_Pedal* layer to be the current layer and draw the pedals of the Bicycle.
- The resulting drawing is shown in Figure 6-13a. For this drawing, by default, the Linetype Scale is 1.
- Make the *Dim* layer to be the current layer and add the dimensions. If the user has not learned the dimensioning techniques, then skip this step.

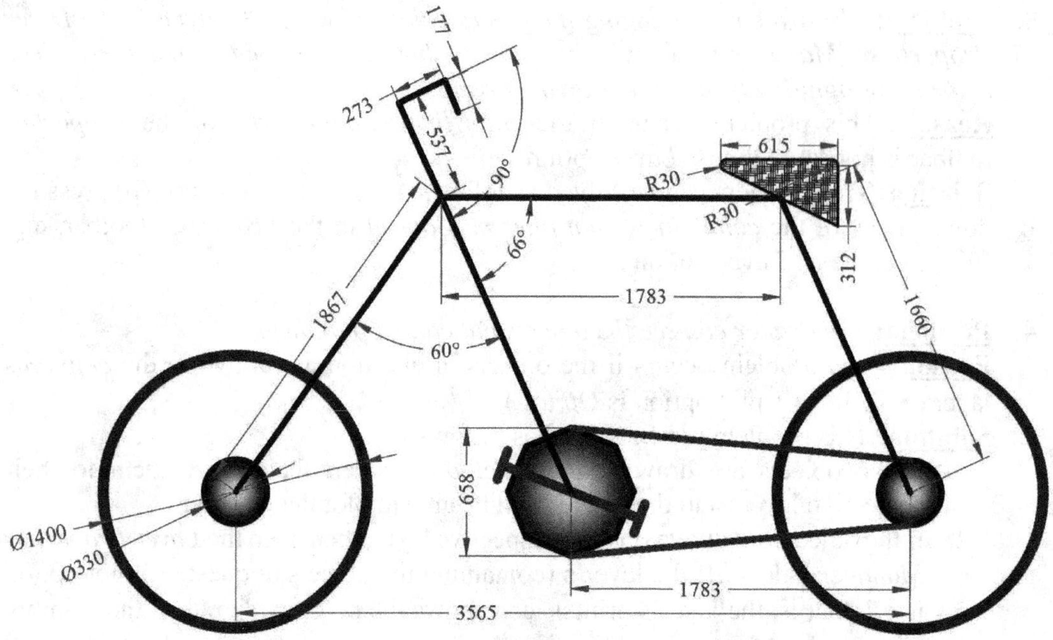

Figure 6-13a

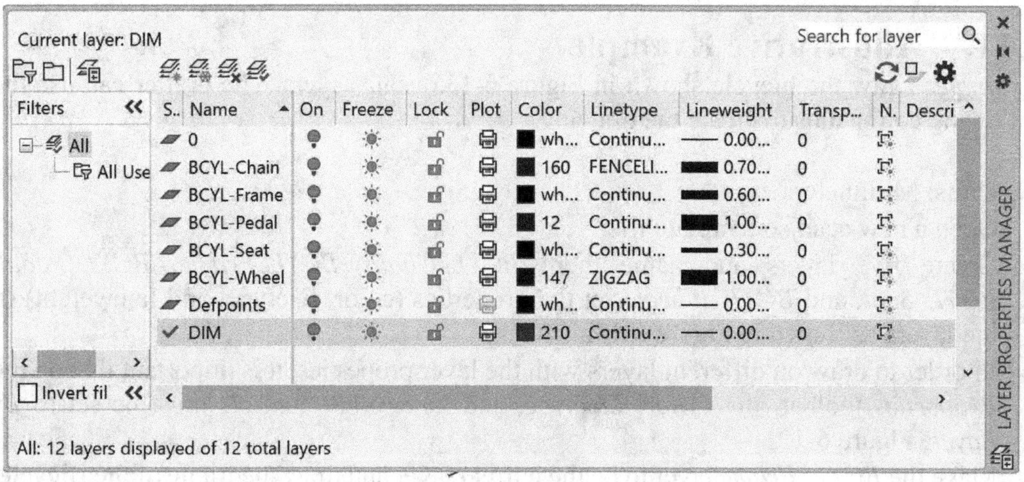

Figure 6-13b

- To change the linetype scale, select the wheels, Figure 6-14a.
    - o Press the right button of the mouse and choose the *Properties* option.
    - o This opens the *Properties* palette, Figure 6-14b.
    - o Select the *Linetype scale* and change the value in the corresponding right column. For the current example, the linetype scale value is changed from 1.00 to 3.00.
    - o Press the *Enter* key on the keyboard.
    - o Similarly, change the linetype scale for the chains. For the current example, the linetype scale value is changed from 1.00 to 4.00.
    - o The resulting drawing is shown in Figure 6-14c.

Figure 6-14a

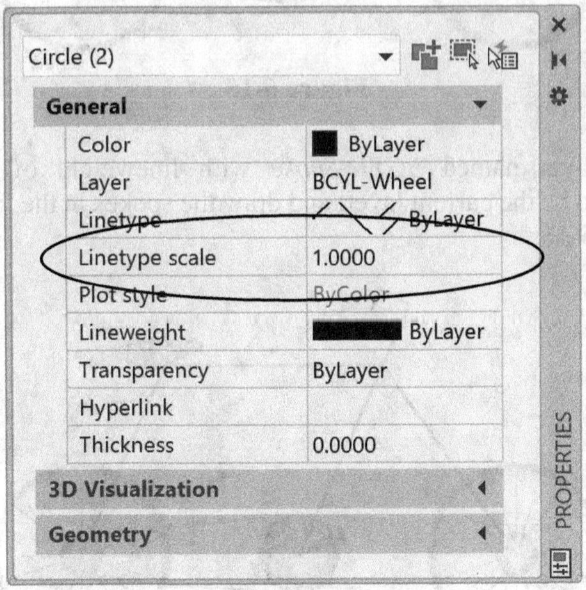

Figure 6-14b

- Note: In Figure 6-14c, the *Color*, *Linetype*, and *Lineweight* is set to “By Layer” option and the hatch's lineweight is set to 0.0.

Figure 6-14c

Now, create a layer named *BCYL_Basket*; make the *BCYL_Basket* layer to be the current layer; and draw the back basket as shown in Figure 6-15. If necessary, set the linetype scale.

Figure 6-15

Finally, create a layer named *BCYL_Spoke* with lineweight of 0.3mm; make the *BCYL_Spoke* layer to be the current layer; and draw the spokes in the front and rear wheels as shown in Figure 6-16.

Figure 6-16

Notes:

7. Blocks

7.1. Learning Objectives

After completing this chapter, the students will show proficiency in the following areas:

- Basics of a block
- Types of blocks
- Create and insert blocks
- Combine blocks
- The Design Center

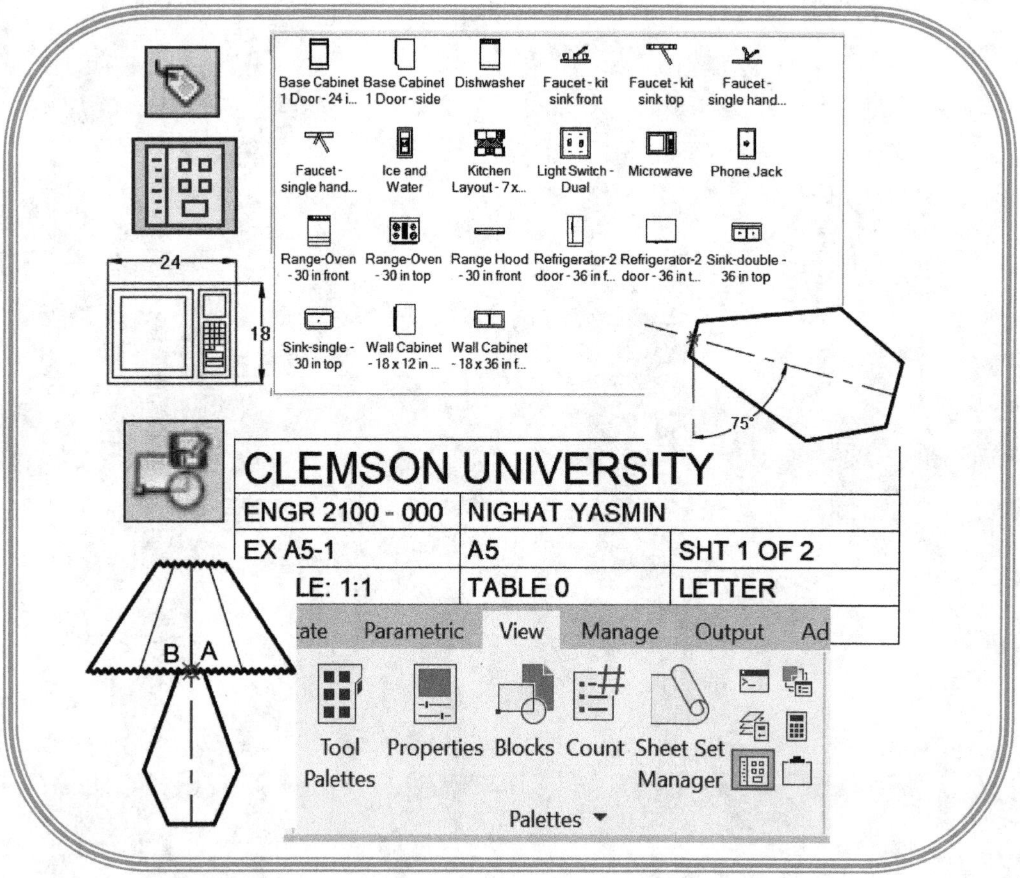

7.2. Introduction

In AutoCAD, block is a general term for one or more objects that are combined to create a single entity. That is, a block is a group of entities saved as a single unit. If an object (or group of objects) is used frequently, then time can be saved if the object is created once and used as many times as needed in the same or a different drawing. A Block can be categorized based on its availability or the nature of its contents as shown in Figure 7-1.

- **Availability:** A basic block is available for insertion only in the native file (that is, in the file in which it is created), the Wblocks (also known as write blocks) can be inserted in any AutoCAD's ".dwg" file, and the dynamic blocks can be updated in real time.
- **Contents:** A drawing block contains only the drawing objects (circle, line, polyline, etc.). A text block is composed of text objects. An attributes block is created using attributes (attributes are the sections of text added to a block that prompts the user to add information to the drawing). A miscellaneous block can contain any combination of drawing objects, texts, and attributes.

A drawing, text, attributes, or combination block can be saved as a basic or Wblock. This chapter discusses in detail the creation of basic and Wblock using drawing, text, and attributes and their insertion in native or other files.

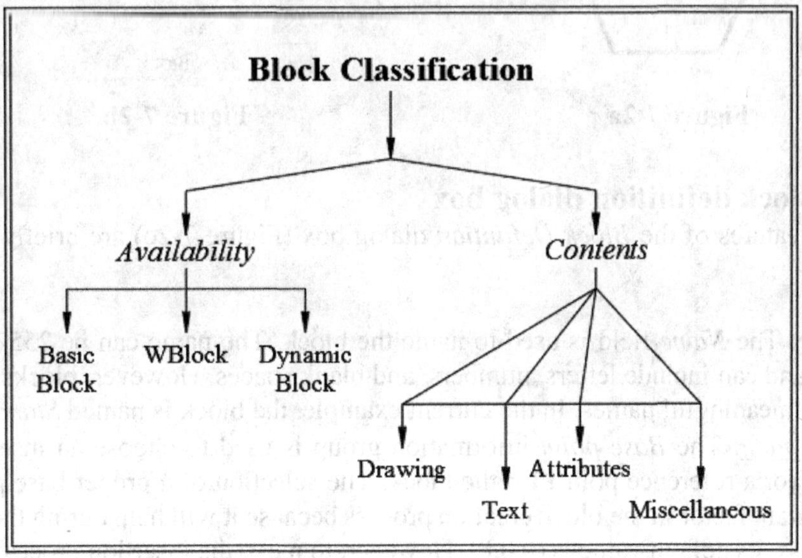

Figure 7-1

7.3. Basic Block

A basic block is a block that can be inserted only in the native drawing file. That is, it can be inserted only in the drawing file in which it was created. To follow a block creation process, draw the lamp stand shown in Figure 7-2a (the drawing units are in inches). The dimensions, point, and label *A* are added for illustration and are not necessary for the block creation process.

7.3.1. Create a basic block

- The *Make Block* command is activated using one of the following methods:
  1. Panel method: Either from the *Home* tab and *Block* panel select the *Create Block* ( ) tool, or from the *Insert* tab and *Block Definition* panel select the *Create Block* tool, Figure 7-2b.
  2. Command line method: Type "block," "Block," or "BLOCK" on the command line and press the *Enter* key.

- The activation of the command opens the *Block Definition* dialog box as shown in Figure 7-2c.

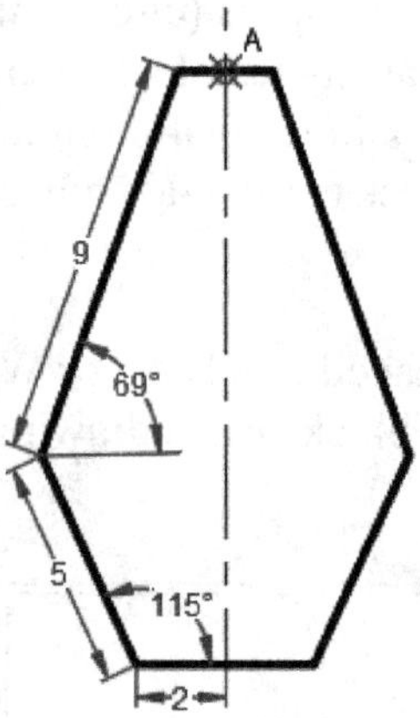

Figure 7-2a

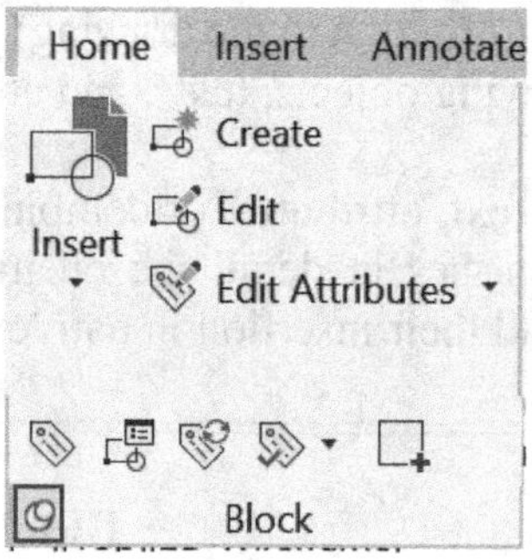

Figure 7-2b

7.3.2. Block definition dialog box

The main features of the *Block Definition* dialog box (Figure 7-2c) are briefly discussed here.

- Name: The *Name* field is used to name the block. The name can be 255 characters long and can include letters, numbers, and blank spaces. However, blocks should be given meaningful names. In the current example, the block is named *Stand.*
- Base point: The *Base point* information group is used to choose an insertion base point (or a reference point) for the block. The selection of a proper base point is an important factor in the block creation process because it will help during the insertion process. Its default value is (0,0,0). However, to make the insertion process efficient, select the base point on the object itself. In the current example, point '*A*' is selected to be the base point. The base point is selected using one of the following techniques.

  - ***Specify On-screen***: The selection of this box makes the other two options inactive. The prompts to specify the base point appear when the *Block Definition* dialog box is closed. In the current example, check this box.
  - ***Pick point***: In order to choose the base point using the pointing device: (i) click on the pointing device button ( ), this temporarily closes the dialog box and

allows the user to select a point; (ii) turn on the *object snap* option and click on the desired point. This reopens the dialog box. In the current example, point '*A*' is selected as the base point using the pointing device.

- ***X, Y, Z***: Specify the coordinates of the base point.

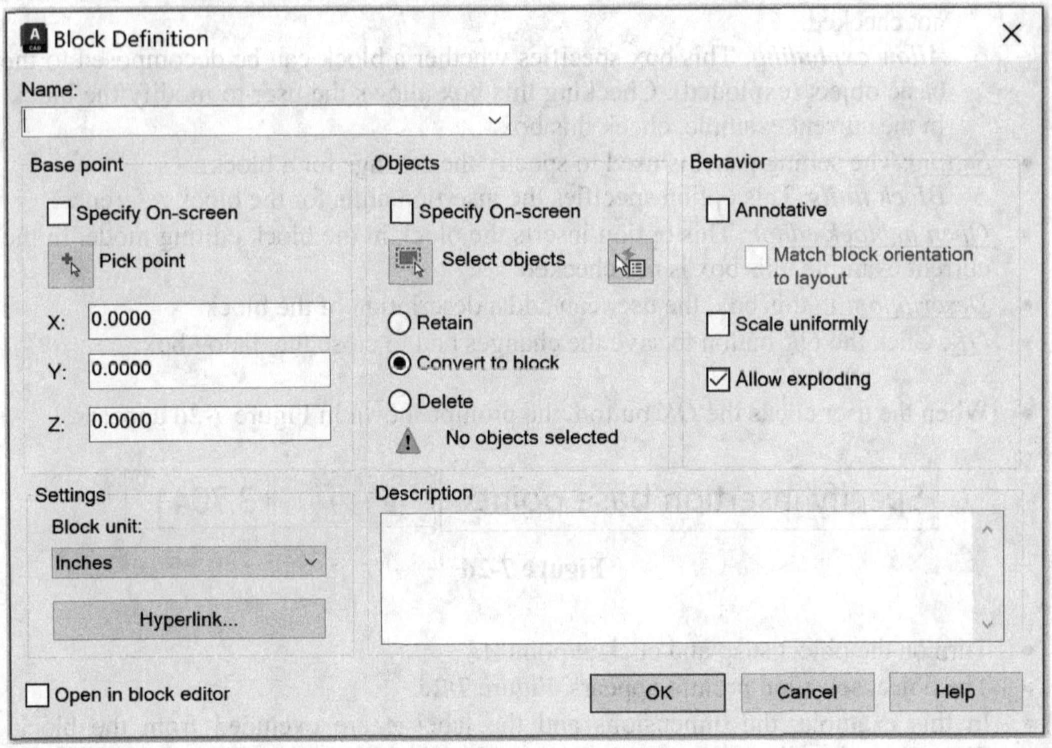

Figure 7-2c

- *Object*: The *Object* panel is used to select the objects to be included in the block.
  - ***Specify On-screen***: The selection of this box makes the other two options inactive. The prompts to select the object appear when the *Block Definition* dialog box is closed.
  - ***Select objects***: In the current example, this option is used. (i) Click on the object selection pointing device button (). This temporarily closes the dialog box and allows the user to select the objects. (ii) Select the objects using one of the object selection methods; this reopens the dialog box. In this example, the dimensions are excluded from the block.
  - ***Retain***: This option retains the selected objects as distinct objects in the drawing after the block is created.
  - ***Convert to block***: This option converts the selected objects to a block in the drawing after the block is created. In the current example, this option is used.
  - ***Delete***: This option deletes the selected objects from the drawing after the block is created.

- Behavior: The behavior panel is used to specify the behavior for a block.
    - ***Scale uniformly***: During the insertion process the user may want to (i) scale the object uniformly (same scale factors in *X*, *Y*, and *Z* direction) or (ii) use different scale factors in *X*, *Y*, and *Z* direction. Since a block can only be scaled uniformly from the second option, do not check this box. In the current example, this box is not checked.
    - ***Allow exploding***: This box specifies whether a block can be decomposed to the basic object (exploded). Checking this box allows the user to modify the block. In the current example, check this box.
- Setting: The setting panel is used to specify the settings for a block.
    - ***Block units***: This option specifies the insertion units for the block reference.
- Open in block editor: This option inserts the block in the block editing mode. In the current example, this box is not checked.
- Description: In this box, the user can add a description of the block.
- OK: Click the *OK* button to save the changes and to close the dialog box.

- When the user clicks the *OK* button, the prompt shown in Figure 7-2d appears.

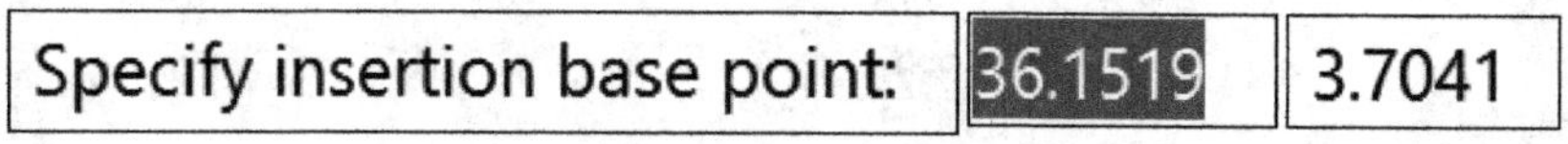

Figure 7-2d

- Turn on the object snap and click at point *A*.
- The object selection prompt appears, Figure 7-2e.
- In this example, the dimensions and the label *A* are excluded from the block. Therefore, the dimension layer is turned off. Select the objects as shown in Figure 7-2e.
- Either press the right button of the mouse or press the *Enter* key.
- This completes the basic block creation process.
- Click on the block; the block only has one grip point. The base point is the only grip point, Figure 7-2f.

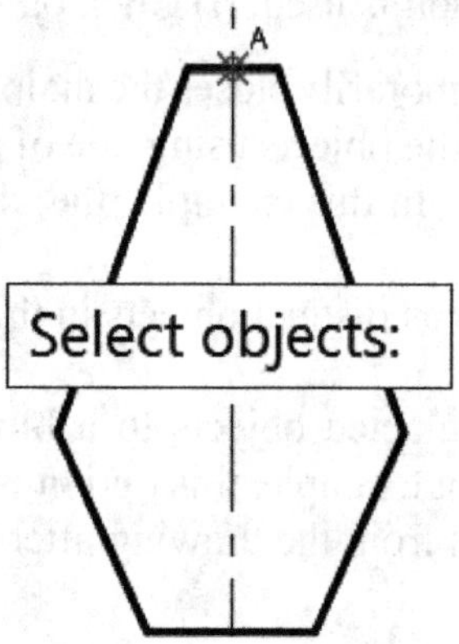

Figure 7-2e

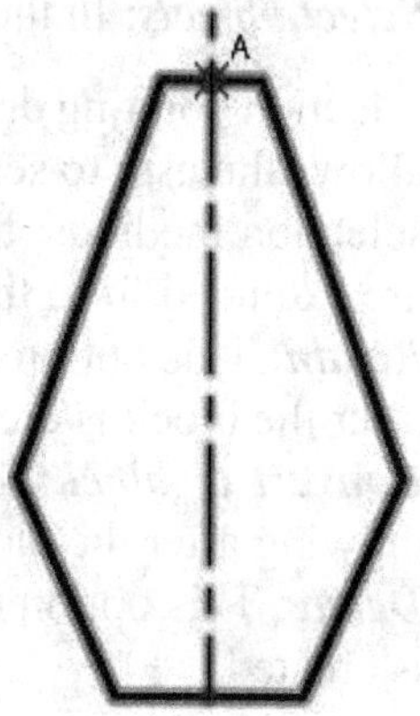

Figure 7-2f

7.4. Wblock

Wblocks (write blocks) are the blocks that can be inserted into any drawing. These blocks are saved as independent drawing files.

7.4.1. Create a Wblock

Create a basic block. This example uses the *Stand* block created in the basic block section.

- The *Wblock* command is activated using one of the following methods:
  1. Panel method: From the *Insert* tab and *Block Definition* panel select the *Write Block* (), Figure 7-3a.
  2. Command line method: Type "wblock," "WBlock," or "WBLOCK" on the command line and press the *Enter* key.

- The activation of the command opens the *Write Block* dialog box as shown in Figure 7-3b.

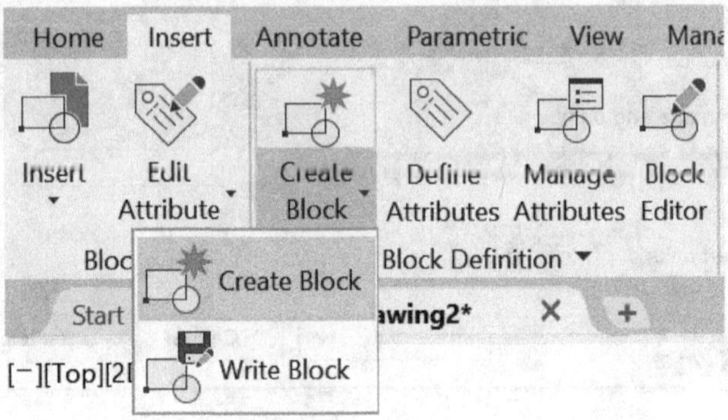

Figure 7-3a

7.4.2. Write block dialog box

In the *Write Block* dialog box, perform the following actions.

- <u>*Source*</u>: Select the *Block* option. The list of blocks (basic or Wblock) in the current file is available. Press the down-arrow to choose the block. Select the *Stand* block created in the basic block section.
- <u>*Base point*</u>: This option is deactivated if the *Block* option is selected in the *Source* panel.
- <u>*Object*</u>: This option is deactivated if the *Block* option is selected in the *Source* panel.
- <u>*Destination*</u>: Select the location to store the Wblock file by clicking the () destination button. This opens *Browse for Drawing File* dialog box, Figure 7-3c. Specify the location and click the *Save* button.
- <u>*OK*</u>: Now, click the *OK* button in the *Write Block* dialog box to save the changes.

- This will close the *Write Block* dialog box, and the *Wblock Preview* window shown in Figure 7-3d pops up for a very short time. This is the indication that the *Wblock* is created properly.

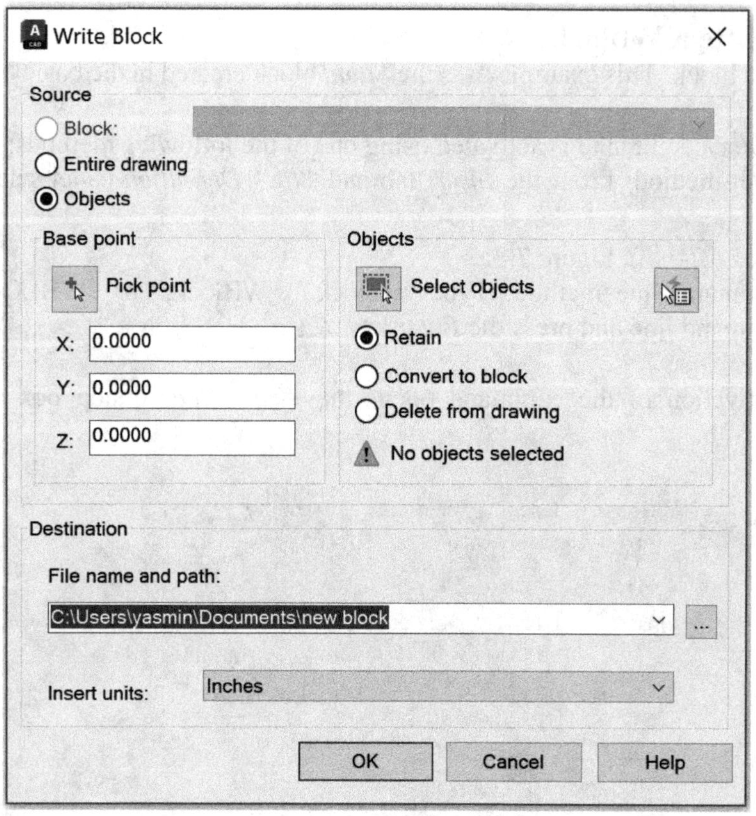

Figure 7-3b

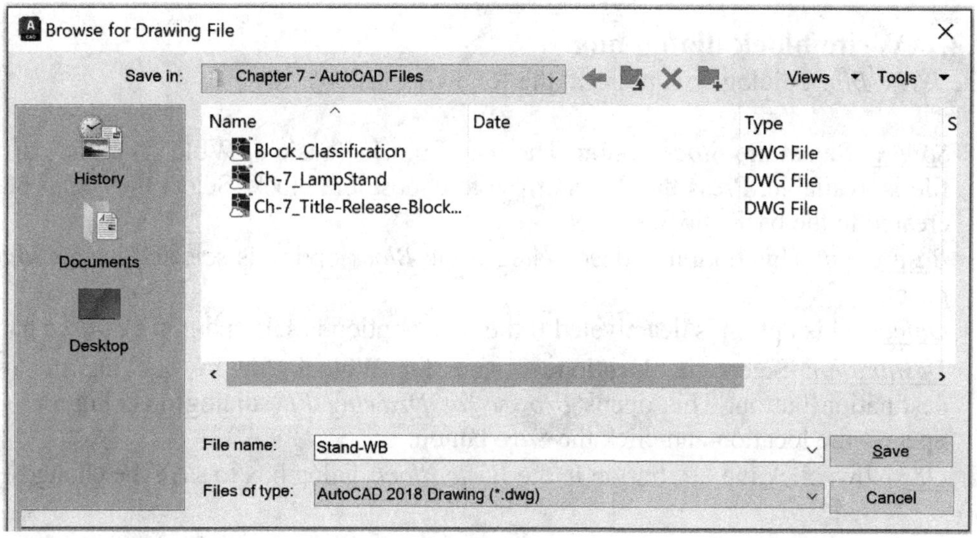

Figure 7-3c

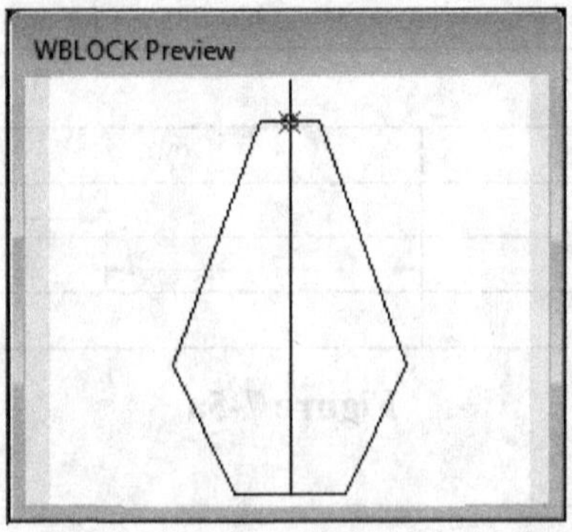

Figure 7-3d

7.5. Block With Attributes

Attributes are the sections of text added to a block that prompt the user to add information to the drawing. This section will create a title block with attributes shown in Figure 7-4. A title block's entries depend on a company and include the information to uniquely identify the drawing. The title block is generally located on the lower right corner of a drawing. The block created in this section is typically used in academic institutions.

CLEMSON UNIVERSITY		
ENGR 2100 - 000	NIGHAT YASMIN	
EX A5-1	A5	SHT 1 OF 2
SCALE: 1:1	TABLE 0	LETTER
05/05/2026	MILLIMETERS	

Figure 7-4

7.5.1. The initial setup

Before creating the attributes, create the initial setup for the title block.

- Open a new acadiso file.
- Create a layer and rename it to be *Title Block*; set the linetype to *Continuous* and lineweight to be *0.0mm*.
- Make the *Title Block* layer to be the current layer.
- Do not add the dimensions.
- Use the *Line* command to draw the lines shown in Figure 7-5a.
- Use the *Offset* command with the offset distance of 3 to create the thin lines (above or to the right of the existing lines) as shown in Figure 7-5b. The thin lines are created to locate the attributes.
- The start point of an attribute is the intersection of the thin lines. The thin lines are deleted after adding the attributes, that is, before creating the block.

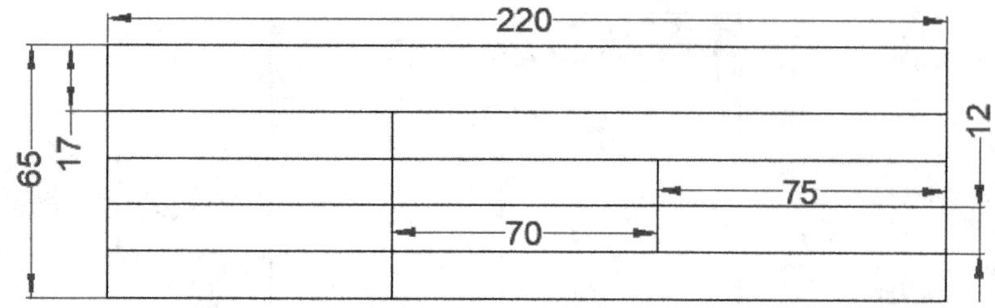

Figure 7-5a

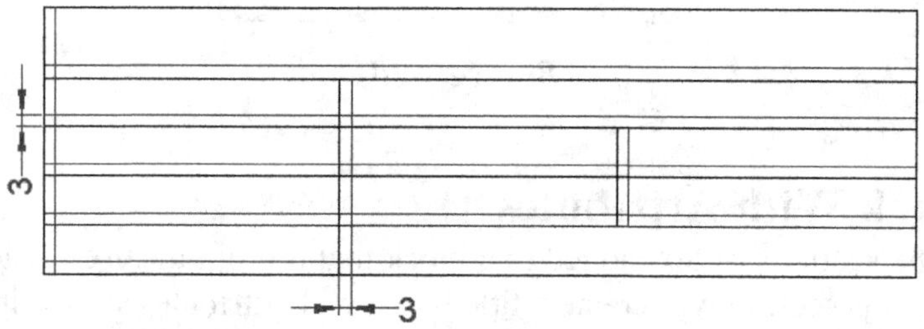

Figure 7-5b

An attribute is defined through the *Attribute Definition* dialog box, Figure 7-5c, and the dialog box is opened using one of the following methods:

1. Panel method: Either from the *Home* tab and expanded *Block* panel select the *Define Attributes* () tool, or from the *Insert* tab and *Block Definition* panel select the *Define Attributes* tool.
2. Command line method: Type "attdef," "Attdef," or "ATTDEF" on the command line and press the *Enter* key.

7.5.2. Attribute definition dialog box

The main features of the *Attribute Definition* dialog box (Figure 7-5c) are briefly discussed here.

- Mode: The *Mode* panel is used to set the options of attribute for inserting the attributes in the drawing.
  - o *Lock position*: This option allows for locking the position of the attribute within the block reference. In the current example, this box is checked.
- Insertion Point: The *Insertion Point* panel is used to set the location of an attribute in the drawing. The user can specify either the coordinates or pick the location in the drawing area. In the current example, the *Specify on-screen* box is checked because the drafter has defined the location of the attributes, the intersection of the thin lines.
- Align below previous attribute definition: If this box is checked then the second and subsequent attribute tags are placed directly below the previously defined attribute. This option is not available for the first attribute. In the current example, this option is not checked because the drafter has defined the location of the attributes, the intersection of the thin lines.

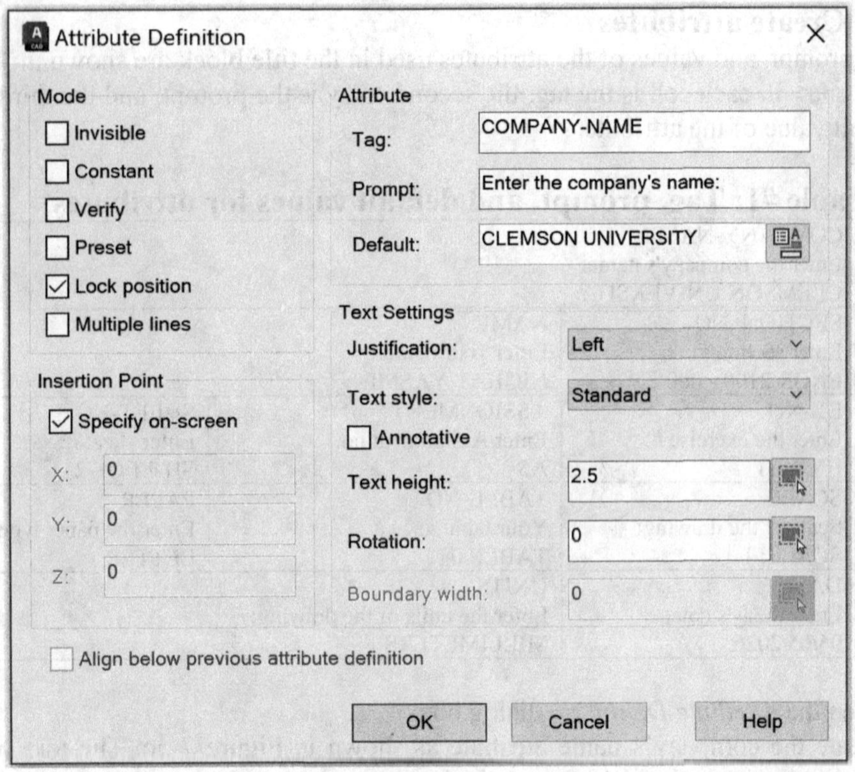

Figure 7-5c

- <u>*Attribute*</u>: The *Attribute* panel is used to set attribute data. An attribute has three components.
  - *Tag*: Tag is the name (one word with no space) of the attribute that identifies an attribute for filing and referencing purposes. The *Tag* field is used to enter the attribute's name using any combination of characters except spaces. Lowercase letters are changed to uppercase letters. If the tag field is left blank and the *OK* button is pressed, then the software displays an error message.
  - *Prompt*: The prompt is the message that is displayed when the block is inserted. The *Prompt* field is used to specify the prompt that is displayed when a block containing attribute is inserted. If the prompt field is left blank, then the tag is used as a prompt.
  - *Value*: The value is the information that is stored in an attribute. The *Value* field is used to specify the default attribute value. Although this field could be left blank, it is good drawing practice to specify a reasonable default value.

- <u>*Text Settings*</u>: The *Text* panel is used to set the justification, style, height, and rotation of the attribute's text.

7.5.3. Create attributes

The tag, prompt, and values of the attributes used in the title block are shown in Table #1. The first entry in each cell is the tag, the second entry is the prompt, and the third entry is the default value of the attribute.

Table #1: Tag, prompt, and default values for attributes

COMPANY-NAME Enter the company's name: CLEMSON UNIVERSITY		
SECTION_NO Enter section #: ENGR 2100 - 000	NAME Enter your name: NIGHAT YASMIN	
EX-NO Enter the exercise #: EX A5-1	ASSIGNMENT Enter Assignment no.: A5	SHEET-NO Enter sheet #: SHT 1 OF 2
SCALE Scale of the drawing: SCALE: 1:1	TABLE-NO. Your table #: TABLE 0	PAPER Enter the paper type: LETTER
DATE Enter today's date: 05/05/2026	UNITS Enter the units of the drawing: MILLIMETERS	

1. Open the *Attribute Definition* dialog box.
2. Create the company's name attribute as shown in Figure 7-5c. The text style and height are standard and 10, respectively.
3. Press the *Enter* key. This closes the *Define Attributes* dialog box.
4. The prompt to specify the start point of the attribute appears, Figure 7-6a.

Figure 7-6a

5. Click at the lower left corner of the thin lines intersection in the topmost cell, Figure 7-6b.

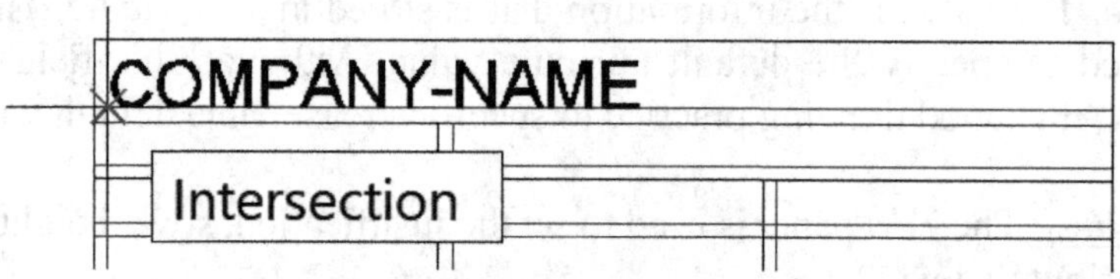

Figure 7-6b

6. Repeat steps #2 to #5 to create the remaining attributes. Set the text height to 6, Figure 7-6c.

7. The resulting title block is shown in Figure 7-6c.
8. Delete the thin lines, and the final version of the title block is shown in Figure 7-6d.

COMPANY-NAME		
SECTION_NO	NAME	
EX-NO	ASSIGNMENT	SHEET-NO
SCALE	TABLE-NO.	PAPER
DATE	UNITS	

Figure 7-6c

COMPANY-NAME		
SECTION_NO	NAME	
EX-NO	ASSIGNMENT	SHEET-NO
SCALE	TABLE-NO.	PAPER
DATE	UNITS	

Figure 7-6d

7.5.4. Create block with attributes

1. Activate the *Make Block* command to open the *Block Definition* dialog box.
2. Set the *Name* of the block to be the Title Block; choose the lower right corner of the block as the base point. Press the *OK* button.
3. This closes the *Block Definition* dialog box and opens the *Edit Attributes* dialog box, Figure 7-7b. This box can display at most eight attributes; therefore, use the *Next* button to see the remaining attributes.
4. Make any changes (if necessary) and press the *OK* button.
5. This closes the *Edit Attributes* dialog box. The block displays the default values of the various attributes, Figure 7-7a.

CLEMSON UNIVERSITY		
ENGR 2100 - 000	NIGHAT YASMIN	
EX A5-1	A5	SHT 1 OF 2
SCALE: 1:1	TABLE 0	LETTER
05/05/2026	MILLIMETERS	

Figure 7-7a

7.5.5. Convert to Wblock

The process to convert a block with attributes into a Wblock is identical to converting a basic block into a Wblock.

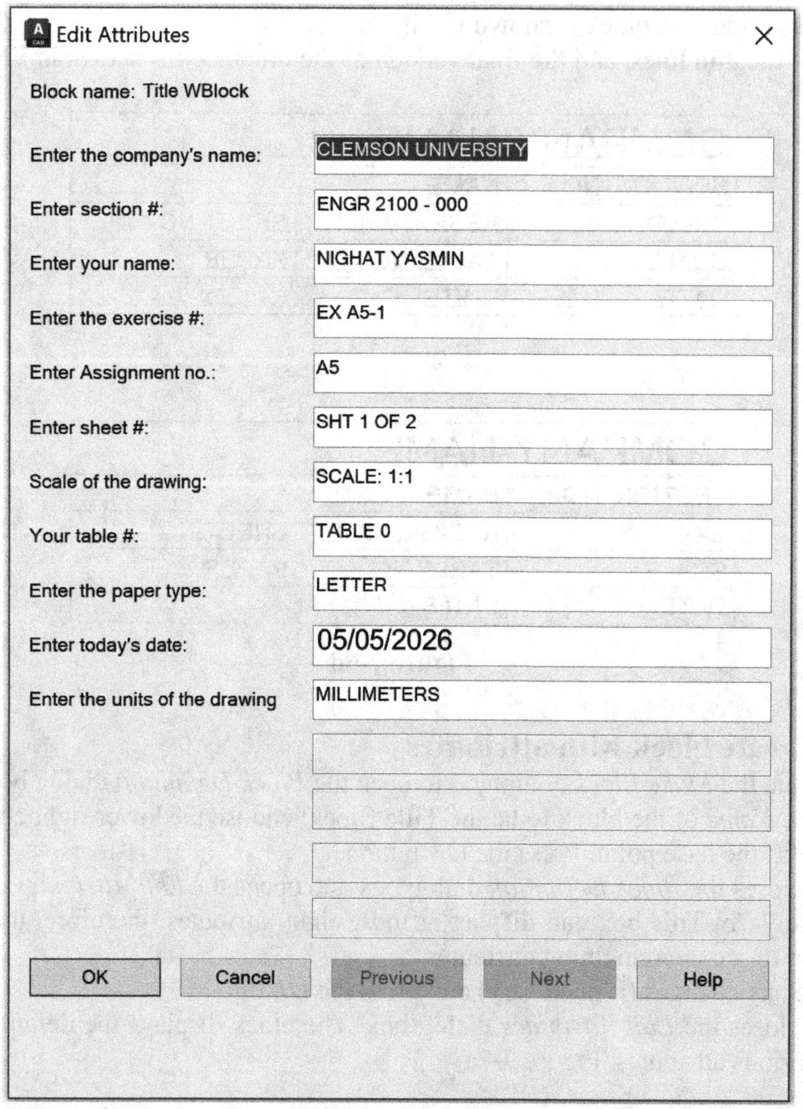

Figure 7-7b

7.6. Block With Text Boxes

This section will create a block that contains several text boxes. This example will create a release block. A release block contains a list of approval signatures or initials required before the drawing is released for the production. Create a release block as follows.

- Open a new acadiso file.
- Create a layer and rename it to be a *Release Block*; set the linetype to *Continuous* and lineweight to be *0.0mm*.
- Make the *Release Block* layer the current layer.
- Do not add the dimensions.
- Use the *Line* command to draw the lines shown in Figure 7-8a.

- Use the *Offset* command with the offset distance of 3 to create the thin lines (above or to the right of the existing lines) as shown in Figure 7-8a. The thin lines are created to place the texts.

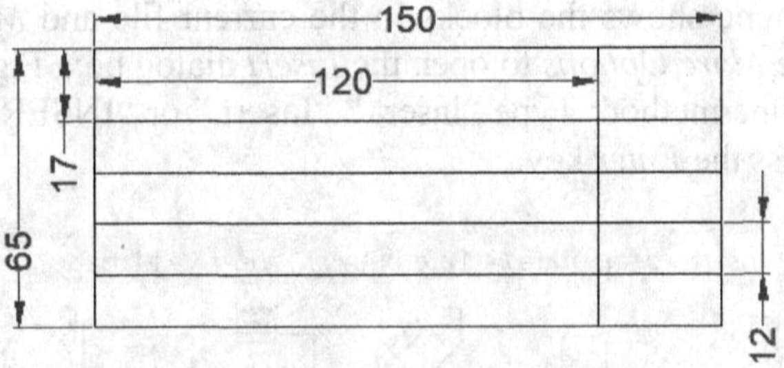

Figure 7-8a

- Use the *Text* command to create the text shown in Figure 7-8b. Select the font type as Arial and the text height as 10 for the team manager and 6 for the others.

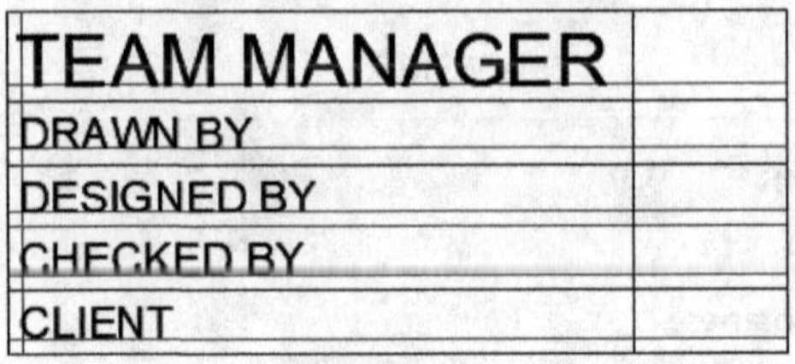

Figure 7-8b

- Remove the thin lines, Figure 7-8c.
- Create a basic block, set the *Name* of the block to be the Release Block, and choose the lower right corner of the block as the base point.
- Convert it to a Wblock.

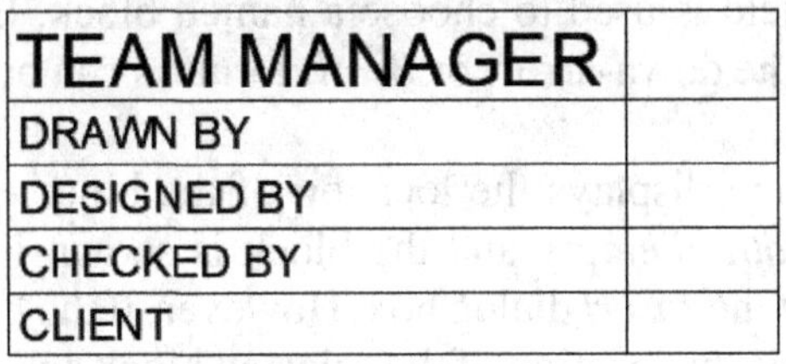

Figure 7-8c

7.7. Basic Block Insertion

The basic block, *Stand*, created earlier is used to demonstrate the block insertion process. The blocks are inserted using the *Insert Block* command.

- The *Insert Block* command is activated using one of the following methods:

1. Panel method: Either from the *Home* tab and *Block* panel, select the *Insert Block* tool, Figure 7-9a; or from the *Insert* tab and *Block* panel, select the *Insert Block* tool. If one or more blocks are available to insert in the current file, then the activation of the command expands the drop-down menu, Figure 7-9a. The expanded menu shows the blocks in the current file and *More Options* option. Click on the *More Options* to open the *Insert* dialog box, Figure 7-9b.
2. Command line method: Type "insert," "Insert," or "INSERT" on the command line and press the *Enter* key.

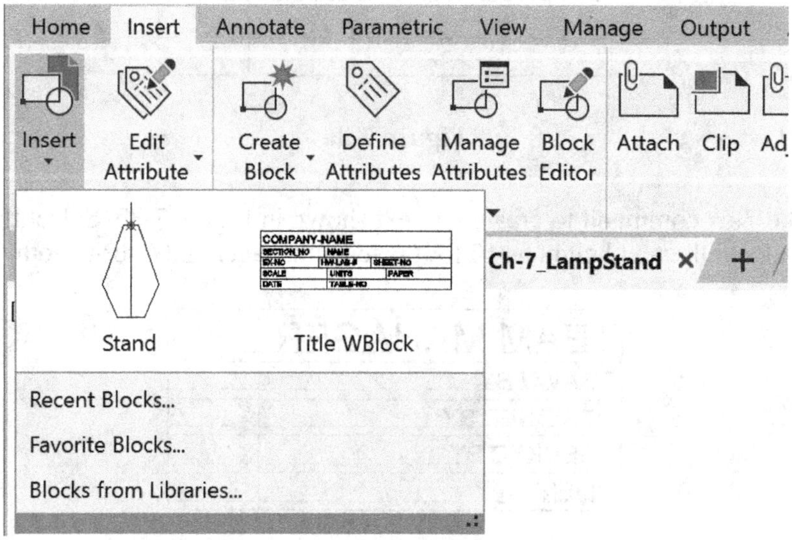

Figure 7-9a

7.7.1. Insert dialog box

The activation of the *Insert Block* command opens the *Insert* dialog box shown in Figure 7-9b. The main features of the *Insert* dialog box are briefly discussed here.

- *Name*: The *Name* field is used to choose a named block. By default, it displays the block just created. The down-arrow or *Browse* button can be used to choose any other block.
- *Path*: The *Path* option displays the location of the block. If the selected block is a basic block, then *Path* is empty and the block is shown in the preview area in the upper right corner of the *Insert* dialog box. However, if the block is saved as a Wblock then the *Path* displays the location of the selected block and the preview area is blank, Figure 7-9b.

- *Insertion point*: This panel is used to specify the insertion point in the drawing for the block.
    - o *Specify On-screen*: Check this box to choose the insertion point using the pointing device.
    - o *X, Y, Z*: These boxes are used to set the coordinate values. If the *Specify On-screen* option is selected, then these boxes are not available.

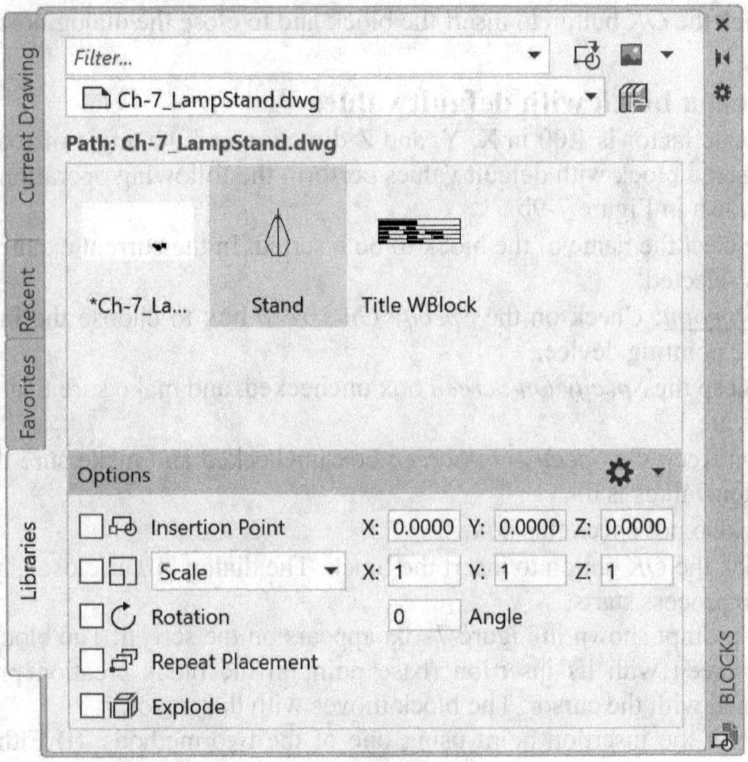

Figure 7-9b

- Scale: This panel is used to specify the scale for the inserted block. The negative value for the X, Y, and Z scale factors inserts a mirror image of the block.
    - *Specify On-screen*: Check this box to specify scale factors during the insertion process using the pointing device.
    - *X, Y, Z*: These boxes are used to set the scale factors in the respective directions. If the *Specify On-screen* option is selected, then these boxes are not available.
    - *Uniform Scale*: This box is checked to specify a single scale value for the *X*, *Y*, and *Z* coordinates. In this case, the *Y* and *Z* fields are deactivated by the software and the value specified for X is displayed in the *Y* and *Z* fields, too.

- Rotation: This panel is used to specify the rotation angle for the inserted block.
    - *Specify On-screen*: Check this box to specify the angle during the insertion process using the pointing device.
    - *Angle*: Specify the value of the rotation in the dialog box.
- Block Unit: This panel is used to display the information regarding the inserted block. The user cannot control the content of this panel.
    - *Unit*: Displays the unit's value for the inserted block.
    - *Factors*: Displays the unit scale factor, which is calculated based on the units used in the block creation and the drawing units.

- Explode: If this box is checked, then the block is exploded and its parts are inserted as individual objects. Generally, this box is not checked.

- *OK*: Click the *OK* button to insert the block and to close the dialog box.

7.7.2. Insert a block with default values

The default scale factor is 1.00 in X, Y, and Z direction and the angle of rotation is zero. In order to insert a block with default values perform the following operation. The default options are shown in Figure 7-9b.

- *Name*: Select the name of the block to be inserted. In the current example, the *Stand* block is selected.
- *Insertion point*: Check on the *Specify On-screen* box to choose the insertion point using the pointing device.
- *Scale*: Keep the *Specify On-Screen* box unchecked, and make sure that the *X*, *Y*, and *Z* values are 1.
- *Rotation*: Keep the *Specify On-Screen* box unchecked and make sure that the angle of rotation values is 0.
- *Explode*: Do not check this box.
- *OK*: Click the *OK* button to insert the block. The dialog box is closed, and the block insertion process starts.
    - The prompt shown in Figure 7-10a appears on the screen. The block appears on the screen with its insertion (base point in the block creation process) point aligned with the cursor. The block moves with the cursor.
    - Specify the insertion point using one of the two methods. (i) Either move the cursor to the desired location and press the left button of the mouse. Or (ii) type the values of the x and y coordinates of the insertion point and press the *Enter* key.

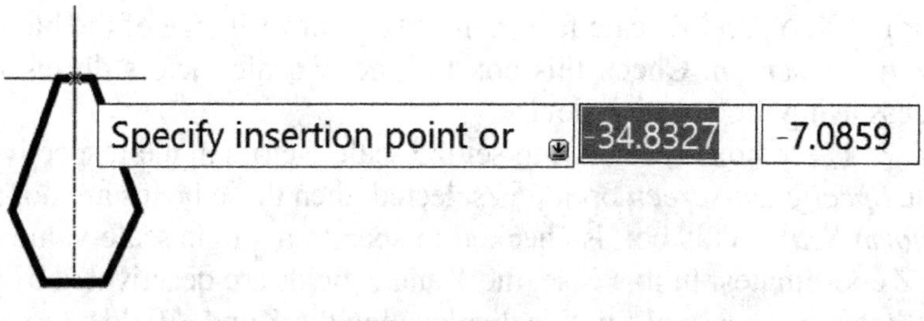

Figure 7-10a

- The block shown in Figure 7-10b appears on the screen. Recall that the dimensions are not selected as a part of the block.

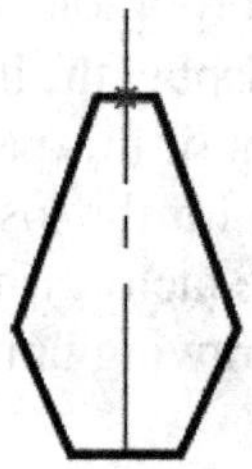

Figure 7-10b

7.7.3. Change the scale of the block at the insertion

Figure 7-11c shows the effect of changes in the scale factors. Activate the *Insert Block* command.

- Name: Select the name of the block to be inserted. In the current example, the *Stand* block is selected.
- Insertion point: Check the *Specify On-screen* box to choose the insertion point using the pointing device.
- Scale: Check the *Specify On-Screen* box.
- Rotation: Keep the *Specify On-Screen* box unchecked and make sure that the angle of rotation values is 0.
- Explode: Do not check this box.
- OK: Click the *OK* button to insert the block. The dialog box will be closed, and the block insertion process will start.
  - The prompt to specify the insertion point appears on the screen.
  - Specify the insertion point.
  - The prompt to specify the scale factor appears on the screen, Figure 7-11a. Specify the *X* scale factor and press the *Enter* key. In the current example, the scale factor is 2.
  - The prompt to specify the *Y* scale factor appears on the screen, Figure 7-11b. Specify the Y scale factor and press the *Enter* key. In the current example, the scale factor is 0.5.
  - The block is inserted at the specified insertion point and at the specified scale factor, Figure 7-11c.

Figure 7-11a

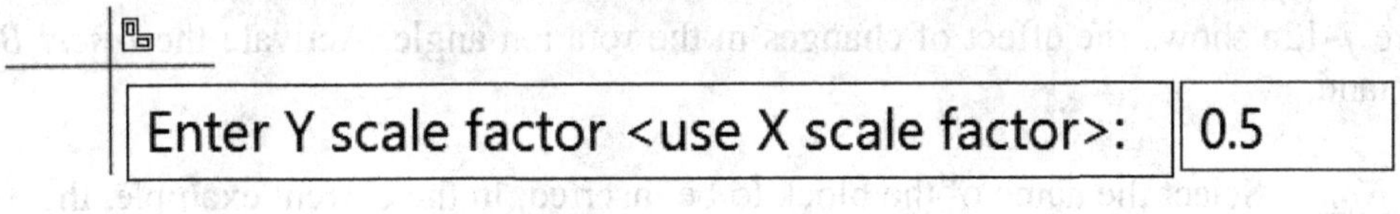

Figure 7-11b

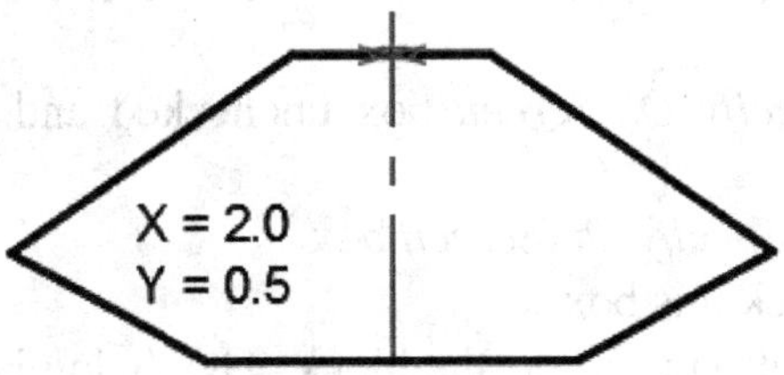

Figure 7-11c

- Repeat the process with the following changes: (i) in the *Scale* panel, do not check the *Specify On-Screen* box; (ii) type the values (1,0, 1.0,1.0) for the (x, y, z) fields. The representations are shown in Figure 7-11d.
- Repeat the process with the following changes: (i) in the *Scale* panel, do not check the *Specify On-Screen* box; (ii) type the values (0.5, 2.0,1.0) for the (x, y, z) fields. The representations are shown in Figure 7-11e.

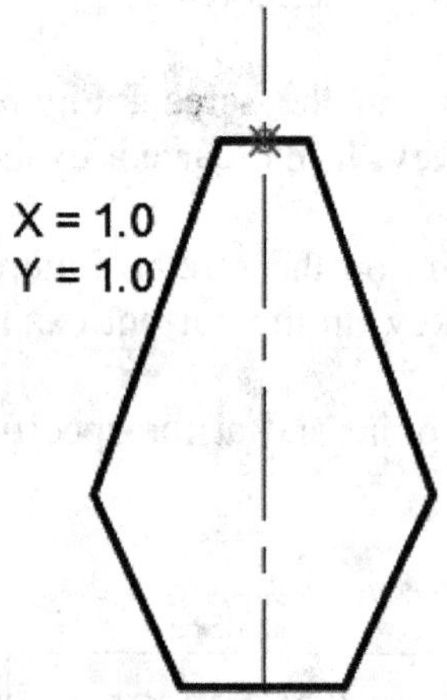

Figure 7-11d

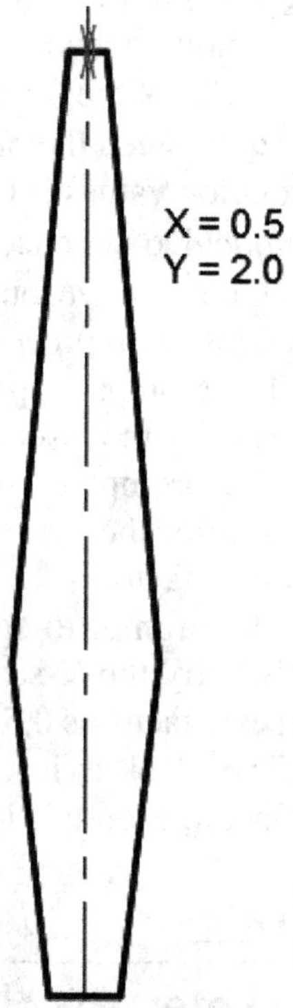

Figure 7-11e

7.7.4. Rotate the block at the insertion

Figure 7-12a shows the effect of changes in the rotation angle. Activate the *Insert Block* command.

- Name: Select the name of the block to be inserted. In the current example, the *Stand* block is selected.
- Insertion point: Check the *Specify On-screen* box to choose the insertion point using the pointing device.
- Scale: Keep the *Specify On-Screen* box unchecked and make sure that the scale factors value is 1.
- Rotation: Check the *Specify On-Screen* box.
- Explode: Do not check this box.
- OK: Click the *OK* button to insert the block. The dialog box will be closed, and the block insertion process will start.

- o The prompt to specify the insertion point will appear on the screen; specify the insertion point.
- o The prompt to specify the rotation angle will appear on the screen; specify the angle and press the *Enter* key, Figure 7-12a. In the example, the angle is 75.
- o The block will be inserted at the specified insertion point and rotated at the specified angle, Figure 7-12b.

- Repeat the process with the following changes: (i) in the *Scale* panel, do not check the *Specify On-Screen* box and keep the default scale; (ii) in the *Rotation* panel, check the *Specify On-Screen* box and type -75 in the *Angle* field; figure not shown.

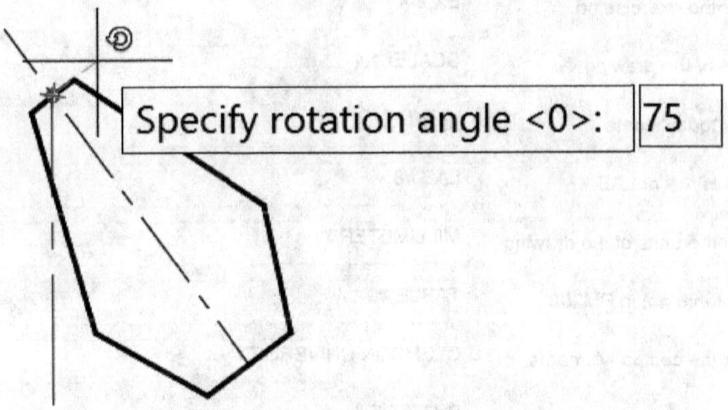

Figure 7-12a

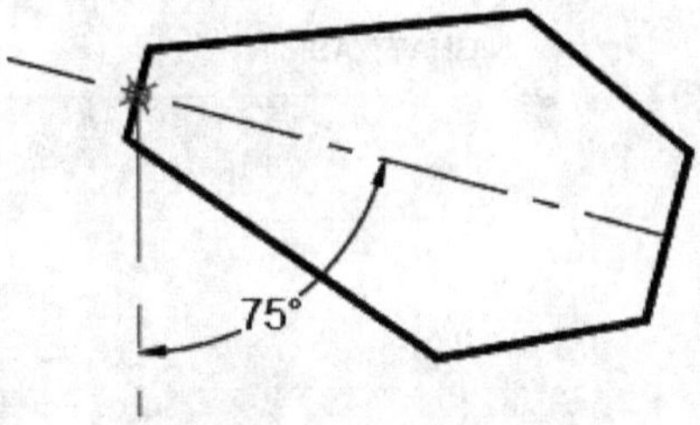

Figure 7-12b

7.7.5. Insert a Wblock

The insertion process of a Wblock is similar to the insertion process of a basic block. In the *Name* field of the *Insert* dialog box, use the browse button to load the Wblock created and saved earlier. Furthermore, the Wblocks can be combined or exploded in a manner similar to a basic block.

7.7.6. Insert a block with attributes

1. Activate the *Insert Block* command to open the *Insert* dialog box.
2. Choose the *Title Block* and set the various options as discussed earlier. Press the *OK* button.
3. Specify the insertion point.
4. The *Edit Attributes* dialog box appears on the screen, Figure 7-13.

5. If necessary, change the value of the data field. This box can display at most fifteen attributes; therefore, use the *Next* button to see the remaining attributes.
6. Press the *OK* button to close the box. The *Title Block* appears with the specified value.

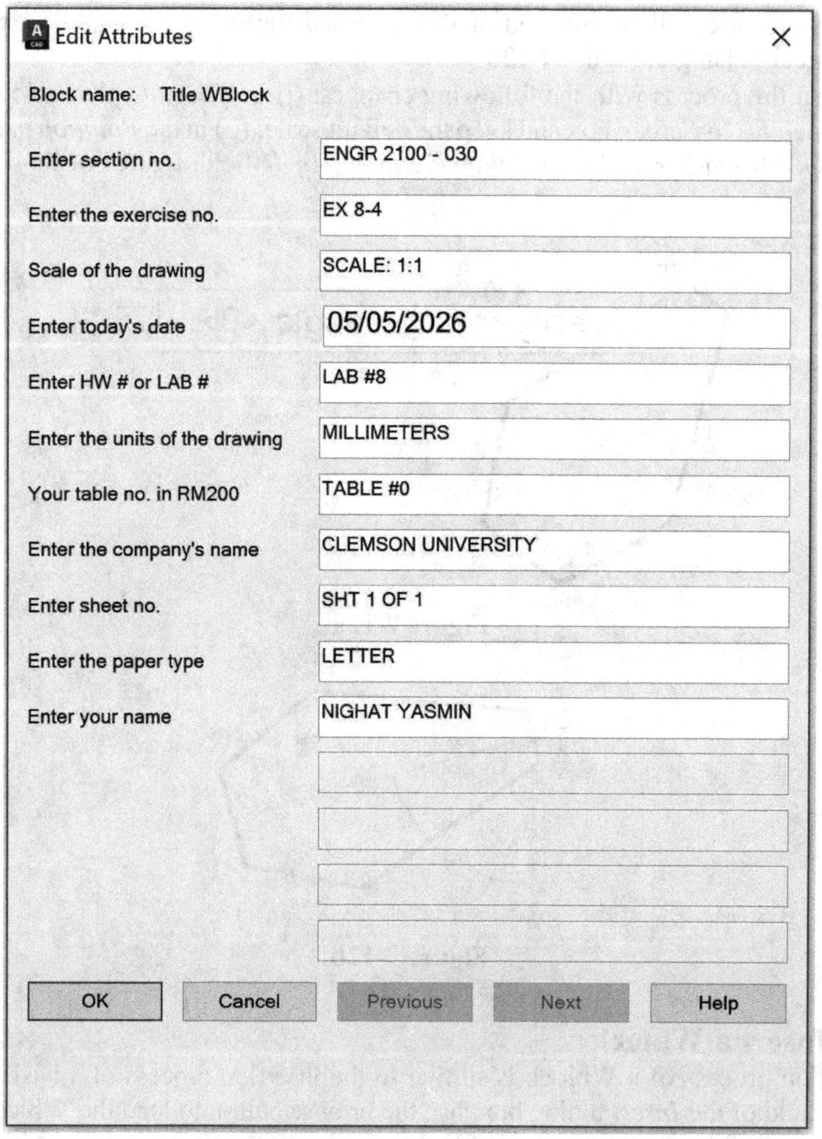

Figure 7-13

7.7.7. Insert a block with text boxes

The insertion process of a block with the text boxes is similar to the insertion process of a basic block. In the *Name* field of the *Insert* dialog box, use the browse button to load the respective block created and saved earlier. Furthermore, a block with the text boxes can be combined or exploded in a manner similar to a basic block.

7.8. Combine Blocks

Complicated shaped objects can be created by inserting different blocks at the desired locations. Figure 7-14c shows a lamp created by combining a *Stand* and a *Shade* block.

Blocks can be combined as follows.

- Create the *Stand* block with point *A* selected as the base point, Figure 7-14a.
- Create the *Shade* block with point *B* selected as the base point, Figure 7-14b.
- Insert the *Stand* block with desired scale factors.
- Insert the *Shade* block on top of the *Stand* block with the desired scale factors, Figure 7-14c. Points A and B should overlap.

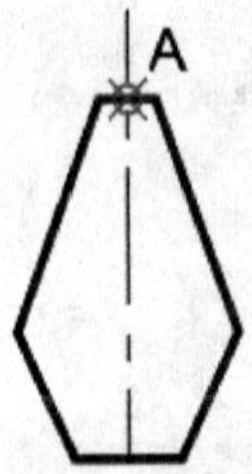

Figure 7-14a

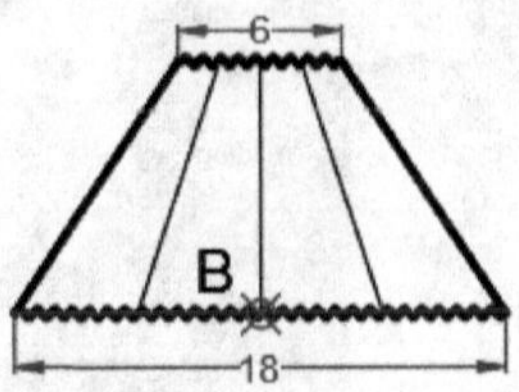

Figure 7-14b

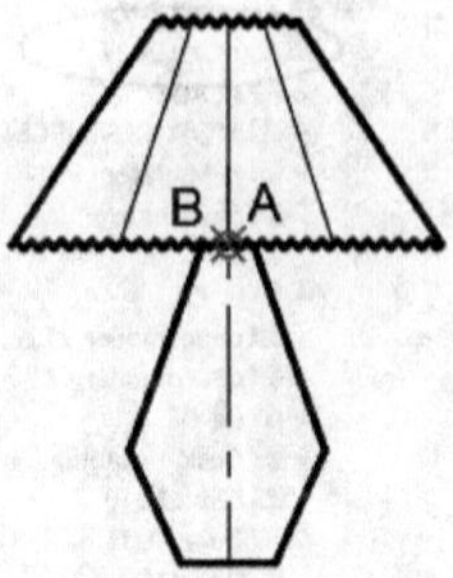

Figure 7-14c

7.9. Modify Block

In some situations, a user of the block is required to modify the block. Figure 7-15 shows the modification of *Shade* block's top and bottom rims (remove the zig-zag linetype). The process is given as:

- Create the lamp (Figure 7-14c) and it becomes part of the current drawing.
- From the Home tab and *Modify* toolbar, use the *Explode* command to explode the block.
- Edit the block as desired; that is, change the linetype of the top and bottom rims.
- If the new shape is used frequently then save it as *Lamp* block (a new block).

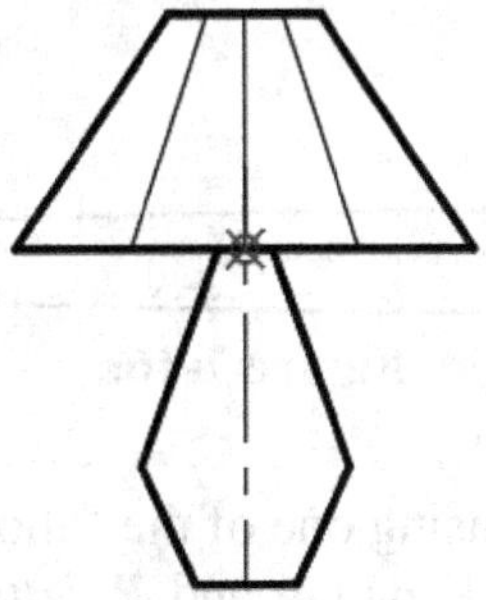

Figure 7-15

7.10. Design Center

AutoCAD provides a *Design Center* (Figure 7-16a), a blocks and symbols library. The *Design Center* is the collection of blocks and symbols that can be inserted in both ANSI and ISO files.

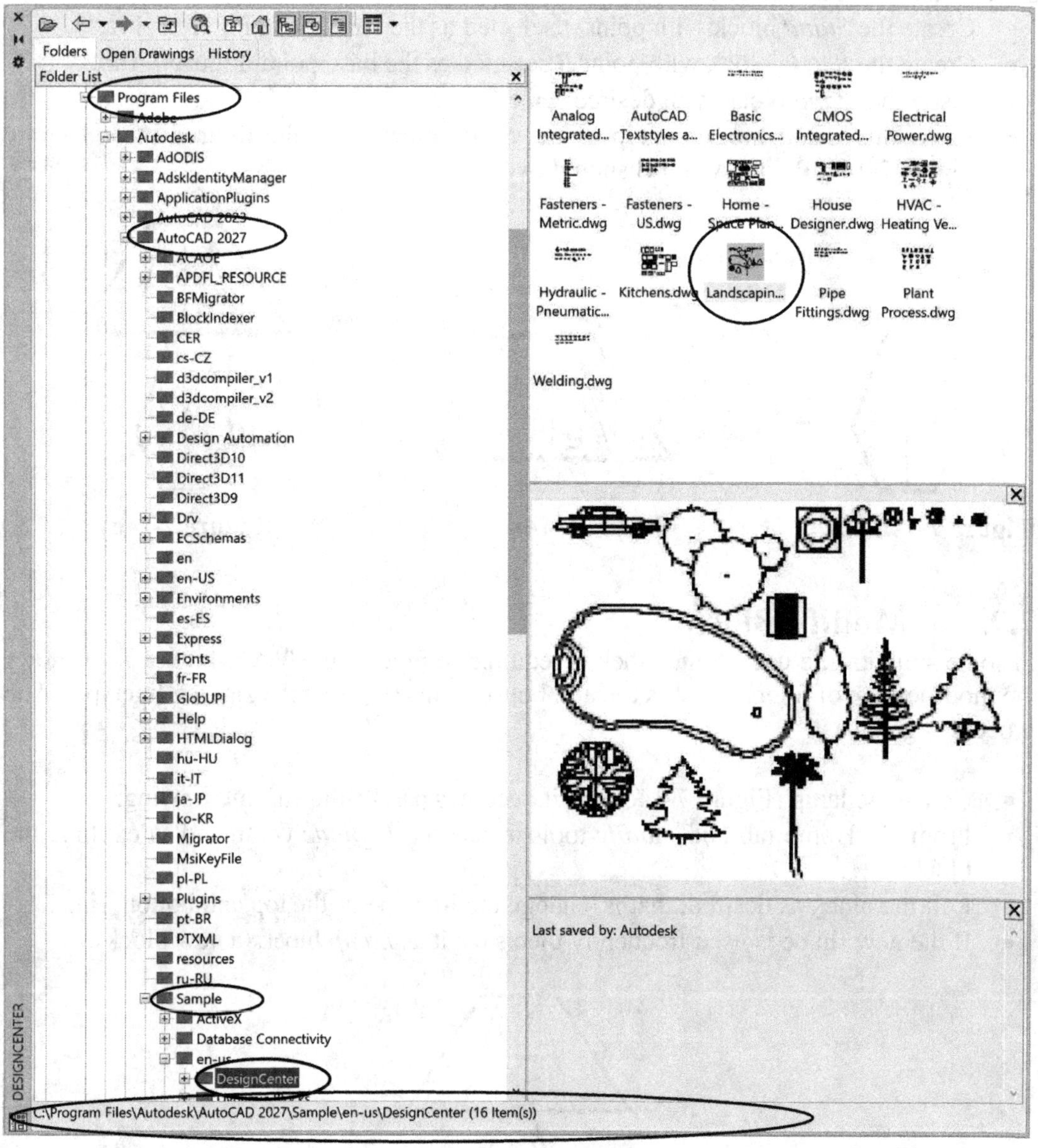

Figure 7-16a

The *Design Center* can be opened using one of the following methods:

1. Panel method: From the *View* tab and *Palettes* panel select the *Design Center* tool, Figure 7-16b.
2. Command line method: Type "adCenter," "Adcenter," or "ADCENTER" on the command line and press the *Enter* key.

3. Hold the *Ctrl* key and press the '*2*' key.
4. Open the *Design Center* option by expanding *Program File* → *Autodesk* → *AutoCAD 2027* → *Sample* → *en-us* → *Design Center*, Figure 7-17a. The path is also shown on the lower edge of the dialog box, Figure 7-17b.

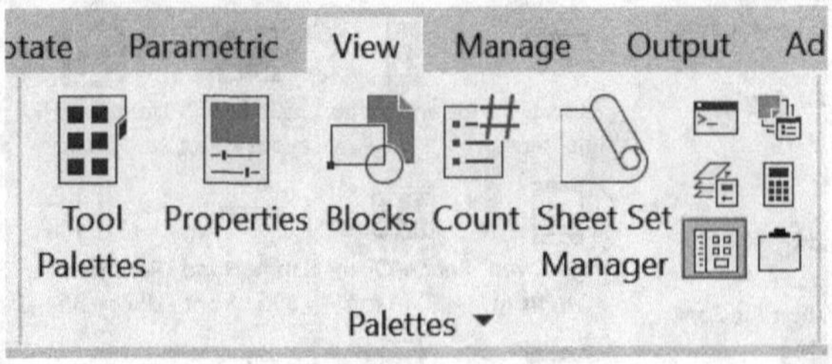

Figure 7-16b

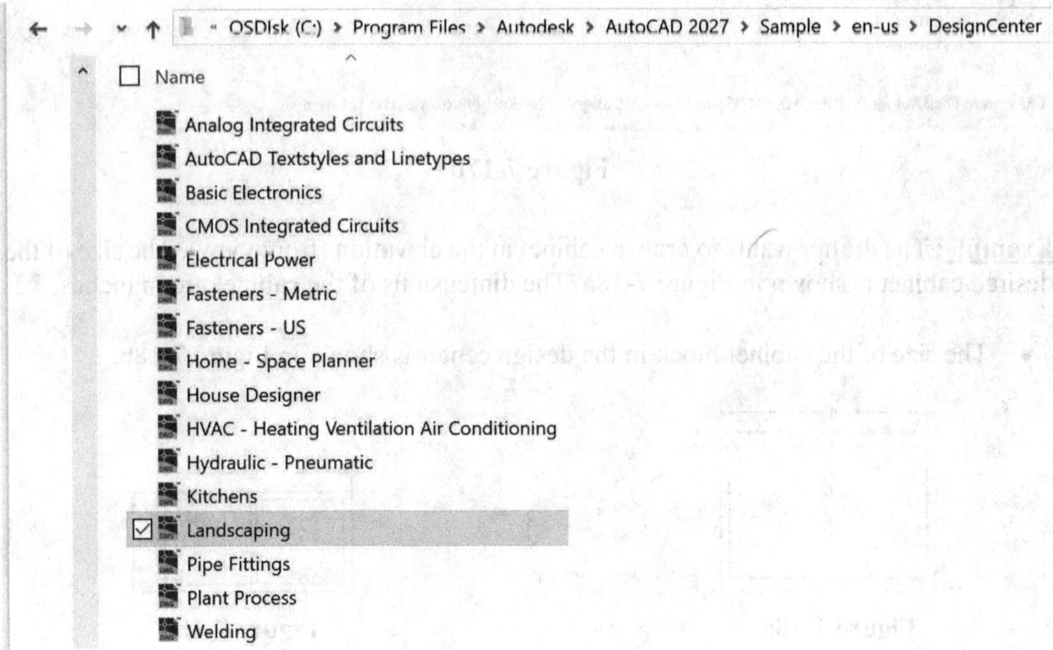

Figure 7-17a

- The remainder of this section explains how to insert a block from the *Kitchens.dwg* of the *Design Center*.
- Expand the *Design Center* and select the *Kitchens.dwg*, Figure 7-17b.
- Either click on the *Blocks* in the left column or double click on the *Blocks* in the preview window; the content of the drawing appears in the preview window, Figure 7-17b. The figure displays the available blocks under the *Kitchen.dwg* file.

7.10.1. Insert a block (known dimension) 

This section explains how to insert a block from the *Design Center* whose dimensions are known by explaining the insertion process of the "*Wall Cabinet 18 X 36 in front*" block.

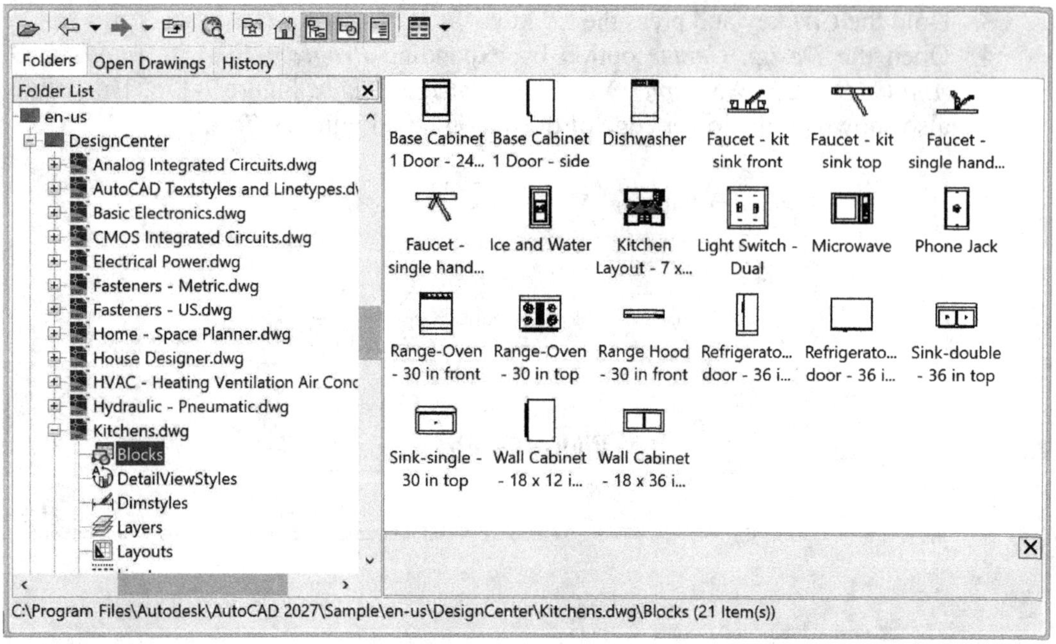

Figure 7-17b

Example: The drafter wants to draw a cabinet in the elevation (front view). The size of the desired cabinet is shown in Figure 7-18a. The dimensions of the cabinet are in inches.

- The size of the cabinet block in the design center is shown in Figure 7-18b.

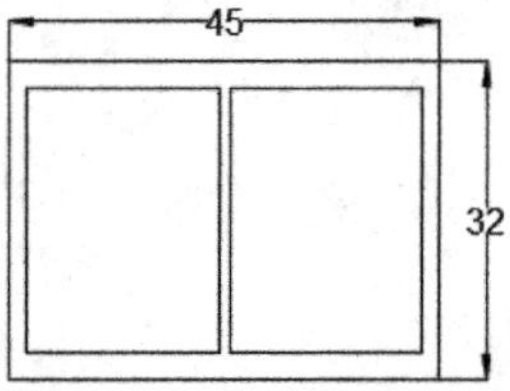

Figure 7-18a

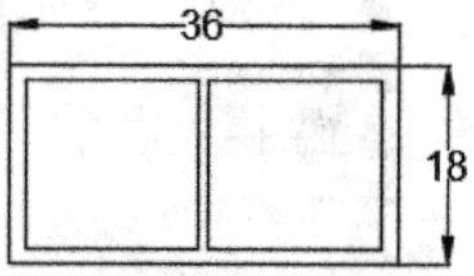

Figure 7-18b

- Insert the cabinet as follows (Figure 7-18c). (i) Click with the left button of the mouse on the cabinet; this highlights the cabinet icon and displays it in the preview window. (ii) Press the right button of the mouse. (iii) Click on the *Insert Block* option. The Insert block dialog box appears on the screen. (iv) Follow the procedure to insert a block.
- In this example, the desired size is different than the actual size. Hence, the cabinet must be scaled before the insertion. The scale factor is calculated as:

  Scale factor = (Desired size) / (Actual size in the *Design Center*)

  Therefore,

  X-Scale factor = 45 / 36

  Y-Scale factor = 32 / 18 and

  Z-Scale factor = 1

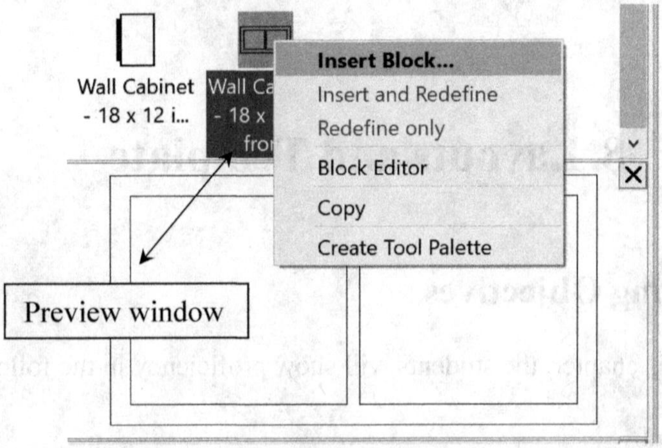

Figure 7-18c

7.10.2. Insert a block (unknown dimension)

This section explains how to insert a block from the *Design Center* whose dimensions are unknown by explaining the insertion process of the "*Microwave*" block.

Example: The drafter wants to draw a microwave in the elevation (front view). The size of the desired microwave is shown in Figure 7-19a. The dimensions of the microwave are in inches.

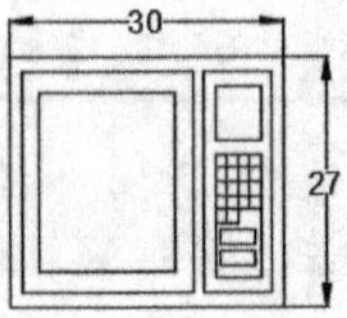

Figure 7-19a

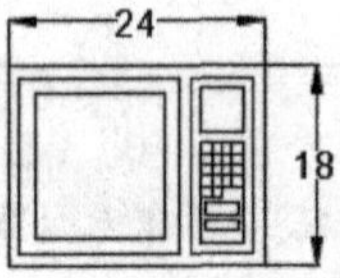

Figure 7-19b

- The microwave's block in the Design Center does not contain any dimension. Therefore, the first step is to find out the block size.
- To find the block size, (i) insert the block in question at the scale factor of 1.0 in X-, Y-, and Z-directions and Angle = 0, and (ii) add the dimensions to the block. Figure 7-19b shows the trial block.

- Now insert the microwave block at the desired location and the desired scale factor.

  Scale factor = (Desired size) / (Actual size in the *Design Center*)

  Therefore,

  X-Scale factor = 30 / 24

  Y-Scale factor = 27 / 18 and

  Z-Scale factor = 1

- Finally, delete the trial block and its dimensions.

Notes:

8. Layouts and Template

8.1. Learning Objectives

After completing this chapter, the students will show proficiency in the following areas:

- Basics of layouts
- Layout manipulation (add, delete, rename, and move)
- Layouts and viewports
- Layers in layouts
- Template files
- Scale list
- Viewport scaling
- Plotting from a layout

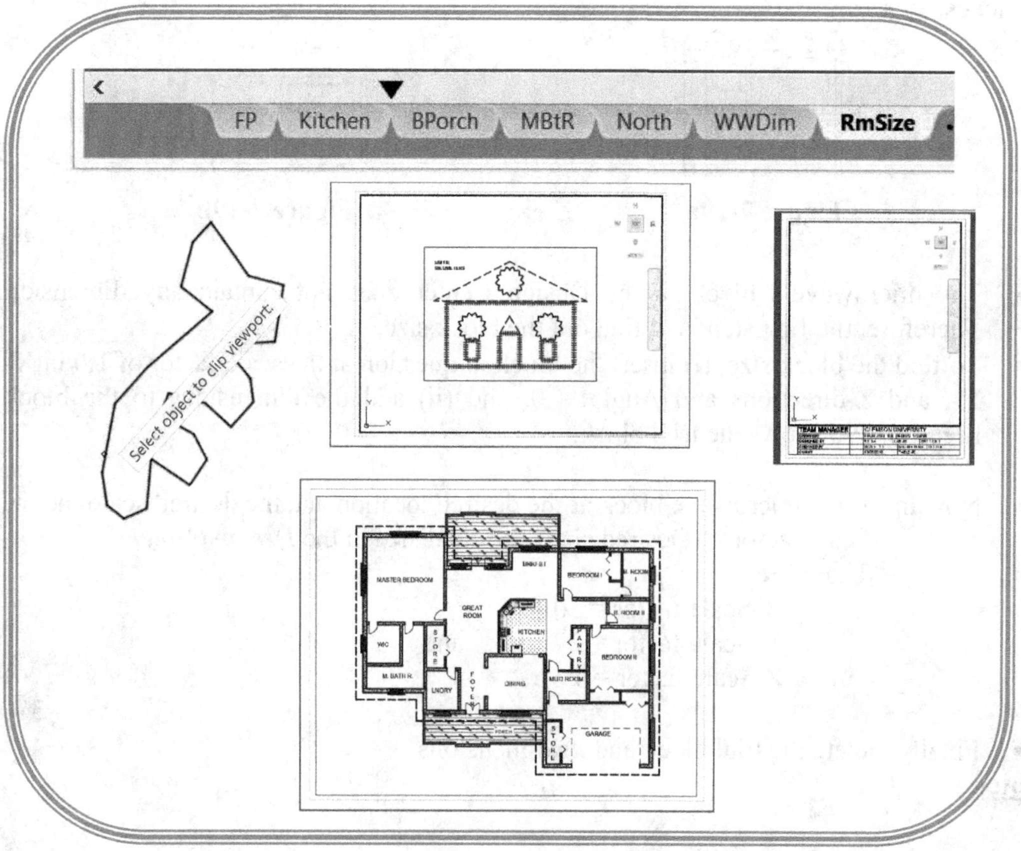

8.1. Introduction

In AutoCAD, paper space is a drawing environment mainly used for printing or plotting the drawing. The paper space is accessed through the layouts, and the layout's viewports allow users to create different views of the Model space. New layouts can be created, and existing layouts can be modified. This chapter explains the usage and advantages of layouts. Furthermore, this chapter creates template files using layouts and the title and release blocks created in the previous chapter.

8.2. Layout

Generally, layouts are used for printing or plotting the drawing. By default, AutoCAD creates two layouts. The user can switch to a layout by selecting the *Layout1* or *Layout2* tab, respectively, from the lower left corner of the AutoCAD's interface, Figure 8-1a.

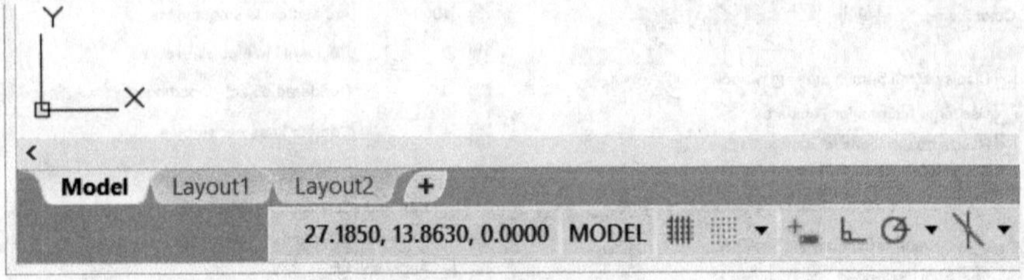

Figure 8-1a

When a user clicks on a layout tab, the drawing area appears as shown in Figure 8-1b. The dashed rectangle is the limit of the printing area. The solid rectangle is the boundary of the viewport. A viewport is a bounded area that displays a portion of the Model space of a drawing in a layout. The user can change the size and location of the viewport.

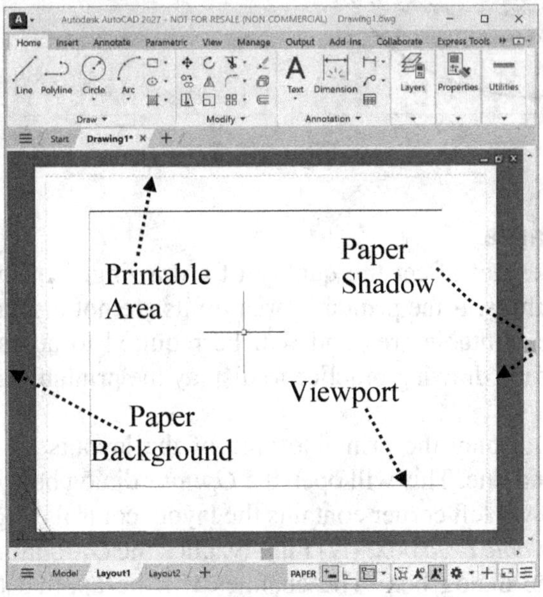

Figure 8-1b

8.2.1. Paper background and shadow

The paper background and shadow do not affect the quality or efficiency of a drawing. However, it is good drawing practice to keep the two options *On*. The user can hide or display the paper background and/or shadow of the layouts as follows. (i) Type the *Options* in the command line. This opens the *Options* dialog box. (ii) Select the *Display* tab, Figure 8-2. The lower left corner contains the layout controls, Figure 8-2. (iii) Clear or check the appropriate boxes. (iv) Finally, click the *OK* button to make the changes effective and close the dialog box. The changes are applied to each layout in the current drawing file.

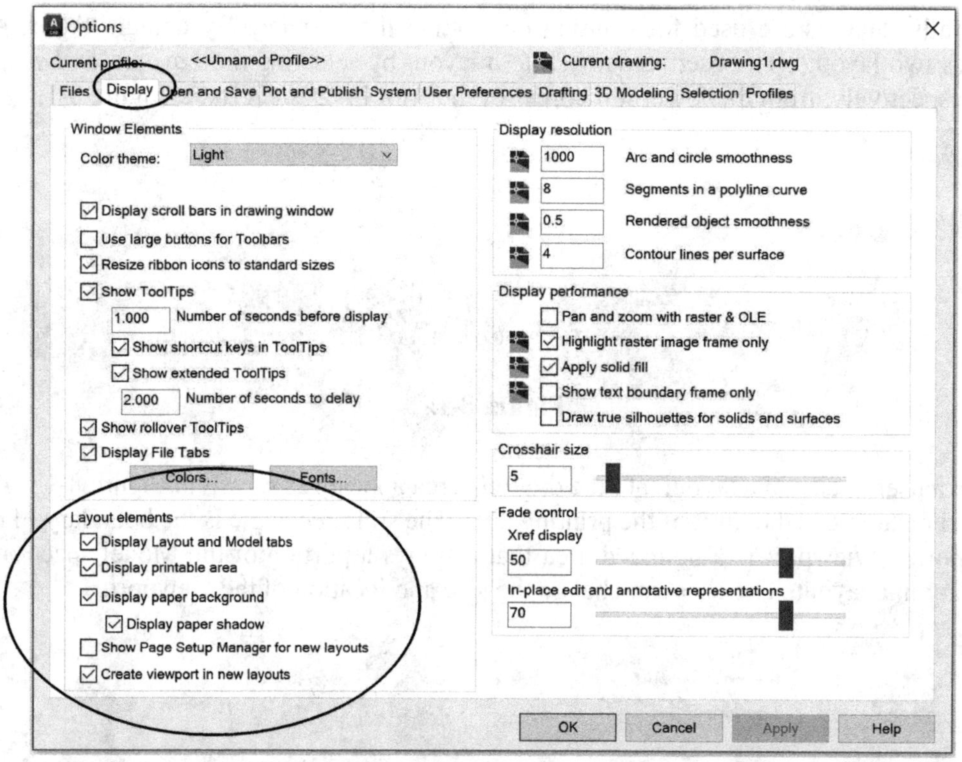

Figure 8-2

8.2.2. Printable area

The printable area does not affect the quality of a drawing. However, it may affect the productivity of the drafters. If the printable area limits are not displayed, then the drafters may draw outside the printable area and will be required to adjust the drawing before printing. Hence, it is good drawing practice to display the printable area in layouts.

The user can hide or display the printable area of the layouts as follows. (i) Type the *Options* in the command line. This will open the *Options* dialog box. (ii) Select the *Display* tab, Figure 8-2. The lower left corner contains the layout controls, Figure 8-2. (iii) Clear or check the *Display printable area* box. (iv) Finally, click the *OK* button to make the changes effective and close the dialog box. The changes will be applied to each layout in the drawing file.

The user can adjust the printable area of the layouts as follows.

- (i) Click the *Layout1* tab. (ii) Bring the cursor on the *Layout1* tab. (iii) Press the right button of the mouse and the option selection panel, Figure 8-3a, appears. (iv) Move the cursor to the *Page Setup Manager* option and press the left button of the mouse. This opens the *Page Setup Manager* dialog box, Figure 8-3b.

- Click the *Modify* button of the *Page Setup Manager* dialog box. This opens the *Page Setup – Layout1* dialog box, Figure 8-3c.

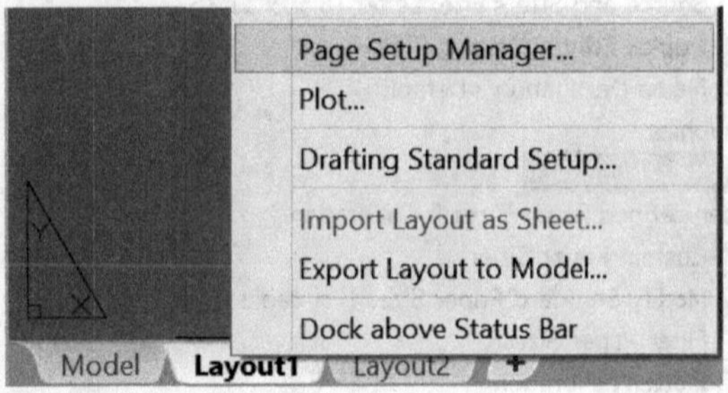

Figure 8-3a

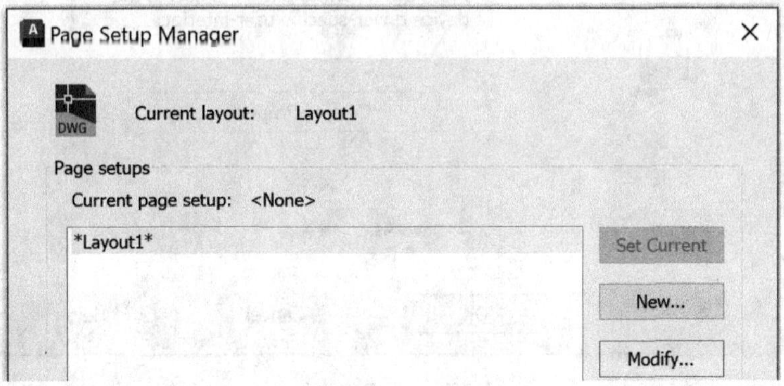

Figure 8-3b

- Select the printer from the *Page Setup – Layout1* dialog box in the *Printer/plotter* panel and click the *Properties* button. This opens the *Plotter Configuration Editor* dialog box, Figure 8-3d.

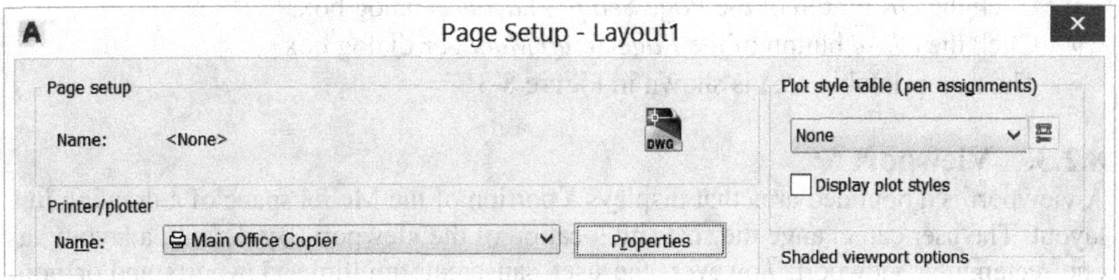

Figure 8-3c

- Select the *Modify Standard Paper Sizes (Printable Area)* from the *Plotter Configuration Editor* dialog box, Figure 8-3d, and click the *Custom Properties* button. This opens the *Custom Paper Sizes - Printable Area* dialog box, Figure 8-3e.

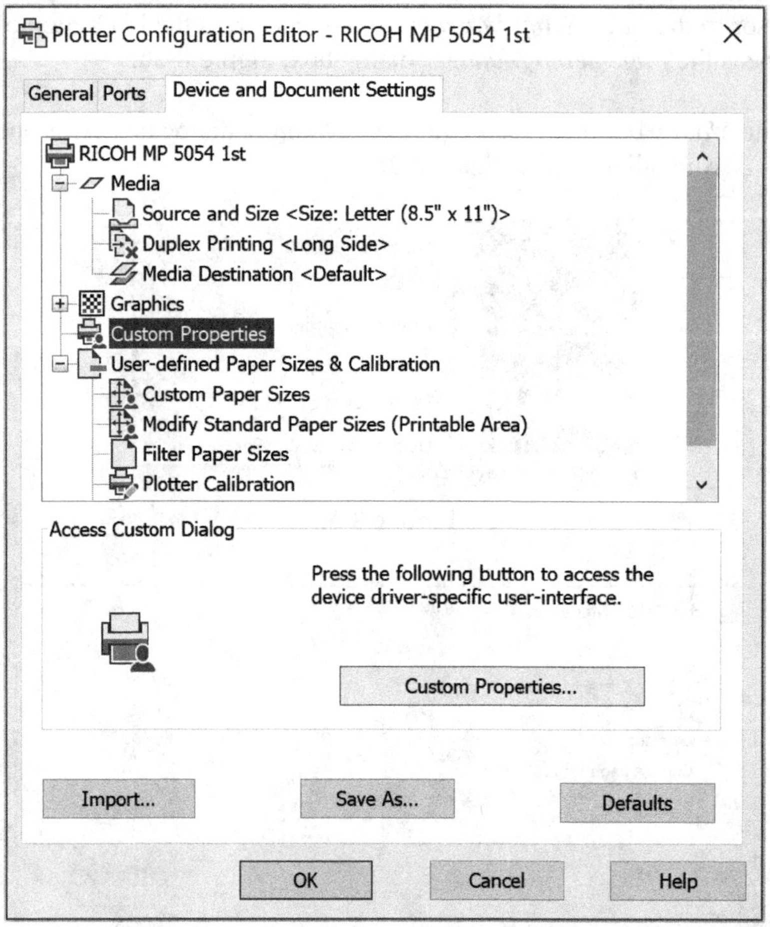

Figure 8-3d

- In the *Custom Paper Sizes - Printable Area* dialog box, Figure 8-3e, set the value for the desired options and click the *OK* button.

- Click the *OK* button of the *Plotter Configuration Editor* dialog box.
- Click the *OK* button of the *Page Setup – Layout1* dialog box.
- Click the *Close* button of the *Page Setup Manager* dialog box.
- The new printable area is shown in Figure 8-3f.

8.2.3. Viewport

A viewport is a bounded area that displays a portion of the Model space of a drawing in a layout. The user can change the size and location of the viewport. By default, a layout has one rectangular viewport; however, the user can create multiple viewports and/or non-rectangular viewports. Generally, a drafter needs to scale the viewport before plotting.

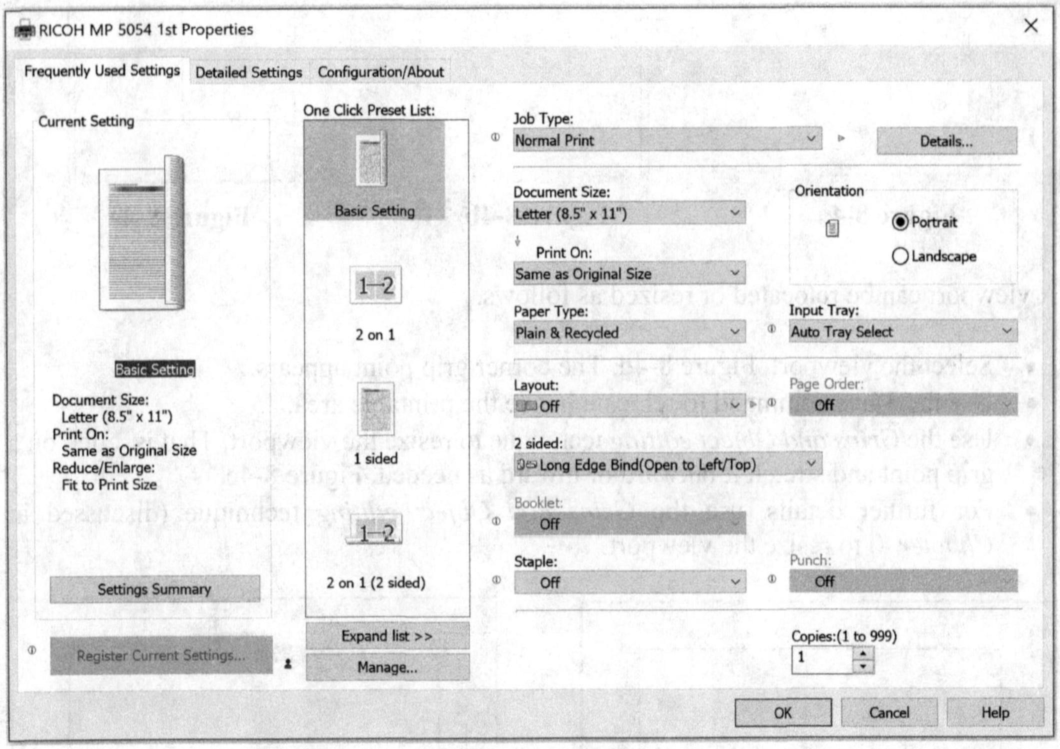

Figure 8-3e

Figure 8-3f

8.2.3.1. Viewport resizing

The user can increase or decrease the viewport size (Figure 8-4a), change its shape (Figure 8-4b), and change its location (Figure 8-4c). In these three figures, the outer rectangle is the boundary for the printable area. The user must keep the viewport inside the printable area.

Figure 8-4a

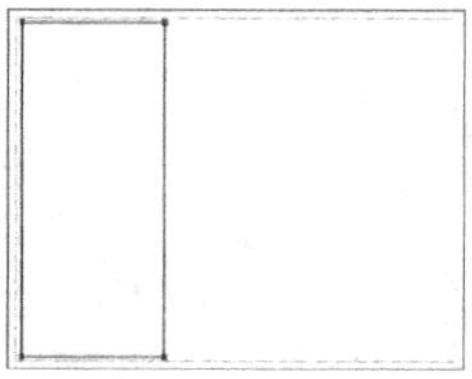

Figure 8-4b

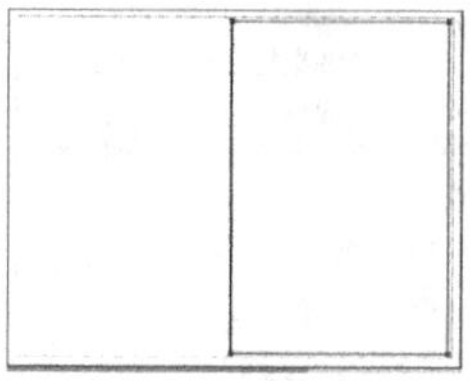

Figure 8-4c

A viewport can be relocated or resized as follows.

- Select the viewport, Figure 8-4d. The corner grip point appears.
- Use the *Move* command to relocate inside the printable area.
- Use the *Grips and Object editing* technique to resize the viewport. That is, click on a grip point and stretch it outward or inward as needed, Figure 8-4e.
- For further details, use the *Grips and Object editing* technique (discussed in *Chapter 4*) to resize the viewport.

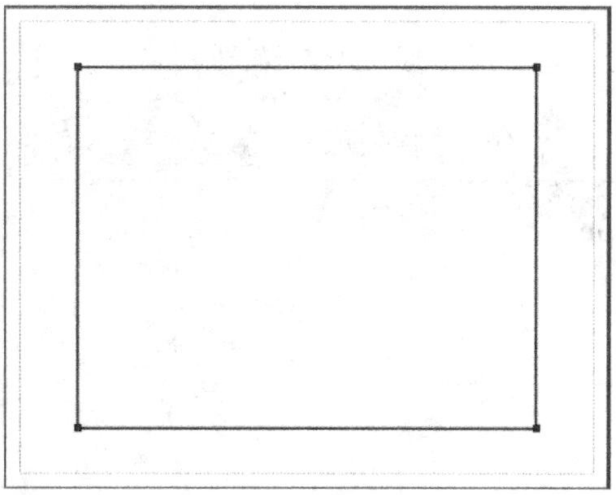

Figure 8-4d

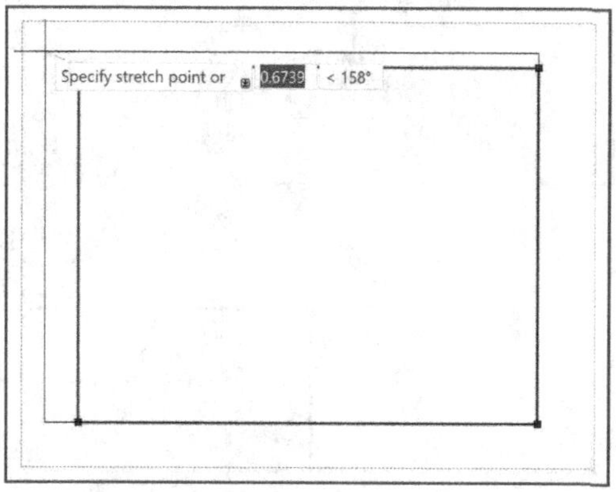

Figure 8-4e

8.2.3.2. Multiple viewports

By default, a layout has one rectangular viewport; however, the user can create multiple viewports, Figure 8-5f. A user can create multiple viewports as follows.

- Select the current viewport, Figure 8-4d. The corner grip point appears.
- Delete the current viewport.
- Activate the *MVIEW* command. (i) Type "mview," "Mview," or "MVIEW" on the command line and press the *Enter* key. The prompt shown in Figure 8-5a appears.
- *Specify corner of viewport or*, Figure 8-5a: Press the down-arrow of the prompt and an option list appears. Click on *4*; the prompt shown in Figure 8-5b appears.
- *Specify first corner or*, Figure 8-5b: Click near the upper left corner of the layout. The prompt shown in Figure 8-5c appears.
- *Specify opposite corner*, Figure 8-5c: Click at a diagonally opposite corner as shown in Figure 8-5c.
- The resulting viewports are shown in Figure 8-5d.

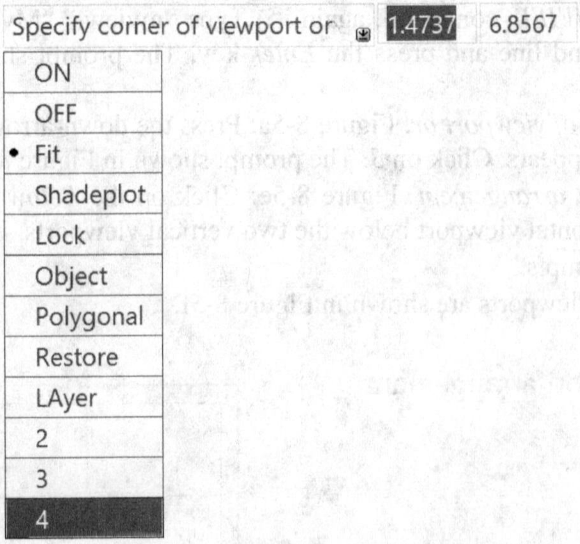

Figure 8-5a

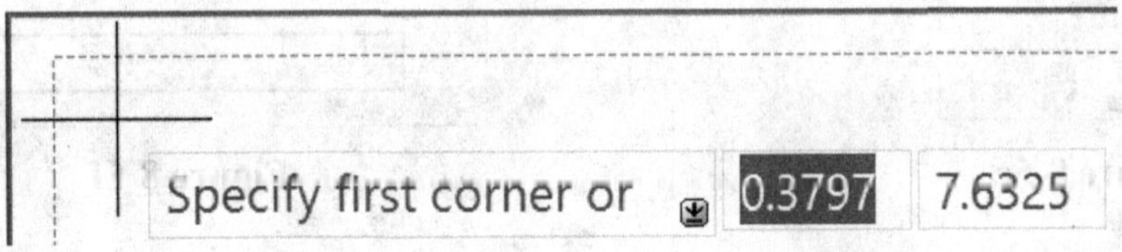

Figure 8-5b

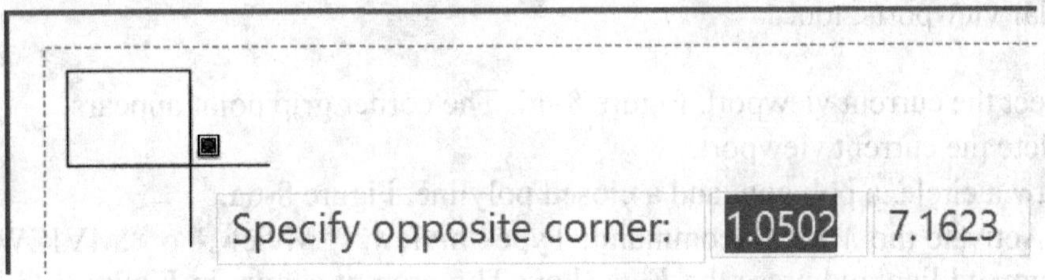

Figure 8-5c

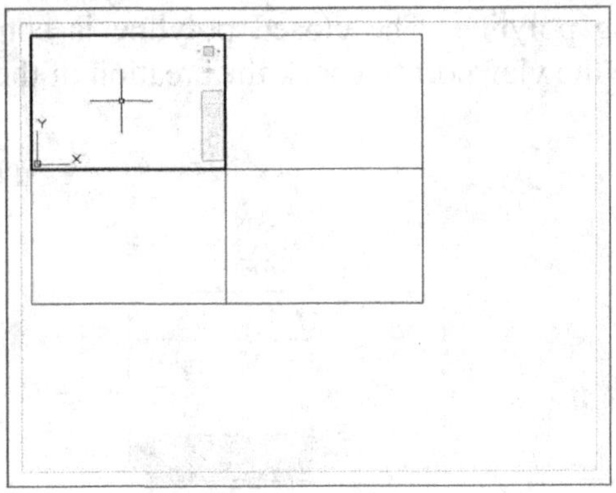

Figure 8-5d

- Activate the *MVIEW* command, again. (i) Type "mview," "Mview," or "MVIEW" on the command line and press the *Enter* key. The prompt shown in Figure 8-5a appears.
- *Specify corner of viewport or*, Figure 8-5a: Press the down-arrow of the prompt and an option list appears. Click on *3*. The prompt shown in Figure 8-5e appears.
- *Enter viewport arrangement*, Figure 8-5e: Click on the *Below* option. This option creates a horizontal viewport below the two vertical viewports.
- Follow the prompts.
- The resulting viewports are shown in Figure 8-5f.

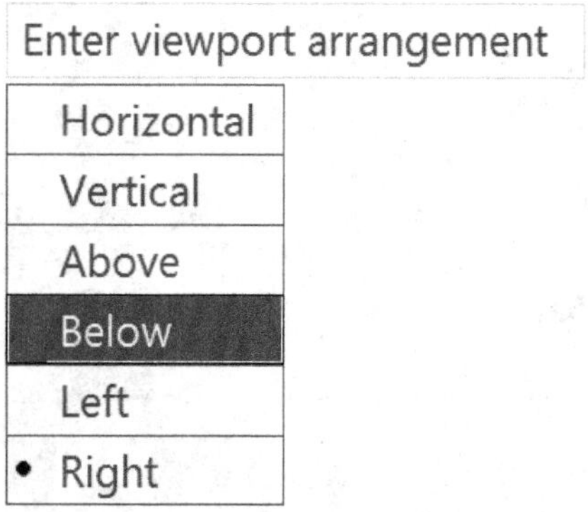

Figure 8-5e

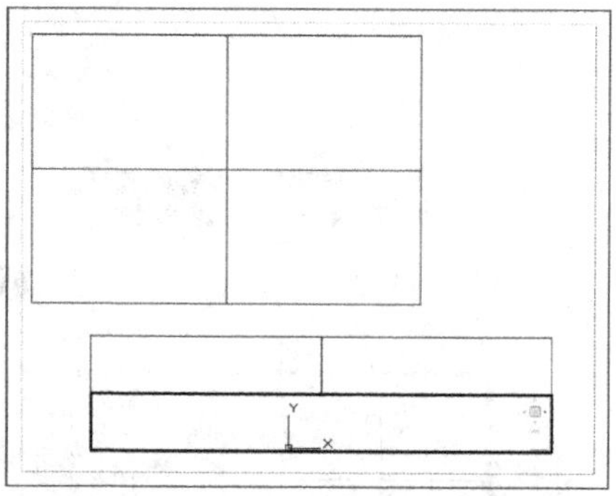

Figure 8-5f

8.2.3.3. Non-rectangular viewports

By default, a layout has one rectangular viewport; however, the user can create non-rectangular viewports, too.

- Select the current viewport, Figure 8-4d. The corner grip point appears.
- Delete the current viewport.
- Draw a circle, a polygon, and a closed polyline, Figure 8-6a.
- (i) Activate the *MVIEW* command: Type "mview," "Mview," or "MVIEW" on the command line and press the *Enter* key. The prompt shown in Figure 8-6b appears. (ii) Press the down-arrow of the prompt, and an option list appears. (iii) Click on the *Object* option. (iv) The prompt shown in Figure 8-6c appears. (v) Click on the closed shape created using polyline. The closed polyline is converted into a viewport. Double click inside the viewport to check the creation of the viewport, Figure 8-6d.

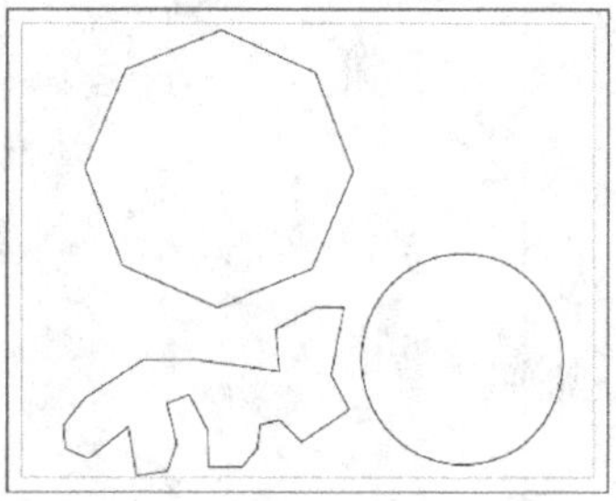

Figure 8-6a

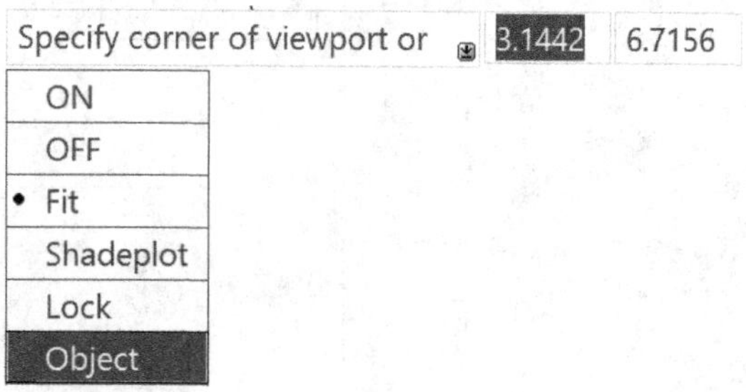

Figure 8-6b

- Repeat the above process with the polygon and the circle.
- The resulting viewports are shown in Figure 8-6d.

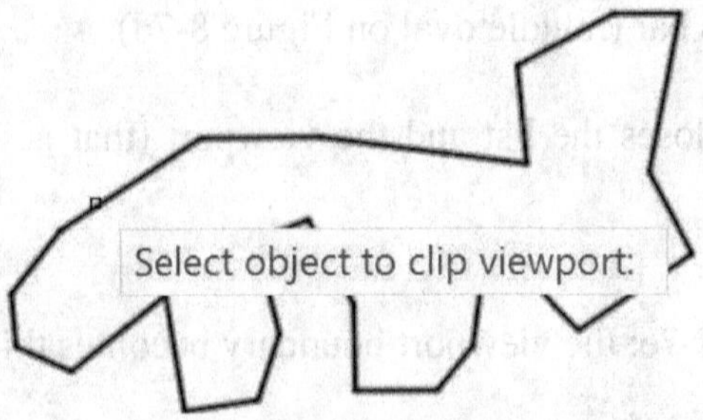

Figure 8-6c

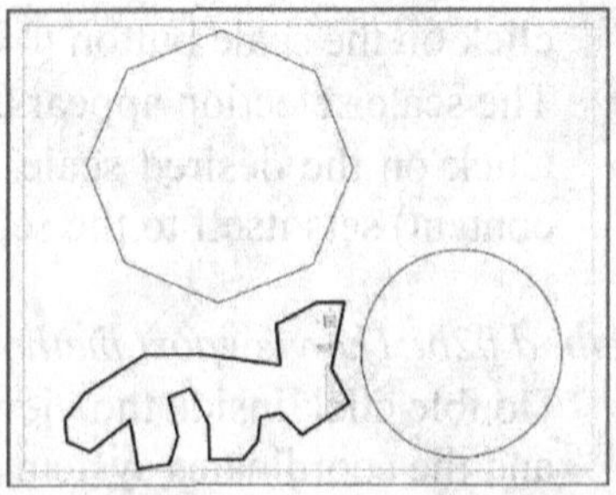

Figure 8-6d

8.2.3.4. Viewport scaling

Consider the floor plan of a three-bedroom house shown in Figure 8-7a. The architect wants to show the client the entire floor plan and the details of the kitchen as shown in Figure 8-5a and Figure 8-7b, respectively. The architect can achieve the desired goal by creating two layouts at two different scale factors. In the figures, the floor plan is at the scale of 1:132 and the kitchen plan is at the scale of 1:40.

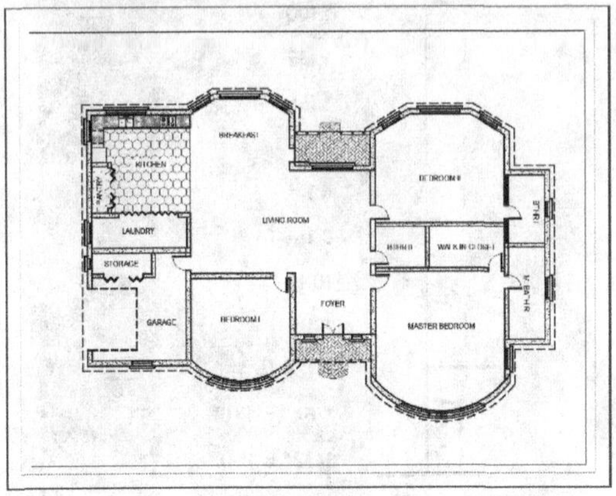

Figure 8-7a

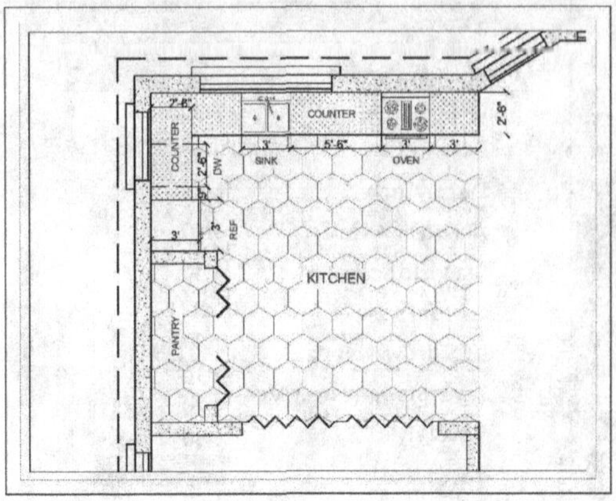

Figure 8-7b

8.2.3.5. Rescale a viewport

A viewport can be rescaled using one of the following two methods.

Method #1: The Properties Palette

- Select the viewport, Figure 8-4d. The corner grips point appears.
- Press the right button of the mouse and select the *Properties* from the options list.
- The above selection opens the *Properties* palette, Figure 8-7c.
- From the *Misc* panel, click the down-arrow in front of the *Standard scale*.
- Click on the desired scale. This action closes the list and the viewport (that is, its content) sets itself to the selected scale.

Method #2a: The Status bar

- Select the viewport, Figure 8-4d. The corner grips point appears.
- Either click on the down-arrow beside the scale factor (right oval on Figure 8-7d) or click on the scale button ( ) on the status bar (middle oval on Figure 8-7d).
- The scale selection appears.
- Click on the desired scale. This action closes the list and the viewport (that is, its content) sets itself to the selected scale.

Method #2b: The viewport method

- Double click inside the viewport, Figure 8-7e; the viewport boundary becomes thick and the coordinates system appears.
- Either click on the down-arrow beside the scale factor (right oval on Figure 8-7d) or click on the scale button ( ) on the status bar (middle oval on Figure 8-7d).
- The scale selection appears.
- Click on the desired scale. This action closes the list and the viewport (that is, its content) sets itself to the selected scale.

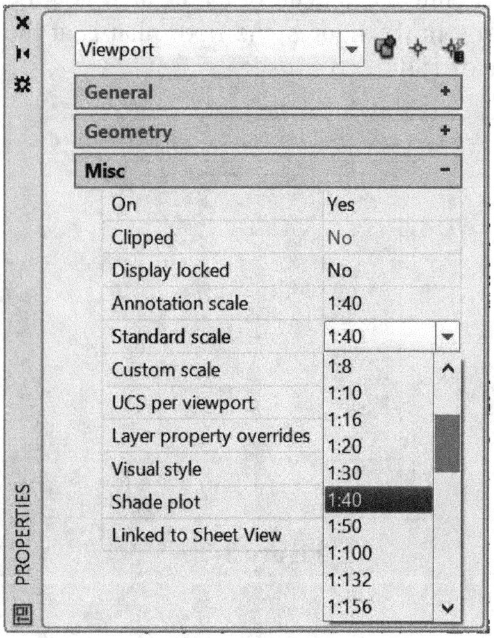

Figure 8-7c

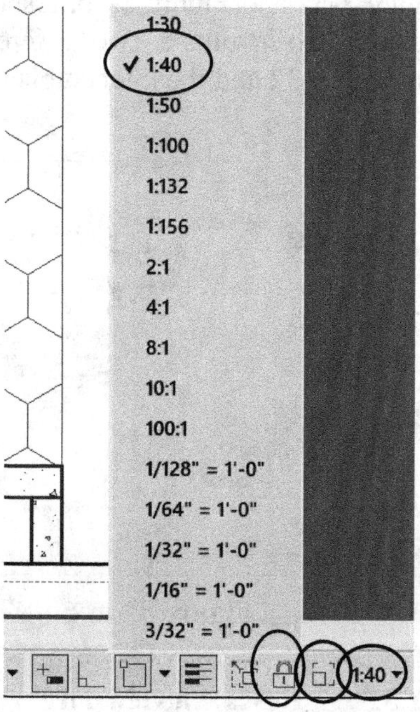

Figure 8-7d

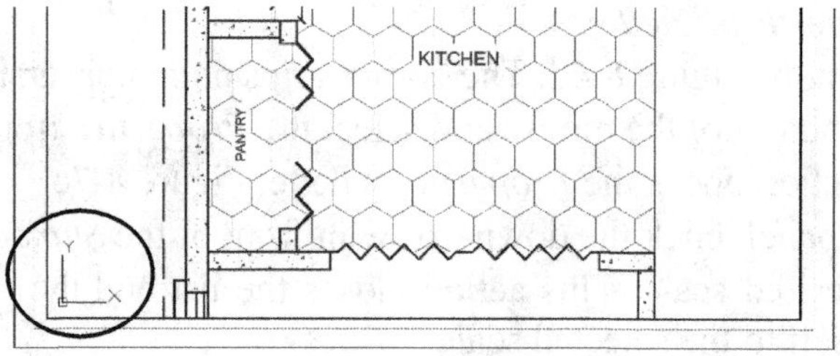

Figure 8-7e

8.2.3.6. Lock the scale of a viewport

The drafter should lock the viewport scale to avoid rescaling of the viewport accidentally using zoom/unzoom commands. By locking the viewport scale, the user can zoom into the viewport (or zoom out) at different levels of detail without altering the viewport (or drawing) scale. A viewport can be locked using one of the following two methods.

Method #1: *The Properties Palette*

- Select the viewport; the corner grips point appears, Figure 8-4d.
- Press the right button of the mouse and select the *Properties* from the options list.
- The above selection opens the *Properties* palette, Figure 8-8a.
- From the *Misc* panel, click in the cell on the right side of the *Display locked*, Figure 8-8b.
- A down-arrow appears in the cell labeled as *No*.
- Press the down-arrow and select the *Yes* option, Figure 8-8c. Notice that the scale is greyed; that is, the user cannot change it.

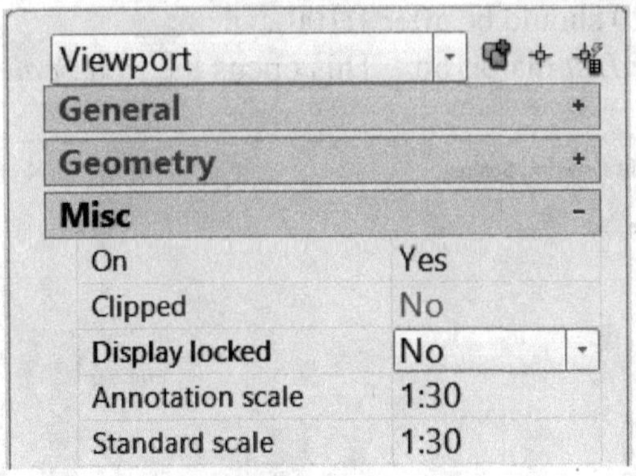

Figure 8-8a

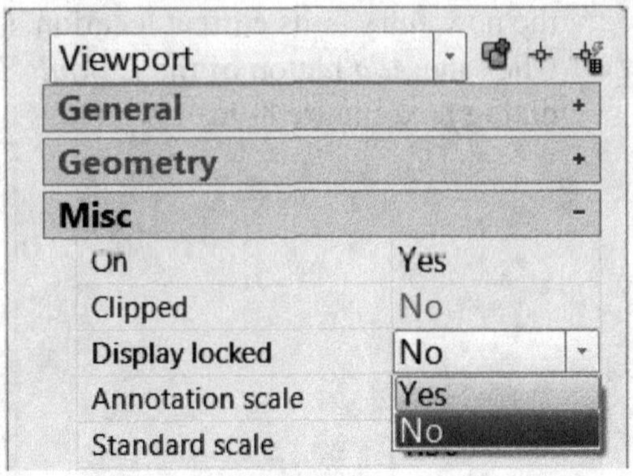

Figure 8-8b

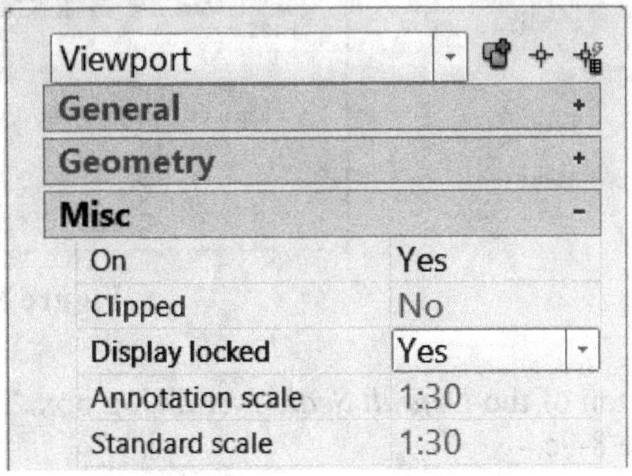

Figure 8-8c

Method #2a: *The Status bar*

- Select the viewport, Figure 8-4d. The corner grips point appears.
- Click on the lock button (🔒) on the status bar (left oval on Figure 8-7d).

Method #2b: *The viewport method*

- Double click inside the viewport, Figure 8-4e; the viewport boundary becomes thick, and the coordinates system appears.
- Click on the lock button (🔒) on the status bar (left oval on Figure 8-7d).

8.3. Add An Entry In The Scale List

A situation may arise when the user needs to use a scale factor not available in the default scale list of AutoCAD.

Example: Add *1:120* entry in the scale list. The user can add a new scale factor in the edit scale list as follows.

- From the *Annotate* tab and *Annotation Scaling* panel, select the *Scale List*, Figure 8-9a. This opens the *Edit Drawing Scales* dialog box, Figure 8-9b.
- On the dialog box, select the entry labeled as 1:100. This helps with the addition of the new entry at its correct location. (1:120 should be after 1:100).
- Click the *Add* button of the *Default Scale List* dialog box. This opens the *Add Scale* dialog box, Figure 8-9c.

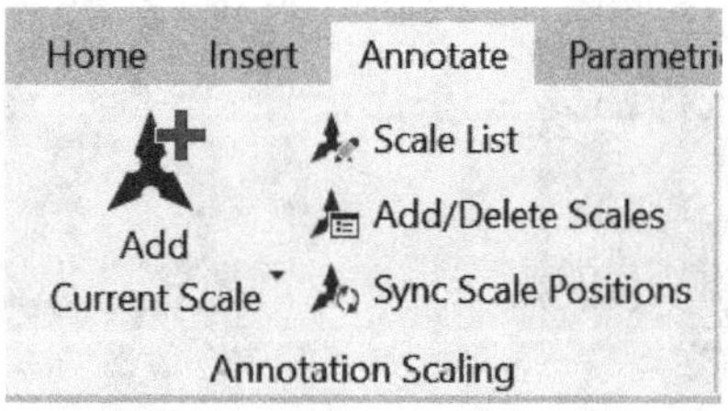

Figure 8-9a

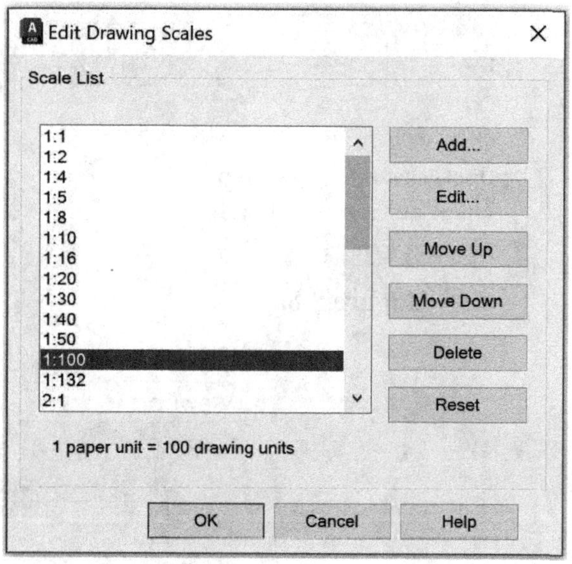

Figure 8-9b

- Click the *Add* button of the *Default Scale List* dialog box. This opens the *Add Scale* dialog box, Figure 8-9c.
- Enter the desired values, Figure 8-9c. Press the *OK* button on the *Add Scale* dialog box. This action will accept the new scale factor and close the dialog box.
- The new scale will appear in the *Edit Scale List* dialog box, Figure 8-9d.
- If the new scale is not created at its correct location, then use the *Move Up* or *Move Down* button to move the newly created scale to the appropriate location.
- Click the *OK* button to close the *Edit Drawing Scale* dialog box.

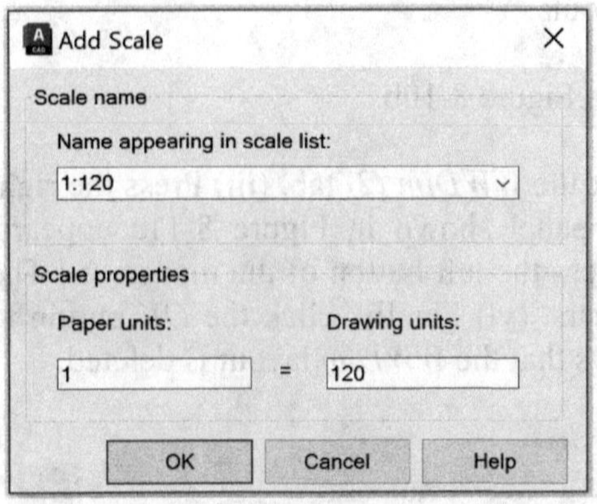

Figure 8-9c

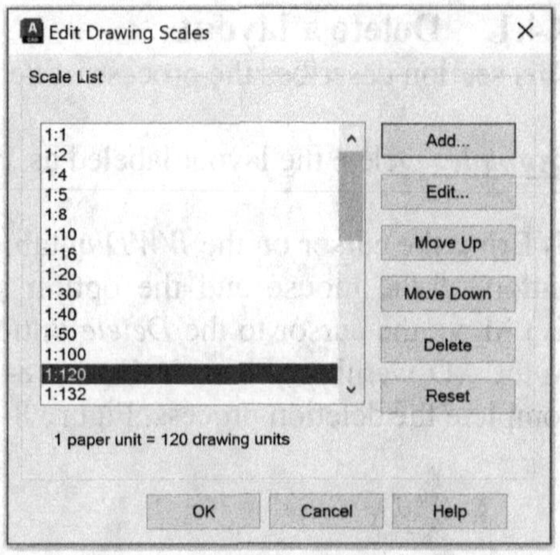

Figure 8-9d

8.4. Layout Manipulation

By default, AutoCAD creates two layouts: *Layout1* and *Layout2*, Figure 8-10a. However, a user can delete, move, copy, or rename existing layouts and insert more layouts. Figure 8-10b shows the layouts created for the floor plan drawing shown in Figure 8-7a and renamed based on their functionality.

If the labels of the layouts cannot fit on the lower left side of the interface, then the labels are collapsed in a list. The user can visualize the list by pressing the  button (not shown in the figure) on the right side of the layout's labels, Figure 8-10b.

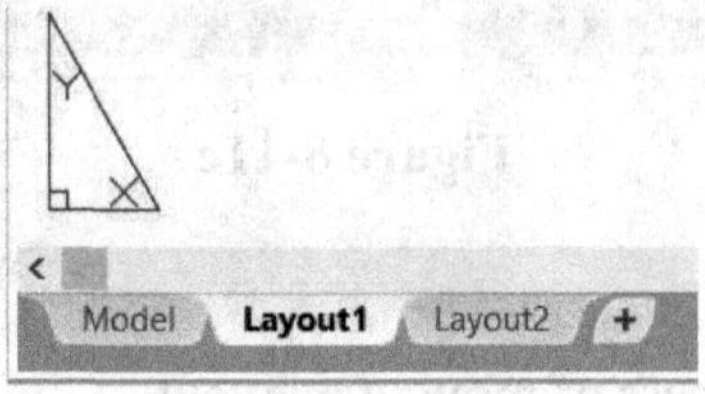

Figure 8-10a

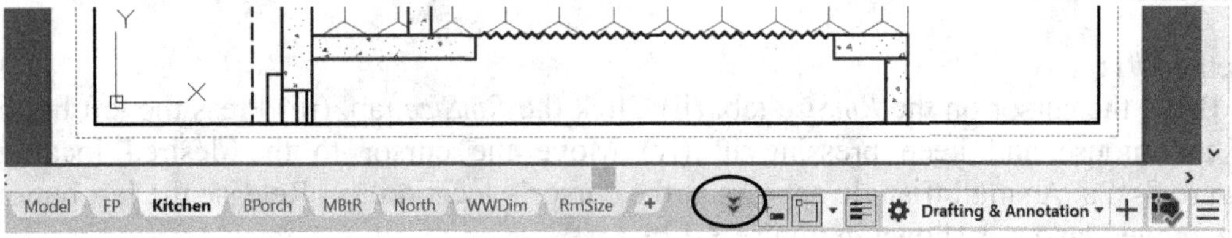

Figure 8-10b

8.4.1. Delete a layout

This section describes the process of deleting layouts.

Example: Delete the layout labeled as *WWDim* in Figure 8-10b.

(i) Bring the cursor on the *WWDim* tab. (ii) Click the *WWDim (2)* tab. (iii) Press the right button of the mouse and the option selection panel shown in Figure 8-11a appears. (iv) Move the cursor to the *Delete* option and press the left button of the mouse. (v) The AutoCAD warning shown in Figure 8-11b appears. (vi) Finally, click the *OK* button to complete the deletion process. Figure 8-11c shows that the *WWDim* layout is deleted.

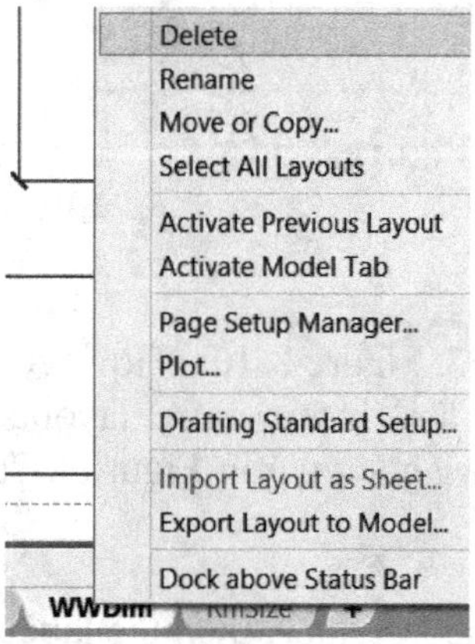

Figure 8-11a

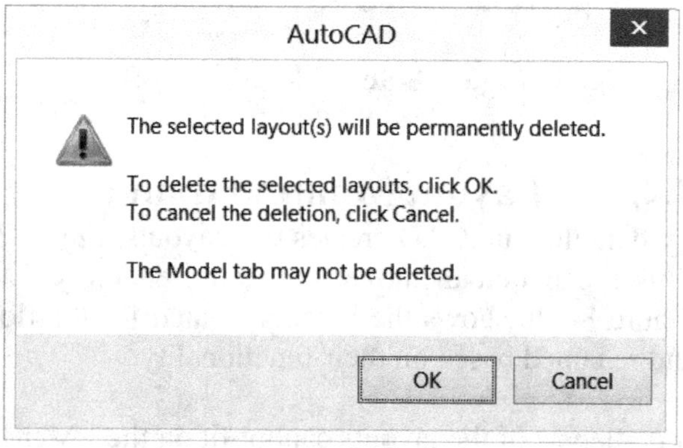

Figure 8-11b

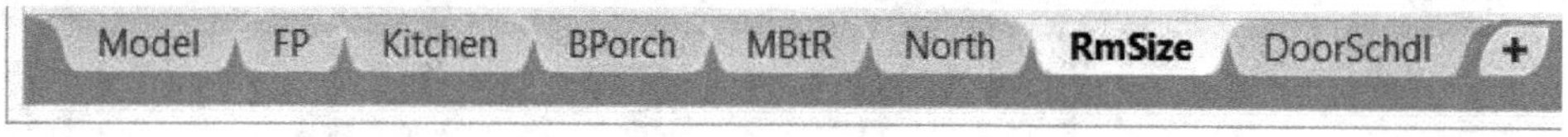

Figure 8-11c

8.4.2. Move a layout

This section describes the process of moving a layout.

Example: In Figure 8-10b, move the *RmSize* layout in front of *BPorch* layout.

Method #1:
(i) Bring the cursor on the *RmSize* tab. (ii) Click the *RmSize* tab. (iii) Press the left button of the mouse and keep pressing it. (iv) Move the cursor to the desired location, Figure 8-12a. A small triangle appears at the cursor's location. (v) Release the left button. The moved layout is shown in Figure 8-12b.

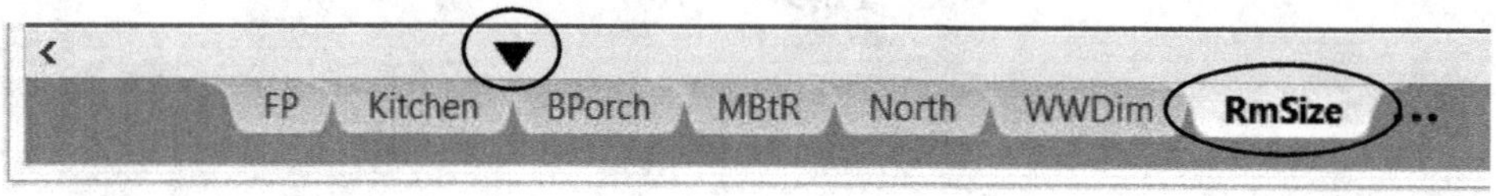

Figure 8-12a

Figure 8-12b

Method #2:
(i) Bring the cursor on the *RmSize* tab. (ii) Click the *RmSize* tab. (iii) Press the right button of the mouse and the option selection panel shown in Figure 8-12d appears. (iv) Move the cursor to the *Move or Copy* option (Figure 8-12c) and press the left button of the mouse. This opens the *Move or Copy* dialog box, Figure 8-12d. (v) Select the new location. Since the *RmSize* is required to move in front of *BPorch*, *BPorch* is selected. (vi) Click the *OK* button to complete the Move command. The moved layout is shown in Figure 8-12b.

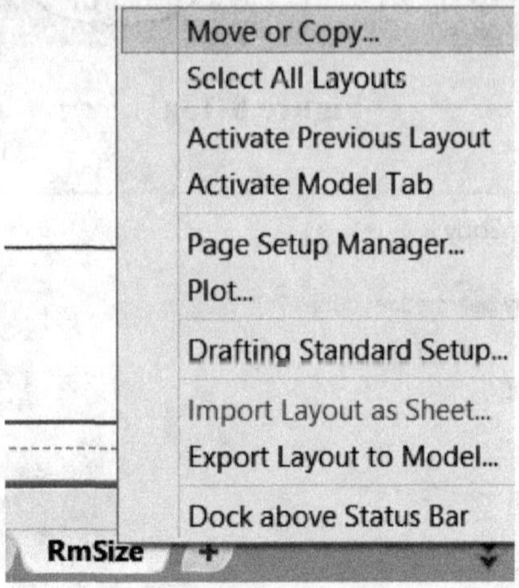

Figure 8-12c

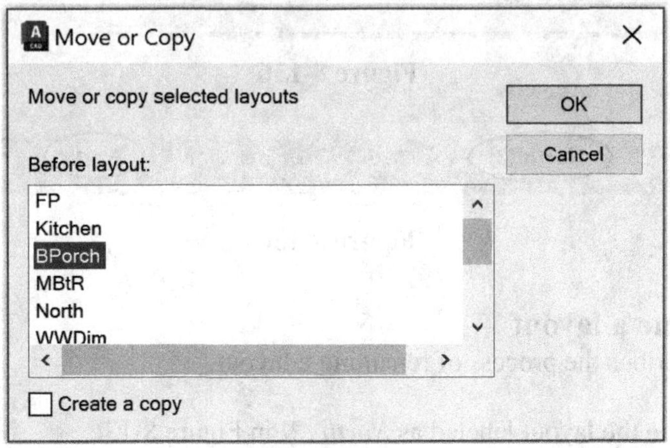

Figure 8-12d

8.4.3. Copy a layout

This section describes the process of copying a layout.

Example: Make a copy of the *North* layout and place the copy before the *Kitchen* layout.

(i) Bring the cursor on the *North* tab, Figure 8-13a. (ii) Click the *North* tab. (iii) Press the right button of the mouse and the option selection panel shown in Figure 8-12c appears. (iv) Move the cursor to the *Move or Copy* option (Figure 8-12c) and press the left button of the mouse. This opens the *Move or Copy* dialog box, Figure 8-13b. (v) Check the *Create a copy* box. (vi) Select the location of the copy. Since the *copy* is required to be on the layout before the *Kitchen, Kitchen* is selected. (vii) Click the *OK* button to complete the copy command. The copied layout, *North (2)*, is shown in Figure 8-13c.

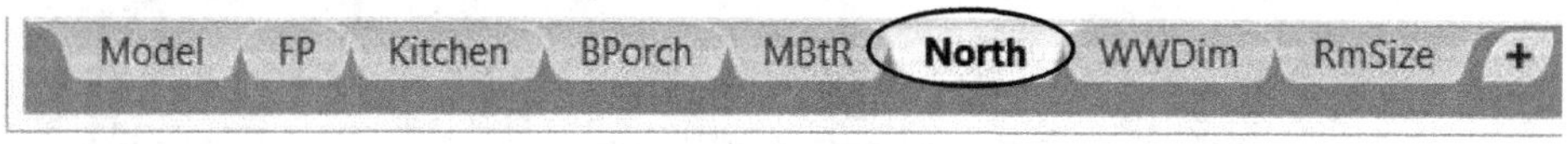

Figure 8-13a

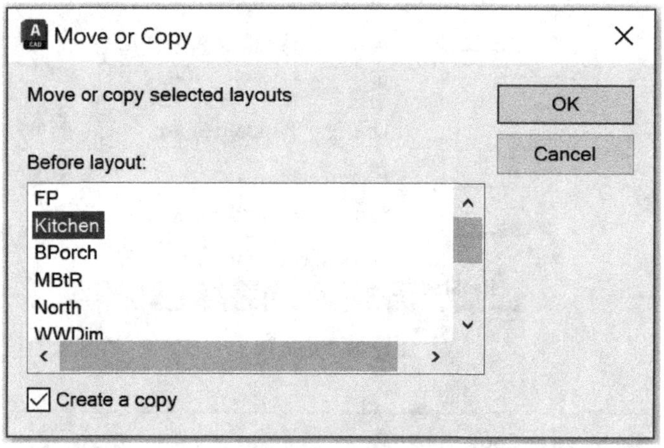

Figure 8-13b

Figure 8-13c

8.4.4. Rename a layout

This section describes the process of renaming a layout.

Example: Rename the layout labeled as *North (2)* in Figure 8-13c.

Method #1:

Double click on the name of the layout *North (2)* and its name is highlighted, Figure 8-14. Type the new name and press the *Enter* key.

Method #2:
(i) Bring the cursor on the *North (2)* tab. (ii) Click the *North (2)* tab. (iii) Press the right button of the mouse and the option selection panel shown in Figure 8-11a appears. (iv) Move the cursor to the *Rename* option. The selected layout is highlighted, Figure 8-14. Type the new name and press the *Enter* key.

Figure 8-14

8.4.5. Insert a layout

AutoCAD allows its user to insert two types of layouts: a default layout or a layout from a specific template file. Template files are discussed in the later sections of this chapter.

8.4.5.1. Default layout

Example: Insert a default layout.

The user can insert a default layout as follows: (i) Bring the cursor on any of the layout tabs. (ii) Press the right button of the mouse and the option panel appears, Figure 8-15. (iii) Move the cursor to the *New layout* option. (iv) Finally, press the left or right button of the mouse. (v) The option panel is closed, and a new layout is added to the drawing.

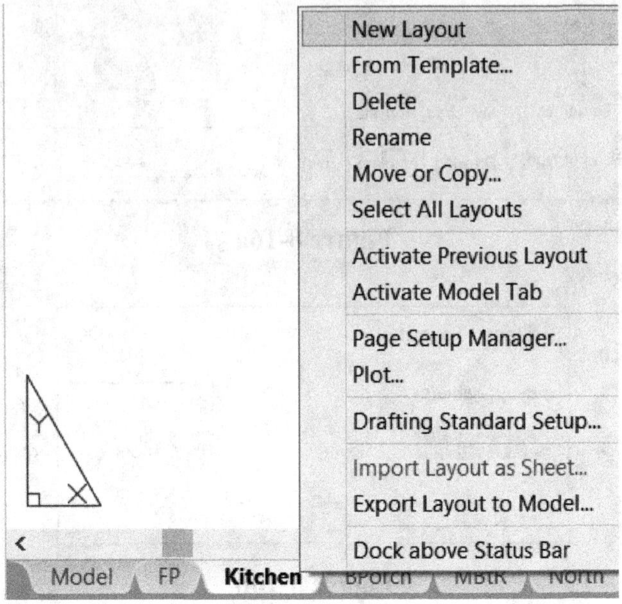

Figure 8-15

8.4.5.2. Layout from template

Example: Insert a "*My_acad_Landscape*" from "My_Template.".

The user can insert a layout from a template as follows: (i) Bring the cursor on any of the layout tabs. (ii) Press the right button of the mouse and the option panel appears, Figure 8-15. (iii) Move the cursor to the *From Template...* option. (iv) This opens the *Select Template From File* dialog box, Figure 8-16a. (v) Choose the appropriate template and press the *Open* button. (iv) This opens the *Insert Layout(s)* dialog box, Figure 8-16b. (v) Select the desired layout, *My_acad_Landscape* in the example. (vi) Press the *OK* button in *Insert Layout(s)* dialog box. (vi) Press the *Open* button in *Select Template From File* dialog box to complete the layout insertion process.

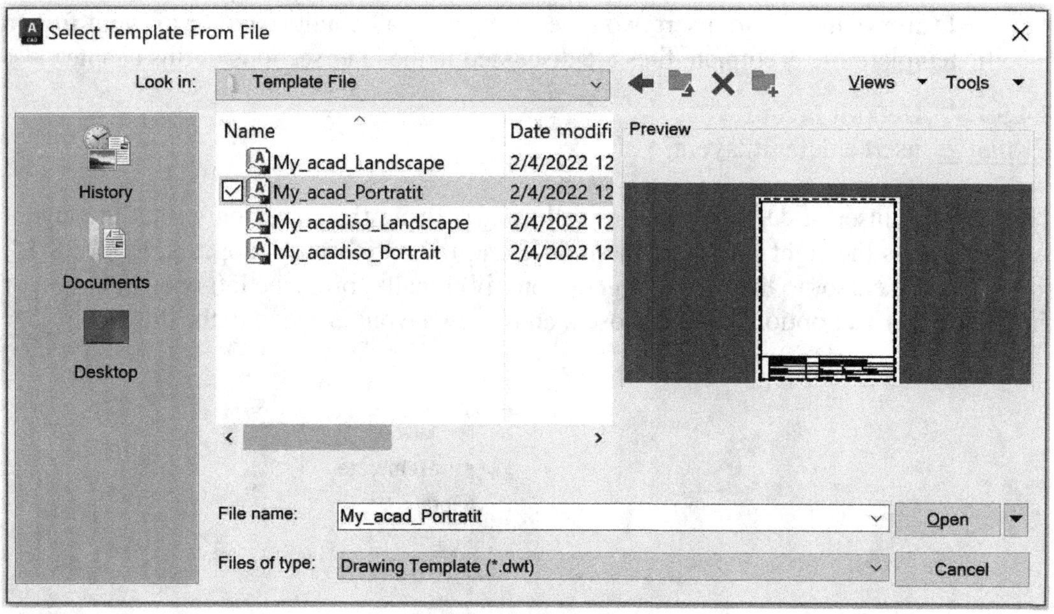

Figure 8-16a

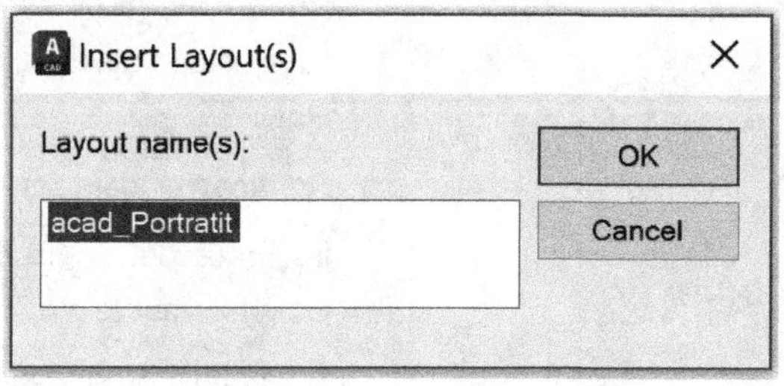

Figure 8-16b

8.4.6. Grid and Snap commands

The *Grid* command is used to display the visible grid (similar to graph or engineering paper) background on the drawing screen. The *Snap* command is used to set an invisible grid background on the drawing screen and to limit the movement of the cursor to the snap grid's points only. The snap grid is completely independent of the visible grid. The process of grid and snap manipulation in the layout is the same as in the Model space and is discussed in detail in *Chapter 2*.

8.4.7. An Example

Example: Create a drawing of the model shown in Figure 8-17a using layers; also create and rename multiple layouts; the dimensions are in millimeters. A drafter can create the drawing using the following steps.

- Important point: The names of the layers and layouts should be small and descriptive. The naming of a layer and layouts are independent processes. The names can be the same or different; note the names of the layouts in Figure 8-17b and the layers in Figure 8-17c. In the example, only two layers and two layouts have the same name.
- File: Open a new acadiso file.
- Layers: Create the layers and label them as shown in Figure 8-17b.
- Layouts: Create the layouts and label them as shown in Figure 8-17c.
- Create the drawing: In the *Model* space, (i) make the *Rectangles* layer to be the current layer and draw the rectangles; (ii) make the *Circles* layer to be the current layer and draw the circles; and (iii) make the *Triangles* layer to be the current layer and draw the triangles. However, the user can skip the dimensioning step.
- Create the views: (i) Select the layout tab labeled as *Layout 1* and rename it to *Rect*. (ii) Select the layout tab labeled as *Layout 2* and rename it to *Circles*. (iii) Either use Copy layout command or Insert layout command to create the remaining two layouts.

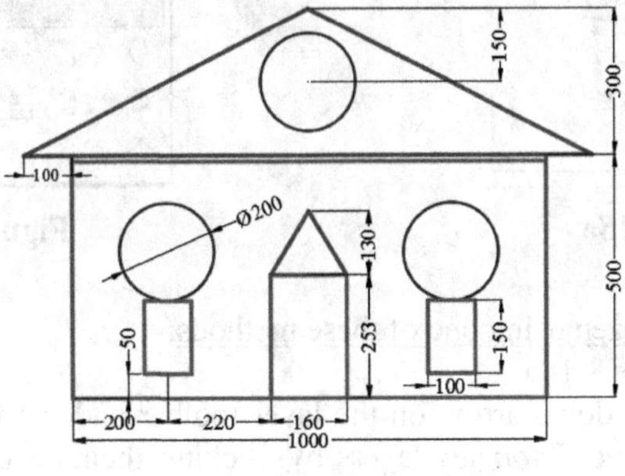

Figure 8-17a

Current layer: 0 — Search for layer

Status	Name	On	Freeze	Lock	Color	Linetype	Lineweight
✓	0				white	Continuous	0.00 mm
	Circles				160	ZIGZAG	0.50 mm
	Defpoints				white	Continuous	0.00 mm
	Rectangles				92	TRACKS	0.50 mm
	Triangles				210	HIDDEN	0.50 mm

Filters: All; All Used

Figure 8-17b

Figure 8-17c

8.5. Layers Freezing And Layouts

Example: Using the drawing shown in Figure 8-17c, display the layouts as shown in the left column of *Table #1*.

The drafter needs to display different parts of the drawing in different layouts. The drafter has two choices: (i) create multiple drawings specific to each layout (wastage of resources and time) or (ii) create one drawing with multiple layers and create the desired views of the layouts by hiding the unnecessary objects. The drafter has decided to follow the second choice. This section explains the process of freezing layers to create the desired views.

- Create the views: (i) Select the layout tab labeled as *Rect*. (ii) Either double click inside the viewport or click on PAPER button on the status bar (lower right corner of the interface). The layout appears as shown in Figure 8-18a. **Note that the viewport boundary is bold and the coordinate and the viewcube appear inside the viewport.**

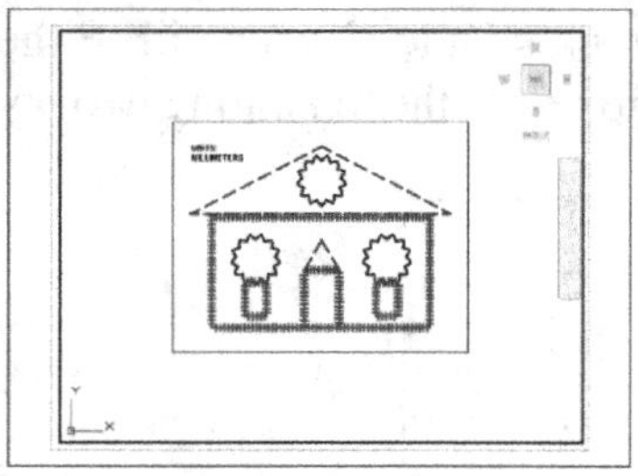

Figure 8-18a

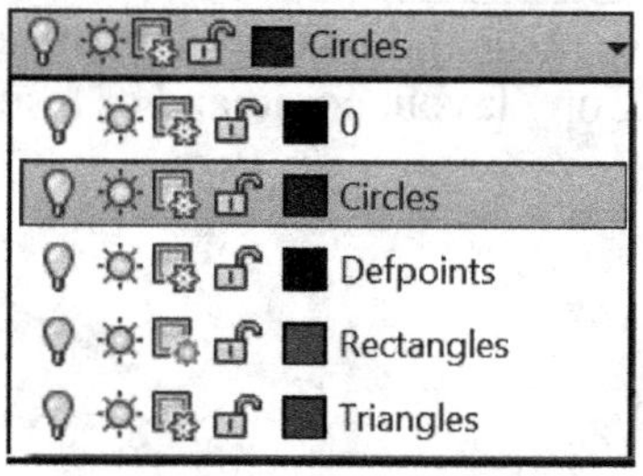

Figure 8-18b

- A layer can be frozen using one of these methods:
  Method #1: Figure 8-18a
  - (i) Press the down-arrow on the layer toolbar and (ii) freeze the '*0*', *Circles, Defpoints*, and *Triangles* layers by clicking their *Freeze or thaw in current viewport* button as shown in Figure 8-18b.

  Method #2: Figure 8-18c
  - (i) Click the layer *Freeze* button, Figure 8-18d. (ii) The prompt shown in Figure 8-18e will appear. (iii) Click on one of the circles and the circles will disappear. (iv) Repeat the process with the big outer rectangle (for '*0*' layer) and one of the triangles (for the '*Triangles*' layer).
- Repeat the process: Repeat the above process with each layout. The layouts and corresponding layers' manipulation are shown in Table #1.
- Important point: Freezing a layer is an independent process from the current layer. In the layers of Table #1, *Circle* is the current layer in all four cases; it is frozen in the *rectangles* and *Triangles* layouts.

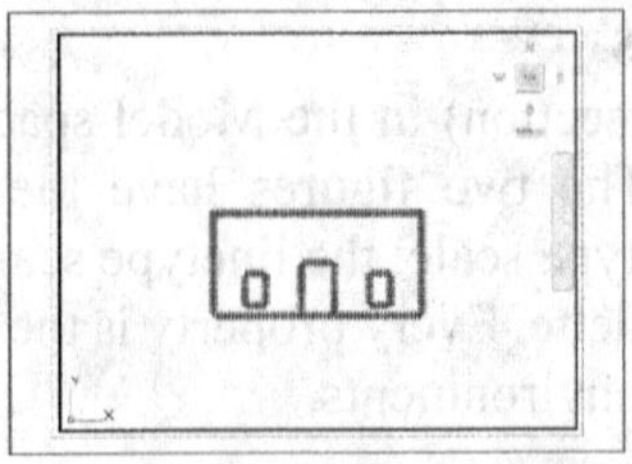

Figure 8-18c

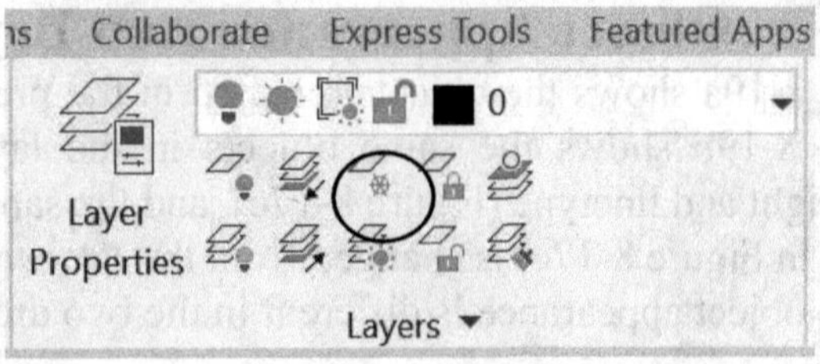

Figure 8-18d

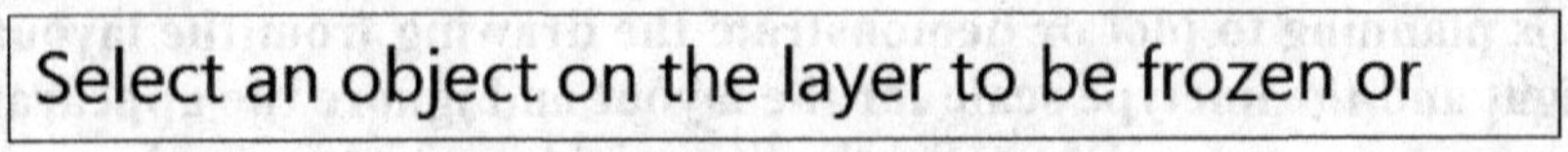

Figure 8-18e

Table #1: Layouts and layers

Layouts	Layers
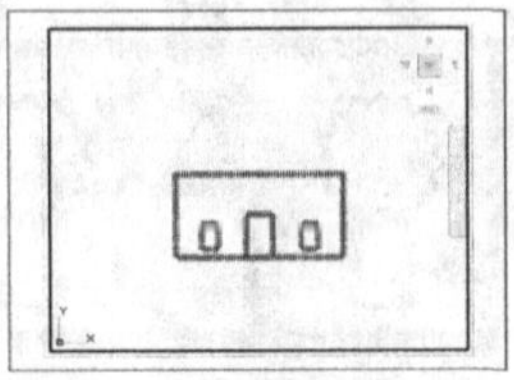 **Rect**	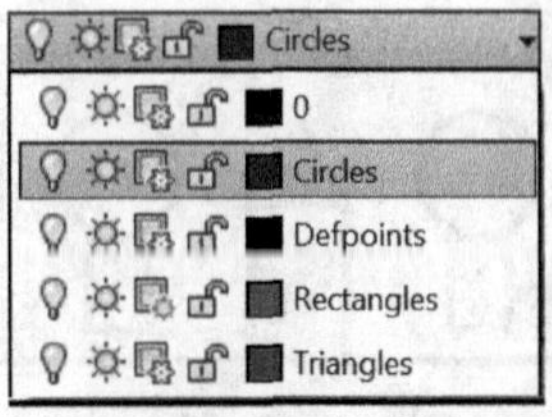
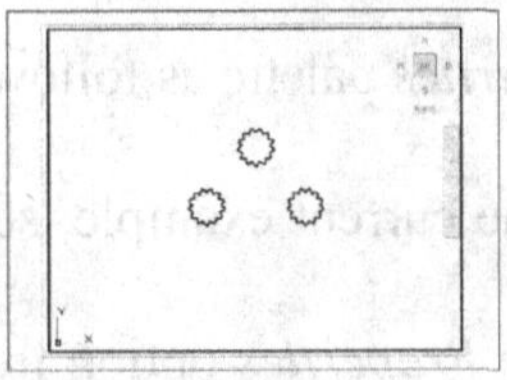 **Circles**	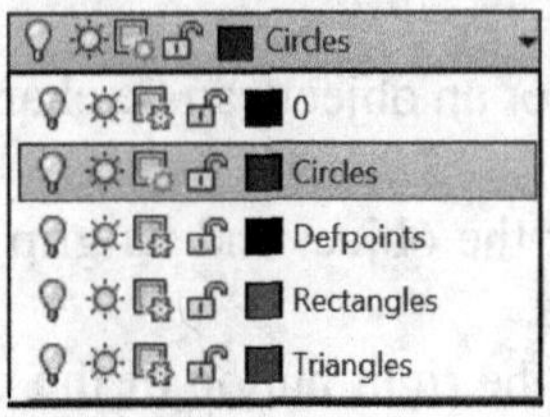
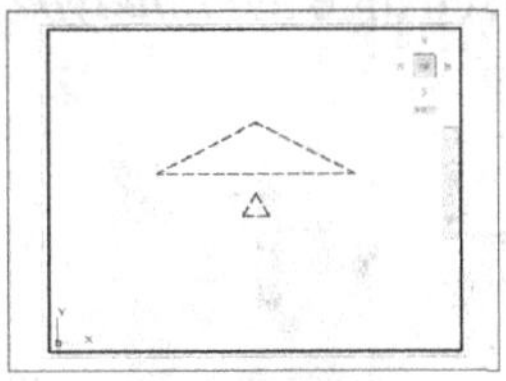 **Triangles**	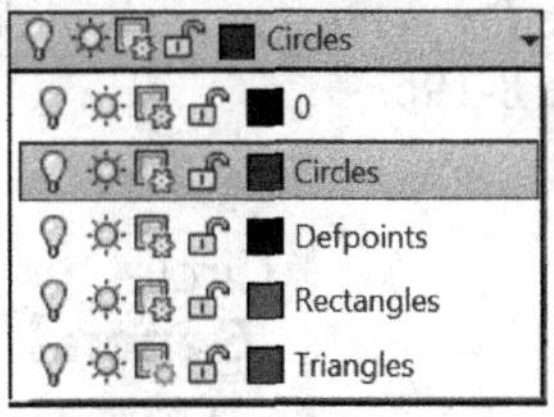
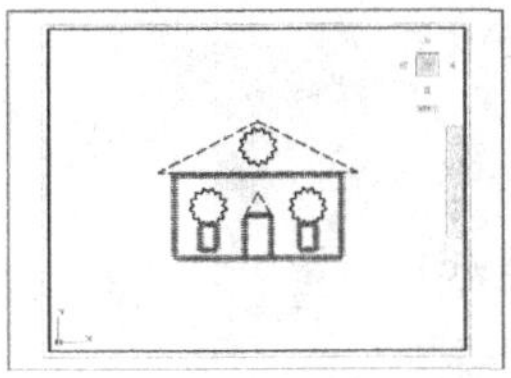 **ShowAll**	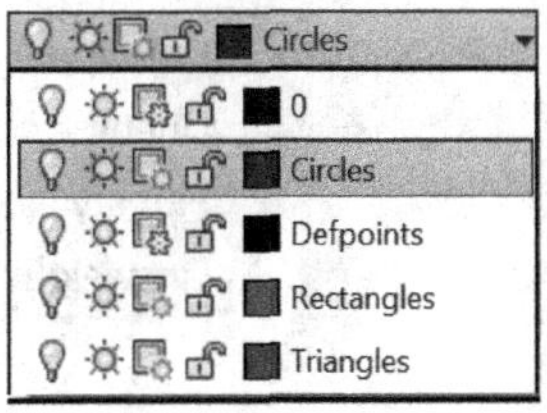

8.6. Object Appearance And Layouts

Figure 8-19a shows the objects (created in the previous section) in the Model space and Figure 8-19b shows the same objects in the layout. The two figures have the same lineweight and linetype (Figure 8-17c), and the same linetype scale; the linetype scale (not shown in Figure 8-17c) is changed from the *Properties* palette. Every property is the same, yet the object appearance is different in the two drawing environments.

The user must decide about the drawing environment for the demonstration of the drawing and activation of the plotting command before setting the lineweight and the linetype scale. **If the user is planning to plot or demonstrate the drawing from the layout, then set the lineweight and the linetype scale for the layout and ignore the appearance in the Model space and vice versa.** Generally, the lineweight is a higher number in the layout; however, the linetype scale is a pattern and the lineweight a dependent number. Lineweight can be changed for a layer from the layer manager. On the other hand, the linetype scale is changed from the *Properties* palette.

Figure 8-19a

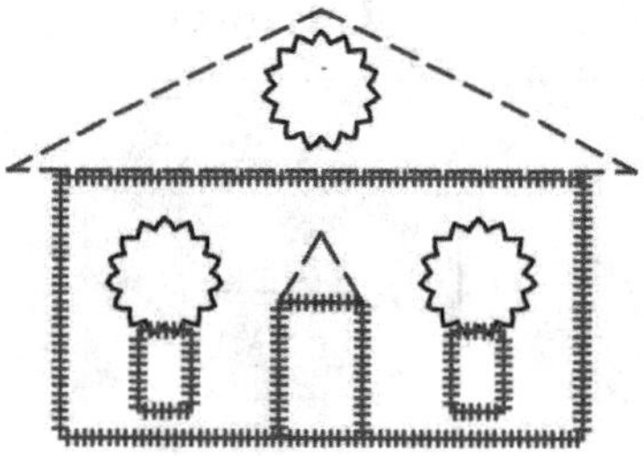

Figure 8-19b

A property of an object can be changed using the *Properties* palette as follows.

- Select the object and its grip points appear. In the current example, select all three circles.
- Press the right button of the mouse and select the *Properties* option from the list of options.
- On the *Properties* palette, under the *General* panel, change the *Linetype scale* to 0.25, Figure 8-19c.

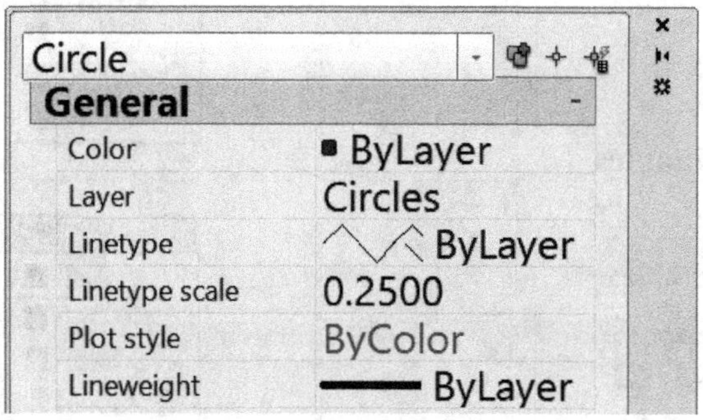

Figure 8-19c

8.7. Template File

A template file is a mold or a pattern file that gives consistency to every drawing file in the company. AutoCAD provides a few template files for its users. However, this section creates a typical template file used in academia.

This section creates template files for ISO (millimeters) and ANSI (inch) units. The title and release blocks created in the previous chapters are inserted in a layout and then the file is saved as a template file.

8.7.1. Landscape template for ISO units

A landscape template for ISO units is created using the following steps. The template file is shown in Figure 8-22c.

1. Open a new acadiso.dwt file.
2. Create a layer *TemplateFile*; set its color to be *White*, linetype to be *Continuous*, and lineweight to be *0.0*.
3. Make the *TemplateFile* layer to be the current layer.
4. Select the *Layout1*; double click inside the viewport and turn *Off* the grid.
5. Click on the *Layout1* tab and rename it to My_acadiso_Landscape. Figure 8-20a shows the viewport and the printable area of the layout.
6. *Add the border*: Every drawing requires a border and the viewport's boundaries are not printed; therefore, the drafter must draw the border. The border of a drawing is 1/2 inches from the edge of the plotting paper. However, in this section the border is created with respect to the printable area. Hence, draw a rectangle slightly smaller than the printable area, Figure 8-20b.

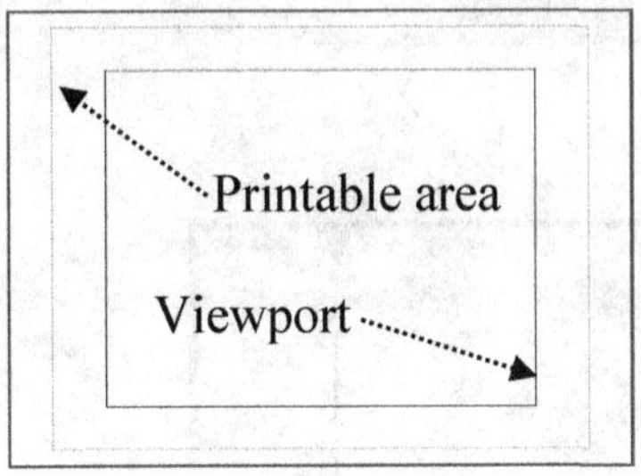

Figure 8-20a

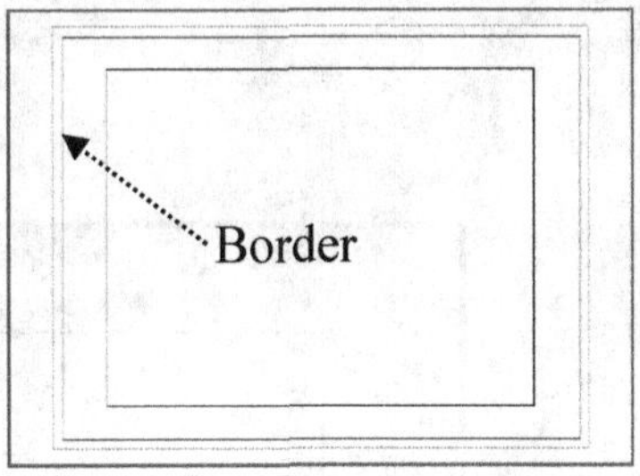

Figure 8-20b

7. *Insert the title block*: Using the *Insert* dialog box settings shown in 7-20d, insert the title block created in *Chapter 7* in the lower right corner as shown in Figure 8-20c. Press the *Enter* key for the prompts; and match the base point of the block to the lower right corner of the border.

8. *Scale down the title block*: If the title block is overpowering the drawing, then scale it down; if it is too small then scale it up. As a rule of thumb, the height of the title block should be about 1/6 of the height of the printable area. If necessary, scale the block as follows: (i) Activate the *Scale* command. (ii) In response to the prompt *Select objects*, click on the title block and press the *Enter* key. (iii) In response to the prompt

Specify the base point, click on the lower right corner of the title block and press the *Enter* key. (iv) In response to the prompt *Specify scale factor*, type 0.5 and press the *Enter* key. (v) The title block is reduced by 50%, Figure 8-20e.

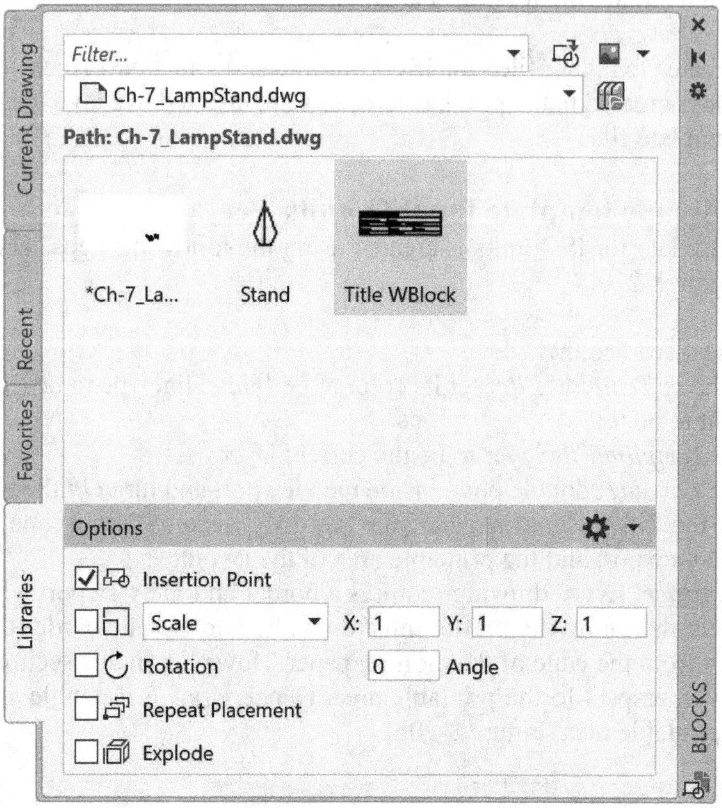

Figure 8-20c

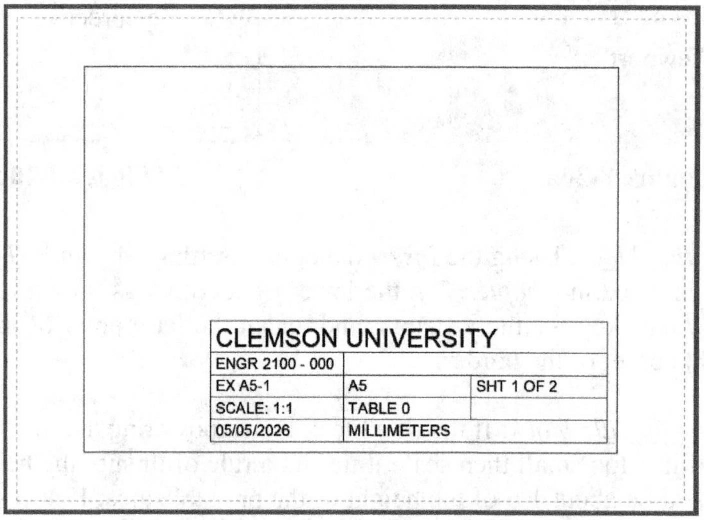

Figure 8-20d

9. *Insert the release block*: Insert the release block in the lower left corner of the title block, Figure 8-20f. The *Insert* block dialog box shows the entries for the release block insertion. Notice that the release block is scaled down during the block insertion process, Figure 8-20g.

10. *Adjust the viewport*: (i) Select the upper left grip point of the viewport and move it to the upper left corner of the border rectangle, Figure 8-21a. (ii) Select the lower right grip point of the viewport and move it to the upper right corner of the title block, Figure 8-21b.

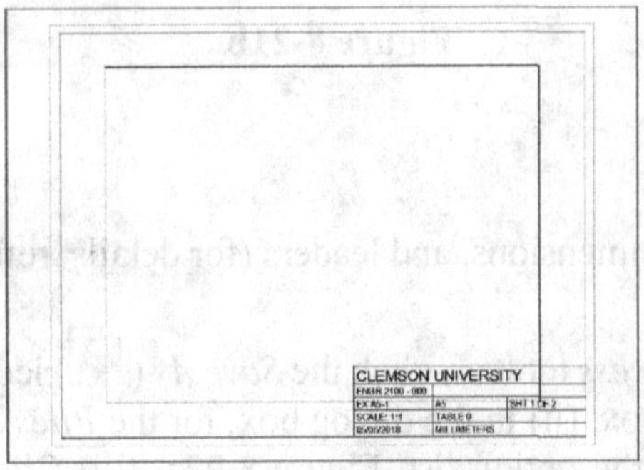

Figure 8-20e

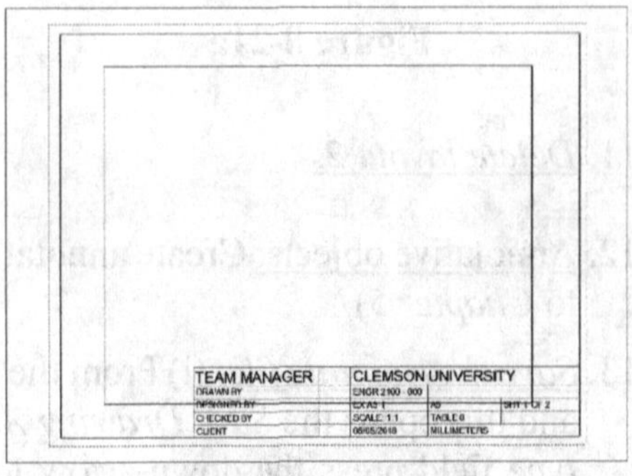

Figure 8-20f

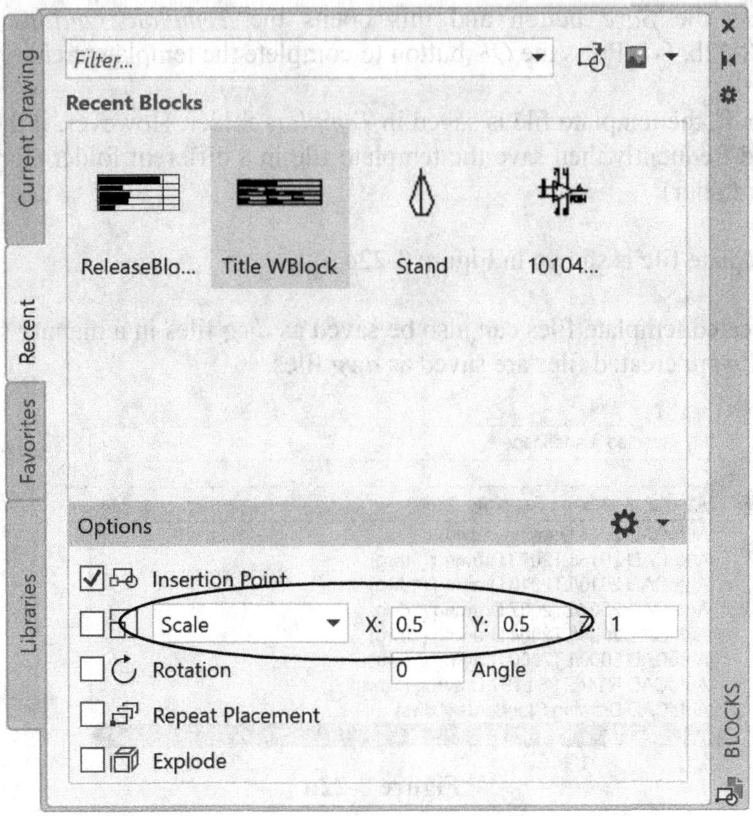

Figure 8-20g

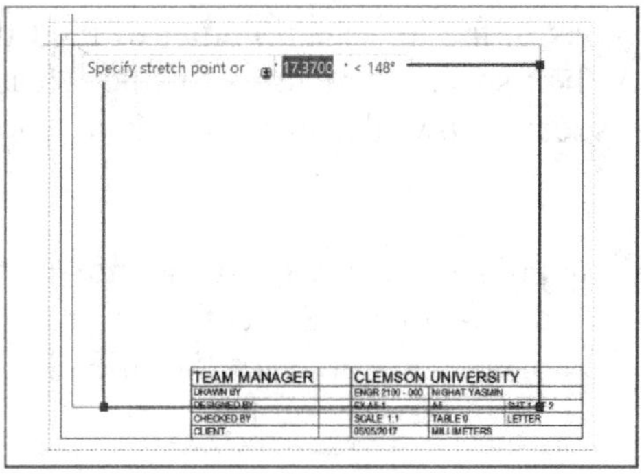

Figure 8-21a

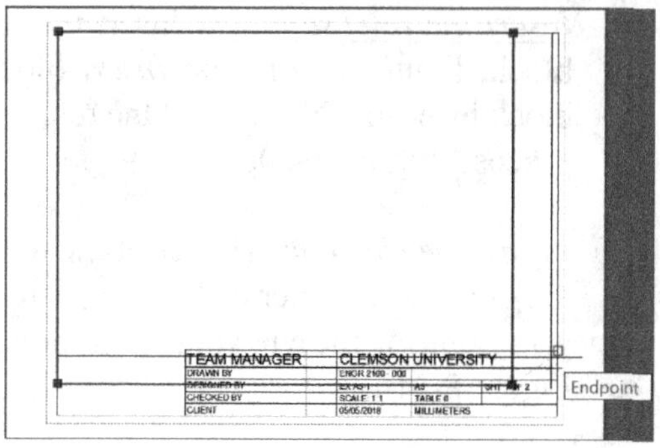

Figure 8-21b

11. *Delete layout 2.*

12. Annotative objects: Create annotative text, dimensions, and leaders (for details, refer to *Chapter 5*)

13. *Save the template file*: (i) From the *Quick Access* toolbar, click the *Save As* ( ) icon and this opens the *Save Drawing As* dialog box. (ii) In the dialog box, for the *Files of type* field press the down-arrow to display the option list, Figure 8-22a. (iii) Click with the left mouse button on *dwt* type, Figure 8-22a, and this opens the template folder. (iv) Specify the template file name, for example, My_acadiso_Landscape. (v) Press the *Save* button and this opens the *Template Options* dialog box, Figure 8-22b. (vi) Press the *OK* button to complete the template creation process.

14. By default, the template file is saved in *Template* folder. However, if the software is reloaded frequently then save the template file in a different folder (for example, in the user folder).

15. The template file is shown in Figure 8-22c.

16. User-created template files can also be saved as *dwg* files in a manner similar to the way software created files are saved as *dwg* files.

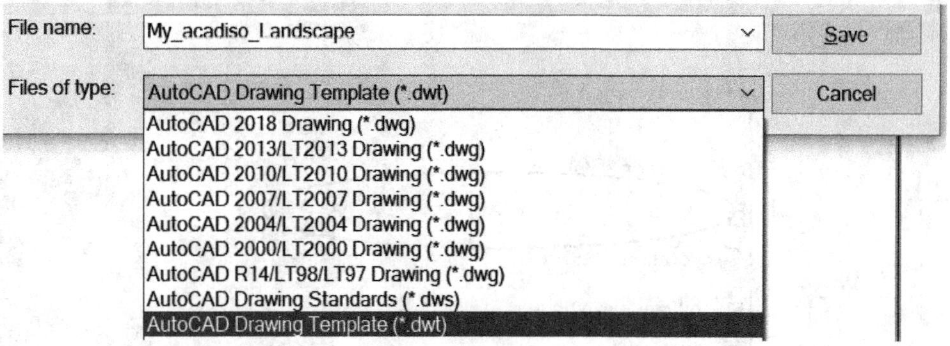

Figure 8-22a

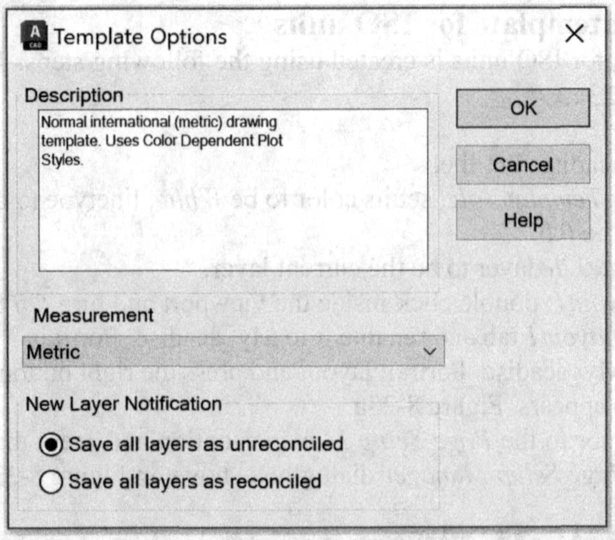

Figure 8-22b

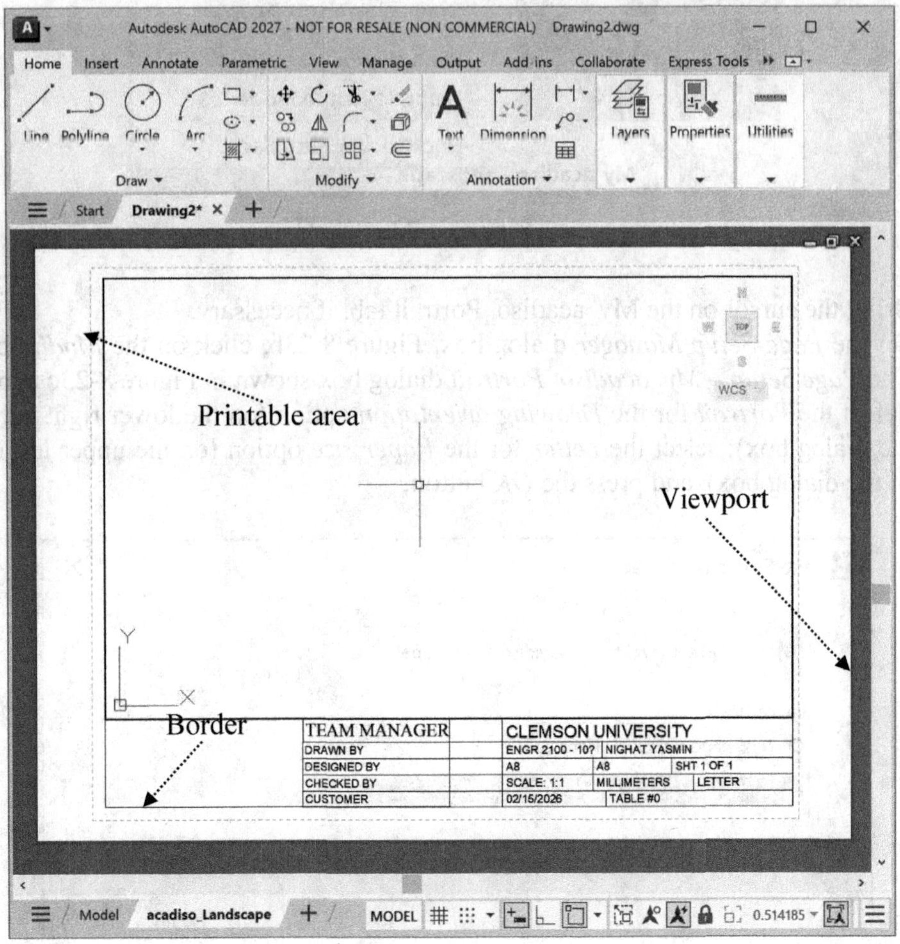

Figure 8-22c

8.7.2. Portrait template for ISO units

A portrait template for ISO units is created using the following steps. The template file is shown in Figure 8-23e.

1. Open a new acadiso.dwt file.
2. Create a layer *TemplateFile*; set its color to be *White*, linetype to be *Continuous*, and lineweight to be *0.0*.
3. Make *TemplateFile* layer to be the current layer.
4. Select the *Layout1*; double click inside the viewport and turn *Off* the grid.
5. Click on the *Layout1* tab and rename it to My_acadiso_Portrait.
6. Click on the My_acadiso_Portrait layout and press the right button of the mouse. The options panel appears, Figure 8-23a.
7. Move the cursor to the *Page Setup Manager* option and press the left button of the mouse. The *Page Setup Manager* dialog box shown in Figure 8-23b appears.

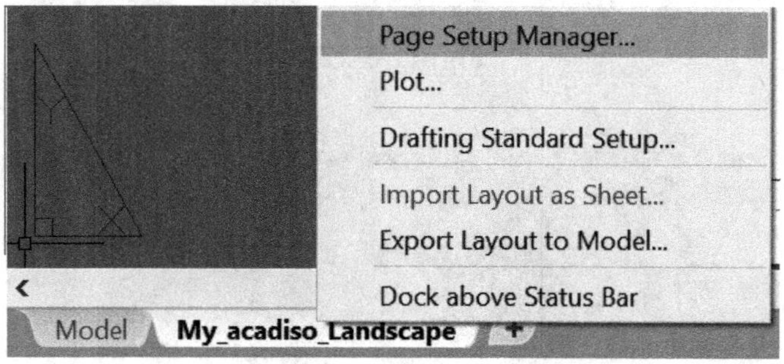

Figure 8-23a

8. Bring the cursor on the My_acadiso_Portrait tab, if necessary.
9. On the *Page Setup Manager* dialog box, Figure 8-23b, click on the *Modify* button. The *Page Setup – My_acadiso_Portrait* dialog box shown in Figure 8-23c appears.
10. Select the *Portrait* for the *Drawing orientation* option (on the lower right corner of the dialog box), select the *Letter* for the *Paper size* option (on the upper left corner of the dialog box), and press the *OK* button.

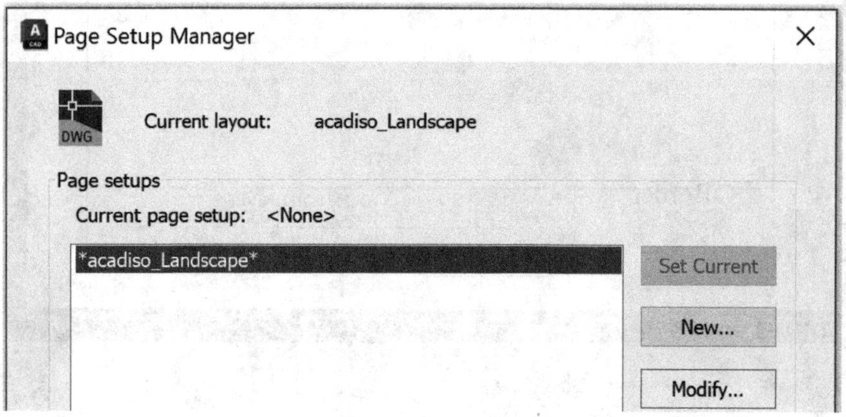

Figure 8-23b

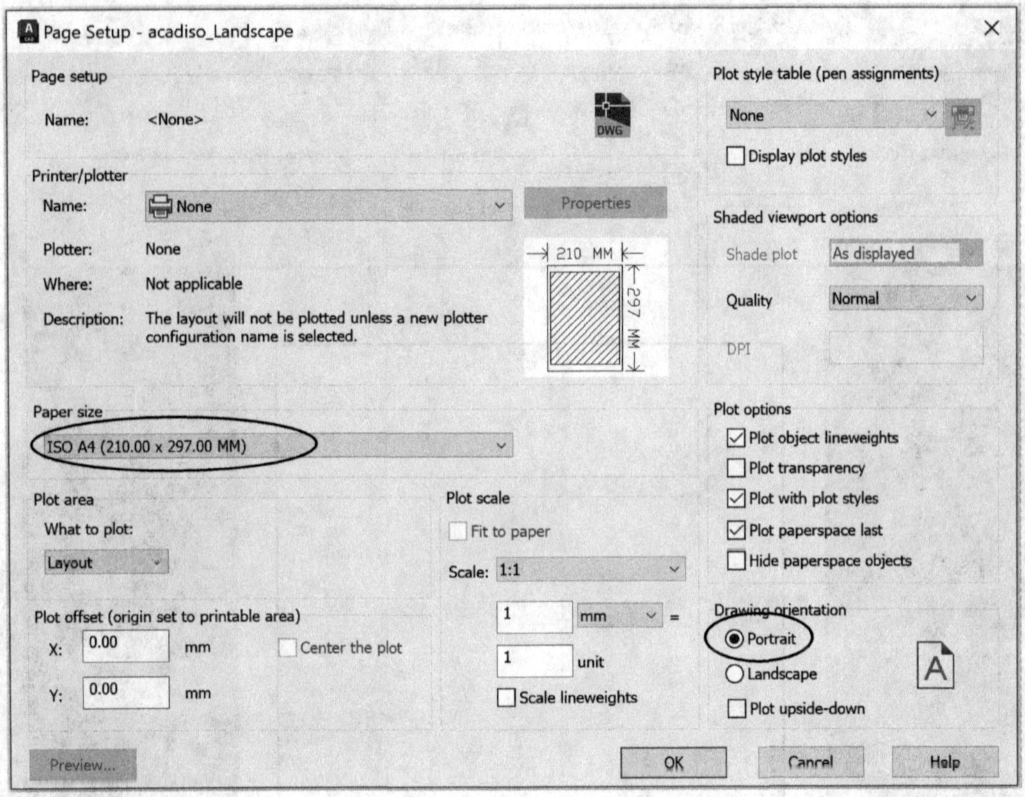

Figure 8-23c

11. Press the *Close* button on the *Page Setup Manager* dialog box.
12. The layout format changes to the portrait style as shown in Figure 8-23d; and the viewport is outside the layout. This is corrected in the template creation process.
13. Now, follow step #6 to step #13 from the procedure used for the landscape template file and save the portrait template file.
14. Save the template file as *My_acadiso_Portrait*.
15. Figure 8-23e shows the portrait template file.

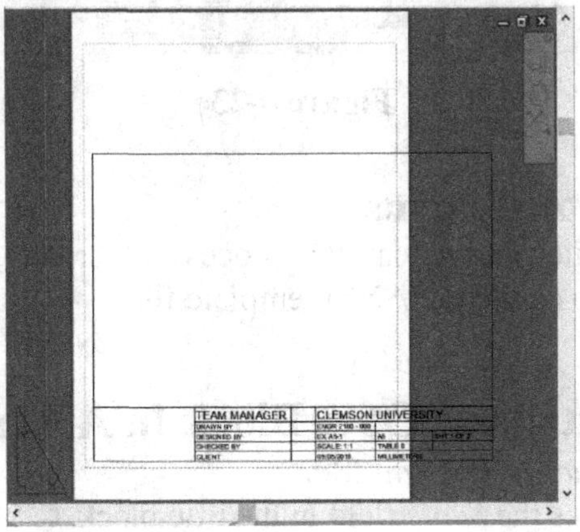

Figure 8-23d

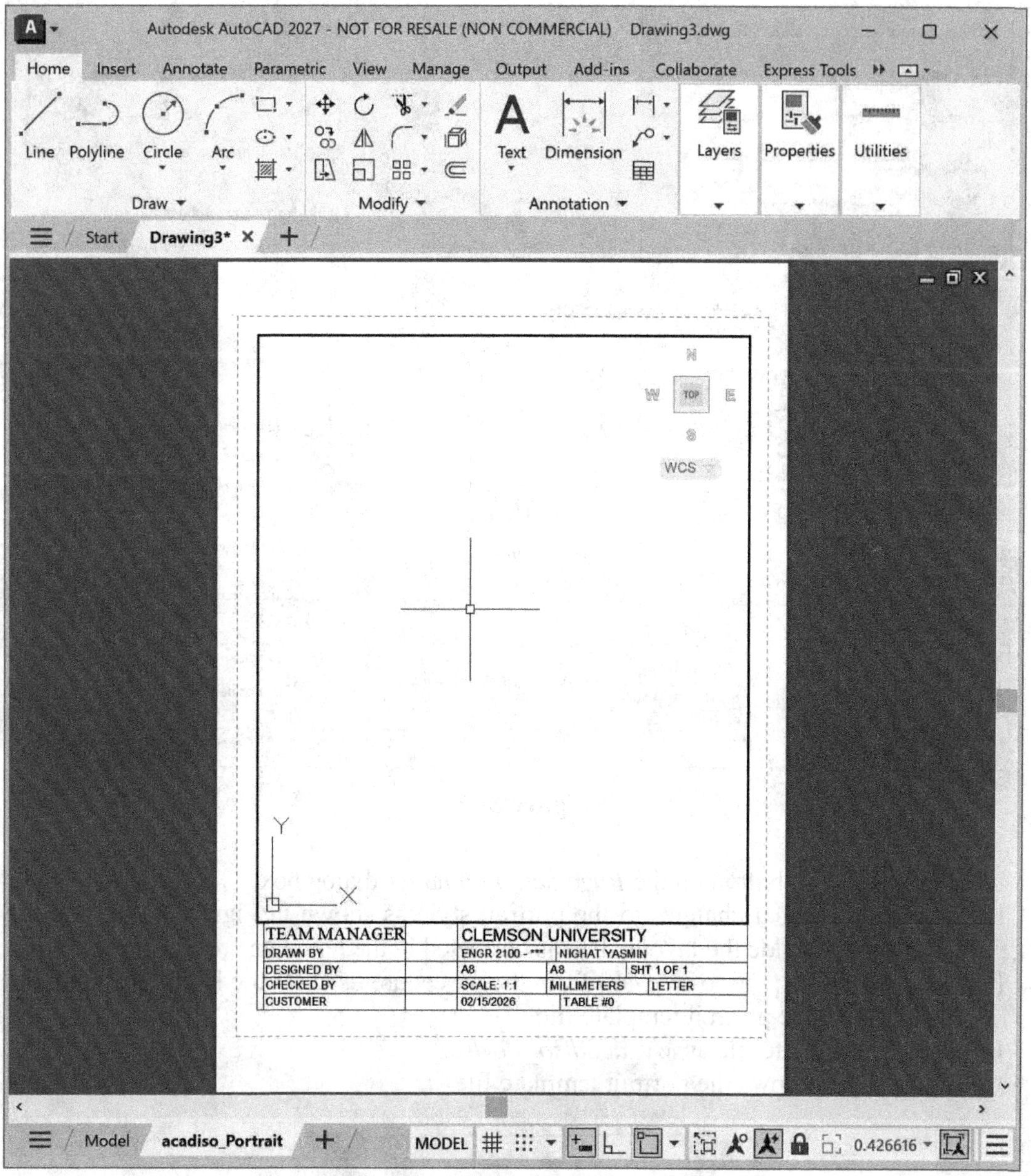

Figure 8-23e

8.7.3. Template for ANSI units

Open a new acad.dwt file and repeat the process of creating acadiso template files (landscape and portrait) to create the ANSI template files.

8.8. Modify Attribute Of A Block In A Template File

1. Open a new *My_acadiso_Portrait* file.
2. This example changes the *Scale* field in the title block.

a. Bring the cursor on top of the *Scale* field in the title block (Figure 8-24a) and double click with the left button of the mouse; this opens the *Enhanced Attribute Editor* dialog box, Figure 8-24b.
b. Select the *Attribute* tab.
c. If necessary, click the desired attribute and change its value in the *Value* field. This activates the *Apply* button.
d. If necessary, change the value of the other attributes, too.
e. Press the *Apply* or the *OK* button. The *Apply* button makes the changes permanent and does not close the dialog box. However, the *OK* button makes the changes permanent and closes the dialog box, too.

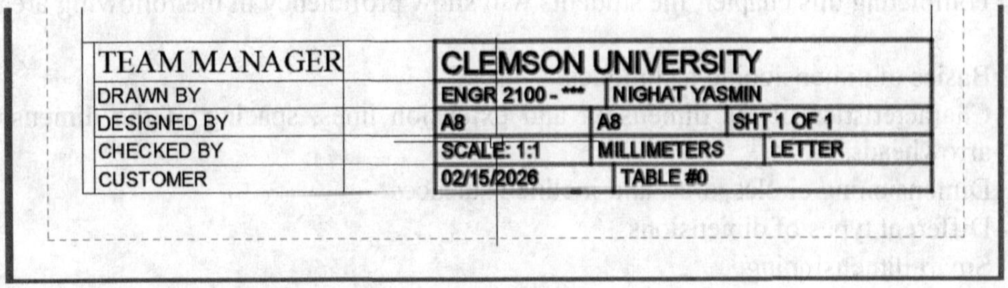

Figure 8-24a

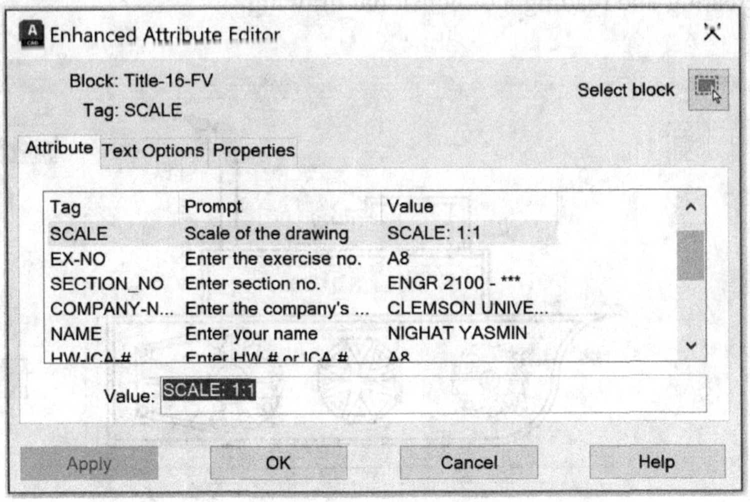

Figure 8-24b

Notes:

9. Dimensions

9.1. Learning Objectives

After completing this chapter, the students will show proficiency in the following areas:

- Basics of dimensioning techniques
- Characteristics of the dimension and extension lines, spacing of the dimensions, arrowheads, etc.
- Dimensioning circles, arcs, and inclined surfaces
- Different types of dimensions
- Smart dimensioning
- Quick dimensioning
- Annotative dimensioning
- Art of creating and reading a dimensional drawing

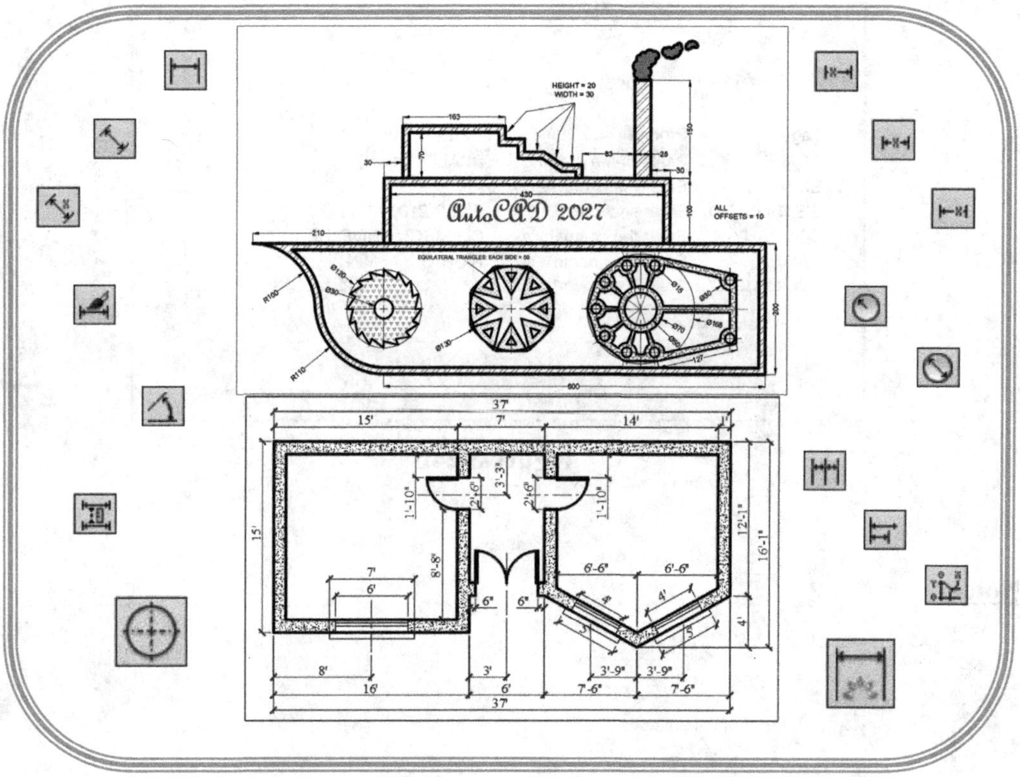

9.2. Introduction

A dimension describes the size and location of the feature of a model. Irrespective of the type of the drawing (architectural, mechanical, etc.) and units used (ANSI, ISO) in the drawing, a dimension is given in the form of a distance, an angle, and/or a note. In AutoCAD, a drafter can add dimensions to a drawing, from the *Home* tab using *Annotation* panel (Figure 9-1a) and from the *Annotate* tab using the *Dimension* panel (Figure 9-1b). This chapter explains the concepts and techniques used to add dimensions to a drawing.

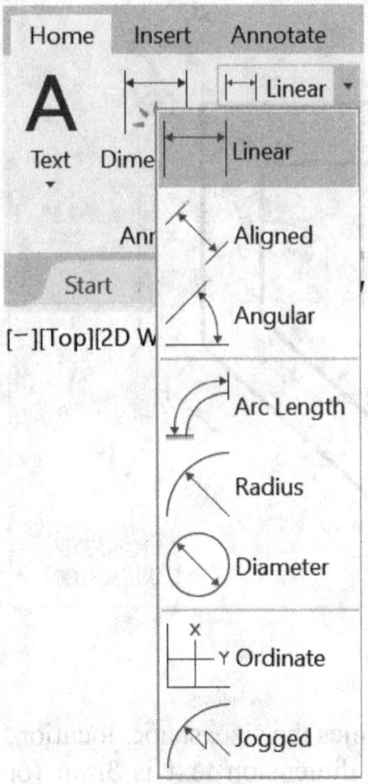

Figure 9-1a

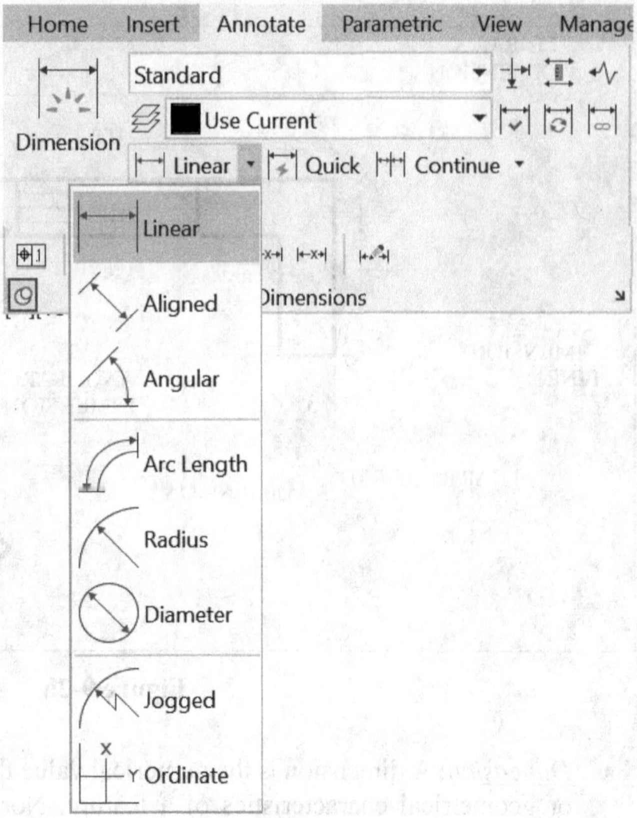

Figure 9-1b

9.3. Dimensioning In General

In addition to visually representing the shape of objects, an engineering drawing must also show the sizes of the objects so that the workers can build the structure or fabricate the parts that fit together. This is accomplished by placing the required values (measurements) along the dimension lines and by giving additional information in the form of notes which are referenced to the parts in question by angled lines called leaders.

A dimensioned drawing should provide all the information necessary for a finished product or part to be manufactured. Dimensions are always drawn using continuous thin lines. Two projection lines indicate where the dimension starts and ends. The projection lines do not touch the object and are drawn perpendicular to the element being dimensioned. In general, units can be omitted from the dimensions if a statement of the units is included in the drawing. All notes and dimensions should be clear and easy to read. In general, all notes should be written in capital letters to aid legibility, and all lettering should be of the same size.

9.4. Terminology

For the following terms, refer to Figure 9-2a and Figure 9-2b.

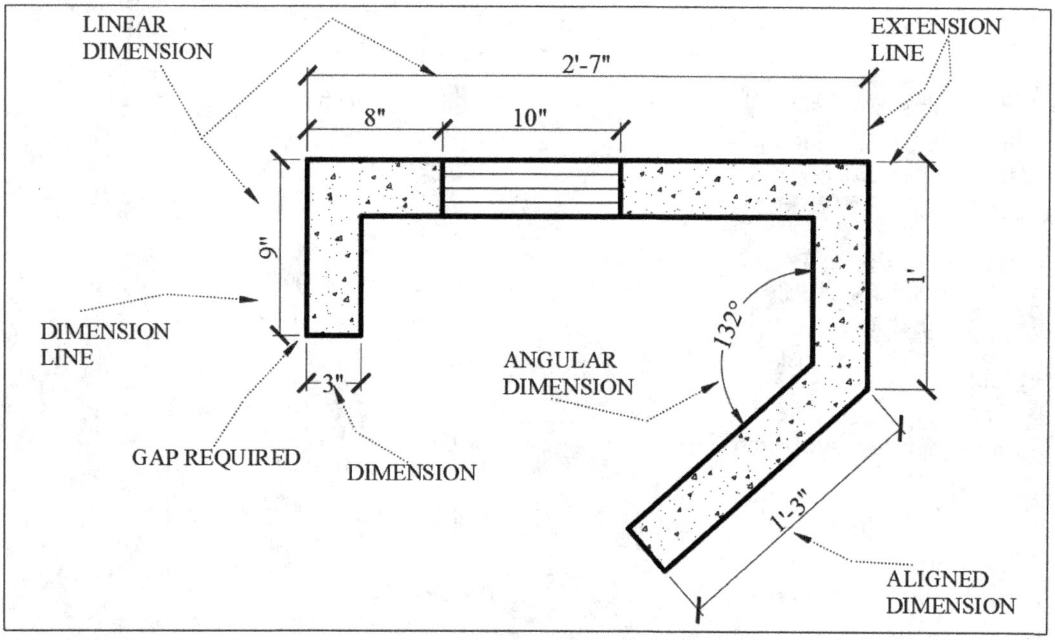

Figure 9-2a

- *Dimension*: A dimension is the numerical value that defines the size, shape, location, or geometrical characteristics of a feature. Normally, dimension text is 3mm (or 0.125") high and the space between lines of text is 1.5mm (or 0.0625").
- *Dimension lines*: A dimension line is a thin continuous line that shows the extent and direction of the dimension, usually located outside the outlines of the object.
- *Extension lines*: An extension line is a thin, continuous line positioned perpendicular to the dimension line that extends from the object. It allows the dimension to be located off the object.
- *Centerlines*: A centerline is a thin line with alternate long and short dashes.
- *Linear dimensions*: A linear dimension is a straight-line distance between two points; it can only be horizontal and/or vertical.
- *Align dimensions*: An align dimension is a straight-line distance between two points and can be horizontal, vertical, or inclined (that is, it is always parallel to the feature).
- *Angular dimensions*: An angular dimension is a dimension that defines the angular value, measured in degrees, between two straight lines.

- *Diameter symbol*: The diameter symbol is ϕ, which precedes a numerical value, to indicate that the dimension shows the diameter of a circle or a circular arc. (The symbol can be created by typing %%c in the text object.) The circles and circular arcs equal or greater than 180° are dimensioned using the diameter symbol.
- *Radius symbol*: The radius symbol is *R*, which precedes a numerical value, to indicate that the dimension shows the radius of a circular arc. The circular arcs less than 180° are dimensioned using the radius symbol.
- *Leader lines*: A leader line is a thin, continuous line used to indicate the feature with which a dimension, note, or symbol is attached. Leader lines begin with an arrowhead or dot.
  - o *For the best appearance make leader lines*
    - ▪ near each other and parallel, and
    - ▪ across as few lines as possible.
  - o *Do not make leader lines*
    - ▪ parallel to the nearby line,
    - ▪ through the corner of the view,
    - ▪ longer than needed, and
    - ▪ horizontal or vertical.
- *Architectural drawing*: In an architectural drawing:
  - o The dimension lines end with tick marks, and the dimension value is located above the dimension line, Figure 9-2a.
  - o The leader lines can end with a dot or an arrow.

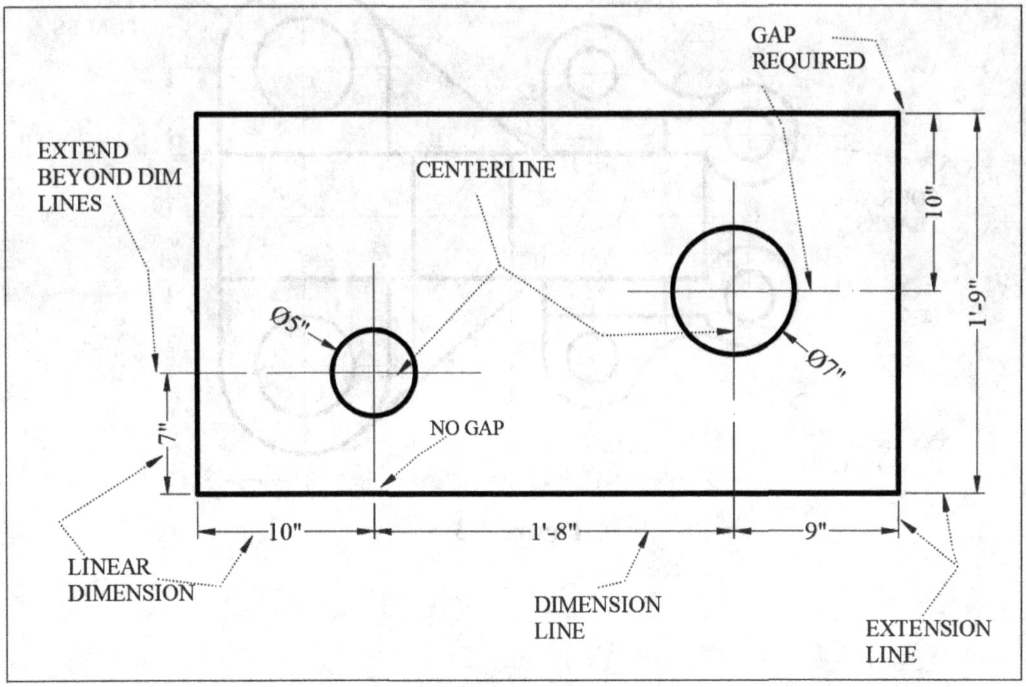

Figure 9-2b

9.5. Dimensions: Basic Rules

Figure 9-2a, Figure 9-2b, and Figure 9-3 show rules for placing dimensions. If possible, turn on the *Grid* so dimension placement becomes faster.

- Space between dimension lines: Dimension lines should be uniformly spaced.
- Alignment of the dimensions: Align and group dimensions for neatness and easy understanding.
- Centerline used as an extension line: For the circled and circular arcs, use the end of the centerline as the beginning of the extension lines.
- Dimension placement:
    - Place dimensions near the features they are dimensioning.
    - Do not place dimensions on the surface of the object.
    - Avoid crossing extension lines.
    - Place smaller dimensions closer to the object than the larger ones.
    - Always place overall dimensions the farthest away from the object.
- Gap between the object and the extension line: There should be a noticeable gap between the object and the extension line to create a visual break. The visual effects can also be enhanced by using a different color for the dimensions.
- Line of symmetry: If a drawing is symmetrical at a certain axis (two sides are mirror images) then show the line of symmetry. It is enough to show the dimension for one side.

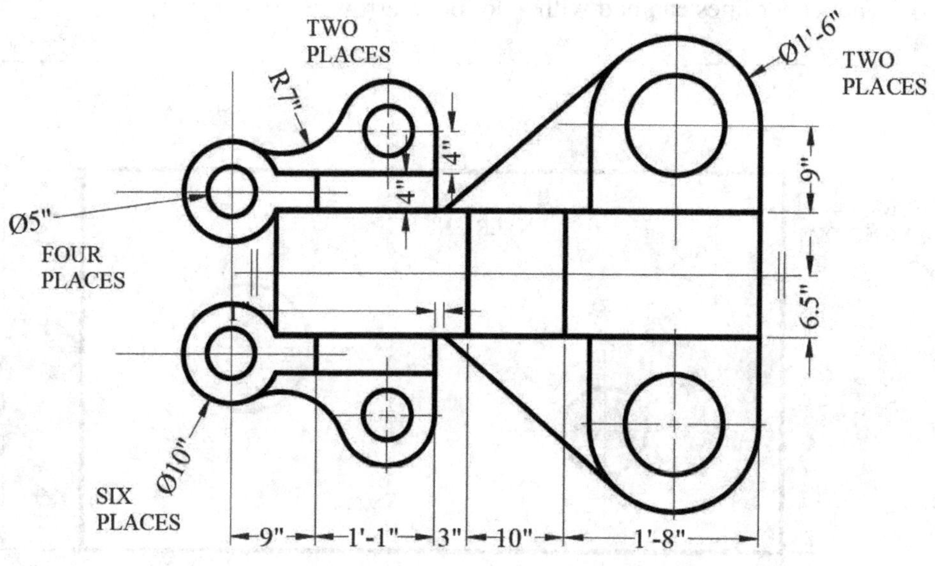

Figure 9-3

9.6. Dimensions Styles

AutoCAD provides two styles for the dimensions, *Standard* and *Annotative*. The user can select either of the two options from the *Home* tab and the *Annotate* panel: (i) click the down arow of the *Dimension Style* tool and (ii) select the desired option. That is, select *Standard* option for the *Standard* dimensions and select *Annotative* option for the *Annotative* dimensions. Figure 9-4a shows the selection of the *Annotative* dimension style.

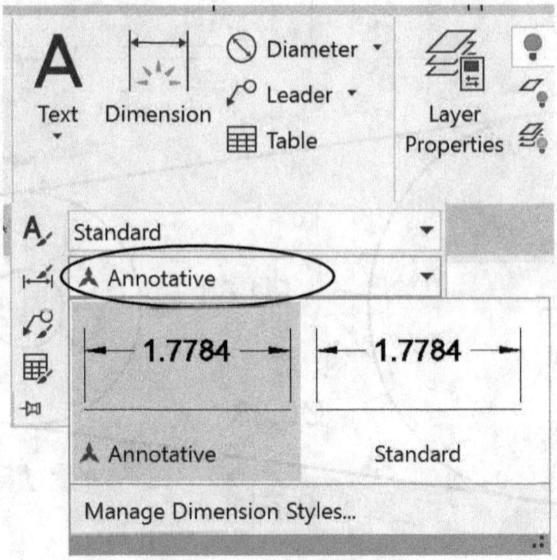

Figure 9-4a

9.6.1. Standard dimensions

The standard dimensions appearance depends on the displayed scale in the Model space and layouts. The standard dimensions appeared to be of different sizes depending on the viewport scale. Figure 9-4b shows three viewports with different viewport scales. The scales are shown in the lower right corners of the viewports. It is clear from the figure that the dimension size depends on the viewport scale factor. If a dimension location is changed in one viewport, it will also be changed in the other viewports.

9.6.2. Annotative dimensions

The annotative dimensions are used to control the size at which the annotative dimensions are displayed in the Model space and layouts. The annotative dimensions always appeared to be of the same size regardless of the viewport scale. Figure 9-4c shows three viewports with different viewport scales. The scales are shown in the lower right corners of the viewports. It is clear from the figure that the dimension size is independent of viewport scale factor. If a dimension location is changed in one viewport, it will not change in the other viewports. For example, the location of the ϕ1.88 and ϕ0.38 are different in viewports with the scale factor of 1:2 and 1:1 (this effect is created by ghost dimensions).

For the ghost object and characteristic of the annotative objects, refer to *Chapter 5*.

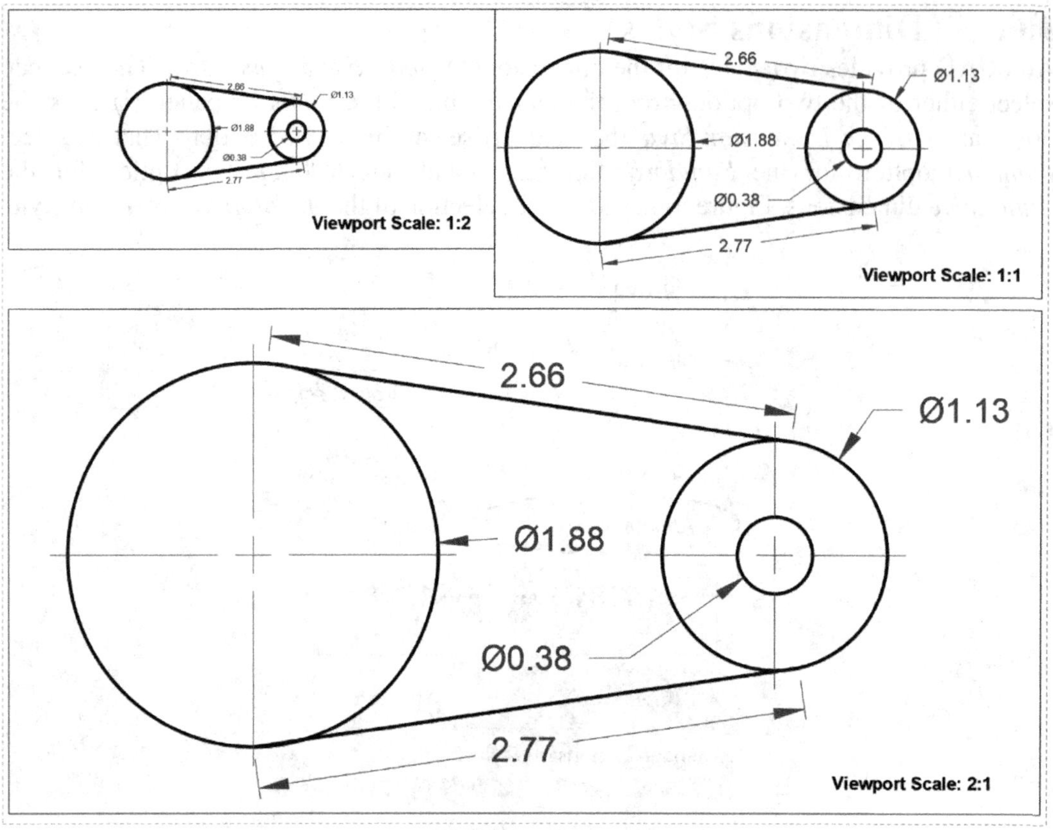

Figure 9-4b

9.7. Illustrative Example

This section explains the steps to add annotative dimensions.

- Launch AutoCAD 2027.
- Open a new *acad* template file.
- Draw one of the drawings from this chapter or draw two circles; two arcs one greater than 180 degrees and one less than 180 degrees; and a few horizontal, vertical, and slanted lines.
- Add dimensions as discussed in the current chapter.
- Add the scales to the dimension's properties: The process of adding multiple scale factors to an annotative object is explained in *Chapter 5: Section 5.3.1*.
- Update the viewports scales. For details, refer to *Chapter 8*.

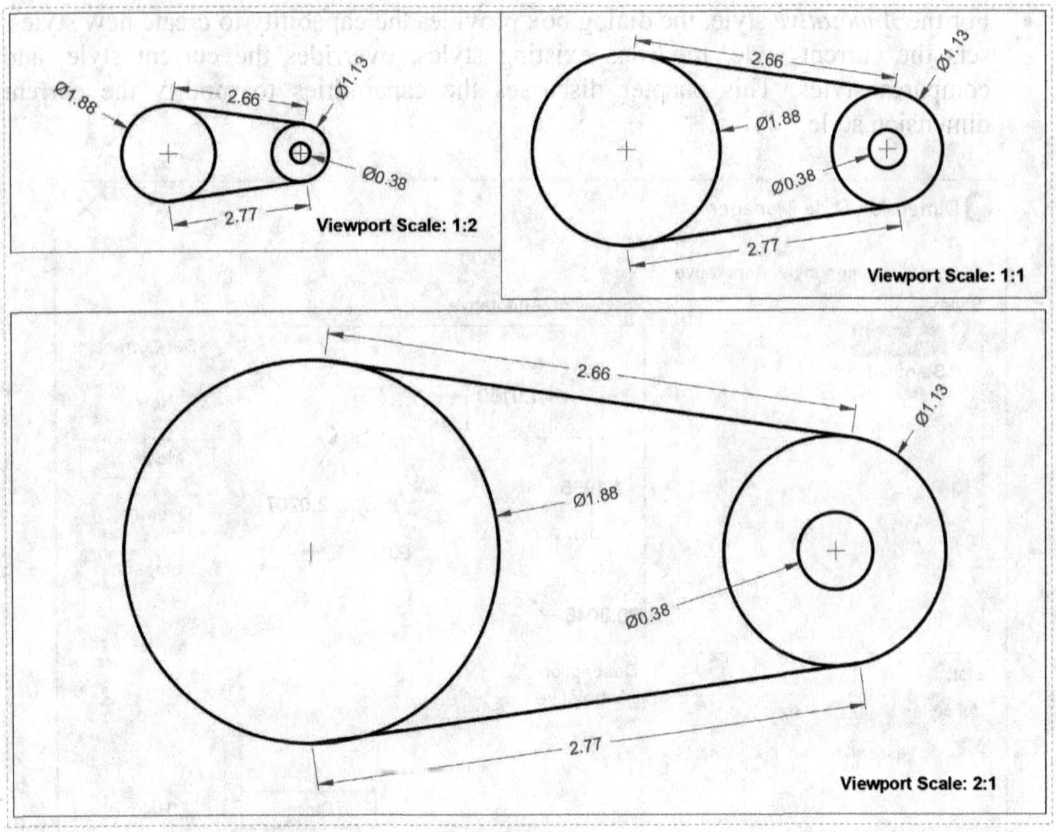

Figure 9-4c

9.8. Dimension Style Manager

The appearance of dimensions can be controlled by changing various settings using the *Dimension Style Manager* dialog box or the *Properties* palette.

- The *Dimension Style Manager* dialog box can be launched using one of the following methods:
    1. Panel method 1: From the *Annotate* tab and the *Dimension* panel, click on the dialog box launcher (the small arrow on the lower right corner of the panel).
    2. Panel method 2: From the *Home* tab, expand the *Annotation* panel, and select the *Dimension Style* tool or click Manage Dimension Styles, Figure 9-4a.
    3. Command line method: Type "dimstyle," "Dimstyle," or "DIMSTYLE" on the command line and press the *Enter* key.

- The activation of the command opens the *Dimension Style Manager* dialog box, Figure 9-5.
- The dialog box provides the capability to select *Annotative* or *Standard* style. The current chapter explains the *Annotative* style.

- For the *Annotative* style, the dialog box provides the capability to create new styles, sets the current style, modifies existing styles, overrides the current style, and compares styles. This chapter discusses the capabilities to modify the current dimension style.

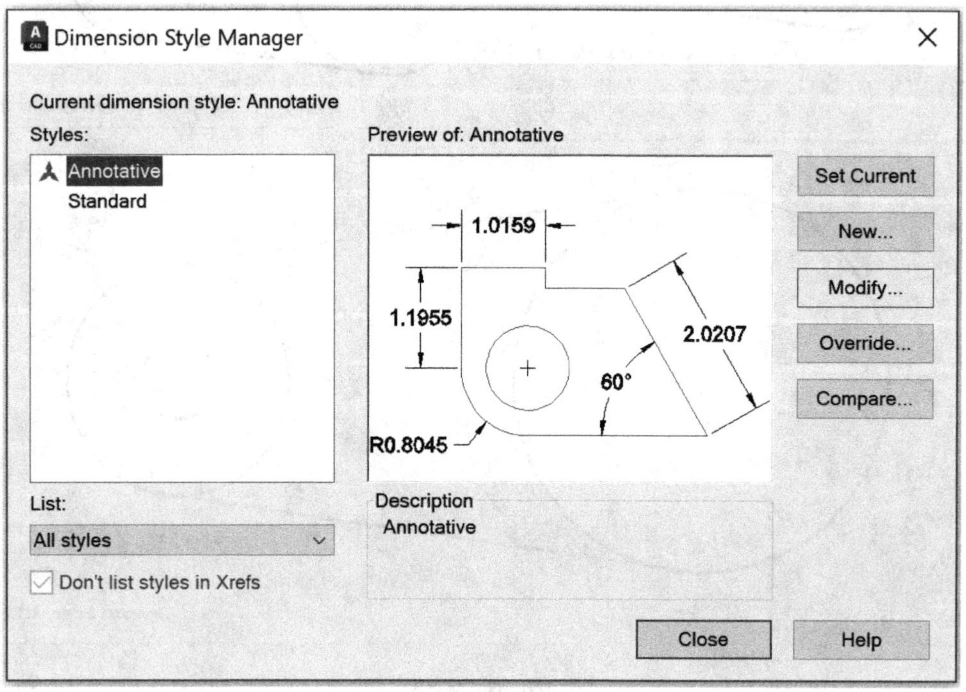

Figure 9-5

- Click on the *Modify* button (Figure 9-5) to modify an existing style. This opens the *Modify Dimension Style* dialog box for the *Annotative* dimensions, Figure 9-6a. Also, the *New Dimension Style* and *Override Current Style* dialog boxes provide these capabilities.

9.9. Modify Dimension Style Dialog Box

The *Modify Dimension Style* dialog box allows for changes in the lines (dimension and extension); symbol and arrows (arrowheads, center mark, jog dimension etc.); text (appearance, placement, and alignment); fit (placement of the dimension text and arrowheads); primary units (linear and angular, measurement, and zero suppression); and tolerance (format, alignment, and zero suppression).

9.9.1. Lines

The *Lines* tab (Figure 9-6a) sets the format and properties for the dimension and extension lines. The commonly used features are shown in Figure 9-2a, Figure 9-2b, and Figure 9-6a; set the color, linetype, and lineweight by *ByLayer*. The effect of some of the commonly used features are shown in Figure 9-6b.

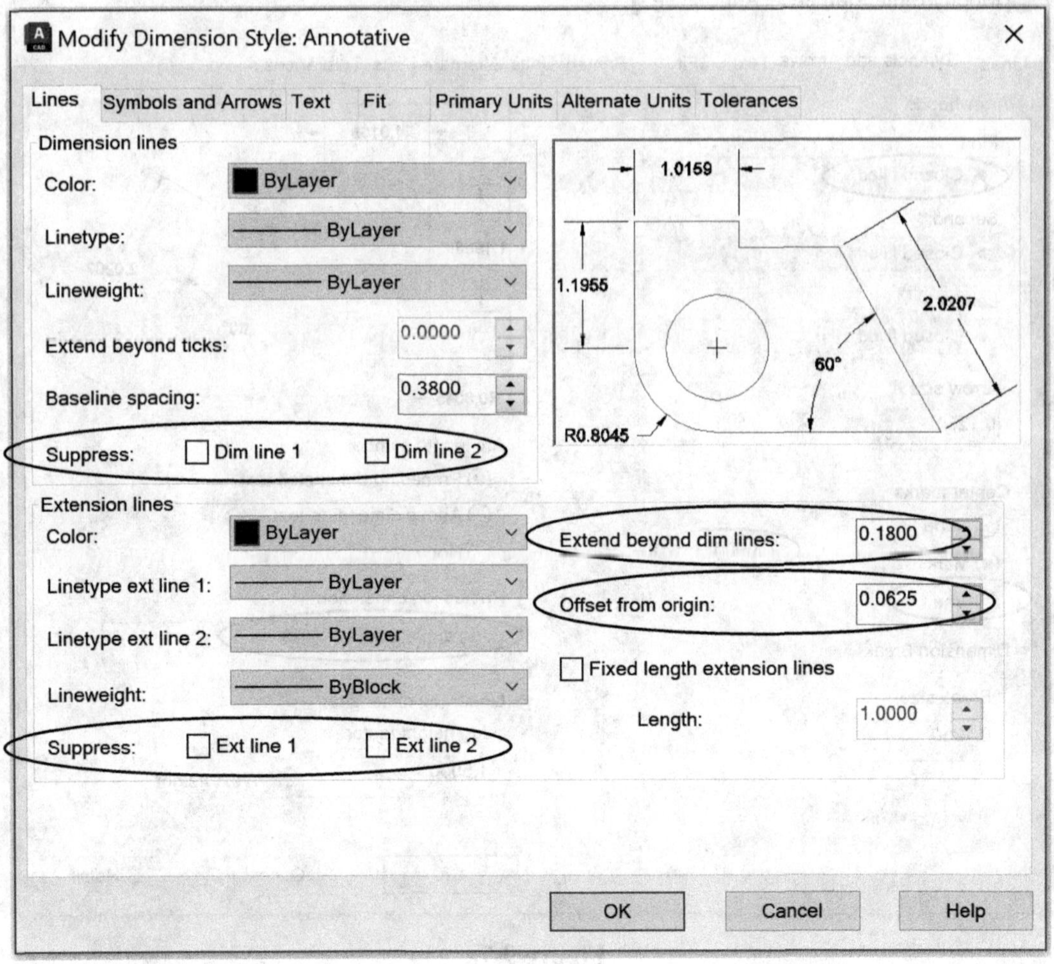

Figure 9-6a

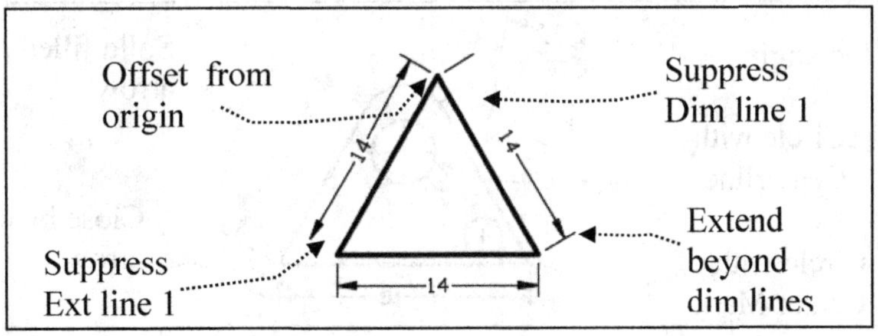

Figure 9-6b

9.9.2. Symbols and arrows

The *Symbols and Arrows* tab, Figure 9-7a, sets the format and size of the arrowhead, center marks, dimension break, arc length symbol, radius jog dimension, and linear jog dimension. The effects of some of the commonly used features are shown in Figure 9-7b.

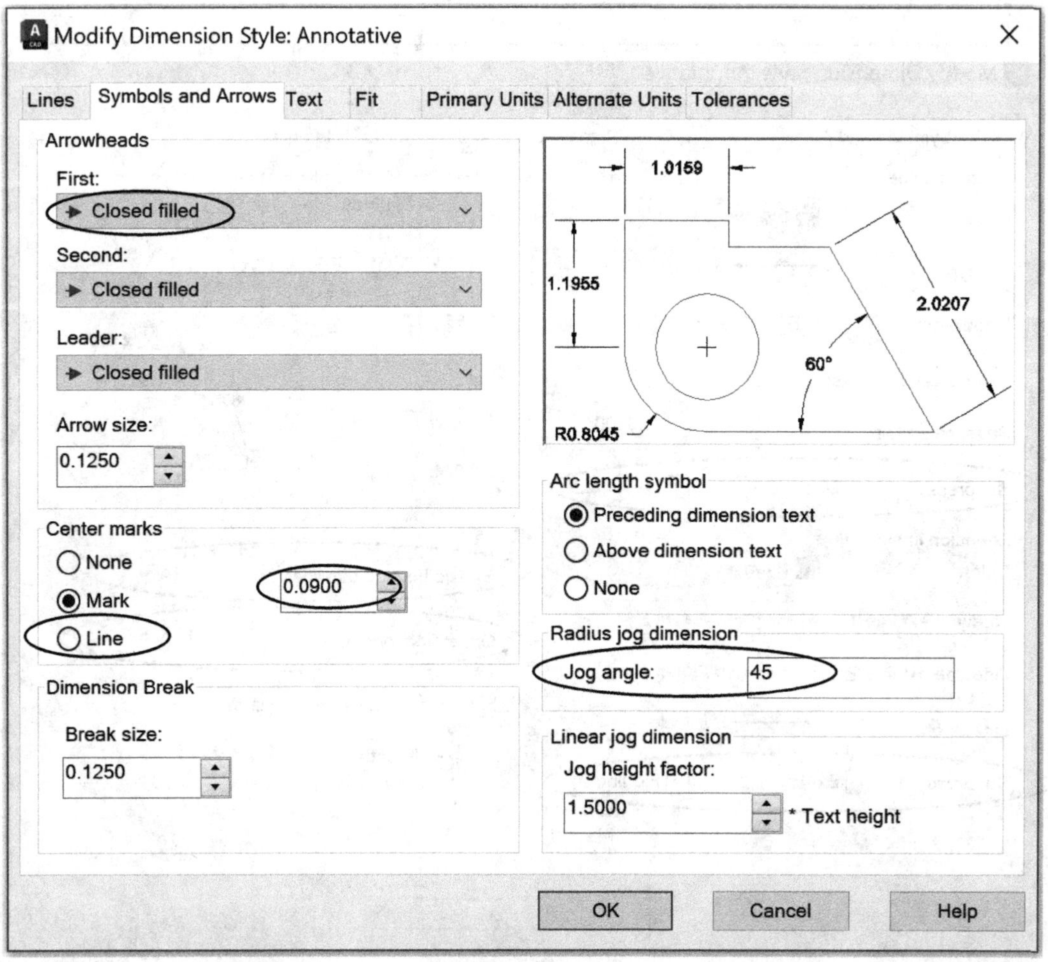

Figure 9-7a

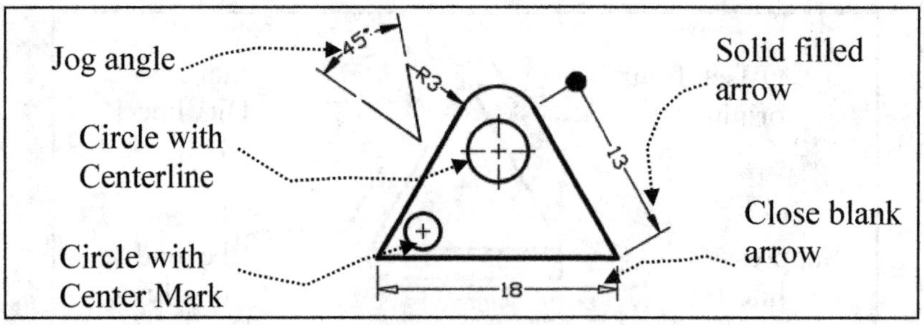

Figure 9-7b

9.9.3. Text

The selection of the *Text* tab (Figure 9-8a) sets the format, placement, alignment, and size of the dimension text. For the annotative dimensions, the user must select *Text style* to be *Annotative*. The effect of some of the commonly used features is shown in Figure 9-8b; set the text color by *ByLayer*. If necessary, set the text style for annotative text before setting the dimension style dialog box. For details, refer to *Chapter 5*.

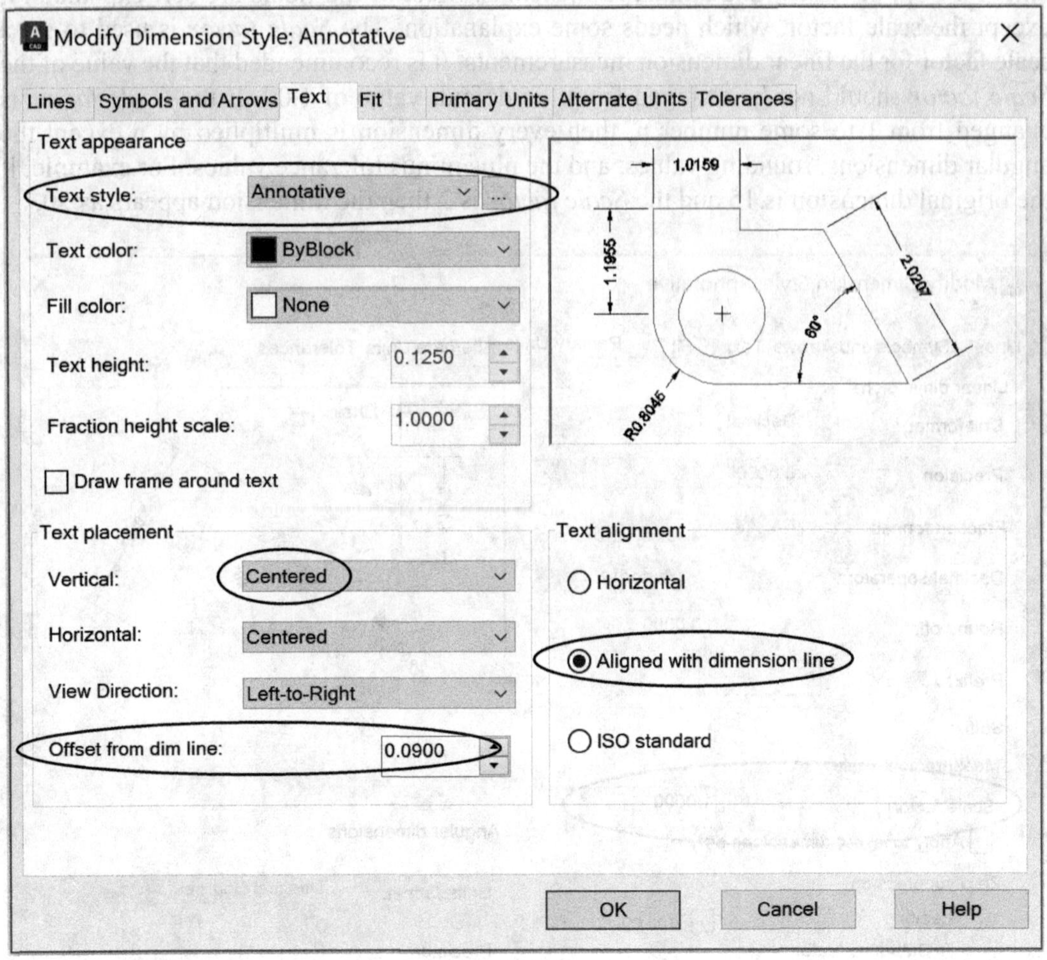

Figure 9-8a

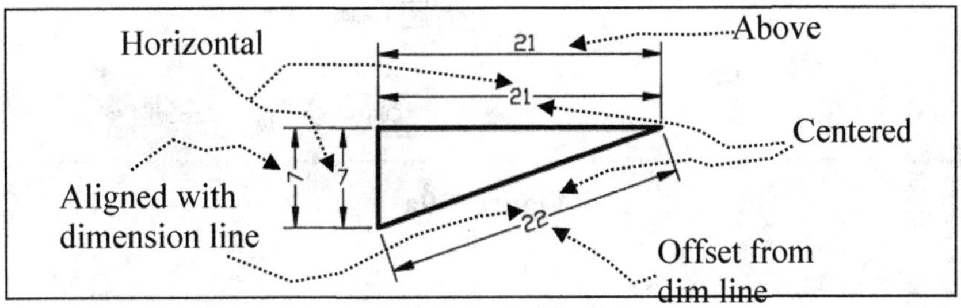

Figure 9-8b

9.9.4. Fit

The *Fit* tab controls the placement of the dimension text and arrowheads based on the space available between the extension lines, leader lines, and dimension lines.

9.9.5. Primary units

The *Primary Units* tab, Figure 9-9a, sets the format and precision of the primary dimension units for both the linear and angular dimensions. Most of the fields are self-explanatory, except the scale factor, which needs some explanation. The *Scale factor* is used to set a scale factor for the linear dimension measurements. It is recommended that the value of the *Scale factor* should not be changed from the default value of 1.00. If the *Scale factor* is changed from 1 to some number n, then every dimension is multiplied by n except the angular dimensions, rounding values, and the plus/minus tolerance values. For example, if the original dimension is 15 and the *Scale factor* is 2 then the dimension appears as 30.

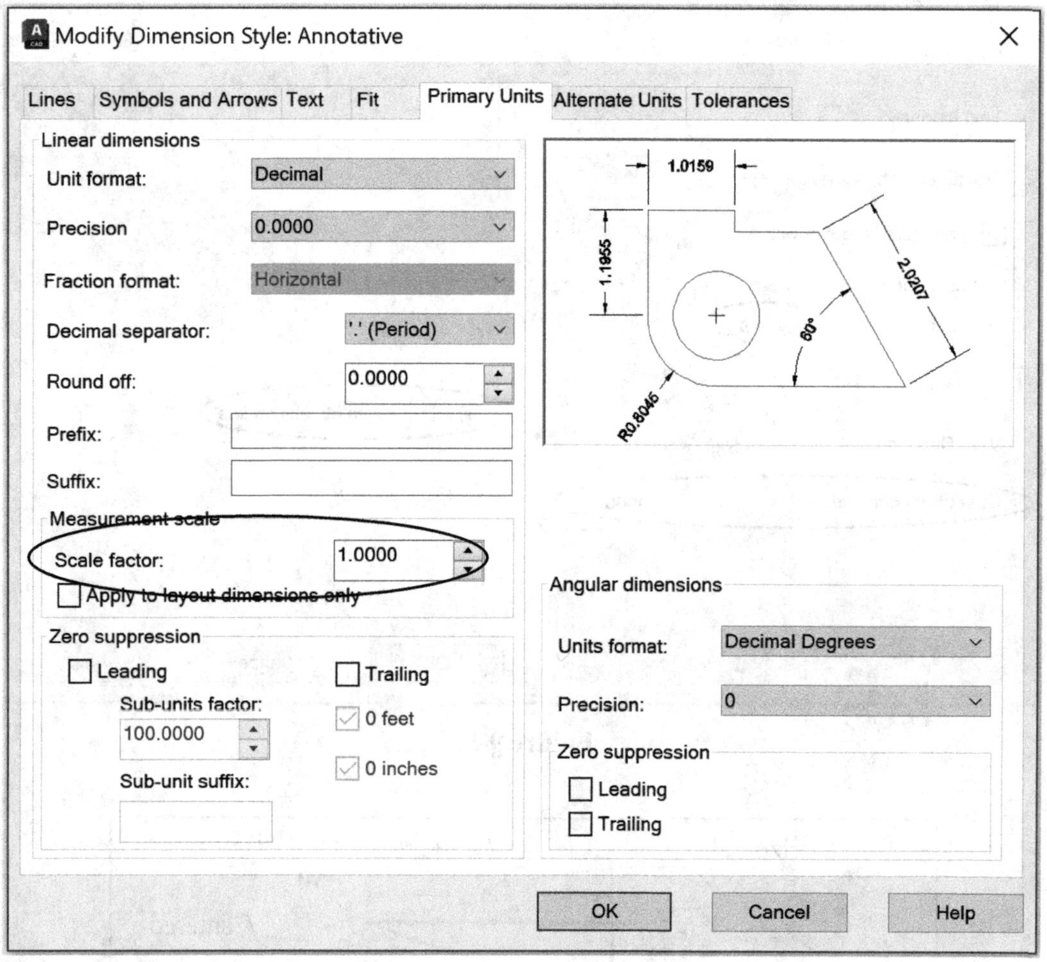

Figure 9-9a

For the linear (length) dimensions, AutoCAD 2027 provides six different types of unit formats, Figure 9-9b. It is left for the user to explore the corresponding updates to the precision.

1. Scientific: Used for highly specialized technical or mechanical drawings.
2. Decimal: Default unitless format.
3. Engineering: This format uses feet and decimal inches. For example, dimension will appear as 3'-2.8".
4. Architectural: This format uses feet and inches in fraction format. For example, dimension will appear stacked ($3' - 2\frac{3''}{4}$ or $3' - 2\,{}^{3''}/_{4}$) or unstacked dimensions (3'-2 3/4").
5. Fractional: Used for highly specialized technical or mechanical drawings.
6. Window Desktop: This format is a specific unit format that sets dimension text to a standard decimal format based on the Microsoft Windows Control Panel of the computer. For example, it may use commas separator for number in thousands (234,56.789).

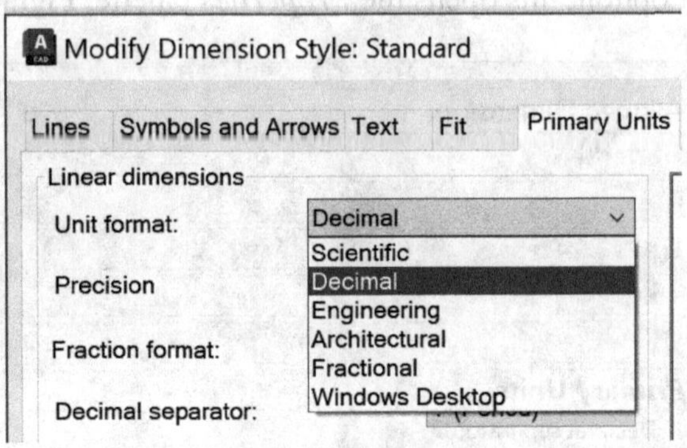

Figure 9-9b

9.9.6. Alternate units

The selection of the *Alternate Units* tab specifies the display of alternate units in dimension measurements and sets their format and precision.

9.9.7. Tolerance

The selection of the *Tolerances* tab controls the display and format of dimension text tolerances. Although theoretically possible, it is economically unfeasible to manufacture products to the exact dimensions displayed on an engineering drawing. The cost of a part rapidly increases as an absolute correct size is approached. Hence, accuracy depends largely on the manufacturing process used and the care taken to manufacture a product. Since different companies make different parts of a system; it is very important that these parts should be interchangeable. A tolerance value shows the manufacturing department the maximum permissible variation from the basic dimension. Tolerance is discussed in detail in Chapter 10.

9.10. Modify Dimension Style

A user can modify the dimension style using the dialog box or the properties palette.

9.10.1. Modify dimension style using the dialog box

If the user desires to change the settings for all the dimensions in the drawing, then open the *Modify Dimension Style* dialog box. Using the functionality of the dialog box, change the dimension setting. For example, if *Suppress Dim line 1* option under the *Lines* tab is selected, then the first-dimension line is suppressed from every dimension (both linear and angular dimensions).

9.10.2. Modify dimension style using the properties palette

If the user desires to change the settings for one (or more but not all) dimension then use the *Properties* palette, Figure 9-10, and perform the following steps.

- Select the desired dimension(s) by clicking with the left mouse button.
- Open the option panel by pressing the right button of the mouse.
- Click on the last option; this opens the *Properties* palette, Figure 9-10a.

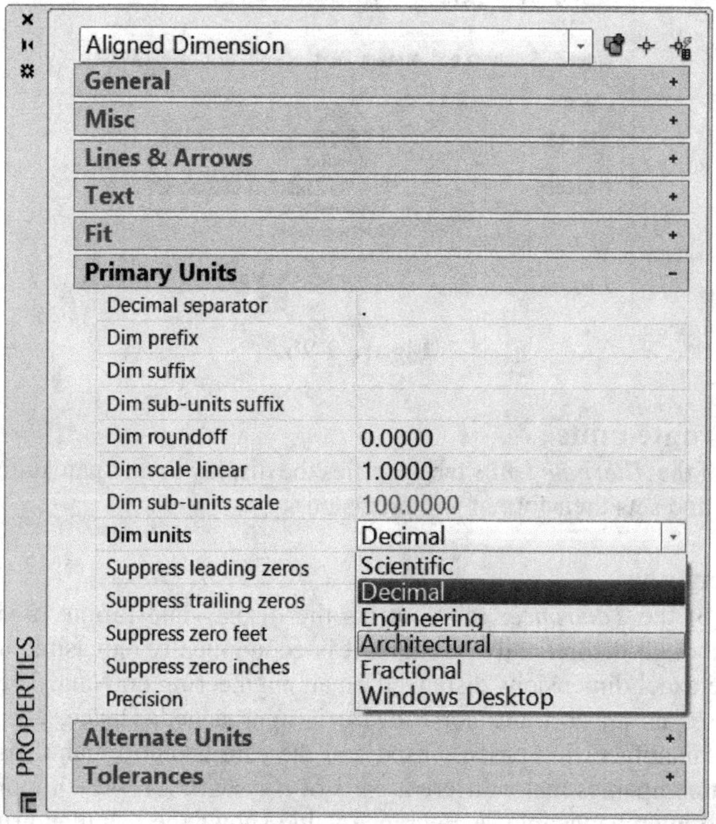

Figure 9-10a

- The *Properties* palette has a panel for every tab in the *Modify Dimension Style* dialog box.
- On the *Properties* palette, select the desired panel.
- In Figure 9-10a under the *Primary Units* panel and *Dim units* command, the current option is *Decimal*. The user is changing it to the *Architectural* type of unit. Modifying the desired option will only affect the selected dimension(s).
- In Figure 9-10b under the *Lines & Arrow* panel and *Dim line 1*, the current option is *on*. The user is changing it to *off*. Modifying the desired option will only affect the selected dimension(s).
- In Figure 9-10c under the *Text* panel and *Text view direction*, the current option is *Left-to-Right*. The user can change it to *Right-to-Left*. Modifying the desired option will only affect the selected dimension(s).

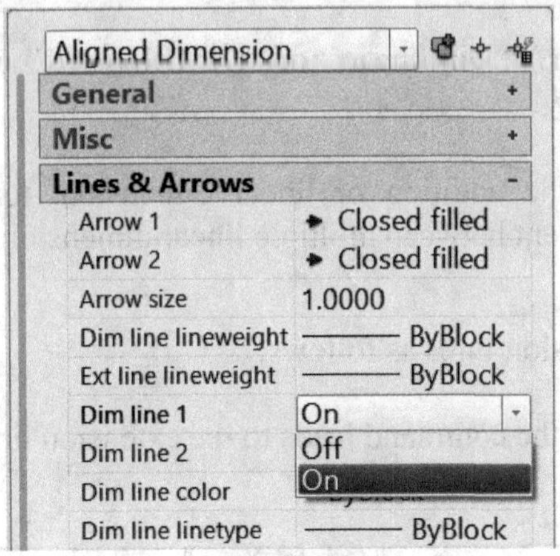

Figure 9-10b

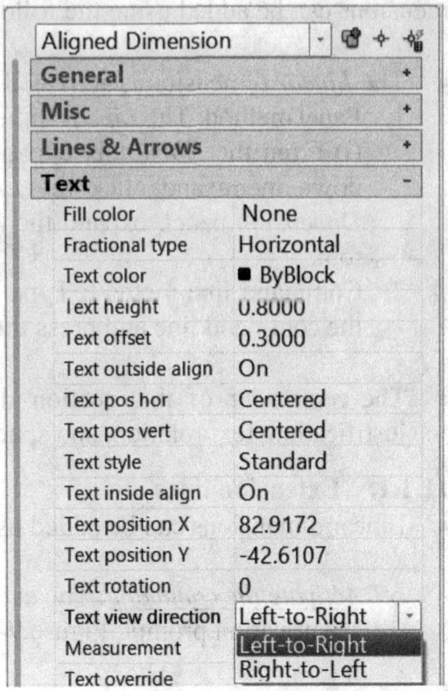

Figure 9-10c

9.11. Dimensioning Techniques

This section describes basic techniques of dimensioning. For example, how to dimension a horizontal or vertical line, sloping lines, angles, circles, etc.

9.11.1. Linear dimensions

The *Linear* dimension command is used to create only horizontal and vertical dimensions. In Figure 9-11a, the dimensions for the sides labeled as A, B, C, and D are the linear dimensions.

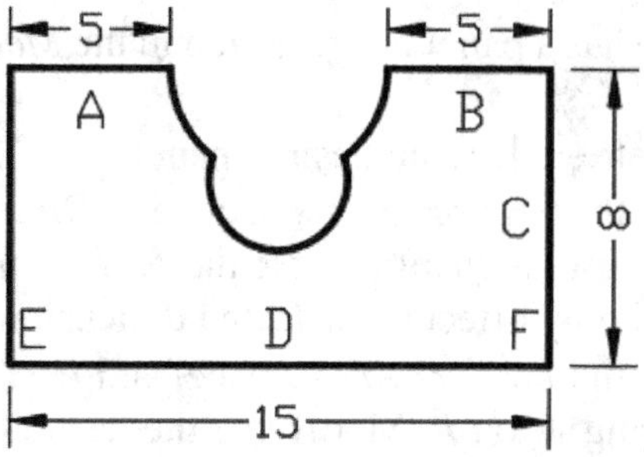

Figure 9-11a

Example: Add the linear dimensions for the sides A, B, C, and D, Figure 9-11a. The linear dimensions can be added using the following procedure.

- The *Linear* dimension is activated using one of the following methods.
  1. Panel method: The *Linear* dimension command can be activated from two panels. (i) From the *Home* tab, expand the *Annotation* panel, expand the *Linear* drop-down menu and click the *Linear* tool. (ii) From the *Annotate* tab and the *Dimension* panel, expand the *Dimension* drop-down menu and click the *Linear* tool.
  2. Command line method: Type "dimlinear," "Dimlinear," or "DIMLINEAR" on the command line and press the *Enter* key.

- The remainder of this section discusses the addition of linear dimension, text justification, text rotation, and space adjustment between multiple linear dimensions.

9.11.1.1. Extension lines

- Linear dimensions can be added using extension lines as follows:

  - *Activate the command*: The activation of the command leads to the extension line specification prompt, Figure 9-11b.

Figure 9-11b

  - *Specify first extension line origin*, Figure 9-11a: Turn on the object snap with *Endpoints* option. Click on point *F* and a rubber band appears originating from point *F* and terminating at the cursor, Figure 9-11c.

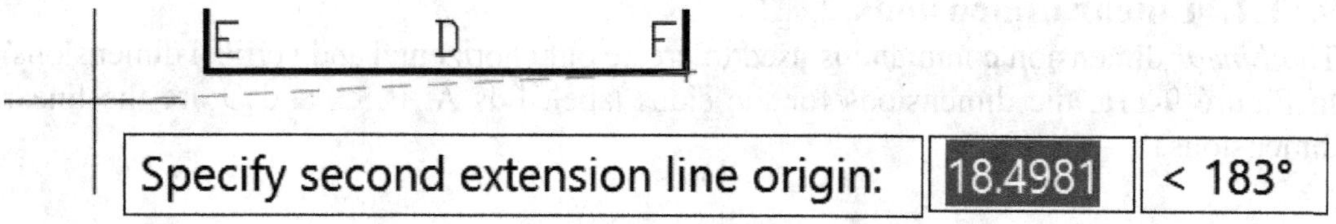

Figure 9-11c

- *Specify second extension line origin* Figure 9-11c: Click on point *E*; the resulting prompt is shown in Figure 9-11d.

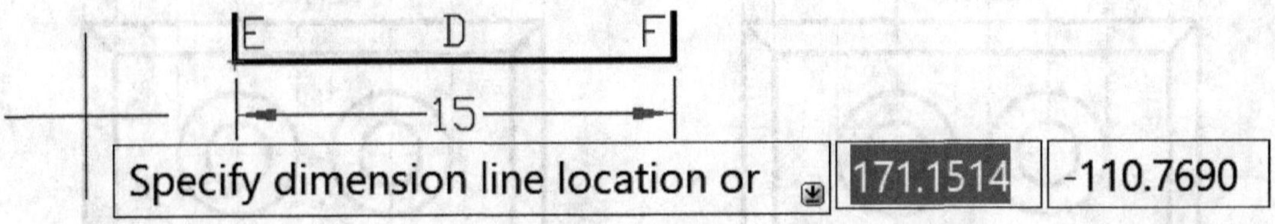

Figure 9-11d

- *Specify the dimension line location*, Figure 9-11d: Locate the dimension line by moving the crosshairs, following the dimension placement rules. Press the left mouse button at the desired location, Figure 9-11e.
- Figure 9-11a: Similarly, add dimensions to sides A, B, and C.

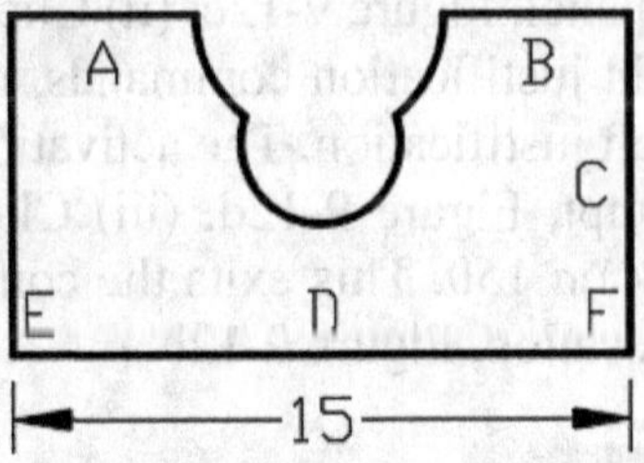

Figure 9-11e

9.11.1.2. Object selection

- Linear dimensions can be added by selecting the object to be dimensioned as follows:
  - *Activate the command*: The activation of the command leads to the extension line specification prompt, Figure 9-11b.
  - Press the *Enter* key, Figure 9-11f.
  - *Select object to dimension*, Figure 9-11f: Bring the cursor on the side D and press the left mouse button, Figure 9-11d.
  - *Specify dimension line location*, Figure 9-11d: Locate the dimension line by moving the crosshairs, following the dimension placement rules. Press the left mouse button at the desired location.

Figure 9-11f

9.11.1.3. Text relocation

Figure 9-12a shows a part of a drawing with several linear dimensions. The user can increase the readability by relocating the dimension's text as shown in Figure 9-12b.

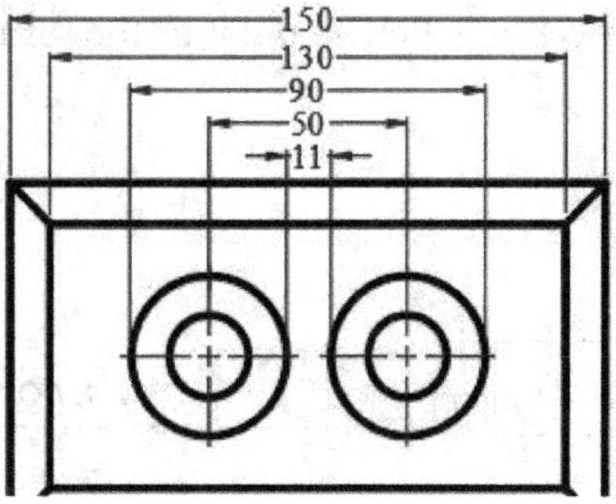

Figure 9-12a

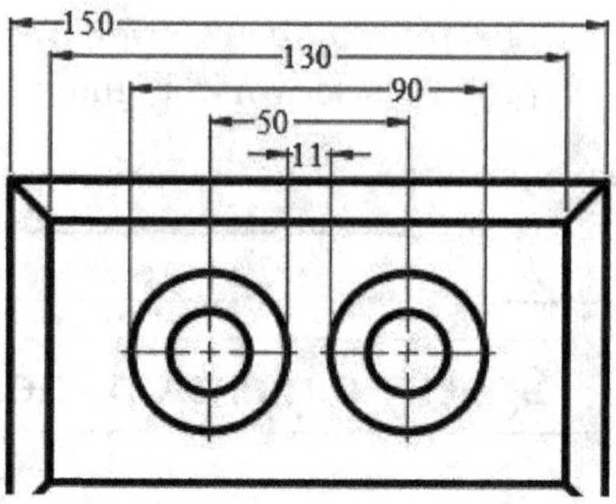

Figure 9-12b

- Justification commands are used as follows:
- The text can be relocated using three different methods as follows:
  1. Panel method: (i) Activate the justification command from the *Annotate* tab, and expanded *Dimension* panel, Figure 9-12c. (ii) Click on , , or tools for the left, center, or right justification commands, respectively. The figure shows the activation of the left justification. The activation of the command leads to the *Select dimension* prompt, Figure 9-12d. (iii) Click on the desired text. In the current example, click on 150. This exits the command and the selected text is relocated to the new location, Figure 9-12b.

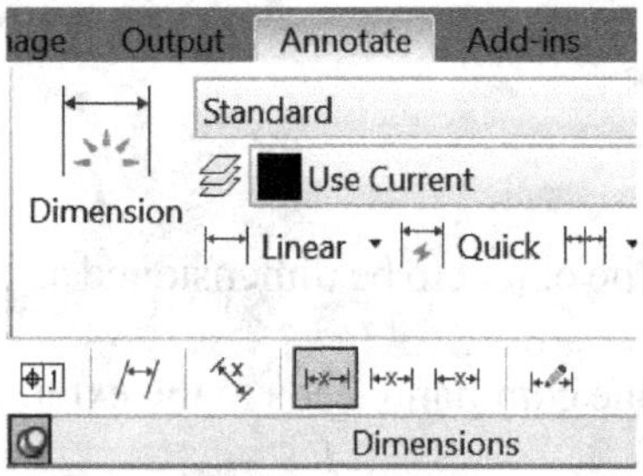

Figure 9-12c

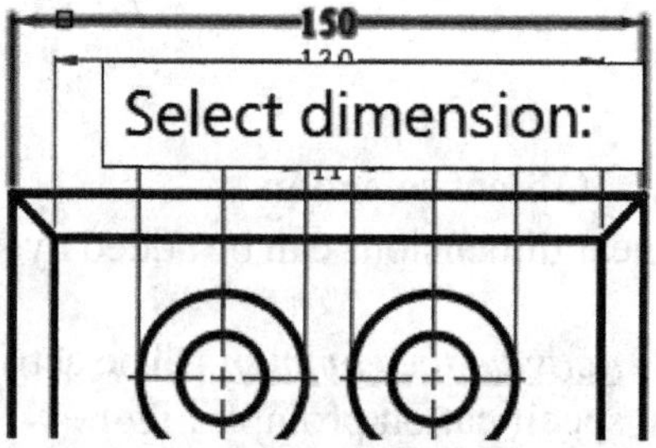

Figure 9-12d

  2. Command line method: (i) Type "dimtedit," "Dimtedit," or "DIMTEDIT" on the command line and press the *Enter* key. (ii) The activation of the command leads to the *Select dimension* prompt, Figure 9-12d. (ii) Click on the desired text. In the current example, click on 150. The cursor is attached to the text and the prompt shown in Figure 9-12b appears. (iii) Click at the desired location. This exits the command, and the selected text is relocated to the new location.

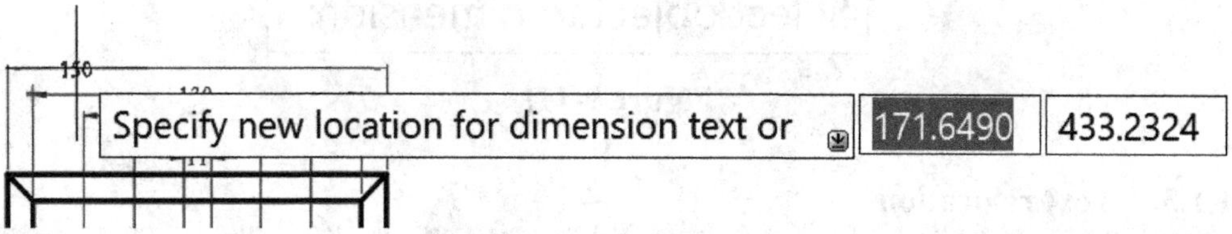

Figure 9-12e

3. Grip point method: (i) Click the desired dimension, 150 in the current example, and its grip points appear, Figure 9-12f. (ii) Click on the grip point on the text. The grip point's color is changed, and the prompt shown in Figure 9-12f appears. (iii) Click at the desired location. This exits the command, and the selected text is relocated to the new location.

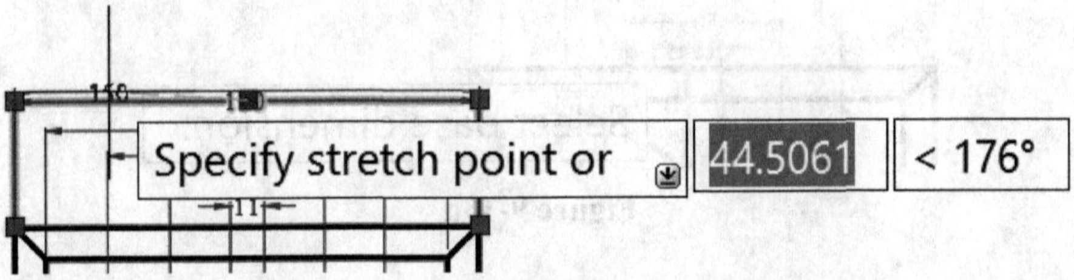

Figure 9-12f

9.11.1.4. Space adjustment

Figure 9-13a shows a part of a drawing with unevenly spaced horizontal dimensions and the scattered vertical dimensions. The same drawing is shown in Figure 9-13b with evenly spaced horizontal dimensions and properly aligned vertical dimensions.

- The user can convert Figure 9-13a into Figure 9-13b using *Adjust Space* command as follows:

1. Panel method: Activate the *Adjust Space* command from the *Annotate* tab, and *Dimension* panel and click on *Adjust Space* tool. The activation of the command leads to the prompt shown in Figure 9-13c.
2. Command line method: Type "dimspace," "Dimspace," or "DIMSPACE" on the command line and press the *Enter* key. The activation of the command leads to the prompt shown in Figure 9-13c.
3. Grip point method: Exhaustive approach! Match the grip points manually, one dimension at a time.

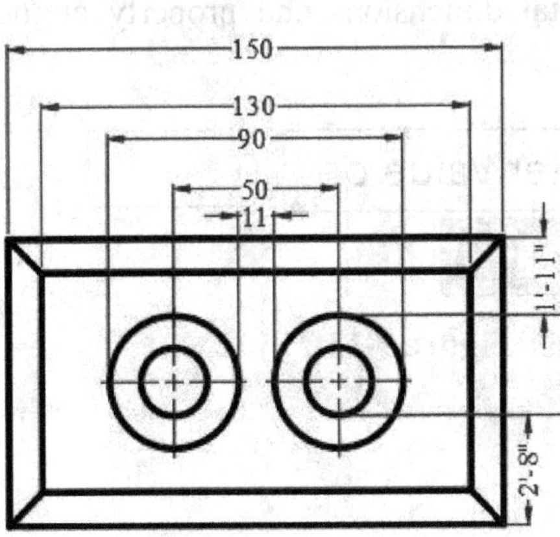

Figure 9-13a

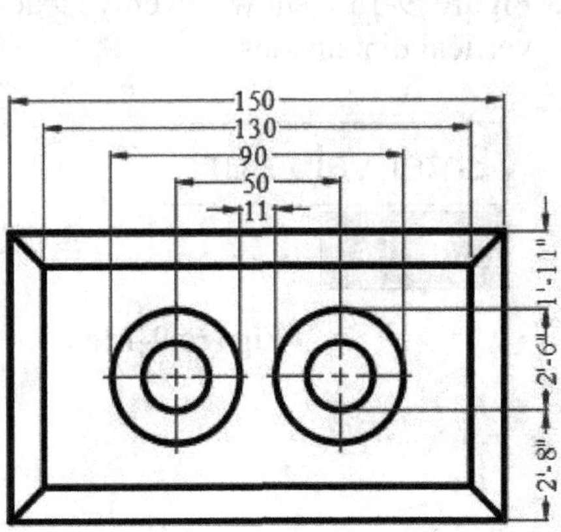

Figure 9-13b

- *Select base dimension*: Click on the dimension 11, Figure 9-13c; and the prompt shown in Figure 9-13d appears.

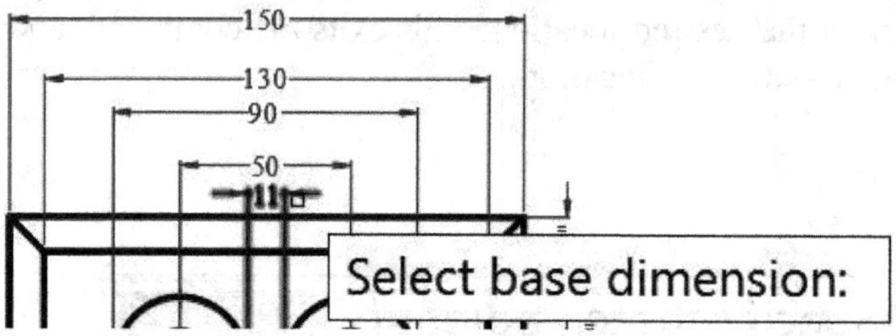

Figure 9-13c

- *Select dimension to space*: Select the remaining horizontal dimensions as shown in Figure 9-13d. Press the *Enter* key and the prompt shown in Figure 9-13e appears.

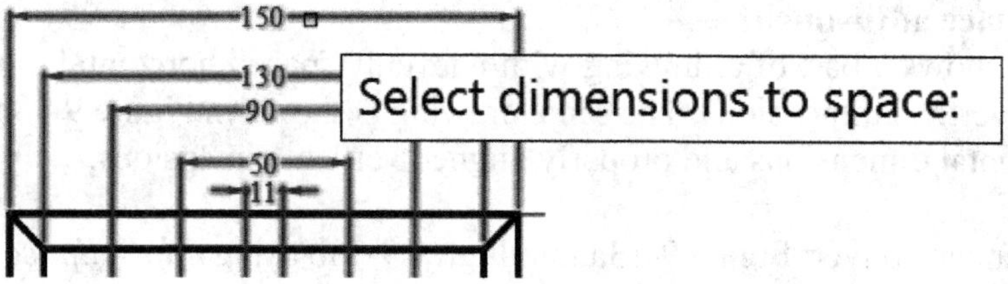

Figure 9-13d

- *Enter value or*: Click on the *Auto* option. This exits the command and evenly spaces the horizontal dimensions. For the *Auto* option, the software automatically calculates the spacing, and the spacing is equal to twice the text height. If desired, the user can specify the spacing.
- Repeat the above process for the vertical dimensions as follows. (i) Select 1'-11" dimension as the base dimension. (ii) In response to *Enter value or* prompt, type 0 as shown in Figure 9-13f.
- Figure 9-13b shows evenly spaced horizontal dimensions and properly aligned vertical dimensions.

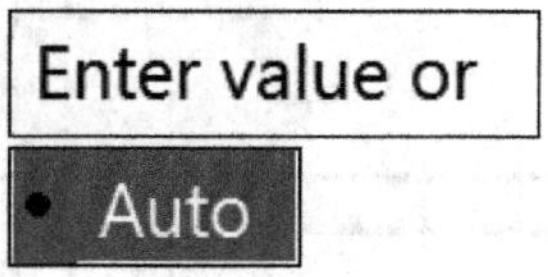

Figure 9-13e

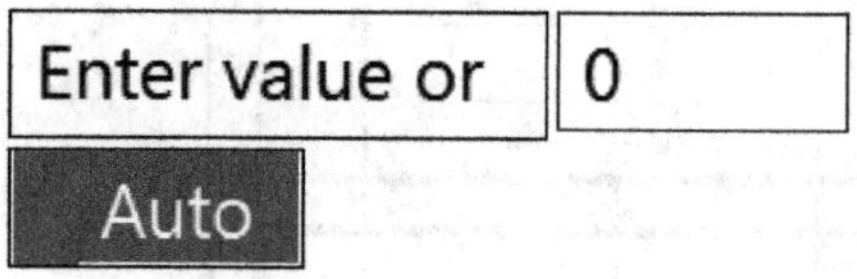

Figure 9-13f

9.11.2. Aligned dimensions

The *Aligned* dimension command is used to create dimensions parallel to the object being dimensioned. In Figure 9-14, every dimension is an aligned dimension. Every linear dimension (dimensions 5, 10, and 23) is an aligned dimension. However, every aligned dimension (dimensions for the side dimensions for the sides AB, BC, and CD) is NOT a linear dimension.

Example: Add the dimension for the sides AB, BC, and CD, Figure 9-14.

- The process of creating aligned dimensions is the same as the linear dimensions.
- The *Aligned* command is activated using one of the following methods:
  1. Panel method: The *Aligned* dimension command can be activated from two panels. (i) From the *Annotate* tab and the *Dimension* panel, expand the *Dimension* drop-down menu and click the *Aligned* tool. (ii) From the *Home* tab, expand the *Annotation* panel, expand the *Linear* drop-down menu and click the *Aligned* tool.
  2. Command line method: Type "dimaligned," "Dimaligned" or "DIMALIGNED" on the command line and press the *Enter* key.

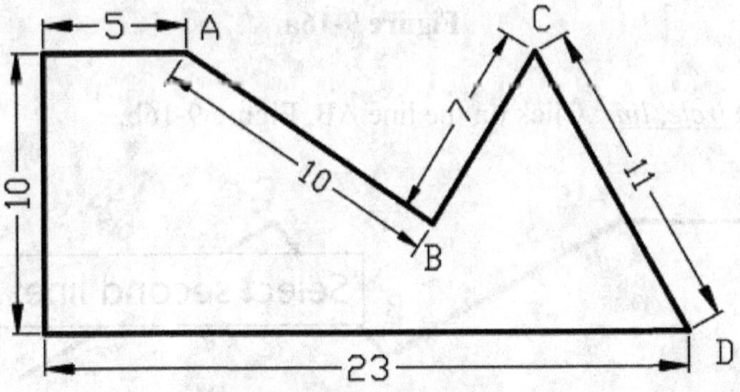

Figure 9-14

9.11.3. Angular dimensions

The *Angular* dimension command is used to create angular dimensions. Figure 9-15 shows two angular dimensions for the path labeled as ABC; one of the angles is less than 180° and the other is greater than 180°. This section explains how to add the two angles.

- The *Angular* command is activated using one of the following methods:

  1. Panel method: The *Angular* dimension command can be activated from two panels. (i) From the *Home* tab, expand the *Annotation* panel, expand the *Linear* drop-down menu and click the *Angular* tool. (ii) From the *Annotate* tab and the *Dimension* panel, expand the *Dimension* drop-down menu and click the *Angular* tool.
  2. Command line method: Type "dimangular," "Dimangular" or "DIMANGULAR" on the command line and press the *Enter* key.

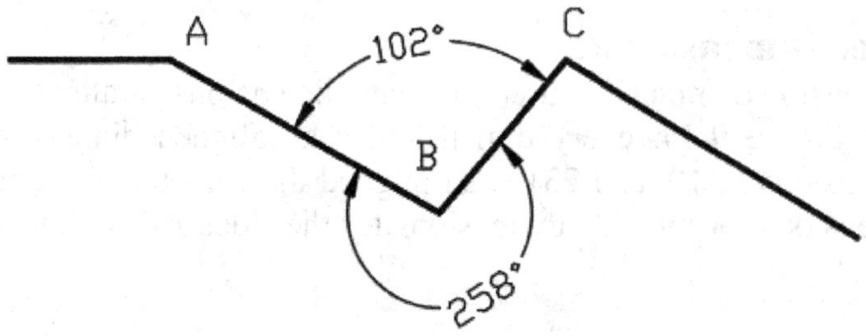

Figure 9-15

9.11.3.1. Angles < 180°

Example: Add the angle 102° as shown in Figure 9-15.

- Activate the *Angular* command. The activation of the command leads to the line selection prompt, Figure 9-16a.

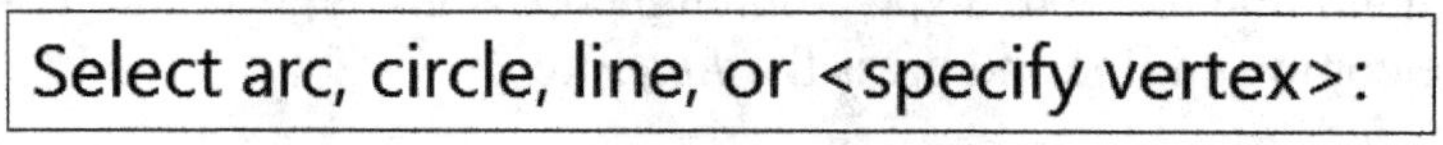

Figure 9-16a

- *Select arc, circle, line*: Click on the line AB, Figure 9-16b.

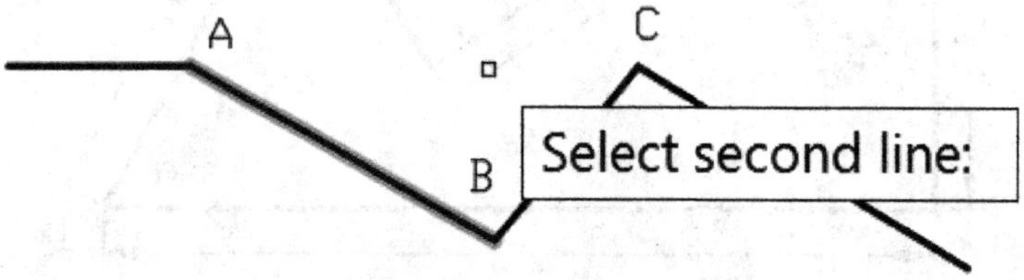

Figure 9-16b

- *Select second line*: Click on the line BC, Figure 9-16c.
- *Specify dimension line location*: Locate the dimension line by moving the crosshairs, following the dimension placement rules. Press the left mouse button at the desired location, Figure 9-16d.
- Figure 9-16d shows the angled dimensions added to the drawing.

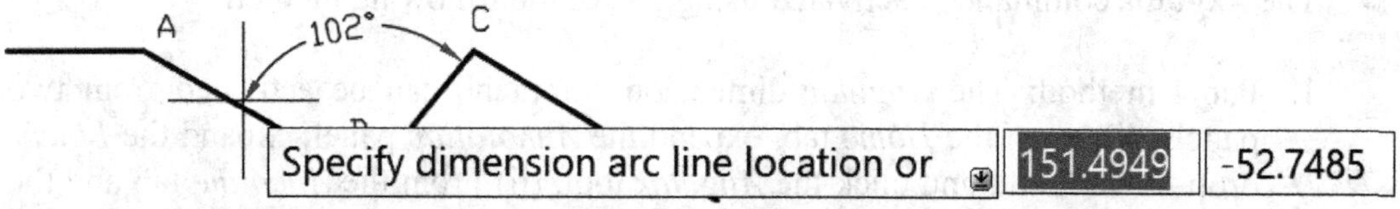

Figure 9-16c

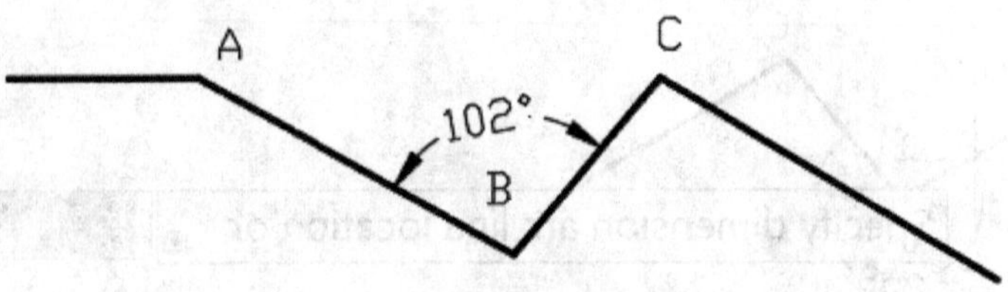

Figure 9-16d

9.11.3.2. Angles > 180°

Example: Add the angle 258° as shown in Figure 9-15.

- Activate the *Angular* command. The activation of the command leads to the line selection prompt, Figure 9-17a.

- Select arc, circle, line or <specify vertex>: Press the *Enter* key and the prompt shown in Figure 9-1a appears. This option allows the specification of three points for an angular dimension.

Figure 9-17a

- Turn on the object snap with *Endpoint* option. Click at point B (the intersection of the AB and BC) and the prompt shown in Figure 9-17c appears.

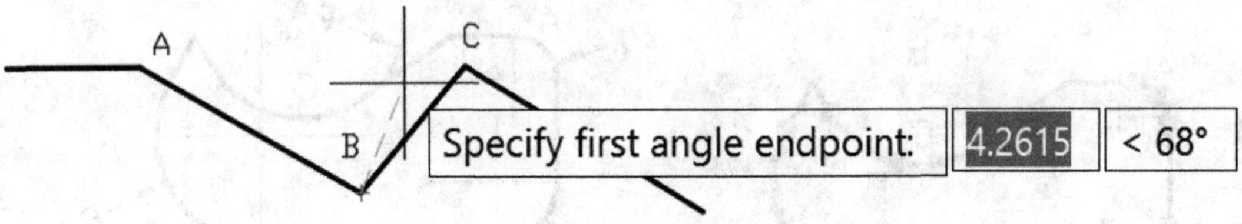

Figure 9-17b

- Click at point C (the endpoint of line BC) and the prompt shown in Figure 9-17c appears.
- Click at point A (the endpoint of line BA) and the prompt shown in Figure 9-17d appears.

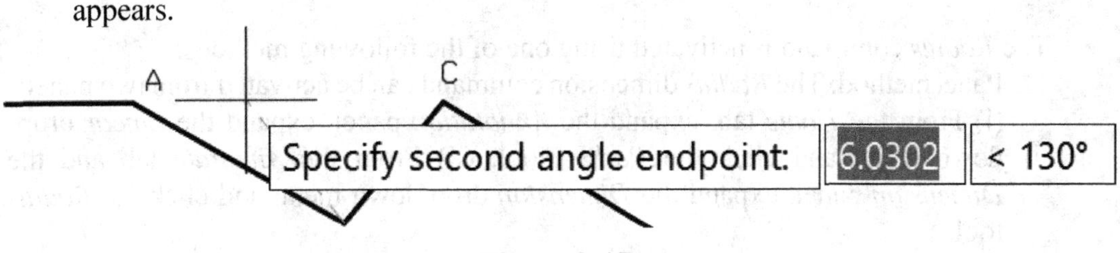

Figure 9-17c

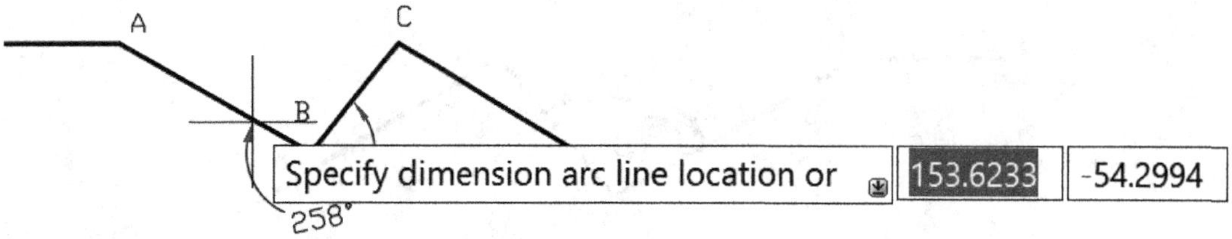

Figure 9-17d

- Finally click a point on the side that the angle is desired as shown in Figure 9-17e.

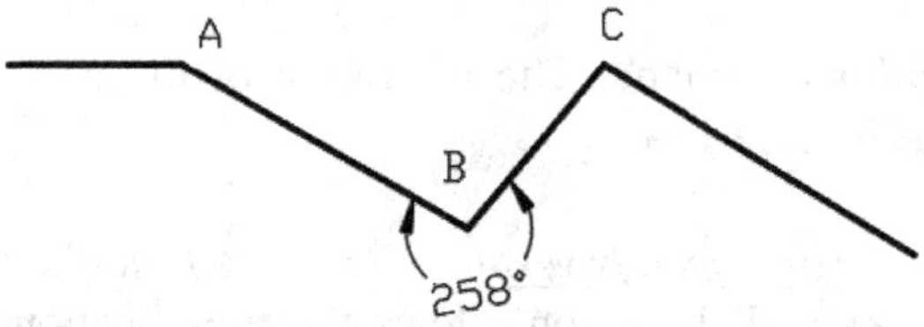

Figure 9-17e

9.11.4. Dimensioning radii

The *Radius* dimension command is used to create radius dimensions. Circular arcs less than 180° are dimensioned using the radius. Figure 9-18a shows four circular arcs less than 180° (notice the grip points). Figure 9-18b shows the arcs' dimensions; all radial dimensions are preceded by the uppercase *R*. Notice, in the figure, the arc labeled as C extends itself to show the radial dimensions.

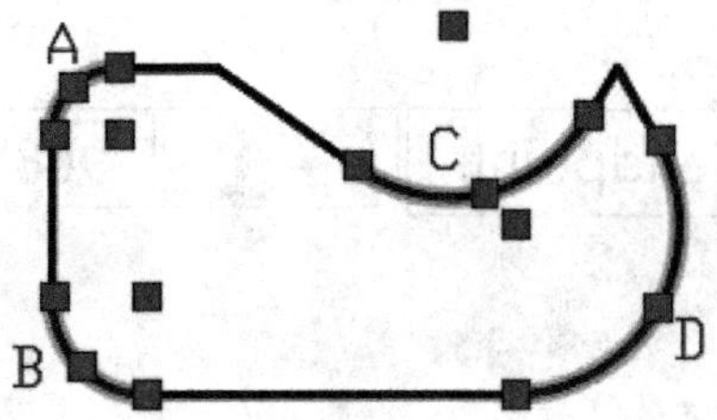

Figure 9-18a

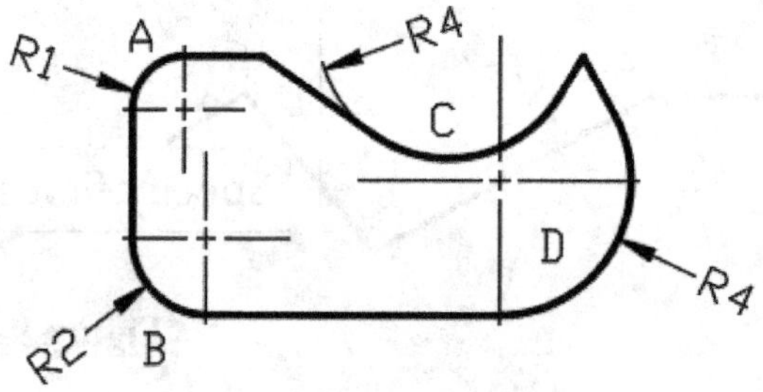

Figure 9-18b

Example: Add the dimension for the arcs A, B, C, and D as shown in Figure 9-18a.

- The *Radius* command is activated using one of the following methods:
  1. Panel method: The *Radius* dimension command can be activated from two panels. (i) From the *Home* tab, expand the *Annotation* panel, expand the *Linear* drop-down menu and click the *Radius* tool. (ii) From the *Annotate* tab and the *Dimension* panel, expand the *Dimension* drop-down menu and click the *Radius* tool.
  2. Command line method: Type "dimradius," "Dimradius" or "DIMRADIUS" on the command line and press the *Enter* key.

- The activation of the command leads to the arc/circle selection prompt, Figure 9-18c.

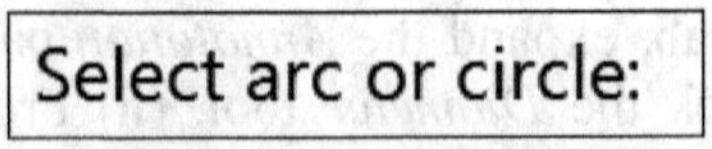

Figure 9-18c

- *Select arc or circle*: Click on the arc A.
- *Specify dimension line location*, Figure 9-18d: Locate the dimension line by moving the crosshairs, following the dimension placement rules. Press the left mouse button at the desired location.
- Position the radius dimension so that the leader line is neither horizontal nor vertical, Figure 9-18b.
- The radius tool automatically includes the center mark or centerline based on the option selected in the *Dimension Style* dialog box → *Modify Dimension Style* dialog box → *Arrow and Symbol* tab.

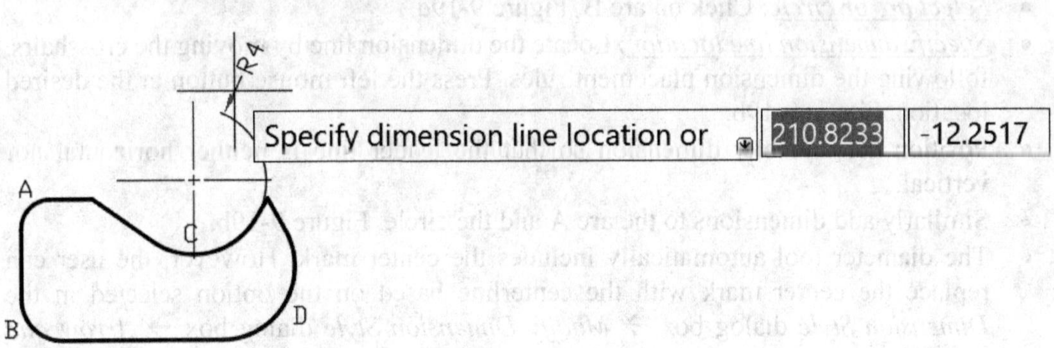

Figure 9-18d

9.11.5. Dimensioning circles

The *Diameter* dimension command is used to create diameter dimensions. The circles, semicircles, or arcs greater than 180 degrees are dimensioned using the diameter, Figure 9-19b. All of the diameter dimensions are preceded by the symbol ϕ. The symbol ϕ can be created by typing %%c in a text box.

Example: Draw a circle and circular arcs, Figure 9-19a; and add the dimension, Figure 9-19b. In the figures, the arc A is greater than 180°, and B is a semicircle (notice the grip points).

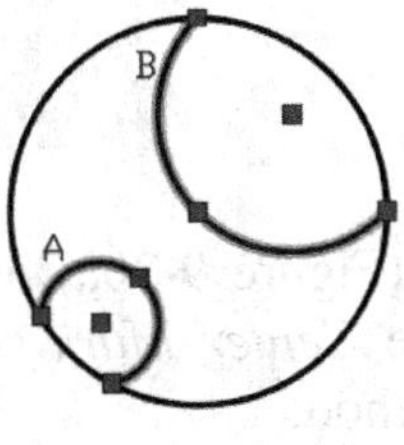

Figure 9-19a

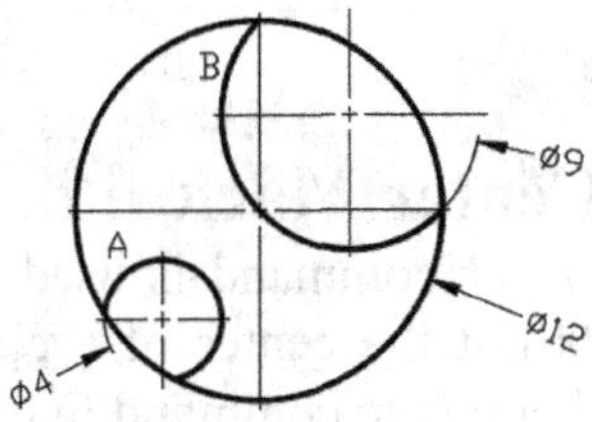

Figure 9-19b

- The *Diameter* command is activated using one of the following methods:
  1. Panel method: The *Linear* dimension command can be activated from two panels. (i) From the *Home* tab, expand the *Annotation* panel, expand the *Linear* drop-down menu and click the *Diameter* tool. (ii) From the *Annotate* tab and the *Dimension* panel, expand the *Dimension* drop-down menu and click the *Diameter* tool.
  2. Command line method: Type "dimdiameter," "Dimdiameter" or "DIMMETER" on the command line and press the *Enter* key.

- The activation of the command leads to the arc/circle selection prompt, Figure 9-19b.

Select arc or circle:

Figure 9-19c

- <u>*Select arc or circle*</u>: Click on arc B, Figure 9-19d.
- <u>*Specify dimension line location*</u>: Locate the dimension line by moving the crosshairs, following the dimension placement rules. Press the left mouse button at the desired location, Figure 9-19b.
- Position the diameter dimension so that the leader line is neither horizontal nor vertical.
- Similarly add dimensions to the arc A and the circle, Figure 9-19b.
- The diameter tool automatically includes the center mark. However, the user can replace the center mark with the centerline based on the option selected in the *Dimension Style* dialog box → *Modify Dimension Style* dialog box → *Arrow and Symbol* tab.

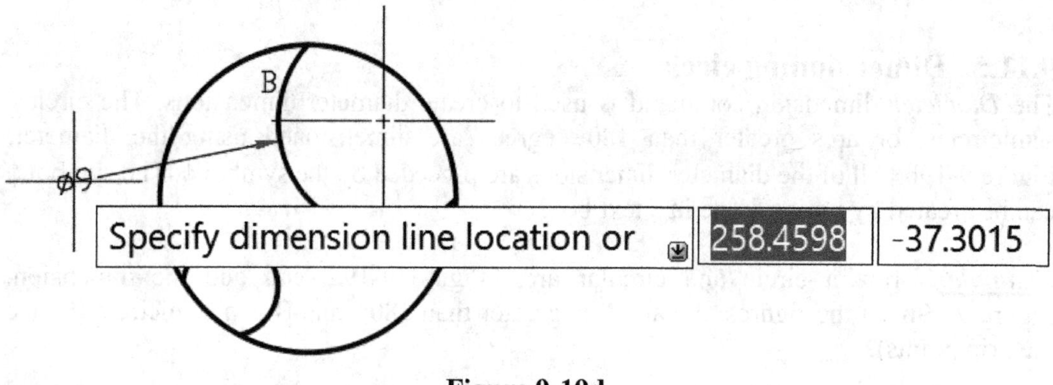

Figure 9-19d

9.12. Center Mark

The *Center mark* command is used to draw a center mark (Figure 9-20a) or centerline (Figure 9-20b) at the center of a circle or circular arc. The *Center Mark* command is activated either by the command line method or the panel method.

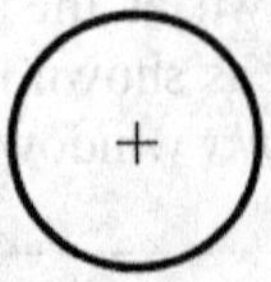

Figure 9-20a

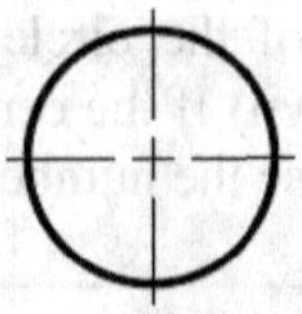

Figure 9-20b

9.12.1. Command line method

The advantages of the command line method are that (i) it allows the user to create both the center mark and centerline and (ii) the user can change the diameter of the circle or circular arc after adding the centerlines (in Figure 9-20c, the diameter of the circle labeled as A is reduced). However, the drawback of this method is that the user is required to activate the command for each circle or circular arc in the drawing. For example, for Figure 9-20c, the user is required to activate the command five times.

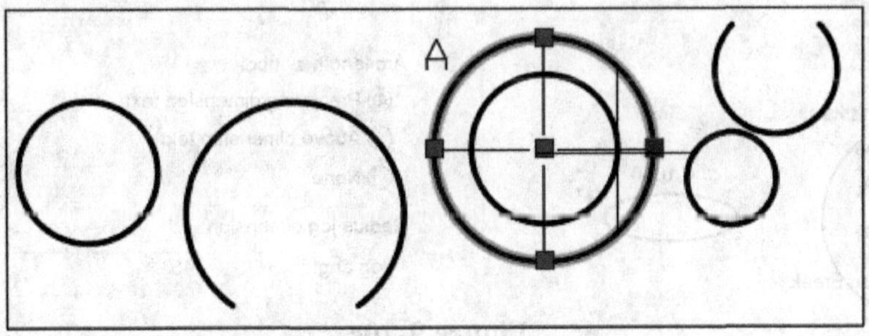

Figure 9-20c

In the command line method, the *Center Mark* command is activated by typing "dimcenter," "Dimcenter" or "DIMCENTER" on the command line and pressing the *Enter* key.

- The activation of the command leads to the prompt for the arc or circle selection, Figure 9-20d.

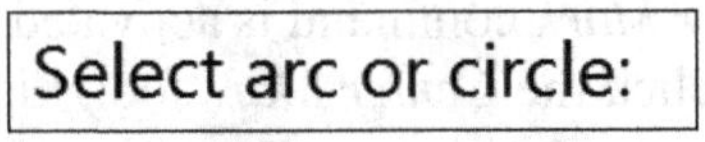

Figure 9-20d

- Click at the circumference of the circle and the center mark is drawn at the center of the circle, Figure 9-20a.
- However, if the user wants to display the centerline, Figure 9-20b, then perform the following steps. (i) Delete the center mark from the circle. (ii) Open the *Dimension Style Manager* dialog box (Section 9.7). (iii) Click on the *Modify* button to open *Modify Dimension Style* dialog box (Section 9.8.2), Figure 9-20e. (iv) Click on the *Symbols and Arrow* tab. (v) Under the *Center marks* panel, select the *Line* option; press the *OK* button. (vi) Activate the *Center marks* command and click at the

circumference of the circle. The centerline is drawn at the center of the circle, Figure 9-20b. (vii) If the centerline does not appear as shown in Figure 9-20b, then increase/decrease the number field in the *Center marks* window.

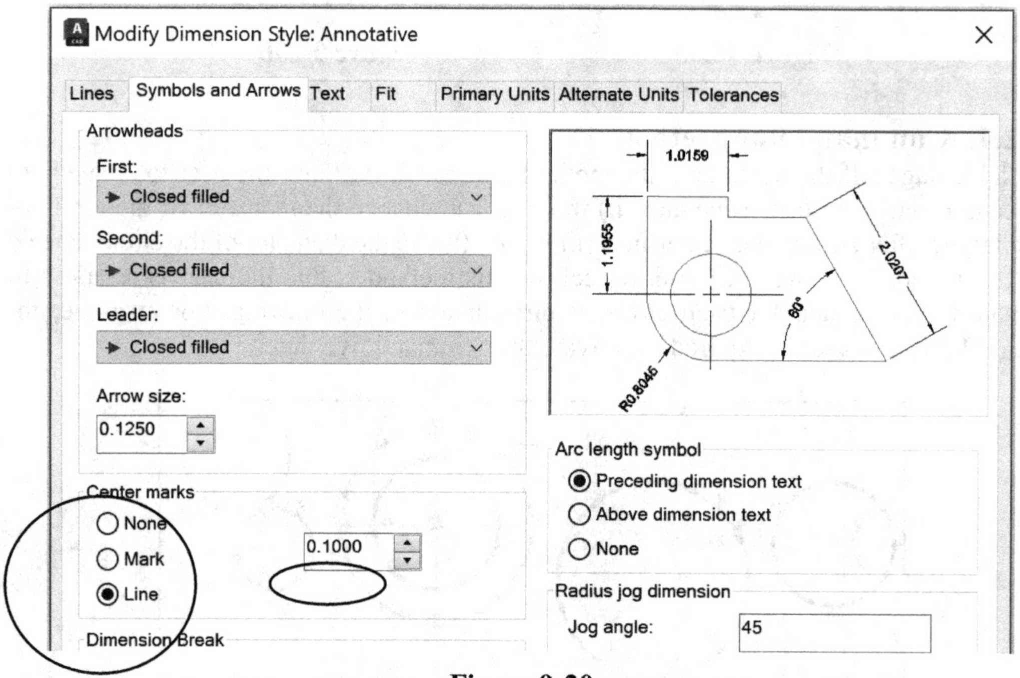

Figure 9-20e

9.12.2. Panel method 

The advantage of the panel method is that the user can add centerlines to multiple circles or circular arcs in a single activation of the command. For example, for Figure 9-20c the user is required to activate the command only once. However, the drawbacks of this method are that (i) it allows the user to create only the centerline and (ii) the user cannot change the diameter of the circle or circular arc after adding the centerlines.

In the panel method, the *Center Mark* command is activated as follows: from the *Annotate* tab and the *Centerlines* panel click the *Center Mark* tool, Figure 9-21a.

- The activation of the command leads to the prompt for the arc or circle selection, Figure 9-21b.

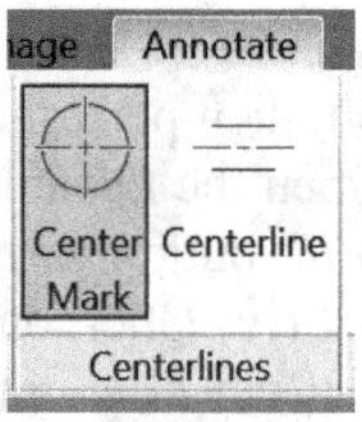

Figure 9-21a

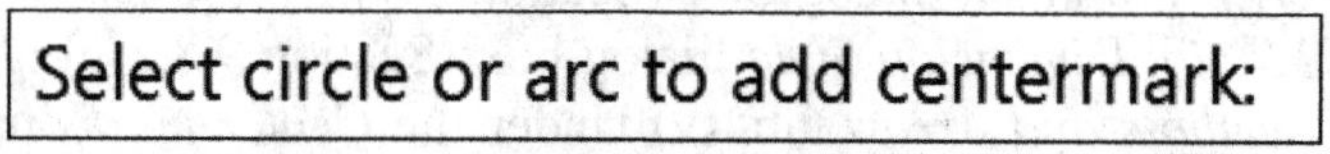

Figure 9-21b

- Click at the boundary of the desired circle or circular arc.
- To exit the command, press either the *Esc* key or the *Enter* key on the keyboard.

9.13. Smart Dimension

Consider a simple object shown in Figure 9-22a. In order to dimension the object, the user needs to activate the dimension commands **eight** times (2**Angular* + 2**Aligned* + 2**Circle* + *Linear* + *Radius*). The user productivity can be greatly enhanced by using the smart dimensioning techniques. In this technique, the user is required to activate only **ONE** command to add the above-mentioned dimensions as follows: (i) hover over the object; (ii) the software recognizes the geometry and will display the appropriate dimension. The remainder of this section describes the smart dimensioning technique.

- The smart dimension command (named *Dimension*) is activated using one of the following methods:
  1. Panel method: From the *Annotate* tab and the *Dimension* panel, click the *Dimension* tool.
  2. Command line method: Type "dim," "Dim" or "DIM" on the command line and press the *Enter* key.

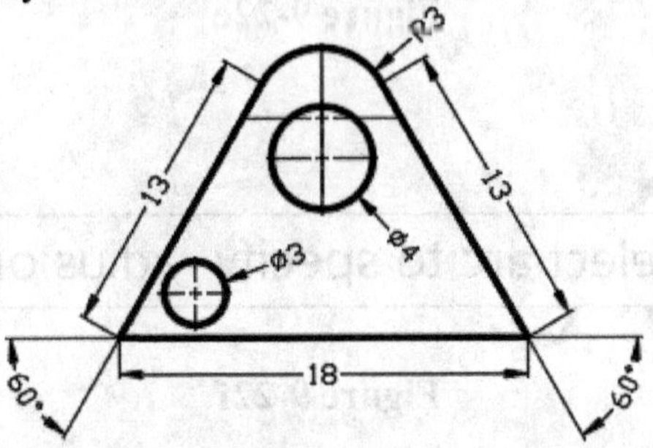

Figure 9-22a

- The user must turn *Off* the ORTHO option by clicking button on the status bar.
- Activate the *Dimension* command; the resulting prompt is shown in Figure 9-22b.

Figure 9-22b

- Bring the cursor on top of the object to be dimensioned and the software displays the appropriate dimensions as shown in Figure 9-22c (align), Figure 9-22d (linear), Figure 9-22e (circular), and Figure 9-22f (radial) dimensions. Click at the desired location to place the dimension; and the prompt is changed to the prompt shown in Figure 9-22b. Continue the dimensioning process.

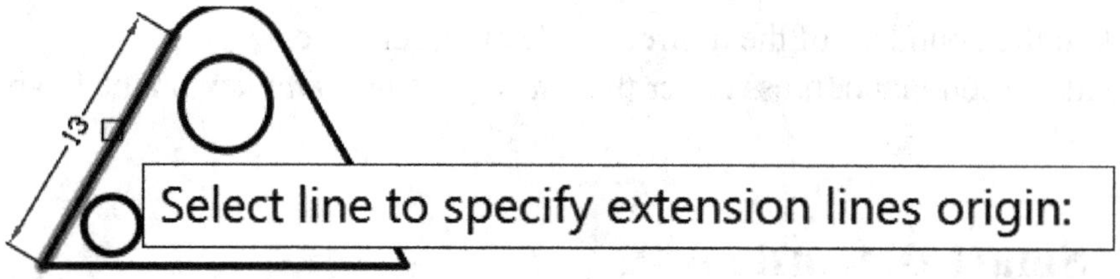

Figure 9-22c

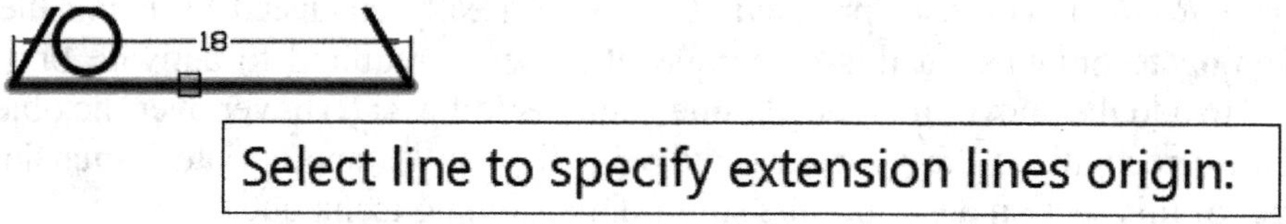

Figure 9-22d

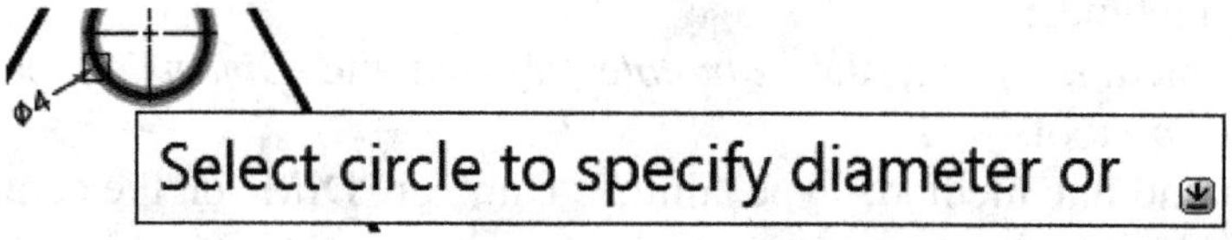

Figure 9-22e

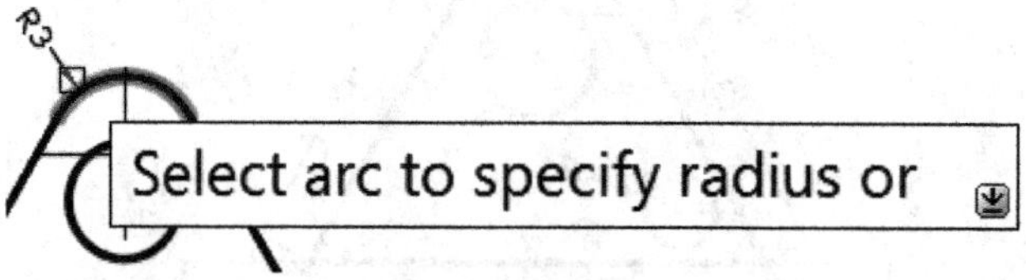

Figure 9-22f

- The angular dimension can be added as follows. (i) Bring the cursor on one of the lines of the angle to be dimensioned, Figure 9-23a. (ii) Click on the line, Figure 9-23b. (iii) Bring the cursor on the second line of the angle to be dimensioned, Figure 9-23c; angles are displayed. (iv) Click on the line, Figure 9-23d. (v) Click at the desired location to place the angle, and the prompt is changed to the prompt shown in Figure 9-22b. Continue the dimensioning process.

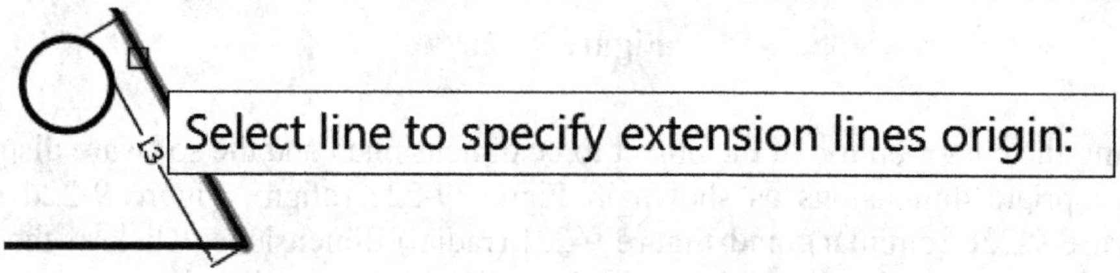

Figure 9-23a

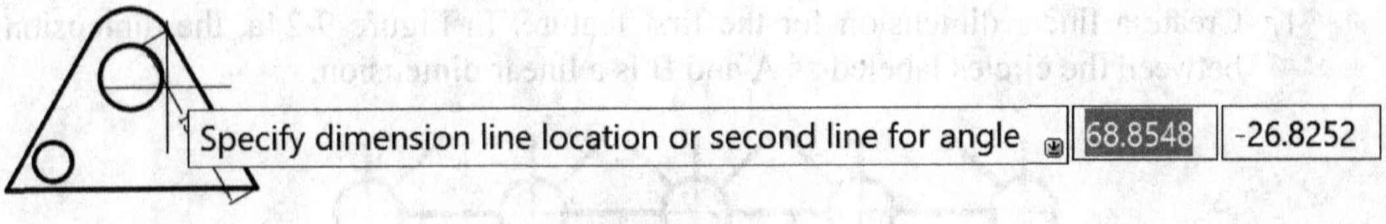

Figure 9-23b

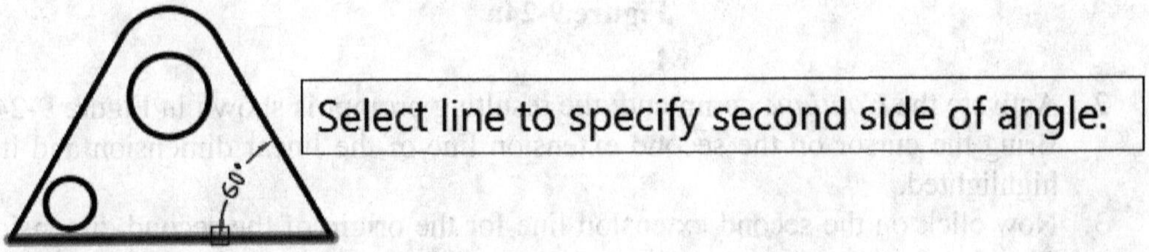

Figure 9-23c

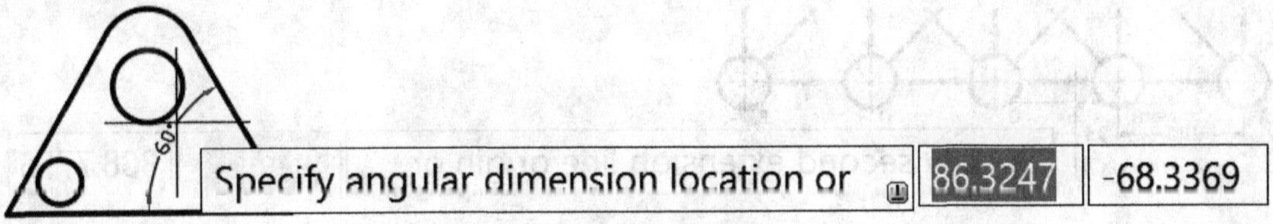

Figure 9-23d

9.14. Types Of Dimensions

This section describes different types of dimensions (continues, baseline, ordinate, tabular, and combine dimensions) used in a drawing.

9.14.1. Continue dimension

The *Continue* dimension is a type of linear dimension that uses the second extension line's origin (of a selected dimension) as the first extension line's origin for the next dimension, Figure 9-24c. This type of dimensioning is also known as the *Chains of dimensions*. This technique breaks one long dimension into shorter segments that add up to the total measurement. However, the continue dimension should only be used if the functionality of the object is not affected by the accumulation of the error.

- The *Continue* dimension command is activated using one of the following methods:
  1. Panel method: From the *Annotate* tab and the *Dimension* panel, expand the *Continue* drop-down menu and click the *Continue* tool.
  2. Command line method: Type "dimcontinue," "Dimcontinue" or "DIMCONTINUE" on the command line and press the *Enter* key.

- In Figure 9-24c, the object is dimensioned using the continue dimensioning technique. The *Continue* dimensions can be added as follows.

1. Create a linear dimension for the first feature. In Figure 9-24a, the dimension between the circles labeled as A and B is a linear dimension.

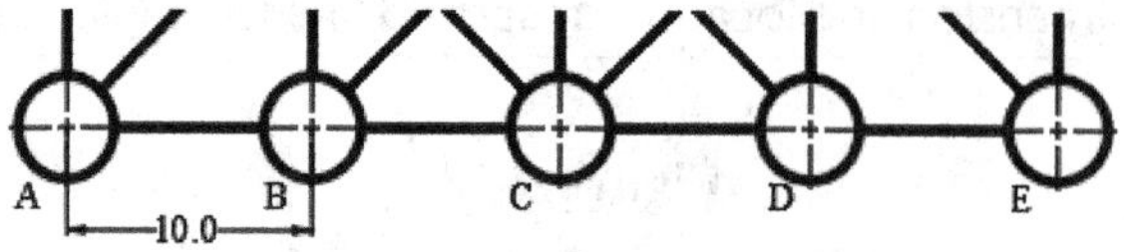

Figure 9-24a

2. Activate the *Continue* command; the resulting prompt is shown in Figure 9-24b. Bring the cursor on the second extension line of the linear dimension and it is highlighted.
3. Now click on the second extension line for the origin of the second dimension. That is, for the second extension line, click at the center of the circle C, Figure 9-24b.

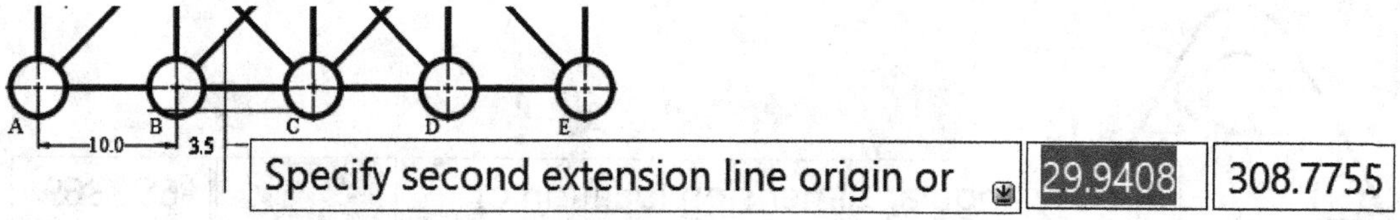

Figure 9-24b

4. Since circles D and E can be dimensioned with respect to the dimensions of circles A and B, repeat step #3 for circles D and E, Figure 9-24c.
5. Press the *Esc* key to exit the command.
6. The location of the text and arrowheads can be changed using the *Fit* tab of the *Modify Dimension Style* dialog box.
7. The current example is based on the linear dimension. However, the continued dimension option can be used with the aligned and angular (Figure 9-24d) dimensions, too.

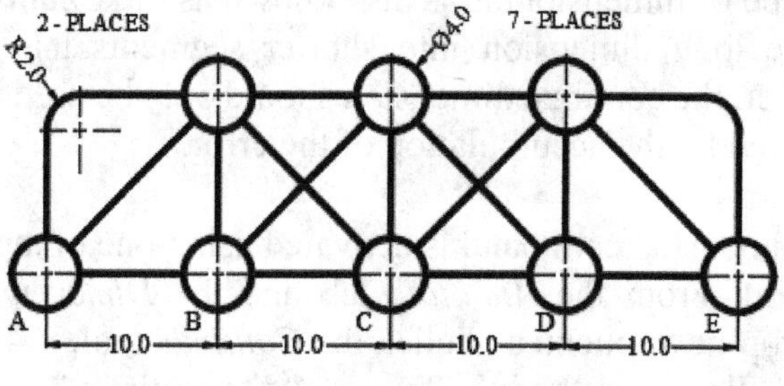

Figure 9-24c

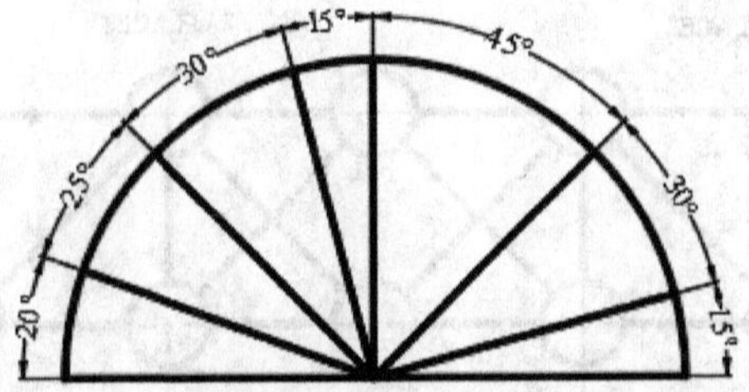

Figure 9-24d

9.14.2. Baseline dimensions

The *Baseline* dimension is a dimensioning technique in which multiple dimensions are measured from the same baseline or datum; that is, several dimensions originate from one extension line as shown in Figure 9-25b and Figure 9-25c. This dimensioning technique is also called *parallel dimensions* and *datum dimensions*. The baseline dimensions are useful because they help eliminate error build up associated with each dimension. However, it requires a large area on the drawing.

- The *Baseline* dimension command is activated using one of the following methods:
  1. Panel method: From the *Annotate* tab and the *Dimension* panel, expand the *Continue* drop-down menu and click the *Baseline* tool.
  2. Command line method: Type "dimbaseline," "Dimbaseline" or "DIMBASELINE" on the command line and press the *Enter* key.

- In Figure 9-25b and Figure 9-25c, the object is dimensioned using the baseline dimensioning technique. The *Baseline* dimensions can be added as follows.
  1. Create a linear dimension for the first feature. In Figure 9-25a, the dimension between the circles labeled as A and B is a linear dimension.
  2. Activate the *Baseline* command; the resulting prompt is shown in Figure 9-20a.

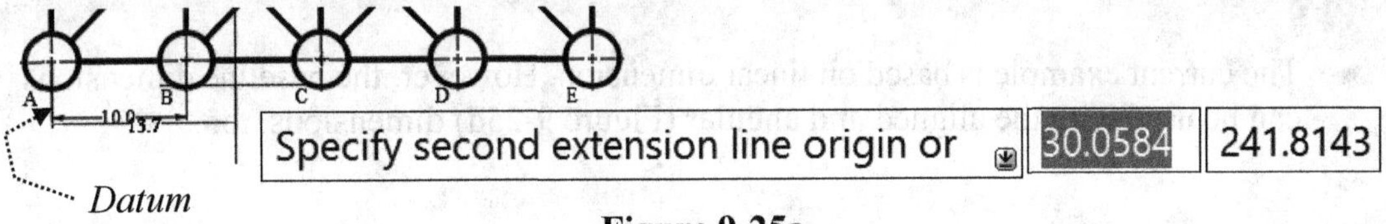

Figure 9-25a

3. Now click at the center of circle C; this causes the dimension from the datum line to be created.
4. Repeat step #3 for circles D and E, Figure 9-25b.
5. Press the *Esc* key to exit the command.

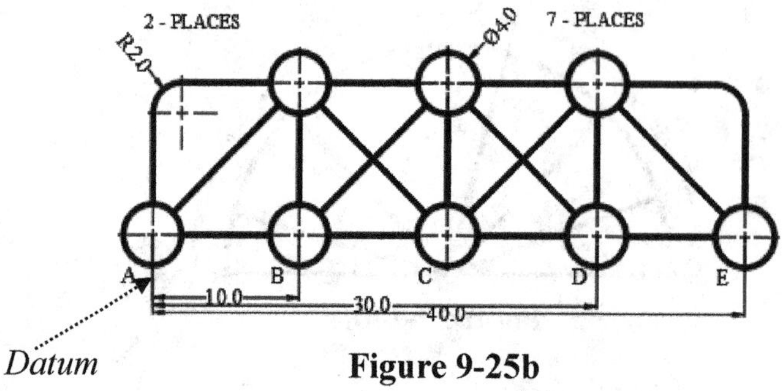

Figure 9-25b

- The appearance of the baseline dimension can be enhanced using one of the following two methods.
- Figure 9-25b, perform the following procedure:
- To enhance the appearance of Figure 9-25b, perform the following procedure:
  1. Use the *Adjust space* command.
  2. Dialog box method.
     a. Open the *Dimension Style Manager* and *Modify Dimension Style* dialog boxes.
     b. Select the *Text* tab under the *Text Alignment* panel and choose the *Aligned with dimension line* option.
     c. Select the *Lines* tab under the *Dimension lines* panel and increase the *Baselines spacing*.
     d. Click the *OK* and *Close* buttons to close the two dialog boxes, respectively.
     e. This changes the alignment of every dimension in the drawing. However, it does not update the baseline spacing.
     f. To reflect the change in the baseline spacing, delete the baseline dimensions and re-dimension the object.
- Figure 9-25c shows the updated version.
- Also, the vertical baseline dimensions are added, Figure 9-25c.

- The current example is based on linear dimension. However, the baseline dimensions can be used with the aligned and angular (Figure 9-25d) dimensions, too.

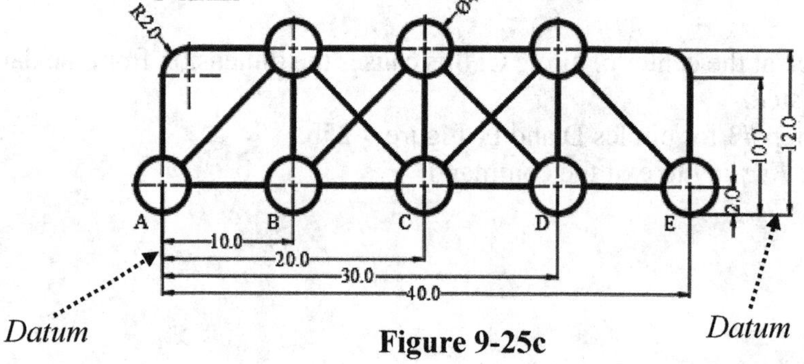

Figure 9-25c

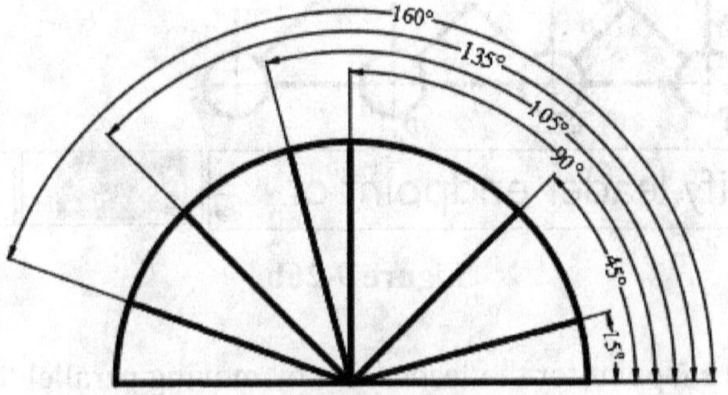

Figure 9-25d

9.14.3. Ordinate dimensions

The *Ordinate* dimensions are based on the X, Y coordinates; and the ordinates are calculated from user defined origin. The technique is useful when dimensioning an object with many holes. Instead of using extension and dimension lines and arrowheads, the ordinate dimensioning includes horizontal and vertical leader lines originating directly from the features of the object.

Since the ordinates are based on the origin, it is important that the origin of the coordinate system is located on the object, as shown in Figure 9-26c. This can be achieved in two ways: (i) either start the drawing from the origin (the center of the lower left circle at the origin of WCS) or (ii) move the drawing to origin (the center of the lower left circle at the origin).

- The *Ordinate* dimension command is activated using one of the following methods:
  1. Panel method: (ii) From the *Home* tab, expand the *Annotation* panel and click the *Ordinate* tool.
  2. Command line method: Type "dimordinate," "Dimordinate" or "DIMORDINATE" on the command line and press the *Enter* key.

- In Figure 9-26c, the object is dimensioned using the ordinate dimensioning technique. The *Ordinate* dimensions can be added as follows.

  1. Relocate the origin (if necessary).
  2. Turn the ORTHO command *On* by clicking the button on the status bar.
  3. Activate the *Ordinate* command. The prompt is shown in Figure 9-26a.

Figure 9-26a

  4. Select the center point for the lower left circle. The prompt shown in Figure 9-26b appears.

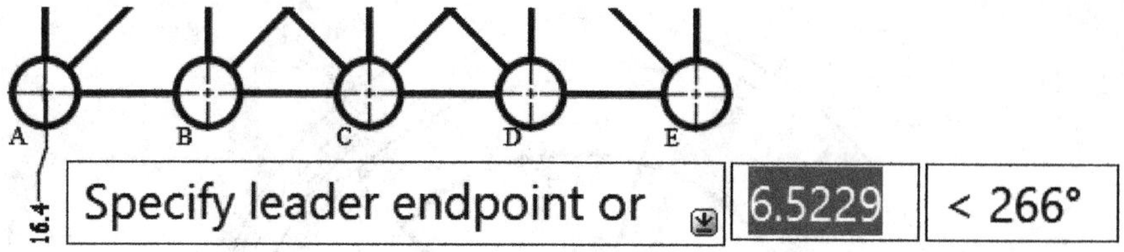

Figure 9-26b

5. Specify the endpoint for the leader line by moving parallel to the y- or x-axis for the x- or y-ordinate, respectively.
6. Repeat steps #4 - #6 for every hole in the drawing and any other feature in the drawing.
7. The dimensioned drawing is shown in Figure 9-26c.

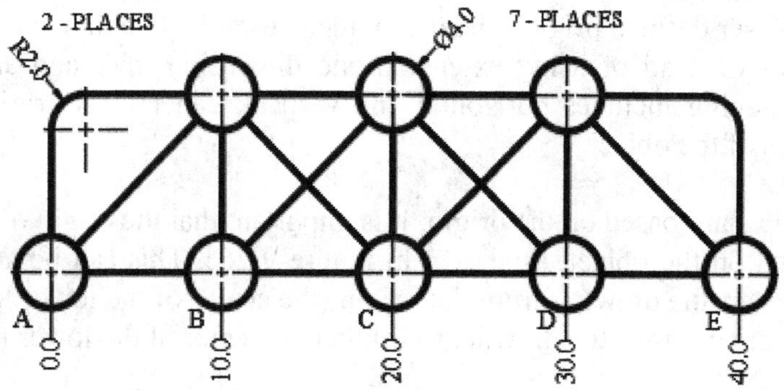

Figure 9-26c

9.14.4. Tabular dimensions

The tabular dimension stores the *coordinate* dimensions in a table. The tabular or *coordinate* dimensions are useful when dimensioning an object that has many holes. The coordinate dimension uses a chart (or a table), Figure 9-27a and Figure 9-27b. Holes are labeled by letters and numbers; holes of the same diameter are labeled with the same letters.

The coordinate dimension can be added as follows:

- Define X and Y-axis as baselines.
- Label the circles (or holes).
- Create a table, Figure 9-27b.
- Populate the table using the coordinates for the centerlines of the circles.
- The diameter symbol is created by typing %%c in the text box.

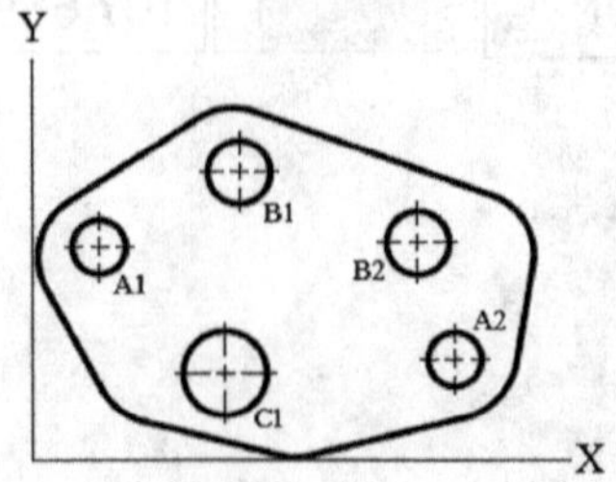

Figure 9-27a

COORDINATE TABLE FOR HOLES			
HOLE	X-COORD	Y-COORD	Ø
A1	3.2100	10.2100	2
A2	21.1200	4.8000	2
B1	9.9400	13.7600	3
B2	18.5300	10.3700	3
C1	9.2800	4.1400	4

Figure 9-27b

9.14.5. Combined dimensions

A combined dimension uses the combination of the dimensioning techniques discussed in the previous sections.

9.15. Quick Dimension 

The *Quick* dimension command is useful to create series of dimensions in a single step.

- The *Quick* dimension command is activated using one of the following methods:
  1. Panel method: (ii) From the *Home* tab, expand the *Annotation* panel and click the *Quick* tool.
  2. Command line method: Type "qdim," "Qdim" or "QDIM" on the command line and press the *Enter* key.

- Activation of the *Quick* dimension command leads to the prompt shown in Figure 9-28a.
- *Select geometry to dimension,* Figure 9-28a: Select the objects to be dimensioned. In the current example, select the circles and press the *Enter* Key. The prompt shown in Figure 9-28b appears.
- *Specify dimension line position, or,* Figure 9-28b: Press the down-arrow and display the available options. The default option is the baseline dimensions. Select the desired option. This closes the option list, and the prompt does not change.

Select geometry to dimension:

Figure 9-28a

- *Specify dimension line position, or,* Figure 9-28b: Click for the dimension location. This exits the command and the selected type dimensions appear.
- If necessary, adjust the dimension spacing and text and arrow size.

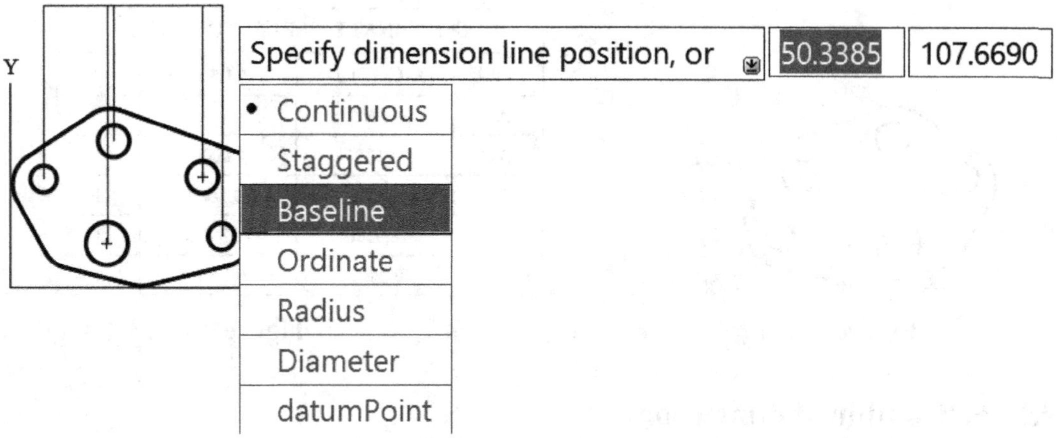

Figure 9-28b

9.16. Dimensioning Fillets And Rounds

Fillets and rounds may be dimensioned individually or by a note. Figure 9-29a to Figure 9-29e show different methods of dimensioning fillets and rounds.

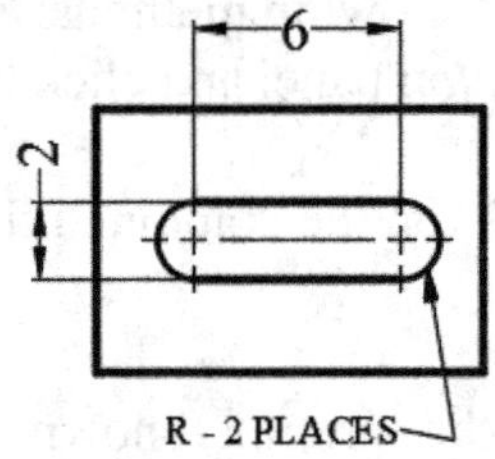

Figure 9-29a

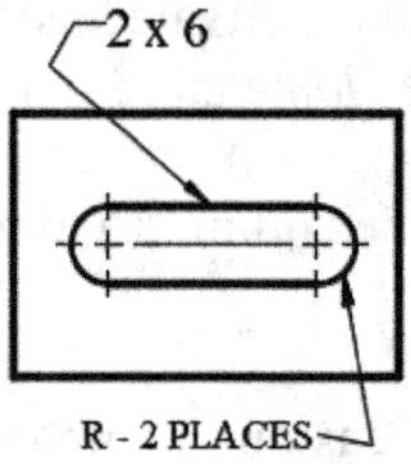

Figure 9-29b

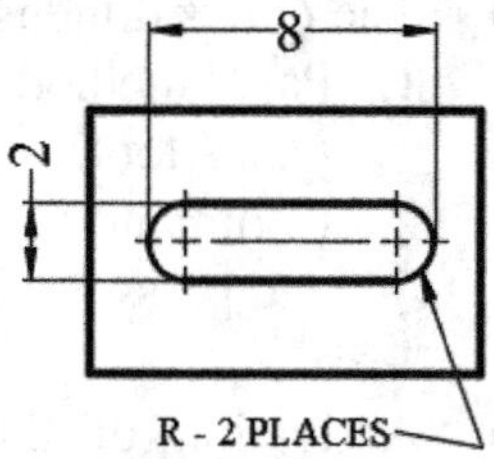

Figure 9-29c

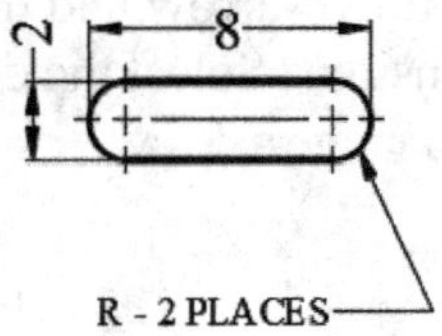

Figure 9-29d

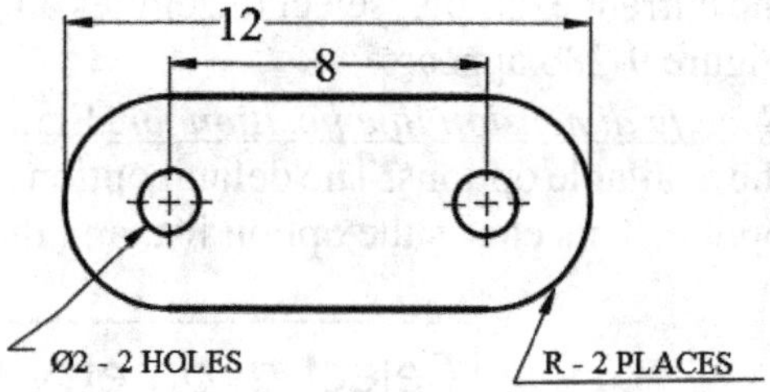

Figure 9-29e

9.17. Centerline

The centerlines are used to indicate the center of an individual component or the entire object. A centerline has two parts: the line and its label, Figure 9-30. A centerline can be drawn as follows.

- <u>*For the centerline*</u>: (i) Load linetype *Center*, (ii) either select linetype *Center* and then draw a line in the center or draw a line and then change its type to *Center*. The user may need to change the linetype scale (from the *Properties* palette).

- *For the centerline symbol*: (i) Activate the *Text* command, (ii) select the font "gdt", and (iii) type lowercase q. The centerline symbol (℄) is created.

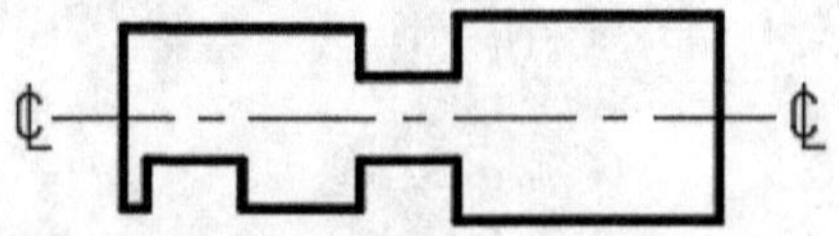

Figure 9-30

9.18. Line Of Symmetry

The line of symmetry indicates that the object is a mirror image on either side of the line of symmetry. The advantage of the line of symmetry is that it reduces the time to draw the object; only draw the repeating part of the object and then use the mirror command to complete the object, Figure 9-31a, Figure 9-31b, Figure 9-31c, and Figure 9-31d.

Figure 9-31a

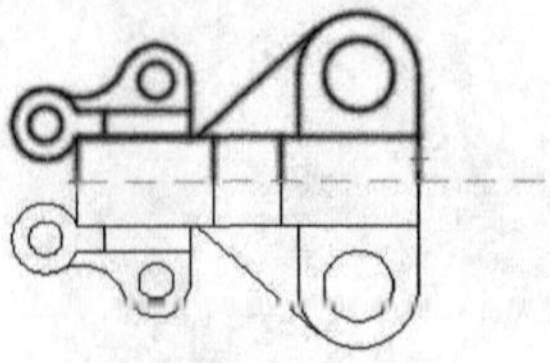

Figure 9-31b

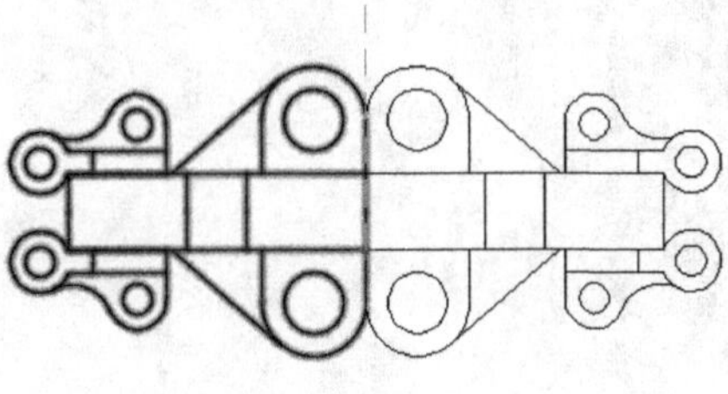

Figure 9-31c

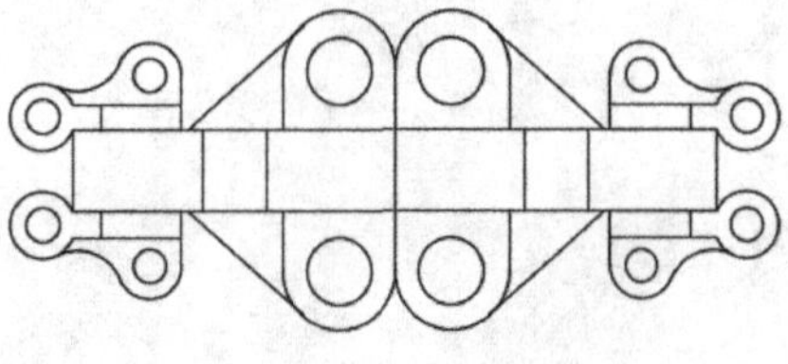

Figure 9-31d

The line of symmetry can be shown in two ways.

- Method #1: Draw two parallel lines perpendicular to the line passing through the axis of symmetry, Figure 9-32a.
- *Method #2*: Write a note OBJECT IS SYMMETRICAL ABOUT THIS AXIS pointing to the line passing through the axis of symmetry, Figure 9-32b.

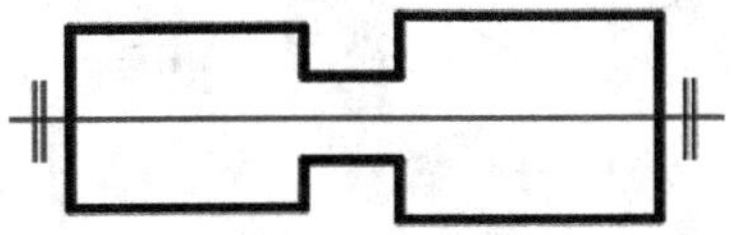

Figure 9-32a

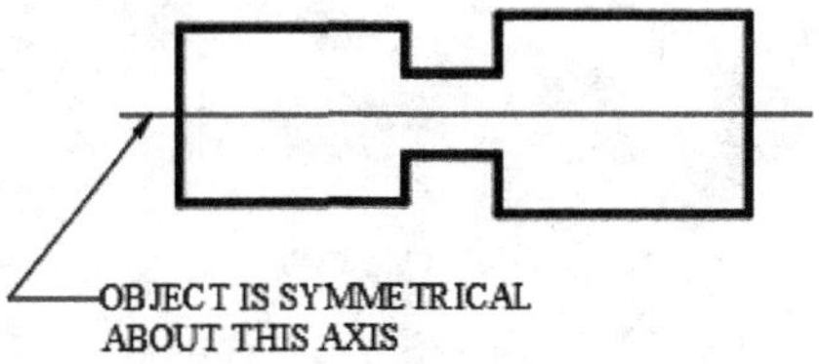

Figure 9-32b

9.19. Dimensioning An Architectural Drawing

The major reason for adding dimensions to an architectural drawing is to provide communication between the architect and the builder. For the details of architectural drawing refer to Chapter 17.

Notes:

10. Tolerance

10.1. Learning Objectives

After completing this chapter, the students will show proficiency in the following areas:

- Basics of tolerance
- Placement of the tolerance text
- Different types of tolerance format
- Selection of tolerance
- Art of creating and reading dimensions appended with tolerances

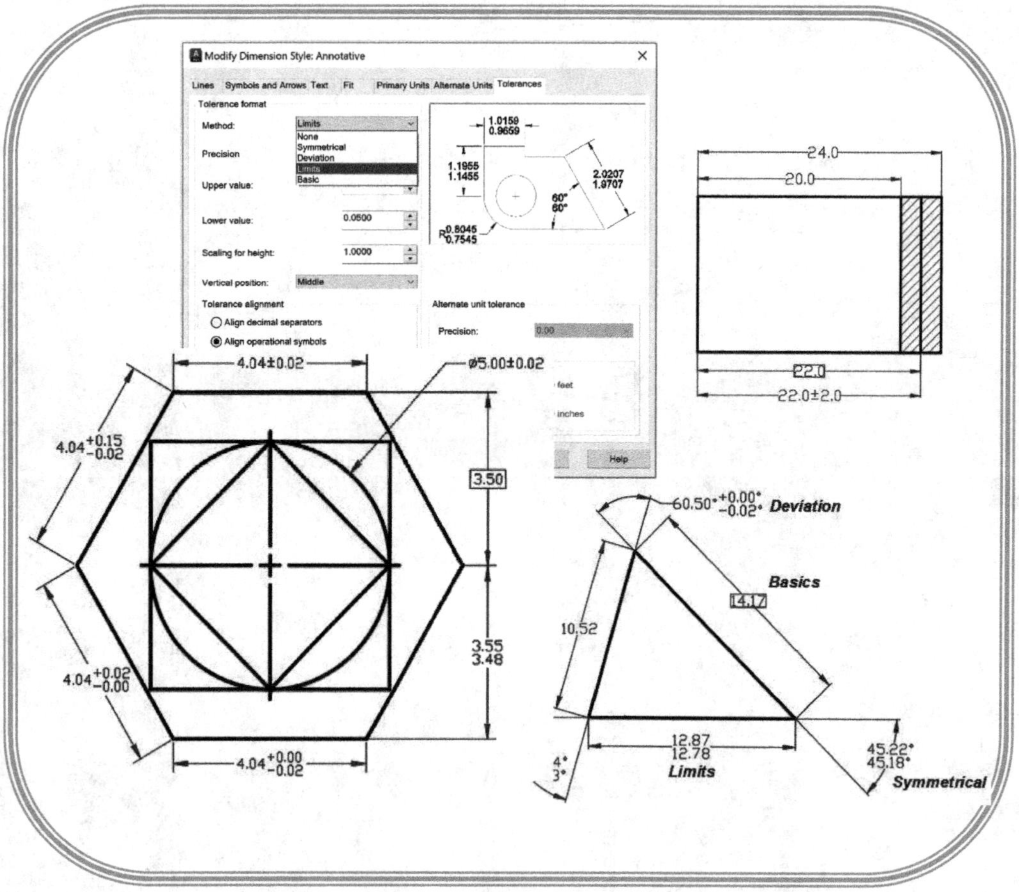

10.2. Introduction

A dimension describes the size and location of features of an object; therefore, dimensions are given in the form of distance, angle, and/or notes irrespective of the units used in the drawing. Although theoretically possible, it is economically unfeasible to manufacture products to the exact numbers displayed on an engineering drawing. The cost of a part rapidly increases as an absolute correct size is approached. Hence, accuracy depends largely on the manufacturing process used and the care taken to manufacture a product. Since different companies make different parts of a model, it is very important that these parts should be interchangeable. A tolerance value shows the manufacturing department the maximum permissible variation from the basic dimension. The size and location of a tolerance depend on the design objective of the model, how it is manufactured, how it is inspected, and how it is used.

In AutoCAD, a drafter can add tolerance to a dimension using the *Tolerance* tab from the *Modify Dimension Style: Annotative* dialog box, Figure 10-1.

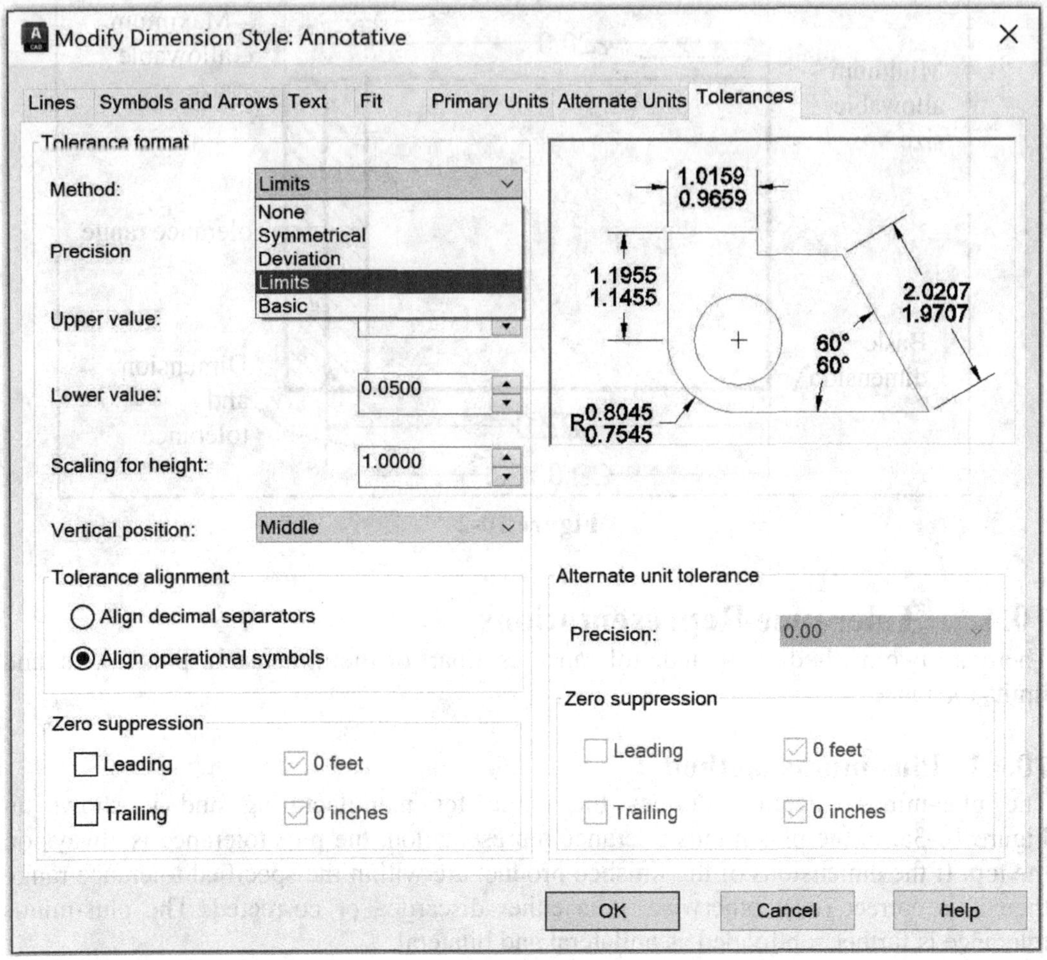

Figure 10-1

10.3. Terminology

Use Figure 10-2 with the following definitions.

- *Basic dimension*: The basic dimension is the theoretical dimension of an object.
- *Actual dimension*: The actual dimension is the measured size of the finished product.
- *Allowance*: The allowance is the minimum clearance or maximum interference between parts.
- *Tolerance*: The tolerance is the total amount by which a given dimension may vary, known as plus-minus or limits (the difference between the maximum and minimum acceptable sizes).
- *Tolerance range*: The tolerance range is the difference between the maximum and minimum allowable sizes of the feature, and is given as
  Tolerance range = maximum allowable size - minimum allowable size

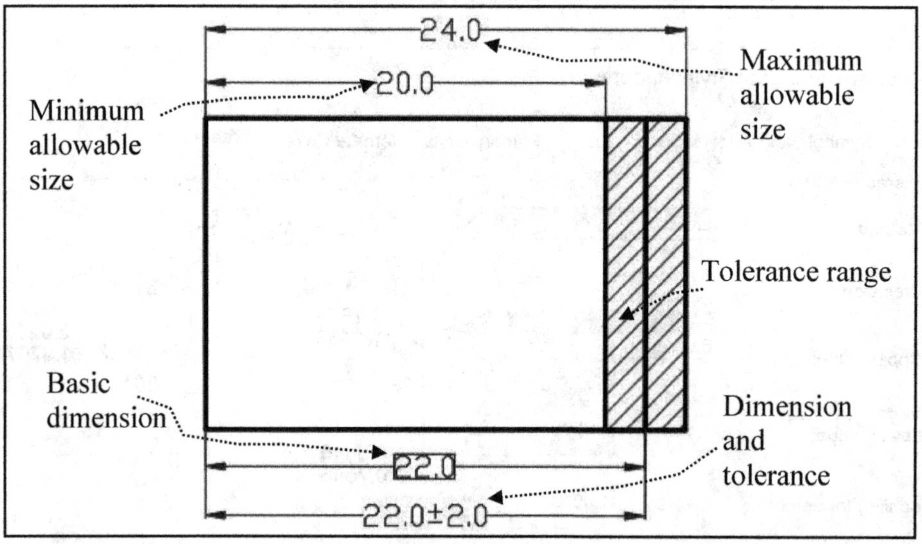

Figure 10-2

10.4. Tolerance Representations

There are two methods to include tolerance as a part of the dimension: plus-minus, and limits tolerance.

10.4.1. Plus-minus method

The plus-minus tolerance defines the range for manufacturing and is shown in Figure 10-3a. In the plus-minus tolerance representation, the plus tolerance is always on the top. If the dimensions of the finished product are within the specified tolerance range then it is correct (ok); otherwise, it is either discarded or corrected. The plus-minus tolerance is further subdivided as unilateral and bilateral.

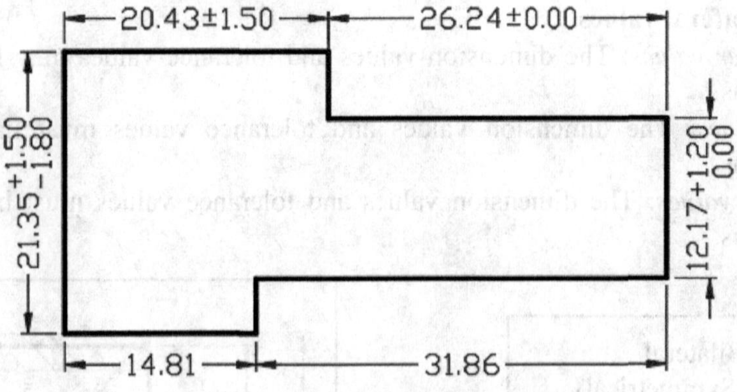

Figure 10-3a

10.4.1.1. Unilateral

When the dimension can vary only in one direction from the basic dimension, either larger or smaller, then the tolerance is known as unilateral (known as *Deviation* in AutoCAD, Figure 10-1). That is, the tolerance is either plus (Figure 10-3b) or minus (Figure 10-3c) but not both.

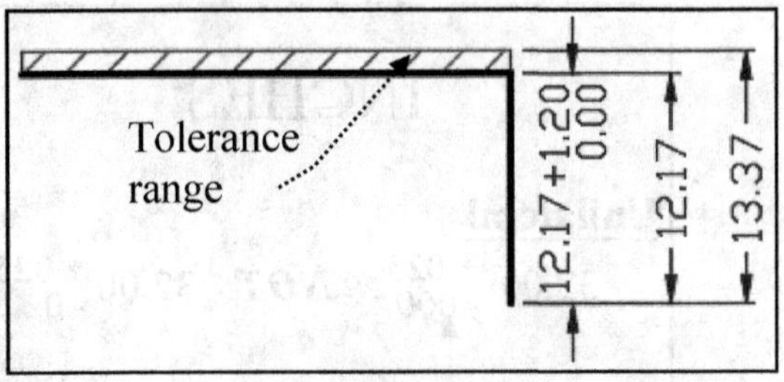

Figure 10-3b

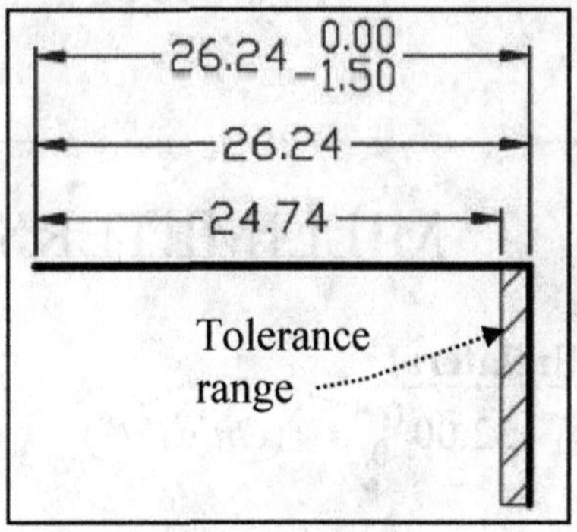

Figure 10-3c

10.4.1.2. Bilateral

When the dimension can vary in both directions from the basic dimension (larger and smaller), then the tolerance is known as a bilateral. The tolerance in both directions can have the same value (known as *Symmetrical* in AutoCAD, Figure 10-1 and Figure 10-3d) or different (known as *Deviation* in AutoCAD, Figure 10-1 and Figure 10-3e).

10.4.1.3. Tolerance expression

The dimension and tolerance values are written differently for inch and millimeter dimension values, Figure 10-4.

10.4.1.4. Unilateral values

- *Millimeter values*: Specify zero limit with one zero only.
- *Inch values*: The zero limits must include the same number of decimal places as given for the dimension.
- *Angular values*: A single "0" can be used for zero limits.

10.4.1.5. Bilateral values

- *Millimeter values*: The dimension values and tolerance values may have different precisions.
- *Inch values*: The dimension values and tolerance values must have the same precisions.
- *Angular values*: The dimension values and tolerance values must have the same precisions.

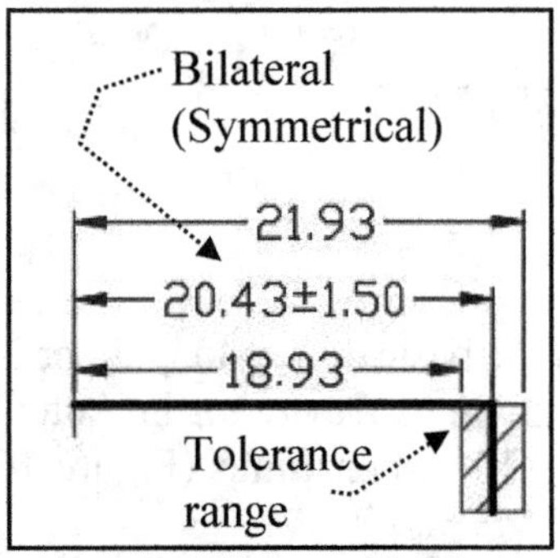

Figure 10-3d

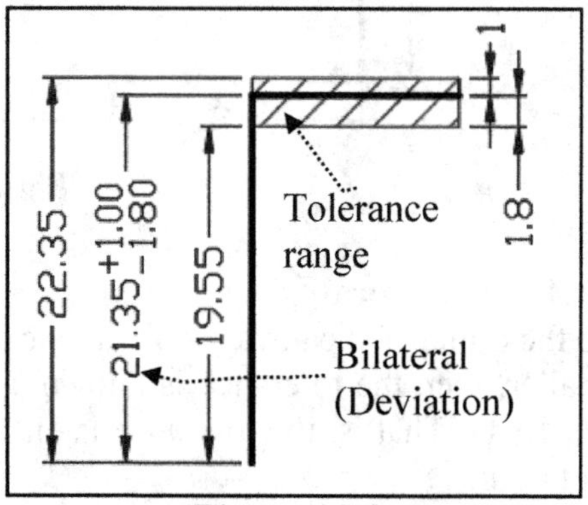

Figure 10-3e

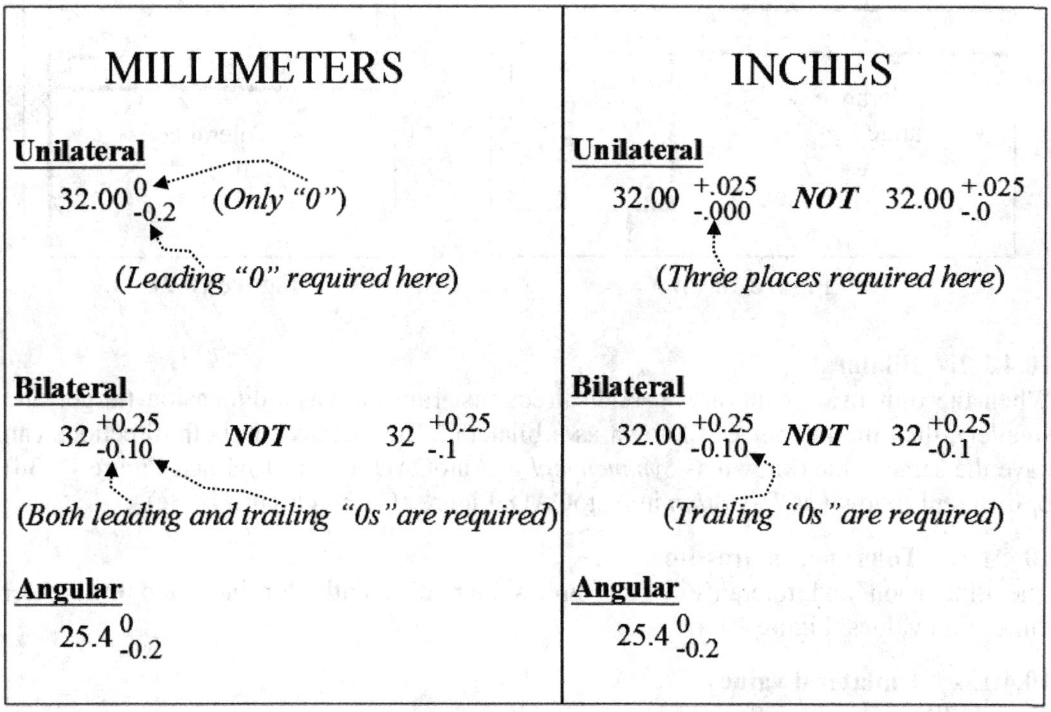

Figure 10-4

10.4.1.6. Usage of plus-minus tolerance

In Table #1 the dimension is in millimeters. Consider a basic dimension (Bd) of 60 with the tolerance values of *+0.25* and *-0.12*. The maximum and minimum allowable sizes and the tolerance range can be calculated as follows:

Maximum allowable size (Mx): 60 + 0.25 = 60.25
Minimum allowable size (Mn): 60 – 0.12 = 59.88
Tolerance range (Tr):
60.25 – 59.88 = 0.37 OR 0.25 - (-0.12) = 0.25 + 0.12 = 0.37

After the object is manufactured and inspected, if *Mn* <= *Bd* <= *Mx* then the object is *OK* (that is, it is accepted), otherwise it is rejected, Table #1. Objects larger than the *Mx* can be reworked to fit the acceptable size; and the objects smaller than the *Mn* are rejected.

Table #1

Given (mm)	**Object**	**Measured Size (mm)**	**Acceptable**
60 +0.25 -0.12	1	60.160	OK
	2	60.020	OK
That is: Max. allowable size = 60.25	3	60.253	Too long (can be fixed)
Min. allowable size = 59.88	4	59.920	OK
Tolerance range = (60.25 – 59.88) = 0.37	5	59.79	Too short (Rejected)

10.4.2. Limits tolerance

When the dimensions are represented by the largest and smallest possible sizes of a feature (that is, upper and lower limits), then the tolerance is in the *limit* format, Figure 10-5. The two limiting values are stacked on top of each other with the larger limit always on the top. Generally, the limit tolerance is considered easier to read than the plus-minus tolerance. For example, if the basic dimension is 60 and the tolerance is ± 0.2 then the upper and lower limits are 60.02 and 59.98, respectively. The final distance should lie between the two limits. The limit tolerance gives the range for manufacture.

10.5. Standard Tolerance

Generally, manufacturers create a table of standard tolerances that can be used if a dimension does not include a specific tolerance. Figure 10-6 shows some standard tolerances. If the dimension is given as *60.000*, then the implied tolerance is *0.005* and if the dimension is given as *60.0*, then the implied tolerance is *0.1*.

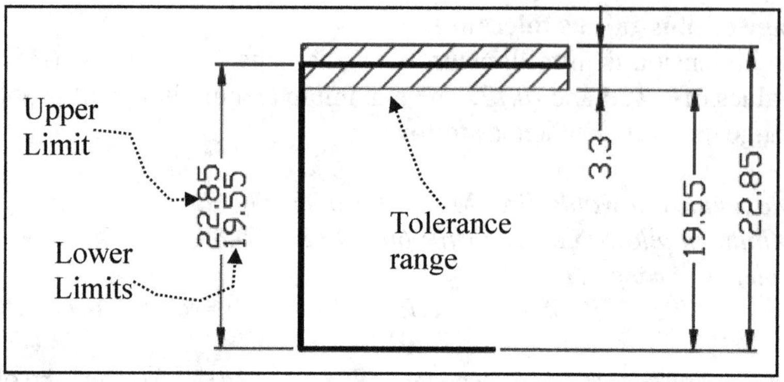

Figure 10-5

x	± 1
.x	± .1
.xx	± .01
.xxx	± .005
x°	± 1°
.x °	± .1°

Figure 10-6

10.6. Double Dimensioning

If the dimension of a feature is given twice then it is called a double dimensioning. In Figure 10-7a, the lower edge is dimensioned twice. (i) The overall length is given as 34. (ii) The overall length can also be calculated from the dimensions on the top (5 + 5 + 12 + 12 = 34).

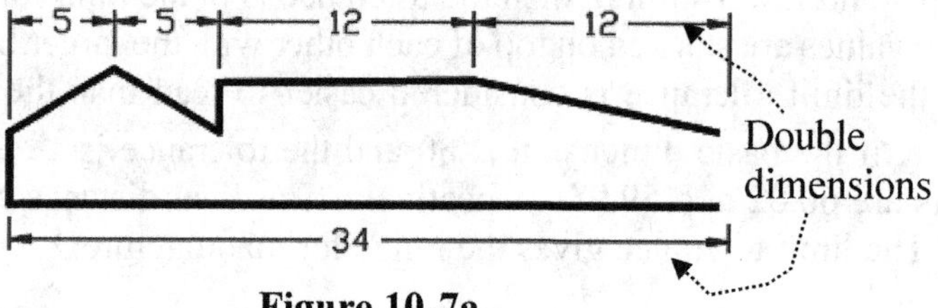

Figure 10-7a

10.6.1. Double dimensioning: an error

In technical drawings, double dimensioning is an error. Mathematically the two dimensions (34 and 5 + 5 + 12 + 12) are equal, Figure 10-7a. On the other hand, in technical drawings these dimensions are not equal when tolerance is applied. Assume the tolerance is "1" then

Sum of top dimensions = (5+1) + (5+1) + (12+1) + (12+1) = 38
Bottom dimension = (34+1) = 35

10.6.2. Solution #1

One possible solution to the double dimensioning problem is to make one of the top dimensions a floating dimension; that is, do not provide its dimension, Figure 10-7b. Instead of providing "12" for one side, called A in the figure, allow that side to have floating dimension; it absorbs the cumulated tolerance. In this case, *A* is equal to (34 + 1) – (5 + 1) – (5 + 1) – (12 + 1) = 10 (the assumption is that every side has the maximum error).

10.6.3. Solution #2

A different possible solution is to use a reference dimension, Figure 10-7c. Keep the dimension "12" and change the overall dimension to a reference dimension by enclosing it in parentheses, Figure 10-7c. In this case, the top three dimensions are used for manufacturing and inspecting the object. The reference dimension is used only for the mathematical convenience.

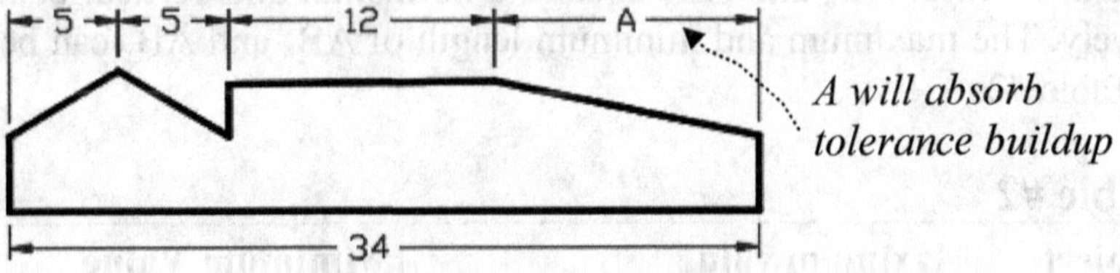

Figure 10-7b

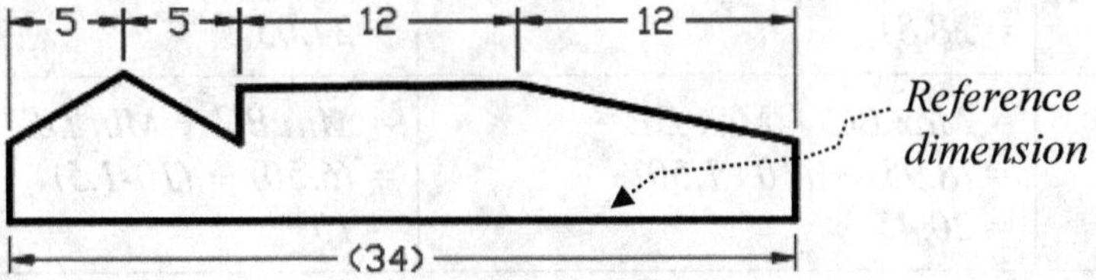

Figure 10-7c

10.7. Chain And Baseline Dimension

The chain dimension relates the dimension of one feature to the next feature, and the baseline dimension relates all features to a single baseline or datum.

- The drawback of the chain dimension is that it accumulates tolerance. The tolerance buildup can be eliminated by using floating dimension (Figure 10-7b), reference dimension (Figure 10-7c) or baseline dimension (Figure 10-7d).
- If the distance between individual features is more important, then use the chain dimension because the error between the two consecutive features is the least. If the distance of a feature from the baseline is more important, then use baseline dimension.

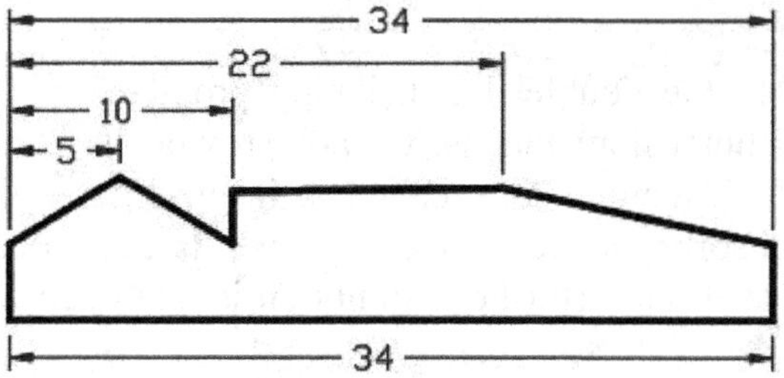

Figure 10-7d

10.8. Tolerance Study

The tolerance study is the process of analyzing the effects of tolerances of different features on each other and on the object. In Figure 10-8 the inclined distance AB is not dimensioned. Its length depends on the tolerances of horizontal distances AE and CD and the vertical distance BC and DE. Let AB_x and AB_y equal the horizontal and vertical components of AB, respectively. The maximum and minimum length of AB_x and AB_y can be calculated as shown in Table #2.

Table #2

Object	Maximum value	Minimum Value
AB_x	= *Max AE – Min CD* = *(34+1.50) – (8-1.31)* = *28.81*	= *Min AE – Max CD* = *(34-1.10) – (8+0.85)* = *24.05*
AB_y	= *Max BC + Max DE* = *(8.95) + (10+1.50)* = *20.45*	= *Min BC + Min DE* = *(6.50) + (10-1.5)* = *15*

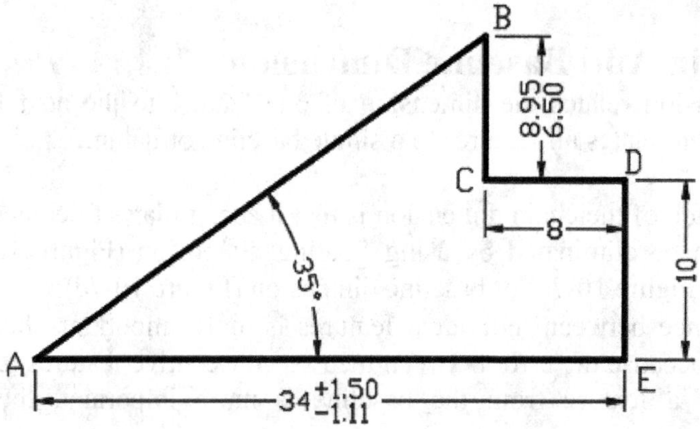

Figure 10-8

10.9. Tolerance In AutoCAD

The appearance of tolerance can be controlled by changing the settings in *Dimension Style Manager* and *Modify Dimension Style* dialog boxes or the *Properties* palette.

- The *Dimension Style Manager* dialog box can be launched using one of the following methods:

  1. Panel method: (ii) From the *Home* tab, expand the *Annotation* panel, and select the *Dimension Style* tool. (ii) From the *Annotate* tab and the *Dimension* panel, click on the dialog box launcher (the small arrow on the lower right corner of the panel).
  2. Command line method: Type "dimstyle," "Dimstyle" or "DIMSTYLE" on the command line and press the *Enter* key.

- The activation of the command opens the *Dimension Style Manager* dialog box, Figure 10-9a. The dialog box provides the capability to create new styles, sets the current style, modifies existing styles, overrides the current style, and compares styles. This chapter discusses the capabilities to modify the current dimension style.
- Click on the *Modify* button to modify an existing style. This opens the *Modify Dimension Style Manager* dialog box, Figure 10-9b. The *: Standard* means that the standard style will be modified. Also, the *New Dimension Style* and *Override Current Style* dialog boxes provide these capabilities.

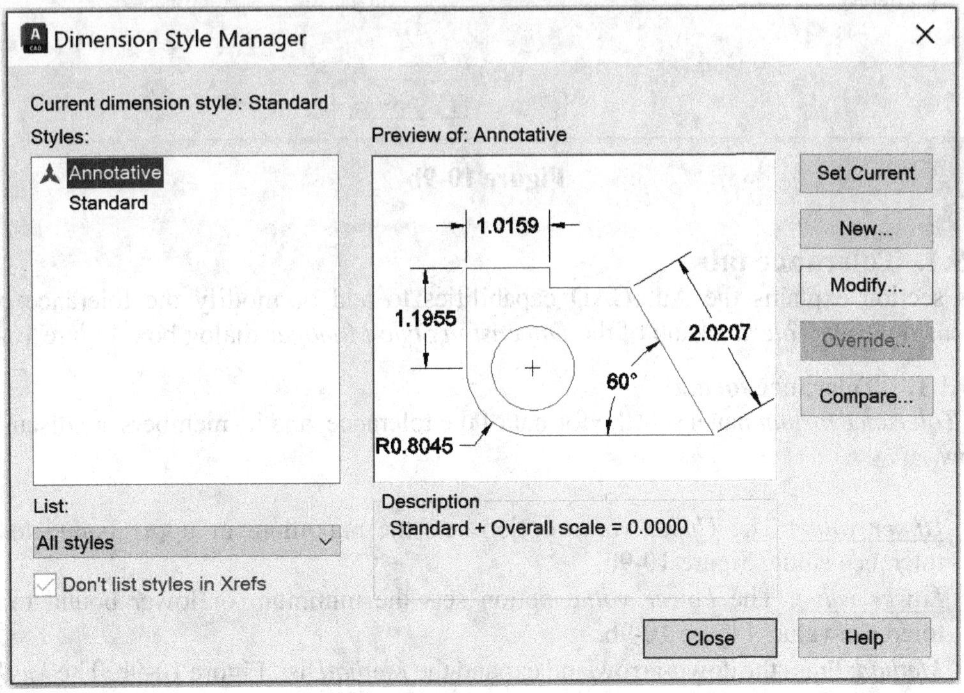

Figure 10-9a

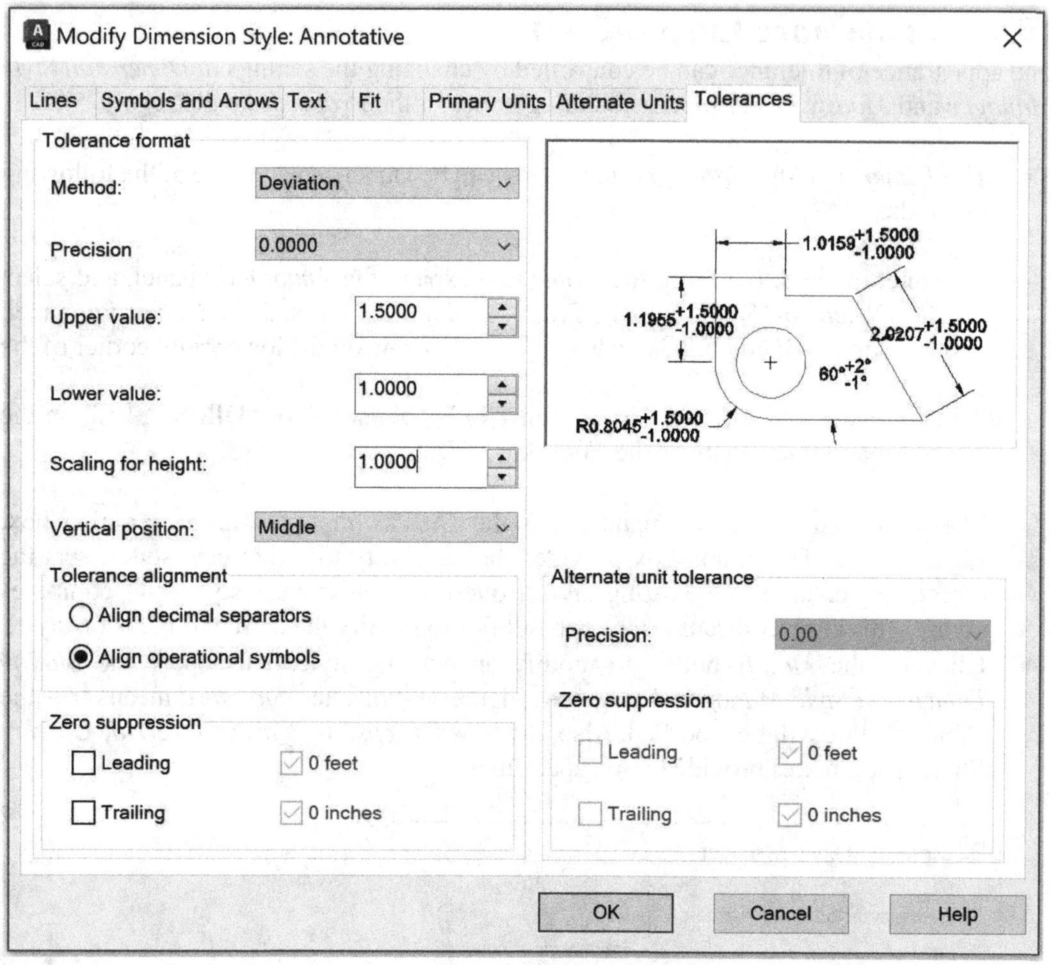

Figure 10-9b

10.9.1. Tolerance tab

This section explains the AutoCAD capabilities to add or modify the tolerance of a dimension using *Tolerance* tab of the *Dimension Style Manager* dialog box, Figure 10-9b.

10.9.1.1. Tolerance format

The *Tolerance format* panel sets the format of the tolerance, and its members are discussed below.

- *Upper value*: The *Upper value* option sets the maximum or upper bound to the tolerance value, Figure 10-9b.
- *Lower value*: The *Lower value* option sets the minimum or lower bound to the tolerance value, Figure 10-9b.
- *Method*: Press the down-arrow and expand the *Method* list, Figure 10-9b. The *Method* list allows the selection of the method to calculate and represent the tolerance. AutoCAD provides five different options, Figure 10-10a.

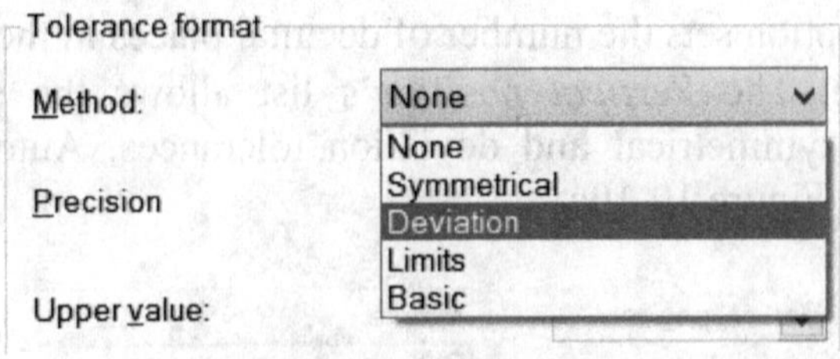

Figure 10-10a

1. *None*: The *None* option indicates that the tolerance is not added to the dimension, Figure 10-10a and Figure 10-10b.
2. *Symmetrical*: The *Symmetrical* option adds a bilateral (symmetrical) tolerance to the dimension measurement, Figure 10-10a and Figure 10-10b. A plus-minus sign appears automatically. For this option, specify the tolerance value in the *Upper value* box: either type the number and press the *Enter* key or use up/down-arrow to increase/decrease the value; the *Lower value* box is deactivated.
3. *Deviation*: The *Deviation* option adds a bilateral (asymmetrical) and unilateral tolerance to the dimension measurement, Figure 10-10a and Figure 10-10b. For this option, specify the tolerance value in the *Upper* and *Lower value* boxes: either type the numbers and press the *Enter* key or use the up/down-arrow to increase/decrease the values. Do not type the plus-minus signs in the *Upper* and *Lower value* boxes; the software adds these signs automatically. **Note**: To create unilateral tolerances, type *0* in the *Upper* or *Lower value* box.
4. *Limits*: The *Limits* option creates a limit dimension and displays a maximum and a minimum value, Figure 10-10a and Figure 10-10b; the maximum value is on top of the lower value. The maximum value is the dimension value plus the value entered in the *Upper value* box, and the minimum value is the dimension value minus the value entered in *Lower value* box.
5. *Basic*: The *Basic* option creates a basic dimension, which displays a box around the dimension, Figure 10-10a and Figure 10-10b.

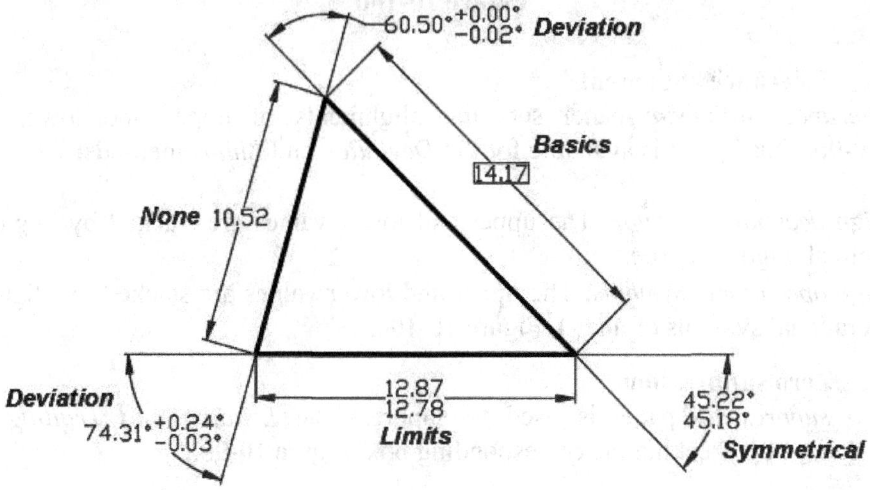

Figure 10-10b

- <u>*Precision*</u>: This option sets the number of decimal places in the tolerance value.
- <u>*Vertical position*</u>: The *Vertical position*'s list allows the selection of the text justification for symmetrical and deviation tolerances. AutoCAD provides three different options, Figure 10-10c.

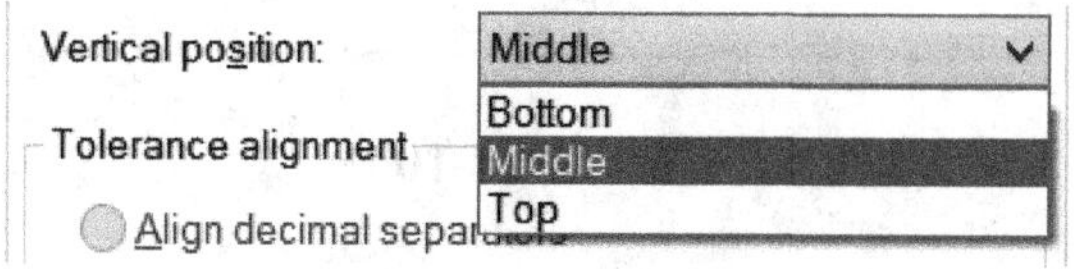

Figure 10-10c

1. <u>*Top*</u>: The *Top* option aligns the tolerance text with the top of the main dimension text, Figure 10-10d.
2. <u>*Middle*</u>: The *Middle* option aligns the tolerance text with the middle of the main dimension text, Figure 10-10d.
3. <u>*Bottom*</u>: The *Bottom* option aligns the tolerance text with the bottom of the main dimension text, Figure 10-10d.

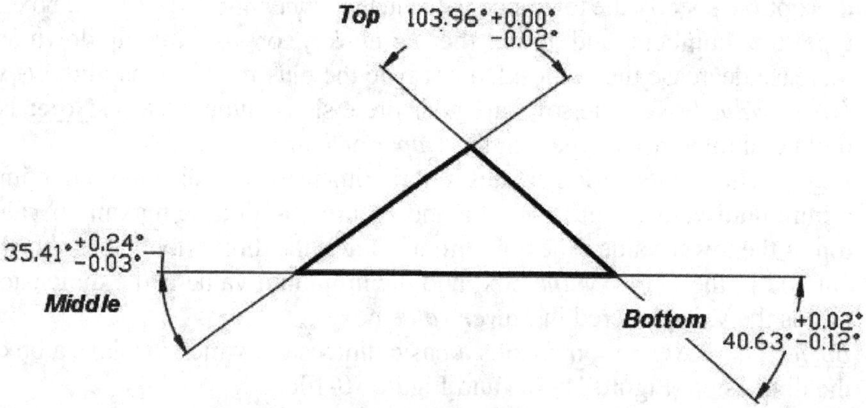

Figure 10-10d

10.9.1.2. Tolerance alignment

The *Tolerance Alignment* panel sets the alignments of upper and lower values, Figure 10-9b. This option is available for the *Deviation* and *Limits* methods.

- *Align decimal separator*: The upper and lower values are stacked by aligning the decimal, Figure 10-10e.
- *Align operational symbols*: The upper and lower values are stacked by aligning the operational symbols (+ and -), Figure 10-10e.

10.9.1.3. Zero suppression

The *Zero suppression* panel is used to suppress the *Leading and Trailing* zeroes (independently) by checking the corresponding box, Figure 10-9b.

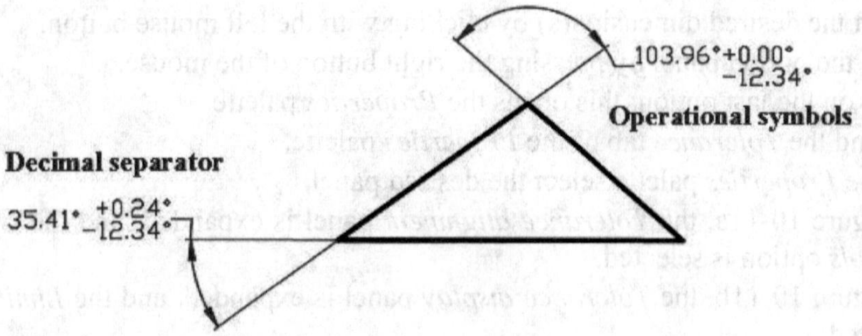

Figure 10-10e

10.9.2. Add or modify tolerance

A user can add or modify the tolerance value and style using the dialog box or the property palette.

10.9.2.1. Add or modify tolerance using the dialog box

If the user desires to change the settings for the tolerance of all the dimensions, then open the *Modify Dimension Style* dialog box; using the functionality of the dialog box, change the tolerance setting. For example, if the *Limits* option under the *Tolerance format* panel is selected, then the tolerance for all the dimensions is set to limits format.

10.9.2.2. Add or modify tolerance using the property palette

If the user desires to change the settings for one (or more but not all) tolerance, then use the *Properties* palette, Figure 10-11a, Figure 10-11b, and Figure 10-11c, and perform the following steps.

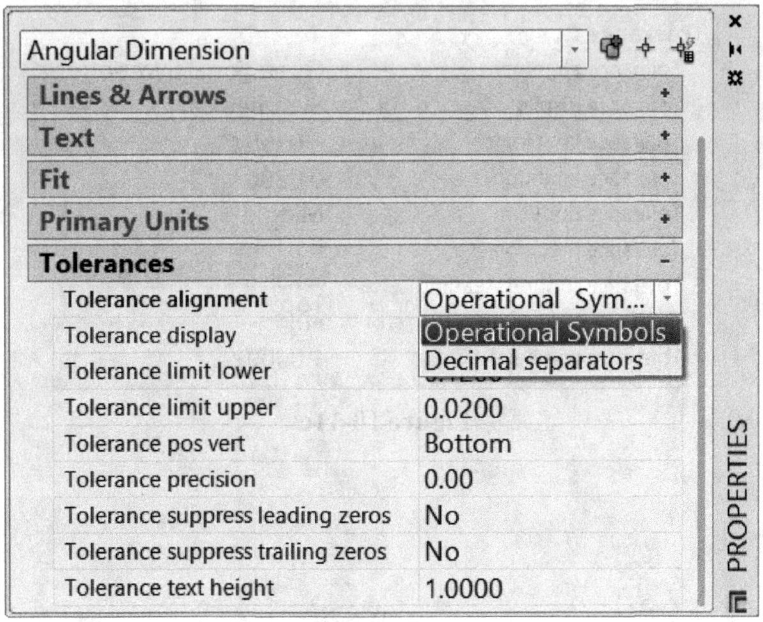

Figure 10-11a

- Select the desired dimension(s) by clicking with the left mouse button.
- Open the option panel by pressing the right button of the mouse.
- Click on the last option; this opens the *Properties* palette.
- Expand the *Tolerance* tab of the *Properties* palette.
- On the *Properties* palette select the desired panel.
- In Figure 10-11a, the *Tolerance alignment* panel is expanded, and the *Operational symbols* option is selected.
- In Figure 10-11b, the *Tolerance display* panel is expanded, and the *Limits* option is selected.
- In Figure 10-11c, the *Tolerance position vertical* panel is expanded, and the *Middle* option is selected.

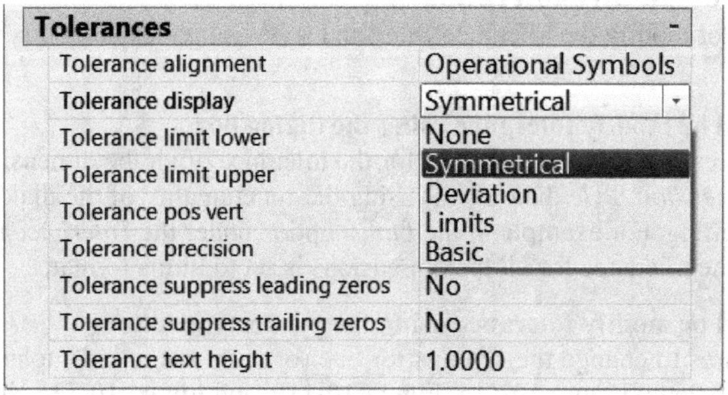

Figure 10-11b

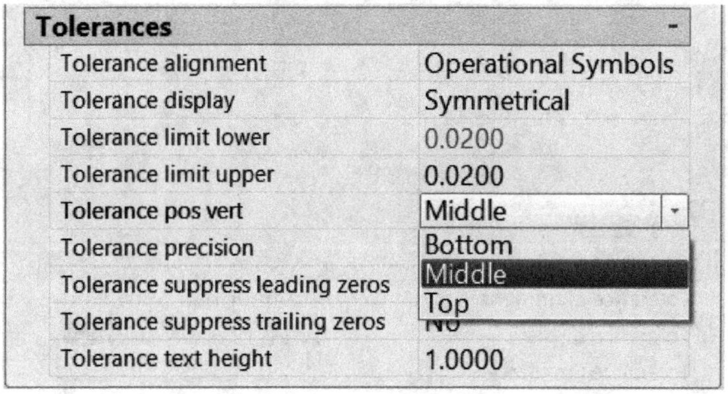

Figure 10-11c

Notes:

11. Land Survey

11.1. Learning Objectives

After completing this chapter, the students will show proficiency in the following areas:

- Basics of land survey
- Angular measurements (azimuth, bearing, and conversion)
- Traverses (open and closed, courses and stations)
- Deed and parcel of land
- Find/calculate area of a parcel
- Different types of survey systems
- Draw survey data using AutoCAD

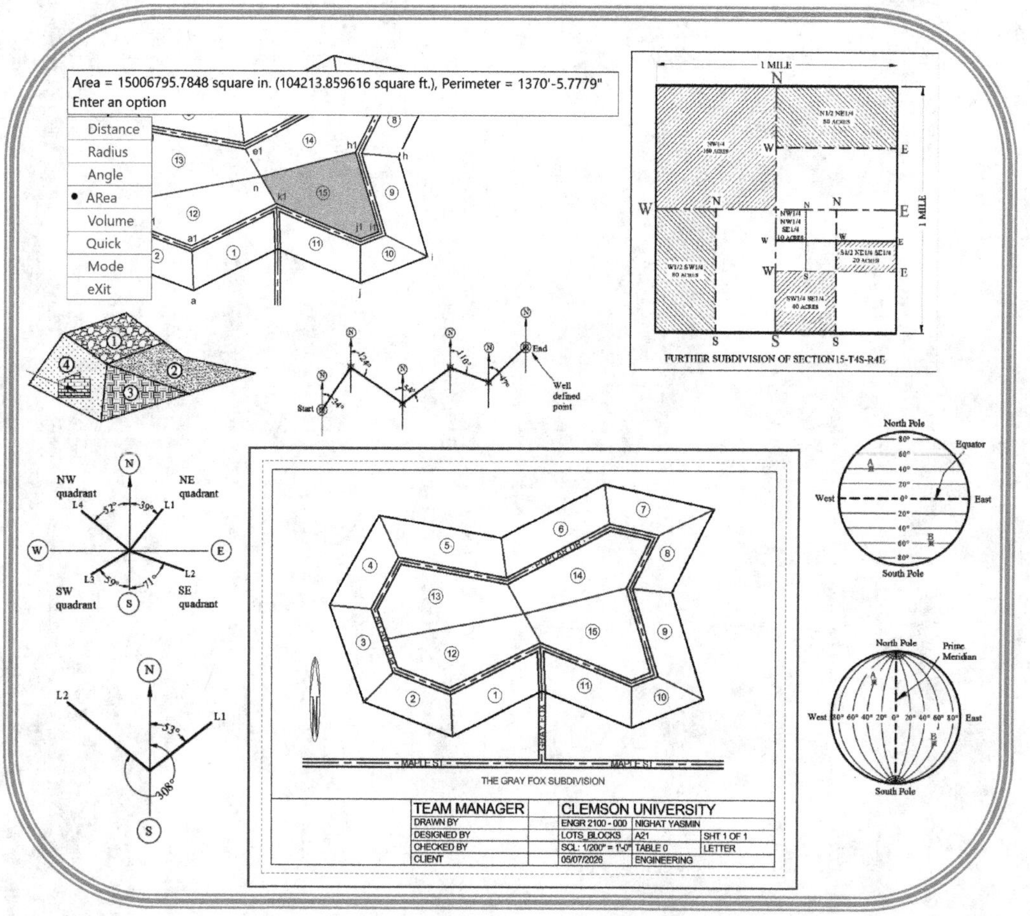

11.2. Introduction

According to Webster New Collegiate Dictionary, the word **survey** is defined as "*to determine and delineate the form, extent, position, of (as a tract of land) by taking linear and angular measurements and by applying the principles of geometry and trigonometry*". Thus, surveying is an art of measuring (angles, distances, etc.), calculating quantities (area, volume, etc.), and plotting of the measurements (profile, contour maps, etc.). Generally, in surveying the point of measurement is known as a station and stations are identified using their position and direction with respect to a reference location.

11.3. Location

The position of a station on the surface of the earth can be specified by its longitude and latitude.

11.3.1. Longitudes

The longitudes, or meridians, are imaginary lines connecting the North Pole to the South Pole, Figure 11-1a. Longitudes are an angular distance measured in degrees towards east or west. The 0° longitude is known as the prime meridian and passes through Greenwich, England. The angles going east are measured as positive and angles going west are measured as negative. For example, station A is at *40° W* longitude, whereas station B is at *60° E* longitude, Figure 11-1a.

11.3.2. Latitudes

Latitude represents the position of a station measured north or south of the equator, Figure 11-1b. The equator is at zero-degree latitude. The north and south poles are 90° north and south latitude, respectively. The angles toward the north are measured as positive, and angles toward the south are measured as negative. However, the latitudes are generally written with N or S. For example, the latitude of station A is *40° N*, whereas the latitude of station B is *60° S*, Figure 11-1b.

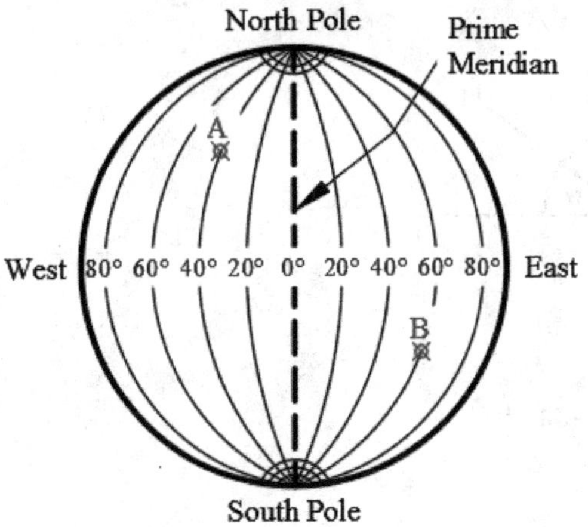

Figure 11-1a

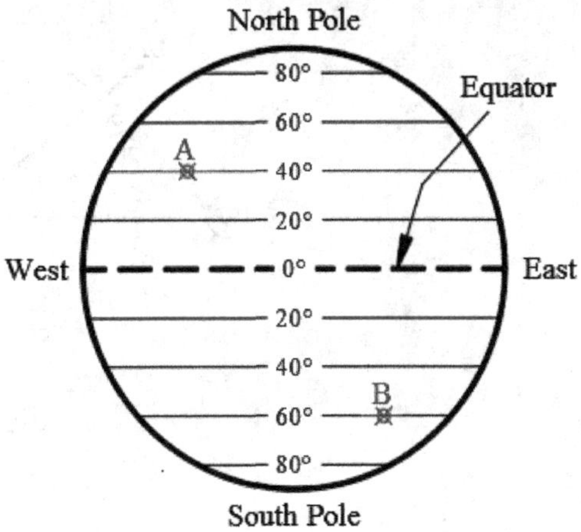

Figure 11-1b

11.3.3. Location on a map

The latitudes and longitudes can be used as a coordinate system to find the location of a station on a map. Figure 11-1c shows a map with two longitudes (85° and 75°), two latitudes (27° and 23°), and four stations (*R*, *H*, *T*, and *C*). For example, C is located east of 85° longitude and to the south of 27° latitude. Also, latitudes and longitudes can be used to find the location of places with respect to each other. For example, Figure 11-1c shows that *R* is to the north of every other station and *C* is to the east of every other station (on the map). It is clear from Figure 11-1c, that both *H* and *T* are to the north of 23° latitude and south of 27° latitude; and *H* is to the west of *T*.

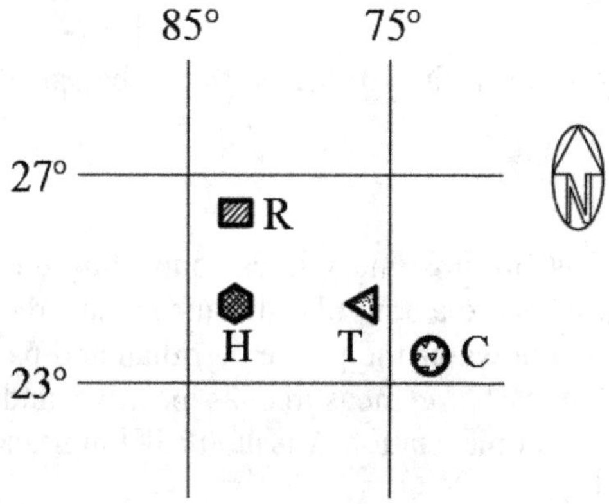

Figure 11-1c

11.4. Angular Measurement

In land survey, the direction of a line represents the angular relationship between the given line and a reference (or datum) line. Generally, either the North-South or the East-West line is used as the reference line. In Figure 11-2a, α is the angle of line *L1* with respect to the East-West line, and β is the angle of the same line with respect to the North-South line.

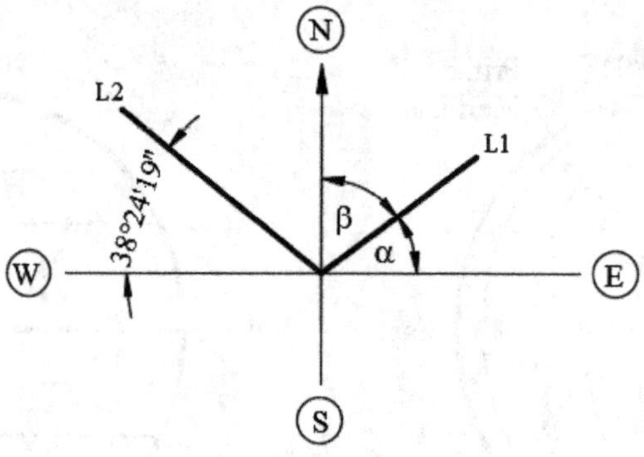

Figure 11-2a

11.4.1. Units of measurement

The angles are measured in degrees or radians. The degrees are denoted by the symbol '°'. Each degree is divided into 60 minutes (denoted by the symbol ') and each minute is subdivided into 60 seconds (denoted by the symbol "). In Figure 11-2a, angle of the line *L2* with respect to the East-West datum line is 38 degrees, 24 minutes, and 19 seconds (or 38° 24' 19").

11.4.2. Direction

The angular measurement is represented either as an azimuth or a bearing.

11.4.2.1. Azimuth

The azimuth of a line is the horizontal angle between the given line and the datum line. Generally, the datum is the north-south line. An azimuth is measured clockwise from the north with its value ranges from 0° to 360°. In Figure 11-2b, the azimuth of L1 is 53° and of L2 is 308°.

11.4.2.2. Bearing

The bearing of a line is the angle between the line and a datum line. Generally, the datum can be either the north or south meridian. Hence, the angle can be measured clockwise or counterclockwise ranging from 0° to 90°. To measure the bearing of a line, the angle of a circle (360°) is divided into four quadrants: NE, SE, SW, and NW, Figure 11-2c. Therefore, the value of the bearing angle is preceded by *N* or *S* and followed by *E* or *W*. For example, the bearing of line *L1* in Figure 11-2c is N39°E and of *L2* is S71°E.

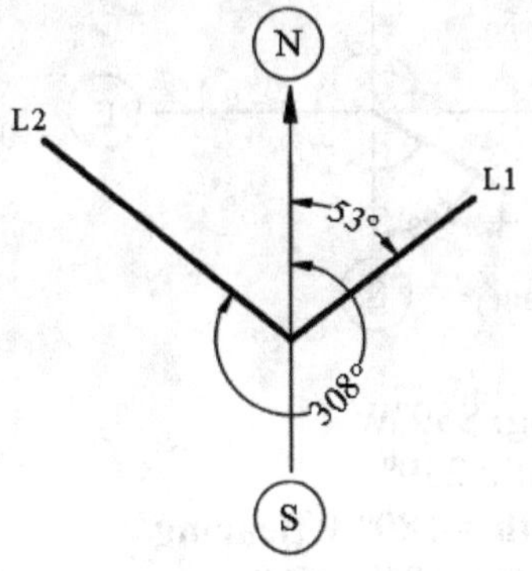

Figure 11-2b

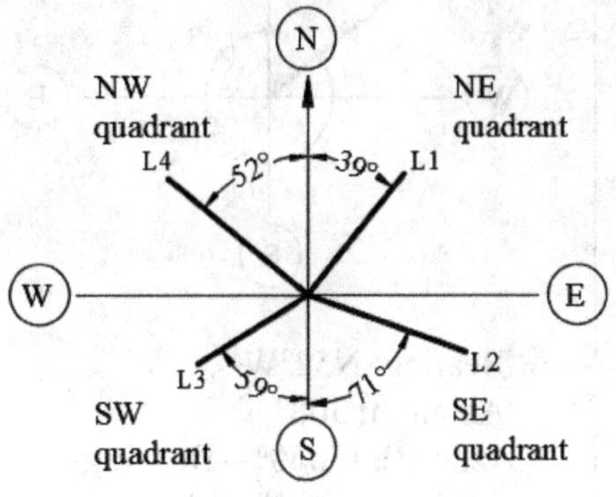

Figure 11-2c

11.4.2.3. Relationship between azimuth and bearing

If necessary, a user can convert a bearing into azimuth and vice versa. To convert a bearing into an azimuth, follow the steps listed below.

- Sketch the line and the reference line.
- Table #1 shows the process for converting bearings into the corresponding azimuths. In the figures of the Table #1, the angles with the dimension lines ending with dots are the azimuths and the angles with the dimension lines ending with arrowheads are the corresponding bearings.

Table #1: Conversion of bearing to azimuth

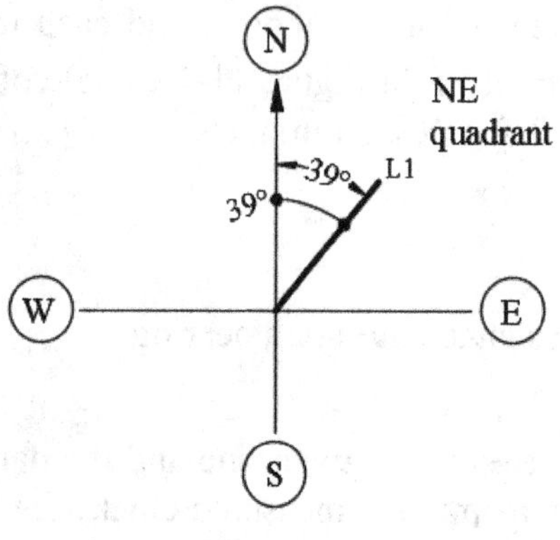

Bearing: N39°E
Azimuth: 39°
Azimuth = Bearing
39° = 39°

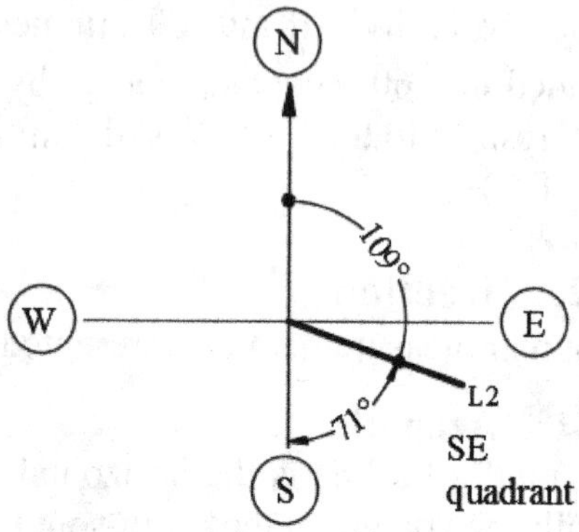

Bearing: S71°E
Azimuth: 109°
Azimuth = 180° – Bearing
109° = 180° – 71°

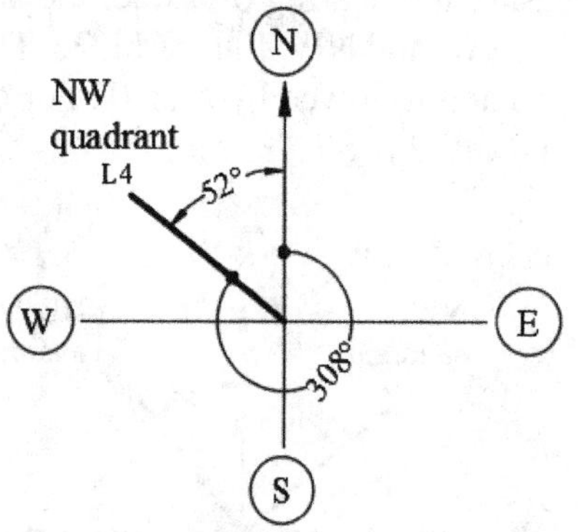

Bearing: N52°W
Azimuth: 308°
Azimuth = 360° – Bearing
308° = 360° – 52°

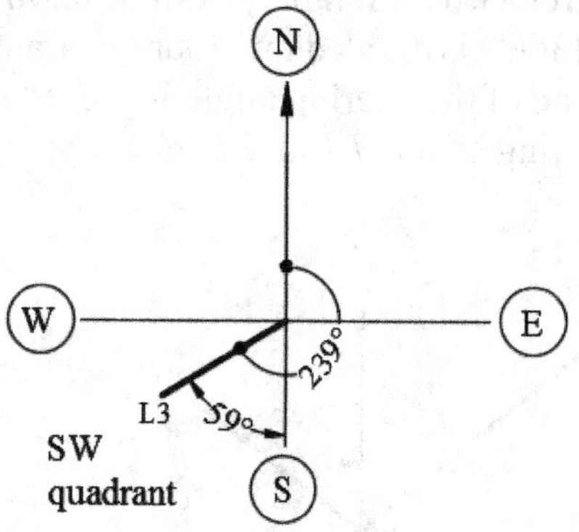

Bearing: S59°W
Azimuth: 239°
Azimuth = 180° + Bearing
239° = 180° + 59°

11.5. Traverse

Traverse is a series of interconnected lines between a series of points. The connecting lines are called courses, and the points are called traverse stations. The main purpose of a traverse survey is to find out the distance between the traverse stations and angle of the courses. A traverse can be classified as an open or a closed traverse.

11.5.1. Open traverse

This type of survey is commonly used for exploratory purposes. As the name suggests, the open traverse neither creates a loop nor does it end at a point of known position, Figure 11-3a. This type of traverse cannot be checked for accuracy. Therefore, if possible, try to avoid this type of survey. If it is necessary to use this survey, then the survey should be repeated at least twice to minimize the errors.

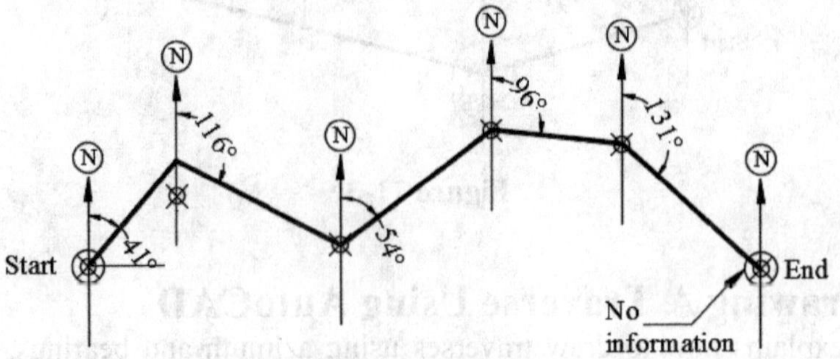

Figure 11-3a

11.5.2. Closed traverse

A close traverse starts and ends at a well defined station. A closed traverse is further subdivided into connecting (Figure 11-3b) and loop traverses (Figure 11-3c).

11.5.2.1. Connecting traverse

A connecting traverse is a type of closed traverse. Although this type of traverse does not end at the starting station, it ends at a well-defined station, Figure 11-3b. Hence, this type of traverse can be checked for accuracy. This type of survey can be used for the planning and designing of highways, railroads, pipelines, etc.

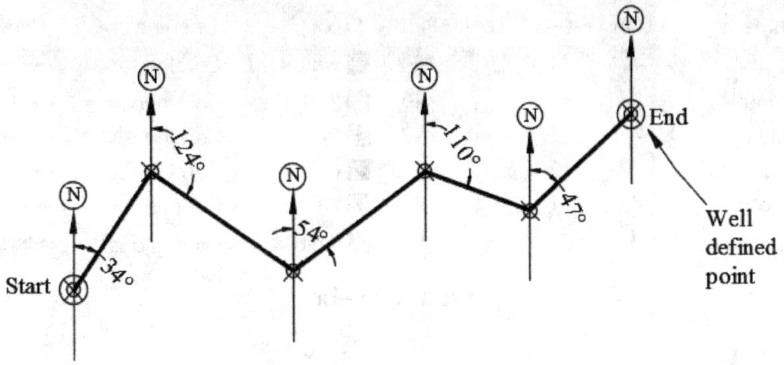

Figure 11-3b

11.5.2.2. Loop traverse

A loop traverse is a type of closed traverse that starts and ends at the same station, thus creating a closed path, Figure 11-3c. This type of traverse can be checked for its accuracy. This type of survey is used for the boundary line of a piece of land.

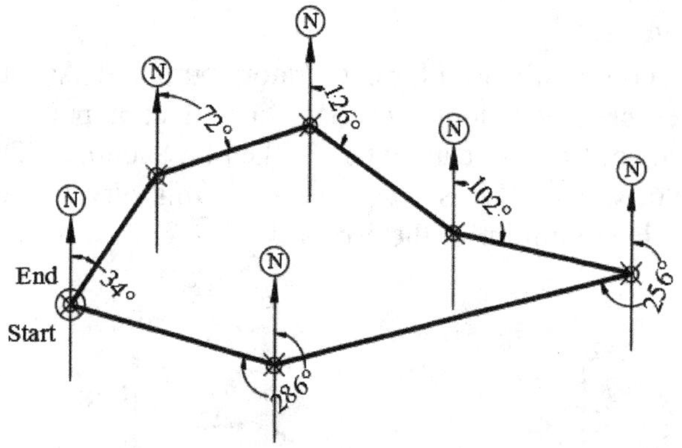

Figure 11-3c

11.6. Drawing A Traverse Using AutoCAD

This section explains how to draw traverses using azimuth and bearings. Although the examples create loop traverses, the process is similar for any other traverse.

11.6.1. Traverse for the given azimuths

In the current section, a closed traverse is drawn using the length of the courses and their azimuth (Figure 11-4d) and bearing (Figure 11-5) and the drawing units are Engineering (Feet-Inches).

- Launch AutoCAD 2027.
- Open the drawing and set the units as follows.

1. Open a new landscape template file for ANSI units created in *Chapter 8*.
2. Create the layers as shown in Figure 11-4a.

Status	Name	On	Freeze	Lock	Plot	Color	Linetype	Lineweight
✔	0					white	Continuous	Default
	Azimuth					210	Continuous	0.00 mm
	Bearing					94	Continuous	0.00 mm
	Defpoints					white	Continuous	Default
	Length					24	Continuous	0.00 mm
	Traverse					white	Continuous	0.50 mm

Figure 11-4a

3. Type *Units* in the command line and press the *Enter* key. This opens the *Drawing Units* dialog box, Figure 11-4b.
4. In the *Length*'s panel, choose the *Engineering*'s option, Figure 11-4b. Now the user can specify the information in engineering units (feet and inches). For example, the length 5'-6" is entered as follows: (i) activate the *Line* or *Polyline* commands; (ii) type 5; (iii) type the apostrophe (') key; (iv) type 6; (v) press the *Enter* key; (vi) DO NOT TYPE hyphen (-) to separate feet from inches and double apostrophe to represent inches.

5. Click on the *Direction* button and the *Direction Control* dialog box opens, Figure 11-4c. Choose the *North* option for the *Base Angle*; and press the *OK* buttons on both dialog boxes.
6. The clockwise angles are specified with negative signs because the positive angles are measured counterclockwise.

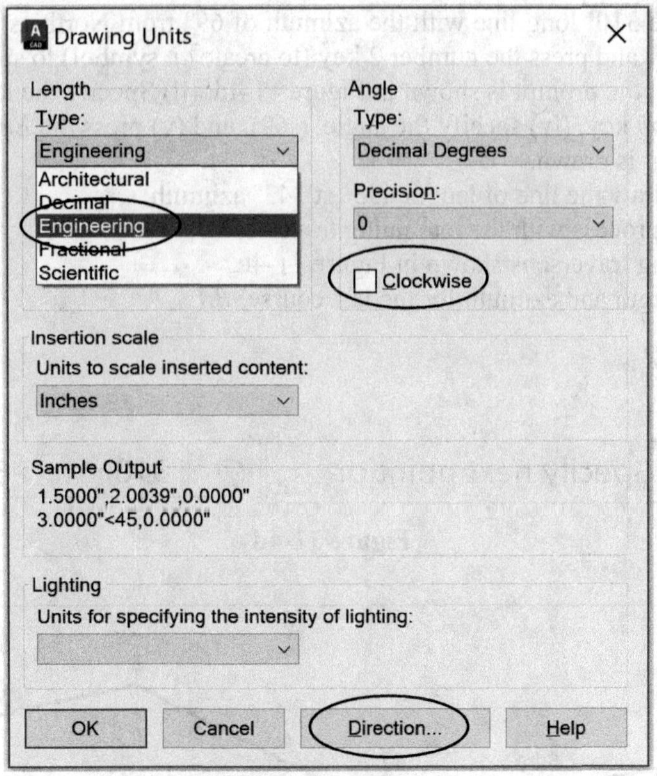

Figure 11-4b

Figure 11-4c

- Create the traverse as follows.

1. Make the Traverse layer to be the current layer.
2. To draw the traverse, the clockwise angles are specified with negative signs because positive angles are measured in the counterclockwise direction.
3. To draw the traverse, activate the *Polyline* command and click at point in the drawing area; this point represents station A of the traverse.
4. To draw the 310' long line with the azimuth of 69° from North as follows. (i) Hold the *Shift* key and press the number 2 key (to create @ symbol) to specify the relative coordinates; the prompt is shown in Figure 11-4d. (ii) Specify the length (310'), (iii) press the *Tab* key, (iv) specify the angle (-69), and (v) press the *Enter* key. The first line segment is drawn.
5. Similarly, draw the line of length 433' at 343° azimuth.
6. Repeat the process with the remaining traverse.
7. The resulting traverse is shown in Figure 11-4e.
8. Find the length and azimuth for the last course, *BA*.

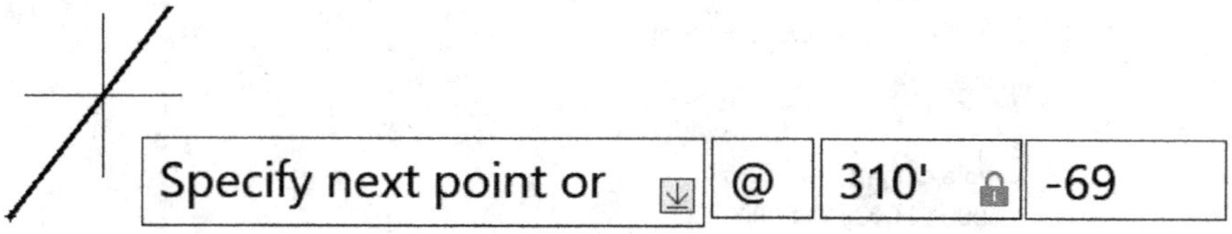

Figure 11-4d

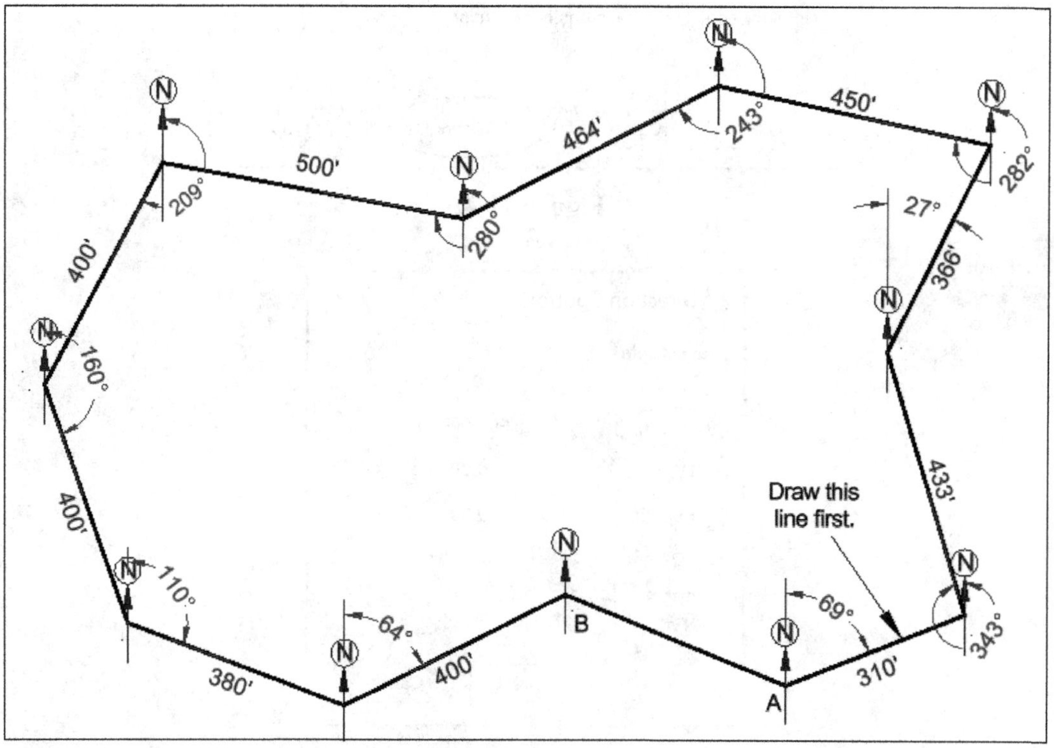

Figure 11-4e

11.6.2. Traverse for the given bearings

In the current section, a closed traverse shown in Figure 11-5 is drawn. The drawing units are Engineering (Feet-Inches), and the angles are the bearing from North or South (that is, the angles are measured in the clockwise or counterclockwise direction).

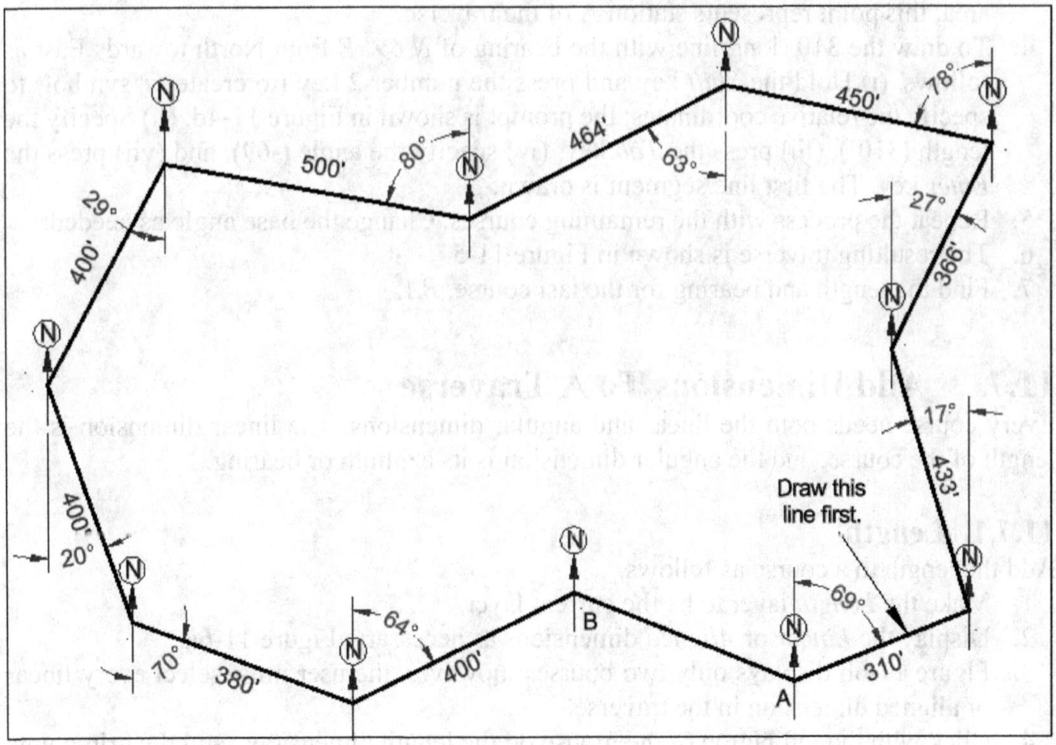

Figure 11-5

Create the drawing as follows.

- Open the drawing and set the units as follows.

1. Open a new landscape template file for ANSI units created in *Chapter 8*.
2. Type *Units* in the command line and press the *Enter* key. This opens the *Drawing Units* dialog box, Figure 11-4b.
3. Click on the *Direction* button and the *Direction Control* dialog box opens, Figure 11-4c. Choose the *North* option for the *Base Angle* and press the *OK* buttons on both dialog boxes.
4. The clockwise angles are specified with negative signs because the positive angles are measured counterclockwise.
5. The *Direction* control box can be activated even if the line command is active. (i) Type *Units* in the command line and press the *Enter* key. This opens the *Drawing Units* dialog box. (ii) Click on the *Direction* button and the *Direction Control* dialog box opens. (iii) Choose the *South* option for the *Base Angle*. (iv) Press the *OK* button on both of the dialog boxes.

- Create the traverse as follows:

1. Make the Traverse layer to be the current layer.
2. To draw the traverse, the clockwise angles are specified with negative signs because positive angles are measured in the counterclockwise direction.
3. To draw the traverse, activate the *Polyline* command and click at point in the drawing area; this point represents station A of the traverse.
4. To draw the 310' long line with the bearing of *N 69º E* from North towards East as follows. (i) Hold the *Shift* key and press the number 2 key (to create @ symbol) to specify the relative coordinates; the prompt is shown in Figure 11-4d. (ii) Specify the length (310'), (iii) press the *Tab* key, (iv) specify the angle (-69), and (vii) press the *Enter* key. The first line segment is drawn.
5. Repeat the process with the remaining courses. Change the base angle as needed.
6. The resulting traverse is shown in Figure 11-5.
7. Find the length and bearing for the last course, *BA*.

11.7. Add Dimensions To A Traverse

Every course needs both the linear and angular dimensions. The linear dimension is the length of the course, and the angular dimension is its azimuth or bearing.

11.7.1. Length

Add the length to a course as follows.

1. Make the *Length* layer to be the current layer.
2. Display the *Linear* or *Aligned* dimensions as necessary, Figure 11-6a.
3. Figure 11-6b displays only two courses; however, the user must select every linear or aligned dimension in the traverse.
4. Click with the left button of the mouse on the length dimensions, and the grip points appear, Figure 11-6b.
5. Press the right button of the mouse, and options list appears.
6. Select the *Properties* option with the left button of the mouse.
7. In the *Properties* palette, under the *Lines & Arrows* panel, turn *Off* the *Dim line 1*, *Dim line 2*, *Ext line 1*, and *Ext line 2*; press the down-arrow in the right column and then choose the *Off* option, Figure 11-7.
8. The resultant dimensions are shown in Figure 11-6c.

Figure 11-6a

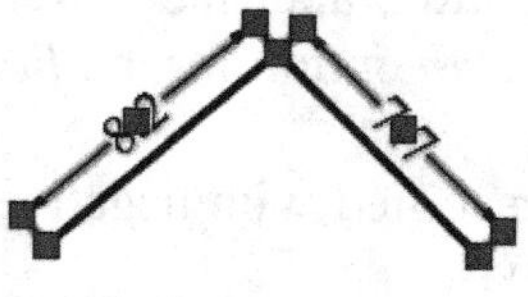

Figure 11-6b

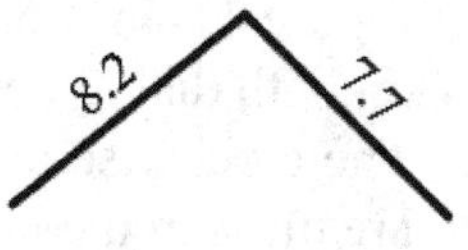

Figure 11-6c

11.7.2. Add reference line to a traverse

To make the dimensioning process faster and accurate draw an arrow, north label, and the reference line at every traverse station using the following steps. The reference line is necessary because the leader (arrow) cannot be used for angular dimensions.

1. Make the *North* layer to be the current layer.
2. The North direction is created by drawing a leader. (i) Turn on the ORTHO option by clicking the icon on the status bar. (ii) Activate the *QLEADER* command and draw a vertical arrow with the arrowhead pointing upward. (iii) Press the *Esc* key from the keyboard to exit the *QLEADER* command without completing it, Figure 11-8a.

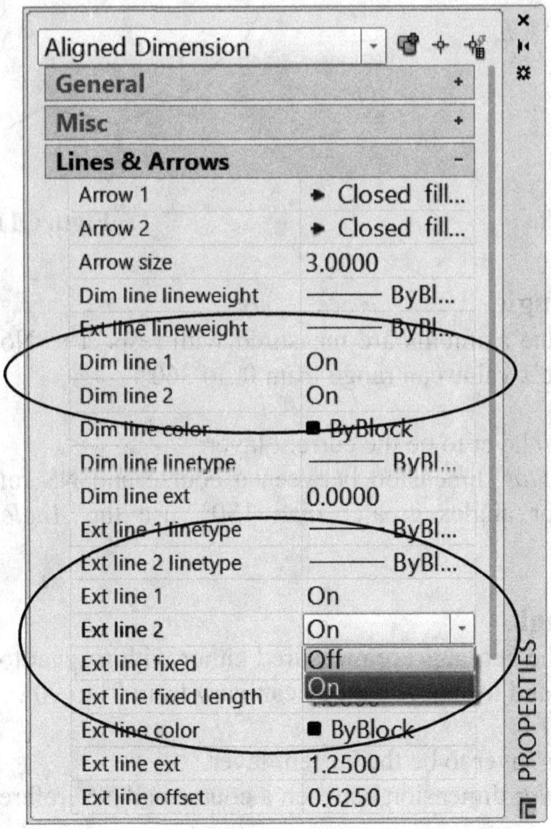

Figure 11-7

3. Make the *North* layer to be the current layer.
4. The North direction is created by drawing a leader. (i) Turn on the ORTHO option by clicking the icon on the status bar. (ii) Activate the *QLEADER* command and draw a vertical arrow with the arrowhead pointing upward. (iii) Press the *Esc* key from the keyboard to exit the *QLEADER* command without completing it, Figure 11-8a.
5. Activate the *Line* command and draw a line on top of the arrow. The user must draw a straight line on top of the arrow because the angular dimension does not recognize an arrow created using *QLEADER* command.
6. Write N using a text command, Figure 11-8a.
7. Enclose N in a circle using *Express Tool* tab → *Text* panel → *Enclose in Object* command; use circle option, Figure 11-8a.
8. Activate the *Copy* command and paste the north at each station, Figure 11-8b.

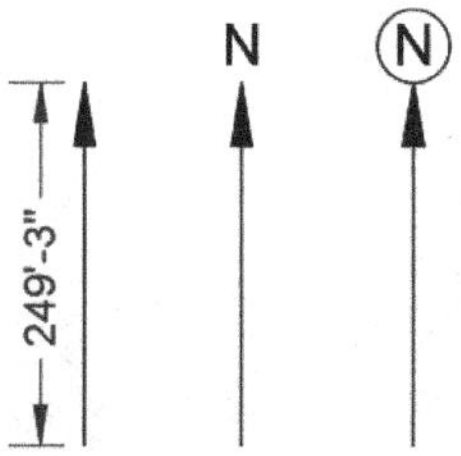

Figure 11-8a

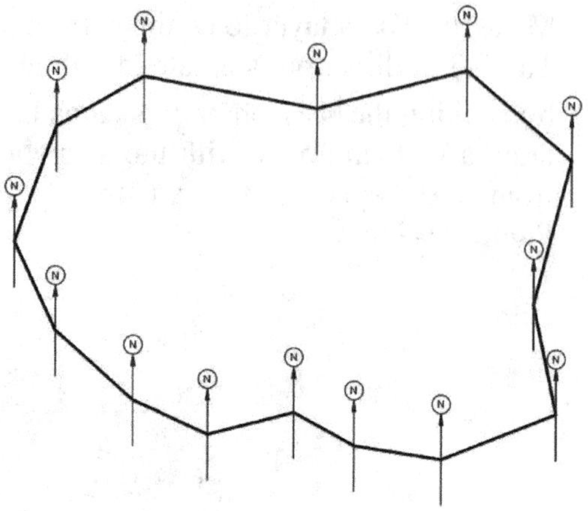

Figure 11-8b

11.7.3. Azimuth angle

As explained earlier, the azimuths are measured with respect to North in the clockwise direction, and the angle's value can range from 0° to 360°.

1. Make the *Azimuth* layer to be the current layer.
2. Display the *Angular* dimension between a course and NS reference as shown in Figure 11-4e; for angles greater than 180°, use the *Angle > 180° technique* (*Chapter 9*).

11.7.4. Bearing angle

As explained earlier, the bearings are measured either with respect to North or South and towards East or West; and the angle's value can vary from 0° to 90°.

1. Make the *Bearing* layer to be the current layer.
2. Display the *Angular* dimension between a course and NS_reference, Figure 11-5.

11.7.5. Save the file

Save the traverse file as *Traverse.dwg*.

11.8. Parcel

In real estate terminology, a parcel is defined as a contiguous area of land, with or without buildings, owned by one or multiple owners and described by a single deed. For example, a residential area plot owned by a single owner and a farmland owned by multiple owners (maybe one family) is a parcel. In Figure 11-9, person X is the owner of lot #3 and person Y is the owner of lot #4, whereas lot #1 and #2 are owned by multiple (A, B, and C) owners.

11.9. Deed

A deed is a legal document (written certificate) indicating ownership of land. In terms of real estate, a deed shows the ownership of a parcel of land. It is also used to convey ownership from the previous owner to the current owner. A deed must show the limits and the detailed description of the boundary of the property. A deed uses specific phrases such as "*Commencing at,*" "*Point-of-Beginning,*" "*thence,*" ";", "*in a* _____*ly direction*" (for example, northerly, northeasterly, easterly, etc.), "*–most,*" "*along,*" "*a distance of,*" "*to,*" "*to a point,*" etc. Due to the importance of a deed, the landowner keeps the original deed, and the local courthouse keeps its copy.

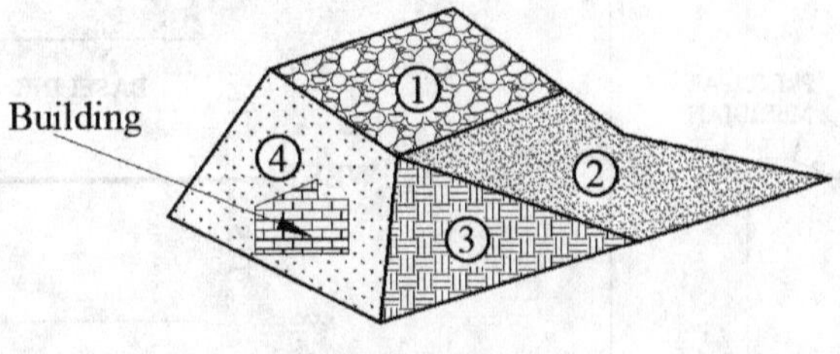

Figure 11-9

11.10. Land Survey

The basic purpose of the land survey is to measure existing boundaries and lay out new boundaries. Based on the size of the area to be surveyed, the survey is carried out by government agencies or private surveyors. In the United States, a parcel of land is usually described using the *rectangular* system, *metes and bound*, and *lots and blocks* methods.

11.11. Rectangular System

The rectangular system is used by the Public Land Survey System (PLSS) of the United States. The system was created by the *Land Ordinance of 1785*. It has been expanded and slightly modified but is still in use in the states of Alabama, Alaska, Arizona, Arkansas, California, Colorado, Florida, Idaho, Illinois, Indiana, Iowa, Kansas, Louisiana, Michigan, Minnesota, Mississippi, Missouri, Montana, Nebraska, Nevada, New Mexico, North Dakota, Ohio, Oklahoma, Oregon, South Dakota, Utah, Washington, Wisconsin, and Wyoming. In the rectangular system, the basic units of the land are the township and range. The townships and ranges are formed by the intersection of the reference lines (baseline and meridians).

11.11.1. Reference lines

In the rectangular system, the baseline and meridians are the two commonly used reference lines. The baseline (or latitude) runs east-west, and the principal meridian (or longitude) runs north-south. Lines parallel to the principal meridian and the baseline with six miles' interval are created, Figure 11-10a and Figure 11-10b. The intersection of these lines forms a grid of 6 miles by 6 miles which is used as the base for the rectangular survey, Figure 11-10c.

The initial point of PLSS survey is the intersection of the meridian and baselines or lines running parallel to the baseline and meridian. The parallel lines to the principal meridian are named. The first surveys in the rectangular system were carried out in eastern Ohio; hence, its west boundary is the first principal meridian. The first six principal meridians are labeled as first, second, third, fourth, fifth, and sixth principal meridians. The rest of the meridians are named using local names. For example, in Louisiana the PLSS uses *Louisiana meridian*.

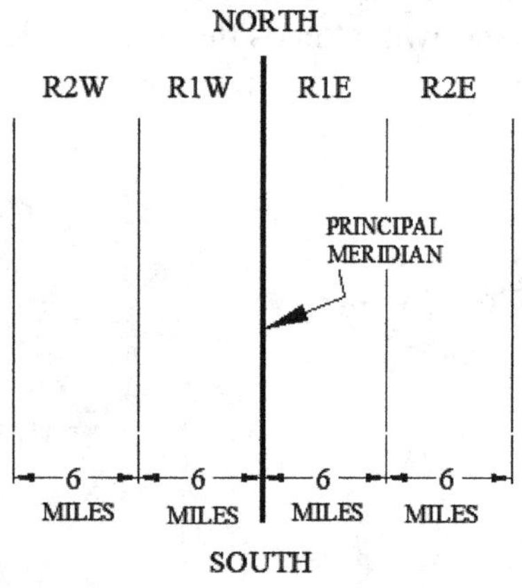

Figure 11-10a

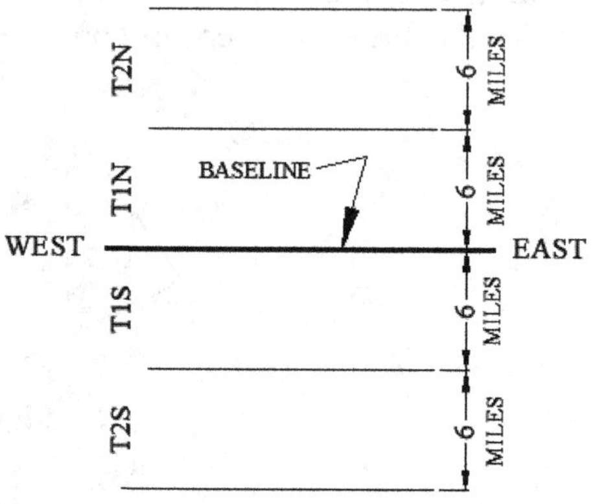

Figure 11-10b

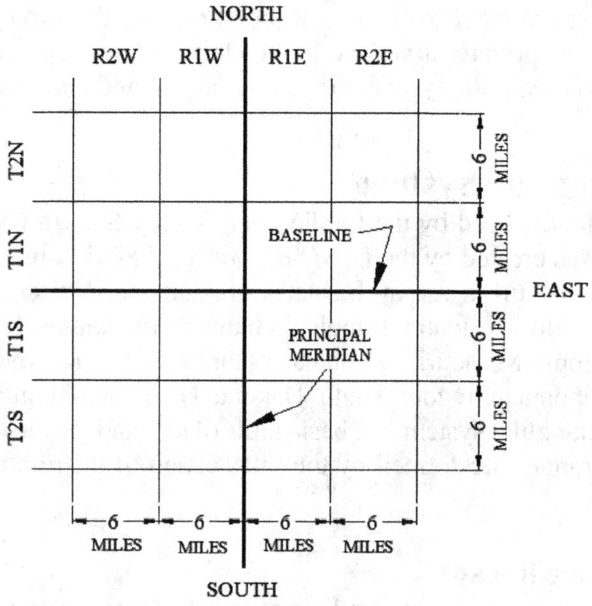

Figure 11-10c

11.11.2. Township and range

The columns of the grid shown in Figure 11-10c are called range, and the rows are called township. Each cell of the grid is called a township. Each township is further subdivided into 36 sections of one square mile (area equal to 640 acres), Figure 11-11a. The numbering of the sections (of a township) starts from the upper right corner and follows the zigzag pattern as shown in Figure 11-11a. Each section can be further subdivided into two half-sections of 0.5 square mile (320 acres) each. Each section can also be further subdivided into four quarter-sections of 0.25 square miles (160 acres) each. The federal government typically surveys only to the quarter-section level. If necessary, smaller parcels are usually surveyed later by private surveyors. In governmental surveys, the township corner is established every six miles and followed by the marking of the section, half-section and the quarter-section corners, denoted as T, S, $\frac{1}{2}$, and $\frac{1}{4}$ as shown in Figure 11-11b.

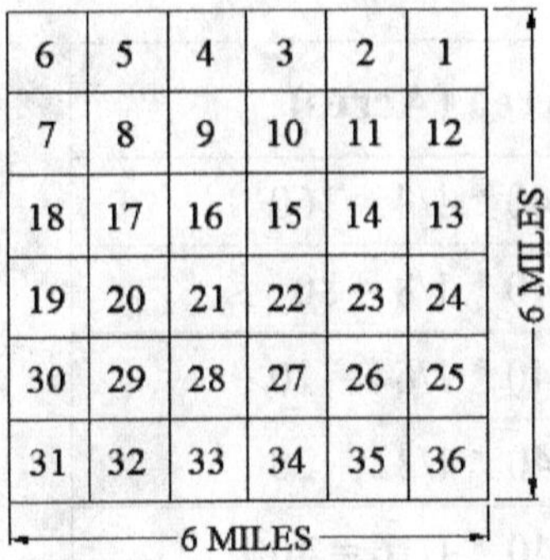

Figure 11-11a

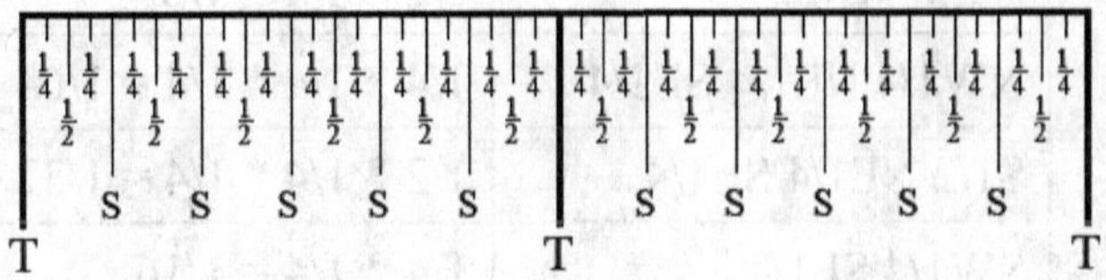

Figure 11-11b

This technique allows for the identification of any parcel of land by specifying section, township, and range numbers. This format is used in deeds to delineate the property. For example, a parcel located in range R1E, township T4S, and in section 15 is shown in Figure 11-11c, and the deed contains the entry 15-4S-1E.

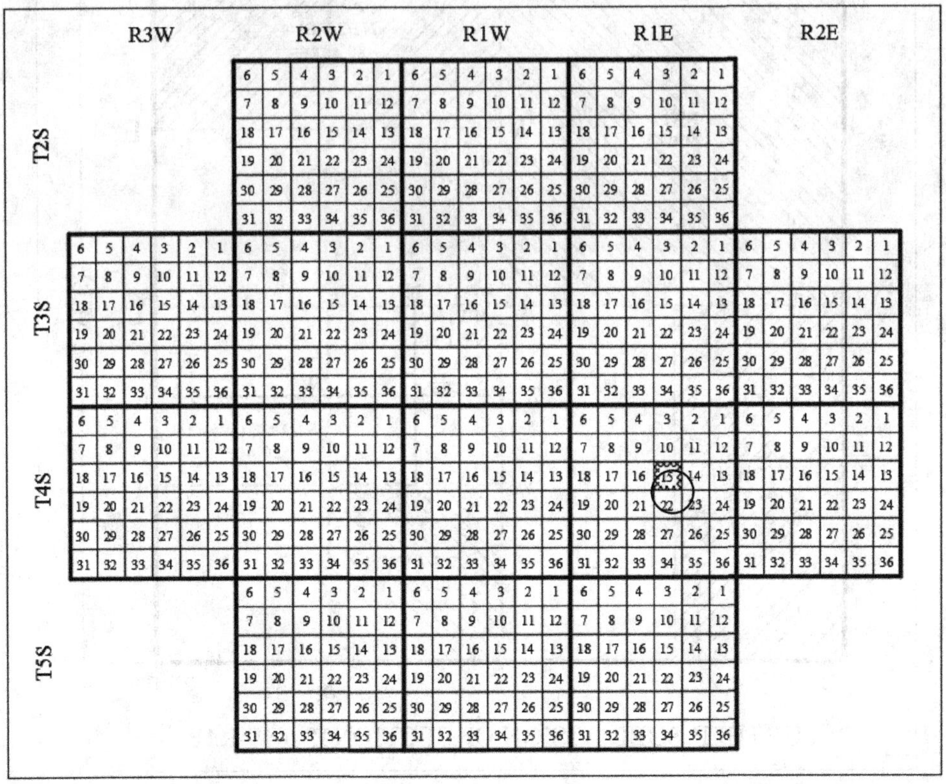

Figure 11-11c

Figure 11-11d shows the further subdivisions of *15-4S-1E*. Since 1sq. mile is equal to 640 acres, the area of the subdivisions can be obtained by multiplying "the product of the factors" with "640 ACRES". The area calculations of the subsections shown in Figure 11-11d are shown in Table #2.

Table #2: Area calculation

Subdivision	Product of Factors	Area (Acres)
NW1/4	1/4	640 * 1/4 = 160
N1/2 NE1/4	1/2 * 1/4 = 1/8	640 * 1/8 = 80
NW1/4 NE1/4 SE1/4	1/4 * 1/4 * 1/4 = 1/64	640 * 1/64 = 10
S1/2 NE1/4 SE1/4	1/2 * 1/4 * 1/4 = 1/32	640 * 1/32 = 20
SW1/4 SE1/4	1/4 * 1/4 = 1/16	640 * 1/16 = 40
W1/2 NW1/4	1/2 * 1/4 = 1/8	640 * 1/8 = 80

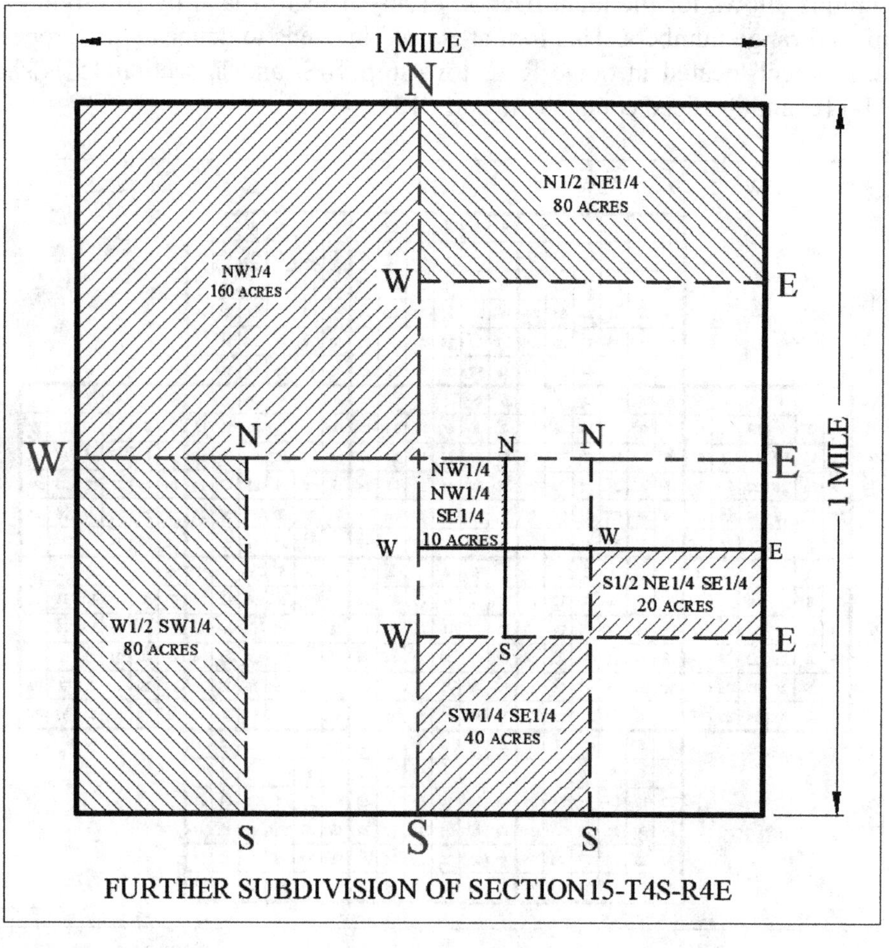

Figure 11-11d

11.12. Metes And Bounds

The term ***metes*** refers to a boundary defined by the measurement of each straight run. A run is specified by the distance between the terminal points and an orientation (or direction). A direction may be a simple compass bearing or a precise orientation determined by accurate survey methods. The term ***bounds*** refers to a more general boundary description, such as along a certain watercourse, a stone wall, an adjoining public roadway, or an existing building.

The *Metes and Bounds* system is often used to define larger pieces of property (e.g. farms), and political subdivisions (e.g. town boundaries) where a precise definition is not required or would be far too expensive, or previously designated boundaries can be incorporated into the description.

Typically, the system uses physical features of the local geography, directions, and distances, to define and describe the boundaries of a parcel of land. The boundaries are described in a running style (from a point of beginning) working around the parcel of the land in sequence (returning to the same point). It may include references to other adjoining parcels of land (and their owners), and it in turn could also be referred to in later surveys. At the time the description was compiled, it may have been marked on the ground with permanent monuments placed where there were no suitable natural monuments.

In many deeds, the angle is described not by a degree measure out of 360 degrees, but instead by indicating a direction north or south (N or S) followed by a degree measure out of 90 degrees and another direction west or east (W or E). For example, such a bearing might be listed as *N 42°35′ W*, which means that the bearing is 42°35' counterclockwise (to the west) from north. This has the advantage of providing the same degree measure regardless of which direction a particular boundary is being followed; the boundary can be traversed in the opposite direction simply by exchanging N for S and E for W. In other words, *N 42°35′ W* describes the same boundary as *S 42°35′ E* but is traversed in the opposite direction.

Once such a survey takes place, traditionally long use establishes the boundaries. The description might refer to *landmarks* such as the *large oak tree* which could die, rot, and disappear. Streams might dry up or change course. Man-made features such as roads, walls, markers, or stakes also have been used to determine the real boundaries. But these features move, change, and disappear over time. When it comes time to re-establish these boundaries (for sale, subdivision, or building construction) it can become difficult, even impossible, to determine the original location of the boundary. Court cases are sometimes required to settle the matter.

11.12.1. Land description using Metes and Bounds

A small parcel of land is shown in Figure 11-12a; and its description using metes and bounds can be written as shown in Figure 11-12b. In the description, POB is the abbreviation for the *Point Of Beginning*.

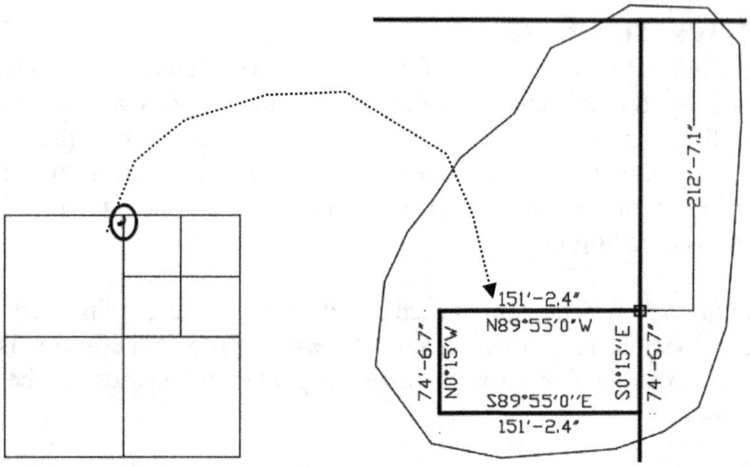

Figure 11-12a

Beginning at a point 212' 7.1" south of the NW corner NW/4 NE/4 of section13-T8N-R1E, Thence S0° 15' 0" E a distance of 74' 6.7", Thence S89° 55' 0" W a distance of 151' 2.4", Thence N0° 15' 0" W a distance of 74' 6.7", Thence N89° 55' 0" E a distance of 151' 2.4" to POB.

Figure 11-12b

11.12.2. AutoCAD And Metes and Bounds

If the surveyor's angles are used when specifying the polar coordinates, then clearly indicate whether the surveyor's angles are in the north or south direction and towards east or west direction.

Example: Draw the boundary of the parcel described using metes and bounds as follows.

1. Open a new file landscape template file for ANSI units created in *Chapter 8*.
2. Type *Units* in the command line and press the *Enter* key. This opens the *Drawing Units* dialog box, Figure 11-12c.
3. In the *length*'s panel, choose the *Engineering*'s option, Figure 11-12c.
4. Now the user can specify the information in engineering units (feet and inches). The length 5'-6" is entered as follows: (i) activate the *Line* or *Polyline* commands. (ii) Type 5. (iii) Type the apostrophe (') key. (iv) Type 6. (v) Press the *Enter* key. (vi) DO NOT TYPE hyphen (-) to separate feet from inches and double apostrophe to represent inches.
5. In the *Angle*'s panel, choose the *Surveyor's Units* option, Figure 11-12d. Using image editing techniques, this figure shows multiple selections; however, AutoCAD allows for only one selection at a time.
6. Click on the *Direction* button, Figure 11-12d, and the *Direction Control* dialog box opens, choose the *North* option for the *Base Angle*, and press the *OK* buttons on both dialog boxes.
7. Open the *Drafting Settings* dialog box and select *Dynamic Input* tab, Figure 11-12e.

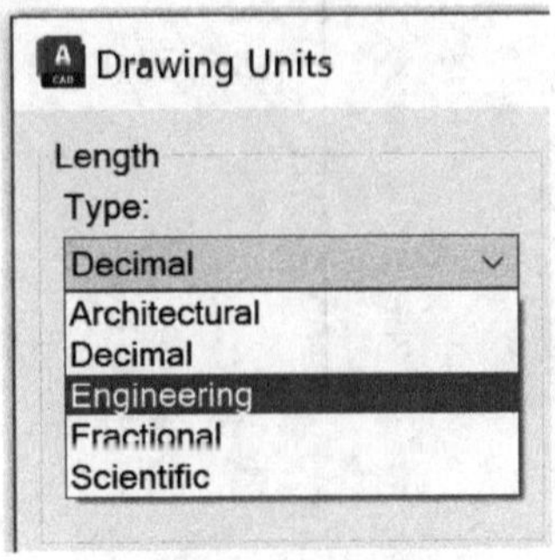

Figure 11-12c

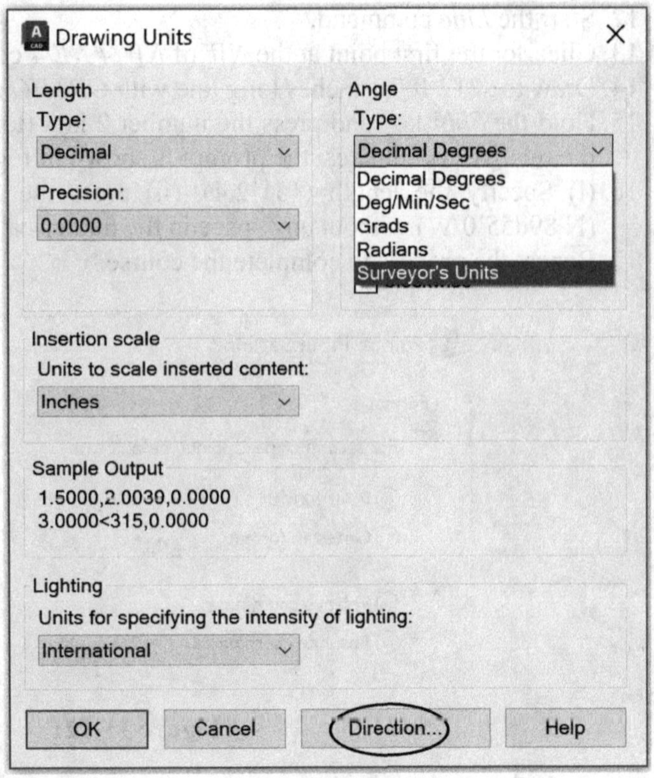

Figure 11-12d

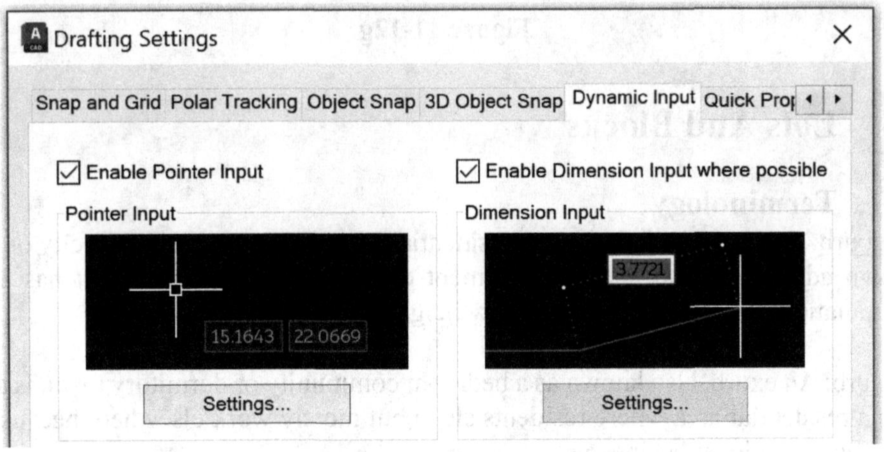

Figure 11-12e

8. Click on the *Settings* option under the *Pointer Input* panel. This opens the *Pointer Input Settings* dialog box, Figure 11-12f.
9. In the *Pointer Input Settings* dialog box, under the Format panel, select the Polar format option, Figure 11-12f.
10. Click on *OK* buttons on both dialog boxes.
11. For further details, refer to *Chapter 3*.

12. Start the *Line* command.
13. Click for the first point at the *NW* of *NW/4 NE/4* corner.
14. Draw the 212 ft 7.1 inches long line with *ORTHO* mode *On*.
15. Hold the *Shift* key and press the number 2 key (to create @ symbol) key to specify the relative coordinates; the prompt is shown in Figure 11-12g.
16. (i) Specify the length (151'2.4), (ii) press the *Tab* key, (iii) specify the angle (N 89d55'0 W) without any space in the numerical value and press the *Enter* key.
17. Repeat the process to complete the course.

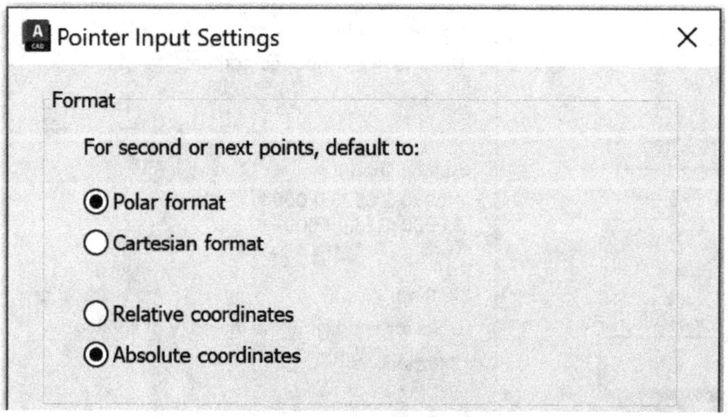

Figure 11-12f

Figure 11-12g

11.13. Lots And Blocks

11.13.1. Terminology

- Suburb: A suburb is defined as a residential area on the outskirts of a city or a large town adjacent to the main employment centers. Most of the time it has a lower population density than the inner-city neighborhoods.

- Exurb: An exurb, also known as a bedroom community or dormitory town, is defined as a residential area where residents sleep but mostly work elsewhere because there are very few local businesses.

- Subdivision: Subdivision is the act of dividing land into pieces that are easier to sell or otherwise develop. If it is used for housing it is typically known as a housing subdivision or housing development, although some developers tend to call these areas communities.

11.13.2. Lots And Blocks

The *Lots and Blocks* Survey System is used in the United States and Canada to locate and identify land, particularly for lots in densely populated metropolitan areas, suburban areas, and exurbs. It is sometimes referred to as the Recorded Plat Survey System or the Recorded Map Survey System.

This system is the most recent and may be the simplest of the three main survey systems. In this system, a large parcel is defined by *Metes and Bounds* or the PLSS. The owners of the parcel would divide the land into smaller parcels known as blocks. Blocks are further subdivided into even smaller parcels known as lots. *Blocks and Lots* can be of any size. However, usually the municipality restricts their sizes. Each *Block and Lots* is given identification (a number or a letter). In some cases, blocks may be part of a subdivision. All surveys and identification are recorded with an official government record keeper. The officially recorded map then becomes the legal description of all of the lots in the subdivision.

A legal description of a lot in a Lots and Blocks system must identify the following:

i. an individual lot number,
ii. the block in which the lot is located, if applicable,
iii. a reference to a platted subdivision or a phase thereof,
iv. a reference to find the cited plat map (i.e., a page and/or volume number), and
v. a description of the map's place of official recording (e.g., recorded in the files of the County Engineer).

The legal description of a 2.7724 acres property under the *Lots and Blocks* system may be something like (i) Lot 10 of (ii) Block 8 of the (iii) The Gray Fox Subdivision (iv) as recorded in Map Book 35, Page 64 (v) at the Recorder of Deeds office, Figure 11-13. Some simple maps may only contain a lot and map numbers, such as Lot C of the Riverside Subdivision map as recorded in Map Book 12, Page 8 in the office of the City Engineer. The more technical details of the legal description are contained in the recorded plat map and there is no need to reiterate them in a deed or other legal description.

11.13.3. AutoCAD And Lots & Blocks

In AutoCAD, a *Lots and Blocks* system can be created by following the step-by-step directions given below.

1. Launch AutoCAD 2027.
2. Units: Engineering (i.e. ANSI).
3. Open file
    - Open the *Traverse.dwg* file created in Section 11.6 and saved in Section 11.7.
4. Layers
    - Create the layers as shown in Figure 11-14.
5. Outline: Draw the outline of the subdivision.
    - The close traverse will be used as the outline for the Lots and Block drawing file.
    - Freeze the layers displaying the angles and north direction.
    - The complete outline is shown in Figure 11-15.

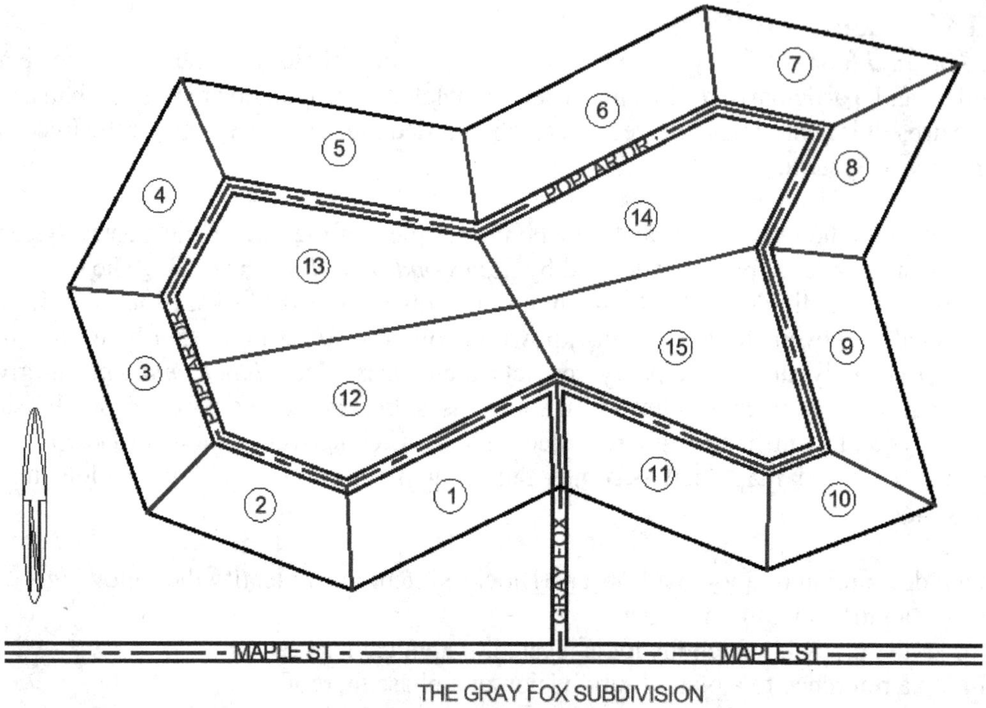

Figure 11-13

Status	Name	On	Freeze	Lock	Plot	Color	Linetype	Lineweight
✓	0					white	Continuous	0.00 mm
	Area					blue	Continuous	0.00 mm
	Azimuth					210	Continuous	0.00 mm
	Bearing					94	Continuous	0.00 mm
	Defpoints					white	Continuous	0.00 mm
	Lots					210	Continuous	0.50 mm
	Lots_L_DIM					160	Continuous	0.00 mm
	Lots_Label					14	Continuous	0.00 mm
	North					blue	Continuous	0.00 mm
	Outline_DIM					24	Continuous	0.00 mm
	Road					12	Continuous	0.50 mm
	Road_CL					10	CENTER	0.50 mm
	Road_Dim					12	Continuous	0.00 mm
	Road_Label					12	Continuous	0.00 mm
	Subdivision_Label					84	Continuous	0.50 mm
	Title Block					white	Continuous	0.00 mm
	Traverse					white	Continuous	0.50 mm

Figure 11-14

6. Outline Dimension: Add the dimensions to the outline of the subdivision.
   - The linear dimensions to the outline of the traverse were added in the *Traverse.dwg*, Figure 11-15.

7. Save the subdivision: Save the subdivision.
   - Save the subdivision as *LotsBlocks.dwg*.

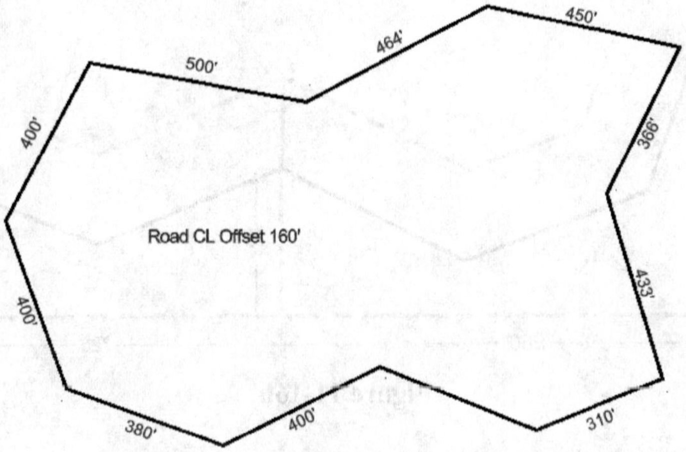

Figure 11-15

8. The road: Draw the roads and add the roads' labels.
   - If the traverse was not created as a single polyline, then use the *Join* command (*Home* tab → *Modify* panel) to make the traverse as a single closed polyline.
   - Using the Offset command, draw an offset at 160' inside the boundary's outline, Figure 11-16a. This will be the centerline of the road. Move the offsets to the *Road_CL* layer.

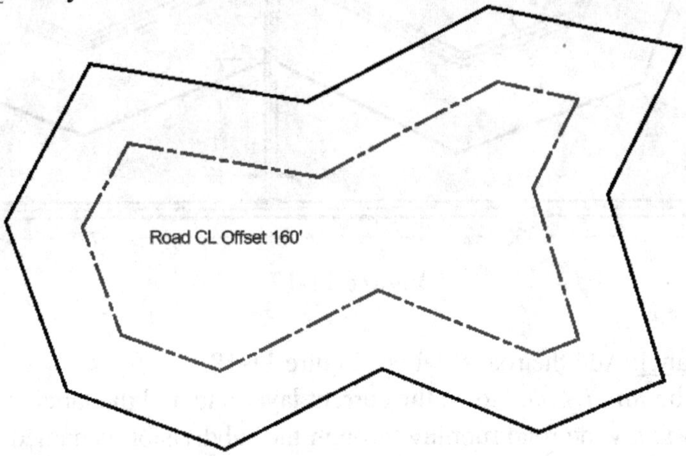

Figure 11-16a

- Draw the centerlines for the remaining roads of the subdivision, Figure 11-16b. If necessary, set the linetype scale (from the *Property* palette) to 0.5.
- The road in the subdivision and the connecting road is 24' wide and the nearest road running parallel to the subdivision is 30' wide
- Using the Offset command, draw the roads, Figure 11-17.

- Move the offsets to the *Road* layer.
- Using the Trim command, trim the extra part of the centerline and road at the intersection of the two roads, Figure 11-18.

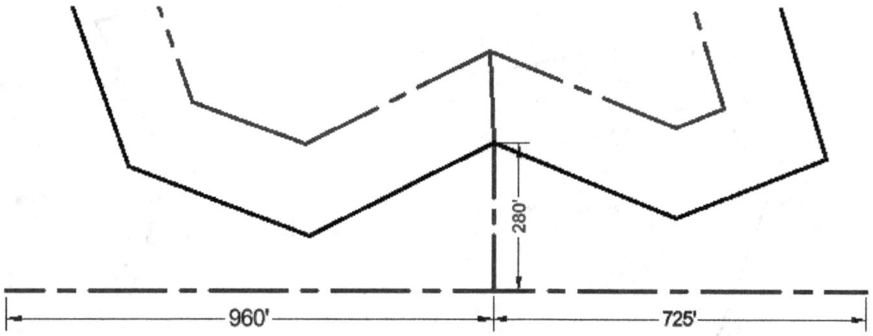

Figure 11-16b

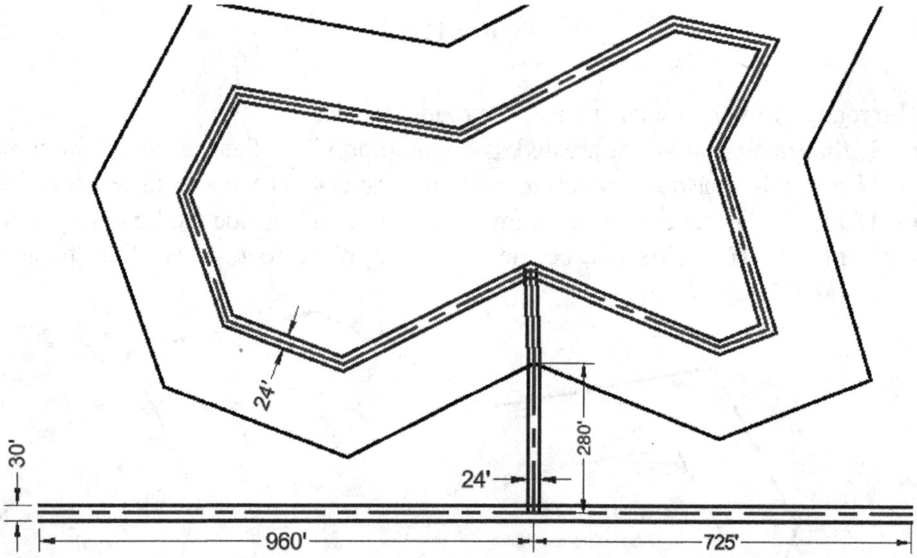

Figure 11-17

9. The road label: Add the roads' labels, Figure 11-18.
   - Make the *Road_Label* to be the current layer and add the labels to the roads.
   - The 24 feet wide road running through the subdivision is named *Poplar Dr.*; the 30 feet wide road running outside and parallel to the subdivision is named *Maple Street*; and the 24 feet wide road connecting *Poplar Dr* and *Maple St* is named *Gray Fox*.
   - Trim the centerline and road lines at the intersection of the roads.

10. The subdivision label: Add the dimensions to the outline of the subdivision.
    - Make the *Subdivision_Label* the current layer. Add the label to the subdivision of the subdivision using the annotative *Text* command, Figure 11-18.

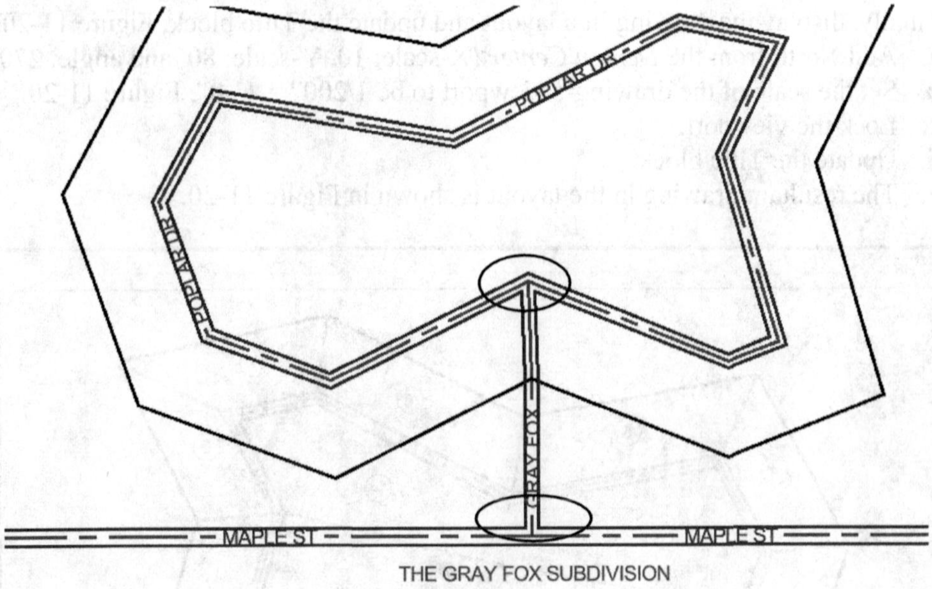

Figure 11-18

11. The Lots: Draw the lots of the subdivision.
    - Make the *Lots* to be the current layer and connect the corners aa1, bb1, …, as shown in Figure 11-19.
    - Make the *Lots_Label* to be the current layer and add the labels. (i) Create a label using annotative *Text* command. (ii) Encircle the text: either from *Express tools* tab → Text panel → *Enclose in Object* command with the *Circle* option or simply draw a circle around the label, Figure 11-20.

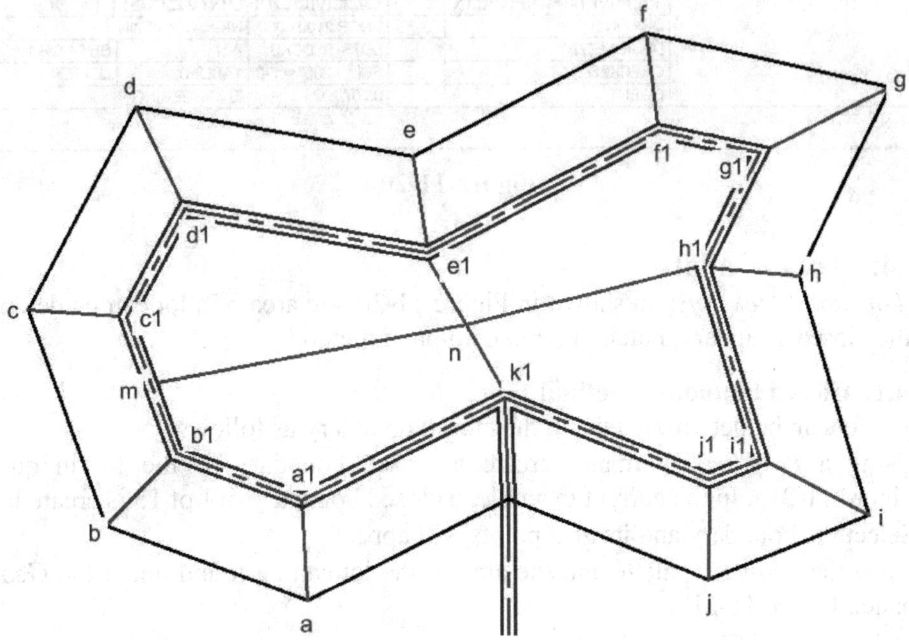

Figure 11-19

12. Finally, display the drawing in a layout and update the Title block, Figure 11-20.
    a. Add North from the *Design Center* (X-scale: 10, Y-scale: 80, and angle: 270º).
    b. Set the scale of the drawing's viewport to be 1/200" = 1'-0", Figure 11-20.
    c. Lock the viewport.
    d. Update the Title block.
    e. The resultant drawing in the layout is shown in Figure 11-20.

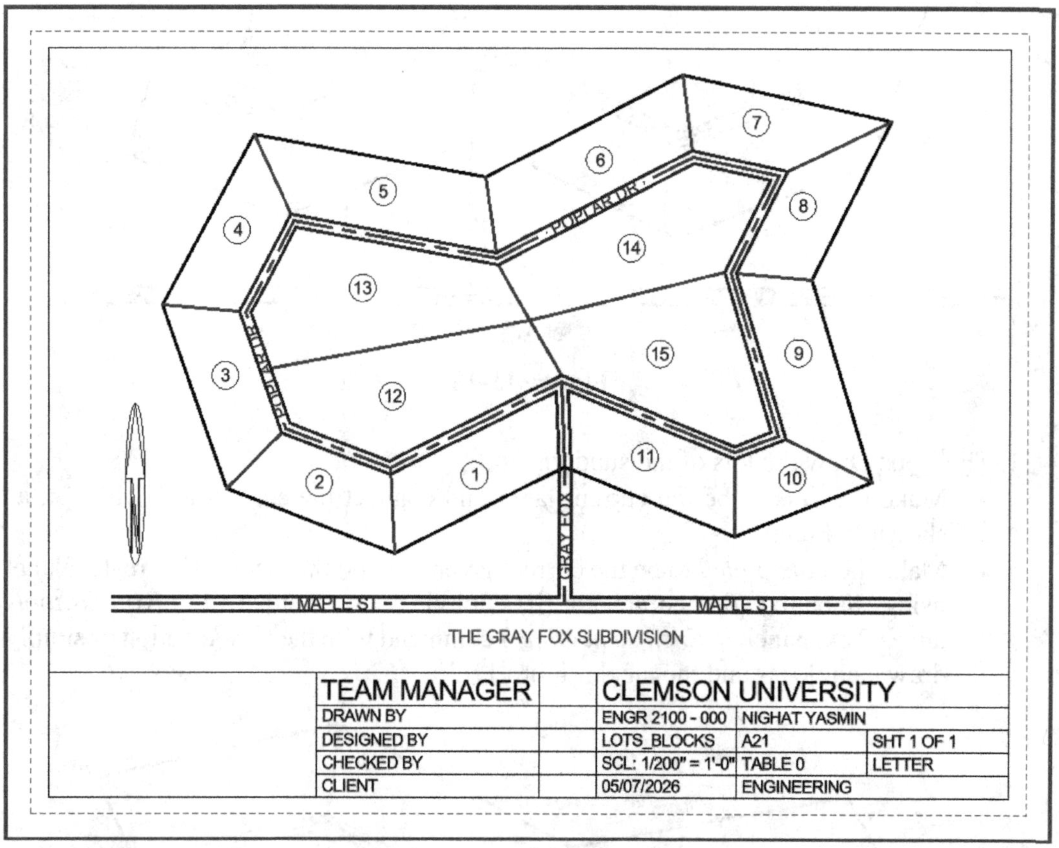

Figure 11-20

11.13.4. Area of a lot

In the *Lots and Blocks* system shown in Figure 11-20, the area of a lot can be determined using the closed boundary, hatch or *Area* command method.

11.13.4.1. Closed boundary method

Area of a lot can be determined using the closed boundary as follows.

- Using a *Polyline* command, create a closed boundary of the lot in question, Figure 11-21a. In the current example, a closed boundary of Lot 15 is created.
- Select the boundary and its grip points will appear.
- Open the *Property* palette and the area of the lot can be found under the *Geometry* panel, Figure 11-21b.

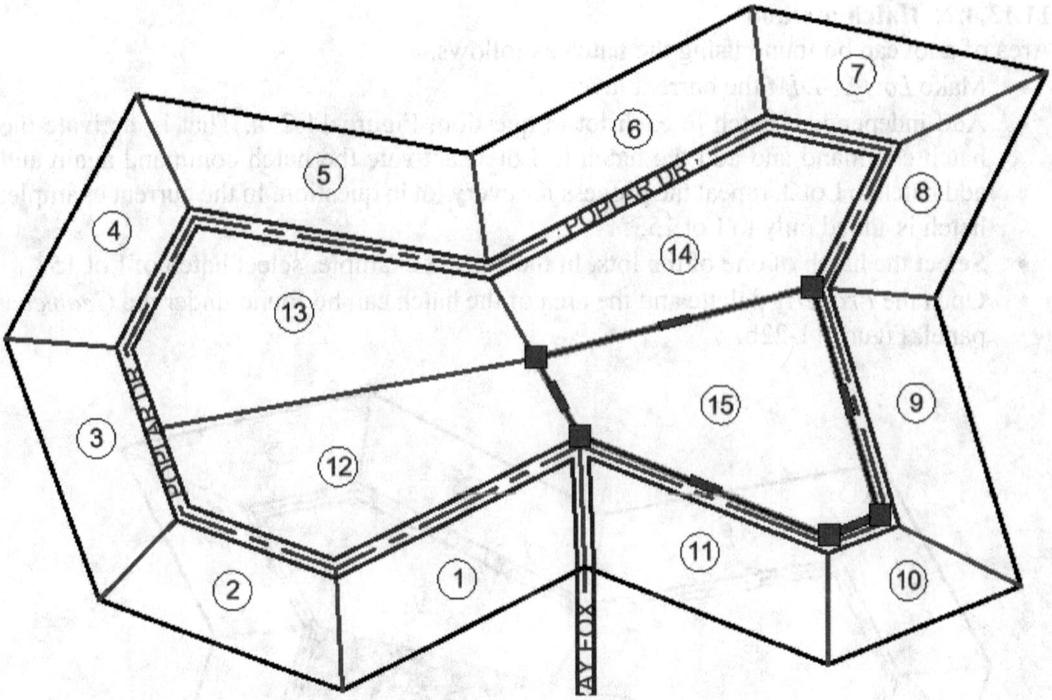

Figure 11-21a

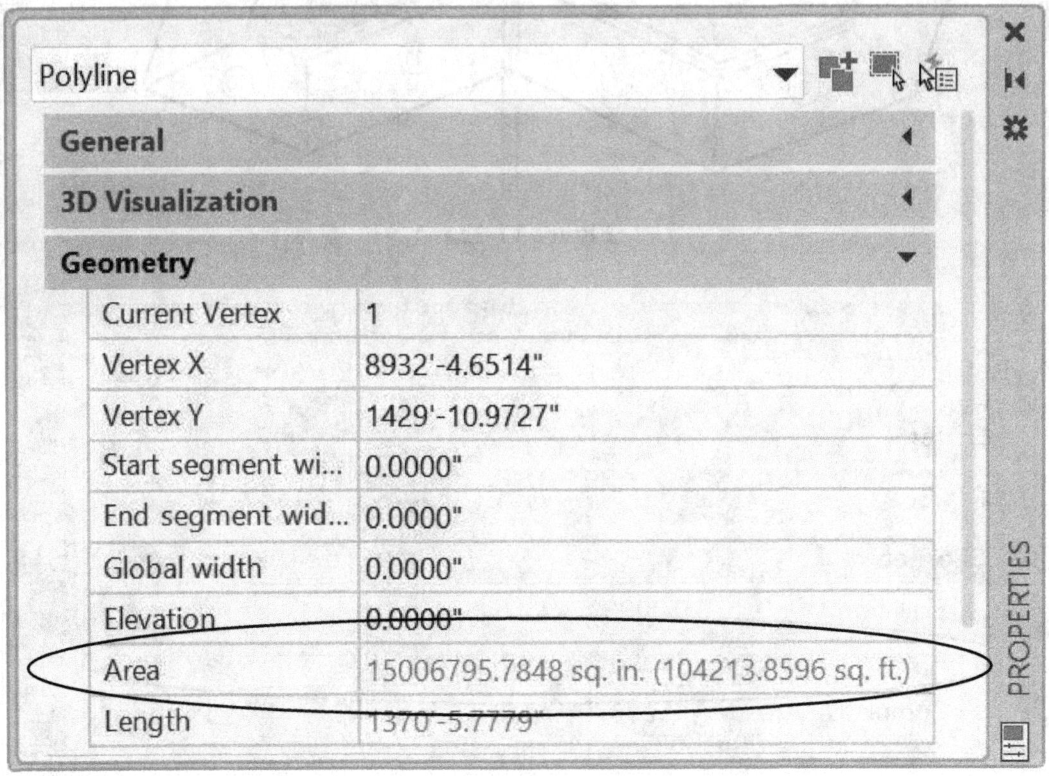

Figure 11-21b

11.13.4.2. Hatch method

Area of a lot can be found using the hatch as follows.

- Make *Lots_A-DIM* the current layer.
- Add independent hatch to each lot in question, Figure 11-22a. That is, activate the hatch command and add the hatch to Lot 1; activate the hatch command again and add hatch to Lot 2; repeat the process for every lot in question. In the current example, hatch is added only to Lot 15.
- Select the hatch of one of the lots. In the current example, select hatch of Lot 15.
- Open the *Property* palette and the area of the hatch can be found under the *Geometry* panel, Figure 11-22b.

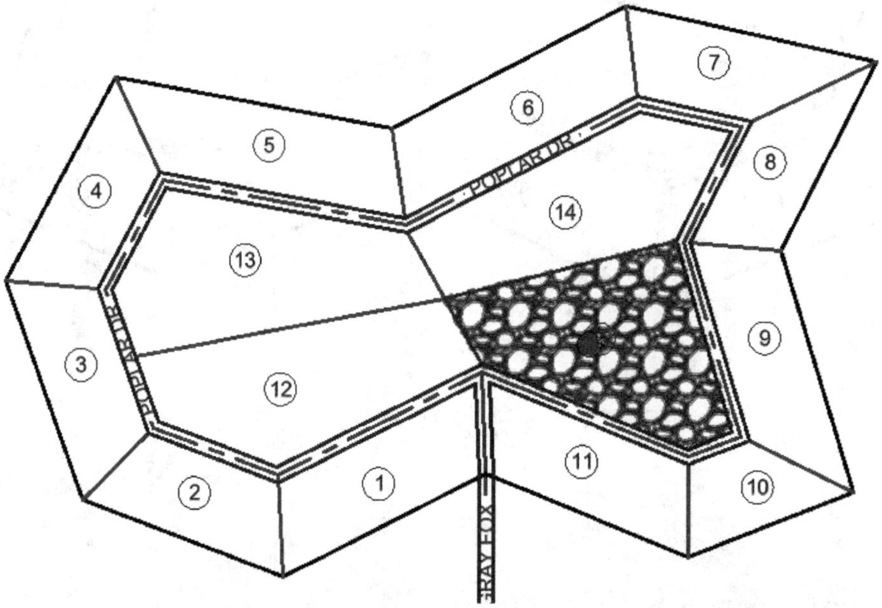

Figure 11-22a

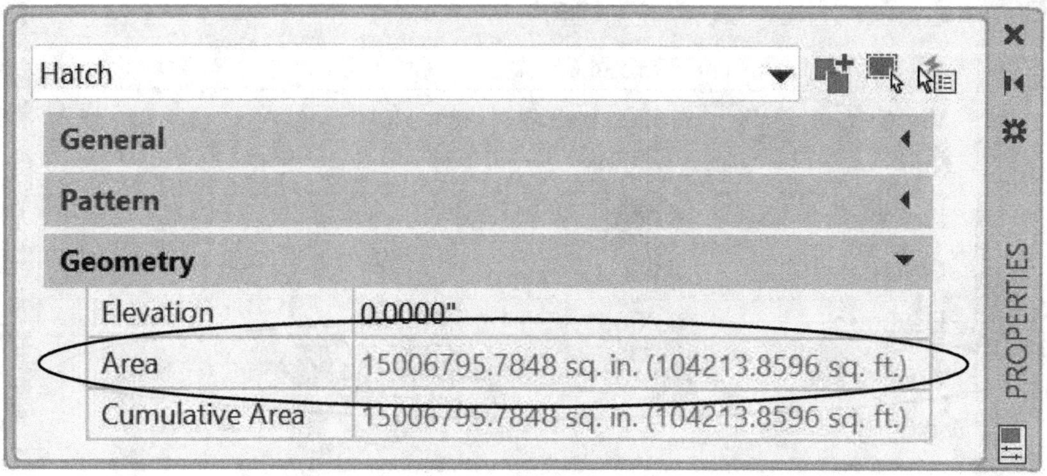

Figure 11-22b

11.13.4.3. Area command method

The *Area* command uses the points on the boundary. All the points must lie in a plane parallel to the XY plane of the UCS.

- The *Area* command is activated using one of the following methods:
  1. Panel method: from the *Home* tab and the *Utilities* panel, expand the *Measure* drop-down menu and click the *Area* option, Figure 11-23a.
  2. Command line method: Type "area," "Area" or "AREA" in the command line and press the *Enter* key.
- The activation of the command results in the prompt shown in Figure 11-23b.
- This example measures the area of Lot 9 shown in Figure 11-20.
- Turn on the object snap.

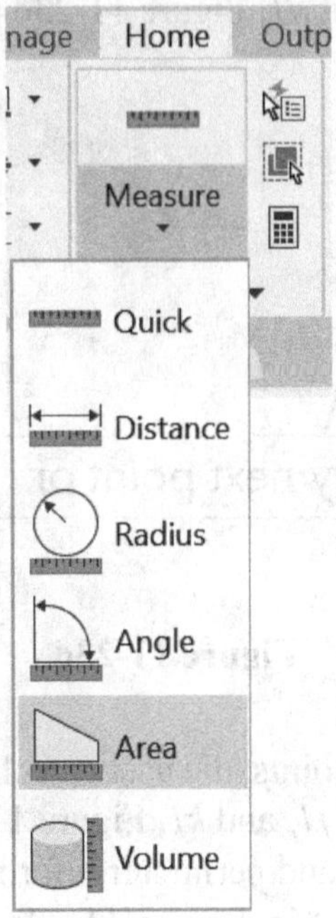

Figure 11-23a

Figure 11-23b

- For the first corner point, the user can click at any point on the boundary of the area. In the current example, click the corner labeled as *n*, Figure 11-23c.

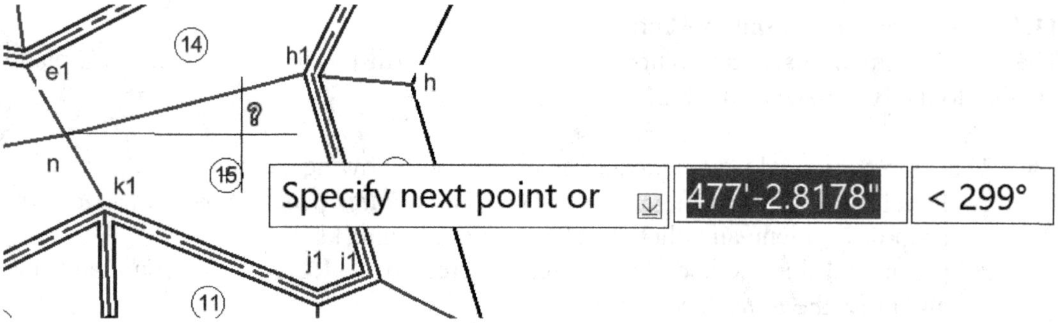

Figure 11-23c

- For the second point, the user can click on the two adjacent points (*h1* or *j1*). In the current example, click at point *h1*, Figure 11-23d.

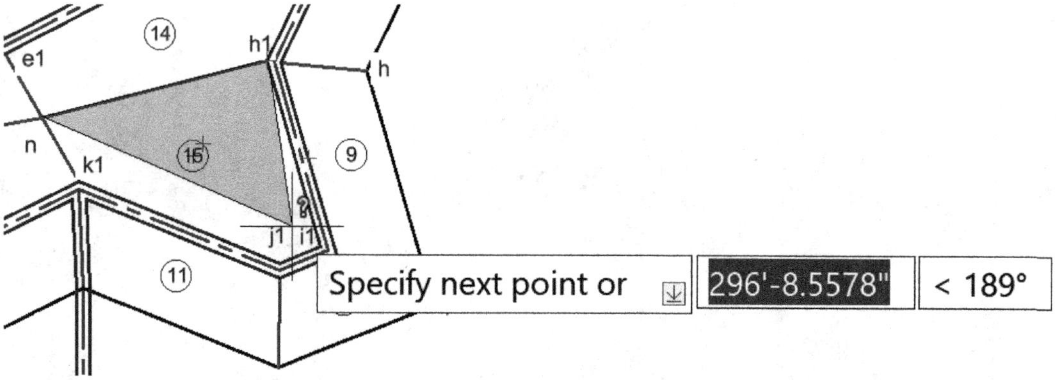

Figure 11-23d

- For the third and subsequent points, the user can click only on the next adjacent point. Click at point *i1*, followed by *j1,* and *k1*, Figure 11-23e.
- Press the *Enter* key. The area and perimeter information are shown in Figure 11-23e.
- Either choose the *eXit* option in Figure 11-20e or press the *Esc* key to exit the command.
- The area and perimeter are also available on the command line.
- If the green area is not closed, then the area is calculated as if a straight line is drawn from the last point to the first. For the perimeter calculation, the length of that line is added to the existing lines.
- Convert the area into acres using the relationship: 1 acre = 43560 sq. ft.
- Save the drawing!

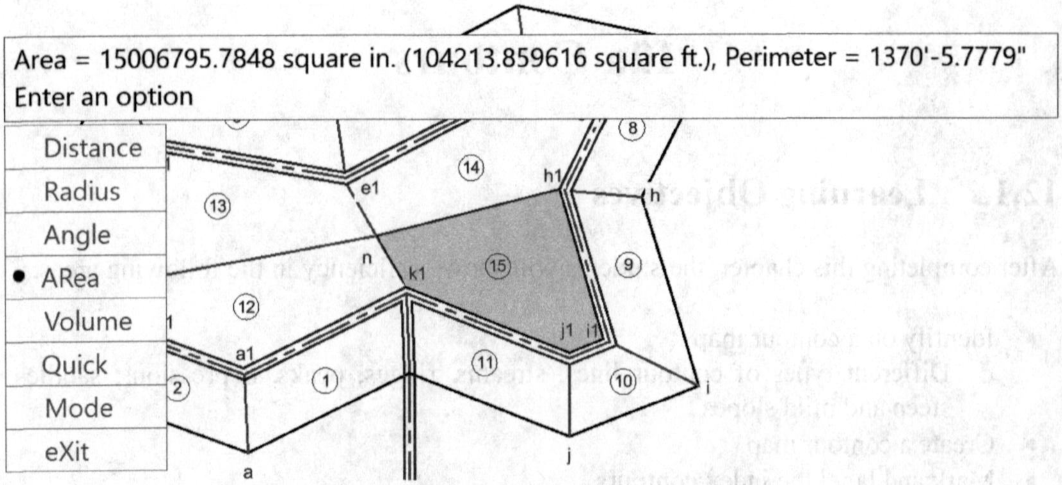

Figure 11-23e

Notes:

12. Contours

12.1. Learning Objectives

After completing this chapter, the students will show proficiency in the following areas:

- Identify on a contour map
    - Different types of contour lines, streams, ridges, peaks, depressions, saddles, steep and mild slopes
- Create a contour map
- Mark and label the index contours

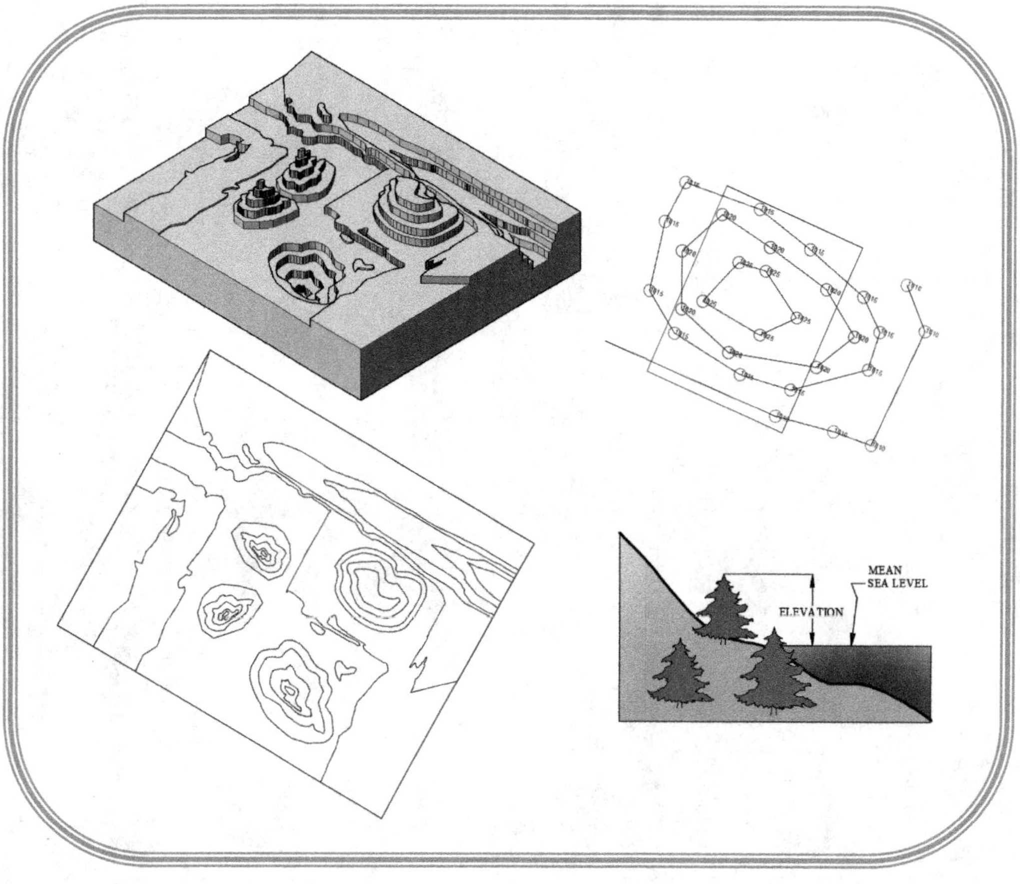

12.2. Introduction

Consider a cup of coffee and assume that the coffee has evaporated. Figure 12-1a shows the coffee marks as circular rings in the top view and straight lines in the front view. In the coffee marks plotting, the parameter is the time when the coffee was evaporated. Similarly, isobars and isotherms are wavy or closed looped lines representing constant pressure and constant temperature, respectively. These wavy or looped lines, representing a constant value of a parameter, are called contour lines. In a land survey, a contour line is an imaginary horizontal line passing through the points of the same elevation drawn on a topographic map, Figure 12-1b. Shorelines are a good example of contour lines, since the water receding marks create non-intersecting loops, Figure 12-1c.

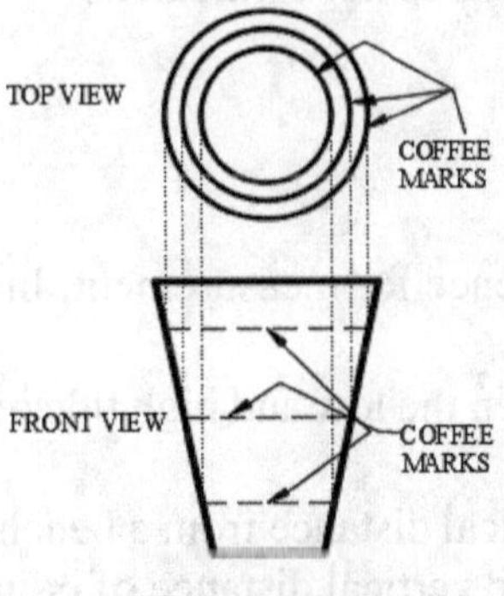

Figure 12-1a

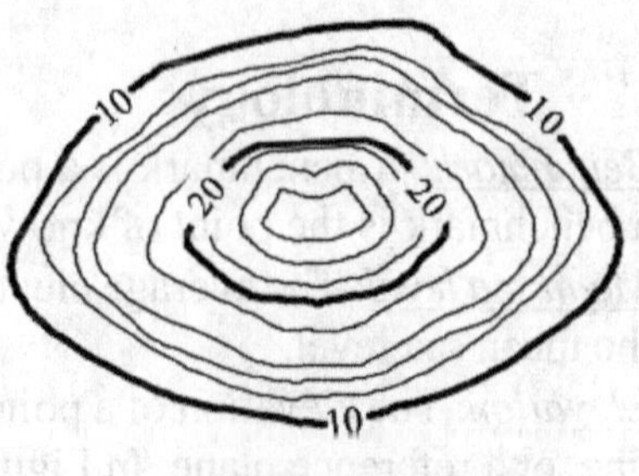

Figure 12-1b

Figure 12-1c

12.3. Characteristics of a Contour Line

A contour line is an imaginary line representing a constant value of a parameter. Some of the characteristics of contour lines are listed here.

- A contour line represents a constant parameter. For example, Figure 12-1b represents elevation contours. The elevation is 10 units for every point on the loop labeled as 10 in the figure.
- If a large enough area is available, then the contour lines loop around and join themselves.
- Contour lines never end.
- Contour lines neither join with other contour lines nor bifurcate.
- Contour lines never cross each other.

12.4. Terminology

- <u>Benchmark</u>: A benchmark is a point of reference for measurement. In a land survey, a benchmark is the point of known elevation.
- <u>Mean sea level</u>: The average elevation between the low and high tide of a sea is called the mean sea level.
- <u>Elevation</u>: The elevation of a point is the vertical distance from a benchmark, a datum line, or a reference plane. In Figure 12-2a, the vertical distance of point *A* is 5ft from the datum line *aa*. Generally, the elevation of a geographic location is its height above (or depth below) the mean sea level. The mean sea level is the datum line. Figure 12-2b shows the elevation of one of the trees on the shore with respect to the mean sea level (datum).

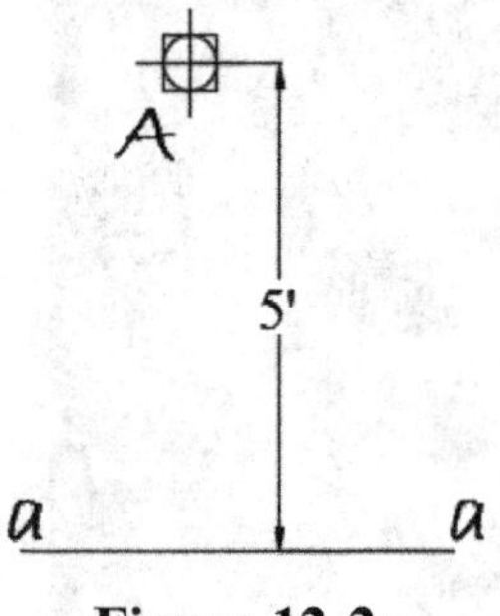

Figure 12-2a

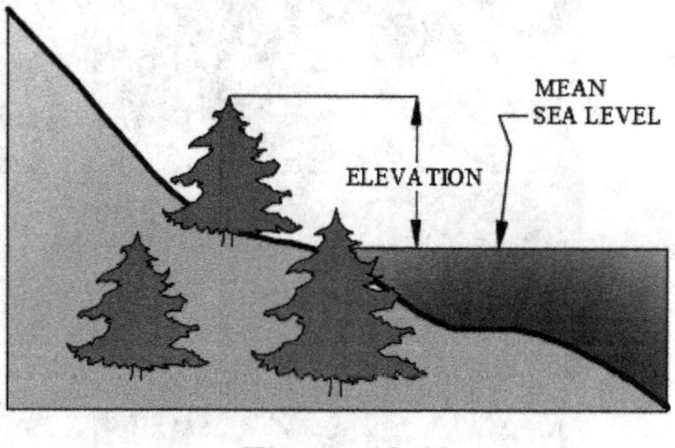

Figure 12-2b

- <u>Contour interval</u>: The contour interval of a map is the vertical distance between two consecutive contour lines. The contour intervals are closely related to the terrain, purpose of the map, and scale of the drawing. On a given map, the contour interval should be constant. Assuming the unit of measurement is feet, the contour interval is 2ft in Figure 12-1b.

- <u>Types of contour lines</u>: Contour lines can be classified into three groups.
  - <u>Index contour</u>: To make reading contour maps easy, every fifth contour is labeled. The labeled contour lines are called index contour, Figure 12-3a. The labels

represent the elevations with respect to the mean sea level. Usually, the index contours are drawn thicker than the other contour lines. The index contours can be marked as follows: (i) Identify the elevation of the first index contour (FIC). (ii) Specify the contour interval (CI). (iii) If the elevation is increasing, then the elevation of the second index contour (SIC) is calculated as:

Elevation of SIC = FIC + 5*CI.

If the elevation is decreasing, then the second index contour (SIC) is calculated as *Elevation of SIC = FIC + 5*(-CI) = FIC - 5*CI.* In Figure 12-3, the contour interval is 10 feet.

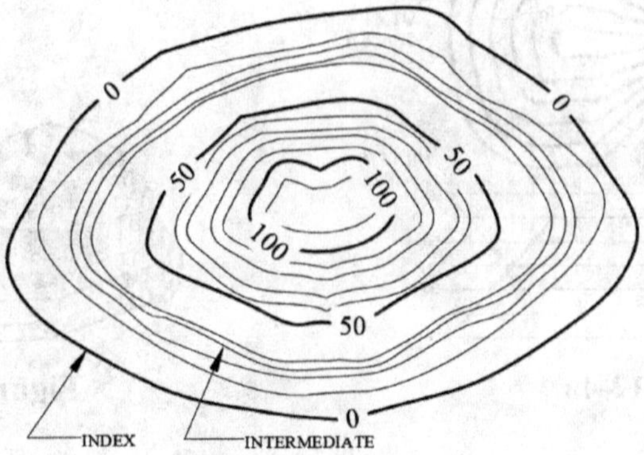

Figure 12-3a

- o *Intermediate contour*: The unlabeled contour lines between any two index contours are called intermediate contours. Conventionally, these contours are not labeled but can be labeled in special cases. Usually, the intermediate contours are drawn lighter than the index contours, Figure 12-3a.

- o *Supplementary contour*: The supplementary contours are the special type of contour lines and are drawn only when the contour interval is large and a user wishes to display the features between two consecutive contour lines. As a rule of thumb, the elevation of the supplementary contour is the average of the two contours on either side, Figure 12-3b.

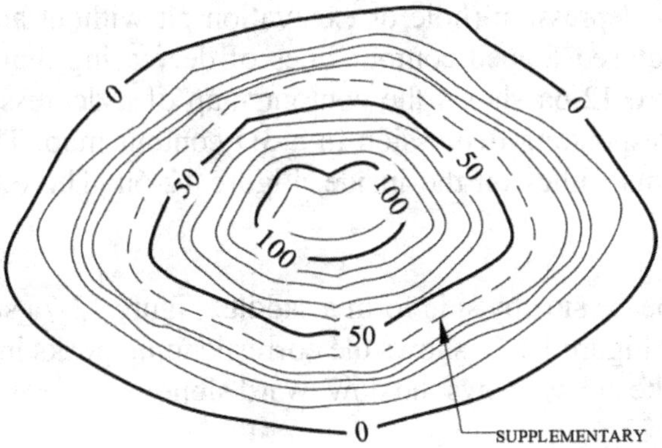

Figure 12-3b

- *Slope versus space*: The closely spaced contour lines represent steep slope, and widely spaced contour lines represent mild slopes. The top portion of Figure 12-4a shows a contour map and the lower parts show the profile indicating slope. On the left side of the top part, the contour lines are closely spaced, and its lower parts show the profile indicating the steep slope. Similarly, on the right side of the top part, the contour lines are widely spaced, and its lower parts show the profile indicating the mild slope. Figure 12-4b shows the corresponding 3D contour map.

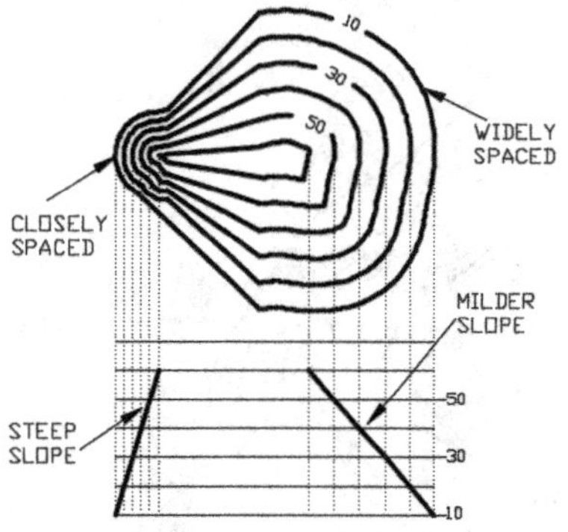

Figure 12-4a

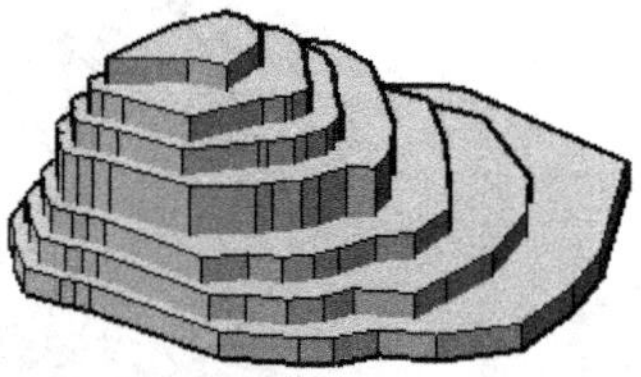

Figure 12-4b

- *Peak*: The peak of a hill or mountain is shown by the closed looped contour lines of decreasing diameters and increasing elevation. Figure 12-5a shows the contour map of a peak and Figure 12-5b shows the corresponding peak in a 3D contour map.

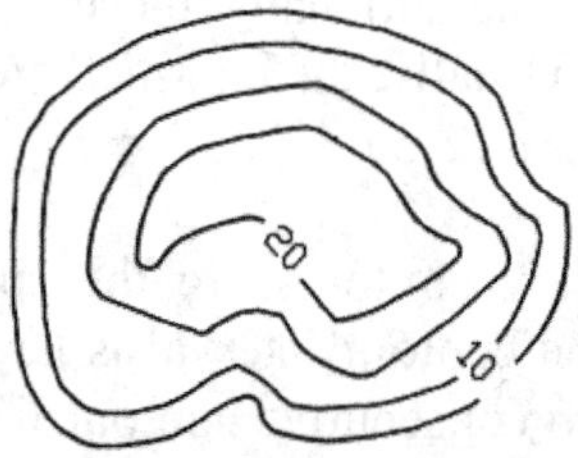

Figure 12-5a

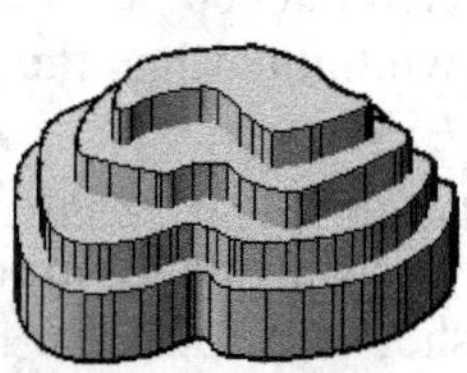

Figure 12-5b

- *Depression*: A depression (hole or excavation pit without any drainage outlets) is shown by the closed looped contour lines of decreasing diameters and decreasing elevation. Figure 12-6a shows the contour map of a depression and Figure 12-6b shows the corresponding depression in a 3D contour map. The innermost circle is marked with small lines on the inside, Figure 12-6a. These small lines are called hachures.

- *Saddle*: Two peaks side by side form a saddle. Figure 12-7a shows the contour map of a saddle and Figure 12-7b shows the corresponding peaks in a 3D contour map. In Figure 12-6a, the arrow shows the downward slope.

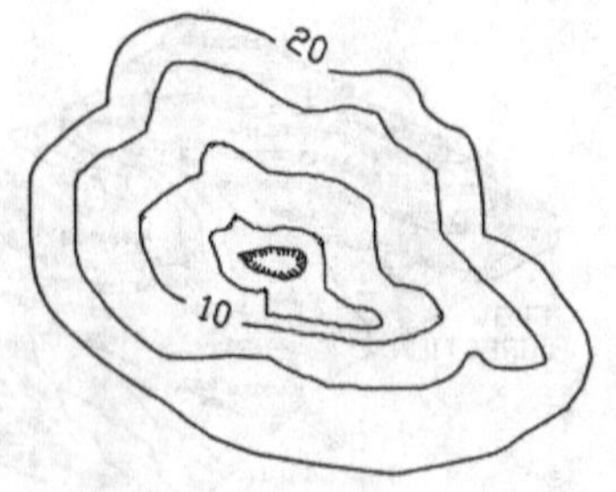

Figure 12-6a

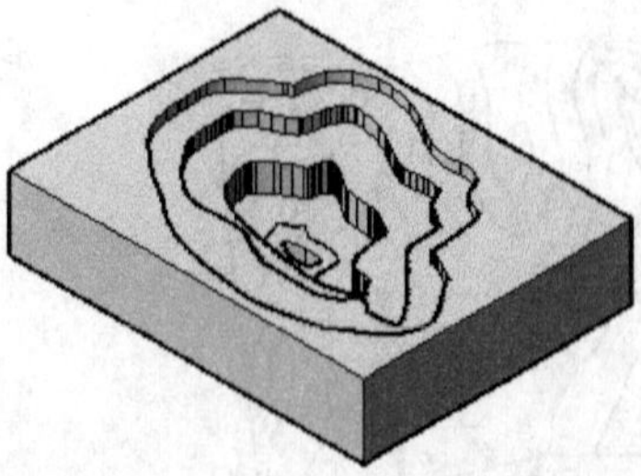

Figure 12-6b

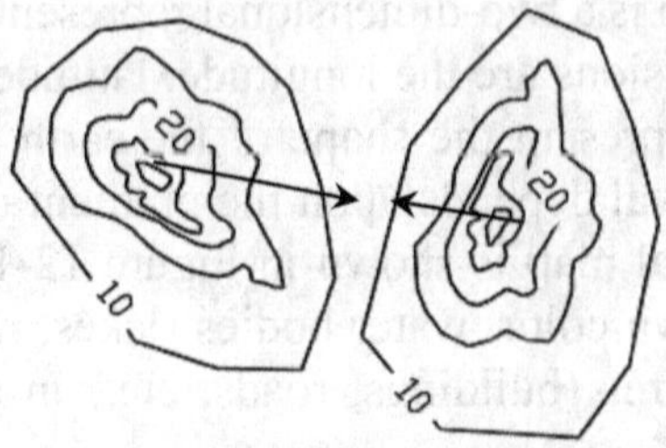

Figure 12-7a

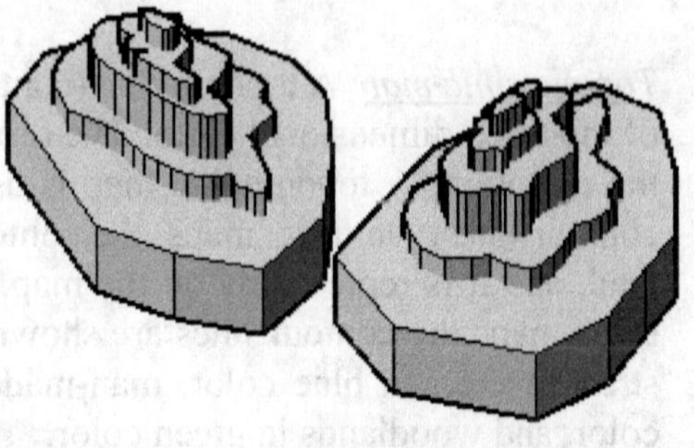

Figure 12-7b

- *Streams*: Contour lines are roughly parallel to stream. The contour lines cross the streambed upstream by creating V's with the closed end of the V's pointing upstream and the open end of the V's pointing downstream. Figure 12-8a shows a contour map of a stream, and Figure 12-8b shows the corresponding stream in a 3D contour map.

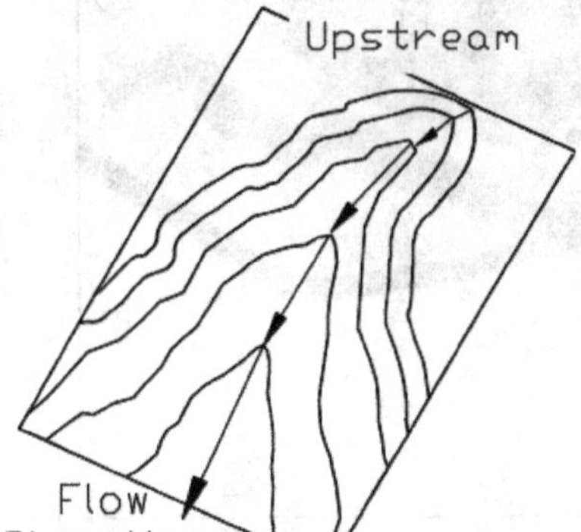

Figure 12-8a

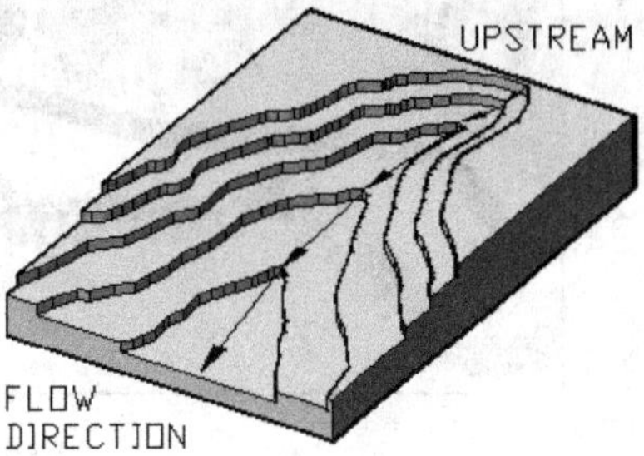

Figure 12-8b

- *Ridge or hill or mountain*: Contour lines are roughly parallel to a ridge, and the contour lines cross the ridge downstream by creating V's or U's. The closed end of the V's or U's points downstream and the open end of the V's or U's points upstream. Figure 12-9a shows a contour map of a stream and ridge line and Figure 12-9b shows the corresponding stream and ridge in a 3D contour map.

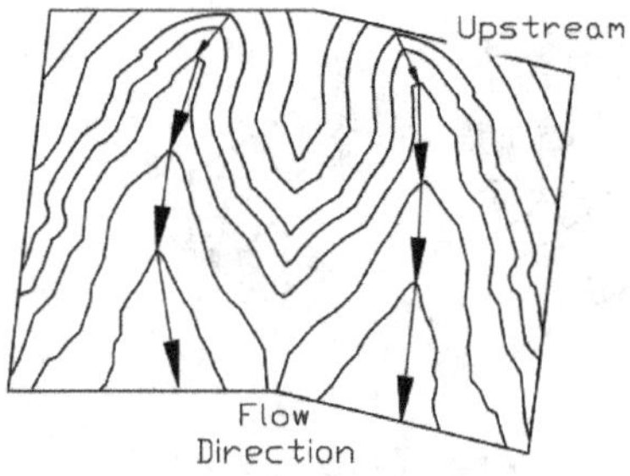

Figure 12-9a

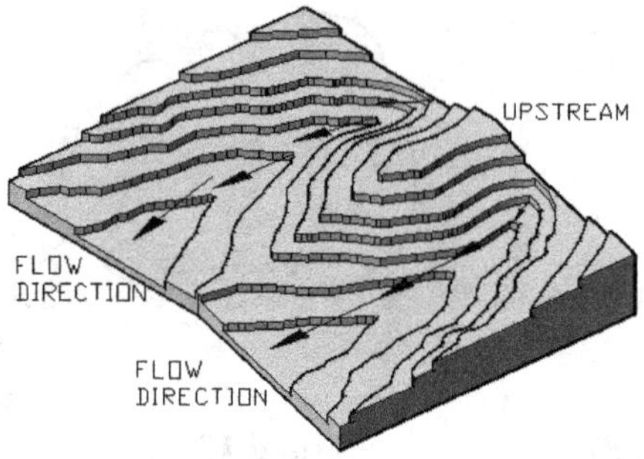

Figure 12-9b

- *Topographic map*: A topographic (contour) map is a two-dimensional representation of the three-dimensional earth. The three dimensions are the longitude, latitude, and the elevation. A topographic map is used to represent the shape of the earth using contour lines. On these maps, the contour interval depends upon the gradient of the land, and it is represented on the map. A typical map is shown in Figure 12-10. In these maps the contour lines are shown in brown color, water bodies (lakes, rivers, streams, etc.) in blue color, man-made structures (buildings, roads, etc.) in black color, and woodlands in green color.

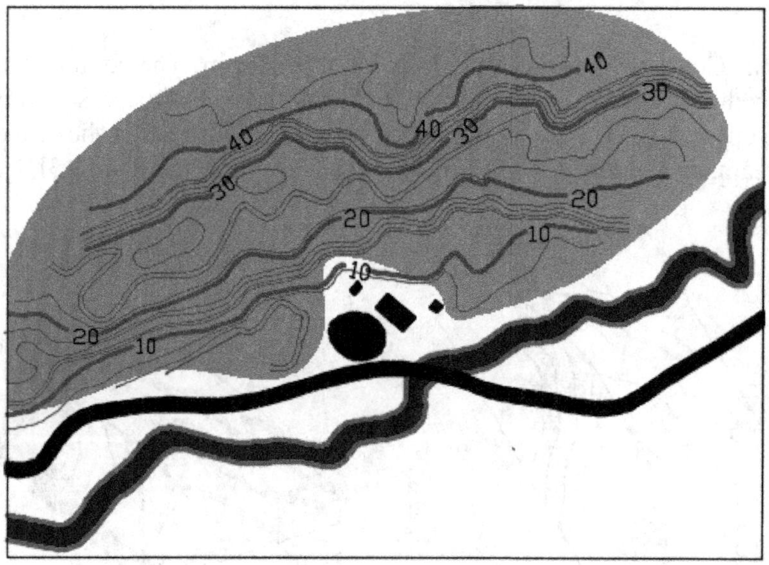

Figure 12-10

12.5. Script File

A script is a text file, and each line of the script file contains a command that can be executed at the Command prompt. A script can execute any command at the Command prompt except a command that displays a dialog box. In most cases, an alternative version of the command exists that displays Command prompts instead of a dialog box; hence, use the alternate version of the command in the script file.

12.5.1. Create script file

- For the current example, download the script file.
- If required, create the script file using the following steps:
    - o Create a script file outside AutoCAD using Notepad on Windows (TextEdit on Mac OS), or a text editor that saves in ASCII format. The script file is saved with file extension "*.scr*". Figure 12-11a shows part of a script (Script.scr) file and Figure 12-11b explains the contents of the script file.
    - o Make sure that the last line of the script file is blank.
    - o The commands in a script file are treated as a unit of commands that can be undone using a single **Undo** command. However, each command in the script file creates an entry in the undo log, which can slow the execution of a script.

color 20 *point* *13.20,8.80,00.00* *text* *13.20,8.80* *0.20 0 930* *point* *12.00,9.67,00.00* *text* *12.00,9.67* *0.20 0 930*	• "color 20" assigns color to a point • Blank line is an error because script file execution will assume that the user pressed the Enter key. • "point" activates the *Point* command. • "13.20,8.80,00.00" (no spaces) are the coordinates of the point. • "text" activates the *Text* command. • "13.20,8.80" is the coordinate of the first corner of the text box. • "0.20" is the text height. • "0" is the rotation of the text . • "930" is the text that appears in the text box. • Blank space after the text is an error. • ……

Figure 12-11a **Figure 12-11b**

12.5.2. Common errors in the script file

- A blank line or a blank space in a script file has a significant effect because it is like pressing the Enter key or the Spacebar. Therefore, the user must be familiar with the command sequence of prompts for the correct execution of the commands that will lead to the correct execution of the script file. *This error can be resolved by deleting the blank lines and the blank spaces.*
- Scripts file can contain comments. Any line that begins with a semicolon (;) is considered a comment and is ignored while the script is being processed.

12.6. AutoCAD And Contour Map

In AutoCAD contour maps can be created by drawing polylines through elevation data. This section assumes that the user has interpolated the field data and has created a script file. To draw a contour map, the color of the point is not important. However, for better understanding, every elevation is assigned to its distinct color. The remainder of this section provides step-by-step instructions to create a contour map.

12.6.1. Create layers

- Launch AutoCAD 2027.
- Open a new portrait file (your template file for the ANSI units).
- (i) Create a *Data* layer for the elevation data points. (ii) Create a *Contour* layer for the contour lines. (iii) Create a *Label* layer for the contours' labels.

12.6.2. Change point style

- From the *Home* tab and the expanded *Utilities* panel click at *Point Style...* tool. This opens the *Point Style* dialog box.
- Change point style to circle (second style in the second row), Figure 12-12.
- Change the point size to 0.5 *Units*.
- Select the *Set Size in Absolute Units* option.
- Press the *OK* button.

12.6.3. Read the script files

- Make the *Data* layer to be the current layer.
- Make sure that the script file is error free.
- Read the script file by activating the script command.
  - Command line method: Type "script," "Script" or "SCRIPT" on the command line and press the *Enter* key.
- Figure 12-13a shows the close-up of the selected elevation data points.
- The complete elevation data is shown in Figure 12-13b.

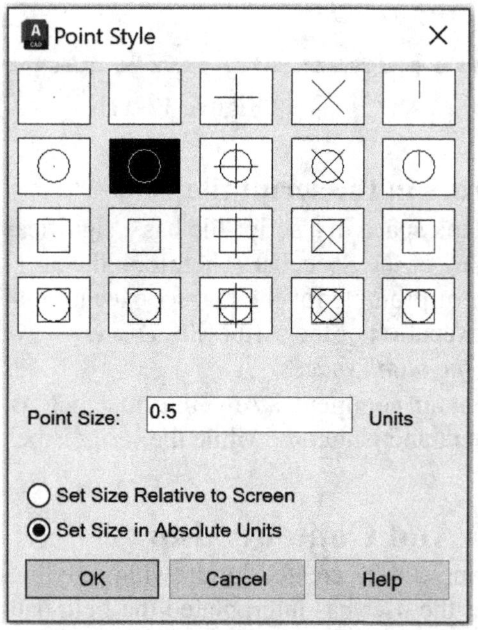

Figure 12-12

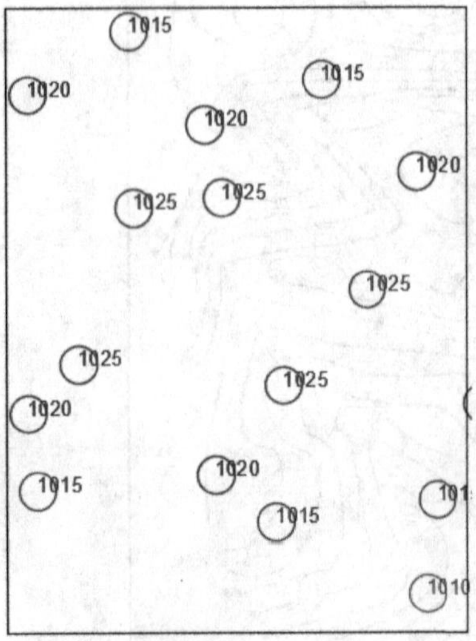

Figure 12-13a

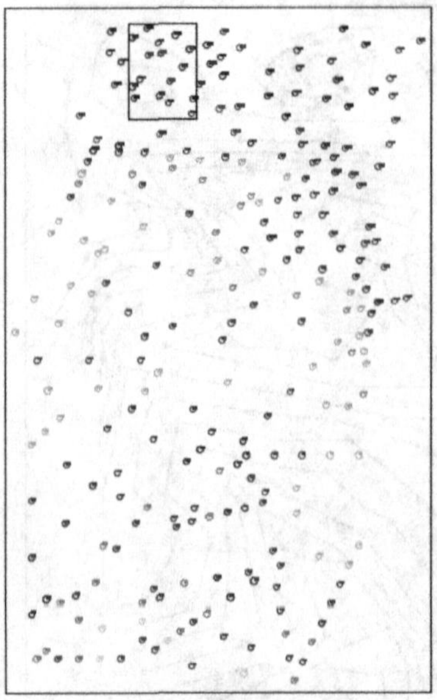

Figure 12-13b

12.6.4. Create the contour map

- Select the 'Contour' layer.
- Activate the *Polyline* command and draw a polyline through the points of the same elevation without intersecting any contour line. Figure 12-14a shows the contour line for the points shown in 11-13a.
- Repeat the process with the remaining data points, Figure 12-14b.
- Fit a curve through each polyline, Figure 12-14c. Curve fitting is discussed in the next section.
- If polylines are created in the multiple activations of the command, then first join the line and then perform the curve fitting operation. The *Join* operation is described in detail in *Chapter 4*.

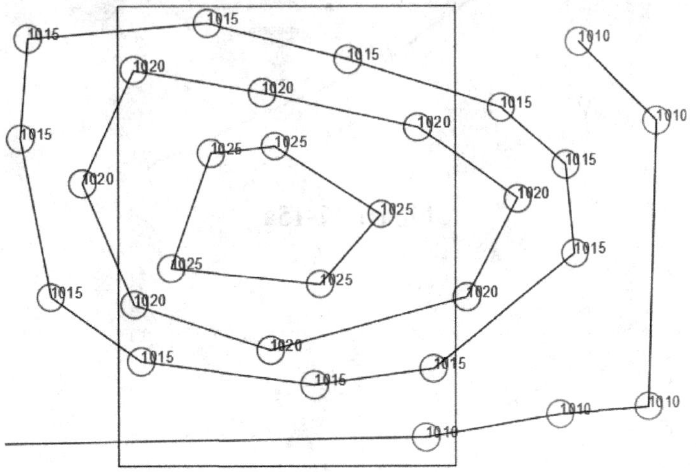

Figure 12-14a

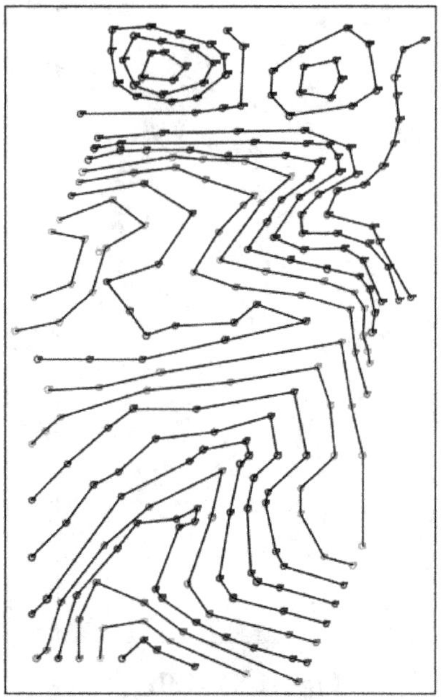

Figure 12-14b

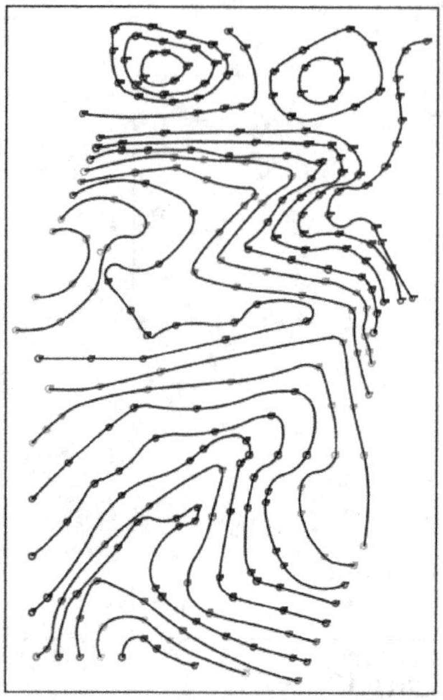

Figure 12-14c

12.6.5. Curve fitting

Curve fitting is optional; however, this section explains the curve fitting technique.

- Select a polyline for the elevation 930 (the grip points appear), Figure 12-15a.
- Press the right button of the mouse, and the options list appears.
- Choose the *Polyline* from the list, Figure 12-15a.
- Another list of options appears; choose the *Curve Fit* option, Figure 12-15a.
- The *Curve Fit* option passes the curve through the data points. A smooth curve is drawn through the points, Figure 12-15b.
- Repeat the process with the other contour lines, Figure 12-14c.

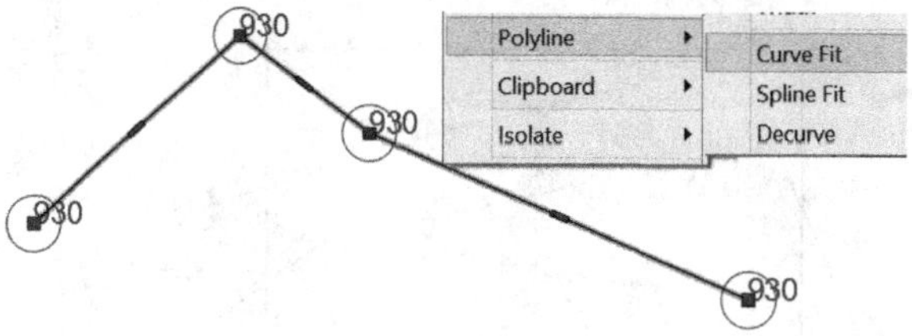

Figure 12-15a

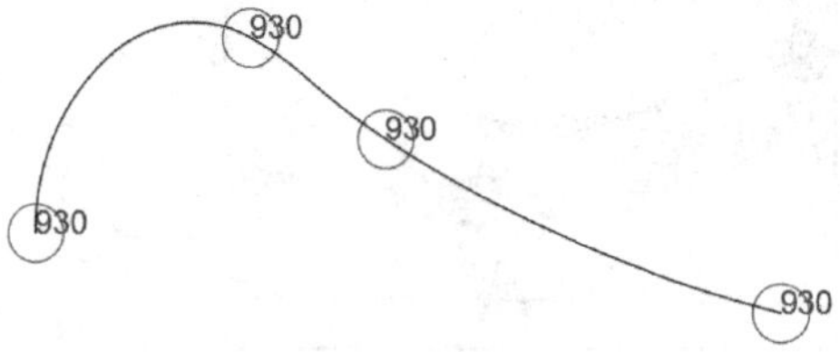

Figure 12-15b

12.6.6. Add the labels to the index contours

- If polylines are created in the multiple activations of the commands, then first join the line, and then perform the labeling and masking operation. The *Join* operation is discussed in detail in *Chapter 4*.
- Mark the index contours (that is, increase the lineweight for the index contours).
- Use the *Annotative Text* command from the *Home* tab and *Annotate* panel to create the text of the label. The text should be parallel to the polyline. If necessary, use the *Rotate* command from the *Home* tab and *Modify* panel to rotate the text.
- Figure 12-16 shows a contour map with only two labeled index contours.
- Similarly add labels to the other contours.
- Hide the contour line behind the label using the *Background mask* option from the *Properties* palette. The *Background mask* command is discussed in *Chapter 5*.
- Finally, add the *North* direction block from the *Design Center* → *Landscaping.dwg* → *North Arrow*; scale the north block appropriately, Figure 12-16.

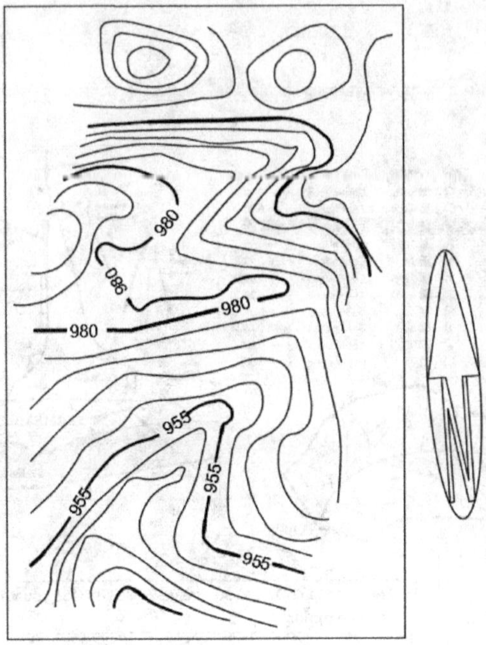

Figure 12-16

Notes:

13. Drainage Basin

13.1. Learning Objectives

After completing this chapter, the students will show proficiency in the following areas:

- Learn basics of a water cycle
- Understand fundamentals of a drainage basin
- Delineate a drainage basin of a channel using AutoCAD

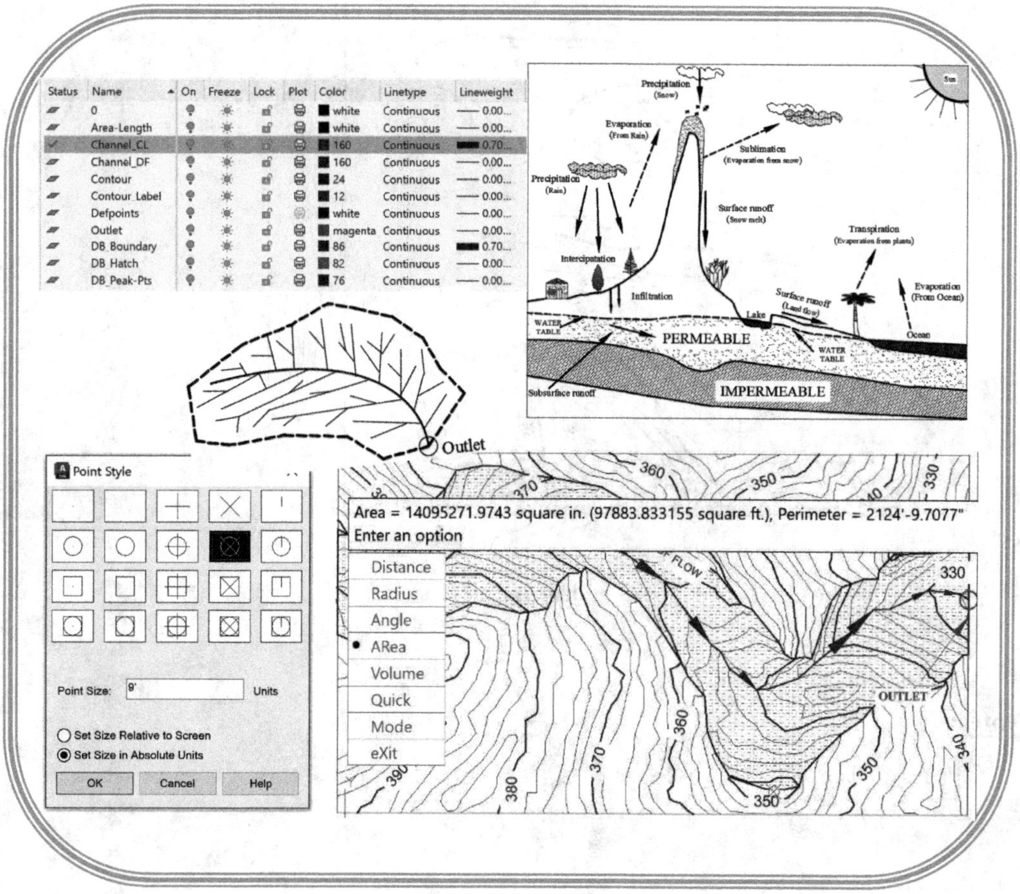

13.2. Introduction

Hydrology is a Greek word, and it means the study of water. In the engineering community, hydrology is the scientific study of the movement, distribution, and quality of water throughout the earth. Hydrology addresses both the hydrologic cycle and water resources.

13.3. Hydrologic Cycle

The hydrologic cycle, also known as the water cycle, is the continuous movement of the water above, on, and below the surface of the earth. Hence, there is no beginning or ending of this cycle. In the various stages of this cycle, water is available in one of the three different possible states: gas (water vapor), liquid, and solid (snow, ice). The most simplified representation of the hydrologic cycle (Figure 13-1) is as follows. *The major driving force of the hydrologic cycle is the sun. It heats the water in the oceans, lakes, rivers, streams, etc. and causes some of it to evaporate. The vapors rise into the air where cooler temperatures cause vapors to condense into clouds. These clouds drift over the land and the vapors fall as precipitation (rain, hail, snow, fog, etc.). The rainwater flows into lakes, rivers, or aquifers. The water in lakes, rivers, and aquifers then either evaporates back to the atmosphere or eventually flows back to the ocean, completing the cycle.*

The hydrological cycle can be affected by environmental effects and by humans. The following list shows some of the human factors affecting the water cycle.

- Agriculture
- Alteration of the chemical composition of the atmosphere
- Construction of dams
- Deforestation and afforestation
- Removal of groundwater from wells
- Water abstraction from rivers
- Urbanization

13.4. Terminology

Refer to Figure 13-1 for the terms discussed in this section.

- Condensation: Condensation is the transformation of water vapor to liquid water, for example, the droplets in the air that produce clouds and fog.
- Precipitation: Precipitation is the process of condensed water vapor falling to the earth's surface. Generally, precipitation occurs as rain. It also occurs as snow, sleet, hail, and fog drip.
- Interception: Interception is the precipitation that is intercepted by buildings, plant foliage, etc. Part of the intercepted precipitation reaches the ground surface, and the remaining part evaporates back to the atmosphere.
- Snowmelt: Snowmelt is the runoff produced by the melting snow.
- Groundwater: Groundwater is the water found below the ground surface. It may be available as soil moisture, in liquid form, or frozen form.

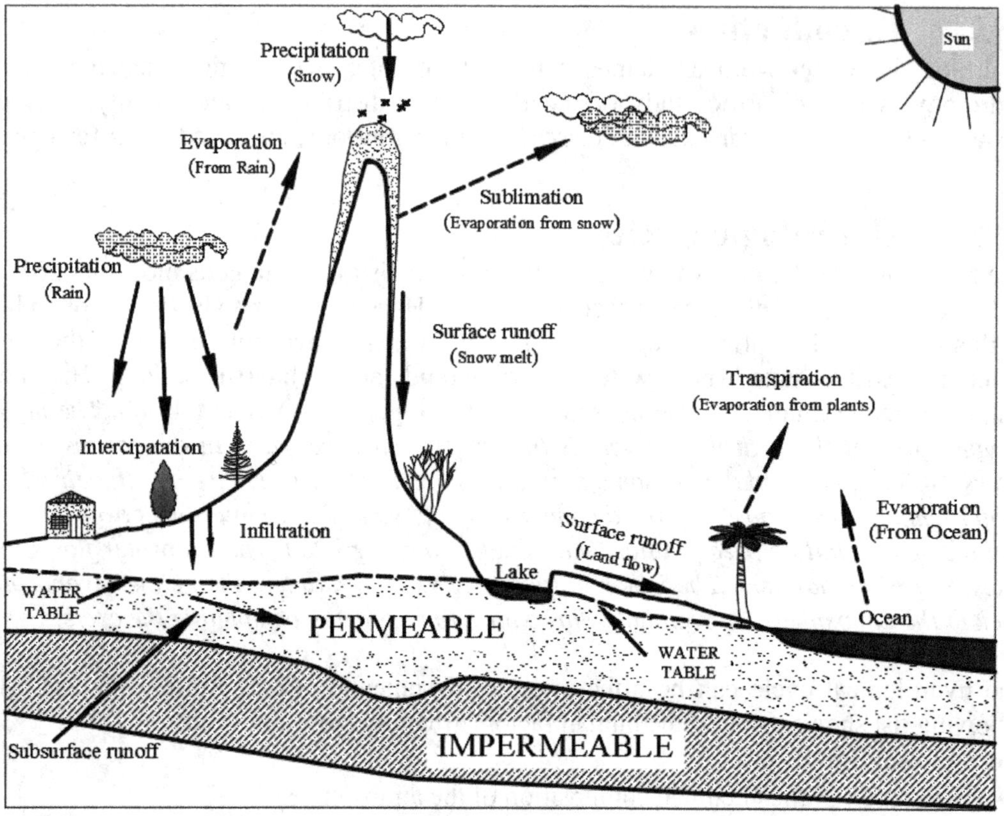

Figure 13-1

- Runoff: Runoff is the method by which water moves across the land. This includes both surface runoff and channel runoff. As water flows, it may infiltrate into the ground, evaporate into the air, become stored in lakes or reservoirs, or be extracted for agricultural or other human uses.
- Infiltration: Infiltration is the percolation of the water from the ground surface into the ground. Once infiltrated, the water becomes soil moisture or groundwater.
- Subsurface flow: Subsurface flow is the underground flow of water. It may return to the surface as a spring or by extraction using pumps.
- Advection: Advection is the movement of water (in solid, liquid, or vapor states) through the atmosphere. Without advection, water that evaporated over the oceans could not precipitate over the land.
- Evaporation: Evaporation is the transformation of water from a liquid to a gaseous state.
- Sublimation: Sublimation is the transformation of water from a solid (ice) to gaseous (vapor) state.
- Transpiration: Transpiration is the evaporation of water from vegetation.
- Evapotranspiration: Evaporation and transpiration are collectively known as evapotranspiration.
- Water table: Water table is the underground water level at which the ground water pressure is equal to the atmospheric pressure.

13.5. Drainage Basin or Watershed

A drainage basin is the area of land that drains into a stream at a given location; that is, it is an area of land bounded by a hydrologic system. A drainage basin is also known as a watershed. Generally, a drainage basin is defined in terms of a point or outlet and all the land area that sheds (pours) water into the outlet during a rainstorm. Using the concept that "water runs downhill," a drainage basin is defined by all points enclosed within an area from which the rain falling at these points contributes water to the outlet. Figure 13-2 represents the delineation of a drainage basin boundary. Drainage basins come in all shapes and sizes and cross state and national boundaries. For example, the Mississippi river drainage basin covers more than 30 states in US and two Canadian provinces.

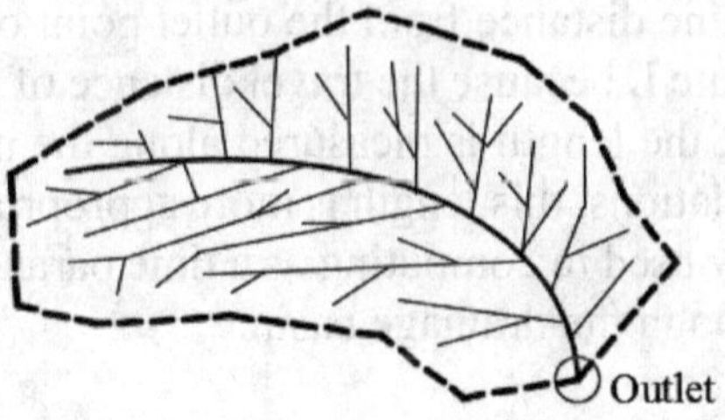

Figure 13-2

A drainage basin is a region of land where the precipitation's water flows downhill into a river, lake, dam, or ocean. The drainage basin includes both the channels and the land from which water drains into those channels. Each drainage basin is separated topographically from adjacent basins by a ridge, hill, or mountain, which is known as a water divide. In Figure 13-2, the dashed line is the main water divide of the hydrographic basin. In North America, watershed refers to the drainage basin itself. The terms catchments, catchment area, catchment basin, drainage area, river basin, and water basin are also used to represent the same concept.

Most of the water that discharges from the basin outlet originated as the precipitation falling on the basin. In hydrology, the drainage basin is a logical unit of focus for studying the movement of water within the hydrological cycle. A portion of the water that enters the groundwater system beneath the drainage basin may flow towards the outlet of another drainage basin because groundwater flow directions do not always match those of their overlying drainage network. The measurement of the discharge of water from a basin may be made by a stream gauge located at the basin's outlet.

13.6. Drainage Basin Characteristics

13.6.1. Drainage area

The drainage area (A) is probably the single most important drainage basin characteristic for a hydrologic design. It reflects the volume of water that can be generated from rainfall. The drainage area is used to indicate the potential for rainfall to provide a volume of water. It is common in hydrologic design to assume a constant depth of rainfall occurring over the drainage basin. Under this assumption, the volume of water available for the runoff would be the product of rainfall depth and the drainage area. Thus, the drainage area is required as input to models ranging from simple linear prediction equations to complex computer models.

13.6.2. Drainage basin length

The length (L) of a drainage basin is the second greatest characteristic of interest. While the length increases as the drainage increases, the length of a drainage basin is important in hydrologic computations. The drainage basin length is usually defined as the distance measured along the main channel from the drainage basin outlet to the basin divide. Since the channel does not extend to the basin divide, it is necessary to extend a line from the end of the channel to the basin divide following a path where the greatest volume of water would travel. The straight-line distance from the outlet point on the drainage basin divide is not usually used to compute L because the travel distance of floodwaters is conceptually the length of interest. Thus, the length is measured along the principal flow path. Since it is used for hydrologic calculations, this length is more appropriately labeled the hydrologic length. The length is usually used in computing as a time parameter, which is a measure of the travel time of water through the drainage basin.

13.6.3. Drainage basin slope

The flood magnitudes reflect the momentum of the runoff. The slope is an important factor in the momentum. Both drainage basin and channel slope may be of interest. The drainage basin slope reflects the rate of change of elevation with respect to distance along the principal flow path. Typically, the principal flow path is delineated, and the drainage basin slope (S) is computed as the difference in elevation (ΔE) between the endpoints of the principal flow path divided by the hydrologic length of the flow path (L).

The elevation difference, ΔE, may not necessarily be the maximum elevation difference within the drainage basin since the point of highest elevation may occur along a side boundary of the drainage basin rather than at the end of the principal flow path.

13.6.4. Miscellaneous

Some of the other important drainage basin factors are listed here.

- Land cover and use
- Surface roughness
- Hydrologic soil groups
- Soil characteristics such as texture, structure, and moisture contents

13.7. Major Steps In A Drainage Basin Delineation Process

The major steps in the drainage basin delineation process are listed below.

Step 1: Create a contour map of the area.
Step 2: Mark the centerline of the channel by joining the V's. For a channel, the tip of the V is upstream.
Step 3: Show the direction of flow. A channel flows from a higher elevation (upstream) to the lower elevation (downstream).

Step 4: Delineate the drainage basin boundary by connecting the ridge lines in the elevation contour lines map. For a ridge, the tip of the V or U is downstream.
Step 5: Choose and label the point of the drainage basin outlet. The outlet is usually a monitoring location or hydraulic structure.
Step 6: Hatch the watershed.
Step 7: Find the length of the channel and the area of the drainage basin watershed.

13.8. Drainage Basin Delineation Using AutoCAD

In AutoCAD the drainage basin delineation can be performed using the following steps.

1. Launch AutoCAD 2027.
2. Contour map
   - Open the contour map previously created or the downloaded map, Figure 13-4.
3. Contour layers
   - Create the layers as shown in Figure 13-3.
   - Change the color, linetype, and lineweight of the layers.

Status	Name	On	Freeze	Lock	Plot	Color	Linetype	Lineweight
	0					white	Continuous	0.00...
	Area-Length					white	Continuous	0.00...
✓	Channel_CL					160	Continuous	0.70...
	Channel_DF					160	Continuous	0.00...
	Contour					24	Continuous	0.00...
	Contour_Label					12	Continuous	0.00...
	Defpoints					white	Continuous	0.00...
	Outlet					magenta	Continuous	0.00...
	DB_Boundary					86	Continuous	0.70...
	DB_Hatch					82	Continuous	0.00...
	DB_Peak-Pts					76	Continuous	0.00...

Figure 13-3

4. Contour labels, Figure 13-4
   - Make the *Contour_Label* layer to be the current layer.
   - Label the index contour using the *Text*, *Background Mask*, and the *Rotate* commands. The annotative text height is 0.15 inches in the current drainage basin.

5. Centerline, Figure 13-5
   - Make *Channel_CL* to be the current layer.
   - A channel flows from the higher elevation to the lower elevation. As mentioned earlier, the contour lines cross the streambed upstream by creating V's with the bottom of the V's pointing upstream.
   - Draw the centerlines for the channel.
     - Activate the *Polyline* command.
     - Draw a polyline through the bottom of the V's as shown in Figure 13-5.

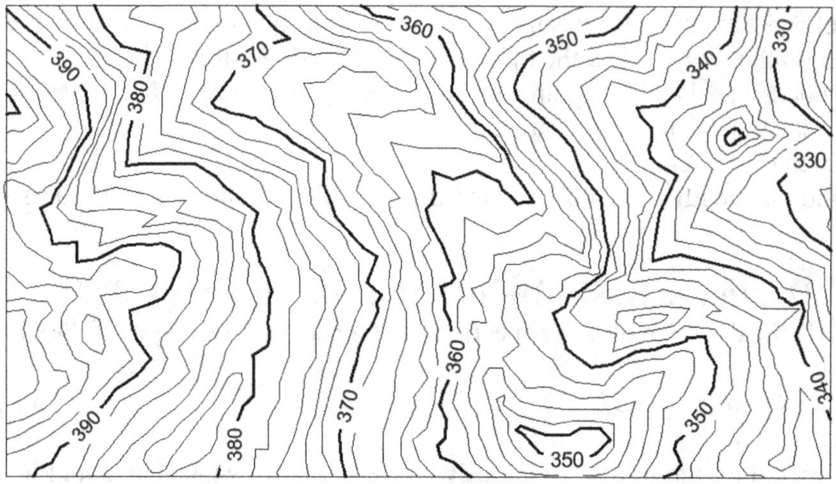

Figure 13-4

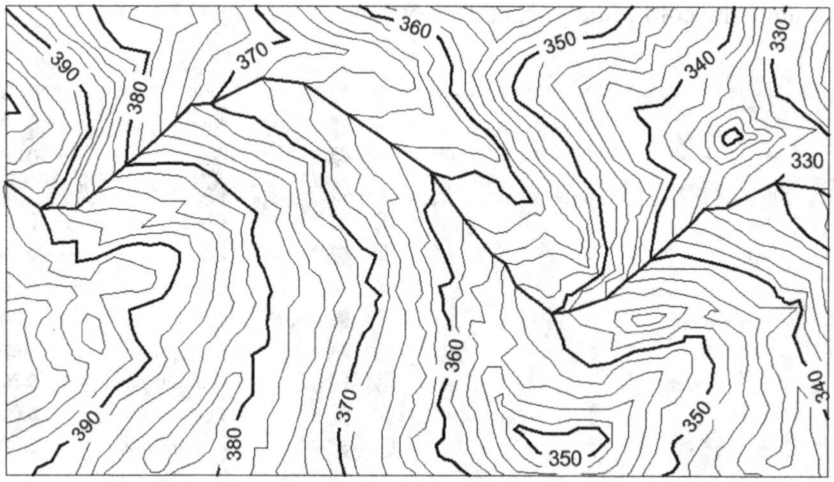

Figure 13-5

6. Direction of the flow, Figure 13-6
   - Make *Channel_DF* to be the current layer.
   - Show the direction of the flow for the channels using the leader line. Use the first part of the *qleader* command to draw arrows; set the arrowhead size appropriately.
   - The direction of flow label's annotative text height is 0.125 inches.

7. Outlet point
   - Make the *Outlet* layer to be the current layer.
   - In Figure 13-6, the intersection of the channel's centerline and the edge of the contour map is selected as the outlet point for the drainage basin.
   - Draw a point at the outlet and label it.
   - The outlet label's annotative text height is 0.125 inches.

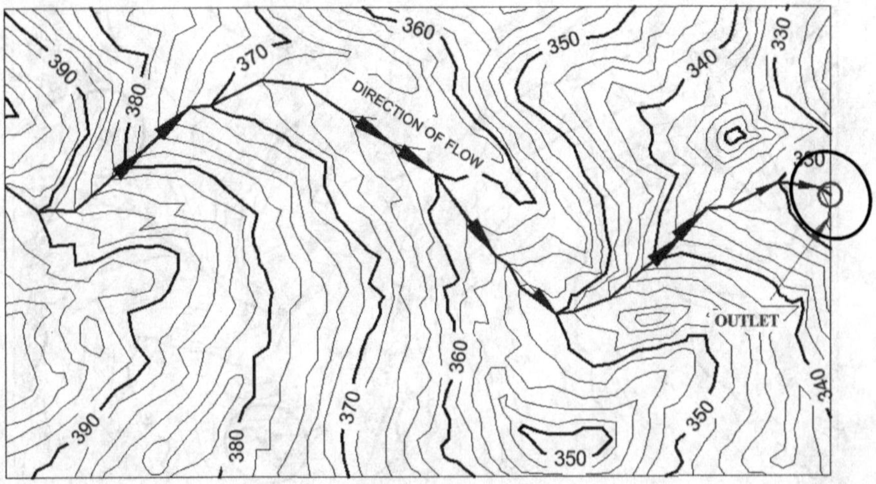

Figure 13-6

8. Delineate the drainage basin
   - The contour lines cross the ridge downstream by creating V's or U's pointing downstream.
   - Make the *DB_Peak-Pts* layer to be the current layer.
   - Mark the peaks that surround the channel
     - From the *Home* tab and *Utilities* panel, activate from the *Point Style* command and select the point style as shown in Figure 13-7a; and set the point size to be 144 inches; that is type 144 if the desired size is 12'.

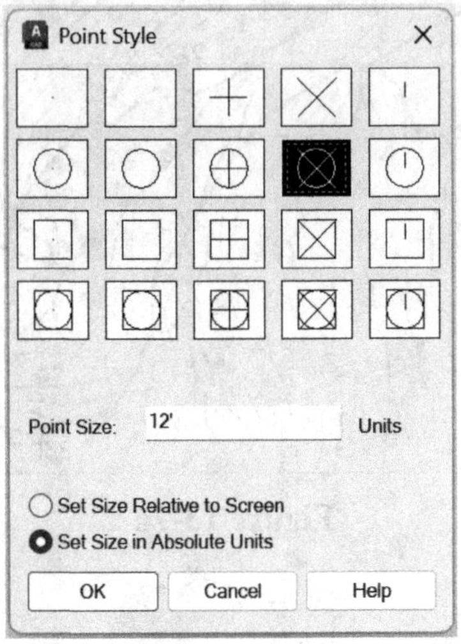

Figure 13-7a

     - Activate the *Points* command.
     - Draw points at the peaks as shown in Figure 13-7b.

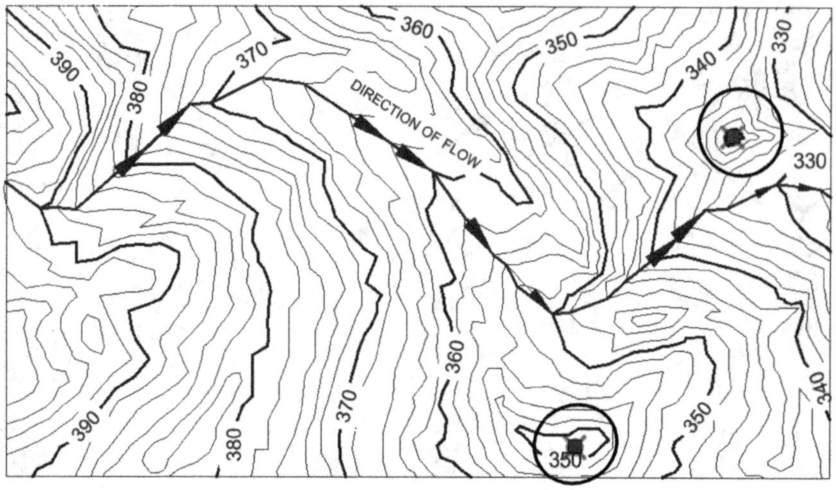

Figure 13-7b

- Make the *DB_Boundary* layer to be the current layer.
- Draw the boundary lines for the channel.
  - o Activate the *Polyline* command.
  - o Draw a polyline through the bottom of *U's* and connect the peaks from the previous step as shown in Figure 13-7c.

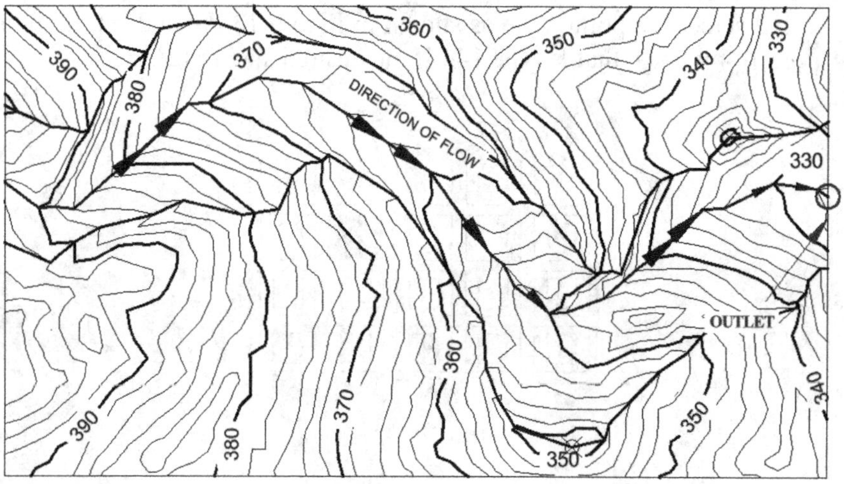

Figure 13-7c

9. <u>Hatch the drainage basin</u>
   - Make the *DB_Hatch* layer to be the current layer.
     - o Turn *Off* all the layers except the *DB_Boundary*, Figure 13-8a, and *DB_Hatch* layers.
     - o Draw polylines to close the open ends of the drainage basin boundary, Figure 13-8b.

- o Join the polylines (using the polyline edit command) to form a single closed polyline.
- o Activate the *Hatch* command.
- o Hatch the drainage basin, Figure 13-8b and Figure 13-8c, using *MUDST* pattern and the scale of 0.125". Do not forget to select *Annotative* option from the hatch Editor.

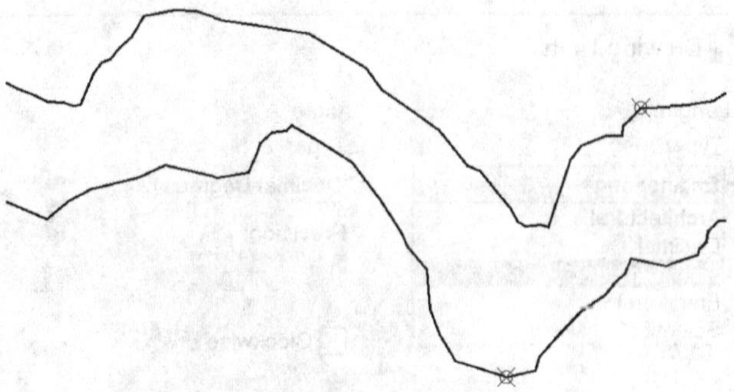

Figure 13-8a

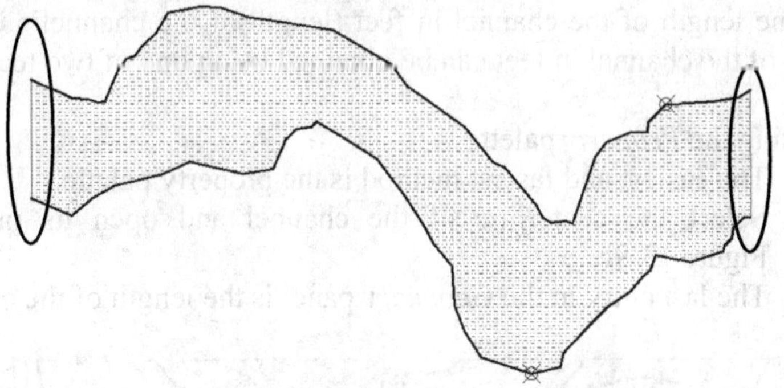

Figure 13-8b

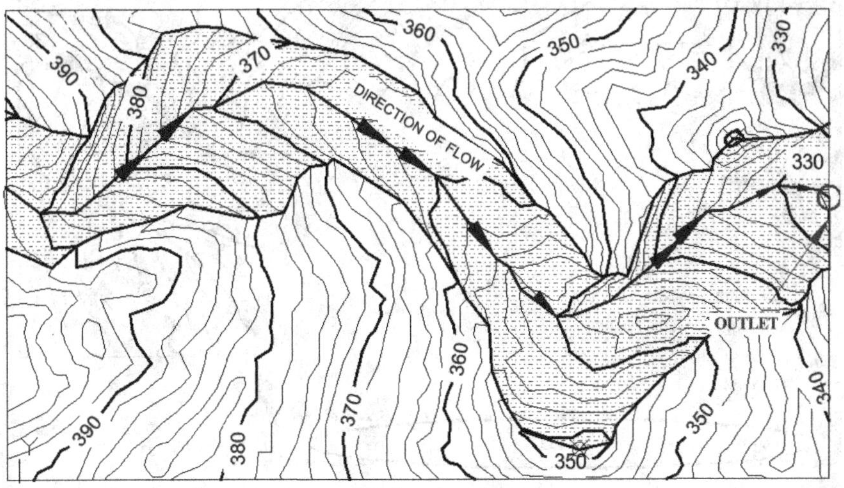

Figure 13-8c

10. Channel length
- Make the *Area-Length* layer to be the current layer.
- Set the drawing units to engineering as follows. (i) Type *Units* on the command line and press the *Enter* key. This opens *Drawing Units* dialog box. (ii) In the *Drawing Units* dialog box, under the *Length* panel, select the *Engineering* units, Figure 13-9a.

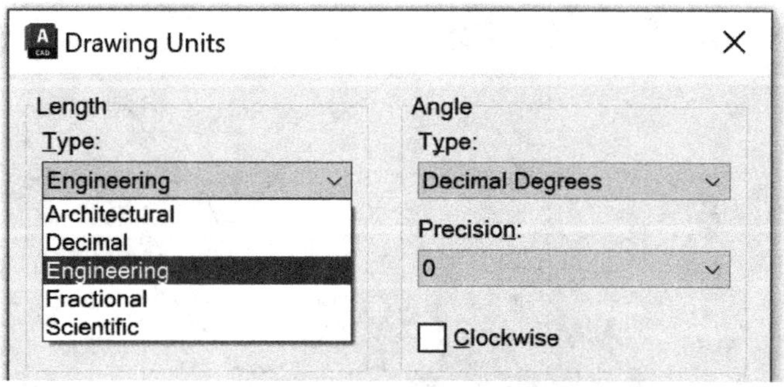

Figure 13-9a

- Find the length of the channel in feet (length of the channel's centerline). The length of the channel in feet can be obtained using one of two techniques.

  (a) Using the *Property* palette
  - o The easiest and fastest method is the property palette.
  - o Select the centerline of the channel and open its property palette, Figure 13-9b.
  - o The last entry in the *Geometry* panel is the length of the channel.

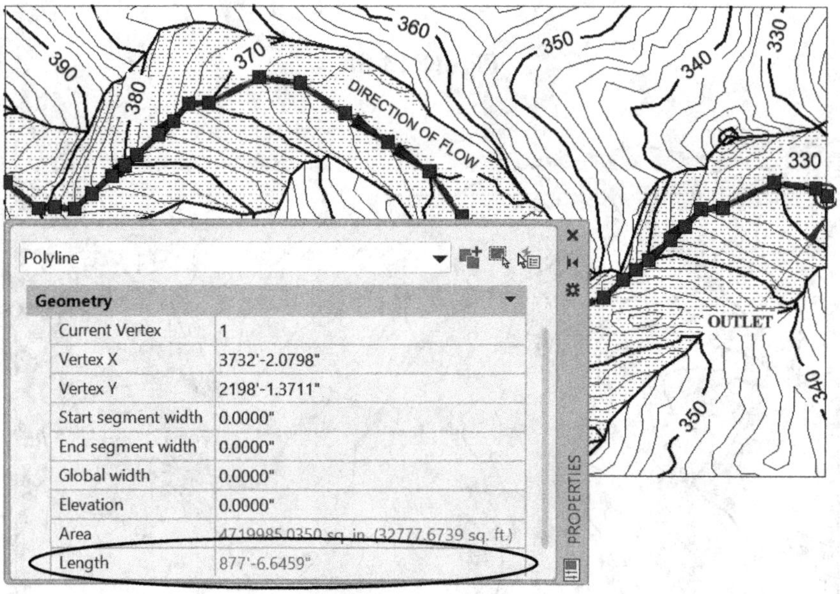

Figure 13-9b

(b) Using the *Distance* command
- o Lengthy method!
- o From the *Home* tab and *Utilities* panel, expand the *Measure* drop-down menu and select the *Distance* (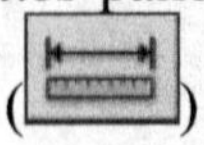) tool.
- o Follow the prompts.

11. Drainage basin area
- Make the *Area-Length* to be the current layer.
- Find the area of the drainage basin in acres. The area of the drainage basin can be obtained using one of the following two techniques.

(a) Using the *Property* palette
- o Select the boundary of the drainage basin, and connect and close the polyline, Figure 13-10.
- o Open its property palette, Figure 13-10.
- o The second to last entry in the *Geometry* panel is the area of the drainage basin.
- o The area is displayed in the units of square feet.

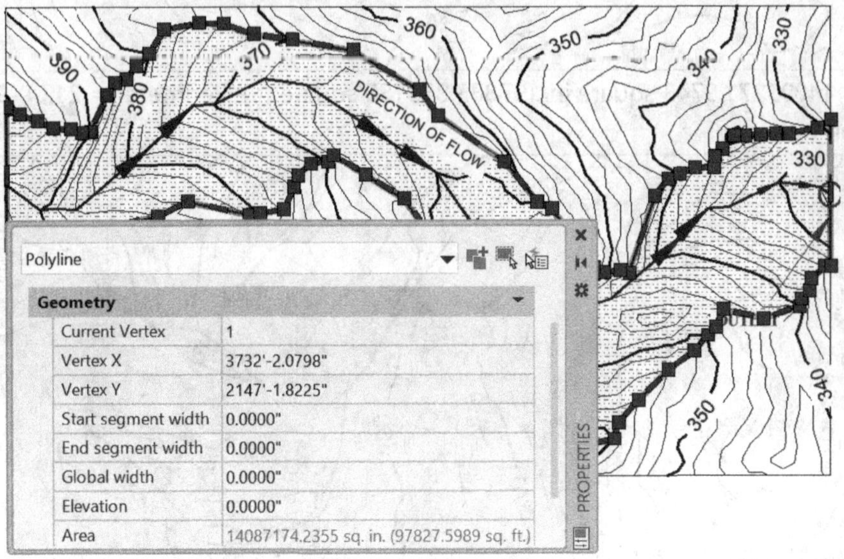

Figure 13-10

(b) Using the *Area* command
- o From the *Home* tab and *Utilities* panel, expand the *Measure* drop-down menu and select the *Area* () tool.
- o The prompt shown in Figure 13-11a appears.
- o Use the down-arrow and choose the *Object* option.

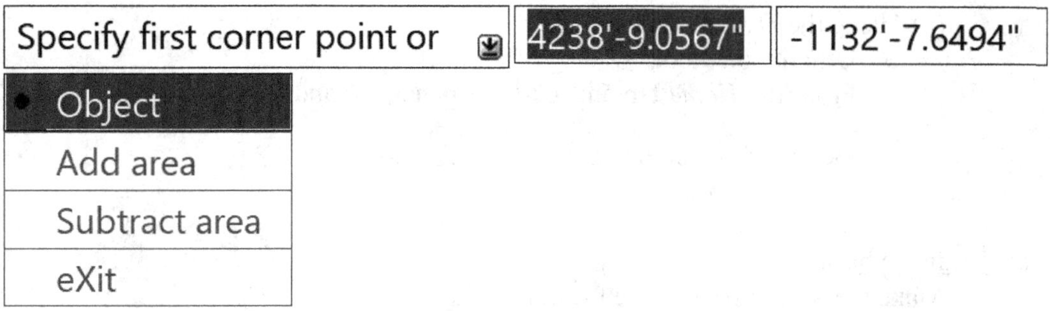

Figure 13-11a

- Click on the drainage basin boundary (make sure the boundary is represented by a single closed polyline, Figure 13-11).
- The area information appears on the screen, Figure 13-11b.
- Press the *Esc* key to exit the command.

- Convert the area into acres using the conversion factor of *1 Acres = 43560 sq. ft.*

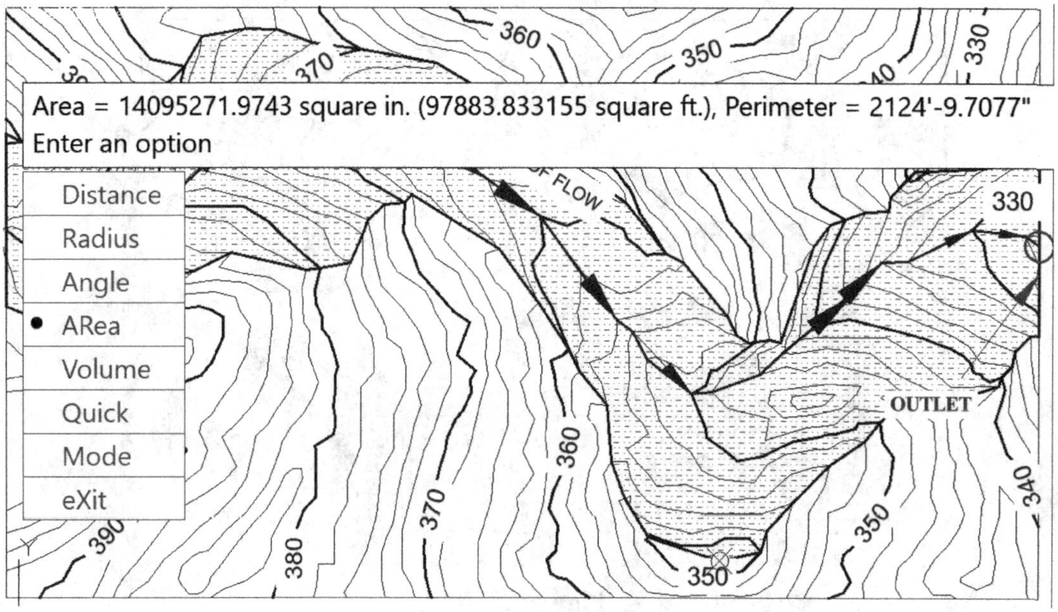

Figure 13-11b

12. <u>Display the length and area on the drawing</u>
    - Create two text boxes (or two tables) to show the length in feet and the area in acres on the drawing, Figure 13-12.

13. <u>Insert Template file</u>
    - Finally, insert the *Landscape* layout from the template file labeled as "*My_acad Landscape.dwt.*"

- Set the viewport scale to 1/72" = 1'-0".
- Lock the viewport scale.
- Update the title block.
- The resultant drawing in the layout is shown in Figure 13-12.

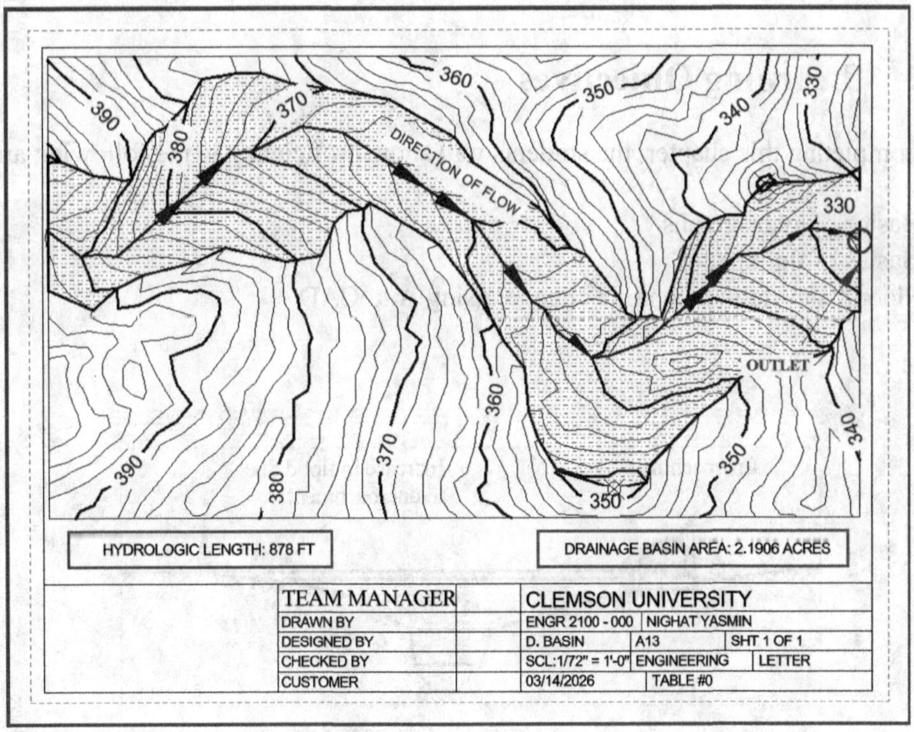

Figure 13-12

<u>**Notes:**</u>

14. Floodplains

14.1. Learning Objectives

After completing this chapter, the students will show proficiency in the following areas:

- Basics of hydrographs
- Basics of floodplains
- Floodplains delineation of a channel using AutoCAD

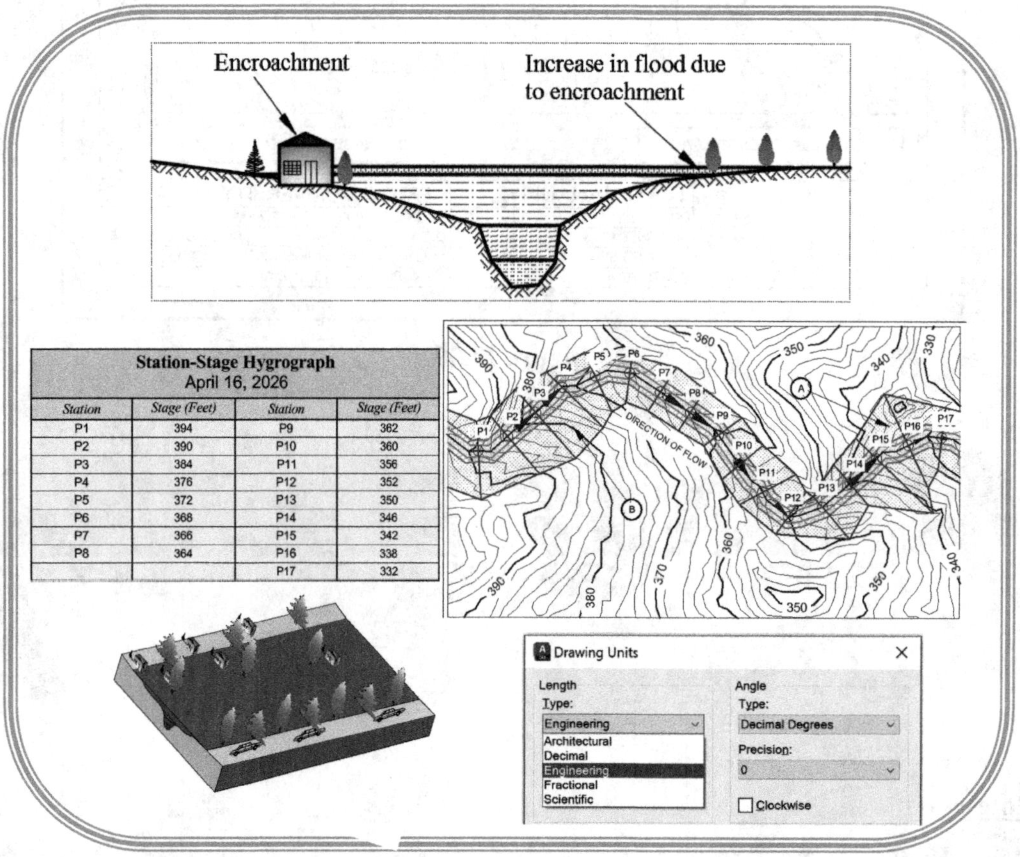

Station-Stage Hygrograph April 16, 2026			
Station	*Stage (Feet)*	*Station*	*Stage (Feet)*
P1	394	P9	362
P2	390	P10	360
P3	384	P11	356
P4	376	P12	352
P5	372	P13	350
P6	368	P14	346
P7	366	P15	342
P8	364	P16	338
		P17	332

14.2. Introduction

Generally, a floodplain is the dry and flat (or mild sloped) land area adjacent to a river, stream, creek, or lake which is subject to inundation by floodwater from the source. In order to save life and property on the floodplain, it is important to estimate their extent and geometry. The area of the floodplain can be determined by delineating the boundaries of the floodplain. The focus of this chapter is floodplain delineation.

14.3. Terminology

- Open channel flow: An open channel flow is a surface water flow with a free surface, e.g., flow in rivers, streams, or partially filled pipes.
- Flooding/flood: A flood, also known as flooding, is the phenomenon by which water level exceeds the capacity of a stream, river, or a drainage channel. Flooding occurs due to excessive rainfall, snowmelt, or dam break upstream.
- Main channel: The main channel is referred to as the normal capacity of a channel, Figure 14-1a and Figure 14-1b.
- Bankfull: The bankfull capacity of a channel is referred to as the maximum capacity of a channel without overflowing, Figure 14-1a and Figure 14-1c.
- Floodplain: A floodplain is defined as the dry and flat (or mild slope) land area adjoining a river, stream, creek, or lake which is subject to inundation by floodwater from the source, Figure 14-1a and Figure 14-1d.

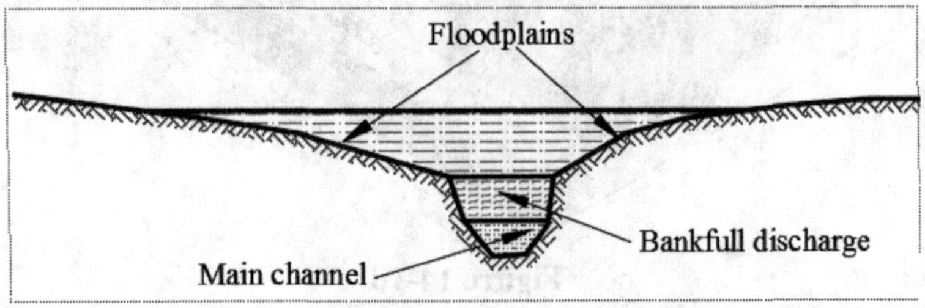

Figure 14-1a

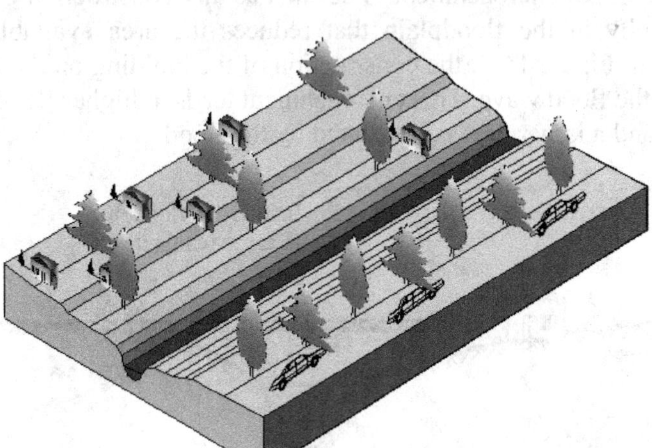

Figure 14-1b

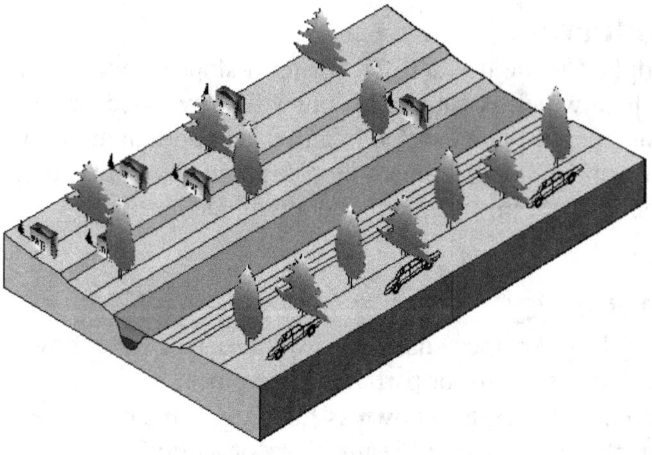

Figure 14-1c

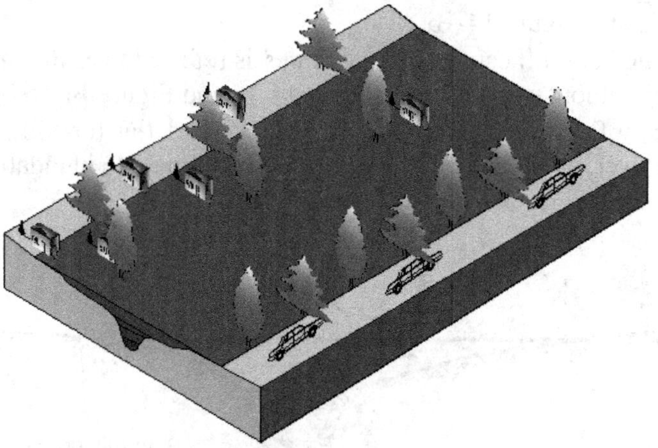

Figure 14-1d

- Encroachment: An encroachment is defined as any construction or modification of the topography in the floodplain that reduces the area available to convey the floodwater. In Figure 14-2, the construction of thc building on the left bank reduces the area for the flood wave. This encroachment leads to higher flood elevation on the right bank, and a larger area is inundated by the flood.

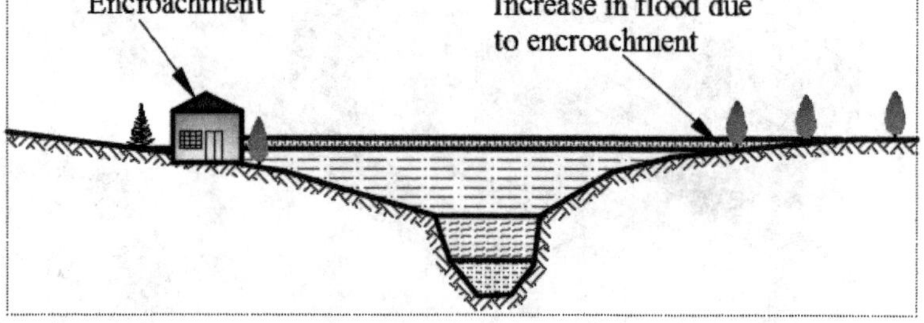

Figure 14-2

- Hydrograph: Hydrograph is the flow data represented as a graph (Figure 14-3a) or in a tabular format (Figure 14-3b). Hydrographs are classified as discharge, stage, and station-stage hydrographs.
  - Discharge hydrograph: A discharge hydrograph, at a gauging station, represents the rate of flow with respect to time usually as cubic feet per second (cfs). Figure 14-3a shows a discharge hydrograph in a graphical representation and its equivalent tabular form is shown in Figure 14-3b.
  - Stage hydrograph: A stage (or elevation) hydrograph represents water surface elevation of flow at a gauging station with respect to time, Figure 14-3c.
  - Station-Stage hydrograph: A station-stage hydrograph represents water surface elevation of flow at a given time for several gauging stations, Figure 14-4.

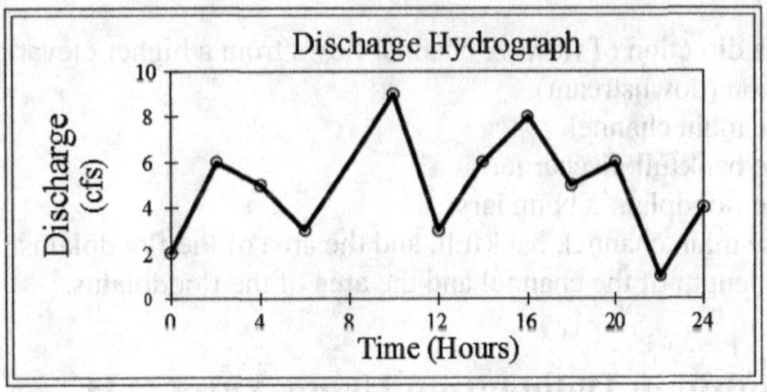

Figure 14-3a

Discharge Hydrograph

Time (Hour)	Discharge (cfs)
0	2
2	6
4	5
6	3
8	6
10	9
12	3
14	6
16	8
18	5
20	6
22	1
24	4

Figure 14-3b

Stage Hydrograph

Time (Hour)	Stage (Feet)
0	1
2	2
4	3
6	4
8	5
10	6
12	7
14	6
16	5
18	4
20	3
22	2
24	1

Figure 14-3c

- 100 years' flood: A 100 years' flood is defined as the flood water level expected to occur only once in a 100-year period. More precisely the 100 years' flood is known as a 1% flood because this is the probability of the occurrence of the flood in a year. Although very unlikely, depending on rainfall or snowmelt in an area it is possible that two 100 years floods occur in the same year.

- Floodplain study: Due to the continuous change in the floodplain, these areas need to be examined in order to find out how they might affect or be affected by the development. The purpose of a floodplain study is to delineate the 100-year floodplain limits within or near a development. The study helps to preserve the natural resources within the 100-year floodplain, to protect property and people, and to apply a unified, comprehensive approach to floodplain management.

14.4. Major Steps In A Floodplain Delineation Process

The major steps in the watershed delineation process are listed below.
Step 1: Create a contour map of the area.
Step 2: Mark the centerline of the channel by joining the V's. For a channel, the tip of the V is upstream.
Step 3: Show the direction of flow. A channel flows from a higher elevation (upstream) to the lower elevation (downstream).
Step 4: Draw the main channel.
Step 5: Draw the bankfull discharge.
Step 6: Draw the floodplain's boundary.
Step 7: Hatch the main channel, bankfull, and the area of the floodplains.
Step 8: Find the length of the channel and the area of the floodplains.

14.5. Floodplain Delineation Using AutoCAD

The term delineate is defined as outlining the boundary. The floodplain delineation is the technique to mark the floodplain for the given stage. This section provides step-by-step instructions to delineate a floodplain. The station-stage hydrograph for a 100-year flood shown in Figure 14-4 is used to delineate the floodplain.

Station-Stage Hygrograph April 16, 2026			
Station	*Stage (Feet)*	*Station*	*Stage (Feet)*
P1	394	P9	362
P2	390	P10	360
P3	384	P11	356
P4	376	P12	352
P5	372	P13	350
P6	368	P14	346
P7	366	P15	342
P8	364	P16	338
		P17	332

Figure 14-4

1. Launch AutoCAD 2027.
   - Open the previously created contour map or the downloaded map.

2. Create layers
   - Open the previously created contour map or the downloaded map.
   - Create the layers as shown in Figure 14-5.
   - Change the color, linetype, and lineweight of the layers.

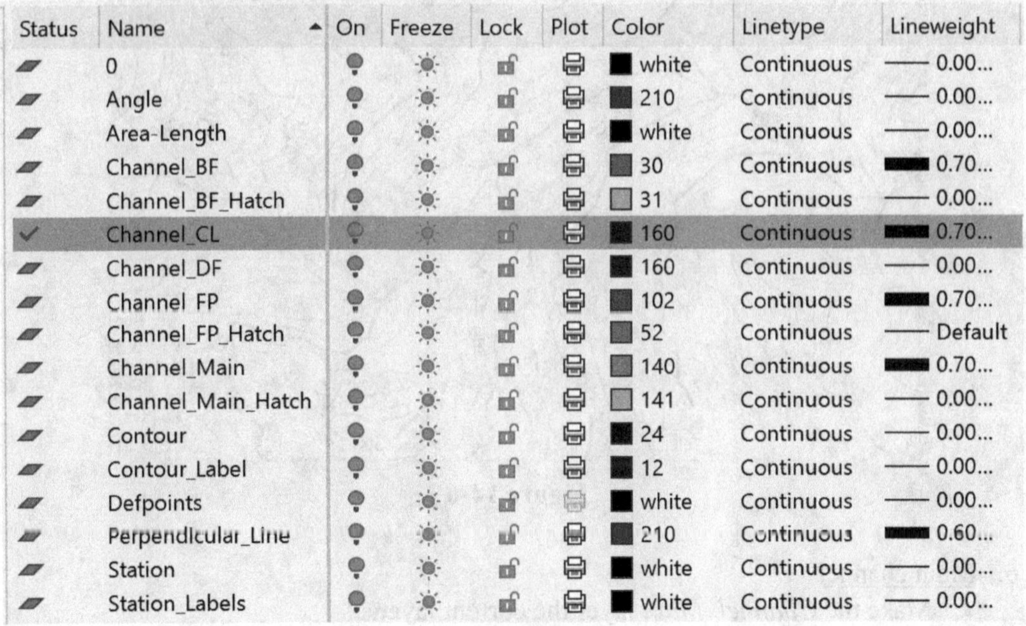

Status	Name	On	Freeze	Lock	Plot	Color	Linetype	Lineweight
	0					white	Continuous	0.00...
	Angle					210	Continuous	0.00...
	Area-Length					white	Continuous	0.00...
	Channel_BF					30	Continuous	0.70...
	Channel_BF_Hatch					31	Continuous	0.00...
✓	Channel_CL					160	Continuous	0.70...
	Channel_DF					160	Continuous	0.00...
	Channel FP					102	Continuous	0.70...
	Channel_FP_Hatch					52	Continuous	Default
	Channel_Main					140	Continuous	0.70...
	Channel_Main_Hatch					141	Continuous	0.00...
	Contour					24	Continuous	0.00...
	Contour_Label					12	Continuous	0.00...
	Defpoints					white	Continuous	0.00...
	Perpendicular_Line					210	Continuous	0.60...
	Station					white	Continuous	0.00...
	Station_Labels					white	Continuous	0.00...

Figure 14-5

3. Contour map
   - Open the previously created contour map or the downloaded map.
   - Create the Index contours shown in Figure 14-6.
   - Make the *Contour_Labels* layer to be the current layer.
   - Label the index contour using the *Annotative Text*, *Background Mask*, and the *Rotate* commands, Figure 14-6. The annotative text height is 0.15 inches in the sample contour map.

4. Centerline
   - Make the *Channel_CL* layer to be the current layer.
   - A channel flows from the higher elevation to the lower elevation. From *Chapter 12*, the contour lines cross the streambed upstream by creating V's with the closed end of the V's pointing upstream.
   - Draw the centerline for the channel, Figure 14-6.
     - Activate the *Polyline* command.
     - Draw a polyline through the closed end of the V's as shown in Figure 14-6.

5. Direction of the flow
   - Make the *Channel_DF* layer to be the current layer.

- Show the direction of the flow for the channels using the quick leader. Use the first part of the *qleader* command to draw the arrows, Figure 14-6.
- Set the arrowhead sizes appropriately.
- The direction of flow label's annotative text size is 0.125 inches.

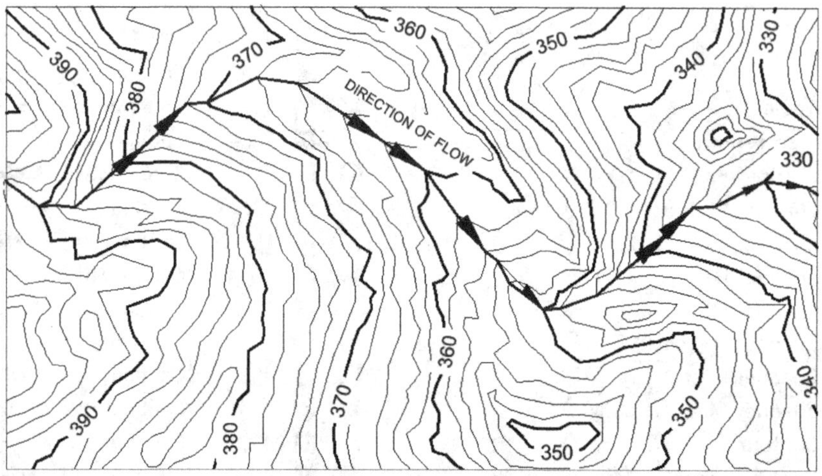

Figure 14-6

6. <u>Main channel</u>
   - Make the *Channel_Main* layer the current layer.
   - The main channel is 30ft wide, Figure 14-7.
     - Activate the *Offset* command.
     - Set the offset distance to 15ft.
     - Create an offset on either side of the centerline.
     - Move the offsets to the *Channel_Main* layer.
     - If necessary, use *Trim* and *Extend* commands near the left and right edges of the contour map.

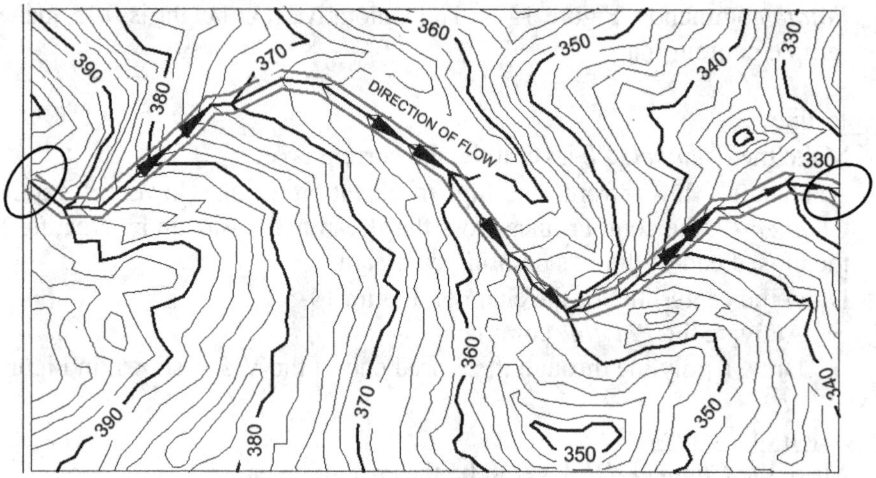

Figure 14-7

7. Bankfull
   - Make the *Channel_BF* layer the current layer.
   - The bankfull is 60ft, Figure 14-8.
     - o Activate the *Offset* command.
     - o Set the offset distance to 30ft.
     - o Create an offset on either side of the centerline of the channel.
     - o Move the offsets to the *Channel_BF* layer.
     - o If necessary, use *Trim* and *Extend* commands near the left and right edges of the contour map.

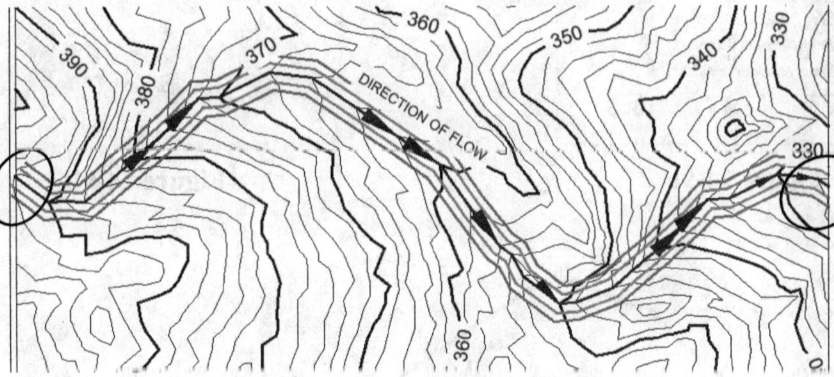

Figure 14-8

8. Gauging station
   - Turn *Off* the *Contour*, *Contour_Label*, *Channel_DF*, *Channel_Main*, and *Channel_BF* layers. Only the *Channel_CL* layer should be *On*.
   - Make the *Station* layer the current layer.
   - Add the stations' locations shown in Figure 14-10 as follows.
     - o From the *Home* tab and the expanded *Utilities* panel, click on the *Point Style…* tool to open the *Point Style* dialog box, Figure 14-9a.
     - o Change the point style and size. In the figure, the point size is set to be 168. For ANSI units, the *Point Style* dialog box takes input ONLY in inches. So set the size to 168 (**DO NOT TYPE 14'!**); however, it displays it in feet.
     - o From the *Home* tab and the expanded *Draw* panel, click on the *Point Measure* ( ) tool, Figure 14-9b, to activate the point command to draw points at a regular interval. The prompt shown in Figure 14-9c appears.
     - o Click on the desired polyline. In the current example, click on the left edge of the centerline, Figure 14-9c. The accuracy of the floodplain delineation depends on the accuracy of this point.
     - o The prompt shown in Figure 14-9d appears.
     - o Specify the distance between the stations (in the current example the distance is 50ft) and press the *Enter* key. The software assumes that the distance between the stations is constant, Figure 14-9d.
     - o The points appear on the centerline. The first point is 50' from the beginning of the polyline, Figure 14-9e.

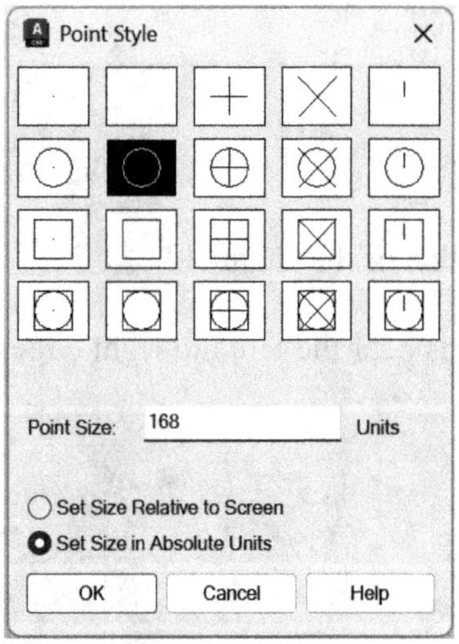

Figure 14-9a

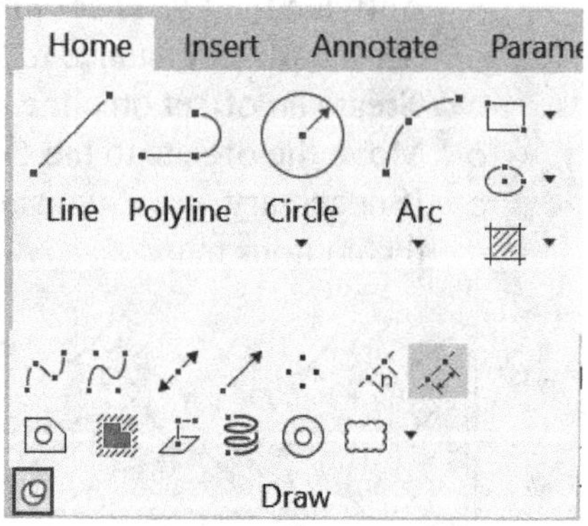

Figure 14-9b

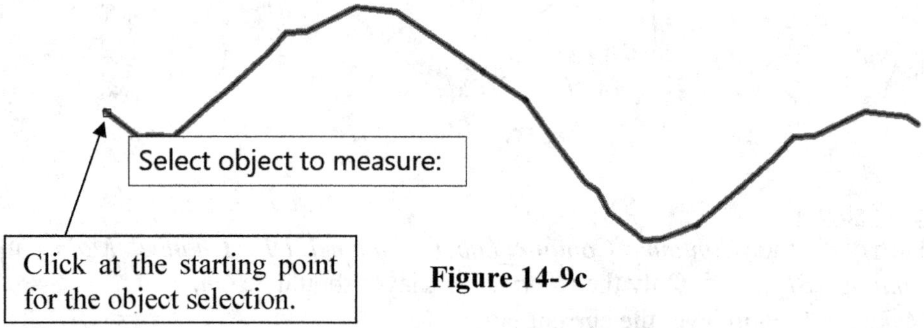

Figure 14-9c

Figure 14-9d

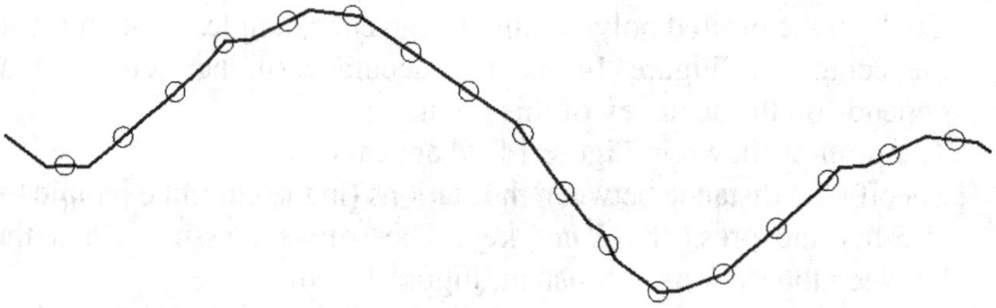

Figure 14-9e

- Make the *Station_Label* layer to be the current layer.
- Label the stations using annotative *Text* with text height of 0.12 inches and *Background Mask* commands, Figure 14-10.

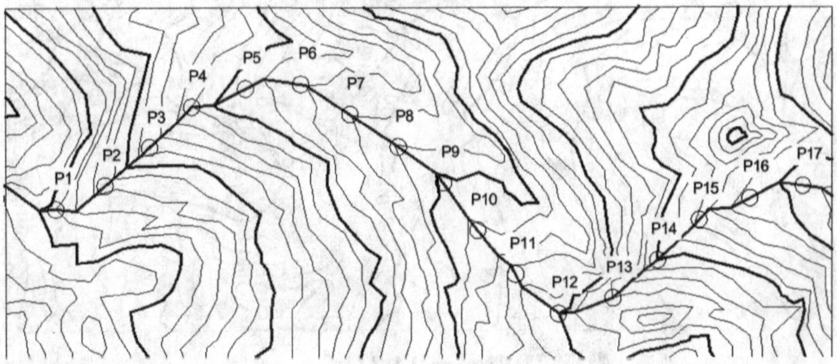

Figure 14-10

9. Perpendicular lines
   - Stage-Station hydrograph of Figure 14-4 shows that the stage (water surface elevation) at station P3 is 384ft.
   - Make the *Perpendicular_Line* layer to be the current layer.
   - Draw a line originating at station P3 and ending at the nearest contour (382ft).
   - Rotate the line at 90 degrees; use the end of the line at P3 as the base point for the rotation. The line will be perpendicular to the centerline, Figure 14-11a.
   - Since the stage at P3 is 384ft, extend the perpendicular line at P3 to the 382ft contour.
   - Refer to the Station-Stage hydrograph shown in Figure 14-4 and repeat the process for all the stations, Figure 14-11b.

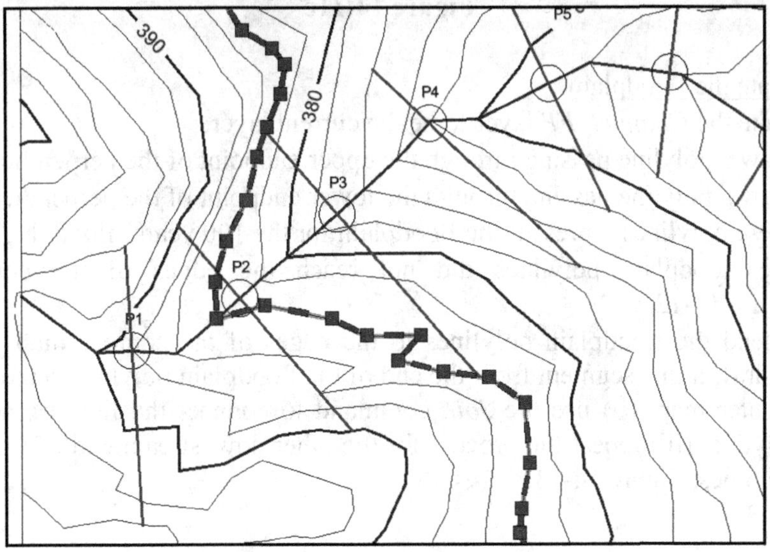

Figure 14-11a

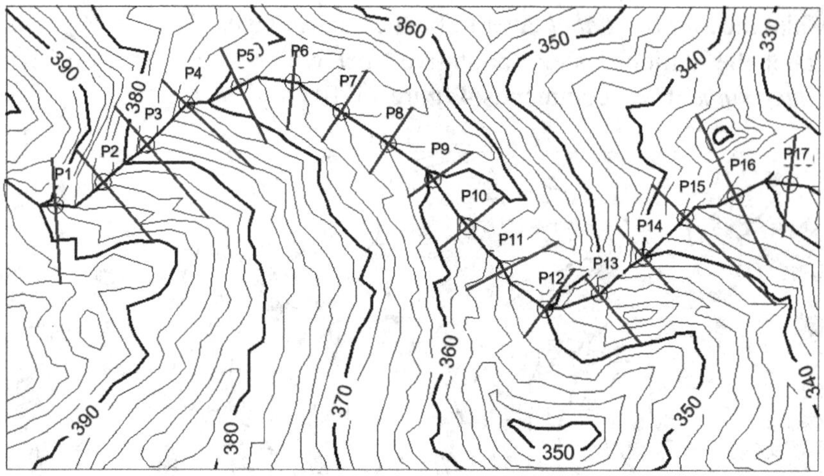

Figure 14-11b

- Make the *Angle* layer to be the current layer.
- Add the angular dimensions to the perpendicular lines, Figure 14-11c.

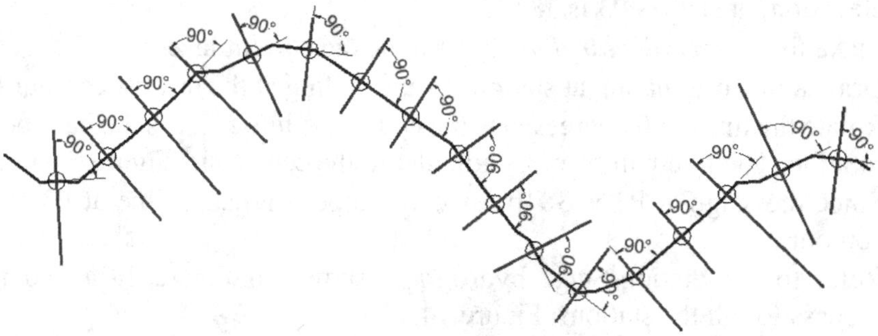

Figure 14-11c

10. Delineate the floodplain
- Make the *Channel_FP* layer to be the current layer.
- Draw a polyline passing through the upper endpoint of the perpendicular lines.
- Draw a polyline passing through the lower endpoint of the perpendicular lines.
- These polylines represent the floodplain for the 100 years' flood, Figure 14-12.
- The floodplain polylines did not reach the edges of the contour map, Figure 14-12.
- Extend the floodplain polylines to the edges of the contour map, as follows: (i) draw a line segment from the end of the floodplain polyline to the edge of the counter map; (ii) use the *Join* command to connect the line segment and the polyline; (iii) repeat the process for the other downstream end of the floodplain polylines, Figure 14-13.

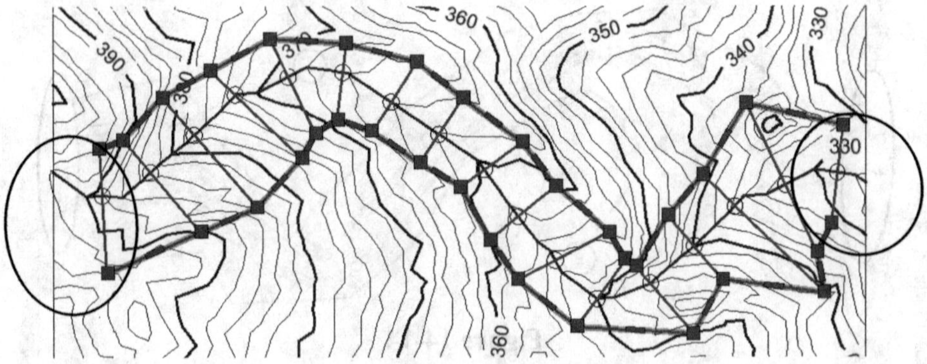

Figure 14-12

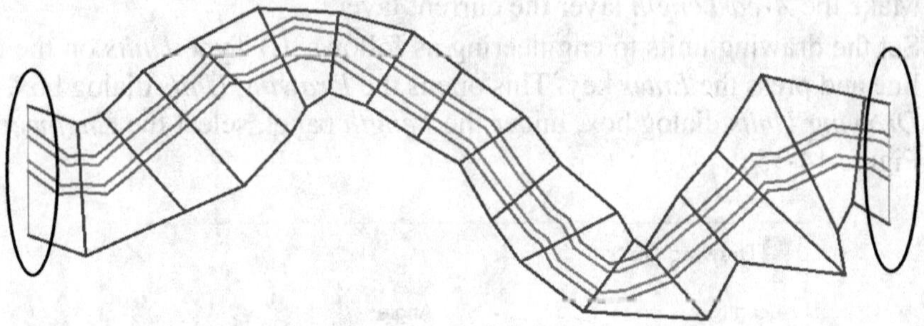

Figure 14-13

11. <u>Display the channel, bankfull, and floodplains</u>
    - Turn on the *Channel_Main, Channel_BF*, and *Channel_FP* layers, Figure 14-13. Turn *Off* the other layers.

12. <u>Hatch:</u> *Do not forget to create associative and annotative hatches.*
    - If necessary, extend the main channel and the bankfull to the edge of the contour map.
    - Make the *Channel_Main_Hatch* layer to be the current layer. Draw a closed boundary for the main channel to be hatched.
    - Activate the *Hatch* command and hatch the main channel. Use *MUDST* and 0.1 for the hatch pattern and the scale, respectively, Figure 14-14.
    - Make the *Channel_BF_Hatch* layer to be the current layer. Draw a closed boundary for the bankfull to be hatched.
    - Activate the *Hatch* command and hatch the bankfull channel. Use *GRAVEL* and 0.2 for the hatch pattern and the scale, respectively, Figure 14-14.
    - Make the *Channel_ FP_Hatch* layer to be the current layer. Draw a closed boundary for the floodplains to be hatched.
    - Hatching the floodplain independently helps in finding the area of the floodplains. Activate the *Hatch* command and hatch the floodplains. For hatching, click on one of the floodplains. Use *GRASS* and 0.05 for the hatch pattern and the scale, respectively, Figure 14-14. Repeat the process for the other floodplain.
    - Label the floodplains as shown in Figure 14-14.

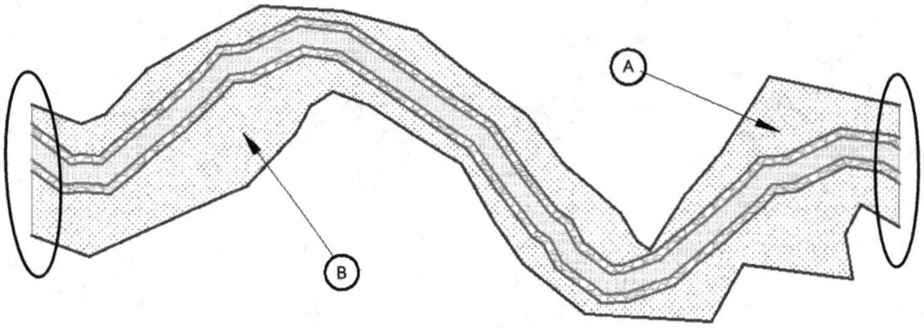

Figure 14-14

13. <u>Channel length</u>
- Make the *Area-Length* layer the current layer.
- Set the drawing units to engineering as follows. (i) Type *Units* on the command line and press the *Enter* key. This opens the *Drawing Units* dialog box. (ii) In the *Drawing Units* dialog box, under the *Length* panel, select the *Engineering* units, Figure 14-15a.

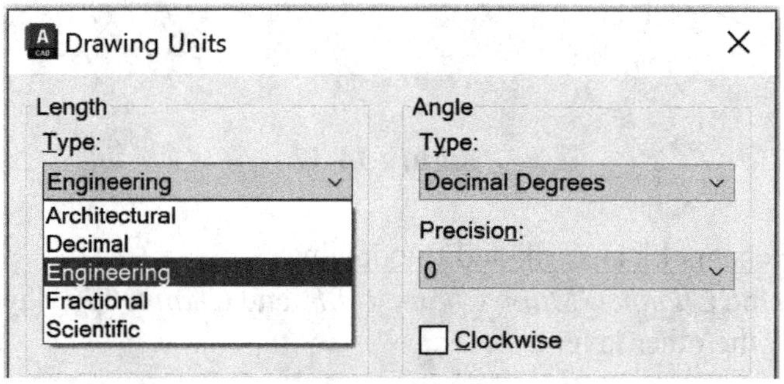

Figure 14-15a

- Find the length of the channel's centerline in feet using one of the following two techniques.

(a) Using the *Property* palette
- o The easiest and most efficient method is the property palette.
- o Select the centerline of the channel and open its property palette, Figure 14-15b.
- o The last entry in the *Geometry* panel is the length of the channel.

(b) Using the *Inquiry* command
- o The lengthy method!
- o From the *Home* tab and *Utilities* panel, expand the *Measure* drop-down menu and select the *Distance* (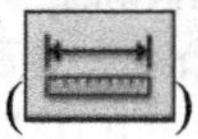) tool.
- o Follow the prompts.

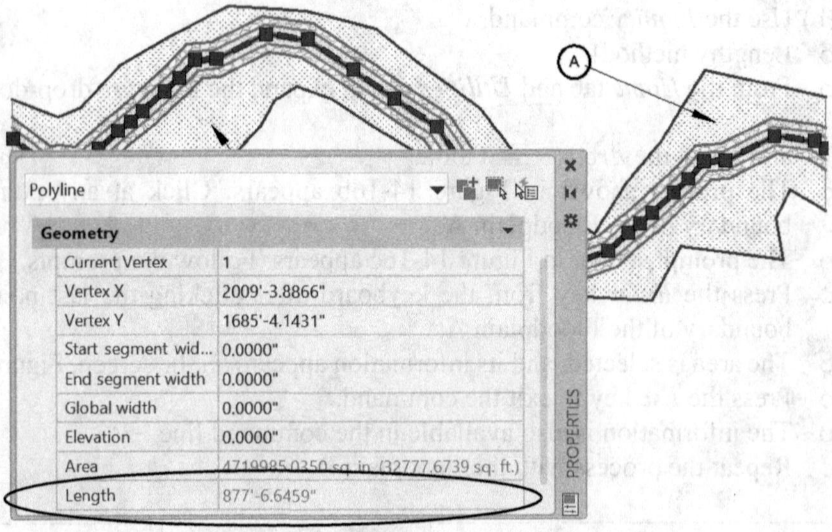

Figure 14-15b

14. Floodplains area

- Make the *Area-Length* layer to be the current layer.
- Find the area of the floodplains in acres.
- The area of the floodplains can be obtained using one of the following two techniques.

(a) Using the *Property* palette

- o Select the hatch of the floodplain labeled as A and open its property palette, Figure 14-16a.
- o The second entry in the *Geometry* panel is the area of the floodplain A.
- o Similarly, find the area of the floodplain labeled as B.

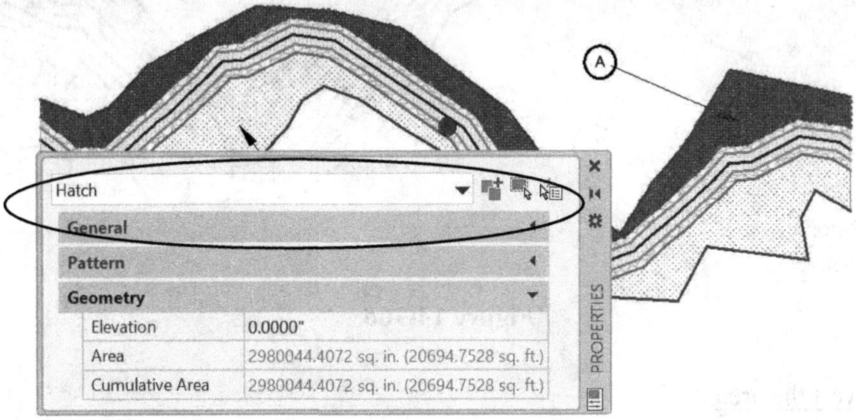

Figure 14-16a

(b) Use the *Inquiry* command.
- Lengthy method!
- From the *Home* tab and *Utilities* panel, expand the *Measure* drop-down menu and select the *Area* () tool.
- The prompt shown in Figure 14-16b appears. Click at any point on the boundary of the Floodplain A.
- The prompt shown in Figure 14-16c appears. Follow the prompts.
- Press the *Enter* key from the keyboard after clicking the last point on the boundary of the Floodplain A.
- The area is selected, and its information appears on the screen, Figure 14-16d.
- Press the *Esc* key to exit the command.
- The information is also available in the command line.
- Repeat the process with the floodplain B.

Figure 14-16b

Figure 14-16c

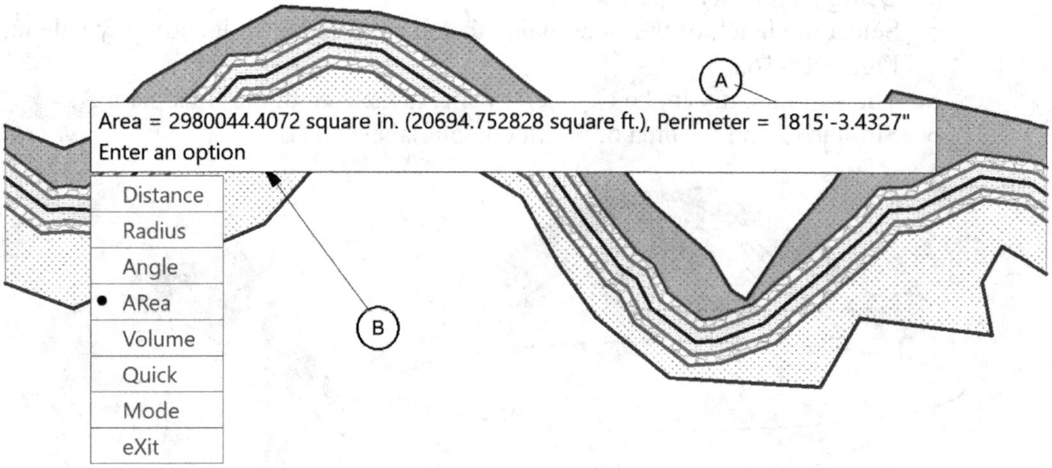

Figure 14-16d

15. <u>Convert the areas</u>
- Convert the areas into acres using the conversion factor of 1 Acres = 43560 sq. ft.

16. Display lengths and areas
    - Display the length of the channel in feet and areas of the floodplains in acres.
    - Either create three text boxes to show the length and the areas in acres on the drawing or create two tables to show the length in one table and areas in the other table. The example creates two tables, Figure 14-17.

17. Insert Template file
    - Finally, insert the landscape layout from the template file labeled as "*My_acad_Landscape.dwt*".
    - Set the viewport scale to 1/72" = 1'-0".
    - Lock the viewport.
    - Update the Title block.
    - The resultant drawing in the layout is shown in Figure 14-17.

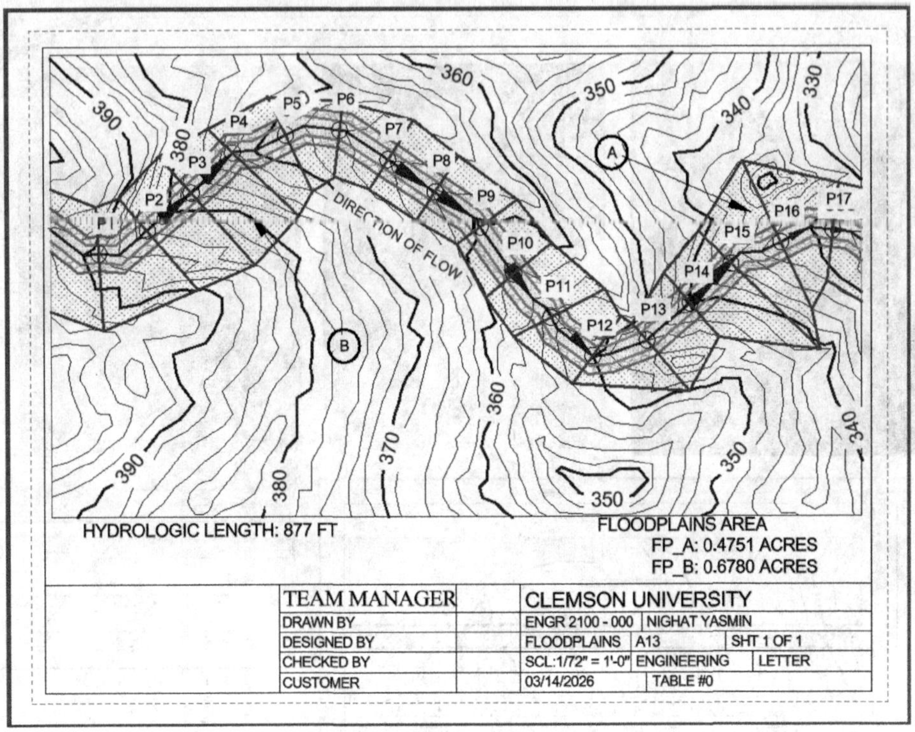

Figure 14-17

Notes:

15. Road Design

15.1. Learning Objectives

After completing this chapter, the students will show proficiency in the following areas:

- Basics of plan, profile, and cross-section of a road
- Drawing plan, profile, and cross-sections using AutoCAD

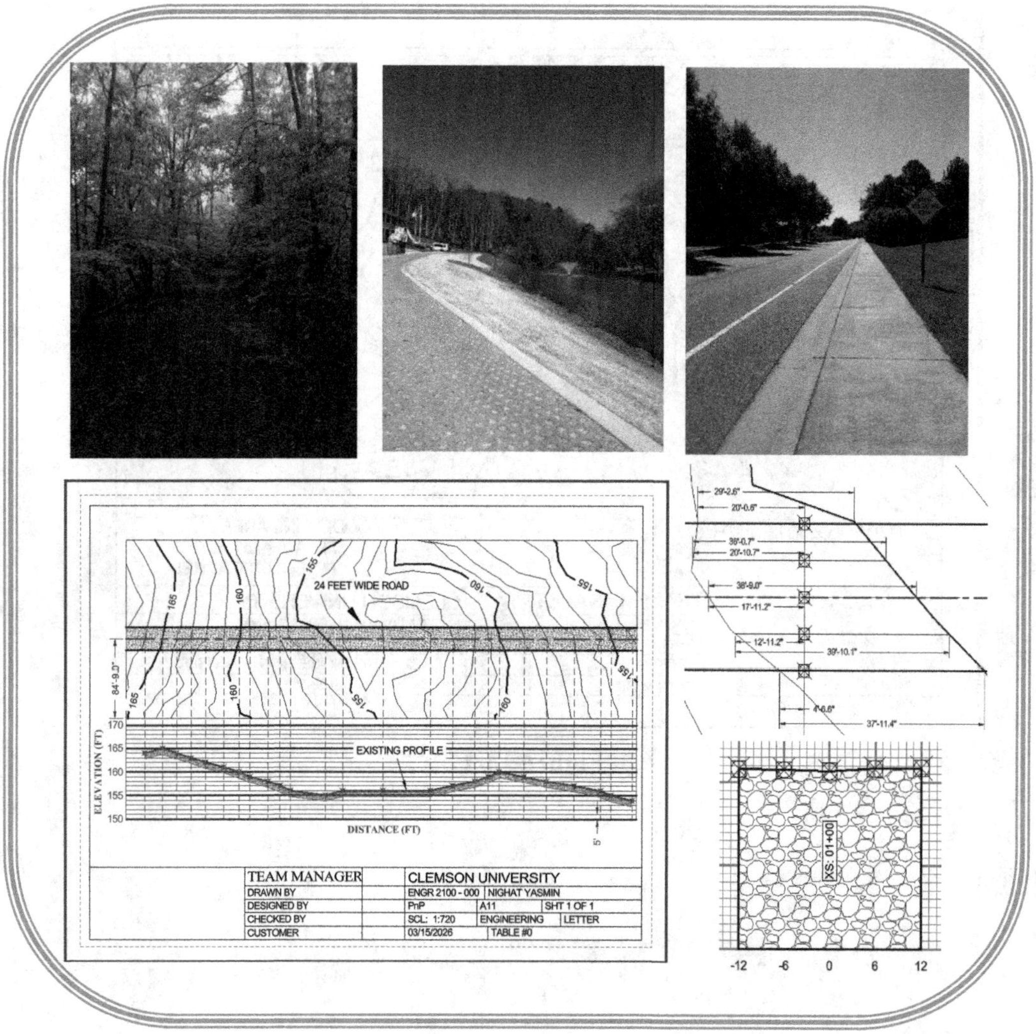

15.2. Introduction

Humans have been using many different modes of transportation on land, from horseback to automobiles (car, bus, truck, etc.). One common feature among these modes is the road. A road can be as simple as a walking trail to a several lanes paved road. Road design is a complicated process. It depends on several factors. Some of the factors are listed here: location of the road, types of vehicles using the road, geometric design, drainage system, and parking facilities. The road location factor is further subdivided into the land topography, soil characteristics, and environmental effects. Once the decision for the road location is made, the area is surveyed, and various drawings are prepared. The focus of this chapter is two of the major drawings: (i) the plan and profile and (ii) the cross-sections drawings.

15.3. Plan And Profile

The plan and profile drawing is commonly known as the PnP drawing. It is a two-view drawing. It is divided into two parts, Figure 15-1. The upper half always displays the plan view (and the contour map), and the lower half displays the profile. The PnP drawing is also an important drawing for most of the civil engineering projects, such as water and sewer pipelines, storm drainage system, curbs, and sidewalk construction.

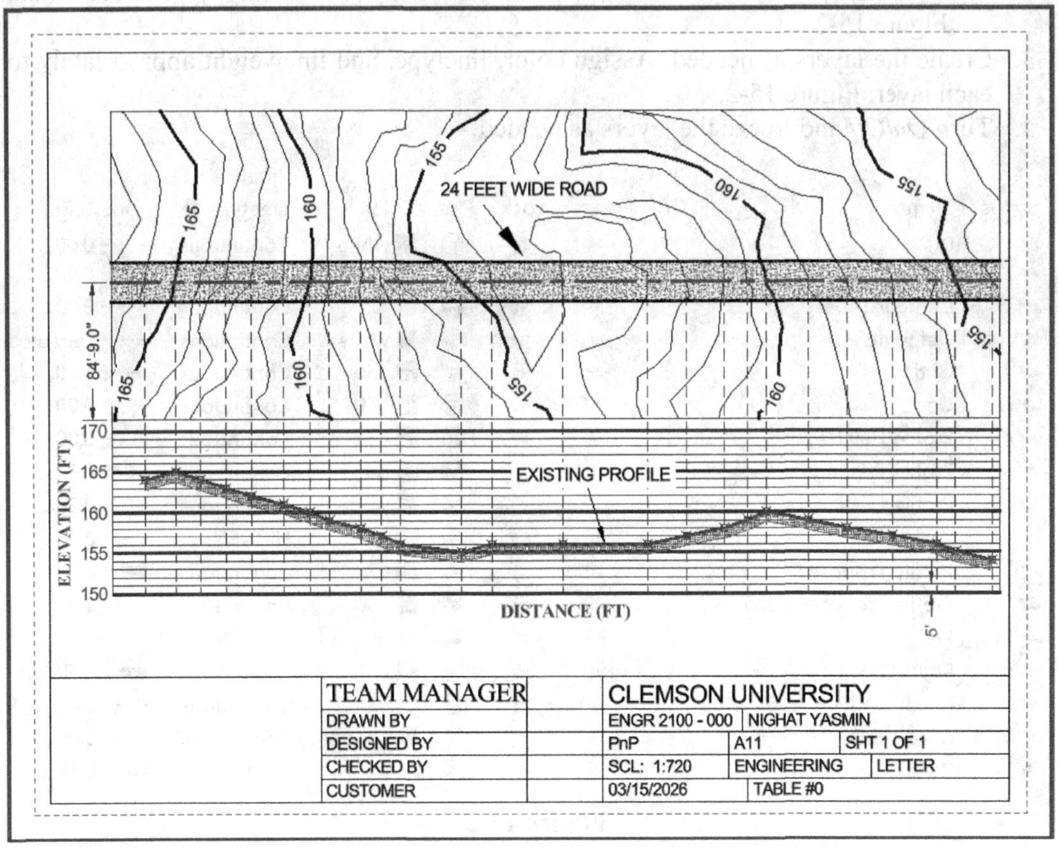

Figure 15-1

15.3.1. Plan

The plan view represents the area as seen from the top or a birds-eye-view. A plan view contains all the necessary information for road construction. The upper half of the Figure 15-1 shows the plan of a road.

15.3.2. Profile

The profile is the representation of the natural ground. It is defined as a display of the elevation of a set of equidistant points along a continuous line, for example, the centerline of a road. It is represented as a graph of elevation with respect to the distance along the centerline. The elevation is represented on the y-axis and the distance along the centerline is shown on the x-axis. The lower half of Figure 15-1 shows the profile of the centerline of the road.

15.4. Draw Road Plan Using AutoCAD

This section provides step-by-step instructions to create a plan of the proposed road.

1. Launch AutoCAD 2027.
2. Contour map
   - Open a previously created or downloaded (*RoadDesign*) contour map, Figure 15-3.
3. Create the layers as needed. Assign color, linetype, and lineweight appropriately to each layer, Figure 15-2.
4. Turn *On/Off* and freeze the layers as needed.

Status	Name	On	Freeze	Lock	Plot	Color	Linetype	Lineweight
	0					white	Continuous	0.00...
	Contour					12	Continuous	0.00...
	Contour_Label					12	Continuous	0.00...
	Defpoints					white	Continuous	Default
	Grid1					150	Continuous	0.00...
	Grid2					150	Continuous	0.00...
	Profile-Hatch					43	Continuous	0.00...
	Profile_Existing					84	Continuous	0.60...
	Profile_Existing-Label					white	Continuous	0.00...
	Profile_Points					11	HIDDEN	0.00...
	Profile_Proposed					12	Continuous	0.60...
	Profile_Proposed-Label					250	Continuous	0.00...
	Proj					magenta	HIDDEN	0.00...
✓	Road-CL					red	CENTER	0.50...
	Road-Hatch					62	Continuous	0.00...
	Road-Label					164	Continuous	0.00...
	Road-Plan					24	Continuous	0.50...

Figure 15-2

5. Add label to the contour map
   - Make the *Contour-Label* layer to be the current layer.
   - Label the index contour using the *Annotative Text* and the *Background Mask* commands, Figure 15-3. Set the annotative text height to be 0.12 inches.

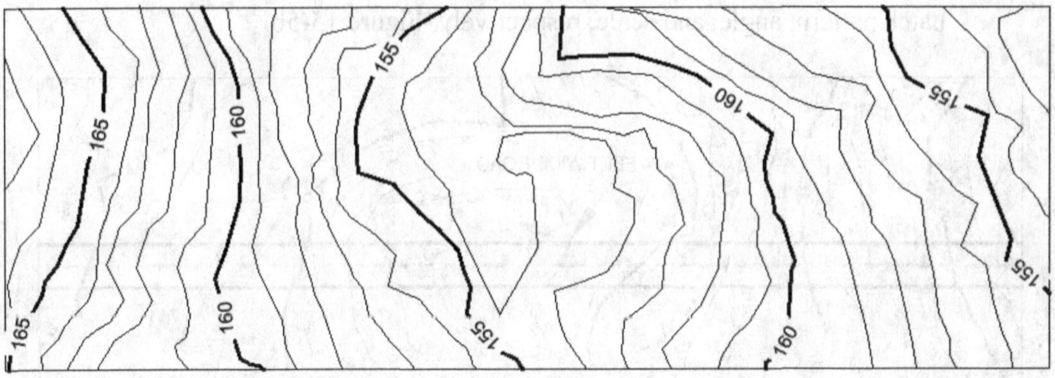

Figure 15-3

6. Centerline
   - Make the *Road-CL* layer to be the current layer.
   - Draw the centerline of the road, Figure 15-4. The centerline of the road is 84'-9" above the lower edge of the counter map.
   - Make the *Road-Dim* layer to be the current layer.
   - Add the dimensions to the centerline of the road.

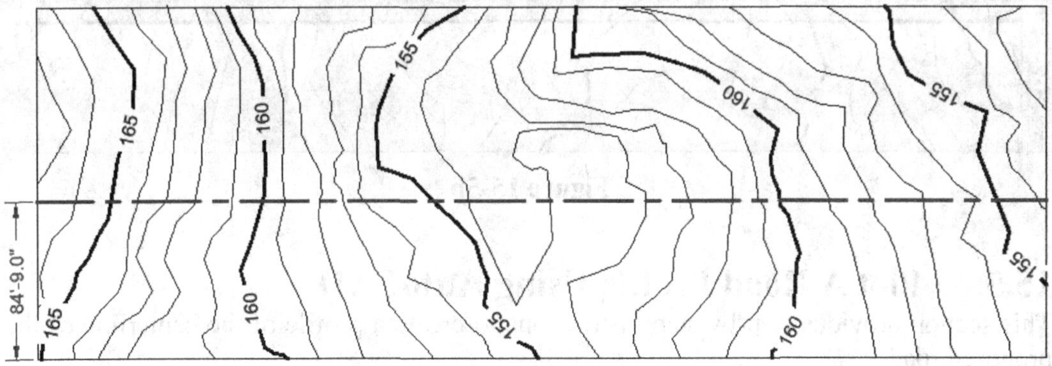

Figure 15-4

7. Road plan
   - Make the *Road-Plan* layer to be the current layer.
   - The road is 24ft wide and the road plan is shown in Figure 15-5a.
     - Activate the *Offset* command. Set the offset distance to 12ft.
     - Create an offset of the centerline on either side of the centerline.
     - Move the offsets to the *Road-Plan* layer.

- Make the *Road-Label* layer to be the current layer.
- Add the road label, Figure 15-5a. The annotative text height is 0.125 inches.

- Make the *Road-Hatch* layer to be the current layer.
- Add the annotative hatch to the road plan. Use AR-CONC, 0, and 0.01 for the hatch pattern, angle, and scale, respectively, Figure 15-5b.

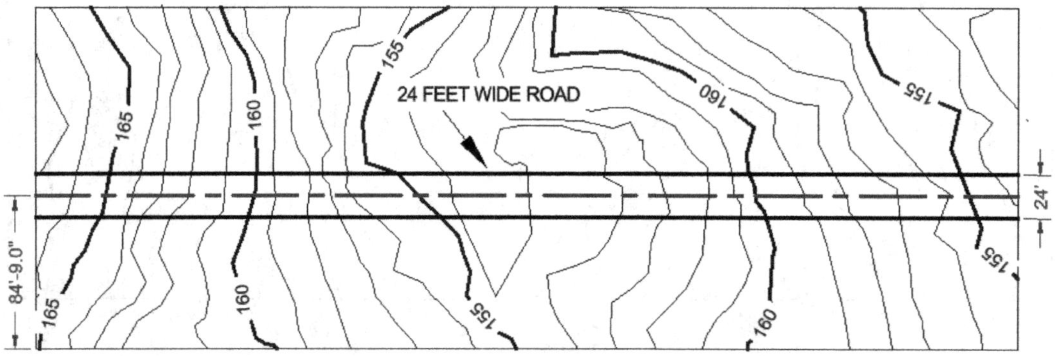

Figure 15-5a

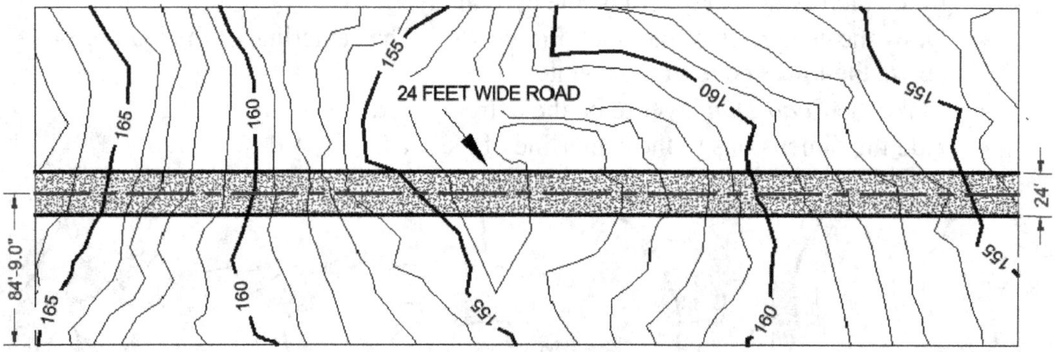

Figure 15-5b

15.5. Plot A Road Profile Using AutoCAD

This section provides step-by-step instructions to create a profile of the centerline of the proposed road.

1. <u>Draw the grid</u>
   - Make the *Grid1* layer to be the current layer. Generally, the grid color is light blue, light green, or light orange.
   - Draw two vertical lines 107ft long originating at the lower corners of the contour map, Figure 15-6a. These lines are highlighted by displaying their grip points.
   - Draw a horizontal line (the length of the line is equal to the width of the counter map) at the lower end of the lines drawn in previous step, Figure 15-6a.

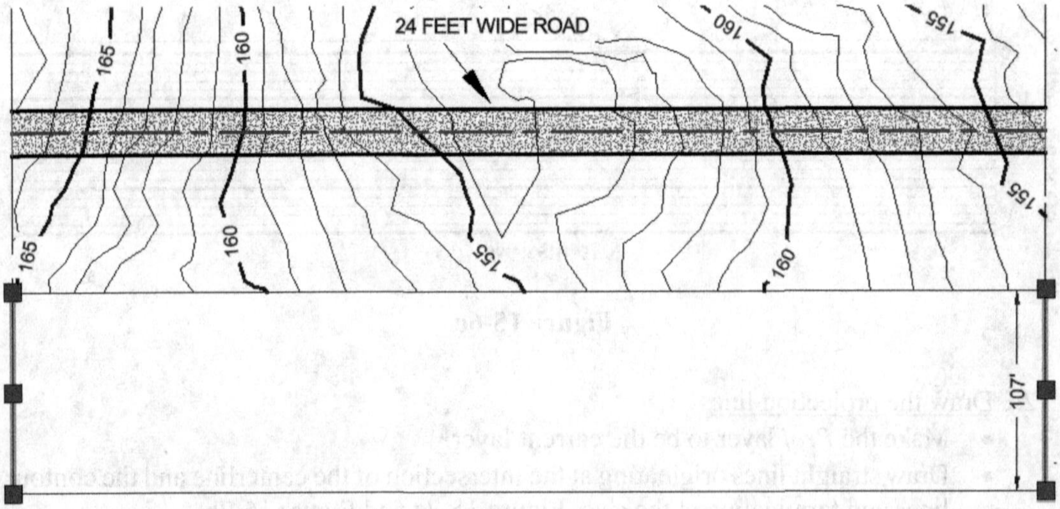

Figure 15-6a

- Use the *Array* command to draw the grid. Activate the *Array* command and create a rectangular array of the horizontal line. The array contains 20 rows with row spacing of 5 and the number of columns is set to 1, in Figure 15-6b.
  Note: Typically, grid row spacing matches the contour interval, but it can be increased to improve profile visibility. In this example, the row spacing is set to 5 feet to enhance the visual presentation, providing clearer differentiation between profile features and improving overall readability.
- Use the *Explode* command to break the array.
- Change the line weight of every fifth row, Figure 15-6c.
- Add the labels as shown in Figure 15-6c. The minimum elevation on the grid is less than the minimum elevation of the contour lines intersecting the centerline; and the maximum elevation on the grid is greater than the maximum elevation of the contour lines intersecting the centerline.

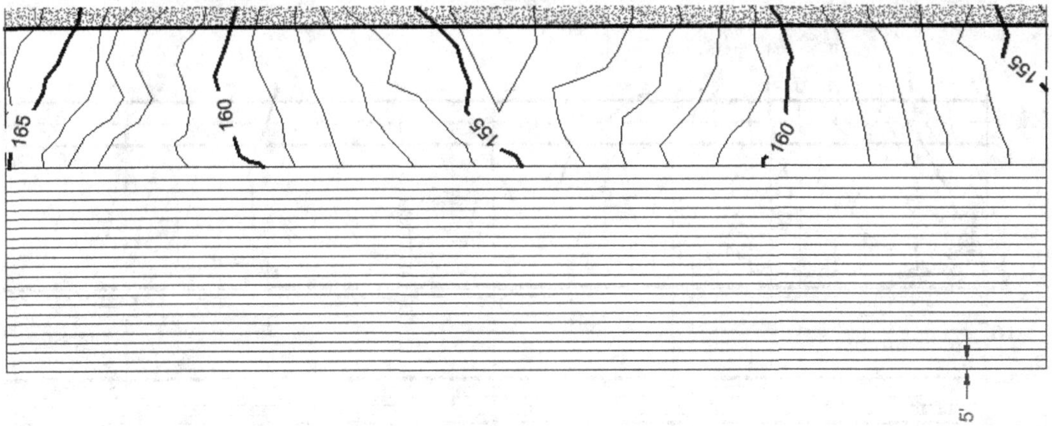

Figure 15-6b

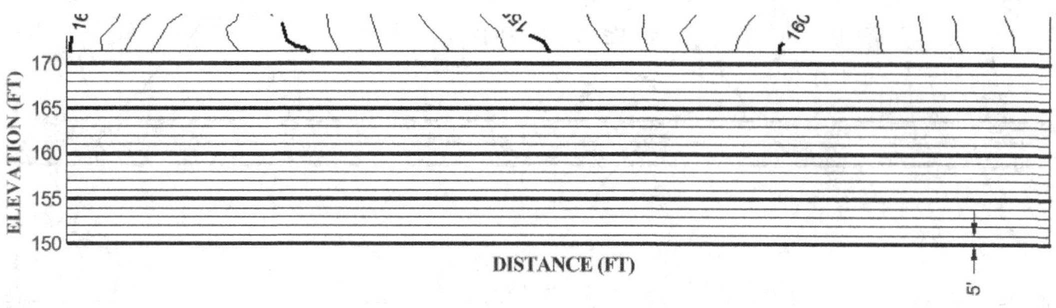

Figure 15-6c

2. Draw the projection line
   - Make the *Proj* layer to be the current layer.
   - Draw straight lines originating at the intersection of the centerline and the contour lines and terminating at the grid, Figure 15-7a and Figure 15-7b.
   - Set the Linetype scale of the projection lines appropriately to match the appearance in Figure 15-7a. In current example, Linetype scale is set to 0.5.

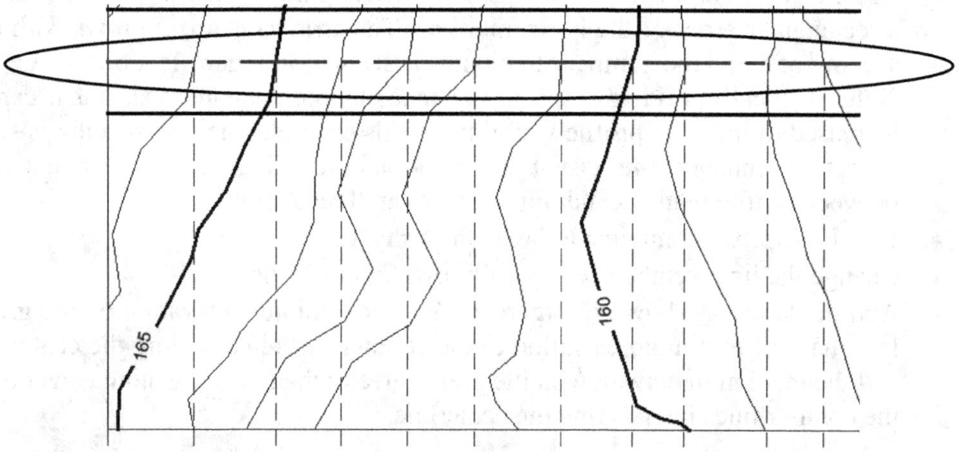

Figure 15-7a

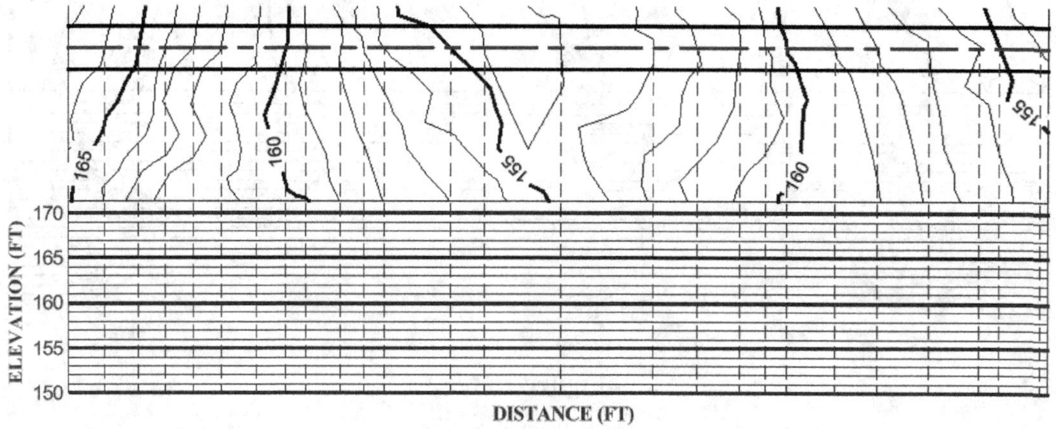

Figure 15-7b

3. Plot the elevation on the grid
    - Make the *Profile-Point* layer to be the current layer.
    - From the *Home* tab and expanded *Utilities* panel, select the *Point Style*... to open the *Point Style* dialog box, Figure 15-8a.
    - Change point style and size, Figure 15-8a. The dialog box shows the point size as 4'. However, the input to the dialog box is always in inches - that is, the input value should be 48.

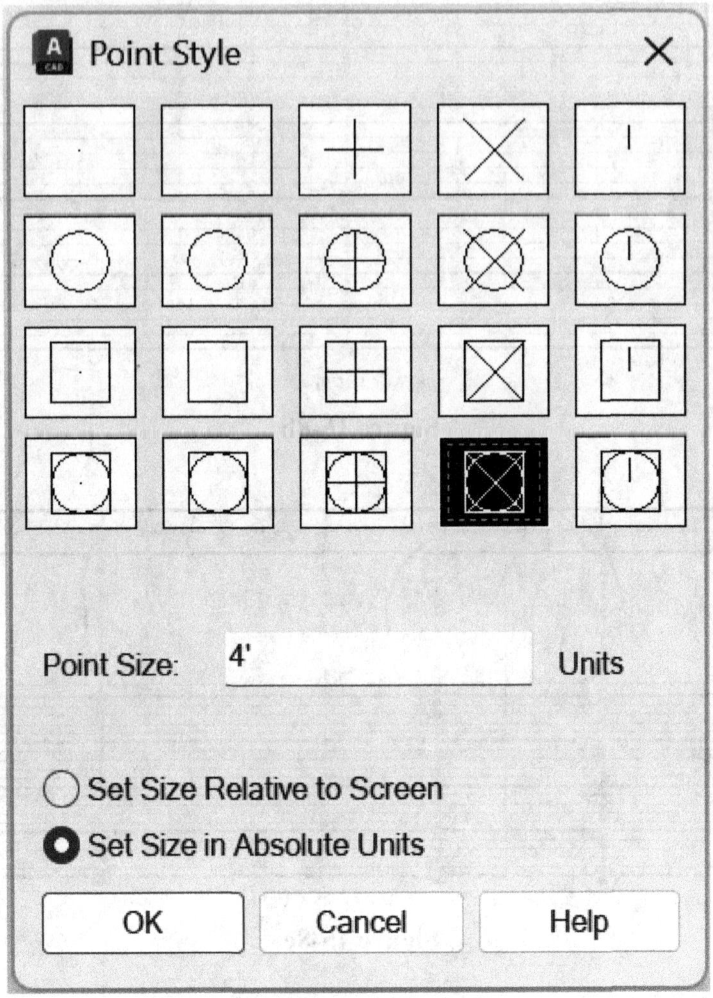

Figure 15-8a

- Figure 15-8b shows the point drawn for the project line for the index contour of 160. On the profile's grid, draw a point on this projection line at the elevation of 160 feet.
- Repeat the process for every index contour line, Figure 15-8c.
- Now, repeat the process for the other projection lines and Figure 15-8c.

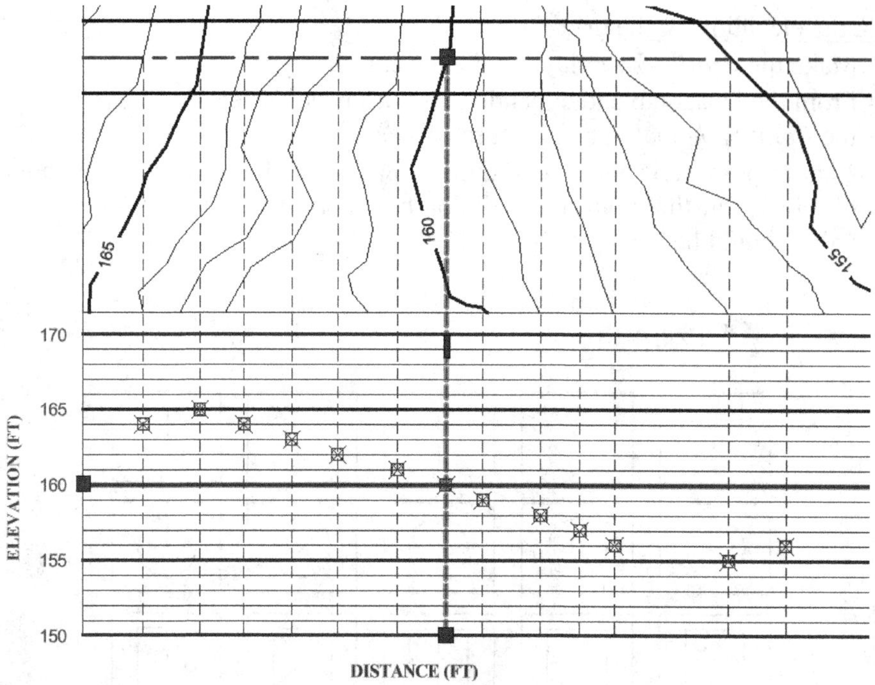

Figure 15-8b

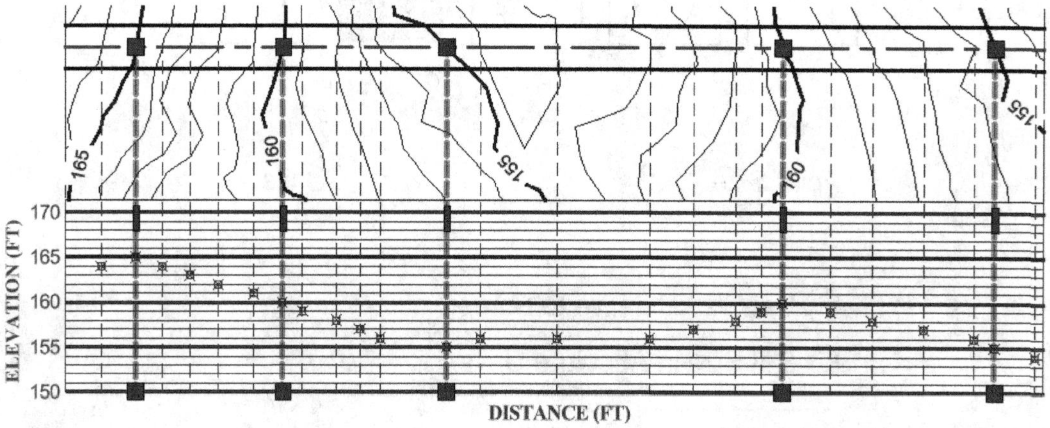

Figure 15-8c

4. Plot the existing profile
   - Make the *Profile-Existing* layer to be the current layer.
   - To create the profile, activate the *Polyline* command and connect the profile points, Figure 15-9. This profile is known as the existing profile or the ground line.
5. Add the label to the existing profile
   - Make the *Profile-Existing_Label* layer to be the current layer.
   - Using the *Annotative Text*, *background Mask* and *qleader* commands, add label to the profile, Figure 15-9. The annotative text height is 0.125 inches.

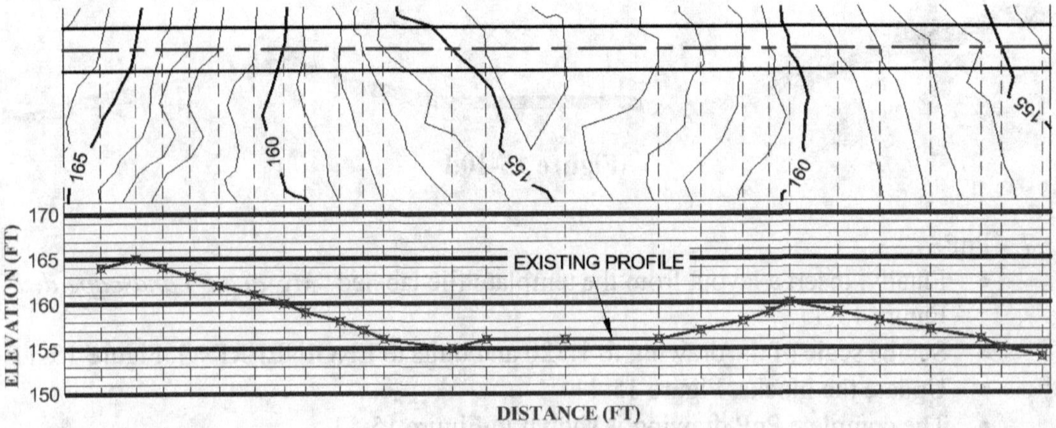

Figure 15-9

6. <u>Hatch the existing profile</u>
   - Make the *Profile-Hatch* layer to be the current layer.
   - Turn *Off* the grid and projection layers.
   - Using an *Offset* command, create an offset of the existing profile with the offset distance of 6'-0", Figure 15-10a.
   - Move the offset to the hatch layer, Figure 15-10b.
   - Connect the ends of the profile using small lines, Figure 15-10c.
   - Activate the *Hatch* command.
   - Add associative and annotative hatch; set the pattern to *EARTH*, angle to 0, and scale to 0.25, Figure 15-10d.

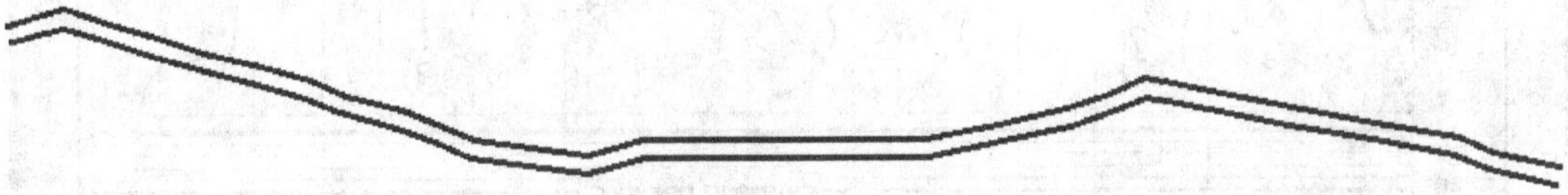

Figure 15-10a

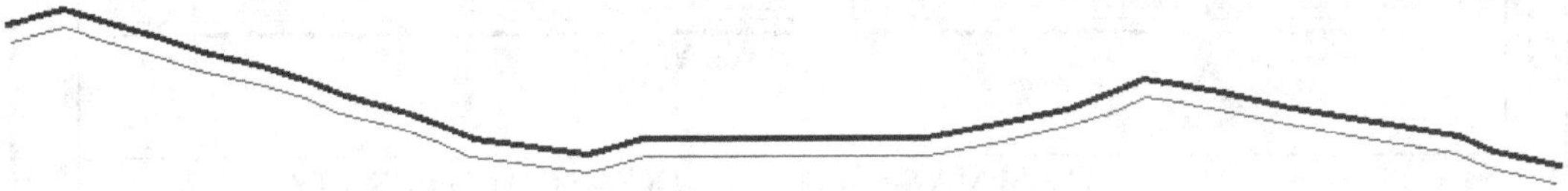

Figure 15-10b

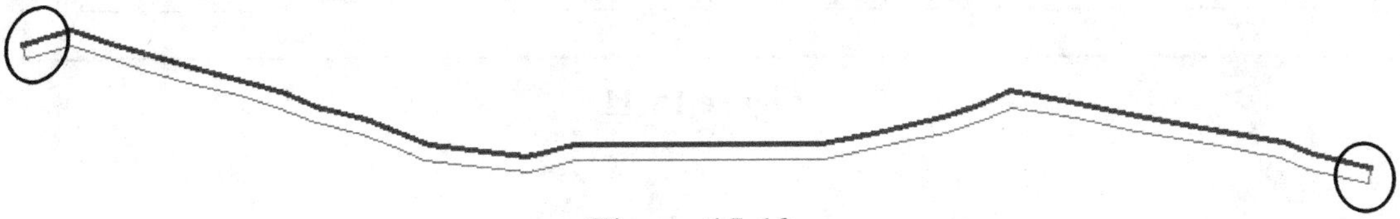

Figure 15-10c

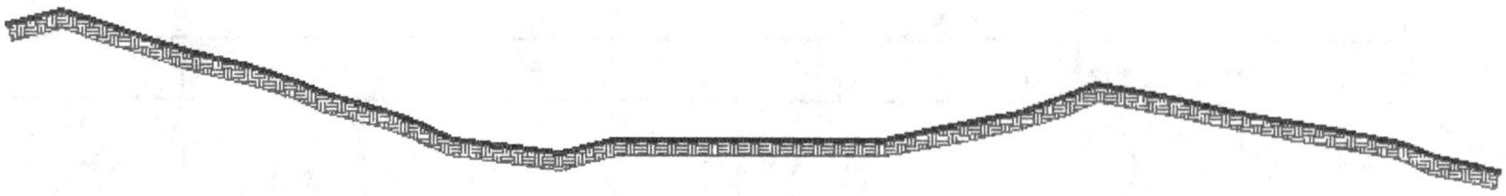

Figure 15-10d

7. PnP
   - Finally, insert a layout from the template file labeled "*My_acad_Landscape.dwt*" Figure 15-11.
   - Set the scale of the drawing to 1:720 and units to ENGINEERING, Figure 15-11.
   - Update the blocks, Figure 15-11.
   - The complete PnP drawing is shown in Figure 15-11.

8. Save the drawing
   - Save the drawing as *PnP.dwg*.

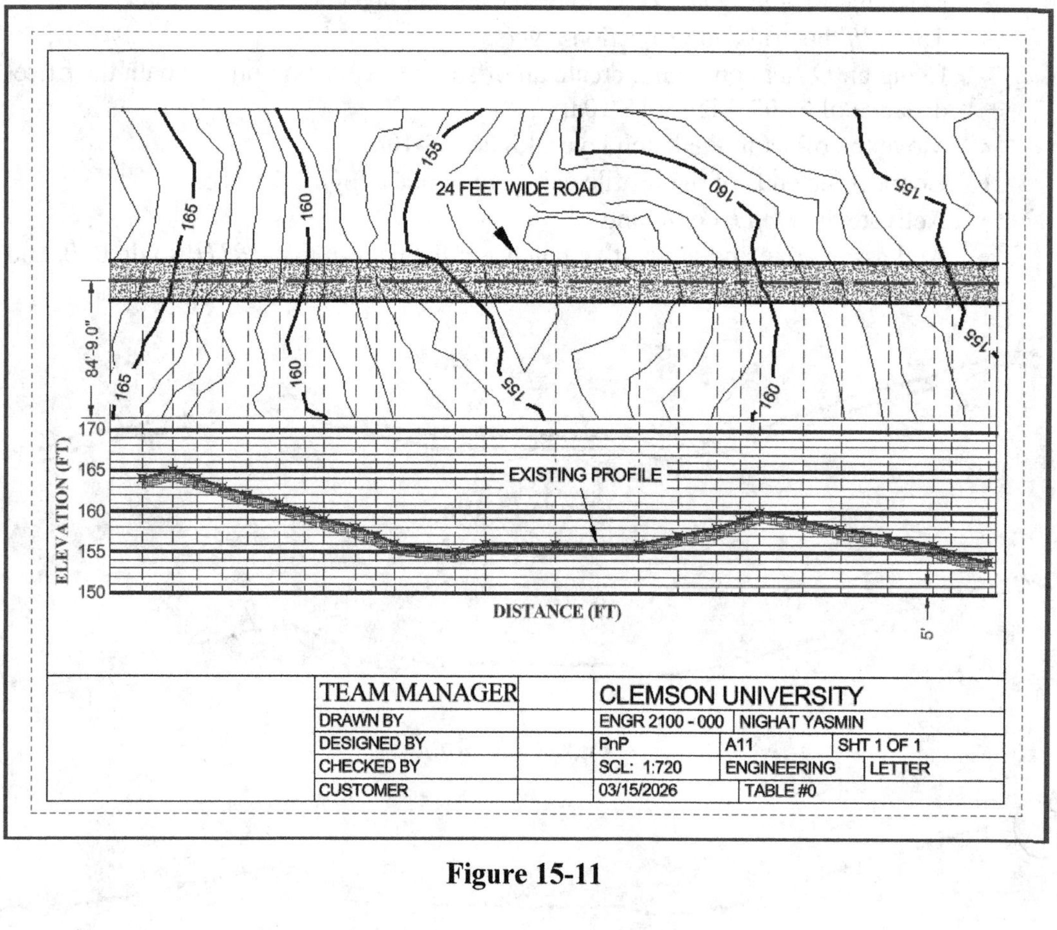

Figure 15-11

15.6. Cross-Section

A cross-section is defined as a display of the elevation of a set of equidistant points along a continuous line that runs perpendicular to the centerline. Usually, the sections are drawn at a regular interval, for example, at every station (and stations are 100' apart). The process for creating cross-sections is the same as for a profile. However, cross-sections are smaller than profiles. Generally, for cross-sections, both the existing and proposed shapes are drawn. For discussion purposes, only the existing shapes are drawn.

15.7. Draw A Cross-Section Using AutoCAD

This section assumes that the user has created the road plan shown in Figure 15-11. This section provides step-by-step instructions to create a cross-section of the centerline of the proposed road.

1. Launch AutoCAD 2027.
2. Open the drawing containing the road plan (*PnP.dwg*). Figure 15-12 shows the plan of the road.
3. Create the layers as needed. Assign color, linetype, and lineweight appropriately to each layer, Figure 15-13.
4. Turn *On*/*Off* and freeze the layers as needed.

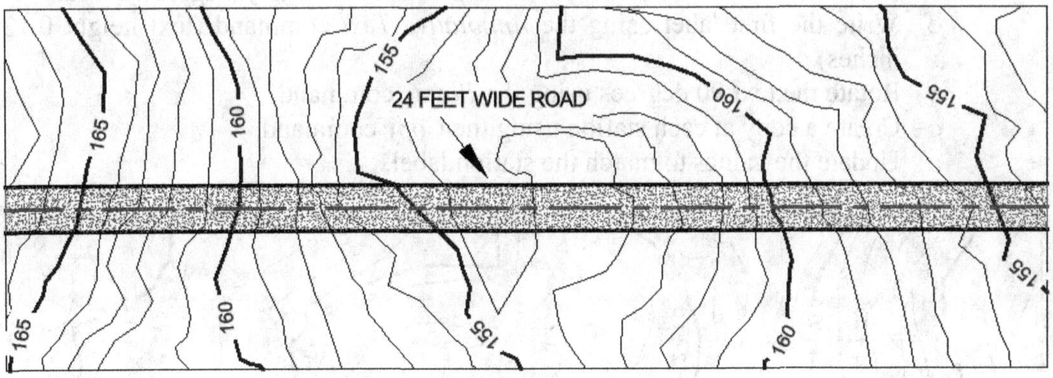

Figure 15-12

Status	Name	On	Freeze	VP Freeze	Lock	Plot	Color	Linetype	Lineweight
✓	Stations						172	Continuous	0.00...
	Stations-Dim						74	Continuous	0.00...
	Stations-Label						white	Continuous	0.00...
	XS-Dist						160	Continuous	0.00...
	XS-PT						white	Continuous	0.00...
	XS-Shape-Grid						140	Continuous	0.00...
	XS-Shape-Hatch						23	Continuous	0.00...
	XS-Shape-Label						white	Continuous	0.00...
	XS-Shape-LN						162	Continuous	0.50...
	XS-Shape-PT						164	Continuous	0.00...

Figure 15-13

5. Draw stations
   - Make the *Stations* layer to be the current layer.
   - Add the stations, Figure 15-14a using *Measure* command; and change the point style and size (*Home* tab → *Utilities* panel→ *Point Style*).

6. Dimension the stations
   - Make the *Station-Dim* layer to be the current layer.
     - Add the dimensions to the stations, Figure 15-14a.

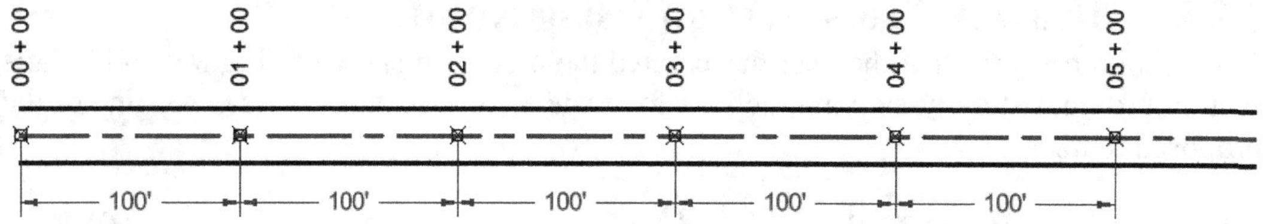

Figure 15-14a

7. Label the stations
   - Make the *Station-Label* layer to be the current layer.
     - The first station is at the left end, hence labeled *00 + 00*. The remaining stations are 100 feet apart, therefore labeled accordingly, Figure 15-14a.
     - Write the first label using the *Annotative Text* command (text height 0.12 inches).
     - Rotate the text 90 degrees using the *Rotate* command.
     - Create a copy at each station using the *Copy* command.
     - Update the values to match the station label.

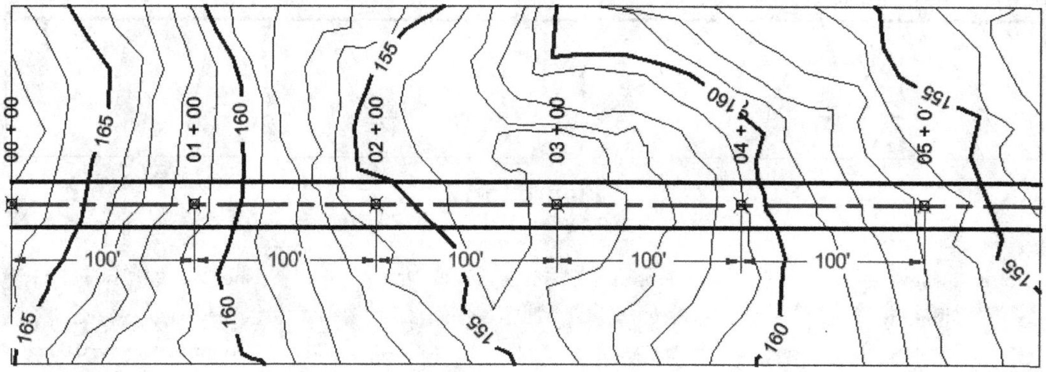

Figure 15-14b

8. Draw the section line perpendicular to the centerline at the selected station.
   - Make the *XS_PT* layer to be the current layer.
   - Turn *Off* the contour and contour labels layers.
   - In the example, the cross-section at *Station 01 + 00* is created.
   - Turn on the *Perpendicular* option in the object snap setting dialog box.

- Start a line at the centerline of the *Station 01 + 00* and move to the outer edge of the road, Figure 15-15a.
- Click at the perpendicular point. A perpendicular line is created from the centerline to the outer edge, Figure 15-15b.
- Repeat the process on the other side of the centerline or use the *Mirror* command. Figure 15-15c shows the perpendicular lines.
- Repeat the process at the other stations or use the *Copy* command.

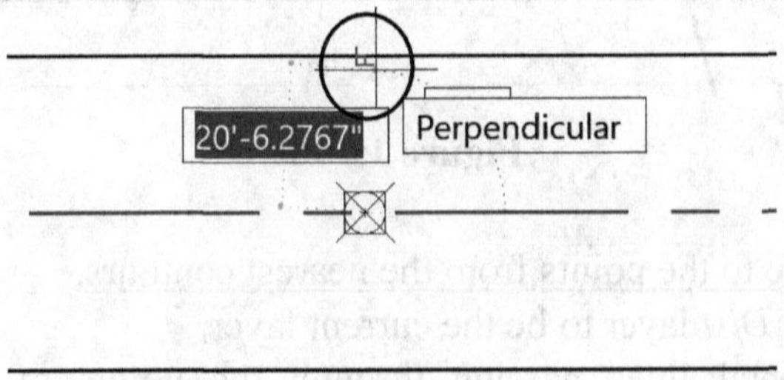

Figure 15-15a

9. Draw points on the perpendicular lines.
   - Make the *XS_PT* layer to be the current layer.
   - Draw four points, two on each line drawn in step #4 as shown in Figure 15-16a (two at the midpoints and two at the outer edges of the road).
   - Repeat the process at the other stations or use the *Copy* command, Figure 15-16b.
   - Details of Station 01+00 and 02+00 are shown in Figure 15-16c.

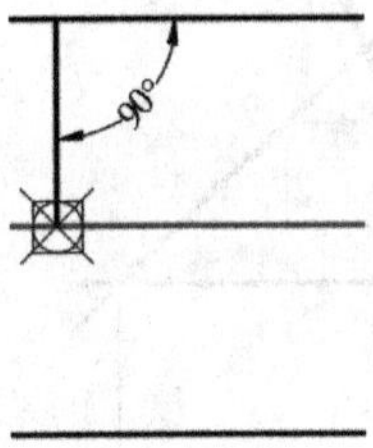

Figure 15-15b

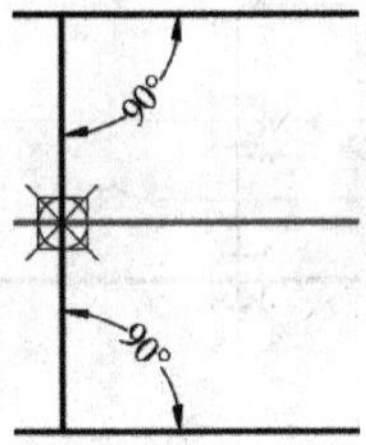

Figure 15-15c

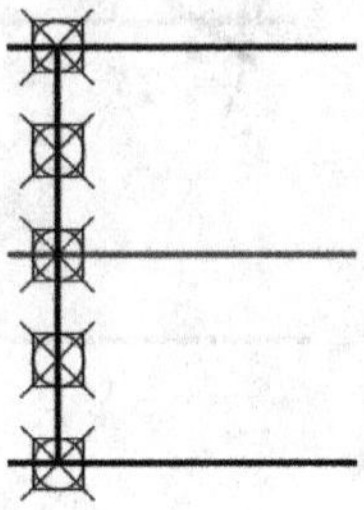

Figure 15-16a

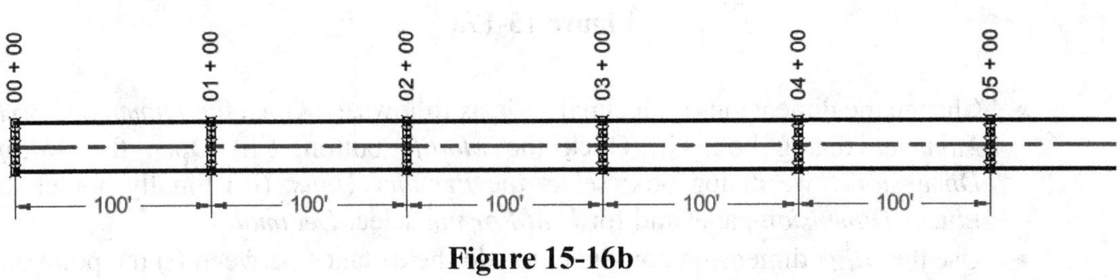

Figure 15-16b

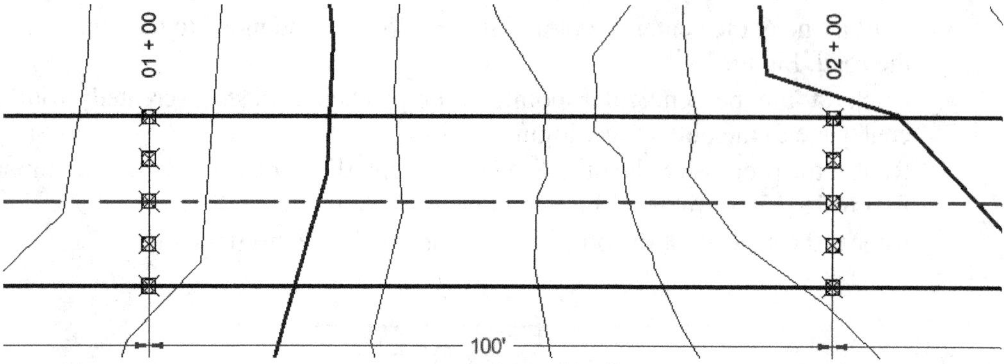

Figure 15-16c

10. Show the distance to the points from the nearest contours.
    - Make the *XS_Dist* layer to be the current layer.
    - Draw horizontal lines passing through the points of the previous points, originating and terminating at the two adjacent contour lines, Figure 15-17b.

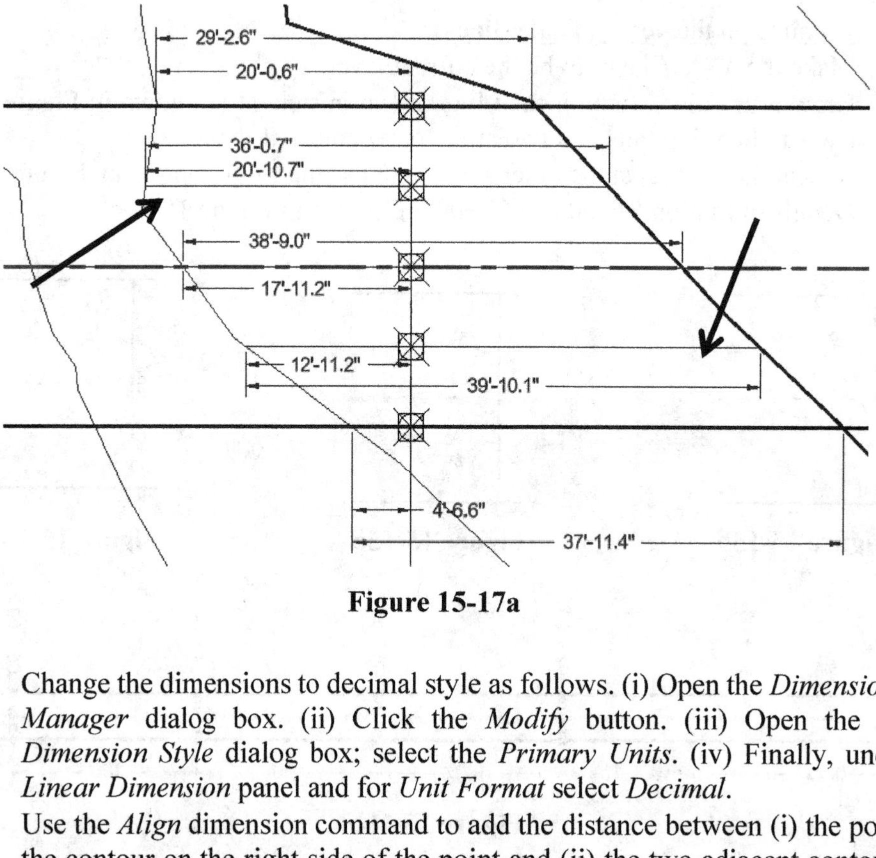

Figure 15-17a

- Change the dimensions to decimal style as follows. (i) Open the *Dimension Style Manager* dialog box. (ii) Click the *Modify* button. (iii) Open the *Modify Dimension Style* dialog box; select the *Primary Units*. (iv) Finally, under the *Linear Dimension* panel and for *Unit Format* select *Decimal*.
- Use the *Align* dimension command to add the distance between (i) the point and the contour on the right side of the point and (ii) the two adjacent contours one on each side of the point. Figure 15-17b shows the dimensions for Stations 01+00 and 02+00.
- The remaining stations are left for the readers.

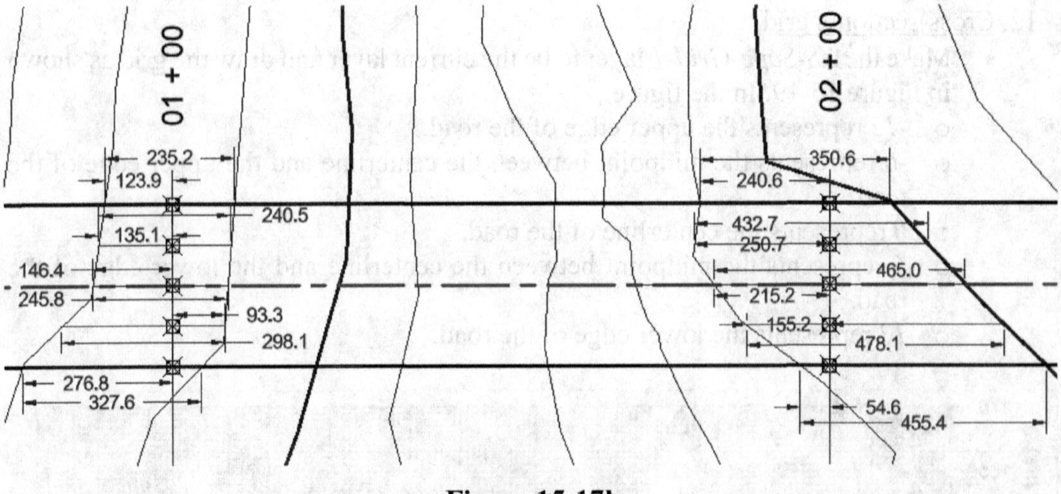

Figure 15-17b

11. Find the elevation of the cross-section points using interpolation.
   - Interpolation is not needed if a contour line passes through a station or if the contour lines on the left and right side of the station have the same value. Hence, skip this step.
   - If a contour line is not passing through a station and the point is not enclosed by the same contour, then find the elevation of the station using linear interpolation.
     - Let ***ep*** be the elevation of a point in question (unknown); ***e1*** and ***e2*** are the elevations of the contours on the left and right side of the point, respectively; and ***d12*** and ***d1p*** are the distance from Figure 15-18. Find the elevation of the station point (***ep***) using the formula: $d12/d1p = (e1 - e2) / (e1 - ep)$.
   - Find the elevation of all the stations.

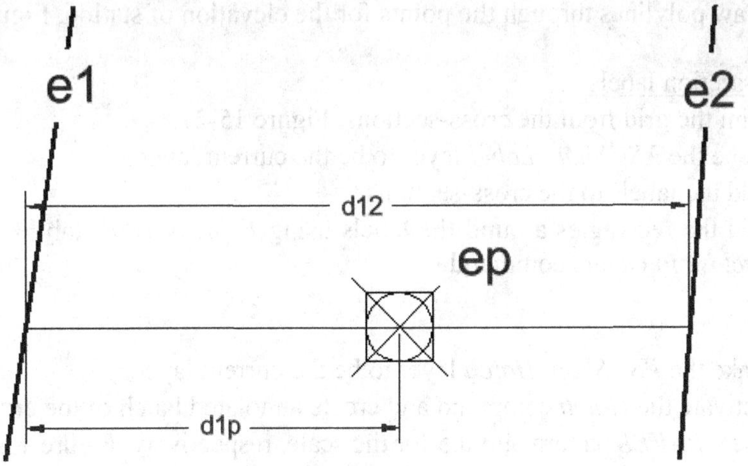

Figure 15-18

12. Cross-section's grid
   - Make the *XS-Sape-Grid-1* layer to be the current layer and draw the grid as shown in Figure 15-19. In the figure:
      - *-12* represents the upper edge of the road.
      - *-6* represents the midpoint between the centerline and the upper edge of the road.
      - *0* represents the centerline of the road.
      - *6* represents the midpoint between the centerline and the lower edge of the road.
      - *12* represents the lower edge of the road.

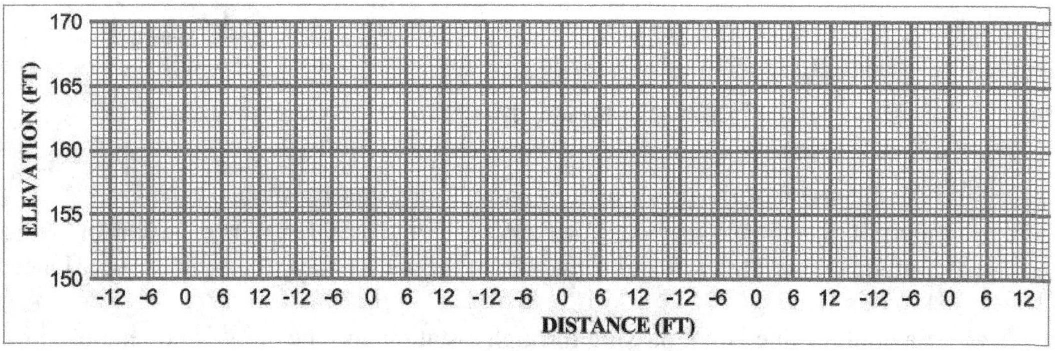

Figure 15-19

13. Cross-section drawing
   - Make the *XS_Shap_PT* layer to be the current layer.
   - Draw points for the elevation of stations across the centerline, Figure 15-20.
   - Make the *XS_ Shap_LN* layer to be the current layer.
   - Draw polylines through the points for the elevation of station, Figure 15-20.

14. Cross-section labels
   - Trim the grid from the cross-sections, Figure 15-21.
   - Make the *XS_ Shap_Label* layer to be the current layer.
   - Add the labels to the cross-sections.
   - Add the rectangles around the labels using *Express Tools* tab → *Text* panel → *Enclose in Object* command.

15. Hatch
   - Make the *XS_ Shap_Hatch* layer to be the current layer.
   - Activate the *Hatch* command and create annotated hatch of the cross-sections.
   - Use *GRAVEL* pattern and 0.5 for the scale, respectively, Figure 15-22.

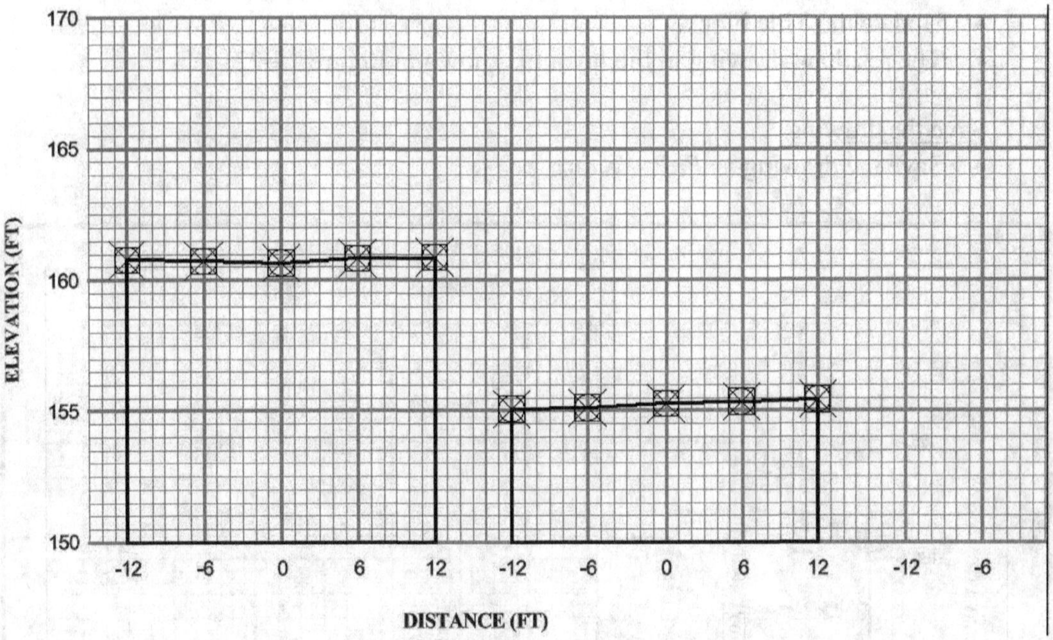

Figure 15-20

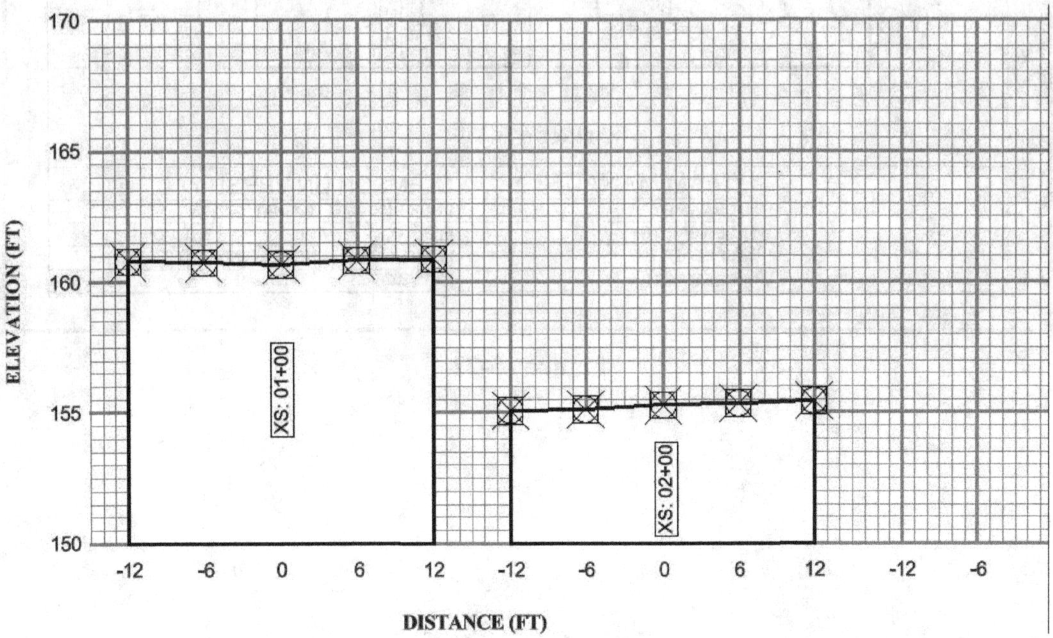

Figure 15-21

16. <u>Insert Template file</u>
   - Finally, insert a layout from the template file labeled "*My_acad_Landscape.dwt*".
   - Set the scale of the drawing to 1:100 and units to Engineering, Figure 15-22.
   - Lock the viewport.

- Update the Title block.
- The resultant drawing in the layout is shown in Figure 15-22.

17. Save the drawing
    - Save the drawing as *PnP_XS.dwg*.

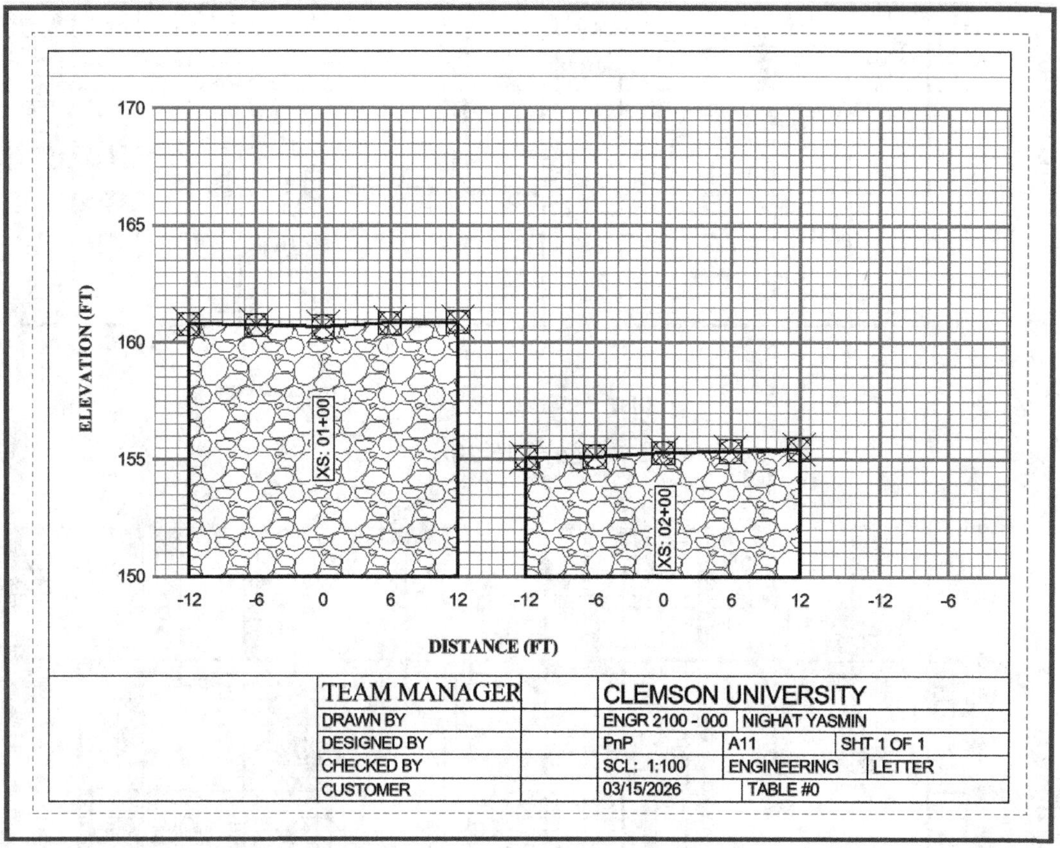

Figure 15-22

Notes:

16. Earthwork

16.1. Learning Objectives

After completing this chapter, the students will show proficiency in the following areas:

- Basics of earthwork (cut-fill) in a road design
- Delineate earthwork using AutoCAD

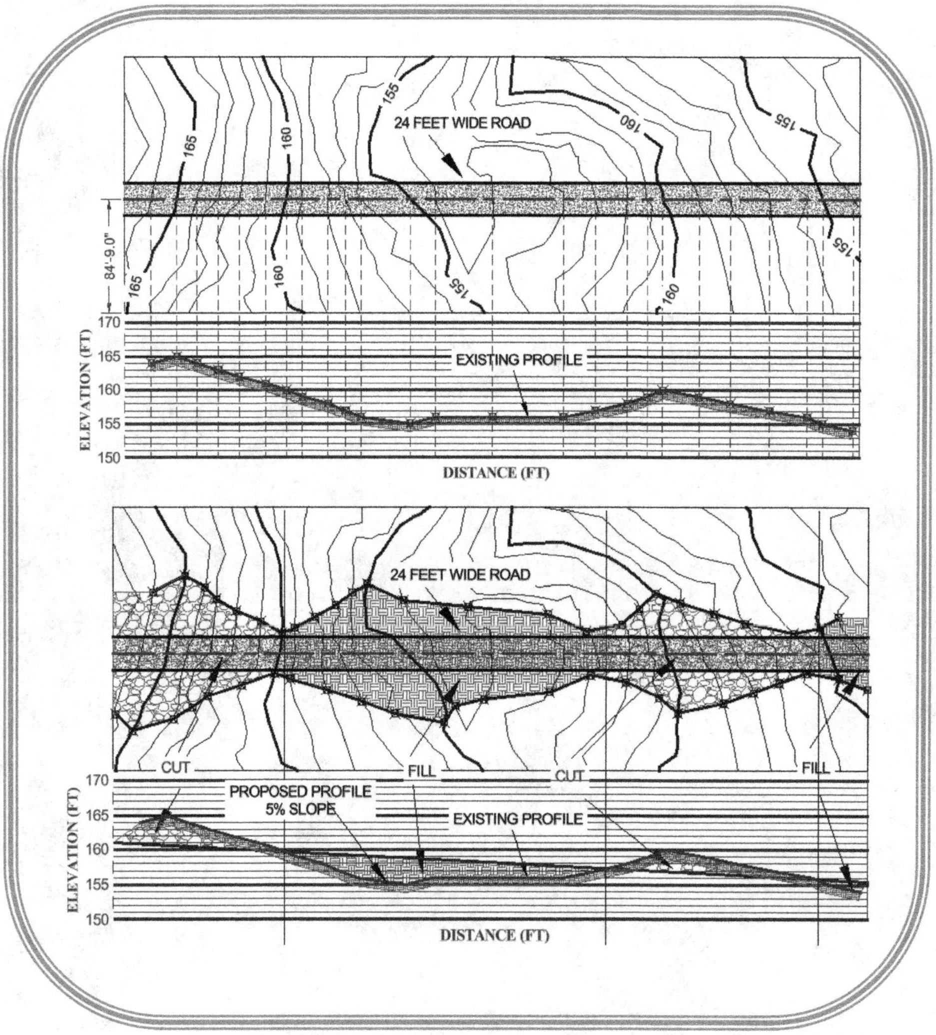

16.2. Introduction

Earthwork, also known as the cut and fill in road construction terminology, refers to the excavation and embankment of the earth. The volume of earthwork plays an important role in the selection of a road location because the cost of the road construction is greatly influenced by the earthwork. The construction cost can be reduced if the volume of cut is equal to the volume of the fill.

16.3. Earthwork

In the plan and profile drawing, the profile represents the natural ground. After developing the PnP, the proposed profile is added to the drawing. The slope of the proposed profile represents the elevation of the centerline of the proposed road.

16.3.1. Cut

If the existing profile is above the proposed profile, then the extra material between the two profiles represents the volume of excavation or cut, Figure 16-1.

16.3.2. Fill

If the existing profile is below the proposed profile, then the empty space between the two profiles represents the volume of embankment or fills, Figure 16-1.

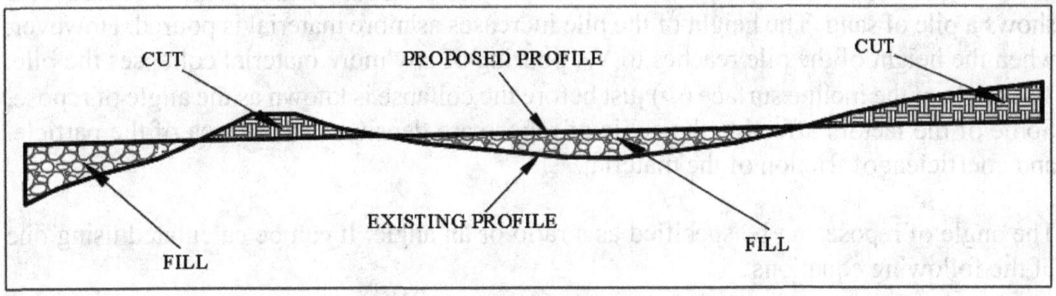

Figure 16-1

16.3.3. Location of a road

The volume of cut and fill greatly affects the cost of road construction. If the volume of cut is more than the volume of fill, then the extra material must be removed from the site. This increases the cost of the project. If the volume of fill is more than the volume of cut, then the extra material must be brought to the site. This increases the cost of the project, too. Generally, the road is located such that the volume of the cut is equal to the volume of fill. However, this is not possible in every road construction.

16.4. Slope

Slope of a line is defined as the ratio of change in altitude (ΔV_d) to the change in horizontal distance (ΔH_d). The slope is positive for an upward line (Figure 16-2a), whereas it is negative for a downward line (Figure 16-2b).

Slope can be specified as an angle or a percentage. It can be calculated using one of the following equations.

- $Slope\ (angle) = tan^{-1}(\Delta V_d / \Delta H_d)$
- $Slope\ (ratio) = (\Delta V_d / \Delta H_d) * 100$

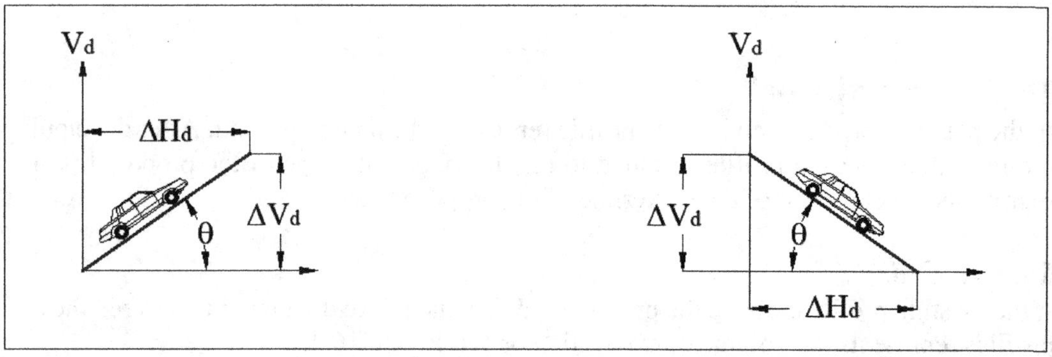

Figure 16-2a **Figure 16-2b**

16.5. Angle Of Repose

When a granular material is poured on a horizontal surface, it makes a pile. Figure 16-3 shows a pile of sand. The height of the pile increases as more material is poured. However, when the height of the pile reaches to V_d, pouring of any more material collapses the pile. The angle of the incline surface (Φ) just before the collapse is known as the angle of repose. Some of the factors affecting the angle of repose are density, surface area of the particle, and coefficient of friction of the material.

The angle of repose can be specified as a ratio or an angle. It can be calculated using one of the following equations.

- $\Phi\ (ratio) = H_d : V_d$
- $\Phi\ (angle) = tan^{-1}(\Delta V_d / \Delta H_d)$

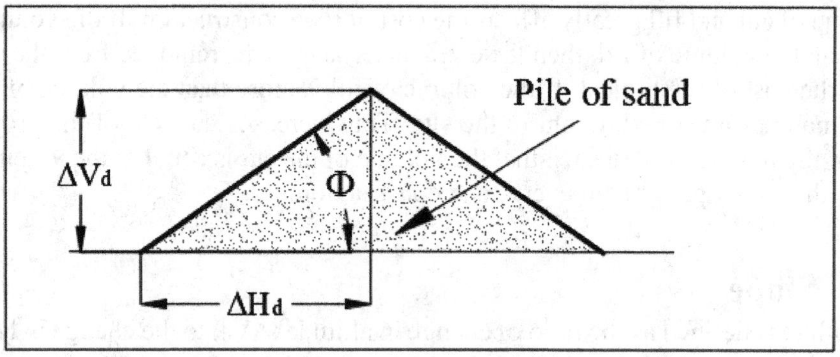

Figure 16-3

16.6. ROAD: Plan And Existing Profile

Create the plan and profile file following the steps from *Chapter 15* and save it as PnP.dwg.

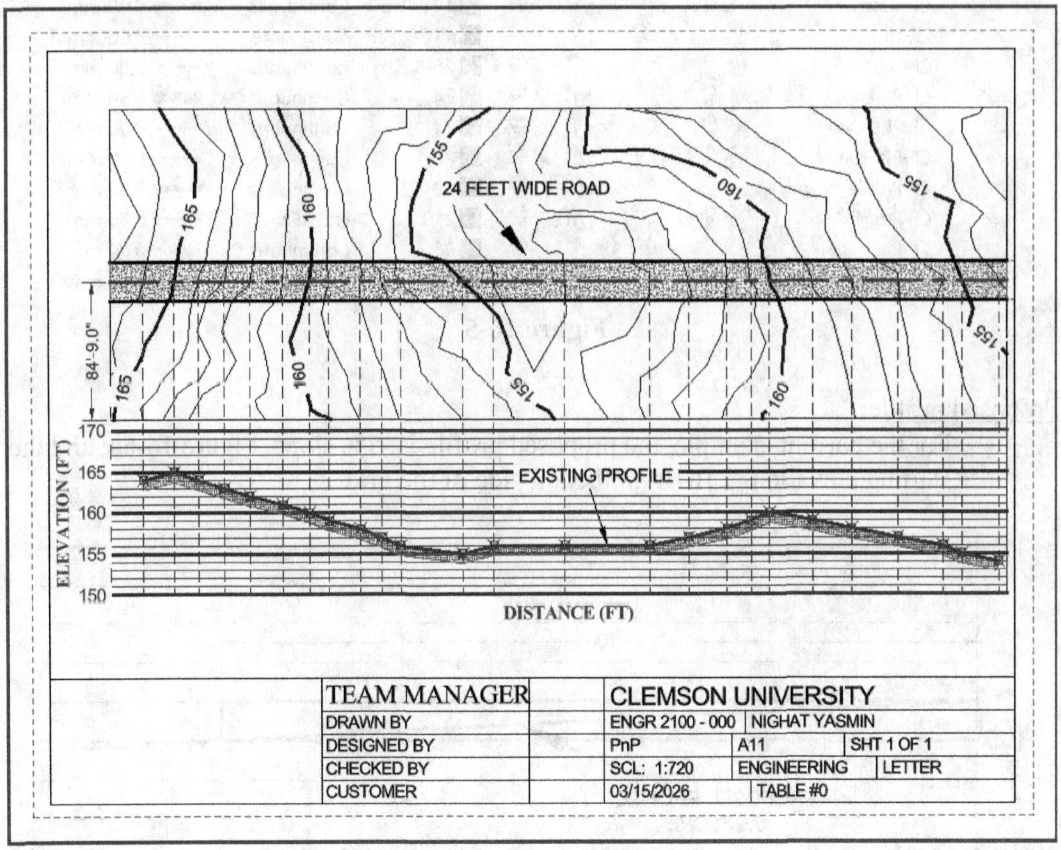

Figure 16-4

16.7. Proposed Profile Of A Road

It is clear from the existing profile of Figure 16-4 that with the current undulation of the road it will not be safe for the drivers and vehicles. Hence, it is very important to provide a safe slope to the road. The new slope is the proposed profile of the road. The proposed profile is also known as the grade line. The proposed profile depends on several factors such as soil condition, vehicle type, budget of the project, environmental issues, etc. This section assumed that the engineers have decided on the slope of the proposed profile. For the current example, the proposed profile is at a slope of +3% grade (that is, for every 100 feet horizontal distance, the road goes up by 3ft).

<u>Layers</u>:

- Create the layers as needed and assign color, linetype, and lineweight appropriately to each layer, or add the layer shown in Figure 16-5 to the profile drawing. **Before using a layer, make the desired layer current.**

Status	Name	On	Freeze	Lock	Plot	Color	Linetype	Lineweight
	0					white	Continuous	Default
✓	CF-Divide					172	Continuous	0.00 mm
	CF-Hatch					191	Continuous	0.00 mm
	CF-HL					170	Continuous	0.00 mm
	CF-Label					26	Continuous	0.00 mm
	CF-PF_Dist					74	Continuous	0.50 mm
	CF-PPF-Dim					74	Continuous	0.00 mm
	CF-PPF-Label					22	Continuous	0.00 mm
	CF-Profile_Proposed					22	Continuous	0.35 mm
	CF-Proj_Ext					210	HIDDEN	0.00 mm
	CF-Pt					96	Continuous	0.00 mm
	CF-Shape					204	Continuous	0.50 mm

Figure 16-5

Proposed profile:

- For the current example, the proposed profile is -5% slope, Figure 16-6a; and the starting elevation is 161ft on the left side of the grid.

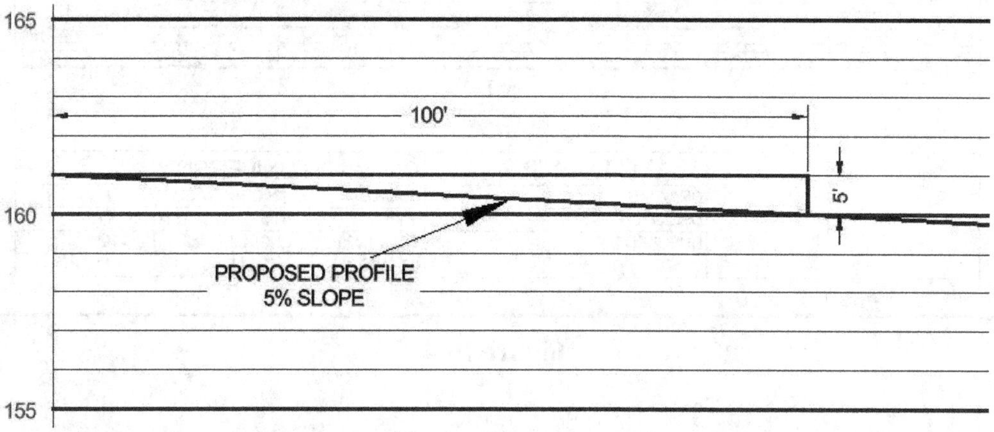

Figure 16-6a

- Draw the proposed profile.
- Make the *CF_Profile-Proposed* layer to be the current layer.
  - o Activate the *Polyline* command.
  - o Starting at the elevation of 161' on the left side of the grid, draw a polyline with -5% slope as follows, Figure 16-6a: (i) starting at the elevation of 161ft on the left side of the grid, draw a 100 ft long horizontal line. (ii) At the end of the horizontal line, draw a 3 ft long vertical line going downward. (iii) Draw a sloping line by connecting the starting point of the horizontal line and the ending point of the vertical line. (iv) Extend the sloping line to the right side's vertical line of the grid, Figure 16-6b.
- Make the *CF_PPF-Label* layer to be the current layer.
- Label the proposed profile as shown in Figure 16-6b.
- Figure 16-6b shows both the existing and proposed profiles.

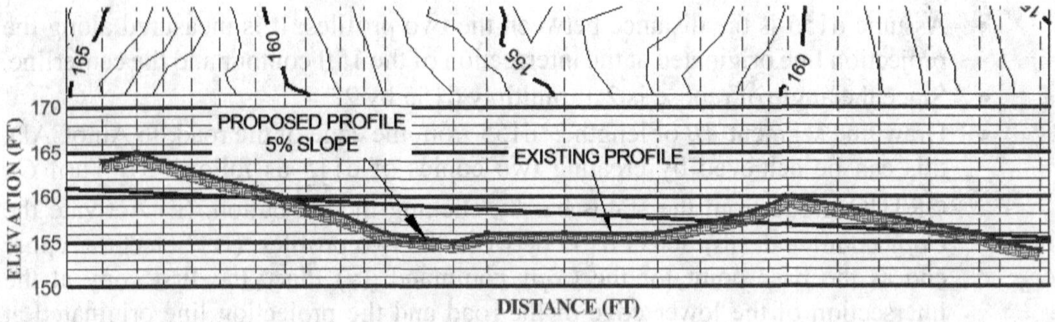

Figure 16-6b

16.8. Delineate The Earthwork Using AutoCAD

This section describes step-by-step process to delineate the Cut-Fill boundary.

1. Distance between two profiles:
   - Make the *CF-PF_Dist* layer to be the current layer.
   - Draw line segments between the proposed and existing profiles. These segments are highlighted by displaying their grip points, Figure 16-7a and Figure 16-7b.

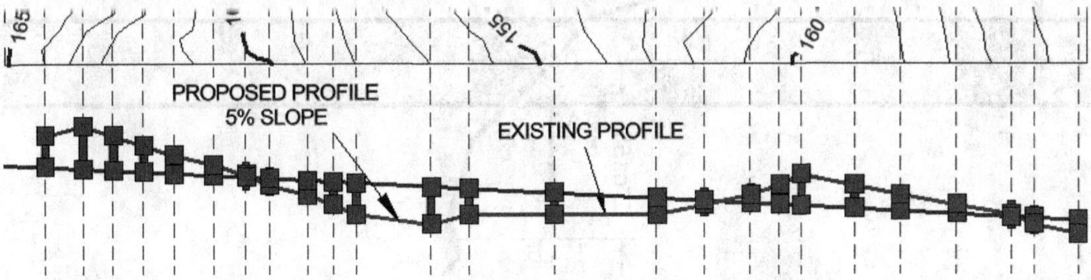

Figure 16-7a

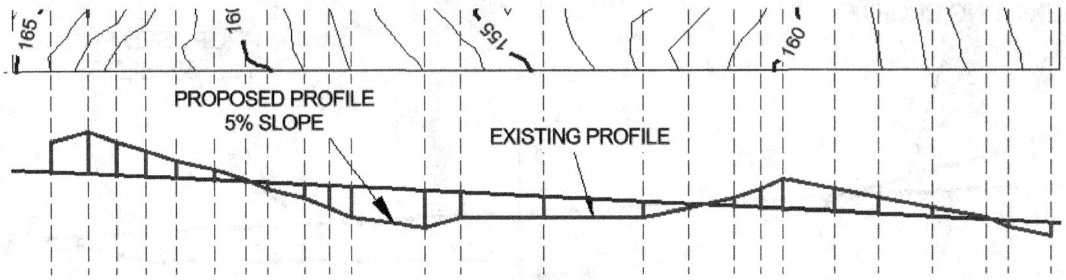

Figure 16-7b

2. Delineation of cut and fill: The angle of repose for both the cut and fill is 2:1.
   - The example shows the delineation of the (cut or fill) boundary for the 155 feet contour, Figure 16-8a.

- Assume d155 is the distance between the two profiles. It is measured along the projection line originated at the intersection of the 15ft contour and the centerline.
- Since the angle of repose is 2:1, multiply d155 by 2.
- Draw line segment *AB* of length 2*d155 from the edge of the road. In AutoCAD, this can be achieved by creating two copies of d115 as follows. (i) Turn *On* ORTHO mode from the status bar by clicking the button. (ii) Activate the *Copy* command. (iii) Select d155 between the two profiles. (iv) Select the upper end as the base point for the *Copy* command. (v) Place the first copy at the intersection of the lower edge of the road and the projection line originated at 155ft contour (point A in Figure 16-8a). (vi) Place the second copy at the lower end of the first copy.
- Make the *CF_HL* layer to be the current layer.
- Draw a horizontal line segment *BC* starting at the lower end of line *AB* and terminating at the 155ft contour (the length of *BC* can be few inches to few feet).
- Make the *CF_Pt* layer to be the current layer.
- Draw a point at C. That is, at the intersection of line *BC* and the 155ft contour.

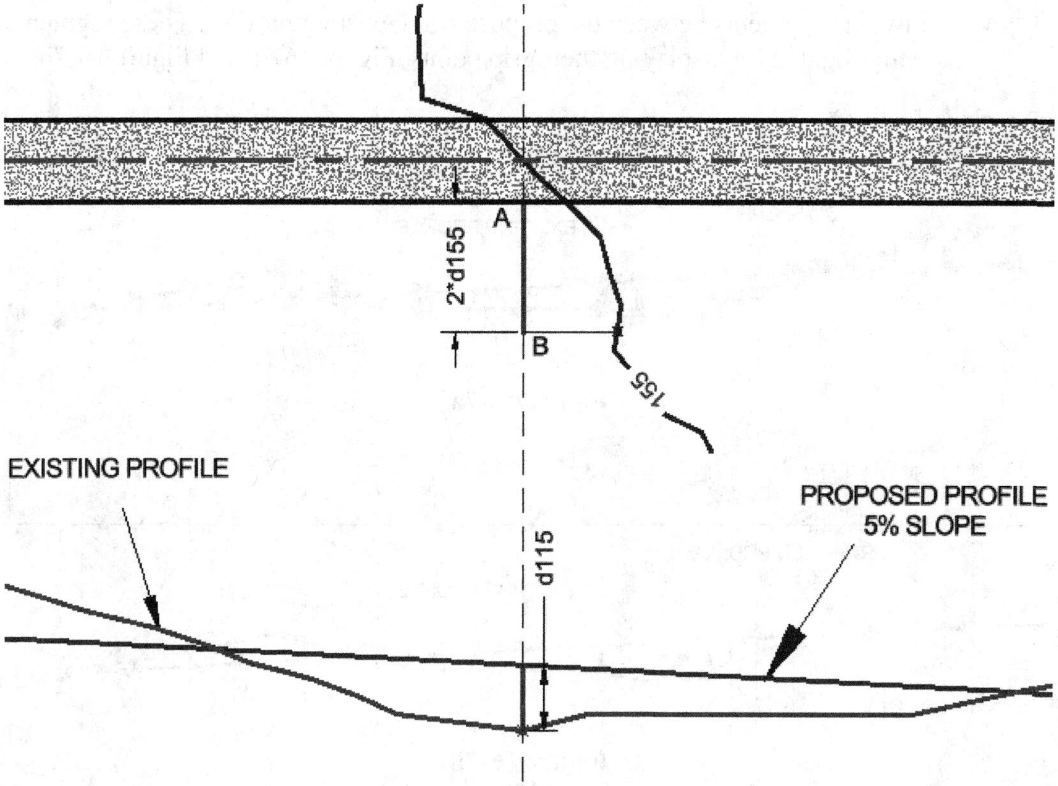

Figure 16-8a

- Repeat the process for the remaining contours. Figure 16-8b shows the left side of the contour map, and Figure 16-8c shows the right side of the contour map.

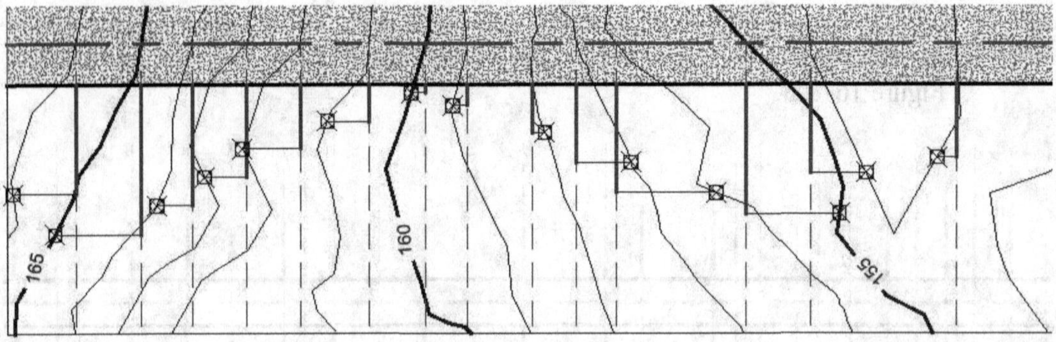

Figure 16-8b

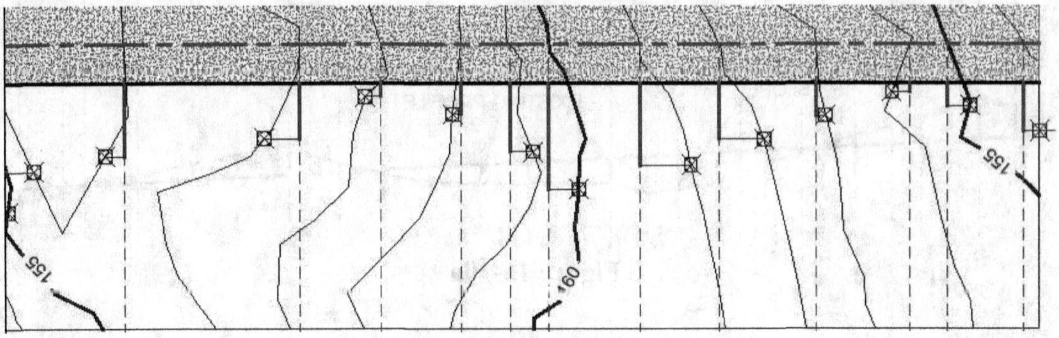

Figure 16-8c

- To repeat the delineation process for the other edge of the road, the first step is to extend the projection lines to the other edge of the road, Figure 16-9.

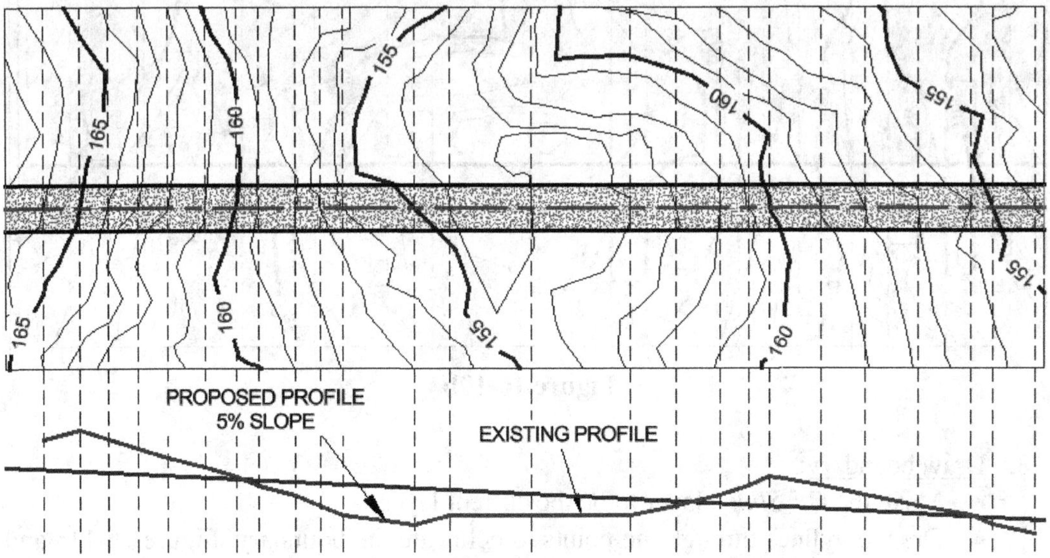

Figure 16-9

- Use the *Mirror* command to mirror the vertical lines (the distance between the two profiles); use the centerline of the road plan as the mirror line, Figure 16-10a.

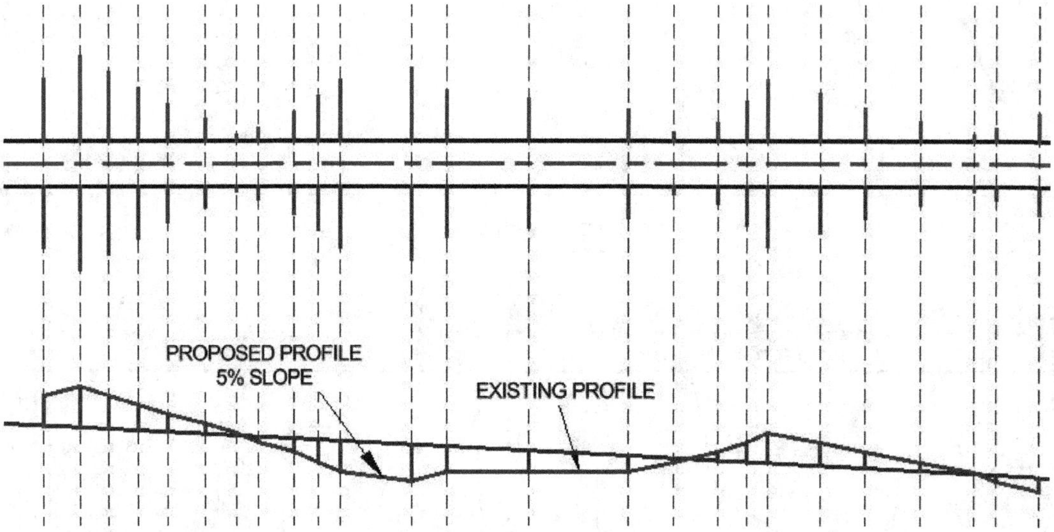

Figure 16-10a

- Make the *CF_HL* layer to be the current layer.
- Draw the horizontal line segment, Figure 16-10b.
- Make the *CF_Pt* layer to be the current layer.
- Draw the points, Figure 16-10b.

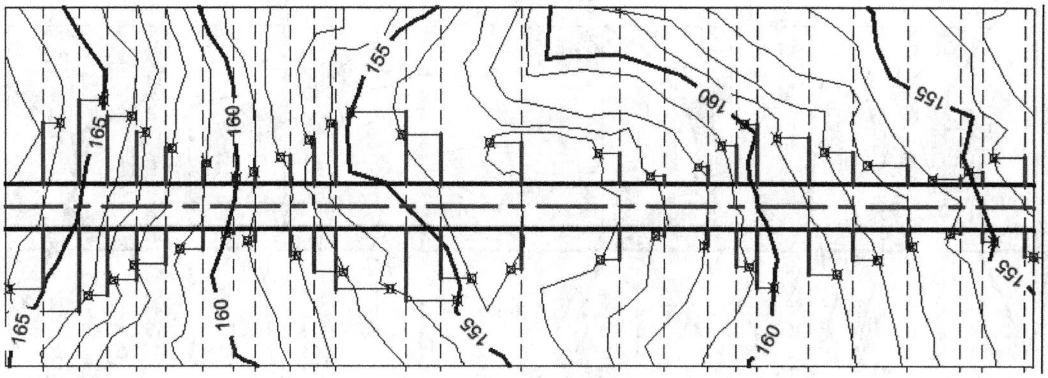

Figure 16-10b

3. Draw boundary:
   - Make the *CF-Shape* layer to be the current layer.
   - Draw polylines through the points to delineate the boundary, Figure 16-11a and Figure 16-11b.
   - If necessary, extend the polylines drawn in the above step to the end of the contour map using the *Extend* command, Figure 16-12.

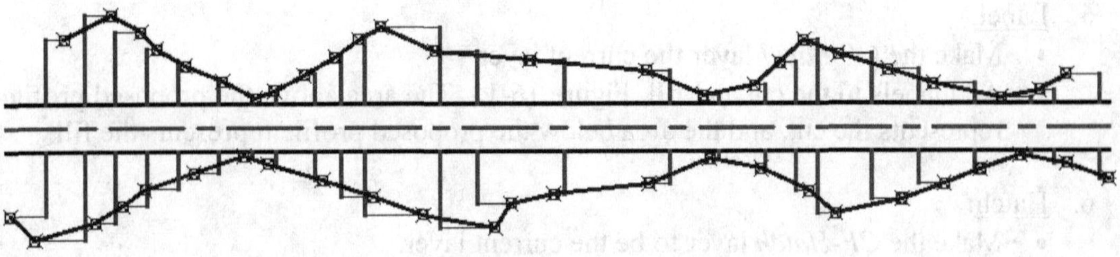

Figure 16-11a

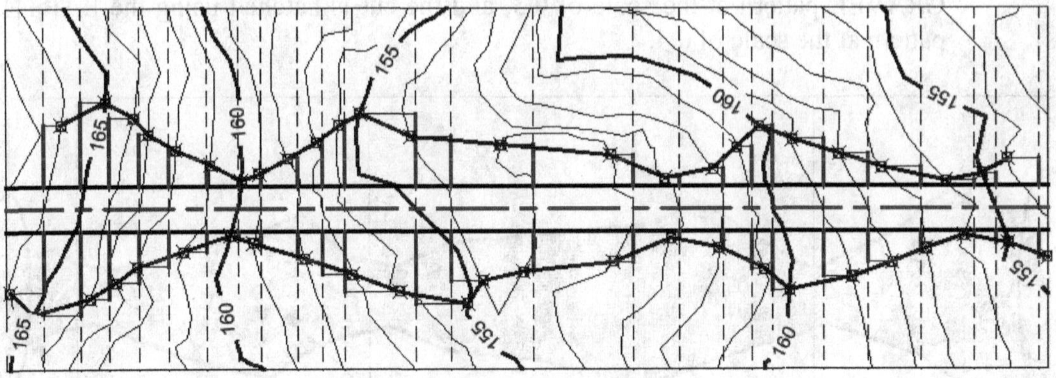

Figure 16-11b

4. Separate the cut and fill area:
   - Make the *CF-Divide* layer be the current layer.
   - Turn *Off* the layers as shown in Figure 16-12.
   - Draw vertical lines originating from the intersection of the two profiles (in the grid area) to the contour map to separate the cut and fill's boundary, Figure 16-12.

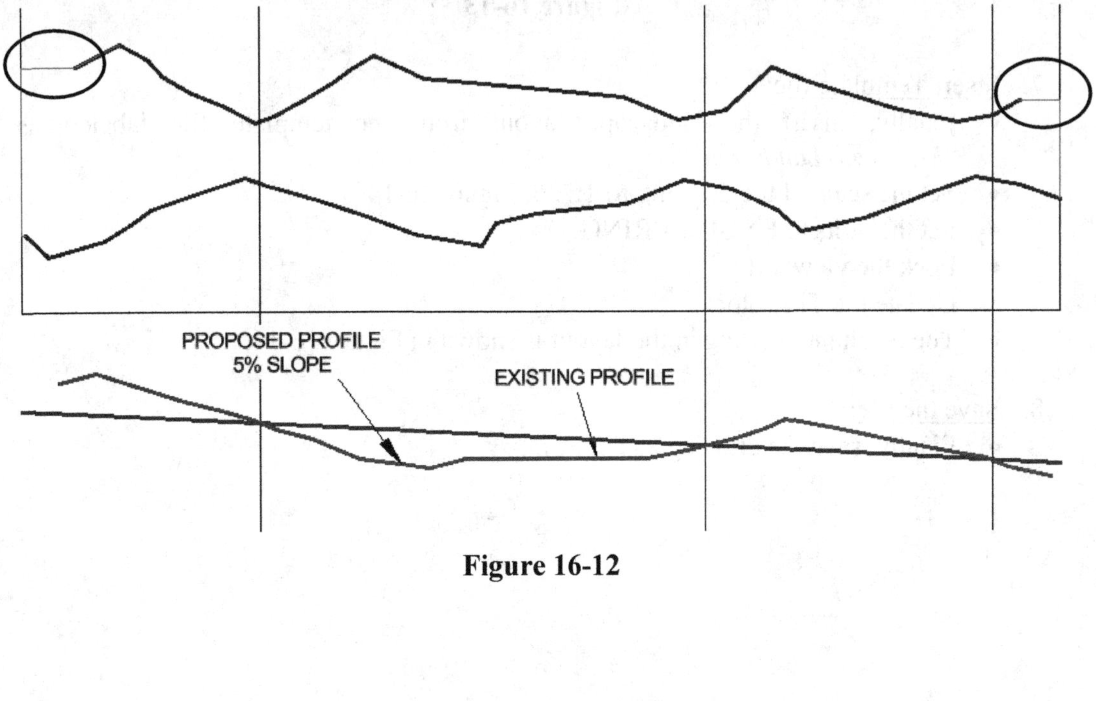

Figure 16-12

5. Label:
   - Make the *CF-Label* layer the current layer
   - Add labels to the cut and fill, Figure 16-13. The area above the proposed profile represents the cut, and the area below the proposed profile represents the fill.

6. Hatch:
   - Make the *CF-Hatch* layer to be the current layer.
   - Draw lines to close the open ends of the cut and fill, Figure 16-13.
   - Annotated hatch the areas as shown in Figure 16-13. The fill is hatched using the GRAVEL pattern at the scale of 0.3, and the cut is hatched using the EARTH pattern at the scale of 0.4.

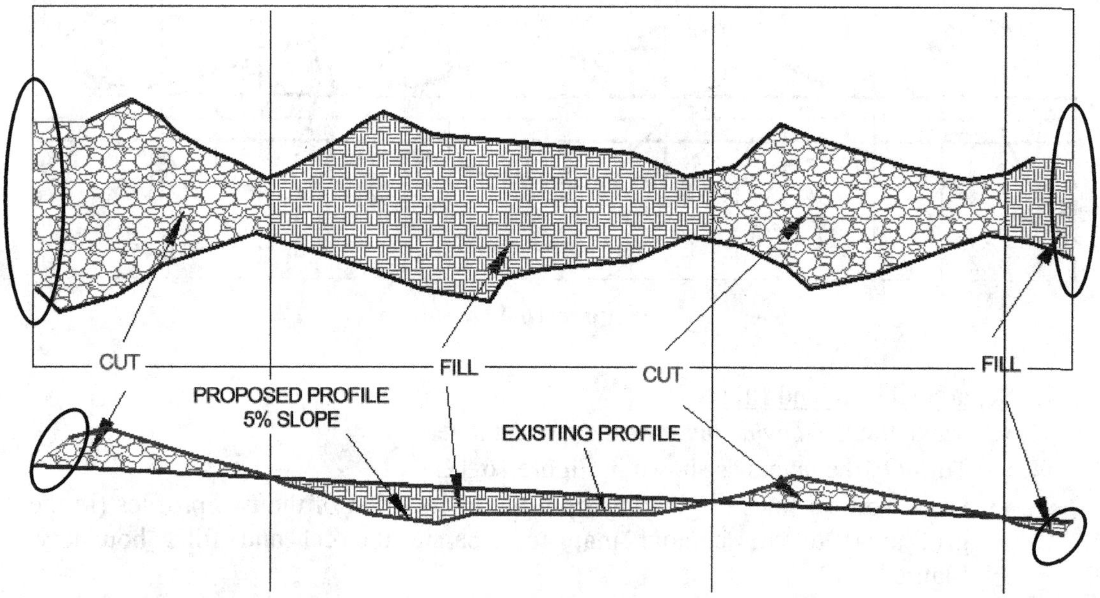

Figure 16-13

7. Insert Template file:
   - Finally, insert the landscape layout from the template file labeled as "*My_acad_Landscape*."
   - Set the scale of the drawing to 1:720, Figure 16-14.
   - Set the units to ENGINEERING.
   - Lock the viewport.
   - Update the Title block.
   - The resultant drawing in the layout is shown in Figure 16-14.

8. Save the file:
   - Finally, save the drawing as *CutFill.dwg*.

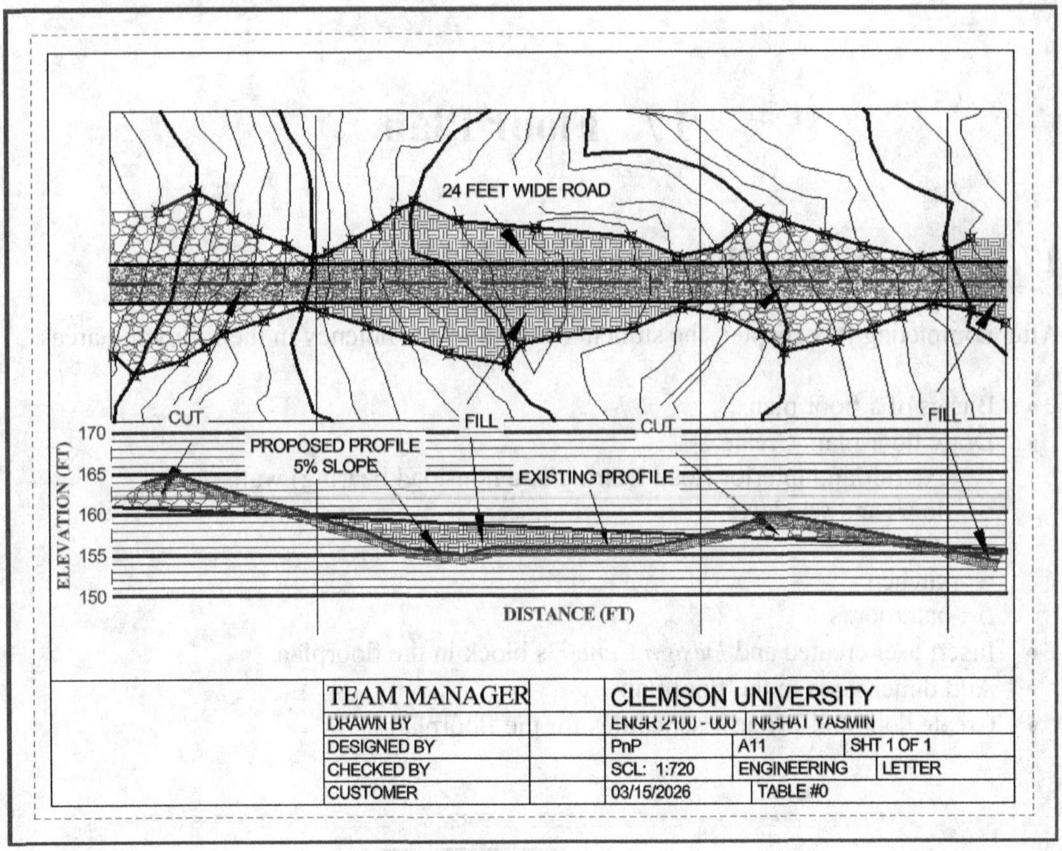

Figure 16-14

Notes:

17. Floor Plan

17.1. Learning Objectives

After completing this chapter, the students will show proficiency in the following areas:

- Basics of a floor plan
- Draw floor plan. Create
  - o exterior and interior (load bearing and non-load bearing) walls
  - o doors and windows
  - o stairs
  - o kitchen
  - o bathrooms
- Insert user created and *Design Center*'s block in the floorplan
- Add dimensions to the floorplan
- Create door and window schedules for the floorplan

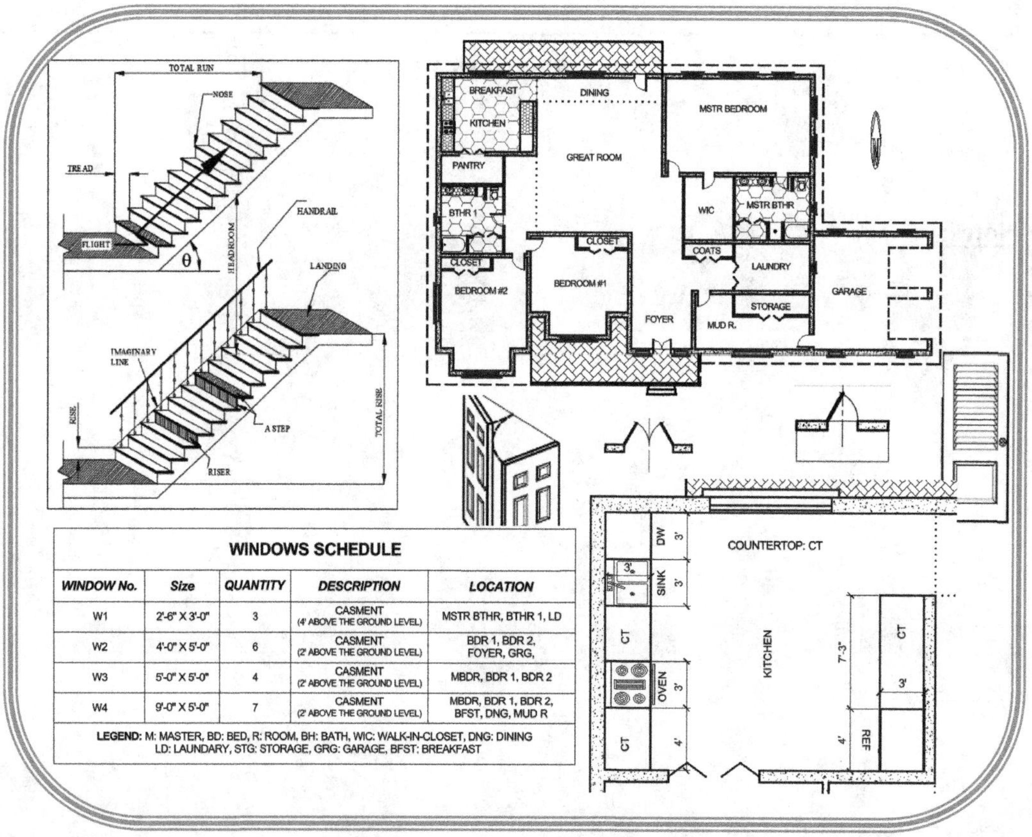

17.2. Introduction

Consider a simple angle bracket shown in Figure 17-1a. The question is *how it can be sketched to convey its three-dimensional shape correctly in two dimensions.*

- The bracket is three-dimensional and describing it in words may be complicated.
- To make the drawing process of a 3D object easier, engineers use a standard system called orthographic projection or orthographic views.
- The orthographic view shows two-dimensional views of three-dimensional objects.

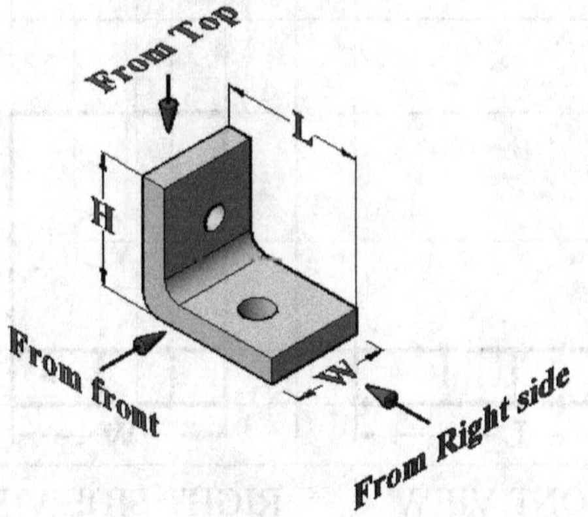

Figure 17-1a

The concept of orthographic projection is similar to the reflection of an object in a mirror. Figure 17-1b shows an image of a bracket in a mirror. Parallel rays from the bracket are creating the image on the mirror; the mirror is perpendicular (orthogonal) to the rays. Similarly, in technical drawing the front view is projected on the frontal plane.

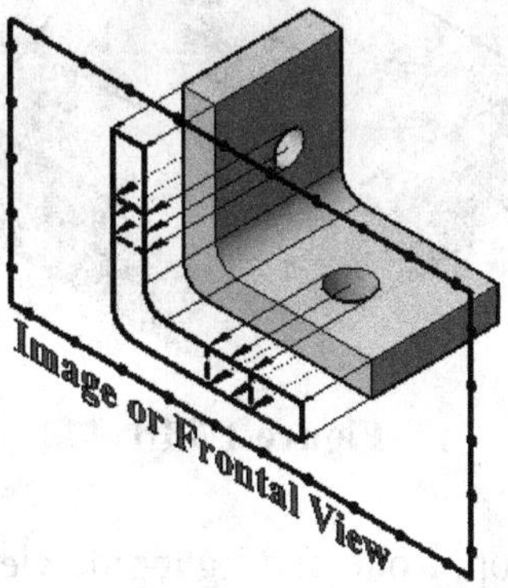

Figure 17-1b

If the bracket is looked at from the top, front, and right sides (Figure 17-1a), then its orthographic projections are two-dimensional views, Figure 17-1c. Vertical lines are used to project information between the top and front views; horizontal lines are used to project information between the front and right-side views; and horizontal and vertical lines are used to project information between the top and right-side views using 45° miter line, Figure 17-1c.

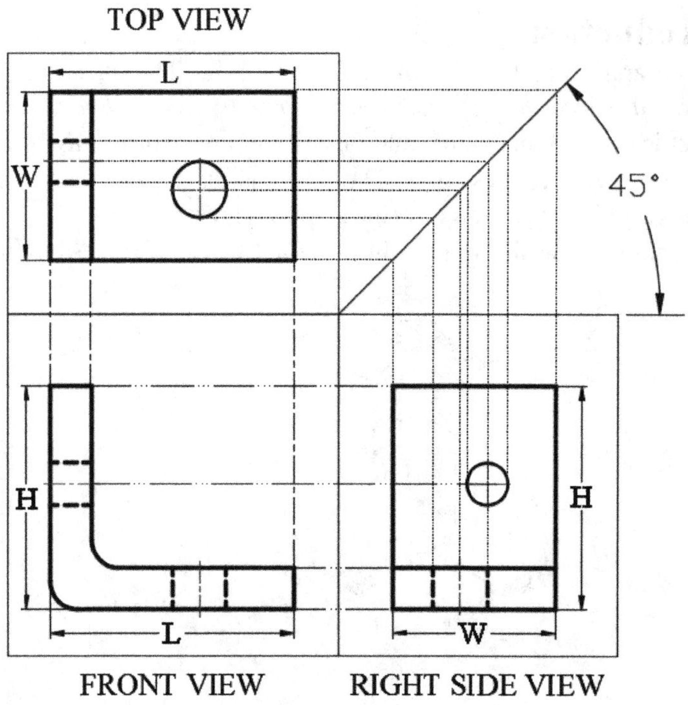

Figure 17-1c

Consider a simple building shown in Figure 17-1d. The figure shows the southeast isometric view of a building.

Figure 17-1d

The three orthographic views (top, front, and right-side views) are shown in Figure 17-1e. Notice the projection of the skylight (the box in the roof), front door, and the gable roof (the triangular roof) in the three orthographic views.

The focus of this chapter is the top view of a building, also known as a floor plan. The front and side views (or elevations) are the focus of the next chapter.

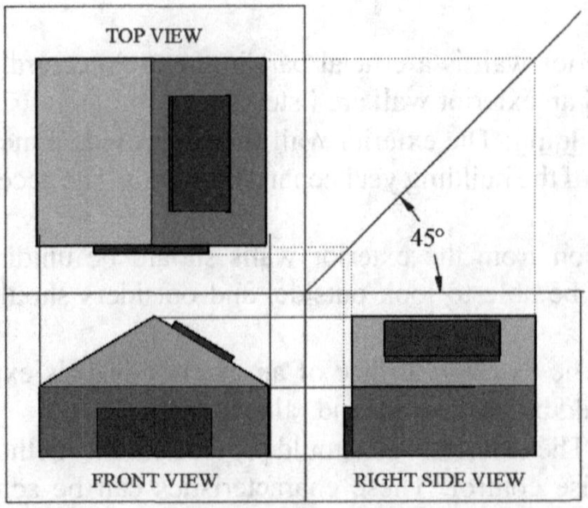

Figure 17-1e

17.3. Floor Plan

In architecture and building engineering terminology, a version of a top view is called a floor plan. A floor plan is a simple two-dimensional line drawing resulting from looking at a building from above (below the ceiling level). It displays the relationship between rooms, windows, doors, walls, stairs, fireplace, and other features at one level of a building as if seen from the top. The focus of this chapter is designing and drawing a floor plan for a residential building with three bedrooms, two bathrooms, and a two-car garage.

The floor plan is the most important and detailed dimensioned drawing of a building. Some of the information included in a floor plan of a residential building is the location and thickness of the exterior and interior walls; size and location of the doors and windows; details of the kitchen, laundry-, storage-, bed- and bath- rooms; ventilation, plumbing, electrical, and mechanical systems; slopes in the floor; etc. For multistory buildings, stairs are also shown on the floor plan. The scale of the drawing depends on the size of the building and size of the printing paper. Generally, the floor plans are printed at a scale of 1:48 or 1:96.

The floor plan design is an iterative process. Usually, it is the first drawing to be started and the last drawing to be completed. It is revised several times to accommodate the decisions made in the elevations and sectional views' design.

17.4. Wall

Walls are the structures that demarcate a building from the surrounding buildings or open spaces and divide the building space into rooms and hallways. They support the load of the superstructure (roof, ceiling, and upper-level floors) of the building. They provide security against intrusion and shelter from the weather. Generally, power outlets, phone connections, lighting switches, thermostats, and plumbing ducts are placed inside the walls. The walls in a building can be grouped as exterior and interior walls or load bearing and non-load bearing walls.

17.4.1. Exterior

The design of an exterior wall is a crucial part in the architectural design of a building. Some basic features of an exterior wall are listed here.

- Access to the building: The exterior wall should provide a method of entry and exit to the occupants of the building yet keep intruders out. The access is achieved through the doors.
- Vision: The vision from the exterior walls should be unidirectional. That is, the residents should be able to look outside, and outsiders should not be able to look inside the house.
- Surface finish: The exterior surface of an exterior wall is exposed to the weather; therefore, it should be heat, wind, and rain resistant.
- Climate control: The exterior wall should provide for the methods of ventilation, heat transfer, and noise control. These characteristics can be achieved by appropriate placement of windows and by properly insulating doors and windows.
- Fire control: The exterior wall should prevent the spreading of fire from inside to outside of the house and vice versa.
- Durability: The walls should be durable for the life of the building.

17.4.2. Interior

The interior walls should also satisfy the vision, fire control, durability, and the characteristics mentioned in the exterior walls.

17.4.3. Load bearing

The load bearing walls not only support the dead load of the wall but also support the load of the roof, ceiling, and upper-level floors.

17.4.4. Non-load bearing

The non-load bearing walls should be strong enough to support their dead load; that is, it should be able to support its own load. The non-load bearing interior walls are called partition walls and the non-load bearing exterior walls are called curtain walls.

17.4.5. Wall thickness

The wall thickness depends on the construction material. For example, usually wood frame exterior walls are 6 inches thick and solid brick are 9 inches or 12 inches thick.

17.5. Doors

Doors are also important parts of a building. They provide access to a building from outside and to different parts of a building from inside and outside.

17.5.1. Types of doors

The doors are classified as exterior and interior based on their location; flush, panel, and louvered doors based on their appearance; hinged, folding, sliding, accordion, and overhead based on the method of door opening. French and Dutch doors are the special purpose doors.

- <u>Classification based on door's location:</u>
  - **Exterior:** As the name suggests, exterior doors are used to enter a building from the outside. The front and rear entrance doors are exterior doors.
  - **Interior:** Interior doors are used to access different parts of a building. These doors include bedroom, bathroom, kitchen, and laundry room doors.

- <u>Classification based on door's appearance:</u>
  - **Flush:** Flush doors have smooth and easy-to-maintain surfaces, Figure 17-2a. These doors are the most commonly used doors due to their low maintenance and construction cost. These doors may be solid- or hollow-cored. The solid-core doors are heavier and denser than the hollow-core doors.
  - **Panel:** Panel doors were developed centuries ago to overcome the dimensional distortions caused by weathering effects because the changes in the moisture content would expand and contract wooden doors. These doors contain built-in panels, which help maintain the door's shape. The panels can be in different shapes and sizes. Figure 17-2b shows a 6-paneled door with two types of panels.
  - **Louvered:** Louvered doors have horizontal stripes placed on the diagonal for the ventilation. These doors are attractive but difficult to maintain (dusting and painting takes a very long time), Figure 17-2c.

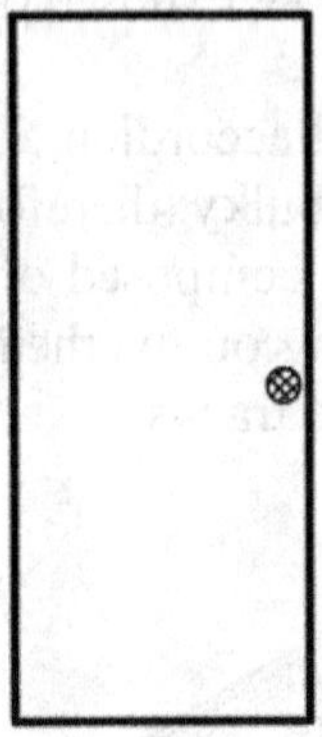

Figure 17-2a

Figure 17-2b

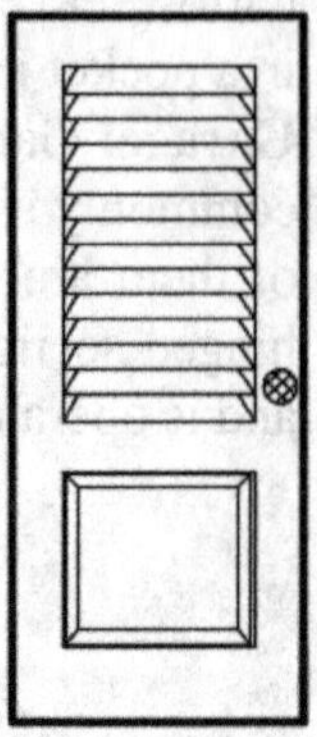

Figure 17-2c

- <u>Classification based on door's operation:</u>
  - **Hinged:** Typically, these doors are hinged at the side; they are also known as swinging doors. These doors may be flush, panel, or louvered. These doors can swing inward or outward for 90° or 180°. These doors can be installed as a double unit or two-leaved, where one is hinged on the left side and the other is hinged on the right side, Figure 17-3a. The minimum swing space requirement for these doors is the width of one panel of the door. The advantage of these doors is that at a given time all of the doorway space is available.
  - **Sliding:** Sliding doors are used to save floor space (because these doors do not swing) and may be flush or panel. A single leaf sliding door slides into a pocket built in the wall. In the case of the two leaves sliding door, one leaf slides in front of the other leaf, Figure 17-3b. The drawback of the two leaves sliding doors is that at a given time only half of the doorway space is available.

- **Folding:** Folding doors are a combination of hinged and sliding doors. The two leaves are hinged together and one of the leaves is also hinged at the side, Figure 17-3c. The advantage of folding doors is that the door can be completely open; thus, all the doorway space is available. These doors can be single (two leaves as shown in Figure 17-3c) or double units (four leaves).

Figure 17-3a

Figure 17-3b

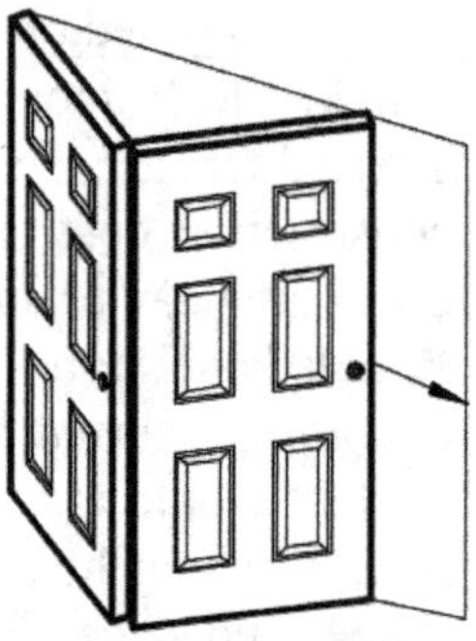

Figure 17-3c

- **Accordion:** Accordion doors are similar to folding doors but consist of several narrow leaves, Figure 17-3d. The folded retracted door can be exposed or hidden in a pocket in the wall.
- **Garage:** Garage doors can be sliding, roll-up, hinged, and accordion. The most commonly used type is the overhead type. These doors are bulky; therefore, most of them are mechanically operated. An overhead door is composed of several hinged sections, Figure 17-3e, that slide up into the ceiling on overhead tracks and is operated with counterweights or springs on overhead tracks.

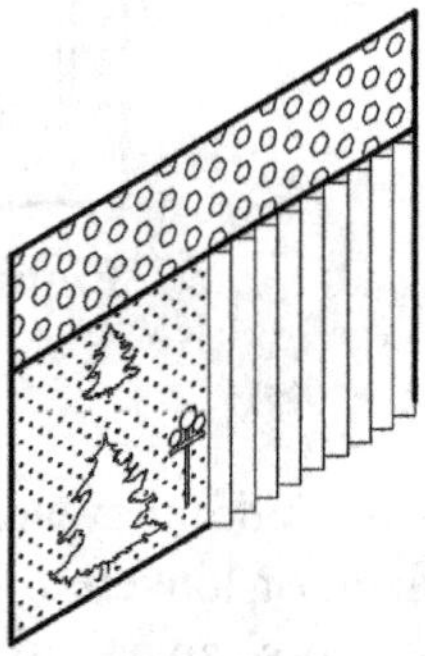

Figure 17-3d

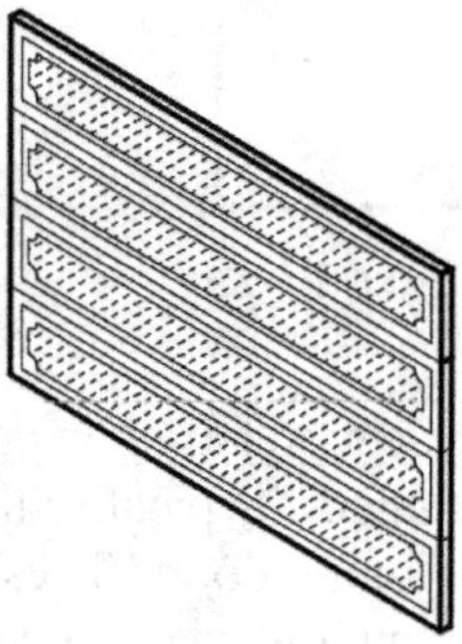

Figure 17-3e

17.5.2. Door sizes

A door can be of any type and size; companies manufacture doors in various shapes and sizes. Nonetheless, the type and size of the door depend on the building style, room type, and the client's requirements. Typically, the door opening is 3 inches wider and 3 inches longer than the size of the door. As a rule of thumb, the width of a door is about half of its height. The commonly used residential door sizes are listed below.

- Front entrance doors: 3'-0" X 6'-8" X 1 3/4"
- Bedroom doors: 2'-6" or 2'-8" X 6'-8" X 1 3/8"
- Bathroom doors: 2'- or 2'-6" X 6'-8" X 1 3/8"
- A garage door is 9'-0" high, and its width can be 8' – 10' for single-car garages and 16' for a double-car garage.

17.5.3. Door selection

The selection of a door depends on the location of the door. Other factors affecting the door selection process in a typical residential building are listed below.

- Weather- and break-resistances are major factors in selecting the exterior doors.
- Fire- and noise-resistance are major factors in selecting the interior doors.
- Solid-core flush doors are typically used for exterior entrances and hollow-core doors are suitable for interior use.
- Louvered doors are the best candidate for closet doors.
- Hinge doors are commonly used for main entrances, bedrooms, and bathrooms.
- Swinging doors are commonly used in kitchens and dining areas for easy operation in both directions.
- Sliding doors are selected for closets and exterior doors (opening in the porch or backyard) from the living area.
- Folding doors are used for closets and laundry rooms.
- Accordion doors are used between dining and living areas.

17.5.4. Door appearance in floor plan

The following list is the plan view of the different types of doors discussed earlier.

- Figure 17-4a: Hinged, single panel, swing inward.
- Figure 17-4b: Hinged, single panel, swing outward.
- Figure 17-4c: Hinged, double panel, swing inward.
- Figure 17-4d: Accordion.
- Figure7-4e: Folding, double panel, 4 leaves.
- Figure 17-4f: Sliding, double panel.

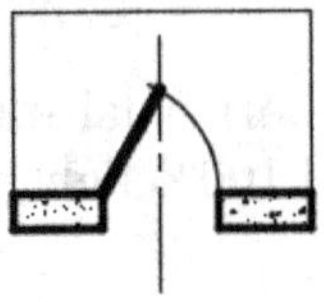

Figure 17-4a

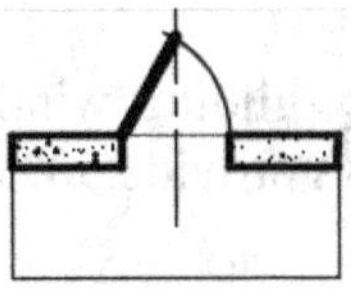

Figure 17-4b

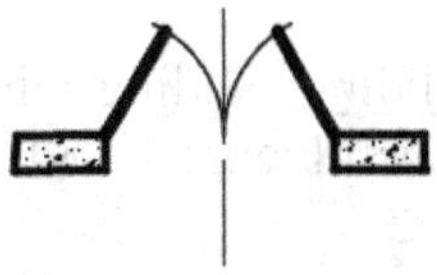

Figure 17-4c

Figure 17-4d

Figure 17-4e

Figure 17-4f

17.6. Windows

Windows are an important part of a building. Windows have evolved over time, from an opening in the wall for fresh air to enter and smoke to leave to the modern-day sophisticated windows. Windows provide light and ventilation to the residents and architectural enhancement to the building; however, improperly placed windows detract from the house's appearance. Generally, 12% of a wall should be windows and the total glass area of the window should be about 10% of the floor area.

17.6.1. Types of windows

Based on the method of opening a window, the commonly used windows are classified as fixed, casement, sliding, and double-hung.

- Casement: Casement windows provide 100% ventilation and 100% light. These windows are hinged.
  - **Side hinge:** Side hinge windows are hinged at the side, Figure 17-5a. Usually these windows are narrow but can be connected to one another, or to a fixed window to fill wider openings.
  - **Awning or top hinge:** Awning windows are hinged at the top, Figure 17-5b. These windows are wider and shorter. Generally, open awning windows swing outward.
  - **Hopper or bottom hinge:** Hopper windows are hinged at the bottom, Figure 17-5c. These windows are commonly used in commercial buildings. Generally, open windows swing inward; otherwise, the rainwater comes inside if it opens outward.

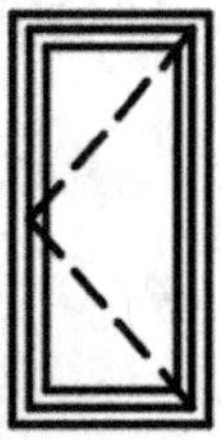

Figure 17-5a

Figure 17-5b

Figure 17-5c

- Sliding: Sliding windows open by gliding window panels on horizontal tracks in pairs, Figure 17-5d. These windows provide 50% ventilation and 100% light.

- Double-hung: Double-hung (also known as vertical-slide) windows open by gliding window panels on vertical tracks, Figure 17-5e. These windows provide 50% ventilation and 100% light. These windows are commonly used in small residential buildings.
- Fixed: Fixed windows are also known as picture windows. These windows do not have any moving parts. Although these windows can provide 100% light, they provide 0% ventilation. These are the cheapest windows.

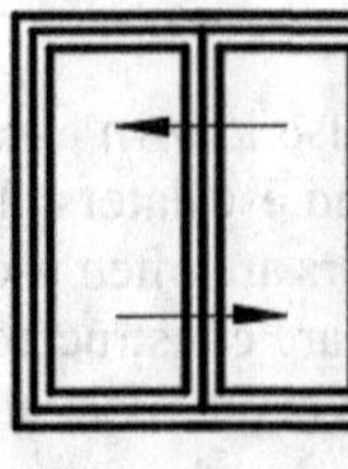

Figure 17-5d

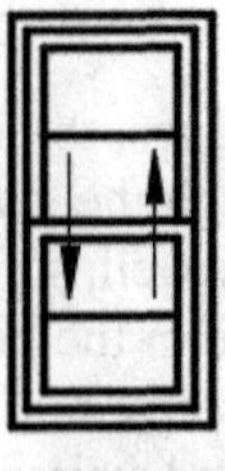

Figure 17-5e

17.6.2. Window sizes

A window can be of any size. Window companies manufacture windows in various shapes and sizes. Nonetheless, the type and size of the windows depend on the building style and the client's requirements. As a rule of thumb, the width of a window is about half of its height. Typically, the top of a window opening is 6'–8" from the floor. The bottom of the opening depends on the type of room. For example, a bedroom, dining, and a living room window's openings are 3'–10", 2'–10", and 1'– 10" above the floor level, respectively.

17.6.3. Window selection

The selection of a window type and its location depend on several factors. The windows should be located to improve the cross ventilation. Also, the hinged window openings in hallways or walkways should be high enough (per se 6 feet) to avoid injuries.

- Site orientation: In the northern hemisphere, the windows should be located in the southern walls, thus allowing sunlight to enter the room during the winter months.
- Insulation: The information regarding thermal performance (how much energy is lost for heating or cooling the building) of a window is very important. Inadequately insulated windows increase the air-conditioning cost, cause discomfort to the residents, and stain and decay the window material due to condensation.
- Operation: The ease of opening, closing, and cleaning a window are important criteria in the selection of the type of window.
- Service: Before deciding about the style and size of a window, it is important to check the services provided by the manufacturer, such as the warranties, accessibility of spare parts, and availability of representatives at the site.
- Floor level: In two-story residential buildings, generally, windows on the first floor are taller than the windows on the second floor.
- Safety: In residential buildings, at least one window should have a clear space big enough for occupants to exit and firefighters to enter the room. The window opening space should be at least 1'–8" wide and 2' high; and its area should be at least six square-feet.
- Security: The windows should be built from break-resistant material.
- Windowsill: The windowsills should be located below the eye level of a seated person. For example, it should be 1' above the floor level in the living room and 4' in the bedrooms.

17.7. Stair

For multilevel buildings, the inter-level movement (also known as vertical movement) is made possible through the stairs, elevators, ramps, and escalators. This section discusses stairs. The terms stairwell, stairway, staircase, and stairs are often used interchangeably. A stairwell is the space in the building where the stairs are constructed. A staircase is often used for the stairs (steps, railings, landings, etc.). The expression stairway is reserved for the entire stairwell and staircase in combination.

The location of the stairs is very important. In case of an emergency, the stairs are used to evacuate the building. In case of a tornado, a stairwell can also be used as an area of refuge.

17.7.1. Terminology

Some of the commonly used terms are explained in this section and are illustrated in Figure 17-6.

- Flight: A flight is an uninterrupted series of steps.
- Landing: A landing is the floor area near the top or bottom step of a stair, or a small platform built as part of the stair used to change the flight's direction, or to provide the user with a resting place.
- Tread (or going): A tread is the horizontal surface part of each step that is stepped on. The tread length is measured from the outer edge of the step to the riser between two adjacent steps.
- Riser: A riser is the vertical portion of the step between two adjacent steps.
- Rise: A rise is the vertical distance between two adjacent treads.
- Total rise: The total rise represents the total vertical distance traveled by a stair; that is, it is the floor-to-floor distance.
- Total run: Total run is the total horizontal length of the stair (from the first riser to the last riser).
- Handrail: A handrail is the round or decorative member of a railing used for hand holding during ascent or descent. It runs parallel to the imaginary line drawn from the top of the first tread to the top of the last tread.
- Step: A step is the combination of a riser and one of the adjacent treads.
- Nose: A nose is the edge part of the tread that protrudes from the riser underneath.
- Headroom: Headroom is the vertical distance from the top of a tread to the ceiling above it.
- Angle of a flight: The angle of a flight (θ) is the ratio of the total rise and the total run: $\theta = tan^{-1}(Total\ rise / Total\ run)$.
- Winders: The winders are the triangular steps used to change the direction of the flight, Figure 17-7b.

17.7.2. Important points

Following is the list of some of the important points that must be considered when designing a staircase in a residential building.

- Flight: For a long flight, provide a break in the flight using landing(s).
- Riser: For comfortable stairs, a riser should be 7 inches. If the riser is too high, then the stairs are very tiring and if it is too low then people will hit their toes against the riser.
- Tread: For comfortable stairs, the tread should be 11 inches. If the tread is too small, then the stairs may not be safe and if it is too long then the horizontal space is wasted.
- Headroom: Headroom should be 7 feet - 4 inches or 6 feet - 8 inches for the major stairs, and 6 feet - 6 inches for the minor stairs (to the basement or attic).
- Handrail: For safe stairs, a railing should be always provided on the open side of the stairs. The height of the railing should not be less than 32 inches and not more than 36 inches.
- Angle of a flight: For residential buildings, the angle of a flight (θ) should be in the range of 30° to 33°.

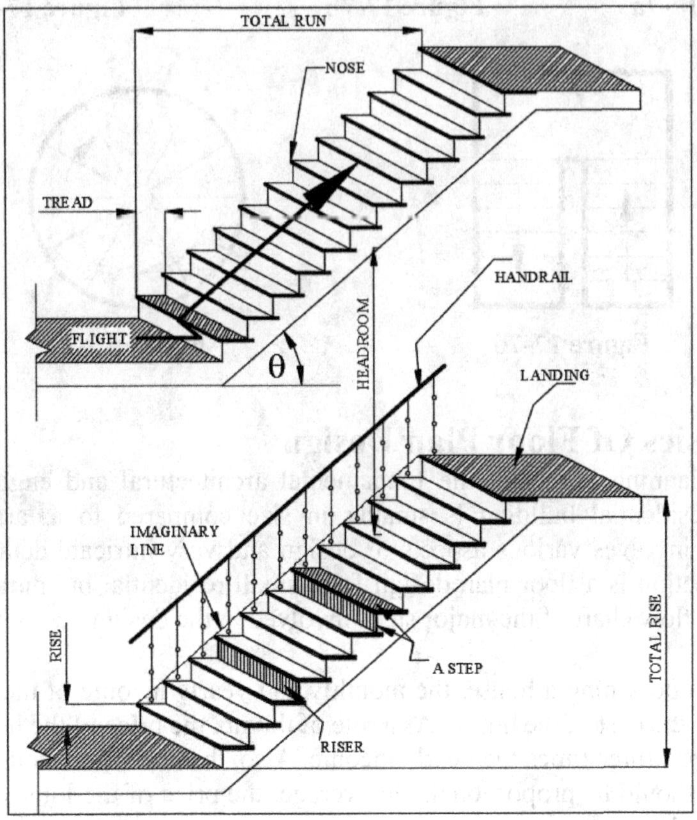

Figure 17-6

17.7.3. Types of stairs

A stair without any wall on its side is called an open stair, and a stair with walls on both sides is called a closed stair.

Based on the availability of the space for the staircase, it can be designed as straight (Figure 17-7a), L-shaped with winders (Figure 17-7b), L-shaped with landing (Figure 17-7c), narrow U (Figure 17-7d), and spiral stairs (Figure 17-7e).

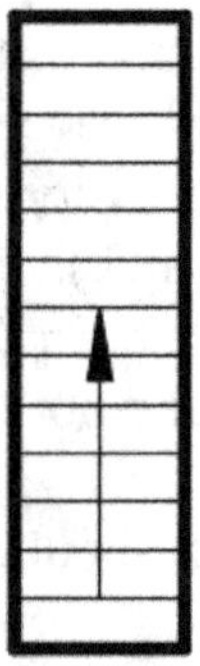

Figure 17-7a

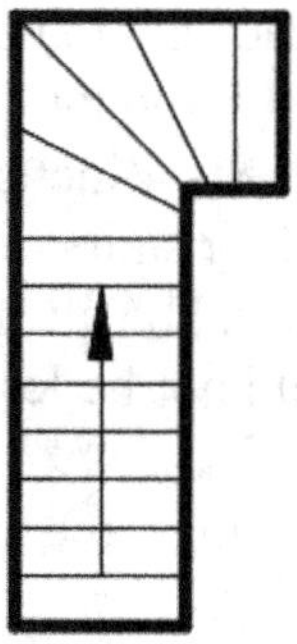

Figure 17-7b

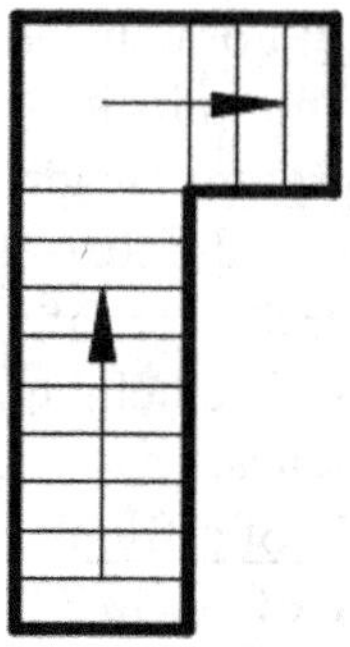

Figure 17-7c

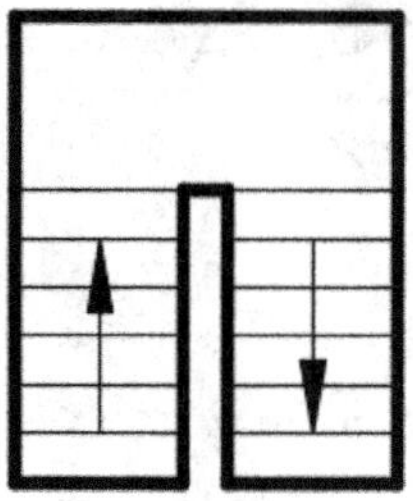

Figure 17-7d

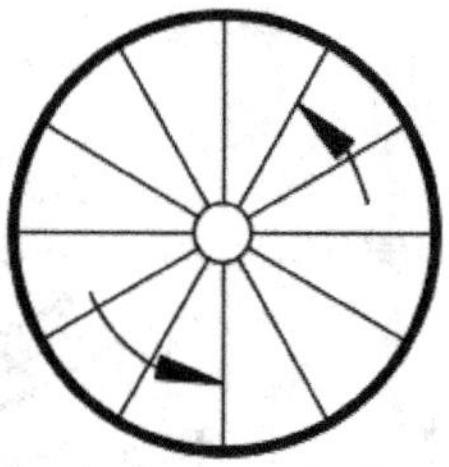

Figure 17-7e

17.8. Basics Of Floor Plan Design

A building's planning is one of the fundamental architectural and engineering design problems. A residential building is smaller in size compared to a large commercial building, yet it involves various aspects of design and very intricate details. Hence, the focus of this section is a floor plan design for a small residential building. Figure 17-8a shows a simple flow chart of the major steps involved in the design.

- <u>Budget</u>: In designing a house, the monthly and yearly income of the family greatly influences the cost of the house. As a rule of thumb, the price of the house should not be more than three times the yearly income. Also, the cost of the house and the price of the lot should be proportional. On average, the price of the lot should be 15% to 20% of the house cost.

- <u>Site</u>: Some of the important features of the lot that must be considered before designing and creating architectural drawings are listed here.
    - *Size*: The size and number of rooms are directly proportional to the lot size. For identical room count and sizes, a single-story house on a larger plot or a multi-story house on a smaller plot might be the most suitable option.
    - *Shape*: The shape of the house depends on the shape of the lot. A house design for a broader lot may not be feasible for a narrow lot.

- *Contours*: Contour lines indicate the change in the elevation. Special design criteria must be considered for steep lots. If the lot is sloped inward, based on the contours, a split-level house may be the only option.
- *Utilities*: The cost of the house may increase if the basic utilities (water, electricity, gas, sewer, trash collection) are not available near the lot under consideration.
- *Orientation*: If possible, the living areas should have southern exposure. Also, if a house is properly planned then the summer breeze can come in and the winter cold air can be kept out.
- *Convenience to amenities*: The cost of the daily commute to school, office, and shopping area may increase or decrease the cost of a lot, which in turn affects the cost of the house.

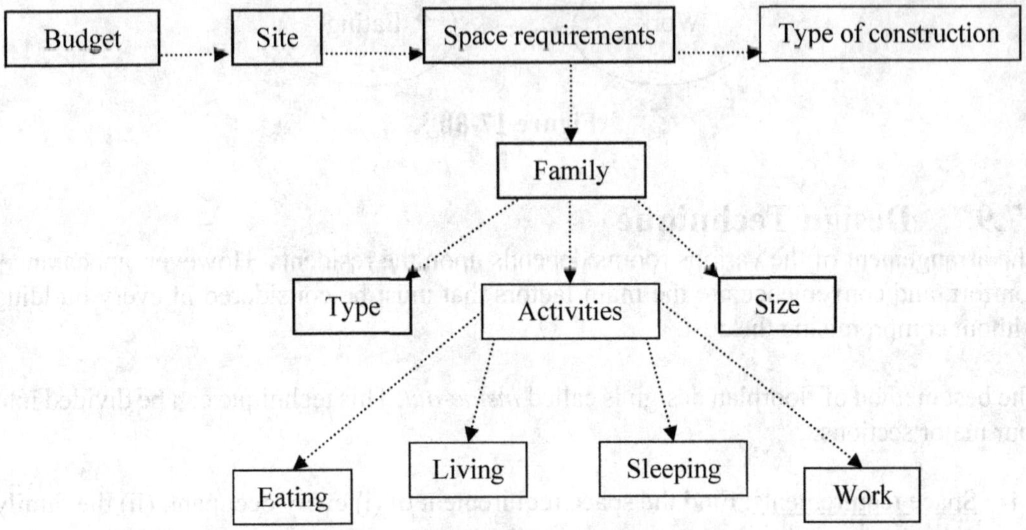

Figure 17-8a

- Space requirements: The space requirement depends on the following factors.
  - *Family type*: The space requirement depends on the building's occupants. For example, a single-story house may be the better option for a family with small children and/or a senior citizen.
  - *Family size*: The number and size of the rooms depend on the number of occupants.
  - *Family activities*: The main activities in a residential building can be grouped into eating, sleeping, living/entertainment, and work zones. Figure 17-8b shows the movement between various zones. The activities zones divide a house into the following rooms.

    - Eating: Kitchen, breakfast room, and dining room
    - Sleeping: Bedrooms and guest rooms
    - Living/entertainment: Living room, exercise room, library, entrance hall
    - Work: Kitchen, pantry, laundry, garage, and storage room

- Type of construction: The type of construction material (for example, wood, brick, steel, etc.) affects the cost of the house.

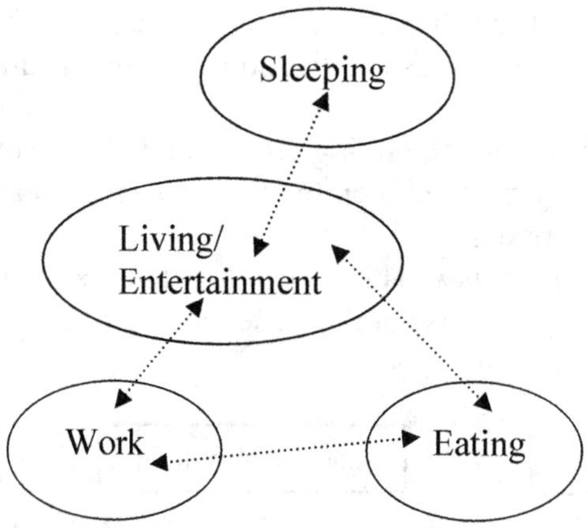

Figure 17-8b

17.9. Design Technique

The arrangement of the various rooms depends upon the residents. However, appearance, comfort, and convenience are the main factors that must be considered in every building without compromising the cost.

The best method of floorplan design is called *inside-out*. This technique can be divided into four major sections.

1. Space requirements: Find the space requirement of (i) every occupant, (ii) the family collectively, and (iii) special needs for the guests.
2. Setup: (i) Find the arrangement of the rooms, size of the rooms, and furnishings. (ii) Revise the plan (if necessary) for comfort, convenience, economy, and appearance.
3. Construction type: Find the method of construction: wood, brick, steel, etc.
4. Finance: Find the method to finance the construction project.

17.10. AutoCAD And Floor Plan

This section provides step-by-step instructions to create a floor plan using AutoCAD 2027.

17.10.1. New file

New file: Open a new "*My_acad_Landscape.dwt*" file. It is one of the template files created in *Chapter 8*. Save the file as *FloorPlan.dwg*.

17.10.2. The input units

Before starting the floor plan, set the input units or the drawing units and the precision.

17.10.2.1. Architectural

Before starting the floor plan, set the input units to the Architectural units. The user inputs lengths in feet and inches as follows:

(i) Type *Units* in the command line and press the *Enter* key. This opens the *Drawing Units* dialog box, Figure 17-9a. (ii) From the *Drawing Units* dialog box, select *Architectural* from the *Length* panel and *Type* sub-panel. (iii) Press the *OK* button.

Now the user can specify the information in architectural units (feet and inches). The length 5'-6" is entered as follows: (i) activate the *Line* or *Polyline* commands. (ii) Type 5. (iii) Type the apostrophe (') key. (iv) Type 6. (v) Press the *Enter* key. (vi) DO NOT TYPE hyphen (-) to separate feet from inches and double apostrophe to represent inches.

17.10.2.2. Precision

Before starting the floor plan, set the drawing precision of the input units as follows:

(i) Type *Units* in the command line and press the *Enter* key. This opens the *Drawing Units* dialog box. (ii) From the *Drawing Units* dialog box, select the *0'-0 1/32* from the *Length* panel and *Precision* sub-panel Figure 17-9b. (iii) Press the *OK* button.

17.10.3. Load linetypes

The floor plan uses solid or visible (known as continuous in AutoCAD), dashed (known as hidden in AutoCAD), and centerlines. Therefore, load *Hidden* and *Center* linetype; *Continuous* is the default linetype. Figure 17-9c shows the loaded linetypes. Refer to *Chapter 3* for loading linetypes.

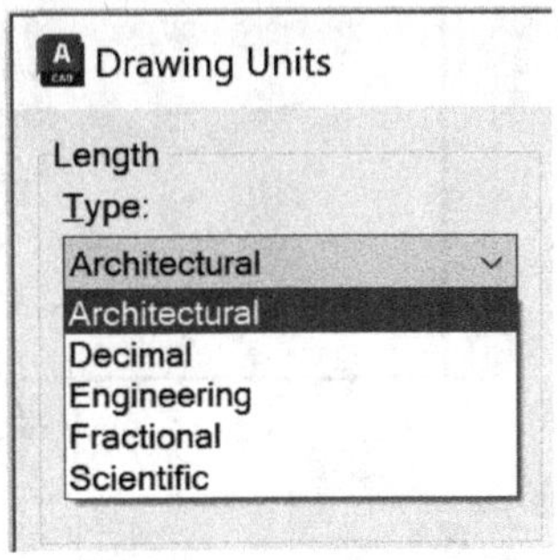

Figure 17-9a

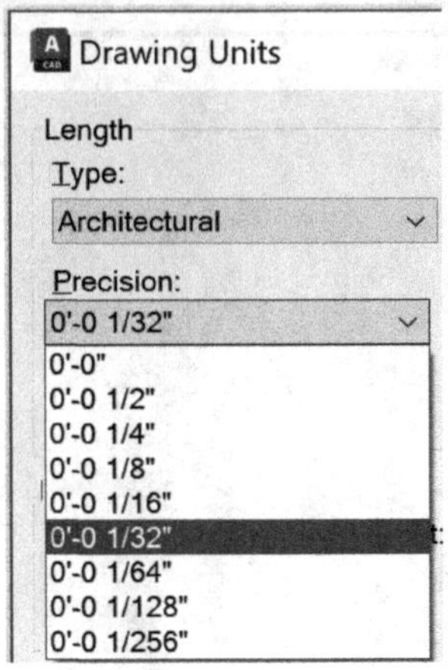

Figure 17-9b

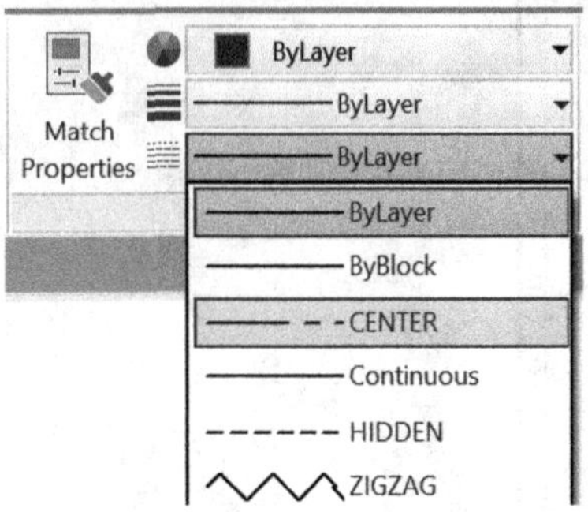

Figure 17-9c

17.10.4. Orthogonal lines

Since most of the lines in a floor plan are either horizontal or vertical, turn *On* the *ORTHO* option by pressing the corresponding button () on the status bar.

17.10.5. Layers

(i) Create layers as necessary. (ii) Set the layers' colors and lineweights. (iii) Before using a layer, make the layer to be the current layer. (iv) Make sure that the current layer is *on* (not frozen or *off*).

17.10.6. The floorplan

This section provides step-by-step instructions for drawing a floor plan of a single-story residential building with three bedrooms, two bathrooms, and a two-car garage.

- Do not add any dimensions! Dimensions are added later.
- The drawing will be printed from the layout! Keep checking the appearance of the linetypes and lineweights in the layouts.

- Create layers as needed.

17.10.6.1. Exterior wall

- Create a layer named *Walls* and set its lineweight to 0.5mm and linetype to be Continuous. This layer is used for the exterior and interior walls.
- Make the *Walls* layer to be the current layer.

- Use the *Polyline* command to draw the exterior face of the exterior wall as shown in Figure 17-10a.

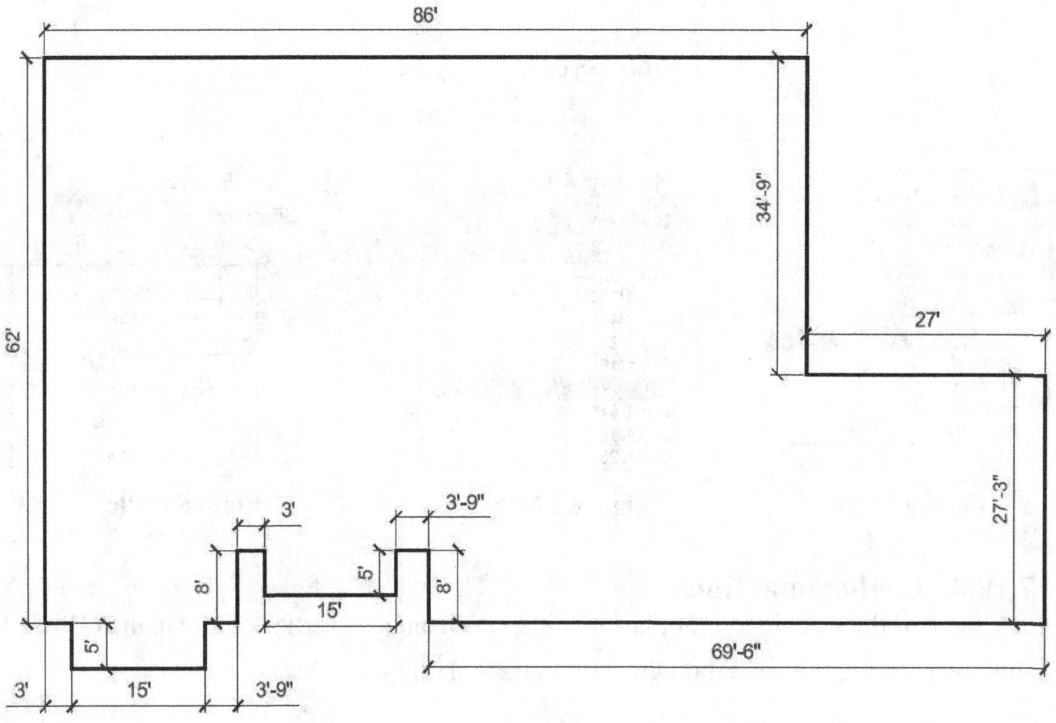

Figure 17-10a

- Draw the interior face of the exterior wall as follows:
  1. The exterior wall thickness is 1'.
  2. Use the *Offset* command with an offset distance of 1' to create the interior face of the exterior wall. To create the offset, click inside the interior face of the exterior wall, Figure 17-10b.

17.10.6.2. Roofline

- Create a layer named *RoofLine* and set its lineweight to 0.5mm and linetype to be Hidden. This layer is used for the roofline.
- Draw the roofline as follows:
  1. The roof overhung is 2'.
  2. Use the *Offset* command with an offset distance of 2' to create the roof overhung from the exterior wall. To create the offset, click outside the exterior face of the exterior wall, Figure 17-10b.
  3. Move the offset to the *RoofLine* layer and turn off the *Roofline* layer.

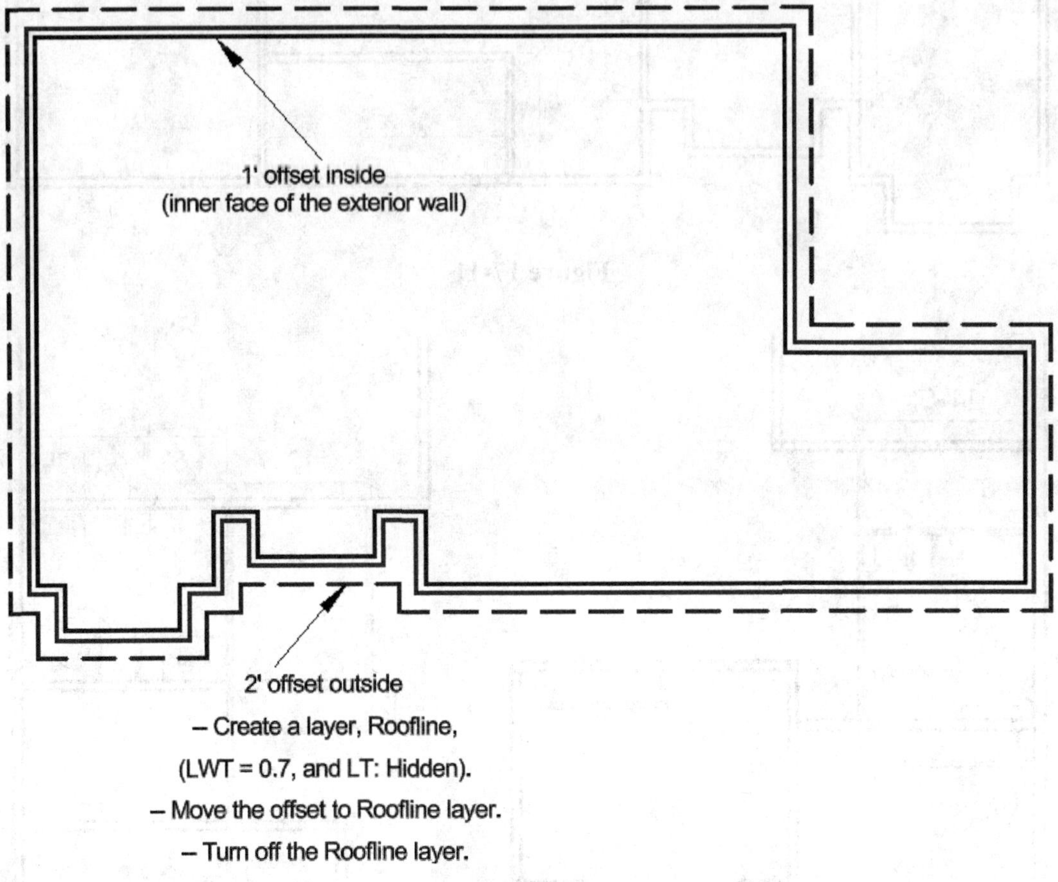

Figure 17-10b

17.10.6.3. Interior walls

The load bearing interior walls' thickness is 9 inches, Figure 17-11; and the non-load bearing interior walls' thickness is 5 inches, Figure 17-12.

- Draw the interior walls as follows:
  1. Make the *Walls* layer to be the current layer.
  2. Use the *Line*, *Offset*, *Trim*, and *Extend* commands to create the interior walls.

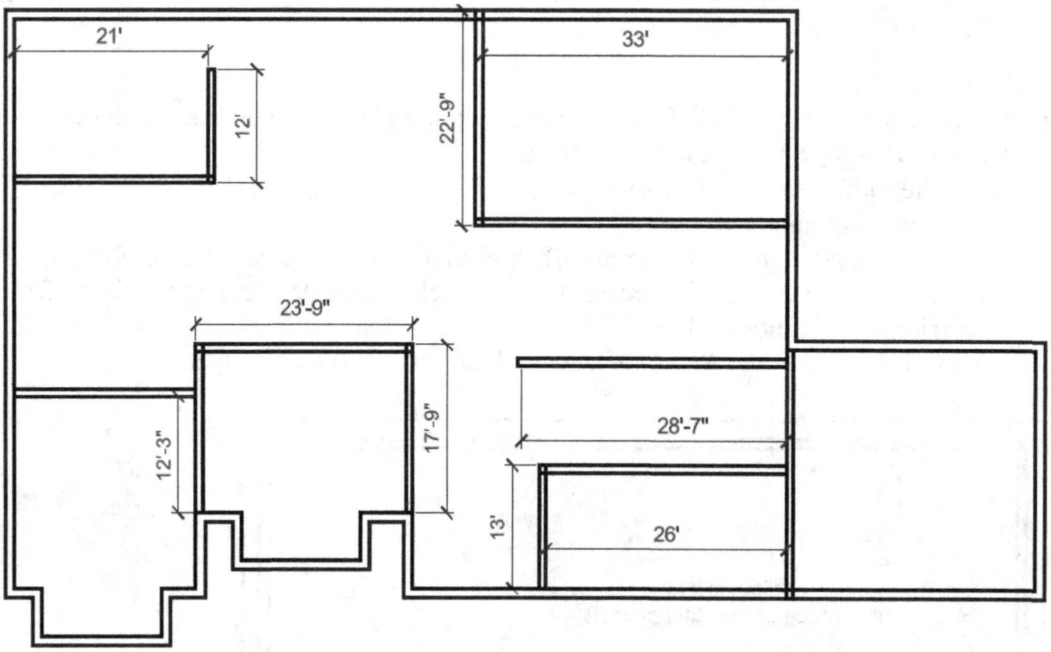

Figure 17-11

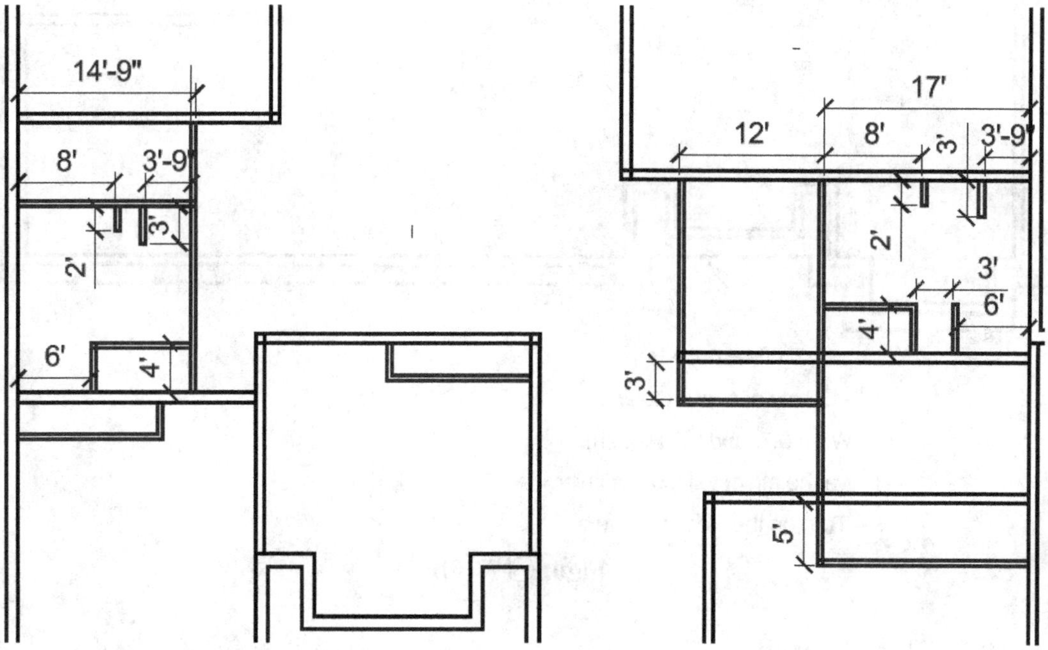

Figure 17-12

17.10.6.4. Label

Label the various parts of the house, Figure 17-13, and place them as shown in the figure. In the figure, MSTR is the abbreviation for master, *WIC* is for walk-in-closet, and *BTHR* is for the bathroom.

- Add the labels as follows:
  1. Create a layer named *Rm_Label* and set its lineweight to 0.0mm and linetype to be Continuous. This layer is used for displaying the names of the various rooms.
  2. Make the *Rm_Label* layer to be the current layer.
  3. Add the label using the *Annotated Text* command.
  4. The labels' annotative text height is 3/32".

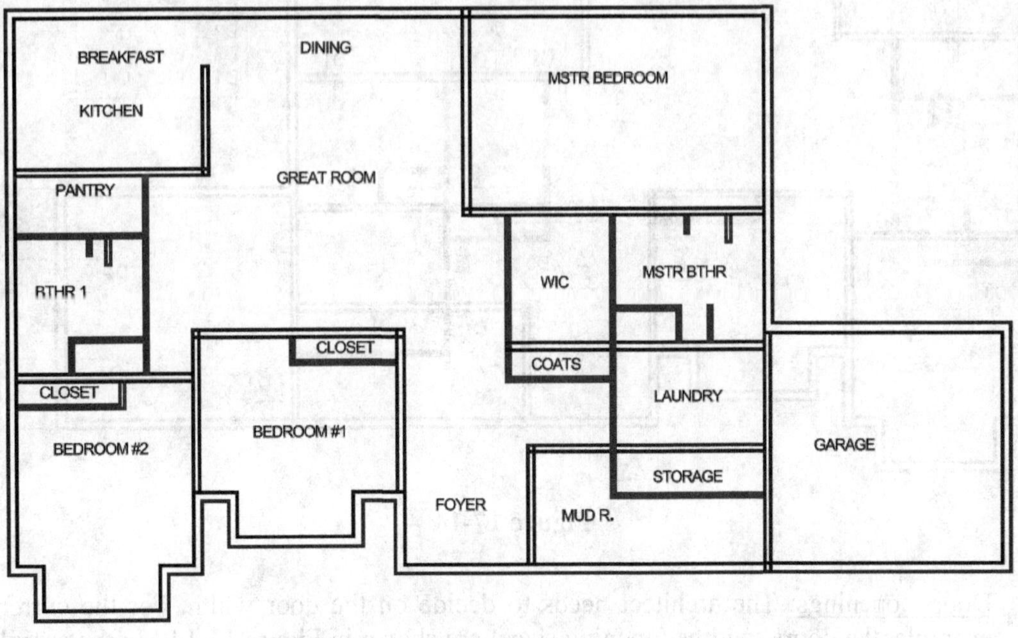

Figure 17-13

17.10.6.5. Doors

The door drawing process can be divided into four major steps: (i) displaying the doors' locations, (ii) writing the doors' labels, (iii) creating the door openings in the walls, and (iv) drawing the door panels. An architect can draw the doors using the following steps.

- <u>Doors' Location</u>: The architect needs to decide on the door location and the distance from the nearest wall. The door location can be shown by drawing the centerline of the door opening, Figure 17-14, using the following steps. The abbreviations used in the figure are SP for Single Panel, DP for Double Panel, FL for Folding, and OH for Overhead.
  1. Create a layer named *DoorCL* and set its lineweight to 0.0mm and linetype to be Center. This layer is used for the centerlines of the doors.
  2. Make the *DoorCL* layer to be the current layer.
  3. Draw 8'-0" long centerlines for the doors' center, Figure 17-14.

- Doors' labels: Figure 17-14.
  1. Create a layer named *DoorLabel* and set its lineweight to 0.0mm and linetype to be Continuous. This layer is used for the labels of the doors.
  2. Make the *DoorLabel* layer to be the current layer.
  3. Using the *Text* command, label the doors as shown in Figure 17-14. The door labels' annotative text height is 1/8".

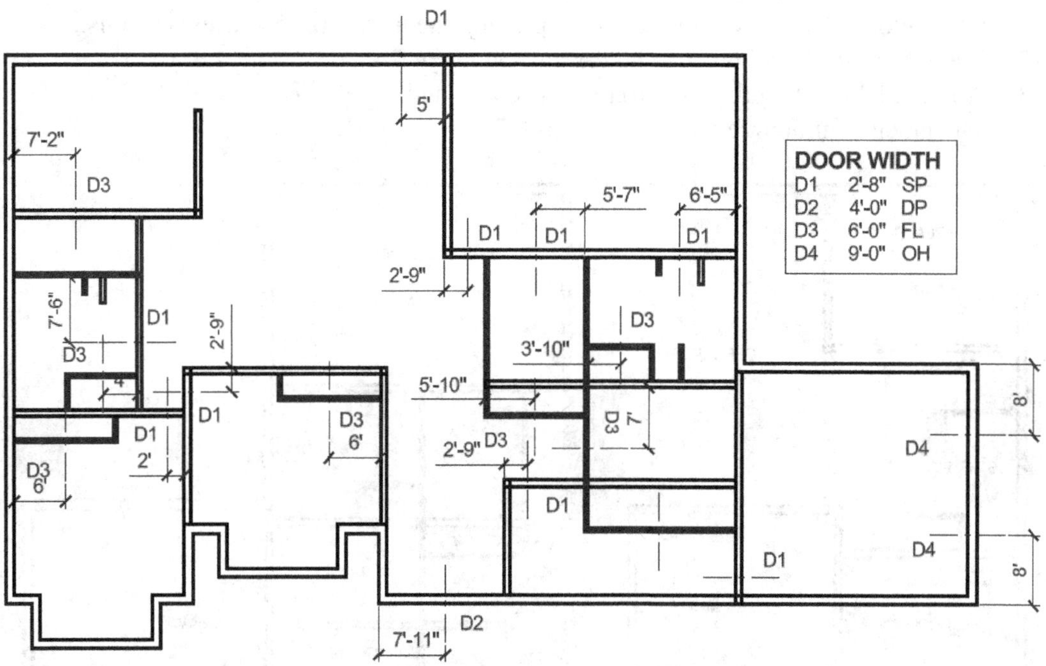

Figure 17-14

- Doors' openings: The architect needs to decide on the door width. For the current example, the doors' widths (opening sizes) are shown in Figure 17-14. In the sample house, the front door is 4 feet wide. The door opening creation demonstration creates the door opening for the front door.
  1. Make the *Walls* layer to be the current layer.
  2. Use the Offset command with the offset distance of 2' (half of the door width) to create a line at a distance of 2', Figure 17-15a. Move this offset line to the *Walls* layer, Figure 17-15b.
  3. Use the *Mirror* command to create a similar line on the right side, Figure 17-15c.
  4. Use the *Trim* command to trim the lines representing the wall and extra portion of the two parallel lines drawn in the previous steps, Figure 17-15d.

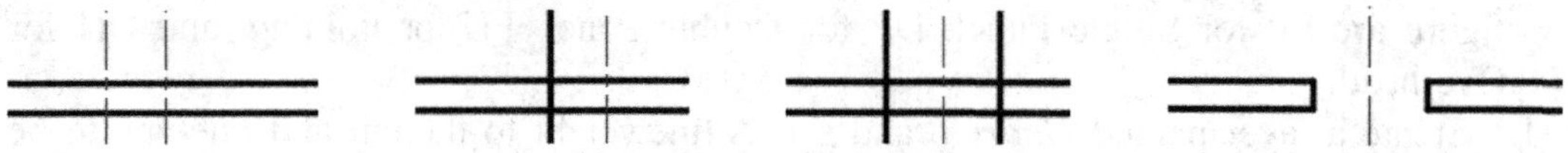

Figure 17-15a **Figure 17-15b** **Figure 17-15c** **Figure 17-15d**

5. Repeat the process for the other doors, Figure 17-16. The door widths are shown in the figure, too.

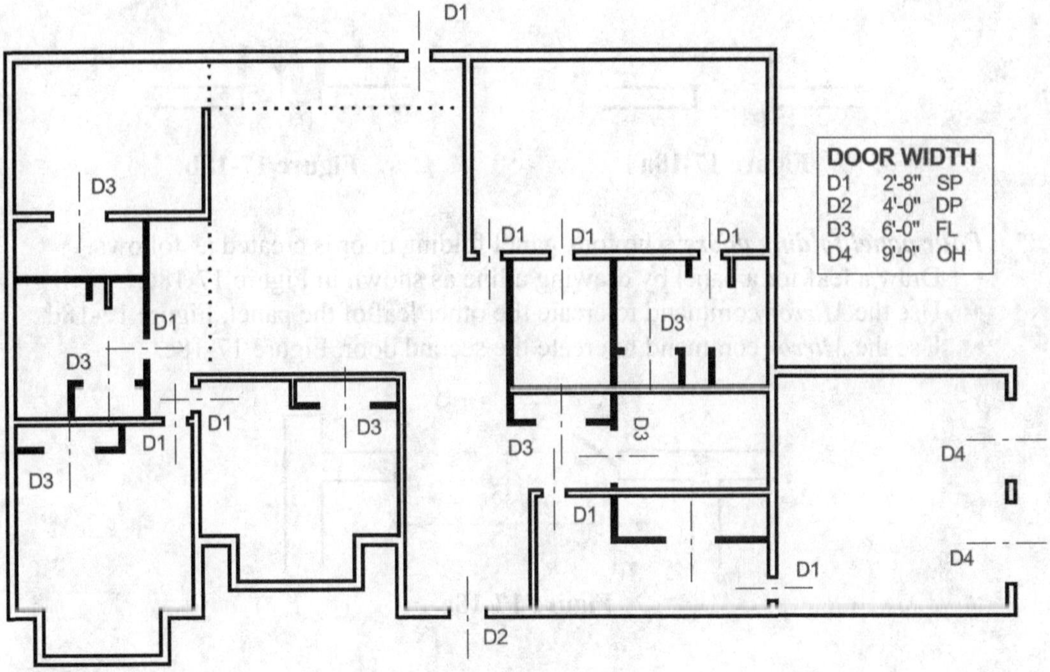

Figure 17-16

- Doors' Panels: Figure 17-19 shows the different types of doors used in the house.
  1. Create a layer named *Doors* and set its lineweight to 1.0mm and linetype to be Continuous. This layer is used for the doors.
  2. Make the *Doors* layer to be the current layer.
  3. ***Single panel swing doors***: Figure 17-17a shows an opening for a single panel swing door. Draw a single panel swing door using the following steps.
     - From the Properties panel, set the LWT to be 0.0mm.
     - Draw a circle of radius equal to the door opening and center as shown in Figure 17-17b.
     - Set the LWT to be *By Layer* option.
     - Draw the door panel using the *Line* command and the *Intersection* option in object snap setting. Also change the line's lineweight to 1.00mm, Figure 17-17c.
     - Use the *Trim* command to create the desired appearance of the door, Figure 17-16c and Figure 17-17d.

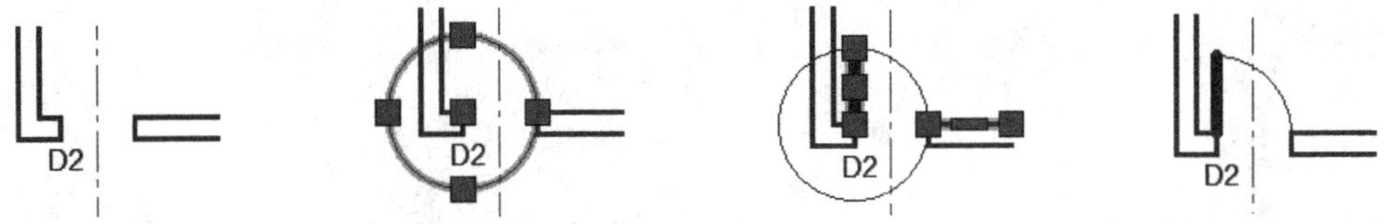

Figure 17-17a **Figure 17-17b** **Figure 17-17c** **Figure 17-17d**

4. ***Double panel swing doors***: The double panel swing door is created as follows. (i) Draw a single panel swing door, Figure 17-18a. (ii) Use the mirror command to create the other panel of the door, Figure 17-18b.

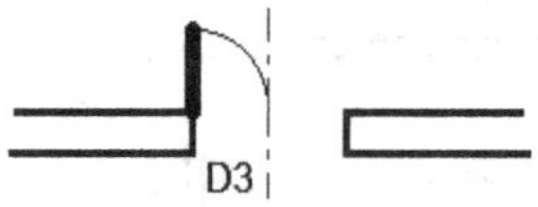

Figure 17-18a

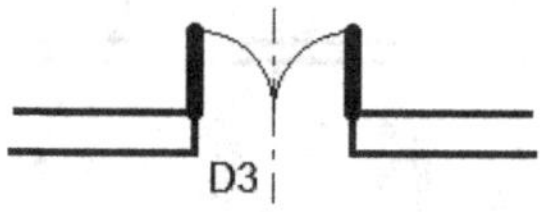

Figure 17-18b

5. ***Four panel folding doors***: The four-panel folding door is created as follows.
   - Draw a leaf for a panel by drawing a line as shown in Figure 17-18c.
   - Use the *Mirror* command to create the other leaf of the panel, Figure 17-18d.
   - Use the *Mirror* command to create the second door, Figure 17-18e.

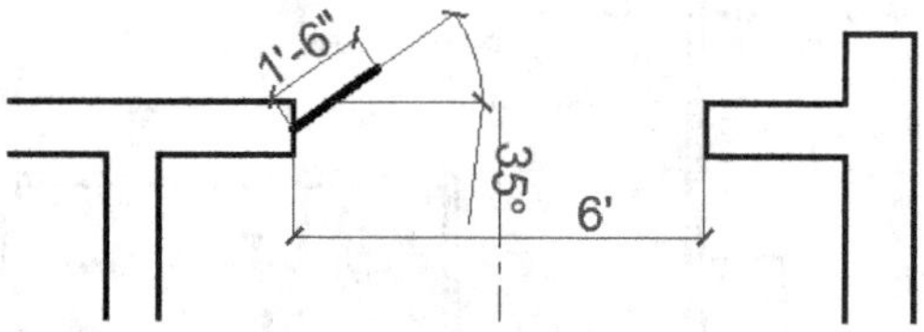

Figure 17-18c

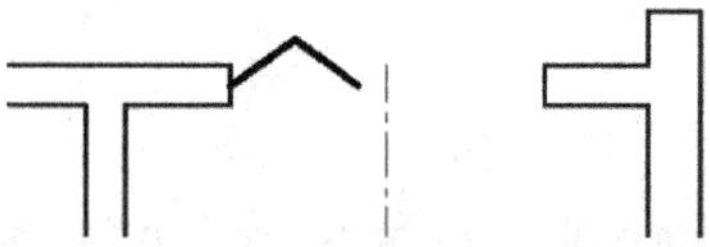

Figure 17-18d

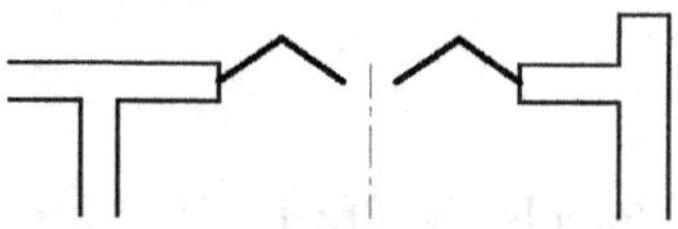

Figure 17-18e

6. ***Front door***: Two panels with inward swing.
   - Draw a single swing door.
   - Use the *Mirror* command to create the other panel.

7. ***Garage door***: The garage door height is 9'; and it is an overhead door.
   - Draw a polyline and change its linetype to *Hidden*. If necessary, set the linetype scale.

8. ***Other doors***: Use *Copy, Mirror*, and *Move* commands to create the remaining doors. Figure 17-19 shows the different types of doors used in the building.

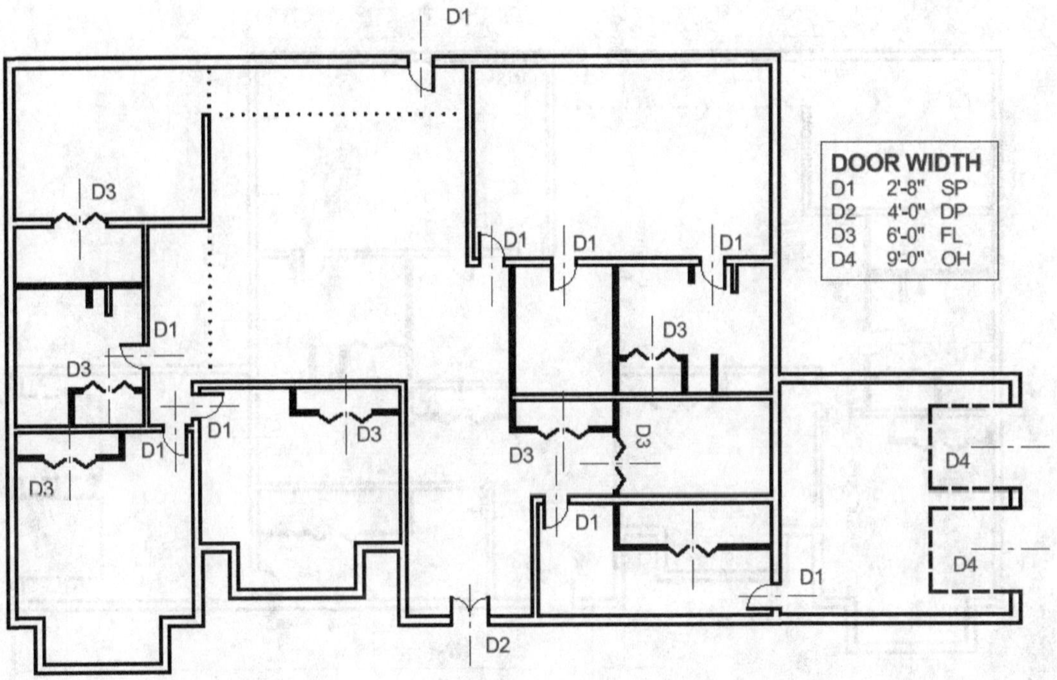

Figure 17-19

17.10.6.6. Windows

The window drawing process can be divided into three major steps: (i) displaying the windows' locations, (ii) writing the windows' labels, (iii) and drawing the windows. An architect can draw windows using the following steps.

- Windows Location: The architect needs to decide on the window location and the distance from the nearest wall, Figure 17-20.
  1. Create a layer named *WindowCL* and set its lineweight to 0.0mm and linetype to be Center. This layer is used for the centerlines of the windows.
  2. Make the *WindowCL* layer to be the current layer.
  3. Draw the centerlines for the windows of length 8'-0'', Figure 17-20.

- Windows' Label: Figure 17-20.
  1. Create a layer named *WindowLabel* and set its lineweight to 0.0mm and linetype to be Continuous. This layer is for the labels of the windows.
  2. Make the *WindowLabel* layer to be the current layer.
  3. Using the *Text* command, label the windows.
  4. The window labels' annotative text height is 1/8".
  5. The windows in Figure 17-21 show the width of W1, W2, W3, and W4.

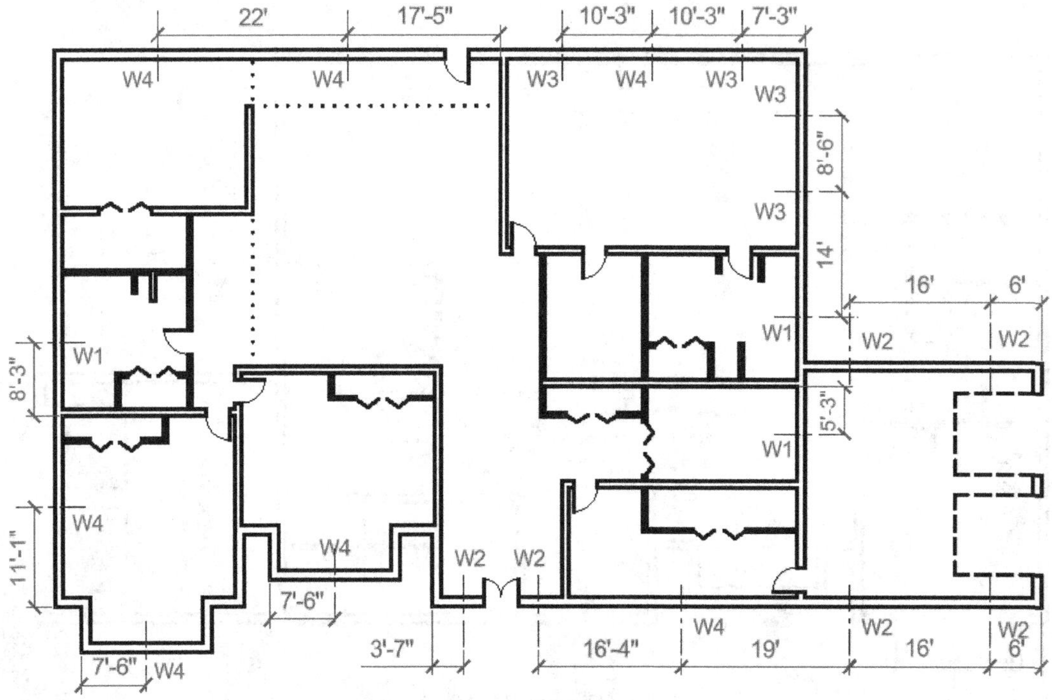

Figure 17-20

- Draw the windows: The details of the windows labeled as W1, W2, W3, and W4 are shown in Figure 17-21a.
  1. Create a layer named *Windows* and set its lineweight to 0.5mm and linetype to be Continuous. This layer is used for the windows.
  2. Make the *Windows* layer to be the current layer.
  3. Draw the windows once.
  4. Use the *Copy*, *Mirror*, and *Rotate* commands to create multiple copies of the windows to place them at appropriate locations, Figure 17-21c.

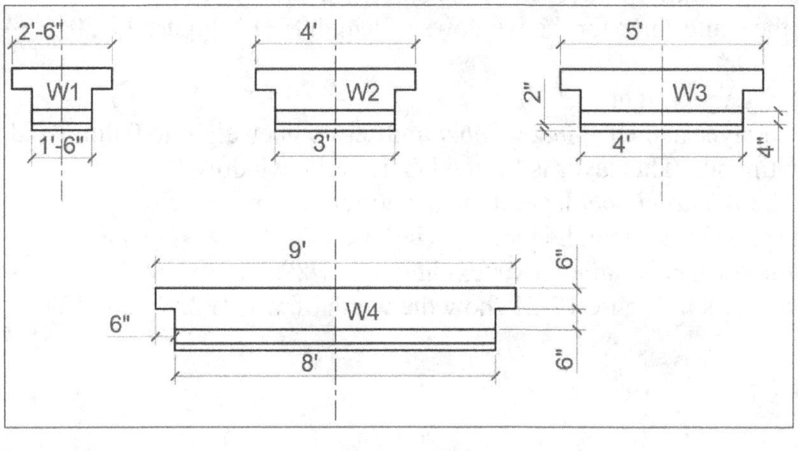

Figure 17-21a

- Figure 17-21b shows the different types of windows used in the building.

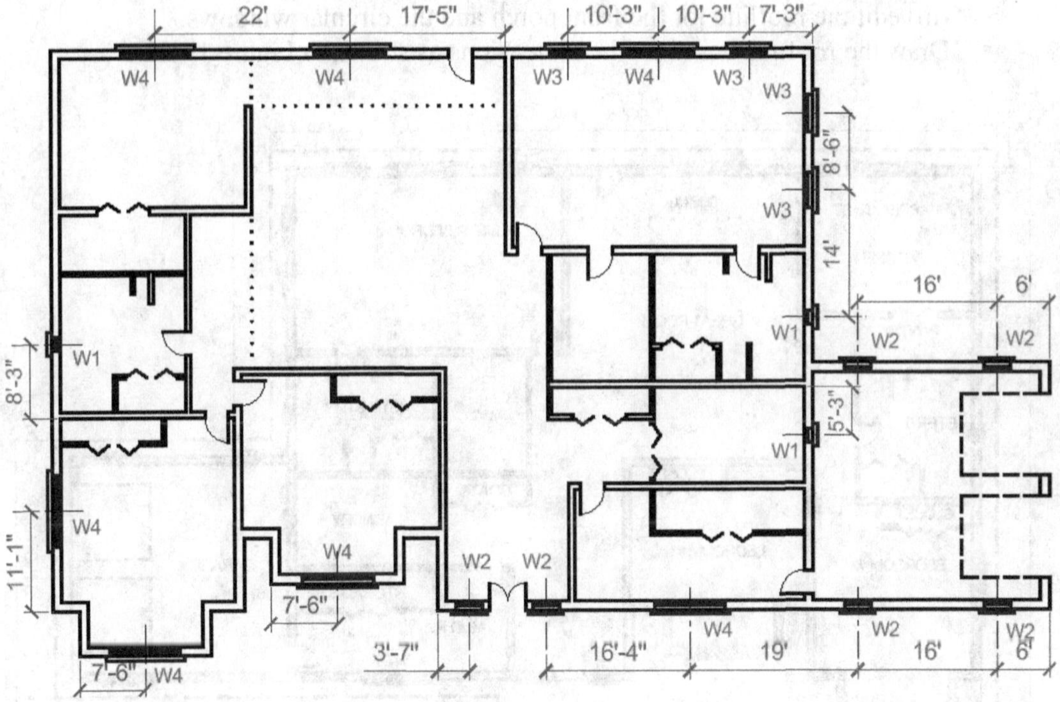

Figure 17-21b

17.10.6.7. Walls cleanup

Clean the walls' intersections Using *Trim* command, Figure 17-22.

17.10.6.8. Wall hatch

- Hatch the walls, Figure 17-22:
  1. Create a layer *Wall_Hatch* and set its lineweight to 0.0mm and linetype to be Continuous. This layer is used for wall hatch.
  2. Make *Wall_Hatch* the current layer.
  3. Activate the *Hatch* command and create annotative hatch.
  4. Select the *AR-CONC* pattern. The scale factor in the current example is 0.005.
  5. Select the exterior and interior walls to hatch, Figure 17-22.

17.10.6.9. Roofline updated

- Add the roof line, Figure 17-22:
  1. If the roofline was created in Section 17.10.6.1, then adjust the roof for the front porch and skip the remainder of this section. Otherwise continue the remainder of this section.
  2. Load the *Hidden* linetype.
  3. Create a layer named *RoofLine* and set its lineweight to 0.5mm and its linetype to be Hidden. This layer is used for the roofline.
  4. Make *RoofLine* the current layer.
  5. Draw the roofline using one of the following two methods:

- Using the *Offset* command with 2' offset distance, (i) create an offset of the exterior face of the exterior wall; (ii) move the offset to *RoofLine* the layer; and (iii) edit the roofline for the front porch and the circular windows.
- Draw the roofline based on the dimensions as shown in Figure 17-22.

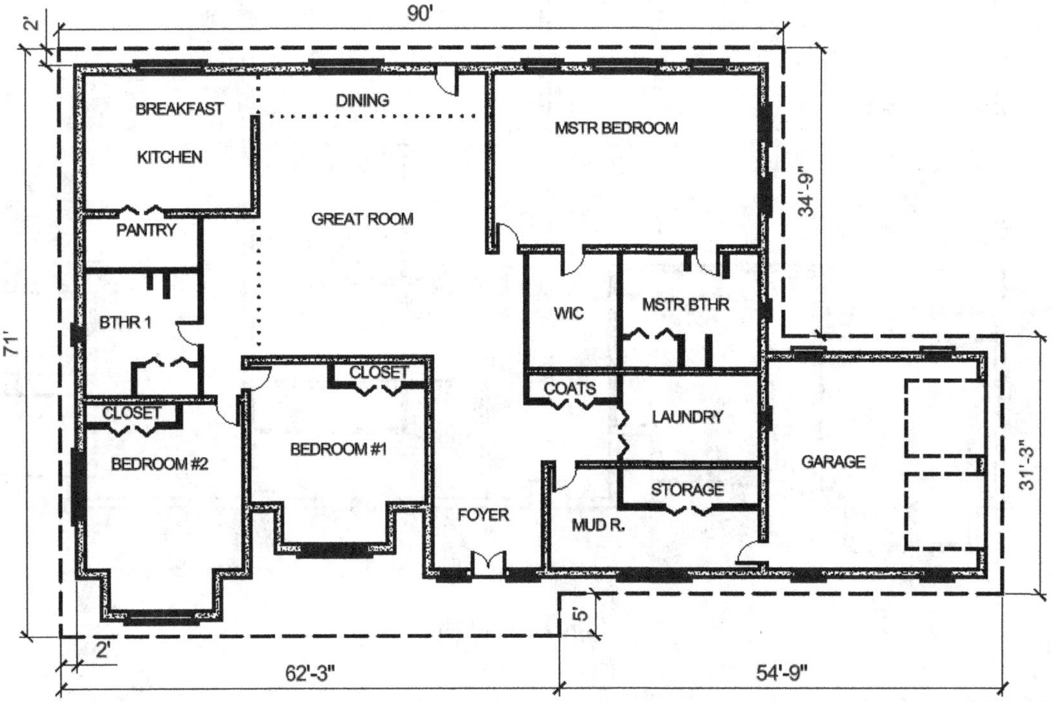

Figure 17-22

17.10.6.10.Front porch

- Draw the front porch, Figure 17-23:
  1. Create a layer named *Porch* and set its lineweight to 0.5mm and its linetype to be Continuous. This layer is used for the porch.
  2. Make *Porch* be the current layer.
  3. The front porch is a covered porch.
  4. (i) Set lineweight to be 0.0mm. (ii) Create the front porch on the *Porch* layer. (iii) Hatch the porch with *AR-HBONE* with a scale factor of 0.025.
  5. (i) Create the columns *Porch* layer. (ii) Hatch the column with solid color.

17.10.6.11.Back patio

- Draw the back porch, Figure 17-24:
  1. Make the *Porch* layer to be the current layer.
  2. The back porch is an uncovered patio and is aligned with the laundry and great room's walls.
  3. (i) Create the back patio on the *Porch* layer. (ii) Hatch the patio with *AR-HBONE* with a scale factor of 0.025.

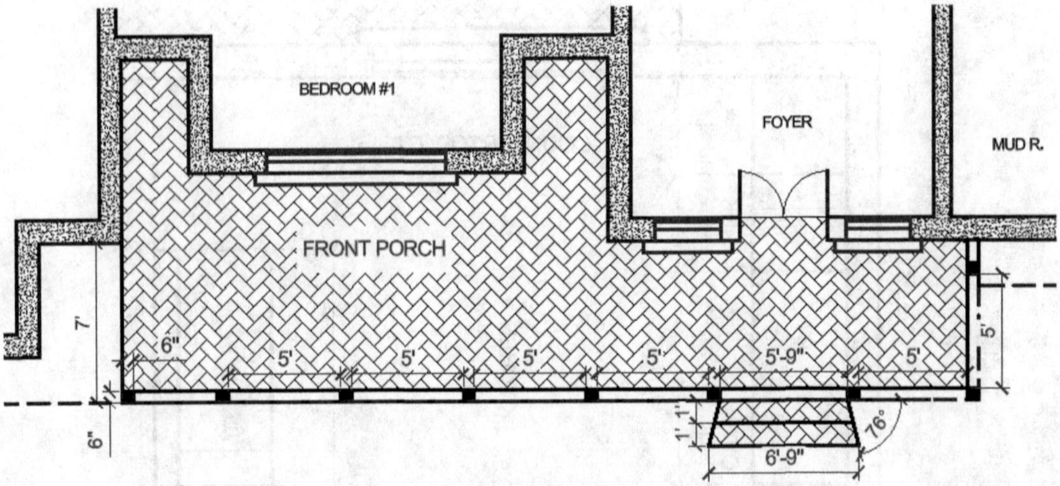

Figure 17-23

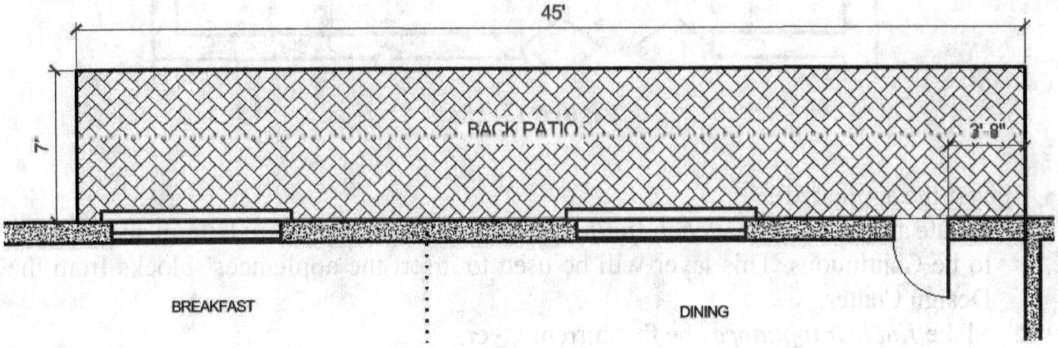

Figure 17-24

17.10.6.12. Kitchen

The kitchen drawing process can be divided into three major steps: (i) specifying the locations of the appliances, (ii) inserting the appliances, (iii) and hatching the kitchen floor and the counters. An architect can draw a kitchen using the following steps.

- <u>Specify the location of appliances and their labels as follows</u>:

1. Create a layer named *KitchenDim* and set its lineweight to 0.0mm and linetype to be Continuous. This layer will be used to specify the appliances' location.
2. Make *KitchenDim* be the current layer.
3. Specify the location for the oven, sink, dishwasher, refrigerator, and the counter space, Figure 17-25a.
4. Create a layer named *KitchenLabel* and set its lineweight to 0.0mm and linetype to be Continuous. This layer will be used for the appliances' labels.
5. Make *KitchenLabel* be the current layer.
6. Using the annotative *Text* command, create the labels as shown in Figure 17-25a. The labels' annotative text height is 1/8".

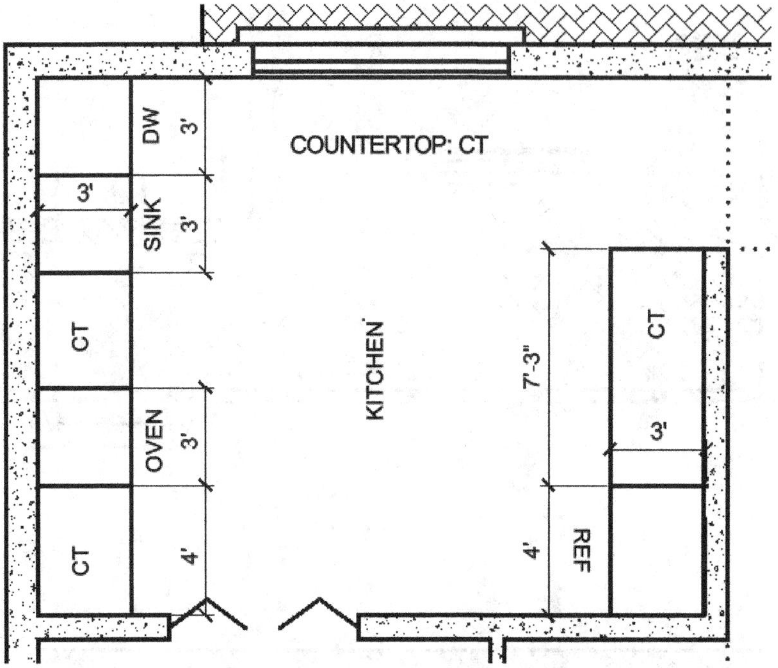

Figure 17-25a

- Insert the appliances:

1. Create a layer named *KitchenAppliances* and set its lineweight to 0.0mm and linetype to be Continuous. This layer will be used to insert the appliances' blocks from the Design Center.
2. Make *KitchenAppliances* be the current layer.
3. Draw the kitchen appliances as follows:
   1. The blocks for the *Range-Oven-Top* (RG), *Refrigerator* (REF), *Sink*, and *Faucet-Kit-Top* are inserted from the *Design Center*. The inserted blocks must be scaled appropriately. Calculate the scale factor as follows:
      Scale factor = Desired size / Size from the Design Center
   2. The blocks are inserted (Figure 17-25c) from the *Design Center → Kitchen.dwg* of AutoCAD 2027. The design center is discussed in detail in *Chapter* 7. The scale factors of the blocks and the angles are listed here.
   3. **Insert the blocks:** The Sink block is inserted for the demonstration; refer to Figure 17-25b. (i) Check the *Insertion point: Check On-screen* option. (ii) For *Scale*, insert the scale factors as shown in the figure. (iii) For *Rotation*, insert the angle values as shown in the figure. (iv) Press the *OK* button of the dialog box. Click for the block insertion location. **Alternate method for rotating the block**: Insert the block and rotate after the insertion.
   - **For scaling, keep the units consistent**. (i) If one of the sizes is the combination of feet and inches then convert both sizes to inches. For example, 2'-4" is entered as 28 and not as 2.25'. For example, the Y-scale = 36/28 for the refrigerator; do not write it as 3/2.25.
   - Specify positive angle for counterclockwise rotation and negative angle for clockwise rotation.

4. The scale factors for the blocks are listed here.

- Sink: X-scale = 1; Y-scale = 36/21; and angle = -90°.
- Faucet: Keep the scale factors the same as used for the corresponding sink; that is, X-scale = 1; Y-scale = 36/21; and angle = -90°.
- Range-Oven: X-scale = 36/30; Y-scale = 3/2; and angle = -90°.
- Refrigerator: X-scale = 4/3; Y-scale = 36/28; and angle = 90°.

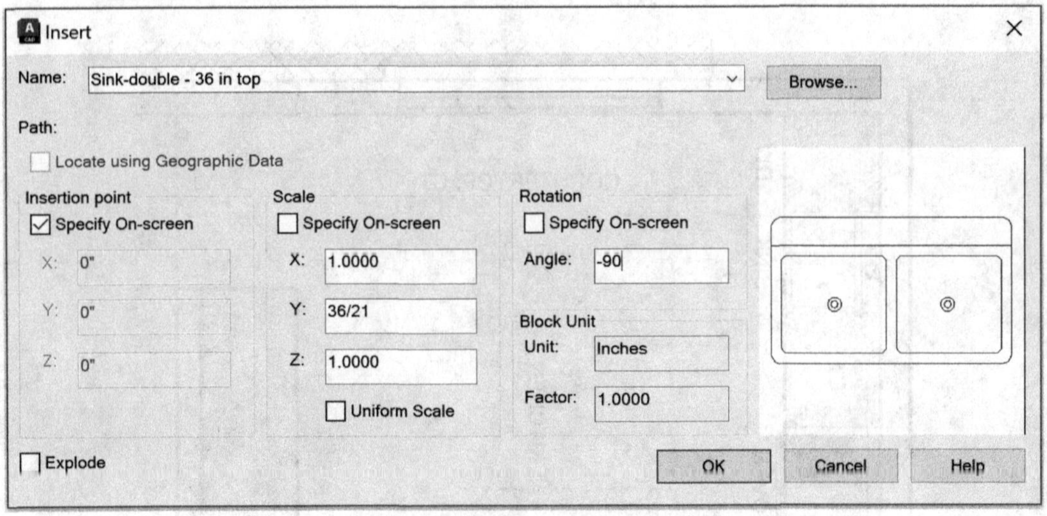

Figure 17-25b

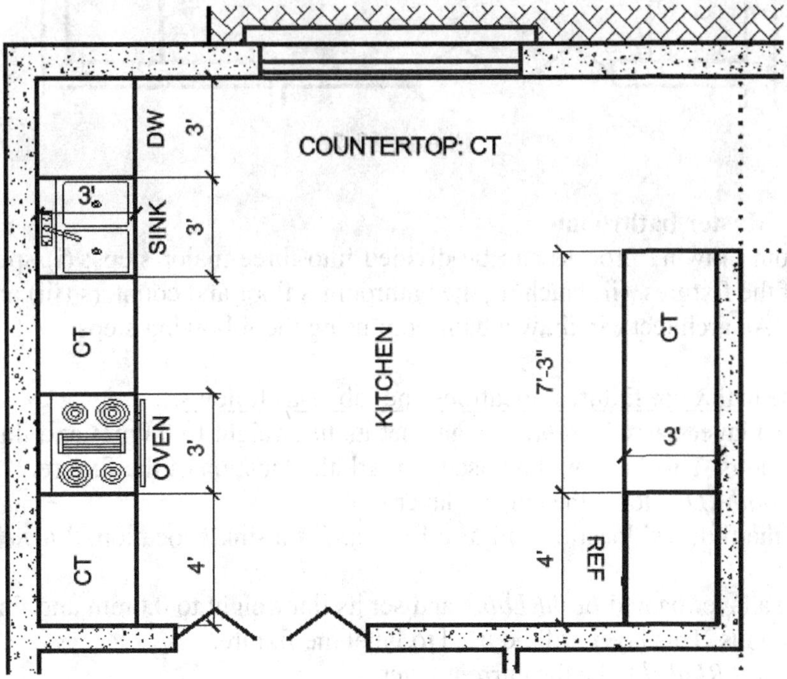

Figure 17-25c

- Hatch the kitchen, Figure 17-26: Hatch the kitchen as follows:
  1. Create a layer named *KitchenHatch* and set its lineweight to 0.0mm and linetype to be Continuous. This layer will be used to hatch the kitchen.
  2. Make *KitchenHatch* to be the current layer.
  3. Create the boundary of the floor area using *Polyline* command.
  4. Hatch the kitchen using annotative *Hatch* command: using *Honey* pattern at the scale of 1.0 for the floor and *Honey* pattern at the scale of 0.4 for the counter tops.

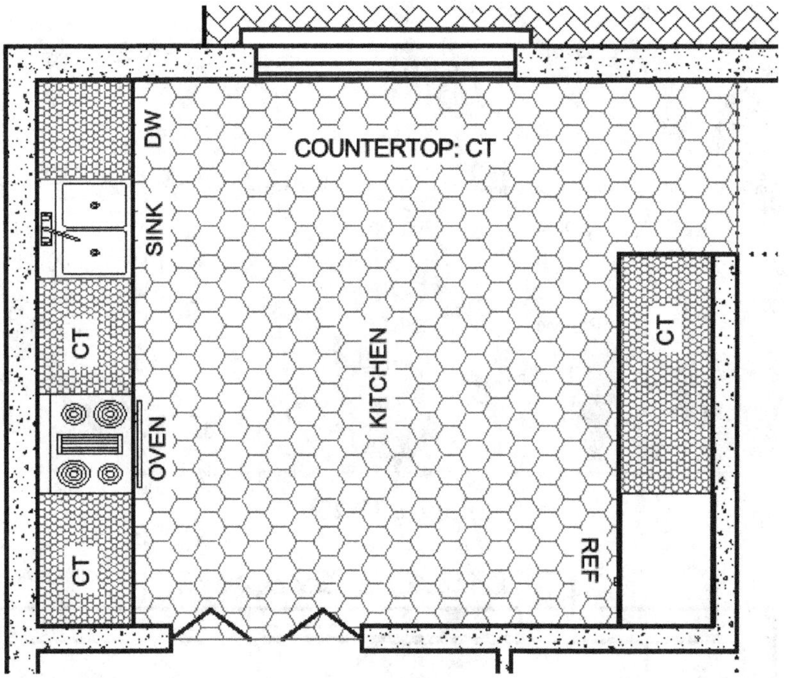

Figure 17-26

17.10.6.13. Master bathroom

The bathroom drawing process can be divided into three major steps: (i) specifying the locations of the fixtures, (ii) hatching the bathroom's floor and counters (iii) and inserting the fixtures. An architect can draw a bathroom using the following steps.

- Draw the bathroom fixtures' locations and labels as follows:
  1. Create a layer named *BathRDim* and set its lineweight to 0.0mm and linetype to be Continuous. This layer will be used to mark the location of the fixture.
  2. Make *BathRDim* to be the current layer.
  3. Draw the fixtures' locations, Figure 17-27a. For a sink's location, draw ellipses.

  4. Create a layer named *BathRLabel* and set its lineweight to 0.0mm and linetype to be Continuous. This layer will be used to label the fixture.
  5. Make *BathRLabel* to be the current layer.
  6. Using the Text command, create the labels as shown in Figure 17-27a. The labels' annotative text height is 1/8".

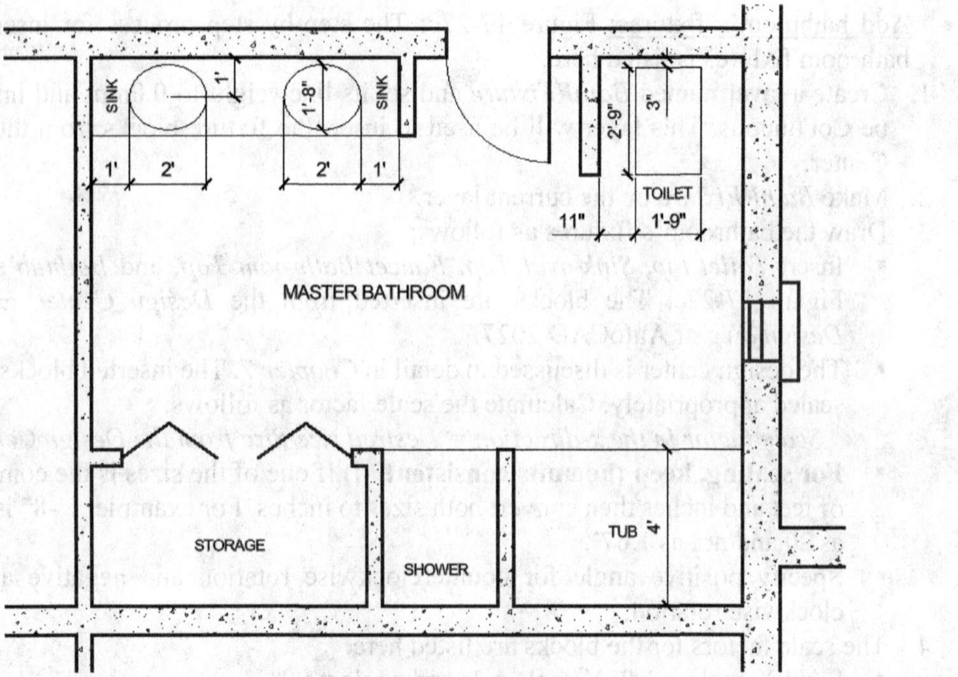

Figure 17-27a

- Add bathroom hatch: Figure 17-27b.
- Create a layer named *BathRHatch* and set its lineweight to 0.0mm and linetype to be Continuous. This layer will be used to hatch the bathroom.
- Make *BathRHatch* to be the current layer.
- Create the boundary of the floor area using *Polyline* command.
- Hatch the bathroom using annotative *Hatch* command: using *Honey* pattern at the scale of 1.0 for the floor and *Honey* pattern at the scale of 0.4 for the counter tops.

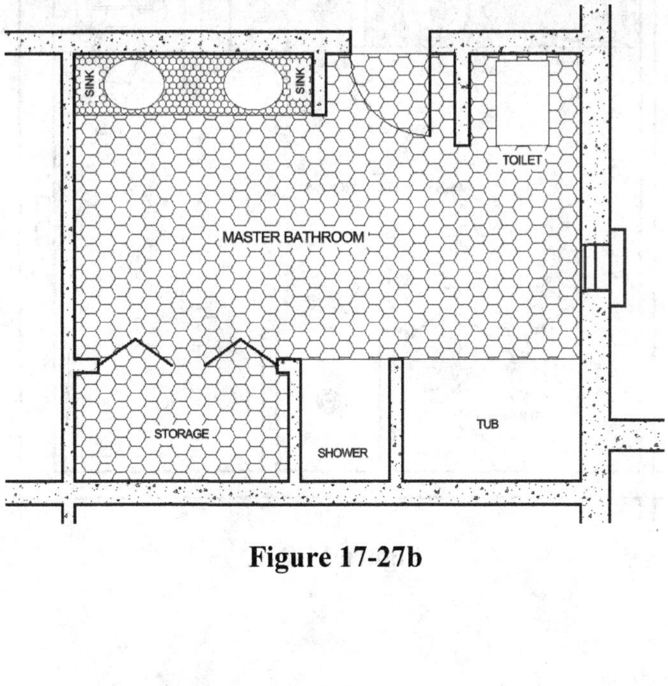

Figure 17-27b

- Add bathroom's fixtures: Figure 17-27c: The step-by-step process for inserting the bathroom fixtures is listed here.

1. Create a layer named *BathRFixture* and set its lineweight to 0.0mm and linetype to be Continuous. This layer will be used to insert the fixture blocks from the Design Center.
2. Make *BathRFixture* be the current layer.
3. Draw the bathroom's fixtures as follows:
   - Insert *Toilet top*, *Sink-oval Top*, *Faucet Bathroom Top*, and *Bathtub*'s blocks, Figure 17-27c. The blocks are inserted from the *Design Center* → *House Design.dwg* of AutoCAD 2027.
   - The design center is discussed in detail in *Chapter 7*. The inserted blocks must be scaled appropriately. Calculate the scale factor as follows:
     Scale factor in the x-direction = Desired size/Size from the Design Center
   - **For scaling, keep the units consistent**. (i) If one of the sizes is the combination of feet and inches then convert both sizes to inches. For example, 1'-8" is entered as 20 and not as 1.67'.
   - Specify positive angle for counterclockwise rotation and negative angle for clockwise rotation.
4. The scale factors for the blocks are listed here.
   - Sink: X-scale = 1.0; Y-scale = 1; and angle = 90°.
   - Faucet Bathroom Top (faucet for sink): Same as sink.
   - Use the mirror command to create the second sink.
   - Bathtub: X-scale = 6/5; Y-scale = 4/3; and angle = 90°.
   - Faucet Bathroom Top (faucet for tub): Same as bathtub.
   - Toilet: X-scale = 1; Y-scale = 1; and angle = 90°.
   - Sink block as drainage hole for the shower: X-scale = 8/24; Y-scale = 8/20; and angle = 0°.

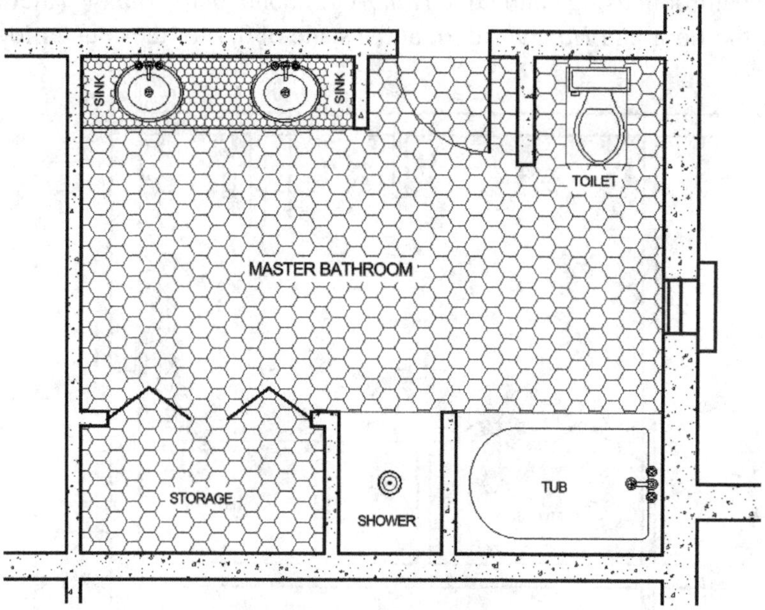

Figure 17-27c

17.10.6.14. Bathroom #1

- Bathroom #1: Complete Bathroom #1 following the master bathroom procedure, Figure 17-27d.

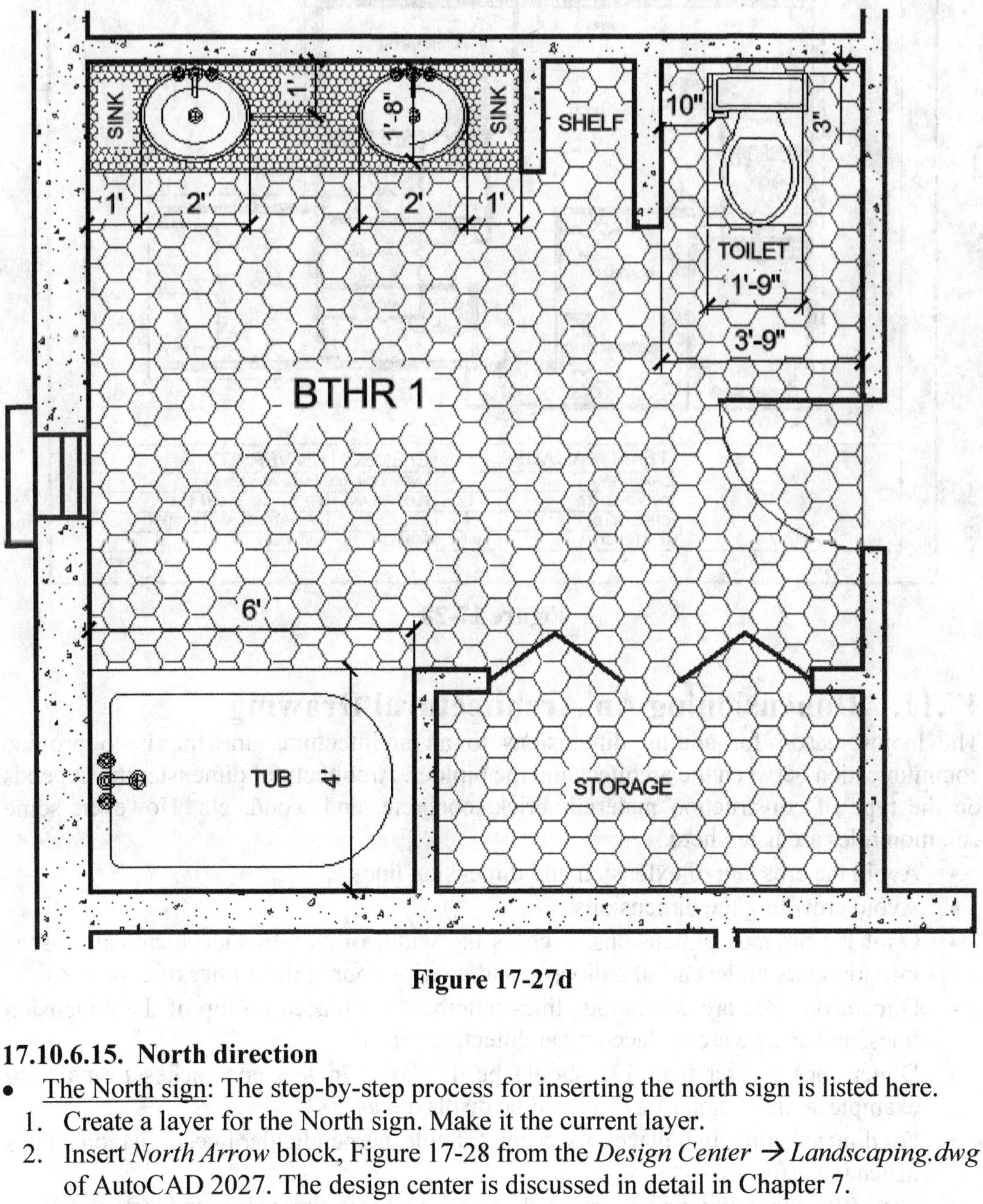

Figure 17-27d

17.10.6.15. North direction

- The North sign: The step-by-step process for inserting the north sign is listed here.
  1. Create a layer for the North sign. Make it the current layer.
  2. Insert *North Arrow* block, Figure 17-28 from the *Design Center → Landscaping.dwg* of AutoCAD 2027. The design center is discussed in detail in Chapter 7.
  3. X-scale = 1 and Y-scale = 6.

17.10.6.16. The complete floor plan

- Update the title block, Figure 17-28.
- Set the scale of the drawing to 1:168 and units to ARCHITECTURAL.

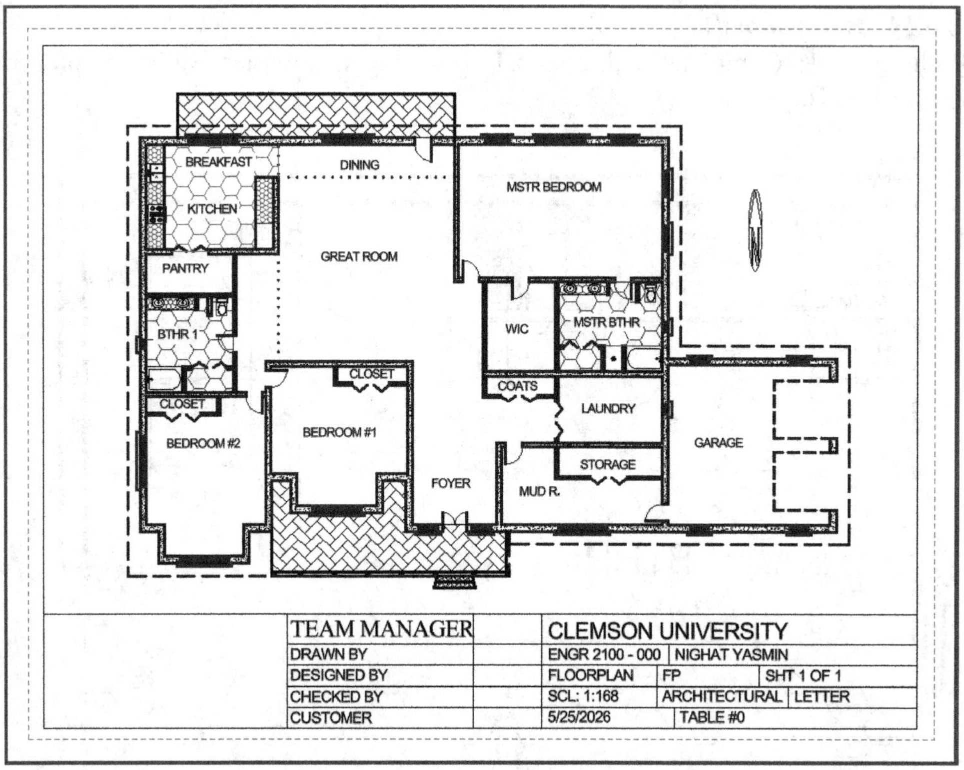

Figure 17-28

17.11. Dimensioning An Architectural Drawing

The major reason for adding dimensions to an architectural drawing is to provide communication between the architect and the builder. Architectural dimensioning depends on the type of construction material: brick, concrete, and wood, etc. However, some common rules are listed here.

- Avoid the crossing of extension and dimension lines.
- Avoid crowding the dimensions.
- Omit the obvious dimensions, such as the width of side-by-side identical closets, interior doors at the end of hallways, and interior door at the corner of a room.
- Dimension lines are continuous lines; numbers are placed on top of the dimension lines; and arrows are replaced by architectural ticks.
- Dimensions greater than 12" should be displayed in feet and inches format. For example, a dimension of 27" should be displayed as 2'-3".
- For dimensioning tight places, use a dot, triangle, perpendicular line, or diagonal lines instead of arrows.
- Generally, three dimensions are used on each wall: (i) dimensions to locate the doors and windows; (ii) dimensions to locate the walls; and (iii) dimensions to show the overall size.
- Irrespective of the scale, the dimensions should always indicate the actual length, that is, the dimensions of a particular item that is constructed.
- Display the scale of the drawing in the title block.

17.11.1. Create layers

Create the following layers. For each layer choose linetype of *Continuous* and lineweight of *0.0*. However, choose different colors for each layer.

1. *Dim_Door* for the location of the centerline of the doors.
2. *Dim_Window* for the location of the centerline of the windows.
3. *Dim_WtoW* for the wall-to-wall distance.
4. *Dim_Overall* for the overall dimension on each side of the building.
5. *Dim_Roomsize* to specify the size of each room.
6. *Dim_Interior* for the sizes of some of the interior walls.
7. *Dim_Porch* for the dimensions of the porch.
8. *Dim_BathRM* for the dimensions of the bathrooms.
9. *Dim_Kitchen* for the dimensions of the kitchen.
10. *Dim_Schedule* for the door and window schedule.

17.11.2. Set Dimension Style dialog box

1. Open the *Dimension Style Manager* dialog box using one of the following methods:
   a. From the *Annotate* tab and *Dimensions* panel, click on the small arrow in the right corner.
   b. From the *Home* tab, expand the *Annotation* tab and click on the button.
2. Select Annotative and click on the *Modify* button, Figure 17-29a.
3. This opens the *Modify Dimension Style* dialog box.

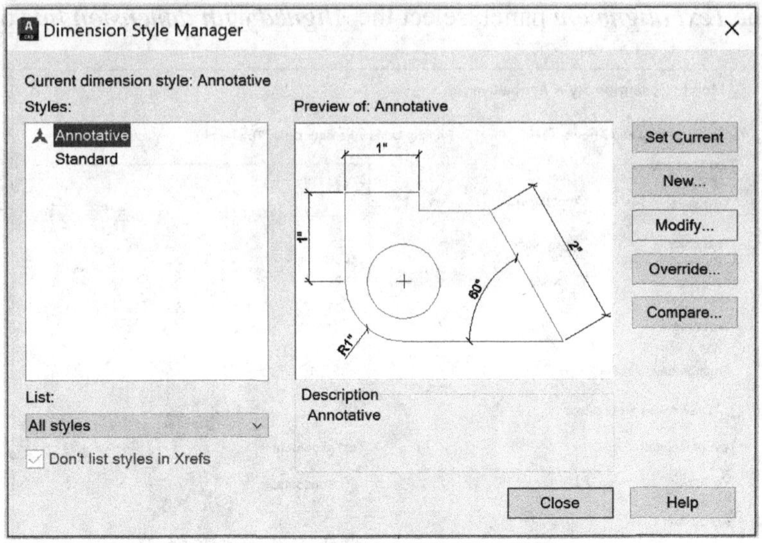

Figure 17-29a

4. Select the *Symbols and Arrows* tab as shown in Figure 17-29b.
   a. In the *Arrowheads* panel, click on the down-arrow under the *First* option and select the *Architectural tick* option.
   b. Make sure that the *Architectural tick* option is also selected for the *Second* arrow.
   c. In the *Arrowheads* panel, set the *Arrowsize* (not shown in the figure).

5. Select the *Primary Units* tab as shown in Figure 17-29c.
   a. In the *Linear dimension* panel, click on the down-arrow under the *Unit format* option and select the *Architectural* option.
   b. Set the *Precision* field to 0'-0" (not shown in the figure).

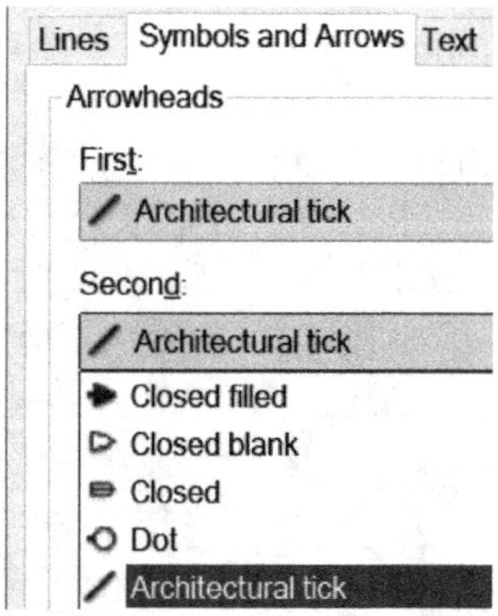

Figure 17-29b

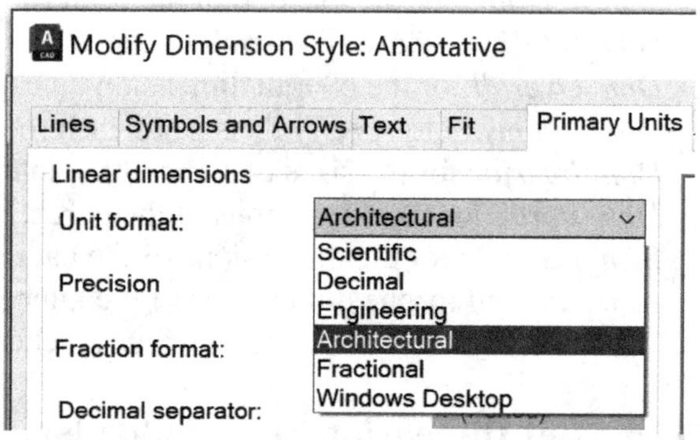

Figure 17-29c

6. Select the *Text* tab as shown in Figure 17-29d.
   a. In the *Text appearance* panel, for the *Text style* select the *Annotative* option. This will set the *Text height* to annotative text height.
   b. In the *Text placement* panel, (i) click on the down-arrow under the *Vertical* option and select the *Above* option; and (ii) set the *Offset from the dim line* to be 1/16".
   c. In the *Text alignment* panel, select the *Aligned with dimension line* option.

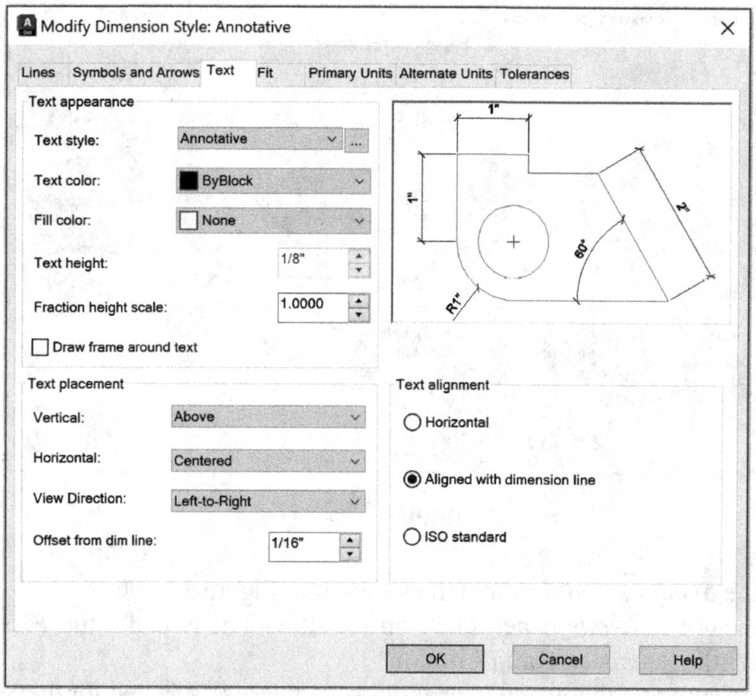

Figure 17-29d

17.11.3. Add dimensions to the floor plan

1. Doors' dimensions:
    a. Turn *On* the door label layer.
    b. Make the *Dim_Door* layer to be the current layer.
    c. Using the *Linear* dimension tool, add the dimensions to the centerline of the doors, Figure 17-30.

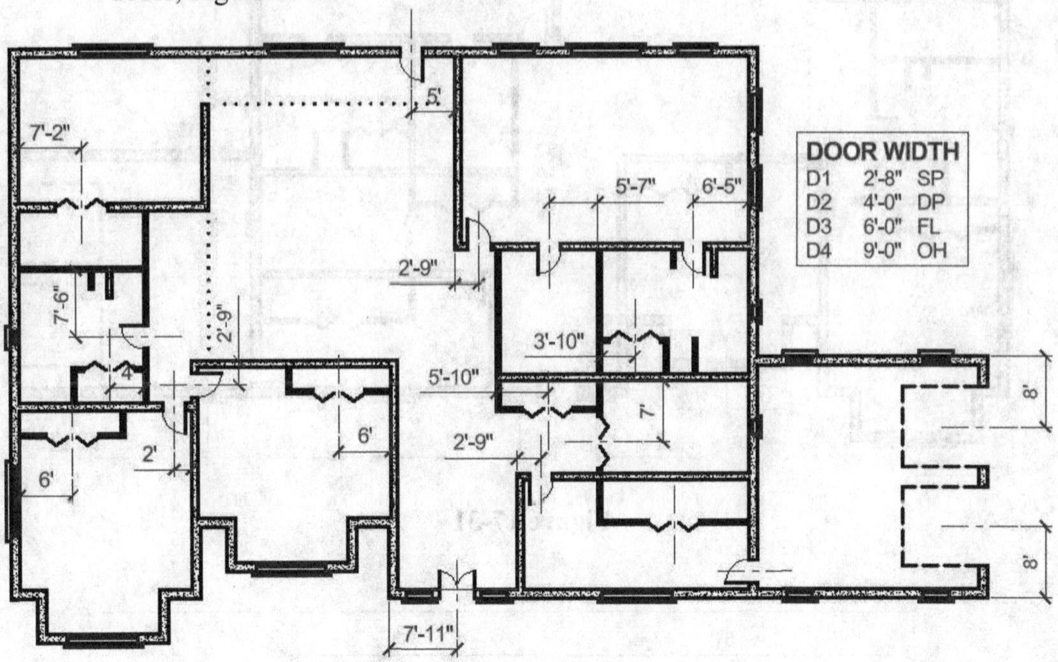

Figure 17-30

2. Windows' dimensions:
    a. Turn *On* the windows' label layer.
    b. Make the *Dim_Window* layer to be the current layer.
    c. Using the *Linear* dimension tool, add the dimensions for the centerlines of all the windows, Figure 17-31.

3. Wall to Wall dimensions:
    a. Make the *Dim_WtoW* layer to be the current layer.
    b. Using the *Linear* dimension tool, add the dimensions for the wall to wall distance, Figure 17-32.

4. Overall dimensions:
    a. Make the *Dim_Overall* layer to be the current layer.
    b. Using the *Linear* dimension tool, add the dimensions for the overall distance, Figure 17-32. Some of the dimensions can be calculated from the other dimensions; the overall dimension of the right side, 76'-0" can be calculated by adding 25'-3", 15'-9", 11'-3", 22'-9", and 1' (wall thickness). However, it is recommended to display the overall dimensions in an architectural drawing and not to omit any useful dimensions.

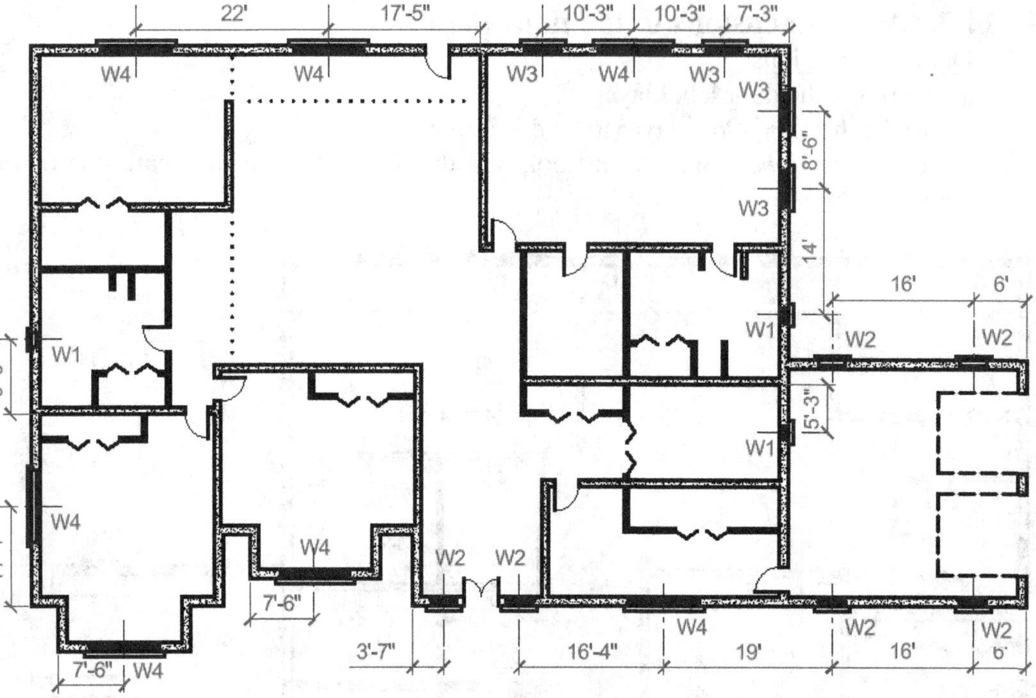

Figure 17-31

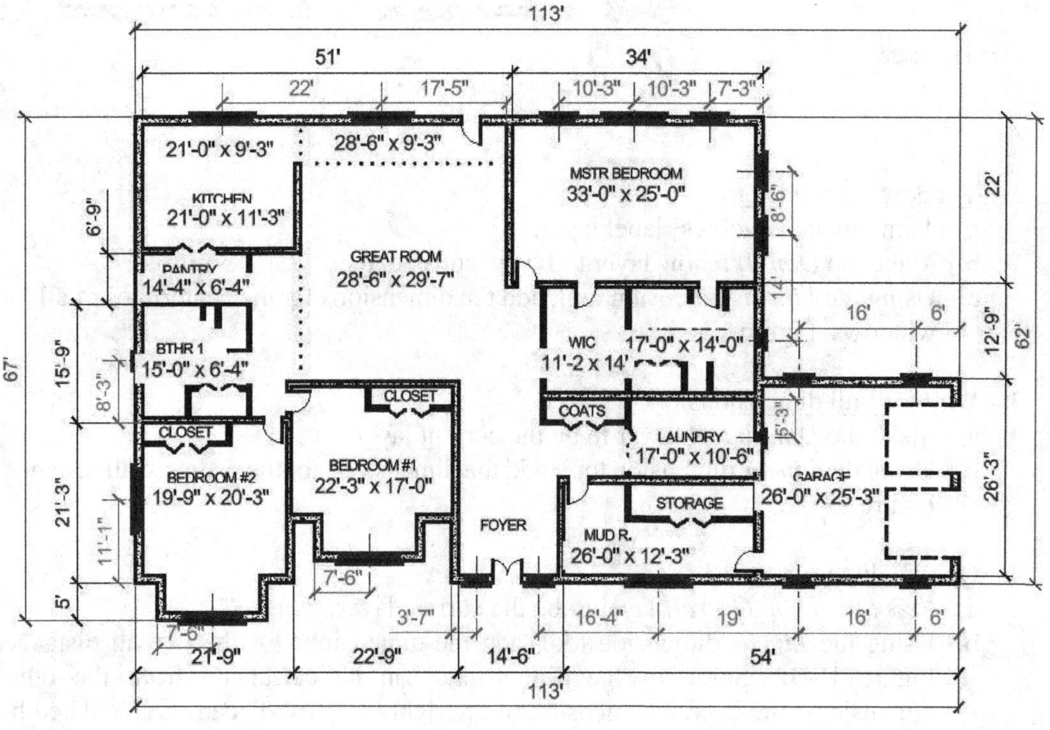

Figure 17-32

5. Room size:
   a. Make the *Dim_Roomsize* layer to be the current layer.
   b. Using the annotative *Text* command with text height of 1/8" 0r 3.32", create text boxes for the room size, Figure 17-32. A room size is written as x-dimension times y-dimension.
   c. Use the four corner grip points of the text to match the four corners of the room to place the text in the center.

6. Interior dimensions:
   a. Make the *Dim_Interior* layer to be the current layer.
   b. Using the *Linear* dimension tool, add the dimensions to the interior walls which are not dimensioned in any of the previous steps, Figure 17-33.

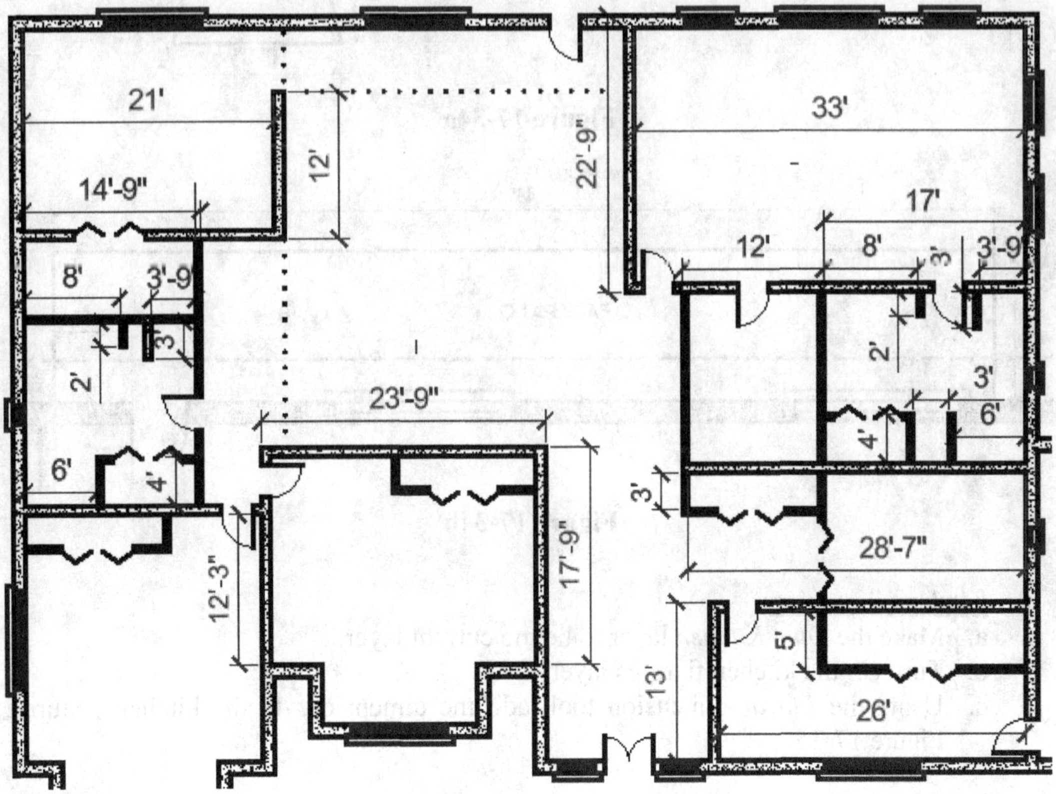

Figure 17-33

7. Porch dimension:
   a. Make the *Dim_Porch* layer to be the current layer.
   b. Turn *On* the porch layer.
   c. Using the *Linear* dimension tool, add the dimensions to the front porch (Figure 17-34a) and back patio (Figure 17-34b).

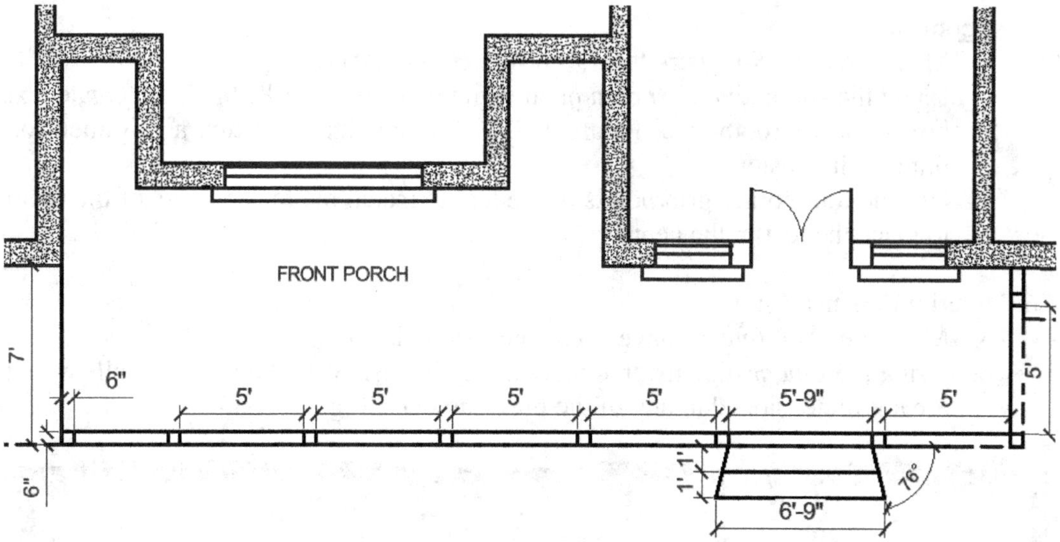

Figure 17-34a

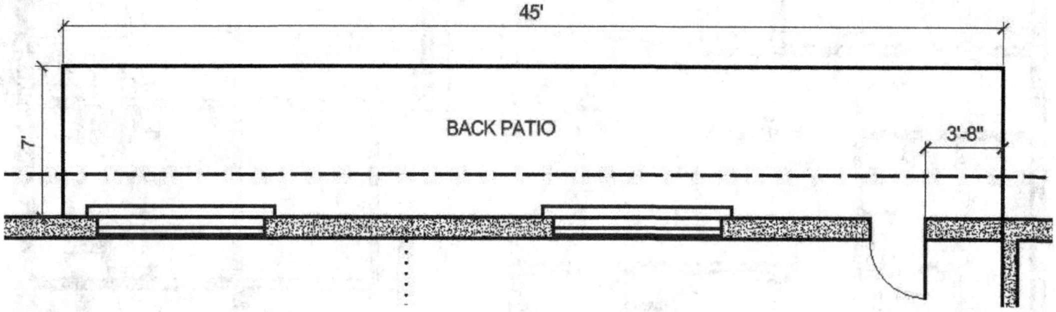

Figure 17-34b

8. Kitchen dimension:
   a. Make the *Dim_Kitchen* layer to be the current layer.
   b. Turn *On* the kitchen fixtures layer.
   c. Using the *Linear* dimension tool, add the dimensions to the kitchen fixtures, Figure 17-35.

9. Bathroom dimension, Figure 17-36a and Figure 17-36b:
   a. Make the *Dim_BathRM* layer to be the current layer.
   b. Turn *On* the bathroom's fixtures layer.
   c. Using the *Linear* dimension tool, add the dimensions to the bathroom's fixtures.

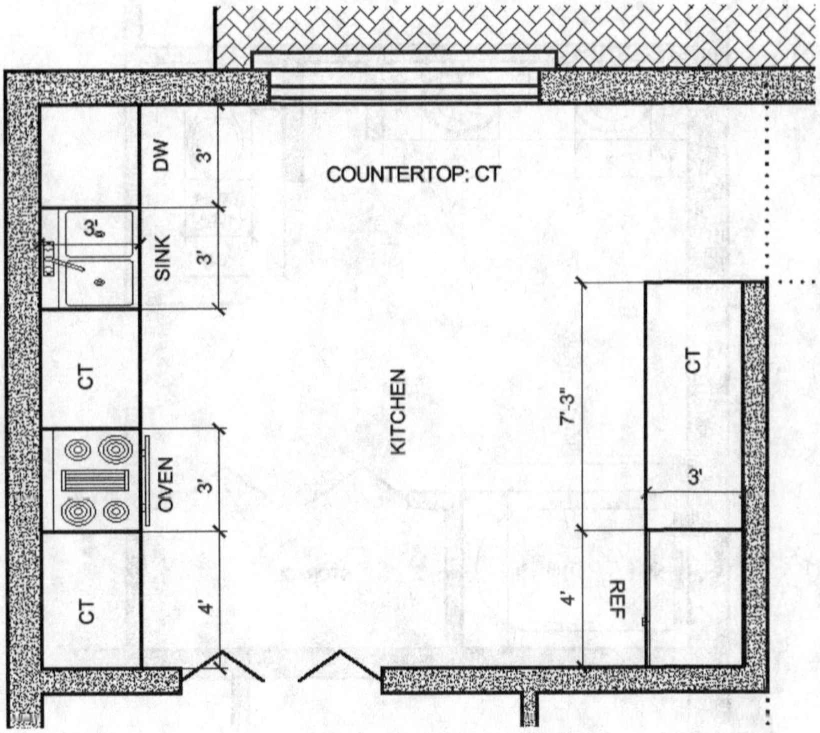

Figure 17-35

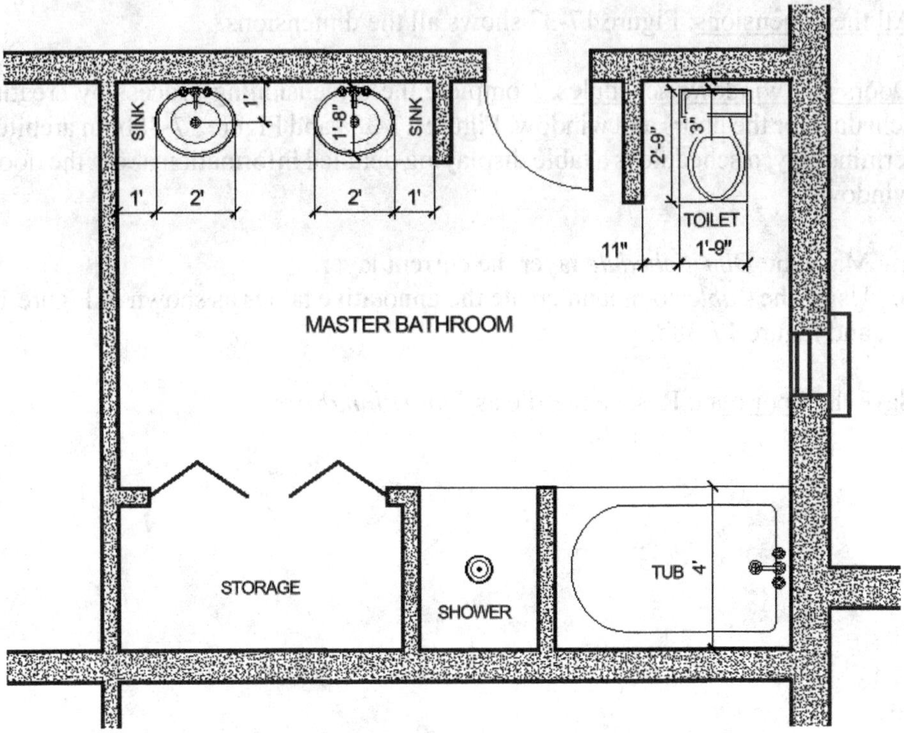

Figure 17-36a

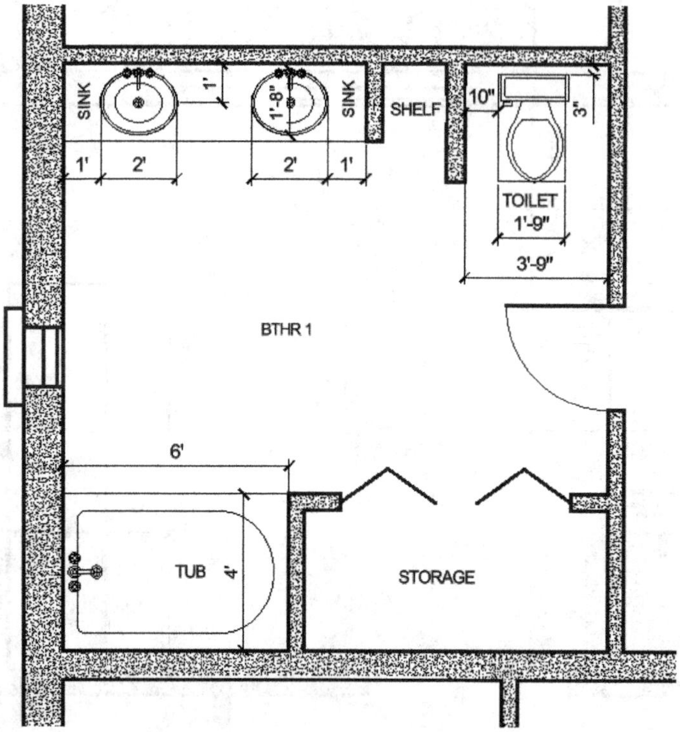

Figure 17-36b

10. <u>All the dimensions</u>: Figure 17-37 shows all the dimensions.

11. <u>Doors and windows schedules</u>: Complete the dimensioning process by creating the schedule for the doors and window, Figure 17-38a and Figure 17-38b. In architectural terminology, a schedule is a table displaying detailed information about the doors and windows.

    a. Make the *Dim_Schedule* layer the current layer.
    b. Using the *Table* command create the annotative tables as shown in Figure 17-38a and Figure 17-38b.

12. <u>Save the floor plan</u>: Resave the file as *FloorPlan.dwg.*

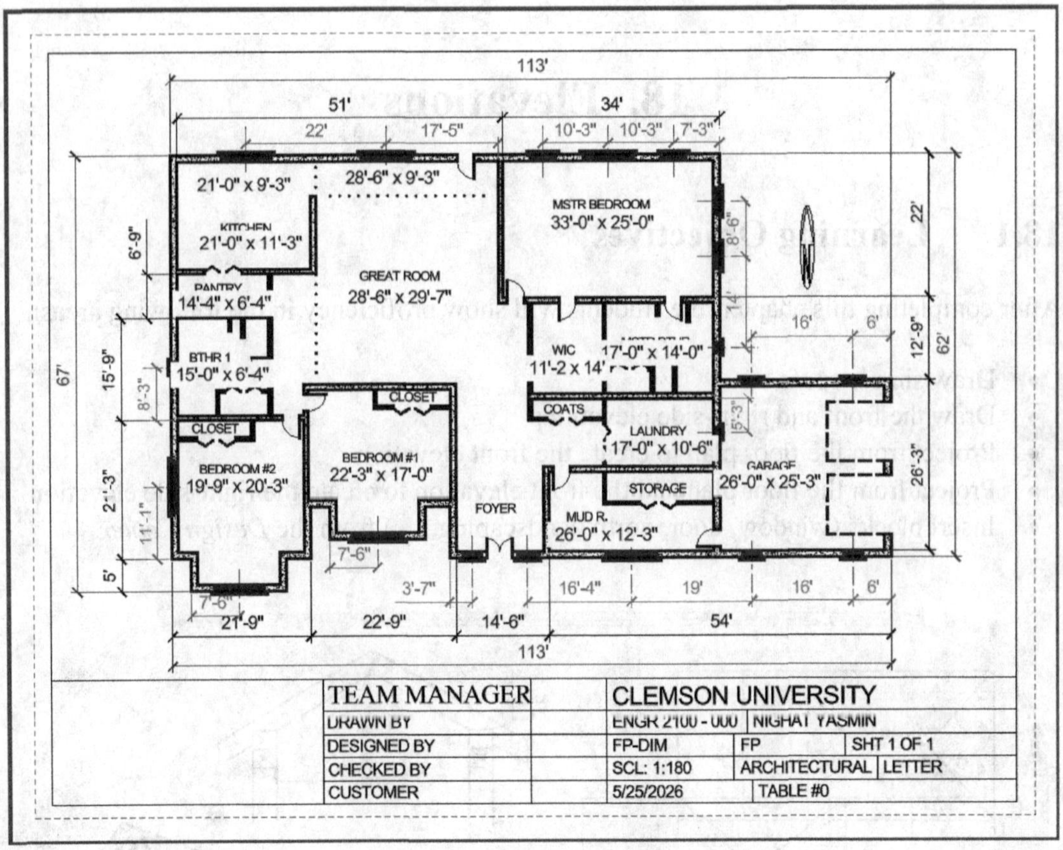

Figure 17-37

DOORS SCHEDULE				
Door No.	***Size***	***QUANTITY***	***DESCRIPTION***	***LOCATION***
D1	2'-8" X 7'-0"	9	INTERIOR SINGLE PANEL	MBDR, BDR 1, BDR 2, , GREAT RM, MSTR BTHR, BTHR 1, WIC, MUD R,
D2	4'-0" X 7'-0"	1	INTERIOR DOUBLE PANEL	FOYER
D3	6'-0" X 7'-0"	8	FOLDING FOUR LEAVES	BDR 1, BDR 2, MSTR BTHR, BTHR 1, PANTRY, COAT, MUD R, LD
D4	9'-0" X 9'-0"	2	OVERHEAD	GRG
LEGEND: M: MASTER, BD: BED, R: ROOM, BH: BATH, WIC: WALK-IN-CLOSET, DNG: DINING LD: LAUNDARY, STG: STORAGE, GRG: GARAGE, BFST: BREAKFAST				

Figure 17-38a

Notes:

18. Elevations

18.1. Learning Objectives

After completing this chapter, the students will show proficiency in the following areas:

- Draw simple roofs
- Draw the front and right-side elevations
- Project from the floor plan to create the front elevation
- Project from the floor plan and the front elevation to create the right-side elevation
- Insert blocks (window, door, north, landscaping, …) from the *Design Center*

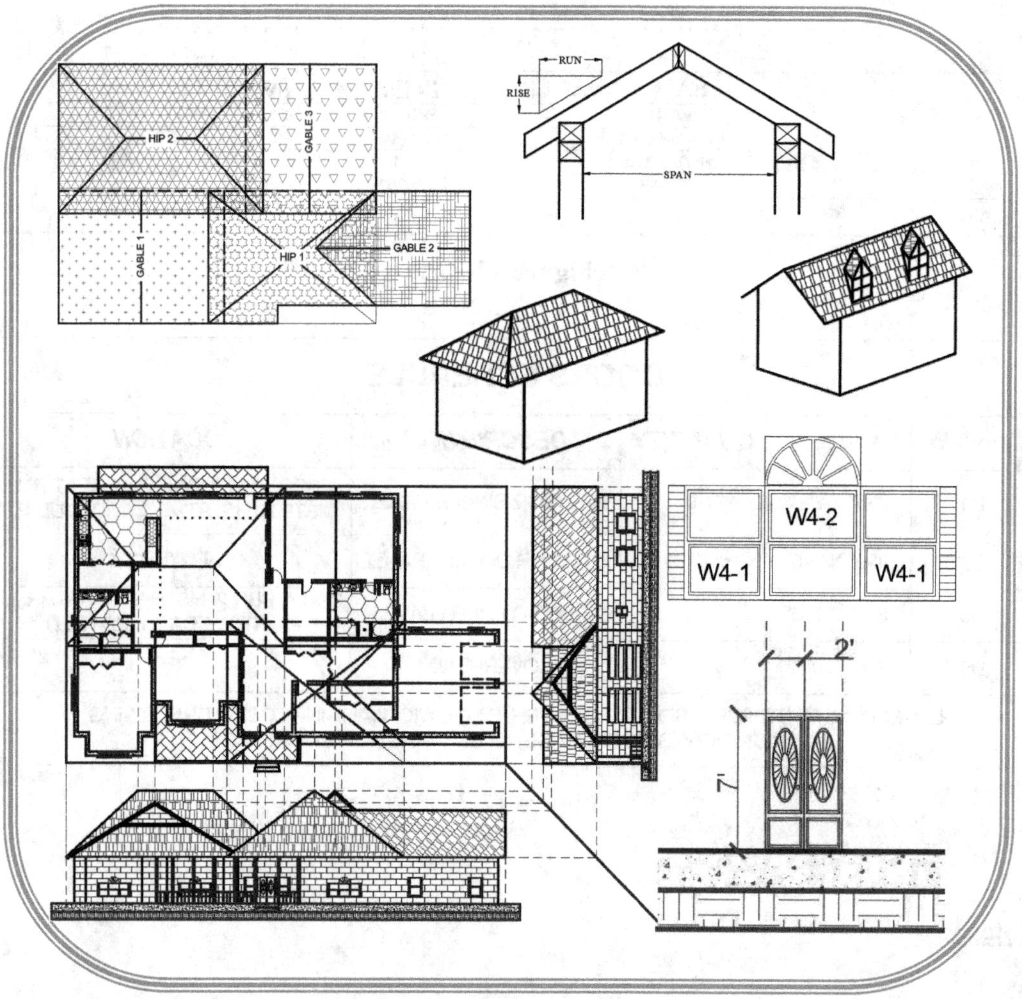

18.2. Introduction

Exterior elevations are commonly used for conveying the appearance of a building from the exterior. Figure 18-1b shows the front elevation of the residential building of the floor plan, Figure 18-1a, created in the previous chapter. In architecture and building engineering terminology, elevation is an orthographic projection of a building from a side. The elevations can be used to envision the building's appearance from all four sides; that is, from the front, rear, left-side, and right-side. Therefore, the architectural drawings of a building include one drawing for each of the front, rear, left-side, and right-side elevations.

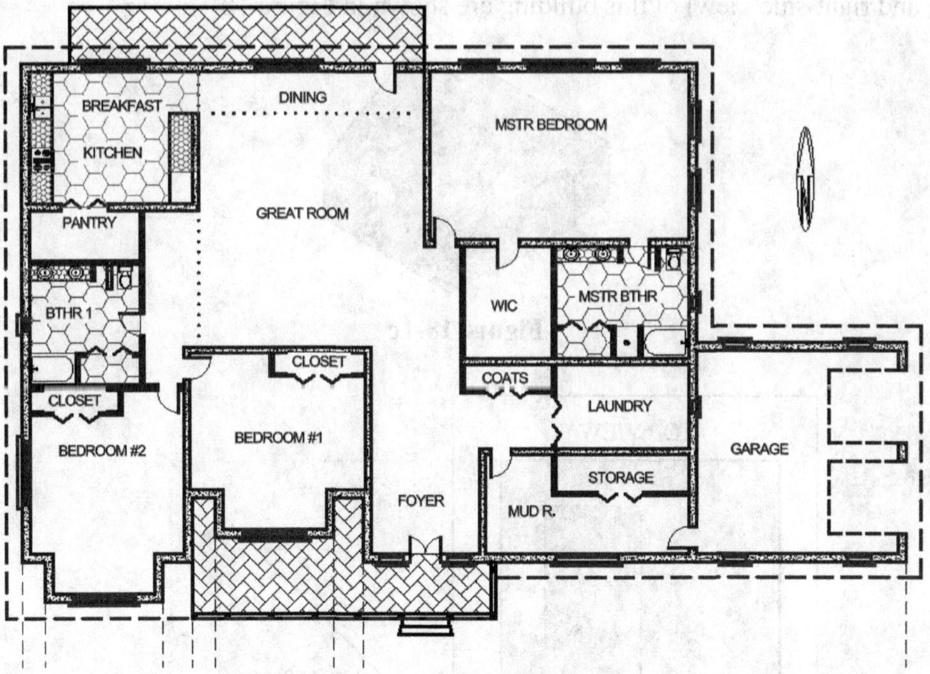

Figure 18-1a

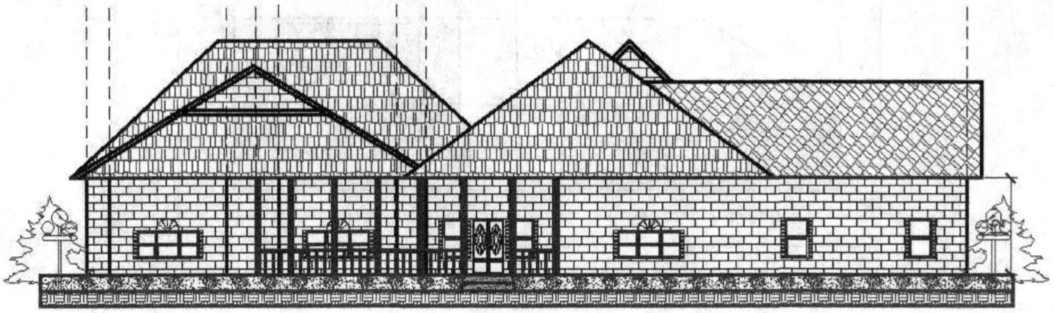

Figure 18-1b

The elevation drawings are simpler than a floor plan. The elevation drawings display the height and appearance of the windows and doors, shape of the roof, floor to floor levels (for multistory buildings), and the exterior walls. A single level building's elevation drawing starts with the ground level. In the drawing, objects below the ground level (foundations and crawl spaces) are shown using dashed (*Hidden*) lines. The next step is the drawing of the floor slab, windows, doors, and walls. Finally, the elevations are finished with the roof. Since the roof is an important part of the elevation design of a building, the next section briefly discusses the basics of roofs.

The focus of this chapter is the front and left side views of a building, also known as the front and left side elevations. Consider a simple building shown in Figure 18-1c. The figure shows the south-east isometric view of the building. The three orthographic views (top, front, and right-side view) of this building are shown in Figure 18-1d.

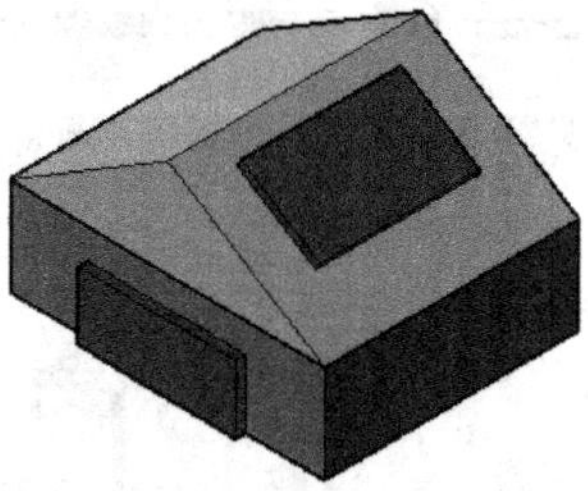

Figure 18-1c

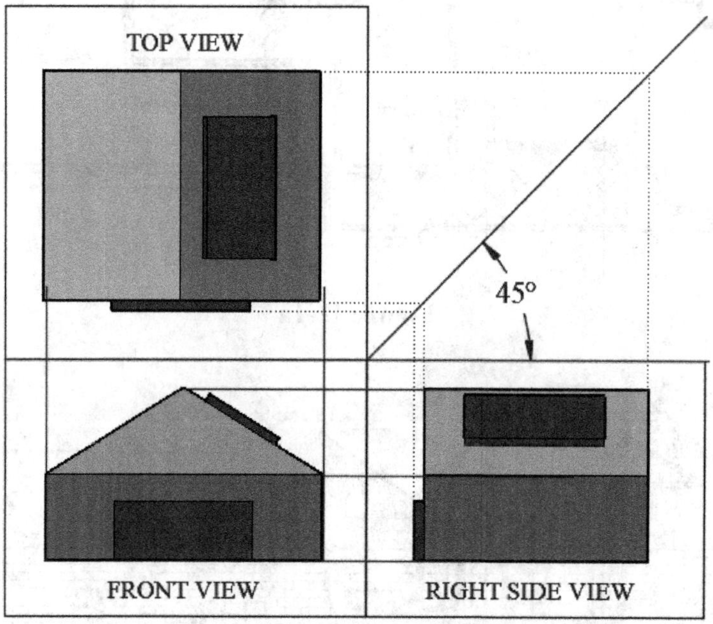

Figure 18-1d

Notice the projection of the skylight (the box in the roof), front door, and the gable roof in the three orthographic views. Vertical lines are used to project information between top (floor plan) and front views. Horizontal lines are used to project information between front and left-side views. Horizontal and vertical lines are used to project information between front and left-side views using a 45 degrees' miter line, Figure 18-1d.

18.3. Roof

18.3.1. Terminology

Some of the commonly used terms are listed here and are shown in Figure 18-2.

- *Span*: The span of a roof is the horizontal distance covered by the roof.
- *Run*: The run of a roof is half of the span.
- *Rise*: The rise of a roof is the vertical distance covered by the roof.
- *Pitch*: The pitch of a roof is the slope of a roof. The pitch is the ratio of the rise and the run (*Pitch* = *Rise/Run*). The steepness of a roof increases as the pitch of the roof increases.

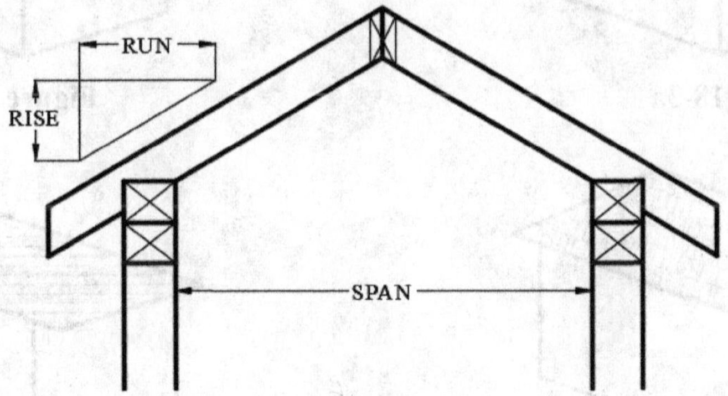

Figure 18-2

18.3.2. Types of roofs

There are many types of roofs based on the type of the house, such as traditional, dormer, contemporary, etc.

- Gable roof: A gable roof is the most common type of roof and is shown in Figure 18-3a. It is easy to construct and is pitched for drainage.
- Dormer gable roof: The dormers are used for the light, Figure 18-3b. The use of a dormer enhances the appearance of the roof but increases the cost of construction and maintenance.
- Hip roof: A hip roof (Figure 18-3c) is more expensive than a gable roof and is commonly used on ranch type houses. It is a low pitch roof. In a hip roof, the chances of leakage increase with an increase in the number of hips.
- Flat roof: A flat roof is shown in Figure 18-3d. Flat roofs are commonly used in commercial buildings. The slope of a flat roof is negligibly small. The slope is used for drainage only.

18.3.3. Important points

The selection of a roof type depends on several factors.

- Low pitched verses high pitched roof: Low pitched roofs are cheaper than high pitched roofs. However, a high pitch roof enhances the appearance of the house.

- Color and material: The color and material of the roof should be selected based on the durability and in accordance with the materials used on the exterior of the building. As a general rule, only two types of material should be used in the exterior finish.

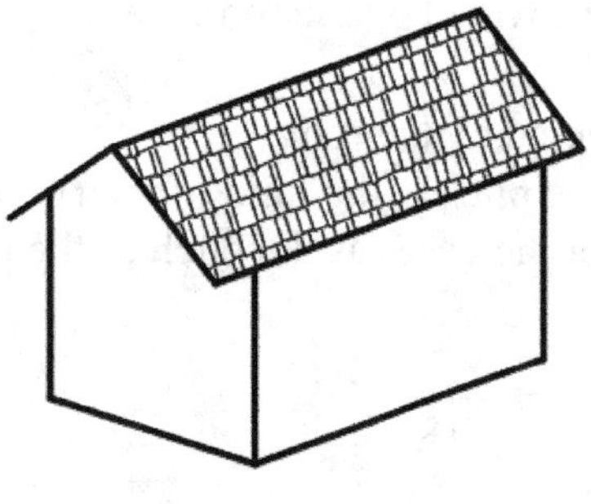

Figure 18-3a

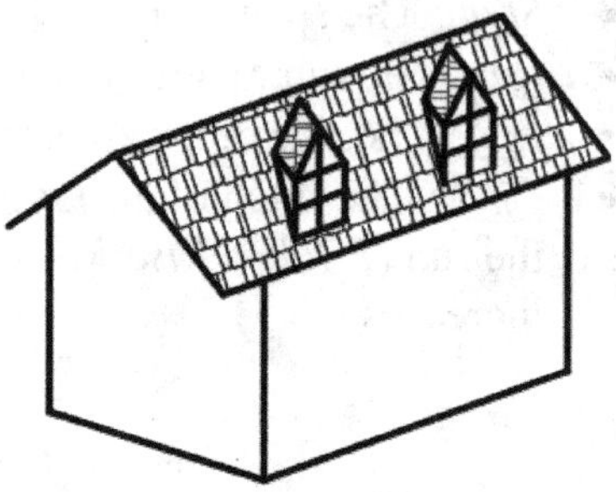

Figure 18-3b

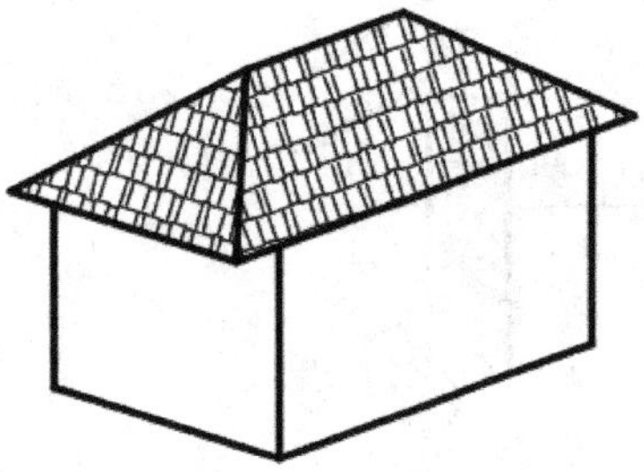

Figure 18-3c

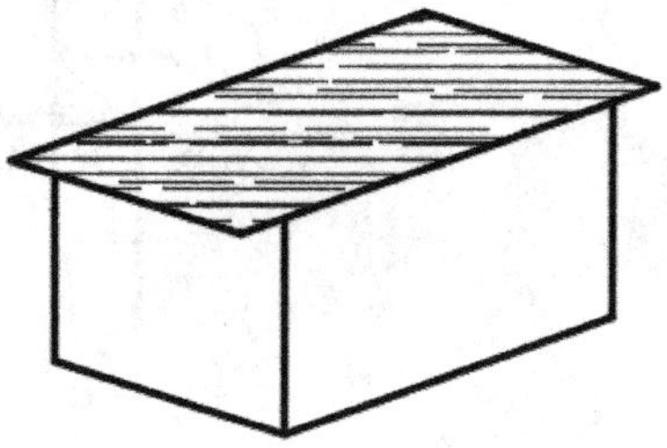

Figure 18-3d

18.4. AutoCAD And Roof Plan

The roof plan drawings of a building are closely related to the floor plan. This section provides step-by-step instructions for drawing the roof plan of the floor plan of the three-bedroom residential building drawn in the previous chapter.

18.4.1. Open file

Open file: Open the floor plan (*FloorPlan.dwg*) file created in the previous chapter and save it as the *RoofPlan.dwg* file.

18.4.2. Load linetypes

The roof plan uses continuous and dashed (known as *Hidden* in AutoCAD) lines. The hidden linetype is loaded for the floor plan. If it is not loaded, then load *Hidden* linetype; *Continuous* is the default linetype.

18.4.3. Layers

Create the layers as necessary and set the layer colors and lineweights. Before using a layer, make it the current layer and ensure that it is *On* (not frozen or *Off*).

18.4.4. The roof plan

Figure 18-4a shows that the house is covered by one hip roof and three gable roofs. This section provides step-by-step instructions to create the roof plan shown in Figures 18-4 (a, b, c, d, and e).

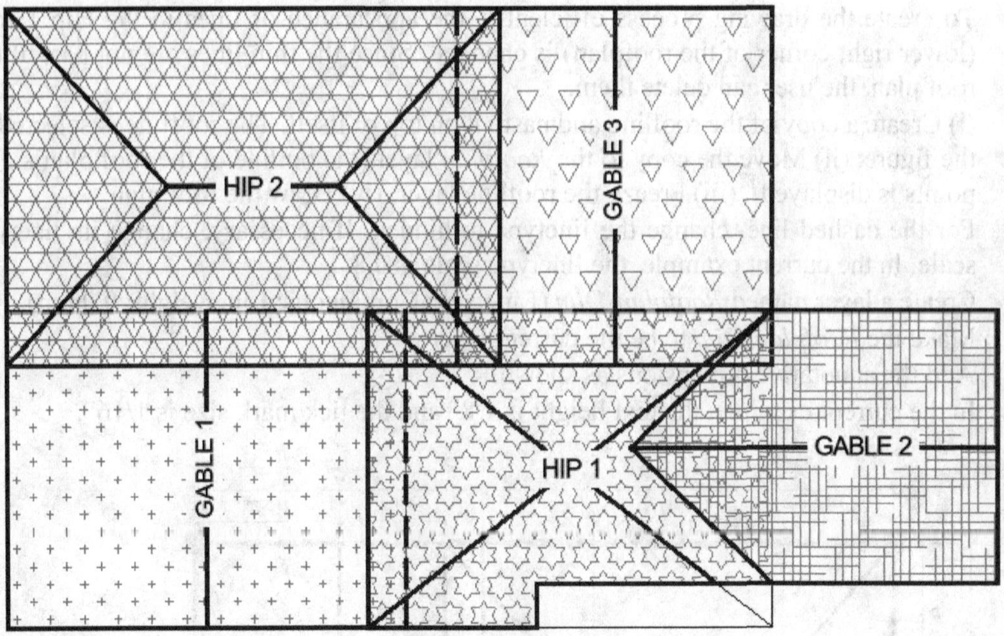

Figure 18-4a

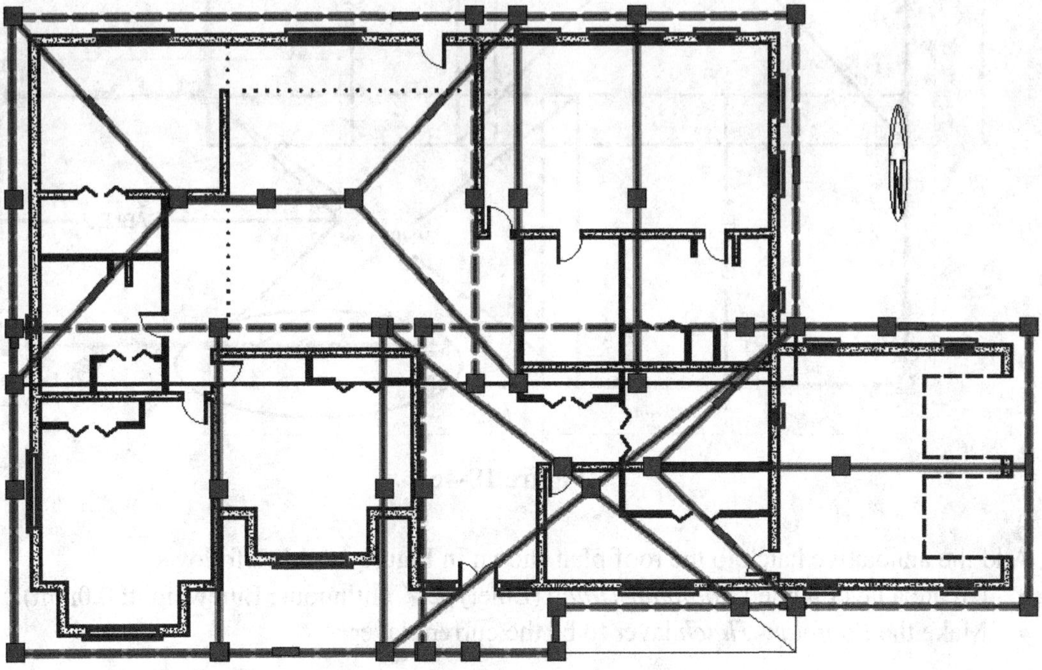

Figure 18-4b

Create the roof plan overlaying the floor plan, Figure 18-b, using the following steps: refer to Figure 18-4c.

- Create a layer named *Roofplan* (Linetype: *Continuous*; Lineweight: 0.5mm).
- Make the *Roofplan* layer to be the current layer.
- To create the drawing process efficiently, the appearance of lines in the Hip 1 roof (lower right corner of the roofplan) is changed. Since the thin lines are not part of the roof plan, the user can delete them.
- (i) Create a copy of the roofline and paste it on top of itself. The roofline is selected in the figure. (ii) Move the copy to the *Roofplan* layer (the outline of the roof plan's grip points is displayed). (iii) Freeze the roofline layer. (iv) Draw the roof plan.
- For the dashed line, change the linetype to hidden. If necessary, change its linetype scale. In the current example, the linetype scale is 0.8.
- Create a layer named *Roofplan-Dim* (Linetype: Continuous; Lineweight: 0.0mm).
- Make the *Roofplan-Dim* to be the current layer.
- Add the annotative dimensions as shown.
- In the current example, the text height is 1/8" and the tick mark size is 1/16".

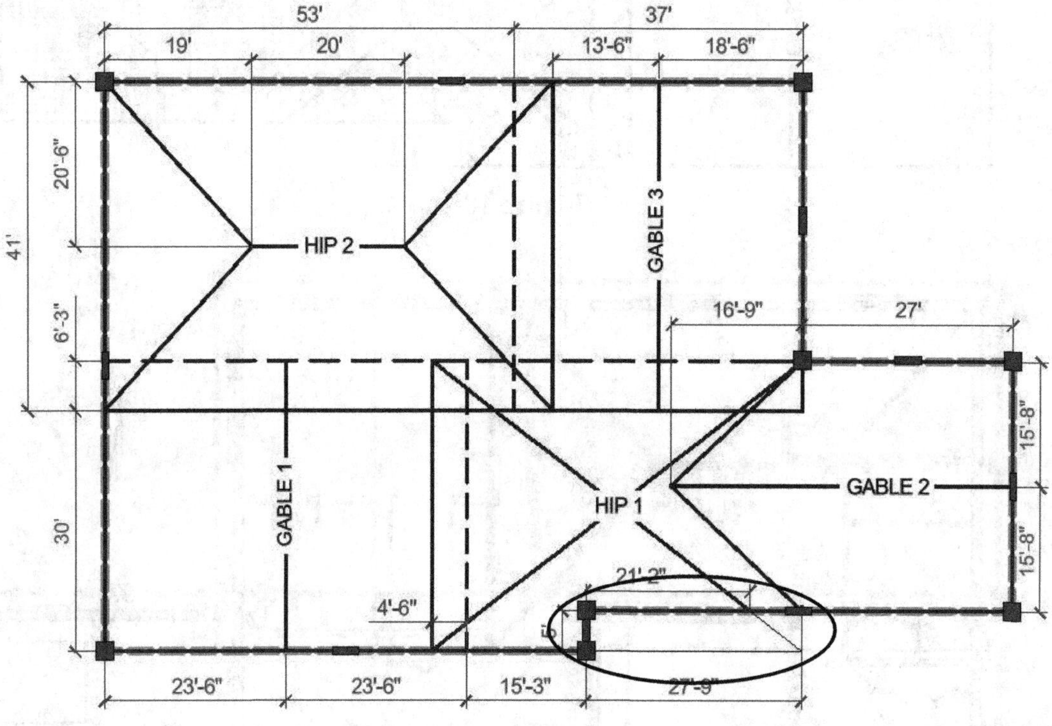

Figure 18-4c

Add the annotative hatch to the roof plan shown in Figure 18-4d as follows.

- Create a layer named *Roofplan-Hatch* (Linetype: Continuous; Lineweight: 0.0mm).
- Make the *Roofplan- Hatch* layer to be the current layer.

- The figure also displays the hatch angles (HA) of the various hatches used in the roof plan. In AutoCAD, the degree symbol can be created by typing %%d in the text command.
- Add the hatch as shown using annotative *Hatch* command with pattern *AR-RSHKE* at the scale value of 0.01; use the hatch angle as shown in the figure. The user must create the hatches independently.
- Using the annotative *Text* command add the hatch labels. In the current example, the annotative text height is 1/8".

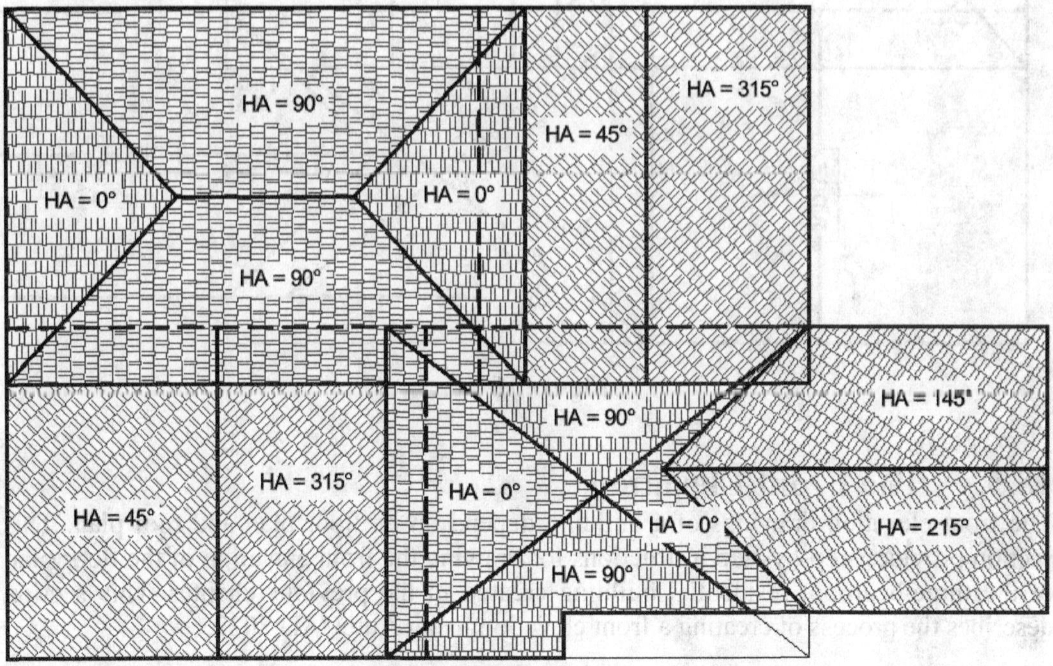

Figure 18-4d

Figure 18-4e shows the location of the ridges, valleys, hip lines, and the slope arrows. In the figure, the arrows adjacent to the ridge labels indicate the direction of the down slope. Add the labels and arrows as follows.

- Create a layer named *Roofplan-Label* (Linetype: Continuous; Lineweight: 0.0mm).
- Make the *Roofplan-Label* layer to be the current layer.
- Using the *Text* command create one label for ridge, one for valley, and one for hip line. The annotative text height is 1/8".
- Enclose the text in a rectangle using the *Enclose in Object* command with the offset factor of 0.35; this command is available from *Express Tool* tab and the *Text* panel.
- The arrows are created using the first two clicks of the annotative *qleader* command (press the *Esc* key after the first two clicks). The arrowhead size is 0.15 inches.
- Rotate the labels using the *Rotate* command.
- Create multiple copies of the labels using the *Copy* command.
- Resave the *RoofPlan.dwg* file.

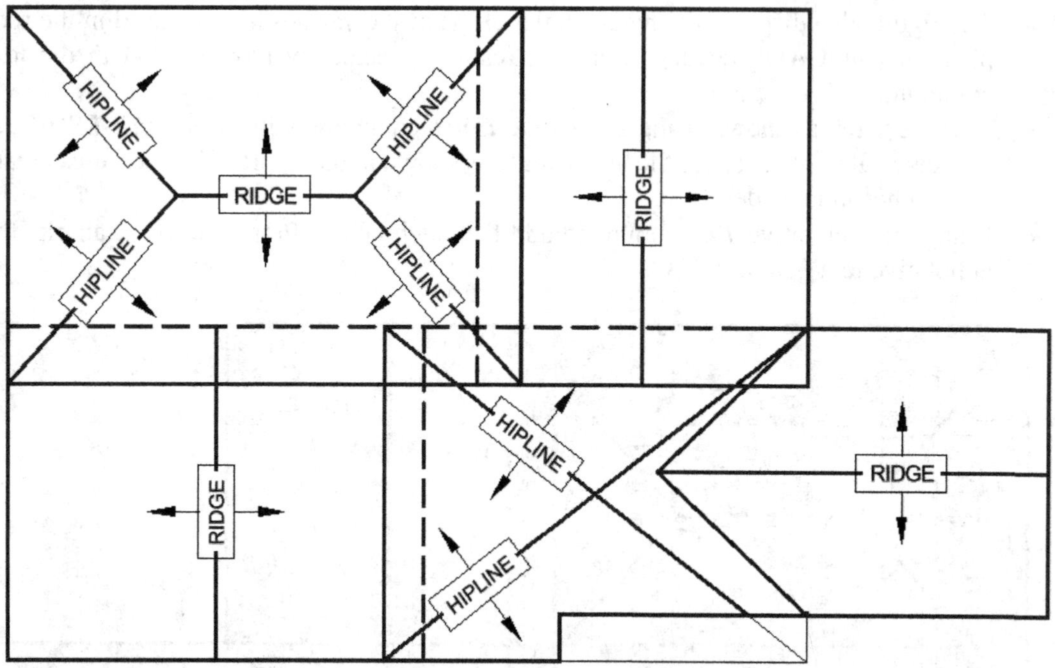

Figure 18-4e

18.5. The Front Elevation

The front elevation drawings of a building depend on its floor plan and roof plan. This section provides step-by-step instructions for drawing the front elevation of the floor plan of the three-bedroom residential building created in the previous chapter. This section describes the process of creating a front elevation using AutoCAD 2027.

18.5.1. Open file

Open file: Open the roof plan file (*RoofPlan.dwg*) created in the previous section and save it as the *FrontElev.dwg* file.

18.5.2. Load linetypes

The front elevation uses continuous and dashed (known as *Hidden* in AutoCAD) lines. The hidden linetype is loaded for the roof plan. If it is not loaded, then load *Hidden* linetype; *Continuous* is the default linetype.

18.5.3. Orthogonal lines

Since most of the lines in the front elevation are either horizontal or vertical, turn *On* the *ORTHO* option by pressing the corresponding button () on the status bar.

18.5.4. Layers

(i) Create layers as necessary. (ii) Set the layers' colors and lineweights. (iii) Before using a layer, make the layer the current layer. (iv) Make sure that the current layer is *on* (not frozen or *off*).

18.5.5. Draw the front elevation

This section provides step-by-step instructions for drawing the front elevation of the given floor plan.

- Do not add any dimensions! Dimensions will be added later.
- The drawing is printed/displayed from the layout! Keep checking the appearance of the linetypes and lineweights in the layouts. The linetype should be clearly and properly visible in the layouts. If necessary, adjust the *Properties* palette →*General* tab → *Linetype Scale* option.

18.5.5.1. Ground level

- Create a layer named *GL* (Linetype: Continuous; Line weight: 0.5mm).
- Make the *GL* layer to be the current layer.
- Draw a horizontal line representing the ground level, below the exterior face of the exterior wall in the floor plan as shown in Figure 18-5a.
- Draw a 2' wide rectangle, Figure 18-5b, representing the ground level.
- Hatch the rectangle using *Earth* pattern at scale of 50, LWT = 0.0, Figure 18-5c.

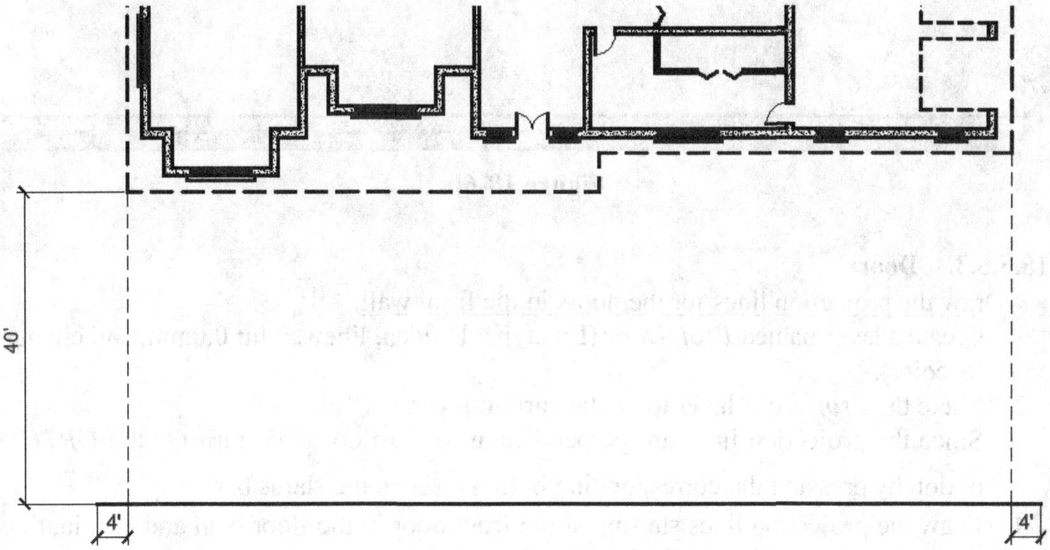

Figure 18-5a

Figure 18-5b

Figure 18-5c

18.5.5.2. Slab level

- Create a layer named *Slab_Line* (Linetype: Continuous; Lineweight: 0.5mm).
- Make the *Slab_Line* layer to be the current layer.
- Generally, for a residential building the slabs are 4" to 8". However, for the demo, the slab is assumed to be 2'. The slab surface is shown as a thick solid line representing the main floor level. Draw a horizontal line representing the main level, 2'-0" above the grade line, as shown in Figure 18-6a.
- Close the edges by drawing vertical lines.
- Hatch the slab using *AR-CONC* pattern at scale 2, LWT = 0.0, Figure 18-6b.

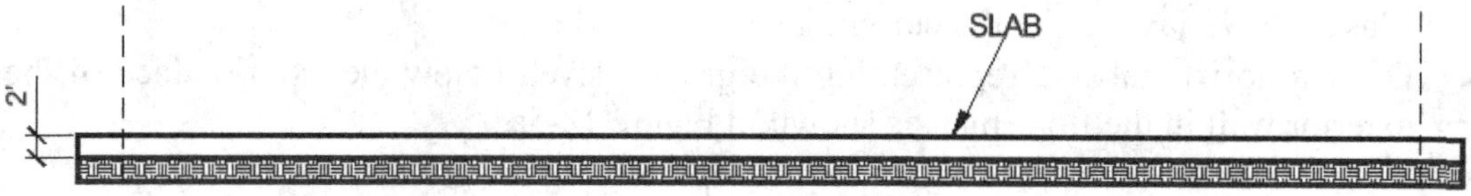

Figure 18-6a

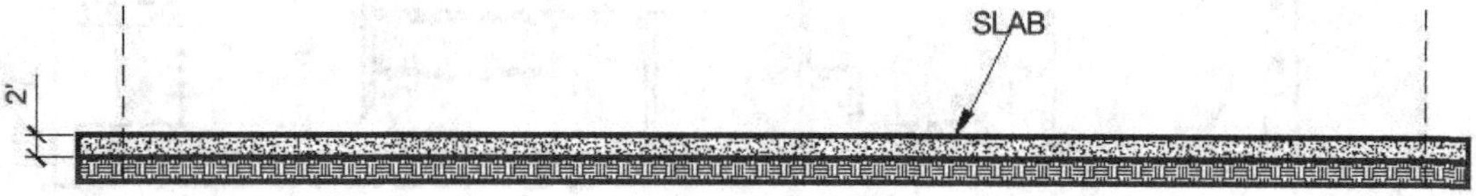

Figure 18-6b

18.5.5.3. Doors

- <u>Draw the projection lines for the doors in the front wall</u>:
  1. Create a layer named *Proj_Door* (Linetype: Hidden, lineweight: 0.0mm, and change its color).
  2. Make the *Proj_Door* layer to be the current layer.
  3. Since the projection lines are perpendicular to the floor plan, turn *On* the *ORTHO* option by pressing the corresponding button () on the status bar.
  4. Draw the projection lines starting at the front door in the floor plan and terminating at the slab line, Figure 18-7a. Use the *Trim* or *Extend* commands as necessary.
  5. Using the *Properties* palette, set the linetype scale to 0.5.

- <u>Draw the front entrance door</u>:
- The front entrance door is 7'-0" high; refer to the *Door Schedule* from *Chapter 17*.
  1. Create a layer named *Elev_Doors* (Linetype: Hidden, lineweight: 0.0mm, and change its color).
  2. Make the *Elev_Doors* layer to be the current layer.

3. From the *Design Center* (*View* tab → *Palette* panel), open the blocks folder of the *House Design.dwg*.
4. Insert the *Door-Fancy 36 inch* block, Figure 18-7b, with the following scale factors:
   - Front door: X-scale = 2/3; Y-scale = 1; Z-scale = 1; and angle = 0º.
5. Use the *Mirror* command to add the second panel, Figure 18-10c and Figure 18-10d.

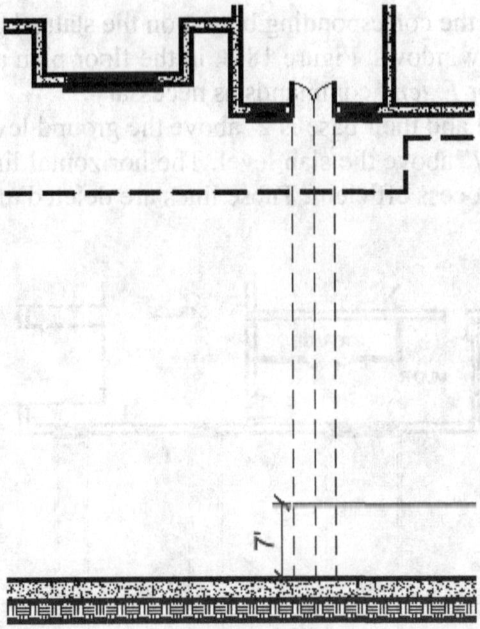

Figure 18-7a

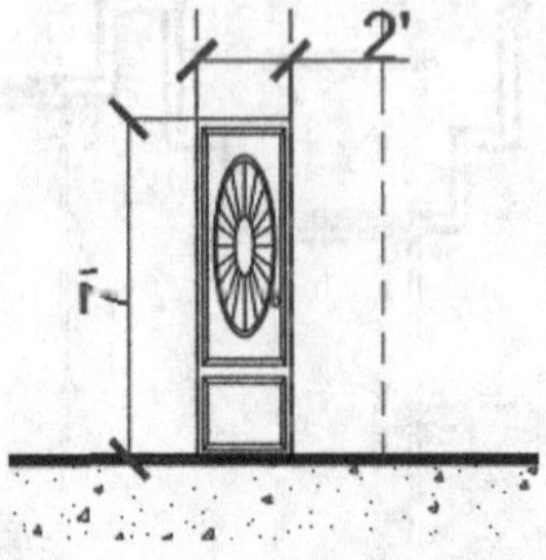

Figure 18-7b

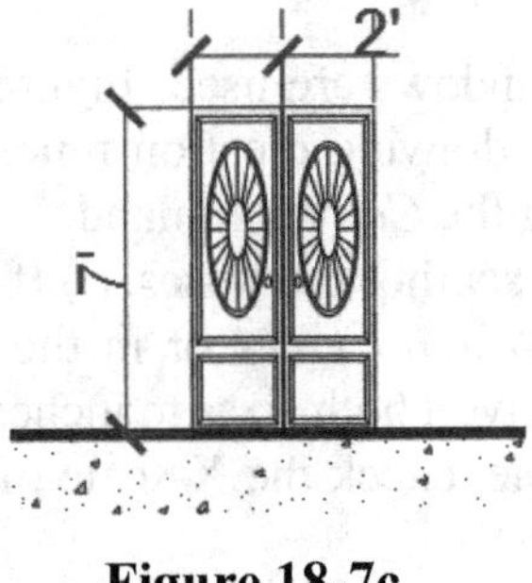

Figure 18-7c

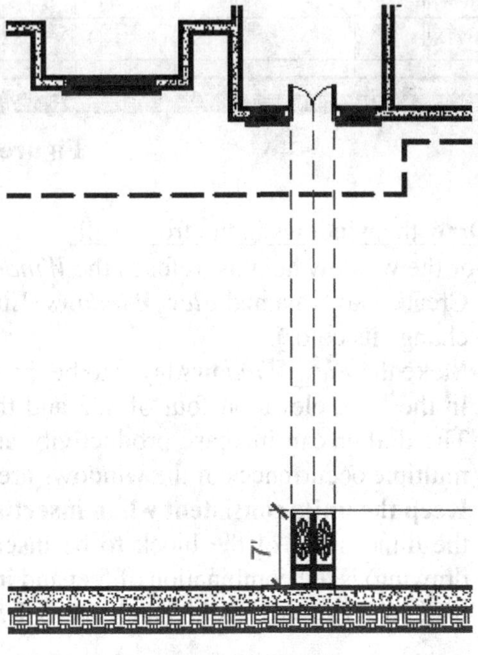

Figure 18-7d

18.5.5.4. Windows

- Draw the projection lines for the windows in the front wall:

1. Turn *Off* the *Proj_Door* layer.
2. Create a layer named *Proj_Window* (Linetype: Hidden, lineweight: 0.0mm, and change its color).
3. Make the *Proj_Window* the current layer.
4. Turn *On* the *ORTHO* option by pressing the corresponding button on the status bar.
5. Draw the projection lines starting at the windows, Figure 18-8, in the floor plan and terminate at the slab line. Use the *Trim* or *Extend* commands as necessary.
6. The windows on the front wall are 5' tall and their base is 2' above the ground level. Therefore, draw horizontal line 2', and 7' above the slab level. The horizontal lines make the block insertion and copying process efficient. These lines are deleted after inserting all the windows.

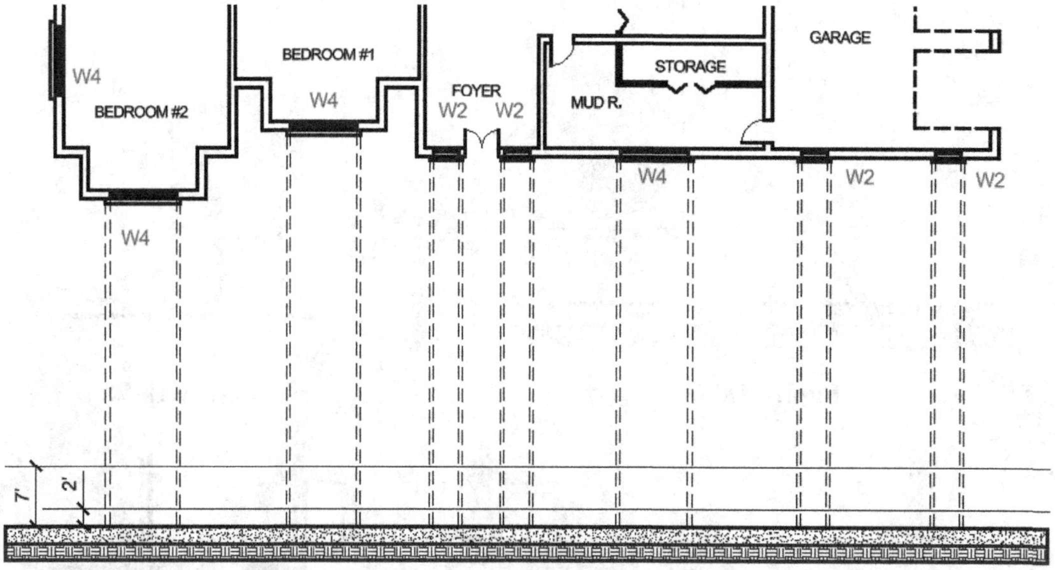

Figure 18-8

- Draw the windows in the front wall:
- For the window heights, refer to the *Window Schedule* from *Chapter 17*.

1. Create a layer named *Elev_Windows* (Linetype: Continuous, lineweight: 0.0mm, and change its color).
2. Make the *Elev_Windows* layer to be the current layer.
3. In the front elevation four of W2 and three of W4 windows are used, Figure 18-8. The drafter can increase productivity and reduce the drawing creation time, if the multiple occurrences of the windows are created using the *Copy* command.
4. **Keep the units consistent when inserting blocks for scaling purposes.** (i) If one of the dimensions of the block to be inserted (in the *Design Center* or in the actual drawing) is the combination of feet and inches, then convert both sizes to inches. That is, 2'-6" is entered as 30" and not as 1.5'. For example, check the X-scale of *W2-1*

below. (ii) If both sizes are in feet then conversion is not necessary. For example, check the X-scale of *front door*, Figure 18-7b.

5. **W4 window**: Refer to Figure 18-9a, Figure 18-9b, and Figure 18-9c. Divide the space for W4 into four compartments as shown in Figure 18-9a.

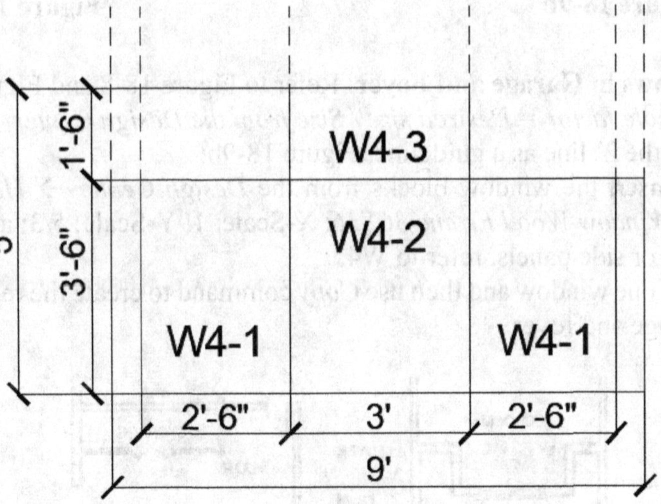

Figure 18-9a

a. **Create W4-1 to W4-3 components**:
- The *Scale factor = Desired size / Size from the Design Center*
- Using the 2' line as a guideline, Figure 18-9b, insert the following scaled window blocks from the *Design Center → House Design.dwg*:
  - W4-1: *Window Wood Frame 36X36*; X-Scale: 30/36; Y-Scale: 42/36; and *Angle* = 0°.
  - W4-2: *Window Wood Frame 36X36*; X-Scale: 1; Y-Scale: 42/36; and *Angle* = 0°.
  - Using the W4-2 block as a guideline, Figure 18-9b, insert the following scaled window blocks from the *Design Center → House Design.dwg*:
  - W4-3: *Window Half-circle 36 in*; X-Scale: 1; Y-Scale: 1; and *Angle* = 0°.
- Use the Mirror command to create the second W4-2 block, Figure 18-9b.

b. **Create W4 side panel**:
- Using the projection lines and the height of the window as guidelines, draw rectangles on either side of the windows, Figure 18-9c. The rectangles are shown by their grip points.
- Activate the *Hatch* command.
- Select *ANS131* pattern, set *Angle* to135° and *Scale* to 20.
- Now, hatch the rectangles on both sides of the windows, Figure 18-9d.

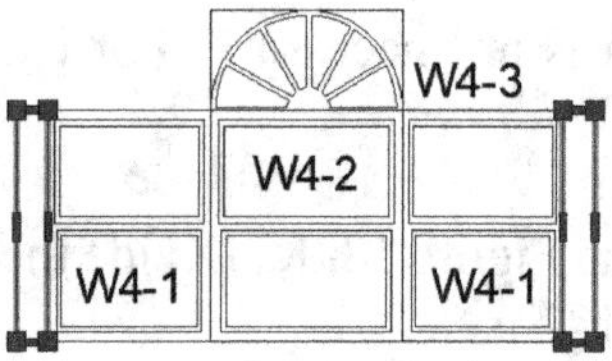

Figure 18-9b

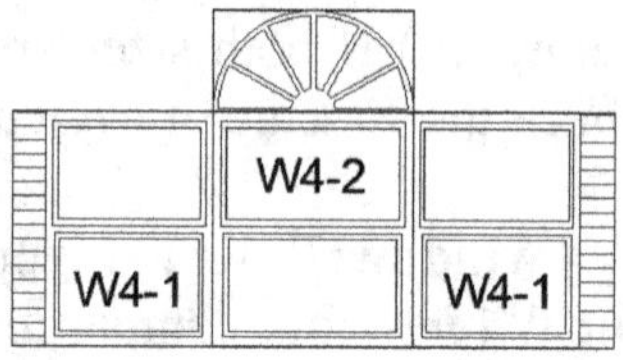

Figure 18-9c

6. **W2 windows in Garage and Foyer**: Refer to Figure 18-8 and Figure 18-9d.
   - The *Scale factor = Desired size / Size from the Design Center*
   - Using the 2' line as a guideline, Figure 18-9b:
     - insert the window blocks from the *Design Center* → *House Design.dwg*: *Window Wood Frame 36X36*; X-Scale: 1; Y-Scale: 5/3; and *Angle* = 0°.
     - For side panels, refer to W4.
   - Create one window and then use *Copy* command to create the remaining windows in garage and foyer.

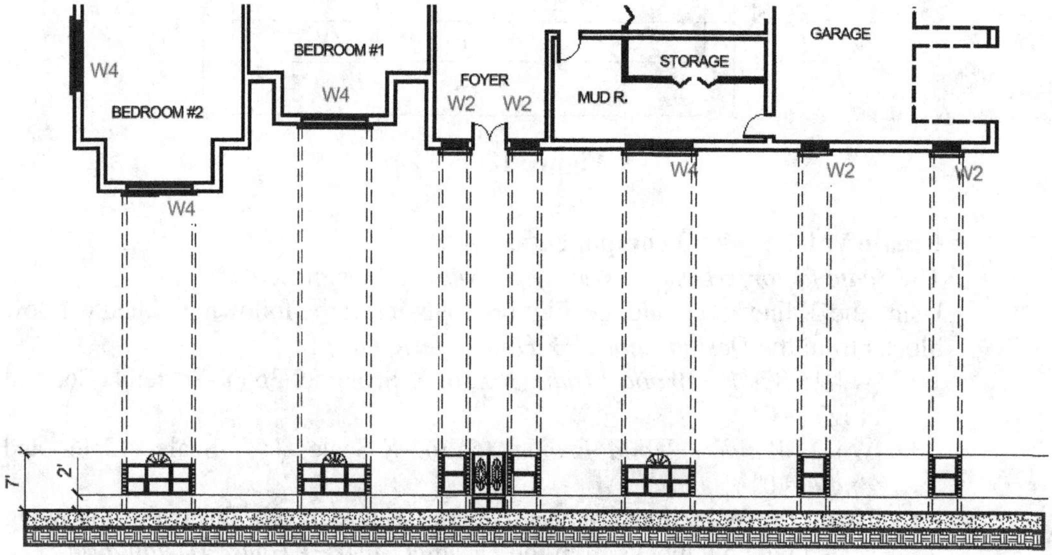

Figure 18-9d

18.5.5.5. Front wall

- Draw the projection lines for the wall:
  1. Create a layer named *Proj_Wall* (Linetype: Hidden, lineweight: 0.0mm, and change its color).
  2. Make the *Proj_Wall* layer to be the current layer.
  3. Turn *On* the *ORTHO* option by pressing the corresponding button on the status bar.
  4. Draw the projection lines, Figure 18-10a, starting at the corners of the wall (that are visible from the outside) in the floor plan and the roofline and terminating at the slab line. Use the *Trim* or *Extend* commands as necessary.

- Add the exterior face of the front wall:
  1. Create a layer named *Elev_Wall* (Linetype: Continuous, lineweight: 0.5mm, and change its color).
  2. Make the *Elev_Wall* layer to be the current layer.
  3. The walls are 12'-0" high.
  4. Draw the exterior face of the exterior wall, Figure 18-10a.
- Add the hatch to the wall:
  1. Create a layer named *Elev_WallHatch* (Linetype: Continuous, lineweight: 0.0mm, and change its color).
  2. Make the *Elev_WallHatch* layer to be the current layer.
  3. Turn *On* the *Proj_Wall* layer, Figure 18-10a.
  4. **Do not create the hatch for the front wall with the wall's projection lines *Off*. It takes a very long time, and the hatch enters inside the doors and window blocks.**
  5. Activate the associative and annotative *Hatch* command.
  6. Select *ARB816* pattern, set *Angle* to 0° and *Scale* to 0.01.
  7. Now, hatch the rectangles created by the doors' and windows' projection lines, Figure 18-10b.
  8. Zoom into the doors and windows to check that the hatch did not enter inside the doors and windows.

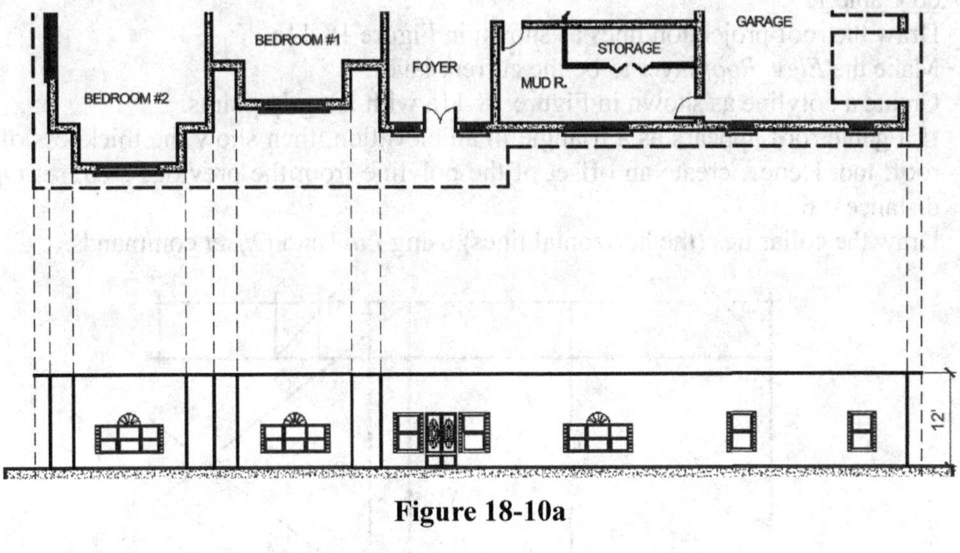

Figure 18-10a

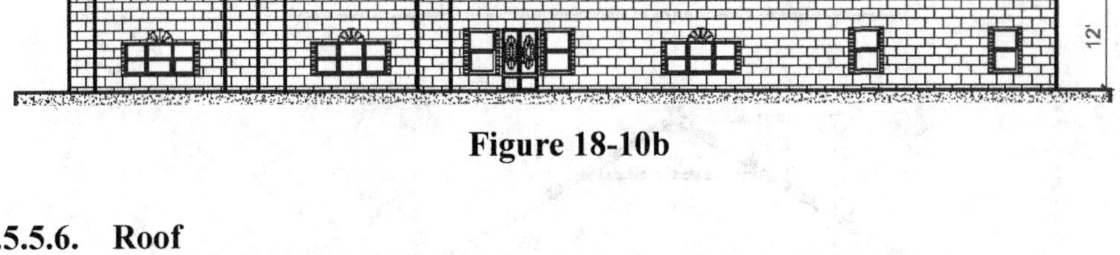

Figure 18-10b

18.5.5.6. Roof

- Turn *On* the layer of the *Roofplan*.
- Turn *Off* the layers of the *floor plan*.

- Create two layers:
  1. Create a layer named *Proj_Roof* (Linetype: Hidden, lineweight: 0.0mm, and change its color).
  2. Create a layer named *Elev_Roof* (Linetype: Continuous, lineweight: 0.5mm, and change its color).

- In the remaining of this section, draw roof projection lines means that execute the following steps:
  1. Make the *Proj_Roof* layer to be the current layer.
  2. Turn *On* the *ORTHO* option by pressing the corresponding button on the status bar.
  3. Draw the projection lines starting at the roof in the roof plan and terminating at the wall height. Use the *Trim* or *Extend* commands as necessary.

- Roof creation in elevations is complex; therefore, each roof is drawn independently. To make the process simpler, always begin with the edge of the roofplan for which the elevation is being developed to ensure proper construction and alignment during the process. Hence, for the front elevation, draw Gable 1, Hip1, and Gable 2 roofs before adding Hip 2 and Gable 3 roofs.
- The roof heights are shown in the respective figures.

- Add Gable 1:
  1. Draw the roof projection lines as shown in Figure 18-11a.
  2. Make the *Elev_Roof* layer to be the current layer.
  3. Create a polyline as shown in Figure 18-11a with the grip points.
  4. If a gable roof appears as a triangle in an elevation, then show the thickness of the roof, too. Hence, create an offset of the polyline from the previous step; set *Offset* distance = 6".
  5. Draw the collar ties (the horizontal lines) using *Line* and *Offset* commands.

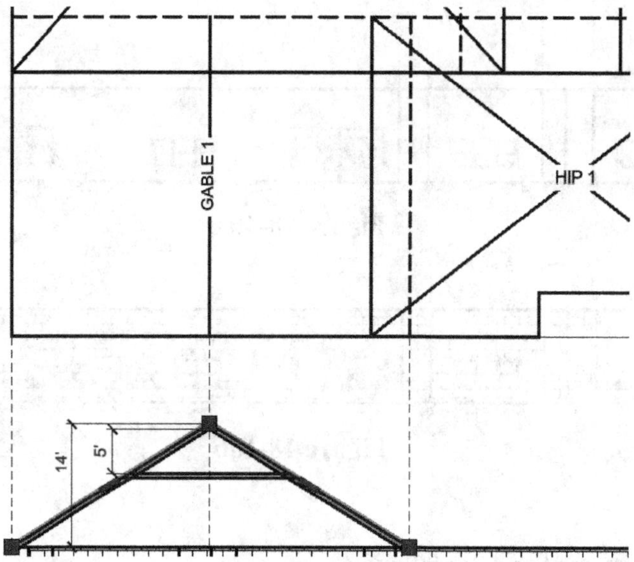

Figure 18-11a

- Add Hip 1:
  1. Draw the roof projection lines as shown in Figure 18-11b.
  2. Make the *Elev_Roof* layer to be the current layer.
  3. Create a polyline as shown in Figure 18-11b with the grip points.
  4. Since the edge of the Gable 1 lies underneath the Hip 1, trim Gabl 1 as shown in Figure 18-11c.

- Add Gable 2:
  1. Draw the roof projection lines as shown in Figure 18-11c.
  2. Make the *Elev_Roof* layer to be the current layer.
  3. Create a polyline as shown in Figure 18-11a with the grip points.

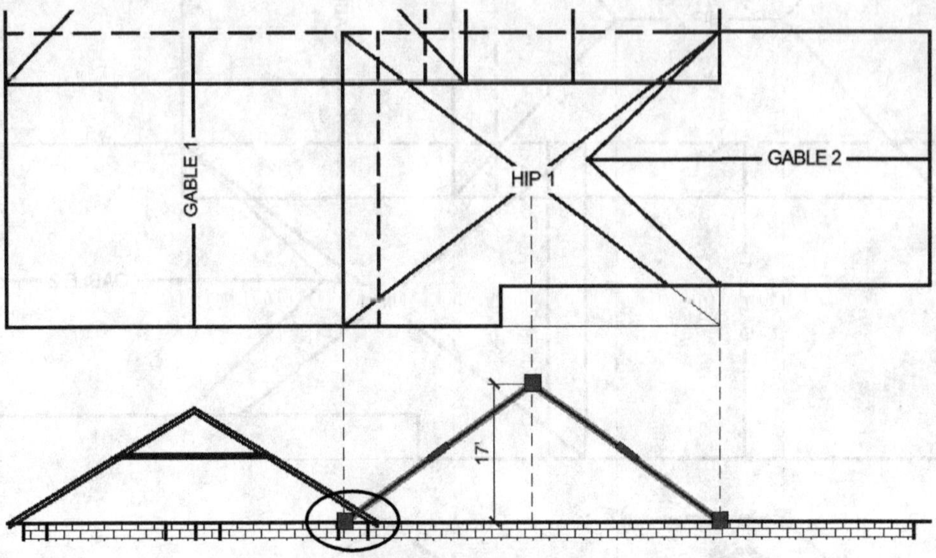

Figure 18-11b

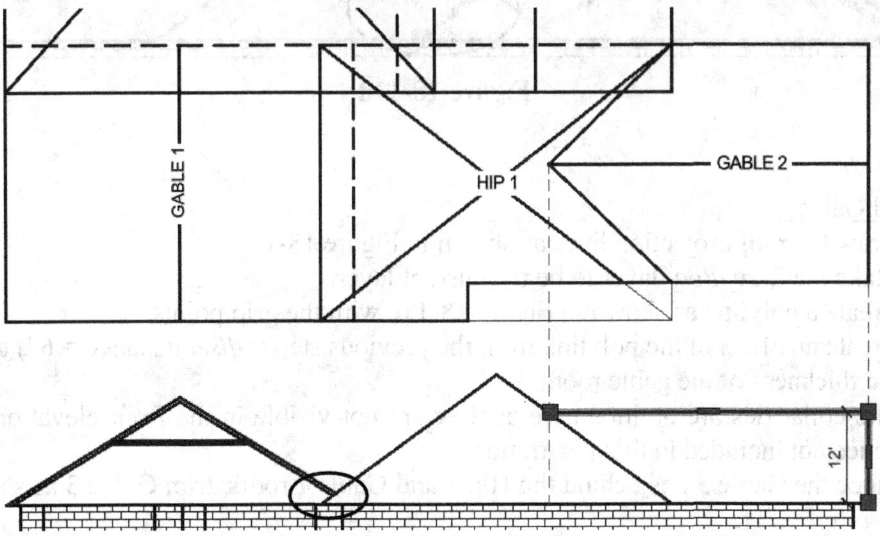

Figure 18-11c

- Add Hip 2:
5. Draw the roof projection lines as shown in Figure 18-11d.
6. Make the *Elev_Roof* layer to be the current layer.
7. Create a polyline as shown in Figure 18-11d with the grip points.
8. Since, the Hip 2 lies behind the Gable 1 and Hip 1 roofs, therefore trim Hip 2 as shown in Figure 18-11e.

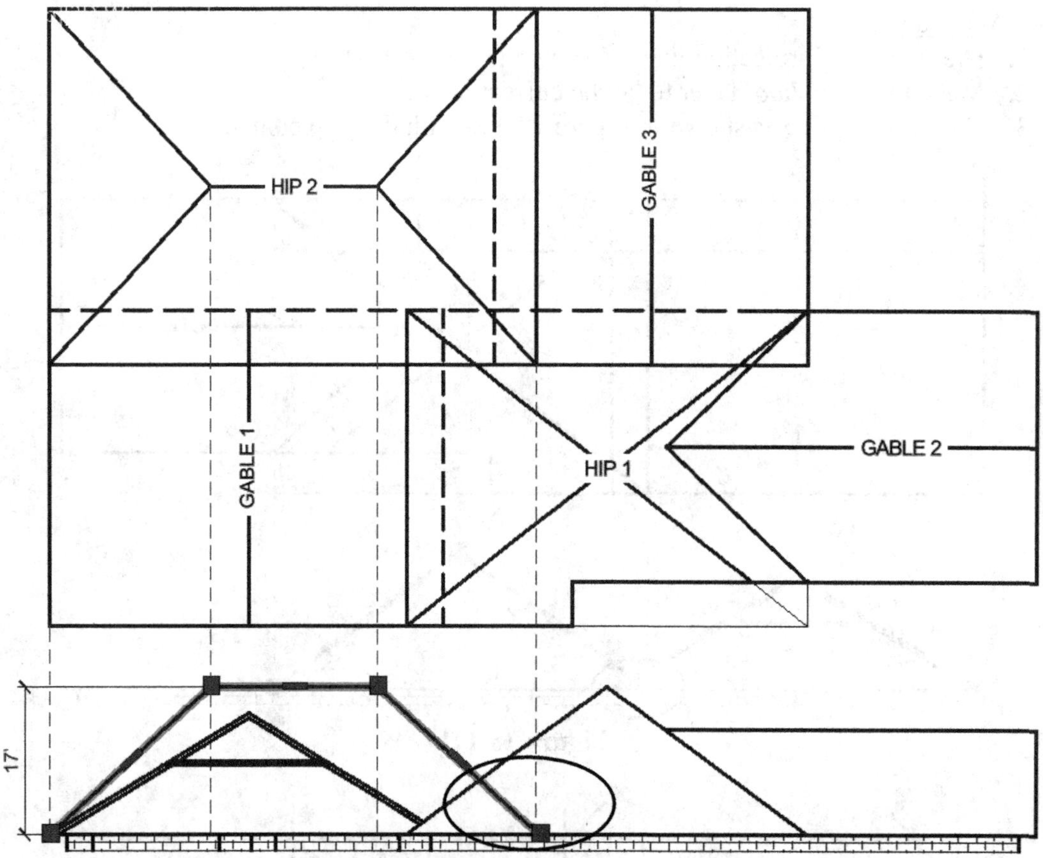

Figure 18-11d

- Add Gable 3:
1. Draw the roof projection lines as shown in Figure 18-11e.
2. Make the *Elev_Roof* layer to be the current layer.
3. Create a polyline as shown in Figure 18-11e with the grip points.
4. Create an offset of the polyline from the previous step (*Offset* distance = 6") to show the thickness of the gable room.
5. The collar ties are omitted here as they are not visible in the front elevation view, hence not included in this illustration.
6. Since the Gable 3 lies behind the Hip 1 and Gable 1 roofs, trim Gable 3 as shown in Figure 18-11f.

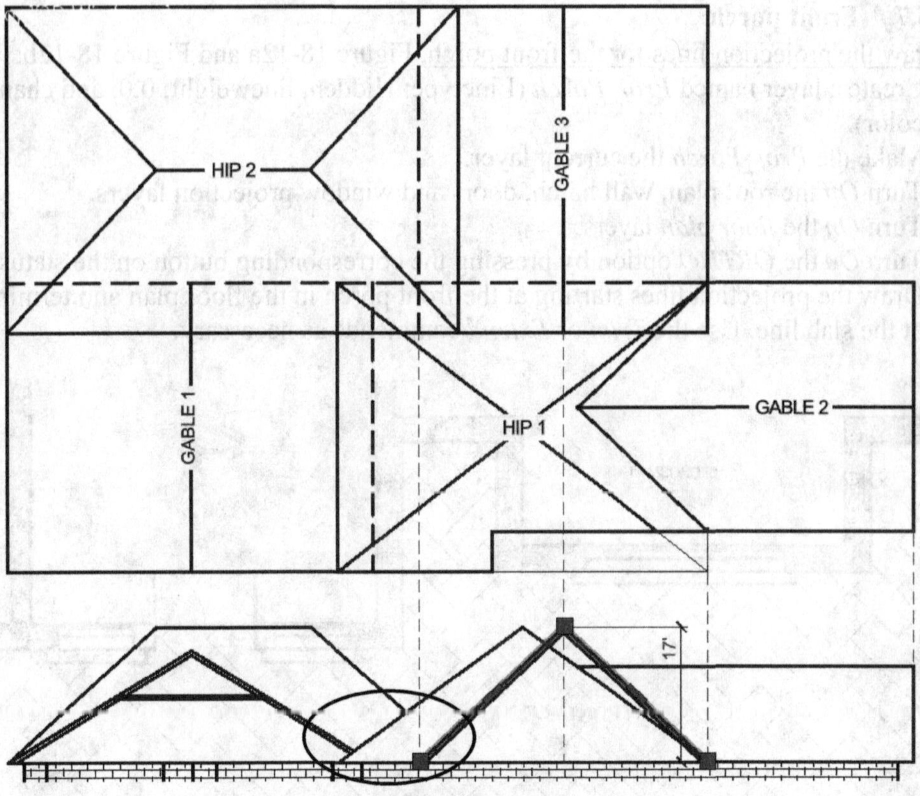

Figure 18-11e

- Add the hatch to the roof.

1. Turn *Off* the *Projection Line*'s layer.
2. Create a layer named *Elev_RoofHatch* (Linetype: Continuous, lineweight: 0.0mm, and change its color).
3. Make the *Elev_RoofHatch* layer to be the current layer.
4. Use the associative and annotative *Hatch* command to hatch the roof. Set the hatch properties as follows, Figure 18-11f.
   - *AR-RSHKE*: Scale = 0.01, angle = 0°, and color = By Layer.
   - *AR-B816*: Scale = 0.01, angle = 0°, and color =204.
   - *Note*: For Gable 2, the angle = 49°.

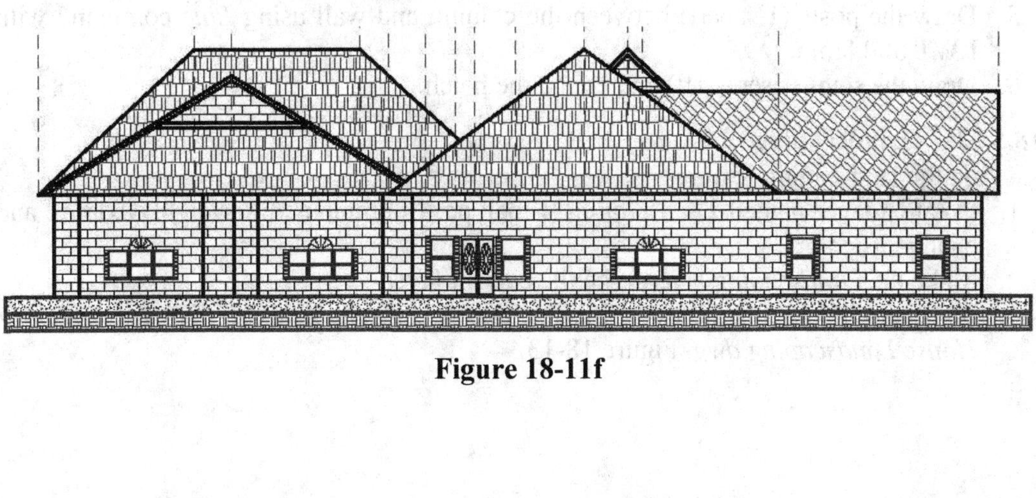

Figure 18-11f

18.5.5.7. Front porch

- Draw the projection lines for the front porch, Figure 18-12a and Figure 18-12b:
  1. Create a layer named *Proj_Porch* (Linetype: Hidden, lineweight: 0.0, and change its color).
  2. Make the *Proj_Porch* the current layer.
  3. Turn *Off* the roof plan, wall hatch, doors and window projection layers.
  4. Turn *On* the *floor plan* layers.
  5. Turn *On* the *ORTHO* option by pressing the corresponding button on the status bar.
  6. Draw the projection lines starting at the front porch in the floor plan and terminating at the slab line. Use the *Trim* or *Extend* commands as necessary.

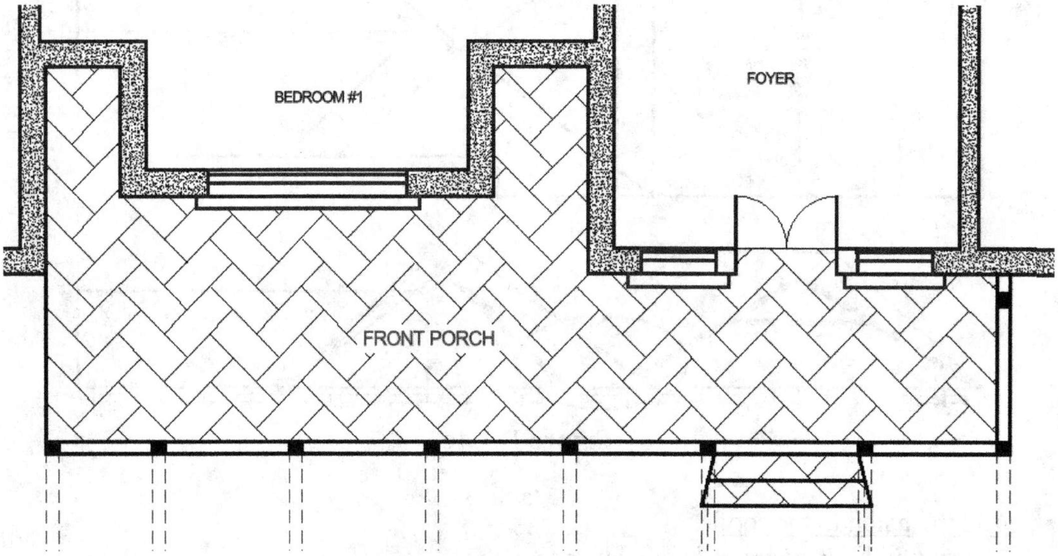

Figure 18-12a

- Draw the front porch, Figure 18-12b:
  1. Create a layer named *Elev_Porch* (Linetype: Continuous, lineweight: 0.5mm, and change its color).
  2. Make the *Elev_Porch* layer to be the current layer.
  3. Draw the columns and create the hatch.
  4. Hatch the columns using *SOLID* pattern for the columns.
  5. Draw the posts (1' apart) between the column and wall using *Line* command with LWT of 0.8mm.
  6. Draw the steps (riser = 1ft) and create the hatch.

18.5.5.8. Landscaping

- Add the landscaping features:
  1. Create a layer named *Landscaping* (Linetype: Continuous, lineweight: 0.0mm, and change its color).
  2. Make the *Landscaping* layer to be the current layer.
  3. Insert the blocks for the trees, bushes, and streetlights from the *Design Center →* *House Landscaping.dwg*, Figure 18-13.

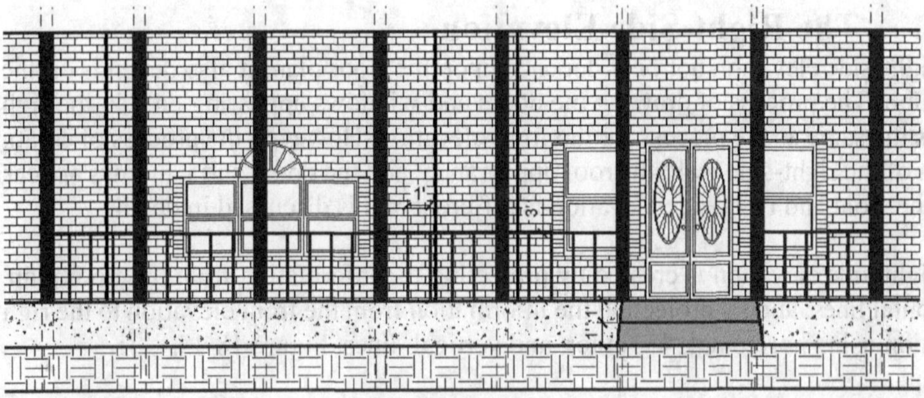

Figure 18-12b

18.5.5.9. Complete front elevation

- The front elevation file: Figure 18-13
  1. Set the scale of the drawing to 1:156.
  2. Update the blocks (units must be updated to architectural).
  3. Save the *FrontElev.dwg* drawing file.
  4. The complete front elevation is shown in Figure 18-13.

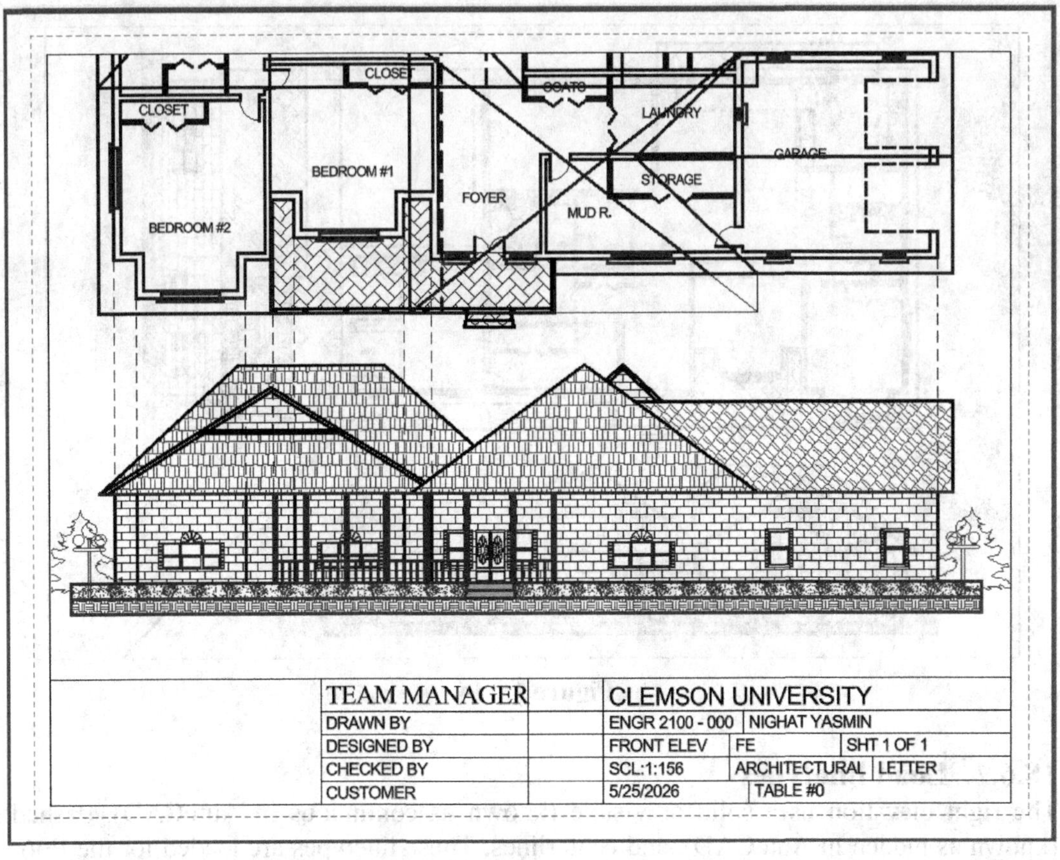

Figure 18-13

18.6. The Right-Side Elevation

The right-side elevation not only depends upon the floor plan; it also depends on the front elevation. The process of drawing the doors and windows appearing only in the right-side wall is the same as the process for the front elevation. However, the process of creating the height of the right-side wall, the roof appearance, and the doors and windows appearing in both the front and right-side elevation is different and is discussed in detail.

The right-side elevation is created by projecting the information from the floor plan using horizontal lines; and by projecting the information from the front elevation to the right-side elevation using horizontal, 45° miter, and vertical, lines, Figure 18-14.

This section provides step-by-step instructions for drawing the right-side elevation of the given floor plan.

- Do not add any dimensions! Dimensions are added later.
- The drawing is printed from the layout! Keep checking the appearance of the linetypes and lineweights in the layouts.

18.6.1. Open file

Open file: Open the front elevation file (*FrontElev.dwg*) created in the previous section and save it as the *RightElev.dwg* file.

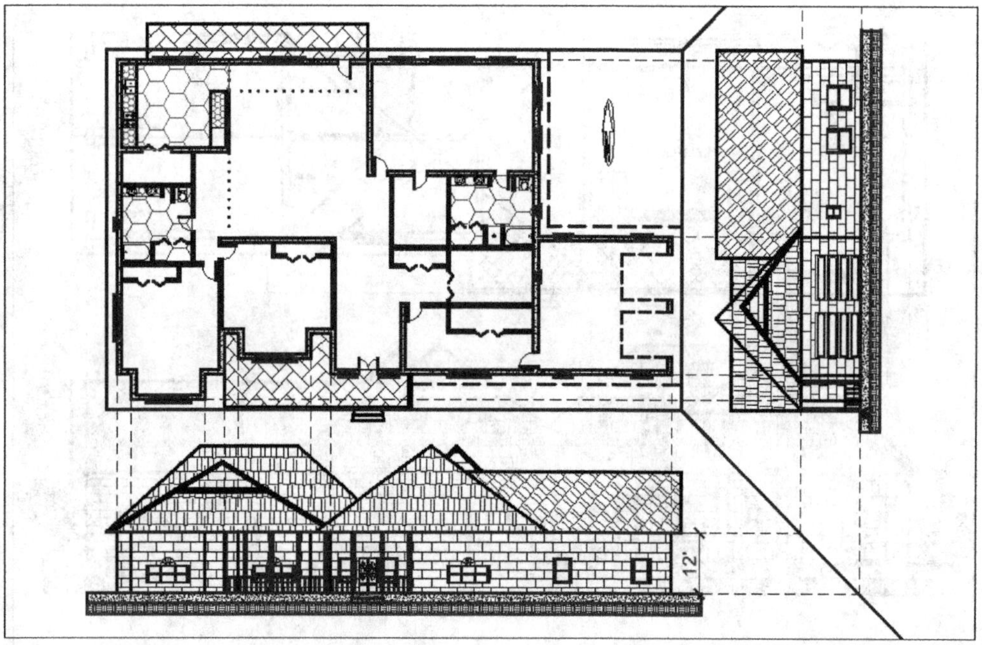

Figure 18-14

18.6.2. Load linetypes

The right elevation uses solid or visible (known as continuous in AutoCAD), dashed (known as hidden in AutoCAD), and centerlines. These linetypes are loaded for the floor plan. If not, then load these linetypes; *Continuous* is the default linetype.

18.6.3. Layers

- Create layers:
  1. Create four layers and name them *Proj_45*, *Proj_45_GL_Slab*, *Proj_45_Door*, *Proj_45_Window*, *Proj_45_Wall*, and *Proj_45_Roof*.
  2. Set their linetype to *Hidden*, lineweight to 0.0, and change their color.
  3. Turn *On* and *Off* these and previously created layers as necessary.

18.6.4. Orthogonal lines

Since most of the lines in the right elevation are either horizontal or vertical, turn *On* the *ORTHO* option by pressing the corresponding button (▭) on the status bar.

18.6.5. Miter line

- Draw a 45 degree miter line, Figure 18-15:
  1. Draw a rectangle using roofline as shown in Figure 18-15.
  2. At the lower right corner of the rectangle, draw a 60' long line at an angle of 45°. This line will be used to project information from the front elevation to the right-side elevation.

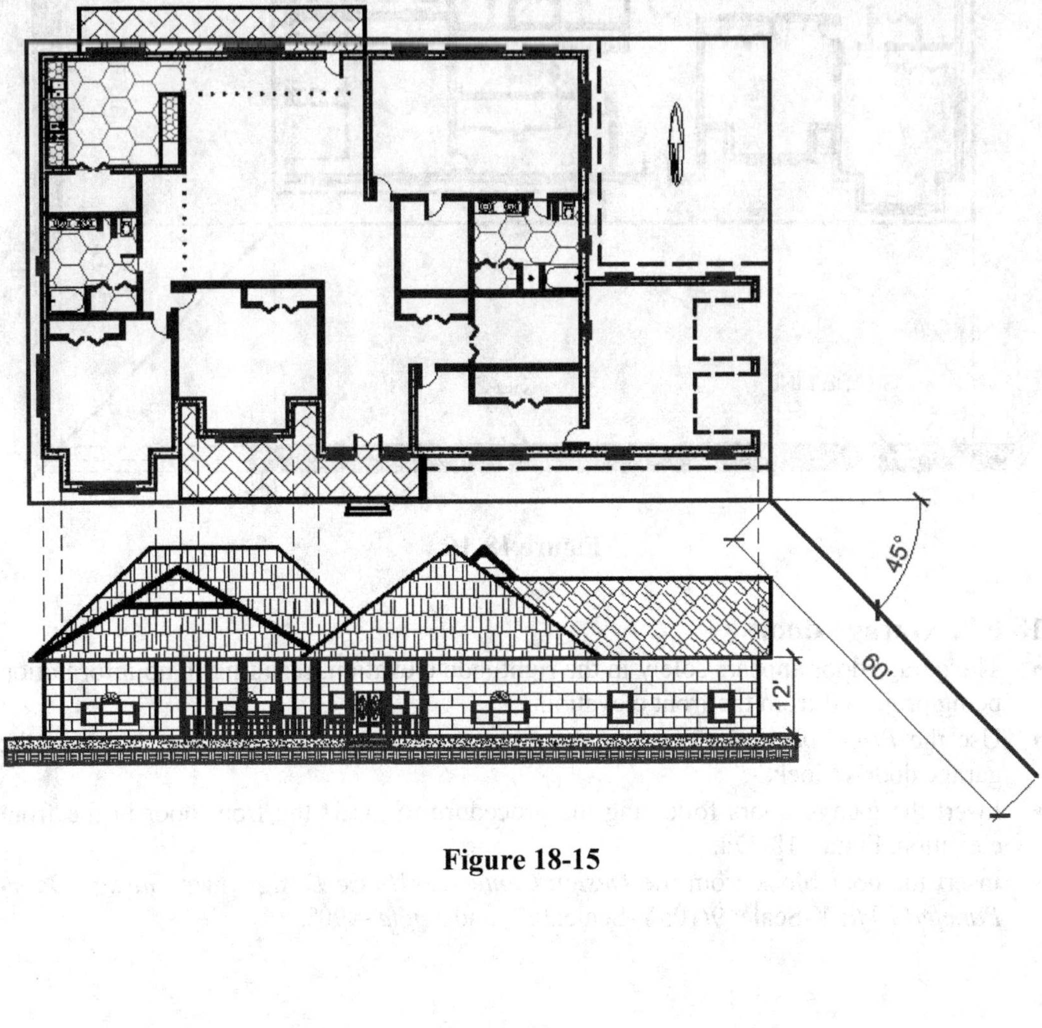

Figure 18-15

18.6.6. Ground and slab level

- Draw ground and slab level, Figure 18-16:
  1. Turn on the *Grade_Line* and *Slab_Line* layers.
  2. Make the *Proj_45_GL_Slab* layer to be the current layer.
  3. Since the slab is drawn in the front elevation, its height is projected from the front elevation. From the front elevation, draw horizontal lines starting at the right end of the grade and slab lines and terminating at the 45° miter line.
  4. Draw vertical lines starting at the 45° miter line (where lines of step #3 terminated) and terminating beyond the floor plan. If necessary, use *Trim* and *Extend* commands.
  5. Now complete the ground and slab level; either use *Mirror* command or the process discussed in the front elevation.

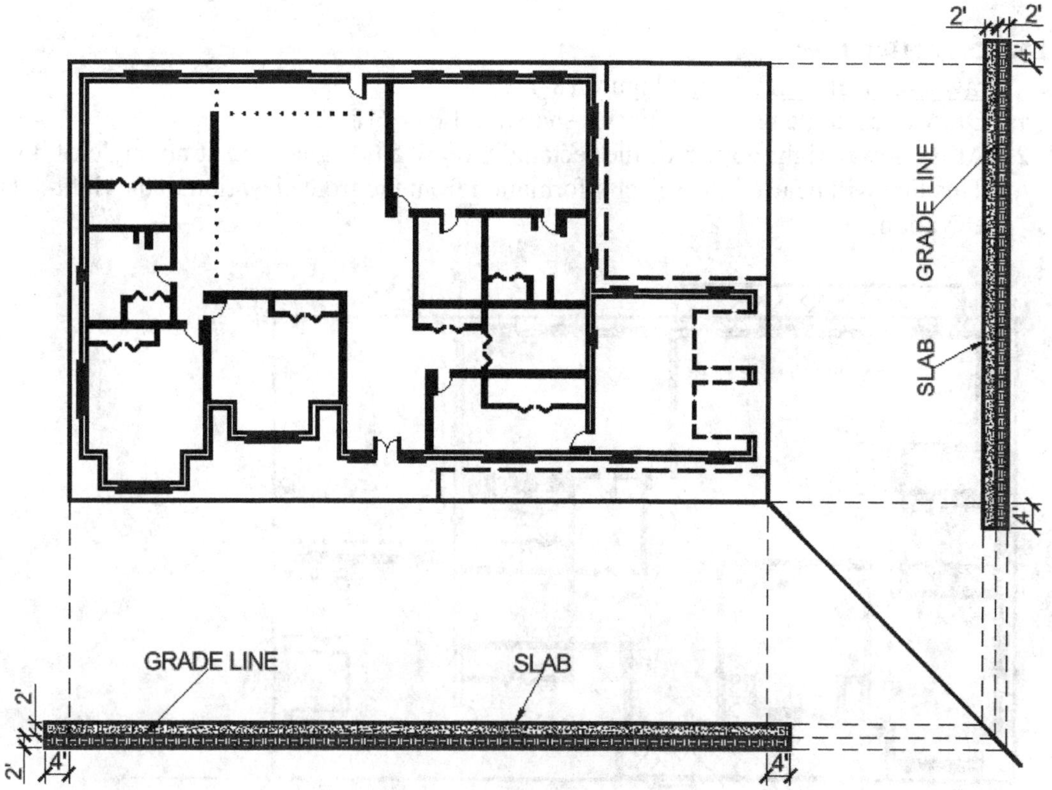

Figure 18-16

18.6.7. Garage doors

- The garage door appears solely in the right-side elevation, resulting in no information being projected from the front elevation.
- Use the *Proj-Door* layer for the projection lines and *Elev-Door* layer to insert the garage door's block.
- Insert the garage doors following the procedure to insert the front door in the front elevation, Figure 18-17a.
- Insert the door block from the *Design Center* → *House Design.dwg*: *Garage Door-Paneled 10 ft*; X-Scale: 9/10; Y-Scale: 9/7; and *Angle* = 90°.

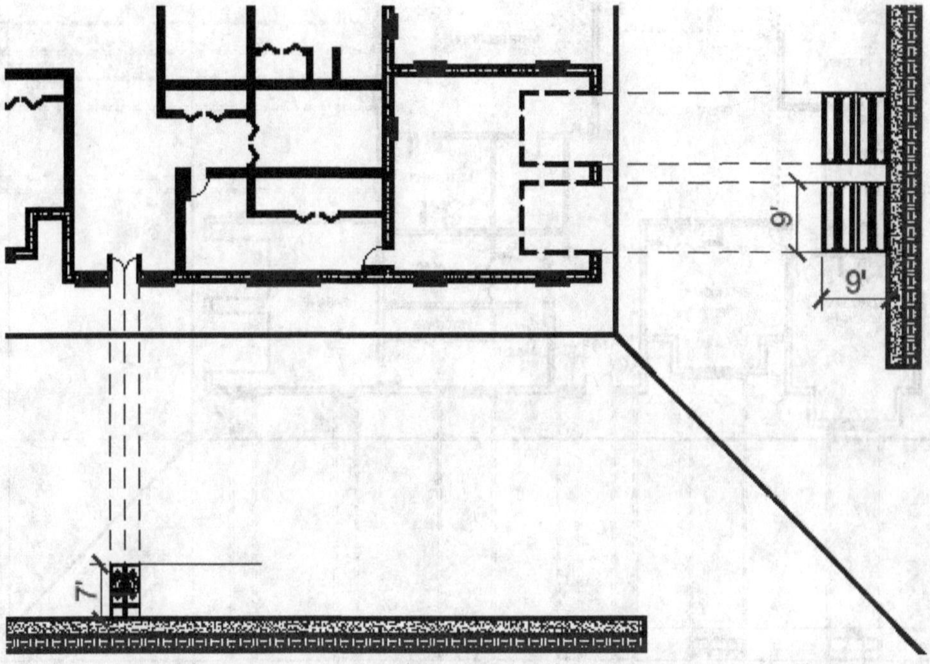

Figure 18-17a

18.6.8. Windows

- Use the *Proj-Window* layer for the projection lines and *Elev-Window* layer to insert the window's block.
- For the windows in the right-side elevation, use the horizontal projection lines from the floor plan to reflect the location and width of the windows.
- For the window heights, refer to the *Window Schedule* from *Chapter 17*.
- Figure 18-17b shows the windows visible in the right-side elevation; and 2', 3', and 7' reference lines. The 2' and 7' lines are projected from the front elevation.
- Figure 18-17b and Figure 18-17c show the windows in the right-side elevation.

1. **W1 window in Master Bathroom:**
   - W1 in the master bathroom is 3' tall and 4' above the ground.
   - Follow the process of W2 created in the garage in the front elevation.
   - X-Scale: 18/36; Y-Scale: 3/3; and *Angle* = 90°.

2. **W3 in MSTR Bedroom**:
   - W3 in the master bathroom is 5' tall and 2' above the ground.
   - Follow the process of W2 created in the garage in the front elevation.
   - X-Scale: 4/3; Y-Scale: 5/3; and *Angle* = 90°.

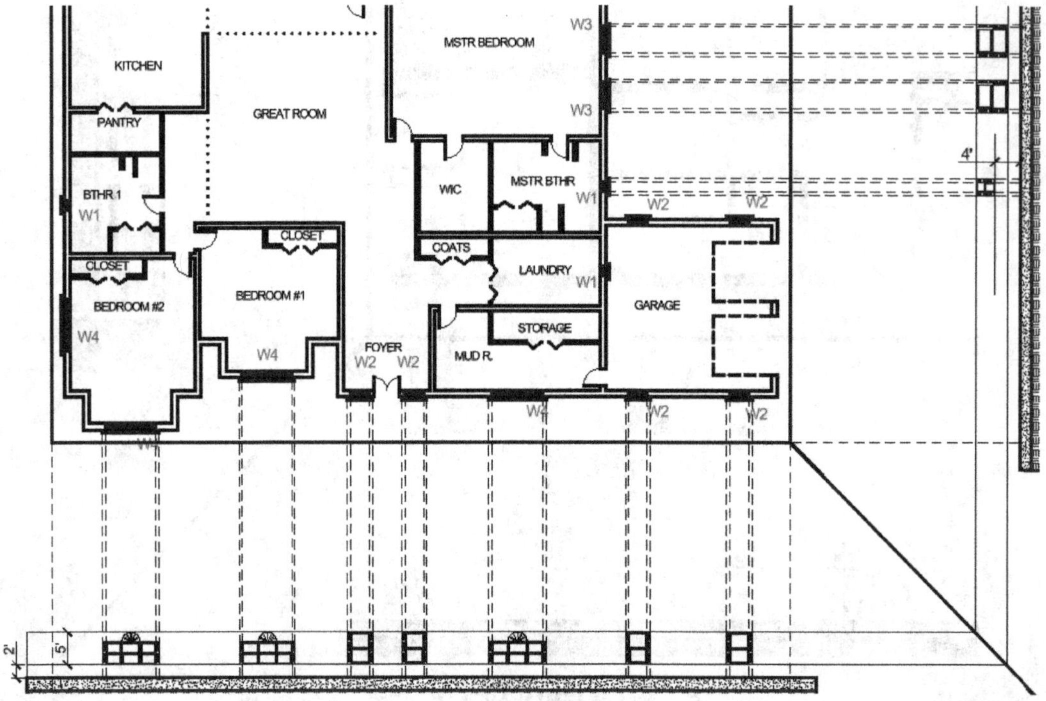

Figure 18-17b

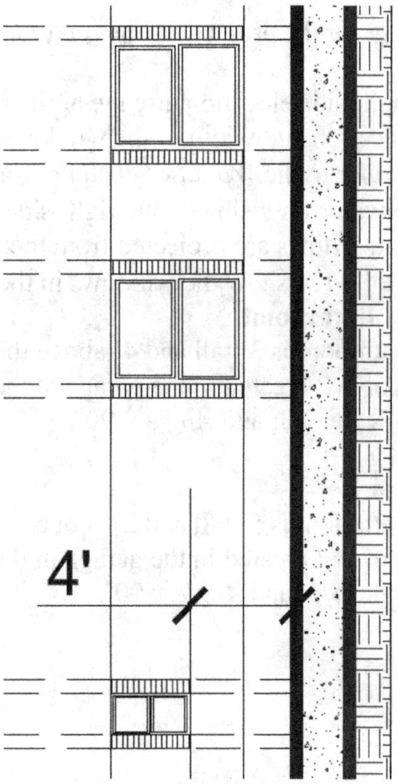

Figure 18-17b

18.6.9. Wall

- For the wall in the right-side elevation refer to Figure 18-18.
- Since the wall is drawn in the front elevation, its height is projected from the front elevation.
  1. Project the length of the wall in right-side elevation; draw horizontal lines starting from the right-side of the floor plan and terminating at the slab level.
  2. From the front elevation, draw horizontal lines starting at the top and bottom ends of the wall and terminating at the 45° miter line.
  3. Draw vertical lines starting at the 45° miter line (where lines of step #2 terminated) and terminating beyond the floor plan. If necessary, use *Trim* and *Extend* commands.
  4. Now complete the wall as discussed in the front elevation.
  5. Use associative and annotative *Hatch* command with *AR-B816* (brick) pattern, set *Angle* to 90° and *Scale* to 0.01.

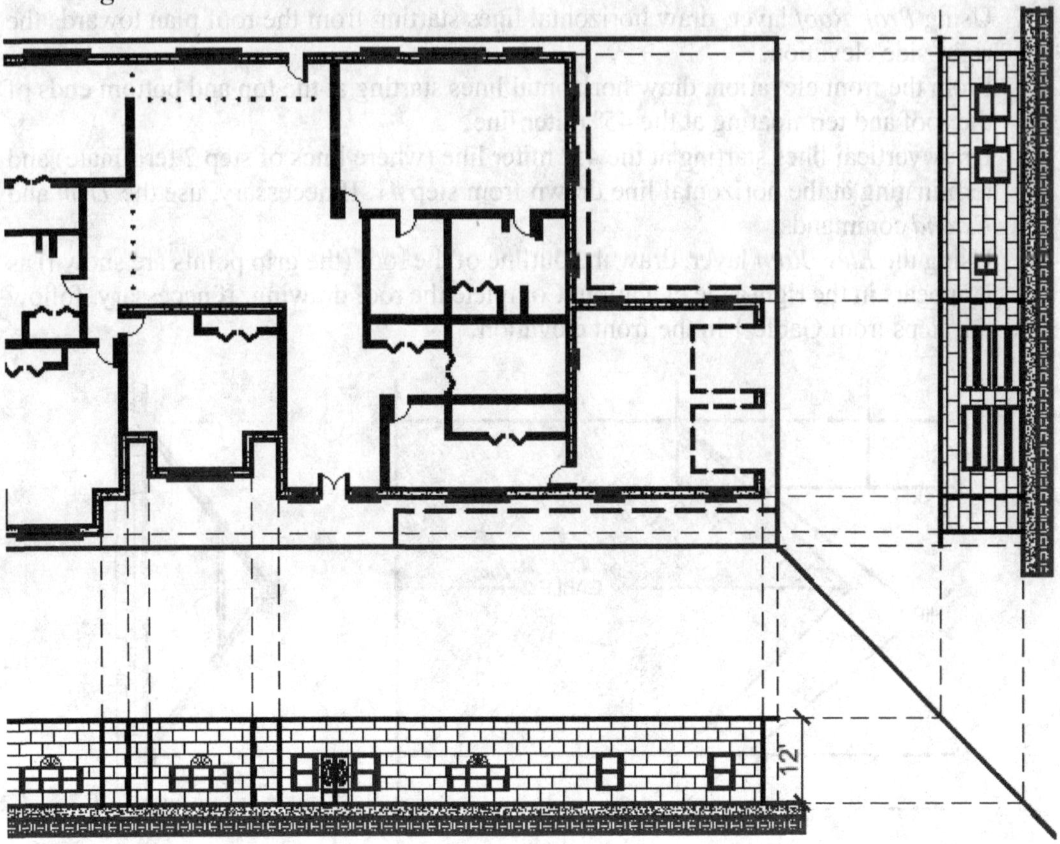

Figure 18-18

18.6.10. Roof

- Turn *On* the layer of the *Roofplan*.
- Turn *Off* the layers of the *floor plan*.

- Roof creation in elevations is complex; therefore, each roof is drawn independently. To make the process simpler, always begin with the edge of the roofplan for which the elevation is being developed to ensure proper construction and alignment during the process. Hence, for the right-side elevation, draw Gable 2 and Gable 3 roofs before adding Gable 1, Hip 1, and Hip 2 roofs.

- Since the roofs are drawn in the front elevation, their heights are projected from the front elevation.
- For demonstration purposes, the projection lines of an individual roof and the corresponding hatches of the roofs are shown.
- The user should hatch the roof in the right-side elevation after drawing the outline of all the roofs visible from the right-side of the house.

Gable 2:

- Create Gable 2 roof, in the right-side elevation as shown in Figure 18-19 and using the following steps.

1. Using *Proj_Roof* layer, draw horizontal lines starting from the roof plan towards the right-side elevation.
2. From the front elevation, draw horizontal lines starting at the top and bottom ends of the roof and terminating at the 45° miter line.
3. Draw vertical lines starting at the 45° miter line (where lines of step 2 terminate) and terminating at the horizontal line drawn from step #1. If necessary, use the *Trim* and *Extend* commands.
4. Using the *Elev_Roof* layer, draw the outline of the roof (the grip points are shown) as it appears in the right-side elevation. Complete the roof drawing. If necessary, follow the steps from Gable 1 in the front elevation.

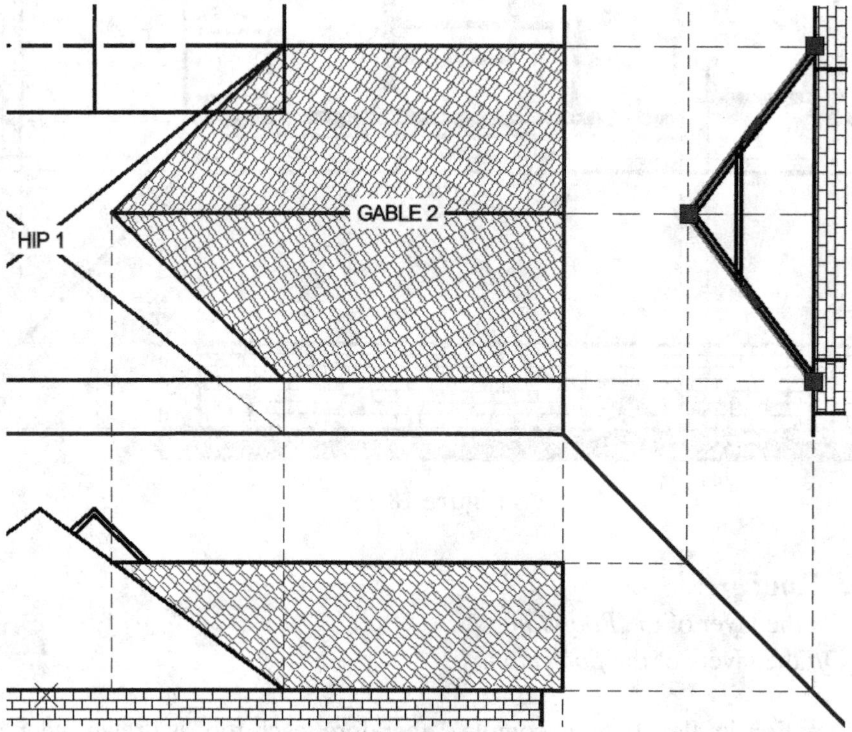

Figure 18-19

Gable 3:

- Create Gable 3 roof, in the right-side elevation as shown in Figure 18-20 and use the following steps.

1. Using *Proj_Roof* layer, draw horizontal lines starting from the roof plan towards the right-side elevation.
2. From the front elevation, draw horizontal lines starting at the top and bottom ends of the roof and terminating at the 45° miter line.
3. Draw vertical lines starting at the 45° miter line (where lines of step 2 terminate) and terminating at the horizontal line drawn from step #1. If necessary, use the *Trim* and *Extend* commands.
4. Using the *Elev_Roof* layer, draw the outline of the roof as it appears in the right-side elevation (the grip points are shown).

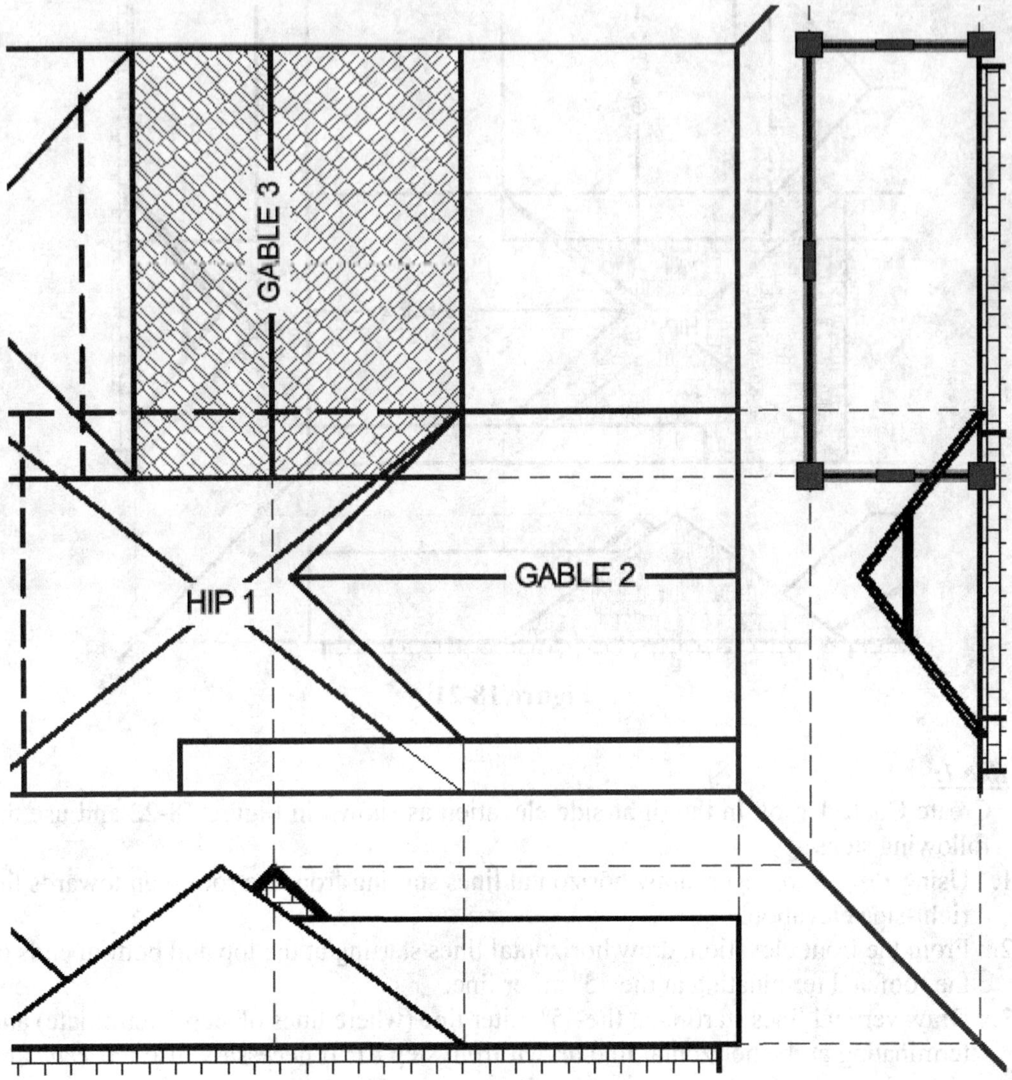

Figure 18-20

Hip 1:

- Create Hip 1 roof, in the right-side elevation as shown in Figure 18-21 and use the following steps.
  1. Using *Proj_Roof* layer, draw horizontal lines starting from the roof plan towards the right-side elevation.
  2. From the front elevation, draw horizontal lines starting at the top and bottom ends of the roof and terminating at the 45° miter line.
  3. Draw vertical lines starting at the 45° miter line (where lines of step 2 terminate) and terminating at the horizontal line drawn from step #1. If necessary, use the *Trim* and *Extend* commands.
  4. Using the *Elev_Roof* layer, draw the outline of the roof as it appears in the right-side elevation (the grip points are shown).

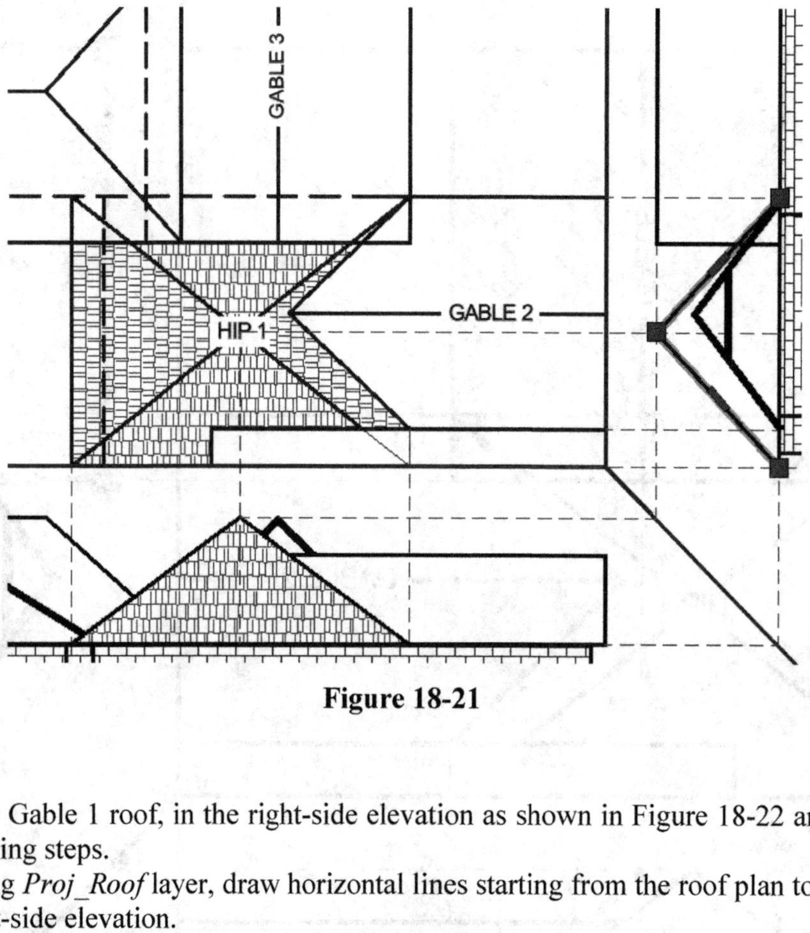

Figure 18-21

Gable 1:

- Create Gable 1 roof, in the right-side elevation as shown in Figure 18-22 and use the following steps.
  1. Using *Proj_Roof* layer, draw horizontal lines starting from the roof plan towards the right-side elevation.
  2. From the front elevation, draw horizontal lines starting at the top and bottom ends of the roof and terminating at the 45° miter line.
  3. Draw vertical lines starting at the 45° miter line (where lines of step 2 terminate) and terminating at the horizontal line drawn from step #1. If necessary, use the *Trim* and *Extend* commands.
  4. Using the *Elev_Roof* layer, draw the outline of the roof as it appears in the right-side elevation (the grip points are shown).

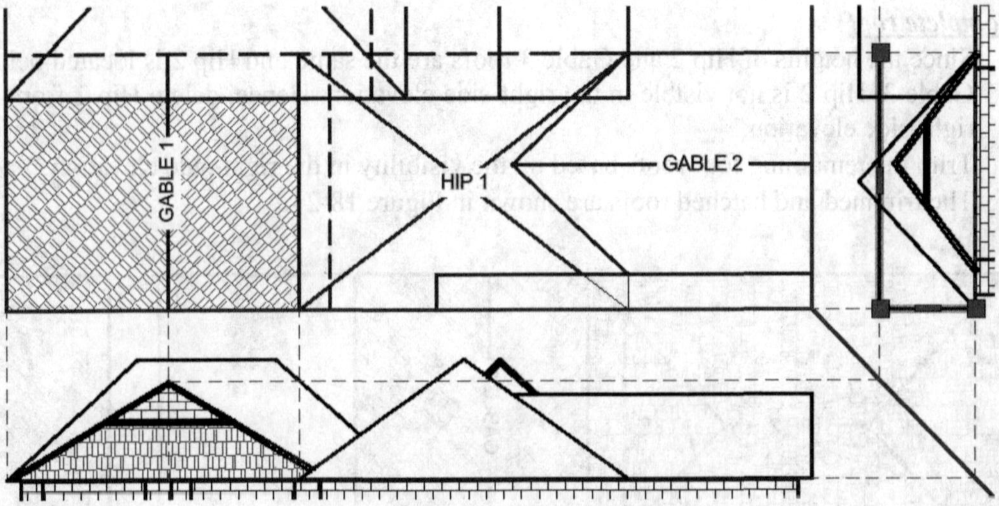

Figure 18-22

Hip 2:

- Create Hip 2 roof, in the right-side elevation as shown in Figure 18-23 and use the following steps.

5. Using *Proj_Roof* layer, draw horizontal lines starting from the roof plan towards the right-side elevation.
6. From the front elevation, draw horizontal lines starting at the top and bottom ends of the roof and terminating at the 45° miter line.
7. Draw vertical lines starting at the 45° miter line (where lines of step 2 terminate) and terminating at the horizontal line drawn from step #1. If necessary, use the *Trim* and *Extend* commands.
8. Using the *Elev_Roof* layer, draw the outline of the roof as it appears in the right-side elevation (the grip points are shown).

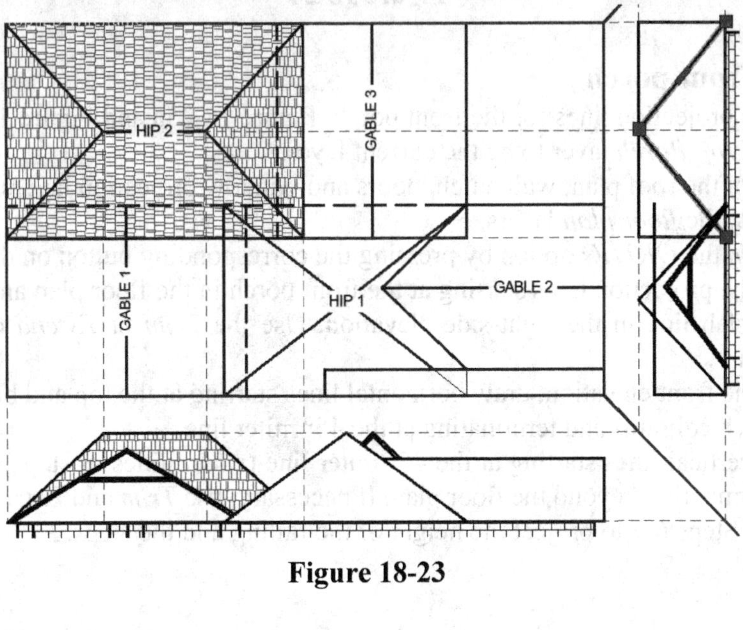

Figure 18-23

Complete roof

- Since the heights of Hip 2 and Gable 3 roofs are the same and Hip 2 is located behind Gable 3, Hip 2 is not visible in the right-side elevation. Hence, delete Hip 2 from the right-side elevation.
- Trim the remaining four roofs based on the visibility in the right-side elevation.
- The trimmed and hatched roofs are shown in Figure 18-24.

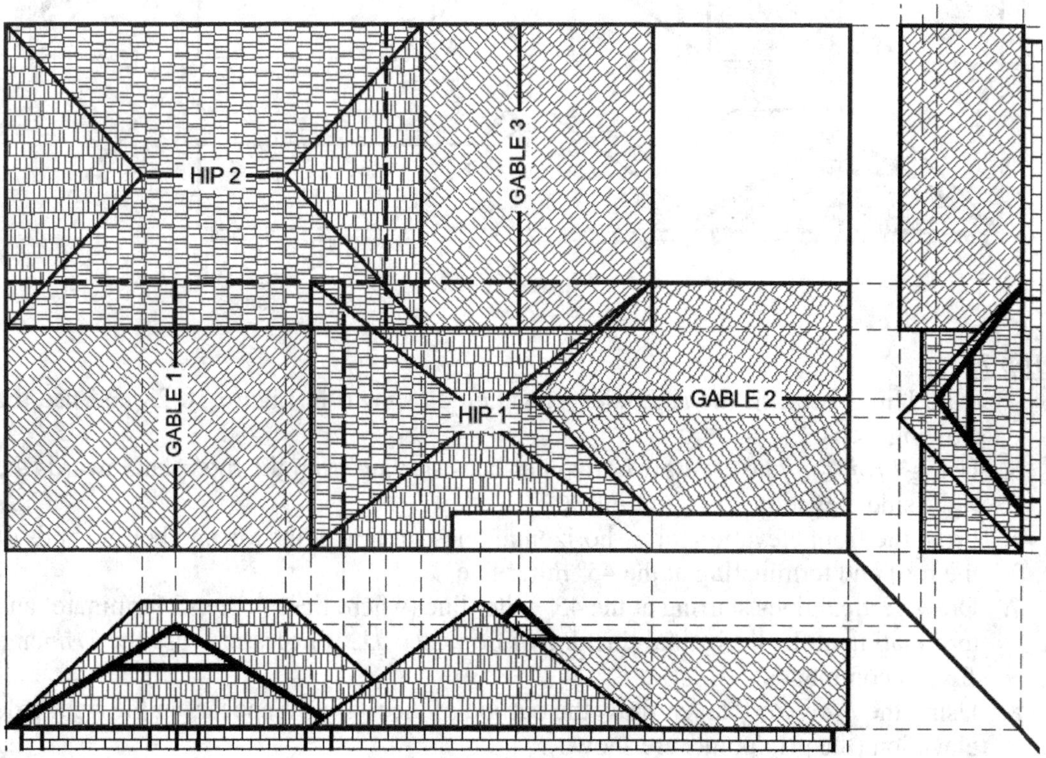

Figure 18-24

18.6.11. Front porch

- Draw the projection lines for the front porch, Figure 18-25a and Figure 18-25b:
  1. Make *Proj_Porch* layer to be the current layer.
  2. Turn *Off* the roof plan, wall hatch, doors and window projection layers.
  3. Turn *On* the *floor plan* layers.
  4. Turn *On* the *ORTHO* option by pressing the corresponding button on the status bar.
  5. Draw the projection lines starting at the front porch in the floor plan and terminating at the slab line in the right-side elevation. Use the *Trim* or *Extend* commands as necessary.
  6. From the front elevation, draw horizontal lines starting at the top and bottom ends of the porch columns and terminating at the 45° miter line.
  7. Draw vertical lines starting at the 45° miter line (where lines of step #6 terminated) and terminating beyond the floor plan. If necessary, use *Trim* and *Extend* commands.
  8. Repeat Steps 6-7 to project the height of the railing and the steps.

- Draw the front porch:
  1. Make *Elev_Porch* layer to be the current layer.
  2. Draw the columns and create the hatch.
  3. Hatch the columns using *SOLID* pattern for the columns.
  4. Draw the posts (1' apart) between the column and wall using *Line* command with LWT of 0.8mm.
  5. Draw the steps (riser = 1ft) and create the hatch.

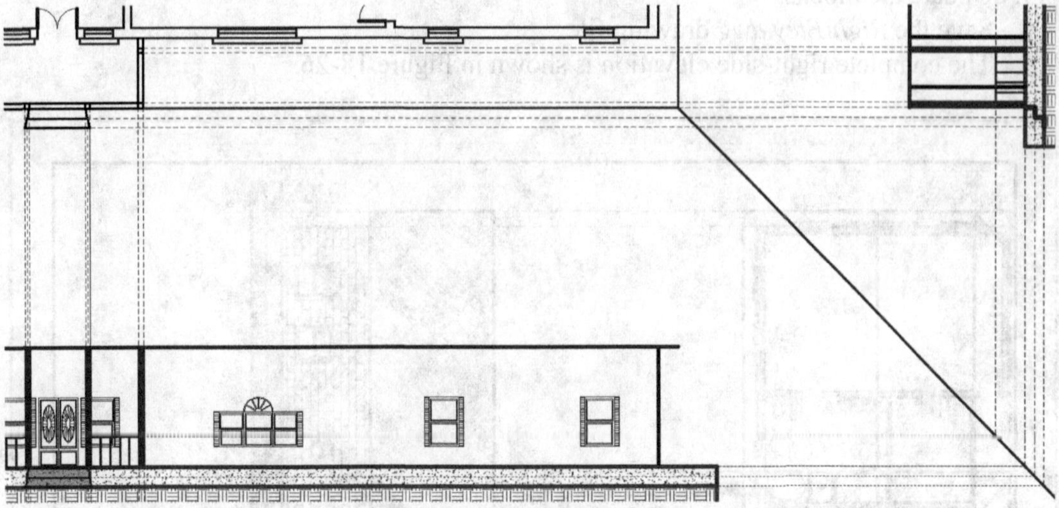

Figure 18-25a

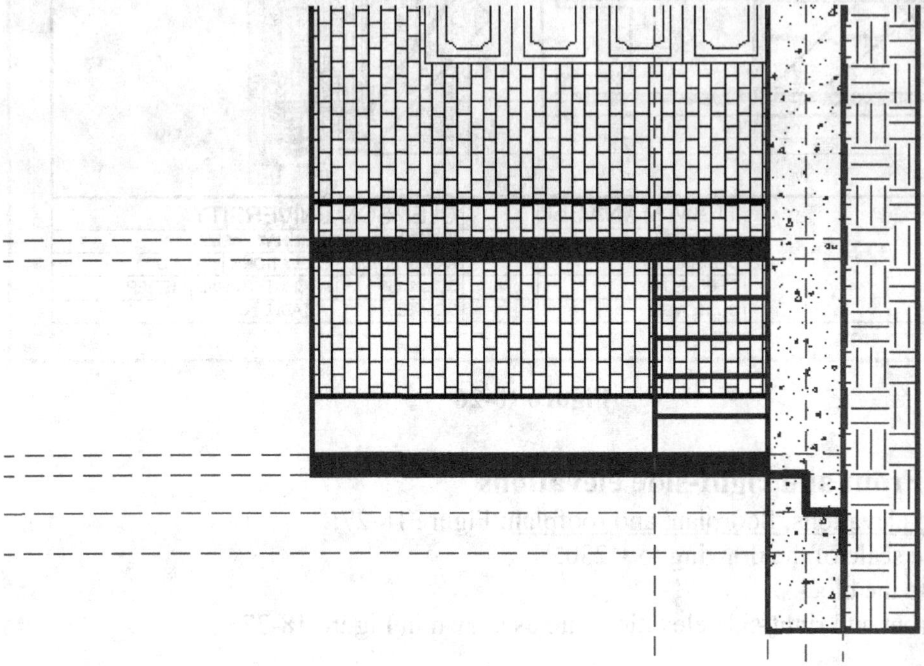

Figure 18-25b

Landscaping:

- Repeat the process from the front elevation.

18.6.12. Complete right-side elevation

- The right-side elevation file: Figure 18-26
  1. Insert an appropriate layout from one of the template files.
  2. Set the scale of the drawing to 1:156
  3. Update the blocks.
  4. Save the *RightElev.dwg* drawing file.
  5. The complete right-side elevation is shown in Figure 18-26.

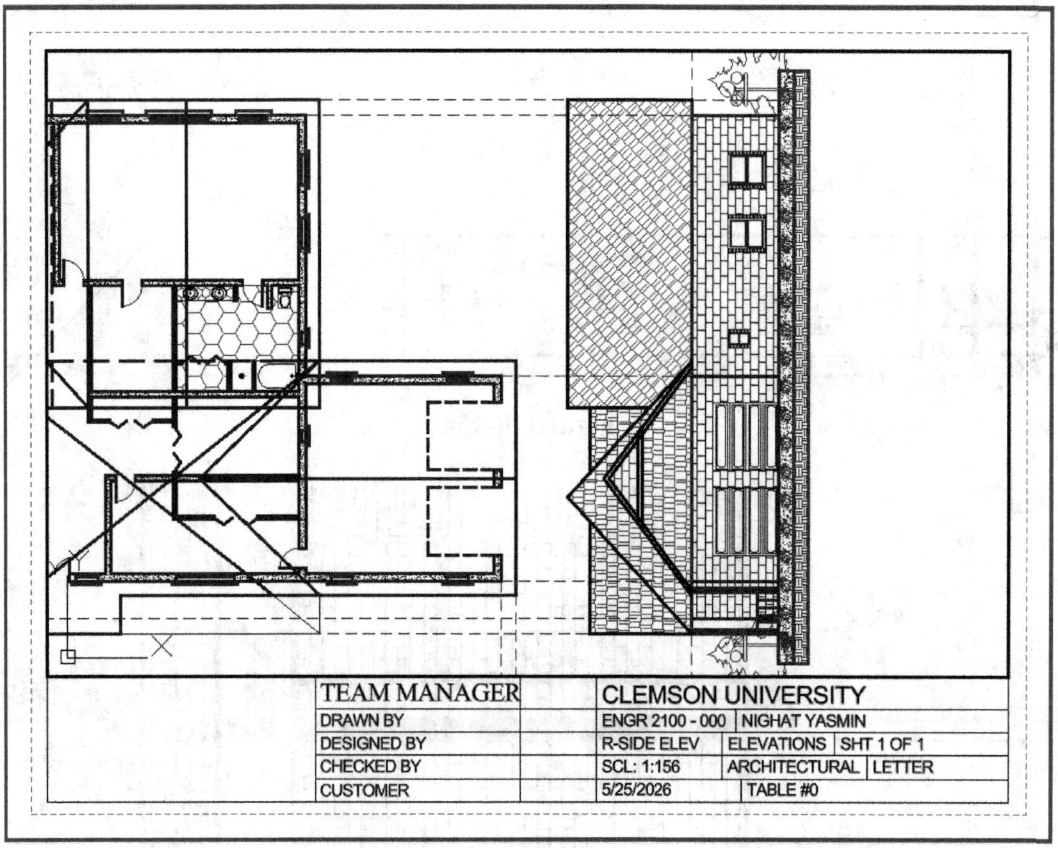

Figure 18-26

18.6.13. Front and right-side elevations

- The two elevations, floorplan, and roofplan: Figure 18-27:
  1. Set the scale of the drawing to 1:230.
  2. Update the blocks.
  3. The front and right-side elevations are as shown in Figure 18-27.

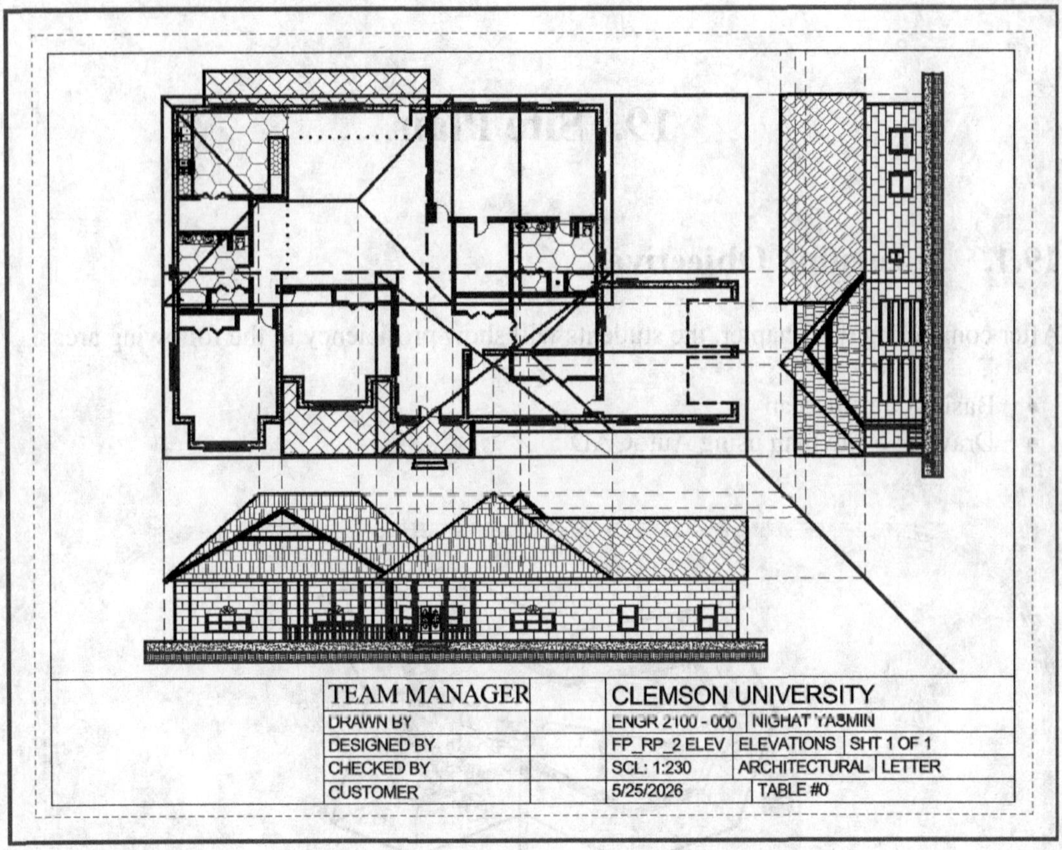

Figure 18-27

18.7. Back And Left-Side Elevations

- The back and the left side elevations are left for the readers.

Notes:

19. Site Plan

19.1. Learning Objectives

After completing this chapter, the students will show proficiency in the following areas:

- Basics of a site plan
- Drawing a site plan using AutoCAD

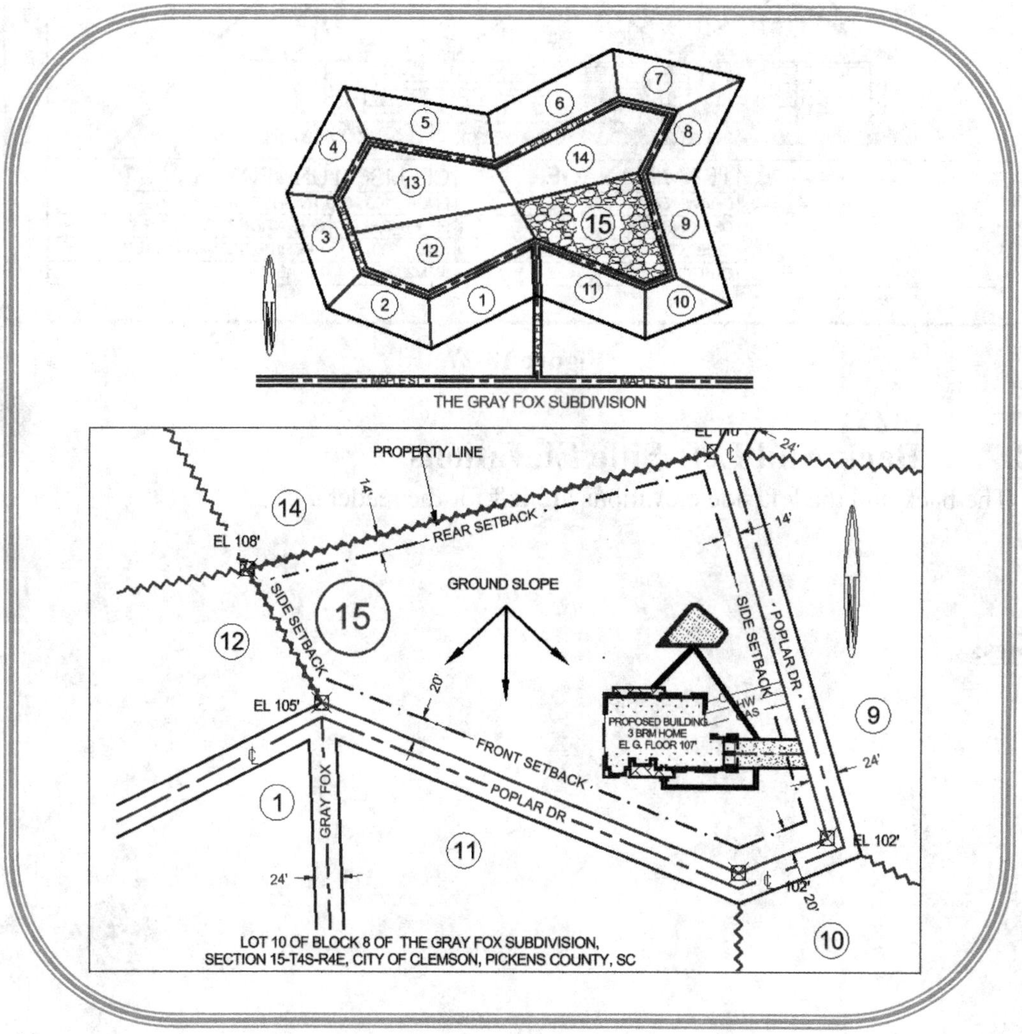

19.2. Introduction

The map of an individual construction site is known as a site plan, plat, or plot. The site plan not only displays the location of the project, it also exhibits other key features. A site plan of a typical building shows an outline of the building, utilities (sewer line, water supply, power lines, gas supply, etc.), driveways, walkways, adjacent roads, adjoining building (if any), etc.

19.3. Terminology

- Property line: A property line is the legal boundary of a parcel of land. It is described as a closed traverse using lengths and bearing (or azimuth) of each course. The boundary is set using one of the survey methods discussed in *Chapter 11*.
- Easement: An easement is defined as a right of way or privilege offered by the property owner to the public or selected users.
- Setback: A setback is the distance from the property line to any structure on the property (site). Setbacks guarantee that sufficient sunlight would reach the street and lower levels of the adjacent buildings. Generally, setbacks are provided on the front and rear of a building. The front setback is typically measured from one foot away from the sidewalk bordering the property. If there is no sidewalk, then the city still owns the area where it normally would be placed. Each street is a different width, so the Department of Public Works must be contacted for detailed information.

19.4. Components Of A Site Plan

The information represented by a site plan may vary from state to state. However, a typical site plan for a residential building contains the following information.

1. Property description, including township, range, section and tax lot number, and property address if available.
2. North arrow.
3. Property line.
4. Dimensions (length and angle) of all the property lines.
5. Direction and percent of the slope.
6. Distance (setbacks) from all structures to the property lines.
7. Names and locations of all the roads adjacent to the property.
8. Names (or labels) and locations of all other properties adjacent to the property in question.
9. Location, size, and intended use of all structures, existing and proposed.
10. Location of driveways, walkways, or any other roads on the property, existing and proposed.
11. Location of any public utility.
12. Location of all major features (e.g., canals, irrigation ditches, or rock ledges).
13. Location of wells or water sources on the property under consideration and adjacent properties.
14. Location of test holes used for the site evaluation during the feasibility process.

15. Height from grade to all shade producing points of roof lines for solar calculation. NOTE: in some cases, plat plans for parcels over 2 acres may need to be scaled for solar purposes.
16. For new septic construction, three elevation shots on each leach line for both the initial and reserve leach field area.
17. Location of proposed septic tank, drain field, and replacement field, showing dimensions and spacing of leach lines. Furthermore, the distance from the septic tank and system to the property lines should be included. NOTE: In some cases, a sanitarian may require the system to be drawn to scale.

19.5. AutoCAD And Site Plan

This section creates a site plan for the residential building designed in *Chapter 16* and *Chapter 17* using Lot 4 from the Lots and Blocks drawing created in *Chapter 11*.

19.5.1. Open file

Launch AutoCAD 2027 and open a file to create the site plan using one of the two methods.

1. Open a new file (the landscape template file for the ANSI units) and work through all the steps listed in this section.
2. (i) Open the lots and blocks drawing, Figure 19-1a, (ii) draw a closed polyline as shown in Figure 19-1b (grip points are shown), and (iii) use the *Trim*, *Delete*, and *Move* commands to modify the drawing as shown in Figure 19-1c. (iv) For the property line, create a layer and move the boundary of Lot 10 to the layer.

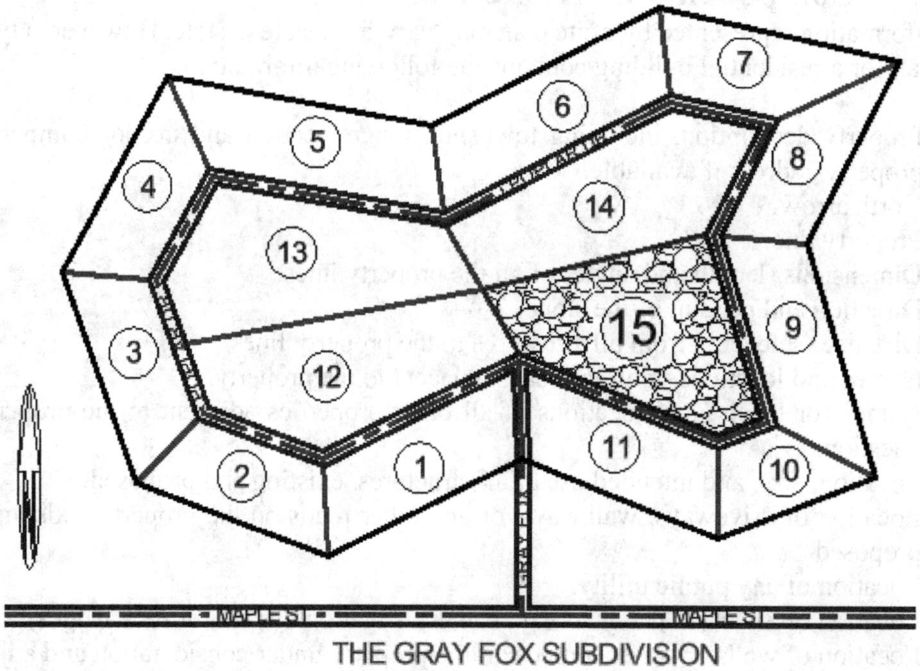

Figure 19-1a

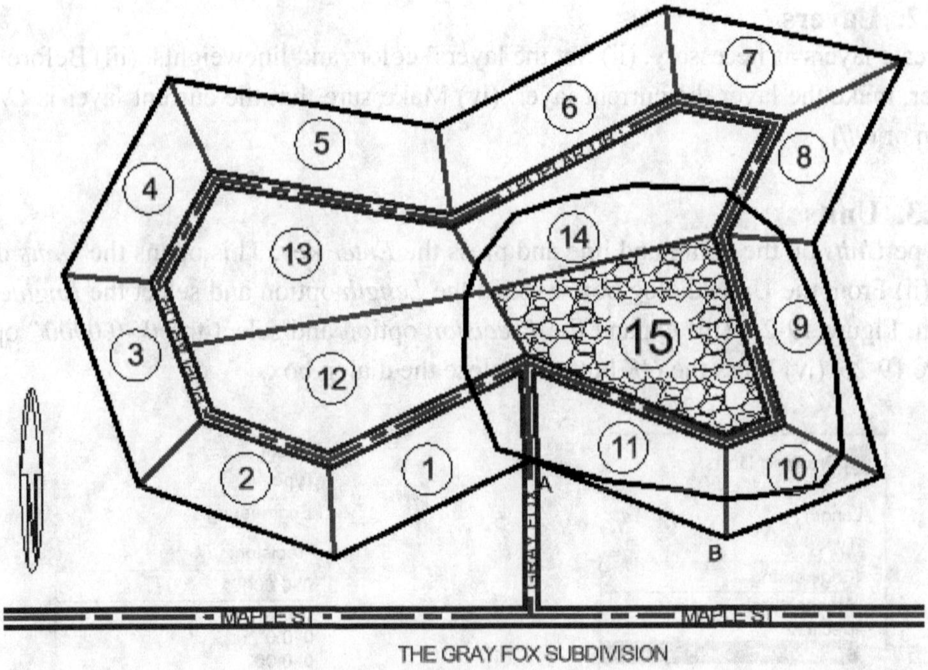

Figure 19-1b

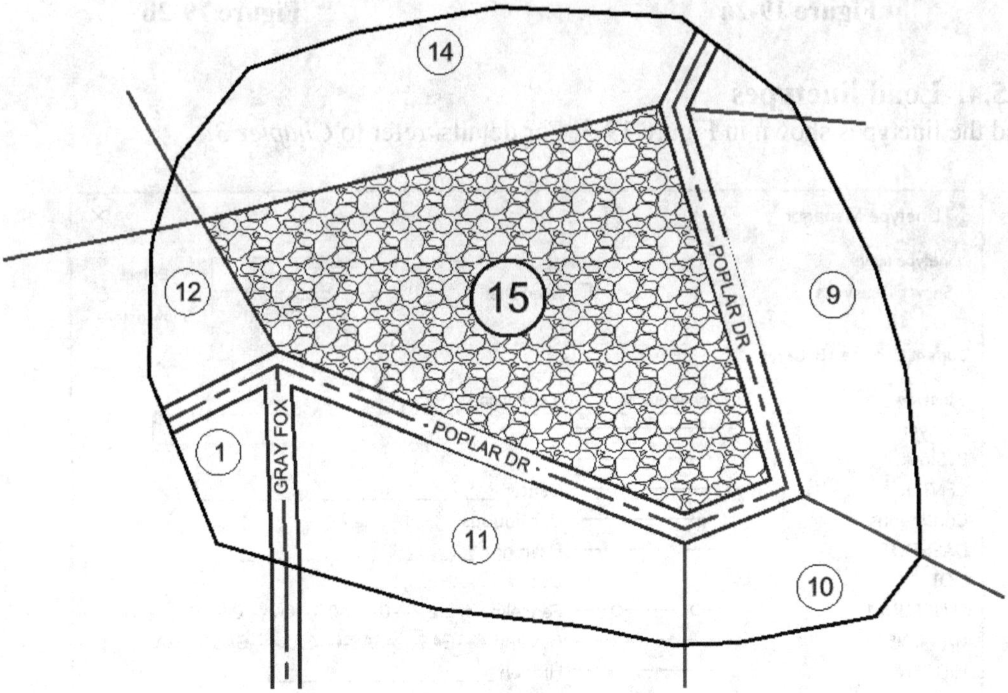

Figure 19-1c

19.5.2. Layers

(i) Create layers as necessary. (ii) Set the layers' colors and lineweights. (iii) Before using a layer, make the layer the current layer. (iv) Make sure that the current layer is *On* (not frozen or *Off*).

19.5.3. Units

(i) Type *Units* on the command line and press the *Enter* key. This opens the *Units* dialog box. (ii) From the Units dialog box, expand the *Length* option and select the *Engineering* option, Figure 19-2a; (iii) expand the *Precision* option and select the *0'-0.0000"* option, Figure 19-2b. (iv) Press the *OK* button to close the dialog box.

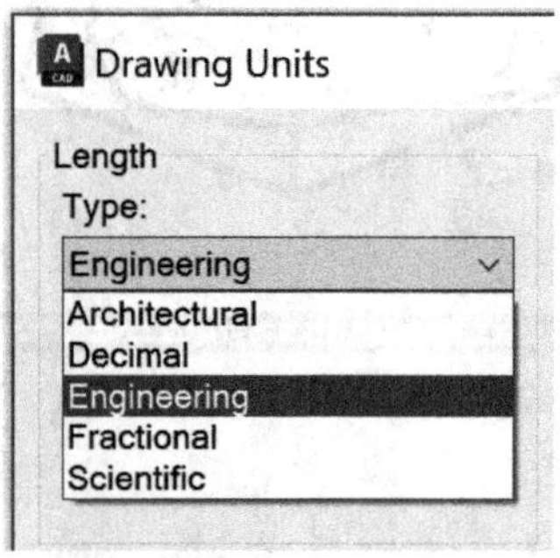

Figure 19-2a

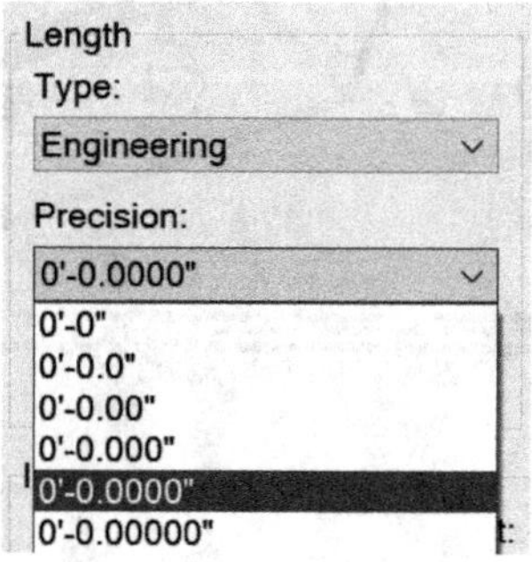

Figure 19-2b

19.5.4. Load linetypes

Load the linetypes shown in Figure 19-3. For details, refer to *Chapter 3*.

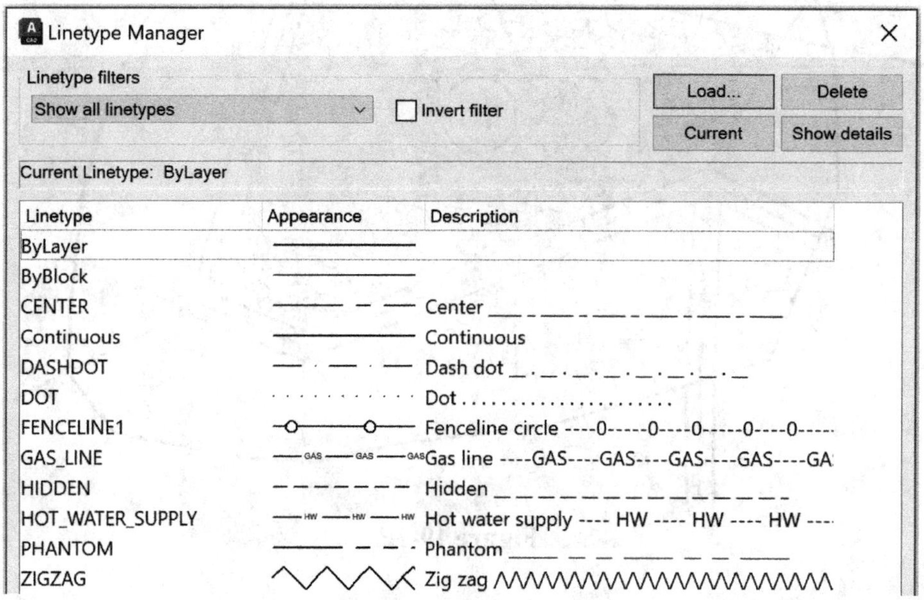

Figure 19-3

19.5.5. Property line

- Create the property line as follows.
  1. Create a layer named *Property_Line*. Set its Linetype to Phantom, Lineweight to 0.7, and change its color.
  2. Make the *Property_Line* layer to be the current layer.
  3. Draw the property's boundary as a closed traverse or trace over Lot 10 of the Lots and Blocks drawing. Make sure that the linetype is clearly visible; if necessary, set the linetype scale, Figure 19-4.

- Add the dimension to the property line as follows.
  1. Create a layer named *Property_Line_Dim*. Set its Linetype to Continuous, Lineweight to *0.0*, and change its color.
  2. Make the *Property_Line_Dim* layer to be the current layer.
  3. Show the dimensions following a closed traverse dimensioning technique, Figure 19-4. The angles are represented as azimuths. The dimension and extension lines are turned *Off* for the length of each course.

- Create the property label as follows.
  1. Create a layer named *Property_ Label*. Set its Linetype to Continuous, Lineweight to 0.0, and change its color.
  2. Make the *Property_Label* layer to be the current layer.
  3. Show the label using the annotative *Text* and *Rotation* commands and arrow using the *qleader* command, Figure 19-4.

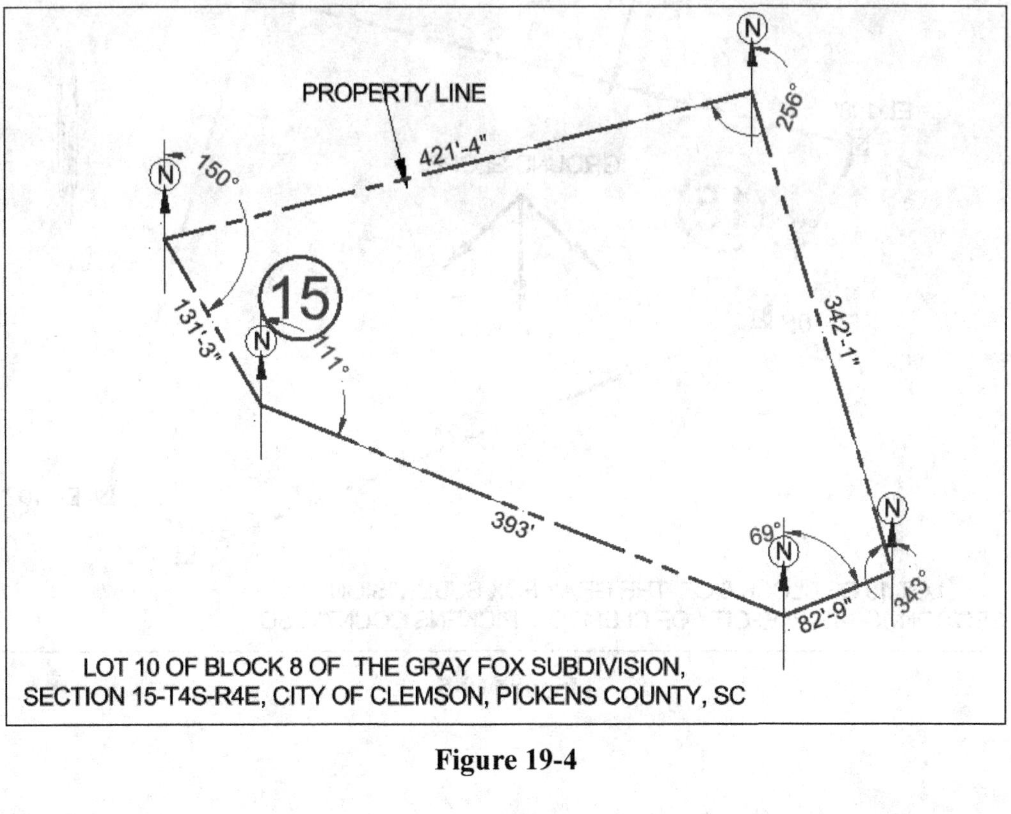

Figure 19-4

19.5.6. North

- The step-by-step process for inserting the north sign is listed here.
  1. Create a layer for the North sign and name it as *North*. Set its Linetype to Continuous, Lineweight to 0.0, and change its color.
  2. Make the *North* layer the current layer.
  3. Insert the *North Arrow* block from the *Design Center* → *Landscaping.dwg* of AutoCAD 2027. The design center is discussed in detail in *Chapter 7*.
  4. Scale the block as: X-scale = 6 and Y-scale = 60, Figure 19-5.

19.5.7. Ground slope

- Create the ground slope as follows.
  1. Create a layer named *Slope*. Set its Linetype to Continuous, Lineweight to 0.5, and change its color.
  2. Make the *Slope* layer to be the current layer.
  3. Draw points using the *Point* command, Figure 19-5. In this example, points are drawn where the property line changes its direction. Change the point style and size using the *Point Style* dialog box from the *Home* tab and the *Utilities* panel.
  4. Using the *Text* command, label the elevation as shown in Figure 19-5.
  5. Using the *Text* and *qleader* commands show the direction of slope. (Activate *qleader* command three times to draw three arrows or use *Add Leader* command.)

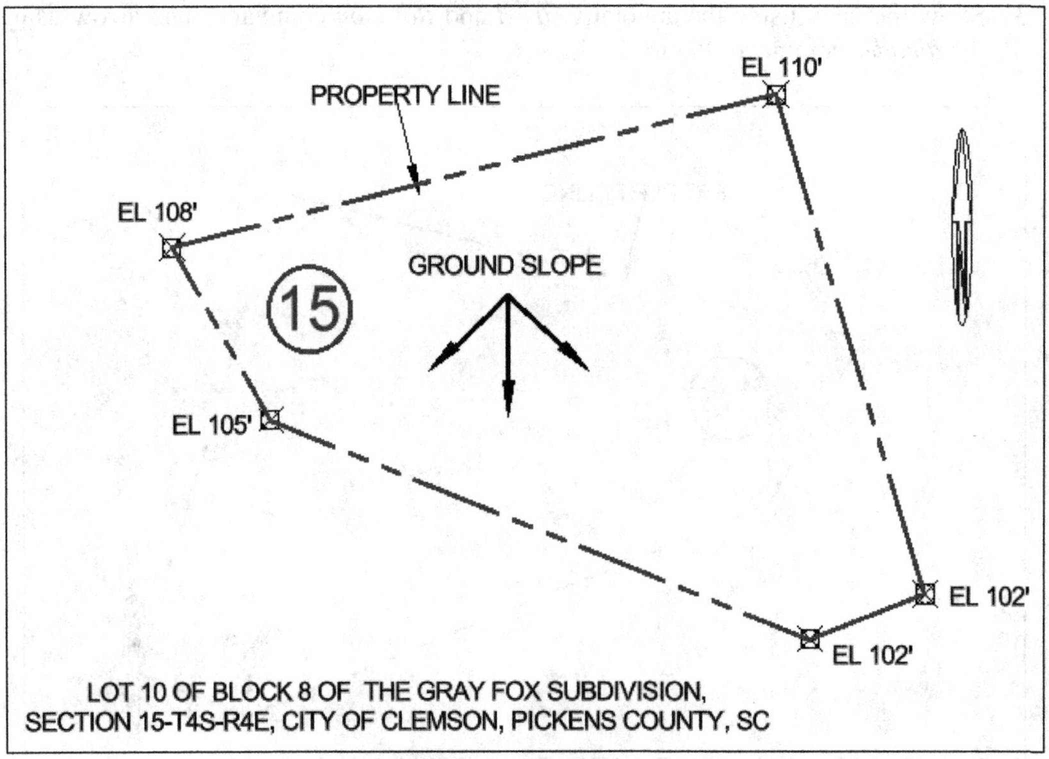

Figure 19-5

19.5.8. Setbacks

- Create the setbacks as follows.
  1. Create a layer named *Setback*. Set its Linetype to Dashdot, Lineweight to 0.5, and change its color.
  2. Make the *Setback* layer to be the current layer.
  3. Draw the setbacks from the property lines as shown in Figure 19-6. In this example, the front setback is 20', the rear, and the side setbacks are 14'. (i) Create two offsets (offset distance 20' and 14') of the property line. (ii) Move the offsets to the *Setback* layer. (iii) Use *Trim* and extend commands to create the setbacks. Make sure the linetype is clearly visible; if necessary, change the linetype scale. (iv) Use the *Join* command to join the parts of the setbacks.

- Add the setbacks' dimension as follows.
  1. Create a layer named *Setback_Dim*. Set its Linetype to Continuous, Lineweight to 0.0, and change its color.
  2. Make the *Setback_Dim* layer to be the current layer.
  3. Show the dimensions, Figure 19-6.

- Create the setbacks' label as follows.
  1. Create a layer named *Setback_Label*. Set its Linetype to Continuous, Lineweight to 0.0, and change its color.
  2. Make the *Setback_Label* layer the current layer.
  3. Add the label using the *Text* and *Rotation* commands, Figure 19-6.

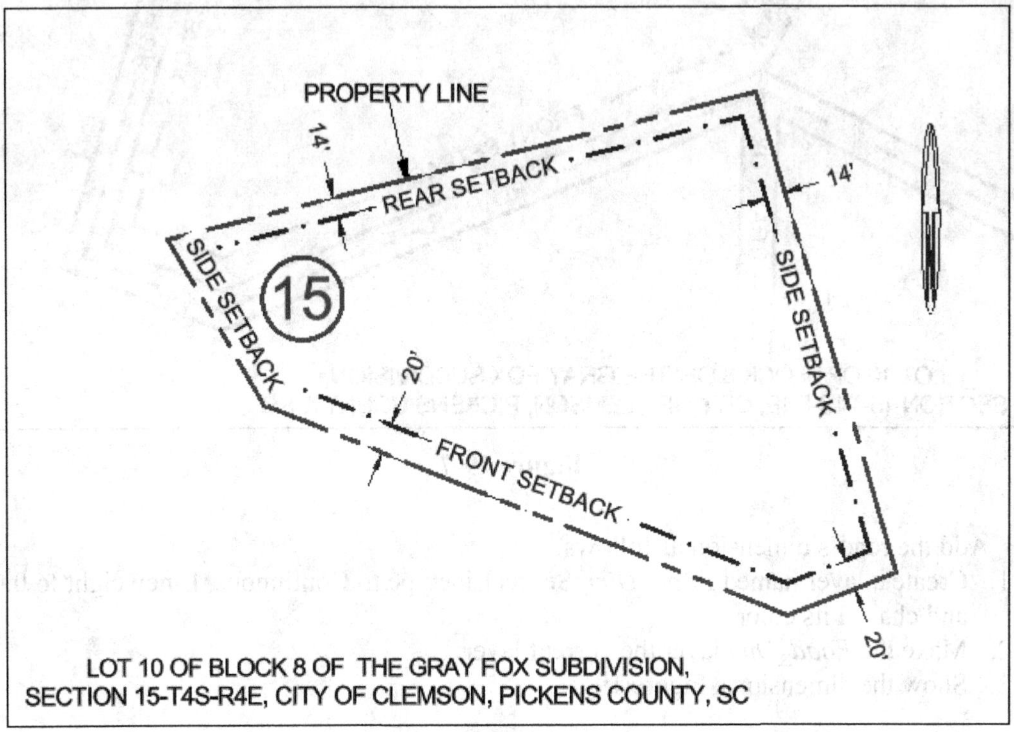

Figure 19-6

19.5.9. Road

- Create the roads as follows.
  1. Create a layer named *Road.* Set its Linetype to Continuous, Lineweight to 0.5, and change its color.
  2. Make the *Road* layer to be the current layer.
  3. Draw the roads. The width of the road is shown in Figure 19-7 or trace over the road drawn in the lots and blocks drawing.

- Create the road's centerline as follows.
  1. Create a layer named *Road_CL.* Set its Linetype to Center, Lineweight to 0.5, and change its color.
  2. Make the *Road_CL* layer to be the current layer.
  3. Add the centerline. Make sure the linetype is clearly visible, Figure 19-7.

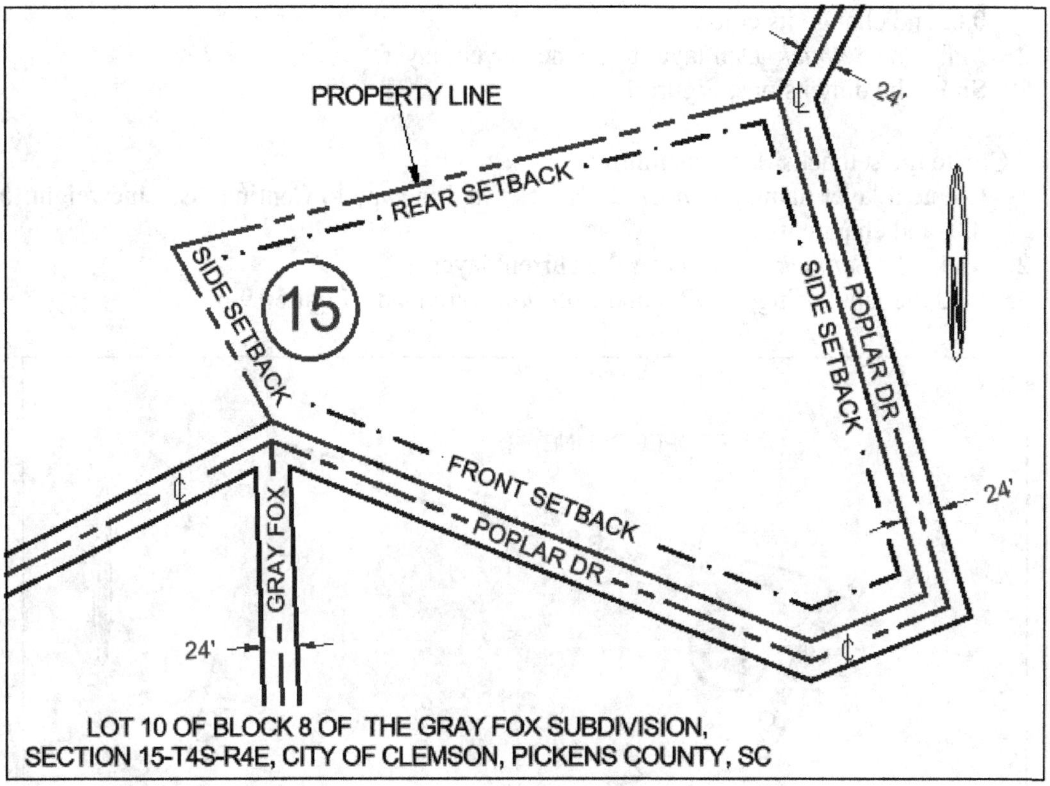

Figure 19-7

- Add the road's dimension as follows.
  1. Create a layer named *Road_Dim.* Set its Linetype to Continuous, Lineweight to 0.0, and change its color.
  2. Make the *Road_Dim* layer the current layer.
  3. Show the dimensions, Figure 19-7.

- Create the roads' labels as follows.
  1. Create a layer named *Road_Label*. Set its Linetype to Continuous, Lineweight to 0.0, and change its color.
  2. Make the *Road_Label* layer to be the current layer.
  3. Add the names of the roads using the *Text* command, Figure 19-7. Remember to use the *Mask Background* option (for further details, check *Chapter 3*).
  4. Add the centerline symbol (Figure 19-7) using the *Text* command as follows: (i) Activate the *Text* command. (ii) Change the font to "gdt." (iii) Type "q". (iv) Set the font size.

19.5.10. Adjacent properties

- Create the adjacent properties as follows.
  1. Create a layer named *AP*. Set its Linetype to Zigzag, Lineweight to 0.5, and change its color.
  2. Make the *AP* layer the current layer.
  3. Draw the adjacent properties or trace over the lots and blocks drawing. Make sure the linetype is clearly visible, Figure 19-8.

- Create the adjacent properties' labels as follows.
  1. Create a layer named *AP_Label*. Set its Linetype to Continuous, Lineweight to 0.0, and change its color.
  2. Make the *AP_Label* layer the current layer.
  3. Add the names of the adjacent properties using the *Text* and *Circle* commands or transfer to the current layer from the lots and blocks drawing, Figure 19-8.

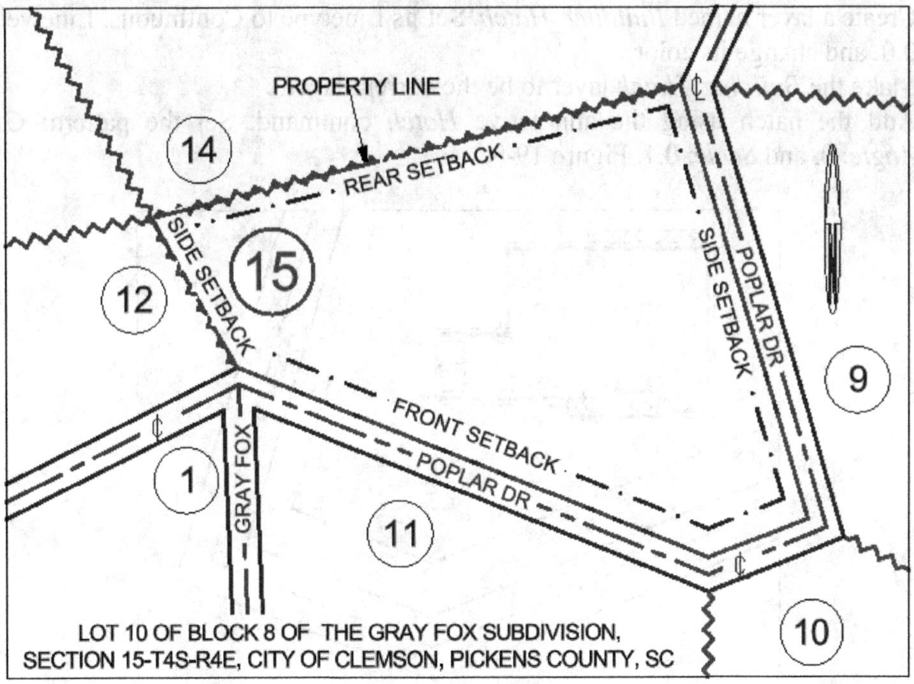

Figure 19-8

19.5.11. Building

- Create the structure as follows.
  1. Create a layer named Building. Set its Linetype to Continuous, Lineweight to 0.0, and change its color.
  2. Make the *Building* layer to be the current layer.
  3. Draw the location and size of all the structures. Copy the exterior face of the exterior wall and the roofline of the residential building created in *Chapter 17* and paste it in the current file. Note that the roof line is drawn inside the setbacks, Figure 19-9.
  4. Garage and front door, and front and back porches are shown in Figure 19-9. This part of the building is used to place the driveway and walkways.

- Add the dimensions as follows.
  1. Create a layer named *Building_Dim*. Set its Linetype to Continuous, Lineweight to 0.0, and change its color.
  2. Make the *Building_Dim* layer to be the current layer.
  3. Add the dimensions of the building's location, Figure 19-9.

- Create the structure's label as follows.
  1. Create a layer named *Building_Label*. Set its Linetype to Continuous, Lineweight to 0.0, and change its color.
  2. Make the *Building_Label* layer to be the current layer.
  3. Add the label using the *Text* command. The label is PROPOSED BUILDING, 3 BEDROOMS HOME, EL MAIN FLOOR 107', Figure 19-9.

- Create the building's hatch as follows.
  1. Create a layer named *Building_Hatch*. Set its Linetype to Continuous, Lineweight to 0.0, and change its color.
  2. Make the *Building_Hatch* layer to be the current layer.
  3. Add the hatch using the annotative *Hatch* command. Set the pattern: *GRASS*, *Angle*: 0, and *Scale*: 0.1, Figure 19-9.

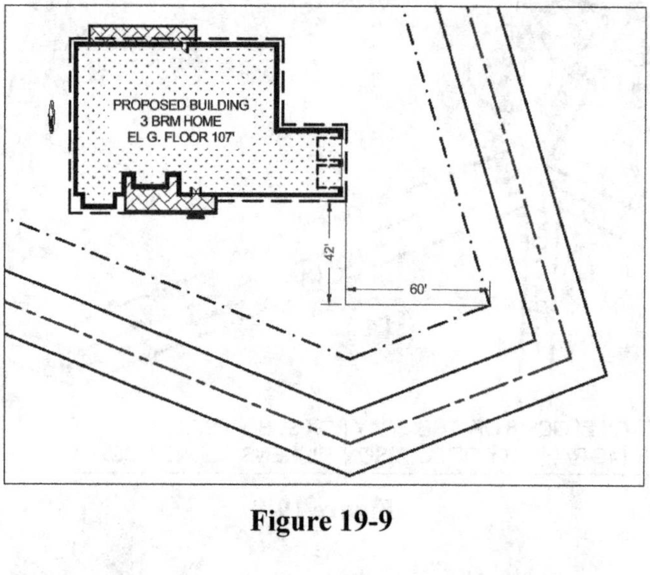

Figure 19-9

19.5.12. Driveway

- The step-by-step process for creating the driveway is listed here.
  1. Create a layer named *Driveway*. Set its Linetype to Continuous, Lineweight to 0.0, and change its color.
  2. Make the *Driveway* layer to be the current layer.
  3. Draw the driveway as follows, Figure 19-10.
     - Draw the centerline. (i) Change the linetype to Center. (ii) Draw a horizontal line originating at the midpoint of the wall between the two garage doors and terminating at the property line.
     - Use the *Offset* command to create the sides of the driveway with the offset distance of 12' on either side of the centerline.
     - Change the linetype of the offsets to *By Layer* option.

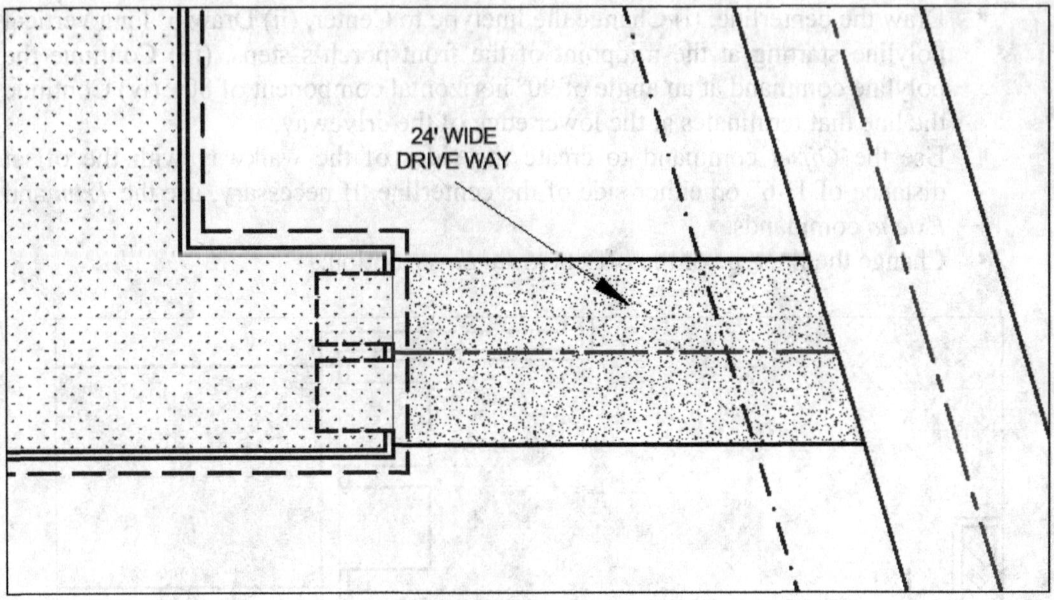

Figure 19-10

- Create the driveway's label as follows.
  1. Create a layer named *Driveway_Label. Set its Linetype to Continuous, Lineweight to 0.0, and change its color.*
  2. Make the *Driveway_Label* layer to be the current layer.
  3. Add the label, Figure 19-10, using the *Text* command and arrow using *qleader* command.

- Create the driveway's dimensions as follows.
  1. Create a layer named *Driveway_Dim*. Set its Linetype to Continuous, Lineweight to *0.0*, and change its color.
  2. Make the *Driveway_Dim* layer to be the current layer.
  3. Add the dimensions.

- Create the driveway's hatch as follows.
  1. Create a layer named *Driveway_Hatch*. Set its Linetype to Continuous, Lineweight to 0.0, and change its color.
  2. Make the *Driveway_Hatch* layer to be the current layer.
  3. Add the associative and annotative hatch using the *Hatch* command, Figure 19-10. Set the pattern: *AR-CONC*, *Angle*: 0, and *Scale*: 0.0125.

19.5.13. Walkway

- The step-by-step process for creating the walkway is listed here, Figure 19-11.
  1. Create a layer and name it *Walkway*. Set its Linetype to Continuous, Lineweight to 0.0, and change its color.
  2. Make the *Walkway* layer to be the current layer.
  3. Draw the walkway as follows.
     - Draw the centerline. (i) Change the linetype to Center. (ii) Draw 6' long vertical polyline starting at the midpoint of the front porch's steps. (iii) Continue the polyline command at an angle of 90° horizontal component of 80'. (iv) Continue the line that terminates at the lower edge of the driveway.
     - Use the *Offset* command to create the sides of the walkway with the offset distance of 1'-6" on either side of the centerline. If necessary, use the *Trim* and *Extend* commands.
     - Change the linetype of the offsets to *By Layer* option.

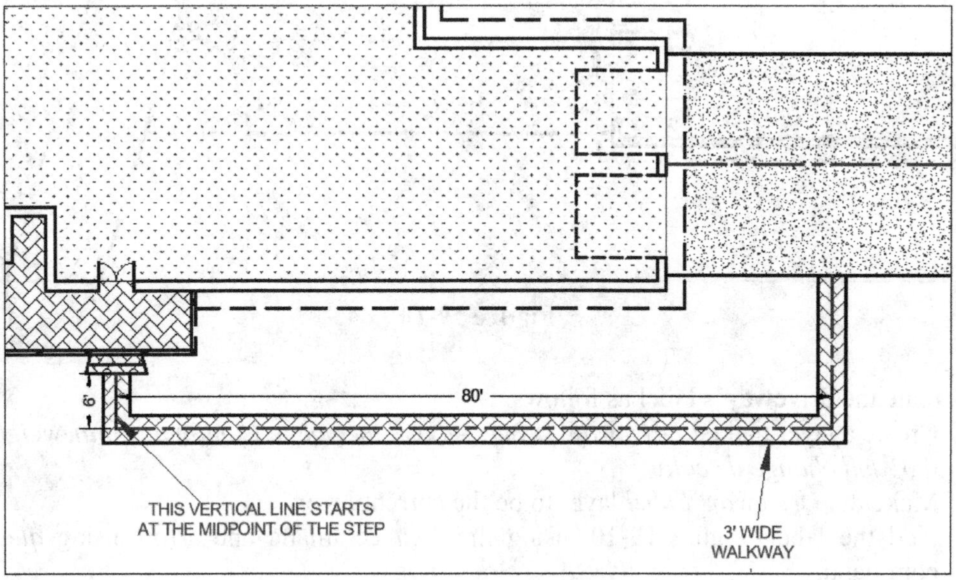

Figure 19-11

- Create the walkway's label as follows.
  1. Create a layer named *Walkway_Label*. Set its Linetype to Continuous, Lineweight to 0.0, and change its color.
  2. Make the *Walkway_Label* layer to be the current layer.
  3. Add the label, using the *Text* command and arrow using the *qleader* command.

- Create the walkway's hatch as follows.
  1. Create a layer named *Walkway_Hatch*. Set its Linetype to Continuous, Lineweight to 0.0, and change its color.
  2. Make the *Walkway_Hatch* layer to be the current layer.
  3. Add the hatch using the *Hatch* command. Set the pattern: *AR-HBON*, *Angle*: 0, and *Scale*: 0.025.

- Add the walkway's dimension as follows.
  1. Create a layer named *Walkway_Dim*. Set its Linetype to Continuous, Lineweight to 0.0, and change its color.
  2. Make the *Walkway_Dim* layer to be the current layer.
  3. Show the dimensions.

- Figure 19-11 shows the driveway and the walkway.

19.5.14. Swimming pool

- The step-by-step process for creating the swimming pool is listed here.
  1. Create a layer named *Swimming_pool*. Set its Linetype to Continuous, Lineweight to 0.5, and change its color.
  2. Make the *Swimming_pool* layer to be the current layer.
  3. Draw the swimming pool. The swimming pool dig is inside the setback. Its location is shown in Figure 19-12a. Draw the swimming pool as follows:
     - Draw the swimming pool boundary as shown in Figure 19-12b.
     - Using the *Fillet* command (radius option), create a fillet of the specified radius, Figure 19-12c.
     - For the finished pool, make an offset of 2' inside, Figure 19-12d.
     - Create circular steps at the upper left corner. The inner circles are created at an offset distance of 2', Figure 19-12d.

- Create the swimming pool's label as follows.
  1. Create a layer and name it *Swimming_pool_Label*. Set its Linetype to Continuous, Lineweight to 0.0, and change its color.
  2. Make the *Swimming_pool_Label* layer to be the current layer.
  3. Add the label, using the *Text* command and arrow using *qleader* command.

- Create the swimming pool's dimensions as follows.
  1. Create a layer named *Swimming_pool_Dim*. Set its *Linetype* to *Continuous*, *Lineweight* to *0.0*, and change its color.
  2. Make the *Swimming_pool_Dim* layer to be the current layer.
  3. Show the dimensions.

- Create the swimming pool's hatch as follows.
  1. Create a layer named *Swimming_pool_Hatch*. Set its Linetype to Continuous, Lineweight to 0.0, and change its color.
  2. Refer to Figure 19-13.
  3. Make the *Swimming_pool_Hatch* layer to be the current layer.

4. For the finished pool, add the associative and annotative hatch using the *Hatch* command. Set the pattern: *MUDST*, Angle: 54 degrees, and Scale: 0.15.
5. For the sides of the pool, add the hatch using the *Hatch* command. Set the pattern: *AR-CONC*, Angle: 0, and Scale: 0.01.

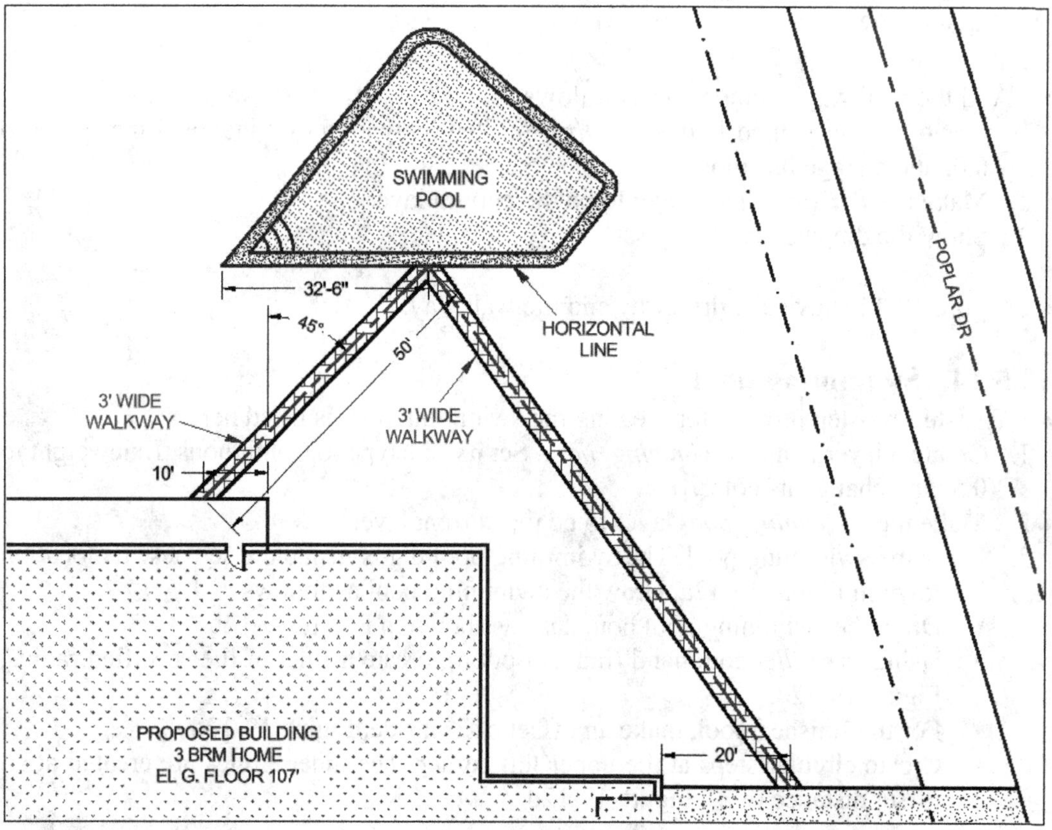

Figure 19-12a

- Create the swimming pool's walkway as follows.

1. Create a layer named *Swimming_pool_walkway*. Set its Linetype to Continuous, Lineweight to 0.5mm, and change its color.
2. Make the *Swimming_pool_walkway* layer to be the current layer.
3. Refer to Figure 19-12a.
4. Draw the walkway as follows.
   - Draw the centerline: (i) Change the linetype to Center. (ii) Draw a 50' long polyline at an angle of 45° originating at the distance of 10' from the right corner of the back patio, continue the line and terminate it at the swimming pool. (iii) Draw another polyline originating from the driveway at the distance of 20' from the garage door wall and terminating at the line from the previous step.
   - Use the *Offset* command to create the walkway with the offset distance of 1'-6" on either side of the centerline.
   - Change the linetype of the offsets to *By Layer* option.
   - If necessary, use trim and/or extend commands.

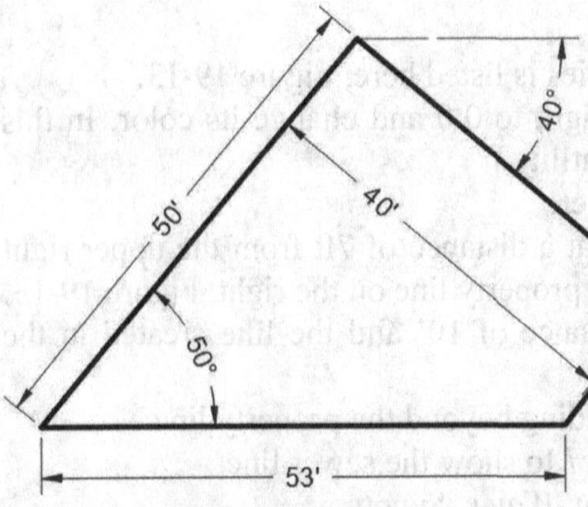

Figure 19-12b

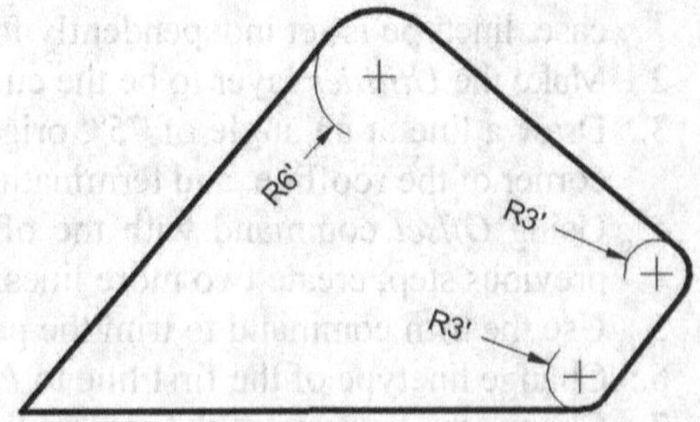

Figure 19-12c

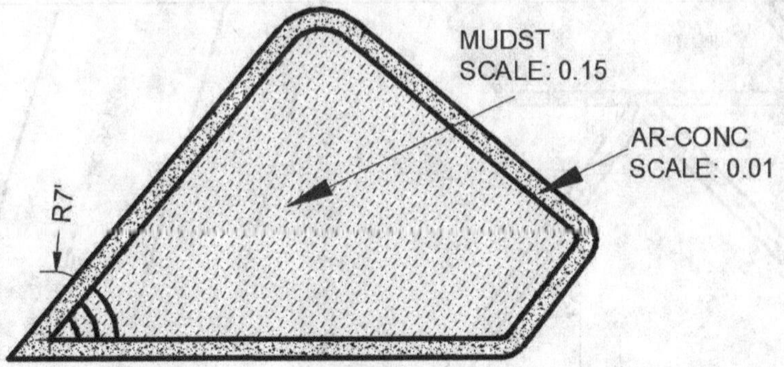

Figure 19-12d

- Create the swimming pool's walkway hatch as follows, Figure 19-12a.
  1. Create a layer named *Swimming_pool_walkway_Hatch*. Set its Linetype to Continuous, Lineweight to 0.0, and change its color.
  2. Make the *Swimming_pool_walkway_Hatch* layer to be the current layer.
  3. For the finished walkway, add the hatch using the associative and annotative *Hatch* command. Set the pattern: *AR-HBON*, *Angle*: 45, and *Scale*: 0.025.

- Add the swimming pool's walkway dimensions as follows, Figure 19-12a.
  1. Create a layer named *Swimming_pool_walkway_Dim*. Set its Linetype to Continuous, Lineweight to 0.0, and change its color.
  2. Make the *Swimming_pool_walkway_Dim* layer to be the current layer.
  3. Show the dimensions.

- Create the swimming pool's walkway label as follows, Figure 19-12a.
  1. Create a layer named d*Swimming_pool_walkway_Label*. Set its Linetype to Continuous, Lineweight to 0.0, and change its color.
  2. Make the *Swimming_pool_walkway_Label* layer to be the current layer.
  3. Add the label, using the *Text* command and the arrow using the *qleader* command.

19.5.15. Utilities

- The step-by-step process for creating the utilities is listed here, Figure 19-13.
  1. Create a layer named *Utilities*. Set Lineweight to 0.0 and change its color. In this case, linetype is set independently for each utility.
  2. Make the *Utilities* layer to be the current layer.
  3. Draw a line at an angle of 75°, originating at a distance of 7ft from the upper right corner of the roofline, and terminating at the property line on the right, Figure 19-13.
  4. Using *Offset* command with the offset distance of 10' and the line created in the previous step, create two more lines.
  5. Use the trim command to trim the part extending beyond the property line.
  6. Change linetype of the first line to *Fenceline1* to show the sewer line.
  7. Change the linetype of the second line to *Hot_Water_Supply*.
  8. Change linetype of the third line to *Gas_Line*.

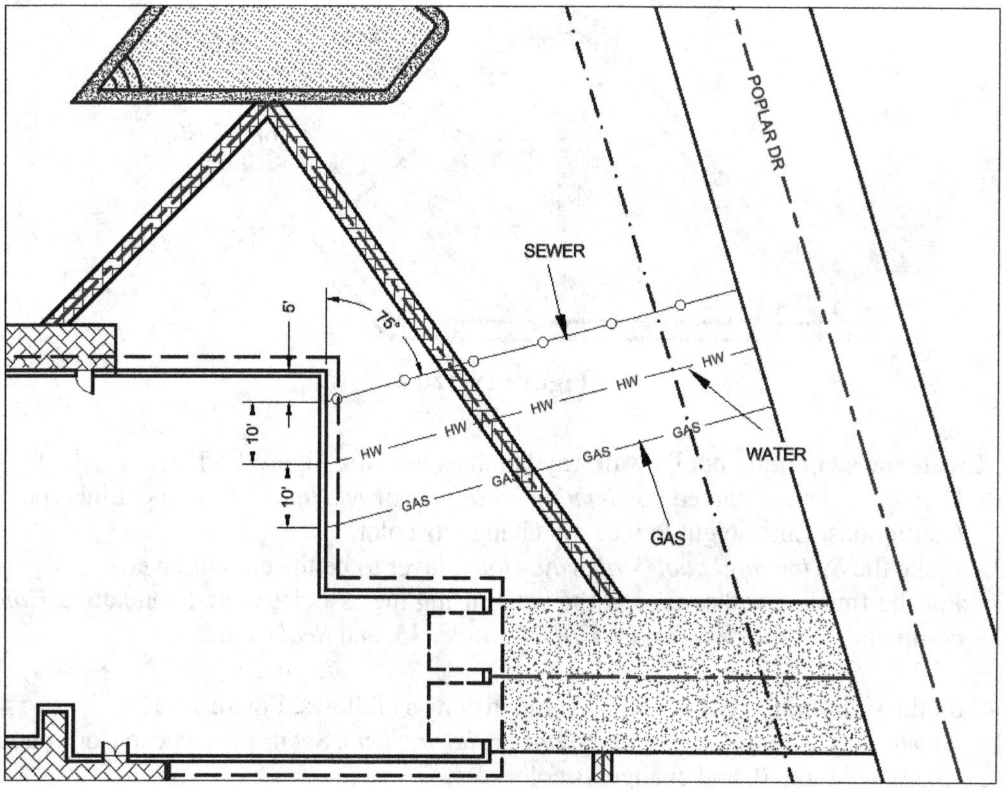

Figure 19-13

- Create the utilities labels as follows.
  1. Create a layer named *Utilities*. Set Lineweight to 0.0 and change its color. In this case, Linetype will be set independently for each utility.
  2. Create a layer named *Utilities_Label*. Set its Linetype to Continuous, Lineweight to 0.0, and change its color.
  3. Make the *Utilities_Label* layer to be the current layer.
  4. Add the labels using the *Text* command and arrows using the *qleader* command.

- Add the utilities dimensions as follows.
  1. Create a layer named *Utilities_Dim*. Set its *Linetype* to *Continuous*, Lineweight to 0.0, and change its color.
  2. Make the *Utilities_Dim* layer the current layer.
  3. Show the dimensions.

19.5.16. Template file

- The step-by-step process for inserting an appropriate layout from one of the template files is listed here, Figure 19-14.
  1. Insert an appropriate layout from one of the template files, Figure 19-14.
  2. Set the scale of the drawing to 1/72" = 1'-0", Figure 19-14.
  3. Update the blocks, Figure 19-14.
  4. The complete site plan is shown in Figure 19-14.

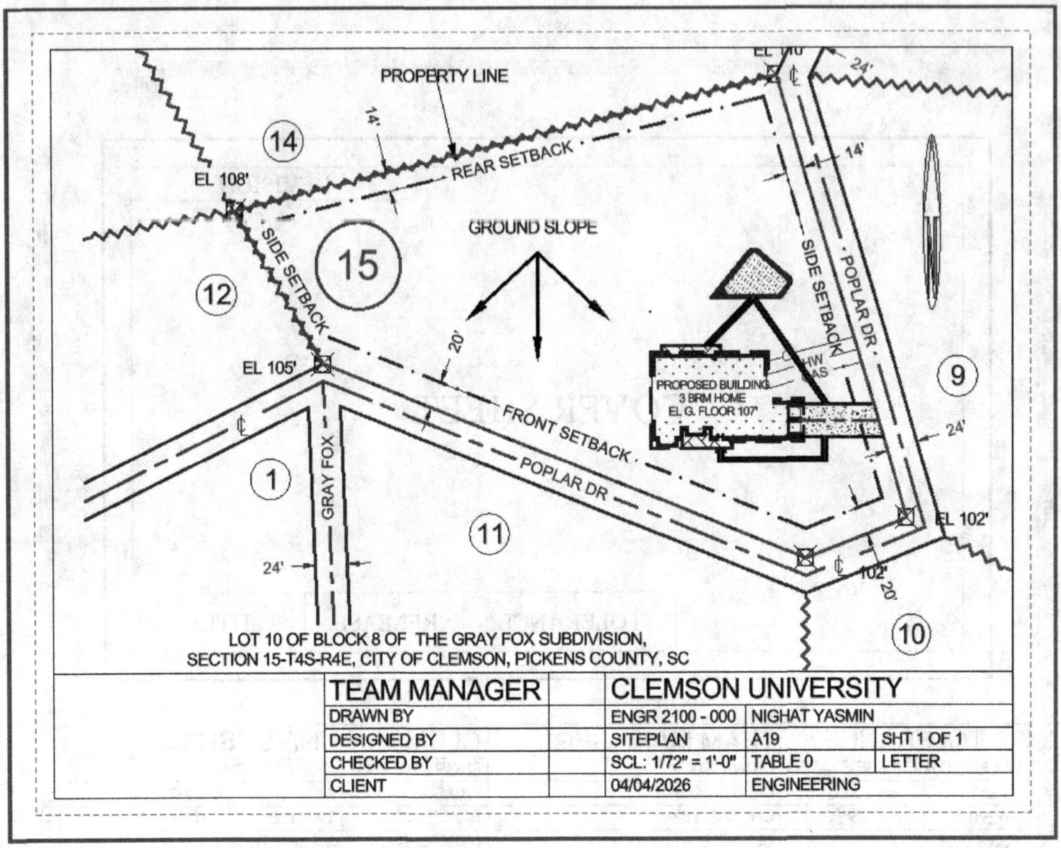

Figure 19-14

Notes:

20. Construction Drawings

20.1. Learning Objectives

After completing this chapter, the students will show proficiency in the following areas:

- Family of drawings

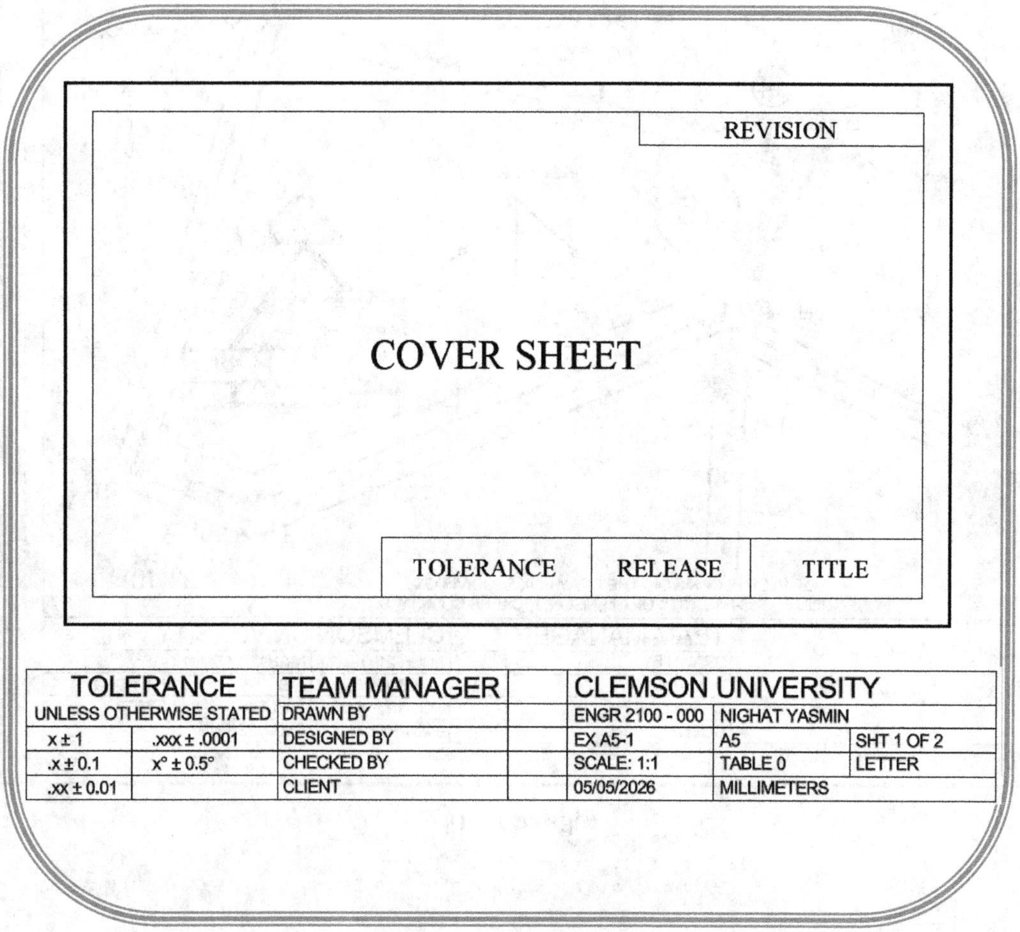

20.2. Introduction

Construction drawings are the collection of several drawings that are used to complete a project. The development of a working drawing is the last step of the design process. The next step is the construction of the project!

Generally, the arrangement and number of the drawings depend on the client's requirement, company, and project type and size. Some of the commonly used drawings are shown in Figure 20-2. For most of the projects at least one of these sheets is created, and for larger projects, there can be more than one of the same types of drawings. For example, for a single-story building, there can be only one floor plan. On the other hand, for a multilevel building there can be as many floor plans as the number of levels. For both of the single and multilevel buildings there can be four exterior elevation drawings (north-, south-, east-, and west-side elevations).

This chapter uses layouts to create different types of the drawing. Hence, to navigate the layouts efficiently, the layouts should be named properly. For example, F_Elev (front elevation), first floor plan (FF_Plan), profile and plane (PnP), etc.

To start a family of drawings based on the dimension of the drawing, open *My_acad_Landscape* or *My_acadiso_Landscape* template file (the templates are created in *Chapter 8*). To create a new layout, click on the *Insert* pull down menu → *Layout* → *Layouts from Template* and follow the prompt. For further details refer to *Chapter 8*.

20.3. Drawing Format

The drawing format varies from company to company, and draftsmen can create their own style. AutoCAD includes many formats known as template files, and the various template files are based on different formats.

20.4. Blocks Used

The members of the family of drawings must have a title block. The drawing may also have release, tolerance, and revision blocks. The title block is located in the lower right corner of the drawing. The release block is placed on the left edge of the title block and the tolerance block is placed on the left edge of the release block, Figure 20-1a.

The title block contains general information about the company and the drawing. A release block contains a list of approval signatures or initials required before the drawing is released for the production. The contents of these blocks may vary from company to company. A typical title and release blocks are shown in Figure 20-1b and Figure 20-1c, respectively. For further details on these blocks, refer to *Chapter 7*.

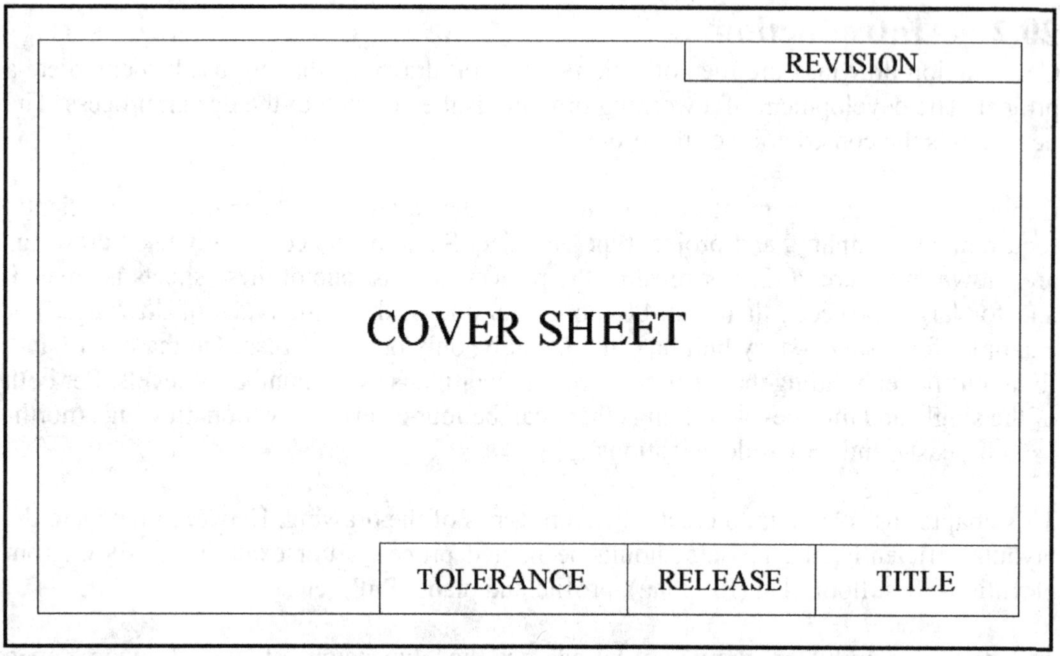

Figure 20-1a

CLEMSON UNIVERSITY		
ENGR 2100 - 000	NIGHAT YASMIN	
EX A5-1	A5	SHT 1 OF 2
SCALE: 1:1	TABLE 0	LETTER
03/03/2026	MILLIMETERS	

Figure 20-1b

TEAM MANAGER	
DRAWN BY	
DESIGNED BY	
CHECKED BY	
CLIENT	

Figure 20-1c

The tolerance block is used to list the standard tolerances. The block is created using line and text commands. In AutoCAD, the plus-minus symbol is created by typing %%p in a text object. The contents of this block may vary from company to company. The tolerance block is placed on the left edge of the release block. A typical tolerance block is shown in Figure 20-1d. The tolerance of "*X plus-minus 1*" implies that if the basic or theoretical dimension of an object is 15 then 16 and 14 are acceptable, too. For further details of blocks in general, refer to *Chapter 7*.

A revision block is used to show the name of the modification made to the drawing, initial or signature of the person responsible for the revision, and the date of the revision. The block is created using line and text commands. The contents of this block may vary from company to company. A revision block is generally located in the upper right corner of the drawing. A typical revision block is shown in Figure 20-1e. For further details of blocks in general, refer to *Chapter 7*.

TOLERANCE	
UNLESS OTHERWISE STATED	
x ± 1	.xxx ± .0001
.x ± 0.1	x° ± 0.5°
.xx ± 0.01	

Figure 20-1d

REVISION	DATE	INITIAL

Figure 20-1e

20.5. Family Of Construction Drawing

This section briefly describes the drawings shown in Figure 20-2.

20.5.1. Cover sheet

As the name suggests, the cover sheet is the title page for the set of drawings. It is always the first sheet. A cover sheet includes the project's title, number, location map, name of the owner, names and signature and stamps of the designers, index of sheets, legend, survey data, perspective drawing, etc.

20.5.2. General information

The general information sheets are also known as G sheets. These sheets include the site data, location map, abbreviations, index to the other drawings, and building code data. In some projects, the cover and general information sheets are merged into one cover sheet.

20.5.3. Quantity sheet

The quantity sheet represents the estimate of the quantities (sod, concrete, lumber, paint, glass, etc.) and the cost of the activities (clearing, digging, hauling, etc.). That is, it represents the estimated cost of the projects. It includes the cost of everything used in the project, ranging from the cost of buying a paper clip to renting heavy machinery.

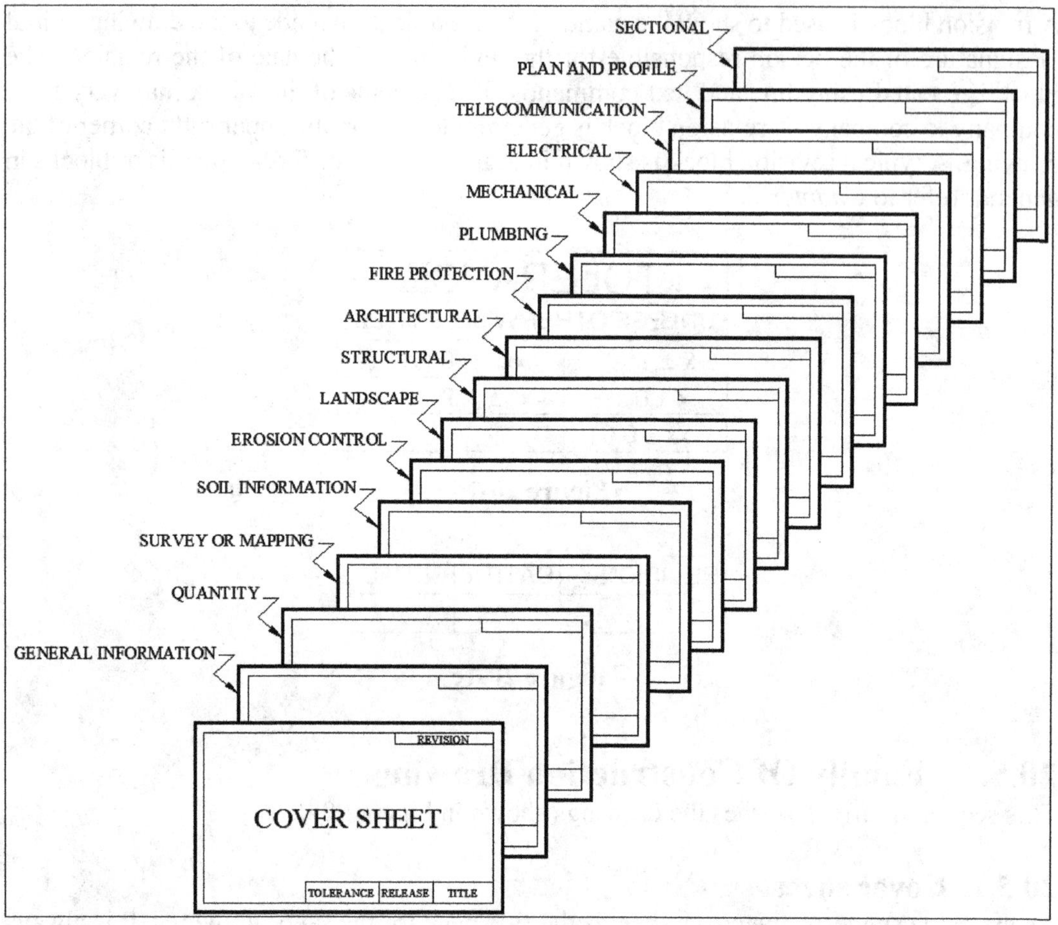

Figure 20-2

20.5.4. Survey or mapping

The survey or mapping sheets are also known as V sheets. The cover and/or general information sheets include brief data. On the other hand, survey sheets represent detailed information. These sheets are used to represent real estate information and vicinity information. These sheets are developed by professionals; however, the data is provided by the owner. The cost of the survey may or may not be included in the estimated cost of the project.

20.5.5. Soil information

The soil information sheets are also known as G sheets. These sheets are used to provide the geotechnical characteristics of the land used for the construction.

20.5.6. Erosion control

The erosion control sheets provide information on the methods and techniques used in the erosion control of the project site. For example, the first step in the construction process is the clearing of the site (cutting the trees and removal of the topsoil). This process will lead to erosion and environmental effects (the eroded material will end up in the stream, lakes, and rivers). Hence, this sheet should be present in every project.

20.5.7. Landscape drawings

The landscape drawings sheets are also known as L sheets. These sheets are used to provide landscaping information such as the plant plan, types of plants, irrigation system, fences, benches, walkways, etc.

20.5.8. Structural drawings

The structural drawings sheets are also known as S sheets. In heavy construction, anything composed of parts is called a structure. These sheets provide information for designing, fabricating, manufacturing, and erecting the structural elements.

20.5.9. Fire protection drawings

The fire protection drawing sheets are also known as F sheets. These sheets are used to provide fire code, access to site, on-site street width and curvature, location of hydrants, power supply, or any other information that will make the fire fighters' jobs effective.

20.5.10. Architectural drawings

The commonly used architectural drawings are floor plans, site plan, elevations, and sectional views.

- *Plan views*: A plan view is a horizontal orthographic view looking from the top. A site plan is the top view of the proposed or existing building situated in the building site. A floor plan is the top view of a building.
- *Elevation views*: An elevation is a vertical orthographic view looking from the side. For example, they include the front, rear, left, and right-side elevations for a building.
- *Sectional views*: Sectional views represent the internal details of the project. As a rule of thumb, the sectional views should be drawn at the same scale as the plan and elevations. In a building, generally the sectional views of the foundations, beams, columns, joints, doors and window jams, etc. are used to display the internal detail.

20.5.11. Plumbing drawings

The plumbing drawings sheets are also known as P sheets. These sheets are used to provide drain waste, hot and cold water supply, and fixtures information for the site as well as for the proposed structure.

20.5.12. Mechanical drawings

The mechanical drawings sheets are also known as M sheets. These sheets are used to provide information regarding the location, size, and type of the units used for distributing, filtering, humidifying/dehumidifying, and cooling and heating air.

20.5.13. Electrical drawings

The electrical drawings sheets are also known as E sheets. These sheets are used to provide information regarding the electrical services (wiring, metering, main switch), distribution (panel boards and switches), branch work (circuitry), and devices used during the construction of the proposed project.

20.5.14. Telecommunication drawings

The telecommunication drawing sheets are also known as T sheets. These sheets are used to provide information regarding how to use computer technology on the site.

20.5.15. Plan and profile drawings

The plan and profiles drawing sheets are also known as PnP sheets. These sheets are used for the water and sewer pipelines, storm drainage system, curbs, sidewalk, and road construction.

- *Plan*: A plan view is a horizontal orthographic view looking from the top.
- *Profile*: A profile is a vertical orthographic view looking from the side.

Notes:

21. Plotting from AutoCAD 2027

21.1. Learning Objectives

After completing this chapter, the students will show proficiency in the following areas:

- Plot/Print the drawing from Model space
- Plot/Print a scaled drawing from layouts
- Email a drawing file as an attachment
- Export a drawing file as a PDF file
- Convert a drawing file to a PDF file

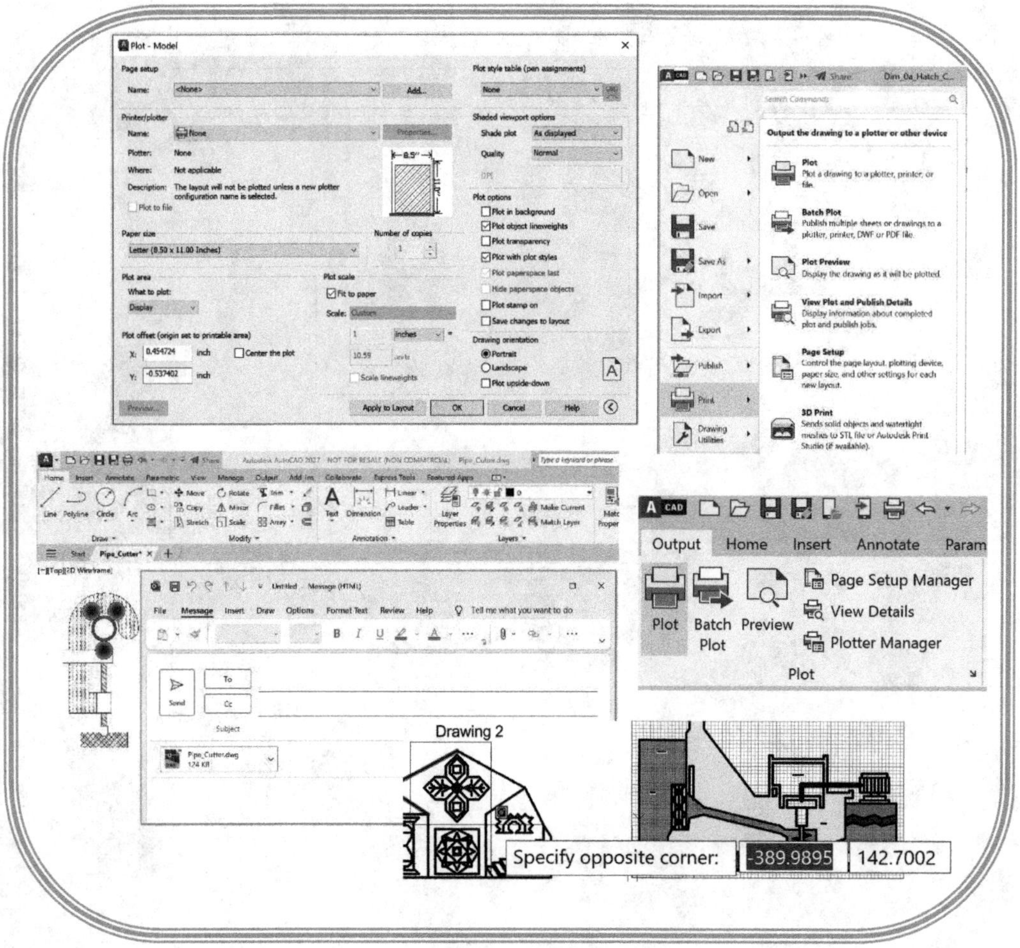

21.2. Introduction

Printing a drawing's hard copy or electronic medium is an important part of AutoCAD users. The focus of this chapter is plotting hard copies, launching email with a drawing file as an attachment, and creating portable document format (pdf) files. The plotting commands can be activated from the Model space and the paperspace (layouts).

21.3. Plotting Problems

Before discussing the plotting techniques, this section discusses the layer issues evident in plotting. The most commonly occurring problem is that *the objects are visible in the Model space or layout, Figure 21-1a; however, some of the objects are missing in the plot preview, Figure 21-1b*. Generally, there are two reasons for this situation: either the layer's plot option is *turned off* or the objects in question are drawn on the *defpoints* layer.

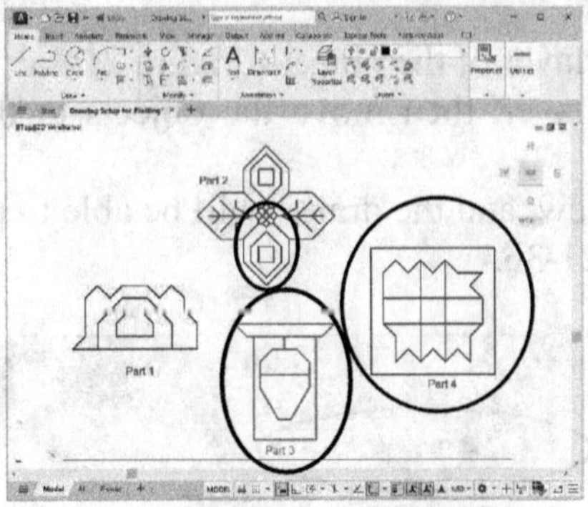

Figure 21-1a

Figure 21-1b

21.3.1. Plot option turned off

The *plot option turned off* problem can be solved as follows:

1. Open the *Layer Properties Manager* palette, Figure 21-2a.
2. If the layer's (containing the objects in question) plot option is *turned off*, that is, the layer's printer icon shows the no entry sign ( ) then click on the printer icon. The no entry sign will disappear ( ).
3. The objects will be visible in the print preview, and the drafter will be able to plot the objects on the layer in question, Figure 21-2b.

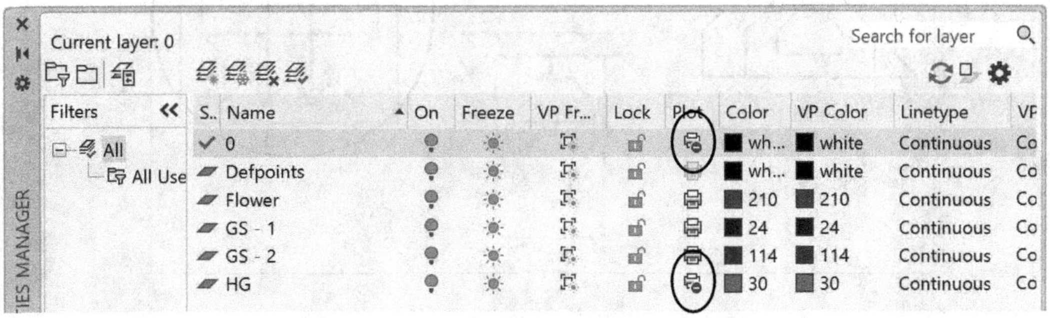

Figure 21-2a

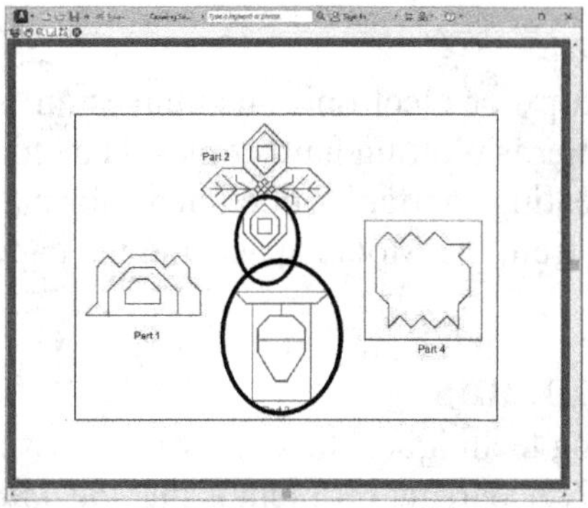

Figure 21-2b

21.3.2. Defpoint layer

The *Defpoint layer* problem can be solved as follows:

1. Select the objects in question and check the layer of the objects, Figure 21-3a.
2. If the objects are drawn on the *defpoints* layer, then move the objects to their respective layers.
3. The objects will be visible in the print preview, and the drafter will be able to plot the objects on the layer in question, Figure 21-3b.

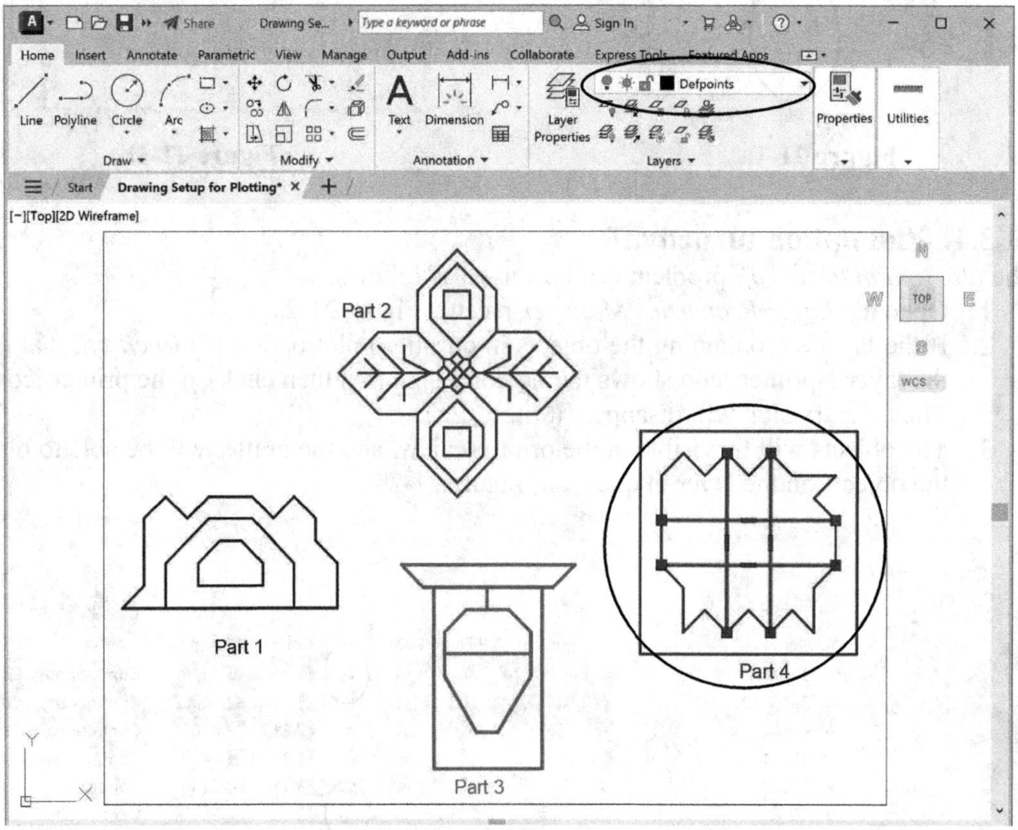

Figure 21-3a

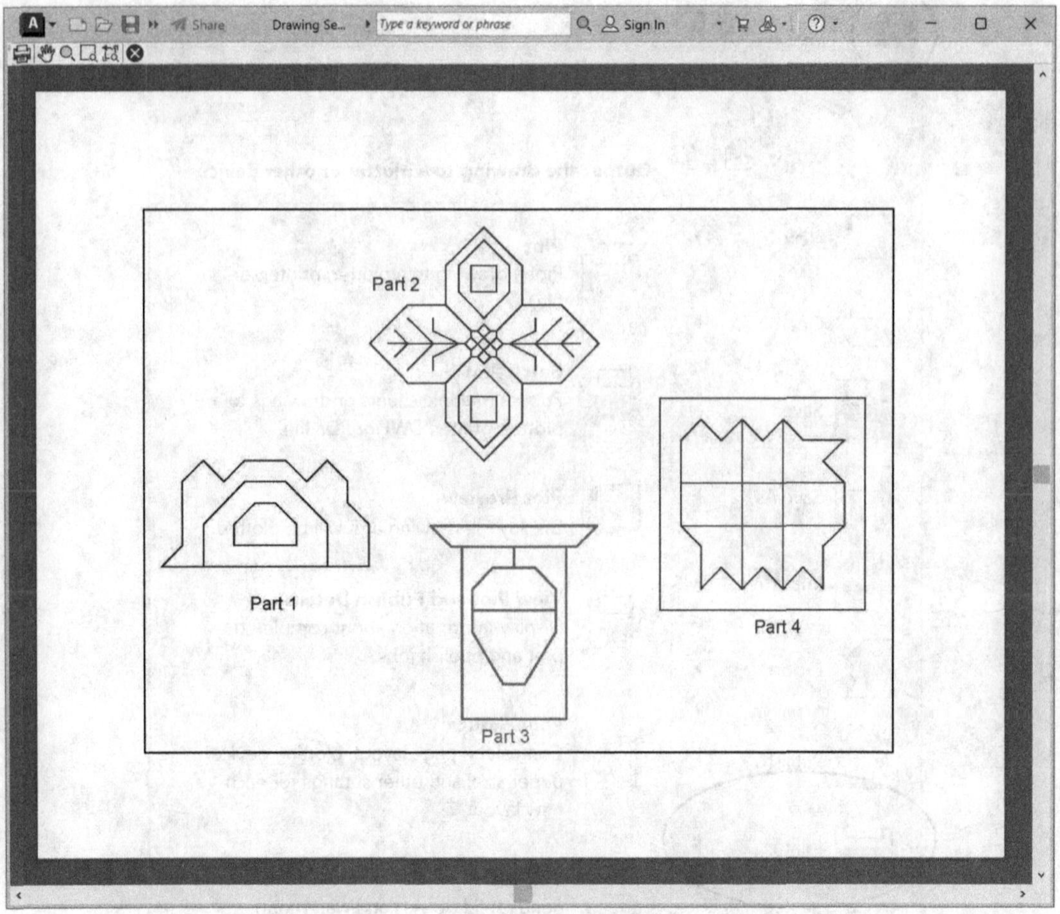

Figure 21-3b

21.4. Plot/Print

The *Plot or Print* command is used to output a drawing file. The output can be sent to a printer/plotter or written to a file for use with another application. The *Plot* command is activated using one of the following methods:

1. Menu method: Select the *Application* pull-down menu, Figure 21-4a, and select the *Print* option.
2. Toolbar method: Select the plot drawing tool ( ), Figure 21-4b, from the quick access toolbar. It is located on the upper left corner of the dialog box.
3. Panel method: Select the *Output* tab, from the *Plot* panel, select the *Plot* ( ) option, Figure 21-4c.
4. Command line method: Type "plot," "Plot" or "PLOT" or "print," "Print" or "PRINT" in the command line and press the *Enter* key.
5. Keyboard method: Hold down the control "Ctrl" key and type "p" or "P".

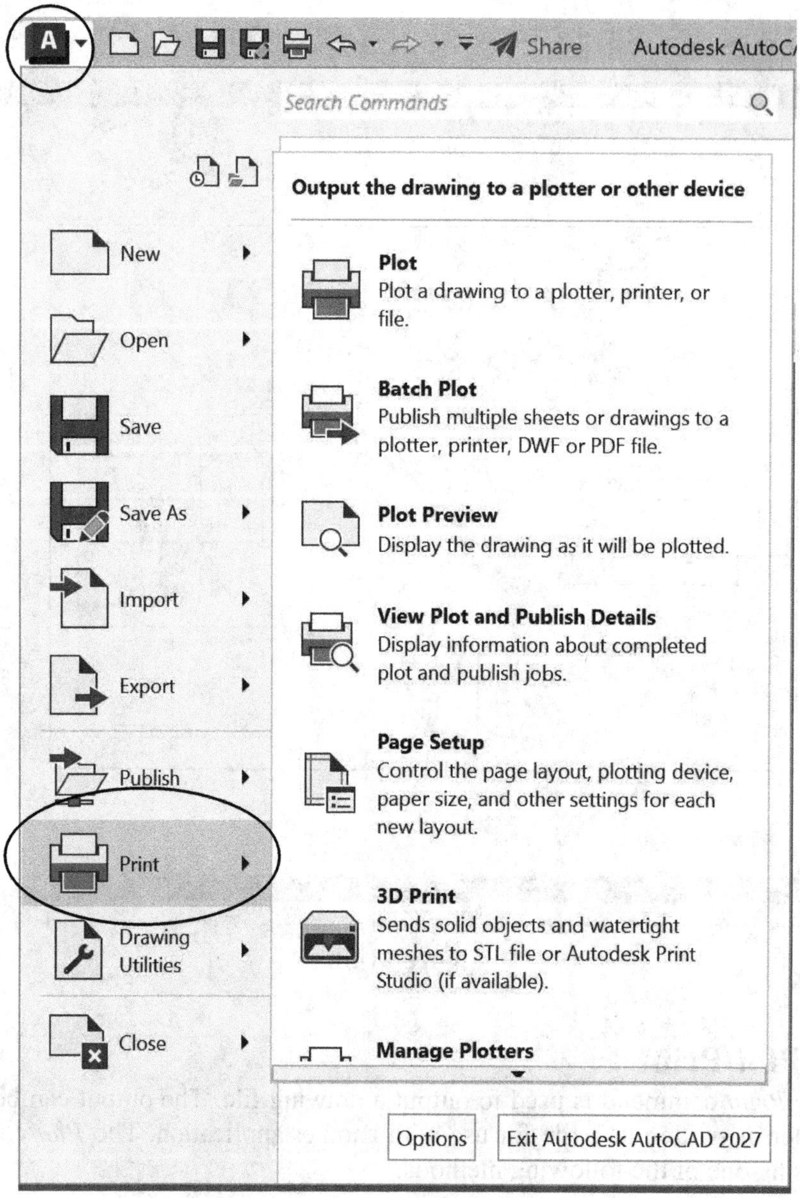

Figure 21-4a

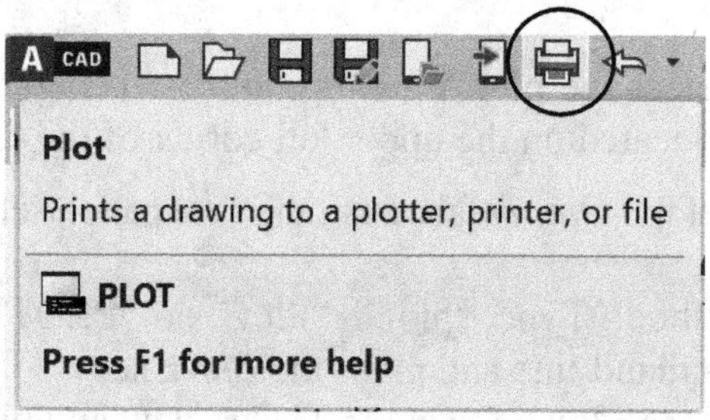

Figure 21-4b

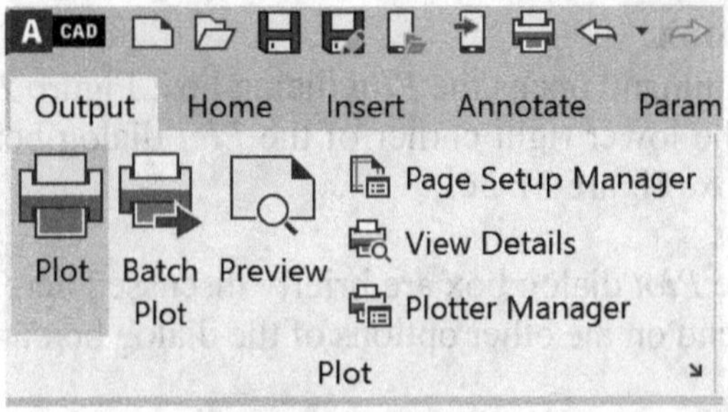

Figure 21-4c

- The activation of the command opens the *Plot* dialog box, Figure 21-5a. If the *Plot* command is activated from the Model space, then it is called *Plot-Model* (Figure 21-5a) and if it is activated from a layout then it is called *Plot – Layout Name*.

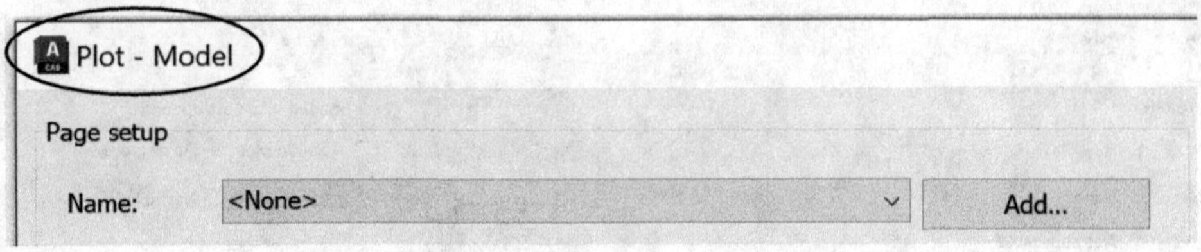

Figure 21-5a

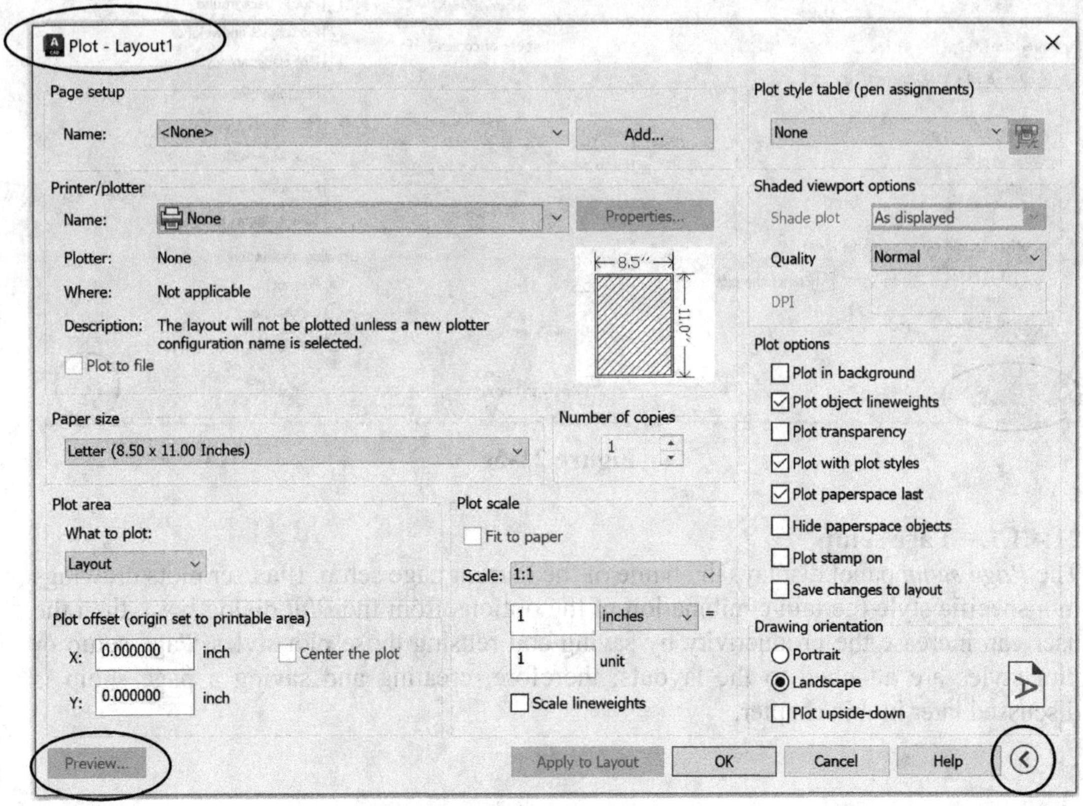

Figure 21-5b

21.4.1. Plot dialog box

The activation of the command opens the *Plot* dialog box, Figure 21-5a and Figure 21-5b. Click on the arrow in the lower right corner of the *Plot* dialog box to display the hidden features of the dialog box, Figure 21-5c.

The main features of the *Plot* dialog box are briefly discussed here. The greyed options of the *Plot* dialog box depend on the other options of the dialog box and are discussed in their respective sections.

The properties of some of the options available from the *Plot* dialog box can be changed from the *Options* dialog box. The Options dialog box is discussed later in this chapter.

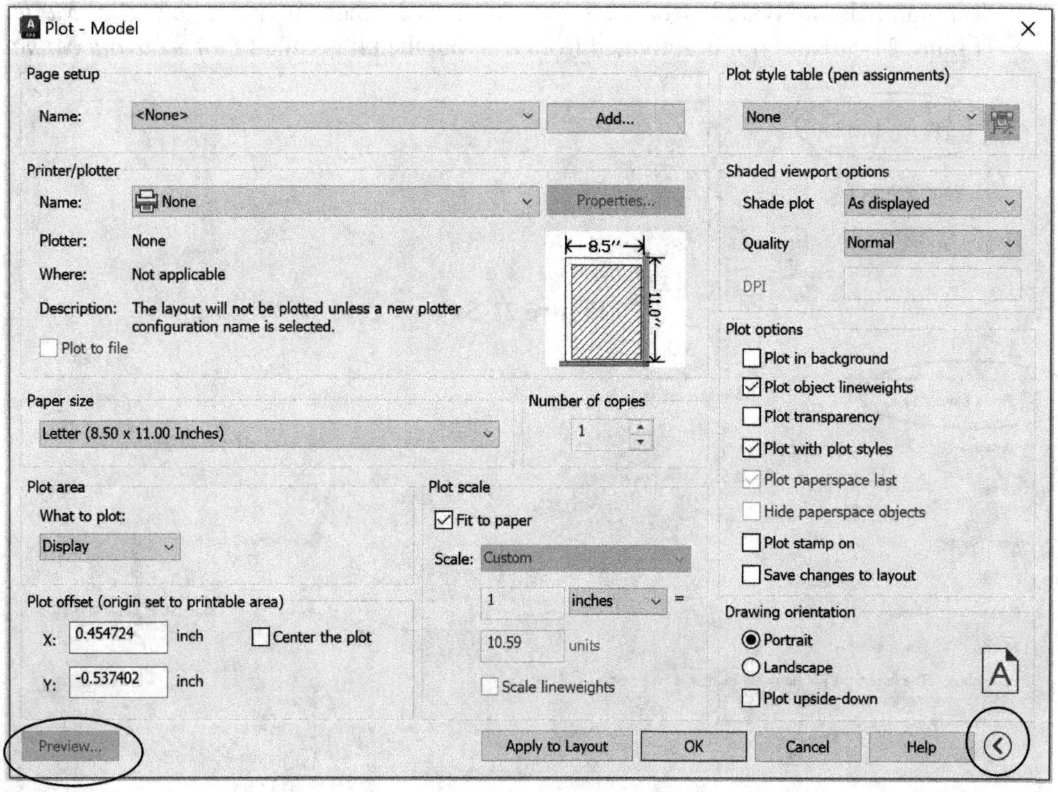

Figure 21-5c

21.4.1.1. Page setup

The *Page setup* panel displays the name of the current page setup. If a user plots drawings in a specific style (certain combination of the options from the *Plot* dialog box), then the user can increase the productivity by saving and reusing those plot styles. Page setup or plot styles are attached to the layouts; therefore, creating and saving a page setup is discussed later in this chapter.

21.4.1.2. Printer/plotter

The *Printer/plotter* panel provides the options for the selection of a configured plotting device to use when plotting or publishing from Model space, layouts, or sheets, Figure 21-5d.

- Name: Lists the available PC3 files or system printers. Press the down-arrow (▾) to display the available printers. If a printer is selected, then the *Preview* button (lower left corner of Figure 21-5b) is activated. Before plotting, confirm that there are no plotting problems, ***refer to Plotting Problem Section.***
- Plot to file: If the *Plot to file box* is checked then the output is saved as a file. This option is discussed in detail later in this chapter under *Portable document format file* and *Option dialog box* sections.
- Partial preview: The partial preview in the printer/plotter panel shows an accurate representation of the effective plot area relative to the paper size and printable area.

21.4.1.3. Paper size

The *Paper size* panel displays standard paper sizes that are available for the selected plotting device. In Figure 21-5e, *Letter* type paper is selected; therefore, the partial preview shows its dimensions, Figure 21-5d. Change the paper size and monitor the change in the partial preview appearance.

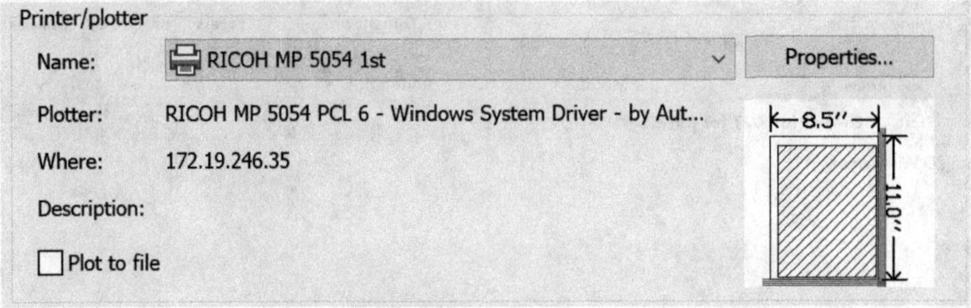

Figure 21-5d

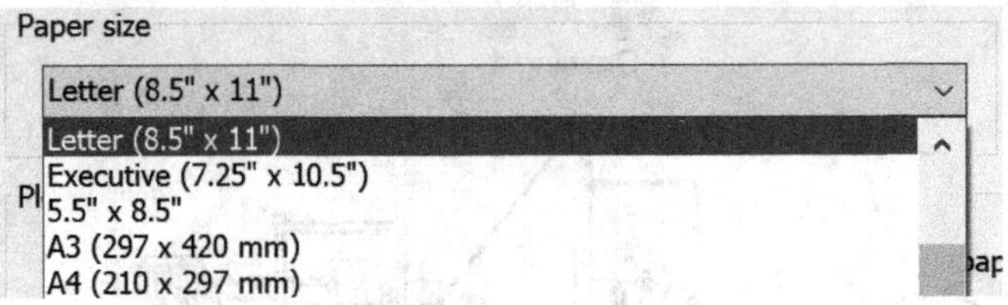

Figure 21-5e

21.4.1.4. Plot area

The *Plot area* panel specifies the area of the drawing to be plotted. The list under *What to Plot* is based on the location (Model space or layout) of the activation of the *Plot* command. If the *Plot* command is activated from the Model space, then the options shown in Figure 21-5f are available. On the other hand, if the *Plot* command is activated from the layout, then the options shown in Figure 21-5g are available.

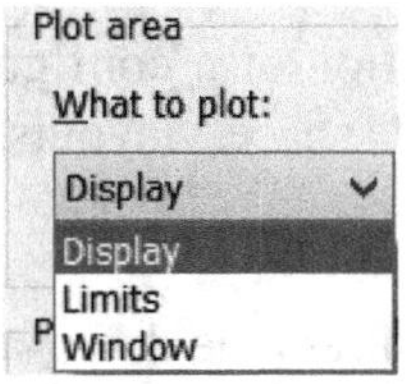

Figure 21-5f

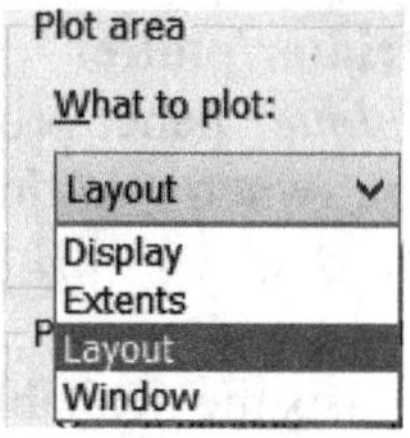

Figure 21-5g

- Display: The *Display* option plots the view in the current viewport in the *Model* tab or in the current paper space view in a layout tab. That is, the drawing is plotted as it appears in the drawing area. Figure 21-6a shows a drawing in the Model space. Figure 21-6b shows the same drawing in the preview window with the selection of the *Display* option in the *Plot* command. Note that the drawing objects are in the lower left corner of the drawing area and printed in the lower left corner of the drawing sheet.

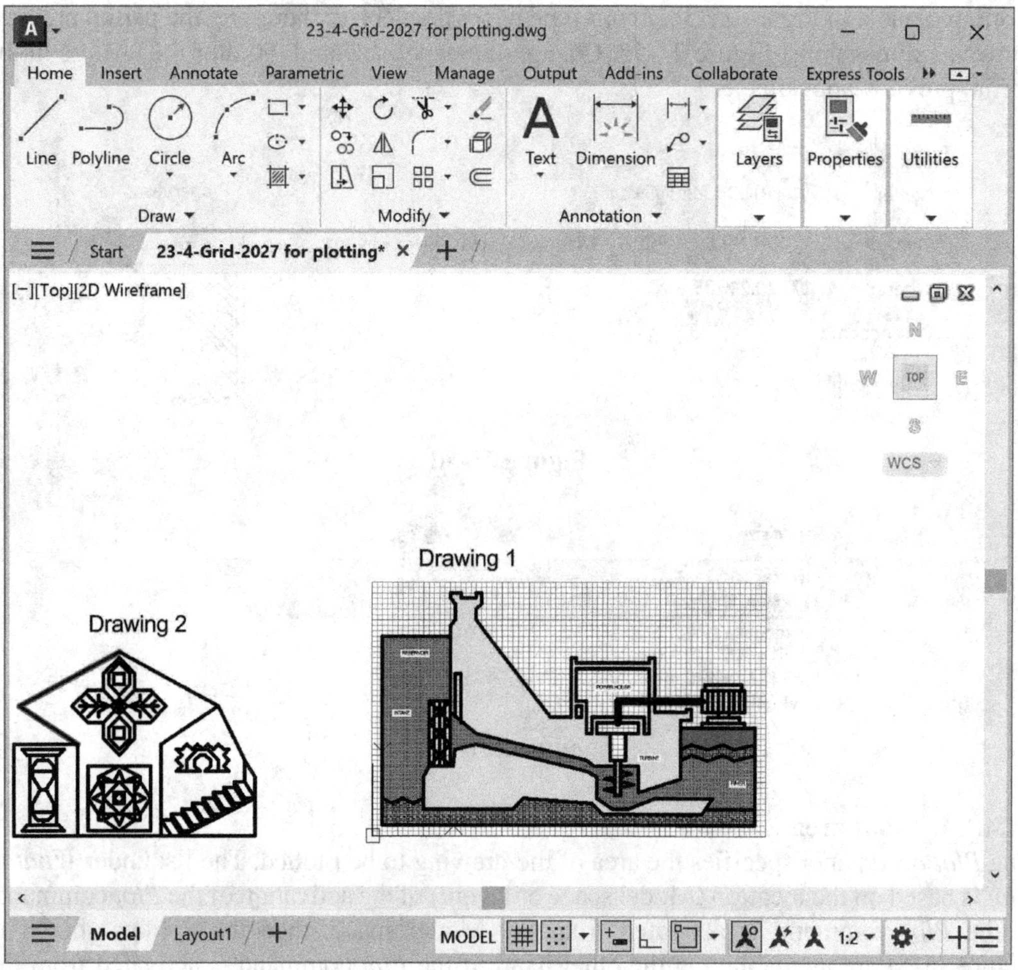

Figure 21-6a

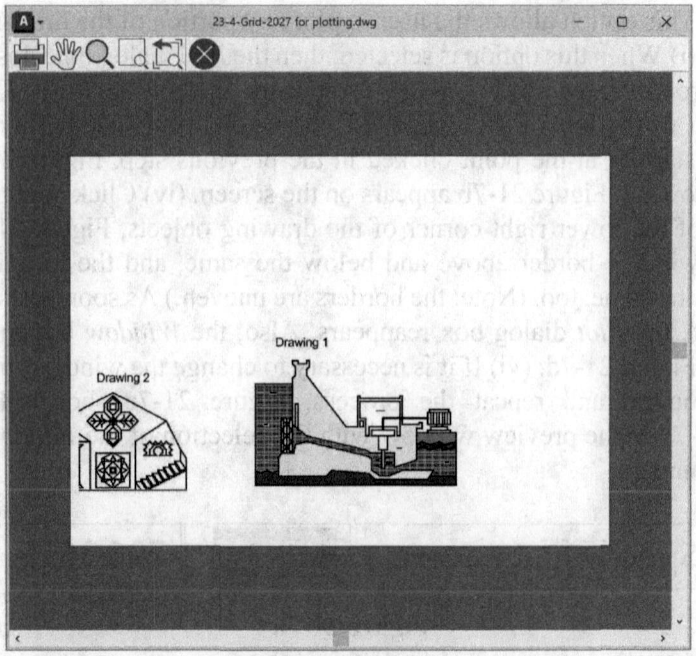

Figure 21-6b

- Limits: When the *Plot* command is activated from the Model space, this option prints every object created on the grid. Figure 21-6a shows two drawings. However, Figure 21-6c shows only one drawing, the dam drawn on the grid. Note that the grid is not appearing in the preview window because it will not be printed.

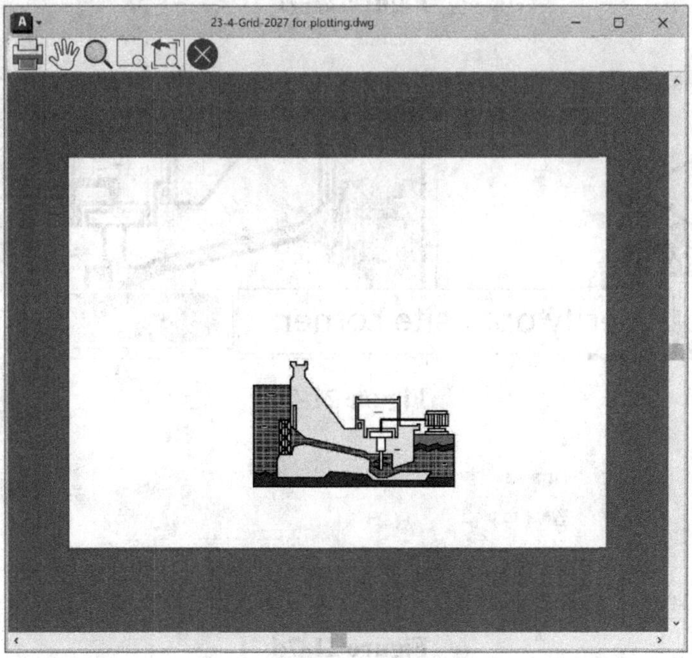

Figure 21-6c

- Window: This option allows the user to plot any portion of the drawing that the user specifies. (i) When this option is selected, then the *Plot* dialog box closes temporarily, and the prompt shown in Figure 21-7a appears on the screen. (ii) Click at slightly above and to the left of the upper left corner of the drawing. (iii) This creates a rectangle starting at the point clicked in the previous step, Figure 21-7b. Also, the prompt shown in Figure 21-7b appears on the screen. (iv) Click slightly below and to the right of the lower right corner of the drawing objects, Figure 21-7c. (v) Try to keep the window border above and below the same, and the left and right border should be the same, too. (Note: the borders are uneven.) As soon as the second corner is selected, the *Plot* dialog box reappears. Also, the *Window* button appears in the plot area, Figure 21-7d. (vi) If it is necessary to change the window, then click on the *Window* button and repeat the process. Figure 21-7e shows the drawing of Figure 21-7a in the preview window with the selection of the *Window* option in the *Plot* command.

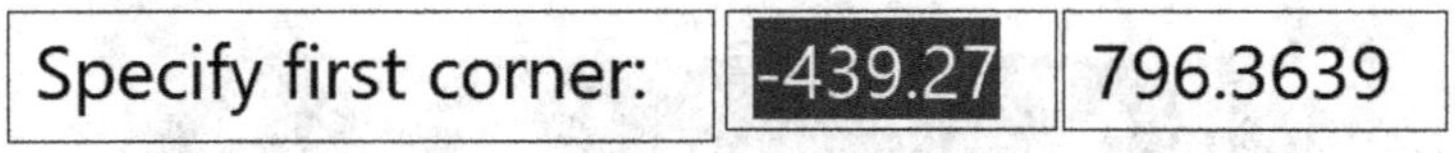

Figure 21-7a

Figure 21-7b

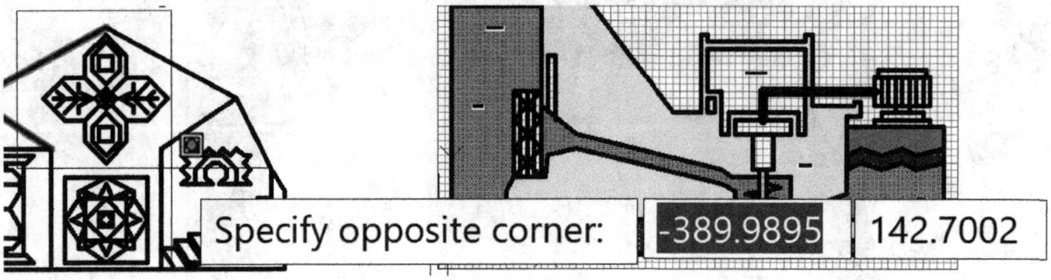

Figure 21-7c

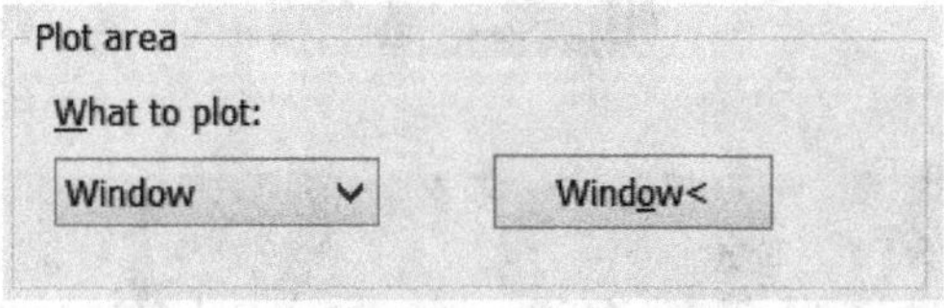

Figure 21-7d

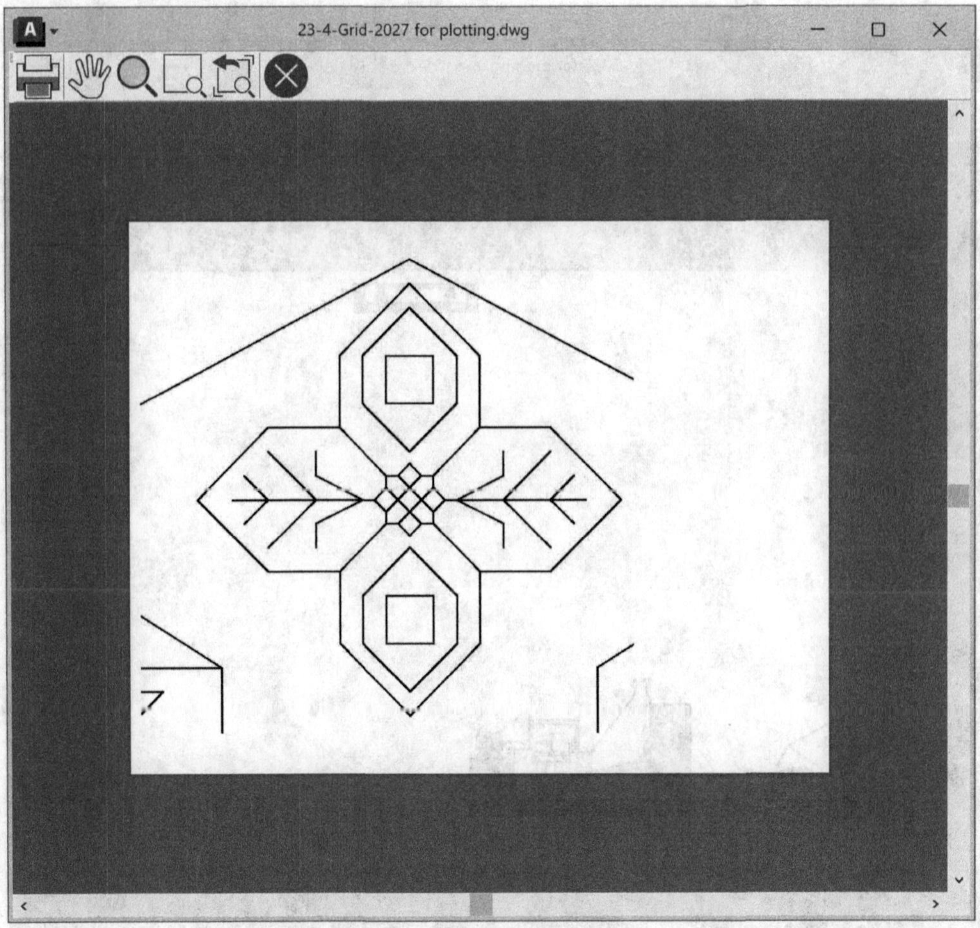

Figure 21-7e

- Extents:
  a) If the *Plot* command is activated from the Model space and *Extent* option is selected, then every object in the current drawing is printed, even if the object is not visible in the drawing window. Figure 21-6a shows two drawings (the drawing of the bridge is not visible). Figure 21-8 shows the sample drawing in the preview window with the selection of the *Extent* option in the *Plot* command and all the three drawings in the drawing area will be printed. However, if this command is activated from a layout, then only the objects visible in the layout are plotted.
  b) *Layout*: This option is available only if the *Plot* command is activated from the *Layout* tab. When plotting a *Layout*, everything within the printable area of the specified paper size is plotted, with the origin calculated from (0, 0) in the layout.

- Layout: This option is available only if the *Plot* command is activated from the *Layout* tab, Figure 21-5g. When this option is selected, then the following two options are not available. (i) Under the *Plot offset*, the *Center the plot* option is not available. (ii) Under the *Plot scale*, the *Fit to paper* option is not available.

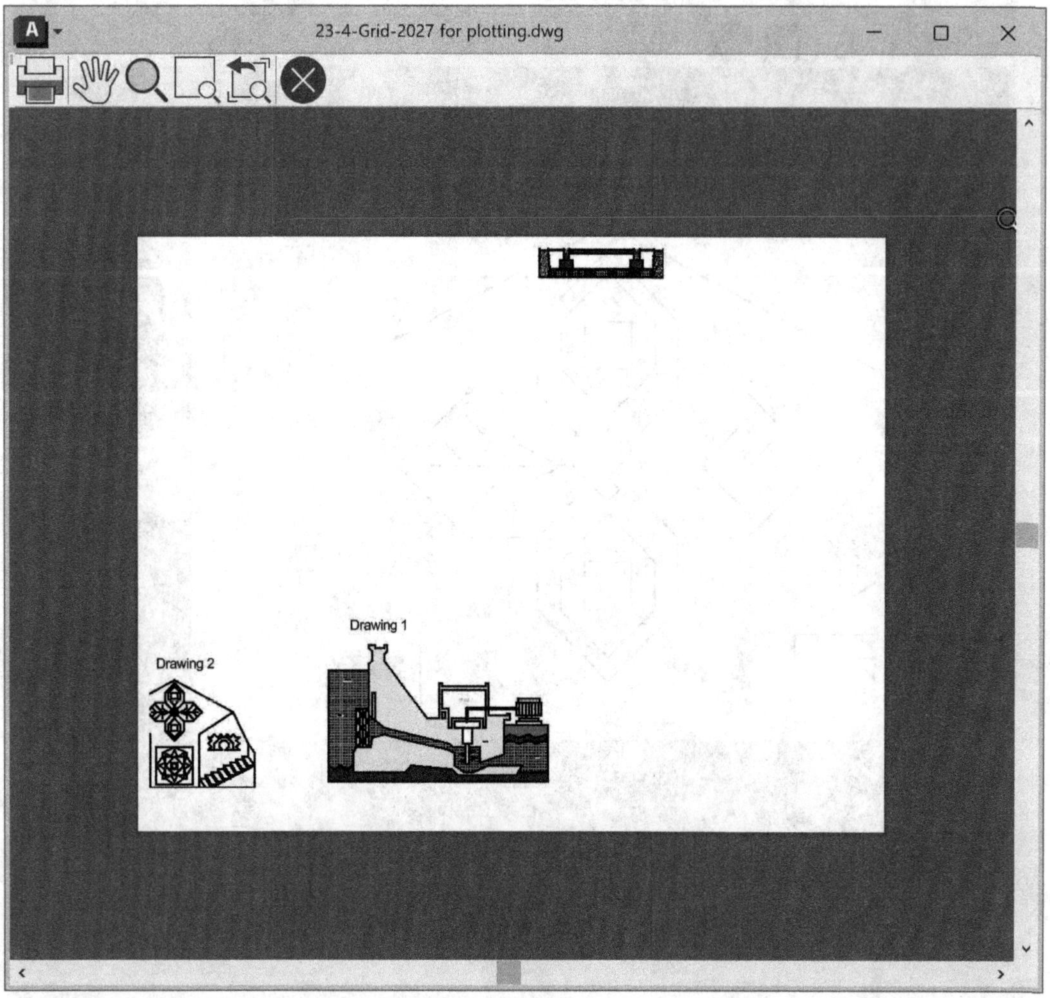

Figure 21-8

21.4.1.5. Plot offset

This option specifies an offset of the plot area relative to the lower-left corner of the printable area or from the edge of the paper. The printable area of a drawing sheet is defined by the selected output device and is represented by a dashed line in a layout.

- X and Y: The X and Y values offset the geometry on the paper by entering a positive or negative value in the respective boxes, Figure 21-9a. The partial preview shows the accurate representation of the effective plot area relative to the paper size, printable area and plot offsets, Figure 21-9b.
- Center the plot: Automatically calculates the X and Y offset values to center the plot on the paper. This option is available only if the *Plot* command is activated from the Model space, Figure 21-9a.
- Repeat the previous examples with *Center the plot* option and observe the difference in the plot preview.

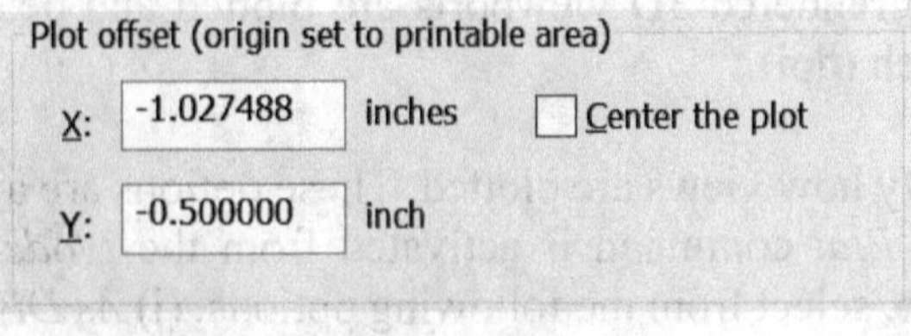

Figure 21-9a

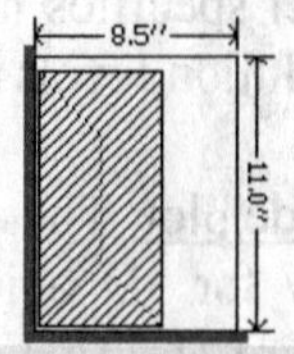

Figure 21-9b

21.4.1.6. Plot scale

This panel controls the relative size of the drawing units to the plotted units. The default setting is *Fit to paper* when the *Plot* command is activated from the *Model* tab, Figure 21-9a. The default scale setting is 1:1 when the *Plot* command is activated from the *Layout* tab, Figure 21-1b.

- Fit to paper: If this box is checked (Figure 21-10a), then the plot is scaled to fit within the selected paper size and the rest of the options in the plot scale window are inactive.
- Scale: The scale list defines the exact scale for the plot. A custom scale can be created by entering the number of inches (or millimeters) equal to the number of drawing units.
- inches = mm =: Specifies the number of inches or millimeters equal to the specified number of units. Pixel is available only when a raster output is selected.
- Units: Specifies the number of units equal to the specified number of inches, millimeters, or pixels, Figure 21-10b.
- Scale lineweights: This option is available only if the plot command is activated from the *Layout* tab. It scales the lineweights in proportion to the plot scale. Lineweights normally specify the line width of the plotted objects and are plotted with the line width size, regardless of the plot scale.

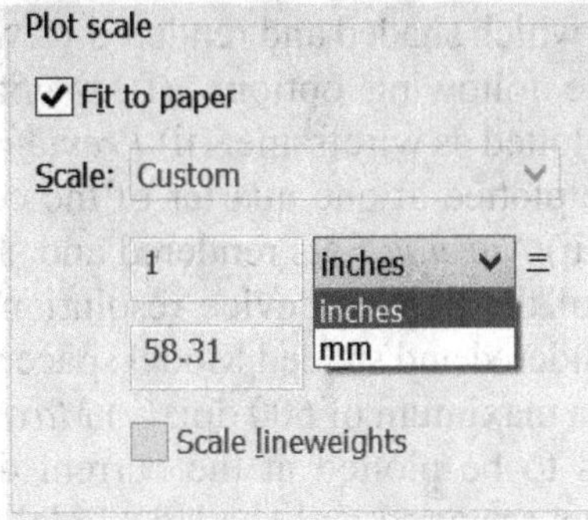

Figure 21-10a

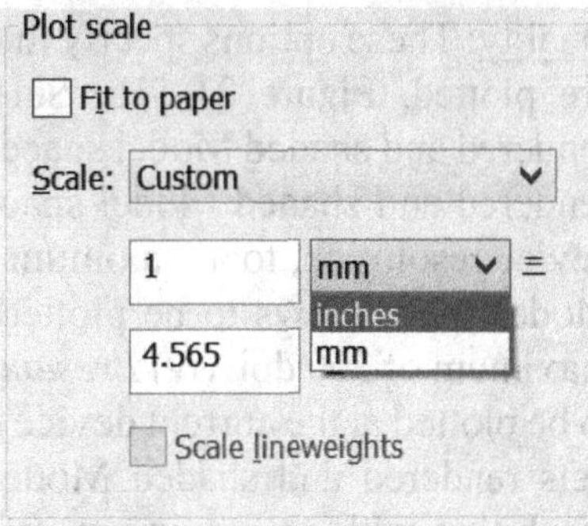

Figure 21-10b

21.4.1.7. Shaded viewport options

This panel specifies how shaded and rendered 3D viewports are plotted and determines their resolution levels and dots per inch (dpi).

- Shade plot: These options specify how views are plotted. These options are available only for 3D objects and if the *Plot* command is activated from the *Model* space, Figure 21-11a. For the *Model* tab, select from the following options: (i) *As Displayed*: Plots objects the way they are displayed on the screen. (ii) *Wireframe*: Plots objects in wireframe regardless of the way they are displayed on the screen. (iii) *Hidden*: Plots objects with hidden lines removed regardless of the way they are displayed on the screen. (iv) *Rendered*: Plots objects as rendered regardless of the way they are displayed on the screen.

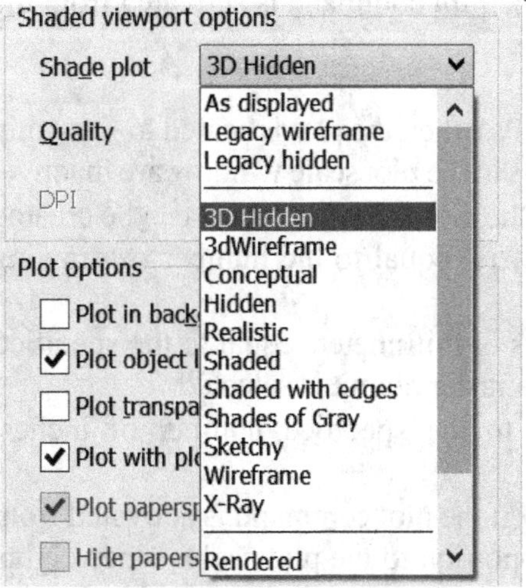

Figure 21-11a

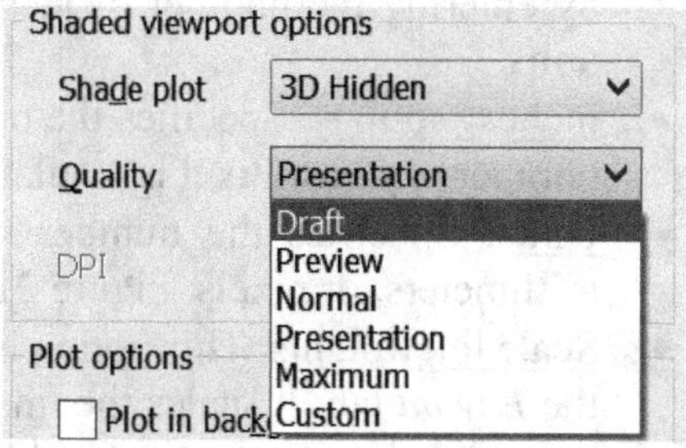

Figure 21-11b

- Quality: These options specify the resolution at which shaded and rendered viewports are plotted, Figure 21-11b. Select one of the following options. (i) *Draft*: Sets rendered and shaded Model space views to be plotted as wireframe. (ii) *Preview*: Sets rendered and shaded Model space views to be plotted at one quarter of the current device resolution, to a maximum of 150 dpi. (iii) *Normal*: Sets rendered and shaded Model space views to be plotted at one half of the current device resolution, to a maximum of 300 dpi. (iv) *Presentation*: Sets rendered and shaded Model space views to be plotted at the current device resolution, to a maximum of 600 dpi. (v) *Maximum*: Sets rendered and shaded Model space views to be plotted at the current device resolution with no maximum. (vi) *Custom*: Sets rendered and shaded Model space views to be plotted at the resolution setting that the user specifies in the DPI box, up to the current device resolution.

- DPI: Specifies the dots per inch for shaded and rendered views, up to the maximum resolution of the current plotting device. This option is unavailable for most of the options under *Shade plot* and *Quality* boxes.

21.4.1.8. Plot options

Plot option specifies the options for lineweights, plot styles, shaded plots, and the order in which objects are plotted, Figure 21-12a. The inactive field in the option list becomes active if the *Plot* command is activated from a layout. Plotting from a layout is discussed in detail later in this chapter.

Figure 21-12a

- Plot in background: The selection of this option allows the user to work in AutoCAD while plotting is processed in background. In some situations, selection of this option makes the computer slow.
- <u>Plot object lineweights</u>: Specifies whether lineweights assigned to objects and layers are plotted.
- <u>Plot with plot styles</u>: Specifies whether plot styles applied to objects and layers are plotted. When the user selects this option, *Plot Object Lineweights* is selected automatically.
- <u>Plot paperspace Last</u>: Plots Model space geometry first. Paper space geometry is usually plotted before Model space geometry.
- <u>Hide paperspace Objects</u>: Specifies whether the HIDE operation applies to objects in the paper space viewport. This option is available only from a layout tab. The effect of this setting is reflected in the plot preview but not in the layout.
- <u>Plot stamp on</u>: Selection of this option allows the plotter to place a stamp with specified information at a specified location on every plot. In addition, a stamp button appears. Click the stamp button ( ) to open the *Plot Stamp* dialog box, Figure 21-12b; if necessary, change the information.
- <u>Save changes to layout</u>: If the *Plot* command is activated from a layout, and the user selects the option for plotting, then those selections can be saved by checking this box. The selections are attached to the layout initiating the plot command.

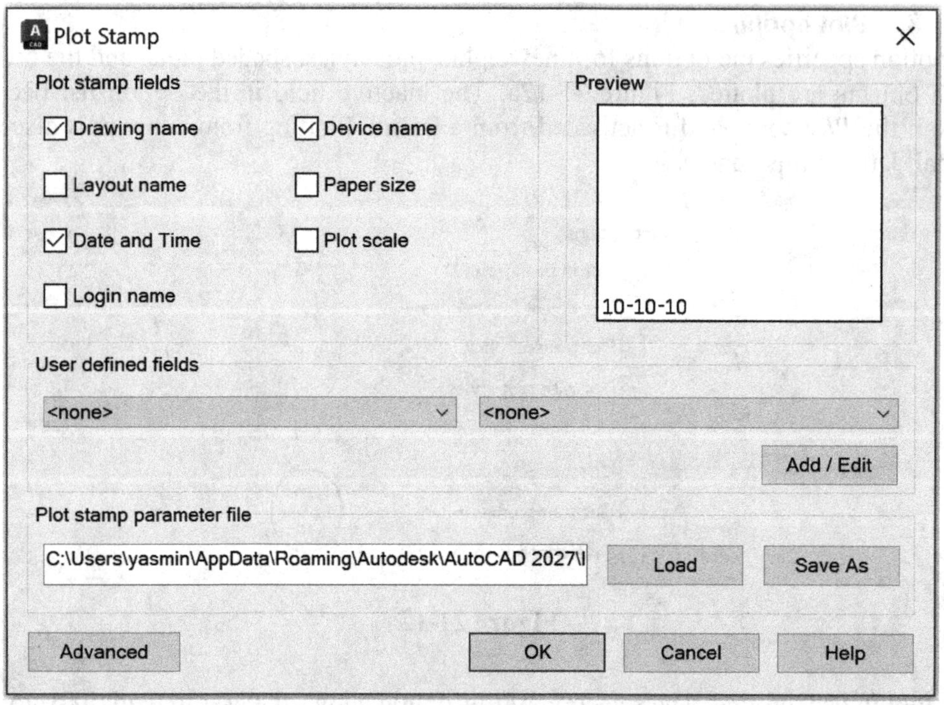

Figure 21-12b

21.4.1.9. Drawing orientation

Specifies the orientation of the drawing on the paper for plotters that support landscape or portrait orientation, Figure 21-13.

- <u>Portrait</u>: Orients and plots the drawing so that the short edge of the paper represents the top of the page.
- <u>Landscape</u>: Orients and plots the drawing so that the long edge of the paper represents the top of the page.
- <u>Plot upside-down</u>: Orients and plots the drawing upside-down.

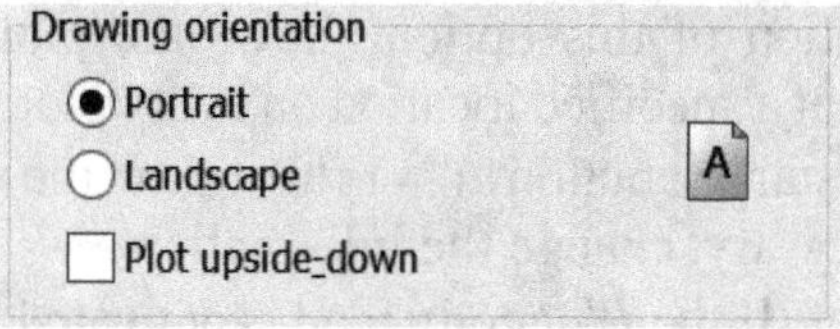

Figure 21-13

21.4.1.10. Preview

The preview command displays the drawing as it appears when plotted on paper. The user must preview the drawing file before clicking the *OK* button! This option is available only if under the *Printer/plotter* panel and *Name* field, a printer is selected. The plot *Preview* button is located in the lower left corner of the *Plot* dialog box. In Figure 21-14a, this option is not available. To exit the print preview and return to the *Plot* dialog box, press the *Esc* or the *Enter* key or click on ⊗ button in the preview window, Figure 21-14b.

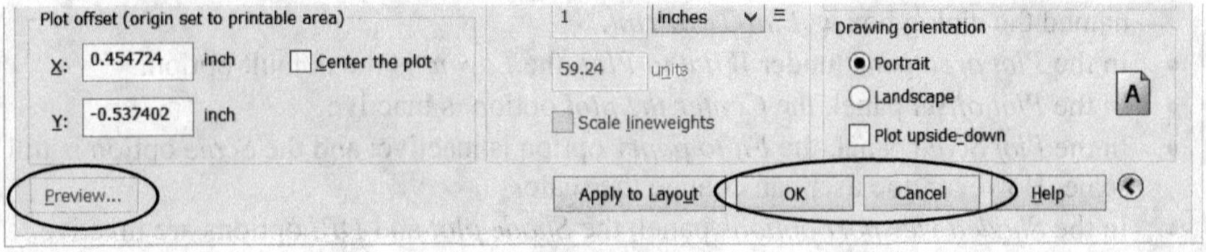

Figure 21-14a

If the preview window is open then to exit the print preview and return to the *Plot* dialog box, press the *Esc* or the *Enter* key or click on ⊗ button on the preview window.

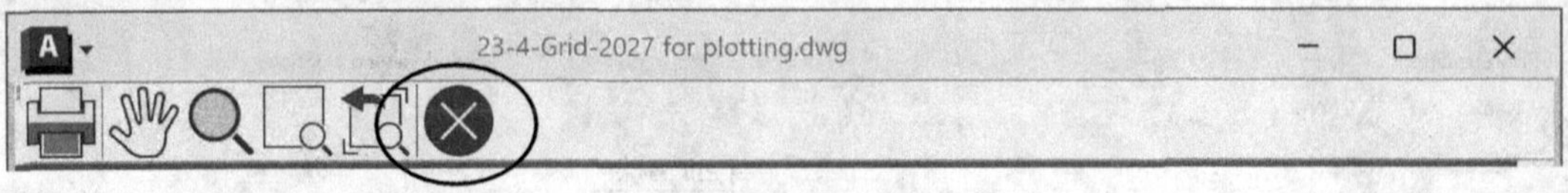

Figure 21-14b

21.4.1.11. Plot to layout

This option is available only if the *Plot* command is activated from a layout and the user has made changes to the *Plot* dialog box. In Figure 21-15, this option is available.

21.4.1.12. OK and cancel

As the name suggests, click the *OK* button to make changes effective, close the *Plot* dialog box, Figure 21-14a, and click the *Cancel* button to ignore changes and close the *Plot* dialog box.

21.4.2. Plot from a layout

The *Print* and *Plot* commands are used to plot a drawing file. When plotting a *Layout*, everything within the printable area of the specified paper size is plotted. Layers and layouts are discussed in detail in *Chapter 6* and *Chapter 8* and are used heavily in the application part of the textbook.

The process of plotting from a layout is summarized in the following steps.

1. Click on the desired layout.
2. Double click INSIDE the viewport (WCS appears) and center the drawing using the scroll bars or pan command.
3. Freeze the unnecessary layers.
4. If necessary, set the linetype scale.
5. Double click OUTSIDE the viewport (WCS disappears).
6. From the *Properties* sheet, set the viewport scale and lock the scale.
7. Update the *Title* block by modifying the block attributes to the desired value.
8. Activate and complete the *Plot* command.
9. On the printout, initial by hand the *Release* block entries.

Figure 21-15 shows the settings of the *Plot* dialog box when the *Plot* command is activated from a layout.

- The *Plot* command is activated from the layout named TestPrint; and the software named the dialog box as *Plot-TestPrint*.
- In the *Plot area* panel under *What to Plot*, the *Layout* is the default option.
- In the *Plot offset* panel, the *Center the plot* option is inactive.
- In the *Plot Scale* panel, the *Fit to paper* option is inactive; and the *Scale* option is full scale. However, the user can change the scale.
- In the *Shaded viewport options* panel, the *Shade plot* and *DPI* options are inactive.
- In the *Plot options* panel, every option is available.

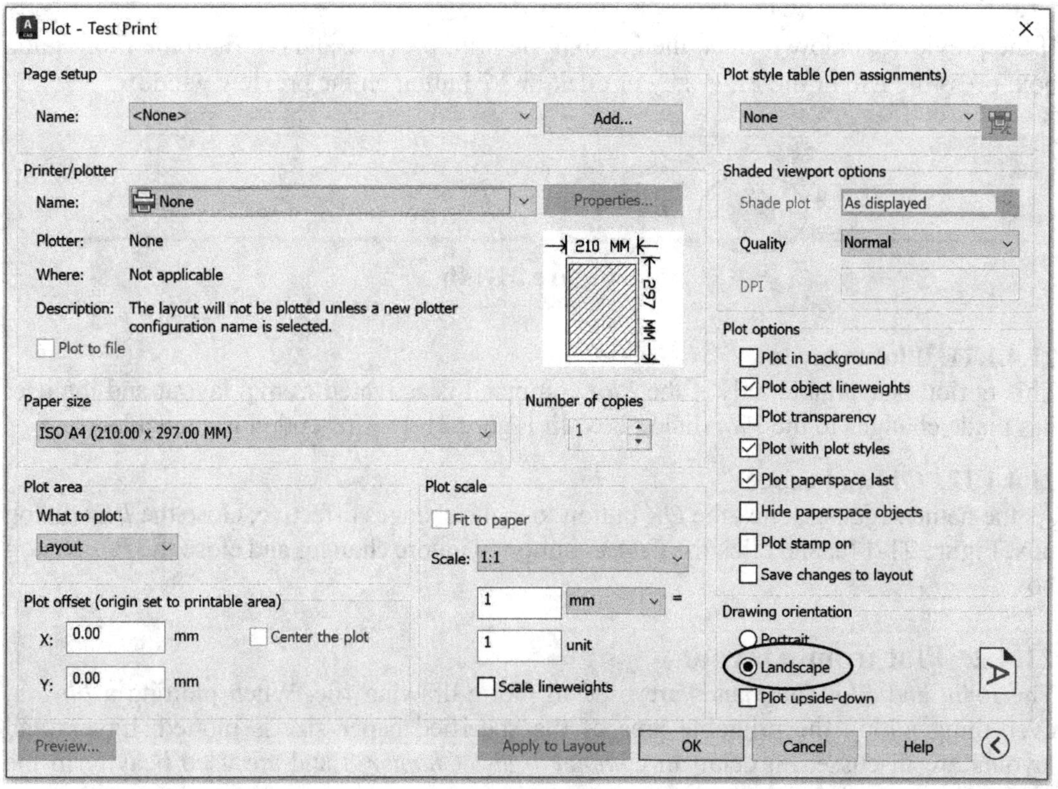

Figure 21-15

- In the *Orientation* panel, AutoCAD selects the *Landscape* option because the *TestPrint* layout is in landscape format, Figure 21-16a. The longest dimension of the pipe cutter in Figure 21-16a is not parallel to the longer side of the paper. Hence, this drawing should be printed in portrait form. Select the *Portrait* option from the *Plot* dialog box and preview the drawing before printing, Figure 21-16b. The pipe cutter is vertical, but the viewport is distorted (it cannot be fixed here). This issue can be resolved by adjusting the orientation of the layout before activating the *Plot* command.

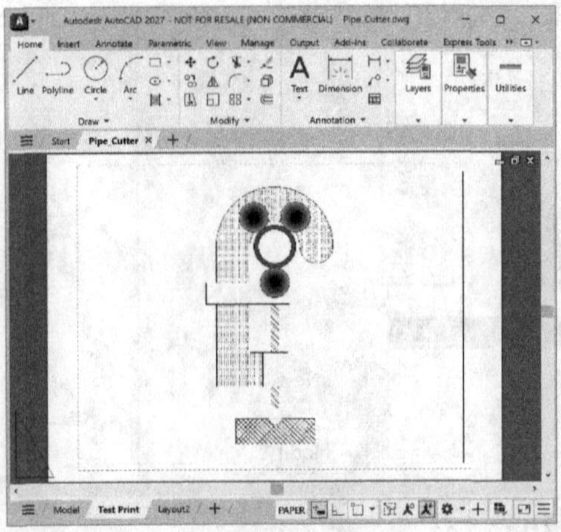

Figure 21-16a

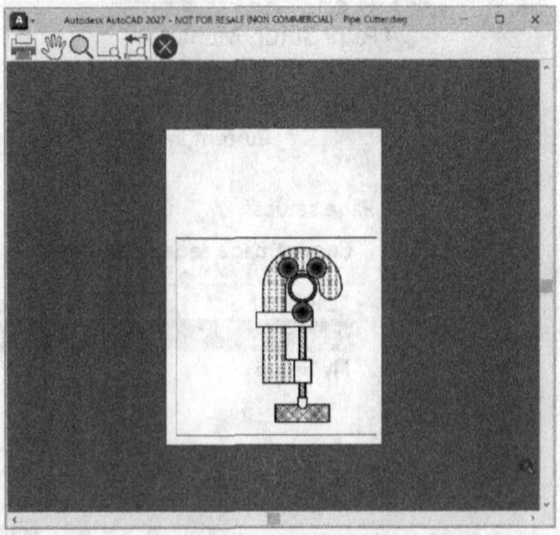

Figure 21-16b

21.4.2.1. Change layout's orientation

A user can change the layout orientation using one of the following two methods. (i) Insert a layout from an appropriate template file (refer to *Chapter 8*), or (ii) change the orientation using the page setup manager.

A user can change the layout orientation using page setup manager as follows.

- Bring the cursor on a layout tab.
- Press the right button of the mouse and the option panel appears, Figure 21-17a.
- Move the cursor to the *Page Setup Manager* option and press the left button of the mouse. The *Page Setup Manager* dialog box shown in Figure 21-17b appears.
- On the *Page Setup Manager* dialog box, click on the *Modify* button. The *Page Setup – TestPrint* dialog box shown in Figure 21-17c appears.

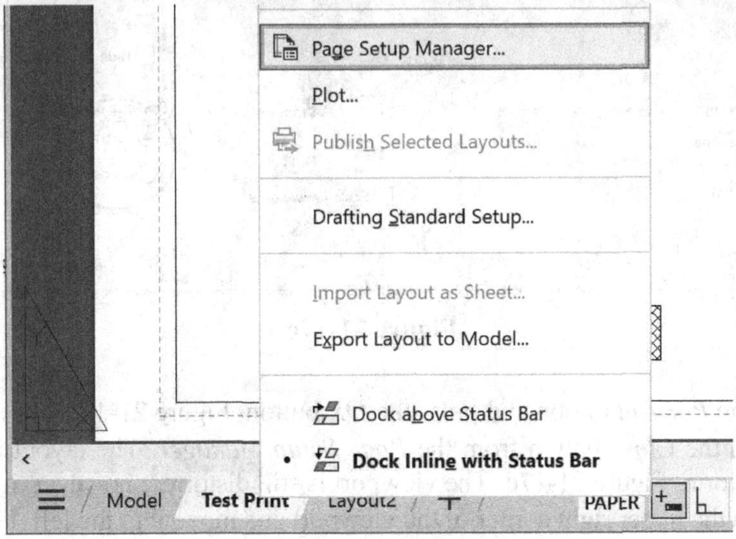

Figure 21-17a

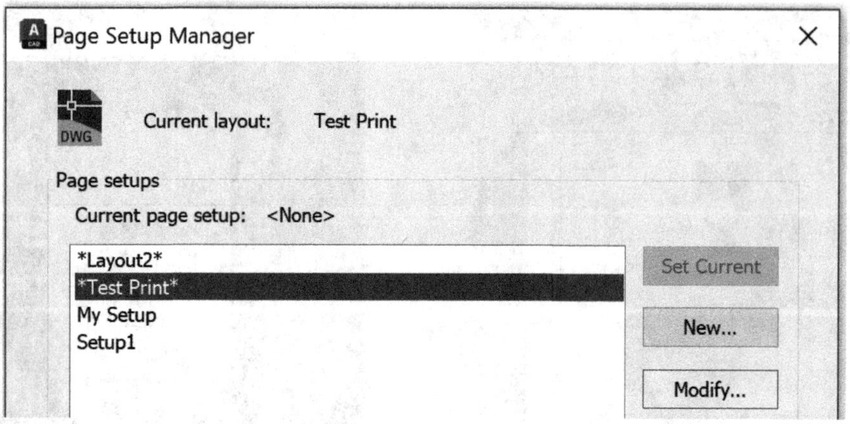

Figure 21-17b

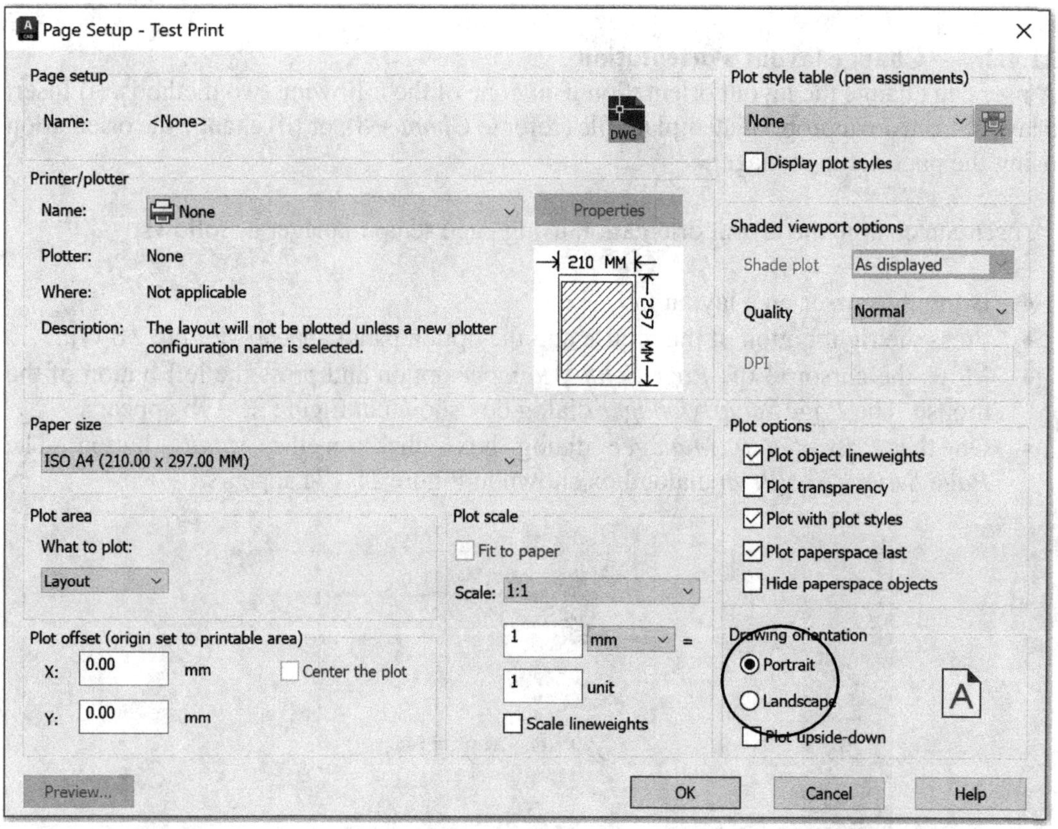

Figure 21-17c

- Select the *Portrait* option and press the *OK* button, Figure 21-17c.
- Click on the *Close* button from the *Page Setup Manager*. The layout is changed to portrait form, Figure 21-17d. The viewport is still distorted; however, it can be fixed.
- Click on the upper right corner of the viewport and move it to the left, Figure 21-17e. Center the viewport and print!

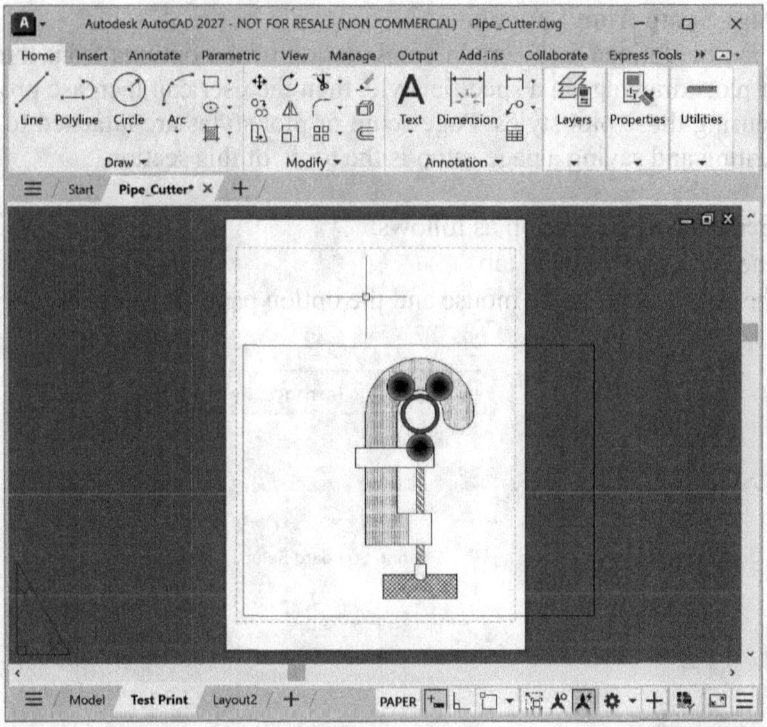

Figure 21-17d

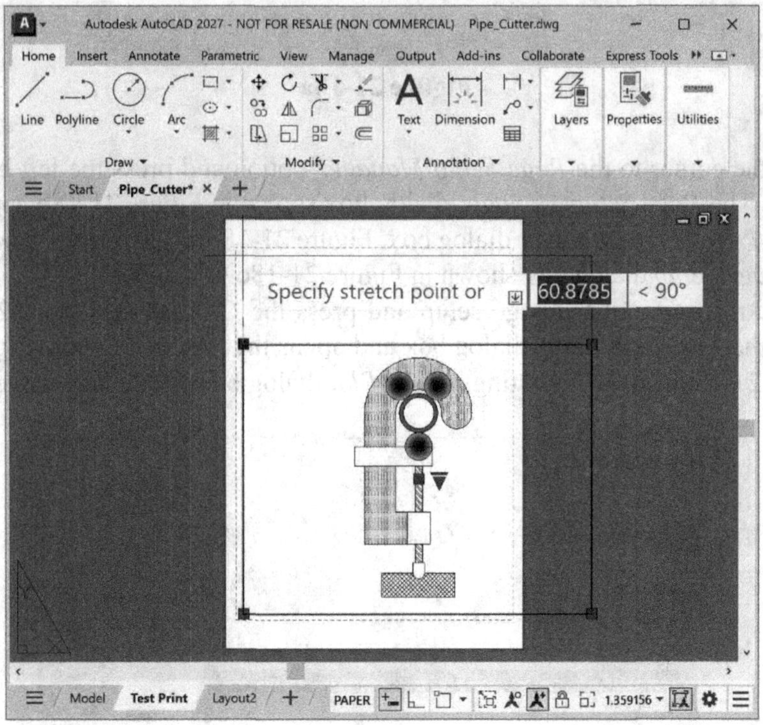

Figure 21-17e

21.4.2.2. Page Setup from Layouts

A plot style can be defined as a certain combination of the options from the *Plot* dialog box. If a user plots drawings in a specific style, then the user can increase productivity by saving and reusing those plot styles. Page setup or plot styles are attached to the layouts; therefore, creating and saving a page setup is the topic of this section.

A user can create a new page setup as follows.

- Bring the cursor on a layout tab.
- Press the right button of the mouse and the option panel appears, Figure 21-18a.

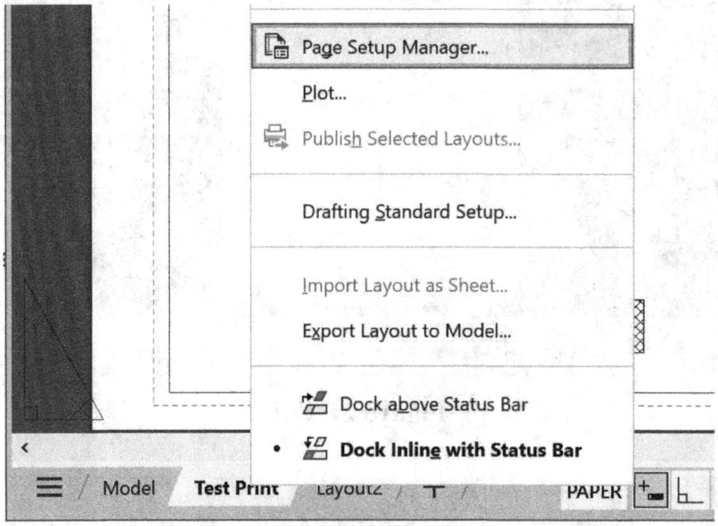

Figure 21-18a

- Move the cursor to the *Page Setup Manager* option and press the left button of the mouse. The *Page Setup Manager* dialog box shown in Figure 21-18b appears.
- On the *Page Setup Manager* dialog box, Figure 21-18b, click on the *New* button. The *New Page Setup* dialog box shown in Figure 21-18c will appear.
- Specify the name of the page setup and press the *OK* button, Figure 21-18c. This closes the *New Page Setup* dialog box and opens the *Plot* dialog box, Figure 21-18d.
- Figure 21-18d shows the settings of the *Plot* dialog box for the new page setup.

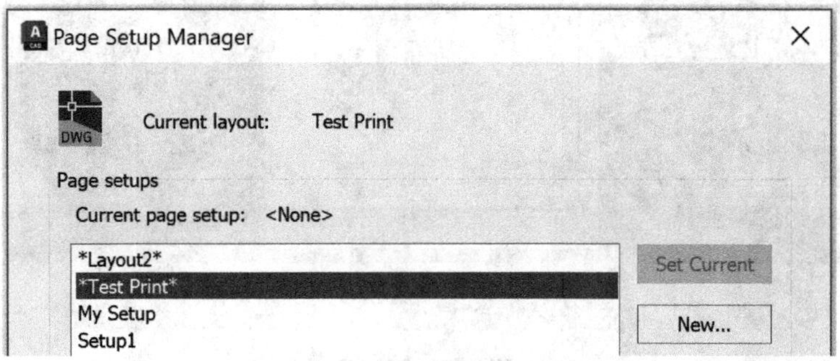

Figure 21-18b

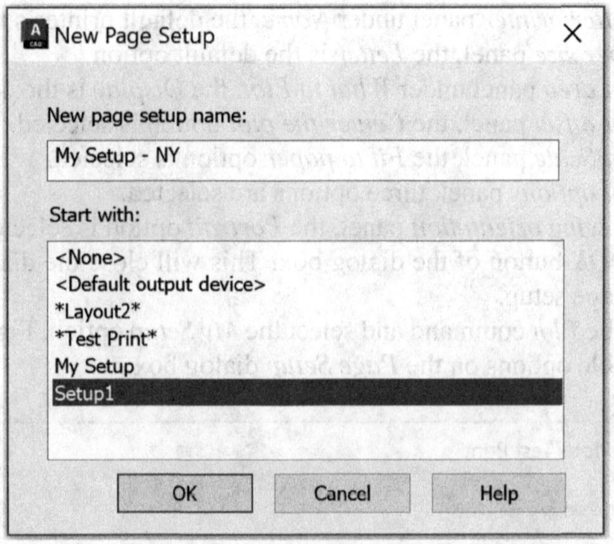

Figure 21-18c

- Note that, in the *Page setup* panel the name is *My Setup - NY*, the newly created page setup's name.

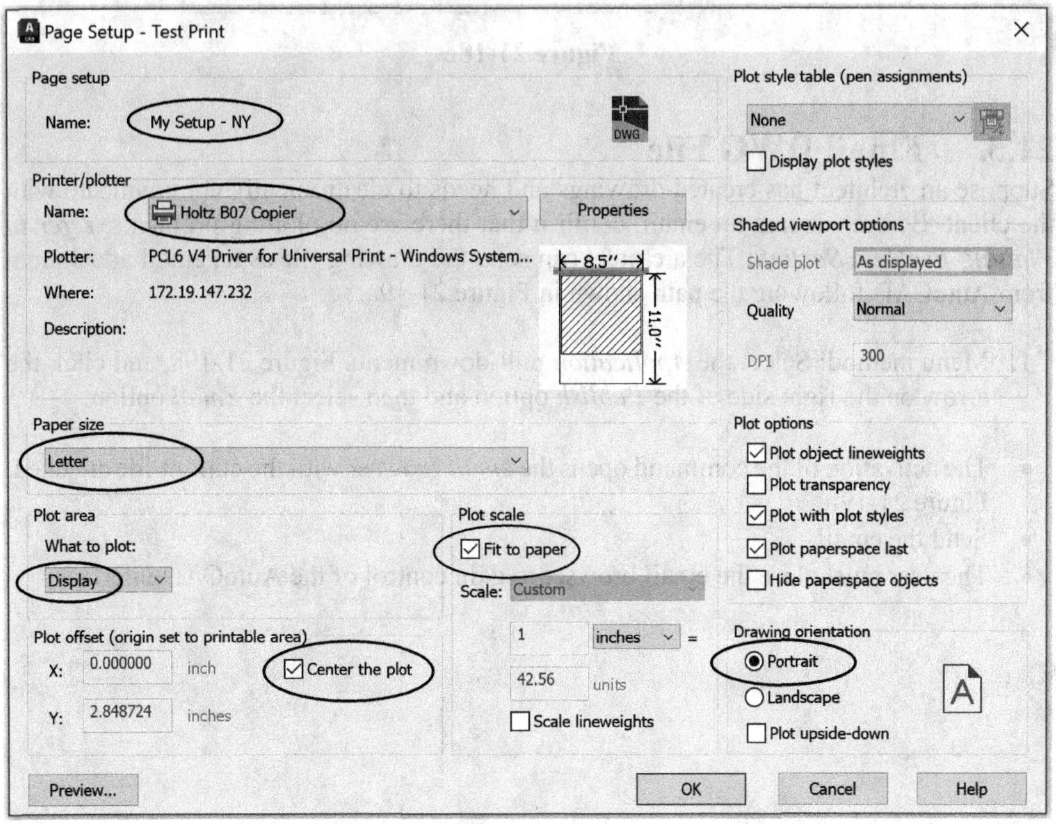

Figure 21-18d

- In the *Plotter/printer* panel under *Name*, the default printer's name is selected.
- In the *paper size* panel, the *Letter* is the default option.
- In the *Plot area* panel under *What to Plot*, the *Display* is the default option.
- In the *Plot offset* panel, the *Center the plot* option is selected.
- In the *Plot Scale* panel, the *Fit to paper* option is selected.
- In the *Plot options* panel, three options are selected.
- In the *Drawing orientation* panel, the *Portrait* option is selected.
- Click the *OK* button of the dialog box. This will close the dialog box and create the new page setup.
- Activate the *Plot* command and select the *My Setup* option, Figure 21-18e. Check the available options on the *Page Setup* dialog box.

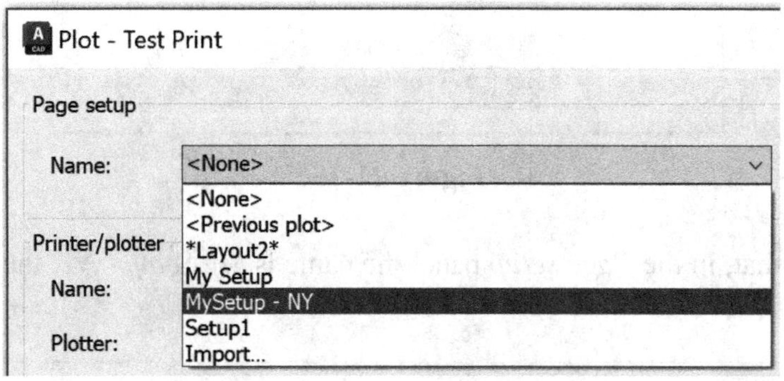

Figure 21-18e

21.5. Email DWG File

Suppose an architect has created drawings and needs to electronically communicate with the client. Before sending an email, confirm that there are no plotting problems, ***refer to Plotting Problem Section.*** The architect can send the drawing file as an email attachment from AutoCAD following the path shown in Figure 21-19a.

1. Menu method: Select the *Application* pull-down menu, Figure 21-19a, and click the arrow on the right side of the *Publish* option and then select the *Email* option.

- The activation of the command opens the *email* browser with the current file attached, Figure 21-19b.
- Send the email.
- The user must close the email browser to gain control of the AutoCAD interface.

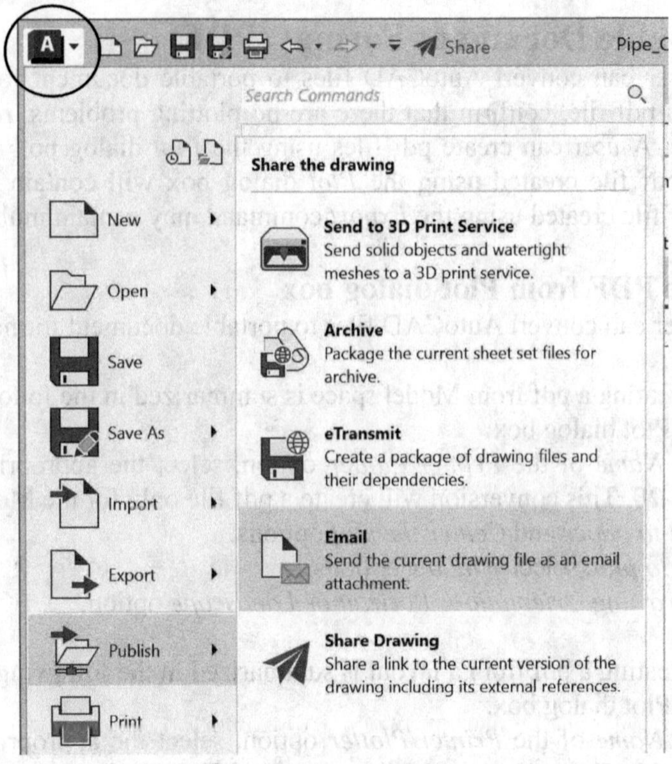

Figure 21-19a

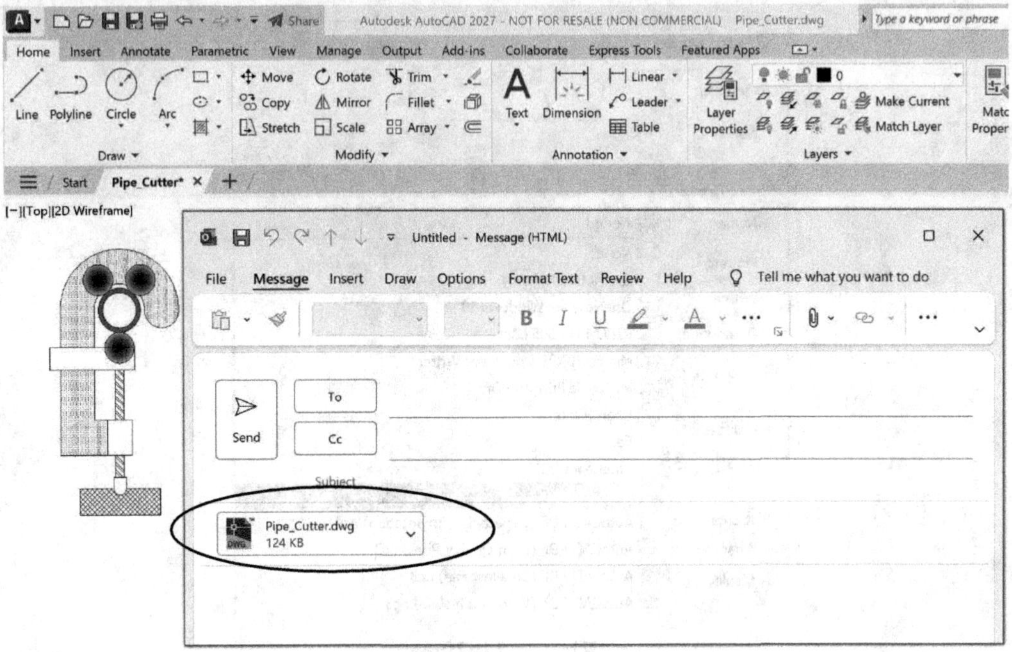

Figure 21-19b

21.6. Portable Document Format (PDF)

An AutoCAD user can convert AutoCAD files to portable document format (pdf) file. Before creating a pdf file, confirm that there are no plotting problems, ***refer to Plotting Problem Section.*** A user can create pdf files using the *Plot* dialog box or using Export command. The pdf file created using the *Plot* dialog box will contain only one page. However, the pdf file created using the *Export* command may contain multiple pages.

21.6.1. Create PDF from Plot dialog box

An AutoCAD user can convert AutoCAD files to portable document format (pdf) file.

The process of creating a pdf from Model space is summarized in the following steps.

1. Open the Plot dialog box.
2. From the *Name* of the *Printer/Plotter* option, select the appropriate pdf format, Figure 21-20. This conversion will create a pdf file only for the Model space.
3. Check *Fit to paper* and *Center the plot* options.
4. For *What to plot*, select *Window* options.
5. Set the *Drawing Orientation: Portrait or Landscape* option.

The process of creating a pdf from a layout is summarized in the following steps.

1. Open the Plot dialog box.
2. From the *Name* of the *Printer/Plotter* option, select the appropriate pdf format, Figure 21-20. This conversion will create a pdf file only for the active layout.
3. Set the *Drawing Orientation: Portrait or Landscape* option.

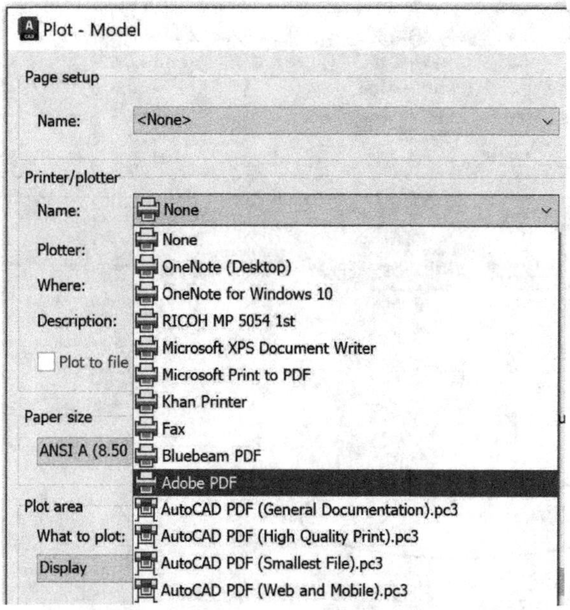

Figure 21-20a

21.6.2. Export a PDF file

An AutoCAD user can export AutoCAD files as a pdf file. Before exporting a file, confirm that there are no plotting problems, ***refer to Plotting Problem Section.*** A user can export drawing files as pdf files using one of the following methods.

21.6.2.1. Export PDF from Model space

The process of exporting a drawing file from Model space is summarized in the following steps.

1. From Model space, select the *Export* command following the path shown in Figure 21-21a.
2. This opens the *Save As PDF* dialog box, Figure 21-21b. For the Page Setup option, select the desired option and follow the prompt.

Figure 21-21a

21.6.2.2. Export PDF from a Layout

The process of exporting a drawing file from a layout is summarized in the following steps.

1. From the layout, select the *Export* command following the path as shown in Figure 21-21a.
2. This opens the *Save As PDF* dialog box, Figure 21-21c. For the Page Setup option, select the desired option and follow the prompt.
3. One key advantage of this method is that the user can create one pdf file for a drawing with multiple layouts using *All layouts* option.

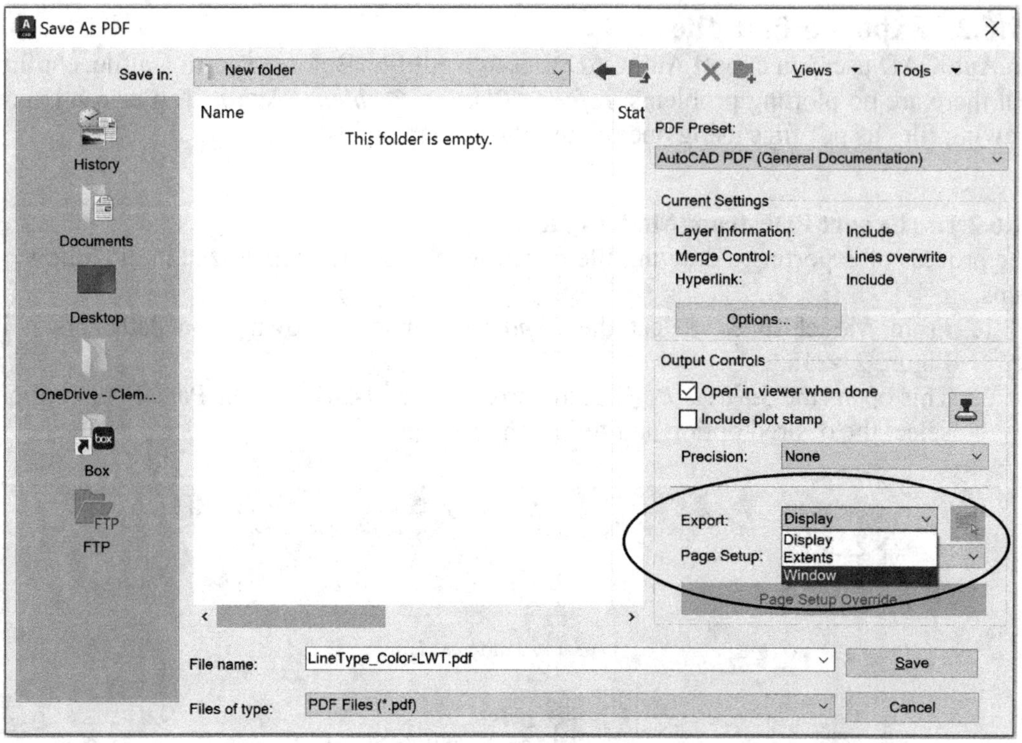

Figure 21-21b

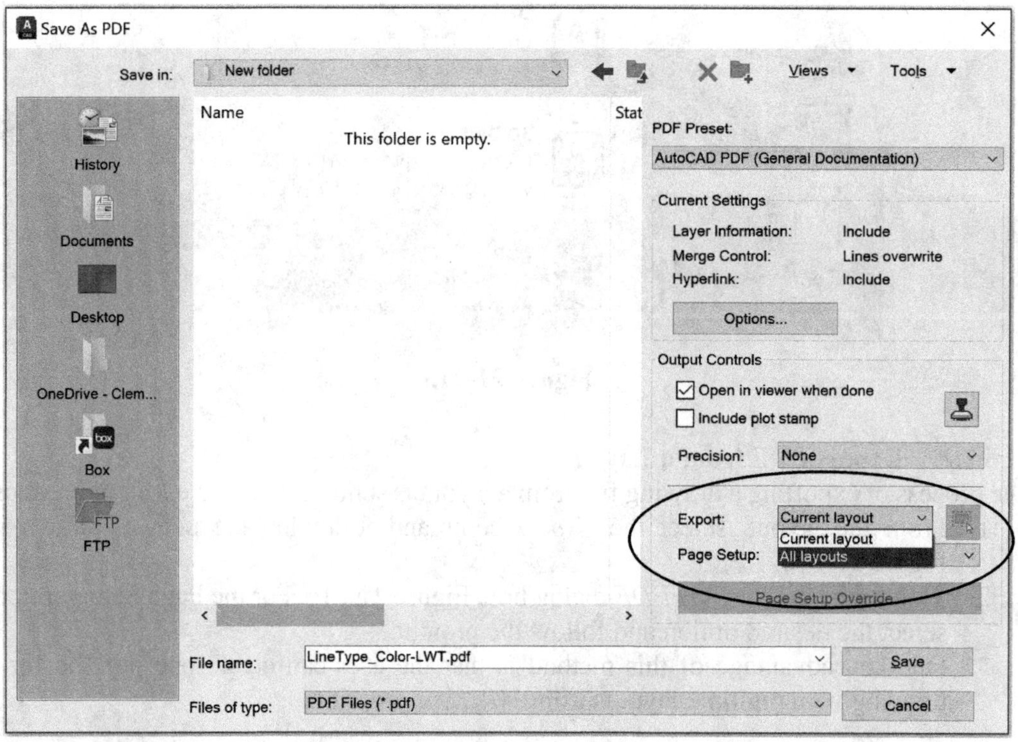

Figure 21-21c

21.7. Import a PDF file into AutoCAD

Import a PDF file command imports data from a PDF file into the current drawing as an AutoCAD object. An AutoCAD user can import a PDF file in AutoCAD using the following steps

1. Open a new file: Check the units of the drawing in the pdf file; for ANSI units open a new *acad.dwg* file and for ISO units open a new *acadiso.dwg* file.

2. Activate the command: Select the *Insert* tab, from the *PDF Import* panel, select the *PDF Import* option, Figure 21-22a. This will open *Select PDF File* dialog box, Figure 21-22b.

3. *Select the PDF file:* Now, select the desired PDF File, Figure 21-22b, and click the *Open* button. This will open *Import PDF* dialog box, Figure 21-22c.

4. Select the options: From the *Import PDF* dialog box, Figure 21-22c, select the desired options and click the OK button. This will transfer the PDF data file into AutoCAD objects.

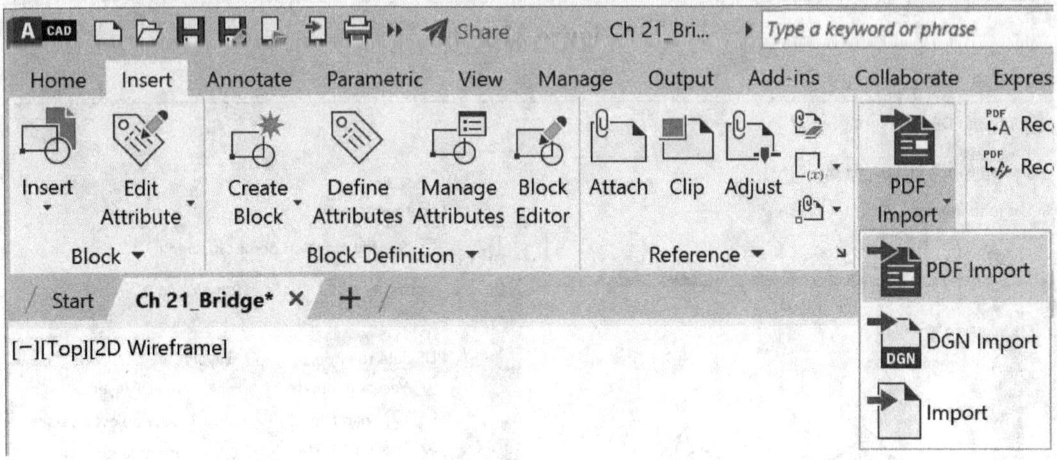

Figure 21-22a

5. Data accuracy is lost: The converted file is shown in Figure 21-22d. Most of the data is transferred correctly; however, some of the data is lost. For example, the hatch is exploded into line segments.

6. Save: Save the newly converted file.

21.8. Option Dialog Box

The properties of some of the options available from the *Plot* dialog box can be changed from the *Plot and Publish* tab of the *Options* dialog box, Figure 21-23. The user should explore the capabilities provided by this dialog box.

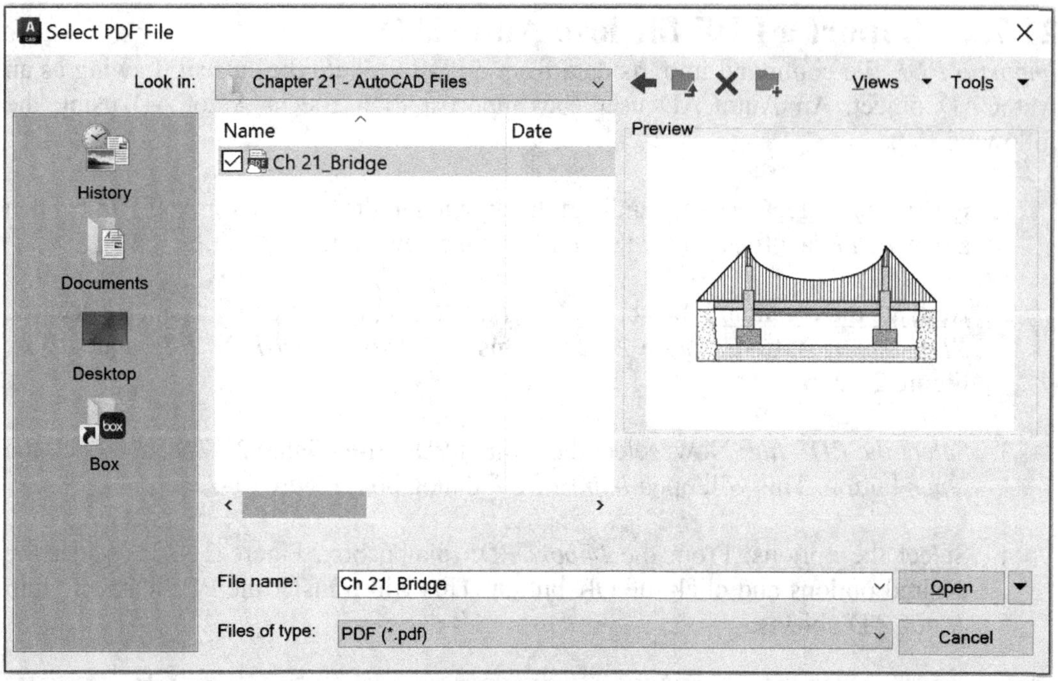

Figure 21-22b

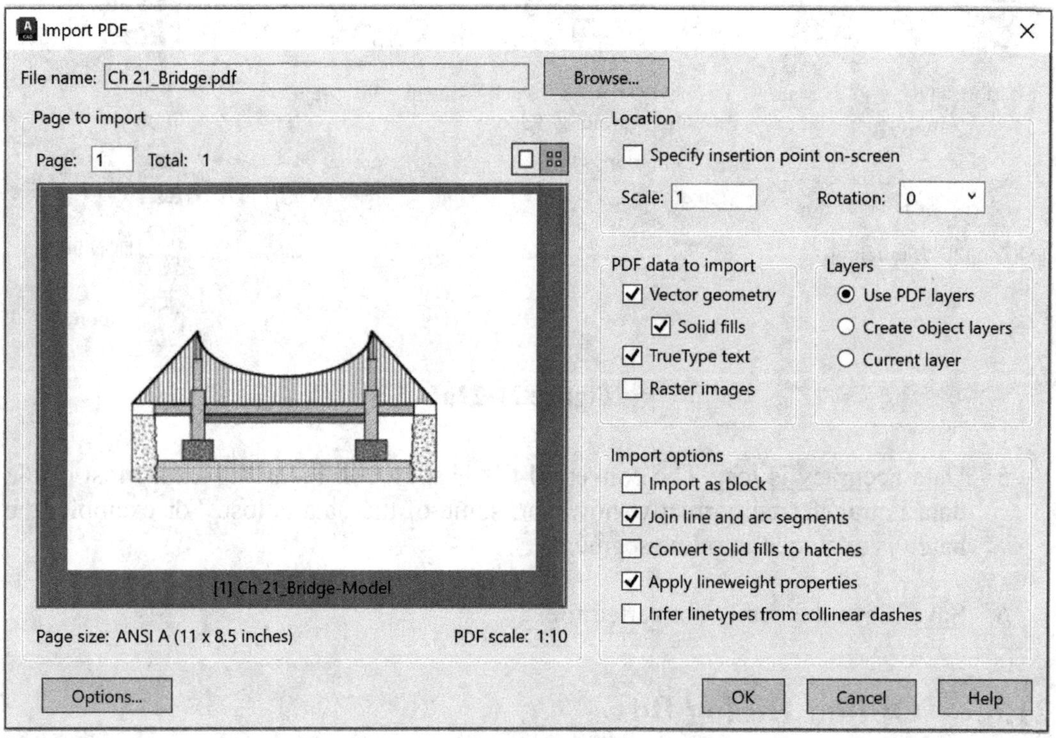

Figure 21-22c

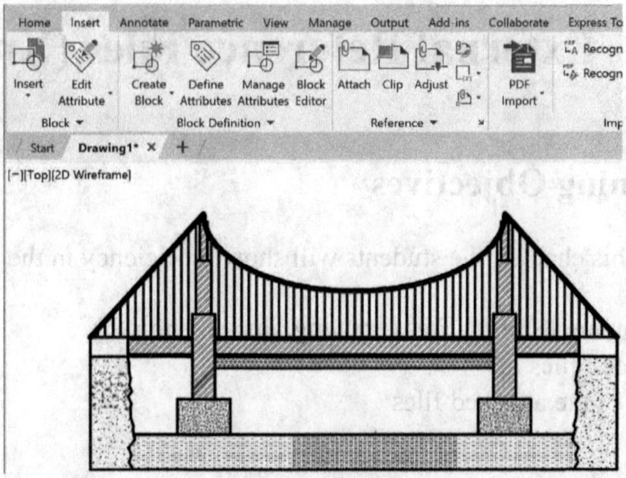

Figure 21-22d

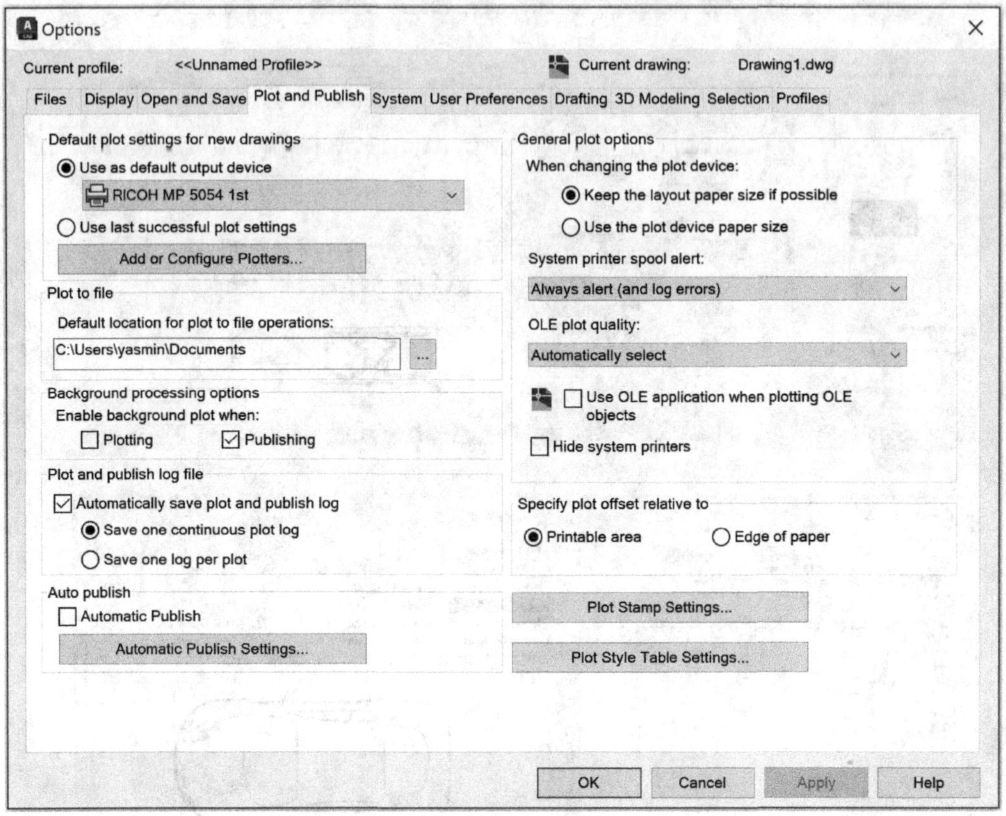

Figure 21-23

Notes:

22. External Reference Files (Xref)

22.1. Learning Objectives

After completing this chapter, the students will show proficiency in the following areas:

- Art of referencing external files (drawing, image, and pdf)
- Crop referenced files
- View details of the attached files

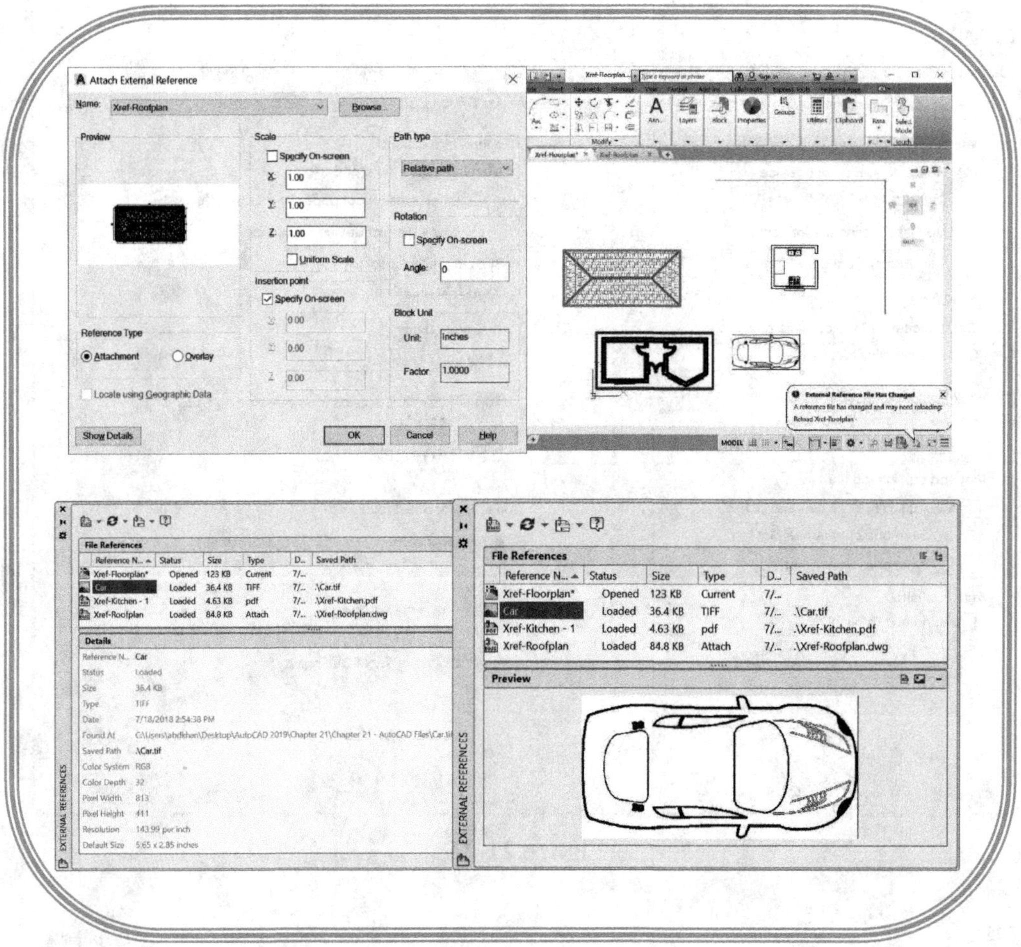

22.2. Introduction

External Reference File (commonly known as Xref) in AutoCAD is the process of referencing external files from the current (or master) file. The user can reference dwg, pdf, dgn, dwf, and image files; Figure 22-2a shows some of the file types that can be referenced.

There are several reasons to reference external files in a large project.

1. Multiple users can work on different parts of the project. For example, in the floor plan (*Chapter 17*) one user can create the kitchen and the other can create the bathrooms.
2. Any change in the referenced file will be visible in the master file.
3. The referenced file does not become part of the master file; therefore, the master file's size does not change.
4. The referenced files are loaded simultaneously when the master file is loaded.
5. The user can open the referenced file from the master file.
6. If necessary, the referenced file can be detached from the master file.

22.3. AutoCAD And Referencing An External File

Referencing an external drawing file in AutoCAD is a four steps process. (i) activate the *Attach* command, (ii) select the options from the *Attach External Reference* dialog box, (iii) insert the file, and finally (iv) reconcile the layers.

This chapter assumes the following:

1. The user has launched AutoCAD 2027.
2. Created (or downloaded and opened) the *Xref-Floorplan.dwg* file.
3. Created or downloaded *Xref-Roofplan.dwg*, *Car.tiff*, and *Xref-Kitchen.pdf*.

22.3.1. Attach command

The *Attach* command is used to reference (or attach) another file to the current file. The *Attach* command is activated using one of the following methods:

1. Panel method: Select the *Insert* tab, from the *Reference* panel, select the *Attach* option ( ), Figure 22-1.
2. Command line method: Type "xfer," "Xfer", "XFER" or "xref," "Xref" or "XREF" in the command line and press the *Enter* key.

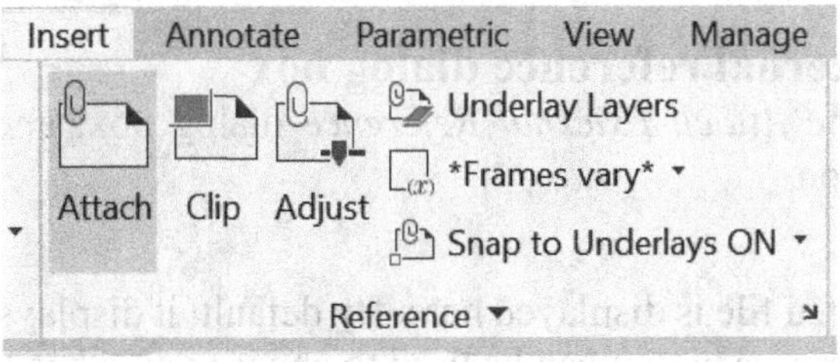

Figure 22-1a

- The activation of the command opens the *Select Reference File* dialog box, Figure 22-1b.
  - The dialog box lists all of the files in the folder. In the current example, the files are grouped based on file type.
  - If under the *View* menu, *Preview* (or *Thumbnail*) option is selected, then the bitmap of the selected file (or thumbnails) is displayed in the *Preview* window. In the current example, the preview option is the default method.
  - Navigate to the desired file and click the *Open* button. In the current example, *Xref-Roofplan.dwg* file is selected.
  - This will close *Select Reference File* dialog box and open *Attach External Reference* dialog box, Figure 22-2.

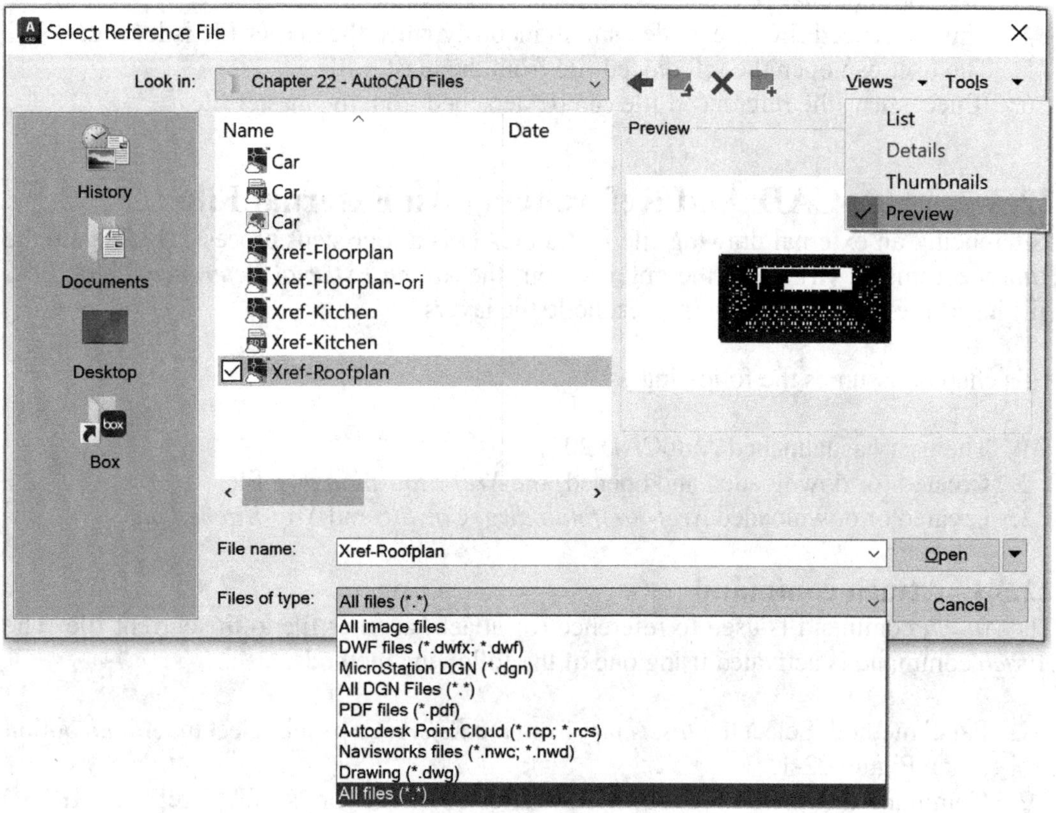

Figure 22-1b

22.3.2. Attach external reference dialog box

Figure 22-2 shows the *Attach External Reference* dialog box; and its components are discussed in this section.

22.3.2.1. Name

The name of the selected file is displayed here. By default, it displays the file just selected. The down-arrow or *Browse* button can be used to choose any other file (this will open the dialog box shown in Figure 22-1b).

22.3.2.2. Preview

The bitmap of the selected file is displayed in this window.

22.3.2.3. Reference type

A file can be referenced as an attachment or an overlay. Consider three drawing files, *B*, *C*, and *D*.

- Attachment: If file *B* is referenced as an attachment in *C* and *C* is used as an attachment in *D*; then *B* will be available in *D*. That is, nested attachment files are supported.
- Overlay: If file *B* is referenced as an overlay in *C* and *C* is used as an attachment/overlay in *D*, then *B* will NOT be available in *D*. That is, nested overlay files are not supported.

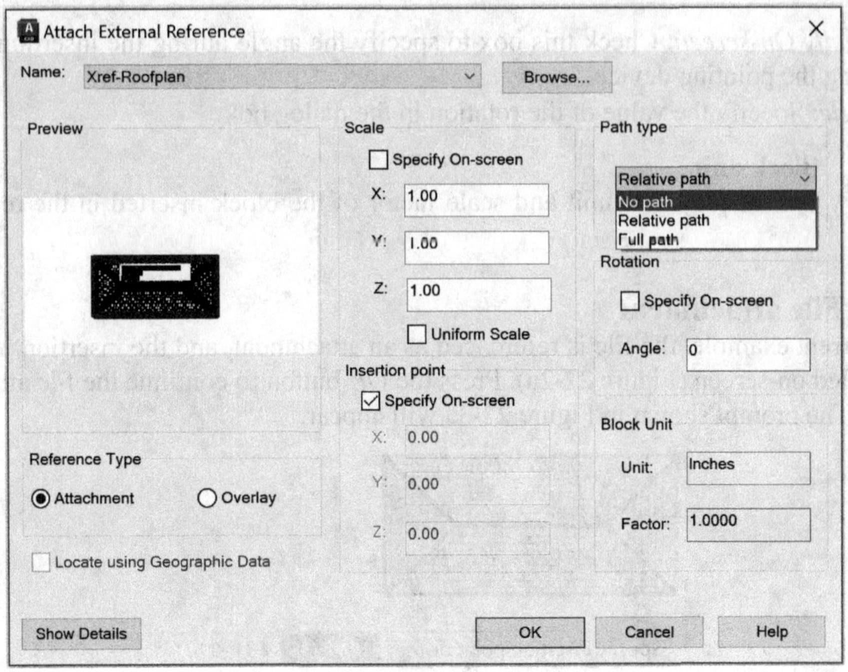

Figure 22-2

22.3.2.4. Scale

This panel is used to specify the scale for the inserted file. The negative value for the X, Y, and Z scale factors inserts a mirror image of the file.

- *Specify On-screen*: Check this box to specify scale factors during the insertion process using the pointing device.
- *X, Y, Z*: These boxes are used to set the scale factors in the respective directions. If the *Specify On-screen* option is selected, then these boxes are not available.
- *Uniform Scale*: This box is checked to specify a single scale value for the *X*, *Y*, and *Z* coordinates. In this case, the *Y* and *Z* fields are deactivated by the software and the value specified for X is displayed in the *Y* and *Z* fields, too.

22.3.2.5. Insertion point

This panel is used to specify the insertion point in the drawing for the referenced file.

- *Specify On-screen*: Check this box to choose the insertion point using the pointing device.
- *X, Y, Z*: These boxes are used to set the coordinate values. If the *Specify On-screen* option is selected, then these boxes are not available.

22.3.2.6. Path type

The *Path* option displays the location of the file Figure 22-2. If both the referenced and the master files are located in the same folder then the path is set to *No path*.

22.3.2.7. Rotation

This panel is used to specify the rotation angle for the referenced file.

- *Specify On-screen*: Check this box to specify the angle during the insertion process using the pointing device.
- *Angle*: Specify the value of the rotation in the dialog box.

22.3.2.8. Block unit

The *Block Unit* displays the unit and scale factor of the block inserted in the referenced file.

22.3.3. File attachment

In the current example, the file is referenced as an attachment, and the insertion point will be specified on-screen (Figure 22-2a). Press the *OK* button to continue the file attachment process. The prompt shown in Figure 22-3a will appear.

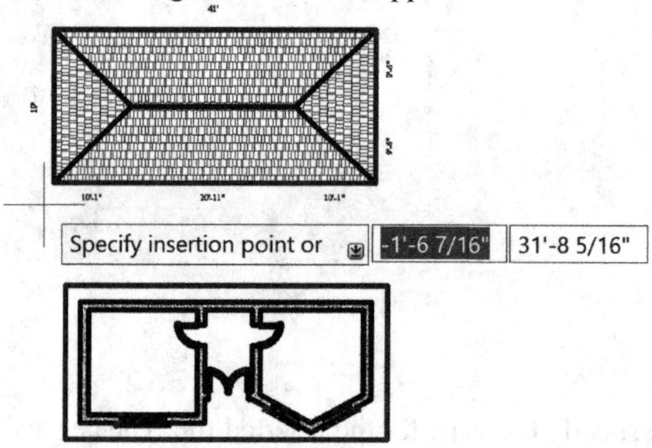

Figure 22-3a

- *Specify insertion point or*: Press the down-arrow of the keyboard to explore the various options, Figure 22-3b. Press the up-arrow of the keyboard to hide the options.
- Type 0, 0 for the insertion point, Figure 22-3c. The referenced file (roof plan) is added to the master file. The roof plan overlaps the floor plan because the origins of the two drawings will match, Figure 22-3d.

- If the referenced file contains layers, then *Unreconciled New Layers* notification will appear in the lower right corner of the interface, Figure 22-3d.

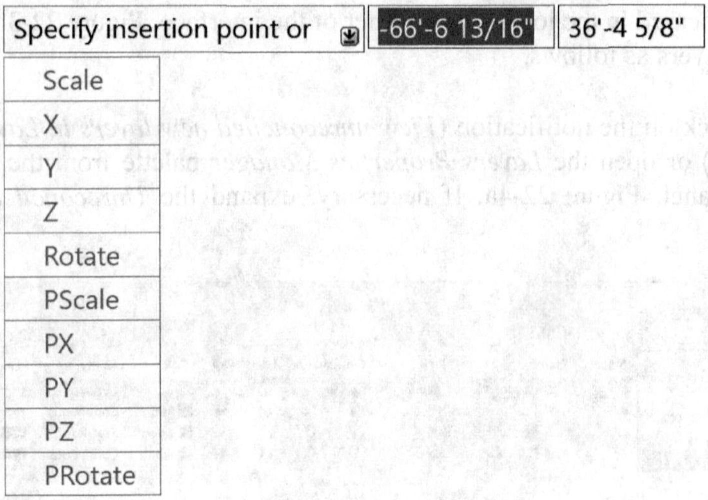

Figure 22-3b

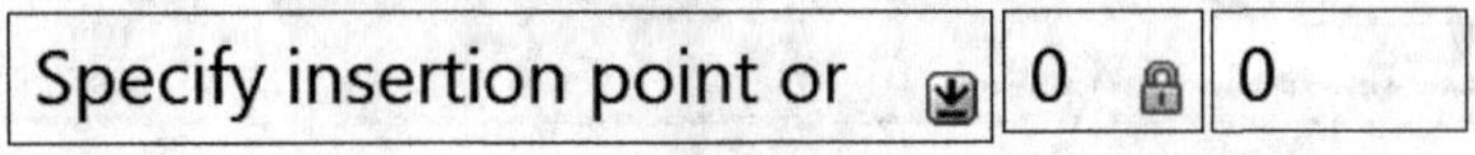

Figure 22-3c

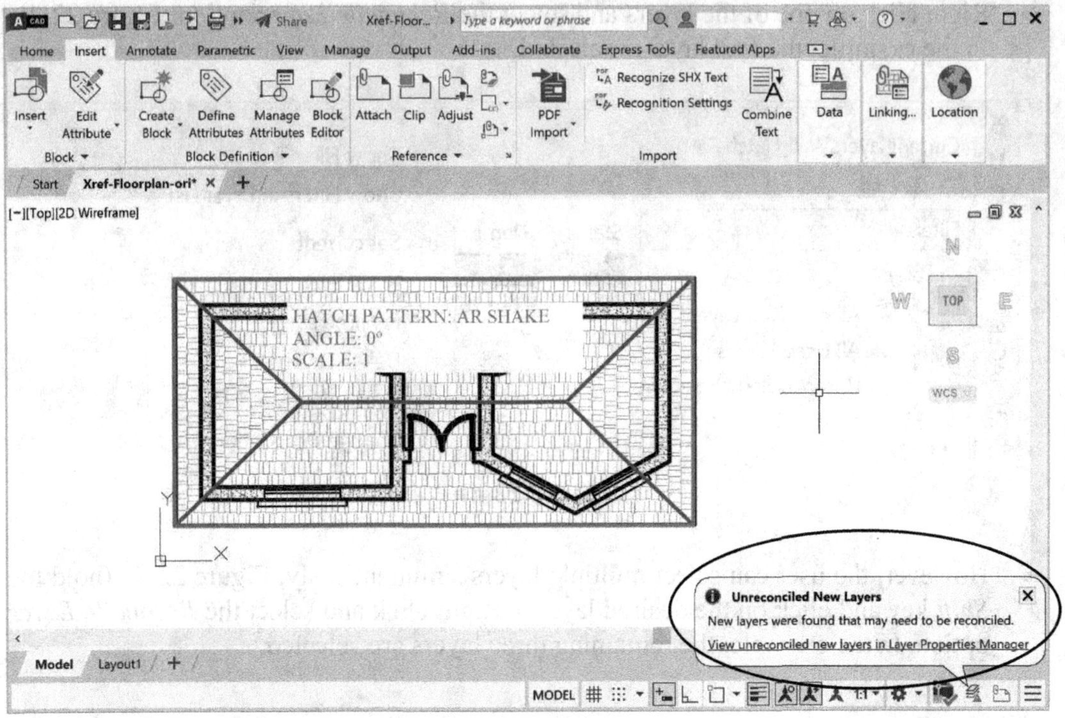

Figure 22-3d

22.3.4. Unreconciled layers

The unreconciled layers are the layers that are added to the drawing after the layer list is updated. Since the referenced drawing contains layers related to the roof plan, the notification appeared in the lower right corner of the interface, Figure 22-3d. The user can reconcile the layers as follows.

- Either click on the notification (*View unreconciled new layers in Layers Properties Manager*) or open the *Layers Properties Manager* palette from the *Home* tab and *Layers* panel, Figure 22-4a. If necessary, expand the *Unreconciled New Layers* option.

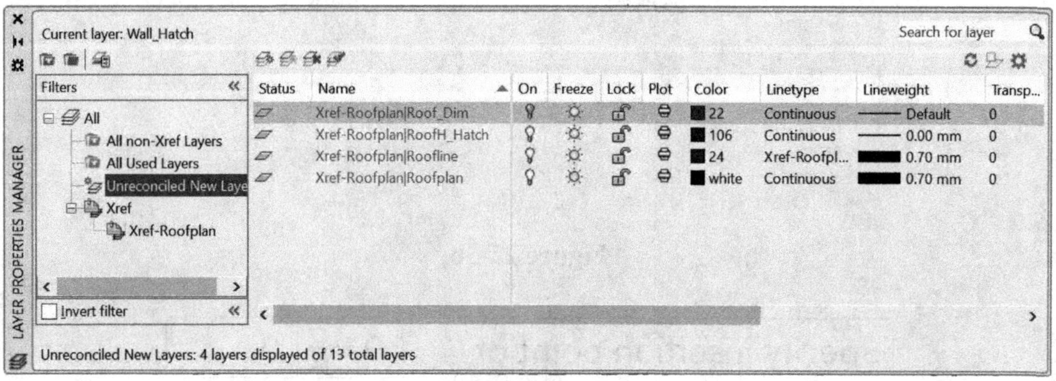

Figure 22-4a

- Right click on one of the layers and select the *Reconcile Layer* option, Figure 22-4b. In the example, the first layer is selected.

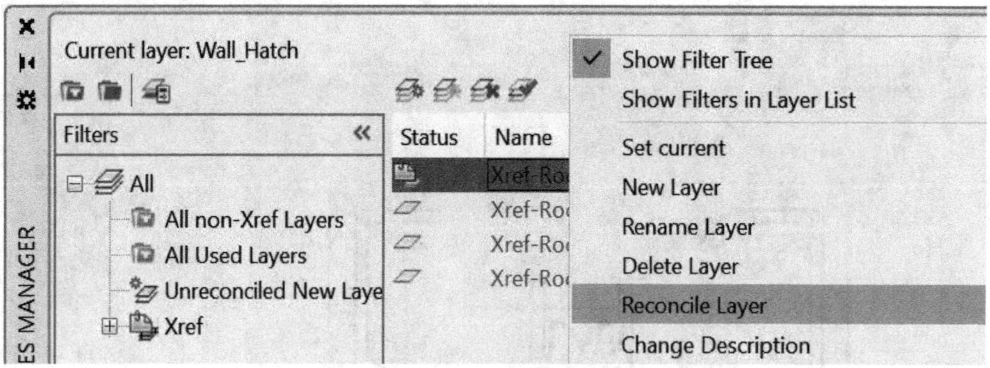

Figure 22-4b

- However, the user can select multiple layers simultaneously, Figure 22-4c (hold the *Shift* key and click on the desired layers). Right click and select the *Reconcile Layer* option. In the example, the remaining three layers are selected.

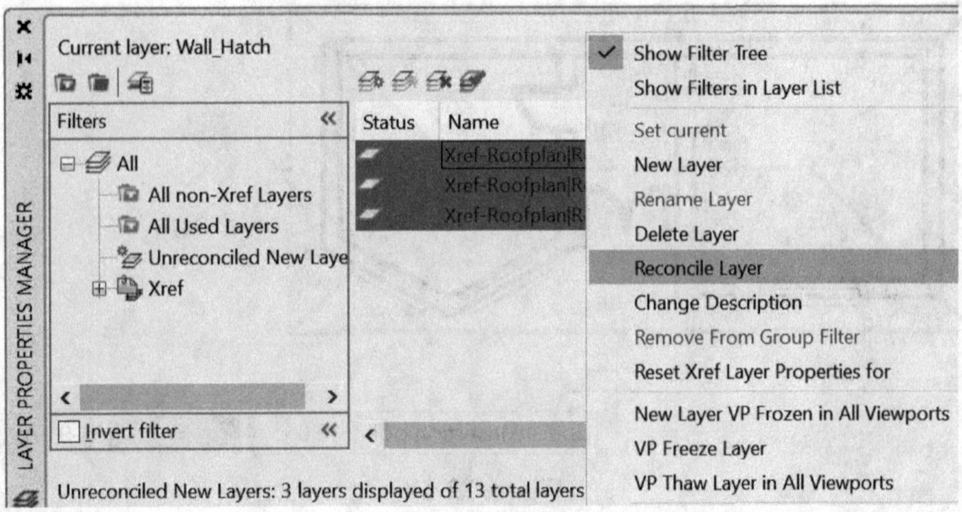

Figure 22-4c

22.4. Reference An Image File

Referencing an external image file in AutoCAD is a two steps process: (i) activate the *Attach* command, and (ii) select the options from the *Attach External Reference* dialog box.

- Activate the *Attach* command: Select the *Insert* tab and from the *Reference* panel select the *Attach* option ().
- The activation of the command opens the *Attach Image* dialog box, Figure 22-5a.
- The image is scaled up from the dialog box. However, the insertion point will be specified on the screen.
- Click at a random point (in front of the house) for the insertion point, Figure 22-5b.
- The referenced file (car) is added to the master file, Figure 22-5c.

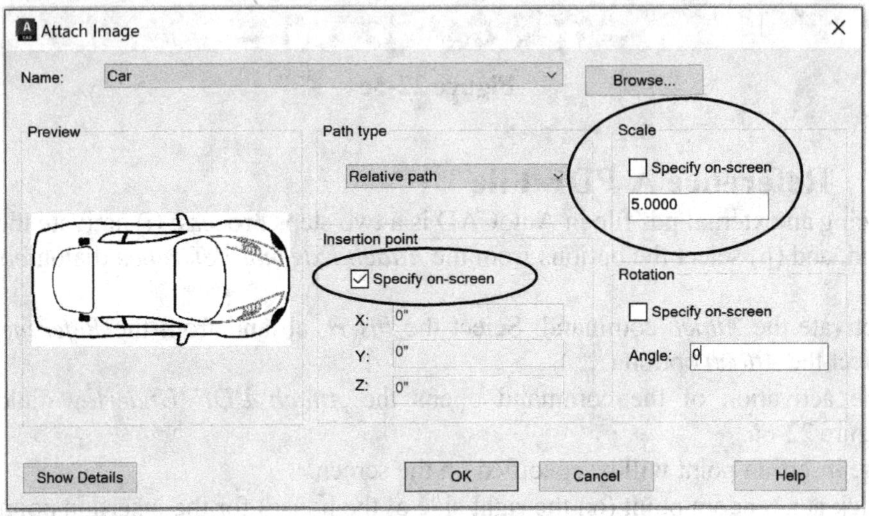

Figure 22-5a

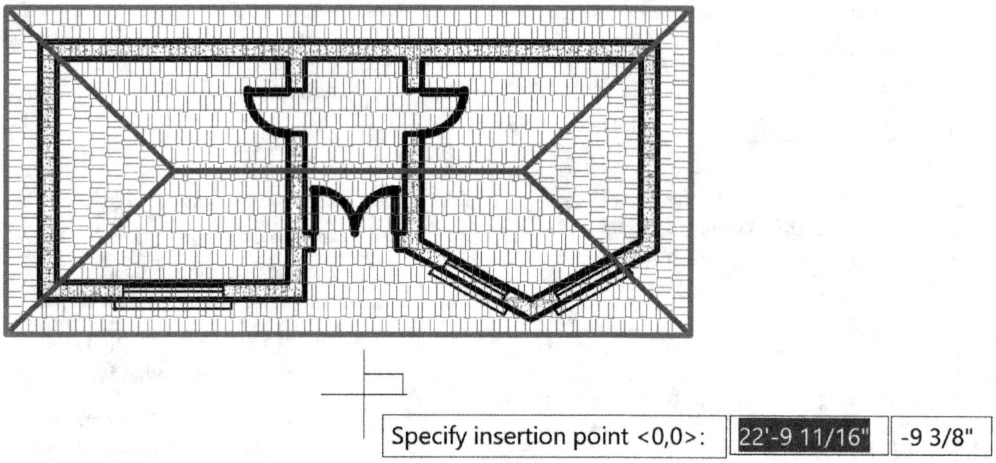

Figure 22-5b

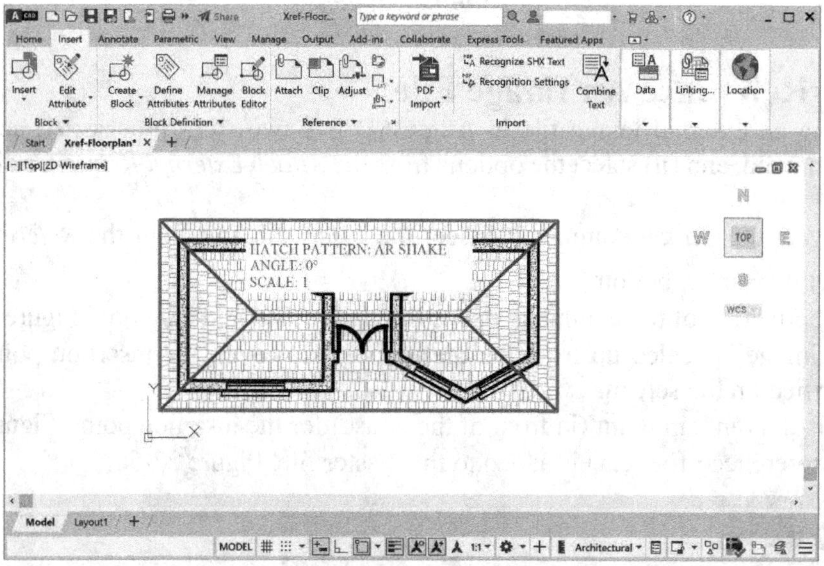

Figure 22-5c

22.5. Reference A PDF File

Referencing an external pdf file in AutoCAD is a two steps process: (i) activate the *Attach* command, and (ii) select the options from the *Attach External Reference* dialog box.

- Activate the *Attach* command: Select the *Insert* tab and from the *Reference* panel select the *Attach* option ( ).
- The activation of the command opens the *Attach PDF Underlay* dialog box, Figure 22-6a.
- The insertion point will be specified on the screen.
- Click at a random point (on the right side of the house) for the insertion point.
- The referenced file (kitchen) is added to the master file, Figure 22-6b.

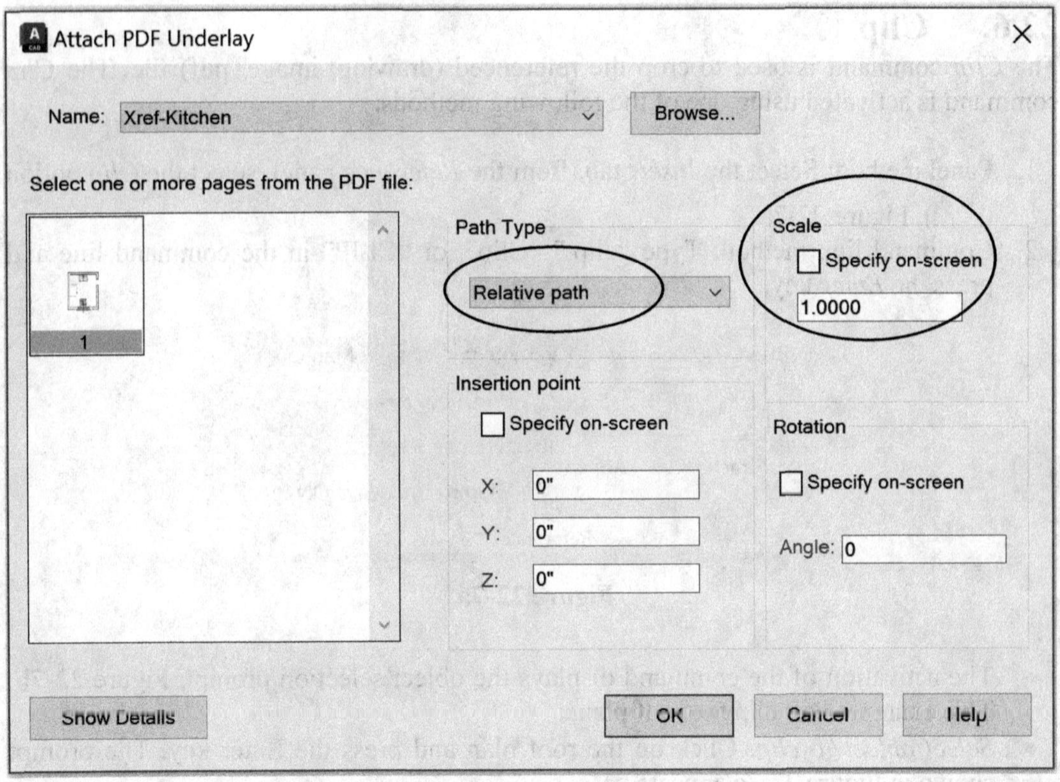

Figure 22-6a

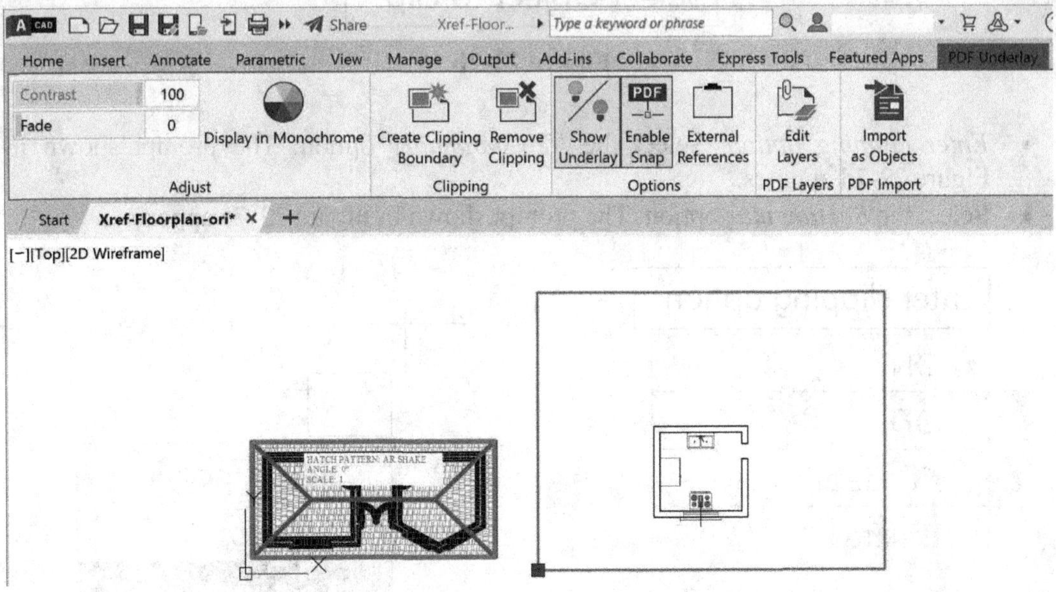

Figure 22-6b

22.6. Clip

The *Clip* command is used to crop the referenced (drawing, image, pdf) file. The *Clip* command is activated using one of the following methods:

1. Panel method: Select the *Insert* tab, from the *Reference* panel, select the *Clip* option ( ), Figure 22-7a.
2. Command line method: Type "clip," "Clip", or "CLIP" in the command line and press the *Enter* key.

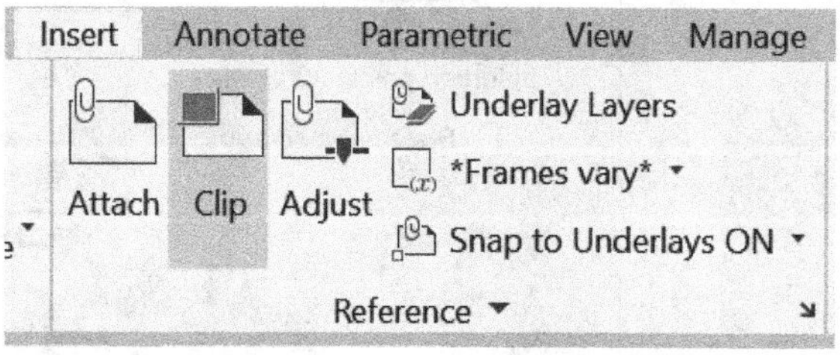

Figure 22-7a

- The activation of the command displays the object selection prompt, Figure 22-7b. This example will clip the roof plan.
- *Select object to clip*: Click on the roof plan and press the Enter key. The prompt shown in Figure 22-7c appears.

Figure 22-7b

- *Enter clipping option*: Select the *New boundary* option. The prompt shown in Figure 22-7d appears.
- Select the *Rectangular* option. The prompt shown in Figure 22-7e appears.

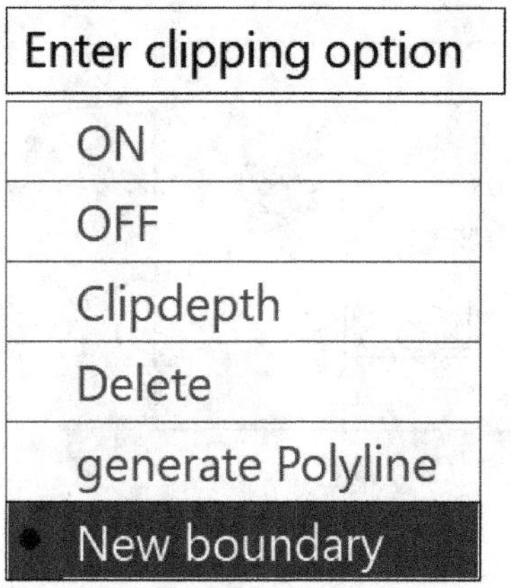

Figure 22-7c

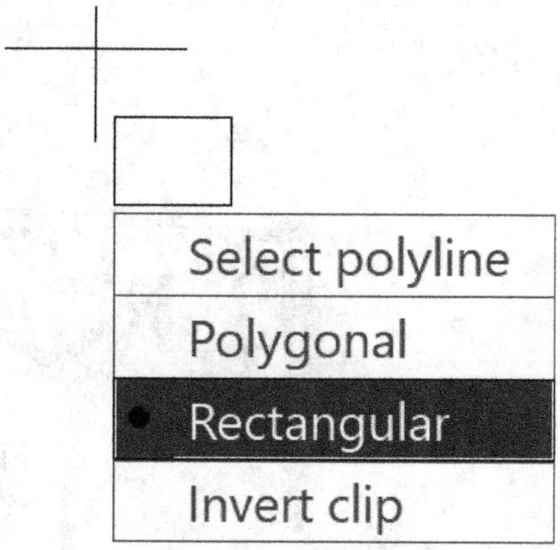

Figure 22-7d

- *Specify first corner*: Click to the left and slightly above the upper left corner of the roof plan. The prompt shown in Figure 22-7f appears.

Figure 22-7e

- *Specify opposite corner*: Click as shown in Figure 22-7f.

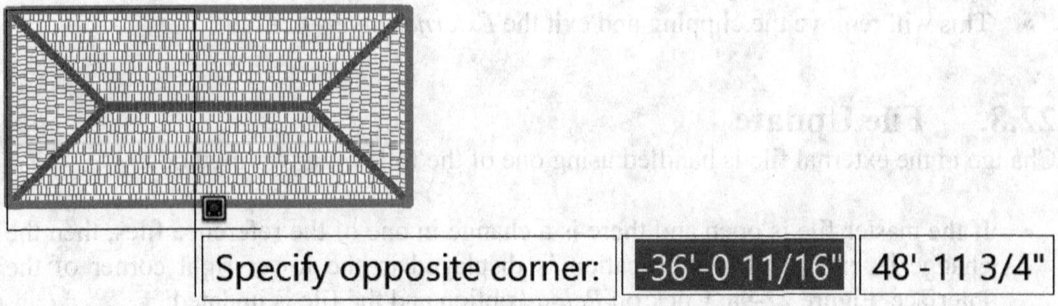

Figure 22-7f

- Figure 22-7g shows the clipped roof plan. The roof plan was moved using *Move* command before executing the *Clip* command.
- Clipping of an image and pdf files are left to the readers.

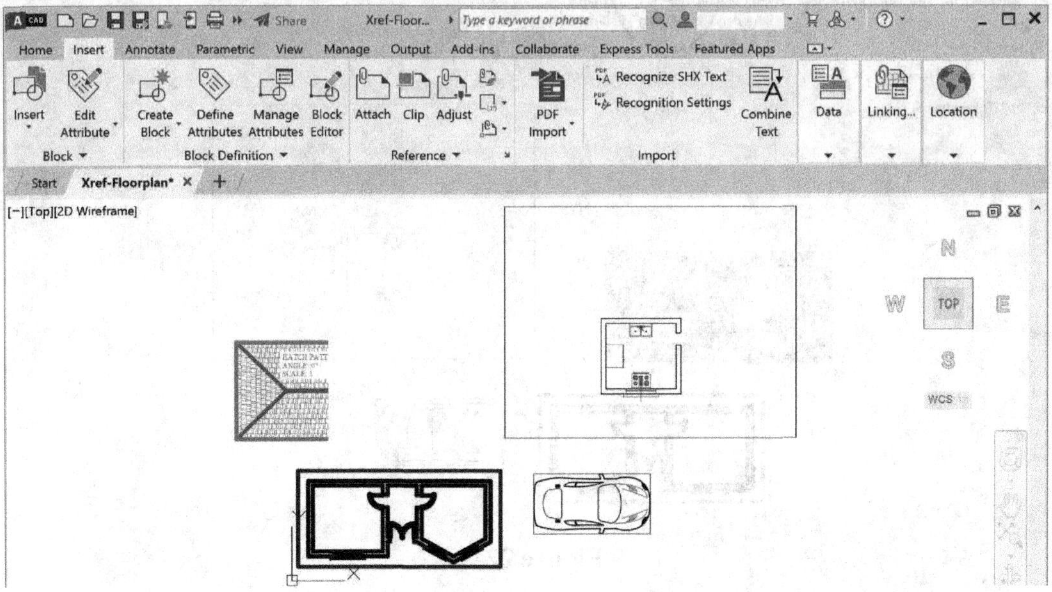

Figure 22-7g

22.7. Remove Clip 

The *Remove Clip* command is used to remove the crop from the referenced (drawing, image, pdf) file. The *Remove Clip* command is activated as follows.

- Click on the cropped object. In the example (Figure 22-7g), the cropped roof plan is selected.
- This will display the *External Reference* tab.
- From the *External Reference* tab and *Clipping* panel, select the *Remove Clip* () option.
- This will remove the clipping and exit the *External Reference* tab.

22.8. File Update

Change in the external file is handled using one of the following two methods.

- If the master file is open and there is a change in one of the reference files, then the change in external file notification is displayed in the lower right corner of the interface, Figure 22-9a. Click on *Reload* option and the file is updated.
- If the master file is opened after the change in the reference file, then the most updated reference file is loaded.

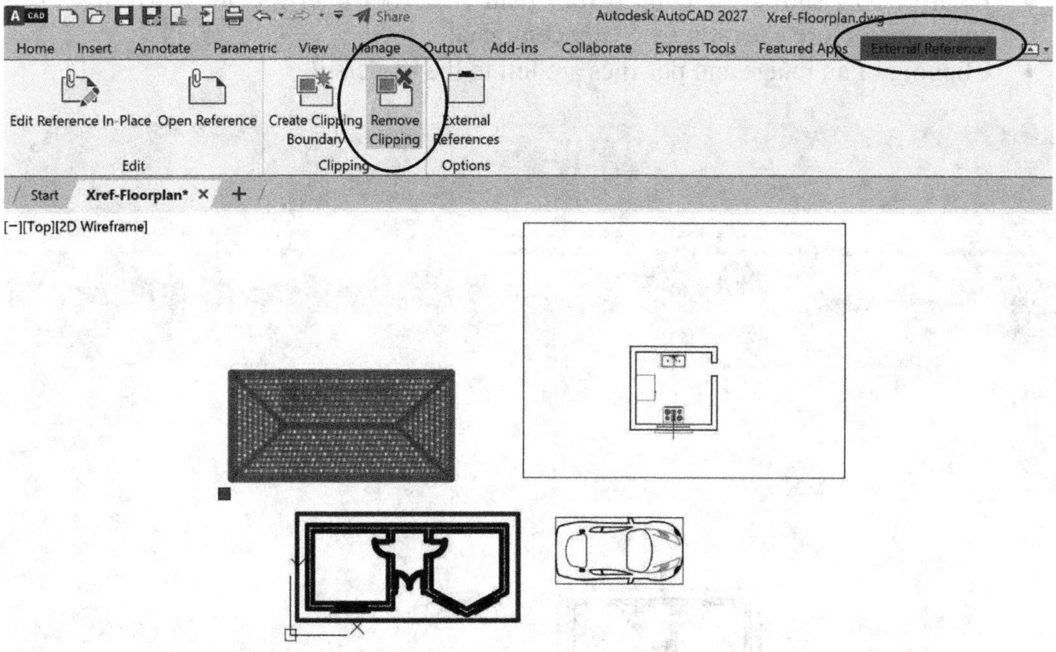

Figure 22-8

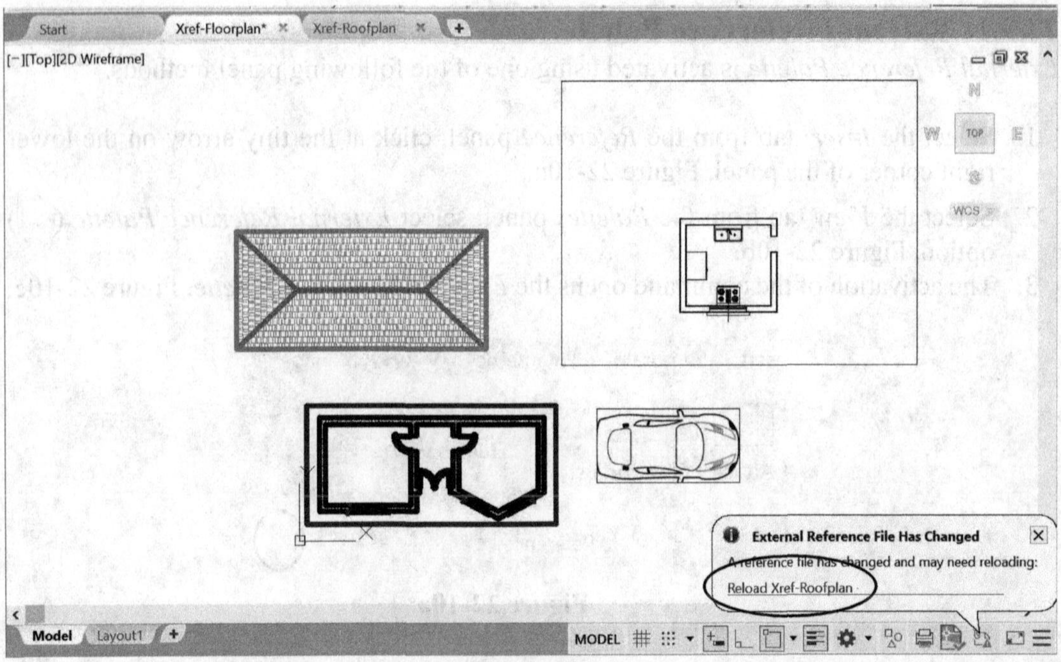

Figure 22-9a

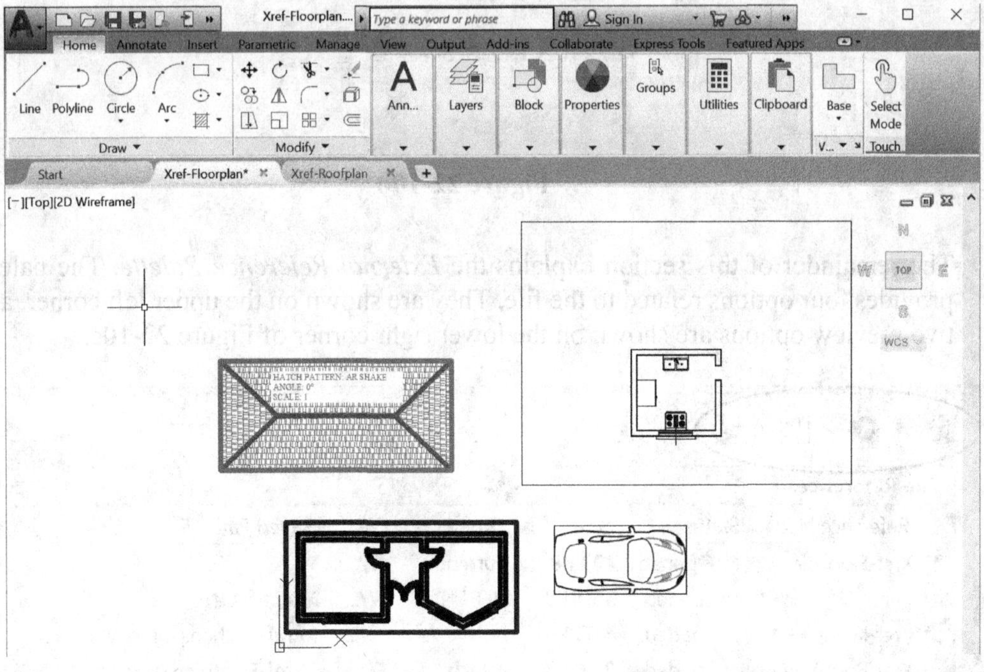

Figure 22-9b

22.9. View Reference Files

The user can list the referenced files using *External Reference Palette*, Figure 22-10a.

22.9.1. External Reference Palette

External Reference Palette is activated using one of the following panel methods.

1. Select the *Insert* tab from the *Reference* panel, click at the tiny arrow on the lower right corner of the panel, Figure 22-10a.
2. Select the *View* tab from the *Palettes* panel, select *External Reference Palette* ( ) option, Figure 22-10b.
3. The activation of the command opens the *External Reference Palette*, Figure 22-10c.

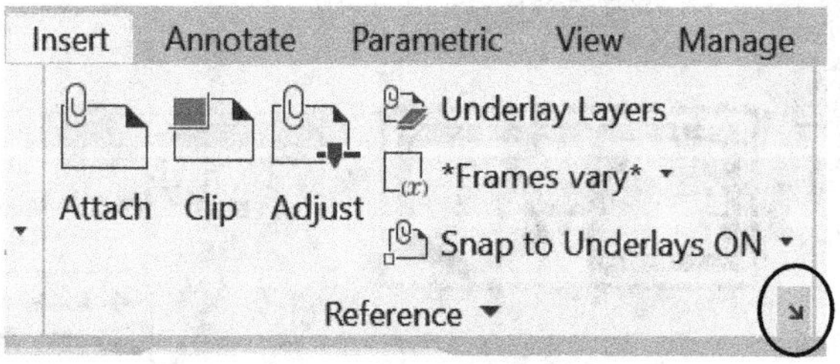

Figure 22-10a

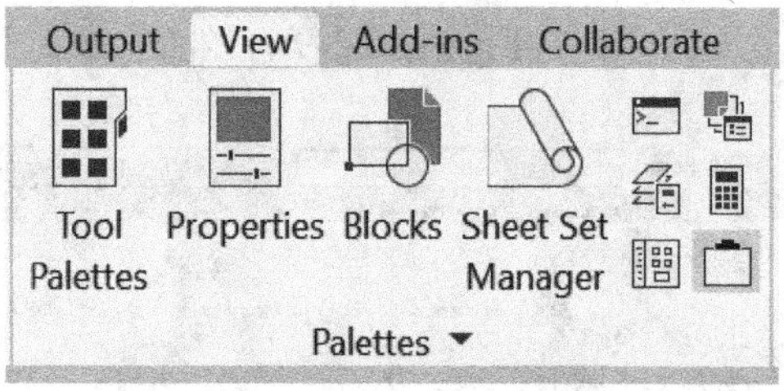

Figure 22-10b

- The remainder of this section explains the *External Reference Palette*. The palette provides four options related to the file. They are shown on the upper left corner, and two preview options are shown on the lower right corner of Figure 22-10c.

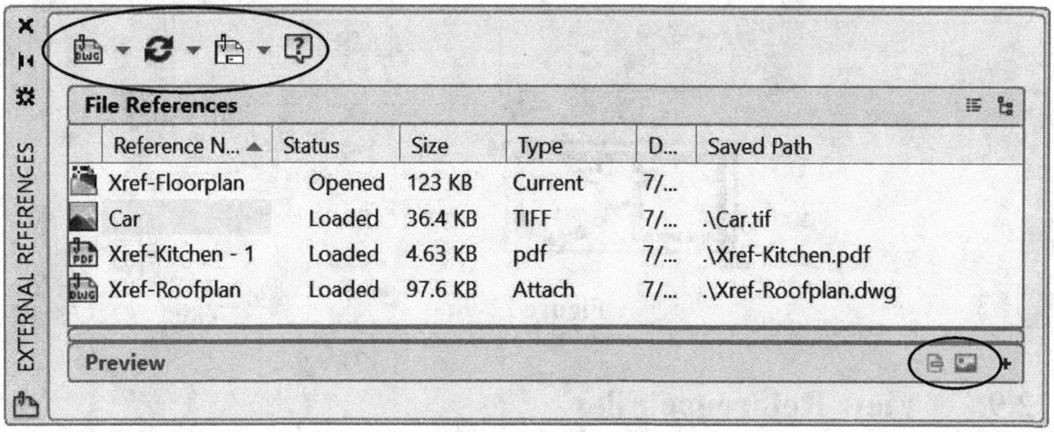

Figure 22-10c

22.9.1.1. Attach

The (*Attach*) option shows the file types that can be attached. Click the down-arrow on the left to display the various options, Figure 22-11a.

22.9.1.2. Refresh

The (*Refresh*) option is used to refresh the files. Click the down-arrow on the left to display the various options, Figure 22-11b.

22.9.1.3. Change path

The (*Change path*) option is used to change the path of the referenced files. Click the down-arrow on the left to display the various options, Figure 22-11c. The file path can be changed as follows: (i) Select the file. (ii) Click the down-arrow and select the desired option. (iii) Follow the prompts.

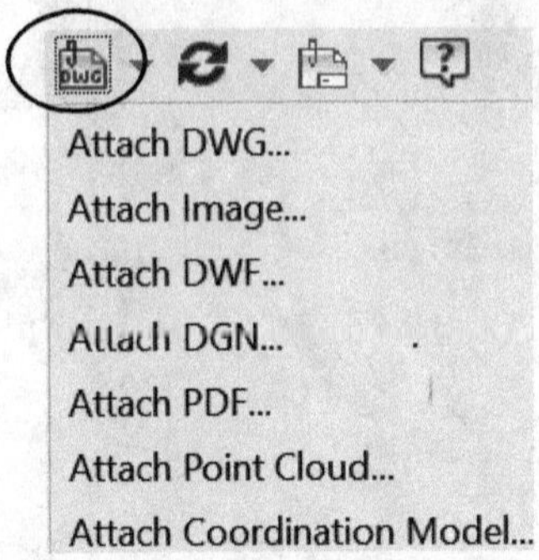

Figure 22-11a

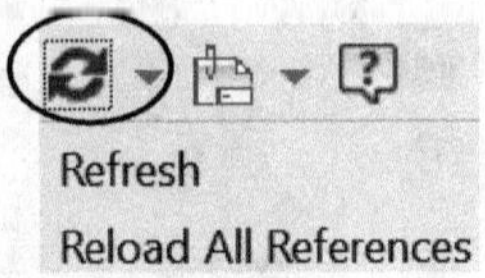

Figure 22-11b

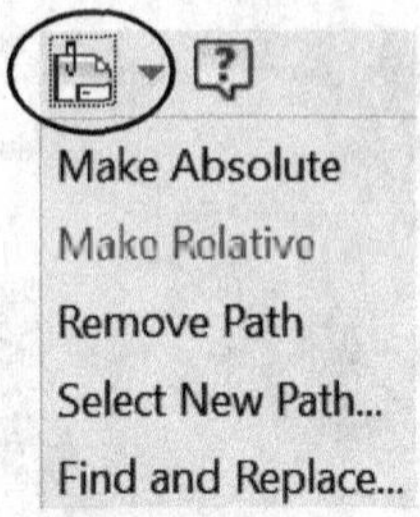

Figure 22-11c

22.9.1.4. Help

The (*Help*) option is used to launch AutoCAD help.

22.9.1.5. Details

The (*Detail*) option is used to display the details of the selected file. Figure 22-12a shows the details of the *Car.tiff*. The details can be displayed as follows: (i) Select the file. (ii) Click the details button.

22.9.1.6. Preview

The (*Preview*) option is used to display the bitmap of the selected file. Figure 22-12b shows the preview of the *Car.tiff*. The preview can be displayed as follows: (i) Select the file. (ii) Click the preview button.

22.10. Open A Referenced File

A user can open the referenced files from the *External Reference Palette* as follows, Figure 22-13: (i) Select the file. (ii) Right click. (iii) Select the *Open* option.

22.11. Detach A Referenced File

A user can detach a referenced file from the *External Reference Palette* as follows, Figure 22-14: (i) Select the file. (ii) Right click. (iii) Select the *Detach* option.

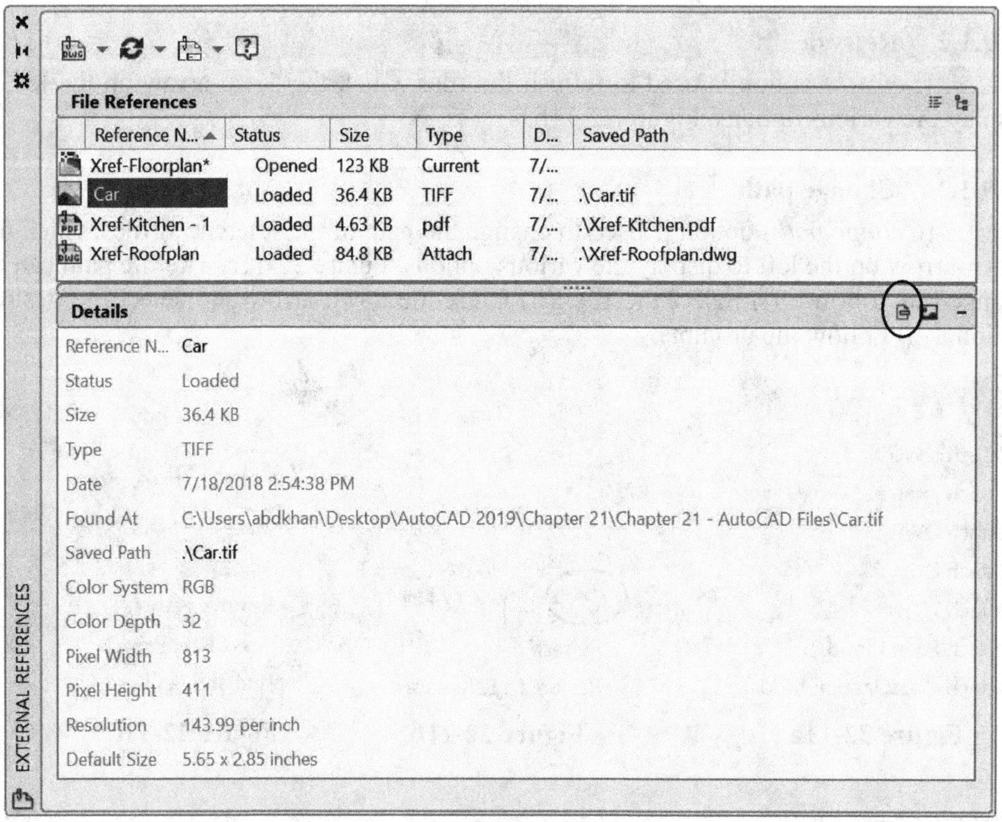

Figure 22-12a

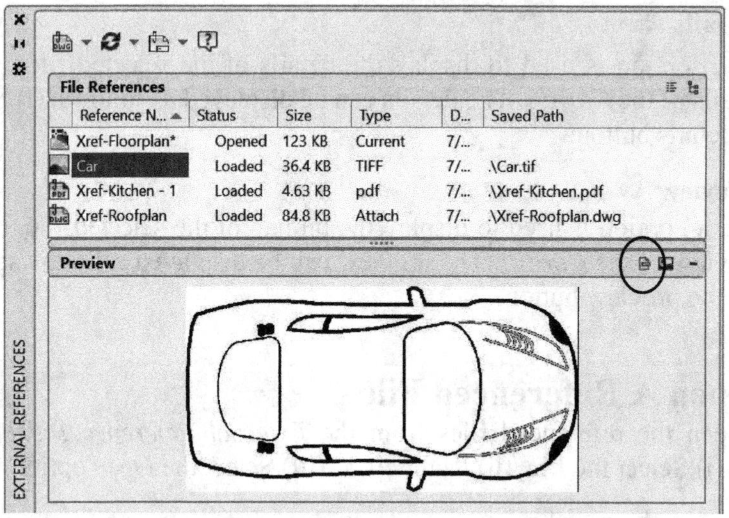

Figure 22-12b

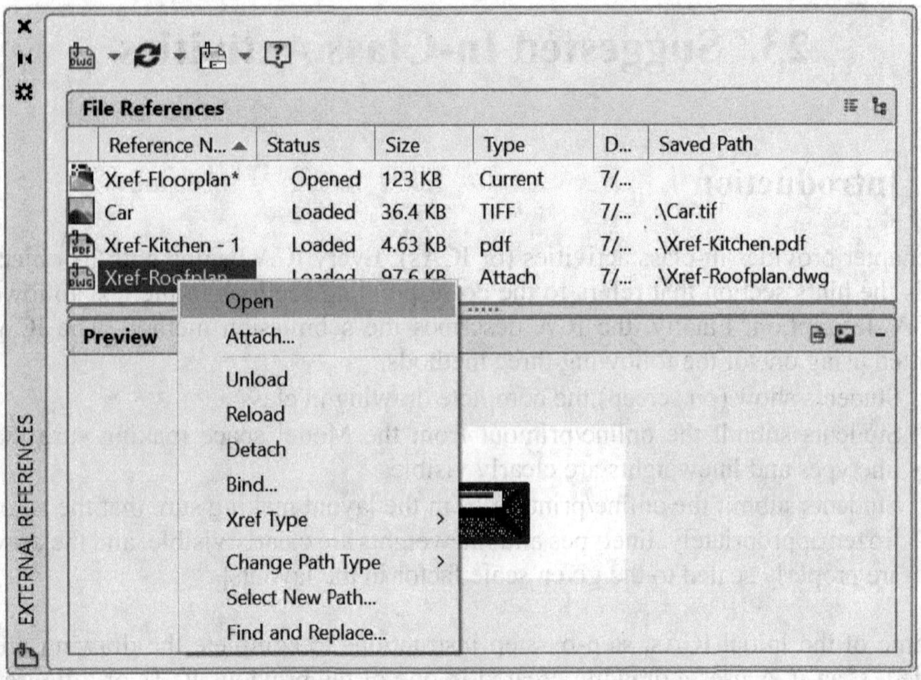

Figure 22-13

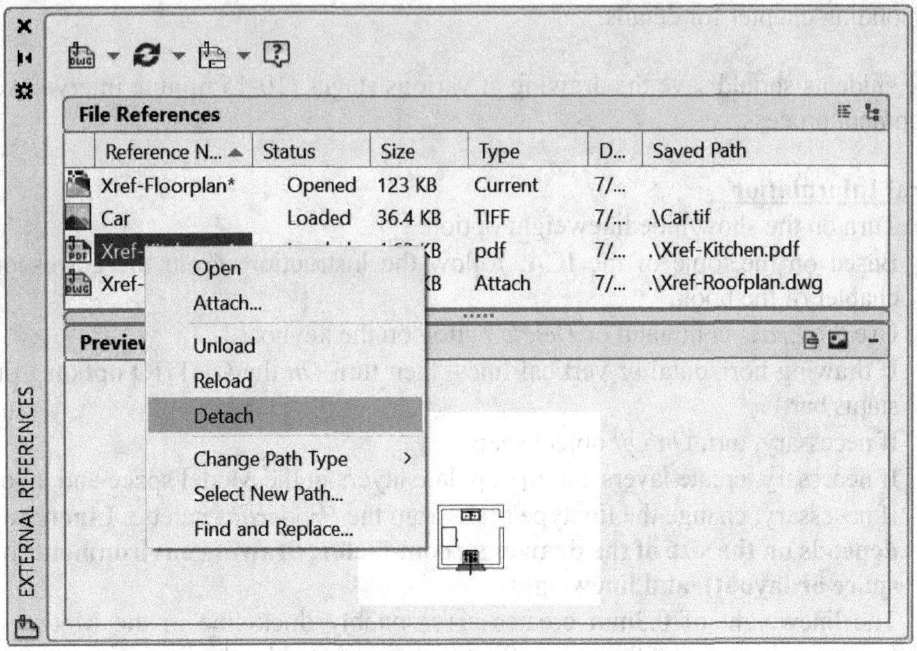

Figure 22-14

<u>Notes:</u>

23. Suggested In-Class Activities

23.1. Introduction

This chapter provides in-class activities (or ICAs). Every ICA begins with its objectives. Next is the hints section that refers to the corresponding sections in the text followed by the ICA description. Finally, the ICA describes the submission method. The ICAs are submitted using one of the following three methods.

- Students show (on screen) the complete drawing in class.
- Students submit the online/printout from the Model space making sure that the linetypes and lineweights are clearly visible.
- Students submit the online/printout from the layout making sure that the layers are frozen appropriately, linetypes and lineweights are clearly visible, and the drawings are properly scaled to the given scale factor in the layouts.

For some of the initial ICAs, step-by-step instructions to complete the drawing are also provided. If an ICA uses a drawing created in one of the previous ICAs or a figure from the text, then a thumbnail (a small size image where dimensions and text may not be clearly visible) is shown at the end of the ICA in question. Therefore, students should check the corresponding chapter for details.

** The students should save the drawing at various stages (10-15 minute intervals) of the development process.

<u>**General Information**</u>

- Turn on the show/hide lineweight option.
- Based on the topic of the ICA, follow the instructions from the corresponding chapter of the book.
- Use the *Erase* command or *Delete* button on the keyboard.
- If drawing horizontal or vertical lines, then turn *On* the ORTHO option from the status bar.
- If necessary, turn *On*/*Off* object snap.
- If necessary, create layers and manipulate layers in the Model space and layouts.
- If necessary, change the linetype scale from the *Properties* palette. **Linetype scale depends on the size of the drawing, zoom factor, drawing environment (Model space or layout), and lineweight.**
- The lineweight of 0.3mm creates a reasonably thick line in the Model space. However, in a layout, the same effect may be created by the lineweight of 0.5mm.

23.2. Download AutoCAD 2027

Objectives

- Learn to download AutoCAD 2027
- Get familiar with AutoCAD 2027
- General information about ICAs

Hints

- Refer to *Chapter 2* for help

ICA Description

1. Download AutoCAD 2027.
2. Start AutoCAD 2027.
3. If you have provided the license numbers correctly, you should be able to perform step 2; otherwise, take the necessary steps to fix the problem.

ICA Submission

1. Launch AutoCAD 2027 in class.
2. Show the default workspace in class to the instructor or TA.

23.3. Customize a Workspace

Objectives

- Learn to customize and save a workspace.

Hints

- Refer to *Chapter 2* for help (*2.14: Ribbon* and *2.15: Workspace*).

ICA Description

1. AutoCAD ribbon and workspace:
    a. Create a tab called MyTab.
    b. Create a panel called MyPanel.
    c. Add the command shown in Figure 23-3.
    d. Save the workspace.

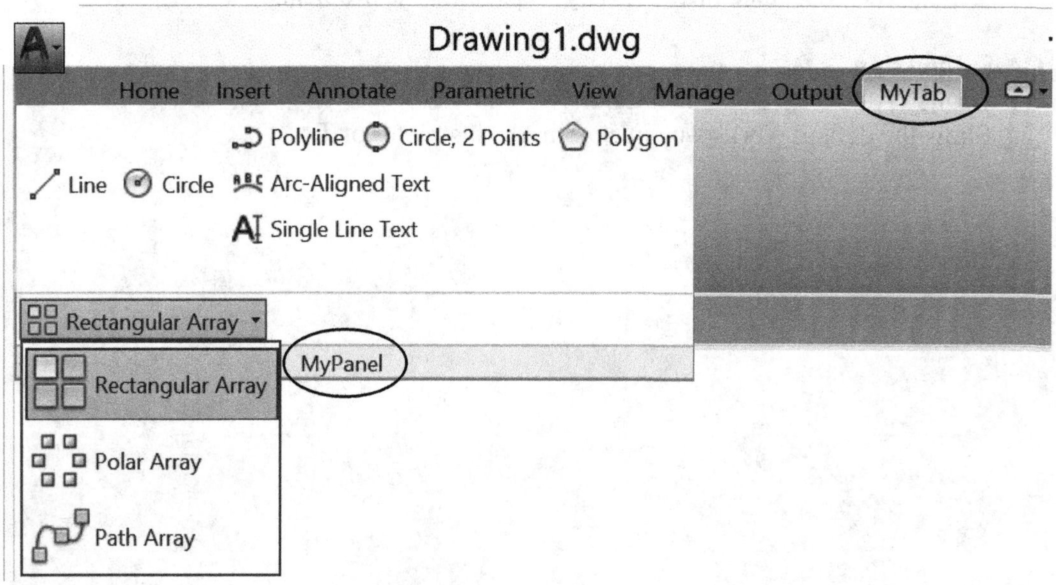

Figure 23-3

ICA Submission

1. Follow the instructor's instructions to submit the ICA.

23.4. Line, Erase, Grid, Snap Commands

Objectives

- Learn how to set and use grid and snap capabilities.
- Learn how to draw lines using grid and snap capabilities.

Hints

- Refer to *Chapter 2* for help (Sections: 2.17, 2.20, 2.21, 3.6.2, 4.13).

ICA Description

1. Drawing units: Millimeters
2. Open *acadiso.dwt* file.
3. Create a grid.
   a. Input format: Decimal units
   b. Drawing limits: 550, 400
   c. Grid: 10
   d. Snap: 5
4. Use the grid created in Step 3 to draw the line diagram of the shapes shown in Figure 23-4.
5. Do not change the thickness of the lines.
6. Save the drawing.

ICA Submission

1. Follow the instructor's instructions to submit the ICA.

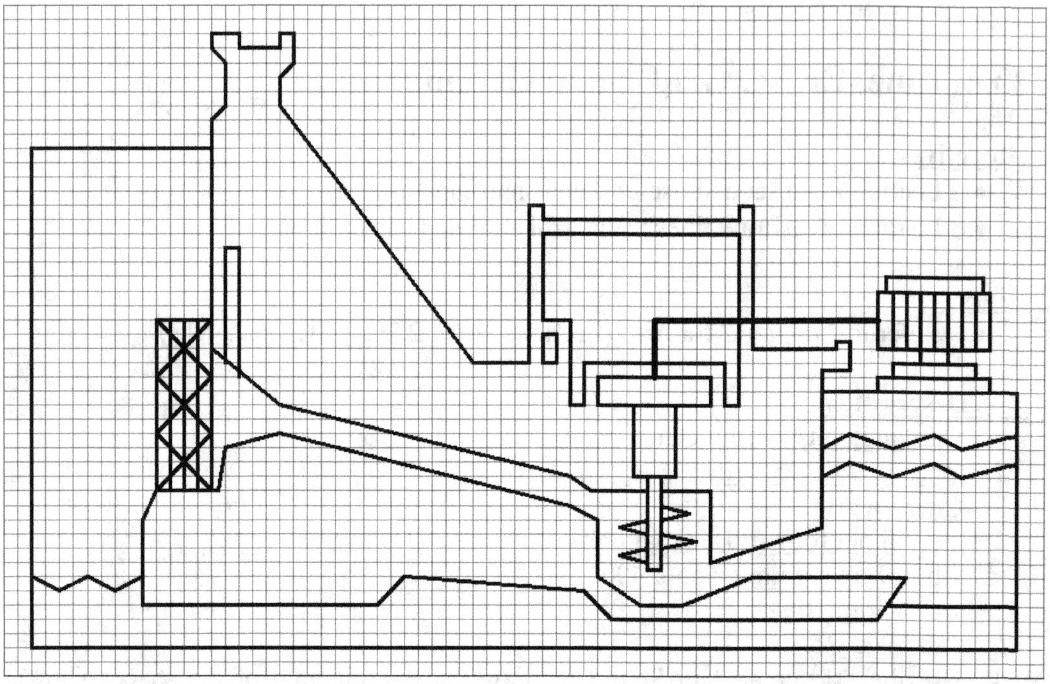

Figure 23-4a

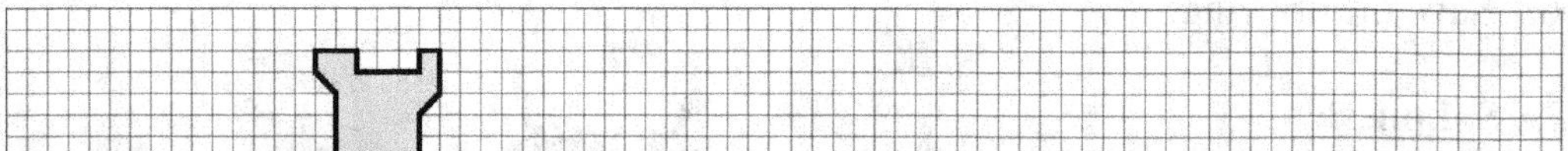

Figure 23-4b

23.5. Line (ORTHO), Polyline, Erase, Offset, and Join

Objectives

- Learn to use Draw commands: *Line* and *Polyline* commands.
- Learn to use Modify commands: *Join*, *Erase*, *Offset*, and ORTHO commands.

Hints

- Refer to *Chapters 3* and *4* for help (Sections: 3.6.5, 3.7, 4.13, 4.21, 4.29).

ICA Description

1. Drawing units: Inches
2. Create and save the drawing shown in Figure 23-5 using *ORTHO*, *Line*, *Polyline*, and *Offset* commands and polar coordinates.
   a. Create the outermost boundary line using *Polyline* command.
   b. Create the first set of inner lines using *Offset* command with the offset distance of 12 inches.
   c. Repeat the *Offset* command to create the remaining set of inner lines. Refer to the figure for the offset distances.
3. Do not add dimensions.
4. Save the drawing.

ICA Submission

1. Follow the instructor's instructions to submit the ICA.

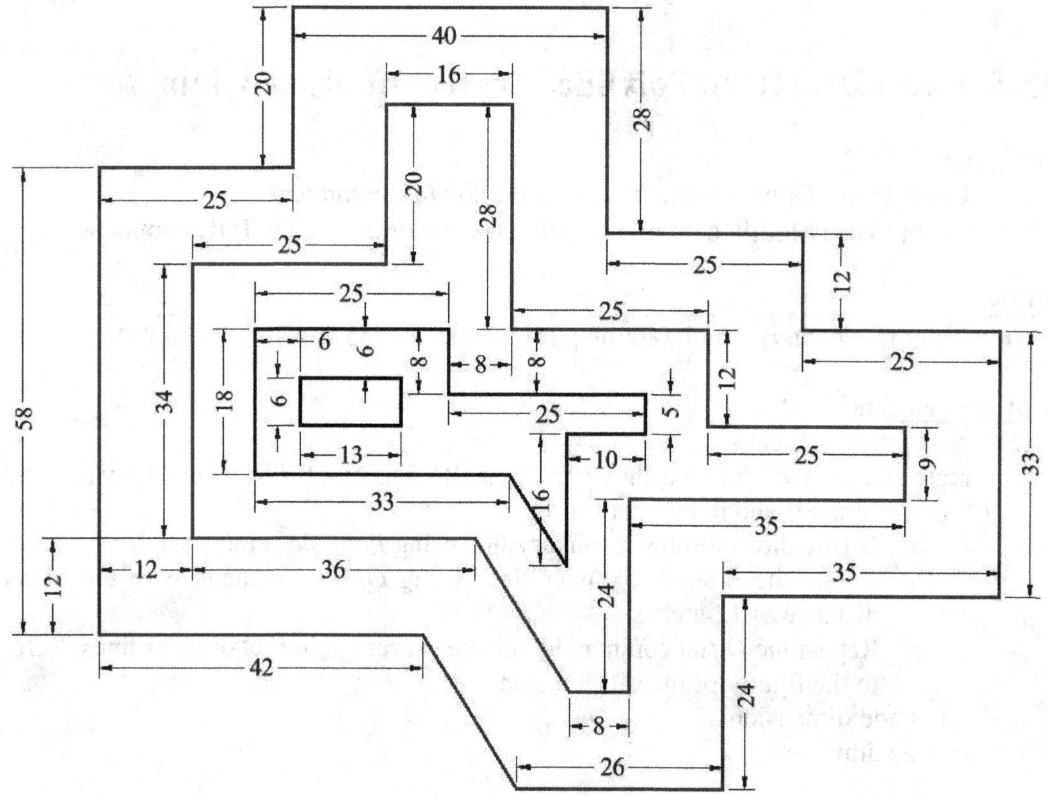
40
16
20
28
20
28
25
25
25
25
25
12
6
6
8
8
8
58
34
18
6
25
5
12
13
10
25
9
33
33
16
35
12
36
35
24
42
24
8
26

Figure 23-5

23.6. Point, Circle, Polygon, Move, Trim, Extend, and Zoom

Objectives

- Learn to use Draw commands: *Point*, *Circle* and *Polygon* commands.
- Learn to use Modify commands: *Move*, *Trim*, *Extend*, *Zoom* commands.

Hints

- Refer to *Chapter 3* and *4* for help (Sections: 3.8, 3.10, 3.14, 4.22, 4.32, 4.33, and 4.6).

ICA Description - Part 1

1. Create the light bulb arrangement shown in Figure 23-6a using *Line* and *Point* commands.
2. Open the drawing created in ICA 5 and save it as ICA 6-a.
3. Add the points (Point size = 4) and *Set size in absolute units*.
4. Save the drawing.
5. Do not add dimension.

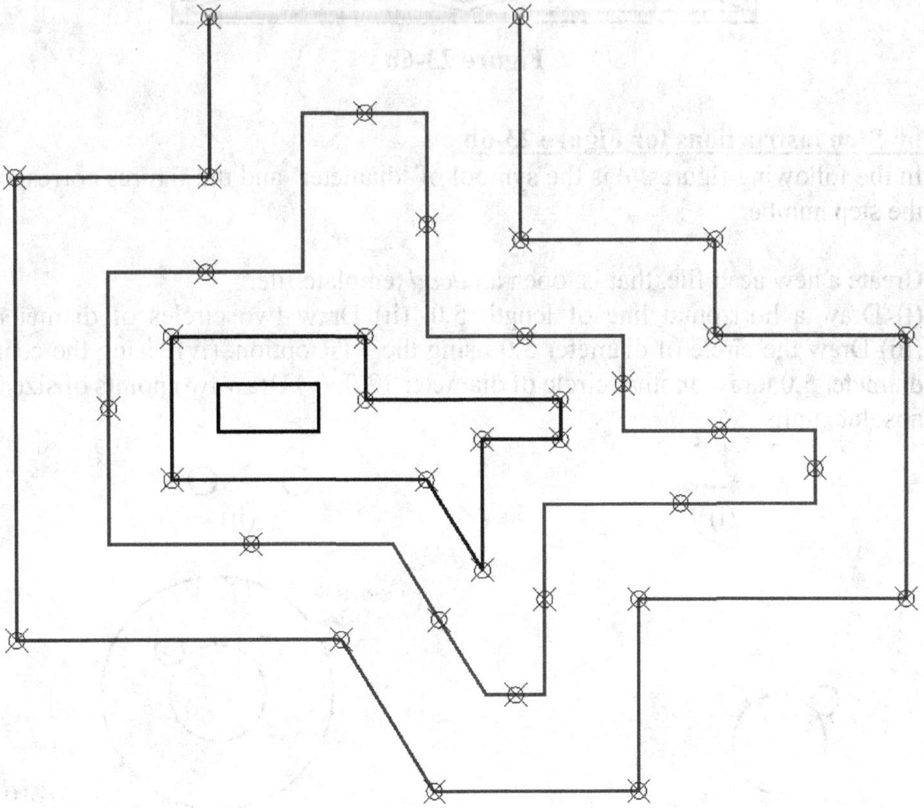

Figure 23-6a

ICA Description - Part 2

1. Drawing units: Inches
2. Create and save the drawing shown in Figure 23-6b using *Line*, *Polyline*, *Polygon*, *Circle*, *Offset*, and *Trim* commands.
3. Save the drawing.
4. Do not add dimension.
5. Follow the step-by-step instructions.

Figure 23-6b

Step-by-Step instructions for Figure 23-6b

1. In the following figures, ϕ is the symbol of 'diameter' and the figures correspond to the step number.

2. Create a new acad file, that is, open an *acad* template file.
3. (i) Draw a horizontal line of length 5.0. (ii) Draw two circles of diameter 1.5. (iii) Draw the circle of diameter 5.0 using the TTR option. (iv) Using the center of diameter 5.0, draw another circle of diameter 12.0. (v) Draw two points of size 0.5 in absolute units.

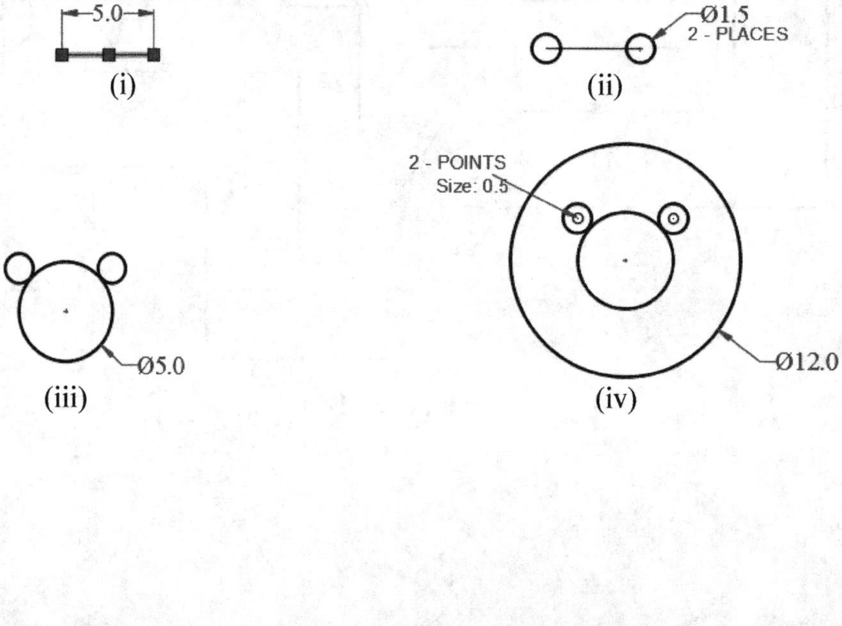

(i) (ii) (iii) (iv)

4. (i) Draw two circles of diameter 6.9 and 3.7 with center at the lower quadrant of circle $\phi 5.0$. The new circle in the figures is selected to display the grip points. These grip points help in locating the center of a circle. (ii) Draw two more circles of $\phi 6.9$.

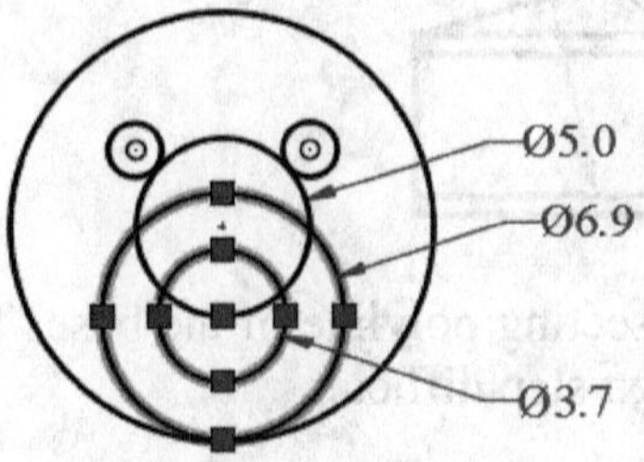

(i)

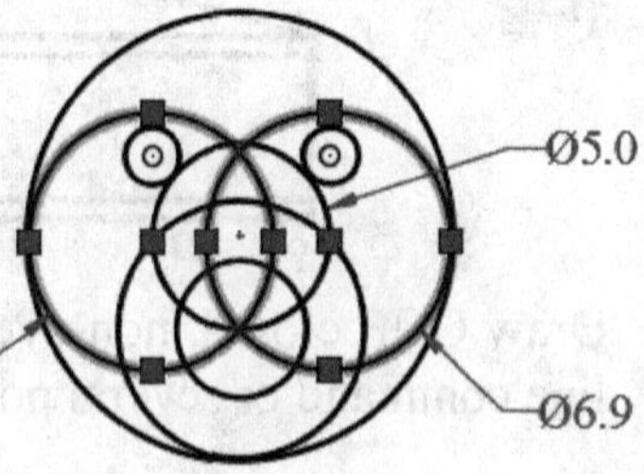

(ii)

5. Use the *Trim* command to create the shape shown below.

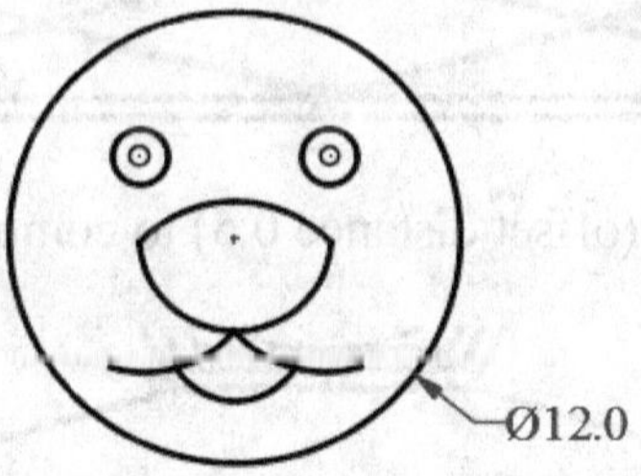

6. Draw a polygon. (i) The center of the polygon is the center of the 12" diameter circle. Select the *Circumscribed about circle* option. (ii) Use the *Offset* command for the outer polygons. Set offset distance to 0.5 inches.

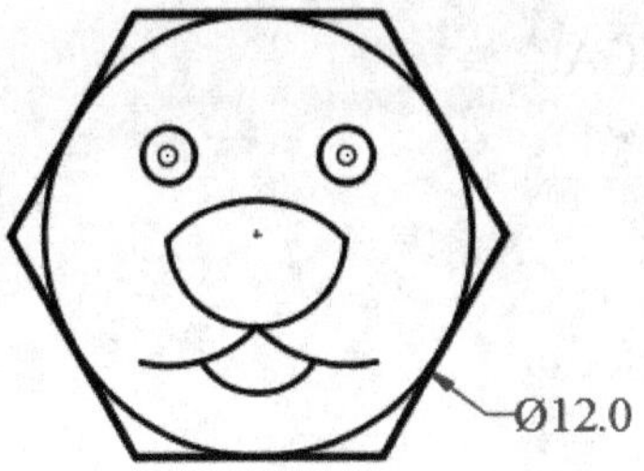

(i)

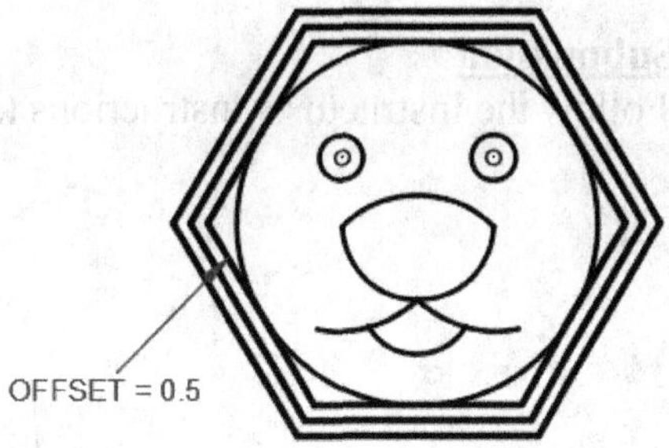

(ii)

7. Use the *Line* command to draw the outline of the base.

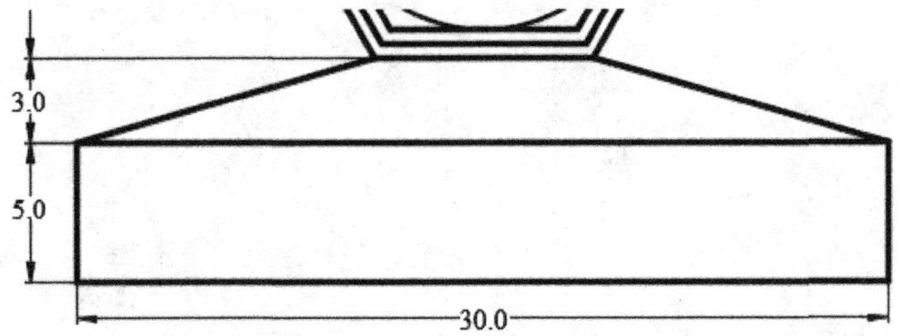

8. Use the *Offset* command for the inside of the base.

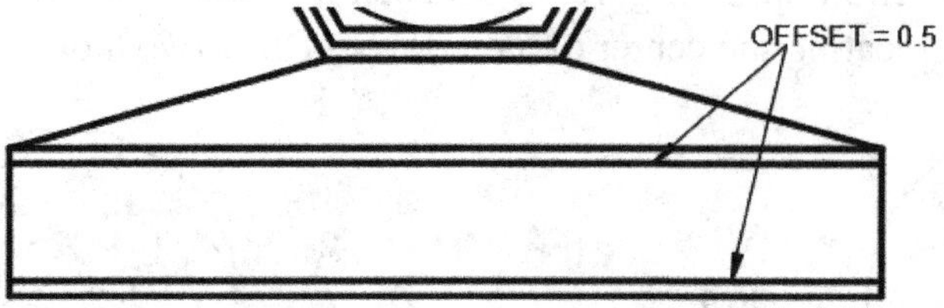

9. Draw ONE closed, non-overlapping, and non-intersecting polyline of the base. The line command or several polylines will make the next step difficult.

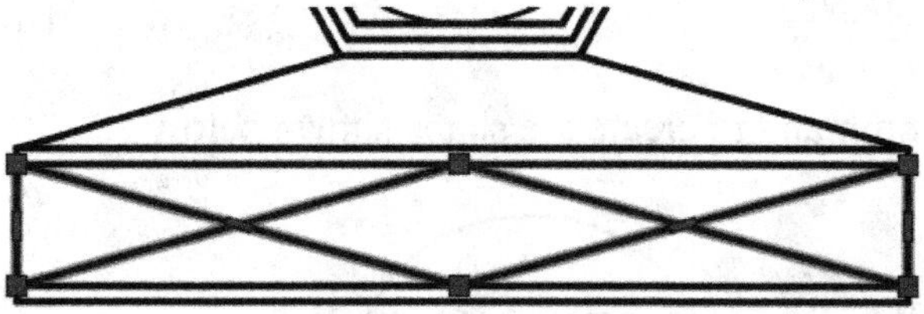

10. Use the *Offset* command (offset distance 0.5) to complete the drawing.

ICA Submission

1. Follow the instructor's instructions to submit the ICA.

23.7. Object appearance

Objectives

- Learn to use *Circle (ttr)* and *Object appearance (linetype, lineweight,* and color) commands.

Hints

- Refer to *Chapter 3* for help (Sections: 3.8, 3.17).

ICA Description

1. Drawing units: Inches
2. Draw the lines and circle as shown in Figure 23-7a.
3. Save the drawing.
4. Do not add the dimensions or centerlines of the circle.
5. Set the lineweight and linetype as shown in the figure.
6. Turn on the LWT option from the status bar.

ICA Submission

1. Follow the instructor's instructions to submit the ICA.

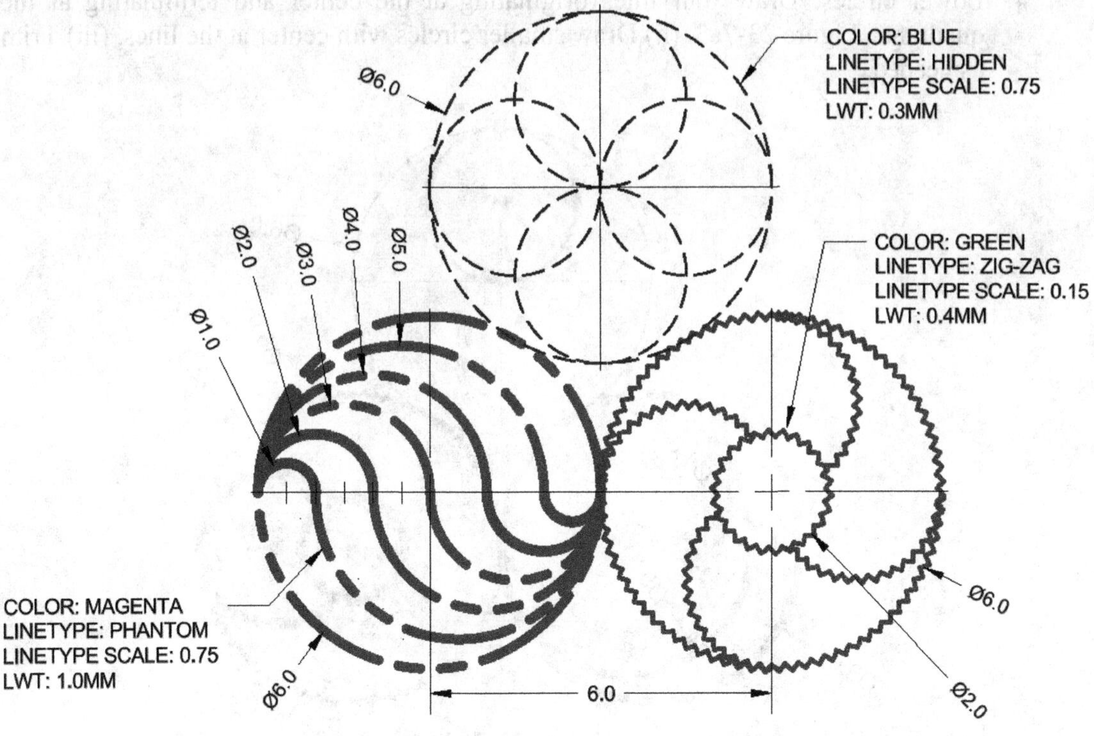

Figure 23-7a

Step-by-Step instructions for Figure 23-7a

1. Draw two circles as shown in Figure 23-7a1.
2. Draw third circle using TTR option as shown in Figure 23-7a2.

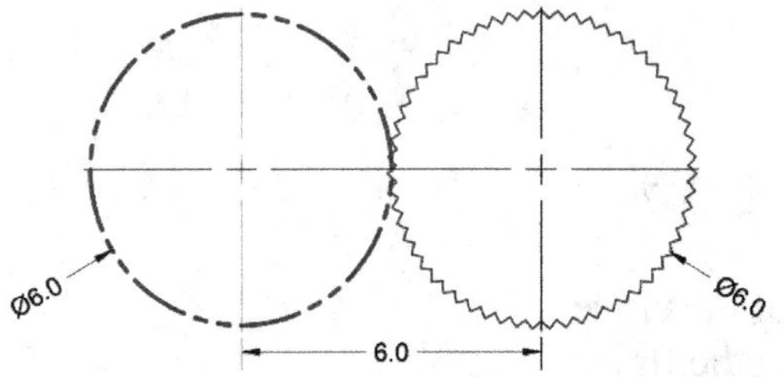

Figure 23-7a1

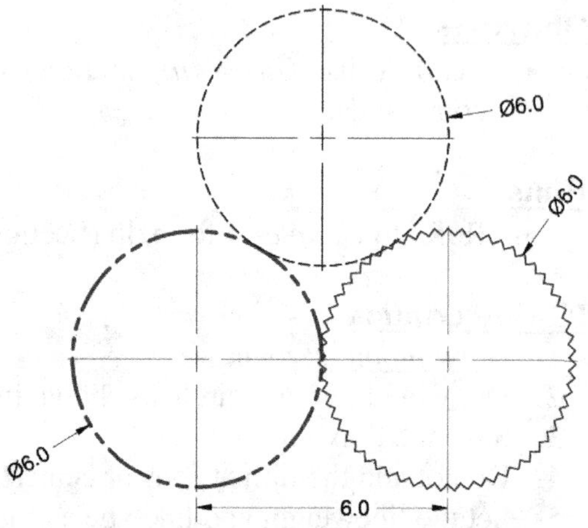

Figure 23-7a2

3. Lower left circle, Figure 23-7a3: (i) Draw two circles of the given diameters. (ii) Trim the extra part of the two circles. (iii) Repeat Steps (i) and (ii) and create the other circles as shown in Figure 23-7a.
4. Lower circles: Draw four lines originating at the center and terminating at the quadrants, Figure 23-7a3. (ii) Draw smaller circles with center at the lines. (iii) Trim as needed.

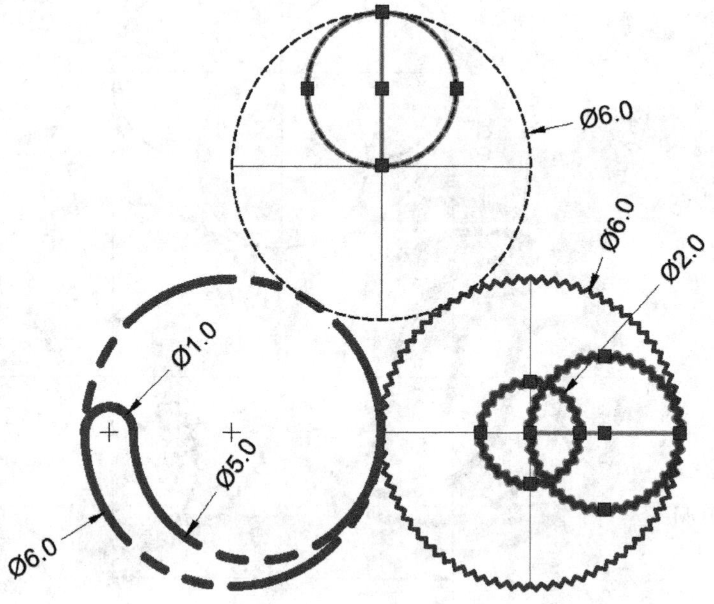

Figure 23-7a3

23.8. Object appearance, Hatch, Copy, Mirror, and Scale

Objectives

- Learn to use Draw commands: *Hatch* command.
- Learn to use Modify commands: *Copy*, *Mirror*, and *Scale* commands.

Hints

- Refer to *Chapters 4* and *5* for help (Sections: 4.18, 4.20, 4.24, 5.6).

ICA Description

1. Drawing units: Inches:
2. Use *Line, offset, Mirror, Copy,* and *Scale* commands to create the objects shown in Figure 23-8f. Do not add dimension.
3. The smaller barn is 60% of the larger barn.
4. Show the complete drawing (both barns) on one screen. Save the drawing.

Step-by-Step by instructions

1. Open an *acad* template file.
2. Draw the lines as shown in Figure 23-8a.
3. Use the *Mirror* command to create the other side of the barn, Figure 23-8b.
4. Use the *Join* command to create one continuous polyline for the outside of the barn.

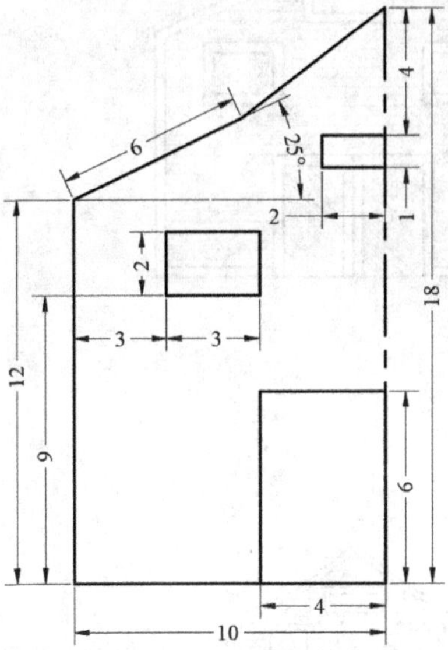

Figure 23-8a

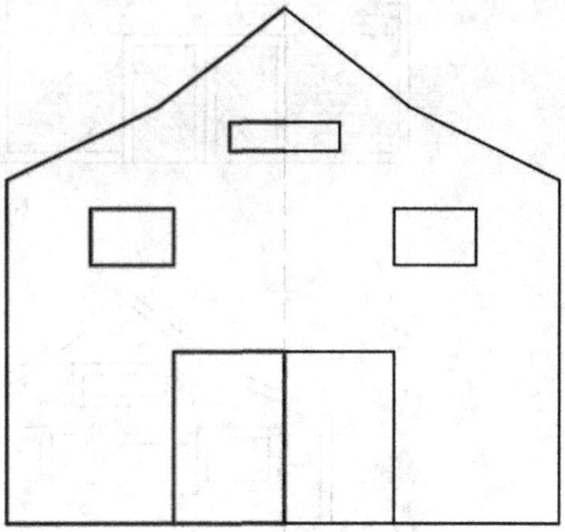

Figure 23-8b

5. Using the *Offset* command with the offset distance of 0.5,
   a. Create rectangles outside the windows (two three rectangles).
   b. Create rectangle inside the door (bottom rectangles).
   c. A line inside the barn boundary line, Figure 23-8c.
6. Use the *Trim* and Extend command as needed on top of the barn, Figure 23-8d.

7. Use the *Hatch* command to hatch the barn, Figure 23-8d.

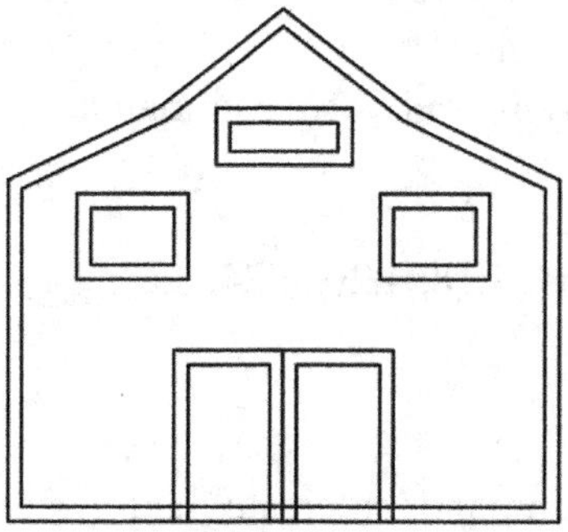

Figure 23-8c

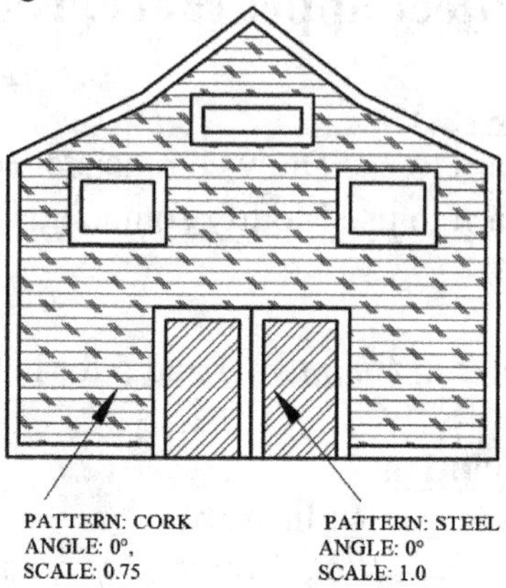

Figure 23-8d

5. Use the *Copy* command to create the second barn, Figure 23-8f.
6. Scale the barn: (i) Activate the *Scale* command, (ii) select the copy created in step 6, (iii) select the lower left corner as the base point, (iv) for the scale factor, type the value 0.60, and (v) press the *Enter* key, Figure 23-8f.

Figure 23-8e

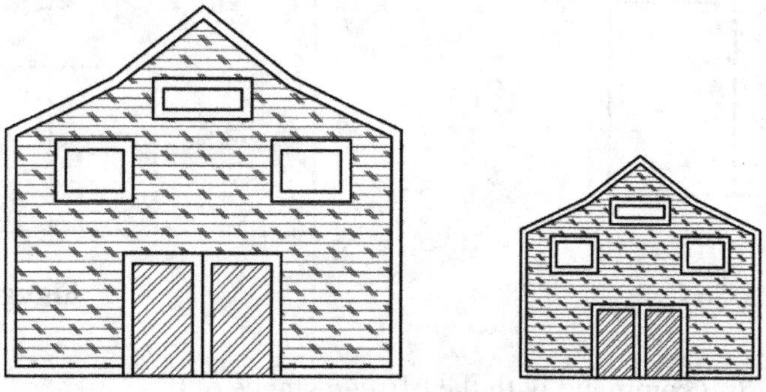

Figure 23-8f

23.9. Ellipse, Array, Text, qleader, and Draw Order

Objectives

- Learn to use *Ellipse*, *Mirror*, *Array Rectangular*, *Text*, and *qleader* commands.
- Learn to use *Draw Order* capabilities.

Hints

- Refer *to Chapters 3*, *4*, *5*, and *8* for help (Sections: 3.11, 4.9, 4.19, 5.5, and 5.7).

ICA Description

1. Drawing units: Inches:
2. Draw the bridge shown in Figure 23-9b using *Array, Text*, *Hatch*, *Mirror*, *Ellipse*, and *qleader* commands.
    a. Figure 23-9a shows the details of the columns used in Figure 23-9b.
    b. The bridge is symmetrical in the center.
3. Add the text boxes and arrows.
4. Save the drawing.
5. Do not add dimensions or centerlines of the circle.

Basic steps

1. Draw the right column as shown in Figure 23-9a.
2. Draw an ellipse with the major axis 40.0" and the minor axis 10" for the central cable of the bridge, Figure 23-9b.
3. Draw the cable on the right side of the bridge.
4. Draw the right-side gravity wall.
5. Use the *Mirror* command to draw the left side of the bridge.
6. Complete the bridge.

ICA Submission

1. Follow the instructor's instructions to submit the ICA.

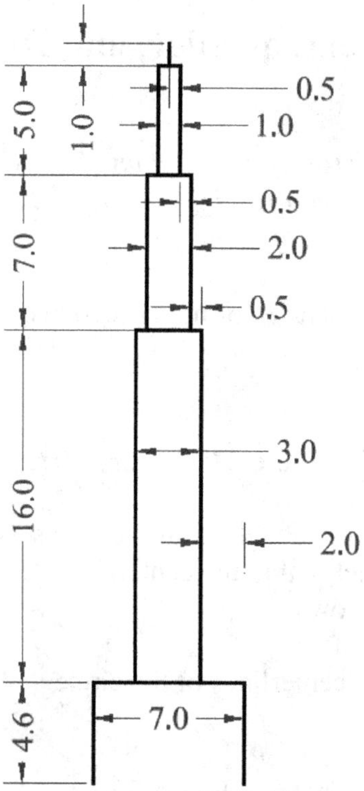

Figure 23-9a

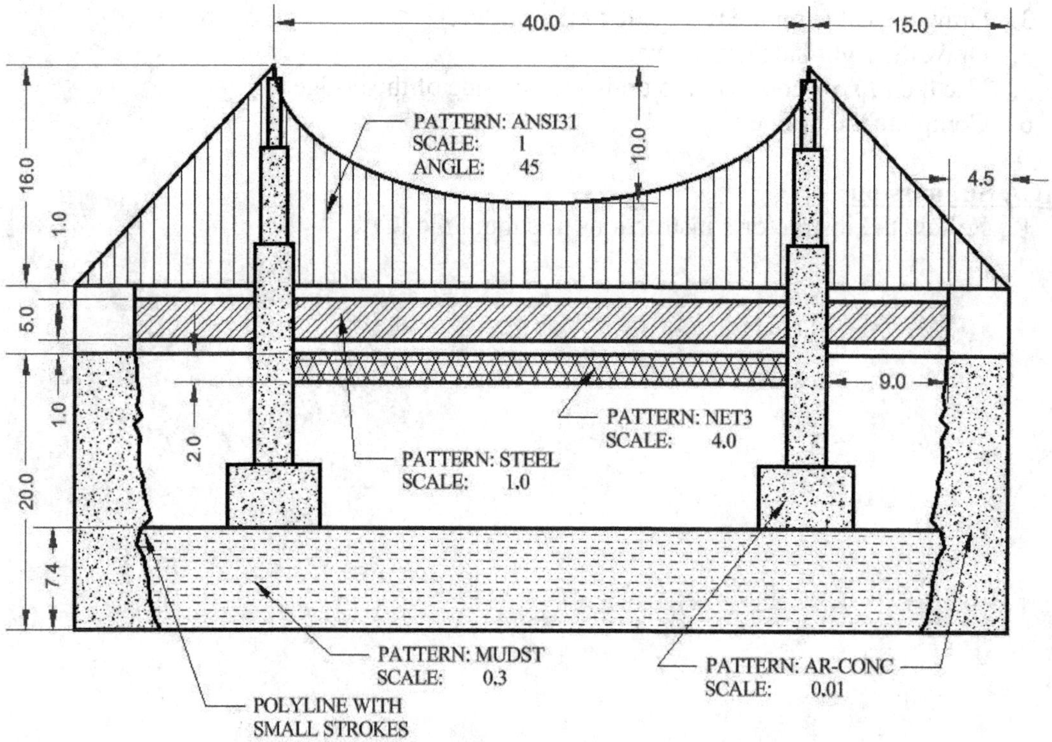

Figure 23-9b

23.10. Layers

Objectives

- Learn to create *Layers* commands.
- Learn to use *Linetype, Linetype Scale, Color*, and *Lineweight (LWT)* commands.

Hints

- Refer to *Chapter 6* for help (Sections: 6.1 - 6.11).

ICA Description - Part 1

1. Drawing units: Inches
2. Draw the object shown in Figure 23-10a using *Line*, *Circle*, and *Polyline* commands.
3. Create appropriate layers.
4. Set the lineweight and linetype as shown in Figure 23-10b.
5. Save the drawing.
6. Do not add dimension and/or centerlines of the circle.
7. Follow the step-by-step instructions.

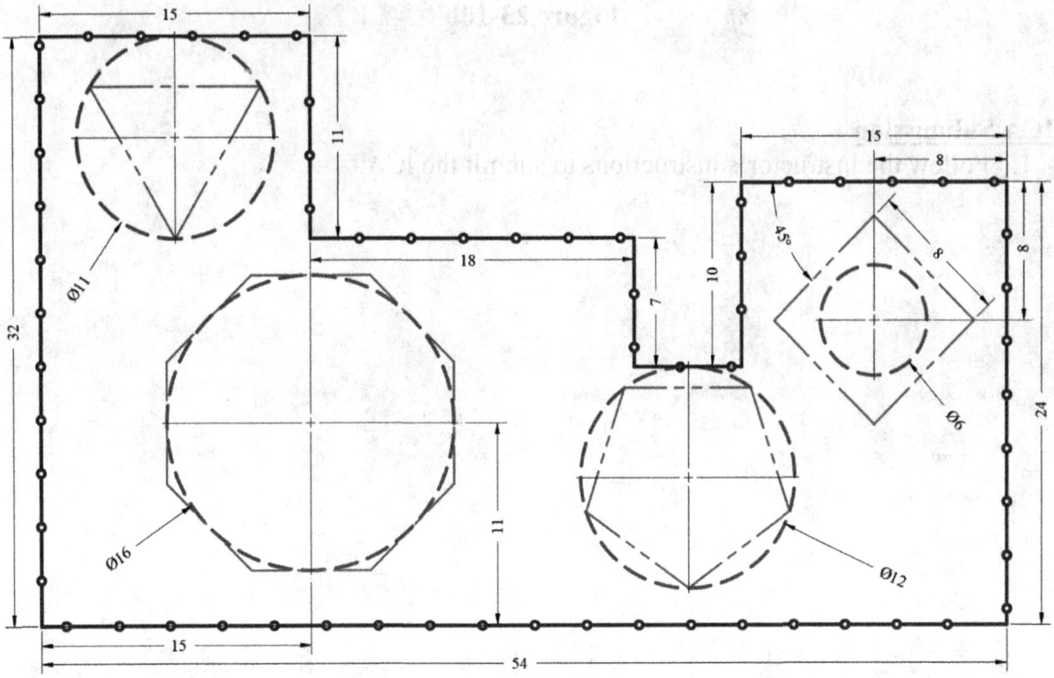

Figure 23-10a

Step-by-Step instructions for Figure 23-10a:

1. Create three layers and name them *Circle*, *Polygon*, and *Rectangle*. Set the properties of the layers as shown in Figure 23-10b.
2. Make the *Rectangle* layer to be the current layer and draw the outline.
3. Make the *Circle* layer to be the current layer and draw the circles.
4. Make the *Polygon* layer to be the current layer and draw the polygon.

5. Set linetype scale (not shown in the figure).
6. Use a reasonable value for *linetype scale* from *Properties* palette.
7. Turn *Off* the *Circle* and *Rectangle* layers; only the polygons will be visible.
8. Turn *On* all of the layers.
9. Turn *Off* the *Circle* and *Polygon* layers; only the outline will be visible.
10. Turn *Off* the *Rectangle* layer; only circles are displayed.

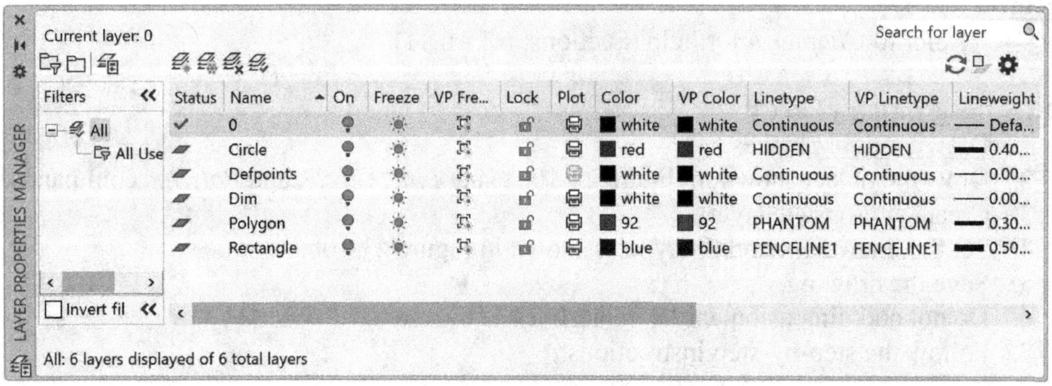

Figure 23-10b

ICA Submission

1. Follow the instructor's instructions to submit the ICA.

23.11. Make & Insert Block, and Template Files

Objectives

- Learn to create and use *Block*, *Block Attribute*, *Make Block*, and *Insert Block* commands.
- Learn to create and use *Template* files.

Hints

- Refer to *Chapter 7* and *Chapter 8* for help (Sections: 7.5 – 7.7, 7.1 – 8.4, 8.8, 8.9).

ICA Description

1. Create the *Title* write block shown in Figure 6-4 following the instructions from Section 7.5 of the textbook.
2. Create the *Release* write block shown in Figure 6-8c following the instructions from Section 7.6 of the textbook.

3. Create the template files following the instructions from Section 8.8 of the textbook. The four template files are shown below.

ICA Submission

1. Follow the instructor's instructions to submit the ICA.

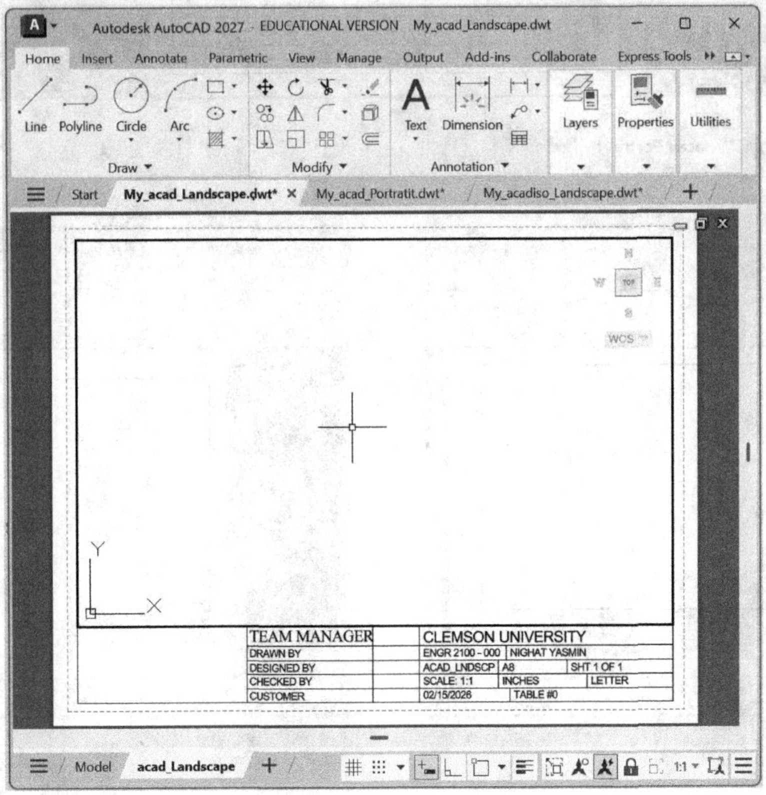

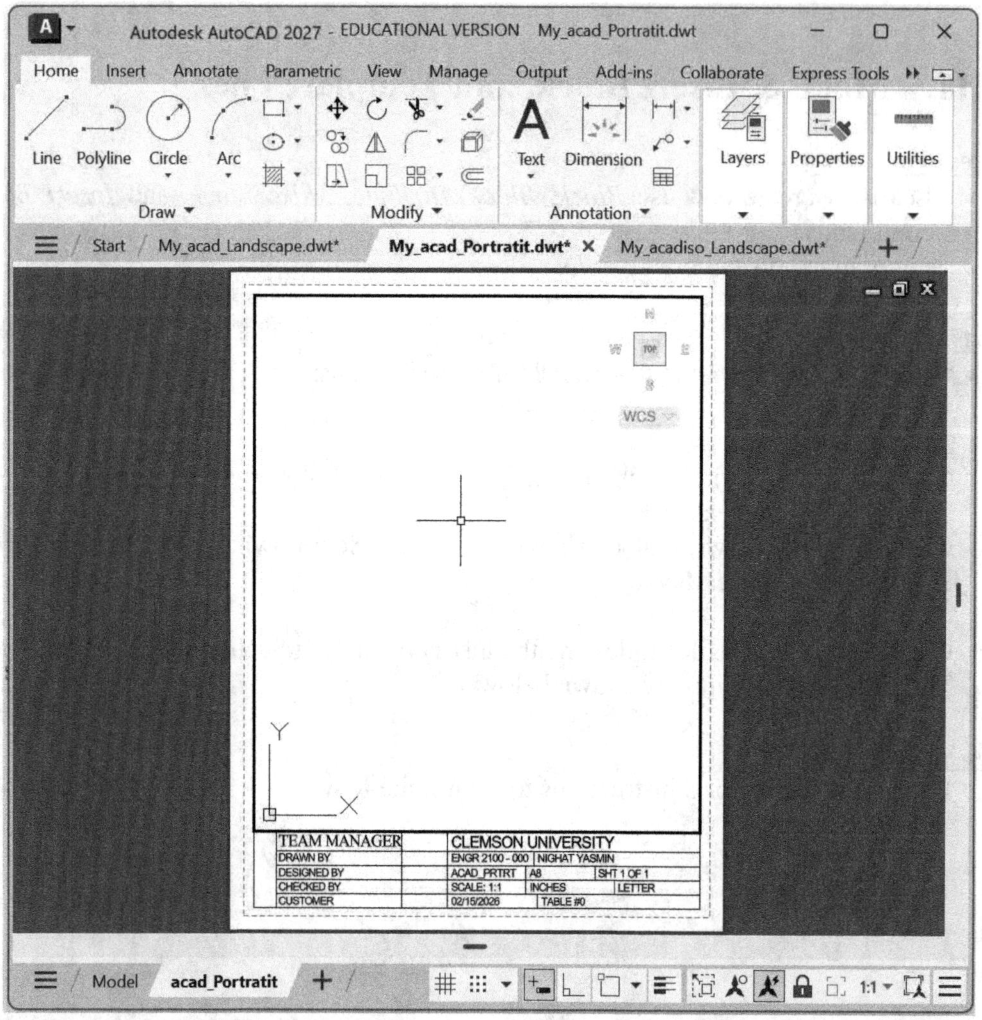
Autodesk AutoCAD 2027 - EDUCATIONAL VERSION My_acad_Portratit.dwt
Home
Insert
Annotate
Parametric
View
Manage
Output
Add-ins
Collaborate
Express Tools
Line
Polyline
Circle
Arc
Draw
Modify
Text
Dimension
Annotation
Layers
Properties
Utilities
Start
My_acad_Landscape.dwt*
My_acad_Portratit.dwt*
My_acadiso_Landscape.dwt*
WCS
Y
X
TEAM MANAGER
CLEMSON UNIVERSITY
DRAWN BY
ENGR 2100 - 000
NIGHAT YASMIN
DESIGNED BY
ACAD_PRTRT
A8
SHT 1 OF 1
CHECKED BY
SCALE: 1:1
INCHES
LETTER
CUSTOMER
02/15/2026
TABLE #0
Model
acad_Portratit
1:1

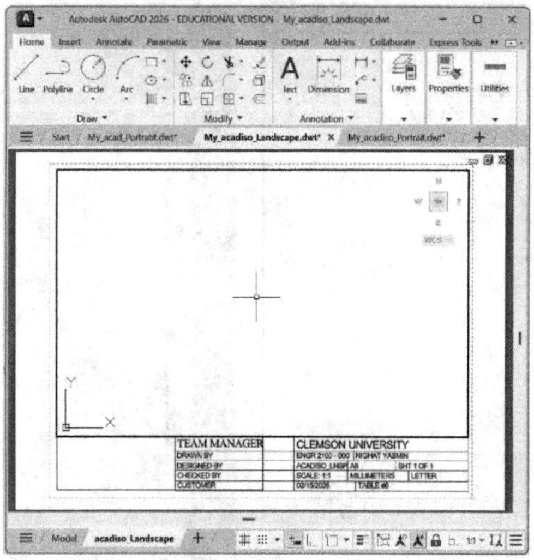
Autodesk AutoCAD 2026 - EDUCATIONAL VERSION My_acadiso_Landscape.dwt
TEAM MANAGER
CLEMSON UNIVERSITY
MILLIMETERS
Model
acadiso_Landscape

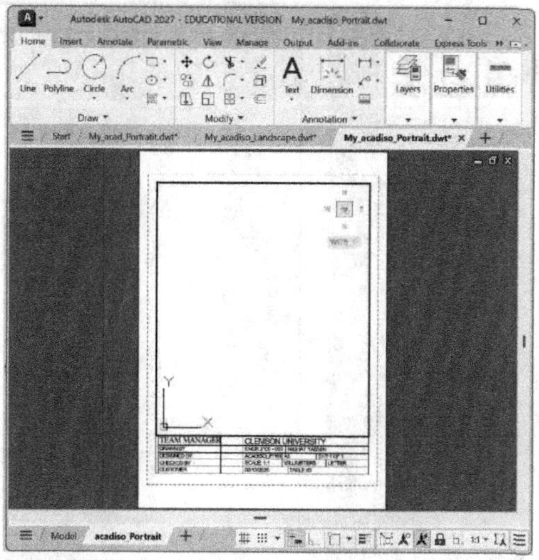
Autodesk AutoCAD 2027 - EDUCATIONAL VERSION My_acadiso_Portrait.dwt
TEAM MANAGER
CLEMSON UNIVERSITY
Model
acadiso_Portrait

23.12. Create layouts and create views by freezing layers

Objectives

- Learn to create *Layout* command.
- Learn to copy, delete, move, and rename a layout.
- Learn to freeze layers in a layout.
- Learn to change the scale of a viewport in a layout.

Hints

- Refer to *Chapter 8* for help (Sections: 8.5, 7.6).

ICA Description – Part 1

1. Units: Inches
2. Create four layers, *Circle Top*, *Circle Left*, *Circle Right*, and *Text*. Set the properties as shown in Figure 23-12a.

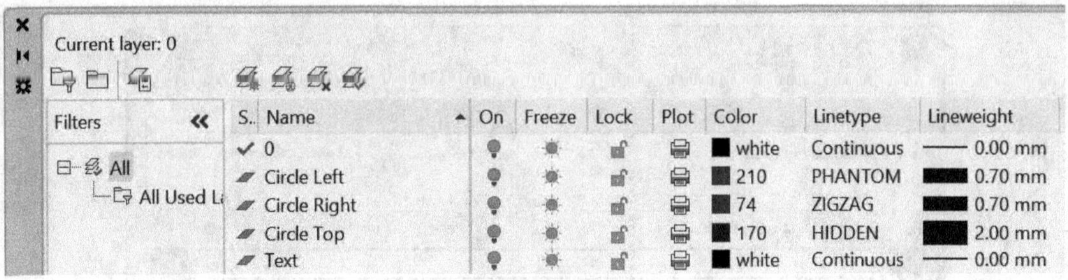

Figure 23-12a

3. Do not add the dimensions.
4. Move the left circle and its smaller circles to the *Circle Left* layer.
5. Move the right circle and its smaller circles to the *Circle Right* layer.
6. Move the top circle and its arcs to the *Circle Top* layer.
7. Move the text labels (color, linetype, …) to the *Text* layer.

8. Set the drawing properties (from the *Properties* panel) to be *By Layers* option, Figure 23-12b.

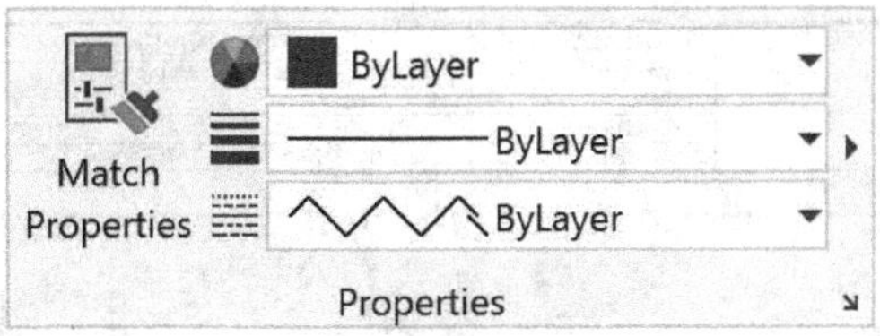

Figure 23-12b

9. Insert *acad_Landscape* layout from corresponding template file (Section 8.5.5.2 of the textbook).
10. Rename the *acad_Landscape* layout to *Show All* (Section 8.5.4 of the textbook).
11. Display the drawing in the *Show All* layout; that is, format the layout as follows:
    a. **Double click inside the viewport** (the coordinate system will appear, and the viewport boundary will become thick).
    b. Using ***Zoom → All*** option, place your layouts in the layout view.
    c. Using ***Zoom → Window*** option, place the three circular patterns in the center of the layout.
    d. Set the linetypes of the patterns such that it appears correctly in the layout.
    e. DO NOT WORRY HOW IT APPEARS IN THE MODEL SPACE!
    f. Set the viewport scale to 1:2 (Section 8.3.3.5, Method 2a of the textbook).
    g. Lock the scale (Section 8.3.3.6 of the textbook).
    h. Freeze the *Text* layer.

12. Update the title block (Section 8.9 of the textbook).
13. The *Show All* layout is shown in Figure 23-12c. *Note: The CirTop, Circle Left, and Cir-LR layouts are not shown here.*

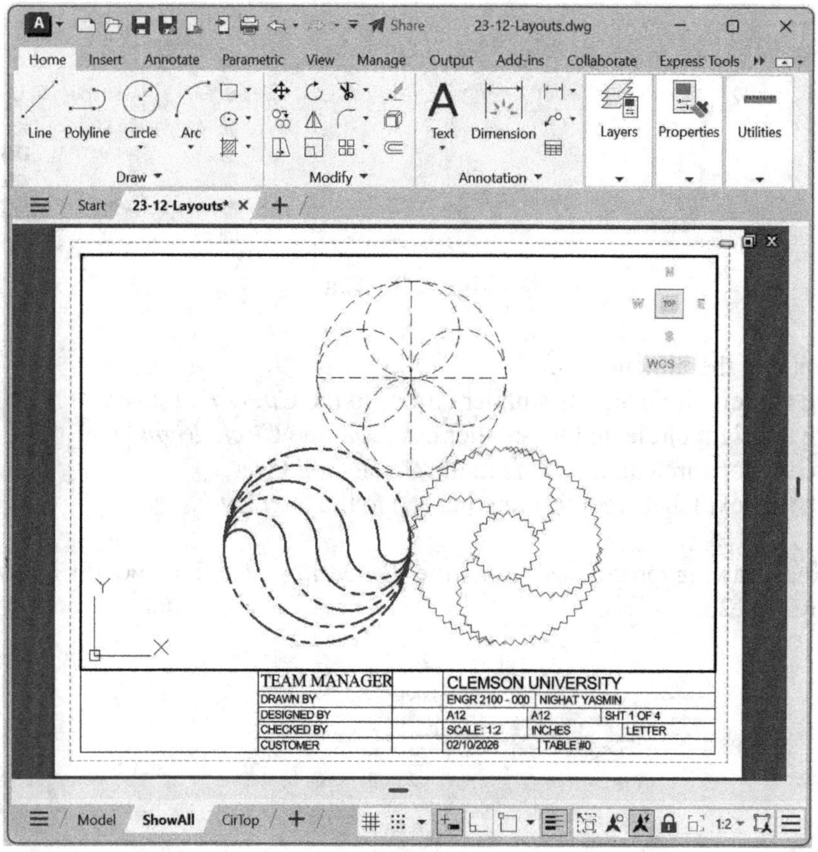

Figure 23-12c

7. Make three copies of the layout labeled as *Show All*.
8. Rename the copied layouts as (Section 8.6.4 of the textbook): *CirTop*, *Circle Left*, and *Cir-LR*, Figure 23-12c.
9. Delete *Layout1* and *Layout2*.

10. Show only the top circular pattern in the layout labeled as *CirTop*. That is, freeze all the layers (Section 7.6 of the textbook) except the layer named *Circle Top*.
    a. Format the layout: (i) Unlock the scale. (ii) Set the viewport scale to 1:1. (iii) Lock the scale.

11. Show only the left circular pattern in the layout labeled as *Circle Left*. That is, freeze all the layers except the layer named *Circle Left*.
    a. Format the layout: (i) Unlock the scale. (ii) Set the viewport scale to 1:1. (iii) Lock the scale.

12. Show both the left and right circular pattern in the layout labeled as *Cir-LR*. Freeze layers as needed.
    a. Format the layout: (i) Unlock the scale. (ii) Set the viewport scale to 1:2. (iii) Lock the scale.

13. Save the drawing file.

ICA Submission

1. Follow the instructor's instructions to submit the ICA.

Notes:

23.13. Dimension

Objectives

- Learn to add *dimensions* to a drawing.

Hints

- Refer to *Chapter 9* for help.

ICA Description - Part 1

1. Open the drawing shown in Figure 23-5 (ICA 5).
   a. Create a layer, *DRAWING*, for the drawing and move the drawing objects to DRAWING layer
   b. Create a layer, *DIM*, for the dimension and make it the current layer.
   c. Add the dimensions to the drawing.
   d. Insert layout from the appropriate template file.
   e. Set the viewport scale to 1:6
   f. Lock the viewport scale.
   g. Update the title block.

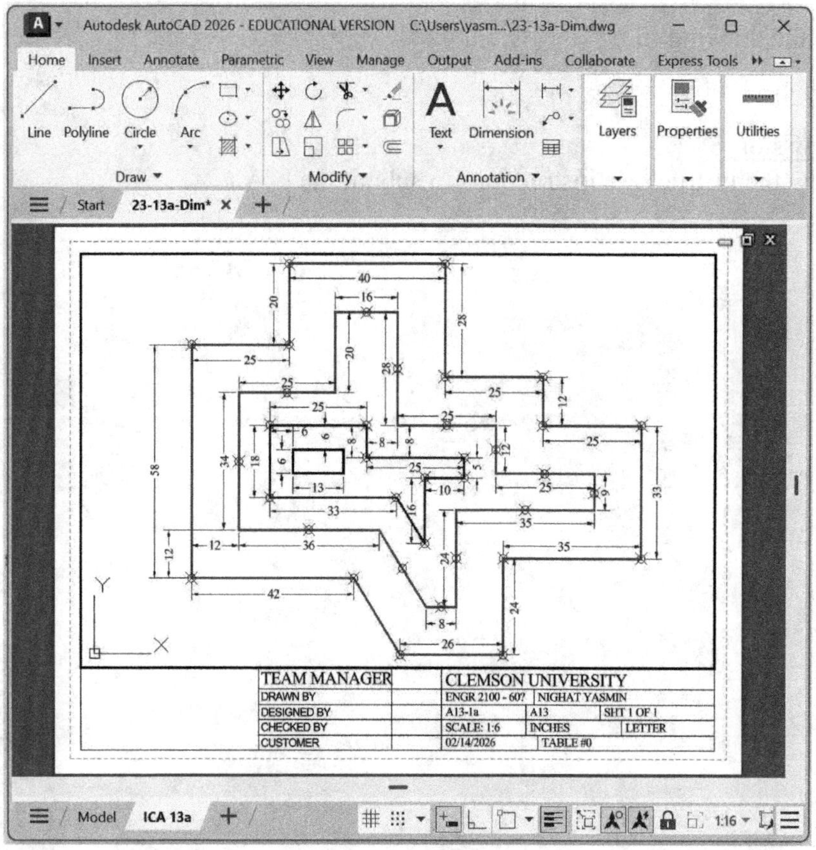

Figure 23-13a

ICA Description - Part 2

1. Open the drawing shown in Figure 23-6b (ICA 6).
   a. Repeat the above process.
   b. Set the viewport scale to 1:4.
   c. Figure of the layout is not shown here.

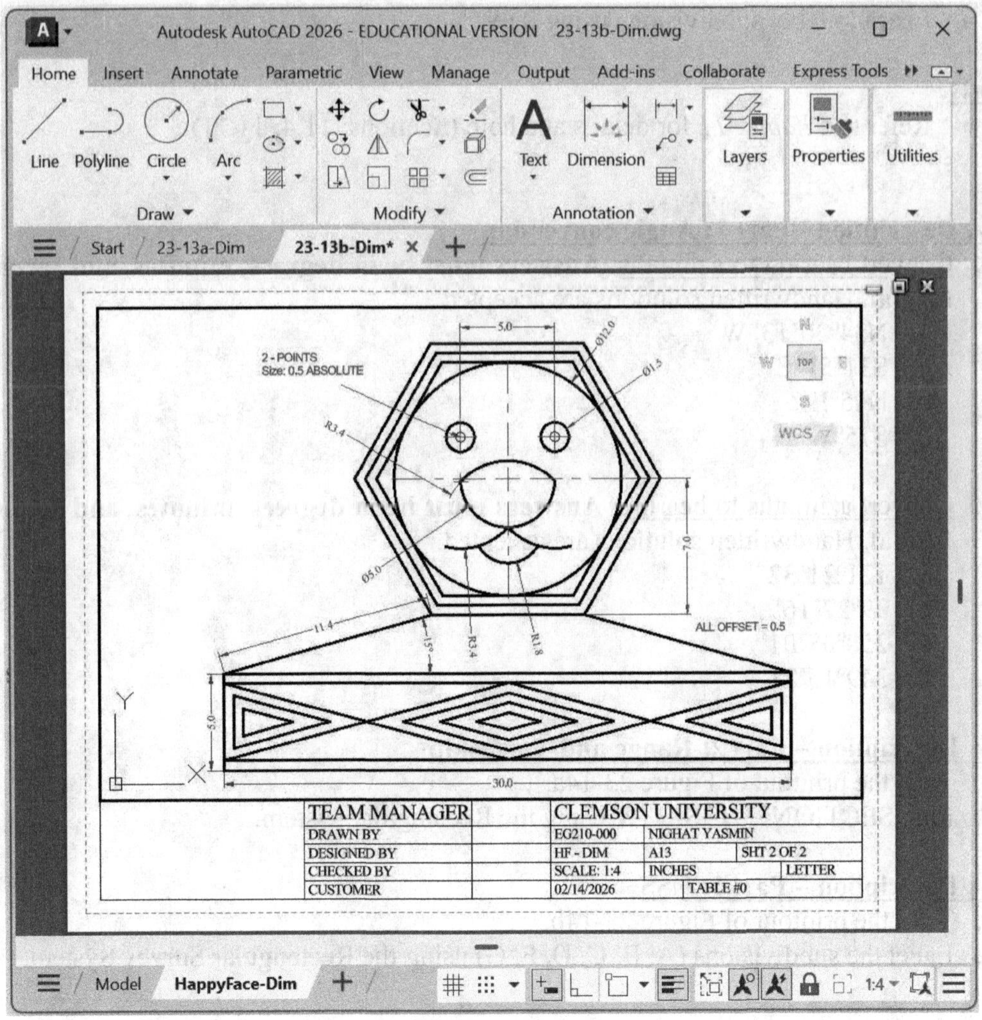

Figure 23-13b

ICA Submission

1. Follow the instructor's instructions to submit the ICA.

23.14. Azimuths, Bearing, and Closed Travers

Objectives

- Learn to convert an azimuth angle into a bearing angle and vice versa.
- Learn to label subdivisions using RSS.

Hints

- Refer to *Chapter 11* for details and help (Sections: 11.4, 11.11).

ICA Description - Part 1: Angle conversion

1. Convert bearing to azimuths: **Answers must be in degrees, minutes, and seconds format.** Handwritten solutions are accepted.
   a. N34°20'13"W
   b. S31°51'E
   c. N15°E
   d. S75°W

2. Convert azimuths to bearing: **Answers must be in degrees, minutes, and seconds format.** Handwritten solutions are accepted.
   a. 121°21'32"
   b. 39°27'16"
   c. 258°08'01"
   d. 349°15'21"

ICA Description – Part 2: Range and Township

1. Take the printout of Figure 23-14a.
2. Find SECTION33-T3S-R3W using the Rectangular system.

ICA Description – Part 3: RSS

1. Take the printout of Figure 23-14b.
2. Label the subdivisions (A, B, C, D, F, G) using the Rectangular Survey System.

ICA Submission

1. Follow the instructor's instructions to submit the ICA.

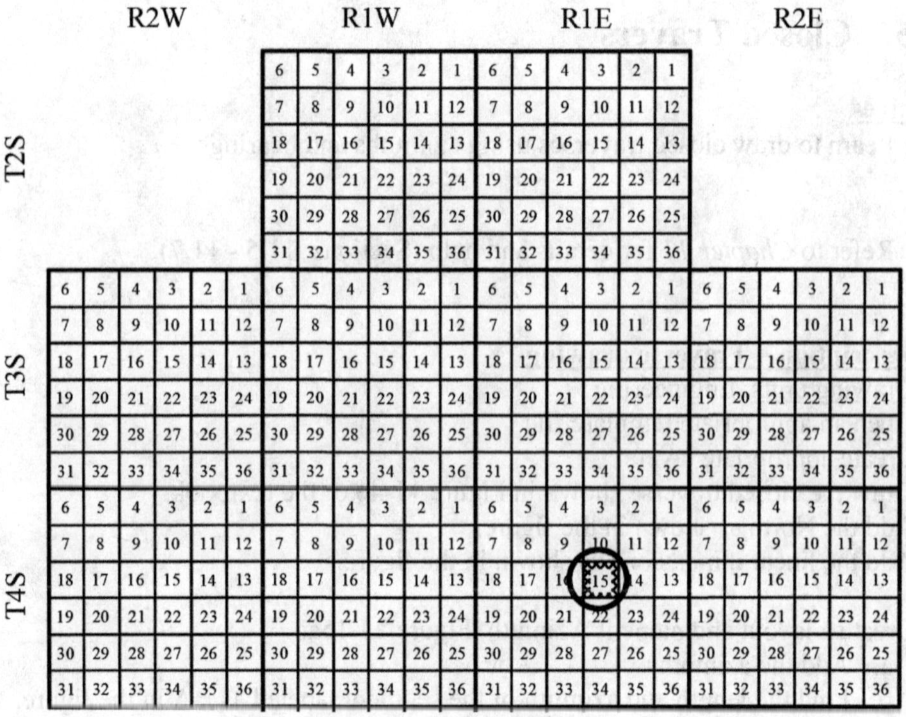

Figure 23-14a

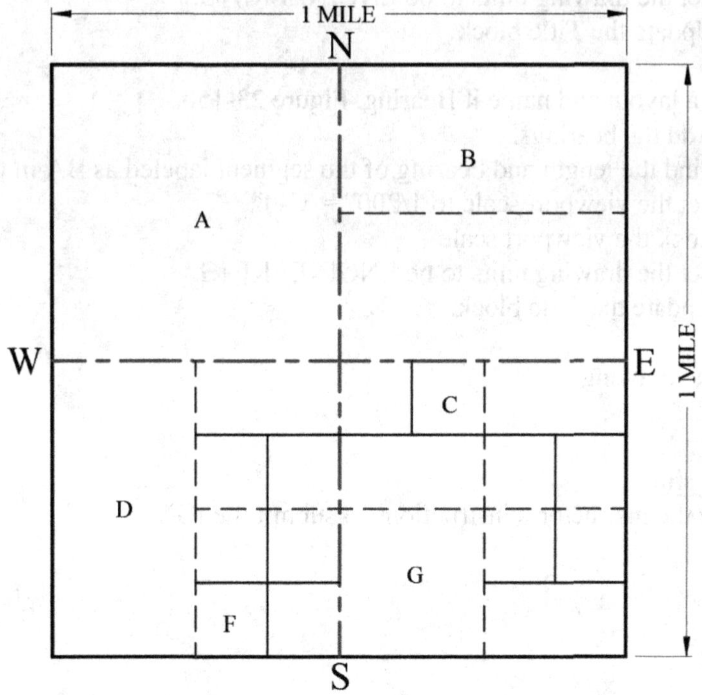

FURTHER SUBDIVISION OF SECTION15-T4S-R4E

Figure 23-14b

23.15. Closed Travers

Objectives

- Learn to draw closed traverses using azimuths and bearings.

Hints

- Refer to *Chapter 11* for details and help (Sections: 11.5 - 11.7).

ICA Description – Traverse drawing

1. Drawing units: Engineering
2. Open an appropriate template file.
3. Create appropriate layers.
4. Draw the closed traverse shown in Figure 11-4e of the textbook.
5. Add the North as shown in the figure.
6. Add the linear dimensions as shown in the figure.

7. Create a layout and name it Azimuth, Figure 23-15a.
    a. Add the azimuths.
    b. Find the length and azimuth of the segment labeled as BA in the figure.
    c. Set the viewport scale to 1/200" = 1'-0".
    d. Lock the viewport scale.
    e. Set the drawing units to be ENGINEERING.
    f. Update the Title block.

8. Create a layout and name it Bearing, Figure 23-15b.
    a. Add the bearings.
    b. Find the length and bearing of the segment labeled as BA in the figure.
    c. Set the viewport scale to 1/200" = 1'-0".
    d. Lock the viewport scale.
    e. Set the drawing units to be ENGINEERING.
    f. Update the Title block.

9. Save the drawing.

ICA Submission

1. Follow the instructor's instructions to submit the ICA.

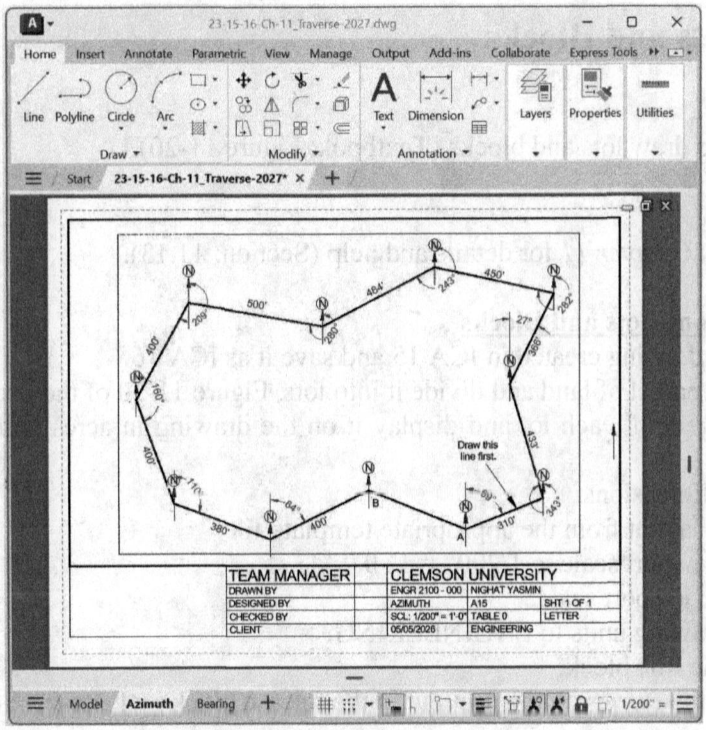

Figure 23-15a

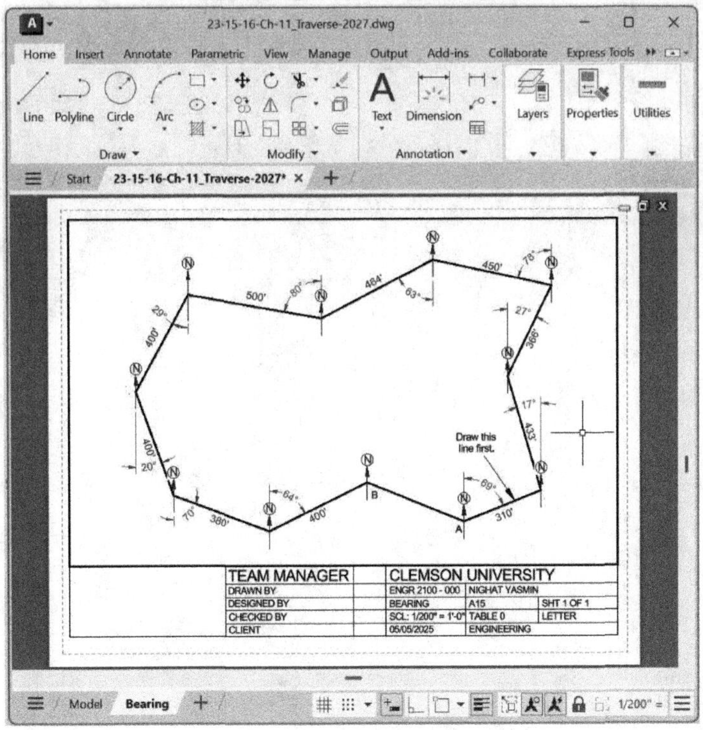

Figure 23-15b

23.16. Lots and Blocks

Objectives

- Learn to draw lots and blocks (Textbook: Figure 11-20).

Hints

- Refer to *Chapter 11* for details and help (Section: 11.13).

ICA Description: Lots and Blocks

1. Open the drawing created in ICA 15 and save it as ICA 16.
2. Draw the parcel of land and divide it into lots, Figure 11-20 of the textbook.
3. Find the area of each lot and display it on the drawing in acres with four decimal places.
4. Add the dimensions.
5. Insert the layout from the appropriate template file.
6. Set the viewport scale to 1/200" = 1'-0".
7. Lock the viewport scale.
8. Set the drawing units to ENGINEERING.
9. Update the title block.
10. Initialize the entries on the printout in the release block by hand (do not type).

ICA Submission

1. Follow the instructor's instructions to submit the ICA.

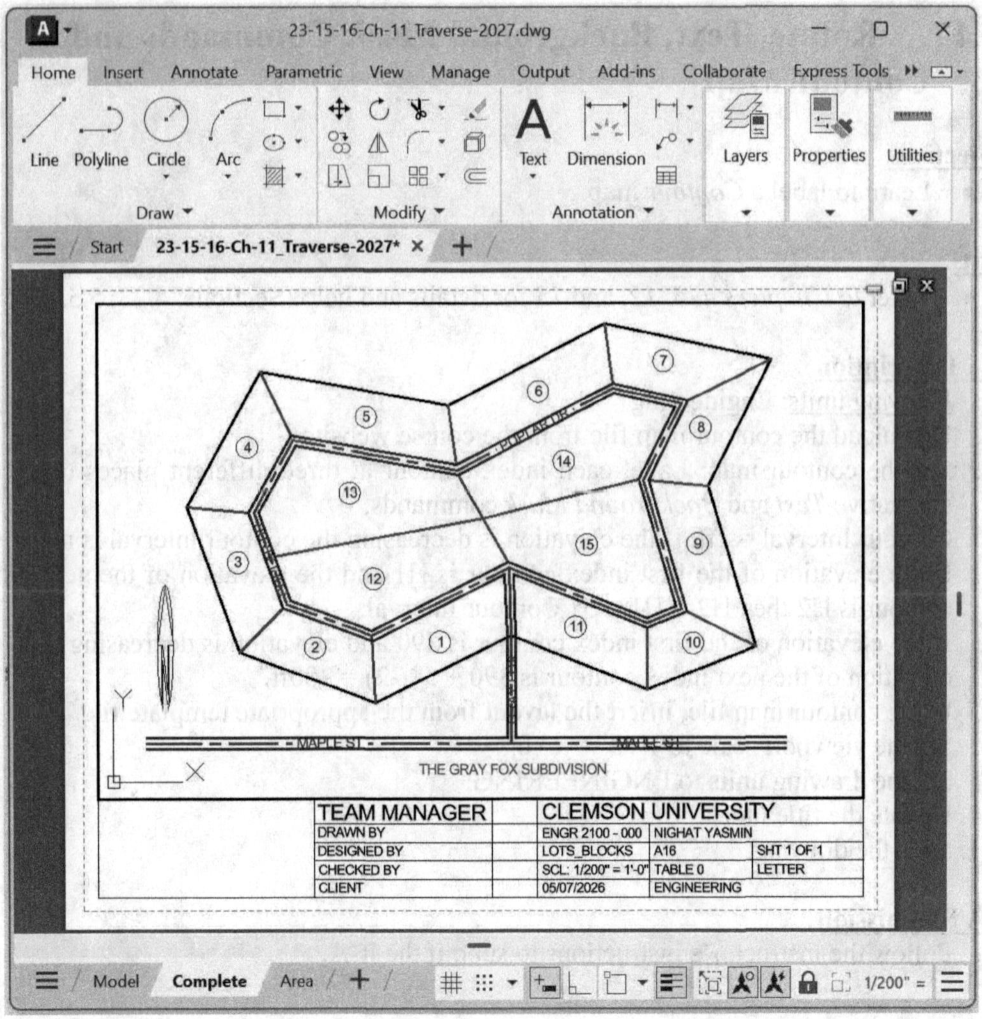
23-15-16-Ch-11_Traverse-2027.dwg
Home
Insert
Annotate
Parametric
View
Manage
Output
Add-ins
Collaborate
Express Tools
Line
Polyline
Circle
Arc
Draw
Modify
Text
Dimension
Annotation
Layers
Properties
Utilities
Start
23-15-16-Ch-11_Traverse-2027*
POPLAR DR
MAPLE ST
MAPLE ST
THE GRAY FOX SUBDIVISION
TEAM MANAGER
CLEMSON UNIVERSITY
DRAWN BY
DESIGNED BY
CHECKED BY
CLIENT
ENGR 2100 - 000
NIGHAT YASMIN
LOTS_BLOCKS
A16
SHT 1 OF 1
SCL: 1/200" = 1'-0"
TABLE 0
LETTER
05/07/2026
ENGINEERING
Model
Complete
Area
1/200" =

Figure 23-16

23.17. Rotate, Text, Background Mask Commands and Contour Map

Objectives

- Learn to label a *Contour* map.

Hints

- Refer to *Chapters 4*, *5*, *12*, and *13* for details and help (Sections: 4.23, 5.5, 12.5).

ICA Description

1. Drawing units: Engineering
2. Download the contour map file from the course website.
3. For the contour map: Label each index contour at three different places using the annotative *Text* and *Background Mask* commands.
4. Contour Interval = 2ft. If the elevation is decreasing the contour interval is negative.
5. If the elevation of the first index contour is H1 and the elevation of the next index contour is H2 then H2 = H1 + 5* Contour Interval.
6. If the elevation of the first index contour is 390 and elevation is decreasing then the elevation of the next index contour is 390 + 5*(-2) = 380ft.
7. In the contour map file, insert the layout from the appropriate template file.
8. Set the viewport scale to 1/72" = 1'-0".
9. Set the drawing units to ENGINEERING.
10. Update the title block.
11. Save the drawing.

ICA Submission

1. Follow the instructor's instructions to submit the ICA.

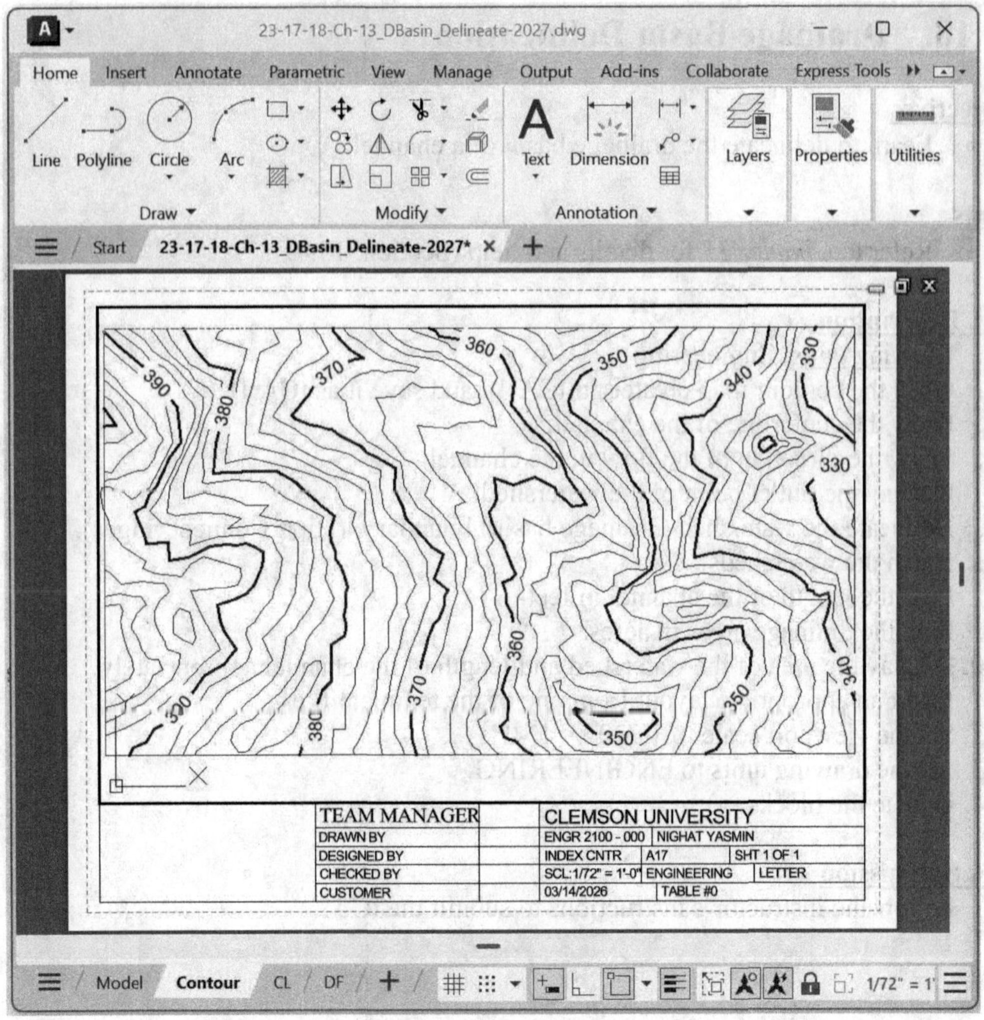
23-17-18-Ch-13_DBasin_Delineate-2027.dwg
Home Insert Annotate Parametric View Manage Output Add-ins Collaborate Express Tools
Line Polyline Circle Arc
Draw
Modify
Text Dimension
Annotation
Layers Properties Utilities
Start 23-17-18-Ch-13_DBasin_Delineate-2027*
360 370 390 380 350 340 330 330 360 370 380 390 350 350 340
TEAM MANAGER
DRAWN BY
DESIGNED BY
CHECKED BY
CUSTOMER
CLEMSON UNIVERSITY
ENGR 2100 - 000 NIGHAT YASMIN
INDEX CNTR A17 SHT 1 OF 1
SCL:1/72" = 1'-0" ENGINEERING LETTER
03/14/2026 TABLE #0
Model Contour CL DF
1/72" = 1'

Figure 23-17

23.18. Drainage Basin Delineation

Objectives

- Learn to delineate the drainage basin of a channel.

Hints

- Refer to *Chapter 13* for details and help (Section: 13.8)

ICA Description

1. Drawing units: Engineering
2. Open the contour map created in ICA 17 and save it as ICA 18.
3. Draw the centerline of the channel.
4. Show the direction of the flow in the channel.
5. Display the outlet point of the watershed.
6. Delineate the watershed (drainage basin) boundary; (Hint: Connect ridges).
7. Hatch the watersheds.
8. Find the length of the channel in feet.
9. Find the drainage areas in acres.
10. Display the area of the watershed and length of the channel appropriately.
11. Insert an appropriate layout from one of the template files.
12. Set the viewport scale to 1/720” = 1’-0”.
13. Set the drawing units to ENGINEERING.
14. Update the blocks.

ICA Submission

1. Follow the instructor’s instructions to submit the ICA.

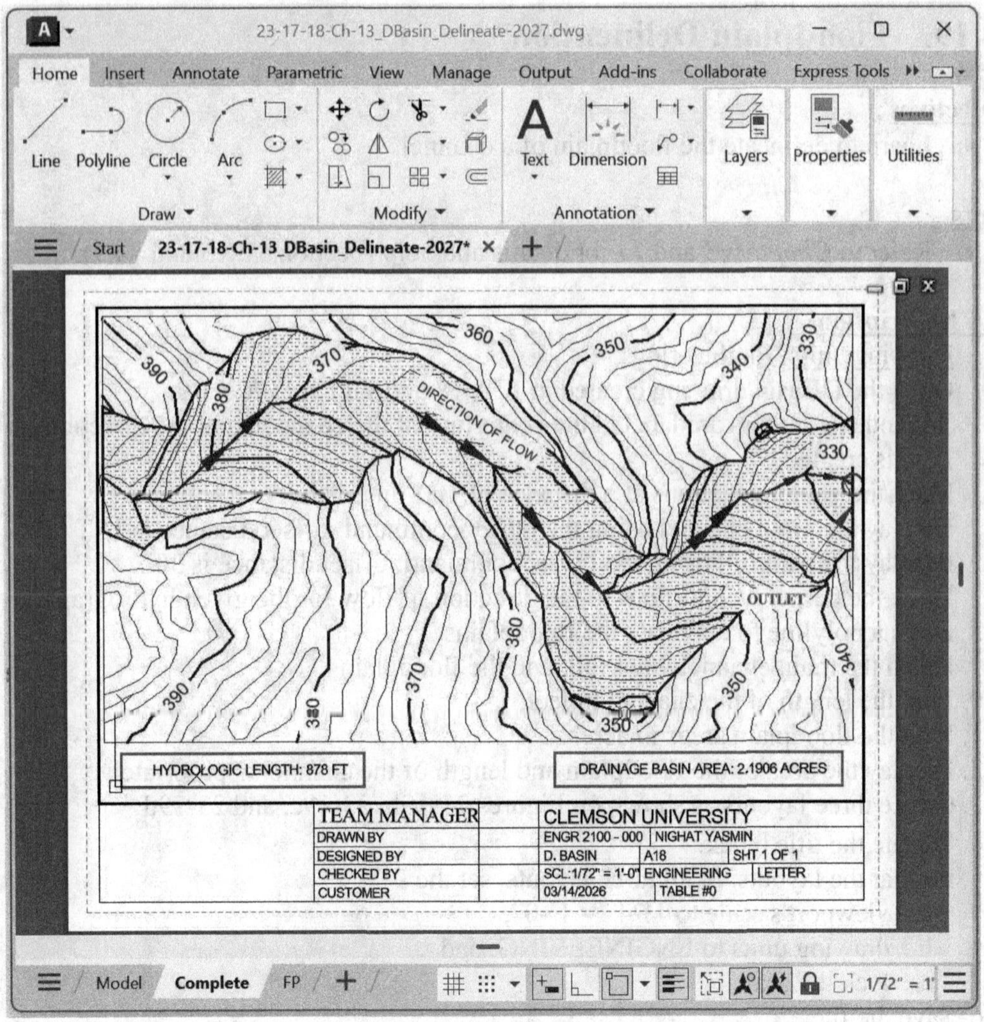
23-17-18-Ch-13_DBasin_Delineate-2027.dwg
Home Insert Annotate Parametric View Manage Output Add-ins Collaborate Express Tools
Line Polyline Circle Arc
Draw
Modify
Text Dimension
Annotation
Layers Properties Utilities
Start 23-17-18-Ch-13_DBasin_Delineate-2027*
DIRECTION OF FLOW
OUTLET
HYDROLOGIC LENGTH: 878 FT
DRAINAGE BASIN AREA: 2.1906 ACRES
TEAM MANAGER
CLEMSON UNIVERSITY
DRAWN BY
ENGR 2100 - 000
NIGHAT YASMIN
DESIGNED BY
D. BASIN
A18
SHT 1 OF 1
CHECKED BY
SCL:1/72" = 1'-0"
ENGINEERING
LETTER
CUSTOMER
03/14/2026
TABLE #0
Model Complete FP
1/72" = 1'

Figure 23-18

23.19. Floodplain Delineation

Objectives

- Learn to delineate the floodplain of a channel.

Hints

- Refer to *Chapters 3* and *14* for details and help (Sections: 3.15 and 14.5).

ICA Description

1. Drawing units: Engineering
2. Open the DBasin drawing created in ICA 18 and save it as ICA 19.
3. The index contours are labeled the centerline of the channel, and the direction of the flow is created.
4. Mark the gauging stations at a distance of 100' intervals.
5. Display the main channel using the *Offset* command; offset distance is 15'.
6. Display the bankfull using the *Offset* command; offset distance is 30'.
7. Draw the perpendicular lines to the direction of flow for the given hydrograph.
8. Draw a polyline to delineate the floodplains.
9. Hatch the main channel, bankfull, and the floodplains.
10. Find the length of the channel in feet.
11. Find the floodplain areas in acres.
12. Display the area of the floodplain and length of the channel appropriately.
13. Create three layouts as shown on Figures 23-19b, 23-19c, and 23-19d.
14. Update the title block.
15. Format the layouts. In all three layouts, set the
    a. viewport's scale to 1/74" = 1'-0",
    b. drawing units to ENGINEERING, and
    c. lock the scale.
16. Save the file.

ICA Submission

1. Follow the instructor's instructions to submit the ICA.

Station-Stage Hygrograph April 16, 2026			
Station	*Stage (Feet)*	*Station*	*Stage (Feet)*
P1	394	P9	362
P2	390	P10	360
P3	384	P11	356
P4	376	P12	352
P5	372	P13	350
P6	368	P14	346
P7	366	P15	342
P8	364	P16	338
		P17	332

Figure 23-19a

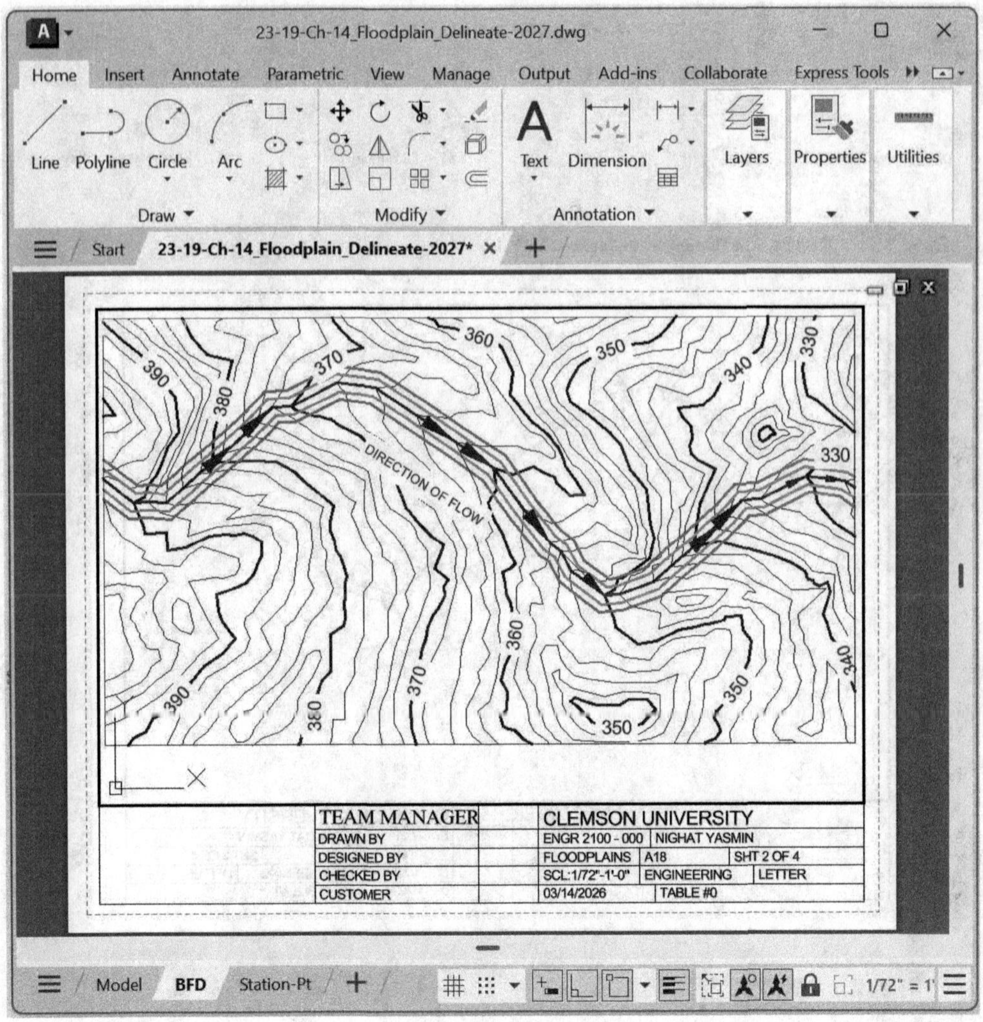

Figure 23-19b

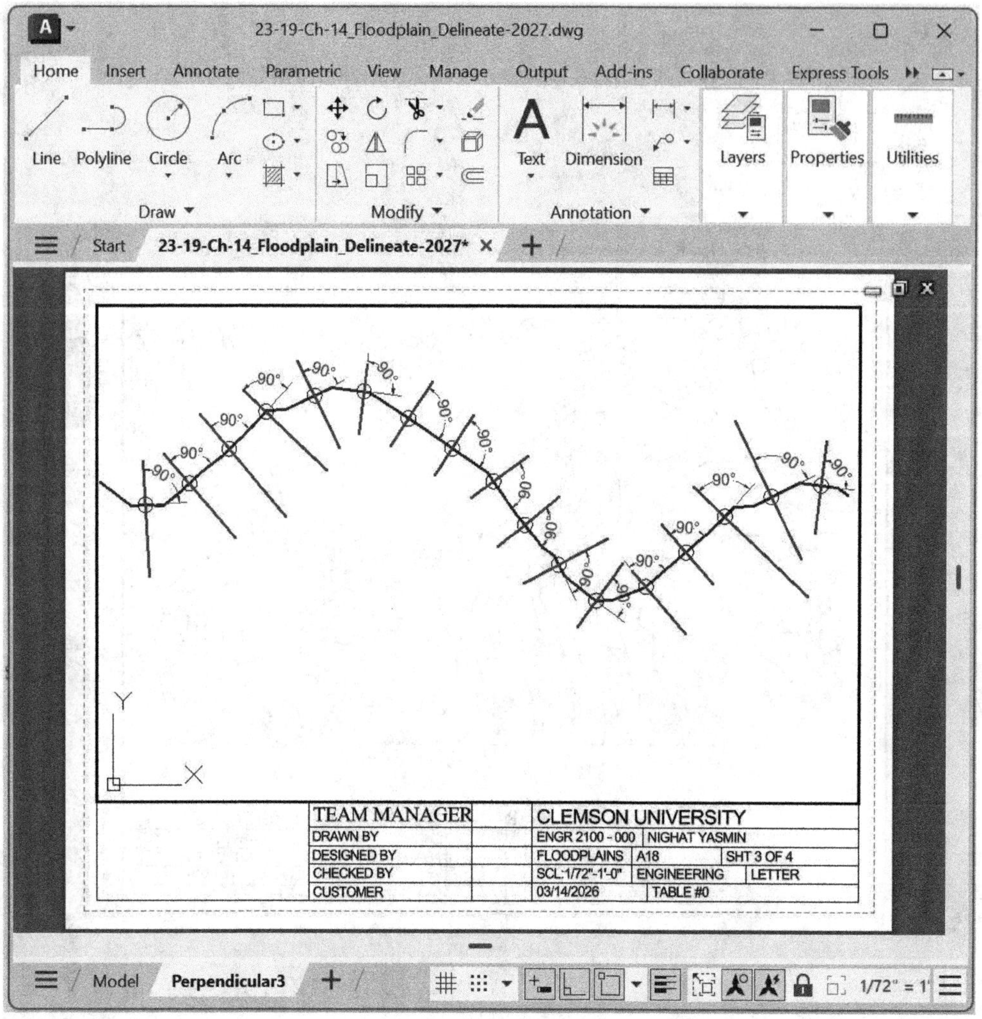

Figure 23-19c

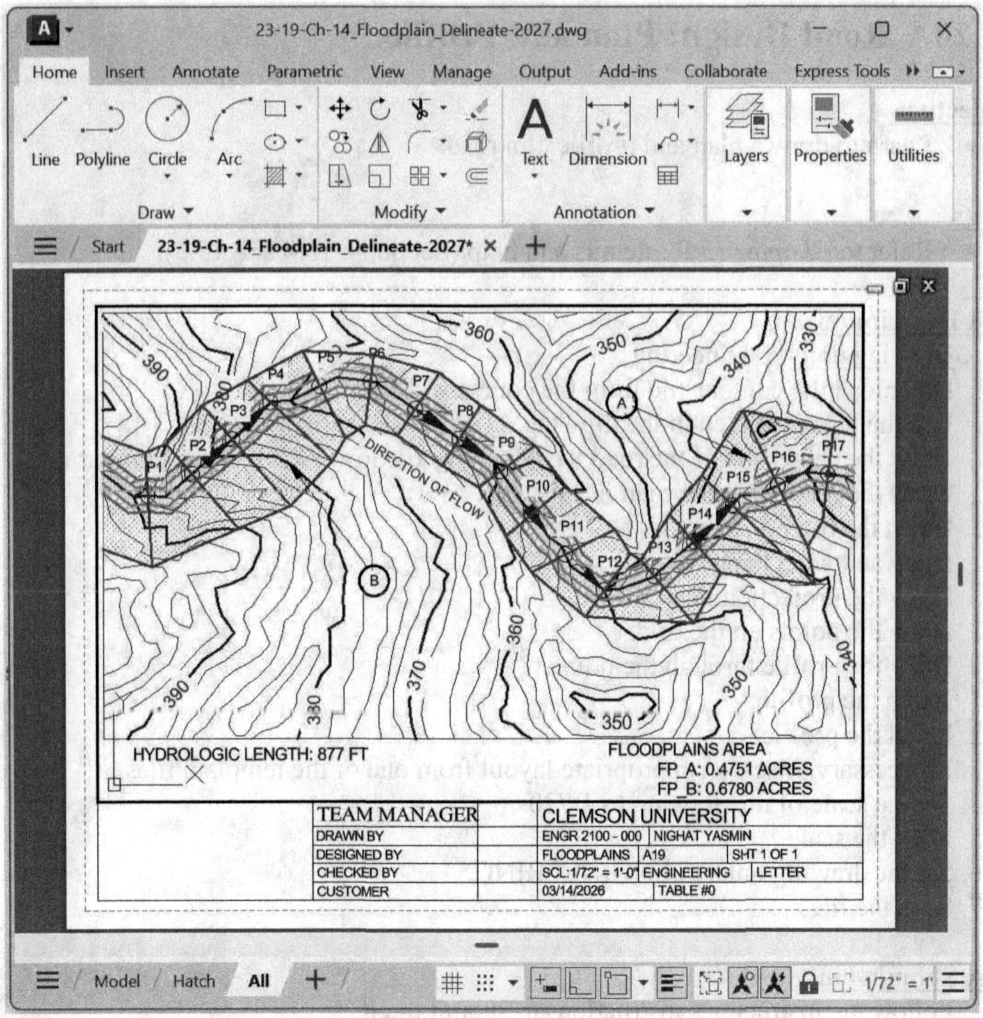

Figure 23-19d

23.20. Road Design: Plan and Profile

Objectives

- Learn to draw a plan and profile of a road.

Hints

- Refer to *Chapter 15* for details and help (Sections: 15.4 and 15.5).

ICA Description

1. Drawing units: Engineering
2. Download the contour file from the course website.
3. Use the layers created in the drawing.
4. Draw the centerline of the road 84'-9" above the lower edge of the contour map.
5. Draw the road plan; the road is 24' wide.
6. Hatch the road plan.
7. Draw and label the grid.
8. Draw the projection lines.
9. Draw the points on the grid.
10. Draw the profile through the points.
11. Hatch the profile.
12. Label the profile.
13. If necessary, insert an appropriate layout from one of the template files.
14. Set the scale of the drawing to 1:720.
15. Lock the scale.
16. Set the drawing units to ENGINEERING.
17. Save the file.

ICA Submission

1. Follow the instructor's instructions to submit the ICA.

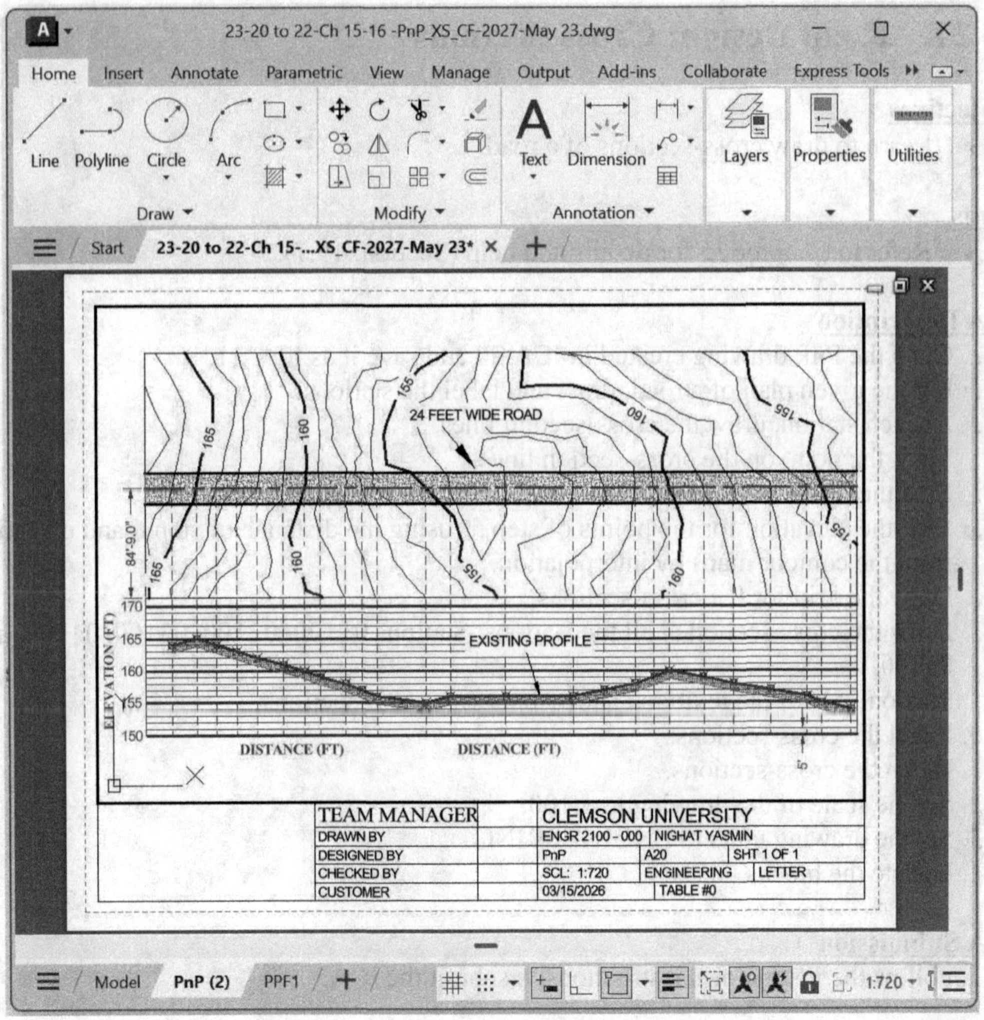

23-20 to 22-Ch 15-16 -PnP_XS_CF-2027-May 23.dwg
Home
Insert
Annotate
Parametric
View
Manage
Output
Add-ins
Collaborate
Express Tools
Line
Polyline
Circle
Arc
Draw
Modify
Text
Dimension
Annotation
Layers
Properties
Utilities
Start
23-20 to 22-Ch 15-...XS_CF-2027-May 23*
24 FEET WIDE ROAD
EXISTING PROFILE
ELEVATION (FT)
DISTANCE (FT)
DISTANCE (FT)
84'-9.0"
TEAM MANAGER
DRAWN BY
DESIGNED BY
CHECKED BY
CUSTOMER
CLEMSON UNIVERSITY
ENGR 2100 - 000
NIGHAT YASMIN
PnP
A20
SHT 1 OF 1
SCL: 1:720
ENGINEERING
LETTER
03/15/2026
TABLE #0
Model
PnP (2)
PPF1
1:720

Figure 23-20

23.21. Road Design: Cross Sections

Objectives

- Learn to draw cross-sections of a road.

Hints

- Refer to *Chapter 15* for details and help (Section: 15.7).

ICA Description

1. Open the PnP drawing created in ICA 20 and save it as ICA 21.
2. For the given plan of a road, draw and label the stations.
3. At each station, draw the cross-section lines.
4. Mark the point on the cross-section lines.
5. Find the distance (for the points of step 5) from the nearest contours.
6. Find the elevation for the points of step 5 (using the distance of step 6 and elevation from the contour map) by interpolation.
7. Draw the grid for the cross-sections.
8. Draw the cross-section at all the stations: Stations 01+00, 02+00, 03+00, 04+00, and 05+00.
9. Section 15.7 of the textbook shows only two cross-sections.
10. Label the cross-sections.
11. Hatch the cross-sections.
12. Set the scale of the drawing to 1:100.
13. Set the drawing units to ENGINEERING.
14. Update the blocks.

ICA Submission

1. Follow the instructor's instructions to submit the ICA.

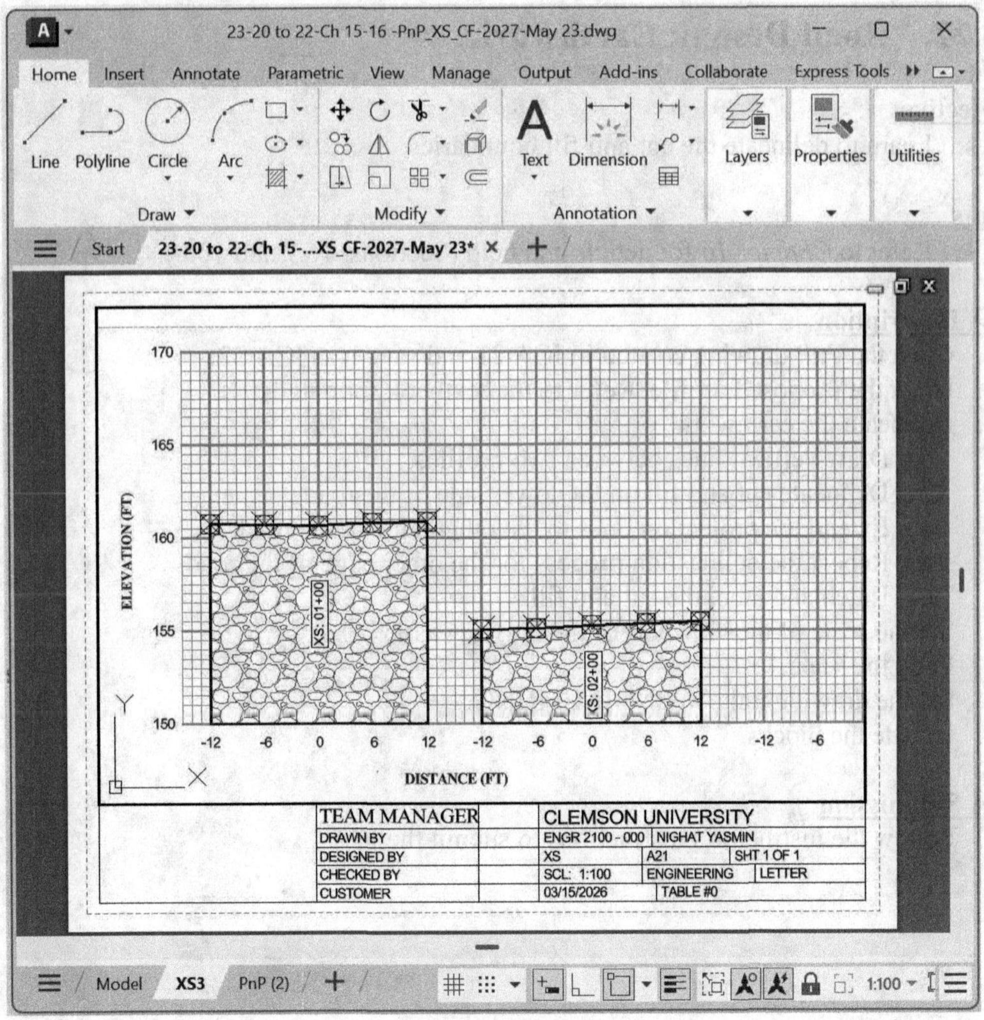
23-20 to 22-Ch 15-16 -PnP_XS_CF-2027-May 23.dwg
Home
Insert
Annotate
Parametric
View
Manage
Output
Add-ins
Collaborate
Express Tools
Line
Polyline
Circle
Arc
Draw
Modify
Text
Dimension
Annotation
Layers
Properties
Utilities
Start
23-20 to 22-Ch 15-...XS_CF-2027-May 23*
170
165
160
155
150
ELEVATION (FT)
XS: 01+00
XS: 02+00
-12
-6
0
6
12
DISTANCE (FT)
TEAM MANAGER
DRAWN BY
DESIGNED BY
CHECKED BY
CUSTOMER
CLEMSON UNIVERSITY
ENGR 2100 - 000
NIGHAT YASMIN
XS
A21
SHT 1 OF 1
SCL: 1:100
ENGINEERING
LETTER
03/15/2026
TABLE #0
Model
XS3
PnP (2)
1:100

Figure 23-21

23.22. Road Design: Earthwork

Objectives

- Learn to delineate the cut and fill boundaries.

Hints

- Refer to *Chapter 16* for details and help (Sections: 16.7 and 16.8).

ICA Description

1. Open the PnP drawing created in ICA 21 and save it as ICA 22.
2. Draw the proposed profile. Refer to the textbook for details.
3. Delineate the earthwork.
    a. Draw vertical lines between two profiles.
    b. Delineate cut and fill on the lower side of the road.
    c. Extend the projection lines to the other edge of the road.
    d. Repeat the delineation process for the other edge of the road.
    e. Hatch and label the cut and fill.
4. Set the scale of the viewport of the drawing as 1:720.
5. Lock the scale.
6. Set the drawing units to ENGINEERING.
7. Update the blocks.

ICA Submission

1. Follow the instructor's instructions to submit the ICA.

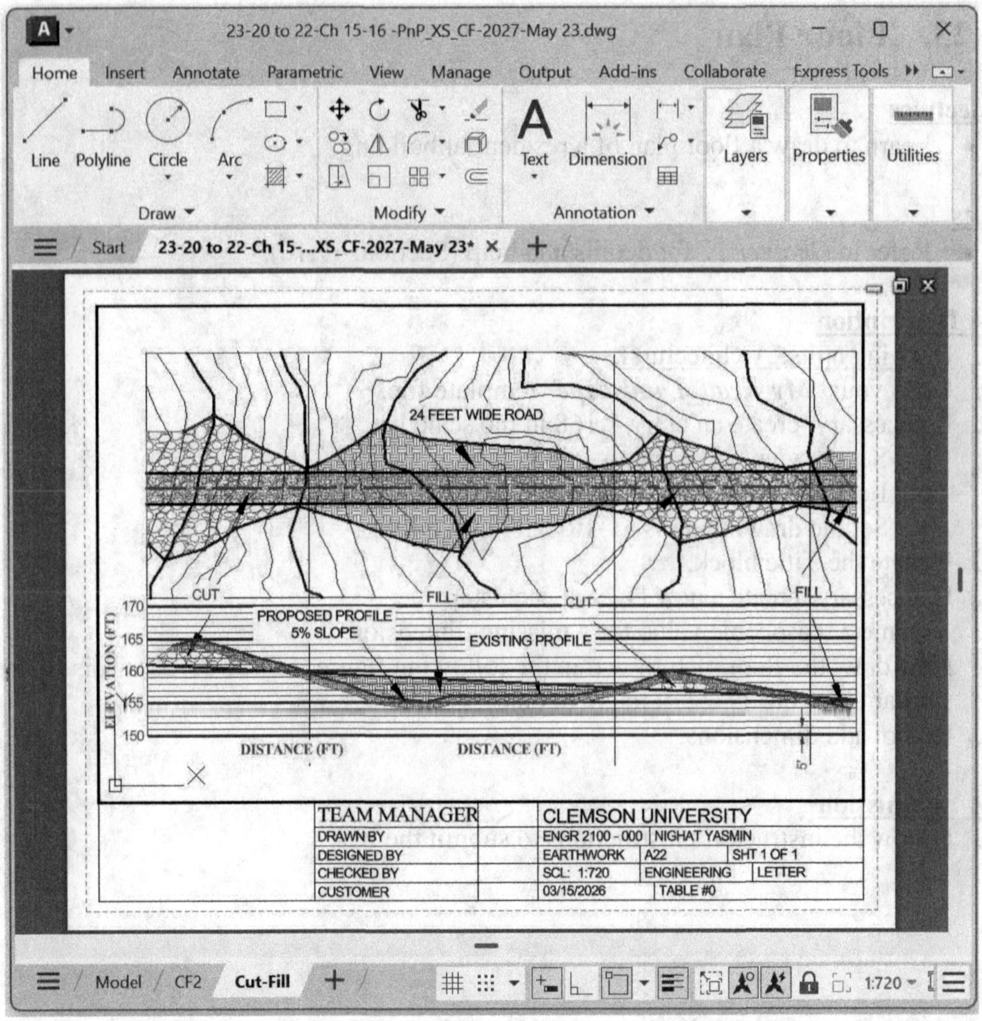
23-20 to 22-Ch 15-16 -PnP_XS_CF-2027-May 23.dwg
Home
Insert
Annotate
Parametric
View
Manage
Output
Add-ins
Collaborate
Express Tools
Line
Polyline
Circle
Arc
Text
Dimension
Layers
Properties
Utilities
Draw
Modify
Annotation
Start
23-20 to 22-Ch 15-...XS_CF-2027-May 23*
24 FEET WIDE ROAD
CUT
FILL
CUT
FILL
PROPOSED PROFILE
5% SLOPE
EXISTING PROFILE
ELEVATION (FT)
170
165
160
155
150
DISTANCE (FT)
DISTANCE (FT)
TEAM MANAGER
CLEMSON UNIVERSITY
DRAWN BY
ENGR 2100 - 000
NIGHAT YASMIN
DESIGNED BY
EARTHWORK
A22
SHT 1 OF 1
CHECKED BY
SCL: 1:720
ENGINEERING
LETTER
CUSTOMER
03/15/2026
TABLE #0
Model
CF2
Cut-Fill
1:720

Figure 23-22

23.23. Floor Plan

Objectives

- Learn to draw a floor plan of a residential building.

Hints

- Refer to *Chapter 17* for details and help (Section: 17.10).

ICA Description

1. Drawing units: Architectural:
2. Open your "***My_acad_Landscape***" template file.
3. If necessary, create an entry 1:168 in the scale list.
    a. Set the viewport scale to 1:168.
    b. Lock the scale.
    c. Set the drawing units to ARCHITECTURAL.
4. Update the Title block.
5. If necessary, create a new layer at each step.
6. Assume a reasonable value for a missing dimension.
7. Now draw the floor plan shown in the following figure (Figure 23-23). This figure is similar to Figure 17-22 of the textbook.
8. Do not add dimensions.

ICA Submission

1. Follow the instructor's instructions to submit the ICA.

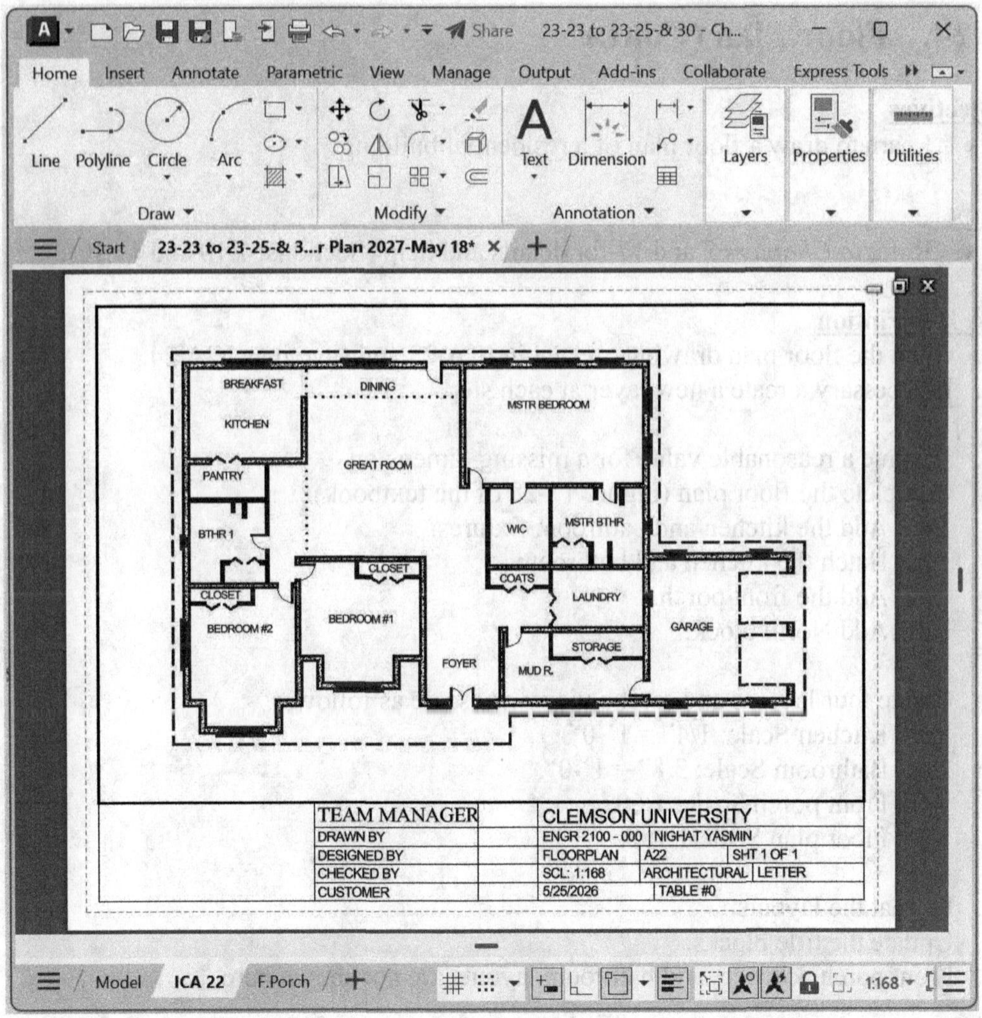
23-23 to 23-25-& 30 - Ch...
Home
Insert
Annotate
Parametric
View
Manage
Output
Add-ins
Collaborate
Express Tools
Line
Polyline
Circle
Arc
Draw
Modify
Text
Dimension
Annotation
Layers
Properties
Utilities
Start
23-23 to 23-25-& 3...r Plan 2027-May 18*
BREAKFAST
DINING
KITCHEN
MSTR BEDROOM
GREAT ROOM
PANTRY
BTHR 1
WIC
MSTR BTHR
CLOSET
COATS
LAUNDRY
BEDROOM #2
BEDROOM #1
GARAGE
STORAGE
FOYER
MUD R.
TEAM MANAGER
DRAWN BY
DESIGNED BY
CHECKED BY
CUSTOMER
CLEMSON UNIVERSITY
ENGR 2100 - 000
NIGHAT YASMIN
FLOORPLAN
A22
SHT 1 OF 1
SCL: 1:168
ARCHITECTURAL
LETTER
5/25/2026
TABLE #0
Model
ICA 22
F.Porch
1:168

Figure 23-23

23.24. Floor Plan (Cont.)

Objectives

- Learn to draw a floor plan of a residential building

Hints

- Refer *to Chapters 7* and 17 for details and help (Sections: 7.10 and 17.10).

ICA Description

1. Open the floor plan drawing created in ICA 23 and save it as ICA 24.
2. If necessary, create a new layer at each step.

3. Assume a reasonable value for a missing dimension.
4. Complete the floor plan (Figure 17-28 of the textbook).
   a. Add the kitchen and bathroom fixtures.
   b. Hatch the kitchen and bathroom.
   c. Add the front porch.
   d. Add North block.

5. Create four layouts and set the viewports scale as follows:
   a. Kitchen Scale: 1/4" = 1'-0".
   b. Bathroom Scale: 3/8" = 1'-0".
   c. Front porch Scale: 1:60.
   d. Floor plan Scale 1:168.

6. Format the layouts.
7. Update the title blocks.
8. Front porch, kitchen, and bathroom layouts are not shown here.

ICA Submission

1. Follow the instructor's instructions to submit the ICA.

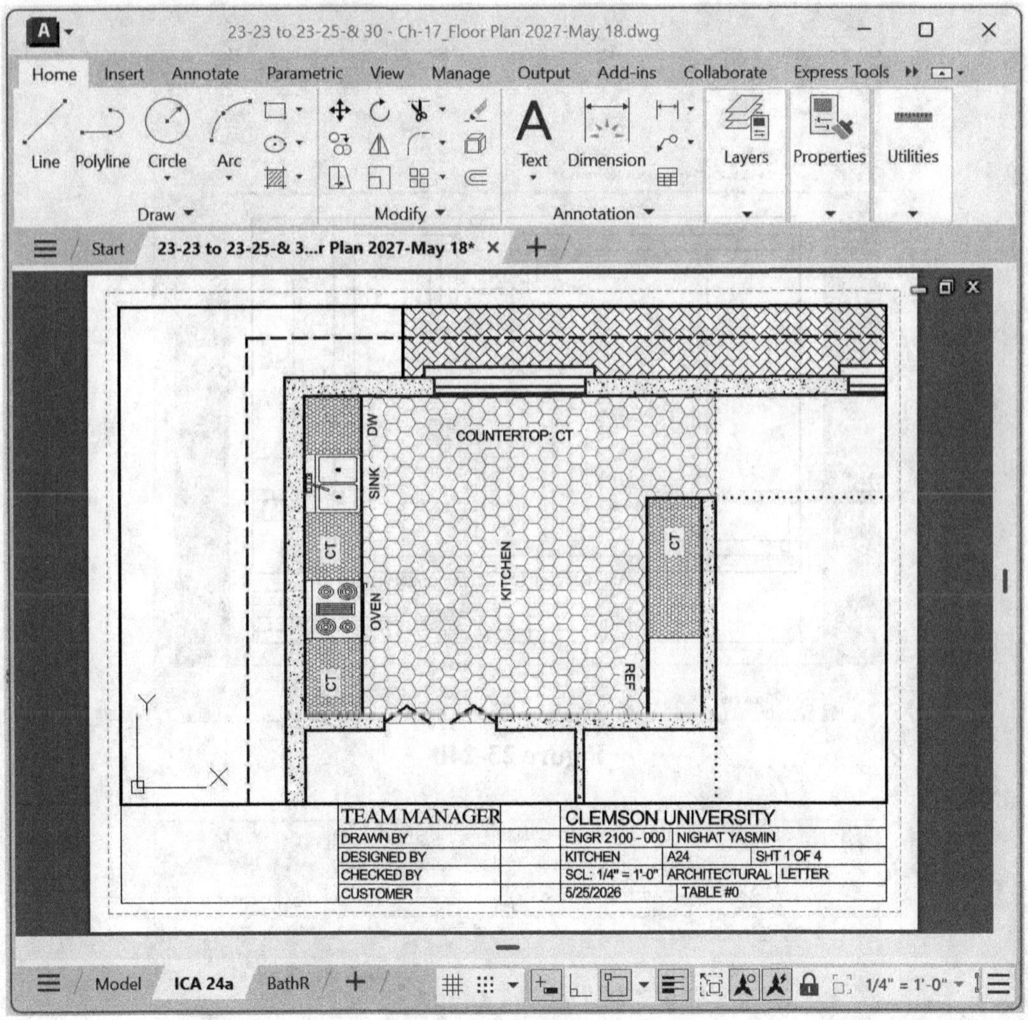

Figure 23-24a

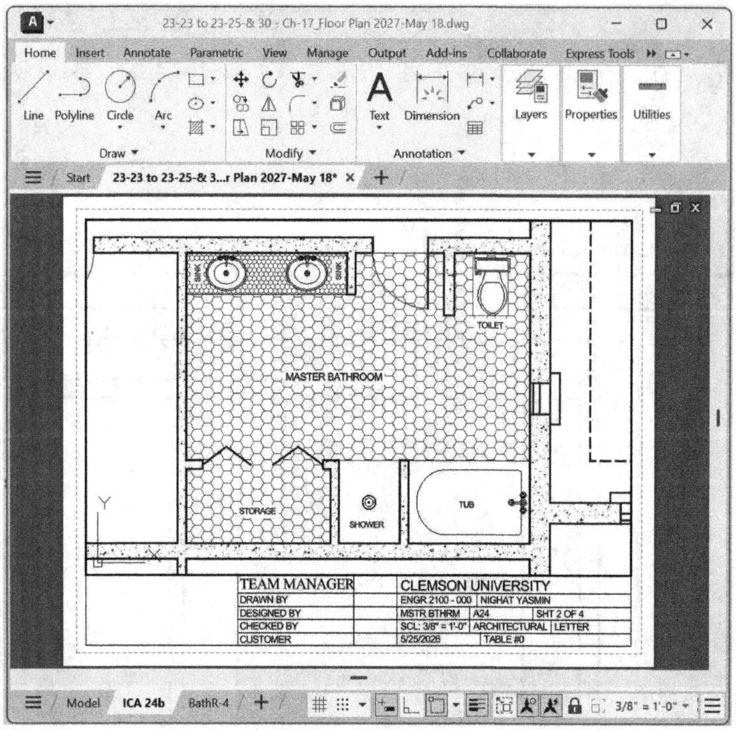

Figure 23-24b

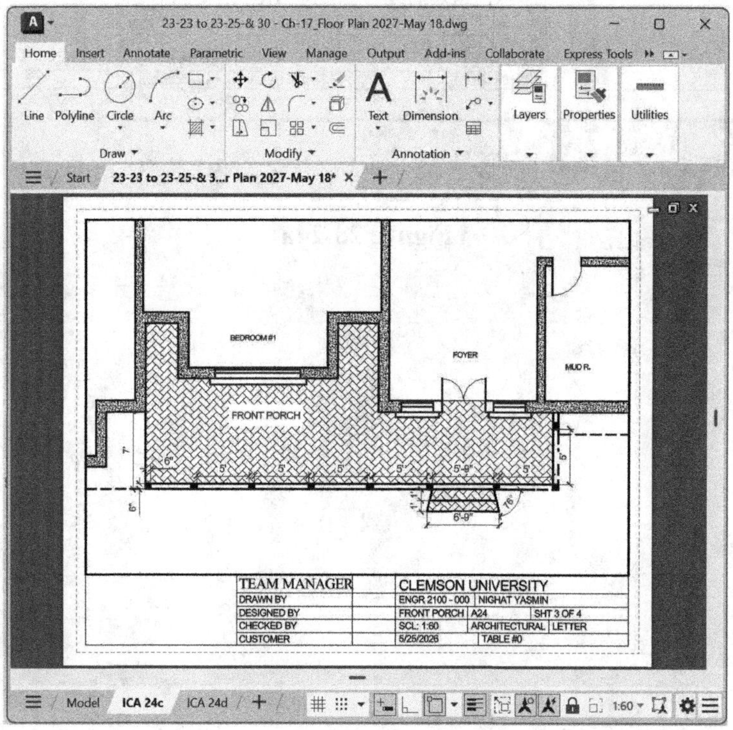

Figure 23-24c

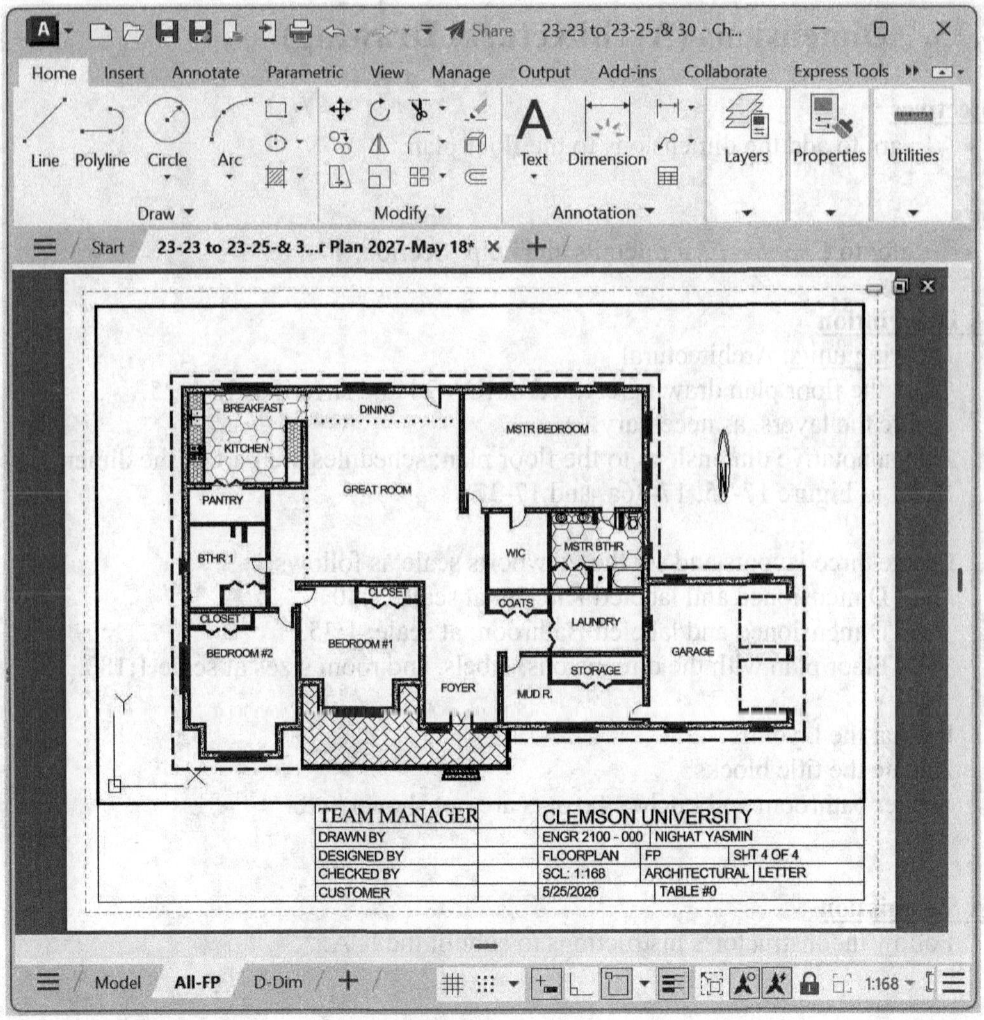

Figure 23-24d

23.25. Dimensions (Architectural Drawing)

Objectives

- Learn to add the dimensions to the floor plan.

Hints

- Refer to *Chapter 17* for details and help (Section: 17.11).

ICA Description

1. Drawing units: Architectural
2. Open the floor plan drawing created in ICA 24 and save it as ICA 25.
3. Create the layers, as necessary.
4. Add annotative dimensions to the floor plan; schedules are part of the dimensions.
5. Refer to Figure 17-35, 17-36a, and 17-37.

6. Create three layouts and set the viewports scale as follows:
   a. Dimensioned and labeled Kitchen at scale: 1:40
   b. Dimensioned and labeled Bathroom at scale: 1:35.
   c. Floor plan with the dimensions, labels, and room sizes at scale 1:180.

7. Format the layouts.
8. Update the title blocks.
9. Master bathroom and kitchen layouts are not shown here.

ICA Submission

1. Follow the instructor's instructions to submit the ICA.

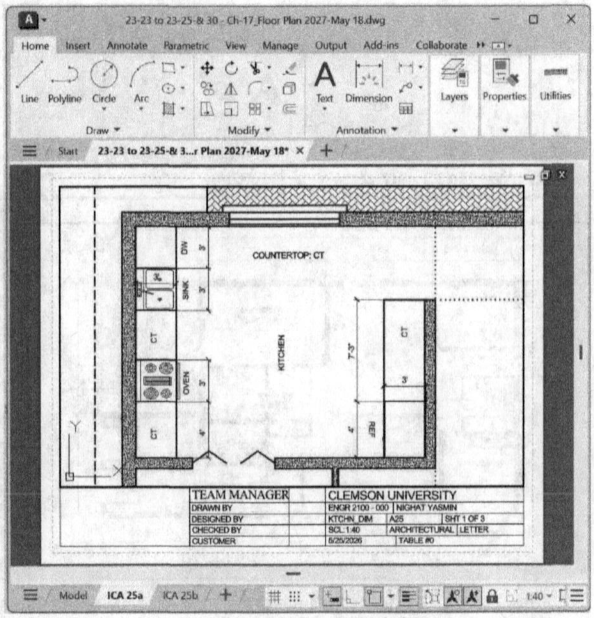

Figure 23-25a

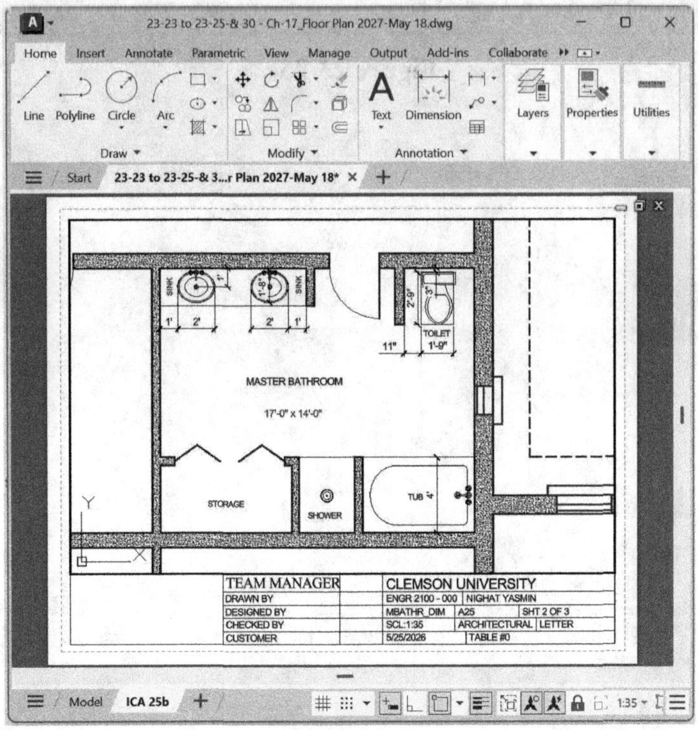

Figure 23-25b

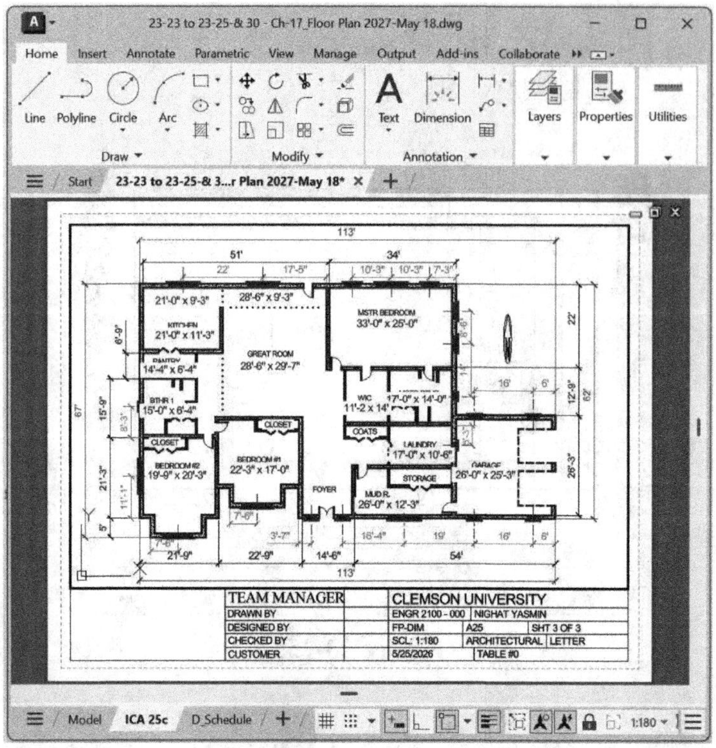

Figure 23-25c

23.26. Roof Plan

Objectives

- Learn to develop a roof plan for the given floorplan.

Hints

- Refer to *Chapter 18* for details and help (Section 18.4).

ICA Description

1. Drawing units: Architectural
2. Create the layers as necessary.
3. Open the floor plan drawing created in ICA 25 and save it as ICA 26.
4. Create the roof plan shown in the following figure (Figure 23-26).
5. Assume a reasonable value for a missing dimension.
6. For details, refer to Figures 18-4b and 18-4c of the textbook.

7. Set the viewport scale to 1:156.

8. Format the layouts.
9. Update the title blocks.

ICA Submission

1. Follow the instructor's instructions to submit the ICA.

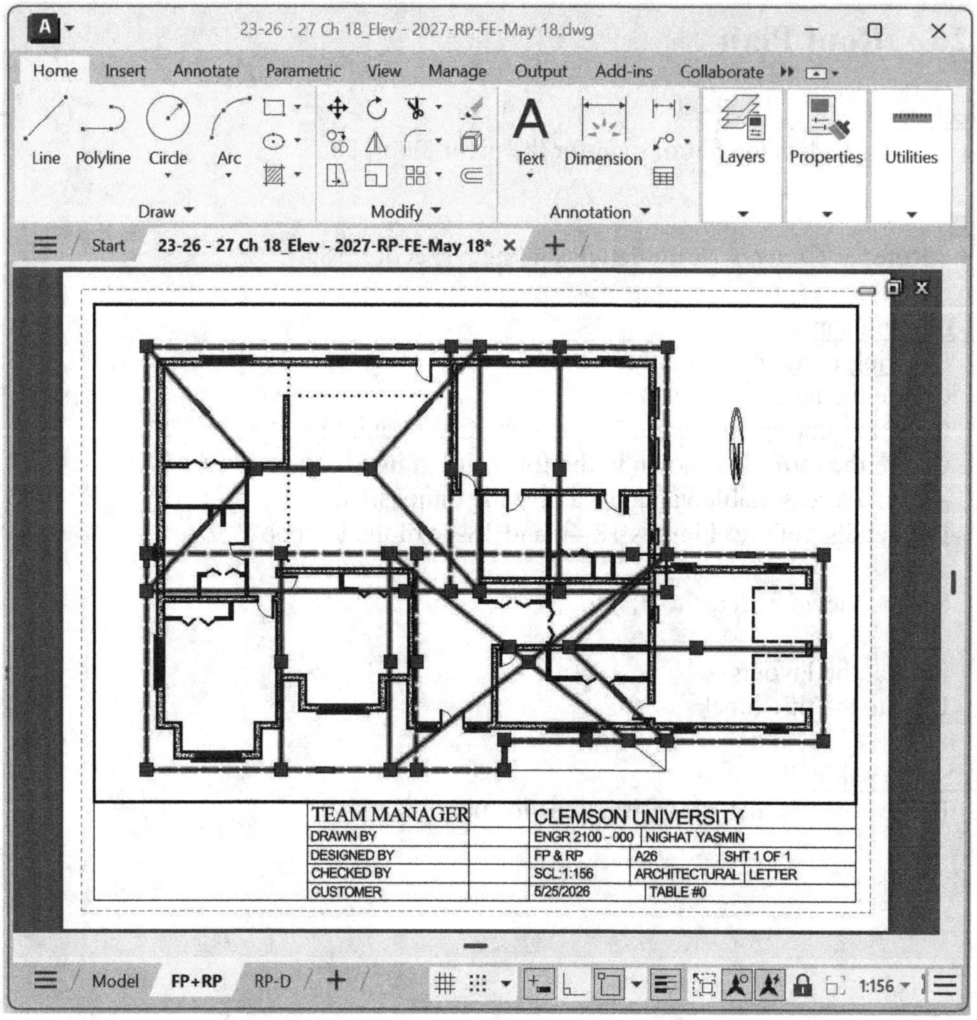
23-26 - 27 Ch 18_Elev - 2027-RP-FE-May 18.dwg
Home
Insert
Annotate
Parametric
View
Manage
Output
Add-ins
Collaborate
Line
Polyline
Circle
Arc
Draw
Modify
Text
Dimension
Annotation
Layers
Properties
Utilities
Start
23-26 - 27 Ch 18_Elev - 2027-RP-FE-May 18*
TEAM MANAGER
DRAWN BY
DESIGNED BY
CHECKED BY
CUSTOMER
CLEMSON UNIVERSITY
ENGR 2100 - 000
NIGHAT YASMIN
FP & RP
A26
SHT 1 OF 1
SCL:1:156
ARCHITECTURAL
LETTER
5/25/2026
TABLE #0
Model
FP+RP
RP-D
1:156

Figure 23-26

23.27. Front Elevation

Objectives

- Learn to insert a block from the *Design Center*.
- Learn to develop front elevation for the given floor and roof plans.

Hints

- Refer to *Chapter 18* for details and help (Sections: 18.5).

ICA Description

1. Drawing units: Architectural:
2. Create the layers, as necessary.
3. Open the drawing created in ICA 26 and save it as ICA 27 (both the floor plan and roof plan in the same file).
4. Create the front elevation shown in Figure 18-13 of the textbook.
5. Do not add dimensions.
6. Landscaping is optional.
7. Set the viewport scale to 1:156.
8. Format the layout.
9. Update the title blocks.

ICA Submission

1. Follow the instructor's instructions to submit the ICA.

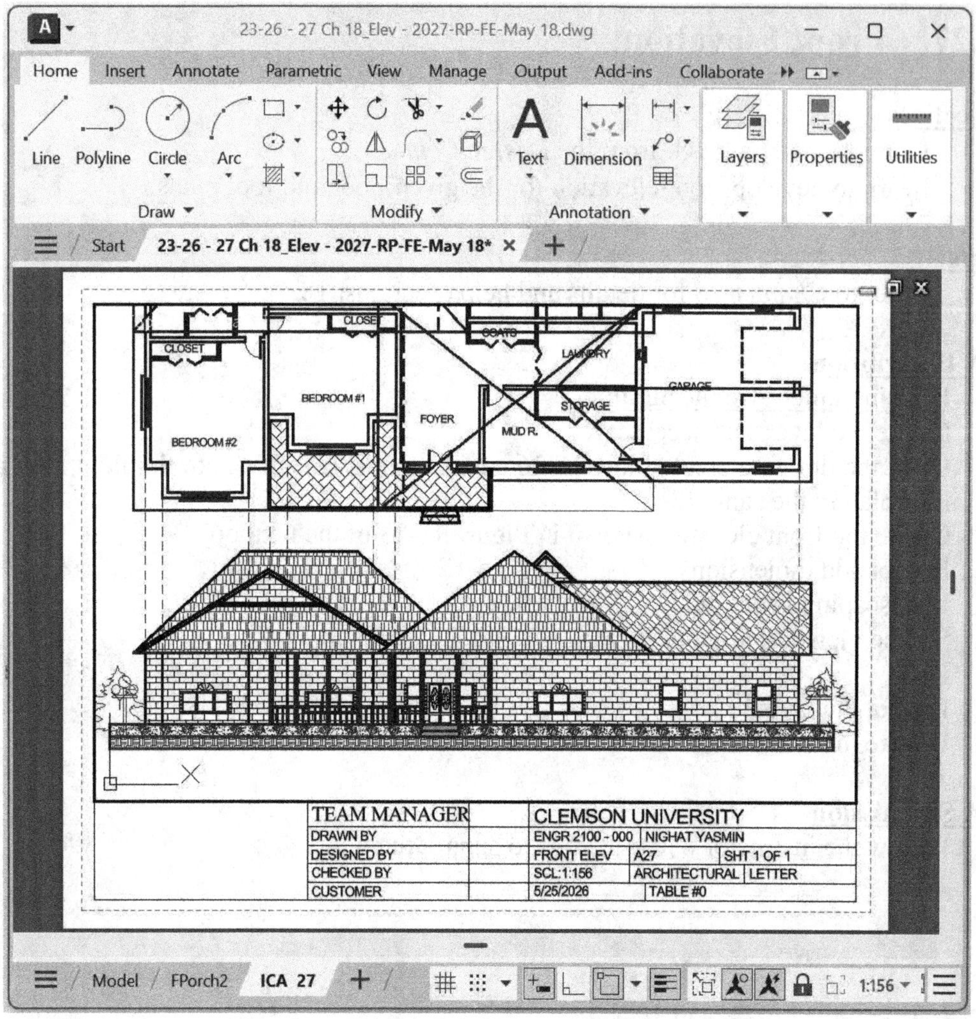
23-26 - 27 Ch 18_Elev - 2027-RP-FE-May 18.dwg
Home
Insert
Annotate
Parametric
View
Manage
Output
Add-ins
Collaborate
Line
Polyline
Circle
Arc
Text
Dimension
Layers
Properties
Utilities
Draw
Modify
Annotation
Start
23-26 - 27 Ch 18_Elev - 2027-RP-FE-May 18*
CLOSET
BEDROOM #1
BEDROOM #2
FOYER
MUD R.
STORAGE
LAUNDRY
GARAGE
TEAM MANAGER
DRAWN BY
DESIGNED BY
CHECKED BY
CUSTOMER
CLEMSON UNIVERSITY
ENGR 2100 - 000
NIGHAT YASMIN
FRONT ELEV
A27
SHT 1 OF 1
SCL:1:156
ARCHITECTURAL
LETTER
5/25/2026
TABLE #0
Model
FPorch2
ICA 27
1:156

Figure 23-27

23.28. Right Side Elevation

Objectives

- Learn to insert blocks from the *Design Center*.
- Learn to develop a front elevation for the given floor and roof plans.

Hints

- Refer to *Chapter 18* for details and help (Section: 18.6).

ICA Description

1. Drawing units: Architectural
2. Create the layers, as necessary.
3. Open the drawing created in ICA 27 and save it as ICA 28 (the floor plan, roof plan, and front elevation in the same file).
4. Create the right-side elevation shown in Figure 18-26 and Figure 18-27 of the textbook.
5. Do not add dimensions.
6. Landscaping is optional.

10. Set the scale as follows:
    a. Right-side elevation, Scale: 1:156.
    b. Front and right-side elevations, Scale: 1:230.

11. Format the layouts.
12. Update the title blocks.

ICA Submission

1. Follow the instructor's instructions to submit the ICA.

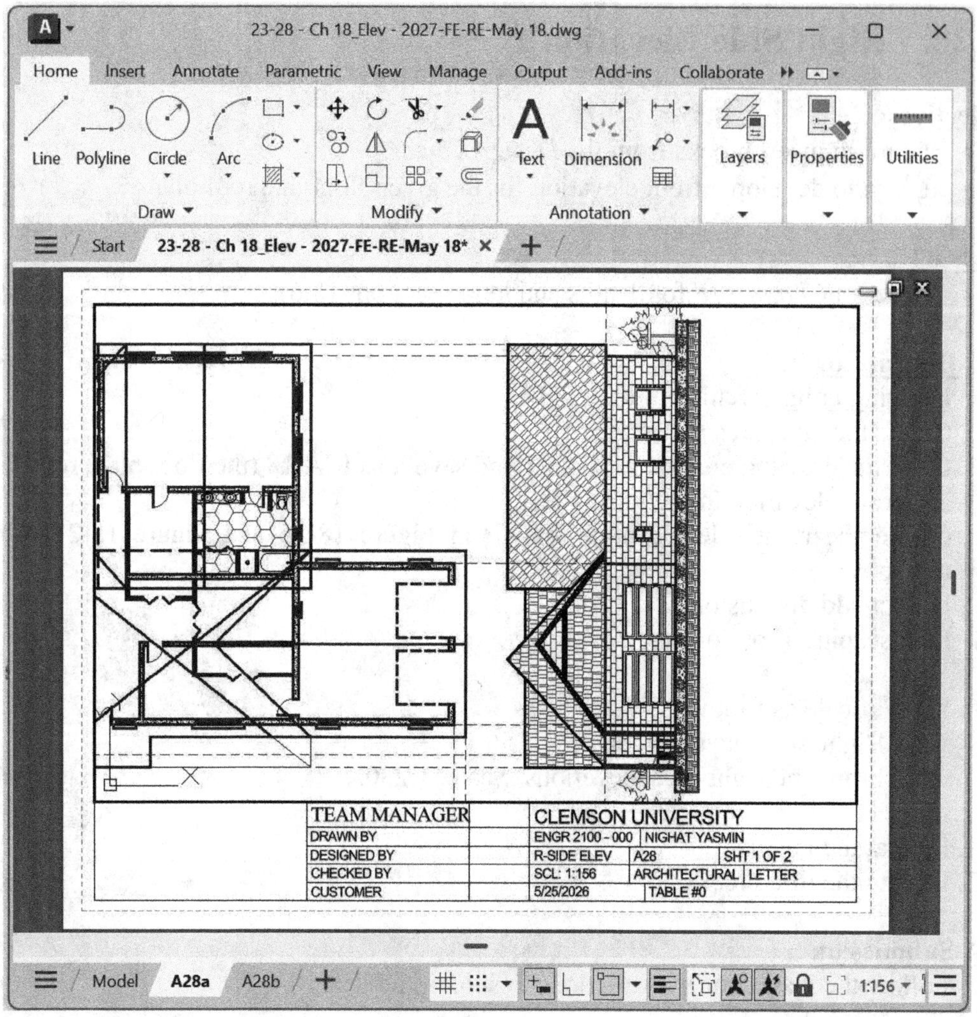

Figure 23-28a

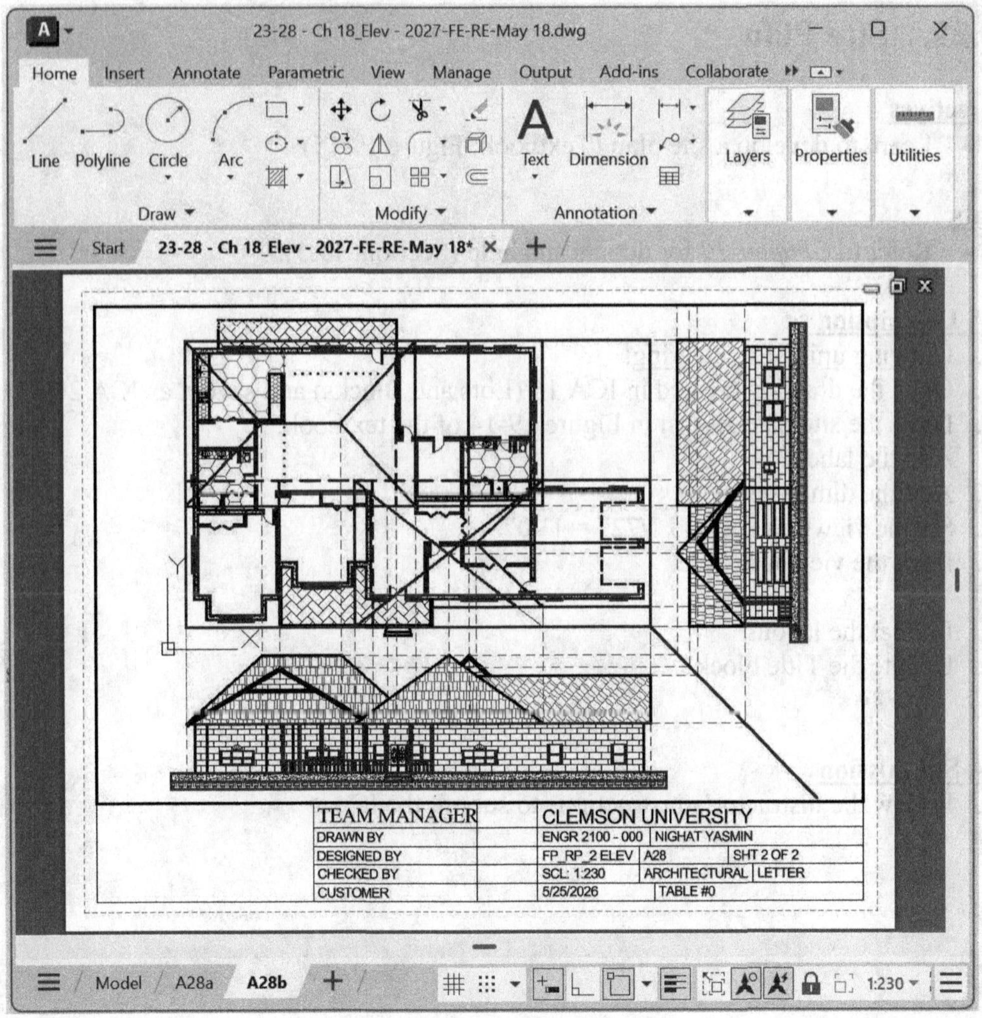

Figure 23-28b

23.29. Site Plan

Objectives

- Learn to develop a site plan (Textbook: Figure 19-15)

Hints

- Refer to *Chapter 19* for details and help (Section: 19.5).

ICA Description

1. Drawing units: Engineering:
2. Open the drawing created in ICA 16 (Lots and Blocks) and save it as ICA 29.
3. Draw the site plan shown in Figure 19-14 of the textbook.
4. Add the labels.
5. Add the dimensions.
6. Set the viewport scale to 1/72” = 1’-0”.
7. Lock the viewport scale.

8. Format the layout.
9. Update the Title block.

ICA Submission

1. Follow the instructor’s instructions to submit the ICA.

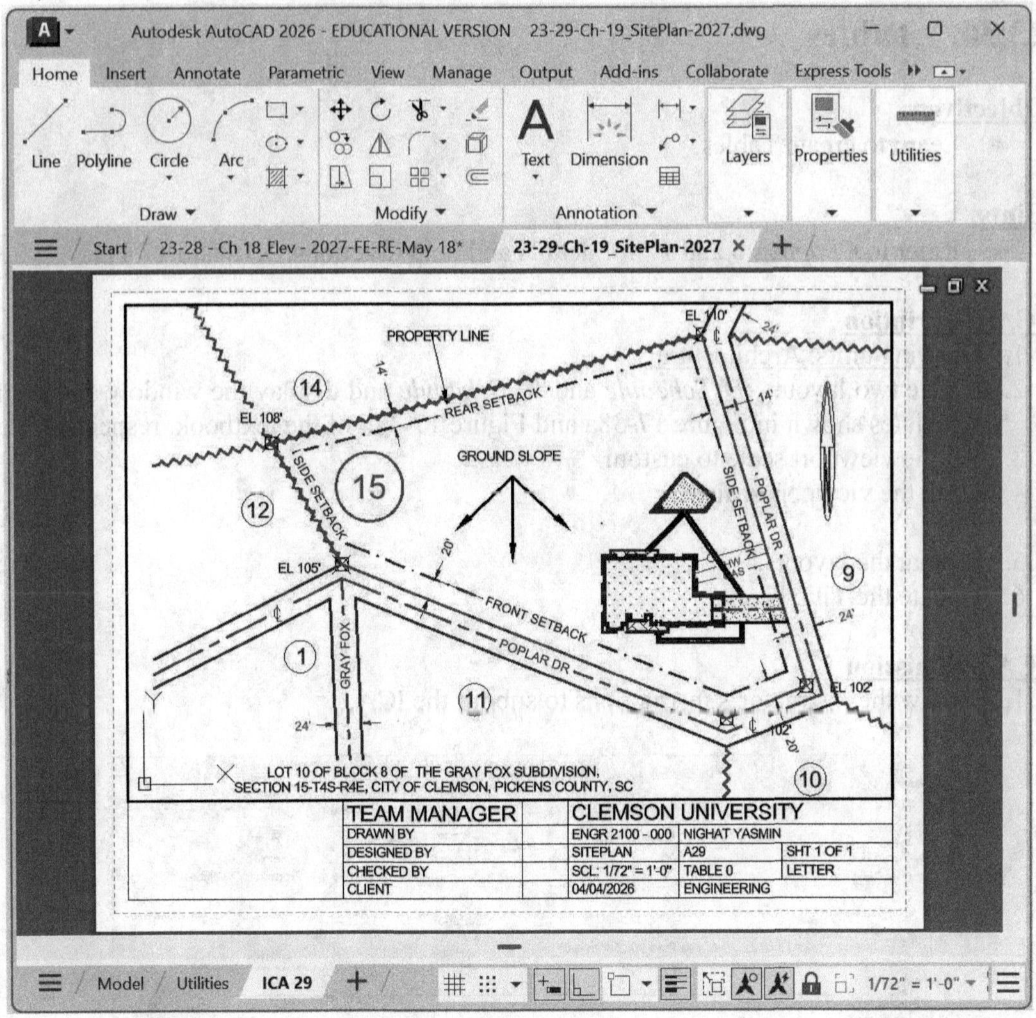
Autodesk AutoCAD 2026 - EDUCATIONAL VERSION 23-29-Ch-19_SitePlan-2027.dwg
Home Insert Annotate Parametric View Manage Output Add-ins Collaborate Express Tools
Line Polyline Circle Arc
Draw
Modify
Text Dimension
Annotation
Layers Properties Utilities
Start 23-28 - Ch 18_Elev - 2027-FE-RE-May 18* 23-29-Ch-19_SitePlan-2027
PROPERTY LINE
REAR SETBACK
GROUND SLOPE
SIDE SETBACK
POPLAR DR
FRONT SETBACK
GRAY FOX
EL 110'
EL 108'
EL 105'
EL 102'
LOT 10 OF BLOCK 8 OF THE GRAY FOX SUBDIVISION,
SECTION 15-T4S-R4E, CITY OF CLEMSON, PICKENS COUNTY, SC
TEAM MANAGER
DRAWN BY
DESIGNED BY
CHECKED BY
CLIENT
CLEMSON UNIVERSITY
ENGR 2100 - 000 NIGHAT YASMIN
SITEPLAN A29 SHT 1 OF 1
SCL: 1/72" = 1'-0" TABLE 0 LETTER
04/04/2026 ENGINEERING
Model Utilities ICA 29
1/72" = 1'-0"

Figure 23-29

23.30. Tables

Objectives

- Learn to create Tables.

Hints

- Refer to *Chapters 3* and *17* for details and help (Sections: 3.18 and 17.11).

ICA Description

1. Drawing units: Architectural
2. Create two layouts: *D_Schedule* and *W_Schedule* and display the window and door schedules shown in Figure 17-38a and Figure 17-38b of the textbook, respectively.
3. Set the viewport scale to custom.
4. Lock the viewport scale.

5. Format the layouts.
6. Update the Title block.

ICA Submission

1. Follow the instructor's instructions to submit the ICA.

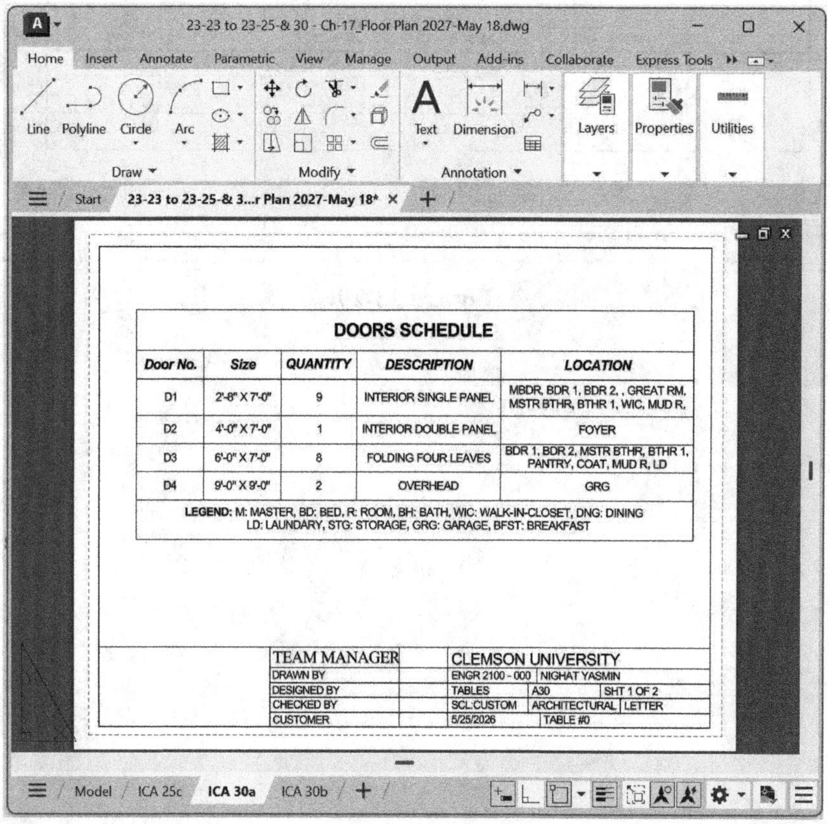

Figure 23-30a

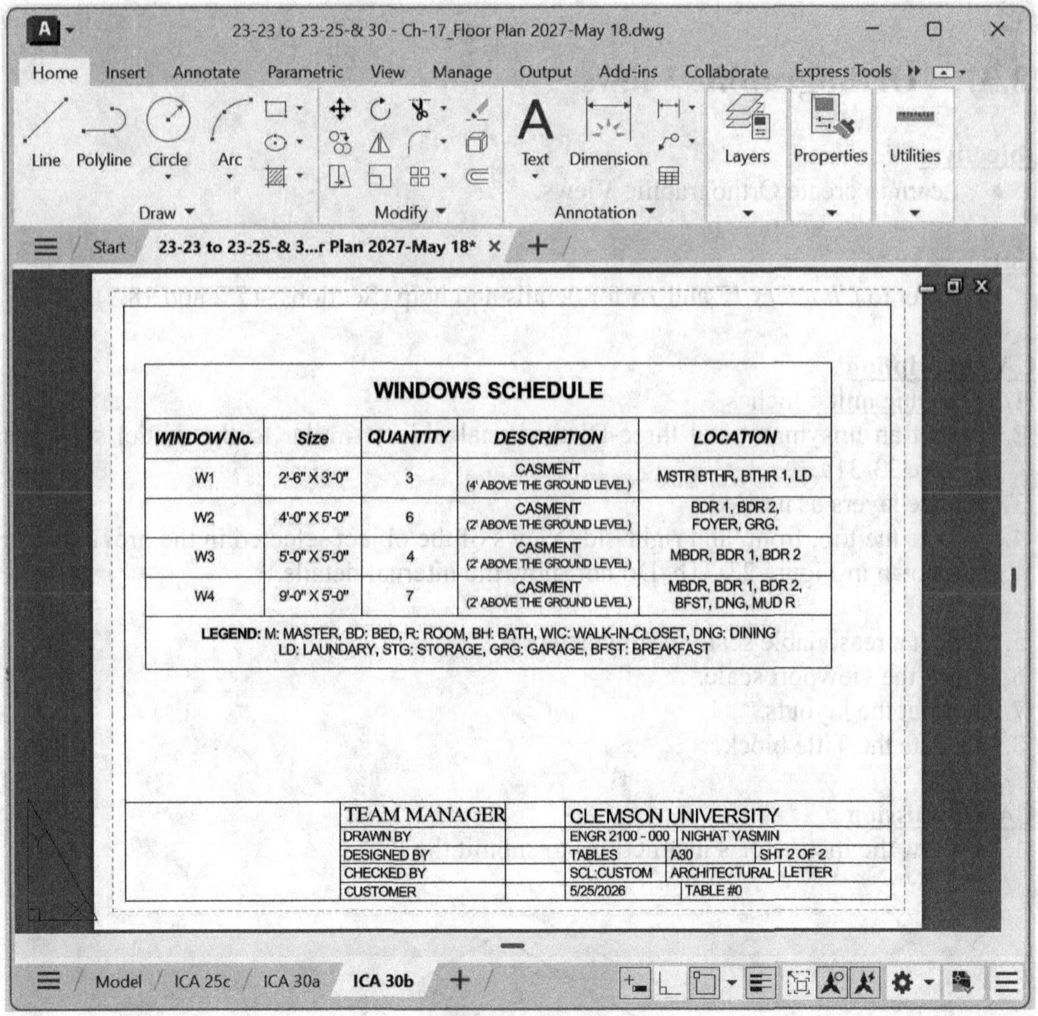

Figure 23-30b

23.31. Orthographic Views

Objectives

- Learn to create Orthographic Views.

Hints

- Refer to *Chapters 17* and *18* for details and help (Sections: 17.2 and 18.2).

ICA Description

1. Drawing units: Inches
2. Select an unsymmetrical three-Dimensional object similar to the model shown in Figure 23-31a.
3. Create layers as needed.
4. Create the top, front, and right-side views of the object selected in the previous step as shown in Figure 23-31b. Do not show the internal details.
5. Select a reasonable scale for the viewport.
6. Lock the viewport scale.
7. Format the layouts.
8. Update the Title block.

ICA Submission

1. Follow the instructor's instructions to submit the ICA.

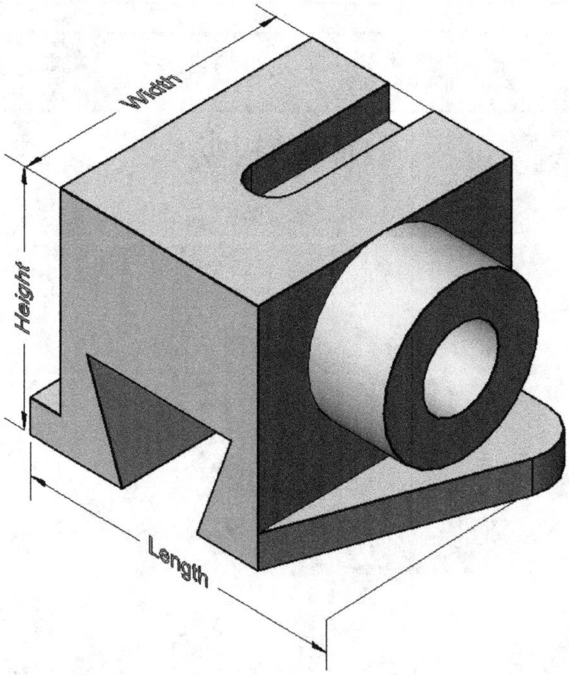

Figure 23-31a

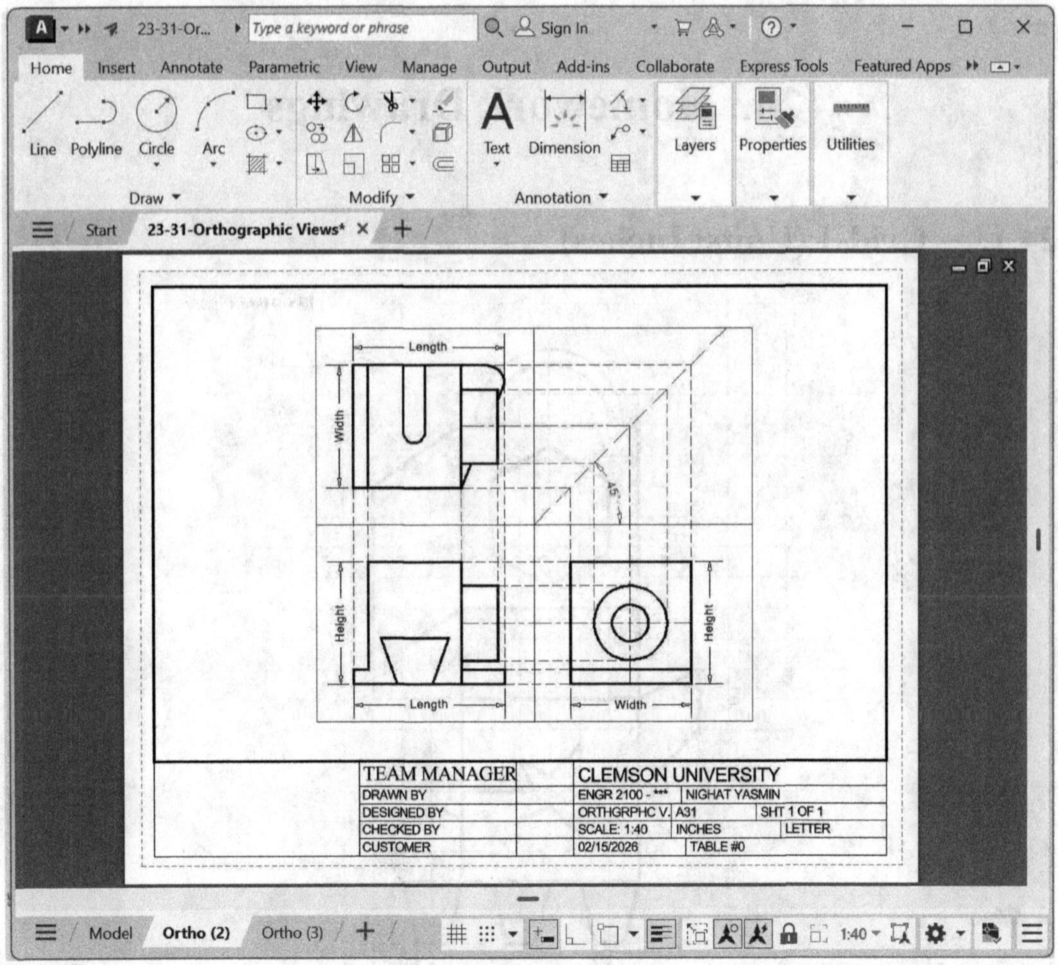

Figure 23-31b

Notes:

24. Homework Drawings

24.1. Grid-1 (Units: Inches)

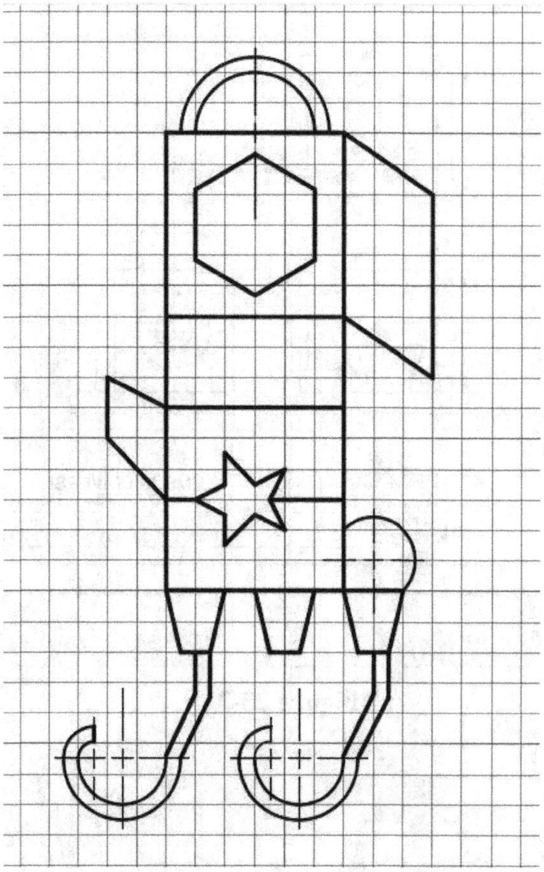

24.2. Grid-2 (Units: Millimeters)

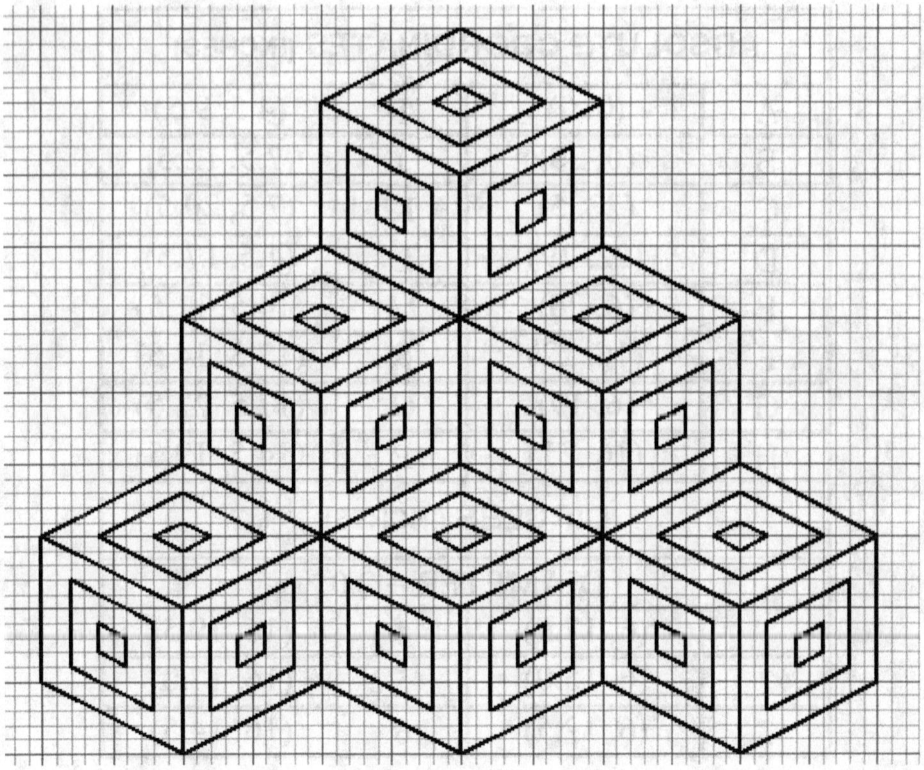

24.3. Circles (Units: Inches)

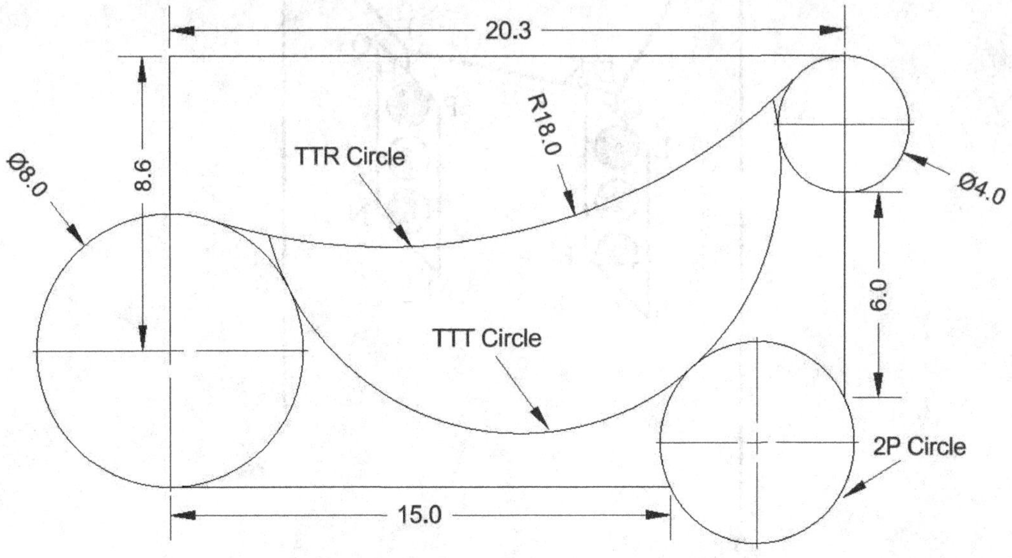

24.4. Light Signal (Units: Inches)

ABSOLUTE COORDINATES (INCHES)			
A	(0, 0)	I	(4.5, 9.5)
B	(0, 30)	J	(7.5, 12.5)
C	(22, 5)	K	(7.5, 20.5)
D	(22, 29)	L	(4.5, 17.5)
E	(6, 20)	M	(14.5, 11.5)
F	(16, 22)	N	(17.5, 14.5)
G	(6, 19)	O	(17.5, 22.5)
H	(16, 21)	P	(14.5, 19.5)
CIRCLES (INCHES)			
DIAMETER = 2.0			
1	(6, 17.5)	4	(16, 19.5)
2	(6, 15.0)	5	(16, 17.0)
3	(6, 12.5)	6	(16, 14.5)

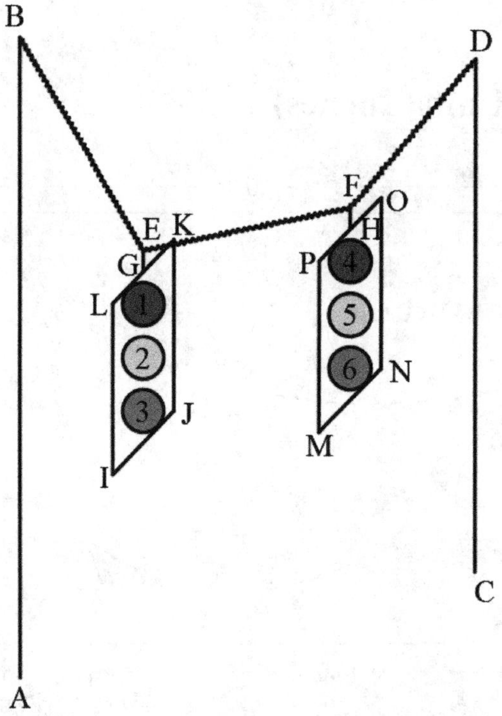

24.5. Plate with holes (Units: Inches)

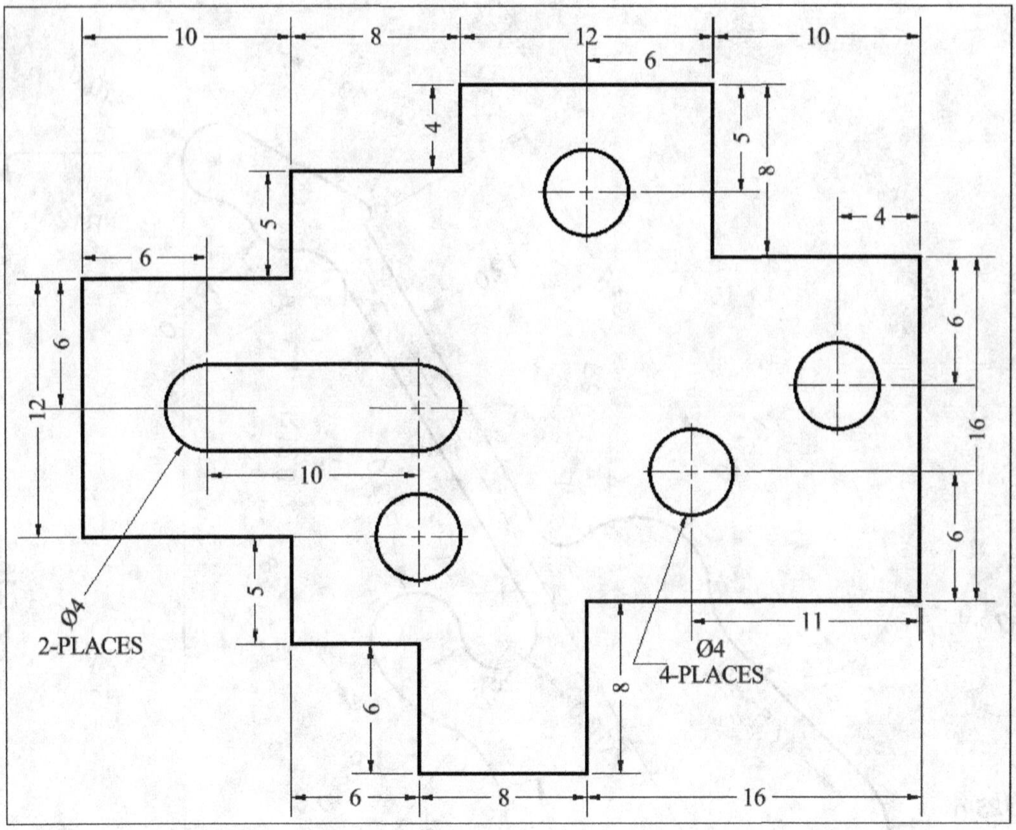

24.6. Circle-TTR (Units: Millimeters)

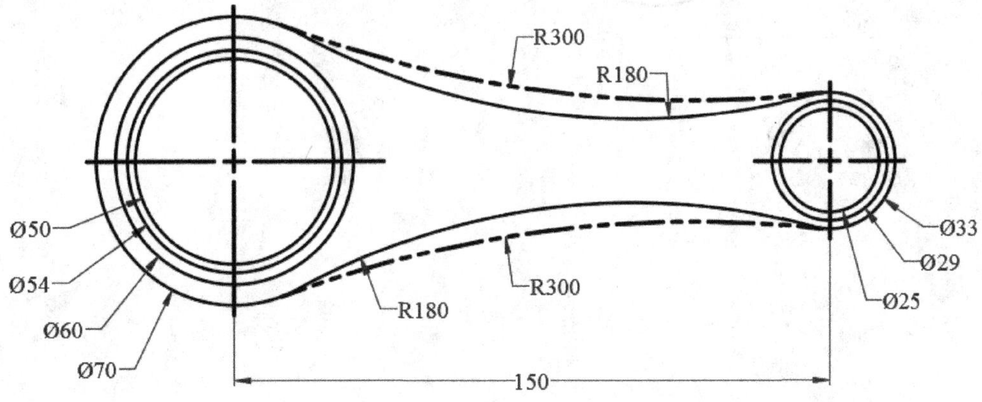

24.7. Guitar: Fillet and circular Arcs (Units: Inches)

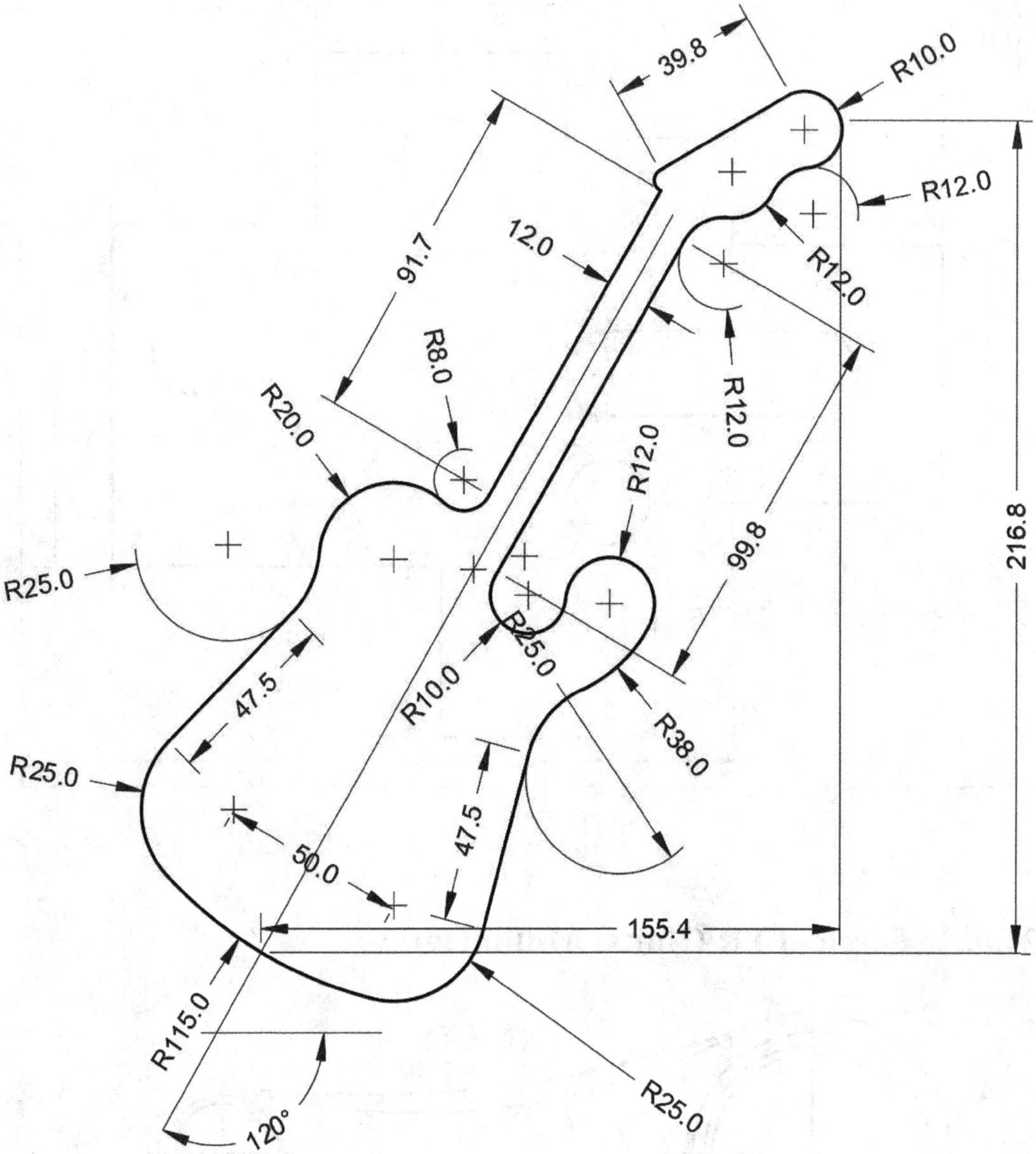

24.8. Bridge Pier (Units: Millimeters)

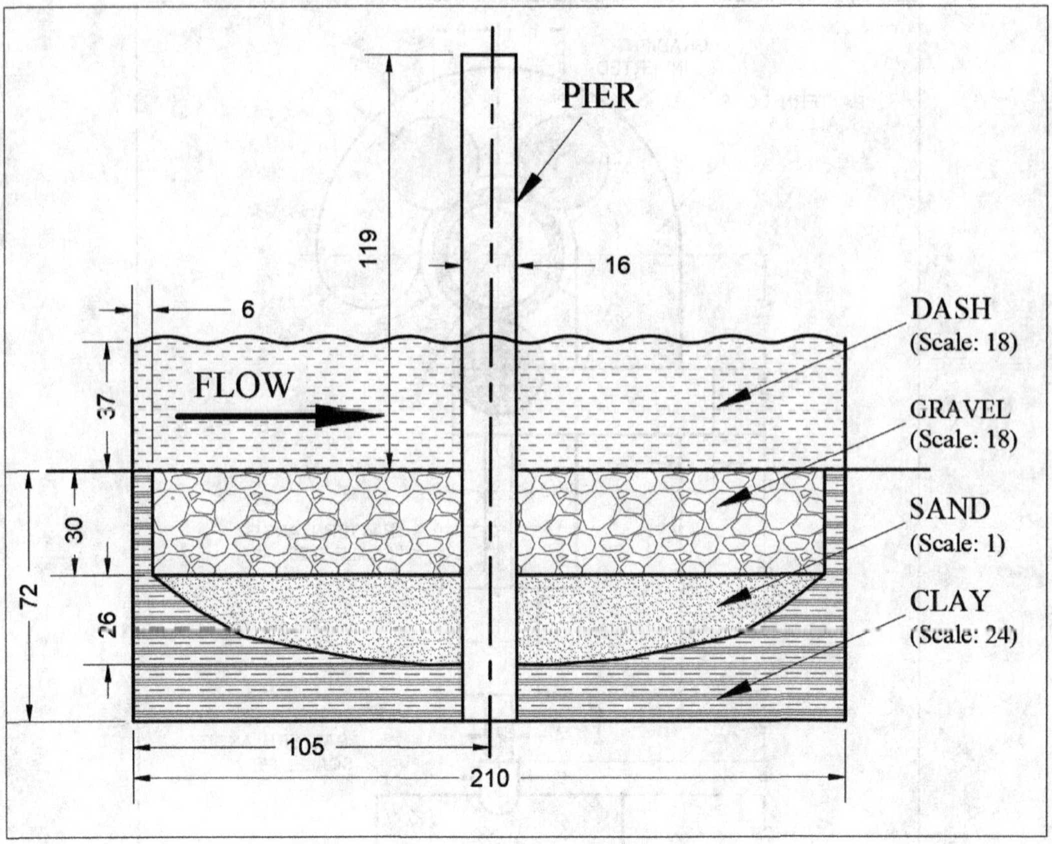

24.9. Object Properties (Units: Inches)

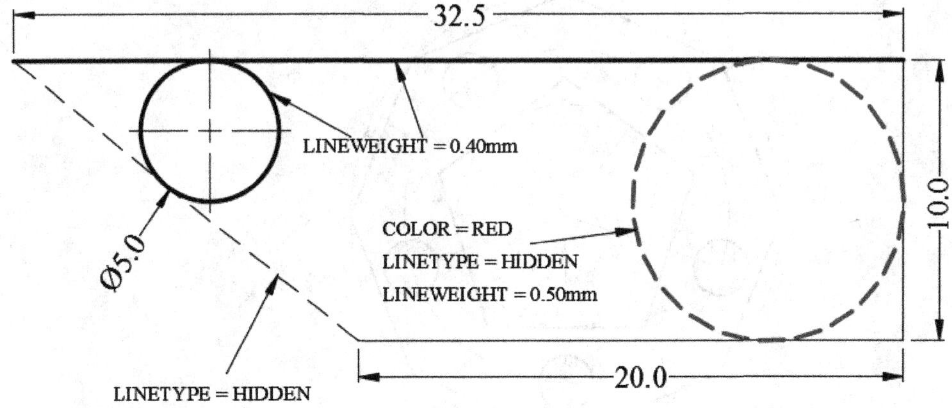

24.10. Pipe Cutter (Units: Millimeters)

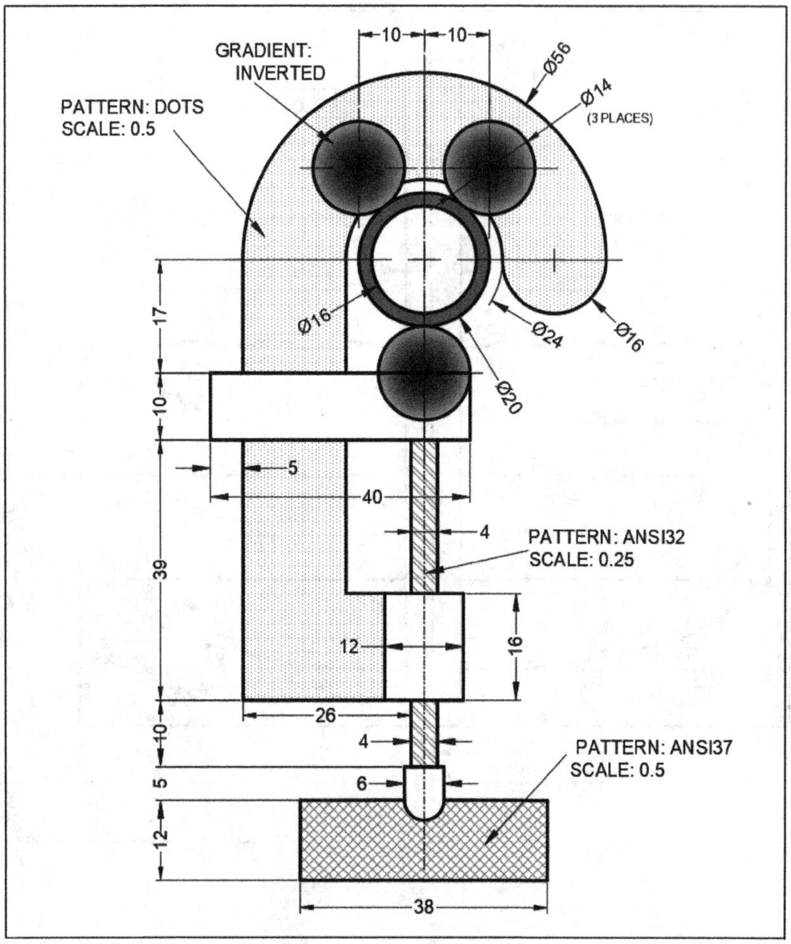

24.11. Polygons and Circles (Units: Inches)

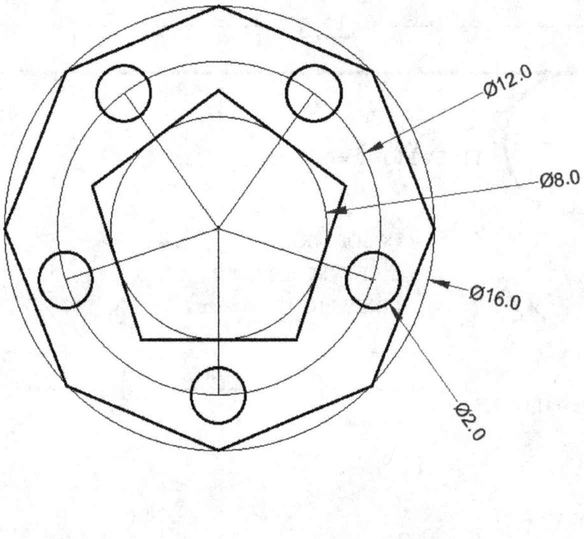

24.12. Rectangular Array (Units: Inches)

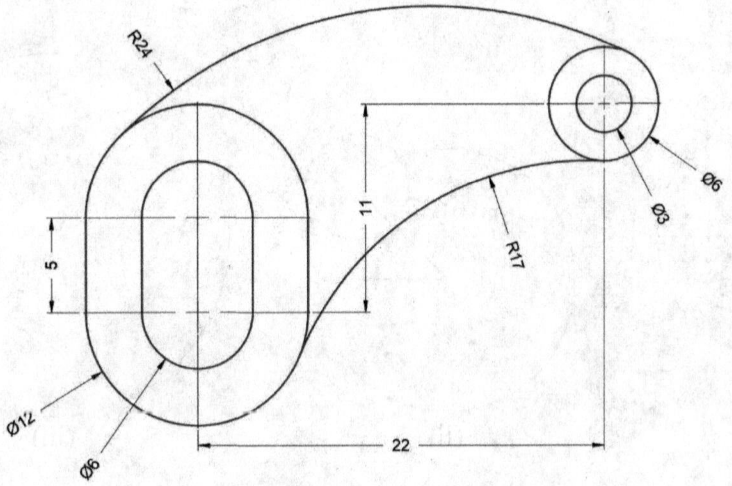

The Basic Element.

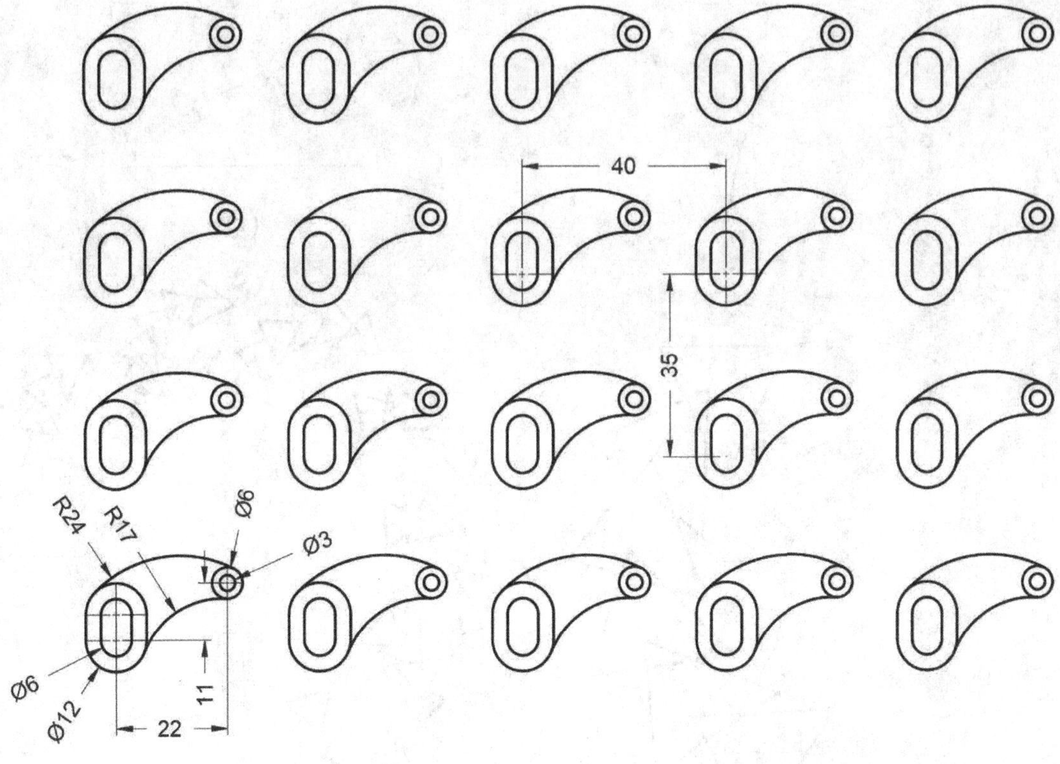

24.13. Polar Array (Units: Inches)

Create the polar array shown in Step (vii) using Steps (i) – (vii)

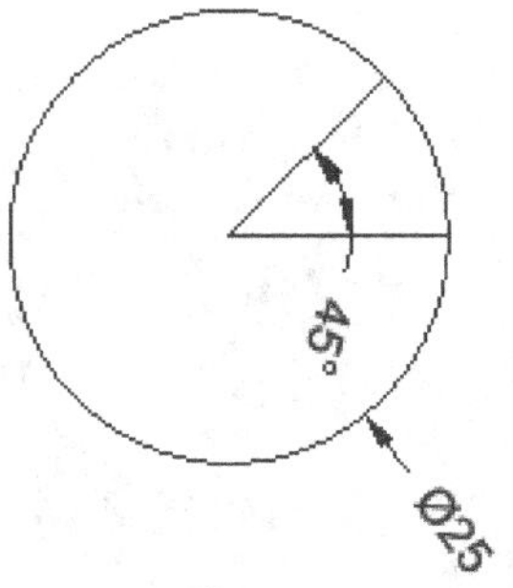

(i)

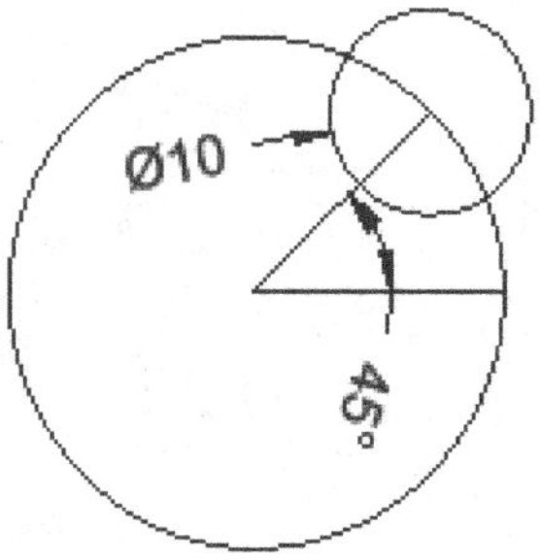

(ii)

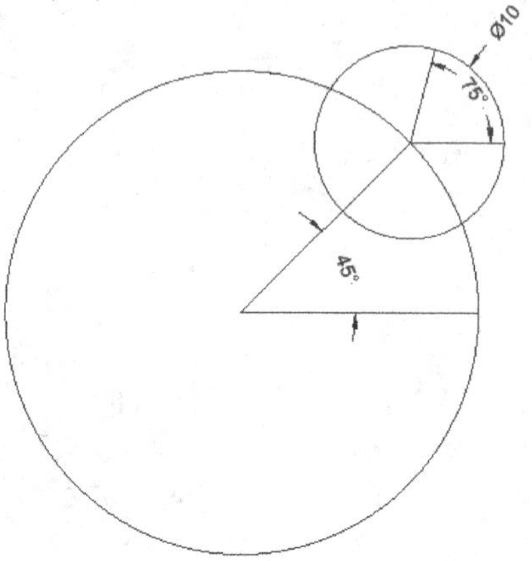

(iii)

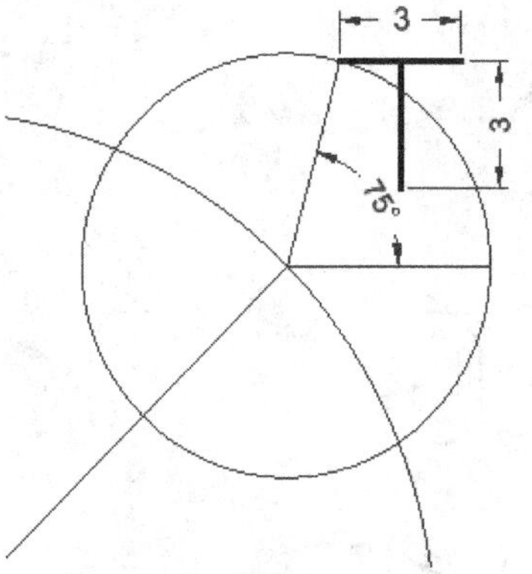

(iv)

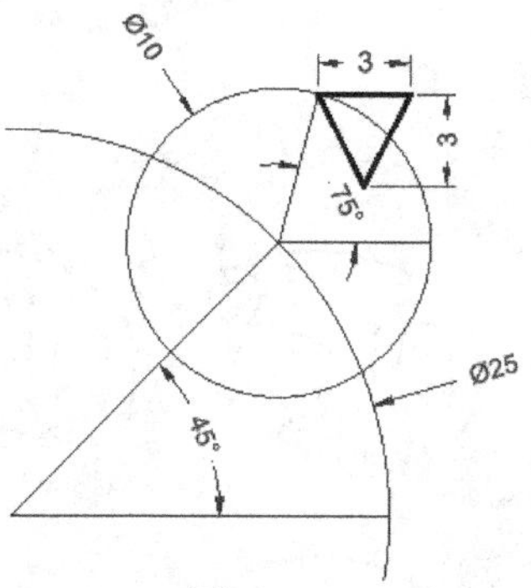

(v)

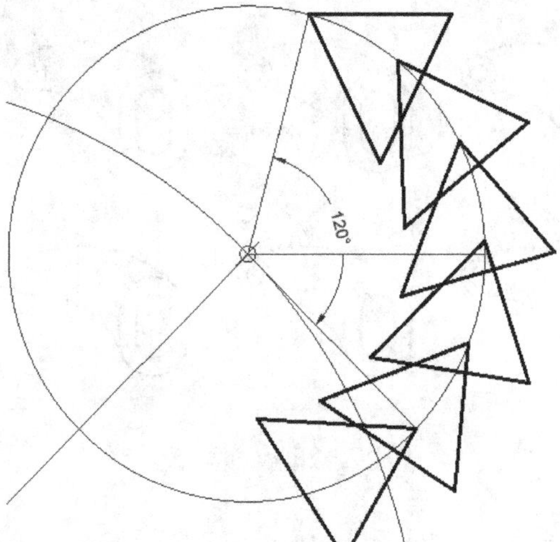

(vi)

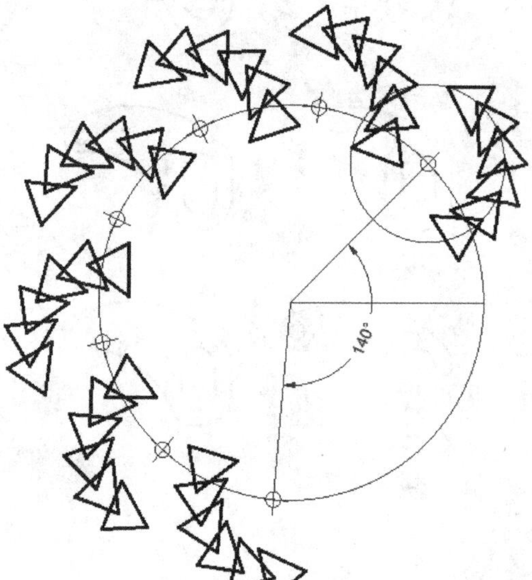

(vii)

24.14. Mirror, Copy, and Scale (Units: Inches)

1. Use the TTR option of the *Circle* (TTR), *Mirror*, *Copy*, and *Scale* commands to create the objects shown in Figure 24-13.
   a. Save the drawing.
   b. Do not add dimensions or centerlines of the circle.
   c. The smaller object is 60% of the bigger object.
   d. Show the complete drawing on one screen.

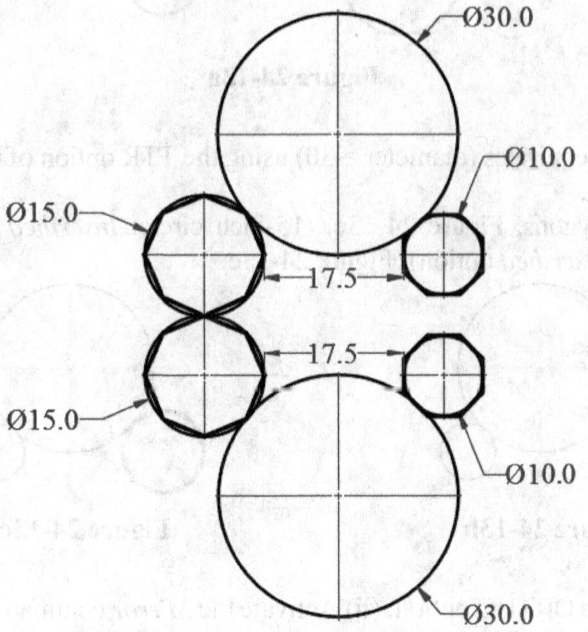

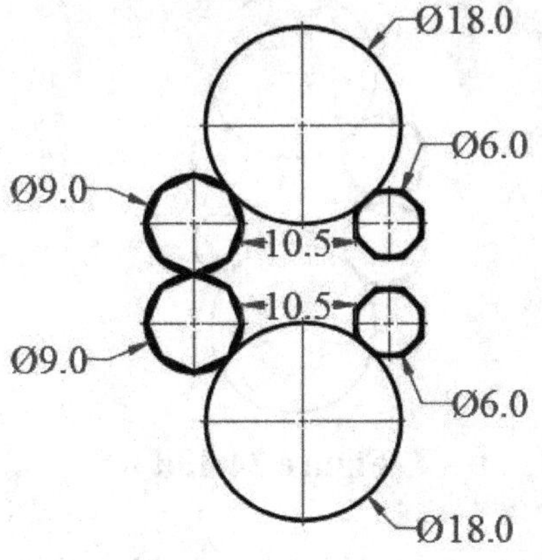

Figure 24-13

Step-by-Step by instructions for Figure 24-13

1. Open an *acad* template file.
2. Draw the circles (ϕ is the symbol of 'diameter'), Figure 24-13a.

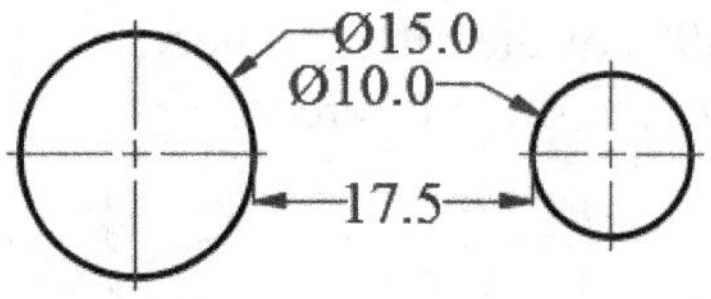

Figure 24-13a

3. Draw the bigger circles (diameter = 30) using the TTR option of the circle command, Figure 24-13b.
4. Draw the polygons, Figure 24-13c. (15-inch circle: *Inscribed* option and 10-inch circle: *Circumscribed* option), Figure 24-13c.

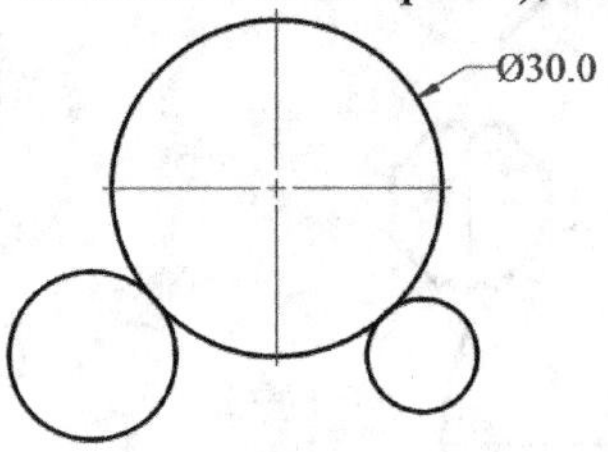

Figure 24-13b

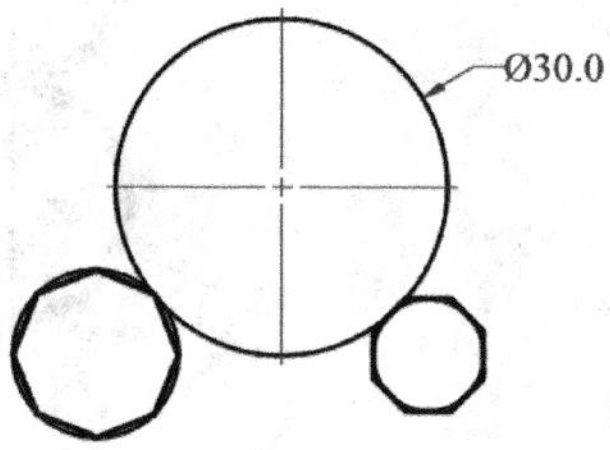

Figure 24-13c

5. (i) Turn *On* the ORTHO option. (ii) Activate the *Mirror* command. (iii) Use the lower quadrant of the circle of diameter = 15 as the base point and complete the *Mirror* command, Figure 24-13d.

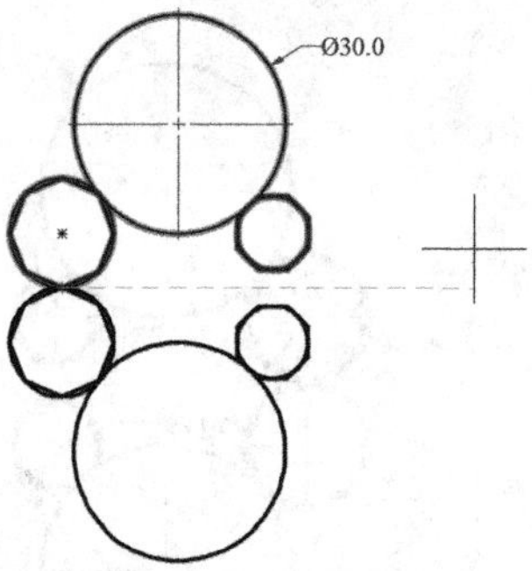

Figure 24-13d

6. Use the *Copy* command to create the second object, Figure 24-13e.
7. Scale the object: (i) Activate the *Scale* command, (ii) select the copy created in step 6, (iii) select the center of one of the large circles as the base point, (iv) for the scale factor, type the value 0.60, and (v) press the *Enter* key, Figure 24-13.

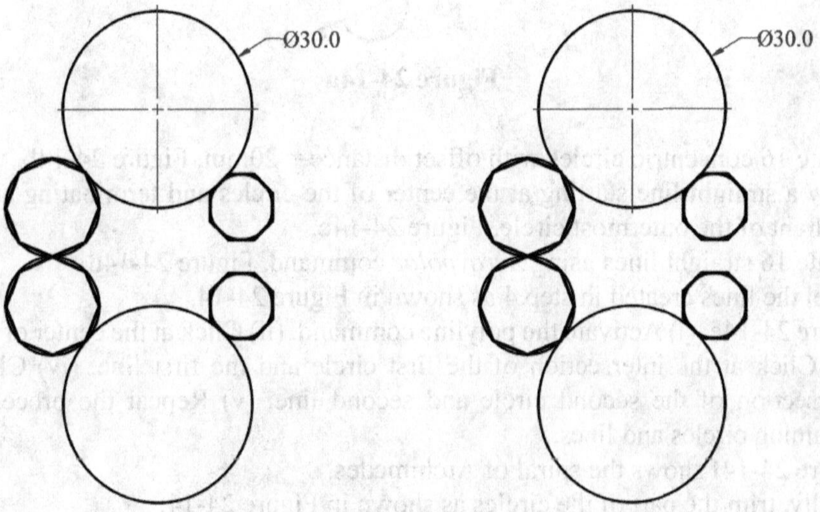

Figure 24-13e

24.15. Spiral of Archimedes (Units: Millimeters)

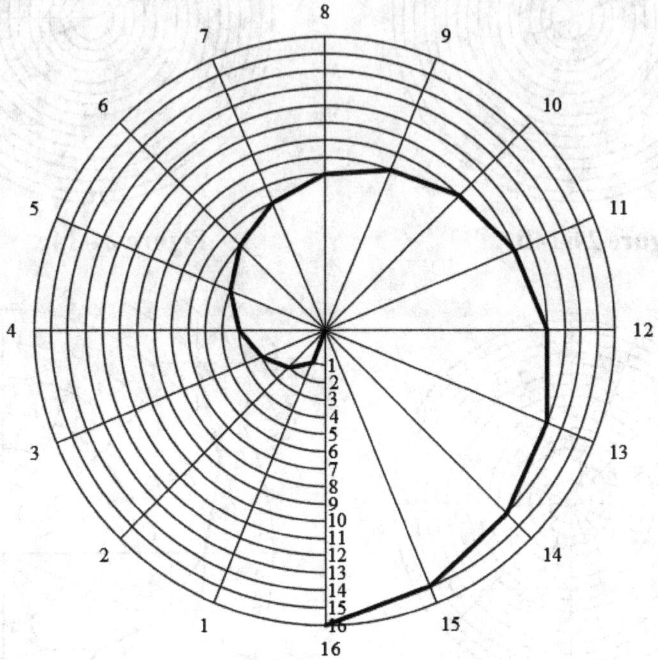

Figure 24-14

Step-by-step instructions for the spiral of Archimedes

1. Draw a circle of the given diameter, Figure 24-14a.

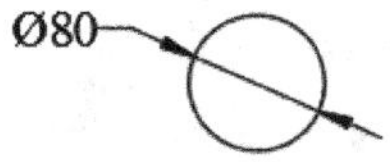

Figure 24-14a

2. Create 16 concentric circles with offset distance = 20mm, Figure 24-14b.
3. Draw a straight line starting at the center of the circles and terminating at the right quadrant of the outermost circle, Figure 24-14c.
4. Create 16 straight lines using *Arraypolar* command, Figure 24-14d.
5. Label the lines created in step 4 as shown in Figure 24-14.
6. Figure 24-14e: (i) Activate the polyline command. (ii) Click at the center of the circle. (iii) Click at the intersection of the first circle and the first line. (iv) Click at the intersection of the second circle and second line. (v) Repeat the process for the remaining circles and lines.
7. Figure 24-14f shows the spiral of Archimedes.
8. Finally, trim the part of the circles as shown in Figure 24-14.

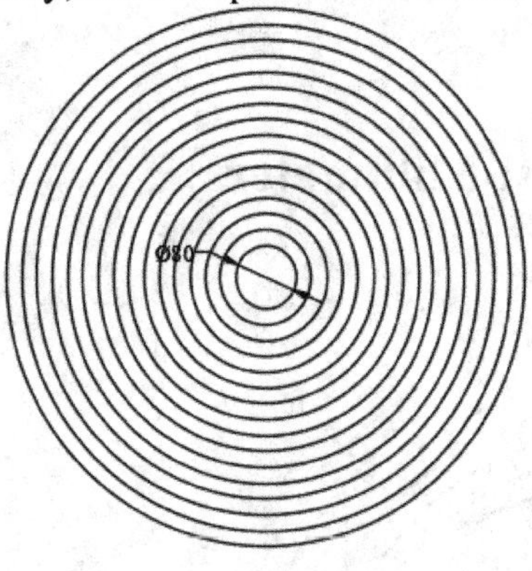

Figure 24-14b

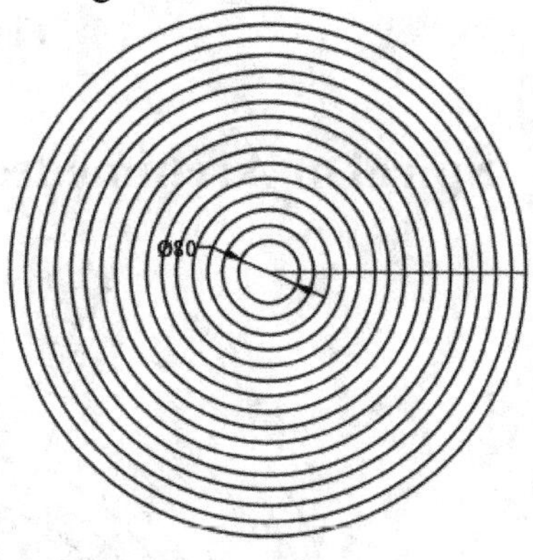

Figure 24-14c

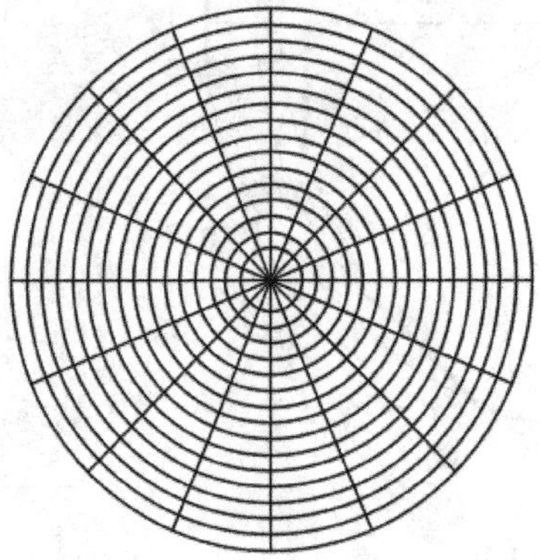

Figure 24-14d

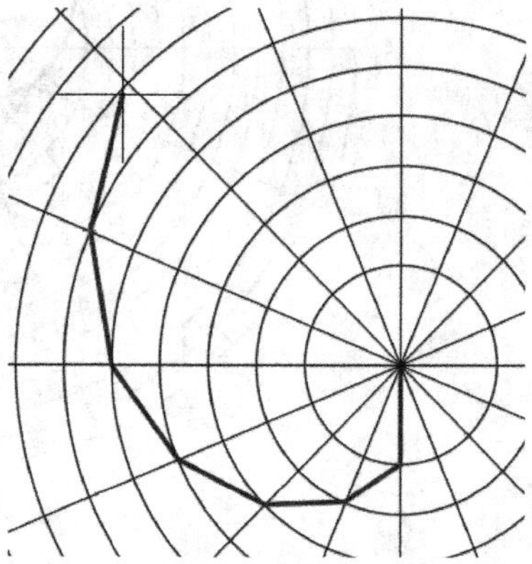

Figure 24-14e

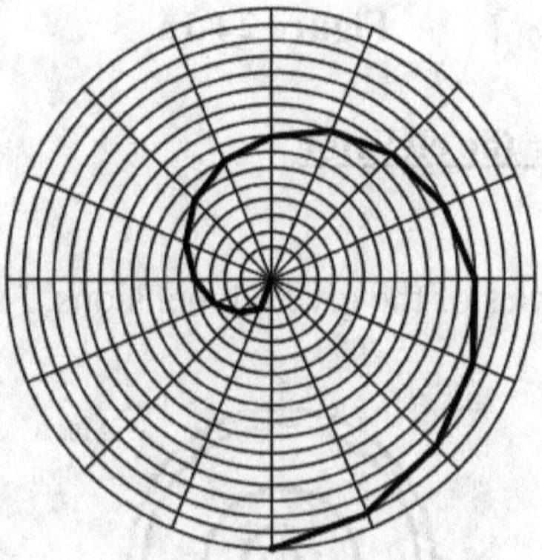

Figure 24-14f

24.16. Elevator system (Units: Millimeters)

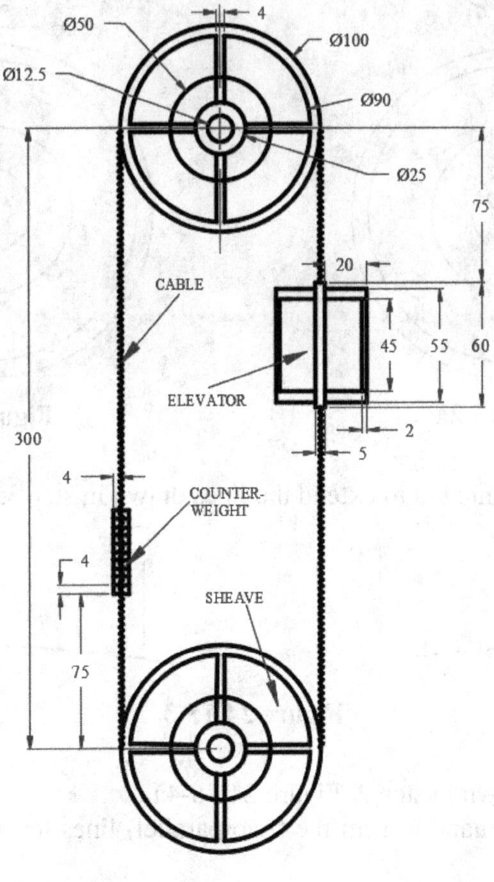

Figure 24-15

Step-by-step instructions for the elevator

First sheave

1. Draw the concentric circles of the given dimensions, Figure 24-15-1.

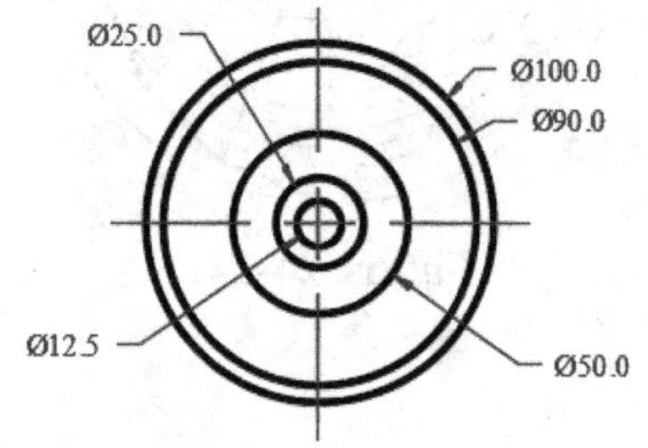

Figure 24-15-1

2. Draw a line of an arbitrary length starting at the top quadrant, Figure 24-15-2a.
3. Use the *Offset* command to create one line on either side, Figure 24-15-2b.

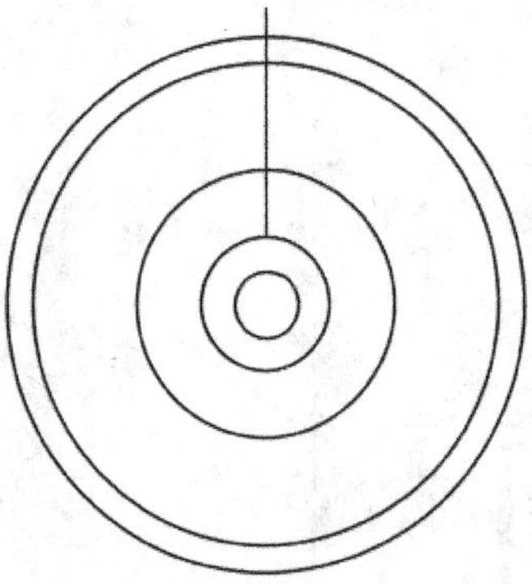

Figure 24-15-2a

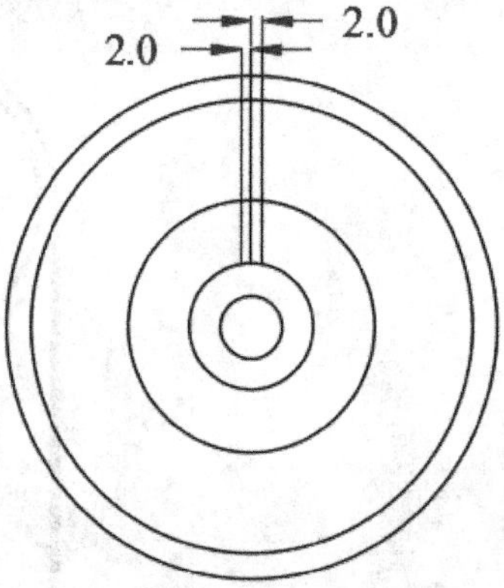

Figure 24-15-2b

4. Use the *Extend* command to extend the lines drawn in step 3, Figure 24-15-3.

Figure 24-15-3

5. Delete the line drawn in step 2, Figure 24-15-4a.
6. Use the *Trim* command to trim the (two parallel) lines to create the desired shape, Figure 24-15-4b.

7. Use the *Arraypolar* command to create the polar array, Figure 24-15-4c.
8. Use the *Trim* command to trim the part of the circle (diameter 90.0) between the two parallel lines to create the desired shape, Figure 24-15-4d.

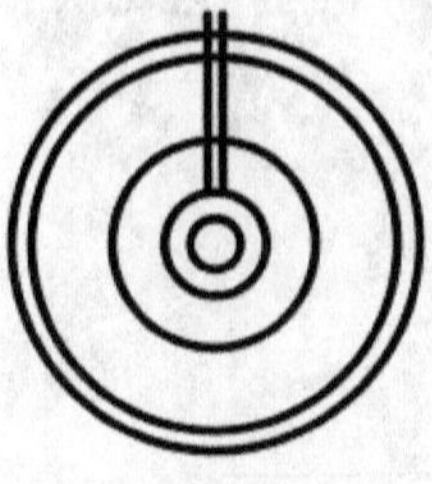
Figure 24-15-4a

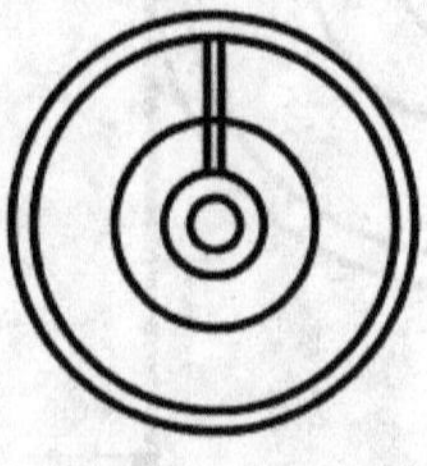
Figure 24-15-4b

Figure 24-15-4c

Figure 24-15-4d

Cable

1. Draw the cable by drawing a line of length 150.0 units starting at the right quadrant, Figure 24-15-5a.
2. Change the linetype of the line drawn in the above step to the "Zig-Zag," Figure 24-15-5b.
3. Change the Linetype scale (using the properties palette) of the line to 0.1, Figure 24-15-5c.
4. Use the *Copy* command to create the copy of the modified line at the left quadrant, Figure 24-15-5d.

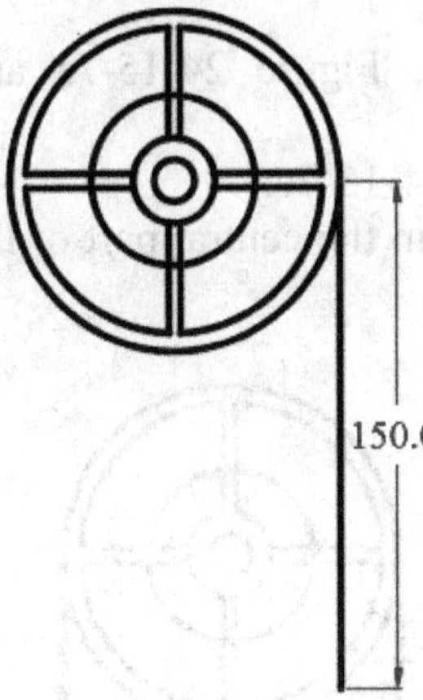

Figure 24-15-5a

Figure 24-15-5b

Figure 24-15-5c

Figure 24-15-5d

Second sheave

1. Use the *Mirror* command to create the mirror image (second sheave), Figure 24-15.6.

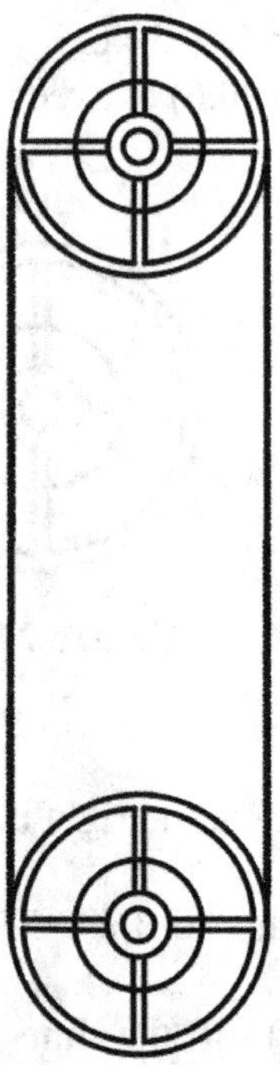

Figure 24-15-6

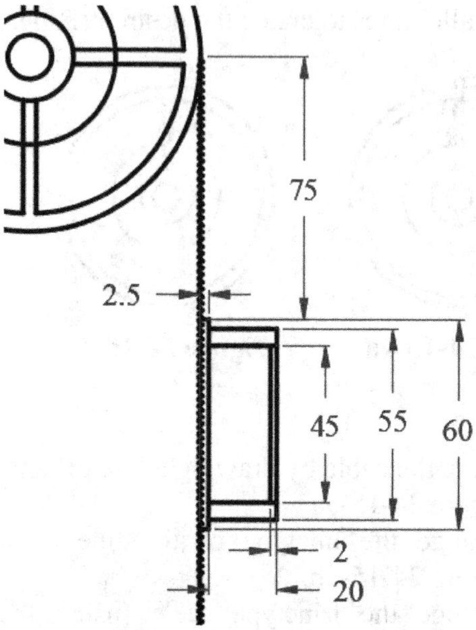

Figure 24-15-7a

Elevator

1. Draw front half of the elevator by drawing the lines, Figure 24-15-7a and Figure 24-15-7b.
2. Use the *Mirror* command to complete the elevator, Figure 24-15-7c.
3. Use the *Trim* command to remove the part of the cable from the central part of the elevator, Figure 24-15-7d.

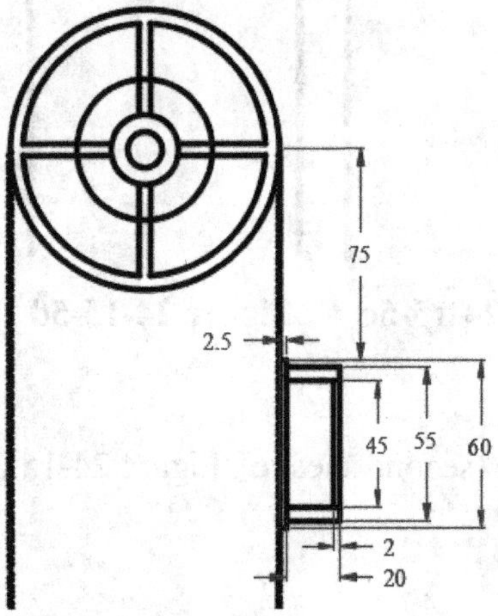

Figure 24-15-7b

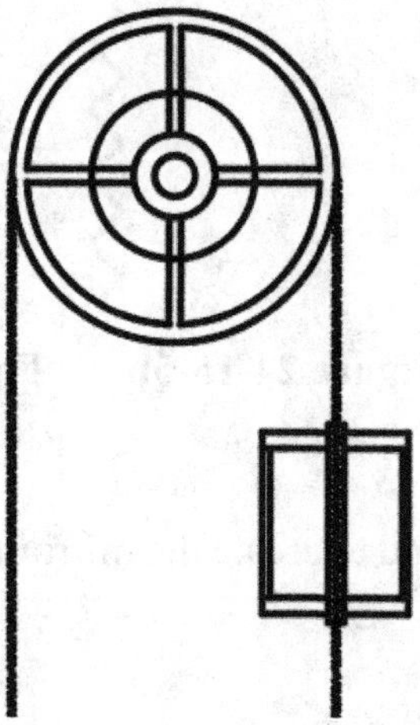

Figure 24-15-7c

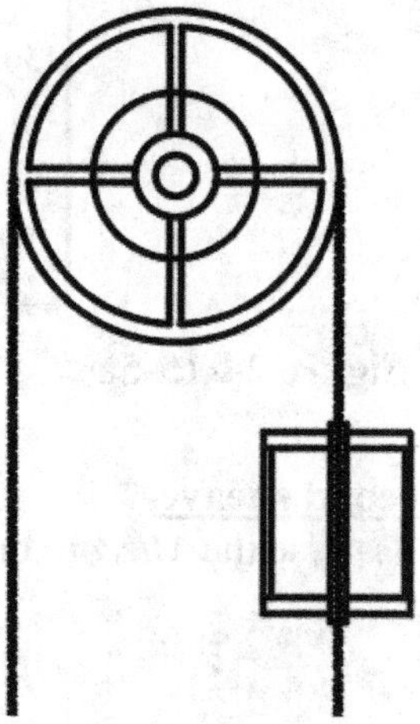

Figure 24-15-7d

Counterweight

1. Draw a small square by drawing the lines, Figure 24-15-8a.
2. Use the *Array* command to create the rectangular array, Figure 24-15-8b.

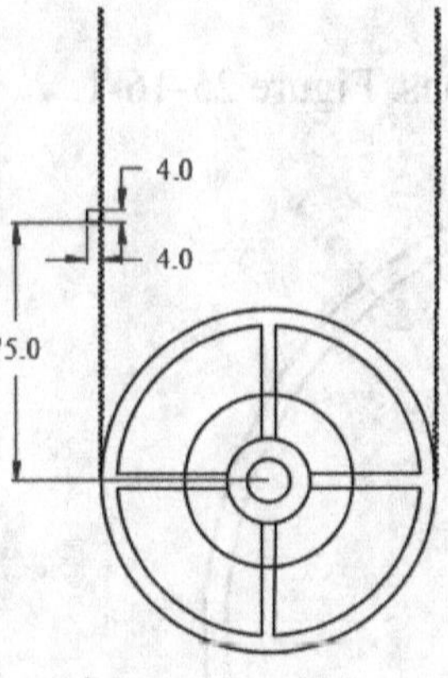

Figure 24-15-8a

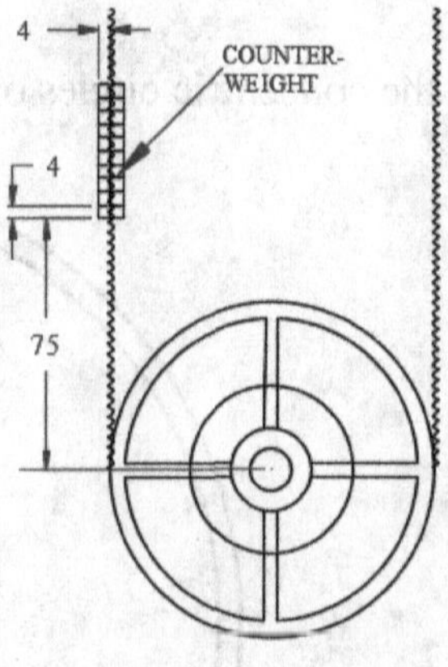

Figure 24-15-8b

Complete system

1. The complete system is shown in Figure 25-13.

24.17. Ferris wheel (Units: Millimeters)

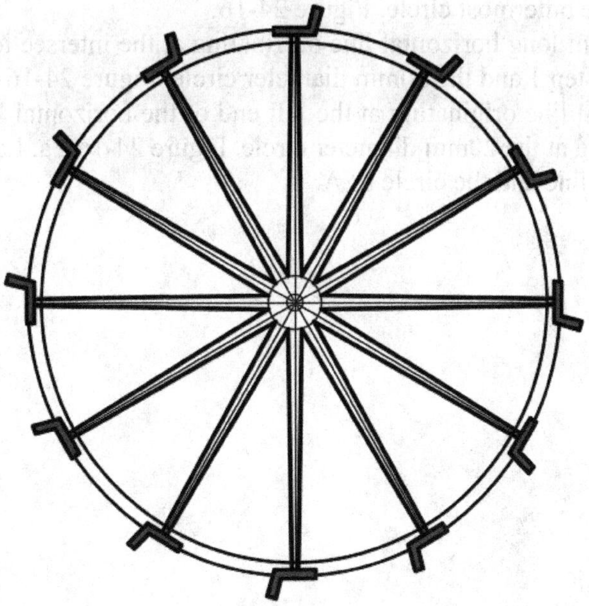

Figure 24-16

Step-by-step instructions for the Ferris wheel

Wheel

1. Draw the concentric circles of the given dimensions, Figure 25-16-1.

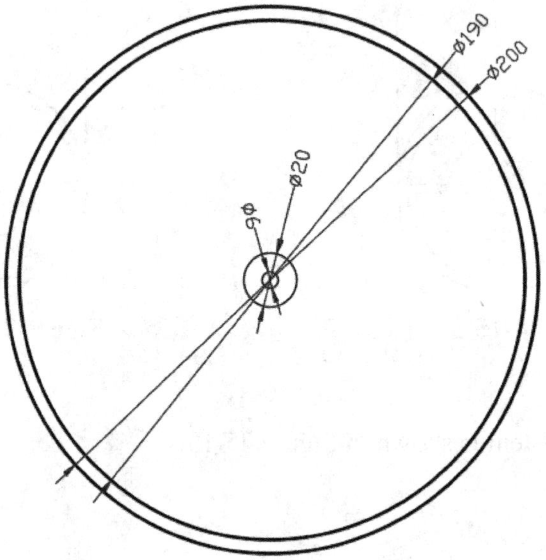

Figure 24-16-1

Spoke

1. Draw a straight line originating at the center of the circles and terminating at the right quadrant of the outermost circle, Figure 24-16.
2. Draw a 0.34mm long horizontal line originating at the intersection of the horizontal line drawn in step 1 and the 20mm diameter circle, Figure 24-16-2a.
3. Draw a vertical line originating at the left end of the horizontal line drawn in step 2 and terminating at the 20mm diameter circle, Figure 24-16-2a. Label the intersection of the vertical line and the circle as A.

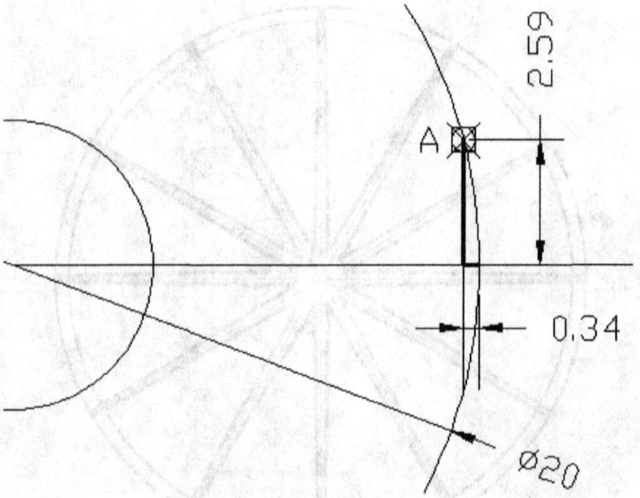

Figure 24-16-2a

4. Draw a straight line originating at point A and terminating beyond the 200mm diameter circle, Figure 24-16-2b.

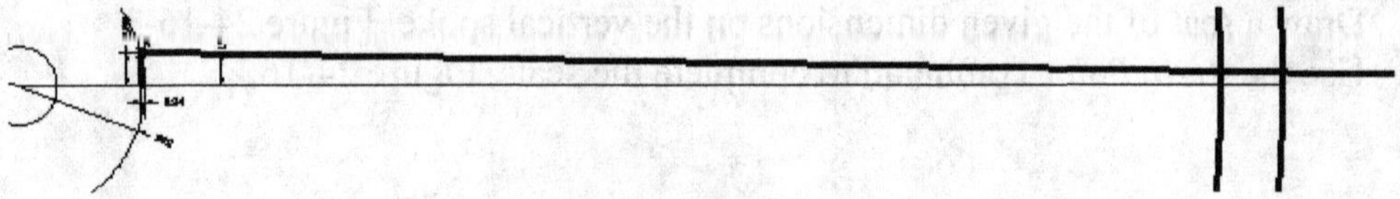

Figure 24-16-2b

5. Trim the line drawn in step 4 with respect to the outermost circle, Figure 24-16-2c.
6. Use the *Mirror* command to create a line below the horizontal line, Figure 24-16-2c.

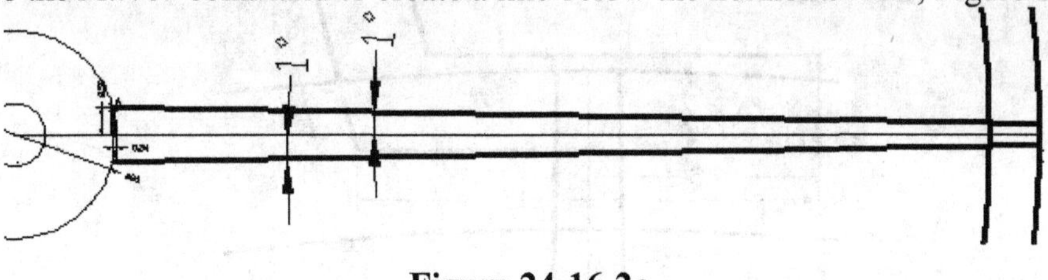

Figure 24-16-2c

7. Use the *ArrayPolar* command to complete the spokes, Figure 24-16-2c.

Figure 24-16-2d

Seats

1. Draw a seat of the given dimensions on the vertical spoke, Figure 24-16-3.
2. Use the *ArrayPolar* command to complete the seats, Figure 24-16.

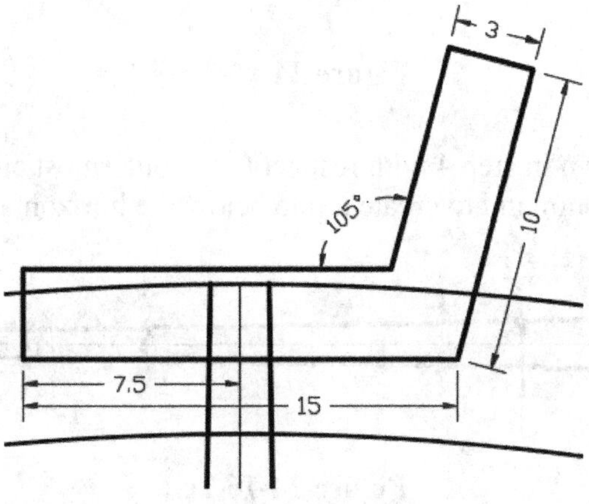

Figure 24-16-3

3. The complete system is shown in Figure 24-16.

Notes:

25. Bibliography

Edward Allen and Joseph Iano, "*Fundamental of Building Construction: materials and methods,*" John Wiley and Sons, Inc, 4th ed., 2004.

James Ambrose, "*Building Construction and Design,*" Van Nostrand Reinhold, 1992.

Gerald Baker, "*Civil Drafting for the Engineering Technician,*" Thomson Delmar Learning, 2006.

Gary R. Bertoline and Eric N. Wiebe, "*Fundamentals of Graphics Communication,*" McGrawHill, 5th ed., 2005.

James D. Bethune, "*Engineering Graphics with AutoCAD 2006,*" Prentice Hall, Pearson Education, 6th ed., 2006.

Wilfried Brutsaert, "*Hydrology: An Introduction,*" Cambridge University Press, 2005.

David A. Chin, "*Water Resources Engineering,*" Prentice Hall, 2nd ed., 1988.

Ven Te Chow, David R. Maidment, and Larry W. Mays, "*Applied Hydrology,*" McGraw-Hill Book Company, 3rd ed., 1988.

Mackenzie L. Davis and David A. Cornwell, "*Introduction to Environmental Engineering,*" McGraw-Hill, 3rd ed., 1998.

Raymond E. Davis, Francis S. Foote, and Joe W. Kelley, "*Surveying: Theory and Practice,*" McGraw-Hill Inc., 5th ed., 1966.

Raymond E. Davis and Joe. W. Kelley, "*Elementary Plane Surveying,*" McGraw-Hill Book Company, 4th ed., 1967.

James H. Earle, "*Fundamentals of Graphics Communication,*" Prentice Hall, Pearson Education, 6th ed., 2002.

Stephen V. Estopinal, "*A Guide to Understanding Land Survey,*" John Wiley and Sons, Inc, 2nd ed., 1993.

David Frey, "*AutoCAD 2002,*" SYBEX, 2002.

Nicholas J. Garber and Lester A. Hoel, "*Traffic and Highway Engineering,*" University of Virginia, Cengage Learning, Toronto, Canada, 4th ed., 2009.

Frederick E. Giesecke, Alva Mitchell, Henry C. Spencer, Ivan L. Hill, and John T. Dygdon, "*Technical Drawing,*" Macmillan Publishing Company and Collier, 8th ed., 1986.

Frederick E. Giesecke, Alva Mitchell, Henry C. Spencer, Ivan L. Hill, John T. Dygdon, and Shawna Lockhart "*Technical Drawing,*" Published by Pearson – Prentice Hall, 13th ed., 2009.

David L. Goetsch, "*Structural, Civil, and Pipe Drafting for CAD Technicians,*" Thomson Delmar Learning, 2003.

David L. Goetsch, "*Technical Drawing,*" Macmillian Publishing Company, 8th ed., 2003.

Randolph P. Hoelscher and Clifford H. Springer, "*Engineering Drawing and Geometry,*" John Wiley & Sons, INC. New York, 1955.

William J. Hornung, "*Architectural Drafting,*" Prentice Hall, 3rd ed., 1960.

Mark Huth, "*Basic Principles for Construction,*" Thomson Delmar Learning, 2004.

Barry F. Kavanagh, "*Surveying Principles and Applications,*" McGraw Hill Inc., Prentice Hall, 6nd ed., 2003.

Philip Kissam, "*Surveying for Civil Engineers,*" McGraw Hill Inc., 2nd ed., 1981.

Philip Kissam and Jerry A. Nathanson, "*Surveying Practice,*" McGraw Hill Inc., 4nd ed., 1987.

A. S. Levens, "*Graphics in Engineering and Science,*" John Wiley & Sons, INC. New York, 2nd Printing, 1957.

Warren J. Luzadder, "*Fundamental of Engineering Drawing for Design, Communication, and Numerical Control,*" Prentice Hall, 6rd ed., 1971.

David A. Madsen and Terence M. Shumaker, "*Civil Drafting Technology,*" Prentice Hall, 3rd ed., 1998.

David A. Madsen and Terence M. Shumaker, "*Civil Drafting Technology,*" Prentice Hall, 6th ed., 2007.

Jack C. McCormac, "*Surveying Fundamentals,*" Prentice Hall, 2nd ed., 1991.
Jack C. McCormac, "*Surveying,*" Prentice Hall, 4nd ed., 1991.

Richard H. McCuen, "*Hydrologic Analysis and Design,*" Prentice Hall, 3rd ed., 2004.

John G. McEntyre, "*Land Survey System,*" John Wiley and Sons, Inc, 1978.

Edward J. Muller, James G. Fausett, and Philip A. Grau III, "*Architectural Drawing and Light construction,*" Prentice Hall, 6th ed., 2002.

Jerry A. Nathanson and Philip Kissam, "*Surveying Practice,*" McGraw-Hill Book Company, 4th ed., 1988.

Ralph W. Liebing and Mimi Ford Paul, "*Architectural Working Drawings,*" John Wiley and Sons, 2nd ed., 1983.

William J. O'Connell, "*Graphic Communications in Architecture,*" Stripes Publishing Company, 1972.

Dave Rosgen, "*Applied River Morphology,*" Wildland Hydrology, Pagosa Springs, Colorado, 1996.

Harry Rubey, George Edward, and Marion Wesley Todd, "*Engineering Surveys: Elementary and Applied,*" The Macmillan Company, 2nd ed., 1950.

George K. Stegman and Harry J. Stegman, "*Architectural Drafting,*" American Technical Society, 2nd ed., 1974.

Warren Viessman, Jr. and Gary L. Lewis, "*Introduction to Hydrology,*" Prentice Hall, 5th ed., 2003.

Harvey W. Waffle, "*Architectural Drawing,*" The Bruce Publishing Company, Revised edition, 1962.

Ernest R. Weidhaas, "*Architectural Drafting and Design,*" Allyn and Bacon, 6th ed., 1989.

"*Webster's New Collegiate Dictionary,*" G. & S. Merriam Co., Publishers, Springfield. MASS, U.S.A.

Notes:

26. Index

A

B

C

D

E

F

G

H

I

J

L

M

O

P

Q

R

S

T

U

V

W

X

Z

9781630578237